The Search for Personal Freedom

Volume 1

The Search for Personal Freedom

seventh edition

Robert C. Lamm
Arizona State University

Neal M. Cross

Rudy H. Turk
Arizona State University

wcb
Wm. C. Brown Publishers
Dubuque, Iowa

Book Team

Karen Speerstra
Senior Developmental Editor

Lynne Niznik
Assistant Developmental Editor

Karen Slaght
Production Editor

Catherine Dinsmore
Designer

Mavis M. Oeth
Permissions Editor

Carol M. Schiessl
Visual Research Editor

group

Wm. C. Brown
Chairman of the Board

Mark C. Falb
*President and Chief
Executive Officer*

wcb
Wm. C. Brown Publishers, College Division

Lawrence E. Cremer
President

James L. Romig
Vice-President, Product Development

David Wm. Smith
Vice-President, Marketing

David A. Corona
Vice-President, Production and Design

E. F. Jogerst
Vice-President, Cost Analysts

Marcia H. Stout
Marketing Manager

Linda M. Galarowicz
Director of Marketing Research

William A. Moss
Production Editorial Manager

Marilyn A. Phelps
Manager of Design

Mary M. Heller
Visual Research Manager

Contents

Illustrations: Colorplates/Figures   ix
Preface/Acknowledgments   xiii

Unit 1
Prologue: The Integrated Humanities   1

  1   Introduction: Human Values and Personal Freedom   3
  2   A Common Basis for Understanding the Arts   9
  3   An Introduction to Music Listening   21
      Record List   29

Unit 2
Greece: The First Humanistic Culture   33

  4   Early Greece: Preparation for the Good Life   35
  5   Hellenic Athens: The Fulfillment of the Good Life   51
      Literary Selections
         Aeschylus, *Agamemnon*   62
         Aeschylus, *Eumenides*   72
         Perikles, *Memorial Oration*   79
         Sophokles, *Oedipus the King*   81
         Euripides, *The Trojan Women*   96
         Euripides, *The Bacchae*   108
  6   Greece: From Hellenic to Hellenistic World   125
      Literary Selections
         Plato, *Apology*   130
         Plato, *Republic*   139
         Aristotle, *Poetics*   156

7 Greek Art: Gods, Temples, and the Greeks   161
8 Music in Greek Life and Thought   195
    Sappho, Poetry   199
    Record List   202
    Time Chart for Greek Civilization   204

Unit 3
Rome: The International Culture   207

9 A Thousand Years of Rome   209
   Literary Selections
    Cicero, Scipio's Dream (Book VI, *On the Republic*)   227
    Virgil, The Lower World (Book VI, *The Aeneid*)   229
    Virgil, Eclogue IV   238
    Lucretius, *On the Nature of Things*   239
    Catullus, Poems   242
    Horace, Odes   243
    Ovid, from *The Art of Love*   243
    Martial, Epigrams   247
    Arrian, Discourses of Epictetus, Book I, Chapter 1   249
    Marcus Aurelius, Meditations, Book II   250
    Juvenal, Against the City of Rome   251
    Lucian, *Philosophies Going Cheap*   255
10 Roman Art and Music: The Arts of Megalopolis   261

Unit 4
Judaism and Christianity: The Star and the Cross   275

11 Faith, Hope, and Love: The Judeo-Christian Tradition   277
   Literary Selections
    The Book of Job   282
    Psalms of David   283
    Ecclesiastes 3   284
    The Sermon on the Mount   284
    Paul's Letter to the Corinthians   286
    Five Parables   287
    Revelation   288
12 The Beginnings of Christian Art   291

Unit 5
The Age of Faith 305

13 Building Medieval Walls 307
    Literary Selections
        Beowulf 317
        Everyman 319
        Aucassin and Nicolette 327
14 The Late Middle Ages: Expansion and Synthesis 337
    Literary Selections
        Songs and Poems of the Wandering Scholars 348
        Our Lady's Juggler 349
        Chaucer, The Prolog to *The Canterbury Tales* 351
        Chaucer, The Reeve's Tale from *The Canterbury Tales* 359
        Andreas Capellanus, from *The Art of Courtly Love* 362
        Sir Thomas Malory, from *Morte Darthur* 363
        Dante, *The Divine Comedy, Hell* 371
        Dante, *Paradiso, Canto XXXIII* 404
15 The Medieval Synthesis in Art 407
16 Medieval Music: Sacred and Secular 429
        Duke William IX of Aquitaine, Troubadour Songs 434
        Bernart de Ventadorn, Lancan Vei per Mei la Landa 435
        Beatritz, Countess of Dia, Troubadour Songs 436
        Record List 442
        Time Chart for the Middle Ages 444

Glossary 447
Credits 461
Index 465

Illustrations

Colorplates

Colorplates follow page indicated.
1   Paul Gauguin, *Where Do We Come From? What Are We? Where Are We Going?*   16
2   Pieter Bruegel, *Winter (Return of the Hunters)*   16
3   Meindert Hobbema, *The Watermill with the Great Red Roof*   16
4   Vincent van Gogh, *The Starry Night*   16
5   Wassily Kandinsky, *Panel (3)* (also known as *Summer*)   16
6   Hyacinthe Rigaud, *Portrait of Louis XIV*   16
7   Pablo Picasso, *Girl Before a Mirror*   16
8   Giovanni Paolo Panini, *The Interior of the Pantheon*   272
9   *Head of Emperor Hadrian*   272
10 Interior view of San Vitale   272
11 *Emperor Justinian and His Courtiers*   272
12 *Empress Theodora and Her Retinue*   272
13 "X–P (Chi-rho) Page," *Lindisfarne Gospels*   416
14 "Crucifixion Cover," *Lindau Gospels*   416
15 Reliquary in shape of head   416
16 "Capture of Christ and the Flagellation," *Psalter of St. Swithin*   416
17 South Rose Window and Lancets, Chartres Cathedral   416
18 Nave, Notre Dame Cathedral of Coutances   416
19 Duccio di Buoninsegna, *The Calling of the Apostles Peter and Andrew*   416
20 Simone Martini, *Annunciation*   416
21 Giotto, *Lamentation*   416

Figures

1.1   Bull, ceiling painting   4
4.1   Portrait bust of Homer   42
4.2   Marble bust identified as Pythagoras   47
5.1   Stone carving of theatrical mask   52
5.2   Marble bust from Tivoli   56
5.3   Athenian silver drachma   57
5.4   Portrait bust of Sophokles   58
5.5   Portrait bust of Euripides   59

6.1   Portrait bust of Demosthanes   126
6.2   Portrait bust of Alexander the Great   126
6.3   Portrait bust of Plato   126
6.4   Portrait bust of Sokrates   130
7.1   Sphinx   162
7.2   *Mycerinus and His Queen*   162
7.3   *Offering Bearers* from Tomb of Sebekhotep   163
7.4   *Colossi of Memnon*   163
7.5   Temple of Amon   164
7.6   Mortuary Temple of Queen Hatshepsut   164
7.7   Temple of Amon-Mut-Khonsu   164
7.8   Floor plan of Temple of Amon-Mut-Khonsu   164
7.9   Cycladic Head   165
7.10   Detail of the south front of the Palace at Knossos   165
7.11   Floor plan of the Palace at Knossos   166
7.12   Throne Room, Palace of Minos, Knossos   166
7.13   Queen's Megaron, Palace of Minos, Knossos   166
7.14   *Snake Goddess*   167
7.15   Mask from Mycenae   167
7.16   Lion Gate at Mycenae   167
7.17   *Amphora of the Dipylon*   168
7.18   Statuette of Youth   169
7.19   *Kore of Auxerre*   170
7.20   *Kouros of Sounion*   170
7.21   *Calf-Bearer (Moschophoros)*   171
7.22   *Hera of Samos*   171
7.23   Exekias, amphora: "Akhilleus Slaying Penthesiles"   171
7.24   Temple of Hera I   172
7.25   *Kore in Dorian Peplos*   172
7.26   *Kore from Chios*   173
7.27   *Anavyssos Kouros*   173
7.28   *Kore (La Delicata)*   174
7.29   Sosias painter, "Akhilleus Bandaging Patrokles' Wound"   174
7.30   *Kritios Boy*   175
7.31   *Delphi Charioteer*   175
7.32   *Delphi Charioteer,* rear view   175
7.33   *Poseidon (Zeus ?)*   176
7.34   Myron, *Discobolus (Discus Thrower)*   176
7.35   Polykleitos, *Doryphoros (Spear Bearer)*   177
7.36   Post and lintel system   177
7.37   Typical Greek temple floor plan   177
7.38   Typical Greek temple facade   177
7.39   Greek orders of columns   178
7.40   Marble drum, Eleusis   179
7.41   Temple of Hera II   179
7.42   View of the akropolis at Athens   179
7.43   Model of classical akropolis at Athens   179
7.44   Iktinus and Kallikrates, Parthenon   180
7.45   Stereobate and stylobate, Parthenon   180
7.46   Schematic drawing of Parthenon refinements   180
7.47   Reconstruction of east pediment of Parthenon   181
7.48   *Dionysos,* from east pediment of Parthenon   181
7.49   Three Goddesses, from east pediment of Parthenon   181
7.50   *Combat between a Lapith and a Centaur*   182
7.51   *Horsemen,* from the west frieze of the Parthenon   182
7.52   Mnesikles, the Erechtheion   182
7.53   Porch of the Maidens, Erechtheion   183
7.54   Kallikrates, Temple of Athena Nike   183
7.55   Temple of Poseidon   184
7.56   Akhilleus Painter, "Muse on Mount Helicon"   184
7.57   *Victory Untying Her Sandal*   185
7.58   Paionios, *Nike*   185
7.59   *Stele of Hegesco*   185
7.60   *Mausolos,* from the Mausoleum at Halikarnassos   186
7.61   Praxiteles, *Hermes with Infant Dionysos*   186
7.62   Praxiteles, *Aphrodite of Knidos*   187
7.63   Marble torso   187
7.64   *Boy from the Bay of Marathon*   188
7.65   Lysippos, *Apoxyomenos (Scraper)*   188
7.66   *The Dying Gaul*   189
7.67   *Child with a Goose*   189
7.68   Pythokritos of Rhodes, *Nike of Samothrace*   190
7.69   Altar of Zeus, west front, from Pergamon   190
7.70   *The Battle of the Gods and Giants*   191

7.71 Cossutius, Temple of the Olympian Zeus 191
7.72 *Aphrodite of Melos* 191
7.73 *Portrait Head,* from Delos 192
7.74 *Laokoön and His Sons* 192
8.1 Lyre player "The Boston Throne" 196
8.2 Aulos Player of the Ludovisi Throne 196
8.3 *Apollo and Marsyas,* marble relief 197
8.4 Orpheus painter, "Orpheus Among the Thracians" 198
8.5 "Alkaios and Sappho with Lyres" 199
8.6 "Young Girls Dancing Around the Altar" 200
8.7 Theatre at Epidauros 201
9.1 *The Capitoline She-Wolf* 210
9.2 Roman Coin, 17 B.C. 215
9.3 Main thoroughfare, Ostia Antica 216
9.4 Great Bath, Roman bath complex 216
9.5 Snack bar, Ostia Antica 216
9.6 Priest of Serapis 218
9.7 Portrait bust of Epicurus 218
9.8 Stadium at Delphi 221
9.9 *Runner at the Starting Point, Two Wrestlers, Javelin Thrower* 222
9.10 Temple of Hera 222
10.1 Etruscan sarcophagus 262
10.2 West portico of the forum, Pompeii 263
10.3 Atrium, House of the Vetti, Pompeii 263
10.4 Bust of Julius Caesar 264
10.5 *Augustus of Primaporta* 264
10.6 Three portrait busts of Caesar Augustus 264
10.7 Maison Carrée 265
10.8 Corinthian capital 265
10.9 Semicircular arch arcade and vault 265
10.10 Pont du Gard 266
10.11 Roman Mausoleum 266
10.12 *Herakles Discovering the Infant Telephos in Arcadia* 267
10.13 Reconstruction of fourth-century Rome 267
10.14 Colosseum, Rome 268
10.15 Colosseum, Rome (aerial view) 268
10.16 Roman amphitheatre, Arles 269
10.17 *Flavian Woman* 269
10.18 Arch of Titus, Rome 269
10.19 Column of Trajan, Rome 270
10.20 Column of Trajan, detail 270
10.21 The Pantheon, Rome 271
10.22 *Equestrian Statue of Marcus Aurelius* 271
10.23 *Head of a Bearded Man* 272
10.24 Arch of Constantine, Rome 272
10.25 *Constantine the Great* 272
10.26 *Diptych of Consul Boethius* 273
11.1 *The Fourth Horseman of the Apocalypse,* Angers Tapestries 289
12.1 *Orant* 292
12.2 *The Good Shepherd* 292
12.3 Anagram as derived from Greek for "Jesus Christ, the Son of God, Savior" 293
12.4 *Crucifixion,* from the door of the Church of Santa Sabina 293
12.5 *Good Shepherd* 294
12.6 *Christ Enthroned* 294
12.7 *The Jonah Sarcophagus* 295
12.8 *The Sarcophagus of Junius Bassus* 295
12.9 Roman basilica, Volubilis, Morocco 296
12.10 Basilica of St. Clement, Rome 296
12.11 Interior, St. Paul's Outside the Walls, Rome 297
12.12 Schematic floor plan of St. Paul's, Rome 297
12.13 *Christ Teaching the Apostles in Heavenly Jerusalem* 298
12.14 *Abraham and the Celestial Visitors* 298
12.15 *The Good Shepherd,* tomb of Galla Placidia 299
12.16 Interior, Church of Sant' Apollinare Nuovo, Ravenna 299
12.17 San Vitale, Ravenna 300
12.18 *Christ Pantocrater* 301
12.19 Anthemius of Tralles and Isodorus of Miletos, Hagia Sophia 301
12.20 Interior of Hagia Sophia 302
12.21 Greek Orthodox church, Naxos, Greece 302
12.22 St. Mark's, Venice (aerial view) 302
12.23 *Crucifixion* 303
13.1 Aigues-Mortes, France 311
13.2 Inside the walls, Carcassonne, France 311
13.3 Aachen, Germany 312

14.1   Boethius, "Music and Her Attendants" 339
14.2   "King David Playing Harp" 350
14.3   Florentine School, *Allegorical Portrait of Dante* 371
15.1   Koca Sinan, Suleymaniye Camii Mosque, Istanbul 408
15.2   Ceiling designs, Suleymaniye Camii Mosque 408
15.3   Courtyard, El Attarin Medersa, Fez, Morocco 408
15.4   Interior, The Great Mosque, Cordoba, Spain 409
15.5   Portal, Great Mosque, Cordoba 409
15.6   Court of the Lions, The Alhambra, Granada, Spain 409
15.7   National Mosque, Kuala Lumpur, Malaysia 410
15.8   "Cross Page," *Lindisfarne Gospels* 410
15.9   "XPI Page," *Book of Kells* 411
15.10   Odo of Metz, Palatine Chapel of Charlemagne 411
15.11   Germigny des Pres, view from east 412
15.12   Interior, Germigny des Pres 412
15.13   "St. Mark," from *Gospel Book of Archbishop Ebbo of Reims* 412
15.14   Interior, St. Martin du Canigou 413
15.15   St.-Benoit-sur-Loire 413
15.16   Capitals and piers, St.-Benoit-sur-Loire 414
15.17   "Flight to Egypt" capital, St.-Benoit-sur-Loire 414
15.18   Choir, St.-Benoit-sur-Loire 414
15.19   Collegiate Church of St. Sernin, Toulouse, France 414
15.20   Nave, St. Sernin 415
15.21   Plan of St. Sernin 415
15.22   West facade, Abbey of Jumièges 415
15.23   St. Etienne, Caen, France 415
15.24   "The Battle Rages," from Bayeux Tapestry 416
15.25   *Mission of the Apostles,* Ste-Madeleine, Vézelay 416
15.26   Nave, Ste.-Madeleine, Vézelay 417
15.27   Schematic drawing of a cross-vault 417
15.28   "The Prophet," Abbey Church of St. Pierre 417
15.29   Busketus, Pisa Cathedral and Campanile 418
15.30   Pisa Cathedral with Baptistery 418
15.31   Benedetto Antelami, *Descent from the Cross* 419
15.32   Mont St. Michel, aerial view 419
15.33   Choir and ambulatory, Abbey Church of St. Denis 420
15.34   Schematic drawings of Romanesque and Gothic arch thrusts 420
15.35   Cross vault of arches of an oblong bay 420
15.36   West facade, Notre Dame, Paris 421
15.37   Apse with flying buttresses, Notre Dame, Paris 421
15.38   West facade, Chartres Cathedral 421
15.39   Central doorway, Royal Portal, Chartres Cathedral 422
15.40   Choir, Notre Dame of Chartres 422
15.41   West facade, Cathedral of Notre Dame of Amiens 423
15.42   Nave, Cathedral of Notre Dame of Amiens 423
15.43   Sainte Chapelle, Paris 424
15.44   Interior, Sainte Chapelle, Paris 424
15.45   Choir of Beauvais Cathedral, aerial view 424
15.46   Nave, Canterbury Cathedral 425
15.47   Giovanni Pisano, Facade, Cathedral of Siena 425
15.48   Cimabue, *Madonna Enthroned* 426
15.49   Giotto, *Madonna Enthroned* 427
15.50   Duccio, *Rucellai Madonna* 427
16.1   "King David as Organist and Pope Gregory the Great" 430
16.2   Guido d'Arezzo 430
16.3   *The Hortus Deliciarum* 433
16.4   "Machaut Receiving Honors of Royalty and Clergy" 439

Preface

This is a text for the integrated humanities: the arts of literature, painting, music, sculpture, and architecture, and the discipline of philosophy. Though not an "art" in the strictest sense, philosophical ideas so consistently permeate each of the arts that theories of major philosophers are, of necessity, interwoven throughout the book. The components of the humanities—philosophy and the arts—are presented not as separate technical disciplines but as interrelated manifestations of human creativity. This is, therefore, a book about people and about "art's eternal victory over the human situation" (André Malraux).

In order to better understand why we are the way we are, we have centered our studies on our cultural heritage, from ancient Greece to the present day. For a better comprehension of the great sweep of Western civilization, the text has been divided into eight units.

Volume 1

1   Prologue: The Integrated Humanities
    1   *Human Values and Personal Freedom*
    2   *A Common Basis for Understanding the Arts*
    3   *An Introduction to Music Listening*

2   Greece: The First Humanistic Culture
    4   *Early Greece: Preparation for the Good Life*
    5   *Hellenic Athens: The Fulfillment of the Good Life*
    6   *Greece: From Hellenic to Hellenistic World*
    7   *Greek Art: Gods, Temples, and the Greeks*
    8   *Greek Music: Music in Greek Life and Thought*

3   Rome: The International Culture
    9   *A Thousand Years of Rome*
    10 *Roman Art and Music: The Arts of Megalopolis*

4   Judaism and Christianity: The Star and the Cross
    11 *Faith, Hope, and Love: The Judeo-Christian Tradition*
    12 *The Beginning of Christian Art*

5   The Age of Faith
      13   *Building Medieval Walls*
      14   *The Late Middle Ages: Expansion and Synthesis*
      15   *The Medieval Synthesis in Art*
      16   *Medieval Music: Sacred and Secular*

Volume 2

6   The Renaissance, 1350–1600
      17   *New Ideas and Discoveries Result from a New Way of Looking at the World*
      18   *Renaissance Art: A New Golden Age*
      19   *Renaissance Music: Court and Church*
      20   *Shadow and Substance: Literary Insights into the Renaissance*

7   The Early Modern World, 1600–1789
      21   *Science, Reason and Absolutism*
      22   *Art: Baroque, Rococo, Neoclassic*
      23   *Music: Baroque, Rococo, Classical*

8   The Middle Modern World, 1789–1914
      24   *Revolution, Romanticism, Reason*
      25   *Romanticism in Music*
      26   *Nineteenth-Century Art: Conflict and Diversity*

9   The Twentieth Century
      27   *Things Fall Apart: The Center Cannot Hold*
      28   *Ideas and Conflicts That Motivate the Twentieth Century*
      29   *Twentieth-Century Art: Shock Waves and Reactions*
      30   *Modern Music*
      31   *Twentieth-Century Literature*

Throughout the book the accomplishments of the past are considered not as museum pieces but as living evidence of enduring responses to the perplexities of life. These achievements have become, in our day, a basic part of our attempts to make sense of the universe.

Because artists naturally respond to the issues of their own time, each unit is prefaced by an overview of the social, scientific, religious, and philosophical climate of the period. Forming the core of these volumes are primary sources, the artworks themselves, many complete works rather than bits and pieces: plays, poetry, short stories, entire sections of large works, hundreds of art illustrations (many in color), and numerous musical examples. Introduced with appropriate commentary, the selections are followed by practical exercises and questions. Additionally, there are maps, graphs, time charts, record lists, and annotated bibliographies, and at the end of each volume, there is a glossary of important terms in philosophy and the arts. An Instructor's Manual is available, highlighting key points and including many supplementary materials: slides, sound filmstrips, sound slidesets, and films. There is more than enough material for a two-semester course based entirely on the book, or the book can be used as a central text embellished by other primary sources.

Since publication of the first edition in 1948, our text has gone through many changes and a whole generation of students and teachers. The framework remains intact; however, some of the parts have changed. While retaining the complete tragedies of Aeschylus *(Agamemnon, Eumenides),* Sophokles *(Oedipus Rex),* and Euripides *(The Trojan Women),* we have added the powerful *The Bacchae* by Euripides (also complete). Other new additions include several selections from Plato's *Republic,* his complete *Apology,* and Aristotle's *Poetics.*

Enlarging our view of Rome's contributions to our culture, we have added "Scipio's Dream" by Cicero and Virgil's *Eclogue IV* and Book VI from *The Aeneid*. We have retained the selections from Lucretius, Catullus, Horace, Ovid, Martial, Epictetus, Marcus Aurelius, Juvenal, and Lucian.

We have broadened our range of selections from the Old and New Testaments, and increased our emphasis on the development of both Judaism and Christianity. In the medieval selections the religious view is provided by art, music, *Everyman*, and Dante's *Inferno*. The secular orientation includes art, music, an added selection from *Beowulf*, the complete *Aucassin and Nicolette*, and the "Prolog" (prefaced by some lines in Middle English) and "Reeve's Tale" from *The Canterbury Tales*. We have added the "Rules of Love" from *The Art of Courtly Love* and retained some complete selections from Malory's *The Morte Darthur*.

In the music chapters technicalities have been pared to a minimum, and appropriate illustrations of sculpture, vase paintings, and illuminated manuscripts have been added. Broadening our treatment of music, we have included some lyric poetry by Sappho and by troubadour poet-musicians like William IX of Aquitaine; Bernart de Ventadorn; and Beatriz, Countess of Dia.

The art chapters have been completely rewritten and now include Greek vases, some Islamic art, and many more illustrations. In reorganizing these chapters, our primary concern has been the overall evolution of artistic styles. No longer are sculpture, painting, and architecture treated as separate categories; rather, artworks are considered chronologically as reflections of an overall cultural evolution. As with literature and music, art is presented as an interrelated component of the integrated humanities.

No longer confined to the art chapters, illustrations are used throughout to point up the text and to help clarify some issues. All in all, this is a broader and richer version of *The Search for Personal Freedom*.

Acknowledgments

This book could not have been written without the patience, forebearance, and expert editorial assistance of Katy Lamm.

We also wish to thank the following professors whose careful reading of the manuscript proved invaluable for this seventh edition.

Lee Ball, Jr.
Southeastern Oklahoma State University

Robert H. Canary
University of Wisconsin–Parkside

Ralph D. Cole
Northeastern Oklahoma A&M College

Charles Davis
Boise State University

Michael A. Jacobsen
University of Georgia, Athens

Katherine Zapantis Keller
Pasco–Hernando Community College

Richard W. Leach
Lakeland College

Carol A. Martin
Boise State University

James V. Mehl
Missouri Western State College

Phil Mullins
Missouri Western State College

William A. Vincent
Michigan State University

Frederick W. Westphal
California State University, Sacramento

Unit **1**

Prologue
The Integrated Humanities

1

Introduction: Human Values and Personal Freedom

> Today, all the normal mischances of living have been multiplied, a million-fold, by the potentialities for destruction, for an unthinking act of collective suicide, which man's very triumphs in science and invention have brought about. In this situation the artist has a special task and duty: the task of reminding men of their humanity and the promise of their creativity.[1]
>
> Lewis Mumford

In Spain and in the modest mountains of southwestern France are numerous caves decorated with paintings that date from the late Old Stone (Paleolithic) Age (ca. 20,000–10,000 B.C.). In the caves of Lascaux there is, for example, a large chamber whose lofty ceiling is covered with paintings of antelope, horses, bulls, and other animals. Too deep and dark for human habitation, this may have been a sanctuary for religious rites or a setting for ritualistic magic to assure successful hunting, but no one knows for sure. No one knows the intentions of the people who created these images, but there is no question about what these people were. They were artists. Using intellect and imagination, late Paleolithic people had invented representation, a momentous step in the evolution of culture.

The invention of art symbolized major changes in the lives of people no longer at the mercy of the elements. Working together and planning ahead ("marking time") for seasonal changes, they hunted and gathered at optimum times and stored food for the long winters. It is now believed that they devoted as little as fifteen to twenty hours a week to the necessities of existence. There was time left over to make more efficient weapons and warmer clothing, to carve ivory and wood, to play, and to decorate cave sanctuaries. Late Paleolithic clans had created what every society must have if it is to advance its culture: free and unstructured time.

---

1. Lewis Mumford, *In the Name of Sanity* (New York: Harcourt, Brace, 1954), p. 141.

Figure 1.1 Bull, ceiling painting, 18′ long, caves of Lascaux near Montignac, France, ca. 12,000 B.C.

The creation of art also signified the emergence of individual artists. Lugging materials down through winding cave passages and erecting a scaffolding were undoubtedly communal efforts, but the artwork was done by an individual. That person, the artist, climbed atop the platform and painted a bull (fig. 1.1) in sweeping, confident lines, elegantly capturing a sense of life and communicating the illusion of powerful motion. In today's high-tech, nuclear-threatened world, the art of Lascaux is a poignant reminder of our kinship with Stone Age artists who, along with a multitude of successors, inspire us to recall our humanity, our intellect and imagination, our creative potential for a better life.

It is because everyone is capable of living a more rewarding life that we study the humanities. From cave art to the present the arts and ideas of humans are beacons of hope, truth, and beauty for a world that needs to pay far more attention to the humanities, to the arts that teach us "nothing except the significance of life" (Henry Miller). In our integrated approach to the humanities, we study literature, painting, music, sculpture, philosophy, and architecture not as separate disciplines but as interrelated manifestations of human creativity. Nor do we study the arts and artists in isolation. Artists are individuals, coping with the stress and strain of everyday life and, perhaps more than other people, influenced by the ideas and values of their society. "Artists are," observed composer Ned Rorem, "like everyone else, only more so."

The humanities engage our intellect, our intuitions, and our emotions. Concerned with human values and the universal need of people to express themselves, they take us on a voyage of discovery. They not only widen our vision and provide insights into the human condition but they also fill us with wonder and delight. They take the materials of earthly existence and reach for the stars. History tells us, in varying degrees, what happened in past ages, but the humanities are individual creations that have outlasted the ages that produced them. Belonging as much to our world as to ancient Athens, Renaissance Florence, or Victorian London, the finest expressions of the human spirit continue to inform and to inspire.

This is a book about the present, the here and now. Only our imagination can take us backwards in time, back to the origins of our cultural heritage in ancient Greece and all the accomplishments since that Golden Age. We study past achievements not as museum pieces but as living evidence of enduring responses to the perplexities of life. In our own day this priceless legacy becomes a basic part of our attempts to make sense of the universe and of our own lives.

In the final analysis, our studies are intended to develop an understanding of cultural diversity as well as cultural achievements. Exposure to a variety of arts and ideas is but the first step towards a lifelong appreciation of the joy, beauty, and artistic truth that are inherent in all the arts. Only the beginning of an open-ended study of human creativity, the humanities are an indispensable part of a liberal, and liberating, education. Equipped with an understanding of some of the accomplishments of Western culture that shape the way we live today, students can begin to realize their full potential as human beings and to shape their own personal freedom.

Using This Book

This book has at least two purposes: (1) to help the student begin to find personal freedom and (2) to help construct a new society with an emphasis on human and life-giving values rather than materialistic and repressive ones. Fortunately, both can be approached through the arts and philosophy, for they are the means to discover human experience and yield new meanings for that experience and new significance for life itself.

First, what do we mean by personal freedom? A very simple analogy may help make this idea clear. One may consider the person first learning to swim and the expert swimmer. The learner does a tremendous amount of splashing and gets almost nowhere. The expert moves through the water with a minimum of disturbance, makes it look easy, and gets to the destination. So the person with a measure of freedom moves through life knowingly, arriving at predetermined goals with a minimum of disturbance.

The freedom we are talking about is not conditioned absolutely by political, social, and economic surroundings, although such factors may help or hinder a person. One can imagine a political prisoner in Siberia whose knowledge and personal values allow a free and independent spirit in the most squalid of surroundings. The prisoner's goals are not those of going somewhere, or of getting some material thing, but of being a particular person. The movement of the person toward Being measures an approach toward the personal freedom of which we are talking.

A person can come to self-knowledge, can establish an ever-expanding personal philosophy and value system, and can know much of life through the arts.

Of course, direct experience with all of life might be better, but waiting for enough immediate sensation would take forever.

Chapter 2 will discuss the personal humanistic value of literature, music, and the visual arts in more detail. The sincere artist confronts great problems of human experience, explores them, cuts away the irrelevancies that confuse us in direct experience, and leads us to new meanings. The greatest artists often present us with visible symbols of the highest human levels of Being or meaning as in Michelangelo's statue of *David,* the Parthenon, or Dante's *Divine Comedy.* Individuals, who make these meanings and these exaltations of the spirit a part of themselves, can make more discriminating value judgments and are on the way in the search for personal freedom.

In approaching the second goal of this book, building a culture based on human values, one needs to know how a culture is built. Philosophers of history have found many patterns that seem to account for the growth, flowering, and decay of civilizations. In this book we are using a modified and simplified form of the *culture-epoch theory* as a framework upon which to arrange our materials. This theory is neither more nor less "true" than any of a half-dozen other theories that attempt to account for changes throughout the recorded story of mankind.

According to the culture-epoch theory, a culture is founded upon whatever conception of reality is held by the great majority of people over a considerable period of time. This is true even though the majority may not be aware of any concept of reality or, more probably take it so much for granted that they are not aware it is simply a human idea, held on faith. Thus, for most people at the time this is written, a typewriter is real, a physical tree is real, and all things which can be seen, heard, smelled, felt, or tasted are real.

As a matter of fact, a number of scientists, philosophers, and religious thinkers have given us different concepts of reality, which have also been widely held. These thinkers have contemplated the millions of forms of life, many of them bearing resemblances to others, yet each one different; they have examined the forms of earth, air, fire, and water; they have wondered about the processes of change by which a tree today may, at some time in the future, disintegrate into earth and reappear in some totally alien form. They have watched such nontangible things as sunlight and air becoming leaf and branch. Pondering these things, they come inevitably to the ultimate question: "What is the nature of reality?"

To reach an answer, they usually focus on a few profound inquiries, some of which may be given here. For example, they might say, "We see change all around us. We see grass eaten and turn into cow. We see cow eaten and turn into human. We see humans disintegrate and turn into earth. If all these changes can take place, what are the universal elements of which all things are composed?" Or they might say, "We see an individual human, John Doe, as baby, as youth, as adult, as senile old man, as corpse. From one moment to the next, he is never the same. Yet he is always the same, John Doe, a distinct being. Can it be that nothing is permanent, that reality is a process rather than a thing or group of things? If we have change, then, how does the process take place? And more important, we know that we live in a world of constant change, but what force directs the process?"

"Nonsense," retorts another group of thinkers. "That which is in a constant state of flow cannot be real. Only that which is permanent and unchanging can be real. What, then, in the universe is permanent, unchanging in itself, yet is able to transform itself, manifest itself, or produce from itself the countless forms we see around us?"

These are some of the basic questions the pure thinker contemplates. The answers are various concepts of reality.

Based upon the idea of reality accepted as "true," specialized thinkers build different thought-structures that underlie visible institutions. These include a philosophy of justice from which particular forms of law and government spring; a philosophy of education that dictates the nature of our schools and the material taught in them; a religious philosophy that becomes apparent in churches and creeds; and an economic philosophy that yields its particular ways of producing and distributing goods and services, including the token-systems used as money. Other philosophies and institutions could be named, but these are some that greatly affect our daily living.

When these are formed, we have a complete culture, but always by the time such a pattern is established, we have forces at work that tend to destroy it. The destroyers are new pure thinkers who note inconsistencies within the idea of reality itself, and who question postulates or find contradictions.

From these new thinkers (philosophers, scientists, theologians) comes a new idea of reality so convincing it cannot be brushed aside. It must be accepted. Suddenly the whole structure of the culture finds itself without foundation. The justice and the law appropriate in the old culture no longer fit on the new foundation; the old education is no longer appropriate; old religious beliefs no longer describe a person's position in relation to God; old ways of making things and distributing them no longer suffice.

At this time people are plunged into a *period of chaos,* the first step in the formation of a new epoch.

The symptoms of the period of chaos lie around us now in such profusion that they scarcely need description. In the latter part of the twentieth century this is where we live. New and shocking ideas, moralities, and beliefs are introduced and discarded; terrorists attack established governments; civil strife and wars of conquest rage; everyone damages the environment; and over everything looms the menace of nuclear obliteration. At the mercy of events beyond their control, some people try to turn back the clock to better, more peaceful days; others seek refuge and security in fundamentalist beliefs; still others retreat to paramilitary armed camps; many just mindlessly camp in front of their television sets, perhaps hoping that all of the problems will somehow vanish. In other words, we see in the late twentieth century a period of chaos that, nevertheless, gives some evidence of resolution.

Out of the turmoil and confusion of chaotic periods of past cultures emerges the *period of adjustment.* At this point, notable artists—whether painters, writers, sculptors, composers, or creators in some other medium—make their important contributions to society. Pheidias and Sokrates of ancient Athens; the master builders of the celebrated Gothic churches; Michelangelo, Beethoven, Goethe—these innovators begin to suggest the new line, shape, and pattern for a new culture.

Two ideas need to be stressed about the role of the artist in the development of a cultural pattern. First, the artist does not necessarily know all about new ideas of reality. For example, the artist in our time does not necessarily know all about Einstein's theory. The artist is simply a person of greater sensitivity than others, and with great skill in one medium. As a sensitive person, the artist probably feels more keenly than the rest of us the tensions of the time—the pulls of this belief and the pulls of another contradictory one. An artist will not rest until he or she has explored this confusing experience and discovered some meaning, some significance, therein. The great artist is always the composer (whether musician, writer, painter, choreographer, architect, or sculptor), the person who puts things together in new relationships and finds new meanings for experience.

A second idea about the artist's contribution to the formation of a cultural pattern is the important role of structure, rather than subject matter, conveying cultural meaning. For example, one may compare the structure of an Egyptian temple (see fig. 7.7) with that of the Parthenon in Athens (see fig. 7.42). The subject matter of both is roughly the same—they are temples built for the worship of a god. But what a difference! The Temple of Amon is enormous, both overpowering and intimidating, reflecting the total control of the populace by the pharaoh and a permanent priesthood. The temple of Athena, the Parthenon, is serene, rational, and exquisitely proportioned. Decorated with sculptured reliefs depicting gods *and* Greek citizens, it is a structure erected by the citizens of a democratic society in which there is no resident priesthood.

It comes down to this: styles in beauty change as the basic characteristics of people change. Or perhaps it works the other way; perhaps as new glimpses of beauty are caught by the artists, people themselves change to conform to the new beauty.

However it may happen, the artist, especially in the period of chaos and early in the period of adjustment within a culture-epoch, personally feels the stresses, tensions, and turmoil of the period. The artist explores conflicts within, which are the conflicts of the general population as well, and creates new structures, new designs, to synthesize the elements of conflict and to give new meaning to experience. Some works of art, probably depending upon the individual artist's breadth of vision and ability to compose insight into significance, are seized upon as symbols of new pattern and new truth in society. They express the new idea of beauty and truth.

At this point another element of the population—we may call them the *intellectuals*—enters the picture. They are people like ourselves, college students and faculty members, government officials, ministers, business executives, and many others who think seriously about things and who, like the artists, have been troubled by the conflict of their times. They still are working within the period of adjustment in an epoch. They become aware of new meanings and patterns produced by the artists, and they start reshaping these designs into new philosophies of justice, of economics, of religion, and the like, and begin to build concrete institutions out of the philosophies that they have created. Through their work, order slowly emerges out of chaos.

When their work is finished, we come to the third period within a culture-epoch, the *period of balance.* At this point, the idea of reality, the philosophies that underlie our basic institutions, and the institutions themselves are all in harmony. Early in a period of balance, life must be very satisfying; everyone must know the reason for getting up in the morning to face the day. But if balance lasts too long, life begins to get dull. The big jobs seem to be done, and decadence, boredom, and deterioration may set in. The long and painful decline of the Roman Empire was just such a period.

But change comes inevitably. At the beginning of the twentieth century, physicists were assuring young scientists that the great discoveries in physics had all been made and that only little tidying-up jobs remained. At the same time, Einstein was beginning his work, which was to supersede all our knowledge in physics. Just when people have been certain of everything in their periods of balance, new pure thinkers come along to upset the whole apple cart into a new epoch.

A word of caution should be appended here. This systematic description of an epoch makes it sound as if artists only function in a time of chaos or adjustment, or as if philosophers quit philosophizing until their proper time comes around. This, of course, is not true. While the epoch does divide itself into three rough periods, all of the functions occur with greater or lesser impact throughout the entire time period.

In this book, the various periods of history will be treated in the following way: The rise of Athenian democracy in the fifth century B.C. and its rapid decline will be treated as one culture-epoch. The Roman period from the time of the rule of Julius Caesar will be regarded as an attempt to maintain rationalistic Greek times, under law, and backed by strong military authority. It does not constitute an epoch of the type we have been describing. Because of their far-reaching importance, Judaism and Christianity will be treated separately, though inadequately because of limited space. Actually the teachings of Jesus represent the work of the pure thinker, and the Christian concept of God was a new concept of reality that served as the foundation for the Middle Ages. The Middle Ages, dating from about A.D. 450 to 1350 will be considered as a complete epoch. The time period from 1350 to the early twentieth century really constitutes another epoch, with the Renaissance as a large segment of the period of chaos within it. Because the Renaissance, using the approximate dates of 1350 to 1600, presents so much of interest for the student of humanities, however, it will be treated as a separate time period. Then, with the clash of rationalism and romanticism and the final emergence of the Faustian man, we will consider the period from about 1600 to the early twentieth century as a complete epoch. The last unit of this book will look as carefully as possible at the cultural changes with which we in the twentieth century are so deeply involved.

Summary

The humanities are the arts of literature, painting, music, sculpture, architecture, and dance, and the discipline of philosophy that permeates all of the arts and finally unites them all. As set forth in chapter 2, the arts, taken together, are a separate field of human knowledge with their own area of exploration and discovery, and with a method of their own. So these volumes will concentrate on the great artistic production of each of the time periods outlined above. Each unit is planned to give a chapter or two to the social, scientific, religious, and philosophic climate of the period in which the artists were working, for the artists usually accept the scientific and social world-picture of their time. Following these introductory discussions, direct attention is given to the arts themselves, with enough examples of each to reveal new answers to the great questions of mankind, new patterns, structures, and meaning the artists found for life in their time. By this treatment, the student will be able to trace the development and changes through history of the problems that plague us so sorely in our own time. Equipped with knowledge of the great answers found in the past that shape the way we live today, having come to know the exalted expressions of humanity revealed at their fullest, students can work to develop their own freedom and assist in the building of a new culture based on a combination of human values and the Greek ideals of *kalos k'agathos:* beauty and goodness.

This idea of discoveries by Shakespeare or any other artist can give us a basis for understanding the arts. In this respect, as Jean Cocteau observed, "art is science in the flesh."

Generally we can think of scientific knowledge and artistic truth in this way: The physical sciences explore the world outside humankind; the social sciences make discoveries about the behavior and activities of people in various groups; and the arts and humanities probe the area of inner meaning: humanity's fears, hopes, loves, delights as the individual and society act and react within their world. "All art is social," as James Adams noted, "because it is the result of a relationship between an artist and his time." Art is also exploration, and the discoveries artists make are expressed as *concepts* and *percepts.* Concepts are ideas that cannot be seen, like friendship, beauty, and justice. Percepts are what we perceive with our senses: line, taste, color, aroma, volume, pitch, and so forth. Artists express concepts by the unique manner in which they choose to arrange the percepts, that is, the sense-apparent objects and materials. Obviously this kind of vivid creativity can never be done by committee: "Art is the most intense mode of individualism that the world has known" (Oscar Wilde).

Because of differences in media and modes of expression, the arts differ from each other in many ways. Certainly a *time-art* such as music, which exists only as long as it is heard, differs from a *space-art* such as painting, which uses visual symbols as its means of expression. Both arts are separated from literature, a *word-art* that must be interpreted by the reader. The differences between Beethoven's Fifth Symphony, the *Mona Lisa,* and *Hamlet* are certainly obvious; what is not so obvious are their similarities. "Painting," wrote Emerson, "was called 'silent poetry,' and poetry 'speaking painting.' The laws of each art are convertible into the laws of any other." The common basis of all the arts is the exploration by means of sensory percepts into the emotion, the mind, the personality of humans; their common goal is to speak directly to our inner being. As Emerson also wrote: "Raphael paints wisdom; Handel sings it, Pheidias carves it, Shakespeare writes it." An examination of this common basis is the purpose of this chapter.

The artist deals subjectively with all materials as he or she draws upon a special store of personal experience. Moreover, artistic production depends as much upon the background and personality of the artist as it does upon the raw material of experience. It follows therefore that each artist is unique, an individual different from all other persons, and that the artist's production is equally unique. One might take, for example, the treatment two literary artists make of the same theme, the emptiness of the life of a woman who, in herself, is virtually a complete blank, but who moves from man to man, living only as a reflection of each man. Read Dorothy Parker's story, "Big Blonde," and Anton Chekov's story, "The Darling" (filmed as *Darling,* starring Julie Christie). Although the experience is the "same" in both stories, the end result is quite different, and the experience of the reader is also very different, while reacting to the general idea in two different forms. The reader might protest, "But one of them must be right about this kind of person and one of them must be wrong." Actually both Parker and Chekov are right, and any other artist who treated the same material with a different insight might also be right. The discovery of multiple truths is a personal matter and the corollary is that the realm of truth in personality, that prime area where the arts are focused, is inexhaustible. The person who understands any work of art grows with each facet of experience shared with the artist. In other words, our boundaries are expanded as we add the artist's experience to our own, thereby increasing the data in our own personal computer bank. Gabriel Marcel expressed a similar idea:

> Thanks to art, instead of seeing one world, our own, we see it multiplied and, as many original artists as there are, so many worlds are at our disposal.

Not always recognized is the fact that the artists in literature, painting, sculpture, music, and the other arts have a method of investigation in their field of knowledge that we may call the method of intuition or insight. In much the same way that scientists start out, artists become aware of a problem in the realm of human experience, or they sense some aspect of the human personality that is dark and unknown. Put more simply, they feel the need to create, and this compulsion is the first step in the artistic method. As a second step, they begin to gather materials, both conceptual (idea-stuff) and perceptual (physical-stuff: visual images, sequences of sound, etc.). The third step is the appropriate arrangement of materials, which comes as an insight or an intuitive perception of new and varied relationships among the materials with which they are working. Since artists are dealing with a problem of relationships, the truth they seek takes the shape of arranging materials in proper order with respect to each other. In other words, the form (arrangement and relationship) is a very necessary part of artistic truth; this form involves the arrangement of incident, character, or images in literature, of visual elements in painting or sculpture, of sounds or themes in musical composition so that they arrive at the point that artists have felt by insight. In other words, this is the step we call *composition,* a term that is common to all of the arts. From this step the art-object emerges—a song, a pot, a picture, a poem—which has both an aesthetic and a utilitarian function in the world (and frequently the best of the utilitarian productions have a very high degree of aesthetic value). But how can artists check results of their exploration? That is the job of the members of their audience. After the composition, artists turn their creations loose in the world. Many people examine these creations, both in terms of subject and explicit meaning, and in terms of the form in which they are presented. If an artwork is composed in such a way that the members of the audience *live through* the experience themselves and find that the artist has made a true statement of the experience in all of its relationships, then the discovery of the artist is accepted as a truth wrested from the dark ignorance of the human condition in the world. Two of the tests that might be applied are these: First, is it new? If the meaning (a combination of idea and formal structure) is old and trite, the artwork may be comfortable, but not of much artistic value. Second, is the emotional content proper for the subject? If the treatment is sentimentalized, then it is probable that the artist lacked either sincerity or a steady view of life.

One caution: The test of artistic truth cannot be made by the general public, although their criticism may be valuable. Scientists, for example, would not allow the validity of their conclusions to be tested by a plumber, a cab driver, and a meat cutter. They ask that these truths be tested by the experiments of scientists who are their equal in scientific knowledge. There is a little difference between scientists and artists, but the difference is not too marked. We could argue that since the butcher, the baker, and the candlestick maker are human personalities, they might be accepted as valid critics of the artist's discovery. To a certain extent this claim is true. On the other hand, certain people can read with more discernment than others. Some are excellent at understanding the language and symbolism of painting, sculpture, or music. Perhaps more important, some people are more sensitive than others to the problems of personality and experience. These people, those who can understand the medium of expression and who are sensitive to human problems, must constitute the group of judges for the validity of a work of art.

The next question for consideration is the nature of the raw materials for artistic investigation. These are sometimes hard to see. Most obvious are the many facets of such emotions as love, hatred, jealousy, contentment, sudden apprehension of the beauty in nature or people, and other emotional reactions. As a matter of fact, these materials from life are so common that it is probable that the great bulk of art is made from them, but there is much more material that has been explored in literature, art, and music. Artists present their explorations as experience that the members of the artistic audience may live through. Take, for example, the psychological experience confronting a young prince who has been humanely educated, who faces a problem of evil involving the murder of his father, the king, and the unfaithfulness, even incest, of his mother. (In other words, the problem Shakespeare explored in *Hamlet.*) The artist feels this problem within himself and composes its elements and its solution. Psychology and literature often run parallel to each other; the former gives facts, the latter gives truth-to-life. This truth is achieved because we become personally involved in the work of literature, live through the complexities of the problem with all their attendant, opposing emotions, and sense the logic, the rightness, and the freedom of the solution when it is reached.

Perhaps one more consideration is necessary before we turn to examples of the explorations and discoveries of the artists. This consideration is that of the place and importance of form. Let us put it this way: human experience is seldom simple or direct. Rather, its importance is usually clouded with events of no importance, many of which are totally irrelevant. Perhaps the best illustration of this may be found in the artist who is painting a landscape. The artist's purpose is not to make a direct copy from nature—a camera might provide a more exact representation than a human being. Rather, the painter is seeking to interpret an experience with beauty. The natural scene, however, is cluttered with objects detracting from the impression the artist seeks. Consequently, the artist leaves many out, rearranges them mentally, and paints on canvas the objects that individual sees, so that the picture, when complete, is not a copy of nature, but a picture of beauty, with the natural objects selected and arranged to make the meaning clear. But no critic, nor commentator, perhaps not even the artist, could give us a definite, final statement as to what that "meaning" is. Perhaps it is a sense of the importance of peace, quiet, repose; perhaps it is the wonder of organization, order, design; perhaps it is the sheer joy of contrasting colors, the delight in appearances of objects, their texture and feel; perhaps the pleasure of a thing of beauty. If it could be expressed definitely in words, the picture would not be necessary, but since it cannot, it is the only means by which the artist can share a delight in the world. And the imperative need to share it, to get it "said," is the quality that makes artists; they not only do what they can, but what they must. Somehow, that creative urge, which everyone shares to some extent, is communicated to an audience; theorists of "aesthetic experience" do not agree on the "how," but something does happen. However little understood the process, the fact remains that people throughout the years have enjoyed (the word is too weak: they have *needed*) the making of pictures and the looking at them.

It is interesting that it is this element of form that all of the arts have in common, and it is this that gives them the "living-through" quality we have noted as distinctive of artistic truth. It is the process, not the end result, that is important. It is the form, not the final statement, that yields artistic truth, though this does not imply that the artist's final point is unimportant. The important thing is having gone through the experience with the artist and arriving at the discovery the artist wishes to communicate.

With this in mind, we are going to examine some examples of art in different mediums to see how the various artists have mined some truth from the darkness and chaos of the experiences of the human personality.

Every art form has much in common with other forms but each also has its own symbols, images, and materials, all used in ways that are unique for each medium. Written or spoken references to a painting, for example, are translations. If, as Gertrude Stein has written, "a rose is a rose is a rose," so also a painting is a painting is a painting. The mixture of paints on the canvas *is* the message; all else is translation in one way or another. "An artist cannot speak about his art," remarked Jean Cocteau, "any more than a plant can discuss horticulture." The literary arts resist translation just as obstinately as do the visual arts. Whether the poet, for example, uses familiar word sets ("Come live with me and be my love") or unconventional combinations ("love is more thicker than forget"), the exact arrangement of the precise words is what the poet has to say and nothing else, or the poet would have said that instead. In both arts a single work may have several levels of meaning, ranging deeper and deeper from the surface meaning, and lookers and readers can uncover greater depths of significance as they work through the symbols created by the artist. In both arts the interpretations are somewhat personal, depending upon the critical ability and background of the reader or the viewer. The response, however, *must be* within the limits set by the artist. In the arts, as in most other things, we can always arrive at some very mistaken interpretations.

Music amounts to pure form and is not amenable to any one "story" interpretation. Many untutored listeners have one of two responses to music. When they think they are listening perceptively they arrive at some sort of story, which usually sounds something like this: This person is in love, and then his girl leaves him, and right at the end she comes back and everything is just dandy. The other listening attitude is simply to be submerged in the sound, to, in other words, take a tonal bath. The latter listeners usually find their attention wandering off in a thousand directions before a musical selection of any length is finished. In other words, they find themselves thinking about everything but the music.

But music, except for program music, which has a story to tell in sound and sometimes employs sounds heard in everyday life (and the composer's "story" is not necessarily that of the listener), is, as said above, form in sound. It is a "time-art," which makes it particularly elusive, since by the time it is heard it is gone. For this reason we are devoting a special chapter to an introduction to music. Music makes greater demands on its audience, both in knowledge and attention, than do any of the other arts. The knowledgeable and attentive listener finds, however, that living through a musical selection yields as much meaning for life's experiences as do any of the other arts. In its structures one may find the grandeur of Bach, the elegance of Mozart, the serenity of Gregorian chant, or the sound of protest, which is sometimes characteristic of jazz. Whatever the significance of a piece of music, it is the composition that counts. As much as in any of the other arts, perhaps more, the composer must arrange materials so that the listener lives through an experience that lies deeper than words or the recognizable subject matter of painting. It is this process of composition that leads to "living through," our concern in this chapter, since it is the common basis for all the arts.

Examples from Literature

In order to see how this intricate interrelation of meaning and form is accomplished in literature, we can use some very simple illustrations for analysis. For example, a creative writing class once tried to make an "absolutely beautiful" line of poetry. This is what they came up with:

Rainy evening. Idle. Only music . . .

Most people would agree that this is a very pretty line. But what makes it so? You might ask yourself where the heavy accents fall. And then, what about the vowel sounds? Suddenly what appears at first to be only a nice lazy line begins to look like the work of a craftsman, for we discover that we are running down the long vowel sounds, exactly as they come in the alphabet *a, e, i, o, u,* and that these sounds occur exactly on the heavy accents. Now what about consonant sounds? The consonants are *r, n, v, ng, dl, l, m,* hard *c* (a *k* sound). We could have had *p, b, k, g,* and all the rest. Are the ones that appear in the line purely accidental choices? Not on your life. Except for the last *c,* all the consonants are *liquid* consonants. The term is self-explanatory; they flow along without creating much stoppage. Only the last one (the *c* in *music*) is of a different sort, and it is put there exactly because it *does* stop the line. We have here a line that doesn't "say" much in terms of making a declaration or asking a question, but it certainly creates a mood. And the mood is created because of a lot of hard work in choosing sounds carefully and distributing them in terms of accentuation.

As another example, a student in the same class wrote a five-line poem about the Cain and Abel story. Here are the first two lines:

Oh Cain, you slay in vain. You may not stay.
East of Eden, East of Eden, flee for. . . .

Notice not only the vowel music, but the change in rhythm between the first and second line. Using the same pattern, you might try to write the last three lines.

The examples given above are really only one-finger exercises in the craft of writing poetry. Now we can choose a complete poem for the same kind of analysis to see the intricate relationships of form that create a sum of meaning greater than the arithmetical addition of the meanings of the words themselves. We might choose A.E. Housman's deceptively simple, eight-line poem, "With Rue My Heart is Laden."

With rue my heart is laden
    For golden friends I had,
For many a rose-lipt maiden
    And many a light-foot lad.
By brooks too broad for leaping
    The lightfoot boys are laid;
The rose-lipt girls are sleeping
    In fields where roses fade.

Of course Housman is saying that he grieves for the friends of his youth, now dead. Where does one attack the *form* of a poem like this? You might ask yourself why he chose the word *boys* in the second stanza when he used *lads* in the first. Then examine the first line of the second stanza:

By *br*ooks too *br*oad for *l*eaping

Perhaps you begin to see that he chose *boys* in the second line to make an alliterative pattern with *brooks* and *broad*. What of the *l* in the first line of the second stanza? Suddenly one discovers that it forms a similar pattern with *lightfoot* and *laid* in the second line. In the first line of the second stanza we have two *b*s, one *l*; in the second line, two *l*s, one *b*. Is this purely accidental on the part of the composer? Try the last two lines of the first stanza, with its *m*s and *l*s. The same pattern reveals itself and, furthermore, the alliterative *l* of the first stanza carries over to repeat itself in the second stanza. In other words, the middle four lines of the poem form a unit by themselves, created by the alliterations.

But that's not all. Examine the rhymes: *laden, maiden; leaping, sleeping; had, lad; laid, fade.* The first four of the rhymes listed here (lines 1, 3, 5, 7 in the poem) are weak endings; that is, they end in a dropping-off syllable that gets almost no accent at all. The second group of rhymes (lines 2, 4, 6, 8 of the poem) are strong endings; they end sharply on the accented syllable. This is strengthened even further by Housman's use of end punctuation after the lines with strong endings. Reason? Look at the subject matter of the lines with weak endings and that of the lines with strong endings.

One more example, this time in prose, for it is easy to jump to the conclusion that poets take this much care with their sounds, but that prose writers do not have to. In a story by Wilbur Daniel Steele,[1] we find the following sentence:

> Accept as he would with the top of his brain the fact of a spherical earth zooming through space, deep in his heart he knew that the world lay flat from modern Illinois to ancient Palestine, and that the sky above it, blue by day and by night festooned with guiding stars for wise men, was the nether side of a floor on which the resurrected trod.

An unskilled writer tried to communicate the "same" meaning with the following sentence:

> Although he accepted in his mind the fact that the earth was a sphere travelling through space, yet in his deepest emotions he knew that it was flat and that the sky was the under-side of the floor of heaven.

Why, for example, does Steele say that the world "lay flat from modern Illinois to ancient Palestine" instead of simply saying that it was flat, as the other writer did? Perhaps he wanted to suggest an expanse of time, from the modern world back to the time of Christ, as well as an expanse of space. Why did he describe the sky as he did rather than plainly using the word *sky*, as the unskilled writer did? There is the possibility that while he was stating a fact about a person's belief concerning the physical structure of the earth he also wanted to suggest a religious significance to the belief. So he mentioned the stars and the wise men to flood our memories with the story of the birth of Christ. The two sentences differ in at least one more phase of meaning. The unskilled writer's sentence has no rhythm, while Steele's sentence reads in long undulations of sound. This kind of rhythm puts us in a philosophic frame of mind, which creates the kind of atmosphere he wanted. It is for such reasons that the author chose exactly the words he did, and arranged them as he did. For its purpose in the story it is a much better sentence than that of the unskilled writer.

An Example from Music

Music is sound moving in time, and therein lies its magical mystery. While listening to an unfamiliar piece of music, the listener does not know where the music is going until it gets there, that is, ceases to sound. From silence to sound to silence and what takes place in between is a mixture of sound and silence comprehended only in retrospect, after one musical section has followed upon another until silence reigns again. Readers can reread difficult passages in a book and art lovers can study a painting for hours, but music listeners have one ride on a merry-go-round. There is no way to stop the music or freeze a beautiful sound, even though some critics are fond of referring to architecture as "frozen music." Nothing is ever that simple.

Music is a structural art built out of a multiplicity of materials by the composer, who picks and chooses tones, colors, textures, rhythms, and patterns just as a writer selects words and phrases that best suit the purpose and the painter chooses lines and colors. Rarely are these infinite choices deliberately calculated or contrived, except in so-called "bad" art. The artist, each in his own way, is seeking expression, to communicate some feeling, truth, or emotion about experience as it is perceived.

Music is the envy of many artists because it is so abstract that it can never pretend to represent anything specific, or exactly portray one iota of the sensible world in which we live. Music is *free,* truly free, to soar to the heights or descend to the depths of intellectual-emotional experiences. This unfettered freedom is the constant delight of all good musicians and experienced nonmusicians (listeners). It is also the cause of utter despair of teachers and students who have yet to learn the basic skills and thus the joys of listening to music with some degree of understanding. Only after understanding can there be any real "appreciation," and this appreciation need not include approbation; many experienced listeners can understand and even appreciate music that they really do not enjoy. But then, how can people who are illiterate know whether or not they dislike a novel?

1. Wilbur Daniel Steele, "The Man Who Saw through Heaven," in *An Anthology of Famous American Stories,* ed. Angus Burrell and Bennett Cerf (New York: Modern Library, 1953).

Literacy in music is no more a common heritage of all humans than is the ability to read and write. To become a reasonably knowledgeable listener is not very difficult because the listener has only to learn to "read"; the "writing" is left to professional musicians. And what is there to read in music: notes, scales, intervals, keys, chords? Not at all; these are merely the "grammar" of music and not its content. The listener begins with the larger units of music, with its structure. In the fullness of time a certain minimal knowledge of musical grammar will fall into place within the overall picture of musical design. For example, the following musical phrase has a beginning and an incomplete and unsatisfying ending:

Ein feste Burg

However, when the next phrase is added we have the completion of a musical idea, even though it is something less than a complete composition:

The two phrases add up to a musical period or a relatively complete musical idea called, for convenience, letter *A*. Then, for purposes of balance, the period (or paired phrases) is repeated before proceeding to the next section (section *B*). This section retains the strong, stern character of the first section, but introduces several new ideas for contrast (phrases indicated by dotted lines):

Formal Structure: *Ein feste Burg*

Bar Form (A-A-B)

Some Examples from Painting

A common plaint among laypeople is that they cannot understand "modern art" and that they prefer "realistic" works, that is, painting and sculpture that tell a story, look like something, and are easy to understand. The sad truth is that most people have never learned to understand much of anything about any kind of art, are very vague as to what "realism" might be, do not know the story related in most figurative painting and sculpture (painting and sculpture presenting natural objects) and, if they do, are unaware that subject matter cannot make the art object beautiful, life-enhancing, or valuable by itself. Most painting, sculpture, and architecture *seem* to be easily understandable, but the qualities that make one work superior to another need to be learned, just as they must be learned in music and literature.

Some people refuse to take art seriously, being convinced that it is all a matter of taste. They fall back on that old bromide "There is no disputing taste." We answer, "Nuts." Taste is a learned, not innate, ability and all statements to the contrary are delusive and established in self-defense to soothe the ego. The vocabulary, subject matter, materials, and techniques of the visual arts cannot be reduced to the confines of this book, which serves a broader purpose. Nevertheless, imparting basic knowledge of the visual arts, stimulating aesthetic response, and encouraging further investigation into the arts are part of that purpose.

It is regrettable that in this century the words *beauty* and *beautiful* have taken on a narrow meaning for the general public, a meaning of prettiness and niceness, which makes the words *beauty* and *beautiful* incomprehensible to many people when they are applied to a highly abstract painting by Picasso; a nonobjective orgy of bright, explosive, and intermingling colors by Kandinsky; miles of earthwork constructions in the wilderness, or mounds of earthworks on the parquet floors of distinguished museums; and sculpture that moves, screeches, or destroys itself. For the moment, then, let us discard these words and investigate a fundamental term, *aesthetics*. A survey of dictionaries to discover the meaning of the word *aesthetics* generally will only add to the confusion, for the word usually is defined as a sense of beauty, love of beauty, or philosophy of beauty. It would seem that we are on a merry-go-round until we realize that the opposite of aesthetic is anaesthetic, which is the diminution and/or loss of communication and excitement of ideas and emotions, irrespective of what these ideas and emotions might be. The quality of art is determined by how well the ideas and emotions have been communicated.

People by nature are sentient, communicative beings—creators, artists. Everyone creates, but few produce anything unique, life-enhancing, or enduring. In this book we are concerned with the fine arts of literature, music, painting, sculpture, and architecture. But we must be aware that there are many other arts, including the art of cooking, the art of dancing, the art of gardening, and the art of living.

The French painter Paul Gauguin (go–GAN; 1848–1903) never saw a scene such as he portrayed in *Where Do We Come From? What Are We? Where Are We Going?* (colorplate 1), nor has or will anyone else. Certainly he drew the images of the gentle islanders, their birds and dogs, the beautiful landscape, from the world about him. But these perceptions could have been captured by a camera, which would have given us a clearer, more detailed, visually accurate representation. Gauguin, however, produced a painting in which his perceptions were simplified, distorted, abstracted, to present his vision of humanity asking the eternal questions. Carefully observe in colorplate 1 that the bodies vary in color from gold to brown to red; that the trees are undulating patterns of blues and purples; that there is a systematic interweaving of shapes and colors. Patterns, shapes, lines, and colors are arranged so as to establish a mood of enduring silence, gentleness, and reflection. Although the title aids us in understanding Gauguin's vision, it is not necessary for understanding the mood and the spirit of the painting. Obviously, this painting could not have been called *Joy and Celebration,* for it does not convey that mood. Likewise, *Natives on the Beach,* its elementary subject matter, fails to express the feeling this painting evokes. Of course philosophers, scientists, theologians, and historians have written books on the very questions Gauguin uses as his title and motif; this text will pursue these questions relentlessly. However, Gauguin painted instead of writing, because line, value, shape, form, color, and texture were his materials, which he used in repetition, opposition, dominance, and subordination, to produce a painting of unique rhythm and harmony.

How different, but equally challenging, is the *Return of the Hunters* (colorplate 2) by the Flemish painter Pieter Bruegel (BROO–gull; 1525–1569). Two moods are conveyed in this painting: the coldness and bleakness of nature, and the warmth and activity of humans. This painting is a wonderful study in linear and aerial perspective, for Bruegel was a master of illusion, convincingly conveying on a two-dimensional surface the illusion of the third dimension. Linear perspective is based on our visual memory, which tells us that two parallel lines eventually seem to meet in the distance; aerial perspective relies again on a visual memory, which tells us that objects seem to become obscure, faint, as we increase our distance from them. Our eyes tell us lies and Bruegel repeated the lies of visual memory. In this painting, which also is called *Winter,* our eyes are directed to the distant snow-covered mountains by strong diagonal lines, which lead away from the picture plane; likewise, people, buildings, even the mountains decrease in size and clarity as we move away from the returning hunters at the lower left-hand side of the painting. We have been brought up to understand perspective and proportion and thus appreciate Bruegel's mastery accordingly. An ancient Egyptian would not have understood this painting, since Egyptian art did not use these principles of perspective, and proportion was determined by the importance of the personages represented. Different cultures see and express themselves with different conventions.

Bruegel's work is considered a masterpiece not only because of his technical virtuosity, but also because the artist presented an image of his time, of life as he saw it. The day may be cold, the hunters and their dogs bent with fatigue after a long and arduous hunt, but within this little hamlet there is a variety of activity that shows the warmth and delights of human life. Bruegel presents a microcosm under the guise of a deceptively simple genre scene.

The Dutch painter Meindert Hobbema (MINE-dirt HOB–a–moh; 1639–1709) records a gentler nature in *The Watermill with the Great Red Roof* (colorplate 3). This scene of a countryside with soft, downy clouds in a baby-blue sky, gnarled trees with fuzzy foliage, sparkling water falling gently into the still pond, has a lyric quality that is enhanced by backlighting the scene. There is a gentle gradation from dark to light from foreground to background. Hobbema refined his work so that we can hardly see the brush strokes. The artist disappears in the image he creates. The artist is concerned with the beauty of domesticated nature as revealed by light. The scene is calm, quiet, and peaceful—a scene such as Wordsworth recounted in many poems.

The Dutch artist Vincent van Gogh (van–GO; 1853–1890) was no pastoral lyricist. He wanted to paint the world, people, and nature, with all the love, passion, and excitement that he failed to convey in personal relationships. In *Starry Night* (colorplate 4), nature is shown to be violent: the moon and stars of brilliant oranges and yellows are glowing, burning whirligigs that leave trails of golden streaks as they speed through the sky, which also moves in dashes, spots, and streaks of a variety of assertive blues. In the foreground the top branches of a cypress shoot into the sky like flames seeking to reach the highest heavens, devouring the very air in their pursuit. No camera could ever reproduce this scene; all knowledge of perspective and of natural color is disregarded; optical illusions and visual truths are forsaken. Van Gogh painted the scene not as he saw it, but as he felt it. And he painted it in heavy pigment (impasto) into which he gouged and scratched, so that in addition to the strength of color and violence of lines, the painting is rich in animated surface texture. Even cursory observation makes us keenly aware of the artist's physical activity in creating the work, and thus heightens our emotional response. Not for a moment, however, should we think of van Gogh as a madman, the popular conception of this great artist. Van Gogh was a driven man, indeed, but he planned his paintings in great detail, as his writings prove; and in this case he purposely established the small hamlet with its buildings composed of quiet squares and rectangles in the lower foreground to contrast with the turbulence of the heavens and the cypress. This painting relies very little on perception, very much on conception, in this case through very personalized abstractions.

The word *abstract* in relation to art is greatly misunderstood and commonly misused. All art is abstract—even the most naturalistic. Take a photo of a friend from your wallet and ask yourself how realistic it is. Quite obviously, your friend's body or head is not flat, not small enough to put in a wallet, and is not black, white, and gray. This photographic likeness is just that: a likeness or an abstraction of your friend. Painters or sculptors have always used abstractions in art; and society, as a group or as individuals, determines the degree to which it will accept these abstractions. Therefore, there are many degrees of abstractions, just as there are many languages, which are oral and written abstractions. Among some primitive tribes a high degree of abstraction from visual reality is so accepted that the primitives cannot recognize photographs of themselves or friends, but do "see" themselves and others in geometric signs and symbols. Some critics persist in claiming that the greatest art is that which is most illusionistic, that is, art that conveys the most convincing illusions of physical bulk and texture, visual recognition, and sense of three-dimensional space. Some of the greatest painters and sculptors in history have been superb illusionists, but illusionism by itself has little merit. There is no art form more illusionistic than the sculptured figures in a wax museum, but these figures lack vitality in that they resemble corpses rather than human beings.

When a painter chooses to forsake the perceptual world completely and paints on canvas with shapes, lines, and colors that draw upon no natural counterpart, the painting is called nonobjective. Wassily Kandinsky (va-SILL-ee can-DIN-ski; 1866-1944), a Russian painter, is often heralded as the first nonobjective artist. Without disclaiming his brilliance and importance to the development of modern art, it is important to note that the pottery painters of the geometric period of ancient Greece, the monks responsible for the medieval *Book of Kells,* the mosaicists who designed and executed the beautifully patterned floors of the public buildings of Byzantium, weavers from all periods of history, and your grandmothers who made patchwork crazy quilts were among the many thousands of artists who worked nonobjectively long before Kandinsky appeared upon the scene.

It was Kandinsky and the Dutch painter Piet Mondrian (Pete MOAN-dree-ahn; 1872-1944) who were the great pioneers of modern nonobjective art. Mondrian became the forerunner of the geometric nonobjective school and Kandinsky of expressionistic nonobjective art, both styles being carried to new and further directions by avant-garde artists today. Kandinsky's *Panel (3)* (colorplate 5) has all the turbulence of van Gogh's *Starry Night* without the subject matter drawn from nature. Colors and shapes move, impinge upon, and obliterate each other in this dynamic composition. For those who say, "I can't understand this kind of painting," here are a few questions: (1) Is this painting quiet or lively? (2) Is this painting somber or gay in mood? (3) Is this painting

dull or bright? If your answers are (1) lively, (2) gay in mood, and (3) bright, you do understand the basic nature and elements of this painting. Keep asking questions of this type about any painting or work of art and you will learn a great deal. All that is needed is time and perseverance. One note of caution: whether or not you understand a work of art has little if any bearing on whether it is a good work.

We are brought to the problem, then, of how does one look at and judge a work of art? Just as with music and literature, there is no easy answer, but perhaps the following guidelines will be of some assistance.

First, look at the work and ask yourself what you *see.* Inventory the painting, not just for the figurative parts but also for all the shapes, colors, lines, textures, and spaces, and notice the manner in which these elements are put together, that is, the composition.

Second, almost at the same time you are asking yourself what you see, ask yourself what you *know.* There is an immense difference between seeing and knowing. For example, you might *see* a figure of a haloed man with a white beard carrying a key, but you might *know,* also, that the halo represents sainthood and that the key is the attribute (or symbol) through which we recognize St. Peter. You might see a tree form, but only special knowledge will define that particular tree as an oak, aspen, or willow.

Third, ask yourself what the artist was attempting to do. It is at this point that most amateurs falter, quite naturally. But the artist sets a mood for a painting, describes items in certain ways through color, shapes, lines, arrangements of many elements to create certain effects. For example, Bruegel bent the backs of his hunters to indicate their weariness, van Gogh painted stars in bright colors to make them seem like glowing orbs, and Kandinsky used white extensively to set off the bright reds, blues, and yellows of his painting. Each artwork, be it painting, sculpture, architecture, or craft item, has a composition that should function to make all parts work together in rhythm and harmony. The rules for judging any work are implicit in the work itself.

Fourth, judge how well the artist solves self-imposed problems. Remember that even the "Divine Michelangelo" goofed sometimes and that some tenth-rate artists turned out single works of inestimable merit. Do not hesitate to be critical. Do Bruegel's hunters give a convincing impression of weariness? Does the little and quiet hamlet afford a balancing contrast for the *Starry Night?* At this point you are evaluating or appreciating the painting, making a judgment on the basis of all that you *see* and *know,* and an analysis of how well the artist resolved the problems.

You have just received an elementary lesson in criticism. Try it often; you'll improve with practice.

Do not be discouraged or embarrassed if some of the world's greatest masterpieces leave you cold. If you can recognize the obvious merit of a work of art but find in it qualities distasteful to your temperament, you are developing discriminating personal

Colorplate 1 Paul Gauguin, *Where Do We Come From? What Are We? Where Are We Going?* signed and dated 1897. Oil on canvas, 54¾ × 147½″. Tompkins Collection. Arthur Gordon Tompkins Fund. Courtesy, Museum of Fine Arts, Boston.

Colorplate 2 Pieter Bruegel the Elder, *Winter (Return of the Hunters)*, 1565. Oil on panel, 46 × 63¾". Kunsthistorisches Museum, Vienna.

Colorplate 3 Meindert Hobbema, *The Watermill with the Great Red Roof,* ca. 1670. Oil on canvas, 32 × 43⅛″. Collection of the Art Institute of Chicago.

Colorplate 4 Vincent van Gogh, *The Starry Night,* 1889. Oil on canvas, 29 × 36¼″. Collection, The Museum of Modern Art, New York. Acquired through the Lillie P. Bliss Bequest.

Colorplate 5 Wassily Kandinsky, *Panel (3)* (also known as *Summer*), 1914. Oil on canvas, 64 × 36¼″. Collection, The Museum of Modern Art, New York. Mrs. Simon Guggenheim Fund.

Colorplate 6 Hyacinthe Rigaud, *Portrait of Louis XIV,* 1701. Oil on canvas, 9′ 1½″ × 6′ 2⅝″. The Louvre, Paris.

Colorplate 7 Pablo Picasso, *Girl Before a Mirror,* 1932. Oil on canvas, 64 × 51¼″. Collection, The Museum of Modern Art, New York. Gift of Mrs. Simon Guggenheim.

taste. It is altogether possible to recognize the greatness of Raphael and van Gogh and at the same time dislike them because Raphael's figures are too saccharine for you and van Gogh's paintings are much too wild for you to live with comfortably. If you find, also, that you like paintings that have little artistic merit but are predominately orange (your favorite color) or whose subject matter is cats (and you love cats), recognize that there often are factors in a work of art that you value over the purely artistic values. In any case, you should begin to know how and why a work moves you. This is part of the process of learning how to judge a painting and yourself. Aesthetic understanding and appreciation is a give-and-take process involving you and the work of art. In undertaking the problem of criticism you should become a more knowledgeable, humanized individual.

Only a historian would know that the portrait (colorplate 6) by Hyacinthe Rigaud (REE-go; 1659–1743) of the imposing old man with the flowing wig, sumptuous robe, and red-heeled and red-ribboned shoes was the famous Louis XIV of France. Still, practically anyone would know that this gentleman was an overdressed, important personage posing in an elaborate setting. The French artist wanted to impress the viewer with the magnificence of the "Sun King," the elegance of his costume, and the majesty of his pose. Observe the artist's mastery in describing the fabrics, which are masterpieces of illusion. This is a beautiful painting of a homely old man, although the artist used every trick in the trade to de-emphasize the face. It is relatively easy to appreciate the quality of this painting, but it is difficult to like it because contemporary taste rejects the overblown extravagance of garb and ceremonial authoritarian poses. Remember that this painting was produced for a palace and now resides in a palace museum. It was not meant to hang over a television set and, despite its beauty as a painting, would have little relevance in most homes.

The Spanish artist Pablo Picasso (PAB-lo pea-KAH-so; 1881–1973) painted the *Girl Before a Mirror* (colorplate 7) in 1932. Like most of his works, it is a very controversial painting, which most people find difficult to understand; and even today it is seldom called beautiful. A cursory examination reveals only a series of circles and triangles in bright colors and patterns working on the picture plane. Perhaps you need to be told that the girl on the left is shown both in full-face and profile. Look carefully and you will see a profile view in pink and then its merging with a yellow side to describe a face frontally, a device now used by many comic strip artists. Picasso told us that he *knew* that each individual has profile views as well as a frontal view, that he painted not only what he actually saw but what he knew exists in a combination or "Picasso-view." That the colors of these sections do not coincide and are different again from the profile reflection in the mirror made no difference to Picasso because, in the last analysis, this painting is a highly abstracted study of a woman presented from many viewpoints and brightly colored and patterned

to achieve a complex decorative composition. Pattern and color are the keys to this painting, but the psychological interpretations that may be made are numerous. This painting still seems new, unique, and very intriguing; Picasso created new forms, a new way of seeing and presenting. Those of us who have been brought up with Picasso's works find them easy to understand, and we enjoy this painting for its decorative qualities, mystery of interpretation, and bold innovations. Art styles change as people's basic ideas and characteristics change. Picasso was one of the great artists of our century who not only reflected but produced these changes. All innovations seem heretical, sometimes even crazy, but often they become part of the mainstream of life, and inevitably are superseded by new and seemingly wilder innovations.

All the works illustrated and discussed were composed to communicate ideas and emotions; all differ from each other in style, degree of abstraction, and perceptual and conceptual understanding of people and nature. It is hoped, even anticipated, that you will appreciate or learn to appreciate each of these works, but it is unlikely you will like each of them. Remember, nevertheless, that each artist is sharing with you a vision of the world, a way of seeing, and in so doing communicates artistic truth.

Summary

In such fashions as those illustrated, artists, whatever their medium—music, painting, literature—have made form the vehicle of idea, have made the raw materials of art acquire significance by arrangement and handling. It is a different kind of meaning from that of scientists, which can be perceived and measured in an objective world, for this sort of meaning can be known only by the individual who can see the relationships the artists have formulated, and who can find them valid in terms of personal experience. It is not an easy process, sometimes; and just as the effectiveness of the scientist depends upon two things—the validity of the discovery, and the ability of the beholder to understand or comprehend it—so the effectiveness of the artist depends upon the validity of the discovery, and the sensitivity of the beholder to apprehend it. "I don't get it" is no refutation of either Einstein or Bach.

Not everyone will derive the same kind or degree of satisfaction from a particular art form, obviously; but the educated person is obligated to know that "there is something in it," even if that "something" does not deeply move that individual. And perhaps, with deeper acquaintance and wider knowledge, that "something" will become clearer and of greater value than before.

In this chapter we have made the assertion that the artist is an explorer and discoverer in the realm of the human personality. The artist uses the method of intuition and composition. The artist's raw material lies in the human personality and in human experience, with their vast and unknown reaches, their disrupting conflicts. The artist gives form to the component elements of personality and experience, and in so doing yields an artistic truth. No matter whether we speak of literature, painting, sculpture, music, or any of the other arts, this concept of creating form out of chaos is the single common basis and foundation for all aesthetics.

Exercises

1. George Meredith's poem, "Dirge in Woods," is given here together with two other versions, which attempt to say the same thing. What differences in the meaning do the differences in form create?

DIRGE IN WOODS
George Meredith

A wind sways the pines
    And below
Not a breath of wild air:
Still as the mosses that glow
On the flooring and over the lines
Of the roots here and there.
The pine-tree drops its dead:
They are quiet as under the sea.
    Overhead, overhead
Rushes life in a race
As the clouds the clouds chase:
    And we go,
And we drop like the fruits of the tree,
    Even we,
    Even so.

A SECOND VERSION

Pines in the wind are swaying.
    It is quiet down below;
Not one wild breath is straying
    Above the mosses that glow
Among the roots in wandering lines
    Upon the forest floor.
The needles quietly fall from the pines,
    Fall, and are no more.
As darkly green, as stilly quiet
    As under the sea, this place.
Look! overhead, in restless riot,
    The rushing clouds' wild chase!
But like the needles we shall fall,
    Nor run in life's swift race;
We all shall die—all, all.

A THIRD VERSION

Above, wind in the pines;
below, stillness—
quiet as the mosses
creeping over roots.
    The pine needles drop, drop,
quiet, dead.
Overhead, the rushing clouds
chasing each other.
    We too die and become
quiet: drop like dead leaves,
like a dying wind
vanish into silence.

Here are three ways of saying the same thing, or nearly the same thing. Yet two of these ways are definitely inferior, although the words repeat, the ideas are like, and the "meaning" is similar. What makes the difference?

Perhaps a fourth way of straight prose without versification, could convey the "meaning" more clearly, if by "meaning" we understand only the words and what they refer to; but there is—or should be—more to a poem than the words and their immediate, surface significance. For part of the stuff of the poem is its pattern, arrangement, and design; the form is significant as well as the meanings of the words. In order to see better the effective form of one, we look at the other poorer versions.

Which one sounds most like a sermon, a teaching with a moral rather than like a poem? Which one is singsong, so monotonous that your ear is distracted from meaning by the regularity of expected sound? Which one most effectively presents the three successive ideas: trees, clouds, ourselves?

In the first version, what is gained by the short second line?

What is the effect of the succession of vowel sounds in "st*I*ll *A*s th*E* m*O*sses that gl*O*w"? (*the* is thə, not thi)

What is the effect of repeated sounds in "glow . . . flooring . . . over"?

Why is "overhead" repeated, and "clouds" (in the eleventh line)? Also the *r* sounds, and the sibilant *s*'s?

What is gained by the short line, "and we go"?

What is the effect of the near repetition in the last two lines?

Again one might ask, what does the poem gain by being a *poem?* It is not merely by the dictionary meanings of the words employed, but by the patterns of sound and arrangement, that the poet has achieved a meaning.

2. Here, again, we might compare the writing of an expert and a rank amateur in terms of meanings that lie beyond pure sense meaning. Both the stanza from Matthew Arnold's "Dover Beach" and the paraphrase of it "mean" the same thing in that they deplore the loss of faith in the world. But what additional overtones and undertones of meaning does Arnold get? In what specific ways does he achieve them?

The Sea of Faith
Was once, too, at the full, and round earth's shore
Lay like the folds of a bright girdle furled.
But now I only hear
Its melancholy, long, withdrawing roar,
Retreating, to the breath
Of the night wind, down the vast edges drear
And naked shingles of the world.

Paraphrase

Once men the world around believed
In other men and God.
But faith's now lost, men are deceived,
And earth's a dusty clod.

3. Here is Robert Frost's lovely poem, "Stopping by Woods on a Snowy Evening."

Whose woods these are I think I know.
His house is in the village, though;
He will not see me stopping here
To watch his woods fill up with snow.

My little horse must think it queer
To stop without a farmhouse near
Between the woods and frozen lake
The darkest evening of the year.

He gives the harness bells a shake
To ask if there is some mistake.
The only other sound's the sweep
Of easy wind and downy flake.

The woods are lovely, dark, and deep,
But I have promises to keep,
And miles to go before I sleep,
And miles to go before I sleep.

Notice how the choice of words in a poem, once it is done, seems right, almost inevitable. In the twelfth line one accepts the word *easy* as an adjective describing the wind. What other adjectives could Frost have chosen? Why do you suppose he selected the rather unusual word *easy?*

In answering these questions, you might notice some of the music of the poem. For example, look at lines three and four. In line three we find the words *will* and *stopping;* in line four, the words *watch* and *fill.* Do you notice the cross-rhyme: *stop* and *watch, will* and *fill?* In lines seven and eight we have something of the same thing with the words *between* and *evening.* Now look at lines eleven and twelve to see why the choice of the word *easy.* You might notice the pattern of end-rhymes, too. Where does the word that ends line three of each stanza find its rhyme? What is the effect, and the author's purpose, of having all four lines of the last stanza rhyme? As one begins to discover these rather hidden elements, a simple-seeming poem becomes a complicated fabric of rhyme and music, most of which has its effect, even though the reader is not conscious of it.

4. Raphael painted *Madonna della Seggiola* within a circle: why he did so does not especially matter—probably because he wanted to! But the decision once made, the problem of the arrangement within that circle was his to solve. (How he did, the picture shows.) Suppose that he had chosen some other arrangement of the mother and child: suppose he had (like Cimabue) presented her and the infant face-on. Suppose he had turned the child the other way. Being Raphael, he probably would have made a better design of it than the following sketches would indicate!—but whatever the design he might have effected, the new picture would not have done what the present one does; it might have been better or worse; it would certainly have been different. The "Madonna of the Chair" is what it is because it was designed the way it is; the flowing curves fitted together with their interweave of movement give the painting its quality of "coziness" (if the word may be forgiven), its intimately human appeal. The mother is not the "Virgin Enthroned," the baby is not God Incarnate, in this picture; the majesty and awe of the subsequent story are foregone to portray the most understandable, the most appealing of human relationships— simply mother and child.

Consider some other possible arrangements, not with a view of bettering or worsening Raphael's design, but in the hope of understanding more fully what this form, this arrangement, accomplishes. (There's even a circle for you to try your hand in.)

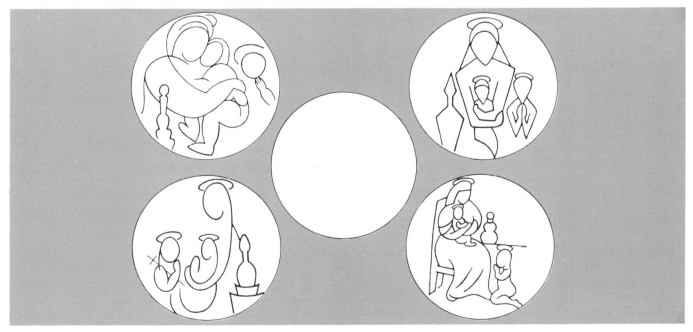

Bibliography

Fiction
Chekov, Anton. "The Darling"
Parker, Dorothy. "Big Blonde"

The Arts in Education

Arts, Education and Americans Panel. *Coming to Our Senses: The Significance of the Arts for American Education.* New York: McGraw-Hill Book Company, 1977. Funded by the U.S. Office of Education and the National Endowment for the Arts, this high-powered panel of leaders from many different fields presents a strong case for the arts at all levels of education, while at the same time implicitly indicting much that is absurd and antihuman in American education.

Brandwein, Paul. *The Permanent Agenda of Man.* Sound Recording. Washington, D.C.: National Education Association, 1973. This is a curriculum design from elementary education upwards that centers on helping every child develop into a well-adjusted adult. Brandwein contends that everyone needs "schooling" to learn how to read, write, and figure.

"Education" is a fundamental need because it gives meaning to our lives. The humanities, he contends, are supposed to teach us about "truth, beauty, justice, faith, and love."

Lockspeiser, Edward. *Music and Painting: A Study in Comparative Ideas from Turner to Schoenberg.* New York: Harper & Row, Publishers, 1973. Using what the author calls the humanities approach, the "why" rather than the "how," this is an interdisciplinary study of some interesting relationships between visual and musical arts.

Munro, Thomas. *The Arts—Their Interrelations.* Western Reserve University Press, 1967. An unusual and fascinating approach to comparative aesthetics by a man who is both a professor of philosophy and professor of art.

Read, Herbert. *Education Through Art.* New York: Pantheon Books, 1974. The author bases his approach to aesthetic education on Plato's thesis that art should be the basis of education. This is certainly a Platonic idea whose time may have finally come.

3

An Introduction to Music Listening

Prelude

Already the most universal of the arts, music can, through modern technology, span either national boundaries or centuries past with effortless ease. Whether rich or poor, all of us can enjoy, in our own homes, the Boston Symphony playing Beethoven or the musical life of medieval Paris or modern China. In fact, we live in a society saturated with music from supermarket to concert hall, however, quantity does not necessarily mean quality. Almost everyone has heard the everyday sounds of popular music and the murmer of Musak; but few know very much about Beethoven, or medieval, Chinese, or any other music that might be called classical.

Classical music is not drastically different from popular music. Both have unity and variety, and both use melody, harmony, rhythm, and tone color structured in recognizable musical forms. Quite simply, classical music just has more of everything: greater length, more unity, increased variety. It follows, then, that anyone who likes popular music—most of us—can learn to enjoy music a step beyond popular songs, music more intricate, complex, and considerably more interesting over a longer period of time. Popular hits are pleasurable and frequently delightful but they are also transitory. Classical music has an appeal that, with repeated listening, extends over months, years, or even a lifetime. And it all begins with nursery jingles, folk songs, hymns, marches, waltzes, and the popular songs of the day.

Music listeners tend to develop their musical tastes up a ladder of progressively more intricate and interesting music, a process usually more intuitive than deliberate. We become music lovers with the songs we sing and whistle as children. As teenagers we generally follow our peers and tune in to popular songs, rock, country-western, bluegrass, and the dance music of the time. At some point, however, nearly everyone develops a liking for more complex music—works like *Fiddler on the Roof, Hello Dolly, My Fair Lady,* and other marvelous American musicals—plus some jazz, which is also America's unique contribution to the world's music. At some other point we add Strauss waltzes, Sousa marches, *Finlandia,* the

Nutcracker Suite, Peter and the Wolf, and, usually, some tuneful symphonies and concertos by Tchaikovsky and Rachmaninoff. At about this time some of the powerful music of Beethoven becomes attractive along with Chopin's romantic piano music. Further exploration leads to the elegance of Mozart and the lyricism of Schubert, and the music goes on and on.

The remarkable and wonderful fact about progressing up a ladder of musical taste is that *we can have it all:* everything we ever enjoyed as children and teenagers *plus* music of countless centuries and cultures. There are so many options when we appreciate a wide spectrum of music: music for romantic candlelight dinners, singing, dancing, jogging, studying, thinking, or dreaming. Modern technology has provided us with an incredible variety of recorded music—a whole world of listening experiences limited only by our musical tastes.

Throughout this book you will be introduced to music as it has developed in Western civilization, from medieval songs and dances to symphonic music by Beethoven, Tchaikovsky, and Stravinsky. As consumers of music—listeners rather than performers—you will have the opportunity to systematically develop your listening skills, to become sophisticated listeners. No one begins music listening from scratch. All our lives we are exposed to all kinds of music, some that we hear and some to which we listen. *Hearing,* sometimes described as taking a tonal bath, is a passive state, whereas *listening* is an active and alert activity. Throughout this text our focus will be on active listening, that is, conscious attention to musical content, melody, harmony, rhythm, tone color, and musical forms. As stated before and reiterated here, these elements are common to all music.

Characteristics of Musical Sounds

Musical tones are sounds of definite pitch and duration, as distinct from noises and other less definite sounds. Musical tones have the four characteristics of *pitch, intensity, tone color,* and *duration,* which may be described as follows:

Pitch   The location of musical sound from low to high or high to low.

Intensity   Relative degree of softness or loudness.

Tone Color   The quality of a sound that distinguishes it from other musical sounds of the same pitch and intensity; for example, the different tone quality of a flute as contrasted with a clarinet. Also called *timbre.*

Duration   The length of time a tone is audible.

The Four Elements of Music

Rhythm, melody, harmony, and *tone color* are the essential elements of music. Composers and performers are concerned with each, while for the listener, they are experienced as a web of sound that makes it difficult to single out any one element. Each can, however, be considered in isolation as a guide to understanding.

Rhythm

Though little is known about prehistoric music, the earliest music was probably the beating out of rhythms long before the existence of either melody or speech. There is rhythm in the universe: our heartbeat, alternating day and night, the progression of the seasons, waves crashing on a beach. Manufactured rhythm can be heard in train wheels clicking on rails, a Ping-Pong game, or the clacking castanets of a Spanish dancer.

Essentially, rhythm is the organization of musical time, that is, everything that takes place in terms of sound and silence, accent and nonaccent, tension and relaxation. Rhythm can also be defined as the "melody of a monotone"; music can be recognized just by hearing its rhythm. For example, tapping out the rhythmic patterns of "Dixie" can bring that familiar melody to mind.

Rhythm is the name of the whole and is not to be confused with *beat,* which results from a certain regularity of the rhythmic patterns. Beat, or pulse, can be compared with the heartbeat or the pulse rate. The beat will usually be steady but it may temporarily speed up or slow down. It may be *explicit* (the uniform thump of a bass drum in a marching band) or *implicit* (resulting from combinations of rhythmic patterns). As soon as one duration follows another, there will be rhythm but not necessarily beat. Certain types of music (such as Gregorian chant) do not produce the regular pulsation called beat.

When beats are produced by the music in a repeating pattern of accents, the result is *meter. Metered* music is *measured* music, with groupings of two, three, or four beats (or combinations of these) in each *measure,* or *bar.*

Time Signatures

When there is a regular pattern of accented and unaccented beats, it is customary to use a *time signature* in which the upper figure indicates the number of beats in a measure and the lower figure (though not in every case), the unit of beat; that is, the note value the composer has selected to symbolize one beat. For example:

2 = two beats per measure (duple meter)
4 = ♩ unit of beat (quarter note receives one beat)

3 = three beats per measure (triple meter)
8 = ♪ unit of beat (eighth note receives one beat)

Melody

A melody is a horizontal organization of pitches or, simply, a succession of musical tones. Melodies may move with:

Conjunct (Stepwise) Motion

Disjunct (Skipping) Motion

Disjunct and Conjunct Motion

Harmony

Harmony exists when two or more pitches are sounded together. Western music has used harmony since about the ninth century. However, harmony is still not commonly used in the music of the Near, Middle, or Far East or Africa.

Individual Harmonies

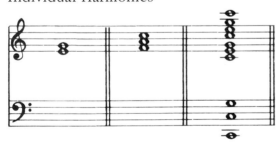

Melody with Harmony

Tone Color

Sometimes called timbre (TAM–ber), tone color is to music what color is to the painter. It is tone color that enables us to distinguish between a flute, a clarinet, and an oboe. A soprano voice is higher in pitch than a bass voice, but the tone color is also different. Through experience, everyone has learned to recognize the unique colors of many instruments. Further study leads to finer discriminations between similar instruments such as violin and viola, oboe and English horn, and so on. Composers select instruments for expressive purposes based largely on their coloration, whether singly or in combination. The full sound of a Beethoven symphony differs from a work by Richard Strauss, for example, because Strauss uses a wider range of instrumental colors.

Musical Literacy

The most abstract of the arts, music is sound moving in time. Factual information about music certainly helps the listener, but all the facts in the world can only assist the listening process; information about music can never replace the sound of music. One extremely useful method of instruction is to present major themes and ideas in musical notation, a practice common to virtually all books on music listening.

A practical approach to intelligent listening must include some instruction in musical literacy sufficient to read a single line of music. This is a simple process that can be quickly learned by young children and can be taught to an adult in a few minutes. The strangely prevalent folklore about musical notation being "too hard" or "too technical" has no foundation in fact, and probably refers to reading music as a performer, which is a very different matter that need not concern us here. As basic to music as the ABC's of written language but easier to understand, musical notation is an indispensable guide for music listeners. Learning to read music well enough to figure out a single line of music and to plunk it out on a piano is simply basic musical literacy.

Educated listeners quickly learn to enjoy picking out musical themes. This turns abstract sounds into tangible tunes, thus giving the listener an opportunity to preview the themes so that they can be anticipated in the music. Equally valuable is the repetition of themes after the listening experience. To summarize, picking out melodies is an aid to understanding, a helpful preview of music to be listened to, and a reminder of music already heard.

Approach the following material not with apprehension but with anticipation. Master the principles of musical notation with the positive attitude that this will materially assist not only in a better understanding of the music in this text but also lead, in time, to a lifetime of pleasurable listening.

Musical Notation

Pitch

The essential elements of our notational system were devised some ten centuries ago and subsequently altered and augmented to become a reasonably efficient means of communicating the composer's intentions to listener and performer. The system is based on the first seven letters of the alphabet and can best be illustrated by using a segment of the piano keyboard. The pitches range from low to high, from A through G in a repeating A–G pattern.

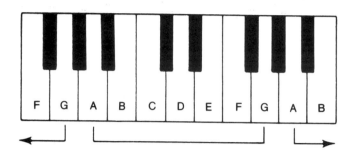

In order to know which of the eight A's available on the piano is the intended note, the following is necessary:

1. Use a musical *staff* of five lines and four spaces.

2. Use a symbol for a musical pitch, i.e., *note*. 𝅝

3. Place the notes on the staff.

4. Indicate by means of a *clef sign* the *names* of the notes.

Clef (French, *key*) implies that the key to precise placement of the notes is the establishment of the letter name of *one* of the lines or spaces of the staff. There are two clefs in common use. Both are ornamental symbols derived from the letters G and F. The solid lines are the present clef signs and the dotted lines their original form:

The clefs are placed on the staff to indicate the location of the letters they represent. The lower portion of the G clef curls around the second line to fix the location of G; the two dots of the F clef are placed above and below the fourth line to show that this is the F line.

Once the five-line staff has received its pitch designations of G or F, the *staff* is subsequently identified as a *treble* or a *bass staff*.

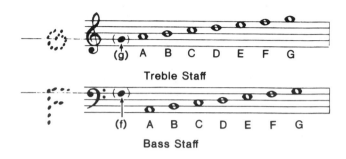

Treble Staff

Bass Staff

Both these staffs are segments of a complete system of lines and spaces called the *great staff*. The following illustration of the great staff includes notes arranged to form words, which is a quick way to learn to read music. Try putting your own words into notation.

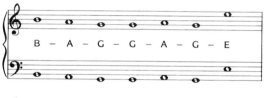

Not all melodies are composed so that they can be played on the white notes only of the piano. Sometimes another *key*, or different set of pitches, is used as demonstrated in the following examples:

Key of C

Key of D

In the second version the *key signature* indicates that all of the F's and C's have been raised a half step to the next closest note. A symbol called a sharp (♯) indicates raised notes. Key signatures can include up to seven sharps or flats.

The other common symbol that changes a note is the *flat* (♭), which lowers a note a half step to the next closest note. Following is the same melody written in the key of B♭. As indicated by the key signature, all the B's and E's have been lowered to B♭ and E♭.

Joy to the World

Key of B

You will note that the staff given above has an added short line, a *ledger line,* used to accommodate the last two notes.

A piano keyboard has *white* keys and *black* keys, with the black keys grouped in alternating sets of two and three. The white note, or key, immediately to the left of the two black keys is always C. There are eight C's; the C closest to the center is *middle C.* It is from this C that you can locate the notes of the themes.

Middle C   Middle C

Below is a guide to the *chromatic scale,* which is all of the white and black keys in one octave.

Duration

The notation of the length of time of musical sounds (and silences) was developed in conjunction, more or less, with the notation of pitch. The modern *note-value* system consists of fractional parts of a whole unit, or *whole note* (𝅝), expressed in mathematical terms as 1/1. A *half note* (𝅗𝅥) is one-half the whole unit, or 1/2; a *quarter note* (♩) is one-quarter the unit, or 1/4; and so forth.

The *name* of the note value indicates the *number* of notes in the whole-note unit. There are four quarter notes ($4 \times 1/4 = 1/1$), eight eighth notes ($8 \times 1/8 = 1/1$), etc.

With note values smaller than the whole note, the relationships remain constant. There are two quarter notes in a half note ($2 \times 1/4 = 1/2$), two eighth notes in a quarter note ($2 \times 1/8 = 1/4$), etc.

Rhythmic notation is both relative and fixed. The duration of a whole note is dependent on the tempo (speed) and notation of music. It may have a duration of one second, eight seconds, or something in between. The interior relationships, however, never vary. A whole note has the same duration as two half notes, four quarter notes, and so forth. The mathematical relationship is fixed and precise. See table 3.1 for an outline of the system.

Table 3.1. Note and Rest Values

Note Value	Symbol
Whole note (basic unit)	𝅝
Half note	𝅗𝅥
Quarter note	♩
Eighth note	♪
Sixteenth note	𝅘𝅥𝅯

Rest Value	Symbol
Whole (note) rest	▬
Half rest	▬
Quarter rest	𝄽
Eighth rest	𝄾
Sixteenth rest	𝄿

Chromatic Scale

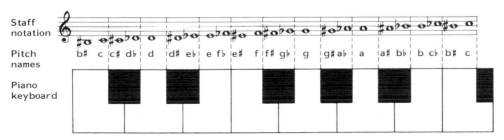

Voices and Instruments

Choral ensembles are usually divided into four voice parts ranging from high to low: soprano and alto (women) and tenor and bass (men).

Instruments of the symphony orchestra and other ensembles are grouped by family, from highest pitch to lowest:

Strings	Woodwinds	Brass	Percussion
violin	piccolo	trumpet	snare drum
viola	flute	(and cornet)	timpani
cello	oboe	French horn	bass drum
bass	clarinet	trombone	cymbals
	bassoon	tuba	many others

Keyboard instruments include piano, harpsichord, and organ. The piano, originally called pianoforte, is based on the principle of hammers striking the strings; the harpsichord has a mechanism that plucks the strings. Built with two or more keyboards called manuals, organs either use forced air to activate the pipes or some version of an electronic reproduction of sound.

Musical Texture

The words for the three kinds of musical texture are derived from Greek and are virtually self-explanatory:

Monophonic (one sound)
Homophonic (same sound)
Polyphonic (many sounds)

Monophonic music has a single unaccompanied melody line. Much of the world's music is monophonic, including Chinese and Hindu music and, in Western civilizations, Gregorian chant and troubadour songs, as discussed in the chapter on medieval music. Homophonic music has a principal melodic line accompanied by harmony, sometimes referred to as chordal accompaniment. While it is relatively unknown outside Western culture, homophonic comprises the bulk of our music including nearly all popular music. Polyphonic music has two or more melodies sounding simultaneously. Familiar rounds like "Three Blind Mice" and "Row, Row, Row Your Boat" are polyphonic, as is most Renaissance music. The music of baroque composers such as Bach, Handel, and many others is basically polyphonic.

Musical Form

Briefly stated, form in music is a balance of unity and variety. Too much unity becomes boring, while excessive variety leads to fragmentation and even chaos. Understanding form in music is a high priority for educated listeners. As Robert Schumann remarked, "Only when the form is quite clear to you will the spirit become clear to you."

The smallest unit of form is the *motive,* which to be intelligible must have at least two notes plus an identifiable rhythmic pattern. The principle motive in

the first movement of Beethoven's Fifth Symphony has two different pitches in a four-note rhythmic pattern:

A musical phrase is a coherent group of notes roughly comparable to a literary phrase and having about the same function. Two related phrases form a *period,* in the manner of a literary sentence. In the period illustrated below, note that the first phrase has a transitional ending called a *half cadence,* while the second phrase ends solidly with a *full cadence.* Note also the extreme unity; the first three measures of both phrases are identical.

In large works the musical periods are used in various combinations to expand the material into sections comparable to paragraphs, and these are then combined to make still larger units.

Musical structure can be comprehended only *after* the music has arrived at wherever the composer intends it to go. Look again at "Ode to Joy." You can "see" its form only because the music is notated, which is why learning some notation is so important. When the music is played, your ear follows the line to the half cadence, which is then heard as a statement that demands completion. As the second phrase begins, there is aural recognition of its relationship to the first phrase. When the second phrase concludes with a gratifying full cadence, there is a kind of flashback to the memory of the first phrase. In other words, the conclusion of the second phrase is satisfying because it completes the thought of the still-remembered first phrase. The music conforms to its own inner logic; that is, the second phrase is a logical consequence of the first.

As a general rule, most music is constructed around two different but logically related (inner logic) musical ideas. We can call one idea *A* and the other *B.* One common musical form is two-part (binary), or simply A–B. An even more common form is three-part (ternary), or A–B–A. In two-part form the composer makes a musical statement (A), which is followed by a new section (B), which is sufficiently different to provide variety but not so different as to destroy the balance. The following hymn tune is a complete composition in two-part form, with two phrases in each section. Section B has the same rhythm as Section A, but the melody is a kind of inversion of the melody in A. The inner logic is maintained through the similarities.

St. Anne

The following complete hymn tune has a form related to two-part form: A–A¹–B, called A, A prime, B. Part A is followed by another A that is varied going into the cadence. Part B is properly different but related to A and A¹ by the similarity of measures 2, 6, and 10. In terms of measures, the structure of the piece can be diagrammed as:

A   A¹   B
2+2   2+2   2+2

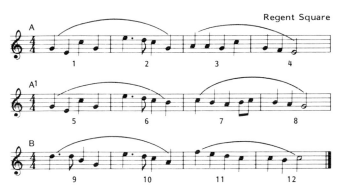

Regent Square

Three-part form operates on the principle of closing with the melody that began the piece, a rounding off of the material: A–B–A. The following example can be analyzed as A–A¹–B–A¹ and diagrammed as:

A   A¹   B   A¹
4 + 4 4 + 4 4 + 4 4 + 4.

This is the thirty-two-measure form most commonly used for popular songs.

There are, of course, other variants of AB and ABA forms as well as several other structures. However, the examples given illustrate the principle of a balance between unity and variety, of which unity is paramount. Perhaps because it is rather amorphous, music, more than any other art, emphasizes repetition, restating the material again and again, but mixing with enough variety to maintain interest. The forms illustrated can also be heard in the larger context of longer compositions. For example, "In the Gloaming" has 32 measures in a basic ABA form; a large symphonic work could have, say, 200 measures and be diagrammed as follows:

A   B   A   A   B   A¹   A   B   A¹
aba aba aba   *or* aba¹ aba aba¹   *or* aa¹ba aba aa¹ba¹

The Listening Experience

Listening to music begins with the question, What do you hear? This is an objective question that has nothing whatever to do with a story you may imagine the music is telling, random associations the music happens to trigger, or any meaning that may be attributed to the music. For the educated listener the procedure is to objectively identify the sounds you hear, to determine how the sounds are produced, and to try to determine how the sounds are organized.

Composers do not pour out notes as if emptying a glass of water on a tabletop. They arrange their sounds in a sort of container in a manner that molds the container to the material it holds. Learning to comprehend the musical structure leads inevitably to the ability to *anticipate* the next melody, cadence, section, or whatever. Being able to anticipate what is to happen next means that you are tuned in to the web of sound, listening along with the pace of the music.

In the Gloaming

Almost everyone has already acquired the ability to follow the progress of popular music and to anticipate what comes next in favorite recordings. As stated before, the larger world of classical music is only a step beyond the listening expertise of most individuals.

The following outline is but the first stage of an objective approach to music listening. (Progressively more detailed outlines conclude chaps. 16, 19, 23, 25, and 30.) Part I specifies some basic categories to listen for; while part II lists three conclusions that can be drawn from listening to the music as objectified by the categories in part I.

Listening Guide (First Stage)

I. Listening outline
- A. Medium
  1. Vocal (Text: English, Latin, German, French, other)
  2. Instrumental
  3. Vocal and instrumental
- B. Tempo—very slow, slow, moderate, fast, very fast
- C. Loudness—soft, medium loud, loud, combination
- D. Number of performers
  1. Solo
  2. Ensemble
     - a) Small (2 to 5)
     - b) Medium (6 to 20)
     - c) Medium large (21 to 59)
     - d) Large (60 to 100 or more)
- E. Rhythm
  1. Regular beat (or pulsation)
  2. Pulsation seems to be either irregular or indistinct
- F. Texture
  1. One melody, unaccompanied
  2. Melody with accompaniment
  3. Simultaneous melodies (two or more)
- G. Form
  1. AB or variant
  2. ABA or variant
  3. Other

II. Conclusions
- A. Period—A.D. 600–1420, 1420–1600, seventeenth century, eighteenth century, nineteenth century, twentieth century
- B. General musical form—symphony, concerto, sonata, mass, cantata, oratorio, opera, jazz, art song, folk song, madrigal, other
- C. National origin—England, France, Germany, Italy, Hungary, United States, Austria, other

Note: See the Glossary for terms that may be unfamiliar.

Exercises

Your first listening experiences based on the Listening Guide will preview some of the musical selections to be studied, music that includes a variety of styles and a time span of about ten centuries. For best results, your listening should be as objective as possible and follow this pattern:

1. Write a vertical column of letters from *A* through *G* corresponding to the categories in the outline below.
2. Follow the Listening Guide, writing down your answers for each letter.
3. Always determine the medium first. It is best to answer each question in the order given, but you may prefer to follow your own sequence. In this case, try to do it the same way every time.
4. Do not leave any blank spaces. An incorrect guess is better than no answer at all. Follow the procedures; correct answers come later as your continued listening experiences are reinforced by an increasing fund of factual knowledge about music and its materials.

Record 1
I. Listening outline
- A.
- B.
- C.
- D.
- E.
- F.
- G.

II. Conclusions
- A.
- B.
- C.

Record 2
(etc.)

The goal of the Listening Guide is to provide you with enough concrete information to make the three educated guesses that are referred to as *conclusions*. Up to this point it is presumed that you have comparatively little information on which to base these educated guesses; however, you can make some logical deductions based on what you are able to hear plus the following clues, which can help you reach your conclusions:

1. The language used in a song usually identifies the country. Names of places (New York, London, etc.) can help pinpoint a locale.
2. The use of Latin usually (but not always) indicates some kind of sacred music.
3. Symphony orchestras, string quartets, and pianos did not exist before the eighteenth century.
4. Opera did not exist before the seventeenth century.

5. Jazz did not exist before about 1890 and is still mostly of American origin.
6. A cappella (unaccompanied) choral music was common in the sixteenth century, but became quite rare until revived in the twentieth century.
7. Solo songs (with instrumental accompaniment) were numerous through the sixteenth century but declined for the next two centuries. They became important again in the nineteenth and twentieth centuries. The instrument used for the accompaniment provides a valuable clue.

After completing the seven listening categories, hazard a guess as to about *when* the music was written, its *general musical form* (not to be confused with musical structure), and the possible *national origin* of the music or the composer.

Record List

The following are some suggested recordings for the music used for Exercises in Listening. These seventeen selections are also used later on in this book to illustrate different periods of music history. *The authors strongly recommend that students invest in their own recordings.* Records, tapes, or cassettes may be ordered through any record store using a Schwann Record and Tape Guide or similar catalog. Except for special records and standard anthologies, no specific recordings are listed. As fluid as the market is, specific listings become an exercise in futility.

1. Bach, J. S. Fugue in G Minor. Biggs, Columbia MS—6261. (Also, recordings of Bach's organ music by Germani, Newman, or Richter.)
2. Bartók, Béla. Concerto for Orchestra.
3. Beethoven, Ludwig van. Symphony no. 5.
4. Bennet, John. "Thyrsis, Sleepest Thou?" In *Masterpieces of Music before 1750.* Vol. 2 (henceforth known as *Masterpieces*). Haydn Society 9039; 3-volume set 9038/9040.
5. Brahms, Johannes. Symphony no. 3.
6. Catch, "Tom the Taylor" *or* "A Catch in the Play of the Knight of Malta." In *Catch That Catch Can.* Musical Heritage Society (Music of the Sixteenth and Seventeenth Centuries, vol. 8). MHS 690.
7. Debussy, Claude. "Voiles." In *Preludes for Piano.*
8. Gabrieli, Giovanni. "Et Ecclesiis." In *Motets.* Columbia MS—7334.
9. Hofstetter (attributed to Haydn). Quartet in F Major.
10. Jazz: Adderley, Cannonball. "This Here." In *San Francisco.* Riverside 6062. (Also, selections from blues, big band, and so forth.)
11. Jazz: "Kyrie Eleison." In *Jazz Suite on the Mass Texts.* RCA LSP—3414.
12. Puccini, Giacomo. *La Boheme.*
13. Scarlatti, Domenico. Sonata in C Major. Longo 104.
14. Schubert, Franz. "Gretchen am Spinnrade." Fischer-Dieskau (Goethe lieder), DG 2530229.
15. Sequence. "Victimae paschali laudes." In *Masterpieces.*
16. Spiritual: "Didn't It Rain." In *Newport 1958: Mahalia Jackson.* Columbia CS—8071.
17. Trouvère song, "Or la truix." In *Masterpieces.*

Many of you have built up a record library of music that you like. If you glance through your collection, you will undoubtedly find records that no longer interest you, but were popular when you bought them. They are not popular now, or have become dated. Now is a good time to start building a permanent library of records that will not go out of style, a library to which you can add over the years for a lifetime of pleasurable listening. Here is a Basic Twenty-Five recordings that will have some initial appeal and that will increase more and more in appeal as you increase your knowledge of this music. (Further suggestions about building a long-term record collection will be made at the end of volume two.)

Few specific recordings are listed because of the chaotic state of the market. Before starting to build a more permanent record or tape library you should check on the latest in recording technology, particularly digital recordings with laser-beam playback units. Whenever possible you should preview each recording you purchase.

A Basic Library of Good Music

Romanticism (ca. 1814–1900)

Much of the music in the romantic style of the nineteenth century is eminently listenable because of its emotional appeal and memorable melodies. The following selections, listed by composer, will provide a variety of solo, orchestral, and chamber music.

Frédéric Chopin (1810–1849) This Polish-born "poet of the keyboard" created a unique piano style. He wrote almost exclusively for the piano, particularly sets of similar pieces all bearing the same title. Listen to some of his polonaises, preludes, nocturnes, mazurkas, and waltzes and select something you particularly like. Try recordings by Arthur Rubinstein, who plays Chopin exceptionally well.

Peter I. Tchaikovsky (1840–1893) Tchaikovsky (notice the different spellings) wrote lush music in a romantic Russian style. His melodies are singable and his orchestra rich and full. He wrote six symphonies, but start with his last two works. *Note:* Sonatas (for solo instruments), concertos (solo instrument and orchestra), and symphonies (orchestra) are generally divided into four different sections called "movements." This is done to achieve some variety. Though there are many ways of structuring symphonies the movements are generally designed as follows: first movement, vigorous; second movement, slow; third movement, from moderate to very fast; fourth movement, fast, strong.

Sergei Rachmaninoff (1873–1943) There are twenty-two different recordings of the Second Piano Concerto by this neo-romantic Russian composer. Listen to Van Cliburn, Stanislav Richter, and Rubinstein. You will notice that each pianist has his own idea of how the music should sound. Select the version you prefer and try to determine why you prefer one interpretation over another.

Franz Schubert (1797–1828) His Symphony no. 8 lacks the last two movements because Schubert was unable to write a third movement that suited him. There are thirty-three recordings of this, the *Unfinished Symphony. Note:* There are many low-grade recordings of popular works like this one. The price is sometimes low because a pickup orchestra is used (assembled just for this recording session) or an old mono record has been reissued as "simulated stereo." Let your ear be the judge.

Schubert had a unique gift for melody; some of his best melodies are in his Quintet in C Major, op. 163. The quintet consists of two violins, a viola, and two cellos and is a small ensemble that plays chamber music. It is said that one cellist had the melody of the second movement engraved on his tombstone. *Note:* That "op. 163" after the title is a way composers have of numbering their work in sequence. This is the one hundred and sixty-third opus (op.) or major work that Schubert wrote.

Felix Mendelssohn (1809–1847) A concerto is a large-scale piece for solo instrument (sometimes two) and orchestra. Mendelssohn wrote only one violin concerto and it became a classic.

The Classical Period (ca. 1760–1827)

This has been called the golden age of music because of the exceptional composers of the time and because it established much of the musical language that we still enjoy today. On the whole the style is less flamboyant than the romantic style, more controlled, and more lucid. This control does not make the music of the classical period less emotional or less moving than music in any other style. In fact, the subtle control that is a hallmark of the classical style can lead to music of enormous power, as in the music of Beethoven.

Ludwig van Beethoven (1770–1827) Beethoven has been called the "Titan" and his Symphony no. 5 the "perfect symphony." Beethoven used a minimum of musical material (one motive and one rhythmic pattern) to generate all four movements of this always inspiring work.

Franz J. Haydn (1732–1809) The "father of the symphony" wrote one hundred and four symphonies, all of which have been recorded in a 46-volume set. Recommended are Symphony no. 94 (*Surprise*) and Symphony no. 101 (*Clock*). The *Surprise* in no. 94 is the unexpectedly loud chord in the second movement. The *Clock* in no. 101 is the tick-tock pattern of the second movement.

Wolfgang A. Mozart (1756–1791) Mozart is almost universally recognized as the greatest musical genius who ever lived, which makes only a few recommendations extremely difficult. Furthermore, there are more Mozart recordings than those of any other composer. Start out with Piano Concerto no. 21 in C Major, K. 467 and concentrate at first on the second movement. Mozart composed so rapidly and sometimes so chaotically that he could never keep track of his work. That "K" after the title means that a man named Köchel determined, after the fact, that this was Mozart's four hundred and sixty-seventh major work.

For a representative small choral work of the period listen to the *Vesperae Solennes de Confessore in C,* K. 339. This was written during the cultural period of the Enlightenment when most sacred music sounded like concert music, as does this piece. Listen especially to the "Adoramus Te," the serene soprano solo with chorus, found near the end of this work.

Mozart was the first major composer to write a lot of music for a newly invented (ca. 1732) instrument called the clarinet. No one has written more effectively for the instrument than he did in Quintet in A for Clarinet and Strings, K. 581.

Impressionism (ca. 1880–1920)

This music has a unique charm all its own as a kind of reverse image of classicism. Classicism tends to be precise, lucid, and energetic; impressionism tends to be vague, obscure, and dreamy. Cool jazz derived much of its inspiration and vocabulary from the lag-a-long mood of impressionism.

Claude Debussy (1862–1918) Debussy referred to his style as *symbolism,* but the impressionistic label appears to be firm. Much of his music can be compared with the painting styles of Monet and Renoir, of which his Prelude to the *Afternoon of a Faun* is a characteristic work. Be sure to study the liner notes so that you can tune in to the tropical torpor of a sleepy faun (not *fawn*).

His *La Mer* is a masterful evocation of the myriad sounds of the sea. Impressionism "does" water very nicely.

Baroque Music (1600–1750)

An introduction to the baroque style has been delayed because the style is so wonderfully complex. Baroque music is usually *monothematic;* that is, it limits itself to one theme. Because there is only one basic melodic idea (theme), baroque composers achieved variety by using a *polyphonic style,* i.e., the simultaneous sounding of two or more different melodies. Romantic-style composers used a main overriding theme with rich harmonies to accomplish their purpose; classical composers contrasted two different thematic ideas; baroque musicians delighted in the complexities of combining three, four, or more melodies. The overall effect of baroque music is generally very vigorous and dynamic with a strong driving beat. When jazz musicians try to "swing the classics," they almost always prefer the dynamic drive of the Baroque.

Johann Sebastian Bach (1685–1750) A powerful composer and one of the greatest, Bach composed a prodigious amount of music. Listen first to the Toccata and Fugue in D minor for organ that he wrote during his late teens. Avoid orchestral versions and stay with pipe organ recordings. If Bach had wanted this piece played by an orchestra he would have written it for an orchestra. As you listen to this brilliant work you may wonder why the film industry is given to showing lunatics playing this piece in a Parisian sewer or at a missile launch site.

Listen to some of the many records entitled *Bach Program,* the *Best of Bach,* or titles of that nature. In particular, try a recording by Ormandy that includes the Moog Synthesizer, a twentieth-century invention that does no disservice to Bach's eighteenth-century style.

George Frederick Handel (1685–1759) Handel, Bach's great contemporary, moved from Germany to England, thereby raising the level of English music. For stimulating music to lift your spirits try his *Water Music* Suite. *Note:* A suite is a series of pieces that contrast with each other but have no other necessary relationship. In this instance the suite is a shorter version of the complete *Water Music.*

Antonio Vivaldi (1678–1741) Vivaldi took special delight in writing for solo instruments and orchestra (including piccolo, guitar, and mandolin) of which the cheerful Concerto for Two Trumpets is a good example of the bright sound of baroque trumpets.

J. S. Bach He wrote six *Brandenburg* Concertos, each of which is actually a *concerto grosso* rather than a solo concerto. A *concerto grosso* is a small group of solo instruments (usually three or four) plus orchestra; it is a favorite device for sharp contrasts in texture and the popular echo effects. Listen to the high-pitched baroque trumpet in the *Brandenburg* Concerto no. 2 in F.

Twentieth Century

You can have anything you want from, say, neo-baroque to twenty radios playing twenty different stations (simultaneously) to wild manipulations of electronic tapes. *Recommendation:* Start with some established works, but check out experimental music from time to time to see what is going on in today's musical world.

Sergei Prokofiev (1891–1953) Prokofiev was the greatest film composer of his age and the Russian film director Sergei Eisenstein was equally outstanding in his field. Eisenstein's cinematic masterpiece, *Alexander Nevsky,* has a Prokofiev score that celebrates the glories of Russian music. Listen to *Alexander Nevsky,* op. 75.

Igor Stravinsky (1882–1971) One of the giants of the century, Stravinsky achieved early fame with his ballets for the Ballet Russe de Monte Carlo, of which *The Firebird* is an early work. Read the story line as you listen to the music.

Charles Ives (1874–1954) Ives is a Yankee original and his music as American as the Fourth of July—and as dissonant as you could want. Read the liner notes before you listen to his orchestral piece, *Three Places in New England,* and then identify the familiar American melodies as you envision the scenes he describes.

Renaissance Music (ca. 1400–1600)

The fifteenth and sixteenth centuries were the golden era of vocal music: lusty English madrigals, sophisticated French chansons, and much more. *Recommended:* All of the following anthologies.

1. *English Madrigals.* Columbia CSP C32160018.
2. *French Renaissance Dances.* Nonesuch 71036.
3. *Game of Love and Other Renaissance Delights.* Orion 7148.
4. *Love and Dalliance in Renaissance France.* Turnabout 34380.
5. *Renaissance Amorous Dialogues.* Nonesuch 71272.
6. *Songs of Shakespeare's Time.* Everett 3348.

Medieval Music (ca. 1100–1400)

Everything from lively dances to spirited sacred music including an overall feeling of freshness and delight. Among the many good recordings now available are the following.

1. *Douce Dame—Music of Courtly Love from Medieval France and Italy.* Vanguard 71179.
2. *Festival of Early Music.* Argo D400.
3. *In a Medieval Garden.* Nonesuch 71120.
4. *Medieval Music & Songs of Troubadours.* Everett 3270.
5. *Voices of Middle Ages.* Nonesuch 71171.

Americana

George Gershwin (1898–1937) America's greatest composer should be on every list. Listen to *Music of George Gershwin* (Columbia MS—7518) and excerpts from the best American opera, *Porgy and Bess.*

Scott Joplin (1868–1917) Joplin is another American original who was relatively unknown until another composer used his music for the score of the film *The Sting.* Joplin's ragtime music is viewed as chamber music by the New England Conservatory Ragtime Ensemble on *Music of Joplin* (Golden Crest GC—31031(Q)).

Summary

It should be pointed out that it takes a long time to learn to speak; it takes about as long to learn to listen. However, listening comes as naturally as speaking, and the music listed in this chapter is just one of the many approaches to good music. You won't like everything at first and you may not start liking some things until a year or two later. You will, however, gradually build up listening skills without even being aware of it. When you hear something that you didn't hear before in the same record, you are indeed sharpening your ear. Moreover, there is no regression with this music; you don't fall out of love with it, so to speak. Instead, your understanding will increase and you will begin to view at least some of the music listed in this chapter as pleasant old friends and lifelong companions.

Unit 2

Greece
The First Humanistic Culture

Early Greece: Preparation for the Good Life

As nearly everyone knows, it was in Greece, particularly in Athens for a short time in the fifth century (ca. 500–400 B.C.), that human life developed a quality that has seldom if ever been equaled. Here for the first time—and most gloriously—personal freedom was achieved for a large percentage of the population, with a sense of justice embodied in laws and a political system that gave individuals the greatest possible freedom compatible with the coherence of the social group. Here, too, there was a sufficient amount of wealth and leisure to allow individuals to develop their capabilities to the fullest. A sufficient challenge in the differences between the various city-states and between the individuals within them kept many persons keenly alive in the development of their full selves.

It would be convenient for the reader, and certainly for the authors, if the development to the apex of culture had proceeded in some sort of regular progression from the beginning of our knowledge about the Greeks until its culmination during the reign of Perikles[1] (PAIR–i–kleez) in Athens or if all of the statesmen who brought change to the Greek social structure had been high-minded men with a clear vision of the ultimate goal of human values. Unfortunately this is not the case. Greek history—even Greek geography—represents the ultimate in confusion, and even the statesmen who made the greatest contributions in the development of the social structure were often self-seeking politicians, not above taking bribes or committing treason to accomplish their purposes. Out of all of this confusing history the evolution of a society devoted, even for a brief time, to human values becomes a tribute to the toughness of the human spirit.

---

1. Greek spelling is used throughout, removing what Robert Fitzgerald, translator of Homer, has called a "Roman screen." Some Latinized spellings have been retained (Helen, Priam, Troy, Crete); other inconsistencies are, we trust, equally deliberate. Rather than include Greek accent marks we have provided phonetic pronunciations, e.g., Hêphaistos = Hephaistos (Hay–FYCE–toss). As Fitzgerald suggests, "Pronounce it slowly and boldly, and savor every syllable."

This chapter will attempt to trace the development of Greek society from its earliest beginnings to the fifth century in what is necessarily an oversimplified version. Eventually the focus will be on the city of Athens, where the highest development took place and where ideas that were generated throughout Greece came into greater conflict than they did in their places of origin. This will necessarily be a long chapter, since the whole Greek period covers 2000 years and this chapter will cope with 1500 of them. This was a lively, even a brawling culture, whose history is hard to trace. Furthermore, during the two millenia of the epoch the seeds—and some of the finest flowers—of all Western art and philosophy reveal themselves.

In the first place, let it be made clear that there never was a nation called Greece. Instead, we find a group of people who called themselves Hellenes (HEL–e–neez), united by a common language, with several dialects; by a common though diversified religion; and a common heritage. Politically these people lived in independent city-states, each with its own form of government. Frequently there were alliances between these small states, and in the fifth century Athens put together a very loose Athenian Empire, opposing a strong coalition of city-states whose allegiance was to Sparta. Greece was not even confined to a single geographical location. The map shows that the mainland of Greece is the tip of the Balkan Peninsula, joined by a narrow isthmus to a fairly large land mass known as the Peloponnesus (pel–uh–puh–NEES–us). This is the heartland. But Greece was invaded from the north in the twelfth and eleventh centuries (1199–1000 B.C.), and many of the mainlanders fled to the Asiatic coast of the Aegean (i–JEE–an) Sea and the islands off the Asian coast to form a flourishing Greek cultural center with many important cities. Later, in the seventh and sixth centuries (699–500 B.C.), land poverty on the mainland encouraged many of the city-states to send out colonies to occupy new land. As a result, a great number of Greek cities were formed all the way from Byzantium (bi–ZANT–e–um), now Istanbul, along both shores of the Mediterranean Sea, in Sicily, and in Italy. For example, Syracuse in Sicily, and Sybaris and Paestum in Italy were important Greek cities. Although these cities were widely dispersed and frequently at war with each other, their common culture, heritage, religion, and language gave them a sense of kinship as Hellenes, while all other people were regarded as barbarians or strangers. The Hellenes felt that they were different from and better than the "barbarians" (which means non-Greek), a sense that created unity amid the vast diversity and a pride that led to the remarkable accomplishments of the people we know as the Greeks.

The Geography of Mainland Greece

Mainland Greece was a hard country in which to live. Ranges of mountains divided the area so that communication across the countryside was extremely difficult. Furthermore, the mountains were so eroded that little farmland was available. Only in the north were there any broad and fertile plains. For the remainder, sheep and goats grazed on the mountain slopes and bee-culture was common. The valleys between the mountains offered small plots of arable land on which olives and grapes were the chief crops. It was in these valleys that the first villages appeared that would later unite to become city-states.

Nor was the climate conducive to easy living. In the winter great storms blew down from the north bringing torrential rains and, on the mountain peaks, a good deal of snow. The summers were extremely hot and dry.

There was still another geographical influence on Greek life: the closeness of the sea. Nowhere is the sea more than a few miles distant, and communication by water was frequently much easier than overland travel.

All of these factors contributed to the Greek character. In a hard land, people must be ingenious and clever to survive. In a land where nature yields little, people must turn to manufacturing objects in order to make a living. As compared to other early civilizations, the Greek population contained many more artisans and artists than peasants. Finally, the proximity of the sea always offered the possibility of trade and commerce (and piracy) as a source of livelihood. Such commerce always broadens horizons; in addition to the bartering of goods, the traders barter ideas and bring them home. It is never possible to attribute the character of a people to geography and climate alone, yet the factors mentioned here must have done much to shape the personality of the Hellenes.

Some Steps in Greek History

The first people about whom we have much information and who lived in Greek lands were the Minoans (mi–NO–uns), so named after the fabled King Minos (MI–nus) who lived on the island of Crete. These were probably not "Greek" people, in that their language, as far as one can tell, does not seem to be related to the Indo-European family. (Of this language we have only clay tablets in the "Linear A" writing, which has not yet been deciphered.) This Minoan culture existed from about 2600 B.C. to about 1125 B.C., and reached its peak somewhere around the year 2000 with the building of the great palaces and the surrounding towns of Knossos (KNAWS–us), Phaistos (FEST–us), Mallia (MAL–ya), and others.

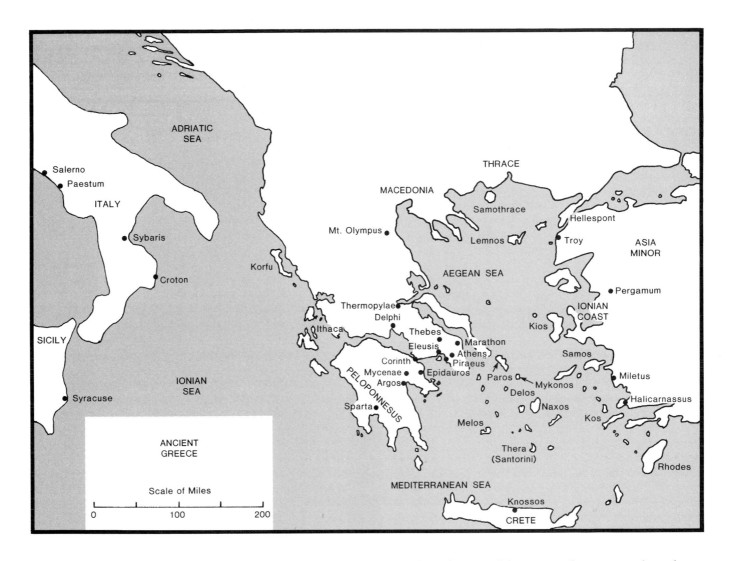

ANCIENT
GREECE

Scale of Miles

0   100   200

Despite the mystery of Linear A, we know a great deal about this culture because of the excavations by Sir Arthur Evans, Spyridon Marinatos, and others. From Evans's excavations and reconstructions at Knossos, we see that this rich and sophisticated culture prospered because of trade and commerce. The excavations of Professor Marinatos at the buried Minoan city of Akrotiri on the island of Thira, beginning in 1967, furnish additional evidence of trade with Egypt and the Asian coast of the Aegean Sea.

Apparently life was peaceful on Crete itself, for the palaces were not fortified, and the Cretans seem to have trusted their maritime power to ward off enemies. This sense of peace is enforced by the art of the time, for the paintings depict athletic contests (the famous bull-dance), women gossiping, cup-bearers, and the like, rather than scenes of war. The designs on jars and vases were ornate and colorful, utilizing fish and animal designs, one of the most common of which is the octopus, as the flowing tentacles offered an infinite possibility for involved and convoluted spirals and circles.

The religion of these people seems to have been a fertility cult and a worship of the earth goddess. This, in turn, led to a matriarchal form of government, with the essential power lying with the queen as the earthly representative, indeed the incarnation, of the earth mother. A part of this worship involved the tradition of the year-king, a tradition that the king married the queen for a specified time—a year, four years, perhaps some other length of time—after which he was killed and the queen took another husband. This custom relates to the concept that the earth (the queen) must be refertilized to maintain continuing prosperity. It is important to mention this here because of the belief by many scholars, particularly Robert Graves, that much of Greek myth arises out of the clash between this earth worship and the matriarchy it produced and the worship of the sky gods, a religion that was brought into Greece by the people we will know as the Mycenaeans (mi–se–NE–uns), the first of the true Greeks, whose worship venerated the male and male symbols rather than the female.

So much has been discovered about the Minoan culture that it could be described at very great length, however, the student is directed to such fictional works as Mary Renault's books *The King Must Die* and *The Bull from the Sea* for a real grasp of the nature of this civilization.

The fact is that for many years (from about 1900 B.C. onwards) a group of tribes from northern Europe had been slowly invading and infiltrating Greece. By the year 1600 they occupied all of the Greek mainland including the Peloponnesus, where, at Mycenae (mi–SEEN–ee), their Great King established his palace and fortress. One of the Great Kings was Agamemnon (ag–a–MEM–non). These were warlike peoples who naturally came into contact and conflict with Cretan culture, and some time after about 1450 B.C. they conquered Crete. A persistent legend and mounting archaeological evidence, particularly at Akrotiri on Thira (Santorini), suggest that the decline of Crete resulted from a cataclysmic eruption of the volcano on Thira in about 1450 B.C. After the volcano's final mighty convulsion, it collapsed into the sea, and tidal waves possibly four hundred or five hundred feet high spread throughout the Aegean Sea, fatally damaging, among other things, the entire Minoan culture. The ongoing excavations on Thira also tend to support the theory that Thira was the legendary Atlantis; most of the island did indeed sink into the sea. Also, there are partially substantiated theories that the Thira catastrophe caused gases and dust clouds to reach Egypt, resulting in the plagues described in the Bible. The parting of the Red Sea has been explained by the tidal waves generated by the eruption. Whatever the cause may have been, the power of Crete was broken and the Mycenaean Greeks became the overlords of the Aegean world.

The deciphering of clay tablets in the "Linear B" script in 1953 showed that the Mycenaeans were true Greeks who not only spoke a Greek language but also worshipped the Greek pantheon of sky gods. They created the heritage that united the Hellenes, for the Mycenaeans fought the Trojan War that centuries later was to become the subject of the Homeric poems and the core of the Hellenic tradition. This Mycenaean culture lasted from the sixteenth century through the twelfth century (1599–1100 B.C.).

As far as the facts of this culture are concerned, we know a considerable amount. The people established themselves in small, warlike independent kingdoms whose kings lived in strongly fortified but rich palaces. Each king was independent, administering his rule through a group of officials who supervised the farmlands, collected taxes in produce, managed religious celebrations and sacrifices, and otherwise handled all the affairs of government. Although each king was independent, each owed a rough allegiance to the high king at Mycenae; although, as seen in Homer's *Iliad* (IL–ee–ad), a local ruler could disobey the high king—as Akhilleus (Ah–KILI–eoos) did with Agamemnon—and not be forced to follow the ruler. Each king had a group of well-armed troops, and the nobles rode chariots into battle, although most of the fighting was done on foot.

These people carried on extensive trade, mostly among the islands and Asia Minor, although their influence extended throughout the Mediterranean world. Gold, ivory, textiles, and spices were bartered for the local products, and the number of gold ornaments and cups found in the royal tombs at Mycenae and at other great palaces attests to the rather barbaric wealth of these kings. In general their prosperity seems to have depended upon trade, commerce, and barter, which is to be remembered as we see this civilization decline in later years.

This was a society in which the masculine virtues were honored, as evidenced in the Homeric poems. Although Homer wrote his epic poems late in the ninth or early in the eighth century, his poetry seems to reflect with considerable accuracy the knowledge we can piece together about the Mycenaeans.

The chief virtues of the early Greeks were physical courage and the preservation of individual honor. These qualities are shown time and time again in the *Iliad*, as when Diomedes (di–uh–MEED–eez) broke from the ranks of his troops and ranged through the Trojan forces risking everything in individual combat. Or by Akhilleus, who by twentieth-century standards appears to be a pouting boy when Agamemnon takes his girl, Briseis (bri–SEE–us), from him, but was in reality the Greek hero whose personal honor had been affronted. He refused to fight, not from cowardice or pique, but simply because Agamemnon had insulted his pride and belittled him in front of the entire Argive (the Greeks, led by the king from Argos) army. The hero must retaliate, and he did so by refusing to fight until he was moved, not by loyalty to his cause or to his king, but by the grief he felt at the loss of his friend Patroklos (Pa–TRO–kloss). The greatest example of all is the death of Hektor in Book XXII of the *Iliad*. Here was a man, the greatest and strongest of the Trojan warriors, who could easily have shirked this last individual battle. His aged father pled with him to stay within the city walls; earlier, in a touching scene with his wife and his little child he admitted he knew that he and his city were doomed. Yet, when the time came, he had to assert himself in a glorious action that would test all of his powers to the utmost, fulfill all of his capacities, and finally bring him immortality, not in heaven, but in the minds of men. For these Greeks, human worth and dignity lay in total self-fulfillment, usually on the battlefield where their exploits would bring death, perhaps, but certainly fame among their fellows and among people to come after them as their deeds were recounted in song and story.

Another aspect of the Greek character, much admired throughout the history of the people, was the use of a wily and tricky intelligence. For this quality, Odysseus (o–DIS–yews) stands as the supreme example. Thus, when Odysseus finally won his way home to his kingdom of Ithaka he was put ashore disguised as a beggar. Here Athena (uh–THEE–nuh) met him and heard his lying tale. Her response was typical of the Greek attitude:

> "What a cunning knave it would take," she said, "to beat you at your tricks! Even a god would be hard put to it."

> "And so my stubborn friend, Odysseus the arch-deceiver, with his craving for intrigue, does not propose even in his own country to drop his sharp practice and the lying tales that he loves from the bottom of his heart. But no more of this: we are both adepts at chicane. For in the world of men you have no rival as a statesman and orator, while I am pre-eminent among the gods for invention and resource."

And a few lines later:

> "How like you to be so wary!" said Athena. "And that is why I cannot desert you in your misfortunes: you are so civilized, so intelligent, so self-possessed."

Perhaps in our time we cannot so admire the man who was so smoothly deceitful to gain his own ends; even in classic Greece Sophokles (SOF-o-kleez) despised these qualities, as he pictured a rather despicable Odysseus in the drama *Philoktetes* (fil–OK-ti-teez). But for the Greek of the heroic age, this was simply another example of the idea of self-fulfillment. Odysseus had been given the quality and the capacity for sharp intelligence, and it was his purpose, a purpose of all people, to utilize all of his capacities to their utmost. He would be a fool, shirking his own fate, not to use this ability.

Greek Religion in the Heroic Age

The worship of the Olympian gods forms one of the most curious religions that we know of. This religion had no "revealer," divine or mortal; no Christ, no Mohammed, no Buddha. Neither did it have any sacred book such as the Bible, the Koran, or the Talmud. As far as we know, it simply grew as a collection of myths that were honored in various ways throughout the Greek world. Even the myths varied greatly, so that no single version of the history and the nature of the gods exists. Hesiod (HEE-see-ud) in his book *Theogony* (thee-OG-uh-nee), and other writers as well, attempted to systematize the story of the gods, but with only minor success. Vastly simplified, the genealogy of the gods can be presented in the following way: In the beginning was Chaos, composed of void, mass, and darkness. From Chaos emerged a male god, Ouranos (YOOR-uh-noss), who represented the heavens, and a female god, Gaea (JEE-ah), who represented earth. These gods had three types of offspring, one of which was the Titans, who represented earthquakes and other cataclysms of the earth. Kronos (KRO-nos), one of the Titans, led a revolt against his father and overthrew him. (It is interesting that from the drops of blood of Ouranos sprang the fearful hags known as the Furies, whose duty it was to pursue anyone who had shed the blood of his kindred; this type of superstition was important because it helped hold the clans together.) Kronos took his sister Rhea (REE-uh), another representation of the earth goddess, as his wife, and from this union, although not without some difficulty, came the Olympian gods. The difficulty alluded to was the fact that Kronos had a prophecy that one of his children would overthrow him; to prevent this, he swallowed all his children at birth (Kronos, of course, may be thought of as Time, which swallows all things). By a trick, Rhea saved Zeus from being swallowed and spirited him away to Crete where he grew to manhood. Then Zeus led the prophesied revolt and, aided by some of the Titans, managed to imprison his father in the dark cave of Tartarus, but not before Kronos had regurgitated the other children, Demeter (di-MEET-er), Hera (HAY-ra), Hades (also called Pluto), Poseidon (po-SIDE-on), and Hestia. Zeus then took Hera as his wife and from this union came such gods and goddesses as Apollo, Aphrodite, Artemis, and others. (See box 4.1.)

In addition to these, many local gods and nymphs presided over particular streams and groves, and were worshipped locally. The whole Greek pantheon represents a most confusing array.

Just as confusing are the stories of the actions of the gods; we see Zeus almost constantly pursuing (and seducing) some mortal girl; all of the gods quarreled jealously among themselves; they all had favorites among the mortals, as we saw Athena protecting Odysseus; and they used all sorts of trickery to foil each other's designs for the success of their favorite mortals. How could such a group possibly be revered and worshipped?

If we can understand this worship, even faintly, then we may come to know something of the Greek character, and particularly some of its love for the very process of living. The gods were regarded as a race infinitely superior to human beings in that they were completely powerful, immortal, and always young and beautiful; they had the same characteristics as humans, but in a higher category. If people sometimes showed wisdom and nobility, so did Athena or Apollo (uh-POL-o), but to a vastly superior degree. If mortals were sometimes lustful, Zeus was much more so, and in his power, much more successful. If people were skilled artisans, so was Hephaistos (hay-FYCE-toss); if humans were crafty and skillful, so was Prometheus (pro-MEE-thee-us)—but the skill, wisdom, lust, or whatever quality one may choose of the gods was infinitely beyond that of mortals. For Greeks, death was a sort of dark oblivion, but the gods had life forever, and life in full beauty, full youth, and complete power.

Box 4.1 The Greek Pantheon

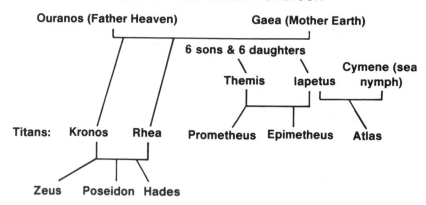

Zeus and his two brothers seized power from Kronos (Saturn) to originate "The Twelve," the Olympians who figure most prominently in Greek life. (The names in parentheses are Roman but these represent only approximations since Greeks and Romans had entirely different attitudes towards their respective gods, and towards most everything else for that matter.)

Zeus (Jupiter, Jove). Leader, god of the thunderbolt, representative of the power principle and chaser of women.

Hera (Juno). Long-suffering wife of Zeus, goddess of marriage and domestic stability.

Poseidon (Neptune). God of the sea and earthshaker (earthquakes).

Demeter (Ceres). Sister of Zeus and goddess of agriculture. Mother of *Persephone* and symbol of fertility.

Hades (Pluto, Dis). God of the underworld. Connected with nature myth by his marriage to Persephone who spends half her time on earth (the growing season) and half in the underworld (fall and winter). *Thanatos* represents death itself.

Pallas Athena (Minerva). Goddess of wisdom, warfare, arts and crafts. Sprang full-armed from the brow of Zeus. Patron goddess of Athens, representing the art of civilized living.

Phoibos Apollo (Sol). Son of Zeus and *Leto,* daughter of the Titans Krios and Phoebe. Sun god, archer, musician, god of truth, light, and healing. Represents principle of intellectual beauty.

Artemis (Diana, Cynthia). Sister of Apollo; virgin goddess of the moon and the hunt.

Aphrodite (Venus). Goddess of love and physical beauty. According to one version she was the daughter of Zeus and Dione; an alternate mythic version has her rising from the waves a la Botticelli.

Hephaistos (Vulcan). Lame blacksmith god who made armor for heroes, forged the thunderbolts of Zeus. Much-deceived husband of Aphrodite.

Hermes (Mercury). Son of Zeus and Maia, daughter of Atlas. Messenger and general handyman of Zeus. God of commerce, traders, travelers, and thieves.

Ares (Mars). Son of Zeus and Hera. God of war.

Hestia (Vesta). Virgin sister of Zeus and goddess of hearth and home. Later replaced among the Twelve by Dionysos.

Dionysos (Bacchus). Son of Zeus and mortal woman Semele. Like Demeter, connected with the principle of fertility and, like Persephone, represented the nature myth by dying in the autumn and being reborn in the spring. The Eleusinian Mysteries were dedicated to all three fertility deities and the festivals of Dionysos were periods of wild, Bacchic rejoicing, scheduled orgies so to speak. Since plays were usually performed at these festivals Dionysos also became god of the theatre. He represents the ecstatic principle as contrasted with the intellectual principle represented by Apollo.

LESSER OLYMPIANS

Eros (Cupid). Eternal child of Aphrodite and Hephaistos. Spirit of love with darts.

Pan (Pan). Son of Hermes, woodland god with goatlike horns and hoofs. Player of the pipes (panpipes).

Nemesis. Avenging goddess, the principle of retribution.

Hebe. Goddess of youth and cupbearer to the gods.

Iris. Goddess of the rainbow and sometimes messenger of the gods.

Hymen. Son of Aphrodite and Dionysos; god of the marriage festival.

The Three Graces: Aglaia (Splendor), *Euphrosyne* (Mirth), and *Thalia* (Good Cheer). Represented the principle of the happy life and always represented as a unit, which is a clear indication of the Greek version of the happy life.

The Nine Muses. Spirits of learning and of the arts. *Clio* (History), *Ourania* (Astronomy), *Melpomene* (Tragedy), *Thalia* (Comedy), *Terpsichore* (Dance), *Calliope* (Epic Poetry), *Erato* (Love Poetry), *Polyhymnia* (Sacred Poetry), and *Euterpe* (Lyric Poetry).

The Erinyes (Furies). *Tisiphone, Megaera,* and *Alecto.* Represented pangs of conscience; relentlessly hounded wrongdoers.

The Three Fates allotted to each man his destiny. *Clotho* spun the thread of life. *Lachesis* wove it into a pattern that determined the kind of life that would be led. *Atropos* cut the thread, terminating existence.

The worship of these gods during Mycenaean times and later may illustrate the point, for the formal ceremonies were always feasts. Animals were sacrificed, and a portion of the meat was burnt upon the fire. The rest was roasted and eaten by those performing the sacrifice. Wine was drunk, with a certain amount poured out first as a libation to the gods. Then the feast proceeded, with the assumption that the god was present as a guest at the meal, and that he enjoyed such things as well as the mortals did.

In what must seem to be a very diverse religious practice, one aspect of the life with the gods is of great importance. The Hellenes were never a priest-ridden group of people, as were the Egyptians. To us their religious practices seem relatively unstructured, almost casual; there was certainly plenty of room for freedom of thought. We will see later that in political organization the Greeks were not oppressed by despots, or at least not for very long. The Persians were, and culturally they produced only the monuments of an authoritarian state. In both religion and politics, the Greeks maintained the widest possible latitude for thought, questioning, and experimentation, which though turbulent and unstable, produced a great humanistic value system.

Such, greatly simplified, was the Olympian religion that existed from the fifteenth century throughout all of Greek history. During classical times and later, doubt may have existed about the nature and the presence of the gods but most people, excluding some of the intellectuals, believed in the gods, and for almost every important state decision one of the oracles was consulted, usually the oracle at Delphi. That the answers given by the oracles were frequently riddles that could be interpreted in any of several ways did not shake the faith of the people in the oracles themselves.

In this bewildering complexity of gods and people, what determined the events and the fate, or doom, of any individual? Here as before, we must rely on Homer, who wrote centuries after the heroic age and was none too certain himself of the answer to the question we have posed. In the first place, they had a vague belief that each of the people, or each of the heroes, had their own *moira* (MOY–ruh), or pattern of life, which they would fulfill. This may be illustrated as a sort of jigsaw puzzle that the hero's life would fill in—with the added complexity that the individual never knew what the picture would be when it was finished nor when it was completed. Within the individual's life we have the three forces of free will as determined by character, accident, and the intervention of the gods. These worked together, and sometimes in opposition, to determine the course of a person's life, and nothing could be counted on as certain until death finished the picture. This problem is considered in greater depth in *Oedipus the King* by Sophokles (see complete work in this volume). Frequently the gods intervened and brought tragedy to a person who overstepped the limits of human action and, out of pride, attempted to act in the realm of the

gods. Such action almost certainly brought about a doom. But for the most part it seems that in the heroic age a person's character *was* fate. The people did the things they did, receiving their attendant consequences, because of the kind of person they were. Thus Akhilleus, in spite of all sorts of ruses to outwit his predicted fate, had his short and glorious life just because he was the kind of person to whom personal honor was all important, because he took great risks in the hope of winning great fame. Odysseus, on the other hand, lived a long life not only because of his heroic strength, but also because of his ability to talk, to deceive, and to plan ahead for survival.

Such, then, is at least a suggestion of the nature of the Mycenaean civilization, the culture in which the Trojan War occurred, in which Agamemnon, Menelaos (men–uh–LAY–us), Helen, and the other fabled Greeks actually lived.

This Mycenaean culture began its decline in the twelfth century (the 1100s) as a result of many factors: a forced closing of trade with the Middle East; a series of wars between the kingdoms within the Mycenaean groups; and, most importantly, an invasion from the north by a group called the Dorians. These last were a people of the same racial stock as the Mycenaeans, but who were just now forced to migrate south because of the complicated folk movements of the time. They slowly occupied the mainland of Greece during the twelfth to the tenth centuries, overcoming the already spent civilization they found there. Two important consequences followed. First, a long "dark ages" descended upon Greece in which there was little cultural or artistic creation. Second, while retreating from the Dorians, the inhabitants of the Greek mainland emigrated to the Asiatic coast of the Aegean Sea where in the course of time, they developed a number of Greek cities in an advanced state of civilization. Because these last people spoke the Ionian dialect of Greek, this region became known as the Ionian coast and was later to become the center of the earliest Greek philosopher-scientists, as well as a land that was a sort of military football between the kingdoms of Lydia and Persia (the great Asiatic powers) and the city-states of Greece.

The Archaic Period (ca. 750–500 B.C.)

These dark ages move almost imperceptibly into the Archaic (ar–KAY–ic) times of historic Greece. We know quite a bit about the life of the period through the poems of Hesiod (HEE–see–ud), *Works and Days.* Hesiod was a farmer in Boeotia who, except for once winning a poetry contest, seems to have known nothing but bad luck. He gives us a picture of a landed aristocracy whose chief occupation was to squeeze the small farmer. Life was a continual round of jobs to be done with little or no reward or future in the work. Justice lay in the hands of the aristocrats who rendered their decisions almost entirely in terms of who could offer the largest bribe. Hesiod was always reverent towards the gods, but he neither expected nor got any reward in this life except for continuous toil, and Hesiod's plight was the common lot of most of the Greeks of his time.

Of course the latter part of the ninth century or the early part of the eighth was also the time when Homer wrote. While Hesiod was describing the life of his own time, Homer's work describes the departed glories of the heroic or Mycenaean period, which has already been discussed. We know little about Homer; computer analysis has shown that a single person, whom we call Homer, composed the tragedy of the *Iliad*. Analysis of the adventure tale that is the *Odyssey* is less conclusive, though Homer is the probable poet. However, precise knowledge about authorship is not as important as the fact that the *Iliad* and the *Odyssey* are at the very heart of the Greek heritage. Greek ideals, the idea of Greek superiority over the barbarians, and the overwhelming desire for personal honor were embodied in these works, and they became as close to a central religious book as the Greeks ever possessed. The works of Homer were memorized by every Greek student; they were recited at all of the great Greek festivals and games throughout the Hellenic world. Homer, of course, did not make up the stories he wrote. The poems were a collection of the legends that had their origins from time out of mind sung or recited by bards in the palaces. But they were brought together by the sure hand of a literary genius and transformed into the works that inspired the Greek mind from the time of their composition (fig. 4.1).

Figure 4.1 Portrait bust of Homer, marble, Roman copy of ca. 150 B.C. Certainly not a likeness, this is an idealized version of how a divinely inspired blind poet should look. National Museum, Naples.

But to return to the times of Hesiod. We witness first the rise of a landed aristocracy who, by force and guile, seized most of the land from the poor farmers. Not the least of the ways of acquiring land by the aristocrat was to lend money to the farmer, who used his own person as security for the loan. When he was unable to pay his debt, his land became the property of the aristocrat and the farmer became a slave. Numerous forms of governments arose at this time. Frequently the most powerful landowner became king; at other times the city-state was ruled by a committee of landowners, constituting an oligarchy. It was during this time that land poverty, simply the fact that there was not enough land to support the population, became painfully evident.

As a result of this land poverty the colonizing process that was mentioned earlier began to take place. Many city-states simply exported fairly large bands of adventurers to found colonies throughout the Aegean and Mediterranean world. Many colonies were established in northern Greece, including Byzantium, and a number of cities on the shores of the Black Sea. The present city of Marseilles in France was originally a Greek colony, as were a number of the cities of Sicily and Italy. The Greek world expanded greatly, and with the expansion came the development of trade and commerce among all of the Hellenic cities and an increasing flow of wealth into the original Greek cities. A large, important, and wealthy commercial class of people also began to form a part of the population of the cities, different from the landed aristocracy and opposed to them and different from the small-farmer group. This new group was to become a political faction to reckon with in the development of new governmental forms.

The first of the political changes came with the rise of *tyrants*. For us in the twentieth century, the term suggests a harsh military dictator, but at first, among the Hellenic cities, it was simply another word meaning "king." The tyrant was simply a man, sometimes chosen by the people, more usually a man who seized power and established himself as absolute ruler as long as he could hold office. Sometimes he came from the members of the old landowning families, a man who discerned the "wave of the future" and grabbed power either by allying himself with the merchant class or the farming class and promising political reforms, which would bring help to his political allies. Sometimes he rose from the merchant group; sometimes he was an outsider who came in to take over the rule of a city-state. No matter what his origin, he had to win over a good part of the population in order to try to hold his position, and he did this by effecting political, judicial, or economic reforms that would make him popular with a fairly large segment of the population. From this movement toward tyranny came the earliest reforms that were to lead, in Athens and some other cities, toward eventual democracy. None of this development was uniform through the cities of the Hellenic world; in none of them was progress a steady evolutionary process.

From this point on in our discussion, we shall focus our attention on governmental changes in the city of Athens, which in most ways was to become the most glorious of the Greek cities. For our purposes in this chapter, we shall consider only the changes made under the rule of four leaders: Draco (DRAY–ko), Solon (SO–lon), Pisistratus (pi–SIS–truh–tus), and Kleisthenes (KLICE–the–neez). They will seem to have appeared in orderly succession but this did not happen. For example, two of Pisistratus's sons attempted to follow their father in the corridors of power but one was assassinated in 514 and the other was exiled in 510. The course of leadership never seems to run smoothly.

The Rise of Athens

In considering the political and economic development of Athens from the sixth century on, it is well to bear in mind a rather curious power structure. Three political factions, largely determined by economic status, struggled for power. They were the old landed aristocracy, the poor farmers who eked out a living on marginal land, and the growing commercial class. In addition to these economic groups, Athenian life was dominated by four family-clans, originally of the aristocracy, who controlled the individual lives of their members, and in a fairly large measure controlled as well the political developments within the city. As long as these four tribes remained powerful, political and economic advances would always be dominated by the traditions of the tribes.

The first of the reformers in the seventh century was an almost legendary figure, Draco (fl. 621 B.C.), one of the early tyrants. His great contribution was to publish a code of laws. This simple act was a great step toward freedom. Hesiod, for example, had complained that the aristocrats who were the judges of his time were the only ones who knew the laws, and it appears that they made up the rules as they went along. An ordinary citizen involved in a legal suit about land or homicide really cast himself on the mercy of the judges who rendered decisions as they saw fit; decisions that depended upon the economic status of the litigants, their family connections, and the size of the bribe that could be offered. Obviously justice cannot prevail in such a system. Draco's Code, although it is reputed to have been very severe, did offer a single standard of justice for *all* people, and since the law was published, individuals within the state could know their legal rights. No matter how harsh the laws may have been, the publication of the laws became a step forward in developing a *rational* system of justice rather than one based upon tradition, privilege, and wealth.

The second of the great reformers was Solon (ca. 639–559 B.C.), a man whose name has come down to us as the synonym for a wise lawgiver. Like Draco, he was a member of the nobility, but evidently in his youth he had travelled extensively and had developed interests in the possibilities of trade and commerce, and he also became aware of the injustice of land distribution in his native state of Attica. Perhaps his most important reform was to free all slaves who had reached that condition because of debt, and to abolish the custom that made debt-slavery possible. A man who sought moderation in all things, he was evidently pressured to break up the great estates and to distribute the land to the farmers, but he did not have sufficient faith in the poor and uneducated masses to take this step. He did, however, allow all people to become involved to some extent with the government. He limited the magistracies and important governmental offices to the upper classes, but he allowed members of the lowest class, even, to serve as jurors, and thus he began a process of educating all people in the processes of social action and social change. In running the day-to-day affairs of Athens he established an administrative council of four hundred members, and thus greatly broadened the civic responsibilities of the citizens. Shrewdly anticipating conservative resistance to change and liberal proclivities for tinkering with reforms, Solon stipulated that all reforms had to remain in force and unchanged for ten years.

In order to encourage trade and commerce, Solon adopted a much lighter coinage than Athens had used in the past, and also he imported many artisans, particularly potters, since pottery manufacture was one of the chief industries of Athens and one of its main exports. These last reforms began a series of developments that were to break Athens away from an economic dependence upon agriculture and land and to establish it as a city whose wealth depended upon manufactured objects that were more or less independent of the uncontrollable forces of nature.

The third great reformer was Pisistratus (ca. 605–527 B.C.), who governed Athens from 546 till his death. In his economic reforms he was to follow the precedent that had already been set by Solon in that he broke up the large estates and distributed the land to the almost landless peasants. Since voting privileges and participation in the government were determined largely by economic status, this single reform did much to broaden the base for government, and it allowed the people who had already been somewhat educated in social action by Solon's changes to take a more important role than before in the actual government of the state. He and his sons further increased employment by starting a number of great public works within the city. Perhaps the most important of Pisistratus's contributions to the city lay in the development of its art. Two of the greatest Hellenic poets of the time, Simonides and Anakreon, were brought to Athens, and Pisistratus and his sons also commissioned the preparation of the first careful edition of Homer's poems, which were later sung and recited at all of the important festivals and sacrifices within the city. This last step may not seem to be of great importance, but its significance is apparent when one realizes that the learning of these poems by most of the citizens and their recitation at public functions gave the people a sense of common heritage and a feeling of unity *as citizens of Athens* not as members of a particular family clan. These tyrants of Athens, consciously or unconsciously, were leading their city toward democracy, and, by educating them through increased responsibility made them ready for active participation in a truly democratic government.

This government came into being with the reforms of Kleisthenes (fl. 582 B.C.) who attempted to abolish the influence of the four old aristocratic tribes whose power had, for years, been the dominant political influence in Athens. To accomplish this he instituted ten new "tribes" whose membership was based simply on place of residence rather than upon heredity. In order to do this he first divided the city into "demes" or neighborhoods. These purely artificial units furnished the basis for the political structure. Then a number of demes were combined to form a tribe, of which there were ten within the city-state. Furthermore, the demes for any single tribe were selected at random, so that within any tribe one found neighborhoods composed of the shore (people connected with shipping and seafaring trades), the city itself, and the rural areas. Thus no tribe was dominated by any single economic group. To make a not-too-exact analogy, we might think of the city of Detroit as divided into ten political groups but within each group one would find neighborhoods from the inner city, neighborhoods from the regularly employed working class, and neighborhoods from suburbs like Grosse Pointe.

Kleisthenes abolished the old Council of Four Hundred, which had come into being with the reforms of Solon, and substituted a Council of Five Hundred, with fifty members representing each of the new political tribes. He did this since the old council had come to be simply the voice of the four traditional tribes, and Kleisthenes wished to break their hold upon political and judicial matters. In the new government, each artificial political tribe nominated a large slate of candidates for the Council, from which fifty were selected by lot, on the theory that any citizen who was nominated (the nomination process eliminated the obviously unfit) was just as capable as any other citizen to administer the affairs of the state, so that actual membership could be left to chance.

The executive branch of the government was placed in the hands of a committee of ten generals who were elected yearly by the Council, and in turn this committee-of-ten was headed by a commander-in-chief whose term was also for a single year.

While Athens was developing its political institutions the mighty Persian Empire was becoming increasingly irritated with the rebellious Greek cities in Asia Minor. Athens supported the Ionian Greeks in their refusal to pay tribute to Darius (da–RYE–us), the Persian King, which gave him all the excuse a despot needs to give rebels a lesson in power, and the free city-state of Athens some instruction in humility. The Persians invaded mainland Greece in 490 B.C., a date that became pivotal for the future of Western culture.

North of Athens, on the plain of Marathon, the mighty army of a totalitarian state was confronted by a badly outnumbered Athenian force. Led by General Miltiades (mil–TIE–uh–deez), the Greeks, like the wily Odysseus, plotted to outwit the Persians and in a swift and stunning dawn attack drove the Persians back into their ships. According to the historian, Herodotos, the Persians lost more than six thousand men, while Greek casualties were minimal. Free people had turned back the Asian hordes and changed the course of history. The messenger who ran the twenty-six plus miles from Marathon to Athens symbolized more than news of an incredible victory. Greek pride in Hellenism, in the superiority of their culture over that of the barbarians, was fully vindicated.

The Persians were not to give up easily, and a second invasion was planned, but held up for ten years while the Persians put down a revolt in Egypt. In 480, however, they effected their second invasion. In the meantime the Athenians had discovered rich silver deposits at Mount Laurium in Attica, and had achieved a fairly high degree of wealth. Themistokles (the–MIS–tuh–kleez), the commander-in-chief in Athens, sent a delegation to Delphi to ask how best to meet the Persians in their second invasion, and was told that they should protect themselves with "wooden walls." Themistokles, with the usual Greek intellectual twist, believed that the Athenians could best protect themselves with a strong navy, and convinced his fellow citizens that the "wooden walls" were ships. Consequently, the money from the silver mines was used to build a strong Athenian navy, which proved to be not only a military force but also the determining factor in establishing Athens as a great commercial center. The Persian invasion of 480 was conducted on an even larger scale than the earlier war, for Herodotos estimates the Persian forces at five million men—an obvious exaggeration—but indicative of the size of the invading army. This army crossed the Aegean Sea far in the north and marched down the Greek peninsula, closely attended by the great Persian navy. The first of the great battles was a Persian victory, but a glorious episode in the history of Greece. This was the battle at the pass of Thermopylai (Ther–MOP–a–lye).

Here, at a narrow pass between the mountains and the sea, three hundred Spartans (now actually allied with Athens as a part of the fighting force) under their king, Leonidas (lee–ON–uh–dus), faced the entire Persian army and fought magnificently. When the Spartans were told to surrender or the sky would be darkened with arrows, Leonidas calmly replied that the Spartans would therefore fight in the shade. As usual in Greek wars, they were betrayed by a traitor who showed the Persians an alternative route through the mountains so that the Spartans were surrounded, but even in the face of such odds, they kept on fighting until they were all killed. The inscription later carved on the tomb of the heroic Spartans, in tremendous understatement and compression of meaning, gives testimony to the spirit of the encounter:

Go tell the Spartans, thou that passest by,
That here, obedient to their laws, we lie.

In the meantime the Persian fleet sailing down the coast in support of the army had suffered defeats from the Greeks and from the storms, but it still overwhelmingly outnumbered the ships of Athens and its allies. Eventually this fleet reached the sea just off Athens near the bay of Salamis (SAL–a–mus), while the land army moved inexorably toward its goal. Themistokles abandoned the city and all of Attica, moved the population to the island of Salamis, and prepared to gamble everything on a single naval battle. By trickery he enticed the Persian fleet into the Bay of Salamis, where the fleet's very size was a disadvantage, since in the narrow waters it was impossible to maneuver so many ships, and the Greek fleet attacked around the edges of the Persian ships and destroyed the Persians. The war continued for a year more on land, but the Persian army was finally defeated by the Spartans at the Battle of Plataca (pla–TEE–uh), and the Persian threat was broken.

It is almost impossible to overestimate the feeling of pride the Greeks felt as a result of these victories. Persia controlled Egypt, the entire eastern end of the Mediterranean Sea, and all of the land as far east as India. The wealth of the Persian kings and their satraps is impossible to estimate. Yet a relatively few Greek men, poverty-stricken in comparison to the Persians, had beaten off the totalitarian enemy. The Greeks rightly felt that their tradition of personal freedom, their pride in personal honor, and the love they felt for their cities had been the decisive factor. As indeed it was. Although the old aristocratic, oligarchical party continued in Athens, the years following the Persian wars marked the complete triumph of democracy in Athens. Suddenly the idea of freedom had worked.

For us in the Western world in the twentieth century, these far-off wars are of equal importance, for the Greek tradition—principally the concept of the worth of the individual person—survived and has given form to the ideas we now hold as of greatest worth. If the Greeks had failed, that tradition might have been snuffed out.

Another Quest for Freedom: The Philosophers

Developments in Greece during these preclassical times were not only political, economic, and military. One important phase of individual freedom is always the liberation of the human mind, allowing the individual to ask all the important questions of the gods and the universe and to formulate new and original answers. This, too, had been going on during the time of more tangible and material progress of which we have been taking note. Curiously, the abstract speculation about the nature of the universe was a Greek phenomenon, one not found in other parts of the Western world. The Egyptians had made astronomical observations, but always for such practical purposes as the prediction of the flooding of the Nile upon which their agriculture depended. So, too, in Babylon a number of astrologers had observed the stars, largely for use in making practical predictions about the affairs of the earth. But pure thought about the nature of things was uniquely Greek; Edith Hamilton attributes it to the loose, nonauthoritarian nature of Greek religion, which was never dominated by a priestly class. The miracle that was ancient Greece will never be satisfactorily explained anyway; the point is that the Greek philosopher-scientists, for whatever reason, were the first true philosophers (pure thinkers) in Western civilization.

The Ionian Philosophers

The first philosopher-scientists lived in the Ionian city of Miletus (my–LEET–us) with Thales (THAY–leez; ca. 636–546 B.C.) as their leading thinker. The *questions* they asked are always more important than the answers they found, for the questions are those that constantly return to challenge people's minds. The answers change as our knowledge of the universe becomes more varied.

One problem consistently bothered the philosophers of the Ionian (or Milesian) School. They were intrigued by the constant change of all the things they could see around them. Earth changed to plant life; plant life changed to animal; wherever one turned, one observed movement from one form of existence to another. They postulated that there must be one single basic substance of which all the forms of being are made, so that the process of change is simply the transformation of the basic element. The first question Thales asked, then, is *What is the single element, the basic stuff, of which the universe is composed?*

His answer was that this basic element is water, for all things need water for their existence, and water itself changes when heated or cooled to a gaseous nature—steam—or to a solid state—ice. These things being true and observable by our relatively coarse sensory equipment, all sorts of other changes and transformations that are not sense-apparent, could take place in water. Other philosophers, following the line of thought first explored by Thales, argued for earth or air as the basic world-stuff. But, as we have said before, the questions are important, not necessarily the answers.

A second of the Ionians, Anaximandros (a–NAKS–uh–man–dros; ca. 611–547 B.C.), a student of Thales, came up with the second question of importance, *How do specific things emerge from the basic element?* His answer, while it may seem unsatisfactory and vague, is probably more scientifically accurate than those of many of his contemporaries or successors. In the first place, he rejected the idea of a physical element such as water, earth, or air, and simply called his basic stuff "the Boundless." This, he suggested, was a form of being we cannot perceive with our senses; that is, it permeates everything and surrounds everything. In specific answer to the question he raised, he simply said that all forms that we can see—trees, living animal bodies, all specific things—are formed by "separating out" of this boundless element. Thus all forms that our senses can know, all physical things, simply coagulate out of the non-sense-apparent boundless and eventually lose their form and disappear back into it.

A later philosopher-scientist, not strictly a Milesian, since his native city was Ephesos on the Ionian coast and since he was doing most of his work right at the end of the sixth century (500 B.C.), was the philosopher Herakleitos (Hair–uh–KLY–toss; ca. 535–475 B.C.). Following the same line of thought as Thales and Anaximandros, he raised a third important question, *What guides the process of change?* He would grant a basic element from which all particular forms emerged, but he felt there must be some sort of controlling force to keep the process of universal change in order so that, let us say, an elm tree always produces elm trees rather than hippopotamuses.

Herakleitos denied the possibility of existence, for he felt that the universe was in a process of flow, not fixed. His basic belief is that nothing *is;* everything is *becoming.* Thus his famous statement that one can never step into the same river twice. The appearance of the river may be the "same," whatever that may mean, but by the time one has taken a foot out of the river and put it back, the water has changed, the bank has changed, nothing is exactly the same. The universe is in the same condition. Between *now* and *now* it has flowed, changed, varied; it is no longer the same even though its appearance may seem to remain.

Perhaps to illustrate this contention, he chose fire as his basic element. Thus one may watch a flame in a fireplace for half an hour and say to one's companion, "I have been watching that same flame for thirty minutes." Actually, though the shape of the flame may remain fairly constant, the burning gas that is the flame is never the same, even for the smallest fraction of a second. Thus is the universe envisioned by Heracleitus.

But such a universe needs a guiding force, for the human mind finds it hard to live with a picture of a changing world without some order and direction. So Herakleitos proposed a great *Logos* as the direct answer to his question of the guiding force. Now *logos* in Greek means *word.* Thus, the Gospel according to John, originally written in Greek, starts with the sentence, "In the beginning was the Word"—*logos* in Greek. But with John, as with Herakleitos, it obviously has a much more important significance than our word, *word.* For Herakleitos it meant a great *Intelligence,* which permeated the world and somehow guided the constant change of its flamelike element of which all things were composed. This sense of all things "knowing" what shapes they should take, what forms they should assume, is one of the great mysteries of the universe. (How does each maple leaf differ from every other maple leaf in the world, yet take a characteristic shape so that we can identify it at a glance? How does it "know" the form it must fulfill?) Herakleitos's assumption of a great Logos or Intelligence is not far from the assumption of a single God as an intellectual Principle in the universe.

The line of thought of these Ionian philosophers seems reasonable enough in their attempt to explain the element that is One and yet so many, which seems to be always the same and yet so varied. However, the basic assumption here is one of constant change, and furthermore, all of the conclusions these thinkers reached are based on the testimony of the human senses. We see, hear, taste, feel, or smell the phenomena of the world and the changing nature of all things. The search for a basic element from which it is all made is essentially a quest for "That Which is Real."

But the human mind can take an entirely different tack in this same quest. For example, our mind can simply say that whatever is *real* cannot always be changing. The mind can equate *permanence* with reality and say that only the things, or thing, that are absolutely permanent and unchanging are real. Furthermore, it can easily be proven that our senses cannot be trusted. We know they give us varying reports about the "same" thing. For example, water at the same temperature as measured by a thermometer will be either "hot" or "cold," depending on the temperature of our hands as we feel the water. Perhaps only the "thought process," independent of the senses, can be trusted as a guide to truth. Here we have the difference between scientists—people who trust their senses as they can be refined through such instruments as they can make—and pure philosophers, those who trust their minds alone to lead them to truth. This distinction appeared early in Greek thought.

Pythagoras

Pythagoras (ca. 582–507 B.C.) was one of the most original, interesting, and least-understood Greek philosophers. He was an Ionian Greek from the Aegean Island of Samos but he was most influential in southern Italy (Magna Graecia), where he established a religious brotherhood in Krotona (fig. 4.2).

Pythagoras taught that number was the essence of all things, in the same sense that his predecessors saw ultimate reality as water or the boundless or fire.

Figure 4.2 Marble bust identified as a portrait of Pythagoras and placed in the Roman Forum in 343 B.C. The identification is probably correct, for what we see here is a religious mystic. Museum, Ostia.

He believed that number was more than a symbolic construction, that all matter was essentially numerical, and that all relationships in the universe could be expressed through number. Pythagoras was the first Greek philosopher to reject the geocentric theory that the sun revolved around the earth. He reduced the earth to the status of a planet that revolved around the fixed point of a central fire; he also saw the sun revolving around what he called the hearth of the universe.

In his search for *that-which-is-most-real,* Pythagoras kept returning to the universality of mathematical relationships. For example, most of us know the formula in plane geometry called the Pythagorean theorem: In right-angle triangles the square of the hypotenuse is equal to the sum of the square of the other two sides. Here are three such triangles:

Although the triangles are dissimilar in appearance, one fact about them is true: $AB^2 + AC^2 = BC^2$. In Euclidean geometry this relationship was true before it was ever discovered, and it will remain true when there is no one on earth to be aware of it. Furthermore, it is true no matter what sensory conditions surround it. In the hottest furnace or the coldest refrigerator it is true. Here is an "idea" that has no substance, that exists entirely apart from people's minds; yet any shape that fulfills the equation is inevitably a right triangle. In this numerical relationship we have the pattern for a physical thing. Pythagoras is therefore credited with the discovery of pure mathematics, with the development of mathematical proofs, and with the awareness that form and structure give objects individual identities. These monumental achievements provide the framework for the Eleatic philosophers and particularly Plato (see chap. 6), upon whom Pythagoras was the single most important influence.

Pythagoras was the first to prove a relationship between mathematics and the harmonies of music. He discovered, through experimentation, that vibrating strings had certain relationships that were dependent on the relative lengths of the strings. These relationships were as consistent and as true as the Pythagorean theorem. For example, a string that is, say, 30 cm long vibrates twice as fast as a string that is 60 cm in length. Further, the 30-cm string produces a tone or musical pitch that is eight notes higher (called *octave*); the name of the note is the same, but the pitch is an octave higher:

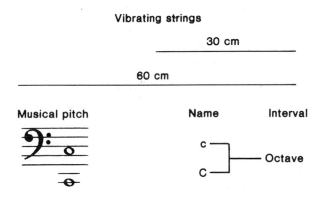

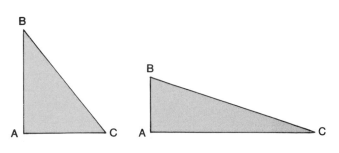

A string 20 cm long vibrates three times as fast as the 60-cm string and produces a pitch a 12th (octave plus five notes) above the lower string. Finally, a string 15 cm long vibrates four times as fast and produces a pitch two octaves higher. Though more and shorter strings can be used, Pythagoras chose to utilize the relationships as illustrated below:

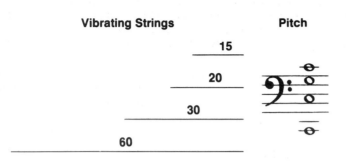

The longest string represents unity to which the other strings are related in vibration ratios of 2:1 (twice as fast), 3:1 (three times as fast), and 4:1 (four times as fast). This is a fact of nature that is always true, and its discovery acted upon Pythagoras like a mystic force. He based his philosophy of numbers upon a permanent reality symbolized by the unchanging relationships of the musical intervals. To Pythagoras these eternal truths proved that there was unity in the universe, that everything had its proper place, and that the universe and all within it could be understood in terms of numerical relationships.

You will notice that three of the four pitches have the same letter name; only the pitch level is different. The bottom *C* represents unity; the two higher *c*'s are derived from unity and related to unity by the even numbers of 2 (2:1) and 4 (4:1). The different note, the *g* represents diversity, for it is the next odd number (3) after unity (1). According to Pythagoras odd numbers are primary, strong, and masculine; even numbers are secondary, weak, and feminine, for they cannot exist independently.

Pythagoras, like most Greeks, considered 3 as the most logical number because it had a "beginning, middle, and end." Pythagoras's perfect number, however, was 10. He used a base 10 mathematical system (just as we do); ten has both a one for unity and a zero, which could be interpreted as representing eternity; ten terminates the one through ten sequence and all beyond this is reiteration of 1–2–3–4–5–6–7–8–9–10.

As previously demonstrated, the ratio of vibrations for the four strings is 1:2, 1:3, 1:4 (or 2:1, 3:1, and 4:1 since ratios can always be reversed). When arranged as superparticular ratios (each whole number differing by one) the three primary musical intervals are included: 1:2 (Perfect Octave), 2:3 (Perfect Fifth), and 3:4 (Perfect Fourth). Moreover, when 1:2:3:4 are added together the sum is ten, thus further confirming the perfection of ten.

Ten is the perfect number for a universe that has, according to Pythagoras, ten planets: sun, moon, Mercury, Venus, Mars, Jupiter, Saturn, the "dome of stars," earth, and counter earth. Of course he postulates a counter earth so that his so-called planets will add up to ten. He is also displaying a typically Greek determination to view the world as it should be rather than as it is. This Greek idealism will be discussed later, particularly in conjunction with Greek art.

Next, Pythagoras considers the 1:2:3:4 from the viewpoint of the "tetractys (tuh–TRACK–tus) of the decad (DEE–cad)," which translates as the "four quality of the ten." This is shown as an equilateral triangle of ten units in a 1:2:3:4 construction from each of the three points:

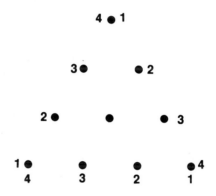

Each of the three sides has four units with a total of ten units in the triangle, and thus the tetractys of the decad. The equilateral triangle is the perfect figure, of course.

Pythagoras further emphasizes the fourness of this figure by pointing out that the figure represents the four mathematical qualities of point, line, plane, and solid. The *point* is one unit, the *line* is an outside lateral of four units, the *plane* (as in plane geometry) is the equilateral triangle (the perfect two-dimensional figure). Finally, the *solid* is the decad envisioned as three dimensional, i.e., as a pyramid, the perfect solid.

The heavenly bodies are pictured as revolving from west to east in an orderly circular orbit around the central fire. Agreement between nature and number has been proven (1:2:3:4) and so orbits are determined by relating them to musical intervals. The predictability of nature, like that of intervals on a vibrating string, was therefore musical and the wheeling arcs of the celestial globes was the *harmonia* of the *kosmos*, the music of the spheres.

From the theory of 10 as the perfect number Pythagoras applied numerical concepts to the world about him, using the concept that odd numbers were strong and masculine and even numbers were weak and feminine. Following are several of the less complicated concepts:

1 = unity
2 = female
3 = male
4 = justice (idea of retribution or 2 × 2)
5 = marriage (2 + 3)
7 = the goddess Athena because it is not generated by the numbers it contains (2 + 5 or 3 + 4). In other words, Athena was a virgin.

A basic thread in Greek thought is the idea that harmony is like a mean between two extremes. One of the first to promote the concepts of balance and control was Pythagoras, who set up the general parameters in his theory of the ten fundamental antitheses:

Odd Numbers (Perfect)	Even Numbers (Imperfect)
Limited	Unlimited
Odd	Even
Right	Left
One	Many
Male	Female
Rest	Motion
Straight	Crooked
Light	Darkness
Good	Evil
Square	Rectangular

A harmony between any of the two extremes listed above is never found precisely halfway in between. Situations change; what was reasonable one day might have to shift towards the other extreme the next day. Furthermore, since the odd numbers are perfect, the tilt will certainly favor the perfect numbers, particularly good over evil and light over darkness. In order to see how the ideas of Pythagoras were applied in everyday life it is now time to turn to the Pythagorean Order.

In the Pythagorean Order philosophy was a central part of a religious way of life, a life-style that was intellectual, political, religious, ethical. Small communities functioned within the larger community, each a social and religious unit as well as a scientific study group. Property was held in common, there was no discrimination based on sex, and music and mathematics were a regular part of social life.

The Pythagoreans are known especially for their doctrine of the transmigration of souls. They believed that souls were reincarnated in a series of lives as they tried to ascend to an ideal existence in a life of divine bliss. The ideal could be approached only through purification, emphasis upon intellectual activity, and renunciation of worldly sensuality. Salvation could be attained only after a final escape from the cycle of intermediate births.

The Pythagoreans were vegetarians who believed in the brotherhood of all living things. They believed in spiritual purification through music and science and physical purification through medicine and gymnastics. They advocated a humane society in which people would live always in harmony and friendship. Eventually they were either killed or forced to flee their communes by neighboring tribes who considered the Pythagoreans a threat to established religious practices.

Summary

In all these developments we see a culture emerging from chaos to a period of adjustment. A new political form, democracy, has appeared but still has to be tested by the stubborn aristocracy. There is great pride in Hellenism, in the great heritage celebrated in the Homeric poems and tremendously enhanced by the victories over the Persians. There is a loose religious structure and much philosophical speculation. Here is all the raw material for a great culture in which we will see the development of the arts and of philosophy as never before, or since.

Bibliography

The following were selected as being particularly useful and interesting with a range from standard works to recent publications.

General Studies of Greek Culture   These works cover the whole period through the Hellenistic Age and will not be listed again.

Asimov, Isaac. *The Greeks: A Great Adventure.* Boston: Houghton Mifflin Company, 1965. Lively and informal.

Barr, Stringfellow. *The Will of Zeus; A History of Greece from the Origins of Hellenic Culture to the Death of Alexander.* Philadelphia: J.B. Lippincott Company, 1961. Whenever possible Barr lets the Greeks tell their own tale. No one can tell it better.

Beye, Charles Rowan. *Ancient Greek Literature and Society.* Anchor Press, 1975. An interesting and sometimes pungent analysis of the beauties of classical Greek and the deficiencies of Latin, among other languages.

Bury, J. B. *History of Greece.* New York: St. Martin's Press, 1975. This is still the standard history, thorough but readable. The history of Alexander and the details of his campaigns are highlights.

Chamoux, Francois. *The Civilization of Greece.* New York: Simon & Schuster, 1965. A handsome cultural history with fine illustrations.

Durant, Will. *The Life of Greece.* Vol. 2, *The Story of Civilization.* New York: Simon & Schuster, 1939. Colorful with true flavor of Greek character.

Eliot, Alexander. *The Horizon Concise History of Greece.* New York: Horizon Press, 1973. This is packed with information and is stimulating to read.

Pollitt, J. J. *The Ancient View of Greek Art: Criticism, History and Terminology.* New Haven, Conn.: Yale University Press, 1974. The Greeks talk about their art in their own words.

Translations of Original Material

Fitzgerald, Robert. *The Iliad of Homer.* Garden City, N.Y.: Doubleday & Company, 1975. And *The Odyssey of Homer.* Garden City, N.Y.: Doubleday & Company, 1961. Each generation should have its translation of Homer and this translation is superb. All the sense of Homer is there and much of the power and the beauty—and the language is idiomatic contemporary American English. Compare this with any other translation and notice the differences. Compare Fitzgerald with the translation of Alexander Pope and marvel at the clear display of cultural differences.

Herodotus. *The Persian Wars,* a new translation by Aubrey de Selincourt. Baltimore, Md.: Penguin Books, 1972. Everyone should read the very first historian of Western culture simply because Herodotus is such a fascinating writer.

Commentaries of One Sort or Another

de Selincourt, Aubrey. *The World of Herodotus.* Boston, Mass.: Little, Brown and Company, 1962. An evaluation of the ancient world and of Herodotus as an historian.

Hogan, James C. *A Guide to the Iliad; based on the translation by Robert Fitzgerald.* Garden City, N.Y.: Doubleday & Company, 1979.

Renault, Mary. *The Bull from the Sea.* New York: Random House, 1962. And *The King Must Die.* New York: Bantam Books, 1964. This is fine historical fiction. Historical facts and archaeological data are accurate and are utilized to bring ancient Crete to life.

Note: New archaeological evidence about the Greeks is constantly appearing. This kind of up-to-date information can be found in periodicals such as: *National Geographic, Smithsonian, Science News, Archaeology.*

Hellenic Athens: The Fulfillment of the Good Life

The city of Athens in 461 B.C. must have been an exciting place in which to live. It was prosperous and strong and, though no one knew it at the time, about to enter its Golden Age, that incredible era (ca. 460–430 B.C.) during which the resident artists, writers, statesmen, and philosophers would establish a society based on human values and on a commitment to truth, beauty, and justice. It was not a perfect society—far from it—but it did aspire to perfection. For a fleeting moment life was enveloped in the lusty embrace of a society that dared to compete with the gods.

Athenian Greeks may have been the most verbal people in the ancient world. Blessed with a sophisticated language rich in vocabulary and capable of infinite subtleties, they talked, discussed, argued, and debated everything under the sun: politics, society, love, and especially philosophy, because the intellectuals of the city were fascinated by the world of ideas. Herakleitean belief in constant change had its supporters, while others contended that reality could be expressed through numerical relationships, as Pythagoras had said. Entering into the debate came new ideas from Elea, the prosperous Greek colony in southern Italy. Led by Parmenides (par–MEN–uh–deez; born ca. 514 B.C.), the Eleatic School refused to accept the Herakleitean idea that nothing *is*, that the universe was in a constant state of *becoming*.

As the very basis of their thought they stated that whatever is *real* must be permanent and unchanging. If one turns the statement around, it may seem more logical: anything that constantly changes its state of Being cannot be real. Furthermore, they attacked the method of the Ionian philosophers by pointing out that the Ionians depended entirely upon their senses for the discovery of truth, trusting their sight, their sense of feeling, their hearing, the senses of smell and taste to lead them to valid conclusions. The Eleatics were quick to point out that the senses cannot be trusted. Of course this contention is easy to support; the sense impression that one receives depends quite as much on the state of the receiving sense organ as upon the thing itself. (The color-blind person sees a green traffic light as a sort of neutral gray; the person with "normal" sight sees it as green. Which is it really? For that matter, when one person sees "green" and another person agrees, are they really seeing the same color?) If the senses cannot be trusted as a guide to truth, what can? The Eleatic philosophers asserted that only the mind is a sure guide, and they could point to such truths as those found by the geometers like Pythagoras to support their theory that the mind, without the aid of the senses, can arrive at truth. As a matter of fact, these thinkers were much like the Pythagoreans, and form a sort of bridge between him and Plato, who will be discussed later. In the middle of the fifth century, Parmenides visited Athens at a time when Sokrates would have been about twenty years old. The two men could have met at that time.

The development of material philosophy reached its high point with the Athenian Leucippus, and his student, Demokritos (Di–MOK–ruh–toss; ca. 460–370 B.C.). Demokritos synthesized the attempts of the Milesians to understand the physical world and developed a theory of the material world that could not be verified until the twentieth century. He postulated Greek atomic theory, apparently using no more and no less than the power of his mind. According to Demokritos all matter consists of minute particles called *atoma* (unable to be cut). These atoms exist in space, combine and separate because of "necessity," and represent a strict conservation of matter and energy, i.e., the same number of atoms always exists; only the combinations differ. Contemporary nuclear physics confirms a strict conservation of matter and energy when taken together but identifies probability rather than necessity in terms of causality. As everyone knows, atoms do exist and some of them can be divided.

Following the Persian wars, Athens was optimistic and hopeful, filled with democratic pride and a confusion of ideas. Furthermore, the entire city had been burned by the Persians and needed to be rebuilt. The possibilities for growth and progress lay everywhere, but direction for human growth was needed. In terms of the development of the spirit, Aeschylus (ESK–i–lus), the playwright-artist in a time of chaos and early adjustment, was to point the way.

The Drama and Aeschylus

Before speaking specifically of the plays of Aeschylus, it might be well to mention something about the history of the drama. It began in Greece, as it was to do later in the Middle Ages in Europe, as a part of the worship service. Originally the priest spoke individual parts, while a chorus chanted responses. An original and almost mythical dramatist, Thespis (THES–pis), began to transform this rite into secular drama during the Archaic period.

The theatres were always in the open air, with the seats for spectators ascending the side of a hill. At the bottom of the hill a round flat area (the orchestra) provided a space in which the chorus danced and sang and chanted, and which had as its center the statue or altar of the god. Back of this and facing the audi-

Figure 5.1 Stone carving of theatrical mask at Ephesos, Turkey, where the Graeco-Roman theatre seated 25,000 spectators.

ence was a long low building (the skene) with a room at either end and a platform between the two rooms. The rooms were for dressing and storage and the chief actors performed on the platform above and behind the chorus. (See fig. 8.7.)

Since they functioned as places of education and entertainment for most of the populace of a city-state, theatres were very large; seating was for 13,000 at Epidauros and 18,000 in Athens. These semicircular stadiums featured acoustics so fine that the actors could be understood fifty rows above the stage; however, because facial expressions could not be seen from this distance, performers wore large masks of easily recognizable character types (fig. 5.1). To compensate for distortions when viewed from high above, actors wore clog shoes that were about eight inches high, a convention that also contributed to the larger-than-life image of the subjects. Violence always took place offstage and was reported either by a messenger or another character. One stage set served throughout the play, and the only stage machinery was the *mechane,* a crane that transported the actors who played gods. This was the celebrated *deus ex machina,* or "god from a machine." Permanent stage sets, masks, clogs, offstage violence, dance, and music all challenged spectators to use their imaginations. (See also "The Art of Dance and Greek Theatre" in chap. 8.)

Drama festivals were held throughout Greece, but the one at Athens in honor of the god Dionysos (Di–uh–NYE–sos, and several other pronunciations) was the most important. Before the festival a number of playwrights would submit their plays to a board of judges, and the plays of four dramatists would be chosen for presentation, each one on a different day. In Aeschylus's time, each dramatist submitted a trilogy (a series of three plays on one theme) and a satyr play, which was a bawdy comedy presented at the end of the trilogy. A wealthy citizen paid the production costs for a playwright in the hope that his dramatist would win the first prize. A slight charge was made for seats at the drama, but in the fifth century the city paid for the admission of any citizens who could not afford it. Thus, if a writer had a message he wished to give to the entire population of his city, the drama was an almost perfect vehicle.

Aeschylus lived from 525 to 456 and was, therefore, a part of the great development of Greece as a whole, and Athens in particular. He was a soldier at the Battle of Marathon, a fact he had recorded on his tomb rather than that he was a dramatist. An aristocrat by birth, his drama presents a synthesis between the old ideas and those of the most enthusiastic democrats. Aeschylus has sometimes been accused of being much more of a preacher than a dramatist, for all of his plays carry a clearly stated message; yet Edith Hamilton points out that he was so much a dramatist that when the dramatic form did not exist, he invented it. Certainly before his time the cast contained only one speaking actor and the chorus. Aeschylus introduced a second speaking actor so that we could have the possibility of dialogue, real conflict, and resolution between two people and two ideas.

Aeschylus wrote about ninety plays, of which seven survive. Of these, only the trilogy called the *Oresteia* (O–res–TYE–ya), the story of Orestes, son of Agamemnon, will be discussed here. The trilogy consists of *Agamemnon,* the *Libation Bearers,* and the *Eumenides* (you–MEN–i–deez). The first and third plays are included in this chapter, but all three will be considered here as if they were three acts of a single drama. They relate the story of the evolution of a system of justice dominated by tradition, fear, and

personal revenge into a new justice administered by the law courts of a free society.

Agamemnon begins in what Aeschylus must have regarded as the rural district of Argos, in front of the palace of Agamemnon, on what should be the most joyous day in ten years, for word has just been received that Troy has fallen, the ten-year Trojan War is over, the Greeks have been victorious, and Agamemnon, the great king, is returning. It should be a day of rejoicing, but the watchman on the palace who first sees the signal fires announcing the victory mutters darkly about the evil deeds that have been going on within the palace; the chorus refuses to believe in the message of the signal fires and spends much of the first part of the play recounting the sacrifice that was a part of the beginning of the war.

Their particular concern is with the death of Iphigeneia (If–i–je–NY–ya), the daughter of Agamemnon and Klytaimestra (Kly–tay–MES–tra) at Aulis (AW–lis) ten years before. The myth tells us that at the beginning of the war the brother kings, Agamemnon and Menelaos (Men–uh–LAY–os), had assembled the Greek army at the port of Aulis for embarkation to Troy, but after the troops were gathered Agamemnon had offended the goddess Artemis (ART–uh–mis) by violating her injunction against hunting. In retaliation she refused to grant favorable winds to the fleet unless Agamemnon offered his daughter as a sacrifice. Faced with a choice of standing firm against restless troops anxious for battle or sacrificing his daughter, Agamemnon, truly the son of his father, made the worst choice. He compounded the evil by sending for Iphigeneia on the pretext that she was to be married. (See box 5.1.)

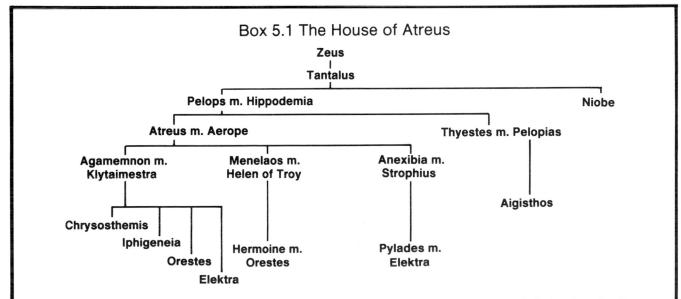

Box 5.1 The House of Atreus

Zeus

Tantalus

Pelops m. Hippodemia — Niobe

Atreus m. Aerope — Thyestes m. Pelopias

Agamemnon m. Klytaimestra — Menelaos m. Helen of Troy — Anexibia m. Strophius

Aigisthos

Chrysosthemis

Iphigeneia

Orestes

Hermoine m. Orestes

Pylades m. Elektra

Elektra

Like most old Greek families the roots go back to Zeus, in this case through Tantalus, a mortal who was permitted nectar and ambrosia at the table of the gods. In order to trick the gods and show them as fallible Tantalus hosted a banquet and served them a stew made of his son Pelops. The furious immortals dispatched Tantalus to Hades to suffer eternal hunger and thirst for he was guilty of *hubris* (overbearing pride), the worst of all sins. The family curse continued with the sons of Pelops. Thyestes (thigh–ES–teez) seduced Aerope, his brother's wife; Atreus, in revenge, killed three of Thyestes' four sons (Aigisthos survived) and served them to their father as a meat course. In his *Oresteia* trilogy Aeschylus dramatizes the working out of the curse.

The chorus also calls our attention to Agamemnon's cousin, Aigisthos (i–JIS–thos), who now occupies the bed of the warring king. Moreover, Klytaimestra has not only taken a lover, she has dared to act as a man, to govern with a firm hand as a man would govern. What should be a day of rejoicing at the return of the victorious king starts as a day when all the dark collective guilt of the past is forced on the awareness of the chorus and the audience.

Finally Agamemnon himself returns, accompanied by Kassandra (Ka–SAN–druh), a princess from Troy who has received the unfortunate gift from Apollo that she can prophesy the future, but that no one will believe her prophesies. The last is not of immediate concern, though it will become important later in the play. What is of importance is that she has come on the same ship with the king, and now appears with him in his chariot. Of course Greek heroes were expected to take captive maidens as their mistresses, but the custom was that they would be brought home in a ship with the rest of the captured booty, and would serve as slaves in the household of their new master. Kassandra's appearance in Agamemnon's chariot is another act that will anger Klytaimestra.

Upon his arrival at the palace, Klytaimestra greets her husband so effusively that one recognizes this as a set speech, the sort of thing that is said when a returning hero is presented the keys to the city on the courthouse steps. Symbolically there follows one of the most important events of the drama, for the wife asks Agamemnon to enter the palace on a carpet dyed with a crimson (or purple) dye, which is so costly that it is reserved for the gods. Agamemnon refuses at first, but is persuaded by his wife. The act shows a pride too great for men; this mortal is stepping out of his proper zone and into the area reserved for the gods. Quite aside from his human errors, which angered his wife, this prideful act alone is sufficient to mark him for death.

After he has gone into the palace, we have one of the most interesting scenes of the play, for Kassandra tries to tell the chorus that Agamemnon is to be killed. Raging back and forth in an almost animal fury, probably in opposition to the strophe and antistrophe of the chorus, she tries to tell them of the murder being committed and urges them to break down the palace doors and prevent the deed. Casting aside all of her prophetic regalia, she finally shouts, "I say you shall see Agamemnon dead!" The chorus remains dumb and stupid, refusing to act. Then Kassandra, knowing she is to be murdered, meekly goes into the palace, hoping only that her death blow will be sure and swift.

Only when they hear Agamemnon cry out that he has been struck does the chorus nearly rouse itself to action. For the first time in Greek drama the members of the chorus speak as individuals, each with a short solo speech. The mood reaches a crescendo in the middle of this brief section when they are almost ready to break in and catch the murderers red-handed. Then apathy takes over, and at the end of the sequence they agree to wait until they really know what has happened. They do not have long to wait.

The palace doors are flung open, revealing the bodies of Agamemnon and Kassandra, with Klytaimestra proudly announcing that she has done this deed. The chorus mutters its protest, and Klytaimestra tries to calm them by suggesting that she is only the instrument of fate and the ancient curse on the house. Finally Aigisthos appears, rattles his sword a bit, and tells them to go home. The play closes as the chorus rather childishly tells the murderers just to wait until Orestes comes home to take his vengeance.

What does all this mean? It is interesting that the image most often presented in the play is that of a net or web. The purple carpet is referred to as a web, and Agamemnon has a net thrown over him in his bath so that he cannot resist while the murderous blows are being struck. Perhaps Aeschylus felt that this net was the old traditionalism, the belief in fate, and the idea of justice as revenge. Certainly the chorus is bound up in this web, since many of their speeches warn against pride, against wealth that breeds pride, and against any sort of innovation. Their wisdom follows the ancestral traditions hindering action. If they had acted by breaking down the door of the palace, they might have done more than merely break through a door; they might have broken the barrier between themselves and freedom. Curiously, Kassandra tries to inspire them to act, but she cannot do it. She, too, is caught in the net. The key to this lies in her entrance into the palace to meet her known fate. Even the chorus admonishes her that to delay her death even by a short time is to gain a small victory, but she answers that the time of her doom has arrived. She, too, is enmeshed by a belief in a fate that rules her life. Of all the characters in the play, only Klytaimestra seems free to act as a human being. True, she falls back upon the curse on the House of Atreus at the end, but this is only to placate the chorus in terms that they can understand. But her action is murderous and destructive, a type of freedom that cannot be permitted to survive in a community of human beings. So, at the end of the first play we have two conditions of human existence: that of the chorus, which is always looking backward to tradition for guidance in their lives, and that of Klytaimestra, whose wild destructive freedom will destroy human society. Aeschylus's job in the remaining two plays of the trilogy is to free one segment of society and restrict the other.

The second play in the trilogy, the *Libation Bearers,* is principally a transition play designed to bring the problem to a head. Orestes as a young man returns from Phocis (rhymes with *focus*) where he has been reared. He bears with him the command of Apollo to kill his mother and Aigisthos to avenge the murder of his father. It is interesting that this is the command of Apollo, a member of the new generation of progressive gods. On the other hand, we have the old tradition coming from clan and tribal governments that anyone who spills kindred blood will be hounded to his death by the Furies. Orestes is caught between two seemingly equally forceful commands; in his killing of his mother, he is damned if he does, and damned if he doesn't. But he does return, and in what must be the most awkwardly handled recognition scene in the history of drama, he is reunited with his sister Elektra (i–LEK–tra) and finally commits the murder. As the play ends he is set upon by the Furies and driven from the stage.

The word *Eumenides* may be translated as the *Gracious Ones,* and the change of the Furies (the Erinyes [i–RIN–e–eez]) to the Eumenides is the point of the third play in the series. The scene opens in Delphi at the shrine of Apollo, with the Furies temporarily sleeping, and with Orestes as a suppliant to the god having performed all the rites for the cleansing of guilt. He is told to go to the Temple of Athena on the Akropolis in Athens where he will receive justice. The movement in the trilogy is interesting to note at this point. *Agamemnon* started in the darkness with the gloomy mutterings of the watchman and the chorus in rural Argos. Now, in *Eumenides* we come to full light in the city of Athens. Because of the clash of ideas, the city is the place where new thought is generated, and Athens is chosen not only because it was the leading city of Greece, but also because it was Aeschylus's own city. The patriotic gesture is the appropriate one.

In Athens the chorus of Furies lament that they, the older gods, are being shamed and dishonored, and predict that if Orestes is allowed to go free, children will murder their parents at will, and that they, the Furies, will bring a blight upon the land. It is at this point that Athena arrives, and after hearing the preliminaries of the case asserts that the cause is too grave for a god to decide, and too grave, also, for a mortal man. She then sends out for a jury of twelve citizens of Athens to hear the case and render a verdict. What appears to be a contradiction may be resolved in this way. A trial by a jury transcends the judgment of a mortal man since, in the course of time, a jury will build up a body of law that will provide a rational basis for judgment, and thus go beyond the limits of on-the-spot mortal judgment.

With the jury selected and sworn in, the evidence in the case is presented, with Apollo acting as attorney for the defense. A modern reader must admit that his case—that the mother is not related to the child, but is only a sort of animated baby carriage—sounds pretty flimsy, but fortunately that is almost beside the point. After the presentation of evidence, Athena establishes the court (which is located at the foot of the Akropolis), the Areopagus (air–ee–OP–uh–gus), and charges it with its duties as the highest court of justice for all time. Her speech, given elsewhere in context, cannot be quoted often enough:

> Here reverence
> For law and inbred fear among my people
> Shall hold their hands from evil night and day,
> Only let them not tamper with the laws,
> But keep the fountain pure and sweet to drink.
> I warn you not to banish from your lives
> All terror but to seek the mean between
> Autocracy and anarchy; and in this way
> You shall possess in ages yet unborn
> An impregnable fortress of liberty
> Such as no people has throughout the world.

The tied vote of the jury follows, with Athena casting her vote for the acquittal of Orestes. There is, however, another interpretation of the voting process that is more closely attuned to the situation, more subtle, more Greek. This second version posits a jury of eleven persons and a vote of six to five for conviction. When Athena casts her vote for acquittal the result is a six–six division, which is, of course, a hung jury. Orestes is acquitted in either case but a hung jury, in a case of matricide, is as close as Orestes can come and still walk out of the court vowing a perpetual alliance between Argos and Athens. We must also consider the curious dramatic structure here when the hero of the drama can walk out with only two-thirds of the play finished. The reader must realize that Orestes is not the hero; *the real hero is an idea of justice*—of people getting along with people in such a way as to promote freedom and happiness for all.

The last third of the play deals with the conversion of the Erinyes to the Eumenides. These ancient and immortal hag-goddesses have real power, which cannot simply be taken from them by force; and they start the dialogue with their usual threats of civil violence and sterility in the city of Athens. But Athena is the goddess of wisdom and also of persuasion, and she slowly reveals to the Furies the role they can play and the worship they will receive as defenders of the city. Finally the Eumenides agree to accept their new role, and the drama closes with a procession, probably including the citizens of Athens, to the altar of the Eumenides on the site of the Areopagus.

As far as the significance of the play is concerned, Aeschylus probably had several specific messages for the Athens of his time. The court Athena founds is the old Areopagus, which represented the conservative element of the city as opposed to the more democratic Council. Four years before the production of the play, the Areopagus had been stripped of much of its authority, and perhaps Aeschylus is protesting this action. On the other hand, he may be considering the development of the Areopagus as the real birth of the polis (PO–lis), the city-state that through law was to give people freedom under a democratic government. For us, this latter is the significant interpretation.

In terms of the problem we noticed at the end of the discussion of *Agamemnon,* we have a much broader and more relevant meaning than the local Athenian one. The problem was that of bringing all the people out of the net of bondage to tradition and fate and, at the same time, limiting the freedom of such a person as Klytaimestra. The universal significance, which is our chief concern, may be described in the following way:

The people, as represented by the old chorus in *Agamemnon,* are set free simply because their eyes are turned forward rather than backward. No longer do they act under the shadow of old tradition and old superstition, since each case is tried in terms of its own evidence, and decided in terms of a law that has been made by human beings. In *Eumenides,* Aeschylus is setting forth the idea that people are to establish the limits for their own zone of action, limits determined by the amount of freedom each person can have while still maintaining the freedom of others. The same thing applies to the Klytaimestras of this new world. Their acts will also be brought to this tribunal to be checked by the same standard. Humanity—at least humanity in Athens—is now free for individual action for the best interests of the person and the state.

One more point is of interest here. The Furies insisted on rule by fear, and one is tempted to discard the element of fear in this new order toward which Aeschylus is pointing. But Athena insists that a certain amount of fear is still necessary. While Aeschylus was optimistic about human nature and human behavior in an atmosphere of freedom, he was not willing to go completely overboard with his hope. He knew that in spite of laws and courts there is in human nature a tendency to act completely selfishly, without any consideration for others. To curb this tendency an inbred fear must remain, more deeply felt than the purely intellectual respect for law. A number of critics have seen in the conversion of the Furies to the Gracious Ones a sort of birth of conscience. If this is true, the conversion must be to a very sophisticated conscience rather than the old primordial cultural fear. This must be an ethical conscience that while incorporating some element of fear, is chiefly concerned with the safety, even the total welfare, of the group. Conscience, of course, is the internal regulating force within each individual by which the morality of the culture is maintained. This may be the type of "fear" Athena maintains; perhaps we do not stretch the meaning of the play to think of the conversion of the old superstitious fears into household gods as the beginning of ethical conscience. At least it is a point to think about.

The Athens of Perikles

After the terms of office of a number of leaders such as Cimon and Ephialtes who made the laws of Kleisthenes ever more democratic, we come to the long and glorious rule of Perikles (PAIR–i–kleez). Perikles was first elected as general-in-chief in 461 and, with the exception of two years when he was voted out of office, directed Athenian affairs until his death in 429 (fig. 5.2).

One historian has estimated the population of Attica (the city of Athens and the surrounding territory it governed) at about two-hundred-thirty thousand people. Of these, forty thousand were free male citizens, the actual voting population that participated in the democracy; forty thousand were women who, at best, were second-class citizens; fifty thousand were foreign-born; and one hundred thousand were slaves. One must remember that in all of our discussion of the glories of Athenian democracy, we are talking

Figure 5.2 Marble bust from Tivoli inscribed with the name of Perikles. Roman copy after a bronze original of 450–425 B.C. The bronze original was possibly by Kresilas and placed on the Akropolis after the death of Perikles. Though the original work was probably a full figure this copy conforms to the Roman tradition of portrait busts, thus accounting for the feeling that this is an incomplete composition. British Museum, London.

about only the forty thousand free men. The rest of the free people participated only on the periphery, and the slaves had no voice at all. Nevertheless it is a miracle of history that a small group of less than a quarter of a million people, in about a single century starting with the second defeat of the Persians, could have produced three of the great writers of tragic drama and one of the great comedy writers in the history of literature, two or more of the philosophers whose ideas still give shape to our lives, great architecture, and magnificent sculpture. The music and the painting of the time are lost, but in the contemporary writings music is regarded as the highest and the best developed of the arts, and sculpture was thought of as a secondary art in comparison with painting.

Finally, and most significant of all, the people, at least in the first generation of this century, produced a life-style that in its freedom for the individual, coupled with a concern for the welfare of the state as a whole, has been envied and emulated by the Western world ever since. This was the life-style toward which the plays of Aeschylus pointed. The ideal of this life-style is nowhere better stated than by C. M. Bowra *(The Greek Experience),* who writes, "A man served his state best by being himself in the full range of his nobility, and not by sacrificing it to some abstract notion of political power or expediency."

Life at this time was largely out-of-doors. The courts and the council met on the Pynx Hill opposite the Akropolis and heard matters of state argued. The town assembly met also on the Pynx, which could seat up to eighteen thousand people. Life was vigorous in the Agora (AG–uh–ruh), a level area at the foot of the Akropolis, the marketplace for the city and also the place where the men went to meet each other and to argue politics and philosophy. Here visiting teachers would lecture to any audience they could attract, and one assumes that they did a thriving business. The Greeks were a dynamic and talkative people, and the issues of the day were thrashed out in the Agora with most of the free men listening and joining in the debate.

When not in the Agora, many men spent their time in the gymnasia. These were parks set aside for physical exercise not far from the city limits of Athens. These provided a running-track, a wrestling-ground, and other facilities for exercise, and provided, as well, for shady walks and places for discussion, since the ideal was the development of the whole man, with full development of both mind and body. Later, Plato's Academy and Aristotle's Lyceum were to be founded in surroundings like those of the gymnasia.

Home was the place where the Greek man went when there was no place else to go, and it is interesting that in all of the archeological remains, we have little indication of the nature of the private houses. Public buildings and palaces were built to last, while individual homes were not. We do know that Greek homes were built in the standard Mediterranean pattern of windowless walls adjoining the street with inner courts for coolness and privacy. The homes to which Greek men retired were, in effect, not their houses but those of their wives. Wives were not citizens and could not vote but they did run the household: raising children, supervising servants, going to market, and keeping household accounts.

Perikles did not make many great changes in the government of the city. His role, instead, was to maintain the democratic values and the human values that had already come into being. In order to do this, he rebuilt the city as a proper home for these ideals. Probably the Agora was first rebuilt, since it formed a marketplace for ideas as well as things, and later he commissioned the building of the Parthenon (447–438) and other temples on the Akropolis. The care with which the architect shaped the building to conform to human standards rather than rigid mathematical and physical rules suggests the complete devotion of the Athenians to the standard of human values.

The balance the Athenians maintained between individualism and the welfare of the state was a most delicate one. During the Age of Perikles there was a shift towards individuality and away from the general, especially in the welfare of other city-states. This was first noticeable in the international relations of the city, for it converted the Delian League into what was really an Athenian empire, and moved the treasury from the island of Delos to Athens. As a matter of fact, the Par-

Figure 5.3 Athenian silver drachma, ca. 450 B.C. Obverse (heads): Archaic head of Athena wearing a crested helmet with three upright olive leaves. Reverse: Owl with olive spray at the left and A θ E at the right, standing for Athens. Known as the "owls of Athens," these coins dominated the Eastern Mediterranean for six hundred years. Museum of Fine Arts, Boston.

thenon and other buildings were constructed with money that belonged to this treasury. When member cities objected, they were simply told that if Athens were to assume the burden of protection for the league as a whole, Athens alone should be able to decide what to do with the money that was paid into the treasury (fig. 5.3).

As an international power, Athens became autocratic, and within the city the older values of reverence to the gods and to the state, ideas that had been triumphant at Marathon and that Aeschylus had preached in his plays, moved toward self-centered individuality. This metamorphosis probably had its start with the teachings of the atomists like Demokritos, who argued for complete materialism, even with the gods, and ascribed all change to accident. In such a world, the only human goal can be material pleasure, since with accident as the ruling force, nothing about the future can be predicted, and the gods who are material and subject to chance offer no guidance or inspiration.

Probably taking their cue from the atomists, the leading teachers of Athens became the sophists (sof [o as in *hot*]–ists). This group had a leader in Protagoras (pro–TAG–uh–rus), a high-minded thinker and teacher whose chief pronouncement was that *man is the measure of all things.* Taken by itself, this is simply a sloganlike reassertion of the idea of human values we have already praised so highly in this Greek state. But dangers also appear. If men, mankind, is the measure, then all may be well; if man the individual is the measure of all, then whatever the individual person may choose to do or believe is proper. The later sophists moved toward this last position, teaching, for example, that the laws were merely a set of people's opinions, so that if any people hold a different opinion, their conviction is as valid for them as are the laws. Much can be said in favor of the sophists' teachings, for they introduced a healthy questioning of the old traditions and the old veneration of the gods. On the other hand, their complete relativism, if taken seriously, undermined any coherence within the group and all thought or action became merely a matter of expediency.

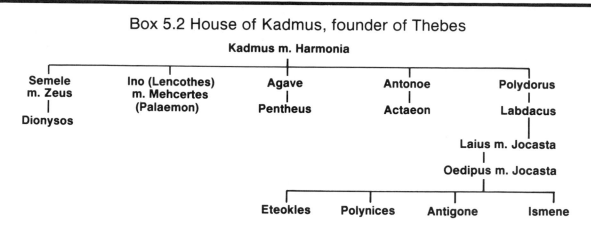

Into this new and changing atmosphere came two of the great tragic writers to direct Athenian thought and feeling: Sophokles (SOF [as in hot]–uh–kleez; 496–406 B.C.) and his younger contemporary, Euripides (you–RIP–uh–deez; 484–406 B.C.).

Sophokles

Sophokles was a general, a priest, and the most popular dramatist in Athenian history (fig. 5.4). He is reputed to have written 123 plays and to have won first prize more than twenty times; he never placed lower than second. Of the seven complete plays that have survived, only *Oedipus the King* (ED–uh–pus, or EED–uh–pus; see complete text in this chapter) will be discussed here.

The plot of *Oedipus the King* concerns a plague in the city of Thebes, which the Delphic oracle says will be lifted only when the murderer of Laius (LYE–us), the former king, is discovered and punished. Oedipus, the new king, who has according to custom married the widowed queen, Jocasta (joe–KAS–ta), swears to find this murderer in order to save the city. This is done in the face of two prophecies. One was known to Jocasta and Laius, that their son would kill his father and marry his mother. Accordingly, when a son was born to them, Laius (without Jocasta's consent) had the baby exposed to die on the slopes of Mount Kithaeron (kee–the–RON). The second prophecy, known to Oedipus when he grew up in Corinth as the son of the king and queen there, was that he would kill his father and marry his mother. To avert this, he had fled the city of Corinth. On his flight he had an altercation with an old man and his

Figure 5.4 Portrait bust of Sophokles. Marble, ca. 340 B.C. British Museum, London.

bodyguard at the place where three roads come together, and in a fit of rage Oedipus had killed the whole group. He had then proceeded to Thebes where he solved the riddle of the Sphinx, was chosen king by the populace, and married Jocasta. The play is riddled with irony, for the audience and the readers know that in the search for the murderer, Oedipus is searching for himself, and that the curse he has pronounced on the killer of King Laius will fulfill itself on him. This expected event comes to pass; Jocasta commits suicide, and Oedipus blinds himself and exiles himself from the city. With these events the play of Oedipus ends.

The play is, of course, subject to a number of interpretations. It can be viewed as an exploration of man's fate; whether Oedipus because of a "fatal flaw" (see Aristotle's *Poetics* in chap. 6) brought disaster upon himself, whether he was just a pawn of the gods, or whether the answer lies somewhere in between.

Professor Bernard Knox sees the play as an example of the power of the gods presented to the Athenians to stop them in their progress toward skepticism and atheism, and certainly this does constitute one level of meaning. Oedipus first quarrels with the ancient prophet, Tiresias (tie–REE–see–us), and ends up shouting angrily that all prophets are cheats. Several times Jocasta entreats Oedipus to put no faith in oracles, each time trying to show him how the oracles have lied. The final statement of her belief is given in the lines:

Why should we be afraid? Chance rules our lives,
And no one can foresee the future, no one.
We live best when we live without a purpose
From one day to the next.

The thought here is almost exactly the day-to-day philosophy of the atomic materialists, but each time Jocasta attempts to prove that the oracles are useless, Oedipus receives a new jolt that points to the fact that he is the murderer whom he is seeking.

This scoffing at the prophecies from the gods has an interesting effect on the populace as represented by the chorus of Thebans. One of their odes is a plea for reverence to the gods, ending with these lines:

If evil triumphs in such ways as these,
    Why should we seek, in choric dance and song,
To give the gods the praise that is their due?
    I cannot go in full faith as of old,
To sacred Delphi or Olympian vale,
    Unless men see that what has been foretold
Has come to pass, that omens never fail.
    All-ruling Zeus, if thou art King indeed,
Put forth thy majesty, make good thy word,
    Faith in these failing oracles restore!
To priest and prophet men pay little heed;
    Hymns to Apollo are no longer heard;
And all religion soon will be no more.

But the oracles are upheld; faith is restored. From the moment of Oedipus's highest hope when the messenger brings news that the king of Corinth has died and that the citizens there have chosen *him* king, he is dashed to the bottom of despair as he finally learns that he was the baby who was exposed to die, and that the old man he killed was his true father. Strained beyond endurance by her burden of knowledge, Jocasta commits suicide, and Oedipus, who has seen external things throughout his life, blinds himself as he comes to see himself and, with clear vision, sees truths that lie beyond the externals. He and the blind Tiresias, also one of the clear-sighted ones, reach equality at the end of the play. On this level of meaning this drama is a clear admonition that the gods are powerful and should receive worship and honor.

Until recently the view that Oedipus did not know he was seeking himself as the murderer was generally accepted. However, a conflicting interpretation, based on the text, is also possible. This alternate view contends that Oedipus had some knowledge (a lot?, a little?) of the truth *before* the fateful day with which the play begins. With this possibility in mind, reread the dialogue between Tiresias and Oedipus beginning with line 302. Also, look at Jocasta's speech, beginning with line 720, and consider who or what Laius's servant is so afraid of. Was it Oedipus?

Euripides

The third great tragedian of Athens, Euripides (484–406 B.C.), directed his tragic vision towards psychological drama with plots revolving around the plight of the underdog: the inferior status of women, the exploitation of peasants, the rejected wife, the exploited wife, those who lose wars. Aristotle said that Aeschylus composed properly without knowing it, that Euripides painted men as they were, and that Sophokles painted men as they should be. Euripides exposed the reality of suffering and suffered the usual fate of the artist who deals with unpopular truths. Euripides wrote ninety-two plays but won only four first prizes; the fourth one was awarded after Sophokles made an issue of the case. However, nineteen plays have survived, more than the combined extant dramas of Aeschylus and Sophokles, an ironic twist Euripides would have appreciated (fig. 5.5).

Figure 5.5 Portrait bust of Euripides. Marble, Roman copy, ca. 320 B.C. Portraits of Euripides survived about as well as his plays; this is one of twenty-five replicas. National Museum, Naples.

Elektra provides a good example of the different styles of the three dramatists. Aeschylus portrays Orestes and Elektra as vehicles for developing an idea of justice; Sophokles writes a classic study of a woman possessed and driven almost mad by the indignities that have been heaped upon her; Euripides presents Elektra and Orestes as cold-blooded butchers bent solely on revenge. Orestes craftily insists upon staying close to the borders of Argos so he can escape should anything go wrong. Elektra is a proud, disdainful aristocrat who looks down upon Pylades, her peasant husband. The nobility of the poor is another of Euripides' themes; the peasant is as good a man as one can find, stoically suffering his wife's scorn.

In *Medea* two more of Euripides' great themes appear: the strength and greatness of a woman, and the hypocrisy and shabby ethics found so often in highly developed cultures. Medea is a raging woman, consumed by love turned to hate because of the sniveling opportunism of her civilized Greek husband. As she arranges for the murder of Kreusa, Jason's intended bride, and then murders her own sons in order to wipe out Jason's line, she is the magnificent Medea, destroyer of a decadent, materialistic civilization.

In *The Trojan Women,* Euripides shows us war as it really is. He does not treat the Trojan War as a glorious victory for the good Greeks; instead, he selects the time immediately after the victory and shows the misery of the women of Troy as they are parceled out to the conquerors and their heartbreak as they see their children murdered by the "heroic" victors (see the complete text near the end of this chapter.)

During the last two years of his life, Euripides exiled himself from civilized Athens and went to live in primitive Macedonia, where he died. There he wrote *The Bacchae* (BOCK–ee), in which he repudiates all of the rationalistic civilization he had known—a civilization that had rejected him and that he had in turn rejected. (See the complete text at the end of this chapter.)

The antagonists in the play are the highly civilized, typically Greek, Pentheus (PEN–thee–us), King of Thebes, and the god Dionysos, who was born in Thebes (see box 5.2). As the play opens, Dionysos has assumed a homosexual role (he was also bisexual or asexual, as he wished) and come to Thebes to demand recognition and worship. The women are quickly enticed into the hills but Pentheus puts the god in prison and assumes that everything will become normal again. Even as Pentheus stands uncomprehendingly in the smoldering ruins of his palace he tries to keep the situation rational. Dionysos responds by tricking Pentheus into wearing women's clothing and then tricks Agave, Pentheus's mother, into tearing off the head of her own son. At the end the kingdom is a total ruin and Dionysos is cooly dispensing justice. The point is that Dionysos is much more than just the god of wine; he also represents the nonrational aspect of human nature, that raging torrent within that man must recognize and to which he

must give proper recognition. Euripides seems to be saying that men and women must maintain a delicate balance between emotion and intellect, and there must be both. Pentheus tried to suppress his emotions and was made a complete fool of before he was killed by his mother. On the other hand, emotion run riot is chaos. Though Dionysos is the god of the nonrational he certainly destroyed Thebes in a cool and calm manner. Euripides did not live to see the play produced. The final irony is that Sophokles used his immense prestige to see that the play received the production it merited, in the city that deserved it.

Athenian Background after Perikles

Throughout the times of these dramatists, the cities of Athens and Sparta had each been growing in power until a confrontation between the two for dominance throughout the Hellenic world was inevitable. In 445 the two city-states signed a pact for a thirty-year truce, which was observed, more or less, for fourteen years. In 431 the Peloponnesian War broke out; it ended in 404 with Sparta's total conquest of Athens. Perikles believed that this would be a long war of attrition, and decided to abandon the land to Sparta, bringing all the people of Attica inside the walls of Athens, and trusting the Athenian navy to attack Sparta and her allies wherever a hit-and-run attack would do the most damage. Athens was almost immediately crippled when, in 430, plague broke out in the city and a third of the population died. Perikles himself died of the disease in 429. The conflict that followed furnishes almost a classic example of the stupidity of war. On two or three occasions Athens obtained the upper hand and could have made peace with Sparta without serious loss of honor, but the hawks within the government demanded total victory.

A number of Athenian acts during the war demonstrate the temper of the times. For example, in 416 the Athenians attacked the neutral island of Melos on the general principle that if you aren't for us, you are against us. The battle lasted a single day, with Athens winning, killing all the men on the island, and selling the women and children into slavery.

In the following year Athens mounted a great attack on the city of Syracuse in Sicily, an attack that was foolhardy and doomed to failure. Of the three generals in command, one of them, Alkibiades (Al–ki–BY–uh–deez), represents an extreme example of the new egocentric individualism that was becoming so prevalent in Athens. His self-indulgent actions and ethical relativism could be construed by the sophists of the city as proper (successful) behavior. In the first place, Alkibiades left Athens under a cloud, for after a series of farewell parties a number of the sacred shrines in the city were defaced, and it was generally supposed that Alkibiades and his followers committed this sacrilege. Before reaching Sicily, he defected to Sparta, and in Sparta became a leading citizen and military adviser. When he felt that his good fortune in Sparta was running out, he deserted to Persia, and even later he returned to Athens where he was greeted as a national hero and reelected to a generalship. This, as we have said, is an extreme case, but when such conduct could be tolerated, the moral fiber of the city must have been extremely weak. After the Sicilian disaster in which the navy and most of the army were lost, the war dragged on to what had become an inevitable victory for Sparta. Then, during the fourth century, the government vacillated between the strong antidemocratic element in the population, the democrats, and a moderate element, which sought to limit the voting power to a few thousand of the upper classes but still maintain some sort of democratic voice.

The Critics of Athens: Sokrates and Aristophanes

Probably the greatest questioner of the new value system in Athens was the philosopher, Sokrates, of whom we know little, since he never wrote and the only reports we have about him are from his pupils, principally Plato and Xenophon (ZEN-oh-fun). It is apparent, however, that he spent most of his life raising embarrassing questions and demanding that the Athenians examine their motives for their way of life. He was an extremely popular teacher for a group of the intellectual young men who shared his views about the decay of the old value systems, but he was certainly not popular with those whose motives were totally selfish. This last group finally had him arrested on the charge of corrupting the youth of Athens; in 399 a jury of his peers found him guilty of impiety and corrupting the youth and sentenced him to death. At his trial he described himself as the gadfly of Athens, and the description is probably very exact. He insisted that the only good life was the well-examined life, and he sought to help others by causing them to examine themselves by asking them what they meant by the words they used—what do you mean, "justice"?—and then by a series of other questions finally revealing to the individuals that they simply didn't know what they were talking about. His method was always the same: to ask a question and arrive at an answer that seemed to be true. Then, by further questions he would test each part of the original answer, paring away those parts that proved themselves to be false, until the original answer was refined to truth by the clear process of thought.

For Sokrates, the end of the good life is happiness, which is not only the avoidance of ignorance and its fruits, but the virtue that comes from knowledge. To know rightly, to make right choices, is virtue, for it alone can satisfy reason. Knowledge and virtue are inseparable. And happiness is the result of worthiness that comes when enlightenment and knowledge result, as necessarily they must in this highest good, which we call virtue.

The other great critic of late fifth-century Athens was Aristophanes (air-i-STOF-uh-neez; ca. 448–388 B.C.), the great writer of Greek Old Comedy. An aristocrat and a conservative, he sought to make Athens aware of its faults through the biting wit of his satires. In *The Clouds* he depicted Sokrates as a sophist who, for a fee, taught either right logic or wrong logic, which did not help matters at the trial of Sokrates. *The Wasps* poked fun at the Athenian passion for litigation and *The Frogs* was a literary satire involving Aeschylus and Euripides; he was sharply critical of Euripides. Perhaps his greatest play was *Lysistrata* (LIS-i-stra-ta or li-SIS-tra-ta) in which the war between Athens and Sparta, or any war for that matter, was satirized. The Athenian woman Lysistrata enlists the cooperation of all the Greek women in a simple and wonderfully effective plan to stop warfare: no sex until all fighting stops. Given a choice between making love and making war the men, after considerable controversy and much pleading, opt for the former.

Thus was the great fifth century in Athens. It had started with the pride of victory over the Persians, with the triumph of democracy, and with the promise of the great life in the plays of Aeschylus. Within the early years of the leadership of Perikles that good life had been realized about as much as it ever can be. It ended in a time of military defeat; a time when selfish individualism was the dominant mood; a time when Athens could no longer listen to the voice of its best critic, and when even criticism-through-comedy turned from biting satire to simple comedy-for-amusement, which we see in the later plays of Aristophanes.

The highest assertion of the human spirit in these exhausted times came at the very end with the trial of Sokrates and a glimpse of the philosopher as hero. In his *Apology* (see chap. 6 for the complete text) he spoke to his jury as a highly urbane and civilized man, disdaining high-flown rhetoric on the one hand, and sentiment on the other. Instead, he speaks almost in a conversational tone about his own life and his devotion to his own highest ideals for human conduct. Perhaps the highest statement comes after the vote has been taken that condemned him to death:

. . . And there are many other ways of avoiding death in every danger if a man is willing to say and to do anything. But, my friends, I think that it is a much harder thing to escape from wickedness than from death, for wickedness is swifter than death. And now I, who am old and slow, have been overtaken by the slower pursuer: and my accusers, who are clever and swift, have been overtaken by the swifter pursuer—wickedness. And now I shall go away, sentenced by you to death; and they will go away, sentenced by truth to wickedness and injustice. I abide by my penalty, they by theirs.

Bibliography

Translations of Original Material
Grene, David, and Richmond Lattimore. *Greek Tragedies.* 3 vols. Chicago: University of Chicago Press, 1960. Good modern translations of the more important plays of Aeschylus, Sophokles, and Euripides. (Available in paperback.)

Plato. *Great Dialogues of Plato.* Translated by W.H.D. Rouse. New York: New American Library. Excellent translation.

Thucydides. *History of the Peloponnesian War.* The Crawley translation in the Modern Library Edition is a good one. Thucydides was an Athenian (or his title would have been *History of the Athenian War.*) However, he was quite objective, very thorough, and he could write. This is good reading by one of history's great historians.

General Works
Bowra, C. M. *The Greek Experience.* New York: New American Library. An interpretation of Greek life at its best.

————. *Classical Greece.* Great Ages of Man Series. Alexandria, Va.: Time-Life Books, 1965. The usual high-quality Time-Life highlights of an age, with good visuals.

Hamilton, Edith. *The Greek Way.* New York: W.W. Norton & Co., 1948. This has become a minor classic.

————. *The Echo of Greece.* New York: W.W. Norton & Co., 1957. The fourth century B.C. in Greece. Nice book with fine writing but does tend to oversimplify. Professor Hamilton just overlooks the flaws that her Greeks had.

Literary Selections
AGAMEMNON
Aeschylus (525–456 B.C.)

This is the first of a series of three plays by Aeschylus, called the *Oresteia.* He investigates in these plays the question of man's relation to other men. He is asking the question, "What is justice?" In the first of the plays he presents the old idea of justice and the individual's freedom of choice as it probably existed in the period of chaos. In the second of the plays (omitted here) he carries the question further. In the last of the series he presents a new idea of justice and explains the meaning of it to his Athenian audience as they approached the period of balance in their epoch. To understand this series of plays, one needs to know a little about the history of the dynasty of the kings who ruled in the land of Argos. Since Atreus (A–tree–us) was one of the early kings in this dynasty, the family line is called the House of Atreus. (See box 5.1.)

The sons of Atreus, Agamemnon and Menelaos, married the sisters, Klytaimestra and Helen, daughters of the King of Lacedemon. Helen left her husband, fleeing to Troy with Paris, and Agamemnon rallied all the forces of Greece to help his brother win her back. The fleet could not leave from Aulis because of adverse winds; the seer, Kalchas (KAL–kus), interpreted omens to mean that the winds would change when Agamemnon sacrificed his daughter, Iphigeneia. That sacrifice was made.

While the war was in progress and Agamemnon fighting before Troy, Aigisthos returned to Argos and became Klytaimestra's lover. He roused discontent among the people and became powerful.

These plays, then, develop a new idea of justice and freedom in the period in which Aeschylus lived. The first one presents the old ideas that made the tragedy of Agamemnon possible. Watch for those ideas.

The Greeks had arranged a series of beacons stretching from Troy to the Grecian mainland to be kindled as a token of victory over Troy. It is with their imminent flaming that the play opens.

The translations of the *Oresteia* are by the twentieth-century scholar George Thomson. His spelling of proper names has been retained.

CHARACTERS
Watchman
Chorus of Old Men
Clytemnestra
Herald
Agamemnon
Cassandra
Aegisthus
Captain of the Guard

The scene is the entrance to the palace of the Atreidae. Before the doors stand shrines of the gods. [A WATCHMAN *is posted on the roof.*]

Watchman: I've prayed God to release me from sentry duty
All through this long year's vigil, like a dog
Couched on the roof of Atreus, where I study
Night after night the pageantry of this vast
Concourse of stars, and moving among them like
Noblemen the constellations that bring
Summer and winter as they rise and fall.
And I am still watching for the beacon signal
All set to flash over the sea the radiant
News of the fall of Troy. So confident
Is a woman's spirit, whose purpose is a man's.
Every night, as I turn in to my stony bed,
Quilted with dew, not visited by dreams,
Not mine—no sleep, fear stands at my pillow
Keeping tired eyes from closing once too often;
And whenever I start to sing or hum a tune,
Mixing from music an antidote to sleep,
It always turns to mourning for the royal house,
Which is not in such good shape as it used to be.
But now at last may the good news in a flash
Scatter the darkness and deliver us. [*The beacon flashes.*]
O light of joy, whose gleam turns night to day,
O radiant signal for innumerable
Dances of victory! Ho there! I call the queen,
Agamemnon's wife, to raise with all the women
Alleluias of thanksgiving through the palace
Saluting the good news, if it is true
That Troy has fallen, as this blaze portends:
Yes, and I'll dance an overture myself.
My master's dice have fallen out well, and I
Shall score three sixes for this nightwatching. [*A pause.*]
Well, come what will, may it soon be mine to grasp
In this right hand my master's, home again! [*Another pause.*]
The rest is secret. A heavy ox has trodden
Across my tongue. These walls would have tales to tell
If they had mouths. I speak only to those
Who are in the know, to others—I know nothing.
[*The* WATCHMAN *goes into the palace. Women's cries are heard. Enter* CHORUS OF OLD MEN.]

Chorus: It is ten years since those armed prosecutors of Justice, Menelaus and Agamemnon, twin-sceptred in God-given sovereignty, embarked in the thousand ships crying war, like eagles with long wings beating the air over a robbed mountain nest, wheeling and screaming for their lost children. Yet above them some god, maybe Apollo or Zeus, overhears the sky-dweller's cry and sends after the robber a Fury. [CLYTEMNESTRA *comes out of the palace and unseen by the elders places offerings before the shrines.*] Just so the two kings were sent by the greater king, Zeus, for the sake of a promiscuous woman to fight Paris, Greek and Trojan locked fast together in the dusty betrothals of battle. And however it stands with them now, the end is unalterable; no flesh, no wine can appease God's fixed indignation.

As for us, with all the able-bodied men enlisted and gone, we are left here leaning our strength on a staff; for, just as in infancy, when the marrow is still unformed, the War-god is not at his post, so it is in extreme old age, as the leaves fall fast, we walk on three feet, like dreams in the daylight. [*They see* CLYTEMNESTRA.]

O Queen, what news? what message sets light to the altars? All over the town the shrines are ablaze with unguents drawn from the royal stores and the flames shoot up into the night sky. Speak, let us hear all that may be made public, so healing the anxieties that have gathered thick in our hearts; let the gleam of good news scatter them! [CLYTEMNESTRA *goes out to tend the other altars of the city.*]

Strength have I still to recall that sign which greeted the
    two kings
Taking the road, for the prowess of song is not yet spent.
I sing of two kings united in sovereignty, leading
Armies to battle, who saw two eagles
Beside the palace
Wheel into sight, one black, and the other was white-
    tailed,
Tearing a hare with her unborn litter.
Cry Sorrow cry, but let good conquer!
Shrewdly the priest took note and compared each eagle
    with each king,
Then spoke out and prefigured the future in these words:
"In time the Greek arms shall demolish the fortress of
    Priam;
Only let no jealous God, as they fasten
On Troy the slave's yoke,
Strike them in anger; for Artemis[1] loathes the rapacious
Eagles of Zeus that have slaughtered the frail hare.
Cry Sorrow cry, but let good conquer!
O Goddess, gentle to the tender whelp of fierce lions
As to all young life of the wild,
So now fulfil what is good in the omen and mend what is
    faulty.
And I appeal unto the Lord Apollo,
Let not the north wind hold the fleet storm-bound,
Driving them on to repay that feast with another,
Inborn builder of strife, feud that fears no man, it is still
    there,
Treachery keeping the house, it remembers, revenges, a
    child's death!"
Such, as the kings left home, was the seer's revelation.
Cry Sorrow cry, but let good conquer!

Zeus, whoe'er he be, if so it best
Please his ear to be addressed,
So shall he be named by me.
All things have I measured, yet
None have found save him alone,
Zeus, if a man from a heart heavy-laden
Seek to cast his cares aside.

Long since lived a ruler of the world,[2]
Puffed with martial pride, of whom
None shall tell, his day is done;
Also, he who followed him
Met his master and is gone.
Zeus the victorious, gladly acclaim him;
Perfect wisdom shall be yours;

Zeus, who laid it down that man
Must in sorrow learn and through
Pain to wisdom find his way.
When deep slumber falls, remembered wrongs
Chafe the bruised heart with fresh pangs, and no
Welcome wisdom meets within.
Harsh the grace dispensed by powers immortal,
Pilots of the human soul.

Even so the elder prince,[3]
Marshal of the thousand ships,
Rather than distrust a priest,
Torn with doubt to see his men
Harbor-locked, hunger-pinched, hard-oppressed,
Strained beyond endurance, still
Watching, waiting, where the never-tiring
Tides of Aulis ebb and flow:

And still the storm blew from mountains far north,
With moorings windswept and hungry crews pent
In rotting hulks,
With tackling all torn and seeping timbers,
Till Time's slow-paced, enforced inaction
Had all but stripped bare the bloom of Greek manhood.
And then was found but one
Cure to allay the tempest—never a blast so bitter—
Shrieked in a loud voice by the priest, "Artemis!" striking
    the Atreidae with dismay, each with his staff smiting
    the ground and weeping.

And then the king spoke, the elder, saying:
"The choice is hard—hard to disobey him,
And harder still
To kill my own child, my palace jewel,
With unclean hands before the altar
Myself, her own father, spill a maid's pure blood.
I have no choice but wrong.
How shall I fail my thousand ships and betray my
    comrades?
So shall the storm cease, and the men eager for war
    clamor for that virginal blood righteously! So pray for
    a happy outcome!"

And when he bowed down beneath the harness
Of cruel coercion, his spirit veering
With sudden sacrilegious change,
He gave his whole mind to evil counsel.
For man is made bold with base-contriving
Impetuous madness, first cause of much grief.
And so then he slew his own child
For a war to win a woman
And to speed the storm-bound fleet from the shore to
    battle.

---

1. Artemis is the goddess of the hunt and all wild things. In this context, the hare is the city of Troy.

2. The reference here is Uranus and Kronos, both kings of the gods. Zeus led a successful revolt against Kronos so that Zeus could become king.

3. This refers to the beginning of the Trojan War when the Greek fleet was delayed in the harbor of Aulis. In order to appease Artemis and secure favorable winds, Agamemnon, "the elder prince," followed the prophecy of the seer, Calchas, and sacrificed his daughter, Iphigenia.

She cried aloud "Father!" yet they heard not;
A girl in first flower, yet they cared not,
The lords who gave the word for war.
Her father prayed, then he bade his vassals
To seize her where swathed in folds of saffron
She lay, and lift her up like a yearling
With bold heart above the altar,
And her lovely lips to bridle
That they might not cry out, cursing the House of Atreus,
With gags, her voice sealed with brute force and crushed.
And then she let fall her cloak
And cast at each face a glance that dumbly craved
    compassion;
And like a picture she would but could not greet
Her father's guests, who at home
Had often sat when the meal was over,
The cups replenished, with all hearts enraptured
To hear her sing grace with clear unsullied voice for her
    loving father.
The end was unseen and unspeakable.
The task of priestcraft was done.
For Justice first chastens, then she presses home her
    lesson.
The morrow must come, its grief will soon be here,
So let us not weep today.
It shall be made known as clear as daybreak.
And so may all this at last end in good news,
For which the queen prays, the next of kin and stay of the
    land of Argos. [CLYTEMNESTRA *appears at the door
    of the palace.*]
Our humble salutations to the queen!
Hers is our homage, while our master's throne
Stands empty. We are still longing to hear
The meaning of your sacrifice. Is it good news?
Clytemnestra: Good news! With good news may the
    morning rise
Out of the night—good news beyond all hope!
My news is this: The Greeks have taken Troy.
Chorus: What? No, it cannot be true! I cannot grasp it.
Clytemnestra: The Greeks hold Troy—is not that plain
    enough?
Chorus: Joy steals upon me and fills my eyes with tears.
Clytemnestra: Indeed, your looks betray your loyalty.
Chorus: What is the proof? Have you any evidence?
Clytemnestra: Of course I have, or else the Gods have
    cheated me.
Chorus: You have given ear to some beguiling dream.
Clytemnestra: I would not come screaming fancies out
    of my sleep.
Chorus: Rumors have wings—on these your heart has
    fed.
Clytemnestra: You mock my intelligence as though I
    were a girl.
Chorus: When was it? How long is it since the city fell?
Clytemnestra: In the night that gave birth to this
    dawning day.
Chorus: What messenger could bring the news so fast?
Clytemnestra: The God of Fire, who from Ida sent
    forth light
And beacon by beacon passed the flame to me.
From the peak of Ida first to the cliff of Hermes
On Lemnos, and from there a third great lamp
Was flashed to Athos, the pinnacle of Zeus;
Up, up it soared, luring the dancing fish
To break surface in rapture at the light;
A golden courier, like the sun, it sped
Post-haste its message to Macistus, thence

Across Euripus, till the flaming sign
Was marked by the watchers on Messapium,
And thence with strength renewed from piles of heath
Like moonrise over the valley of Asopus,
Relayed in glory to Cithaeron's heights,
And still flashed on, not slow the sentinels,
Leaping across the lake from peak to peak,
It passed the word to burn and burn, and flung
A comet to the promontory that stands
Over the Gulf of Saron, there it swooped
Down to the Spider's Crag above the city,
Then found its mark on the roof of this house of Atreus,
That beacon fathered by Ida's far off fires.
Such were the stages of our torch relay,
And the last to run is the first to reach the goal.
That is my evidence, the testimony which
My lord has signaled to me out of Troy.
Chorus: Lady, there will be time later to thank the
    Gods.
Now I ask only to listen: speak on and on.
Clytemnestra: Today the Greeks have occupied Troy.
I seem to hear there a very strange street-music.
Pour oil and vinegar into one cup, you will see
They do not make friends. So there two tunes are heard.
Slaves now, the Trojans, brothers and aged fathers,
Prostrate, sing for their dearest the last dirge.
The others, tired out and famished after the night's
    looting,
Grab what meal chance provides, lodgers now
In Trojan houses, sheltered from the night frosts,
From the damp dews delivered, free to sleep
Off guard, off duty, a blissful night's repose.
Therefore, provided that they show due respect
To the altars of the plundered town and are not
Tempted to lay coarse hands on sanctities,
Remembering that the last lap—the voyage home—
Lies still ahead of them, then, if they should return
Guiltless before God, the curses of the bereaved
Might be placated—barring accidents.
That is my announcement—a message from my master.
May all end well, and may I reap the fruit of it!
Chorus: Lady, you have spoken with a wise man's
    judgment.
Now it is time to address the gods once more
After this happy outcome of our cares.

Thanks be to Zeus and to gracious Night, housekeeper of
heaven's embroidery, who has cast over the towers of Troy
a net so fine as to leave no escape for old or young, all
caught in the snare! All praise to Zeus, who with a shaft
from his outstretched bow has at last brought down the
transgressor!

"By Zeus struck down!" The truth is all clear
With each step plainly marked. He said, Be
It so, and so it was. A man denied once
That heaven pays heed to those who trample
Beneath the feet holy sanctities. He lied wickedly;
For God's wrath soon or late destroys all sinners filled
With pride, puffed up with vain presumption,
And great men's houses stocked with silver
And gold beyond measure. Far best to live
Free of want, without grief, rich in the gift of wisdom.
Glutted with gold, the sinner kicks
Justice out of his sight, yet
She sees *him* and remembers.

As sweet temptation lures him onwards
With childlike smile into the death-trap
He cannot help himself. His curse is lit up
Against the darkness, a bright baleful light.
And just as false bronze in battle hammered turns black
    and shows
Its true worth, so the sinner time-tried stands condemned.
His hopes take wing, and still he gives chase, with foul
    crimes branding all his people.
He cries to deaf heaven, none hear his prayers.
Justice drags him down to hell as he calls for succor.
Such was the sinner Paris, who
Rendered thanks to a gracious
Host by stealing a woman.

She left behind her the ports all astir
With throngs of men under arms filing onto shipboard;
She took to Troy in lieu of dowry death.
A light foot passed through the gates and fled,
And then a cry of lamentation rose.
The seers, the king's prophets, muttered darkly:
"Bewail the king's house that now is desolate,
Bewail the bed marked with print of love that fled!"
Behold, in silence, without praise, without reproach,
They sit upon the ground and weep.
Beyond the wave lies their love;
Here a ghost seems to rule the palace!
Shapely the grace of statues.
Yet they can bring no comfort,
Eyeless, lifeless and loveless.

Delusive dream shapes that float through the night
Beguile him, bringing delight sweet but unsubstantial;
For, while the eye beholds the heart's desire,
The arms clasp empty air, and then
The fleeting vision fades and glides away
On silent wing down the paths of slumber.
The royal hearth is chilled with sorrows such as these,
And more; in each house from end to end of Greece
That sent its dearest to wage war in foreign lands
The stout heart is called to steel itself
In mute endurance against
Blows that strike deep into the heart's core:
Those that they sent from home they
Knew, but now they receive back
Only a heap of ashes.

The God of War holds the twin scales of strife,
Heartless gold-changer trafficking in men,
Consigning homeward from Troy a jar of dust fire-refined,
Making up the weight with grief,
Shapely vessels laden each
With the ashes of their kin.
They mourn and praise them saying, "He
Was practiced well in sword and spear,
And he, who fell so gallantly—
All to avenge another man's wife":
It is muttered in a whisper
And resentment spreads against each of the royal
    warlords.
They lie sleeping, perpetual
Owners each of a small
Holding far from their homeland.
The sullen rumors that pass mouth to mouth
Bring the same danger as a people's curse.
And brooding hearts wait to hear of what the night holds
    from sight.

Watchful are the Gods of all
Hands with slaughter stained. The black
Furies wait, and when a man
Has grown by luck, not justice, great,
With sudden turn of circumstance
He wastes away to nothing, dragged
Down to be food in hell for demons.
For the heights of fame are perilous.
With a jealous bolt the Lord Zeus in a flash shall blast
    them.
Best to pray for a tranquil
Span of life and to be
Neither victor nor vanquished.

—The news has set the whole town aflame.
Can it be true? Perhaps it is a trick.
—Only a child would let such fiery words
Kindle his hopes, then fade and flicker out.
—It is just like a woman
To accept good news without the evidence.
—An old wives' tale, winged with a woman's wishes,
Spreads like wildfire, then sinks and is forgotten.

We shall soon know what the beacon signifies,
Whether it is true or whether this joyful daybreak
Is only a dream sent to deceive us all.
Here comes a messenger breathless from the shore,
Wearing a garland and covered in a cloud
Of dust, which shows that he has news to tell,
And not in soaring rhetoric of smoke and flame,
But either he brings cause for yet greater joy,
Or else—no, let us abjure the alternative.
Glad shone the light, as gladly break the day!
[*Enter* HERALD]

Herald: O joy! Argos, I greet you, my fatherland!
Joy brings me home after ten years of war.
Many the shattered hopes, but this has held.
Now I can say that when I die my bones
Will lie at rest here in my native soil.
I greet you joyfully, I greet the Sun,
Zeus the All-Highest, and the Pythian King,
Bending no more against us his fatal shafts,
As he did beside Scamander—that was enough,
And now defend us, Savior Apollo; all
The Gods I greet, among them Hermes, too,
Patron of messengers, and the spirits of our dead,
Who sent their sons forth, may they now prepare
A joyful welcome for those whom war has spared.
Joy to the palace and to these images
Whose faces catch the sun, now, as of old,
With radiant smiles greet your sovereign lord,
Agamemnon, who brings a lamp to lighten you
And all here present, after having leveled
Troy with the mattock of just-dealing Zeus,
Great son of Atreus, master and monarch, blest
Above all living men. The brigand Paris
Has lost his booty and brought down the house of Priam.

Chorus: Joy to you, Herald, welcome home again!
Herald: Let me die, having lived to see this day!
Chorus: Your yearning for your country has worn you
out.
Herald: So much that tears spring to the eyes for joy.
Chorus: Well, those you longed for longed equally for
you.
Herald: Ah yes, our loved ones longed for our safe
return.
Chorus: We have had many anxieties here at home.
Herald: What do you mean? Has there been
disaffection?

Chorus: Never mind now. Say nothing and cure all.
Herald: Is it possible there was trouble in our absence?
Chorus: Now, as you said yourself, it would be a joy to
die.
Herald: Yes, all has ended well. Our expedition
Has been successfully concluded, even though in part
The issue may be found wanting. Only the Gods
Prosper in everything. If I should tell you all
That we endured on shipboard in the night watches,
Our lodging the bare benches, and even worse
Ashore beneath the walls of Troy, the rains
From heaven and the dews that seeped
Out of the soil into lice-infested blankets;
If I should tell of those winters, when the birds
Dropped dead and Ida heaped on us her snows;
Those summers, when unruffled by wind or wave
The sea slept breathless under the glare of noon—
But why recall that now? It is all past,
Yes, for the dead past never to stir again.
Ah, they are all gone. Why count our losses? Why
Should we vex the living with grievance for the dead?
Goodbye to all that for us who have come back!
Victory has turned the scale, and so before
This rising sun let the good news be proclaimed
And carried all over the world on wings of fame:
"These spoils were brought by the conquerors of Troy
And dedicated to the Gods of Greece."
And praise to our country and to Zeus the giver
And thanks be given. That is all my news.
[CLYTEMNESTRA *appears at the palace door.*]
Chorus: Thank God that I have lived to see this day!
This news concerns all, and most of all the queen.
Clytemnestra: I raised my alleluia hours ago,
When the first messenger lit up the night,
And people mocked me saying, "Has a beacon
Persuaded you that the Greeks have captured Troy?
Truly a woman's hopes are lighter than air."
But I still sacrificed, and at a hundred
Shrines throughout the town the women chanted
Their endless alleluias on and on,
Singing to sleep the sacramental flames,
And now what confirmation do I need from you?
I wait to hear all from my lord, for whom
A welcome is long ready. What day is so sweet
In a woman's life as when she opens the door
To her beloved, safe home from war? Go and tell him
That he will find, guarding his property,
A wife as loyal as he left her, one
Who in all these years has kept his treasuries sealed,
Unkind only to enemies, and knows no more
Of other men's company than of tempering steel. [*Exit*]
Herald: Such a protestation, even though entirely true,
Is it not unseemly on a lady's lips?
Chorus: Such is her message, as you understand,
Full of fine phrases plain to those who know.
But tell us now, what news have you of the king's
Co-regent, Menelaus? Is he too home again?
Herald: Lies cannot last, even though sweet to hear.
Chorus: Can you not make your news both sweet and
true?
Herald: He and his ships have vanished. They are
missing.
Chorus: What, was it a storm that struck the fleet at sea?
Herald: You have told a long disaster in a word.
Chorus: Has no one news whether he is alive or dead?
Herald: Only the Sun, from whom the whole earth
draws life.

Chorus: Tell us about the storm. How did it fall?
Herald: A day of national rejoicing must not be marred
By any jarring tongue. A messenger who comes
With black looks bringing the long prayed-against
Report of total rout, which both afflicts
The state in general and in every household leaves
The inmates prostrate under the scourge of war—
With such a load upon his lips he may fitly
Sing anthems to the Furies down in hell;
But when he greets a prospering people with
News of the war's victorious end—how then
Shall I mix foul with fair and find words to tell you
Of the blow that struck us out of that angry heaven?
    Water and Fire, those age-old enemies,
Made common cause against the homebound fleet.
Darkness had fallen, and a northerly gale
Blew up and in a blinding thunderstorm
Our ships were tossed and buffeted hull against hull
In a wild stampede and herded out of sight;
Then, at daybreak, we saw the Aegean in blossom
With a waving crop of corpses and scattered timbers.
Our ship came through, saved by some spirit, it seems,
Who took the helm and piloted her, until
She slipped under the cliffs into a cove.
There, safe at last, incredulous of our luck,
We brooded all day, stunned by the night's disaster.
And so, if any of the others have survived,
They must be speaking of us as dead and gone.
May all yet end well! Though it is most to be expected
That Menelaus is in some great distress,
Yet, should some shaft of sunlight spy him out
Somewhere among the living, rescued by Zeus,
Lest the whole house should perish, there is hope
That he may yet come home. There you have the truth.
Chorus: Tell us who invented that
Name so deadly accurate?
Was it one who presaging
Things to come divined a word
Deftly tuned to destiny?
Helen—hell indeed she carried
To men, to ships, to a proud city, stealing
From the silk veils of her chamber, sailing seaward
With the Zephyr's breath behind her;
And they set forth in a thousand ships to hunt her
On the path that leaves no imprint,
Bringers of endless bloodshed.

So, as Fate decreed, in Troy,
Turning into keeners kin,
Furies, instruments of God's
Wrath, at last demanded full
Payment for the stolen wife;
And the wedding song that rang out
To greet the bride from beyond the broad Aegean
Was in time turned into howls of imprecation
From the countless women wailing
For the loved ones they had lost in war for her sake,
And they curse the day they gave that
Welcome to war and bloodshed.

An old story is told of an oxherd who reared at his hearth
    a lion-cub, a pet for his children,
Pampered fondly by young and old with dainty morsels
    begged at each meal from his master's table.
But Time showed him up in his true nature after his
    kind—a beast savaging sheep and oxen,
Mad for the taste of blood, and only then they knew what
    they had long nursed was a curse from heaven.
And so it seemed then there came to rest in Troy

A sweet-smiling calm, a clear sky, seductive,
A rare pearl set in gold and silver,
Shaft of love from a glancing eye.
She is seen now as an agent
Of death sent from Zeus, a Fury
Demanding a bloody bride-price. [*Enter* CLYTEMNESTRA]
From ancient times people have believed that when
A man's wealth has come to full growth it breeds
And brings forth tares and tears in plenty.
No, I say, it is only wicked deeds
That increase, fruitful in evil.
The house built on justice always
Is blest with a happy offspring.
And yet the pride bred of wealth often burgeons anew
In evil times, a cloud of deep night,
Spectre of ancient crimes that still
Walks within the palace walls,
True to the dam that bore it.
But where is Justice? She lights up the smoke-darkened
       hut.
From mansions built by hands polluted
Turning to greet the pure in heart,
Proof against false praise, she guides
All to its consummation. [*Enter* AGAMEMNON *in a
       chariot followed by another chariot carrying
       CASSANDRA and spoils of war.*]
Agamemnon, conqueror, joy to our king! How shall my
greeting neither fall short nor shoot too high? Some men
feign rejoicing or sorrow with hearts untouched; but
those who can read man's nature in the book of the eyes
will not be deceived by dissembled fidelity. I declare that,
when you left these shores ten years ago to recover with
thousands of lives one woman, who eloped of her own
free will, I deemed your judgment misguided; but now in
all sincerity I salute you with joy. Toil happily ended
brings pleasure at last, and in time you shall learn to
distinguish the just from the unjust steward.

Agamemnon: First, it is just that I should pay my
       respects
To the land of Argos and her presiding Gods,
My partners in this homecoming as also
In the just penalty which I have inflicted on
The city of Troy. When the supreme court of heaven
Adjudicated on our cause, they cast
Their votes unanimously against her, though not
Immediately, and so on the other side
Hope hovered hesitantly before it vanished.
The fires of pillage are still burning there
Like sacrificial offerings. Her ashes
Redolent with riches breathe their last and die.
For all this it is our duty to render thanks
To the celestial powers, with whose assistance
We have exacted payment and struck down
A city for one woman, forcing our entry
Within the Wooden Horse, which at the setting
Of the Pleiads like a hungry lion leapt
Out and slaked its thirst in royal blood.
As to your sentiments, I take due note
And find that they accord with mine. Too few
Rejoice at a friend's good fortune. I have known
Many dissemblers swearing false allegiance.
One only, though he joined me against his will,
Once in the harness, proved himself a staunch
Support, Odysseus, be he now alive or dead.
All public questions and such as concern the Gods
I shall discuss in council and take steps
To make this triumph lasting; and if here or there

Some malady comes to light, appropriate
Remedies will be applied to set it right.
Meanwhile, returning to my royal palace,
My first duty is to salute the Gods
Who led me overseas and home again.
Victory attends me; may she remain with me!

Clytemnestra: Citizens of Argos, councillors and
       elders,
I shall declare without shame in your presence
My feelings for my husband. Diffidence
Dies in us all with time. I shall speak of what
I suffered here, while he was away at the war,
Sitting at home, with no man's company,
Waiting for news, listening to one
Messenger after another, each bringing worse
Disasters. If all his rumored wounds were real,
His body was in shreds, shot through and through.
If he had died—the predominant report—
He was a second Geryon, an outstretched giant
With three corpses and one death for each,
While I, distraught, with a knot pressing my throat,
Was rescued forcibly, to endure still more.
       And that is why our child is not present here,
As he should be, pledge of our marriage vows,
Orestes. Let me reassure you. He lives
Safe with an old friend, Strophius, who warned me
Of various dangers—your life at stake in Troy
And here a restive populace, which might perhaps
Be urged to kick a man when he is down.
       As for myself, the fountains of my tears
Have long ago run dry. My eyes are sore
After so many nights watching the lamp
That burnt at my bedside always for you.
If I should sleep, a gnat's faint whine would shatter
The dreams that were my only company.
       But now, all pain endured, all sorrow past,
I salute this man as the watchdog of the fold,
The stay that saves the ship, the sturdy oak
That holds the roof up, the longed-for only child,
The shore despaired-of sighted far out at sea.
God keep us from all harm! And now, dearest,
Dismount, but not on the bare ground! Servants,
Spread out beneath those feet that have trampled Troy
A road of royal purple, which shall lead him
By the hand of Justice into a home unhoped-for,
And there, when he has entered, our vigilant care
Shall dispose of everything as the Gods have ordained.

Agamemnon: Lady, royal consort and guardian of our
       home,
I thank you for your words of welcome, extended
To fit my lengthy absence; but due praise
Should rather come from others; and besides,
I would not have effeminate graces unman me
With barbarous salaams and beneath my feet
Purple embroideries designed for sacred use.[4]
Honor me as a mortal, not as a god.
Heaven's greatest gift is wisdom. Count him blest
Who has brought a long life to a happy end.
I shall do as I have said, with a clear conscience.

---

4. The purple dye was extracted from seaweed. It was very rare,
therefore very expensive; a color reserved for the gods.

Clytemnestra: Yet tell me frankly, according to your judgment.

Agamemnon: My judgment stands. Make no mistake about that.

Clytemnestra: Would you not in time of danger have vowed such an act?

Agamemnon: Yes, if the priests had recommended it.

Clytemnestra: And what would Priam have done, if he had won?

Agamemnon: Oh, he would have trod the purple without a doubt.

Clytemnestra: Then you have nothing to fear from wagging tongues.

Agamemnon: Popular censure is a potent force.

Clytemnestra: Men must risk envy in order to be admired.

Agamemnon: A contentious spirit is unseemly in a woman.

Clytemnestra: Well may the victor yield a victory.

Agamemnon: Do you set so much store by your victory?

Clytemnestra: Be tempted, freely vanquished, victor still!

Agamemnon: Well, if you will have it, let someone unlace
These shoes, and, as I tread the purple, may
No far-off god cast at me an envious glance
At the prodigal desecration of all this wealth!
Meanwhile, extend your welcome to this stranger.
Power tempered with gentleness wins God's favor.
No one is glad to be enslaved, and she
Is a princess presented to me by the army,
The choicest flower culled from a host of captives.
And now, constrained to obey you, setting foot
On the sacred purple, I pass into my home.

Clytemnestra: The sea is still there, nothing can dry it up,
Renewing out of its infinite abundance
Unfailing streams of purple and blood-red dyes.
So too this house, the Gods be praised, my lord,
Has riches inexhaustible. There is no counting
The robes *I* would have vowed to trample on,
Had some oracle so instructed, if by such means
I could have made good the loss of one dear soul.[5]
So now your entry to your hearth and home
Is like a warm spell in the long winter's cold,
Or when Zeus from the virgin grape at last
Draws wine, coolness descends upon the house
(For then from the living root the new leaves raise
A welcome shelter against the burning Dog-Star)
As man made perfect moves about his home.
[*Exit* AGAMEMNON]
Zeus, perfecter of all things, fulfil my prayers
And fulfil also your own purposes! [*Exit*]

Chorus: What is this delirious dread,
Ominous, oracular,
Droning through my brain with unrelenting
Beat, irrepressible prophet of evil?
Why can I not cast it out
Planting good courage firm
On my spirit's empty throne?
In time the day came
When the Greeks with anchors plunged
Moored the sloops of war, and troops
Thronged the sandy beach of Troy.

So today my eyes have seen
Safe at last the men come home.

Still I hear the strain of stringless music,
Dirge of the Furies, a choir uninvited
Chanting in my heart of hearts.
Mortal souls stirred by God
In tune with fate divine the shape
Of things to come; yet
Grant that these forebodings prove
False and bring my fears to naught.
If a man's health be advanced over the due mean,
It will trespass soon upon sickness, who stands
Next neighbor, between them a thin wall.
So does the vessel of life
Launched with a favoring breeze
Suddenly founder on reefs of destruction.
Caution seated at the helm
Casts a portion of the freight
Overboard with measured throw;
So the ship may ride the storm.
Furrows enriched each season with showers from heaven
Banish hunger from the door.
But if the red blood of a man spatters the ground,
      dripping and deadly, then who
Has the magical power to recall it?
Even the healer who knew
Spells to awaken the dead,
Zeus put an end to his necromancy.
Portions are there preordained,
Each supreme within its own
Province fixed eternally.
That is why my spirit groans
Brooding in fear, and no longer it hopes to unravel
Mazes of a fevered mind.
[*Enter* CLYTEMNESTRA]

Clytemnestra: You, too, Cassandra, come inside! The merciful
Zeus gives you the privilege to take part
In our domestic sacrifice and stand
Before his altar among the other slaves there.
Put by your pride and step down. Even Heracles
Submitted once to slavery, and be consoled
In serving a house whose wealth has been inherited
Over so many generations. The harshest masters
Are those who have snatched their harvest out of hand.
You shall receive here what custom prescribes.

Chorus: She is speaking to you. Caught in the net, surrender.

Clytemnestra: If she knows Greek and not some barbarous language,
My mystic words shall fill the soul within her.

Chorus: You have no choice. Step down and do her will.

Clytemnestra: There is no time to waste. The victims are
All ready for the knife to render thanks
For this unhoped-for joy. If you wish to take part,
Make haste, but, if you lack the sense to understand,—
[*To the* CHORUS]
Speak to her with your hands and drag her down.

Chorus: She is like a wild animal just trapped.

Clytemnestra: She is mad, the foolish girl. Her city captured,
Brought here a slave, she will be broken in.
I'll waste no words on her to demean myself. [*Exit*]

---

5. Iphigenia

Cassandra: Oh! oh! Apollo!

Chorus: What blasphemy, to wail in Apollo's name!

Cassandra: Oh! oh! Apollo!

Chorus: Again she cries in grief to the god of joy!

Cassandra: Apollo, my destroyer! a second time!

Chorus: Ah, she foresees what is in store for her.
She is now a slave, and yet God's gift remains.

Cassandra: Apollo, my destroyer! What house is this?

Chorus: Do you not know where you have come, poor girl?
Then let us tell you. This is the House of Atreus.

Cassandra: Yes, for its very walls smell of iniquity,
A charnel house that drips with children's blood.[6]

Chorus: How keen her scent to seize upon the trail!

Cassandra: Listen to them as they bewail the foul
Repast of roast meat for a father's mouth!

Chorus: Enough! Reveal no more! We know it all.

Cassandra: What is it plotted next? Horror unspeakable,
A hard cross for kinsfolk.
The hoped-for savior is far away.

Chorus: What does she say? This must be something new.

Cassandra: Can it be so—to bathe one who is travel-tired,
And then smiling stretch out
A hand followed by a stealthy hand!

Chorus: She speaks in riddles, and I cannot read them.

Cassandra: What do I see? A net!
Yes, it is she, his mate and murderess!
Cry alleluia, cry, angels of hell, rejoice,
Fat with blood, dance and sing!

Chorus: What is the Fury you have called upon?
Helpless the heart faints with the sinking sun.
Closer still draws the stroke.

Cassandra: Ah, let the bull[7] beware!
It is a robe she wraps him in, and strikes!
Into the bath he slumps heavily, drowned in blood.
Such her skilled handicraft.

Chorus: It is not hard to read her meaning now.
Why does the prophet's voice never have good to tell,
Only cry woes to come?

Cassandra: Oh, pitiful destiny! Having lamented his,
Now I lament my own passion to fill the bowl.
Where have you brought me? Must I with him die?

Chorus: You sing your own dirge, like the red-brown bird
That pours out her grief-stricken soul,
Itys, Itys! she cries, the sad nightingale.

Cassandra: It is not so; for she, having become a bird,
Forgot her tears and sings her happy lot,
While I must face the stroke of two-edged steel.

Chorus: From whence does this cascade of harsh discords
Issue, and where will it at last be calmed?
Calamity you cry—O where must it end?

Cassandra: O wedding day, Paris accurst of all!
Scamander,[8] whose clear waters I grew beside!
Now I must walk weeping by Acheron.

Chorus: Even a child could understand.
The heart breaks, as these pitiful cries
Shatter the listening soul.

Cassandra: O fall of Troy, city of Troy destroyed!
The king's rich gifts little availed her so
That she might not have been what she is now.

Chorus: What evil spirit has possessed
Your soul, strumming such music upon your lips
As on a harp in hell?

Cassandra: Listen! My prophecy shall glance no longer
As through a veil like a bride newly-wed,
But bursting towards the sunrise shall engulf
The whole world in calamities far greater
Than these. No more riddles, I shall instruct,
While you shall verify each step, as I
Nose out from the beginning this bloody trail.
Upon this roof–do you see them?–stands a choir–
It has been there for generations–a gallery
Of unmelodious minstrels, a merry troop
Of wassailers drunk with human blood, reeling
And retching in horror at a brother's outraged bed.
Well, have I missed? Am I not well-read in
Your royal family's catalogue of crime?

Chorus: You come from a far country and recite
Our ancient annals as though you had been present.

Cassandra: The Lord Apollo bestowed this gift on me.

Chorus: Was it because he had fallen in love with you?

Cassandra: I was ashamed to speak of this till now.

Chorus: Ah yes, adversity is less fastidious.

Cassandra: Oh, but he wrestled strenuously for my love.

Chorus: Did you come, then, to the act of getting child?

Cassandra: At first I consented, and then I cheated him.

Chorus: Already filled with his gift of prophecy?

Cassandra: Yes, I forewarned my people of their destiny.

Chorus: Did your divine lover show no displeasure?

Cassandra: Yes, the price I paid was that no one listened to me.

Chorus: Your prophecies seem credible enough to us.

Cassandra: Oh!
Again the travail of the prophetic trance
Runs riot in my soul. Do you not see them
There, on the roof, those apparitions—children
Murdered by their own kin, in their hands
The innards of which their father ate—oh
What a pitiable load they carry! For that crime
Revenge is plotted by the fainthearted lion,[9]
The stay-at-home, stretched in my master's bed
(Being his slave, I must needs call him so),
Lying in wait for Troy's great conqueror.
Little he knows what that foul bitch with ears
Laid back and rolling tongue intends for him
With a vicious snap, her husband's murderess.
What abominable monster shall I call her—
A two-faced amphisbaene or Scylla that skulks
Among the rocks to waylay mariners,
Infernal sea-squib locked in internecine
Strife–did you not hear her alleluias
Of false rejoicing at his safe return?
Believe me or not, what must be will be, and then
You will pity me and say, She spoke the truth.

Chorus: The feast of Thyestes I recognized, and shuddered,
But for the rest my wits are still astray.

Cassandra: Your eyes shall see the death of Agamemnon.

---

6. She refers to Thyestes' banquet. See introduction.

7. Agamemnon.

8. Scamander is a river near Troy; Acheron (AK-e-ron) is the river of the underworld.

9. Aegisthus.

Chorus: No, hush those ill-omened lips, unhappy girl!

Cassandra: There is no Apollo present, and so no cure.

Chorus: None, if you speak the truth; yet God forbid!

Cassandra: Pray God forbid, while they close in for the kill!

Chorus: What man is there who would plot so foul a crime?

Cassandra: Ah, you have altogether misunderstood,

Chorus: But how will he do it? That escapes me still.

Cassandra: And yet I can speak Greek only too well.

Chorus: So does Apollo, but his oracles are obscure.

Cassandra: Ah, how it burns me up! Apollo! Now
That lioness[10] on two feet pours in the cup
My wages too, and while she whets the blade
For him promises to repay my passage money
In my own blood. Why wear these mockeries,
This staff and wreath, if I must die, then you
Shall perish first and be damned. Now we are quits!
Apollo himself has stripped me, looking upon me
A public laughingstock, who has endured
The name of witch, waif, beggar, castaway.
So now the god who gave me second sight
Takes back his gift and dismisses his servant,
Ready for the slaughter at a dead man's grave.
Yet we shall be avenged. Now far away,
The exile[11] shall return, called by his father's
Unburied corpse to come and kill his mother.
Why weep at all this? Have I not seen Troy fall,
And those who conquered her are thus discharged.
I name this door the gate of Hades: now
I will go and knock, I will take heart to die.
I only pray that the blow may be mortal,
Closing these eyes in sleep without a struggle,
While my life blood ebbs quietly away.

Chorus: O woman, in whose wisdom is so much grief,
How, if you know the end, can you approach it
So gently, like an ox that goes to the slaughter?

Cassandra: What help would it be if I should put it off?

Chorus: Yet, while there is life there's hope—so people say.

Cassandra: For me no hope, no help. My hour has come.

Chorus: You face your end with a courageous heart.

Cassandra: Yes, so they console those whom life has crossed.

Chorus: Is there no comfort in an honorable death?

Cassandra: O Priam, father, and all your noble sons!

[*She approaches the door, then draws back.*]

Chorus: What is it? Why do you turn back, sick at heart?

Cassandra: Inside there is a stench of dripping blood.

Chorus: It is only the blood of their fireside sacrifice.

Cassandra: It is the sort of vapor that issues from a tomb.
I will go now and finish my lament
Inside the house. Enough of life! O friends!
I am not scared. I beg of you only this:
When the day comes for them to die, a man
For a man, woman for woman, remember me!

Chorus: Poor soul condemned to death, I pity you.

Cassandra: Yet one word more, my own dirge for myself.
I pray the Sun, on whom I now look my last,
That he may grant to my master's avengers
A fair price for the slave-girl slain at his side.
O sad mortality! when fortune smiles,
A painted image; and when trouble comes,
One touch of a wet sponge wipes it away. [*Exit*]

Chorus: And her case is even more pitiable than his.
Human prosperity never rests but always craves more, till blown up with pride it totters and falls. From the opulent mansions pointed at by all passersby none warns it away, none cries. "Let no more riches enter!" To him was granted the capture of Troy, and he has entered his home as a god, but now, if the blood of the past is on him, if he must pay with his own death for the crimes of bygone generations, then who is assured of a life without sorrow?

Agamemnon: Oh me!

Chorus: Did you hear?

Agamemnon: Oh me, again!

Chorus:[12]   It is the King. Let us take counsel!
 1 I say, raise a hue and cry!
 2 Break in at once!
 3 Yes, we must act.
 4 *They* spurn delay.
 5 They plot a tyranny.
 6 Must we live their slaves?
 7 Better to die.
 8 Old men, what can we do?
 9 We cannot raise the dead.
10 His death is not yet proved.
11 We are only guessing.
12 Let us break in and learn the truth!

[*The doors are thrown open and* CLYTEMNESTRA *is seen standing over the bodies of* AGAMEMNON *and* CASSANDRA, *which are laid out on a purple robe.*]

Clytemnestra: All that I said before to bide my time
Without any shame I shall now unsay. How else
Could I have plotted against an enemy
So near and seeming dear and strung the snare
So high that he could not jump it? Now the feud
On which I have pondered all these years has been
Fought out to its conclusion. Here I stand
Over my work, and it was so contrived
As to leave no loophole. With this vast dragnet
I enveloped him in purple folds, then struck
Twice, and with two groans he stretched his legs,
Then on his outspread body I struck a third blow,
A drink for Zeus the Deliverer of the dead.
There he lay gasping out his soul and drenched me
In these deathly dew-drops, at which I cried
In sheer delight like newly-budding corn
That tastes the first spring showers. And so,
Venerable elders, you see how the matter stands.
Rejoice, if you are so minded. I glory in it.
With bitter tears he filled the household bowl;
Now he has drained it to the dregs and gone.

Chorus: How can you speak so of your murdered king?

Clytemnestra: You treat me like an empty-headed woman.
Again, undaunted, to such as understand
I say—commend or censure, as you please—
It makes no difference—here is Agamemnon,
My husband, dead, the work of this right hand,
Which acted justly. There you have the truth.

---

10. Clytemnestra.

11. Orestes.

12. To the best of our knowledge, this is the first time in any Greek play when the chorus-members have spoken as individuals. Some translations show the passage as a crescendo through the seventh speech; then a lapse into a do-nothing attitude. What does this movement show about the relation of the chorus to the tradition-ridden, fatalistic society?

Chorus: Woman, what evil brew have you devoured to take
On you a crime that cries out for a public curse?
Yours was the fatal blow, banishment shall be yours,
Hissed and hated of all men.

Clytemnestra: Your sentence now for me is banishment,
But what did you do then to contravene
His purpose, when, to exorcise the storms,
As though picking a ewe-lamb from his flocks,
Whose wealth of snowy fleeces never fails
To increase and multiply, he killed his own
Child, born to me in pain, my best-beloved?
Why did you not drive *him* from hearth and home?
I bid you cast at me such menaces
As make for mastery in equal combat
With one prepared to meet them, and if, please God,
The issue goes against you, suffering
Shall school those grey hairs in humility.

Chorus: You are possessed by some spirit of sin that stares
Out of your bloodshot eyes matching your bloody hands.
Dishonored and deserted of your kind, for this
Stroke you too shall be struck down.

Clytemnestra: Listen! By Justice, who avenged my child,
By the Fury to whom I vowed this sacrament,
No thought of fear shall enter through this door
So long as the hearth within is kindled by
Aegisthus, faithful to me now as always.
Low lies the man who insulted his wedded wife,
The darling of the Chryseids at Troy,
And stretched beside him this visionary seer,
Whom he fondled on shipboard, both now rewarded,
He as you see, and she swanlike has sung
Her dying ditty, his tasty side dish, for me
A rare spice to add relish to my joy.

Chorus: Oh, for the gift of death
To bring the long sleep that knows no waking,
Now that my lord and loyal protector
Breathes his last. For woman's sake
Long he fought overseas,
Now at home falls beneath a woman's hand.
  Helen, the folly-beguiled, having ravaged the city of Troy,
  She has set on the curse of Atreus
  A crown of blood beyond ablution.

Clytemnestra: Do not pray for death nor turn your anger against one woman as the slayer of thousands!

Chorus: Demon of blood and tears
Inbred in two women single-hearted!
Perched on the roof he stands and preens his
Sable wings, a carrion-crow
Loud he croaks, looking down
Upon the feast spread before him here below.

Clytemnestra: Ah now you speak truth, naming the thrice-fed demon, who, glutted with blood, craves more, still young in his hunger.

Chorus: When will the feast be done?
Alas, it is the will of Zeus,
Who caused and brought it all to pass.
Nothing is here but was decreed in heaven.

Clytemnestra: It was not my doing, nor am I Agamemnon's wife, but a ghost in woman's guise, the shade of the banqueter whom Atreus fed.

Chorus: How is the guilt not yours?
And yet the crimes of old may well
Have had a hand, and so it drives
On, the trail of internecine murder.

Clytemnestra: What of *him?* Was the guilt not his, when he killed the child that I bore him? And so by the sword he has fallen.

Chorus: Alas, the mind strays. The house is falling.
A storm of blood lays the walls in ruins.
Another mortal stroke for Justice's hand
Will soon be sharpened.
  Oh me, who shall bury him, who sing the dirge?
  Who shall intone at the tomb of a blessed spirit
  A tribute pure in heart and truthful?

Clytemnestra: No, I'll bury him, but without mourners.
By the waters of Acheron Iphigenia is waiting for him with a kiss.

Chorus: The charge is answered with countercharges.
The sinner must suffer: such is God's will.
The ancient curse is bringing down the house
In self-destruction.

Clytemnestra: That is the truth, and I would be content that the spirit of vengeance should rest, having absolved the house from its madness.

[*Enter* AEGISTHUS *with a bodyguard*]

Aegisthus: Now I have proof that there are Gods in heaven,
As I gaze on this purple mesh in which
My enemy lies, son of a treacherous father.
His father, Atreus, monarch of this realm,
Was challenged in his sovereign rights by mine,
Thyestes, his own brother, and banished him
From hearth and home. Later he returned
A suppliant and found sanctuary, indeed
A welcome; for his brother entertained him
To a feast of his own children's flesh, of which
My father unsuspecting took and ate.
Then, when he knew what he had done, he fell
Back spewing out the slaughtered flesh and, kicking
The table to the floor, with a loud cry
He cursed the House of Pelops. That is the crime
For which the son lies here. And fitly too
The plot was spun by me; for as a child
I was banished with my father, until Justice
Summoned me home. Now let me die, for never
Shall I live to another sight so sweet.

Chorus: Aegisthus, if it was you who planned this murder,
Then be assured, the people will stone you for it.

Aegisthus: Such talk from the lower benches! Even in dotage
Prison can teach a salutary lesson.
Better submit, or else you shall smart for it.

Chorus: You woman, who stayed at home and wallowed in
His bed, you plotted our great commander's death!

Aegisthus: Orpheus led all in rapture after him.[13]
Your senseless bark will be snuffed out in prison.

Chorus: You say the plot was yours, yet lacked the courage
To raise a hand but left it to a woman!

---

13. That is: You are not Orpheus, whose music caused people to follow him.

Aegisthus: As his old enemy, I was suspect.
Temptation was the woman's part. But now
I'll try my hand at monarchy, and all
Who disobey me shall be put in irons
And starved of food and light till they submit.
Chorus: Oh, if Orestes yet beholds the sun,
May he come home and execute them both!
Aegisthus: Ho, my guards, come forward, you have
   work to do.
Captain of the Guard: Stand by, draw your swords!
Chorus: We are not afraid to die.
Aegisthus: Die! We'll take you at your word.
Clytemnestra: Peace, my lord, and let no further
   wrong be done.
Captain, sheathe your swords. And you, old men,
Go home quietly. What has been, it had to be.
Scars enough we bear, now let us rest.
Aegisthus: Must I stand and listen to their threats?
Chorus: Men of Argos never cringed before a rogue.
Aegisthus: I shall overtake you yet—the day is near.
Chorus: Not if Orestes should come home again.
Aegisthus: Vain hope, the only food of castaways.
Chorus: Gloat and grow fat, blacken justice while you
   dare!
Aegisthus: All this foolish talk will cost you dear.
Chorus: Flaunt your gaudy plumes and strut beside
   your hen!
Clytemnestra: Pay no heed to idle clamor. You and I,
Masters of the house, shall now direct it well.

Exercises

1. It might be interesting to read through the speeches of the Chorus without any reference to the other speeches or action of the play. What is your impression of their attitude toward life in general? Do you find many examples of them speaking proverbial wisdom? It is one theme of this discussion of the Greeks that in their early cultural development they were bound by tradition and nature. Does this speaking in proverbs have any relation to this theme?

2. Kassandra, of course, is trying to arouse the Chorus to action. Quite aside from the mythical problem of the curse of Apollo, which caused everyone to disbelieve her prophecies, can you see any other reason why she cannot get these men to act? For example, why, when she was left alone in the chariot, knowing that she faced death as soon as she entered the palace, did she not run away? Certainly the members of the Chorus would not stop her.

3. Below is given a chart dealing with the levels of human freedom of action. It might be interesting to place the characters somewhere above or below the dividing line. Where would you place the Chorus throughout the play? Do they stand still, or does their position fluctuate? Where would you place Kassandra? Agamemnon? Klytaimestra?

The area of conduct
in which people are free
to accomplish their
purposes and desires.

The Dividing Line _____

A not-quite-human
level where the ideas
of justice are bound by
tradition and nature.

4. When the Chorus is telling of the death of Iphigeneia, they speak of her "swathed in folds of saffron." Later they say, "Night . . . who has cast over the towers of Troy a net so fine." Still later, Agamemnon walks on a purple "web," or "net." Why did Aeschylus use this image throughout the play? Does it have any significance beyond its literal meaning?

5. Notice that *Agamemnon* has its beginning in the darkness in the country town of Mycenae. The *Eumenides,* the third play of the trilogy, ends in the bright sunlight of Athens. Does this symbolism have any significance?

EUMENIDES
Aeschylus

This is the third play of the *Oresteia.* In the second one (*Choephori* or *The Libation Bearers*), Orestes has returned to Argos, recognized his sister, Elektra, and the two of them have planned and carried out the murder of Aigisthos and Klytaimestra. In the second play, the two ideas of justice became more apparent, for Orestes felt qualms about the murder of his mother. His sense of filial duty in carrying out revenge, as well as the fact that Apollo had commanded him to the deed, triumphed over his own conscience. Immediately after the murder he was set upon by the old hags, goddesses descended from the blood of Ouranos, whose duty it was to pursue those who had killed their own kindred.

The old idea of justice, revenge or retaliation, was presented in *Agamemnon;* we see in *Eumenides* the development of a new idea of justice and freedom for the city of Athens. Watch how this is handled. When you have finished the play, stop a while and think about the ways in which men and women can live under this new concept.

CHARACTERS:
Priestess
Apollo
Orestes
Ghost of Clytemnestra
Chorus of Furies
Athena
Escort of Women

Before the temple of Apollo at Delphi.
[*Enter the* PRIESTESS]
Priestess: First among all the gods to whom this prayer
Shall be addressed is the first of prophets, Earth;[14]
And next her daughter, Themis, who received
The oracular shrine from her; third, another
Daughter, Phoebe, who having settled here
Bestowed it as a birthday gift, together
With her own name, on Phoebus; whereupon,
Leaving his native isle of Delos and landing
In Attica, he made his way from there
Attended by the sons of Hephaestus, who tamed
The wilderness and built a road for him;
And here Zeus, having inspired him with his art,
Set him, the fourth of prophets, on this throne,
His own son and interpreter, Apollo.
Together with these deities I pay
Homage to Athena and to the nymphs that dwell
In the Corycian caves on the rugged slopes
Of Parnassus,[15] where Dionysus led
His troop of frenzied Bacchants to catch and kill
King Pentheus like a mountain-hare; and so,
After calling on Poseidon and the springs
Of Pleistus, watering this valley, and last
On Zeus the All-Highest, who makes all things perfect,
I take my seat on the oracular throne,
Ready to be consulted. Let all Greeks
Approach by lot according to the custom
And I shall prophesy to them as God dictates. [*She enters
    the temple, utters a loud cry, and returns.*]
O horror, horror! I have been driven back
Strengthless, speechless, a terror-struck old woman,
By such a sight as was never seen before.
Entering the shrine I saw at the navel-stone
In the posture of a suppliant a man
Who held an olive-branch and an unsheathed sword
In hands dripping with blood; and all round him,
Lying fast asleep, a gruesome company
Of women—yet not women—Gorgons rather;
And yet not Gorgons; them I saw once in a picture
Of the feast of Phineus: these are different.
They have no wings, and are all black, and snore,
And drips ooze from their eyes, and the rags they wear
Unutterably filthy. What country could
Have given such creatures birth, I cannot tell.
Apollo is the master of this house,
So let him look to it, healer, interpreter,
Himself of other houses purifier.
[*The inside of the temple is revealed, as described, with
    APOLLO and HERMES standing beside ORESTES.*]
Apollo: I will keep faith, at all times vigilant,
Whether at your side or far away, and never
Mild to your enemies, whom you now see
Subdued by sleep, these unloved virgins, these
Children hoary with age, whose company
Is shunned by God and man and beast, being born
For evil, just as the abyss from which they come
Is evil, the bottomless pit of Tartarus.
Yet you must fly before them, hotly pursued,
Past island cities and over distant seas,
Enduring all without faltering, until
You find sanctuary in Athena's citadel,
And there, embracing her primeval image, you
Shall stand trial, and after healing words
From me, who commanded you to kill your mother,
You shall be set free and win your salvation.

Orestes: O Lord Apollo, you have both wisdom and
    power,
And, since you have them, use them on my behalf!
Apollo: Remember, endure and have no fear! And you,
Hermes, go with him, guide him, guard his steps,
An outcast from mankind, yet blest of Zeus.
[*Exeunt* HERMES *and* ORESTES. *Enter the ghost of*
    CLYTEMNESTRA.]
Clytemnestra: Oho! asleep! What good are you to me
    asleep?
While I, deserted and humiliated,
Wander, a homeless ghost. I warn you that
Among the other spirits of the dead
(The taunt of murder does not lose its sting
In the dark world below) I am the accused
And not the accuser, with none to defend me,
Brutally slain by matricidal hands.
Look on these scars, and remember all
The wineless offerings which I laid upon
The hearth for you at many a solemn midnight—
All now forgotten, all trampled underfoot!
And *he* is gone! Light as a fawn he skipped
Out of your snare and now he laughs at you.
Oh hear me! I am pleading for my soul!
O goddesses of the underworld, awake!
I, Clytemnestra, call you now in dreams!
Chorus: Mu!
Clytemnestra: Ah, you may mew, but he is fled and
    gone.
He has protectors who are no friends of mine.
Chorus: Mu!
Clytemnestra: Still so drowsy, still so pitiless?
Orestes has escaped, the matricide!
Chorus: Oh, oh!
Clytemnestra: Still muttering and mumbling in your
    sleep!
Arise, do evil! is not that your task?
Chorus: Oh, oh!
Clytemnestra: How sleep and weariness have made
    common cause
To disenvenom the foul dragon's rage!
Chorus: Oh, oh! where is the scent? Let us mark it
    down!
Clytemnestra: Yes, you may bay like an unerring
    hound,
But still you are giving chase only in your dreams.
What are you doing? Rise, slothful slugabeds,
Stung by the scourge of my rebukes, arise
And blow about his head your bloody breath,
Consume his flesh in bellyfuls of fire!
Come on, renew the chase and hunt him down! [*Exit*]
Chorus: We have been put to shame! What has befallen
    us?
The game has leapt out of the snare and gone.
In slumber laid low, we slip the prey.

Aha, son of Zeus! pilferer, pillager!
A God, to steal away the matricide!
A youth to flout powers fixed long ago!

---

14. Earth, Themis, Phoebe, and Phoebus Apollo are the gods
who have prophesied at the Oracle of Delphi.

15. Mount Parnassus stands beside Delphi. King Pentheus of
Thebes was killed by the female worshippers of Dionysus either
here or on Mount Kithaeron.

In dream I felt beneath the heart a swift
Charioteer's sharp lash.
Under the ribs, under the flank
It rankles yet, red and sore,
Like the public scourger's blow.

This is the doing of the younger gods.
Dripping with death, red drops
Cover the heel, cover the head.
Behold the earth's navel-stone
Thick with heavy stains of blood!

His own prophetic cell he has himself defiled.
Honoring mortal claims, reckless of laws divine,
And dealing death to Fates born of old.
He injures us and yet *him* he shall never free,
Not in the depths of hell, never shall he have rest
But suffer lasting torment below.

Apollo: Out, out! Be off, and clear this holy place
Of your foul presence, or else from my golden bow
Shall spring a snake of silver and bite so deep
That from your swollen bellies you shall spew
The blood which you have sucked! Your place is where
Heads drop beneath the axe, eyes are gouged out,
Throats slit, and men are stoned, limbs lopped, and boys
Gelded, and a last whimper heard from spines
Spiked writhing in the dust. Such celebrations,
Which fill heaven with loathing, are your delight.
Off with you, I say, and go unshepherded,
A herd shunned with universal horror!

Chorus: O Lord Apollo, hear us in our turn!
You are not an abettor in this business.
You are the culprit. On you lies the whole guilt.

Apollo: Explain yourselves. How do you make that out?

Chorus: It was at your command that he killed his
mother.

Apollo: I commanded him to take vengeance for his
father.

Chorus: So promising the acceptance of fresh blood.

Apollo: I promised to absolve him from it here.

Chorus: Why do you insult the band that drove him
here?

Apollo: This mansion is not fit for your company.

Chorus: But this is the task that has been appointed to
us.

Apollo: What is this privilege that you are so proud of?

Chorus: To drive all matricides from hearth and home.

Apollo: And what of a woman who has killed her
husband?

Chorus: That is not manslaughter within the kin.

Apollo: So then you set at naught the marriage-bond
Sealed by Zeus and Hera, and yet what tie
Is stronger, joined by Fate and watched over
By Justice, than the joy which Aphrodite
Has given to man and woman? If you let those
Who violate that covenant go unpunished,
You have no right to persecute Orestes.
Why anger here, and there passivity?
On this in time Athena shall pass judgment.

Chorus: We shall give chase and never let him go.

Apollo: Pursue him then, and make trouble for
yourselves.

Chorus: No words of yours can circumscribe our
powers.

Apollo: I would not have your powers even as a gift.

Chorus: Then take your proud stand by the throne of
Zeus.
Meanwhile a mother's blood is beckoning to us,
And we must go and follow up the trail.

Apollo: And I will still safeguard the suppliant.
A wrong unheard-of in heaven and on earth
Would be his protest, if I should break faith.
[*A year passes. Before a shrine of Athena at Athens. Enter*
ORESTES.]

Orestes: O Queen Athena, I have come here in
obedience
To the Lord Apollo. Grant me sanctuary,
An outcast, yet with hands no longer sullied, for
The edge of my pollution has been worn
Off on countless paths over land and sea;
And now, in accordance with his word, present
Before your image, I entreat you to
Receive me here and pass the final judgment.

Chorus: Step where our dumb informer leads the way;
For as the hounds pursue a wounded fawn,
So do we dog the trail of human blood.
How far we have traveled over land and sea,
Faint and footsore but never to be shaken off!
He must be somewhere here, for I smell blood.
—Beware, I say, beware!
Look on all sides for fear he find some escape!
—Ah, here he is, desperate,
Clasping that image awaiting trial.
—It cannot be! The mother's blood
That he has spilt is irrecoverable.
—Ravenous lips shall feed upon his living flesh
And on his blood—a lush pasturage.
—And others shall he see in hell, who wronged
Parents, guests or gods;
For Hades is a stern inquisitor of souls,
Recording all things till the hour of judgment.

Orestes: Taught by long suffering, I have learnt at what
Times it is right to keep silence and when
To break it, and in this matter a wise
Instructor has charged me to speak. The stain
Of matricide has been washed out in the flow
Of swine's blood by Apollo. I could tell
Of many who have given me lodging and no
Harm has befallen them from my company;
And now with lips made pure I call upon
Athena to protect me and so join
Our peoples as allies for all time to come.
Wherever she may be, on Libyan shores
Or by the stream of Trito, where she came
To birth, or like a captain keeping watch
On the heights of Phlegra against some enemy,
O may she come—far off, she can still hear me—
And from my sufferings deliver me!

Chorus: Neither Apollo nor Athena can
Save your soul from perdition, a feast for fiends.
Have you no answer? Do you spurn us so,
Fattened for us, our consecrated host?

Let us dance and declare in tune with this grim music
the laws which it is ours to enforce on the life of man.
It is only those that have blood on their hands who need
fear us at all, but from them without fail we exact
retribution.

Mother Night, your children cry! Hear, black Night!
It is ours to deal by day and dark night judgment:
The young god Apollo has rescued the matricide!
    Over the blood that has been shed
    Maddening dance, melody desperate, deathly,
    Chant to bind the soul in hell,
    Spell that parches flesh to dust.

This the Fates who move the whole world through
Have assigned to us, a task for all future ages,
To keep watch on all hands that drip red with kindred
   blood.
      Over the blood that has been shed
      Maddening dance, melody desperate, deathly,
      Chant to bind the soul in hell,
      Spell that parches flesh to dust.

Such are the powers appointed us from the beginning,
None of the Gods of Olympus to eat with us, while we
Take no part in the wearing of white—no,
Other pleasures are our choice—
      Wrecking the house, hunting the man,
      Hard on his heels ever we run,
      And though his feet be swift we waste and wear him
      out.

Hence it is thanks to our zealous endeavor that from such
Offices Zeus and the Gods are exempted, and yet he
Shuns us because we are covered in blood, not
Fit to share his majesty.
      Wrecking the house, hunting the man,
      Hard on his heels ever we run,
      And though his feet be swift we waste and wear him
      out.

Glories of men, how bright in the day is their splendor,
Yet shall they fade in the darkness of hell,
Faced with our grisly attire and dancing
Feet attuned to sombre melodies.
      Nimble the feet leap in the air,
      Skip and descend down to the ground,
      Fugitive step suddenly tripped up in fatal confusion.

Caught without knowing he stumbles, his wickedness
   blinds him,
Such is the cloud of pollution that hangs
Over him and on his house, remembered
Many generations after him.
      Nimble the feet leap in the air,
      Skip and descend down to the ground,
      Fugitive step suddenly tripped up in fatal confusion.
Our task is such. With long memories
We keep constant watch on human sin.
What others spurn is what we prize.

Our heaven their hell, a region of trackless waste,
Both for the quick and dead, for blind and seeing too.

What wonder then that men bow in dread
At these commandments assigned to us
By Fate—our ancient privilege?
We are not without our own honors and dignities,
Though we reside in hell's unfathomable gloom. [*Enter*
   ATHENA]

Athena: I heard a distant cry, as I was standing
Beside Scamander to take possession of
The lands which the Achaean princes have
Bestowed on my people in perpetuity;
And thence I have made my way across the sea
In wingless flight; and now, as I regard
Before my shrine this very strange company,
I cannot but ask, in wonder, not in fear,
Who you may be. I address you all in common,
This stranger here who is seated at my image,
And you, who are not human in appearance
Nor yet divine; but rather than speak ill
Without just cause let me receive your answer.

Chorus: Daughter of Zeus, your question is soon
   answered.
We are the dismal daughters of dark Night,
Called Curses in the palaces of hell.
Athena: I know your names then and your parentage.
Chorus: And now let us inform you of our powers.
Athena: Yes, let me know what office you perform.
Chorus: We drive the matricide from hearth and home.
Athena: Where? In what place does his persecution
   end?
Chorus: A place where joy is something quite
   unknown.
Athena: Is that your hue and cry against this man?
Chorus: Yes, because he dared to kill his mother.
Athena: Was he driven to it perhaps against his will?
Chorus: What force could drive a man to matricide?
Athena: It is clear there are two parties to this case.
Chorus: We challenged him to an ordeal by oath.
Athena: You seem to seek only the semblance of
   justice.
Chorus: How so? Explain, since you are so rich in
   wisdom.
Athena: Do not use oaths to make the wrong prevail.
Chorus: Then try the case yourself and give your
   judgment.
Athena: Will you entrust the verdict to my charge?
Chorus: Yes, a worthy daughter of a worthy father.
Athena: Stranger, what is your answer? Tell us first
Your fatherland and family and what
Misfortune overtook you, and then answer
The charge against you. If you have taken your stand
Here as a suppliant with full confidence
In the justice of your cause, now is the time
To render on each count a clear reply.
Orestes: O Queen Athena, first let me remove one
   doubt.
I am not a suppliant seeking purification.
I was already cleansed before I took
This image in my arms, and I can give
Evidence of this. The manslayer is required
To keep silent until he has been anointed
With sacrificial blood. That has been done,
And I have traveled far over land and sea
To wear off the pollution. So, having set
Your mind at rest, let me tell you who I am.
I come from Argos, and my father's name—
For asking me that I thank you—was Agamemnon,
The great commander, with whom not long ago
You wiped out Troy. He died an evil death,
Murdered on his return by my blackhearted
Mother, who netted him in a bath of blood.
And therefore I, restored from banishment,
In retribution for my father's death,
I killed my mother; and yet not I alone—
Apollo too must answer for it, having
Warned me what anguish would afflict me if
I should fail to take vengeance on the guilty.
Whether it was just or not, do you decide.
Athena: This is too grave a case for mortal minds,
Nor is it right that I should judge an act
Of blood shed with such bitter consequences,
Especially since you have come to me
As one already purified, who has done no wrong
Against this city. But your opponents here
Are not so gentle, and, if their plea
Should be rejected, the poison dripping from
Their angry bosoms will devastate my country.

The issue is such that, whether I let them stay
Or turn them out, it is fraught with injury.
But be it so. Since it has come to this,
I will appoint judges for homicide,
A court set up in perpetuity.
Do you prepare your proofs and witnesses,
Then I, having selected from my people
The best, will come to pass a final judgment. [*Exit*]

Chorus: Now the world shall see the downfall of old
    commandments made
Long ago, if the accurst matricide should win his case.
Many a bitter blow awaits parents from their own children
    in the times to come.

We who had the task to watch over human life shall now
Cease to act, giving free rein to deeds of violence.
Crime shall spread from house to house like a plague,
    and whole cities shall be desolate.

Then let no man stricken cry
Out in imprecation, "Oh
Furies!" Thus shall fathers groan,
Thus shall mothers weep in vain,
Since the house of righteousness
Lies in ruins, overthrown.

Times there are when fear is good,
Keeping watch within the soul.
Needful too are penalties.
Who of those that have not nursed
Wholesome dread within them can
Show respect to righteousness?

Choose a life despot-free yet restrained by rule of law.
God has appointed the mean as the master in all things.
Wickedness breeds pride, but from wisdom is brought
    forth
Happiness prayed for by all men.

So, we say, men must bow down before the shrine of
    Right.
Those who defy it shall fail; for the ancient
    commandments
Stand—to respect parents and honor the stranger.
Only the righteous shall prosper.
The man who does what is right by choice, not constraint,
Shall prosper always; the seed of just men shall never
    perish.
Not so the captain who ships a load of ill-gotten gains.
Caught in the gathering storm his proud sail shall be torn
    from the masthead.
He cries to deaf ears, no longer able to ride
The gale and meanwhile his guardian spirit is close
    beside him
And scoffs to see him despair of ever again making port,
Dashed on the reefs of Justice, unlooked-on and
    unlamented.

[*Enter* ATHENA *with the* JUDGES, *followed by citizens of
Athens.*]

Athena: Herald, give orders to hold the people back,
Then sound the trumpet and proclaim silence.
For while this new tribunal is being enrolled,
It is right that all should ponder on its laws,
Both the litigants here whose case is to be judged,
And my whole people for all generations. [*Enter* APOLLO]

Chorus: Apollo, what is there here that concerns you?
We say you have no authority in this matter.

Apollo: I come both as a witness, the accused
Having been a suppliant at my sanctuary
And purified of homicide at my hands,

And also to be tried with him, for I too
Must answer for the murder of his mother.
Open the case, and judge as you know how.

Athena: The case is open. You shall be first to speak.
    [*To the* CHORUS]
The prosecutors shall take precedence
And first inform us truthfully of the facts.

Chorus: Many in number, we shall be brief in speech.
We beg you to answer our questions one by one.
First, is it true that you killed your mother?

Orestes: I killed her. That is true, and not denied.

Chorus: So then the first of the three rounds is ours.

Orestes: You should not boast that you have thrown me
    yet.

Chorus: Next, since you killed her, you must tell us
    how.

Orestes: Yes, with a drawn sword leveled at the throat.

Chorus: Who was it who impelled or moved you to it?

Orestes: The oracle of this God who is my witness.

Chorus: The God of prophecy ordered matricide?

Orestes: Yes, and I have not repented it to this day.

Chorus: You *will* repent it, when you have been
    condemned.

Orestes: My father shall defend me from the grave.

Chorus: Having killed your mother, you may well trust
    the dead!

Orestes: She was polluted by a double crime.

Chorus: How so? Explain your meaning to the judges.

Orestes: She killed her husband and she killed my
    father.

Chorus: She died without bloodguilt, and you still live.

Orestes: Why did you not hunt her when she was alive?

Chorus: She was not bound by blood to the man she
    killed.

Orestes: And am I then bound by blood to my mother?

Chorus: Abandoned wretch, how did she nourish you
Within the womb? Do you repudiate
The nearest and dearest tie of motherhood?

Orestes: Apollo, give your evidence. I confess
That I did this deed as I have said.
Pronounce your judgment: was it justly done?

Apollo: Athena's appointed judges, I say to you,
Justly, and I, as prophet, cannot lie.
Never from my prophetic shrine have I
Said anything of city, man or woman
But what my father Zeus has commanded me.
This plea of mine must override all others,
Since it accords with our great father's will.

Chorus: Your argument is, then, that Zeus commanded
    you
To charge Orestes with this criminal act
Regardless of the bond between son and mother?

Apollo: It is not the same, to murder a great king,
A woman too to do it, and not in open
Fight like some brave Amazon, but in such
Manner as I shall now inform this court.
On his return from battle, bringing home
A balance for the greater part of good,
She welcomed him with fine words and then, while
He bathed, pavilioned him in a purple robe
And struck him down and killed him—a man and king
Whom the whole world had honored. Such was the crime
For which she paid. Let the judges take note.

Chorus: According to your argument Zeus gives
Precedence to the father; yet Zeus it was
Who cast into prison his own father Kronos.
Judges, take note, and ask him to explain.

Apollo: Abominable monsters, loathed by gods
And men, do you not understand that chains
Can be unfastened and prison doors unlocked?
But once the dust has drunk a dead man's blood,
He can never rise again—for that no remedy
Has been appointed by our almighty Father,
Although all else he can overturn at will
Without so much effort as a single breath.
Chorus: See what your plea for the defendant means.
Is this not what he did—to spill his mother's
Blood on the ground? And shall he then be allowed
To live on in his father's house? What public
Altar can he approach and where find fellowship?
Apollo: The mother is not a parent, only the nurse
Of the seed which the true parent, the father,
Commits to her as to a stranger to
Keep it with God's help safe from harm. And I
Have proof of this. There can be a father
Without a mother. We have a witness here,
This daughter of Olympian Zeus, who sprang
Armed from her father's head, a goddess whom
No goddess could have brought to birth. Therefore,
Out of goodwill to your country and your people
I sent this suppliant to seek refuge with you,
That you, Athena, may find in him and his
A faithful ally for all time to come.
Athena: Enough has now been spoken. Are you agreed
That I call on the judges to record
Their votes justly according to their conscience?
Apollo: Our quiver is empty, every arrow spent.
We wait to hear the issue of the trial.
Athena: And has my ruling your approval too?
Chorus: Sirs, you have heard the case, and now declare
Judgment according to your solemn oath.
Athena: Citizens of Athens, hear my declaration
At this first trial in the history of man.
This great tribunal shall remain in power
Meeting in solemn session on this hill,
Where long ago the Amazons encamped
When they made war on Theseus, and sacrificed
To Ares—hence its name:[16] Here reverence
For law and inbred fear among my people
Shall hold their hands from evil night and day,
Only let them not tamper with the laws,
But keep the fountain pure and sweet to drink.
I warn you not to banish from your lives
All terror but to seek the mean between
Autocracy and anarchy; and in this way
You shall possess in ages yet unborn
An impregnable fortress of liberty
Such as no people has throughout the world.
With these words I establish this tribunal
Grave, quick to anger, incorruptible,
And always vigilant over those that sleep.
Let the judges now rise and cast their votes.[17]
Chorus: We charge you to remember that we have
Great power to harm, and vote accordingly.
Apollo: I charge you to respect the oracles
Sanctioned by Zeus and see that they are fulfilled.
Chorus: By interfering in what is not your office
You have desecrated your prophetic shrine.
Apollo: Then was my Father also at fault when he
Absolved Ixion, the first murderer?
Chorus: Keep up your chatter, but if our cause should
fail,
We shall lay on this people a heavy hand.

Apollo: Yes, you will lose your case, and then you may
Spit out your poison, but it will do no harm.
Chorus: Insolent youth mocks venerable age.
We await the verdict, ready to let loose
Against this city our destructive rage.
Athena: The final judgment rests with me, and I
Announce that my vote shall be given to Orestes.
No mother gave me birth, and in all things
Save marriage I commend with all my heart
The masculine, my father's child indeed.
Therefore I cannot hold in higher esteem
A woman killed because she killed her husband.
If the votes are equal, Orestes wins.
Let the appointed officers proceed
To empty the urns and count the votes.
Orestes: O bright Apollo, how shall the judgment go?
Chorus: O black mother Night, are you watching this?
Orestes: My hour has come—the halter or the light.
Chorus: And ours—to exercise our powers or perish.
Apollo: Sirs, I adjure you to count carefully.
If judgment errs, great harm will come of it,
Whereas one vote may raise a fallen house.
Athena: He stands acquitted on the charge of
bloodshed,
The human votes being equally divided.
Orestes: Lady Athena, my deliverer,
I was an outcast from my country, now
I can go home again and live once more
In my paternal heritage, thanks to you
And to Apollo and to the third, Zeus,
Who governs the whole world. Before I go
I give my word to you and to your people
For all posterity that no commander
Shall lead an Argive army in war against
This city. If any should violate this pledge,
Out of the graves which shall then cover us
We would arise with adverse omens to
Obstruct and turn them back. If, however,
They keep this covenant and stand by your side,
They shall always have our blessing. And so farewell!
May you and your people always prevail
Against the assaults of all your enemies! [*Exit*]
Chorus: Oho, you junior gods, since you have trod
under foot
The laws of old and robbed us of our powers,
We shall afflict this country
With damp contagion, bleak and barren, withering up the
soil,
Mildew on bud and birth abortive. Venomous pestilence
Shall sweep your cornlands with infectious death.
To weep—No! To work? Yes! To work ill and lay low the
people!
So will the maids of Night mourn for their stolen honors.
Athena: Let me persuade you to forget your grief!
You are not defeated. The issue of the trial
Has been determined by an equal vote.
It was Zeus himself who plainly testified
That Orestes must not suffer for what he did.
I beg you, therefore, do not harm my country,
Blasting her crops with drops of rank decay
And biting cankers in the early buds.

---

16. The hill and the court which met on it were called the
Areopagus.
17. It is understood that the members of the jury are dropping
their votes into an urn during the next eight speeches.

Rather accept my offer to stay and live
In a cavern on this hill and there receive
The adoration of my citizens.
Chorus: Oho, you junior gods, etc.
Athena: No, *not* dishonored, and therefore spare my
people!
I too confide in Zeus—why speak of that?—
And I alone of all the Olympian gods
Know of the keys which guard the treasury
Of heaven's thunder. But there is no need of that.
Let my persuasion serve to calm your rage.
Reside with me and share my majesty;
And when from these wide acres you enjoy
Year after year the harvest offerings
From couples newly-wed praying for children,
Then you will thank me for my intercession.
Chorus: How can you treat us so?
Here to dwell, ever debased, defiled!
Hear our passion, hear, black Night!
For the powers once ours, sealed long, long ago
Have by the junior gods been all snatched away.
Athena: You are my elders, and therefore I indulge
Your passion. And yet, though not so wise as you,
To me too Zeus has granted understanding.
If you refuse me and depart, believe me,
This country will yet prove your heart's desire,
For as the centuries pass so there will flow
Such glory to my people as will assure
To all divinities worshipped here by men
And women gathered on festive holidays
More honors than could be yours in any other
City throughout the world. And so, I beg you,
Keep from my citizens the vicious spur
Of internecine strife, which pricks the breast
Of manhood flown with passion as with wine!
Abroad let battle rage for every heart
That is fired with love of glory—that shall be theirs
In plenty. So this is my offer to you—
To give honor and receive it and to share
My glory in this country loved by heaven.
Chorus: How can you, etc.
Athena: I will not weary in my benedictions,
Lest it should ever be said that you, so ancient
In your divinity, were driven away
By me and by my mortal citizens.
No, if Persuasion's holy majesty,
The sweet enchantment of these lips divine,
Has power to move you, please, reside with me.
But, if you still refuse, then, since we have made
This offer to you, it would be wrong to lay
Your hands upon us in such bitter rage.
Again, I tell you, it is in your power to own
This land attended with the highest honors.
Chorus: Lady Athena, what do you offer us?
Athena: A dwelling free of sorrow. Pray accept.
Chorus: Say we accept, what privileges shall we have?
Athena: No family shall prosper without your grace.
Chorus: Will you ensure us this prerogative?
Athena: I will, and bless all those that worship you.
Chorus: And pledge that assurance for all time to come?
Athena: I need not promise what I will not perform.
Chorus: Your charms are working, and our rage
subsides.
Athena: Here make your dwelling, where you shall win
friends.

Chorus: What song then shall we chant in salutation?
Athena: A song of faultless victory—from land and sea,
From skies above let gentle breezes blow
And breathing sunshine float from shore to shore;
Let crops and cattle increase and multiply
And children grow in health and happiness,
And let the righteous prosper; for I, as one
Who tends flowers in a garden, cherish fondly
The seed that bears no sorrow. That is your part,
While I in many a battle shall strive until
This city stands victorious against all
Its enemies and renowned throughout the world.
Chorus: We accept; we agree to dwell with you
Here in Athens, which by grace of Zeus
Stands a fortress for the gods,
Jeweled crown of Hellas. So
With you now we join in prayer
That smiling suns and fruitful soils unite to yield
Lifelong joy, fortune fair,
Light and darkness reconciled.
Athena: For the good of my people I have given homes
in the city to these deities,[18] whose power is so great and
so slowly appeased; and, whenever a man falls foul of
them, apprehended to answer for the sins of his fathers,
he shall be brought to judgment before them, and the
dust shall stifle his proud boast.
Chorus: Free from blight may the early blossom deck
Budding trees, and may no parching drought
Spread across the waving fields.
Rather Pan in season grant
From the flocks and herds a full
Return from year to year, and from the rich
Store which these gods vouchsafe
May the Earth repay them well!
Athena: Guardians of my city, listen to the blessings
they bring, and remember that their power is great in
heaven and hell, and on earth too they bring to some glad
music and to some lives darkened with weeping.
Chorus: Free from sudden death that cuts
Short the prime of manhood, blest
In your daughters too, to whom
Be granted husband and home, and may the dread Fates
Keep them safe, present in every household,
Praised and magnified in every place!
Athena: Fair blessings indeed from powers that so
lately were averted in anger, and I thank Zeus and the
spirit of persuasion that at last there is no strife left
between us, except that they vie with me in blessing my
people.
Chorus: Peace to all, free from that
Root of evil, civil strife!
May they live in unity,
And never more may the blood of kin be let flow!
Rather may all of them bonded together
Feel and act as one in love and hate!
Athena: From these dread shapes, so quick to learn a
new music, I foresee great good for my people, who, if
only they repay their favors with the reverence due, shall
surely establish the reign of justice in a city that will
shine as a light for all mankind.
[*Enter* ESCORT OF WOMEN, *carrying crimson robes and
torches.*]

---

18. This is the transition of the awful goddesses from the *Erinyes*
(the Furies) to the *Eumenides* (the Gracious Ones).

Chorus: Joy to you all in your justly appointed riches,
Joy to all the people blest
With the Virgin's love, who stands
Next beside her Father's throne!
Wisdom man has learnt at last.
Under her protection this
Land enjoys the grace of Zeus.
Athena: Joy to you also, and now let me lead you in torchlight to your new dwelling place! Let solemn oblations speed you in joy to your home beneath the earth, and there imprison all harm while still letting flow your blessings!
Chorus: Joy to you, joy, yet again we pronounce our blessing,
Joy to all the citizens,
Gods and mortals both alike.
While you hold this land and pay
Homage to our residence,
You shall have no cause to blame
Chance and change in human life.
Athena: I thank you for your gracious salutations,
And now you shall be escorted in the light
Of torches to your subterranean dwelling,
Attended by the sacristans of my temple
Together with this company of girls
And married women and others bowed with years.
Women, let them put on these robes of crimson,
And let these blazing torches light the way,
That the goodwill of our new co-residents
Be shown in the manly prowess of your sons!
[*The* CHORUS *put on the crimson robes and a procession is formed led by young men in armor, with the* CHORUS *and the escort following, and behind them the citizens of Athens. The rest is sung as the procession moves away.*]
Chorus of the Escort: Pass on your way, O powers majestic,
Daughters of darkness in happy procession!
People of Athens, hush, speak fair!

Pass to the caverns of earth immemorial
There to be worshipped in honor and glory!
People of Athens, hush, speak fair!

Gracious and kindly of heart to our people,
Come with us, holy ones, hither in gladness,
Follow the lamps that illumine the way!
O sing at the end alleluia!

Peace to you, peace of a happy community,
People of Athens! Zeus who beholds all
Watches, himself with the Fates reconciled.
O sing at the end alleluia!

Exercises

1. Of course all that one has to do to understand this play almost completely is to understand the difference in the meaning of the word *justice* as it is first used in the play by the Furies and as it is used by Athena in her last speech of the play. That difference in meaning is worth analyzing in class. To do so, here are some questions that may guide your discussion:
   a. Insofar as the structure of the play is concerned—and its significance—why can Orestes leave when two-thirds of the play is over?
   b. The Furies insist that *fear* is a necessary part of the idea of justice that people hold. How right are they?
   c. The real turning point of the play probably comes when Athena gives her final instructions to the jury:

   > Here reverence
   > For law and inbred fear among my people
   > Shall hold their hands from evil night and day,
   > Only let them not tamper with the laws,
   > But keep the fountain pure and sweet to drink.
   > I warn you not to banish from your lives
   > All terror but to seek the mean between
   > Autocracy and anarchy; and in this way
   > You shall possess in ages yet unborn
   > An impregnable fortress of liberty . . .

   What principles are involved in this statement?
   d. The actual role of the Eumenides (as they are changed from the Furies) is never made entirely clear. From the evidence in the play itself, what seems to be their role in the maintenance of a new type of justice?
2. What difference will be found in the lives of the people of Athens as they change from the old idea of justice to the new? In what way will the new idea allow for personal freedom?

MEMORIAL ORATION
Perikles (?–429 B.C.)

This portion of Perikles' famous oration is taken from the history of the Peloponnesian War as written by Thucydides (thoo–SID–i–deez). Perikles made this address at the public funeral of a group of Athenian young men who had been killed in the war.

Some scholars contend that Aspasia exerted considerable influence not only on this notable speech but also on the political strategies of Perikles in general. An intelligent and highly educated foreigner from Ionia, Aspasia was a former hetaera (Gk., *hetaira,* female companion), Perikles' concubine (in effect, common-law wife), and the mother of his son Perikles, who was legitimized by vote of the people. The hetaerae of ancient Greece were companions—physically, intellectually, and emotionally—to influential men in Athenian society. Well-educated and adept in music, dancing, conversation, and other social graces, they fulfilled a role generally denied to Greek wives who, though undisputed mistresses of their households, were not permitted to partake fully in life outside the home.

Though criticized by some because of her former profession and her political influence, Aspasia established in the home of Perikles what might be called the first salon. Here she entertained notable artists, philosophers, and political leaders, including the more liberated women of Athens. Breaking with tradition, some men brought their wives to Aspasia's dinner parties to participate in discussions about the need for wives to be better educated and thus better able to be fit companions for their husbands. Since she was credited by Sokrates with teaching Perikles the art of rhetoric, it is likely that the brilliant Aspasia assisted Perikles in the composition of some of his speeches, most especially the Memorial Oration.

As you read this eloquent address, you should remind yourself of the questions about human aspirations that had been raised in the plays of Aeschylus. In the *Agamemnon* the chorus railed against great wealth, insisting that the most humble life was the best. In *Eumenides* we observed the question of whether justice should be by reason or by stern revenge within the family. The question of the conflict between maturing man and an absolute god who ruled through fear had been raised. Other questions we have not yet seen in the literature, but which were present in the Greek mind (and in our own) are whether the state needs to protect itself by universal military training or not, and whether a life of cultural pursuits does not enfeeble people in a nation. Perhaps the greatest question for our time and theirs is whether a democracy can really function. The argument on the one side is that an absolute government gets things done quickly and efficiently, while in a democracy, people talk so much that they have no time for action.

You will find some of the answers in which the Athenians believed in the following selection.

. . . Before I praise the dead, I should like to point out by what principles of action we rose to power, and under what institutions and through what manner of life our empire became great. For I conceive that such thoughts are not unsuited to the occasion, and that this numerous assembly of citizens and strangers may profitably listen to them.

Our form of government does not enter into rivalry with the institutions of others. We do not copy our neighbors, but are an example to them. It is true that we are called a democracy; for the administration is in the hands of the many and not of the few. But while the law secures equal justice to all alike in their private disputes, the claim of excellence is also recognized; and when a citizen is in any way distinguished, he is preferred to the public service, not as a matter of privilege, but as the reward of merit. Neither is poverty a bar, but a man may benefit his country whatever be the obscurity of his condition. There is no exclusiveness in our public life, and in our private intercourse we are not suspicious of one another, nor angry with our neighbor if he does what he likes; we do not put on sour looks at him, which though harmless are not pleasant. While we are thus unconstrained in our private intercourse, a spirit of reverence pervades our public acts: we are prevented from doing wrong by respect for authority and for the laws; having an especial regard to those which are ordained for the protection of the injured, as well as to these unwritten laws which bring upon the transgressor of them the reprobation of the general sentiment.

And we have not forgotten to provide for our weary spirits many relaxations from toil; we have regular games and sacrifices throughout the year; at home the style of our life is refined; and the delight which we daily feel in all these things helps to banish melancholy. Because of the greatness of our city the fruits of the whole earth flow in upon us; so that we enjoy the goods of other countries as freely as of our own.

Then again, our military training is in many respects superior to that of our adversaries. Our city is thrown open to the world; and we never expel a foreigner, or prevent him from seeing or learning anything of which the secret, if revealed to an enemy, might profit him. We rely not upon management of trickery, but upon our own hearts and hands. And in the matter of education whereas they from early youth are always undergoing laborious exercises which are to make them brave, we live at ease, and yet are equally ready to face the perils which they face. . . .

If, then, we prefer to meet danger with a light heart but without laborious training, and with a courage which is gained by habit and not enforced by law, are we not greatly the gainers? Since we do not anticipate the pain, although, when the hour comes, we can be as brave as those who never allow themselves to rest; and thus too our city is equally admirable in peace and in war. For we are lovers of the beautiful, yet simple in our tastes, and we cultivate the mind without loss of manliness. Wealth we employ, not for talk and ostentation, but when there is a real use for it. To avow poverty with us is no disgrace; the true disgrace is in doing nothing to avoid it. An Athenian citizen does not neglect the State because he takes care of his own household; and even those of us who are engaged in business have a very fair idea of politics. We alone regard a man who takes no interest in public affairs, not as a harmless but as a useless character; and if few of us are originators, we are all sound judges, of a policy. The great impediment to action is, in our opinion, not discussion, but the want of that knowledge which is gained by discussion preparatory to action. For we have a peculiar power of thinking before we act, and of acting too; whereas other men are courageous from ignorance but hesitate upon reflection. And they are surely to be esteemed the bravest spirits, who, having the clearest sense both of the pains and the pleasures of life, do not on that account shrink from danger. In doing good, again we are unlike others; we make our friends by conferring, not by receiving favors. Now he who confers a favor is the firmer friend, because he would fain by kindness keep alive the memory of an obligation; but the recipient is colder in his feelings, because he knows that in requiting another's generosity he will not be winning gratitude, but only paying a debt. We alone do good to our neighbors not upon a calculation of interest, but in the confidence of freedom and in a frank and fearless spirit.

To sum up: I say that Athens is the school of Hellas, and that the individual Athenian in his own person seems to have the power of adapting himself to the most varied forms of action with the utmost versatility and grace. This is no passing and idle word, but truth and fact; and the assertion is verified by the position to which these qualities have raised the State. For in the hour of trial, Athens alone among her contemporaries is superior to the report of her. No enemy who comes against her is indignant at the reverses which he sustains at the hands of such a city; no subject complains that his masters are unworthy of him. And we shall assuredly not be without witnesses: there are mightly monuments of our power, which will make us the wonder of this and of succeeding ages; we shall not need the praises of Homer or of any other panegyrist, whose poetry may please for the moment although his representation of the facts will not bear the light of day. For we have compelled every land and every sea to open a path for our valor, and have everywhere planted eternal memorials of our friendship and of our enmity. Such is the city for whose sake these men nobly fought and died: they could not bear the thought that she might be taken from them; and every one of us who survive should gladly toil on her behalf.

Exercises

1. The chorus of *Agamemnon* cautions against the evils of wealth. We, too, have a proverb about money and evil. How have the Greeks grown since Aeschylus wrote of the earlier populace? How would Perikles argue with our own proverb?
2. What stand would Perikles take on the question of universal military training?
3. Here is raised an old question about men of words and men of action. It is frequently said that the democratic ways are terribly slow because people spend their time talking and never act. Is a compromise between words and action possible?
4. Why does Perikles speak of the individual Athenian when he is making a summary of the government?

OEDIPUS THE KING

Sophokles (496–406 B.C.)

This play is perhaps the best known of all the Greek tragedies, since it was taken by Aristotle in his treatise, *Poetics* (see chap. 6), as a model for this form of drama. All of the classic elements of tragedy are here: a man of great stature who falls from high station to low because of a fatal flaw in his personality; the unity of time (one day) and of place (the exterior of the royal palace at Thebes); the calling forth of the emotions of pity and fear in the spectator; and the final sense of catharsis. This last might be defined as the sense that the action has worked itself out to its one inevitable conclusion. In doing so, the emotions of pity and fear are purged in the spectator, who is left at peace. We feel that the ending, though tragic, is right, and that there is no more to be said or done.

In order to understand the play, one should know some of the mythology that lies in its background. The city of Thebes was founded by Kadmus, as we are reminded frequently in the speeches. The history that follows is not of immediate concern until we come to the reign of King Laius and his queen, Jocasta. Two things happened at that time. First, Laius set out on a journey and was murdered on the road by unknown assailants. In the meantime a fearful monster known as the Sphinx (to whom frequent references are made in the play) established itself outside the gate of Thebes and demanded a yearly tribute from the city.

This was to continue until someone could solve the riddle the Sphinx proposed to every passer-by. The riddle, we might think, is a simple one, for it was the old one, "What goes on four legs in the morning, on two legs at noon, and on three legs in the evening?" The answer, of course, is *Man*. The riddle and its answer in this play are symbolic of the idea that the one who could solve the riddle knew the nature of man.

To the city at this time came a young man, Oedipus, supposedly the son of the king and queen of Corinth. The Sphinx posed her riddle and he gave the right answer readily, thus freeing the city of the monster and the tribute she demanded. The king being dead, the people of the city chose Oedipus as their king. As was the custom, he married Jocasta who bore him two sons and two daughters. It is several years after this when the play begins.

One question this play might bring up in the mind of a spectator is whether Oedipus is the victim of fate, or whether he is a man with free will whose character is his fate and produces his doom. Probably one will not find a clear answer to this question. In this connection one might ask what is the fatal flaw in Oedipus's character. Is it his sudden anger? Is it his impulsiveness in all of his actions, an impulsiveness that might be of great value to a ruler who must make quick decisions? Or is it his search for truth that will not be turned aside even when his wife and the chorus suggest that he should leave well enough alone? This last, again, would be a good quality in most men. Another interesting point is that of clear vision: Oedipus sees all things clearly; Tiresias is blind and sees truth with a sort of inner sight. Which one beholds more clearly? And why is the wound Oedipus inflicts upon himself not only *an* appropriate one but *the* appropriate one?

This modern translation is by Theodore Howard Banks, whose spelling of proper names has been retained.

CHARACTERS:
Oedipus, King of Thebes
Jocasta, Queen of Thebes, wife and mother of Oedipus
Creon, brother of Jocasta
Tiresias, a prophet
Boy, attendant of Tiresias
Priest of Zeus
Shepherd
First Messenger, from Corinth
Second Messenger
Chorus of Theban elders
Attendants

Scene: *Before the doors of the palace of* OEDIPUS *in Thebes. A crowd of citizens are seated next to the two altars at the sides. In front of one of the altars stands the* PRIEST OF ZEUS. *[Enter* OEDIPUS*]*

Oedipus: Why are you here as suppliants, my children,
You in whose veins the blood of Cadmus flows?
What is the reason for your boughs of olive,
The fumes of incense, the laments and prayers
That fill the city? Because I thought it wrong,
My children, to depend on what was told me,

I have come to you myself, I, Oedipus,
Renowned in the sight of all. [*to* PRIEST] Tell me—
    you are
Their natural spokesman—what desire or fear
Brings you before me? I will gladly give you   10
Such help as is in my power. It would be heartless
Not to take pity on a plea like this.
Priest: King Oedipus, you see us, young and old.
Gathered about your altars: some, mere fledglings
Not able yet to fly; some, bowed with age;
Some, priests, and I the priest of Zeus among them;
And these, who are the flower of our young manhood.
The rest of us are seated—the whole city—
With our wreathed branches in the market places,
Before the shrines of Pallas, before the fire   20
By which we read the auguries of Apollo.
Thebes, as you see yourself, is overwhelmed
By the waves of death that break upon her head.
No fruit comes from her blighted buds; her cattle
Die in the fields; her wives bring forth dead children.
A hideous pestilence consumes the city,
Striking us down like a god armed with fire,
Emptying the house of Cadmus, filling full
The dark of Hades with loud lamentation.
I and these children have not thronged your altars   30
Because we hold you equal to the immortals,
But because we hold you foremost among men,
Both in the happenings of daily life
And when some visitation of the gods
Confronts us. For we know that when you came here,
You freed us from our bondage, the bitter tribute
The Sphinx wrung from us by her sorceries.
And we know too that you accomplished this
Without foreknowledge, or clue that we could
    furnish.
We think, indeed, some god befriended you,   40
When you renewed our lives. Therefore, great king,
Glorious in all men's eyes, we now beseech you
To find some way of helping us, your suppliants,
Some way the gods themselves have told you of,
Or one that lies within our mortal power;
For the words of men experienced in evil
Are mighty and effectual. Oedipus!
Rescue our city and preserve your honor,
Since the land hails you as her savior now
For your past service. Never let us say   50
That when you ruled us, we were lifted up
Only to be thrown down. Restore the state
And keep it forever steadfast. Bring again
The happiness and good fortune you once brought
    us.
If you are still to reign as you reign now,
Then it is better to have men for subjects
Than to be king of a mere wilderness,
Since neither ship nor town has any value
Without companions or inhabitants.
Oedipus: I pity you, my children. Well I know   60
What hopes have brought you here, and well I know
That all of you are suffering. Yet your grief,
However great, is not so great as mine.
Each of you suffers for himself alone,
But my heart feels the heaviness of my sorrow,
Your sorrow, and the sorrow of all the others.
You have not roused me. I have not been sleeping.
No. I have wept, wept long and bitterly,
Treading the devious paths of anxious thought;
And I have taken the only hopeful course   70

That I could find. I have sent my kinsman, Creon,
Son of Menoeceus, to the Pythian home[19]
Of Phoebus Apollo to find what word or deed
Of mine might save the city. He has delayed
Too long already, his absence troubles me;
But when he comes, I pledge myself to do
My utmost to obey the god's command.
Priest: Your words are timely, for even as you
    speak
They sign to me that Creon is drawing near.
Oedipus: O Lord Apollo! Grant he may bring to us   80
Fortune as smiling as his smiling face.
Priest: Surely he brings good fortune. Look! The
    crown
Of bay leaves that he wears is full of berries.
Oedipus: We shall know soon, for he is close
    enough
To hear us. Brother, son of Menoeceus, speak!
What news? What news do you bring us from the god?
[*Enter* CREON]
Creon: Good news. If we can find the fitting way
To end this heavy scourge, all will be well.
Oedipus: That neither gives me courage nor alarms
    me.
What does the god say? What is the oracle?   90
Creon: If you wish me to speak in public, I will do
    so.
Otherwise let us go in and speak alone.
Oedipus: Speak here before everyone. I feel more
    sorrow
For their sakes than I feel for my own life.
Creon: Then I will give the message of Lord
    Phoebus:
A plain command to drive out the pollution
Here in our midst, and not to nourish it
Till our disease has grown incurable.
Oedipus: What rite will purge us? How are we
    corrupted?
Creon: We must banish a man, or have him put to
    death   100
To atone for the blood he shed, for it is blood
That has brought this tempest down upon the city.
Oedipus: Who is the victim whose murder is
    revealed?
Creon: King Laius, who was our lord before you
    came
To steer the city on its proper course.
Oedipus: I know his name well, but I never saw
    him.
Creon: Laius was killed, and now we are
    commanded
To punish his killers, whoever they may be.
Oedipus: How can they be discovered? Where shall
    we look
For the faint traces of this ancient crime?   110
Creon: In Thebes, the god said. Truth can be
    always found:
Only what is neglected ever escapes.
Oedipus: Where was King Laius murdered? In his
    home,
Out in the fields, or in some foreign land?
Creon: He told us he was journeying to Delphi.
After he left, he was never seen again.

----

19. That is, the oracle at Delphi.

Oedipus: Was no one with King Laius who saw
  what happened?
You could have put his story to good use.
Creon: The sole survivor fled from the scene in
  terror,
And there was only one thing he was sure of.   120
Oedipus: What was it? A clue might lead us far
Which gave us even the faintest glimmer of hope.
Creon: He said that they were violently attacked
Not by one man but by a band of robbers.
Oedipus: Robbers are not so daring. Were they
  bribed
To commit this crime by some one here in Thebes?
Creon: That was suspected. But in our time of
  trouble
No one appeared to avenge the death of Laius.
Oedipus: But your King was killed! What troubles
  could you have had
To keep you from searching closely for his killers?   130
Creon: We had the Sphinx. Her riddle made us
  turn
From mysteries to what lay before our doors.
Oedipus: Then I will start fresh and again make
  clear
Things that are dark. All honor to Apollo
And to you, Creon, for acting as you have done
On the dead King's behalf. So I will take
My rightful place beside you as your ally,
Avenging Thebes and bowing to the god.
Not for a stranger will I dispel this taint,
But for my own sake, since the murderer,   140
Whoever he is, may strike at me as well.
Therefore in helping Laius I help myself.
Come, children, come! Rise from the altar steps,
And carry away those branches. Summon here
The people of Cadmus. Tell them I mean to leave
Nothing undone. So with Apollo's aid
We may at last be saved—or meet destruction.
[*Exit* OEDIPUS]
Priest: My children, let us go. The King has
  promised
The favor that we sought. And may Lord Phoebus
Come to us with his oracles, assuage
Our misery, and deliver us from death.   150
[*Exeunt. Enter* CHORUS]
Chorus: The god's great word, in whose sweetness
  we ever rejoice,
      To our glorious city is drawing nigh,
Now, even now, from the gold of the Delphic shrine.
      What next decree will be thine,
Apollo, thou healer, to whom in our dread we cry?
      We are anguished, racked, and beset by
        fears!
What fate will be ours? One fashioned for us alone,
      Or one that in ancient time was known
      That returns once more with the circling years? 160
Child of our golden hope, O speak, thou immortal
  voice!
Divine Athene, daughter of Zeus, O hear![20]
      Hear thou, Artemis! Thee we hail,
Our guardian goddess throned in the market place.
      Apollo, we ask thy grace.
Shine forth, all three, and the menace of death will
  fail.
      Answer our call! Shall we call in vain?

If ever ye came in the years that have gone before,
      Return, and save us from plague once more,
      Rescue our city from fiery pain!   170
Be your threefold strength our shield. Draw near to
  us now, draw near!
      Death is upon us. We bear a burden of bitter
        grief.
There is nothing can save us now, no device that our
  thought can frame.
      No blossom, no fruit, no harvest sheaf
      Springs from the blighted and barren earth.
Women cry out in travail and bring no children to
  birth;
      But swift as a bird, swift as the sweep of flame,
      Life after life takes sudden flight
To the western god, to the last, dark shore of night.
      Ruin has fallen on Thebes. Without number her
        children
      are dead;   180
Unmourned, unattended, unpitied, they lie polluting
  the ground.
      Grey-haired mothers and wives new-wed
      Wail at the altars everywhere,
With entreaty, with loud lament, with clamor filling
  the air.
      And songs of praise to Apollo, the healer,
        resound.
      Athene, thou knowest our desperate need.
Lend us thy strength. Give heed to our prayer,
  give heed!
      Fierce Ares has fallen upon us. He comes
        unarrayed for war,
Yet he fills our ears with shrieking, he folds us in
  fiery death.
      Grant that he soon may turn in headlong flight
        from our
      land,   190
Swept to the western deep by the fair wind's favoring
  breath,
      Or swept to the savage sea that washes the
        Thracian shore.
We few who escape the night are stricken down in
  the day.
      O Zeus, whose bolts of thunder are balanced
        within thy hand,
Hurl down thy lightning upon him! Father, be swift to
  slay!
      Save us, light-bringing Phoebus! The shower of
        thine arrows let fly;
Loose them, triumphant and swift, from the golden
  string of thy bow!
O goddess, his radiant sister, roaming the Lycian
  glade,
Come with the flash of thy fire! Artemis, conquer our
  foe!
      And thou, O wine-flushed god to whom the
        Bacchantes
      cry,   200

---

20. These appeals to the gods are understandable chiefly as cries
of despair. Ares, referred to in line 188, is the God of War and
here chiefly suggests destruction. Bacchus, or Dionysus (line
200), was the patron god of Thebes, and his devotees, the
bacchantes, held wild revels in the streets of the city.

With thy brilliant torch ablaze amid shouts of thy
  maenad train,
  With thy hair enwreathed with gold, O Bacchus,
  we beg thine aid
Against our destroyer Ares, the god whom the gods
  disdain!
[*Enter* OEDIPUS]
Oedipus: You have been praying. If you heed my
  words
And seek the remedy for your own disease,
The gods will hear your prayers, and you will find
Relief and comfort. I myself know nothing
About this story, nothing about the murder,
So that unaided and without a clue
I could not have tracked it down for any distance.   210
And because I have only recently been received
Among you as a citizen, to you all,
And to all the rest, I make this proclamation:
Whoever knows the man who killed King Laius,
Let him declare his knowledge openly.
If he himself is guilty, let him confess
And go unpunished, except for banishment.
Or if he knows the murderer was an alien,
Let him by speaking earn his due reward,
And thanks as well. But if he holds his tongue,   220
Hoping to save himself or save a friend,
Then let him hear what I, the King, decree
For all who live in Thebes, the land I rule.
No one shall give this murderer shelter. No one
Shall speak to him. No one shall let him share
In sacrifice or prayer or lustral rites.
The door of every house is barred against him.
The god has shown me that he is polluted.
So by this edict I ally myself
With Phoebus and the slain. As for the slayer,   230
Whether he had accomplices or not,
This is my solemn prayer concerning him:
May evil come of evil; may he live
A wretched life and meet a wretched end.
And as for me, if I should knowingly
Admit him as a member of my household,
May the same fate which I invoked for others
Fall upon me. Make my words good, I charge you,
For love of me, Apollo, and our country
Blasted by the displeasure of the gods.   240
You should not have left this guilt unpurified,
Even without an oracle to urge you,
When a man so noble, a man who was your King,
Had met his death. Rather, it was your duty
To seek the truth. But now, since it is I
Who hold the sovereignty that once was his,
I who have wed his wife, who would have been
Bound to him by the tie of having children
Born of one mother, if he had had a child
To be a blessing, if fate had not struck him down—   250
Since this is so, I intend to fight his battle
As though he were my father.[21] I will leave
Nothing undone to find his murderer,
Avenging him and all his ancestors.
And I pray the gods that those who disobey
May suffer. May their fields bring forth no harvest,
Their wives no children; may the present plague,
Or one yet worse, consume them. But as for you,
All of you citizens who are loyal to me,
May Justice, our champion, and all the gods   260
Show you their favor in the days to come.

Chorus: King Oedipus, I will speak to avoid your
  curse.
I am no slayer, nor can I point him out.
The question came to us from Phoebus Apollo;
It is for him to tell us who is guilty.
Oedipus: Yes. But no man on earth is strong
  enough
To force the gods to act against their will.
Chorus: There is; I think, a second course to
  follow.
Oedipus: If there is yet a third, let me know that.
Chorus: Tiresias, the prophet, has the clearest
  vision   270
Next to our Lord Apollo. He is the man
Who can do most to help us in our search.
Oedipus: I have not forgotten. Creon suggested it,
And I have summoned him, summoned him twice.
I am astonished he is not here already.
Chorus: The only rumors are old and half-
  forgotten.
Oedipus: What are they? I must find out all I can.
Chorus: It is said the King was killed by travelers.
Oedipus: So I have heard, but there is no eye-
  witness.
Chorus: If fear can touch them, they will reveal
  themselves   280
Once they have heard so dreadful a curse as yours.
Oedipus: Murderers are not terrified by words.
Chorus: But they can be convicted by the man
Being brought here now, Tiresias. He alone
Is godlike in his knowledge of the truth.
[*Enter* TIRESIAS,[22] *led by a* BOY.]
Oedipus: You know all things in heaven and earth,
  Tiresias:
Things you may speak of openly, and secrets
Holy and not to be revealed. You know,
Blind though you are, the plague that ruins Thebes.
And you, great prophet, you alone can save us.   290
Phoebus has sent an answer to our question,
An answer that the messengers may have told you,
Saying there was no cure for our condition
Until we found the killers of King Laius
And banished them or had them put to death.
Therefore, Tiresias, do not begrudge your skill
In the voice of birds or other prophecy,
But save yourself, save me, save the whole city,
Save everything that the pestilence defiles.
We are at your mercy, and man's noblest task   300
Is to use all his powers in helping others.
Tiresias: How dreadful a thing, how dreadful a
  thing is wisdom,
When to be wise is useless! This I knew
But I forgot, or else I would never have come.

---

21. This whole passage is filled with dramatic irony: that is, the
audience understands the words in another sense than the
speaker means them.

22. Tiresias is a blind prophet, a priest of Apollo. He seems to
have been almost infinitely old, and was both masculine and
feminine. Consequently his wisdom was almost without bounds.
Priests often made their prophecies after observing flights of
birds, listening to the cries of birds, observing the entrails of
sacrificial animals, etc.

Oedipus: What is the matter? Why are you so troubled?

Tiresias: Oedipus, let me go home. Then you will bear
Your burden, and I mine, more easily.

Oedipus: Custom entitles us to hear your message.
By being silent you harm your native land.

Tiresias: You do not know when, and when not to speak.   310
Silence will save me from the same misfortune.

Oedipus: If you can be of help, then all of us
Kneel and implore you not to turn away.

Tiresias: None of you know the truth, but I will never
Reveal my sorrow—not to call it yours.

Oedipus: What are you saying? You know and will not speak?
You mean to betray us and destroy the city?

Tiresias: I refuse to pain you. I refuse to pain myself.
It is useless to ask me. I will tell you nothing.

Oedipus: You utter scoundrel! You would enrage a stone!
Is there no limit to your stubbornness?

Tiresias: You blame my anger and forget your own.

Oedipus: No one could help being angry when he heard
How you dishonor and ignore the state.   320

Tiresias: What is to come will come, though I keep silent.

Oedipus: If it must come, your duty is to speak.

Tiresias: I will say no more. Rage to your heart's content.

Oedipus: Rage? Yes, I will rage! I will spare you nothing.
In the plot against King Laius, I have no doubt
That you were an accomplice, yes, almost
The actual killer. If you had not been blind,
I would have said that you alone were guilty.

Tiresias: Then listen to my command! Obey the edict
That you yourself proclaimed and never speak,   330
From this day on, to me or any Theban.
You are the sinner who pollutes our land.

Oedipus: Have you no shame? How do you hope to escape
The consequence of such an accusation?

Tiresias: I have escaped. My strength is the living truth.

Oedipus: This is no prophecy. Who taught you this?

Tiresias: You did. You forced me to speak against my will.

Oedipus: Repeat your slander. Let me learn it better.

Tiresias: Are you trying to tempt me into saying more?
I have spoken already. Have you not understood?   340

Oedipus: No, not entirely. Give your speech again.

Tiresias: I say you are the killer, you yourself.

Oedipus: Twice the same insult! You will pay for it.

Tiresias: Shall I say more to make you still more angry?

Oedipus: Say what you want to. It will make no sense.

Tiresias: You are living in shame with those most dear to you,
As yet in ignorance of your dreadful fate.

Oedipus: Do you suppose that you can always use
Language like that and not be punished for it?

Tiresias: Yes. I am safe, if truth has any strength.   350

Oedipus: Truth can save anyone excepting you,
You with no eyes, no hearing, and no brains!

Tiresias: Poor fool! You taunt me, but you soon will hear
The self-same insults heaped upon your head.

Oedipus: You live in endless night. What can you do
To me or anyone else who sees the day?

Tiresias: Nothing. I have no hand in your destruction.
For that, Apollo needs no help from me.

Oedipus: Apollo! Is this your trick, or is it Creon's?

Tiresias: Creon is guiltless. The evil is in you.   360

Oedipus: How great is the envy roused by wealth, by kingship,
By the subtle skill that triumphs over others
In life's hard struggle! Creon, who has been
For years my trusted friend, has stealthily
Crept in upon me anxious to seize my power,
The unsought gift the city freely gave me.
Anxious to overthrow me, he has bribed
This scheming mountebank, this fraud, this trickster,
Blind in his art and in everything but money!
Your art of prophecy! When have you shown it?   370
Not when the watch-dog of the gods was here,
Chanting her riddle. Why did you say nothing,
When you might have saved the city? Yet her puzzle
Could not be solved by the first passer-by.
A prophet's skill was needed, and you proved
That you had no such skill, either in birds
Or any other means the gods have given.
But I came, I, the ignorant Oedipus,
And silenced her. I had no birds to help me.
I used my brains. And it is I you now   380
Are trying to destroy in the hope of standing
Close beside Creon's throne. You will regret
This zeal of yours to purify the land,
You and your fellow-plotter. You seem old;
Otherwise you would pay for your presumption.

Chorus: Sir, it appears to us that both of you
Have spoken in anger. Anger serves no purpose.
Rather we should consider in what way
We best can carry out the god's command.

Tiresias: King though you are, I have a right to answer   390
Equal to yours. In that I too am king.
I serve Apollo. I do not acknowledge
You as my lord or Creon as my patron.
You have seen fit to taunt me with my blindness.
Therefore I tell you this: you have your eyesight
And cannot see the sin of your existence,
Cannot see where you live or whom you live with,
Are ignorant of your parents, bring disgrace
Upon your kindred in the world below
And here on earth. And soon the double lash   400
Of your mother's and father's curse will drive you headlong
Out of the country, blinded, with your cries
Heard everywhere, echoed by every hill
In all Cithaeron. Then you will have learned
The meaning of your marriage, learned in what harbor,

After so fair a voyage, you were shipwrecked.
And other horrors you could never dream of
Will teach you who you are, will drag you down
To the level of your children. Heap your insults
On Creon and my message if you choose to.   410
Still no one ever will endure the weight
Of greater misery than will fall on you.
Oedipus: Am I supposed to endure such talk as
this,
Such talk from him? Go, curse you, go! Be quick!
Tiresias: Except for your summons I would never
have come.
Oedipus: And I would never have sent for you so
soon
If I had known you would prove to be a fool.
Tiresias: Yes, I have proved a fool—in your
opinion,
And yet your parents thought that I was wise.
Oedipus: What parents? Wait! Who was my father?
Tell me!   420
Tiresias: Today will see your birth and your
destruction.
Oedipus: You cannot speak unless you speak in
riddles!
Tiresias: And yet how brilliant you are in solving
them!
Oedipus: You sneer at me for what has made me
great.
Tiresias: The same good fortune that has ruined
you.
Oedipus: If I have saved the city, nothing else
matters.
Tiresias: In that case I will go. Boy, take me home.
Oedipus: Yes, let him take you. Here, you are in
the way.
Once you are gone, you will give no further trouble.
Tiresias: I will not go before I have said my say,   430
Indifferent to your black looks. You cannot harm me.
And I say this: the man whom you have sought,
Whom you have threatened, whom you have
proclaimed
The killer of King Laius—he is here.
Now thought an alien, he shall prove to be
A native Theban, to his deep dismay.
Now he has eyesight, now his wealth is great;
But he shall make his way to foreign soil
Blinded, in beggary, groping with a stick.
In his own household he shall be shown to be   440
The father of his children—and their brother,
Son to the woman who bore him—and her husband,
The killer and the bedfellow of his father.
Go and consider this; and if you find
That I have been mistaken, you can say
That I have lost my skill in prophecy.
[*Exeunt* OEDIPUS *and* TIRESIAS]
Chorus: What man is this the god from the Delphic
rock denounces,
Whose deeds are too shameful to tell, whose
murderous hands are red?
Let his feet be swifter now than hooves of horses
racing
The storm-clouds overhead.   450
For Zeus's son, Apollo, leaps in anger upon him,
Armed with lightning to strike and slay;
And the terrible Fates, unflagging, relentless,
Follow the track of their prey.

The words of the god have flashed from the peaks of
snowy Parnassus,
Commanding us all to see this killer as yet
unknown.
Deep in the tangled woods, through rocks and caves
he is roaming
Like a savage bull, alone.
On his lonely path he journeys, wretched, broken by
sorrow,
Seeking to flee from the fate he fears;   460
But the voice from the center of earth that
doomed him
Inescapably rings in his ears.
Dreadful, dreadful those words! We can neither
approve nor deny them.
Shaken, confounded with fears, we know not
what to say.
Nothing is clear to us, nothing—what is to come
tomorrow,
Or what is upon us today.
If the prophet seeks revenge for the unsolved murder
of Laius,
Why is Oedipus charged with crime?
Because some deep-rooted hate divides their
royal houses?
The houses of Laius and Oedipus, son of the
king of
Corinth?   470
There is none that we know of, now, or in
ancient time.
From Zeus's eyes and Apollo's no human secret is
hidden;
But man has no test for truth, no measure his wit
can devise.
Tiresias, indeed, excels in every art of his office,
And yet we too may be wise.
Though Oedipus stands accused, until he is proven
guilty
We cannot blacken his name;
For he showed his wisdom the day the winged
maiden faced him.
He triumphed in that ordeal, saved us, and won our
affection.
We can never believe he stooped to an act of
shame.   480
[*Enter* CREON]
Creon: Thebans, I come here outraged and
indignant,
For I have learned that Oedipus has accused me
Of dreadful crimes. If, in the present crisis,
He thinks that I have wronged him in any way,
Wronged him in word or deed, then let my life
Come to a speedy close. I cannot bear
The burden of such scandal. The attack
Ruins me utterly, if my friends, and you,
And the whole city are to call me traitor.
Chorus: Perhaps his words were only a burst of
anger,   490
And were not meant as a deliberate insult.
Creon: He *did* say that I plotted with Tiresias?
And that the prophet lied at my suggestion?
Chorus: Those were his words. I cannot guess his
motive.
Creon: Were his eyes clear and steady? Was his
mind
Unclouded, when he brought this charge against me?

Chorus: I cannot say. To see what princes do
Is not our province. Here comes the King himself.
[*Enter* OEDIPUS]
Oedipus: So you are here! What brought you to my door?
Impudence? Insolence? You, my murderer! 500
You, the notorious stealer of my crown!
Why did you hatch this plot? What kind of man,
By heaven, what kind of man, could you have
    thought me?
A coward or a fool? Did you suppose
I would not see your trickery take shape,
Or when I saw it, would not counter it?
How stupid you were to reach for royal power
Without a troop of followers or rich friends!
Only a mob and money win a kingdom.
Creon: Sir, let me speak. When you have heard my
    answer, 510
You will have grounds on which to base your
    judgment.
Oedipus: I cannot follow all your clever talk.
I only know that you are dangerous.
Creon: That is the issue. Let me explain that first.
Oedipus: Do not explain that you are true to me.
Creon: If you imagine that a blind self-will
Is strength of character, you are mistaken.
Oedipus: As you are, if you strike at your own
    house,
And then expect to escape all punishment.
Creon: Yes, you are right. That would be
    foolishness. 520
But tell me, what have I done? How have I harmed
    you?
Oedipus: Did you, or did you not, urge me to
    summon
Tiresias, that revered, that holy prophet?
Creon: Yes. And I still think my advice was good.
Oedipus: Then answer this: how long ago was
    Laius—
Creon: Laius! Why how am I concerned with him?
Oedipus: How many years ago was Laius murdered?
Creon: So many they cannot easily be counted.
Oedipus: And was Tiresias just as cunning then?
Creon: As wise and honored as he is today. 530
Oedipus: At that time did he ever mention me?
Creon: Not in my hearing. I am sure of that.
Oedipus: And the murderer—a thorough search
    was made?
Creon: Yes, certainly, but we discovered nothing.
Oedipus: Then why did the man of wisdom hold
    his tongue?
Creon: I cannot say. Guessing is not my habit.
Oedipus: One thing at least you need not guess
    about.
Creon: What is it? If I know it, I will tell you.
Oedipus: Tiresias would not have said I murdered
    Laius,
If you two had not put your heads together. 540
Creon: You best know what he said. But now I
    claim
The right to take my turn in asking questions.
Oedipus: Very well, ask. You never can find me
    guilty.
Creon: Then answer this: my sister is your wife?
Oedipus: I cannot deny that fact. She is my wife.
Creon: And in your rule she has an equal share?
Oedipus: She has no wish that goes unsatisfied.

Creon: And as the third I stand beside you both?
Oedipus: True. That position proves your treachery.
Creon: No. You would see, if you thought the
    matter through 550
As I have done. Consider. Who would choose
Kingship and all the terrors that go with it,
If, with the same power, he could sleep in peace?
I have no longing for a royal title
Rather than royal freedom. No, not I,
Nor any moderate man. Now I fear nothing.
Every request I make of you is granted,
And yet as king I should have many duties
That went against the grain. Then how could rule
Be sweeter than untroubled influence? 560
I have not lost my mind. I want no honors
Except the ones that bring me solid good.
Now all men welcome me and wish me joy.
Now all your suitors ask to speak with me,
Knowing they cannot otherwise succeed.
Why should I throw away a life like this
For a king's life? No one is treacherous
Who knows his own best interests. To conspire
With other men, or to be false myself,
Is not my nature. Put me to the test. 570
First, go to Delphi. Ask if I told the truth
About the oracle. Then if you find
I have had dealings with Tiresias, kill me.
My voice will echo yours in passing sentence.
But base your verdict upon something more
Than mere suspicion. Great injustice comes
From random judgments that bad men are good
And good men bad. To throw away a friend
Is, in effect, to throw away your life,
The prize you treasure most. All this, in time, 580
Will become clear to you, for time alone
Proves a man's honesty, but wickedness
Can be discovered in a single day.
Chorus: Sir, that is good advice, if one is prudent.
Hasty decisions always lead to danger.
Oedipus: When a conspiracy is quick in forming,
I must move quickly to retaliate.
If I sat still and let my enemy act,
I would lose everything that he would gain.
Creon: So then, my banishment is what you want? 590
Oedipus: No, not your banishment. Your
    execution.
Creon: I think you are mad.
Oe.: I can protect myself.
Creon: You should protect me also.
Oe.: You? A traitor?
Creon: Suppose you are wrong?
Oe.: I am the King. I rule.
Creon: Not if you rule unjustly.
Oe.: Thebes! Hear that!
Creon: Thebes is my city too, as well as yours.
Chorus: No more, no more, sirs! Here is Queen
    Jocasta.
She comes in time to help make peace between you.
[*Enter* JOCASTA]
Jocasta: Oedipus! Creon! How can you be so
    foolish?
What! Quarrel now about a private matter 600
When the land is dying? You should be ashamed.
Come, Oedipus, come in. Creon, go home.
You make a trivial problem too important.

Creon: Sister, your husband has made dreadful threats.
He claims the right to have me put to death
Or have me exiled. He need only choose.
Oedipus: Yes. I have caught him at his treachery,
Plotting against the person of the King.
Creon: If I am guilty, may it be my fate
To live in misery and to die accursed. 610
Jocasta: Believe him, Oedipus, believe him, spare him—
I beg you by the gods—for his oath's sake,
For my sake, for the sake of all men here.
Chorus: Consent, O King. Be gracious. Hear us, we beg you.
Oedipus: What shall I hear? To what shall I consent?
Chorus: Respect the evidence of Creon's wisdom,
Respect the oath of innocence he has taken.
Oedipus: You know what this means?
Ch.: Yes.
Oe.: Tell me again what you ask for.
Chorus: To yield, to relent.
He is your friend and swears he is not guilty. 620
Do not act in haste, convicting him out of hand.
Oedipus: When you ask for this, you ask for my destruction;
You sentence me to death or to banishment.
Be sure that you understand.
Chorus: No, by Apollo, no!
If such a thought has ever crossed my mind,
Then may I never find
A friend to love me or a god to save;
And may dark doom pursue me to the grave.
My country perishes, and now new woe 630
Springs from your quarrel, one affliction more
Has come upon us, and my heart is sore.
Oedipus: Let him go free, even though that destroys me.
I shall be killed, or exiled in disgrace.
Not his appeal but yours aroused my pity.
I shall hate him always, no matter where he is.
Creon: You go beyond all bounds when you are angry,
And are sullen when you yield. Natures like yours
Inflict their heaviest torments on themselves.
Oedipus: Go! Go! Leave me in peace!
Cr.: Yes, I will go. 640
You have not understood, but in the sight
Of all these men here I am innocent.
[*Exit* CREON]
Chorus: Take the King with you, Madam, to the palace.
Jocasta: When I have learned what happened, we will go.
Chorus: The King was filled with fear and blind suspicion.
Creon resented what he thought injustice.
Jocasta: Both were at fault?
Ch.: Both.
Joc.: Why was the King suspicious?
Chorus: Do not seek to know.
We have said enough. In a time of pain and trouble
Inquire no further. Let the matter rest. 650
Oedipus: Your well-meant pleading turned me from my purpose,
And now you come to this. You fall so low
As to think silence best.

Chorus: I say again, O King,
No one except a madman or a fool
Would throw aside your rule.
For you delivered us; your single hand
Lifted the load from our beloved land.
When we were mad with grief and suffering,
In our extremity you found a way 660
To save the city, as you will today.
Jocasta: But tell *me* Oedipus, tell *me*, I beg you,
Why you were so unyielding in your anger.
Oedipus: I will, Jocasta, for I honor you
More than I do the elders. It was Creon's plotting.
Jocasta: What do you mean? What was your accusation?
Oedipus: He says I am the murderer of King Laius.
Jocasta: Did he speak from first-hand knowledge or from hearsay?
Oedipus: He did not speak at all. His lips are pure.
He bribed Tiresias, and that scoundrel spoke. 670
Jocasta: Then you can rid your mind of any fear
That you are guilty. Listen to me. No mortal
Shares in the gods' foreknowledge. I can give you
Clear proof of that. There came once to King Laius
An oracle—I will not say from Phoebus,
But from his priest—saying it was his fate
That he should be struck down by his own child,
His child and mine. But Laius, as we know,
Was killed by foreign robbers at a place
Where three roads came together. As for the child, 680
When it was only three days old, its father
Pierced both its ankles, pinned its feet together,
And then gave orders that it be abandoned
On a wild mountainside. So in this case
Phoebus did not fulfill his oracle. The child
Was not its father's murderer, and Laius
Was not the victim of the fate he feared,
Death at his son's hands, although just that fate
Was what the seer predicted. Pay no heed
To prophecies. Whatever may be needful 690
The god himself can show us easily.
Oedipus: What have you said, Jocasta? What have you said?
The past comes back to me. How terrible!
Jocasta: Why do you start so? What has happened to you?
Oedipus: It seemed to me—I thought you said that Laius
Was struck down where three roads came together.
Jocasta: I did. That was the story, and still is.
Oedipus: Where was it that this murder was committed?
Jocasta: In Phocis, where the road from Thebes divides,
Meeting the roads from Daulia and Delphi.
Oedipus: How many years ago did this occur? 700
Jocasta: The news of it was published here in Thebes
Not long before you came to be our king.
Oedipus: Is this my fate? Is this what the gods decreed?
Jocasta: What have I said that has so shaken you?
Oedipus: Do not ask me yet. Tell me about King Laius.
What did he look like? Was he young or old?
Jocasta: His build was not unlike yours. He was tall.
His hair was just beginning to turn grey.

Oedipus: I cannot bear the thought that I called down
A curse on my own head unknowingly.
Jocasta: What is it Oedipus? You terrify me!
Oedipus: I dread to think Tiresias had clear eyesight; 710
But tell me one thing more, and I will know.
Jocasta: And I too shrink, yet I will answer you.
Oedipus: How did he travel? With a few men only,
Or with his guards and servants, like a prince?
Jocasta: There were five of them in all, with one a herald.
They had one carriage in which King Laius rode.
Oedipus: It is too clear, too clear! Who told you this?
Jocasta: The only servant who escaped alive.
Oedipus: And is he still here now, still in the palace?
Jocasta: No. When he came home and found Laius dead 720
And you the reigning king, he pleaded with me
To send him where the sheep were pasturing,
As far as possible away from Thebes.
And so I sent him. He was a worthy fellow
And, if a slave can, deserved a greater favor.
Oedipus: I hope it is possible to get him quickly.
Jocasta: Yes, that is easy. Why do you want to see him?
Oedipus: Because I am afraid, deadly afraid
That I have spoken more than I should have done.
Jocasta: He shall come. But Oedipus, have I no right 730
To learn what weighs so heavily on your heart?
Oedipus: You shall learn everything, now that my fears
Have grown so great, for who is dearer to me
Than you, Jocasta? Whom should I speak to sooner,
When I am in such straits? King Polybus
Of Corinth was my father. Meropé,
A Dorian, was my mother. I myself
Was foremost among all the citizens,
Till something happened, strange, but hardly worth
My feeling such resentment. As we sat 740
One day at dinner, a man who had drunk too much
Insulted me by saying I was not
My father's son. In spite of being angry,
I managed to control myself. Next day
I asked my parents, who were both indignant
That he had leveled such a charge against me.
This was a satisfaction, yet the thing
Still rankled, for the rumor grew widespread.
At last I went to Delphi secretly.
Apollo gave no answer to my question 750
But sent me off, anguished and terrified,
With fearful prophecies that I was fated
To be my mother's husband, to bring forth
Children whom men could not endure to see,
And to take my father's life. When I heard this
I turned and fled, hoping to find at length
Some place where I would know of Corinth only
As a far distant land beneath the stars,
Some place where I would never have to see
The infamies of this oracle fulfilled. 760
And as I went on, I approached the spot
At which you tell me Laius met his end.
Now this, Jocasta, is the absolute truth.

When I had come to where the three roads fork,
A herald met me, walking before a carriage,
Drawn by two colts, in which a man was seated,
Just as you said. The old man and the herald
Ordered me off the road with threatening gestures.
Then as the driver pushed me to one side,
I struck him angrily. And seeing this, 770
The old man, as I drew abreast, leaned out
And brought his driver's two-pronged goad down hard
Upon my head. He paid a heavy price
For doing that. With one blow of my staff
I knocked him headlong from his chariot
Flat on his back. Then every man of them
I killed. Now if the blood of Laius flowed
In that old stranger's veins, what mortal man
Could be more wretched, more accursed than I?
I whom no citizen or foreigner 780
May entertain or shelter, I to whom
No one may speak, I, I who must be driven
From every door. No other man has cursed me,
I have brought down this curse upon myself.
The hands that killed him now pollute his bed!
Am I not vile, foul, utterly unclean?
For I must fly and never see again
My people or set foot in my own land,
Or else become the husband of my mother
And put to death my father Polybus, 790
To whom I owe my life and my upbringing.
Men would be right in thinking that such things
Have been inflicted by some cruel fate.
May the gods' high and holy majesty
Forbid that I should see that day. No! No!
Rather than be dishonored by a doom
So dreadful may I vanish from the earth.
Chorus: Sir, these are terrible things, but there is hope
Until you have heard what the one witness says.
Oedipus: That is the one remaining hope I have, 800
To wait for the arrival of the shepherd.
Jocasta: And when he *has* arrived, what can he do?
Oedipus: He can do this. If his account agrees
With yours, I stand acquitted of this crime.
Jocasta: Was what I said of any consequence?
Oedipus: You said his story was that robbers killed
King Laius. If he speaks of the same number,
Then I am not the murderer. One man
Cannot be several men. But if he says
One traveler, single-handed, did the deed, 810
Beyond all doubt the evidence points to me.
Jocasta: I am quite certain that was what he said.
He cannot change now, for the whole of Thebes
Heard it, not I alone. In any case,
Even supposing that his story *should*
Be somewhat different, he can never make
Laius's death fulfill the oracle.
Phoebus said plainly Laius was to die
At my son's hands. However, that poor child
Certainly did not kill him, for it died 820
Before its father. I would not waste my time
In giving any thought to prophecy.
Oedipus: Yes, you are right. And yet have someone sent
To bring the shepherd here. Make sure of this.
Jocasta: I will, at once. Come, Oedipus, come in.
I will do nothing that you disapprove of.
[*Exeunt* OEDIPUS *and* JOCASTA]

Chorus: May piety and reverence mark my actions;
        May every thought be pure through all my days.
May those great laws whose dwelling is in heaven
        Approve my conduct with their crown of praise: 830
Offspring of skies that overarch Olympus,
        Laws from the loins of no mere mortal sprung,
Unslumbering, unfailing, unforgetting,
        Filled with a godhead that is ever young.
Pride breeds the tyrant. Insolent presumption,
        Big with delusive wealth and false renown,
Once it has mounted to the highest rampart
        Is headlong hurled in utter ruin down.
But pour out all thy blessings, Lord Apollo,
        Thou who alone hast made and kept us great,   840
On all whose sole ambition is unselfish,
        Who spend themselves in service to the state.
Let that man be accursèd who is proud,
In act unscrupulous, in thinking base,
        Whose knees in reverence have never bowed,
In whose hard heart justice can find no place,
        Whose hands profane life's holiest mysteries,
How can he hope to shield himself for long
        From the gods' arrows that will pierce him
        through?
If evil triumphs in such ways as these,   850
        Why should we seek, in choric dance and song,
To give the gods the praise that is their due?
        I cannot go in full faith as of old,
To sacred Delphi or Olympian vale,
        Unless men see that what has been foretold
Has come to pass, that omens never fail.
        All-ruling Zeus, if thou art King indeed,
Put forth thy majesty, make good thy word,
        Faith in these fading oracles restore!
To priest and prophet men pay little heed;   860
        Hymns to Apollo are no longer heard;
And all religion soon will be no more.
[*Enter* JOCASTA]
Jocasta: Elders of Thebes, I thought that I should
        visit
The altars of the gods to offer up
These wreaths I carry and these gifts of incense.
The King is overanxious, overtroubled.
He is no longer calm enough to judge
The present by the lessons of the past,
But trembles before anyone who brings
An evil prophecy. I cannot help him.   870
Therefore, since thou art nearest, bright Apollo,
I bring these offerings to thee. O, hear me!
Deliver us from this defiling curse.
His fear infects us all, as if we were
Sailors who saw their pilot terrified.
[*Enter* MESSENGER]
Messenger: Sirs, I have come to find King
        Oedipus.
Where is his palace, can you tell me that?
Or better yet, where is the King himself?
Chorus: Stranger, the King is there, within his
        palace.
This is the Queen, the mother of his children.   880
Messenger: May all the gods be good to you and
        yours!
Madam, you are a lady richly blessed.
Jocasta: And may the gods requite your courtesy.
But what request or message do you bring us?

Messenger: Good tidings for your husband and
        your household.
Jocasta: What is your news? What country do you
        come from?
Messenger: From Corinth. And the news I bring
        will surely
Give you great pleasure—and perhaps some pain.
Jocasta: What message can be good and bad at
        once?
Messenger: The citizens of Corinth, it is said,   890
Have chosen Oedipus to be their King.
Jocasta: What do you mean? Their King is Polybus.
Messenger: No, madam. Polybus is dead and
        buried.
Jocasta: What! Dead! The father of King Oedipus?
Messenger: If I speak falsely, let me die myself.
Jocasta: [*to* ATTENDANT]
Go find the king and tell him this. Be quick!
What does an oracle amount to now?
This is the man whom Oedipus all these years
Has feared and shunned to keep from killing him,
And now we find he dies a natural death!   900
[*Enter* OEDIPUS]
Oedipus: My dear Jocasta, why have you sent for
        me?
Jocasta: Listen to this man's message, and then tell
        me
What faith you have in sacred oracles.
Oedipus: Where does he come from? What has he
        to say?
Jocasta: He comes from Corinth and has this to
        say:
The King, your father, Polybus is dead.
Oedipus: [*to* MESSENGER]
My father! Tell me that again yourself.
Messenger: I will say first what you first want to
        know.
You may be certain he is dead and gone.
Oedipus: How did he die? By violence or sickness?   910
Messenger: The scales of life tip easily for the old.
Oedipus: That is to say he died of some disease.
Messenger: Yes, of disease, and merely of old age.
Oedipus: Hear that, Jocasta! Why should anyone
Give heed to oracles from the Pythian shrine,
Or to the birds that shriek above our heads?
They prophesied that I must kill my father.
But he is dead; the earth has covered him.
And I am here, I who have never raised
My hand against him—unless he died of grief,   920
Longing to see me. Then I might be said
To have caused his death. But as they stand, at least,
The oracles have been swept away like rubbish.
They are with Polybus in Hades, dead.
Jocasta: Long ago, Oedipus, I told you that.
Oedipus: You did, but I was blinded by my terror.
Jocasta: Now you need take these things to heart
        no longer.
Oedipus: But there is still my mother's bed to fear.
Jocasta: Why should you be afraid? Chance rules
        our lives,
And no one can foresee the future, no one.   930
We live best when we live without a purpose
From one day to the next. Forget your fear
Of marrying your mother. That has happened
To many men before this in their dreams.
We find existence most endurable
When such things are neglected and forgotten.

Oedipus: That would be true, Jocasta, if my mother
Were not alive; but now your eloquence
Is not enough to give me reassurance.

Jocasta: And yet your father's death is a great
comfort. 940

Oedipus: Yes, but I cannot rest while she is living.

Messenger: Sir, will you tell me who it is you fear?

Oedipus: Queen Merope, the wife of Polybus.

Messenger: What is so terrible about the Queen?

Oedipus: A dreadful prophecy the gods have sent
us.

Messenger: Are you forbidden to speak of it, or
not?

Oedipus: It may be told. The Lord Apollo said
That I was doomed to marry my own mother,
And shed my father's blood with my own hands.
And so for years I have stayed away from Corinth, 950
My native land—a fortunate thing for me,
Though it is very sweet to see one's parents.

Messenger: Was that the reason you have lived in
exile?

Oedipus: Yes, for I feared my mother and my
father.

Messenger: Then since my journey was to wish you
well,
Let me release you from your fear at once.

Oedipus: That would deserve my deepest
gratitude.

Messenger: Sir, I *did* come here with the hope of
earning
Some recompense when you had gotten home.

Oedipus: No. I will never again go near my home. 960

Messenger: O son, son! You know nothing. That is
clear—

Oedipus: What do you mean, old friend? Tell me, I
beg you.

Messenger: If that is why you dare not come to
Corinth.

Oedipus: I fear Apollo's word would be fulfilled.

Messenger: That you would be polluted through
your parents?

Oedipus: Yes, yes! My life is haunted by that
horror.

Messenger: You have no reason to be horrified.

Oedipus: I have no reason! Why? They are my
parents.

Messenger: No. You are not the son of Polybus.

Oedipus: What did you say? Polybus not my father? 970

Messenger: He was as much your father as I am.

Oedipus: How can that be—my father like a
stranger?

Messenger: But he was *not* your father, nor am I.

Oedipus: If that is so, why was I called his son?

Messenger: Because he took you as a gift, from me.

Oedipus: Yet even so, he loved me like a father?

Messenger: Yes, for he had no children of his own.

Oedipus: And when you gave me, had you bought
or found me?

Messenger: I found you in the glens of Mount
Cithaeron.

Oedipus: What could have brought you to a place
like that? 980

Messenger: The flocks of sheep that I was tending
there.

Oedipus: You went from place to place, hunting
for work?

Messenger: I did, my son. And yet I saved your
life.

Oedipus: How? Was I suffering when you took me
up?

Messenger: Your ankles are the proof of what you
suffered.

Oedipus: That misery! Why do you speak of that?

Messenger: Your feet were pinned together, and I
freed them.

Oedipus: Yes. From my cradle I have borne those
scars.

Messenger: They are the reason for your present
name.[23]

Oedipus: Who did it? Speak! My mother, or my
father? 990

Messenger: Only the man who gave you to me
knows.

Oedipus: Then you yourself did not discover me.

Messenger: No. A man put you in my arms, some
shepherd.

Oedipus: Do you know who he was? Can you
describe him?

Messenger: He was, I think, one of the slaves of
Laius.

Oedipus: The Laius who was once the King of
Thebes?

Messenger: Yes, that is right. King Laius was his
master.

Oedipus: How could I see him? Is he still alive?

Messenger: One of his fellow Thebans would
know that.

Oedipus: Does anyone here know who this
shepherd is? 1000
Has anyone ever seen him in the city
Or in the fields? Tell me. Now is the time
To solve this mystery once and for all.

Chorus: Sir, I believe the shepherd whom he
means
Is the same man you have already sent for.
The Queen, perhaps, knows most about the matter.

Oedipus: Do you, Jocasta? You know the man we
summoned.
Is he the man this messenger spoke about?

Jocasta: Why do you care? What difference can it
make?
To ask is a waste of time, a waste of time! 1010

Oedipus: I cannot let these clues slip from my
hands.
I must track down the secret of my birth.

Jocasta: Oedipus, Oedipus! By all the gods,
If you set any value on your life,
Give up this search! I have endured enough.

Oedipus: Do not be frightened. Even if my mother
Should prove to be a slave, and born of slaves,
This would not touch the honor of your name.

Jocasta: Listen, I beg you! Listen! Do not do this!

Oedipus: I cannot fail to bring the truth to light. 1020

Jocasta: I know my way is best for you, I know it!

Oedipus: I know your best way is unbearable.

Jocasta: May you be saved from learning who you
are!

Oedipus: Go, someone. Bring the shepherd. As for
her,
Let her take comfort in her noble birth.

Jocasta: You are lost! Lost! That is all I can call you
now!
That is all I will ever call you, ever again!
[*Exit* JOCASTA]

---

23. The name *Oedipus* means "swollen foot."

Chorus: What wild grief, sir, has driven the Queen
　away?
Evil, I fear, will follow from her silence,
A storm of sorrow that will break upon us.
Oedipus: Then let it break upon us; I must learn
My parentage, whatever it may be.
The Queen is proud, far prouder than most women,
And feels herself dishonored by my baseness.
But I shall not be shamed. I hold myself
The child of Fortune, giver of all good.
She brought me forth. And as I lived my life, 1040
The months, my brothers, watched the ebb and flow
Of my well-being. Never could I prove
False to a lineage like that, or fail
To bring to light the secret of my birth.
Chorus: May Phoebus grant that I prove a true
　prophet!
My heart foreknows what the future will bring:
At tomorrow's full moon we shall gather, in chorus
　To hail Cithaeron, to dance and sing
In praise of the mountain by Oedipus honored,
　Theban nurse of our Theban King.
What long-lived nymph was the mother who bore
　you?
　What god whom the joys of the hills invite
Was the god who begot you? Pan? or Apollo? 1050
　Or Hermes, Lord of Cyléné's height?
Or on Helicon's slope did an oread place you
　In Bacchus's arms for his new delight?
Oedipus: Elders, I think I see the shepherd
　coming
Whom we have sent for. Since I never met him,
I am not sure, yet he seems old enough,
And my own slaves are the men bringing him.
But you, perhaps, know more of this than I,
If any of you have seen the man before.
Chorus: Yes, it is he. I know him, the King's
　shepherd, 1060
As true a slave as Laius ever had.
[*Enter* SHEPHERD]
Oedipus: I start with you, Corinthian. Is this man
The one you spoke of?
Mess.: Sir, he stands before you.
Oedipus: Now you, old man. Come, look me in the
　face.
Answer my questions. You were the slave of Laius?
Shepherd: Yes, but not bought. I grew up in his
　household.
Oedipus: What was the work that you were given to
　do?
Shepherd: Sheep-herding. I have always been a
　shepherd.
Oedipus: Where was it that you took your sheep to
　pasture?
Shepherd: On Mount Cithaeron, or the fields near
　by. 1070
Oedipus: Do you remember seeing this man there?
Shepherd: What was he doing? What man do you
　mean?
Oedipus: That man beside you. Have you ever met
　him?
Shepherd: No, I think not. I cannot recollect him.
Messenger: Sir, I am not surprised, but I am sure
That I can make the past come back to him.
He cannot have forgotten the long summers
We grazed our sheep together by Cithaeron,
He with two flocks, and I with one—three years.
From spring to autumn. Then, for the winter months, 1080

I used to drive my sheep to their own fold,
And he drove his back to the fold of Laius.
Is that right? Did it happen as I said?
Shepherd: Yes, you are right, but it was long ago.
Messenger: Well then, do you remember you once
　gave me
An infant boy to bring up as my own?
Shepherd: What do you mean? Why do you ask me
　that?
Messenger: Because the child you gave me stands
　before you.
Shepherd: Will you be quiet? Curse you! Will you
　be quiet?
Oedipus: [*to* SHEPHERD]
You there! You have no reason to be angry. 1090
You are far more to blame in this than he.
Shepherd: What have I done, my Lord? What have
　I done?
Oedipus: You have not answered. He asked about
　the boy.
Shepherd: Sir, he knows nothing, nothing at all
　about it.
Oedipus: And you say nothing. We must make you
　speak.
Shepherd: My Lord, I am an old man! Do not hurt
　me!
Oedipus: [*to* GUARDS]
One of you tie his hands behind his back.
Shepherd: Why do you want to know these fearful
　things?
Oedipus: Did you, or did you not, give him that
　child?
Shepherd: I did. I wish that I had died instead. 1100
Oedipus: You will die now, unless you tell the
　truth.
Shepherd: And if I speak, I will be worse than
　dead.
Oedipus: You seem to be determined to delay.
Shepherd: No. No! I told you that I had the child.
Oedipus: Where did it come from? Was it yours or
　not?
Shepherd: No, it was not mine. Someone gave it to
　me.
Oedipus: Some citizen of Thebes? Who was it?
　Who?
Shepherd: Oh! Do not ask me that! Not that, my
　Lord!
Oedipus: If I must ask once more, you are a dead
　man.
Shepherd: The child came from the household of
　King Laius. 1110
Oedipus: Was it a slave's child? Or of royal blood?
Shepherd: I stand on the very brink of speaking
　horrors.
Oedipus: And I of hearing horrors—but I must.
Shepherd: Then hear. The child was said to be the
　King's.
You can best learn about this from the Queen.
Oedipus: The Queen! She gave it to you?
Shep.: Yes, my Lord.
Oedipus: Why did she do that?
Shep.: So that I should kill it.
Oedipus: Her own child?
Shep.: Yes, she feared the oracles.
Oedipus: What oracles?
Shep.: That it must kill its father.
Oedipus: Then why did you give it up to this old
　man? 1120

Shepherd: I pitied the poor child. I thought the man
Would take it with him back to his own country.
He saved its life only to have it come
At last to this. If you should be the man
He says you are, you were born miserable.
Oedipus: All true! All, all made clear! Let me no longer
Look on the light of day. I am known now
For what I am—I, cursed in being born,
Cursed in my marriage, cursed in the blood I shed.
[*Exit* OEDIPUS]
Chorus: Men are of little worth. Their brief lives last   1130
    A single day.
They cannot hold elusive pleasure fast;
    It melts away.
All laurels wither; all illusions fade;
Hopes have been phantoms, shade on air-built shade,
    Since time began.
Your fate, O King, your fate makes manifest
Life's wretchedness. We can call no one blessed,
    No, not one man.
Victorious, unerring, to their mark   1140
    Your arrows flew.
The Sphinx with her curved claws, her riddle dark,
    Your wisdom slew.
By this encounter you preserved us all,
Guarding the land from death's approach, our tall,
    Unshaken tower.
From that time, Oedipus, we held you dear,
Great King of our great Thebes, without a peer
    In place and power.
But now what sadder story could be told?   1150
A life of triumph utterly undone!
What fate could be more grievous to behold?
    Father and son
Both found a sheltering port, a place of rest,
    On the same breast.
Father and son both harvested the yield
    Of the same bounteous field.
    How could that earth endure such dreadful wrong
    And hold its peace so long?
All-seeing time condemned your marriage lot;   1160
    In ways you least expected bared its shame—
Union wherein begetter and begot
    Were both the same.
This loud lament, these tears that well and flow,
    This bitter woe
Are for the day you rescued us, O King,
    From our great suffering;
For the new life and happiness you gave
    You drag down to the grave.
[*Enter* SECOND MESSENGER]
Second Messenger: Most honored elders, princes of the land,   1170
If you are true-born Thebans and still love
The house of Labdacus,[24] then what a burden
Of sorrow you must bear, what fearful things
You must now hear and see! There is no river—
No, not the stream of Ister or of Phasis—
That could wash clean this house from the pollution
It hides within it or will soon bring forth:
Horrible deeds not done in ignorance,
But done deliberately. The cruelest evils
Are those that we embrace with open eyes.   1180

Chorus: Those we already know of are enough
To claim our tears. What more have you to tell?
Second Messenger: It may be briefly told. The Queen is dead.
Chorus: Poor woman! oh, poor woman! How? What happened?
Second Messenger: She killed herself. You have been spared the worst,
Not being witnesses. Yet you shall learn
What her fate was, so far as I remember.
When she came in, almost beside herself,
Clutching her hair with both her hands, she rushed
Straight to her bedroom and slammed shut the doors   1190
Behind her, screaming the name of Laius—
Laius long dead, but not her memory
Of their own child, the son who killed his father,
The son by whom his mother had more children.
She cursed the bed in which she had conceived
Husband by husband, children by her child,
A dreadful double bond. Beyond this much
I do not know the manner of her death,
For with a great cry Oedipus burst in,
Preventing us from following her fate   1200
To its dark end. On him our gaze was fixed,
As in a frenzy he ran to and fro,
Calling: 'Give me a sword! Give me a sword!
Where is that wife who is no wife, that mother,
That soil where I was sower and was sown?'
And as he raved, those of us there did nothing,
Some more than mortal power directed him.
With a wild shriek, as though he had some sign,
He hurled himself against the double doors,
Forcing the bars out of their loosened sockets,   1210
And broke into his room. There was the Queen,
Hanged in a noose, still swinging back and forth.
When he saw this, the King cried out in anguish,
Untied the knotted cord in which she swung,
And laid the wretched woman on the ground.
What happened then was terrible to see.
He tore the golden brooches from her robe,
Lifted them up as high as he could reach,
And drove them with all his strength into his eyes,
Shrieking, 'No more, no more shall my eyes see   1220
The horrors of my life—what I have done,
What I have suffered. They have looked too long
On those whom they ought never to have seen.
They never knew those whom I longed to see.
Blind, blind! Let them be blind!' With these wild words
He stabbed and stabbed his eyes. At every blow,
The dark blood dyed his beard, not sluggish drops,
But a great torrent like a shower of hail.
A two-fold punishment of two-fold sin
Broke on the heads of husband and of wife.   1230
Their happiness was once true happiness,
But now disgrace has come upon them, death,
Sorrow, and ruin, every earthly ill
That can be named. Not one have they escaped.
Chorus: Is he still suffering? Has he found relief?
Second Messenger: He calls for someone to unbar the doors
And show him to all Thebes, his father's killer,
His mother's—no, I cannot say the word;
It is unholy, horrible. He intends

---

24. Labdacus was a grandson of Cadmus and the father of Laius.

To leave the country, for his staying here
Would bring down his own curse upon his house.   1240
He has no guide and no strength of his own.
His pain is unendurable. This too
You will see. They are drawing back the bars.
The sight is loathsome and yet pitiful.
[*Enter* OEDIPUS]

Chorus: Hideous, hideous! I have seen nothing so
       dreadful,
            Ever before!
            I can look no more.
Oedipus, Oedipus! What madness has come upon
       you?
            What malignant fate
            Has leaped with its full weight.   1250
Has struck you down with an irresistible fury,
       And born you off as its prey?
            Poor wretch! There is much that I yearn
            To ask of you, much I would learn;
But I cannot. The sight of you fills me with horror!
       I shudder and turn away.

Oedipus: Oh, Oh! What pain! I cannot rest in my
       anguish!
            Where am I? Where?
Where are my words? They die away as I speak them,
            Into thin air.   1260
            What is my fate to be?

Chorus: A fate too fearful for men to hear of, for
       men to see.

Oedipus: Lost! Overwhelmed by the rush of
       unspeakable darkness!
            It smothers me in its cloud.
            The pain of my eyes is piercing.
The thought of my sins, the horrors that I have
       committed,
            Racks me without relief.

Chorus: No wonder you suffer, Oedipus, no
       wonder you cry aloud
       Under your double burden of pain and grief.

Oedipus: My friend, my friend! How steadfast you
       are, how ready   1270
            To help me in my great need!
            I feel your presence beside me.
Blind as I am, I know your voice in the blackness
            Of my long-lasting night.

Chorus: How could you put out your eyes, still
       another infamous deed?
       What god, what demon, induced you to quench
       their light?

Oedipus: It was Apollo, my friends, who brought
       me low,
Apollo who crushed me beneath this unbearable
       burden;
            But it was my hand, mine, that struck the blow.
Why should I see? What sight could have given me
       pleasure?   1280

Chorus: These things are as you say.

Oedipus: What is there now to love? What greeting
       can cheer me?
            Lead me away,
Quickly, quickly! O lead me out of the country
To a distant land! I am beyond redemption
Accursed, beyond hope lost, the one man living
            Whom all the gods most hate.

Chorus: Would we had never heard of your
       existence,
            Your fruitless wisdom and your wretched fate.

Oedipus: My curses be upon him, whoever freed   1290
My feet from the cruel fetters, there on the mountain,
       Who restored me from death to life, a thankless
       deed.
My death would have saved my friends and me from
       anguish.

Chorus: I too would have had it so.

Oedipus: Then would I never have been my
       father's killer.
            Now all men know
That I am the infamous son who defiled his mother,
       That I shared the bed of the father who gave me
       being.
And if there is sorrow beyond any mortal sorrow,
       I have brought it upon my head.   1300

Chorus: I cannot say that you have acted wisely.
       Alive and blind? You would be better dead.

Oedipus: Give me no more advice, and do not tell
       me
That I was wrong. What I have done is best.
For if I still had eyesight when I went
Down to the underworld, how could I bear
To see my father and my wretched mother?
After the terrible wrong I did them both,
It would not have been punishment enough
If I had hanged myself. Or do you think   1310
That I could find enjoyment in the sight
Of children born as mine were born? No! No!
Nor in the sight of Thebes with its towered walls
And sacred statues of the gods. For I—
Who is so wretched?—I, the foremost Theban,
Cut myself off from this by my own edict
That ordered everyone to shun the man
Polluting us, the man the gods have shown
To be accursed, and of the house of Laius.
Once I laid bare my shame, could I endure   1320
To look my fellow-citizens in the face?
Never! Never! If I had found some way
Of choking off the fountain of my hearing,
I would have made a prison of my body,
Sightless and soundless. It would be sweet to live
Beyond the reach of sorrow. Oh, Cithaeron!
Why did you give me shelter rather than slay me
As soon as I was given to you? Then
No one would ever have heard of my begetting.
Polybus, Corinth, and the ancient house   1330
I thought my forebears'! You reared me as a child.
My fair appearance covered foul corruption,
I am impure, born of impurity.
Oh, narrow crossroad where the three paths meet!
Secluded valley hidden in the forest,
You that drank up my blood, my father's blood
Shed by my hands, do you remember all
I did for you to see? Do you remember
What else I did when I came here to Thebes?
Oh marriage rites! By which I was begotten,   1340
You then brought forth children by your own child,
Creating foulest blood-relationship:
An interchange of fathers, brothers, sons,
Brides, wives, and mothers—the most monstrous
       shame
Man can be guilty of. I should not speak
Of what should not be done. By all the gods,
Hide me, I beg you, hide me quickly somewhere
Far, far away. Put me to death or throw me
Into the sea, out of your sight forever.
Come to me, friends, pity my wretchedness.   1350
Let your hands touch me. Hear me. Do not fear,
My curse can rest on no one but myself.

Chorus: Creon is coming. He is the one to act
On your requests, or to help you with advice.
He takes your place as our sole guardian.
Oedipus: Creon! What shall I say? I cannot hope
That he will trust me now, when my past hatred
Has proved to be so utterly mistaken.
[*Enter* CREON]
Creon: I have not come to mock you, Oedipus,
Or to reproach you for any evil-doing.   1360
[*to* ATTENDANTS] You there. If you have lost all your
      respect
For men, revere at least the Lord Apollo,
Whose flame supports all life. Do not display
So nakedly pollution such as this,
Evil that neither earth nor holy rain
Nor light of day can welcome. Take him in,
Take him in, quickly. Piety demands
That only kinsmen share a kinsman's woe.
Oedipus: Creon, since you have proved my fears
      were groundless,
Since you have shown such magnanimity   1370
To one so vile as I, grant my petition.
I ask you not for my sake but your own.
Creon: What is it that you beg so urgently?
Oedipus: Drive me away at once. Drive me far off.
Let me not hear a human voice again.
Creon: I have delayed only because I wished
To have the god reveal to me my duty.
Oedipus: But his command was certain: put to
      death
The unholy parricide. And I am he.
Creon: True. But as things are now, it would be
      better   1380
To find out clearly what we ought to do.
Oedipus: An oracle for a man so miserable?
Creon: Yes. Even you will now believe the god.
Oedipus: I will. Creon, I charge you with this duty.
Accept it, I entreat you. Give to her
Who lies within such burial as you wish,
For she belongs to you. You will perform
The proper obsequies. But as for me,
Let not my presence doom my father's city,
But send me to the hills, to Mount Cithaeron,   1390
My mountain, which my mother and my father
Chose for my grave. So will I die at last
By the decree of those who sought to slay me.
And yet I know I will not die from sickness
Or anything else. I was preserved from death
To meet some awful, some mysterious end.
My own fate does not matter, only my children's.
Creon, my sons need give you no concern,
For they are men, and can find anywhere
A livelihood. But Creon, my two girls!   1400
How lost, how pitiable! They always ate
Their daily bread with me, at my own table,
And had their share of everything I touched.
Take care of them! O Creon, take care of them!
And one thing more—if I could only touch them
And with them weep. O prince, prince, grant me this!
Grant it, O noble Creon! If I touched them,
I could believe I saw them once again.
[*Enter* ISMENE *and* ANTIGONE]
What! Do I hear my daughters? Hear them sobbing?
Has Creon had pity on me? Has he sent them,   1410
My children, my two darlings? Is it true?
Creon: Yes. I have had them brought. I knew how
      much
You used to love them, how you love them still.

Oedipus: May the gods bless you, Creon, for this
      kindness;
And may they guard you better on your journey
Than they have guarded me. Children, where are
      you?
Come to your brother's hands, the hands that made
Your father's clear eyes into what these are—
Your father, who saw nothing and knew nothing,
Begetting you where he had been conceived.   1420
I cannot see you, but I weep for you,
Weep for the bitter lives that you must lead
Henceforward. Never, never will you go
To an assembly with the citizens,
Or to a festival, and take your part.
You will turn back in tears. And when you come
To the full bloom of womanhood, what man
Will run the risk of bringing on himself
Your shame, my daughters, and your children's
      shame?
Is there one evil, one, that is not ours?   1430
'Your father killed his father; he begot
Children of his own mother; she who bore you
Bore him as well.' These are the taunts, the insults
That you will hear. Who, then, will marry you?
No one, my children. Clearly it is your fate
To waste away in barren maidenhood.
Creon, Creon, their blood flows in your veins.
You are the only father left to them;
They have lost both their parents. Do not let them
Wander away, unmarried, destitute,   1440
As miserable as I. Have pity on them,
So young, so utterly forlorn, so helpless
Except for you. You are kind-hearted. Touch me
To tell me that I have your promise. Children,
There is so much, so much that I would say,
If you were old enough to understand it,
But now I only teach you this one prayer:
May I be given a place in which to live,
And may my life be happier than my father's.
Creon: Come, come with us. Have done with
      further woe.   1450
Oedipus: Obedience is hard.
Cr.:   No good in life endures beyond its season.
Oedipus: Do you know why I yield?
Cr.:   When I have heard your reason I will know.
Oedipus: You are to banish me.
Cr.:   The gods alone can grant you that entreaty.
Oedipus: I am hated by the gods.
Cr.:   Then their response to you will not be slow.
Oedipus: So you consent to this?
Cr.:   I say no more than I have said already.
Oedipus: Come, then, lead me away.
Cr.:   Not with your children.
      You must let them go.
Oedipus: Creon, not that, not that!
Cr.:   You must be patient. Nothing can restore
      Your old dominion. You are King no more.
[*Exeunt* CREON, OEDIPUS, ISMENE, *and*
ANTIGONE]
Chorus: Behold him, Thebans: Oedipus, great and
      wise,
Who solved the famous riddle. This is he   1460
      Whom all men gazed upon with envious eyes,
Who now is struggling in a stormy sea,
      Crushed by the billows of his bitter woes.
Look to the end of mortal life. In vain
      We say a man is happy, till he goes
Beyond life's final border, free from pain.

Exercises

1. The first question that arises after reading the *Oedipus* is whether the king is brought to his doom through the workings of an inexorable fate, whether he is brought low because of a flaw in his own character, or whether the downfall is the result of the interweaving of the two forces. Can you find evidence in the play itself to support any of these positions?

2. One scholar has suggested that the play was written as an admonition to the increasingly atheistic people of Athens that the gods were powerful. Do you find evidence in the play to support or deny this statement as the central theme of the play?

3. The discussion in chapter 5 ended with the suggestion that Oedipus was at least partially aware of the truth when the play began. The exchange with Tiresias and Jocasta's speech about the servant of Laius were cited. Have you found any additional evidence that would tend to support this alternate theory?

THE TROJAN WOMEN
Euripides (484–406 B.C.)

In his *History of the Peloponnesian War,* Thucydides relates the mournful story of the unprovoked Athenian attack of 416 B.C. on the neutral island of Melos, during which all the men were killed and the women and children enslaved. The only horrified reaction to this terrible deed that has come down to us is *The Trojan Women,* apparently written shortly after the slaughter. *The Trojan Women* is Euripides' passionate protest against this brutal action and against the whole sickening business of war. With no plot and little action, the play is set in the aftermath of the fall of Troy. Except for two subordinate roles, all the characters are women who are also, except for Helen, sorrowing, bereft widows. Waiting on the beach for the victors to divide the spoils of war, including themselves and their children, their situation is hopeless. The ultimate irony, however, is that victors and vanquished suffer equally; those who destroyed the city will themselves be given, in the words of Athena, "a bitter homecoming." Euripides, the "poet of the world's grief," saw clearly that the great god War destroys everything and solves nothing.

This translation is by the noted classical scholar Edith Hamilton, whose spelling of proper names has been retained.

[The scene is a space of waste ground except for a few huts to right and left, where the women selected for the Greek leaders are housed. Far in the background Troy, the wall in ruins, is slowly burning, as yet more smoke than flame. In front a woman with white hair lies on the ground. It is just before dawn. A tall dim figure is seen, back of the woman.]

Poseidon: I am the sea god. I have come
up from the salt sea depths of the Aegean,
from where the sea nymphs' footsteps fall,
weaving the lovely measures of the dance.
For since that day I built the towers of stone
around this town of Troy, Apollo with me,
—and straight we raised them, true by line and
    plummet—
good will for them has never left my heart,
my Trojans and their city.
City? Smoke only—all is gone,
perished beneath Greek spears.
A horse was fashioned, big with arms.
Parnassus was the workman's home,
in Phocia, and his name Epeius.
The skill he had Athena gave him.
He sent it through the walls—it carried death.
The wooden horse, so men will call it always,
which held and hid those spears.
A desert now where groves were. Blood drips down
from the gods' shrines. Beside his hearth
Priam lies dead upon the altar steps
of Zeus, the hearth's protector.
While to the Greek ships pass the Trojan treasure,
gold, gold in masses, armor, clothing,
stripped from the dead.
The Greeks who long since brought war to the town,
—ten times the seed was sown before Troy fell—
wait now for a fair wind for home,
the joyful sight of wife and child again.
Myself defeated by the Argive goddess
Hera and by Athena, both in league together—
I too must take my leave of glorious Troy,
forsake my altars. When a town is turned
into a desert, things divine fall sick.
Not one to do them honor.
Scamander's stream is loud with lamentation,
so many captive women weeping.
Their masters drew lots for them. Some will go
to Arcady and some to Thessaly.
Some to the lords of Athens, Theseus' sons.
Huts here hold others spared the lot, but chosen
for the great captains.
With them, like them a captive of the spear,
the Spartan woman, Helen.
But if a man would look on misery,
it is here to see—Hecuba lies there
before the gates. She weeps.
Many tears for many griefs.
And one still hidden from her.
But now upon Achilles' grave her daughter
was killed—Polyxena. So patiently she died.
Gone is her husband, gone her sons, all dead.
One daughter whom the Lord Apollo loved,
yet spared her wild virginity, Cassandra,
Agamemnon, in the dark, will force upon his bed.
No thought for what was holy and was God's.
O city happy once, farewell.
O shining towers, crumbling now
beneath Athena's hand, the child of God,
or you would still stand firm on deep foundations.
[As he turns to go the goddess PALLAS ATHENA *enters.]*
Athena: Am I allowed to speak to one who is
my father's nearest kinsman,
a god among gods honored, powerful?
If I put enmity aside, will he?
Poseidon: He will, most high Athena. We are kin,
old comrades too, and these have magic power.

Athena: Thanks for your gentleness. What I would say touches us both, great king.

Poseidon: A message from the gods? A word from Zeus? Some spirit, surely?

Athena: No, but for Troy's sake, where we stand, I seek your power to join my own with it.

Poseidon: What! Now—at last? Has that long hatred left you?
Pity—when all is ashes—burned to ashes?

Athena: The point first, please. Will you make common cause
with me? What I wish done will you wish, too?

Poseidon: Gladly. But what you wish I first must know.
You come to me for Troy's sake or for Greece?

Athena: I wish to make my Trojan foes rejoice,
and give the Greeks a bitter home-coming.

Poseidon: The way you change! Here—there—then back again.
Now hate, now love—no limit ever.

Athena: You know how I was outraged and my temple.

Poseidon: Oh that—when Ajax dragged Cassandra out?

Athena: And not one Greek to punish him—not one to blame him.

Poseidon: Even though your power ruined Troy for them.

Athena: Therefore with you I mean to hurt them.

Poseidon: Ready for all you wish. But—hurt them? How?

Athena: Give them affliction for their coming home.

Poseidon: Held here, you mean? Or out on the salt sea?

Athena: Whenever the ships sail.
Zeus shall send rain, unending rain, and sleet,
and darkness blown from heaven.
He will give me—he has promised—his thunderbolt,
to strike the ships with fire. They shall burn.
Your part, to make your sea-roads roar—
wild waves and whirlwinds,
while dead men choke the winding bay.
So Greeks shall learn to reverence my house
and dread all gods.

Poseidon: These things shall be. No need of many words
to grant a favor. I will stir the sea,
the wide Aegean. Shores and reefs and cliffs
will hold dead men, bodies of many dead.
Off to Olympus with you now, and get
those fiery arrows from the hand of Zeus.
Then when a fair wind sends the Greeks to sea,
watch the ships sail.
[*Exit* ATHENA]
Oh, fools, the men who lay a city waste,
giving to desolation temples, tombs,
the sanctuaries of the dead—so soon
to die themselves.
[*Exit* POSEIDON]
[*The two gods have been talking before daylight, but now the day begins to dawn and the woman lying on the ground in front moves. She is* HECUBA, *the aged queen of Troy.*]

Hecuba: Up from the ground—O weary head, O breaking neck.
This is no longer Troy. And we are not
the lords of Troy.
Endure. The ways of fate are the ways of the wind.
Drift with the stream—drift with fate.
No use to turn the prow to breast the waves.
Let the boat go as it chances.

Sorrow, my sorrow.
What sorrow is there that is not mine,
grief to weep for.
Country lost and children and husband.
Glory of all my house brought low.
All was nothing—nothing, always.
Keep silent? Speak?
Weep then? Why? For what?
[*She begins to get up.*]
Oh, this aching body—this bed—
it is very hard. My back pressed to it—
Oh, my side, my brow, my temples.
Up! Quick, quick. I must move.
Oh, I'll rock myself this way, that way,
to the sound of weeping, the song of tears,
dropping down forever.
The song no feet will dance to ever,
for the wretched, the ruined.

O ships, O prows, swift oars,
out from the fair Greek bays and harbors,
over the dark shining sea,
you found your way to our holy city,
and the fearful music of war was heard,
the war song sung to flute and pipe,
as you cast on the shore your cables,
ropes the Nile dwellers twisted and coiled,
and you swung, oh, my grief, in Troy's waters.

What did you come for? A woman?
A thing of loathing, of shame,
to husband, to brother, to home.
She slew Priam, the king,
father of fifty sons,
she wrecked me upon
the reef of destruction.
Who am I that I wait[25]
here at a Greek king's door?
A slave that men drive on,
an old gray woman that has no home.
Shaven head brought low in dishonor.
O wives of the bronze-armored men who fought,
and maidens, sorrowing maidens,
plighted to shame,
see—only smoke left where was Troy.
Let us weep for her.
As a mother bird cries to her feathered brood,
so will I cry.
Once another song I sang
when I leaned on Priam's scepter,
and the beat of dancing feet
marked the music's measure.
Up to the gods
the song of Troy rose at my signal.
[*The door of one of the huts opens and a woman steals out, then another, and another.*]

First Woman: Your cry, O Hecuba—oh, such a cry—
What does it mean? There in the tent
we heard you call so piteously,
and through our hearts flashed fear.
In the tent we were weeping, too,
for we are slaves.

Hecuba: Look, child, there where the Greek ships lie—

Another Woman: They are moving. The men hold oars.

---

25. This is the way Professor Murray translates the line and the one following. The translation is so simple and beautiful, I cannot bear to give it up for a poorer one of my own.

Another: O God, what will they do? Carry me off
over the sea in a ship far from home?
Hecuba: You ask and I know nothing,
but I think ruin is here.
Another Woman: Oh, we are wretched. We shall hear
     the summons.
Women of Troy, go forth from your home,
for the Greeks set sail.
Hecuba: But not Cassandra, oh, not her.
She is mad—she has been driven mad. Leave her within.
Not shamed before the Greeks—not that grief too.
I have enough.
     O Troy, unhappy Troy, you are gone
and we, the unhappy, leave you,
we who are living and we who are dead.
[*More women now come out from a second hut.*]
A Woman: Out of the Greek king's tent
trembling I come, O Queen,
to hear my fate from you.
Not death—They would not think of death
for a poor woman.
Another: The sailors—they are standing on the prow.
Already they are running out the oars.
Another: [*She comes out of a third hut and several
follow her.*]
It is so early—but a terror woke me.
     My heart beats so.
Another: Has a herald come from the Greek camp?
Whose slave shall I be? I—bear that?
Hecuba: Wait for the lot drawing. It is near.
Another: Argos shall it be, or Phthia? or an island of
     the sea?
     A Greek soldier lead me there,
far, far from Troy?
Hecuba: And I a slave—to whom—where—how?
You old gray woman, patient to endure,
you bee without a sting,
only an image of what was alive, or the ghost of one dead.
I watch a master's door?
     I nurse his children?
     Once I was queen in Troy.
One Woman to Another: Poor thing. What are your
     tears
to the shame before you?
The Other: The shuttle will still pass through my
     hands, but the loom will not be in Troy.
Another: My dead sons. I would look at them once
     more.
Never again.
Another: Worse to come.
A Greek's bed—and I—
Another: A night like that? Oh, never—
oh, no—not that for me.
Another: I see myself a water carrier,
dipping my pitcher in the great Pierian spring.
Another: The land of Theseus, Athens, it is known
to be a happy place. I wish I could go there.
Another: But not to the Eurotas, hateful river,
where Helen lived. Not there, to be a slave
to Menelaus who sacked Troy.
Another: Oh, look. A man from the Greek army—
a herald. Something strange has happened,
he comes so fast. To tell us—what?
What will he say? Only Greek slaves are here,
waiting for orders.
[*Enter* TALTHYBIUS *with soldiers.*]

Talthybius: You know me, Hecuba. I have often come
with messages to Troy from the Greek camp.
Talthybius—these many years you've known me.
I bring you news.
Hecuba: It has come, women of Troy. Once we only
     feared it.
Talthybius: The lots are drawn, if that is what you
     feared.
Hecuba: Who—where? Thessaly? Phthia? Thebes?
Talthybius: A different man takes each. You're not to
     go together.
Hecuba: Then which takes which? Has any one good
     fortune?
Talthybius: I know, but ask about each one, not all at
     once.
Hecuba: My daughter, who—who drew her? Tell me—
Cassandra. She has had so much to bear.
Talthybius: King Agamemnon chose her out from all.
Hecuba: Oh! but—of course—to serve his Spartan wife?
Talthybius: No, no—but for the king's own bed at
     night.
Hecuba: Oh, never. She is God's, a virgin, always.
That was God's gift to her for all her life.
Talthybius: He loved her for that same strange purity.[26]
Hecuba: Throw away, daughter, the keys of the temple.
Take off the wreath and the sacred stole.
Talthybius: Well, now—a king's bed is not so bad.
Hecuba: My other child you took from me just now?
Talthybius: [*Speaking with constraint*]
Polyxena, you mean? Or someone else?
Hecuba: Her. Who drew her?
Talthybius: They told her to watch Achilles' tomb.
Hecuba: To watch a tomb? My daughter?
That a Greek custom?
What strange ritual is that, my friend?
Talthybius: [*Speaking fast and trying to put her off*]
Just think of her as happy—all well with her.
Hecuba: Those words—Why do you speak like that?
She is alive?
Talthybius: [*Determined not to tell her*]
What happened was—well, she is free from trouble.
Hecuba: [*Wearily giving the riddle up*]
Then Hector's wife—my Hector, wise in war—
Where does she go, poor thing—Andromache?
Talthybius: Achilles' son took her. He chose her out.
Hecuba: And I, old gray head, whose slave am I,
creeping along with my crutch?
Talthybius: Slave of the king of Ithaca, Odysseus.
Hecuba: Beat, beat my shorn head! Tear, tear my cheek!
His slave—vile lying man. I have come to this—
There is nothing good he does not hurt—a lawless beast.
He twists and turns, this way and that, and back again.
A double tongue, as false in hate as false in love.
Pity me, women of Troy,
I have gone. I am lost—oh, wretched.
An evil fate fell on me,
a lot the hardest of all.
A Woman: You know what lies before you, Queen, but
     I—
What man among the Greeks owns me?

----

26. This line, too, is Professor Murray's, and retained here for the
reason given above.

Talthybius: [*To the soldiers*]
Off with you. Bring Cassandra here. Be quick,
you fellows. We must give her to the chief,
into his very hand. And then these here
to all the other generals. But what's that—
that flash of light inside there?
[*Light shines through the crevices of one of the huts.*]
Set fire to the huts—is that their plan,
these Trojan women? Burn themselves to death
rather than sail to Greece. Choosing to die instead.
How savagely these days the yoke bears down
on necks so lately free.
Open there, open the door. [*Aside*] As well for them
perhaps,
but for the Greeks—they'd put the blame on me.

Hecuba: No, no, there is nothing burning. It is my
daughter,
Cassandra. She is mad.
[CASSANDRA *enters from the hut dressed like a priestess,
a wreath in her hair, a torch in her hand. She does not
seem to see anyone.*]

Cassandra: Lift it high—in my hand—light to bring.
I praise him. I bear a flame.
With my torch I touch to fire this holy place.
Hymen, O Hymen.
Blessed the bridegroom, blessed am I
to lie with a king in a king's bed in Argos.
Hymen, O Hymen.
Mother, you weep
tears for my father dead,
mourning for the beloved country lost.
I for my bridal here
lift up the fire's flame
to the dawn, to the splendor,
to you, O Hymen.
Queen of night,
give your starlight
to a virgin bed,
as of old you did.
Fly, dancing feet.
Up with the dance.
Oh, joy, oh, joy!
Dance for my father dead, most blest to die.
Oh, holy dance!
Apollo—you?
Lead on then.
There in the laurel grove
I served your altar.
Dance, Mother, come. Keep step with me.
Dear feet with my feet tracing the measure this way and
that.
Sing to the Marriage god,
oh, joyful song.
Sing for the bride, too,
joyously all.
Maidens of Troy,
dressed in your best,
honor my marriage.
Honor too him
whose bed fate drives me to share.

A Woman: Hold her fast, Queen, poor frenzied girl.
She might rush straight to the Greek camp.

Hecuba: O fire, fire, when men make marriages
you light the torch, but this flame flashing here
is for grief only. Child, such great hopes once I had.
I never thought that to your bridal bed

Greek spears would drive you.
Give me your torch. You do not hold it straight,
you move so wildly. Your sufferings, my child,
have never taught you wisdom.
You never change. Here! someone take the torch
into the hut. This marriage needs no songs,
but only tears.

Cassandra: O Mother, crown my triumph with a
wreath.
Be glad, for I am married to a king.
Send me to him, and if I shrink away,
drive me with violence. If Apollo lives,
my marriage shall be bloodier than Helen's.
Agamemnon, the great, the glorious lord of Greece—
I shall kill him, Mother, lay his house as low
as he laid ours, make him pay for all
he made my father suffer, brothers, and—
But no. I must not speak of that—that axe
which on my neck—on others' too—
nor of that murder of a mother.
All, all because he married me and so
pulled his own house down.
But I will show you. This town now, yes, Mother,
is happier than the Greeks. I know that I am mad,
but Mother, dearest, now, for this one time
I do not rave.
One woman they came hunting, and one love,
Helen, and men by tens of thousands died.
Their king, so wise, to get what most he hated
destroyed what most he loved,
his joy at home, his daughter, killing her
for a brother's sake, to get him back a woman
who had fled because she wished—not forced to go.
And when they came to the banks of the Scamander
those thousands died. And why?
No man had moved their landmarks
or laid siege to their high-walled towns.
But those whom war took never saw their children.
No wife with gentle hands shrouded them for their grave.
They lie in a strange land. And in their homes
are sorrows, too, the very same.
Lonely women who died, old men who waited
for sons that never came—no son left to them
to make the offering at their graves.
That was the glorious victory they won.
But we—we Trojans died to save our people,
no glory greater. All those the spear slew,
friends bore them home and wrapped them in their
shroud
with dutiful hands. The earth of their own land
covered them. The rest, through the long days they
fought,
had wife and child at hand, not like the Greeks,
whose joys were far away.
And Hector's pain—your Hector. Mother, hear me.
This is the truth: he died, the best, a hero.
Because the Greeks came, he died thus.
Had they stayed home, we never would have known him.
This truth stands firm: the wise will fly from war.
But if war comes, to die well is to win
the victor's crown.
The only shame is not to die like that.
So, Mother, do not pity Troy,
or me upon my bridal bed.

Talthybius: [*Has been held awestruck through all this, but can bear no more*]
Now if Apollo had not made you mad
I would have paid you for those evil words,
bad omens, and my general sailing soon.
[*Grumbles to himself*]
The great, who seem so wise, have no more sense
than those who rank as nothing.
Our king, the first in Greece, bows down
before this mad girl, loves her, chooses her
out of them all. Well, I am a poor man,
but I'd not go to bed with her.
[*Turns to* CASSANDRA]
Now you—you know your mind is not quite right.
So all you said against Greece and for Troy,
I never heard—the wind blew it away.
Come with me to the ship now.
[*Aside*]
A grand match for our general, she is.
[*To* HECUBA, *gently*]
And you, do follow quietly when Odysseus' men come.
His wife's a good, wise woman, so they say.

Cassandra: [*Seeming to see* TALTHYBIUS *for the first time and looking him over haughtily*]
A strange sort of slave, surely.
Heralds such men are called,
hated by all, for they are tyrants' tools.
You say my mother goes to serve Odysseus?
[*She turns away and speaks to herself.*]
But where then is Apollo's word, made clear
to me, that death will find her here?
And—no, that shame I will not speak of.
Odysseus! wretched—but he does not know.
    Soon all these sorrows, mine and Troy's, will seem
compared to his like golden hours.
Ten years behind him here, ten years before him.
Then only, all alone, will he come home,
and there find untold trouble has come first.
But his cares—why let fly one word at him?
Come, let us hasten to my marriage.
We two shall rest, the bridegroom and the bride,
within the house of death.
O Greek king, with your dreams of grandeur yet to come,
vile as you are, so shall your end be,
in darkness—all light gone.
And me—a cleft in the hills,
washed by winter rains,
his tomb near by.
There—dead—cast out—naked—
and wild beasts seeking food—
It is I there—I myself—Apollo's servant.
O flowers of the God I love, mysterious wreaths,
away. I have forgotten temple festival,
I have forgotten joy.
Off. I tear them from my neck.
Swift winds will carry them
up to you, O God of truth.
My flesh still clean, I give them back to you.
Where is the ship? How do I go on board?
Spread the sail—the wind comes swift.
Those who bring vengeance—three are they,
And one of them goes with you on the sea.
Mother, my Mother, do not weep. Farewell,
dear City. Brothers, in Troy's earth laid, my father,
a little time and I am with you.
You dead, I shall come to you a victor.

Those ruined by my hand who ruined us.
[*She goes out with* TALTHYBIUS *and the soldiers.* HECUBA, *motionless for a moment, falls.*]
A Woman: The Queen! See—see—she is falling.
Oh, help! She cannot speak.
Miserable slaves, will you leave her on the ground,
old as she is. Up—lift her up.
Hecuba: Let me be. Kindness not wanted is
    unkindness.
I cannot stand. Too much is on me.
Anguish here and long since and to come—
O God—Do I call to you? You did not help.
But there is something that cries out for God
when trouble comes.
Oh, I will think of good days gone,
days to make a song of,
crowning my sorrow by remembering.
We were kings and a king I married.
Sons I bore him, many sons.
That means little—but fine, brave lads.
They were the best in all Troy.
No woman, Trojan, Greek, or stranger,
had sons like mine to be proud of.
I saw them fall beneath Greek spears.
My hair I shore at the grave of the dead.
Their father—I did not learn from others
that I must weep for him—these eyes beheld him.
I, my own self, saw him fall murdered
upon the altar, when his town was lost.
My daughters, maidens reared to marry kings,
are torn from me. For the Greeks I reared them.
All gone—no hope that I shall look upon
their faces any more, or they on mine.
And now the end—no more can lie beyond—
an old gray slave woman I go to Greece.
The tasks they know for my age hardest, mine.
The door to shut and open, bowing low
—I who bore Hector—meal to grind; upon
the ground lay this old body down that once
slept in a royal bed; torn rags around me,
torn flesh beneath.
And all this misery and all to come
because a man desired a woman.
Daughter, who knew God's mystery and joy,
what strange chance lost you your virginity?
And you, Polyxena—where are you gone?
No son, no daughter, left to help my need,
and I had many, many—
Why lift me up? What hope is there to hold to?
    This slave that once went delicately in Troy,
take her and cast her on her bed of clay,
rocks for her pillow, there to fall and die,
wasted with tears. Count no one happy,
however fortunate, before he dies.
Chorus: Sing me, O Muse, a song for Troy,
a strange song sung to tears,
a music for the grave.
O lips, sound forth a melody for Troy.

A four-wheeled cart brought the horse to the gates,
brought ruin to me, captured, enslaved me.
Gold was the rein and the bridle,
deadly the arms within,
and they clashed loud to heaven as the threshold was
    passed.

High on Troy's rock the people cried,
"Rest at last, trouble ended.
Bring the carven image in.
Bear it to Athena,
fit gift for the child of God."
Who of the young but hurried forth?
Who of the old would stay at home?
With song and rejoicing they brought death in,
treachery and destruction.

All that were in Troy,
hastening to the gate,
drew that smooth-planed horse of wood
carven from a mountain pine,
where the Greeks were hiding,
where was Troy's destruction,
gave it to the goddess,
gift for her, the virgin,
driver of the steeds that never die.

With ropes of twisted flax,
as a ship's dark hull is drawn to land,
they brought it to her temple of stone,
to her floor that soon would run with blood, to Pallas
    Athena.

      On their toil and their joy
the dark of evening fell,
but the lutes of Egypt still rang out to the songs of Troy.
And girls with feet light as air
dancing, sang happy songs.
The houses blazed with light
through the dark splendor, and sleep was not.
A Girl: I was among the dancers.
I was singing to the maiden of Zeus,
the goddess of the hills.
A shout rang out in the town,
a cry of blood through the houses,
and a frightened child caught his mother's skirt
and hid himself in her cloak.
Then War came forth from his hiding place—
Athena, the virgin, devised it.
Around the altars they slaughtered us.
Within on their beds lay headless men,
young men cut down in their prime.
This was the triumph-crown of Greece.
We shall bear children for her to rear,
grief and shame to our country.
[*A chariot approaches, loaded with spoils. In it sits a
woman and a child.*]
A Woman: Look, Hecuba, it is Andromache.
See, in the Greek car yonder.
Her breast heaves with her sobs and yet
the baby sleeps there, dear Astyanax, the son of Hector.
Another: Most sorrowful of women, where do you go?
Beside you the bronze armor that was Hector's,
the spoil of the Greek spear, stripped from the dead.
Will Achilles' son use it to deck his temples?
Andromache: I go where my Greek masters take me.
Hecuba: Oh, our sorrow—our sorrow.
Andromache: Why should you weep? This sorrow is
   mine.
Hecuba: O God—
Andromache: What has come to me is mine.
Hecuba: My children—
Andromache: Once we lived, not now.
Hecuba: Gone—gone—happiness—Troy—
Andromache: And you bear it.

Hecuba: Sons, noble sons, all lost.
Andromache: Oh, sorrow is here.
Hecuba: For me—for me.
Andromache: For the city, in its shroud of smoke.
Come to me, O my husband.
Hecuba: What you cry to lies in the grave.
My son, wretched woman, mine.
Andromache: Defend me—me, your wife.
Hecuba: My son, my eldest son,
whom I bore to Priam,
whom the Greeks used shamefully,
come to me, lead me to death.
Andromache: Death—oh, how deep a desire.
Hecuba: Such is our pain—
Andromache: For a city that has fallen, fallen.
Hecuba: For anguish heaped upon anguish.
Andromache: For the anger of God against Paris,
your son, who fled from death,
who laid Troy's towers low to win an evil love.
Dead men—bodies—blood—
vultures hovering—
Oh, Athena the goddess is there, be sure,
and the slave's yoke is laid upon Troy.
Hecuba: O country, desolate, empty.
Andromache: My tears fall for you.
Hecuba: Look and see the end—
Andromache: Of the house where I bore my children.
Hecuba: O children, your mother has lost her city,
and you—you have left her alone.
Only grief is mine and mourning.
Tears and more tears, falling, falling.
The dead—they have forgotten their pain.
They weep no more.
A Woman: [*Aside to another*]
Tears are sweet in bitter grief,
and sorrow's song is lamentation.
Andromache: Mother of him whose spear of old
   brought death
to Greeks unnumbered, you see what is here.
Hecuba: I see God's hand that casts the mighty down
and sets on high the lowly.
Andromache: Driven like cattle captured in a raid,
my child and I—the free changed to a slave.
Oh, changed indeed.
Hecuba: It is fearful to be helpless. Men just now
have taken Cassandra—forced her from me.
Andromache: And still more for you—more than
   that—
Hecuba: Number my sorrows, will you? Measure them?
One comes—the next one rivals it.
Andromache: Polyxena lies dead upon Achilles' tomb,
a gift to a corpse, to a lifeless thing.
Hecuba: My sorrow! That is what Talthybius meant—
I could not read his riddle. Oh, too plain.
Andromache: I saw her there and left the chariot
and covered her dead body with my cloak,
and beat my breast.
Hecuba: Murdered—my child. Oh, wickedly!
Again I cry to you. Oh, cruelly slain!
Andromache: She has died her death, and happier by
   far
dying than I alive.
Hecuba: Life cannot be what death is, child.
Death is empty—life has hope.

Andromache: Mother, O Mother, hear a truer word.
Now let me bring joy to your heart.
I say to die is only not to be,
and rather death than life with bitter grief.
They have no pain, they do not feel their wrongs.
But the happy who has come to wretchedness,
his soul is a lost wanderer,
the old joys that were once, left far behind.
She is dead, your daughter—to her the same
as if she never had been born.
She does not know the wickedness that killed her.
While I—I aimed my shaft at good repute.
I gained full measure—then missed happiness.
For all that is called virtuous in a woman
I strove for and I won in Hector's house.
Always, because we women, whether right or wrong,
are spoken ill of
unless we stay within our homes, my longing
I set aside and kept the house.
Light talk, glib women's words,
could never gain an entrance there.
My own thoughts were enough for me,
best of all teachers to me in my home.
Silence, a tranquil eye, I brought my husband,
knew well in what I should rule him,
and when give him obedience.
And this report of me came to the Greeks
for my destruction. When they captured me
Achilles' son would have me.
I shall be a slave to those who murdered—
O Hector, my beloved—shall I thrust him aside,
open my heart to the man that comes to me,
and be a traitor to the dead?
And yet to shrink in loathing from him
and make my masters hate me—
One night, men say, one night in a man's bed
will make a woman tame—
Oh, shame! A woman throw her husband off
and in a new bed love another—
Why, a young colt will not run in the yoke
with any but her mate—not a dumb beast
that has no reason, of a lower nature.
O Hector, my beloved, you were all to me,
wise, noble, mighty, in wealth, in manhood, both.
No man had touched me when you took me,
took me from out my father's home
and yoked a girl fast to you.
And you are dead, and I, with other plunder,
am sent by sea to Greece. A slave's yoke there.
Your dead Polyxena you weep for,
what does she know of pain like mine?
The living must have hope. Not I, not any more.
I will not lie to my own heart. No good will ever come.
But oh, to think it would be sweet.

A Woman: We stand at the same point of pain. You
   mourn your ruin,
and in your words I hear my own calamity.

Hecuba: Those ships—I never have set foot on one,
but I have heard of them, seen pictures of them.
I know that when a storm comes which they think
they can ride out, the sailors do their best,
one by the sail, another at the helm,
and others bailing.
But if great ocean's raging overwhelms them,
they yield to fate.
They give themselves up to the racing waves.
So in my many sorrows I am dumb.
I yield, I cannot speak.
The great wave from God has conquered me.
But, O dear child, let Hector be,
and let be what has come to him.
Your tears will never call him back.
Give honor now to him who is your master.
Your sweet ways—use them to allure him.
So doing you will give cheer to your friends.
Perhaps this child, my own child's son,
you may rear to manhood and great aid for Troy,
and if ever you should have more children,
they might build her again. Troy once more be a city!
Oh—one thought leads another on.
But why again that servant of the Greeks?
I see him coming. Some new plan is here.
[Enter TALTHYBIUS *with soldiers. He is troubled and
advances hesitatingly.*]

Talthybius: Wife of the noblest man that was in Troy,
O wife of Hector, do not hate me.
Against my will I come to tell you.
The people and the kings have all resolved—

Andromache: What is it? Evil follows words like those.

Talthybius: This child they order—Oh, how can I say
   it—

Andromache: Not that he does not go with me to the
   same master—

Talthybius: No man in Greece shall ever be his master.

Andromache: But—leave him here—all that is left of
   Troy?

Talthybius: I don't know how to tell you. What is bad,
words can't make better—

Andromache: I feel you kind. But you have not good
   news.

Talthybius: Your child must die. There, now you know
the whole, bad as it is.

Andromache: Oh, I have heard an evil worse
than a slave in her master's bed.

Talthybius: It was Odysseus had his way. He spoke
to all the Greeks.

Andromache: O God. There is no measure to my pain.

Talthybius: He said a hero's son must not grow up—

Andromache: God, on his own sons may that counsel
   fall.

Talthybius: —but from the towering wall of Troy be
   thrown.
Now, now—let it be done—that's wiser.
Don't cling so to him. Bear your pain
the way a brave woman suffers.
You have no strength—don't look to any help.
There's no help for you anywhere. Think—think.
The city gone—your husband too. And you
a captive and alone, one woman—how
can you do battle with us? For your own good
I would not have you try, and draw
hatred down on you and be shamed.
Oh, hush—never a curse upon the Greeks.
If you say words that make the army angry
the child will have no burial, and without pity—
Silence now. Bear your fate as best you can.
So then you need not leave him dead without a grave,
and you will find the Greeks more kind.

Andromache: Go die, my best beloved, my own, my
   treasure,
in cruel hands, leaving your mother comfortless.
Your father was too noble. That is why
they kill you. He could save others,
he could not save you for his nobleness.

My bed, my bridal—all for misery—
when long ago I came to Hector's halls
to bear my son—oh, not for Greeks to slay,
but for a ruler over teeming Asia.
Weeping, my little one? There, there.
You cannot know what waits for you.
Why hold me with your hands so fast, cling so fast to me?
You little bird, flying to hide beneath my wings.
And Hector will not come—he will not come,
up from the tomb, great spear in hand, to save you.
Not one of all his kin, of all the Trojan might.
How will it be? Falling down—down—oh, horrible.
And his neck—his breath—all broken.
And none to pity. You little thing,
curled in my arms, you dearest to your mother,
how sweet the fragrance of you.
All nothing then—this breast from where
your baby mouth drew milk, my travail too,
my cares, when I grew wasted watching you.
Kiss me—Never again. Come, closer, closer.
Your mother who bore you—put your arms around my
    neck.
Now kiss me, lips to lips.
O Greeks, you have found out ways to torture
that are not Greek.
A little child, all innocent of wrong—
you wish to kill him.
O Helen, evil growth, that was sown by Tyndareus,
you are no child of Zeus, as people say.
Many the fathers you were born of,
Madness, Hatred, Red Death, whatever poison
the earth brings forth—no child of Zeus,
but Greece's curse and all the world's.
God curse you, with those beautiful eyes
that brought to shame and ruin
Troy's far-famed plains.
Quick! take him—seize him—cast him down—
if so you will. Feast on his flesh.
God has destroyed me, and I cannot—
I cannot save my child from death.
Oh hide my head for shame and fling me into the ship.
[She falls, then struggles to her knees.]
My fair bridal—I am coming—
Oh, I have lost my child, my own.
A Woman: O wretched Troy, tens of thousands lost
for a woman's sake, a hateful marriage bed.
Talthybius: [Drawing the child away]
Come, boy, let go. Unclasp those loving hands,
poor mother.
Come now, up, up, to the very height,
where the towers of your fathers crown the wall,
and where it is decreed that you must die.
[To the soldiers]
Take him away.
A herald who must bring such orders
should be a man who feels no pity,
and no shame either—not like me.
Hecuba: Child, son of my poor son, whose toil was all
    in vain,
we are robbed, your mother and I, oh, cruelly—
robbed of your life. How bear it?
What can I do for you, poor piteous child?
Beat my head, my breast—all I can give you.
Troy lost, now you—all lost.
The cup is full. Why wait? For what?
Hasten on—swiftly on to death.

[The soldiers, who have waited while HECUBA speaks, go
out with the child and TALTHYBIUS. One of them takes
ANDROMACHE to the chariot and drives off with her.]
Chorus: The waves make a ring around Salamis.
The bees are loud in the island.
King Telamon built him a dwelling.
It fronted the holy hills,
where first the gray gleaming olive
Athena showed to men,
the glory of shining Athens,
her crown from the sky.
He joined himself to the bowman,
the son of Alcmena, for valorous deeds.
Troy, Troy he laid waste, my city,
long ago when he went forth from Greece.
When he led forth from Greece the bravest
in his wrath for the steeds[27] withheld,
and by fair-flowing Simois stayed his oar
that had brought him over the sea.
Cables there made the ship fast.
In his hand was the bow that never missed.
It brought the king to his death.
Walls of stone that Phoebus had built
he wrecked with the red breath of fire.
He wasted the plain of Troy.
Twice her walls have fallen. Twice
a blood-stained spear struck her down, laid her in ruin.

In vain, O you who move
with delicate feet where the wine-cups are gold,
son of that old dead king,
who fill with wine the cup Zeus holds,
service most fair—
she who gave you birth is afire.
The shores of the sea are wailing for her.
As a bird cries over her young,
women weep for husbands, for children,
for the old, too, who gave them birth.
Your dewy baths are gone,
and the race-course where you ran.
Yet your young face keeps the beauty of peace
in joy, by the throne of Zeus.
While Priam's land
lies ruined by Greek spearsmen.

Love, O Love,
once you came to the halls of Troy,
and your song rose up to the dwellers in heaven.
How did you then exalt Troy high,
binding her fast to the gods, by a union—
No—I will not speak blame of Zeus.
But the light of white-winged Dawn, dear to men,
is deadly over the land this day,
shining on fallen towers.
And yet Dawn keeps in her bridal bower
her children's father, a son of Troy.
Her chariot bore him away to the sky.
It was gold, and four stars drew it.
Hope was high then for our town.

---

27. When Troy was destroyed the first time, the reason was that
the Trojan king had promised two immortal horses to Hercules
("the son of Alcmena") but did not give them to him. Hercules
in revenge ruined the city. The son of this king was Ganymede,
cup bearer to Zeus.

But the magic that brought her the love of the gods
has gone from Troy.
[As the song ends MENELAUS enters with a bodyguard of
soldiers.]
Menelaus: How bright the sunlight is today—
this day, when I shall get into my power
Helen, my wife. For I am Menelaus,
the man of many wrongs.
I came to Troy and brought with me my army,
not for that woman's sake, as people say,
but for the man who from my house,
and he a guest there, stole away my wife.
Ah, well, with God's help he has paid the price,
he and his country, fallen beneath Greek spears.
I am come to get her—wretch—I cannot speak her name
who was my wife once.
In a hut here, where they house the captives,
she is numbered with the other Trojan women.
The men who fought and toiled to win her back,
have given her to me—to kill, or else,
if it pleases me, to take her back to Argos.
And it has seemed to me her death in Troy
is not the way. I will take her overseas,
with swift oars speeding on the ship,
and there in Greece give her to those to kill
whose dearest died because of her.
[To his men]
Attention! Forward to the huts.
Seize her and drag her out by that long blood-drenched
      hair—
[Stops suddenly and controls himself]
And when fair winds come, home with her to
Greece.
[Soldiers begin to force the door of one of the huts.]
Hecuba: [Comes slowly forward]
O thou who dost uphold the world,
whose throne is high above the world,
thou, past our seeking hard to find, who art thou?
God, or Necessity of what must be,
or Reason of our reason?
Whate'er thou art, I pray to thee,
seeing the silent road by which
all mortal things are led by thee to justice.
Menelaus: What have we here? A queer prayer that.
Hecuba: [She comes still nearer to him and he
recognizes her.]
Kill her, Menelaus? You will? Oh, blessings on you!
But—shun her, do not look at her.
Desire for her will seize you, conquer you.
For through men's eyes she gets them in her power.
She ruins them and ruins cities too.
Fire comes from her to burn homes,
magic for death. I know her—so do you,
and all these who have suffered.
[HELEN enters from the hut. The soldiers do not touch
her. She is very gentle and undisturbed.]
Helen: [With sweet, injured dignity. Not angry at all.]
Menelaus, these things might well make a woman fear.
Your men with violence have driven me from my room,
have laid their hands upon me.
Of course, I know—almost I know—you hate me,
but yet I ask you, what is your decision,
yours and the Greeks? Am I to live or not?
Menelaus: Nothing more clear. Unanimous, in fact.
Not one who did not vote you should be given me,
whom you have wronged, to kill you.

Helen: Am I allowed to speak against the charge?
To show you if I die that I shall die
most wronged and innocent?
Menelaus: I have come to kill you, not to argue with
      you.
Hecuba: Oh, hear her. She must never die unheard.
Then, Menelaus, let me answer her.
The evil that she did in Troy, you do not know.
But I will tell the story. She will die.
She never can escape.
Menelaus: That means delay. Still—if she wants to
      speak,
she can. I grant her this because of what you say,
not for her sake. She can be sure of that.
Helen: And perhaps, no matter if you think I speak
the truth or not, you will not talk to me,
since you believe I am your enemy.
Still, I will try to answer what I think
you would say if you spoke your mind,
and my wrongs shall be heard as well as yours.
First: who began these evils? She, the day
when she gave birth to Paris. Who next was guilty?
The old king who decreed the child should live,
and ruined Troy and me—Paris, the hateful,
the firebrand.
What happened then? Listen and learn.
This Paris—he was made the judge for three,
all yoked together in a quarrel—goddesses.
Athena promised he should lead the Trojans
to victory and lay all Greece in ruins.
And Hera said if he thought her the fairest
she would make him lord of Europe and of Asia.
But Aphrodite—well, she praised my beauty—
astonishing, she said—and promised him
that she would give me to him if he judged
that she was loveliest. Then, see what happened.
She won, and so my bridal brought all Greece
great good. No strangers rule you,
no foreign spears, no tyrant.
Oh, it was well for Greece, but not for me,
sold for my beauty and reproached besides
when I deserved a crown.
But—to the point. Is that what you are thinking?
Why did I go—steal from your house in secret?
That man, Paris, or any name you like to call him,
his mother's curse—oh, when he came to me
a mighty goddess walked beside him.
And you, poor fool, you spread your sails for Crete,
left Sparta—left him in your house.
Ah well—Not you, but my own self I ask,
what was there in my heart that I went with him,
a strange man, and forgot my home and country?
Not I, but Aphrodite. Punish her,
be mightier than Zeus who rules
the other gods, but is her slave.
She is my absolution—
One thing with seeming justice you might say.
When Paris died and went down to the grave,
and when no god cared who was in my bed,
I should have left his house—gone to the Greeks.
Just what I tried to do—oh, many times.
I have witnesses—the men who kept the gates,
the watchmen on the walls. Not once, but often
they found me swinging from a parapet,
a rope around this body, stealthily
feeling my way down.

2 A Common Basis for Understanding the Arts

In the humanities we take art seriously because, as Aristotle observed, "art is a higher type of knowledge than experience." Earlier in this century the arts were regarded as "the finer things of life" and were respected as a sort of polish the upper classes received as a part of their education. Art was show-off stuff, valuable precisely because it was of no practical good. The upper middle-class child showed his status by wearing braces on his teeth and by taking piano lessons until he eventually learned to plunk out the *Moonlight Sonata* with little thought beyond the mechanical problem of getting the right fingers on the right notes. Another domestic status symbol was having a beautifully bound volume of the *Complete Works of Swinburne* (an "important" writer) resting casually on the coffee table, never opened let alone read, but advertising the good taste of the owner. As a matter of fact, this whole attitude towards art might well be called the coffee-table school of appreciation. The attitude still exists. But, as indicated in our description of a culture-epoch in chapter 1, we now recognize that eminent artists actually help create patterns for a way of life; "The object of art is to give life a shape" (Jean Anouilh).

One might ask what area of the universe is the darkest, the most unknown. The universe itself? Einstein once said that the most incomprehensible fact about the universe is that it is so comprehensible. No, the most bewildering portion of the universe is yourself. As a member of the human race, you are (or should be) asking yourself such questions as "Who am I?" "What am I?" "Why am I here?" It is the artist who persists in reacting to these questions, who seeks answers from within, and who discovers answers that strike responsive chords in the rest of us. As Henry Miller said, "art teaches nothing, except the significance of life."

A Shakespearean scholar once made the statement that in his plays Shakespeare had made discoveries as important as those made by any scientist. At first, such an assertion seems to be an overreaction to the dominance of science in the modern world. Consider, however, Shakespeare's treatment of love and hate in *Romeo and Juliet,* good and evil in *King Lear,* and murder and revenge in *Macbeth,* for example. These aspects of the human condition, as they are dramatized on the stage, are artistic truths.

9

The Trojans then no longer wanted me,
but the man who next took me—and by force—
would never let me go.
My husband, must I die, and at your hands?
You think that right? Is that your justice?
I was forced—by violence. I lived a life
that had no joy, no triumph. In bitterness
I lived a slave.
Do you wish to set yourself above the gods?
Oh, stupid, senseless wish!

A Woman: O Queen, defend your children and your
country.
Her soft persuasive words are deadly.
She speaks so fair and is so vile.
A fearful thing.

Hecuba: Her goddesses will fight on my side while
I show her for the liar that she is.
Not Hera, not virgin Athena, do I think
would ever stoop to folly great enough
to sell their cities. Hera sell her Argos,
Athena Athens, to be the Trojan's slave!
playing like silly children there on Ida,
and each one in her insolence demanding
the prize for beauty. Beauty—why was Hera
so hot for it? That she might get herself
a better mate than Zeus?
Athena—who so fled from marriage that she begged
one gift from Zeus, virginity.
But she would have the prize, you say. And why?
To help her hunt some god to marry her?
Never make gods out fools to whitewash your own evil.
No one with sense will listen to you.
And Aphrodite, did you say—who would not laugh?
—must take my son to Menelaus' house?
Why? Could she not stay quietly in heaven
and send you on—and all your town—to Troy?
My son was beautiful exceedingly.
You saw him—your own desire was enough.
No need of any goddess.
Men's follies—they are Aphrodite.
She rose up from the sea-foam; where the froth
and foam of life are, there she is.
It was my son. You saw him in his Eastern dress
all bright with gold, and you were mad with love.
Such little things had filled your mind in Argos,
busied with this and that.
Once free of Sparta and in Troy where gold,
you thought, flowed like a river, you would spend
and spend, until your spendthrift hand
had drowned the town.
Your luxuries, your insolent excesses,
Menelaus' halls had grown too small for them.
Enough of that. By force you say he took you?
You cried out? Where? No one in Sparta heard you.
Young Castor was there and his brother too,
not yet among the stars.
And when you came to Troy and on your track the Greeks,
and death and agony in battle,
if they would tell you, "Greece has won today,"
you would praise this man here, Menelaus,
to vex my son, who feared him as a rival.
Then Troy had victories, and Menelaus
was nothing to you.
Looking to the successful side—oh yes,
you always followed there.
There was no right or wrong side in your eyes.
And now you talk of ropes—letting your body down
in secret from the wall, longing to go.

Who found you so?
Was there a noose around your neck?
A sharp knife in your hand? Such ways
as any honest woman would have found,
who loved the husband she had lost?
Often and often I would tell you, Go,
my daughter. My sons will find them other wives.
I will help you. I will send you past the lines
to the Greek ships. Oh, end this war
between our foes and us. But this was bitter to you.
In Paris' house you had your insolent way.
You liked to see the Eastern men fall at your feet.
These were great things to you.
Look at the dress you wear, your ornaments.
Is that the way to meet your husband?
You should not dare to breathe the same air with him.
Oh, men should spit upon you.
Humbly, in rags, trembling and shivering,
with shaven head—so you should come,
with shame at last, instead of shamelessness,
for all the wickedness you did.
King, one word more and I am done.
Give Greece a crown, be worthy of yourself.
Kill her. So shall the law stand for all women,
that she who plays false to her husband's bed,
shall die.

A Woman: O son of an ancient house, O King, now
show
that you are worthy of your fathers.
The Greeks called you a woman, shamed you
with that reproach. Be strong. Be noble. Punish her.

Menelaus: [*Impatiently*]
I see it all as you do. We agree.
She left my house because she wanted to—
went to a stranger's bed. Her talk of Aphrodite—
big words, no more. [*Turns to* HELEN] Go. Death is near.
Men there are waiting for you. In their hands are stones.
Die—a small price for the Greeks' long suffering.
You shall not any more dishonor me.

Helen: [*Kneeling and clinging to him*]
No! No! Upon my knees—see, I am praying to you.
It was the gods, not me. Oh, do not kill me.
Forgive.

Hecuba: The men she murdered. Think of those
who fought beside you—of their children too.
Never betray them. Hear that prayer.

Menelaus: [*Roughly*]
Enough, old woman. She is nothing to me.
Men, take her to the ships and keep her safe
until she sails.

Hecuba: But not with you! She must not set foot on
your ship.

Menelaus: [*Bitterly*]
And why? Her weight too heavy for it?

Hecuba: A lover once, a lover always.

Menelaus: [*Pauses a moment to think*]
Not so when what he loved has gone.
But it shall be as you would have it.
Not on the same ship with me. The advice is good.
And when she gets to Argos she shall die
a death hard as her heart.
So in the end she will become a teacher,
teach women chastity—no easy thing,
but yet her utter ruin will strike terror
into their silly hearts,
even women worse than she.

Chorus: And so your temple in Ilium,
your altar of frankincense,
are given to the Greek,
the flame from the honey, the corn and the oil,
the smoke from the myrrh floating upward,
the holy citadel.
And Ida, the mountain where the ivy grows,
and rivers from the snows rush through the glens,
and the boundary wall of the world
where the first sunlight falls,
the blessed home of the dawn.

The sacrifice is gone, and the glad call
of dancers, and the prayers at evening to the gods
that last the whole night long.
Gone too the golden images,
and the twelve Moons, to Trojans holy.
Do you care, do you care, do you heed these things,
O God, from your throne in high heaven?
My city is perishing,
ending in fire and onrushing flame.

A Woman: O dear one, O my husband,
you are dead, and you wander
unburied, uncared for, while over-seas
the ships shall carry me,
swift-winged ships darting onward,
on to the land the riders love,
Argos, where the towers of stone
built by giants reach the sky.

Another: Children, our children.
At the gate they are crying, crying,
calling to us with tears,
Mother, I am all alone.
They are driving me away
to a black ship, and I cannot see you.

Another: Where, oh where? To holy Salamis,
with swift oars dipping?
Or to the crest of Corinth,
the city of two seas,
where the gates King Pelops built
for his dwelling stand?

Another: Oh, if only, far out to sea,
the crashing thunder of God
would fall down, down on Menelaus' ship,
crashing down upon her oars,
the Aegean's wild-fire light.
He it was drove me from Troy.
He is driving me in tears
over to Greece to slavery.

Another: And Helen, too, with her mirrors of gold,
looking and wondering at herself,
as pleased as a girl.
May she never come to the land of her fathers,
never see the hearth of her home,
her city, the temple with brazen doors
of goddess Athena.
Oh, evil marriage that brought
shame to Greece, the great,
and to the waters of Simois
sorrow and suffering.
[TALTHYBIUS *approaches with a few soldiers. He is carrying the dead child.*]

Another Woman: Before new sufferings are grown old
come other new.
Look, unhappy wives of Troy,
the dead Astyanax.
They threw him from the tower as one might pitch a ball.
Oh, bitter killing.
And now they have him there.

Talthybius: [*He gives the body into* HECUBA'S *arms.*]
One ship is waiting, Hecuba, to take aboard
the last of all the spoil Achilles' son was given,
and bear it with the measured beat of oars
to Thessaly's high headlands.
The chief himself has sailed because of news
he heard, his father's father
driven from his land by his own son.
So, more for haste even than before,
he went and with him went Andromache.
She drew tears from me there upon the ship
mourning her country, speaking to Hector's grave,
begging a burial for her child, your Hector's son,
who thrown down from the tower lost his life.
And this bronze-fronted shield, the dread of many a
    Greek,
which Hector used in battle,
that it should never, so she prayed,
hang in strange halls, her grief before her eyes,
nor in that bridal chamber where she must be a wife,
Andromache, this dead boy's mother.
She begged that he might lie upon it in his grave,
instead of cedar wood or vault of stone.
And in your arms she told me I must lay him,
for you to cover the body, if you still
have anything, a cloak left—
And to put flowers on him if you could,
since she has gone. Her master's haste
kept her from burying her child.
So now, whenever you have laid him out,
we'll heap the earth above him, then
up with the sails!
Do all as quickly as you can. One trouble
I saved you. When we passed Scamander's stream
I let the water run on him and washed his wounds.
I am off to dig his grave now, break up the hard earth.
Working together, you and I,
will hurry to the goal, oars swift for home.

Hecuba: Set the shield down—the great round shield
    of Hector.
I wish I need not look at it.
[TALTHYBIUS *goes out with the soldiers.*]
You Greeks, your spears are sharp but not your wits.
You feared a child. You murdered him.
Strange murder. You were frightened, then? You thought
he might build up our ruined Troy? And yet
when Hector fought and thousands at his side,
we fell beneath you. Now, when all is lost,
the city captured and the Trojans dead,
a little child like this made you afraid.
The fear that comes when reason goes away—
Myself, I do not wish to share it.
[*She dismisses the Greeks and their ways.*]
Beloved, what a death has come to you.
If you had fallen fighting for the city,
if you had known strong youth and love
and godlike power, if we could think
you had known happiness—if there is
happiness anywhere—
But now—you saw and knew, but with your soul
you did not know, and what was in your house
you could not use.
Poor little one. How savagely our ancient walls,
Apollo's towers, have torn away the curls
your mother's fingers wound and where she pressed
her kisses—here where the broken bone grins white—
Oh no—I cannot—

Dear hands, the same dear shape your father's had,
how loosely now you fall. And dear proud lips
forever closed. False words you spoke to me
when you would jump into my bed, call me sweet names
and tell me, Grandmother, when you are dead,
I'll cut off a great lock of hair and lead my soldiers all
to ride out past your tomb.
Not you, but I, old, homeless, childless,
must lay you in your grave, so young,
so miserably dead.
Dear God. How you would run to greet me.
And I would nurse you in my arms, and oh,
so sweet to watch you sleep. All gone.
What could a poet carve upon your tomb?
"A child lies here whom the Greeks feared and slew."
Ah, Greece should boast of that.
Child, they have taken all that was your father's,
but one thing, for your burying, you shall have,
the bronze-barred shield.
It kept safe Hector's mighty arm, but now
it has lost its master.
The grip of his own hand has marked it—dear to me
    then—
His sweat has stained the rim. Often and often
in battle it rolled down from brows and beard
while Hector held the shield close.
Come, bring such covering for the pitiful dead body
as we still have. God has not left us much
to make a show with. Everything I have
I give you, child.
        O men, secure when once good fortune comes—
fools, fools. Fortune's ways—
here now, there now. She springs
away—back   and away, an idiot's dance.
No one is ever always fortunate.
[*The women have come in with coverings and garlands.*]
A Woman: Here, for your hands, they bring you
        clothing for the dead,
got from the spoils of Troy.
Hecuba: [*Shrouding the body and putting garlands
beside it*]
Oh, not because you conquered when the horses raced,
or with the bow outdid your comrades,
your father's mother lays these wreaths beside you,
and of all that was yours, gives you this covering.
A woman whom God hates has robbed you,
taken your life, when she had taken your treasure
and ruined all your house.
A Woman: Oh, my heart! As if you touched it—touched
    it.
Oh, this was once our prince, great in the city.
Hecuba: So on your wedding day I would have dressed
    you,
the highest princess of the East your bride.
Now on your body I must lay the raiment,
all that is left of the splendor that was Troy's.
And the dear shield of Hector, glorious in battle,
mother of ten thousand triumphs won,
it too shall have its wreath of honor,
undying it will lie beside the dead.
More honorable by far than all the armor
Odysseus won, the wicked and the wise.
A Woman: You, O child, our bitter sorrow,
earth will now receive.
Mourn, O Mother.
Hecuba: Mourn, indeed.
A Woman: Weeping for all the dead.

Hecuba: Bitter tears.
A Woman: Your sorrows that can never be forgotten.
[*The funeral rite is now begun,* HECUBA *symbolically
healing the wounds.*]
Hecuba: I heal your wounds; with linen I bind them.
Ah, in words only, not in truth—
a poor physician.
But soon among the dead your father
will care for you.
A Woman: Beat, beat your head.
Lift your hands and let them fall,
moving in measure.
Hecuba: O Women. Dearest—
A Woman: Oh, speak to us. Your cry—what does it
    mean?
Hecuba: Only this the gods would have,
pain for me and pain for Troy,
those they hated bitterly.
Vain, vain, the bulls we slew.
And yet—had God not bowed us down,
not laid us low in dust,
none would have sung of us or told our wrongs
in stories men will listen to forever.
Go: lay our dead in his poor grave,
with these last gifts of death given to him.
I think those that are gone care little
how they are buried. It is we, the living,
our vanity.
[*Women lift the shield with the body on it and carry it
out.*]
A Woman: Poor mother—her high hopes were stayed
    on you
and they are broken.
They called you happy at your birth,
a good man's son.
Your death was miserable exceedingly.
Another: Oh, see, see—
On the crested height of Troy
fiery hands. They are flinging torches.
Can it be
some new evil?
Something still unknown?
Talthybius: [*Stops as he enters and speaks off stage*]
Captains, attention. You have been given charge
to burn this city. Do not let your torches sleep.
Hurry the fire on.
When once the town is level with the ground
then off for home and glad goodbye to Troy.
And you, you Women—I will arrange for you
as well, one speech for everything—
whenever a loud trumpet-call is sounded,
go to the Greek ships, to embark.
Old woman, I am sorriest for you,
follow. Odysseus' men are here to get you.
He drew you—you must leave here as his slave.
Hecuba: The end then. Well—the height of sorrow, I
    stand there.
Troy is burning—I am going.
But—hurry, old feet, if you can,
a little nearer—here, where I can see
my poor town, say goodbye to her.
You were so proud a city, in all the East
the proudest. Soon your name the whole world knew,
will be taken from you. They are burning you
and leading us away, their slaves.
O God—What makes me say that word?
The gods—I prayed, they never listened.

Quick, into the fire—Troy, I will die with you.
Death then—oh, beautiful.
Talthybius: Out of your head, poor thing, with all
you've suffered.
Lead her away—Hold her, don't be too gentle.
She must be taken to Odysseus.
Give her into his hands. She is his—
[*Shakes his head*]
his prize.
[*It grows darker.*]
A Woman: Ancient of days, our country's Lord,
Father, who made us,
You see your children's sufferings.
Have we deserved them?
Another: He sees—but Troy has perished, the great
city.
No city now, never again.
Another: Oh, terrible!
The fire lights the whole town up.
The inside rooms are burning.
The citadel—it is all flame now.
Another: Troy is vanishing.
War first ruined her.
And what was left is rushing up in smoke,
the glorious houses fallen.
First the spear and then the fire.
Hecuba: [*She stands up and seems to be calling to
someone far away.*]
Children, hear, your mother is calling.
A Woman: [*Gently*]
They are dead, those you are speaking to.
Hecuba: My knees are stiff, but I must kneel.
Now, strike the ground with both my hands—
A Woman: I too, I kneel upon the ground.
I call to mine down there.
Husband, poor husband.
Hecuba: They are driving us like cattle—taking us
away.
A Woman: Pain, all pain.
Another: To a slave's house, from my country.
Hecuba: Priam, Priam, you are dead,
and not a friend to bury you.
The evil that has found me—
do you know?
A Woman: No. Death has darkened his eyes.
He was good and the wicked killed him.
Hecuba: O dwellings of the gods and O dear city,
the spear came first and now
only the red flame lives there.
A Woman: Fall and be forgotten. Earth is kind.
Another: The dust is rising, spreading out like a great
wing of smoke.
I cannot see my house.
Another: The name has vanished from the land,
and we are gone, one here, one there.
And Troy is gone forever.
[*A great crash is heard.*]
Hecuba: Did you hear? Did you know—
A Woman: The fall of Troy—
Another: Earthquake and flood and the city's end—
Hecuba: Trembling body—old weak limbs,
you must carry me on to the new day of slavery.
[*A trumpet sounds.*]
A Woman: Farewell, dear city.
Farewell, my country, where once my children lived.
On to the ships—
There below, the Greek ships wait.
[*The trumpet sounds again and the women pass out.*]

Exercises

1. Why did Euripides stage an argument between
Hecuba and Andromache about who had the
greater grief? What does this scene tell us about
each woman? About human nature?
2. All the women are tear-stained and disheveled,
except Helen; Euripides implies that Helen has
tidied up before making her grand entrance.
Why did Euripides do this? Is he sympathetic to
Helen? How does Helen come off when
compared with the vindictive women? When
compared with Menelaus?
3. What is implied when Helen says to Menelaus,
"And you, poor fool, you spread your sails for
Crete, left Sparta—left him in your house"?
What kind of a husband was Menelaus? What
kind of a marriage was this?

THE BACCHAE
Euripides (484–406 B.C.)

The Bacchae (BOCK–ee) is probably more "contemporary" than most of the twentieth-century literature presented in volume 2 of this text. It was one of the last two plays that Euripides wrote after he had exiled himself from "civilized" Athens to Macedonia.

According to the myth, Dionysos was the son of Zeus by the mortal woman, Semele, daughter of Kadmus the first king of Thebes. Semele uttered a wish to see Zeus in all his glory as the god of lightning, and as her wish was granted, she was blasted by the lightning-stroke. The unborn god, Dionysos, was saved from his mother's womb and hidden by Zeus (in his thigh) until the time of his birth.

Euripides follows the belief that the worship of Dionysos moved through Asia before it took root in Greece. This is the account that Dionysos gives of himself as he comes to his native city of Thebes to inaugurate his cult in Hellas, bringing with him a chorus of Asian women.

The conventional interpretation of this play is that a person or a society must recognize the fact that the human personality contains much of the Dionysiac (nonrational and emotional) element, and must give this part of the character adequate expression in order to develop a healthy individual or culture. This healthy group is represented by the Asian women. Certainly Pentheus is a caricature of the "rational" man, particularly as he stands amid what seems to be the ruins of his palace and carries on his discussion with the god, not even noticing the chaos around him. Perhaps Pentheus, the traditional rational Greek, deserves punishment, but what of Agave, Kadmus, and the others who have accepted the god and honored him?

This modern translation is by Philip Vellacott, whose spelling of proper names has been retained.

CHARACTERS:

Dionysus (die–uh–NIE–sus)
Chorus of Oriental women, devotees of Dionysus
Teiresias (tie–REE–see–us), *a blind seer*
Cadmus (KAD–mus), *founder of Thebes, and formerly king*
Pentheus (PEN–thee–us), *his grandson, now king of Thebes*
A Guard attending Pentheus
A Herdsman
A Messenger
Agaue (ah–GAH–vee), *daughter of Cadmus and mother of Pentheus*

Scene: Before the palace of Pentheus in Thebes. At one side of the stage is the monument of Semele (SEM–uh–lee); above it burns a low flame, and around it are the remains of ruined and blackened masonry.

[Dionysus enters on stage right. He has a crown of ivy, a thyrsus²⁸ in his hand, and a fawnskin draped over his body. He has long flowing hair and a youthful, almost feminine beauty.]

Dionysus: I am Dionysus, son of Zeus. My mother was
Semele, Cadmus' daughter. From her womb the fire
Of a lightning-flash delivered me. I have come here
To Thebes and her two rivers, Dirce and Ismenus,
Veiling my godhead in a mortal shape. I see
Here near the palace my mother's monument, that
      records
Her death by lightning. Here her house stood; and its
      ruins
Smoulder with the still living flame of Zeus's fire—
The immortal cruelty Hera wreaked upon my mother.
Cadmus does well to keep this ground inviolable,
A precinct consecrated in his daughter's name;
And I have decked it round with sprays of young vine-
      leaves.
From the fields of Lydia and Phrygia,²⁹ fertile in gold,
I travelled first to the sun-smitten Persian plains,
The walled cities of Bactria, the harsh Median country,
Wealthy Arabia, and the whole tract of the Asian coast
Where mingled swarms of Greeks and Orientals live
In vast magnificent cities; and before reaching this,
The first city of Hellas I have visited,
I had already, in all those regions of the east,
Performed my dances and set forth my ritual
To make my godhead manifest to mortal men.

The reason why I have chosen Thebes as the first place
To raise my Bacchic shout, ³⁰ and clothe all who respond
In fawnskin habits, and put my thyrsus in their hands—
The weapon wreathed with ivy-shoots—my reason is this:
My mother's sisters said—what they should have been the
      last
To say—that I, Dionysus, was not Zeus's son;
That Semele, being with child—they said—by some
      mortal,
Obeyed her father's prompting, and ascribed to Zeus
The loss of her virginity; and they loudly claimed
That this lie was the sin for which Zeus took her life.
Therefore I have driven those same sisters mad, turned
      them
All frantic out of doors; their home now is the mountain;
Their wits are gone. I have made them bear the emblem
      of
My mysteries; the whole female population of Thebes,
To the last woman, I have sent raving from their homes.
Now, side by side with Cadmus' daughters, one and all
Sit roofless on the rocks under the silver pines.

For Thebes, albeit reluctantly, must learn in full
This lesson, that my Bacchic worship is a matter
As yet beyond her knowledge and experience;
And I must vindicate my mother Semele
By manifesting myself before the human race
As the divine son whom she bore to immortal Zeus.

Now Cadmus has made over his throne and kingly
      honours
To Pentheus, son of his eldest daughter Agaue. He
Is a fighter against gods, defies me, excludes me from
Libations, never names me in prayers. Therefore I will
Demonstrate to him, and to all Thebes, that I am a god.
When I have set all in order here, I will pass on
To another place, and manifest myself. Meanwhile
If Thebes in anger tries to bring the Bacchants home
By force from the mountain, I myself will join that army
Of women possessed and lead them to battle. That is why
I have changed my form and taken the likeness of a man.
Come, my band of worshippers, women whom I have
      brought
From lands of the east, from Tmolus,³¹ bastion of Lydia,
To be with me and share my travels! Raise the music
Of your own country, the Phrygian drums invented by
Rhea³² the Great Mother and by me. Fill Pentheus' palace
With a noise to make the city of Cadmus turn and look!
—And I will go to the folds of Mount Cithaeron,³³ where
The Bacchants are, and join them in their holy dance.
[DIONYSUS *goes out towards the mountain. The*
CHORUS *enter where* DIONYSUS *entered, from the road by which they have travelled.*]

Chorus: From far-off lands of Asia,   *Strophe 1*
From Tmolus the holy mountain,
We run with the god of laughter;
Labour is joy and weariness is sweet,
And our song resounds to Bacchus!

Who stands in our path?   *Antistrophe 1*
Make way, make way!
Who in the house? Close every lip,
Keep holy silence, while we sing
The appointed hymn to Bacchus!

Blest is the happy man   *Strophe 2*
Who knows the mysteries the gods ordain,
And sanctifies his life,

Joins soul with soul in mystic unity,
And, by due ritual made pure,
Enters the ecstasy of mountain solitudes;
Who observes the mystic rites
Made lawful by Cybele³⁴ the Great Mother;
Who crowns his head with ivy,
And shakes aloft his wand in worship of Dionysus.

---

28. A thyrsus is a light stick of reed or fennel with fresh strands of ivy twined about it. It was carried by every devotee of Dionysus.

29. These are the names of Asian countries in which the worship of Dionysus has been accepted in its progress toward Greece (Hellas).

30. Dionysus is also known by the name of Bacchus (his worshippers are Bacchantes), and also by the name of Bromius.

31. An Asian mountain in Lydia.

32. The earth mother, wife of Kronus. Notice the alliance between the female fertility-worship and that of Dionysus.

33. kee-the-RON. A mountain just outside the city of Thebes.

34. KI-buh-lee. The original earth mother, wife of the first god, Uranus.

On, on! Run, dance, delirious, possessed!
Dionysus comes to his own;
Bring from the Phrygian hills to the broad streets of
    Hellas
The god, child of a god,
Spirit of revel and rapture, Dionysus!

Once, on the womb that held him   *Antistrophe 2*
The fire-bolt flew from the hand of Zeus;
And pains of child-birth bound his mother fast,
And she cast him forth untimely,
And under the lightning's lash relinquished life;
And Zeus the son of Cronos
Ensconced him instantly in a secret womb
Chambered within his thigh,
And with golden pins closed him from Hera's sight.

So, when the Fates had made him ripe for birth,
Zeus bore the bull-horned god
And wreathed his head with wreaths of writhing snakes;
Which is why the Maenads[35] catch
Wild snakes, nurse them and twine them round their hair.

O Thebes, old nurse that cradled Semele,   *Strophe 3*
Be ivy garlanded, burst into flower
With wreaths of lush bright-berried bryony,
Bring sprays of fir, green branches torn from oaks,
Fill soul and flesh with Bacchus' mystic power;
Fringe and bedeck your dappled fawnskin cloaks
With wooly tufts and locks of purest white.
There's a brute wildness in the fennel-wands—
Reverence it well. Soon the whole land will dance
    When the god with ecstatic shout
    Leads his companies out
    To the mountain's mounting height
    Swarming with riotous bands
    Of Theban women leaving
    Their spinning and their weaving
    Stung with the maddening trance
        Of Dionysus!

O secret chamber the Curetes knew![36]   *Antistrophe 3*
O holy cavern in the Cretan glade
Where Zeus was cradled, where for our delight
The triple-crested Corybantes[37] drew
Tight the round drum-skin, till its wild beat made
Rapturous rhythm to the breathing sweetness
Of Phrygian flutes![38] Then divine Rhea found
The drum could give her Bacchic airs completeness;
    From her, the Mother of all,
    The crazy Satyrs[39] soon,
    In their dancing festival
    When the second year comes round,
    Seized on the timbrel's tune
    To play the leading part
    In feasts that delight the heart
        Of Dionysus.

O what delight is in the mountains!   *Epode*
There the celebrant,[40] wrapped in his sacred fawnskin,
Flings himself on the ground surrendered,
While the swift-footed company streams on;
There he hunts for blood, and rapturously
Eats the raw flesh of the slaughtered goat,
Hurrying on to the Phrygian or Lydian mountain heights.
Possessed, ecstatic, he leads their happy cries;
The earth flows with milk, flows with wine,
Flows with nectar of bees;
The air is thick with a scent of Syrian myrrh.
The celebrant runs entranced, whirling the torch

That blazes red from the fennel-wand in his grasp,
And with shouts he rouses the scattered bands,
Sets their feet dancing,
As he shakes his delicate locks to the wild wind.
And amidst the frenzy of song he shouts like thunder:
'On, on! Run, dance, delirious, possessed!
You, the beauty and grace of golden Tmolus,
Sing to the rattle of thunderous drums,
Sing for joy,
Praise Dionysus, god of joy!
Shout like Phrygians, sing out the tunes you know,
While the sacred pure-toned flute
Vibrates the air with holy merriment,
In time with the pulse of the feet that flock
To the mountains, to the mountains!'
And, like a foal with its mother at pasture,
Runs and leaps for joy every daughter of Bacchus.
[*Enter* TEIRESIAS. *Though blind, he makes his way*
    unaided to the door, and knocks.]
Teiresias: Who keeps the gate? Call Cadmus out,
    Agenor's son,
Who came from Sidon here to build these walls of
    Thebes.[41]
Go, someone, say Teiresias is looking for him.
He knows why; I'm an old man, and he's older still—
But we agreed to equip ourselves with Bacchic wands
And fawnskin cloaks, and put on wreaths of ivy-shoots.
[*Enter* CADMUS]
Cadmus: Dear friend, I knew your voice, although I
    was indoors,
As soon as I heard it—the wise voice of a wise man.
I am ready. See, I have all that the god prescribes.
He is my daughter's son; we must do all we can
To exalt and honour him. Where shall we go to dance
And take our stand with others, tossing our grey heads?
You tell me what to do, Teiresias. We're both old,
But you're the expert. (*He stumps about, beating his
    thyrsus on the ground.*] I could drum the ground all
    night
And all day too, without being tired. What joy it is
To forget one's age!
Teiresias: I feel exactly the same way,
Bursting with youth! I'll try it—I'll dance with the rest.
Cadmus: You don't think we should go to the mountain
    in a coach?

---

35. MEE–nad. Another name for the female worshippers of
Dionysus.

36. The reference here is to the cave on the island of Crete
where Zeus was hidden from his father and raised to manhood
(or godhood).

37. kore-uh–BAN-teez. The priests of Cybele.

38. Flutes. The aulos, the reedy, two-pronged musical instrument
used in conjunction with Greek tragedies and Dionysian rites
(see Chap. 8).

39. SAYT–ur. Half-animal gods; part of the worship of Dionysus.

40. The celebrant. Dionysus and the Chorus comprise the typical
group of Bacchic worshippers, a male leader with a devoted band
of women and girls. The leader flings himself on the ground in
the climax of ecstasy when the power of the god enters into him
and he becomes possessed.

41. Cadmus was the original king of Thebes. He planted the
dragon's teeth from which grew a group of warriors who built the
city. Pentheus' father, Echion (ee–KEY-on), who is referred to
later in the play, was one of the warriors who grew from the
dragon's teeth.

Teiresias: No, no. That would not show the god the
same respect.

Cadmus: I'll take you there myself then—old as we
both are.

Teiresias: The god will guide us there, and without
weariness.

Cadmus: Are we the only Thebans who will dance to
him?

Teiresias: We see things clearly; all the others are
perverse.

Cadmus: We're wasting time; come, take my hand.

Teiresias: Here, then; hold tight.

Cadmus: I don't despise religion. I'm a mortal man.

Teiresias: We have no use for theological subtleties.
The beliefs we have inherited, as old as time,
Cannot be overthrown by any argument,
Not by the most inventive ingenuity.
It will be said, I lack the dignity of my age,
To wear this ivy-wreath and set off for the dance.
Not so; the god draws no distinction between young
And old, to tell us which should dance and which should
not.
He desires equal worship from all men; his claim
To glory is universal; no one is exempt.

Cadmus: Teiresias, I shall be your prophet, since you
are blind.
Pentheus, to whom I have resigned my rule in Thebes,
Is hurrying here towards the palace. He appears
Extremely agitated. What news will he bring?

[*Enter* PENTHEUS. *He addresses the audience, without at
first noticing* CADMUS *and* TEIRESIAS, *who stand at
the opposite side of the stage.*]

Pentheus: I happen to have been away from Thebes;
reports
Of this astounding scandal have just been brought to me.
Our women, it seems, have left their homes on some
pretence
Of Bacchic worship, and now are gadding about
On the wooded mountain-slopes, dancing in honour of
This upstart god Dionysus, whoever he may be.
Amidst these groups of worshippers, they tell me, stand
Bowls full of wine; and our women go creeping off
This way and that to lonely places and give themselves
To lecherous men. They are Maenad priestesses, if you
please!
Aphrodite supplants Bacchus in their ritual.
Well, those I've caught, my guards are keeping safe; we've
tied
Their hands, and lodged them at state expense. Those
still at large
On the mountain I am going to hunt out; and that
Includes my own mother Agaue and her sisters
Ino and Autonoe. Once they're fast in iron fetters,
I'll put a stop to this outrageous Bacchism.

They tell me, too, some oriental conjurer
Has come from Lydia, a magician with golden hair
Flowing in scented ringlets, his face flushed with wine,
His eyes lit with the charm of Aphrodite;[42] and he
Entices young girls with his Bacchic mysteries,
Spends days and nights consorting with them. Once let
me
Get that fellow inside my walls—I'll cut his head
From his shoulders; that will stop him drumming with his
thyrsus,
Tossing his long hair. *He's* the one—this foreigner—
Who says Dionysus is a god; who says he was
Sewn up in Zeus's thigh. The truth about Dionysus

Is that he's dead, burnt to a cinder by lightning
Along with his mother, because she said Zeus lay with
her.
Whoever the man may be, is not his arrogance
An outrage? Has he not earned a rope around his neck?

[PENTHEUS *turns to go, and sees* CADMUS *and*
TEIRESIAS.]

Why, look! Another miracle! Here's Teiresias
The prophet—in a fawnskin; and my mother's father—
A Bacchant with a fennel-wand! Well, there's a sight
For laughter! [*But he is raging, not laughing*]
Sir, I am ashamed to see two men
Of your age with so little sense of decency.
Come, you're my grandfather: throw down that ivy-wreath,
Get rid of that thyrsus!—*You* persuaded him to this,
Teiresias. By introducing a new god, you hope
To advance your augurer's business, to collect more fees
For inspecting sacrifices. Listen: your grey hairs
Are your protection; otherwise you'd be sitting now
In prison with all these crazy females, for promoting
Pernicious practices. As for women, I tell you this:
Wherever the sparkle of sweet wine adorns their feasts,
No good will follow from such Bacchic ceremonies.

Chorus: Have you no reverence, Sir, no piety? Do you
mock
Cadmus, who sowed the dragon-seed of earth-born men?
Do you, Echion's son, dishonour your own race?

Teiresias: When a good speaker has a sound case to
present,
Then eloquence is no great feat. Your fluent tongue
Promises wisdom; but the content of your speech
Is ignorant. Power and eloquence in a headstrong man
Spell folly; such a man is a peril to the state.

This new god, whom you ridicule—no words of mine
Could well express the ascendancy he will achieve
In Hellas. There are two powers, young man, which are
supreme
In human affairs: first, Demeter[43]—the same goddess
Is also Earth; give her which name you please—and she
Supplies mankind with solid food. After her came
Dionysus, Semele's son; the blessing he procured
And gave to men is counterpart to that of bread:
The clear juice of the grape. When mortals drink their fill
Of wine, the sufferings of our unhappy race
Are banished, each day's troubles are forgotten in sleep.
There is no other cure for sorrow. Dionysus,
Himself a god, is thus poured out in offering
To the gods, so that through him come blessings on
mankind.
And do you scorn this legend, that he was sewn up
In Zeus's thigh? I will explain the truth to you.
When Zeus snatched Dionysus from the lightning-flame
And took the child up to Olympus as a god,
Hera resolved to cast him out of heaven. But Zeus
Found such means to prevent her as a god will find.
He took a fragment of the ether that surrounds
The earth, fashioned it like a child, presented it
To Hera as a pledge[44] to soothe her jealousy,
And saved Dionysus from her. Thus, in time, because

---

42. af–ro–DIE–tee. The goddess of love and beauty.

43. di–MEET–ur. The third personification of the earth goddess.

44. The ancient word for pledge: the translation necessarily
expands the original. *Homeros* means "pledge," and *meros*
means thigh.

The ancient words for 'pledge' and 'thigh' are similar,
People confused them, and the 'pledge' Zeus gave to
    Hera
Became transformed, as time went on, into the tale
That Dionysus was sewn up in Zeus's thigh.

And this god is a prophet; the Bacchic ecstasy
And frenzy hold a strong prophetic element.
When he fills irresistibly a human body
He gives those so possessed power to foretell the future.
In Ares' province too Dionysus has his share;
Sometimes an army, weaponed and drawn up for battle,
Has fled in wild panic before a spear was raised.
This too is an insanity sent by Dionysus.

Ay, and the day will come when, on the very crags
Of Delphi,[45] you shall see him leaping, amidst the blaze
Of torches, over the twin-peaked ridge, waving aloft
And brandishing his Bacchic staff, while all Hellas
Exalts him. Pentheus, pay heed to my words. You rely
On force; but it is not force that governs human affairs.
Do not mistake for wisdom that opinion which
May rise from a sick mind. Welcome this god to Thebes,
Offer libations to him, celebrate his rites,
Put on his garland. Dionysus will not compel
Women to be chaste, since in all matters self-control
Resides in our own natures. You should consider this;
For in the Bacchic ritual, as elsewhere, a woman
Will be safe from corruption if her mind is chaste.

Think of this too: when crowds stand at the city gates
And Thebes extols the name of Pentheus, you rejoice;
So too, I think, the god is glad to receive honour.

Well, I at least, and Cadmus, whom you mock, will wear
The ivy-wreath and join the dancing—we are a pair
Of grey heads, but this is our duty; and no words
Of yours shall lure me into fighting against gods.
For a most cruel insanity has warped your mind;
While drugs may well have caused it, they can bring no
    cure.
Chorus: What you have said, Teiresias, shows no
    disrespect
To Apollo; at the same time you prove your judgment
    sound
In honouring Dionysus as a mighty god.
Cadmus: My dear son, Teiresias has given you good
    advice.
Don't stray beyond pious tradition; live with us.
Your wits have flown to the winds, your sense is
    foolishness.
Even if, as you say, Dionysus is no god,
Let him have *your* acknowledgment; lie royally,
That Semele may get honour as having borne a god,
And credit come to us and to all our family.

Remember, too, Actaeon's miserable fate—
Torn and devoured by hounds which he himself had
    bred,
Because he filled the mountains with the boast that he
Was a more skilful hunter than Artemis herself.
Don't share his fate, my son! Come, let me crown your
    head
With a wreath of ivy; join us in worshipping this god.
Pentheus: Keep your hands off! Go to your Bacchic
    rites, and don't
Wipe off your crazy folly on me. But I will punish
This man who has been your instructor in lunacy.
Go, someone, quickly to his seat of augury,
Smash it with crowbars, topple the walls, throw all his
    things

In wild confusion, turn the whole place upside down,
Fling out his holy fripperies to the hurricane winds!
This sacrilege will sting him more than anything else.
The rest of you—go, comb the country and track down
That effeminate foreigner, who plagues our women with
This new disease, fouls the whole land with lechery;
And once you catch him, tie him up and bring him here
To me; I'll deal with him. He shall be stoned to death.
He'll wish he'd never brought his Bacchic rites to Thebes.
                                            [*Exit* PENTHEUS]
Teiresias: Foolhardy man! You do not know what you
    have said.
Before, you were unbalanced; now you are insane.
Come, Cadmus; let us go and pray both for this man,
Brutish as he is, and for our city, and beg the god
To show forbearance. Come, now, take your ivy staff
And let us go. Try to support me; we will help
Each other. It would be scandalous for two old men
To fall; still, we must go, and pay our due service
To Dionysus, son of Zeus. Cadmus, the name
Pentheus means *sorrow*. God grant he may not bring
    sorrow
Upon your house. Do not take that as prophecy;
I judge his acts. Such foolish words bespeak a fool.
                                [*Exeunt* TEIRESIAS *and* CADMUS]
Chorus: Holiness, Queen of heaven,
Holiness, golden-winged ranging the earth,
Do you hear his blasphemy?
Pentheus dares—do you hear?—to revile the god of joy,
The son of Semele, who when the gay-crowned feast is
    set,
Is named among gods the chief;
Whose gifts are joy and union of soul in dancing,
Joy in music of flutes,
Joy when sparkling wine at feasts of the gods
Soothes the sore regret,
Banishes every grief,
When the reveller rests, enfolded deep
In the cool shade of ivy-shoots,
On wine's soft pillow of sleep.

The brash, unbridled tongue,   *Antistrophe 1*
The lawless folly of fools, will end in pain.
But the life of wise content
Is blest with quietness, escapes the storm
And keeps its house secure.
Though blessed gods dwell in the distant skies,
They watch the ways of men.
To know much is not to be wise.
Pride more than mortal hastens life to its end;
And they who in pride pretend
Beyond man's limit, will lose what lay
Close to their hand and sure.
I count it madness, and know no cure can mend
The evil man and his evil way.

O to set foot on Aphrodite's island,   *Strophe 2*
On Cyprus, haunted by the Loves, who enchant
Brief life with sweetness; or in that strange land
Whose fertile river carves a hundred channels
To enrich her rainless sand;

---

45. Delphi was the shrine sacred to Apollo, a god of the rational
Greeks. The twin-peaked ridge is Mount Parnassus, the home of
the Muses.

Or where the sacred pastures of Olympus slant
Down to Pieria, where the Muses dwell—
Take me, O Bromius, take me and inspire
Laughter and worship! There our holy spell
And ecstasy are welcome; there the gentle band
Of Graces have their home, and sweet Desire.
Dionysus, son of Zeus, delights in banquets;

Antistrophe 2

And his dear love is Peace, giver of wealth,
Saviour of young men's lives—a goddess rare!
In wine, his gift that charms all griefs away,
Alike both rich and poor may have their part.
His enemy is the man who has no care
To pass his years in happiness and health,
His days in quiet and his nights in joy,
Watchful to keep aloof both mind and heart
From men whose pride claims more than mortals may.
The life that wins the poor man's common voice,
His creed, his practice—this shall be my choice.

[*Some of the guards whom* PENTHEUS *sent to arrest*
DIONYSUS *now enter with their prisoner.*
PENTHEUS *enters from the palace.*]

Guard: Pentheus, we've brought the prey you sent us
out to catch;
We hunted him, and here he is. But, Sir, we found
The beast was gentle; made no attempt to run away,
Just held his hands out to be tied; didn't turn pale,
But kept his florid colour, smiling, telling us
To tie him up and run him in; gave us no trouble
At all, just waited for us. Naturally I felt
A bit embarrassed. 'You'll excuse me, Sir,' I said,
'I don't want to arrest you; it's the king's command.'
Another thing, sir—those women you rounded up
And put in fetters in the prison, those Bacchants;
Well, they're all gone, turned loose to the glens; and
there they are,
Frisking about, calling on Bromius their god.
The fetters simply opened and fell off their feet;
The bolts shot back, untouched by mortal hand; the doors
Flew wide. Master, this man has come here with a load
Of miracles. Well, what happens next is your concern.

Pentheus: Untie this man's hands. [*The* GUARD *does
so.*] He's securely in the trap.
He's not so nimble-footed as to escape me now.
Well, friend: your shape is not unhandsome—for the
pursuit
Of women, which is the purpose of your presence here.
You are no wrestler, I can tell from these long curls
Cascading most seductively over your cheek.
Your skin, too, shows a whiteness carefully preserved;
You keep away from the sun's heat, walk in the shade,
So hunting Aphrodite with your lovely face.
Ah, well; first tell me who you are. What is your birth?

Dionysus: Your question's easily answered, it is no
secret.
Perhaps you have heard of Tmolus, a mountain decked
with flowers.

Pentheus: A range that curves round Sardis? Yes, I
know of it.

Dionysus: That is my home. I am a Lydian by birth.

Pentheus: How comes it that you bring these rituals to
Hellas?

Dionysus: Dionysus, son of Zeus, himself instructed
me.

Pentheus: Is there a Lydian Zeus, then, who begets
new gods?

Dionysus: I speak of Zeus who wedded Semele here in
Thebes.

Pentheus: Did he possess you in a dream, or visibly?

Dionysus: Yes, face to face; he gave these mysteries to
me.

Pentheus: These mysteries you speak of: what form do
they take?

Dionysus: To the uninitiated that must not be told.

Pentheus: And those who worship—what advantage do
they gain?

Dionysus: It is not for you to learn; yet it is worth
knowing.

Pentheus: You bait your answer well, to arouse my
eagerness.

Dionysus: His rituals abhor a man of impious life.

Pentheus: You say you saw him face to face: what was
he like?

Dionysus: Such as he chose to be. I had no say in that.

Pentheus: Still you side-track my question with an
empty phrase.

Dionysus: Just so. A prudent speech sleeps in a foolish
ear.

Pentheus: Is Thebes the first place where you have
introduced this god?

Dionysus: No; every eastern land dances these
mysteries.

Pentheus: No doubt. Their moral standards fall far
below ours.

Dionysus: In this they are superior; but their customs
differ.

Pentheus: Do you perform these mysteries by night or
day?

Dionysus: Chiefly by night. Darkness promotes
religious awe.

Pentheus: For women darkness is deceptive and
impure.

Dionysus: Impurity can be pursued by daylight too.

Pentheus: You must be punished for your foul and
slippery tongue.

Dionysus: And you for blindness and impiety to the
god.

Pentheus: How bold this Bacchant is! A practised
pleader too.

Dionysus: Tell me my sentence. What dread pain will
you inflict?

Pentheus: I'll start by cutting off your delicate long
hair.

Dionysus: My hair is sacred; I preserve it for the god.

Pentheus: And next, that thyrsus in your hand—give it
to me.

Dionysus: Take it from me yourself; it is the god's
emblem.

Pentheus: I'll lock you up in prison and keep you
there.

Dionysus:
                                                    The god
Himself, whenever I desire, will set me free.

Pentheus: Of course—when you, with all your
Bacchants, call to him!

Dionysus: He is close at hand here, and sees what is
done to me.

Pentheus: Indeed? Where is he, then? Not visible to my
eyes.

Dionysus: Beside me. You, being a blasphemer, see
nothing.

Pentheus: [*To the* GUARDS]
Get hold of him; he's mocking me and the whole city.
Dionysus: [*To the* GUARDS]
Don't bind me, I warn you. [*To* PENTHEUS] I am sane,
and you are mad.
Pentheus: My word overrules yours. [*To the* GUARDS] I
tell you, bind him fast.
Dionysus: You know not what you are saying, what you
do, nor who
You are.[46]
Pentheus: Who? Pentheus, son of Echion and Agaue.
Dionysus: Your name points to calamity. It fits you
well.
Pentheus: Take him away and shut him in my stables,
where
He can stay staring at darkness.—You can dance in there!
As for these women you've brought as your accomplices,
I'll either send them to the slave-market to be sold,
Or keep them in my own household to work the looms;
And that will stop their fingers drumming on
tambourines!
Dionysus: I'll go. Nothing can touch me that is not
ordained.
But I warn you: Dionysus, who you say is dead,
Will come in swift pursuit to avenge this sacrilege.
You are putting *him* in prison when you lay hands on me.
[GUARDS *take* DIONYSUS *away to the stables;*
PENTHEUS *follows.*]
Chorus: Dirce, sweet and holy maid,   *Strophe*
Acheloüs' Theban daughter,
Once the child of Zeus was made
Welcome in your welling water,
When the lord of earth and sky
Snatched him from the undying flame,
Laid him safe within his thigh,
Calling loud the infant's name:
'Twice-born Dithyrambus! Come,
Enter here your father's womb;
Bacchic child, I now proclaim
This in Thebes shall be your name.'
Now, divine Dirce, when my head is crowned
And my feet dance in Bacchus' revelry—
Now you reject me from your holy ground.
Why should you fear me? By the purple fruit
That glows in glory on Dionysus' tree,
His dread name yet shall haunt your memory!

Oh, what anger lies beneath   *Antistrophe*
Pentheus' voice and sullen face—
Offspring of the dragon's teeth,
And Echion's earth-born race,
Brute with bloody jaws agape,
God-defying, gross and grim,
Slander of his human shape!
Soon he'll chain us limb to limb—
Bacchus' servants! Yes, and more:
Even now our comrade lies
Deep on his dark prison floor.
Dionysus! Do your eyes
See us? O son of Zeus, the oppressor's rod
Falls on your worshippers; come, mighty god,
Brandish your golden thyrsus and descend
From great Olympus; touch this murderous man,
And bring his violence to a sudden end!

Where are you, Dionysus? Leading your dancing bands
          Epode
Over the mountain slopes, past many a wild beast's lair,
Or on Corycian crags, with the thyrsus in their hands?

Or in the wooded coverts, maybe, of Olympus, where
Orpheus once gathered the trees and mountain beasts,
Gathered them with his lyre, and sang an enchanting air.
Happy vale of Pieria! Bacchus delights in you;
He will cross the flood and foam of the Axius river, and
there
He will bring his whirling Maenads, with dancing and
with feasts,
Cross the father of waters, Lydias, generous giver
Of wealth and luck, they say, to the land he wanders
through,
Whose famous horses graze by the rich and lovely river.
[*Suddenly a shout is heard from inside the building—the
voice of* DIONYSUS.]
Dionysus: Io, Io! Do you know my voice, do you hear?
Worshippers of Bacchus! Io. Io!
Chorus: Who is that? Where is he?
The shout of Dionysus is calling us!
Dionysus: Io, Io! hear me again:
I am the son of Semele, the son of Zeus!
Chorus: Io, Io, our lord, our lord!
Come, then, come to our company, lord of joy!
Dionysus: O dreadful earthquake, shake the floor of
the world!
Chorus: [*With a scream of terror*]
Pentheus' palace is falling, crumbling in pieces! [*They
continue severally.*]
          —Dionysus stands in the palace; bow before him!
          —We bow before him.—See how the roof and pillars
          Plunge to the ground!—Bromius is with us,
          He shouts from prison the shout of victory!
[*The flame on Semele's tomb grows and brightens.*]
Dionysus: Fan to a blaze the flame the lightning lit;
Kindle the conflagration of Pentheus' palace!
Chorus: Look, look, look!
Do you see, do you see the flame of Semele's tomb,
The flame that lived when she died of the lightning-
stroke?
[*A noise of crashing masonry is heard.*]
Down, trembling Maenads! Hurl yourselves to the ground.
Your god is wrecking the palace, roof to floor;
He heard our cry—he is coming, the son of Zeus!
[*The doors open and* DIONYSUS *appears.*]
Dionysus: Women of Asia, why do you cower thus,
prostrate and terrified?
Surely, you could hear Dionysus shattering Pentheus'
palace? Come,
Lift yourselves up, take good courage, stop this trembling
of your limbs!
Chorus: We are saved! Oh, what a joy to hear your
Bacchic call ring out!
We were all alone, deserted; you have come, and we
rejoice.
Dionysus: Were you comfortless, despondent, when I
was escorted in,
Helpless, sentenced to be cast in Pentheus' murky prison-
cell?
Chorus: Who could help it? What protector had we,
once deprived of you?
Tell us now how you escaped the clutches of this wicked
man.
Dionysus: I alone, at once, unaided, effortlessly freed
myself.

---

46. Compare this speech with that of Teiresias as he predicts the
fate of Oedipus in Sophokles' *Oedipus the King.*

Chorus: How could that be? Did not Pentheus bind
your arms with knotted ropes?

Dionysus: There I made a mockery of him. He thought
he was binding me;
But he neither held nor touched me, save in his deluded
mind.
Near the mangers where he meant to tie me up, he found
a bull;
And he tied his rope round the bull's knees and hooves,
panting with rage,
Dripping sweat, biting his lips; while I sat quietly by and
watched.
It was then that Dionysus shook the building, made the
flame
On his mother's tomb flare up. When Pentheus saw this,
he supposed
The whole place was burning. He rushed this way, that
way, calling out
To the servants to bring water; every slave about the place
Was engaged upon this futile task. He left it presently,
Thinking I had escaped; snatched up his murderous
sword, darted indoors.
Thereupon Dionysus—as it seemed to me; I merely
guess—
Made a phantom hover in the courtyard. Pentheus flew at
it,
Stabbing at the empty sunlight, thinking he was killing
me.
Yet a further humiliation Bacchus next contrived for him:
He destroyed the stable buildings. Pentheus sees my
prison now
Lying there, a heap of rubble; and the picture grieves his
heart.
Now he's dazed and helpless with exhaustion. He has
dropped his sword.
He, a man, dared to take arms against a god. I quietly
walked
Out of the palace here to join you, giving Pentheus not a
thought.
But I hear his heavy tread inside the palace. Soon, I think,
He'll be out here in the forecourt. After what has
happened now,
What will he have to say? For all his rage, he shall not
ruffle *me.*
It's a wise man's part to practise a smooth-tempered self-
control.

[*Enter* PENTHEUS]

Pentheus: This is outrageous. He has escaped—that
foreigner.
Only just now I had him locked up and in chains.

[*He sees* DIONYSUS *and gives an excited shout.*]

He's there! Well, what's going on now? How did you get
out?
How dare you show your face here at my very door?

Dionysus: Stay where you are. You are angry; now
control yourself.

Pentheus: You were tied up inside there. How did you
escape?

Dionysus: I said—did you not hear?—that I should be
set free—

Pentheus: By whom? You're always finding something
new to say.

Dionysus: By him who plants for mortals the rich-
clustered vine.

Pentheus: The god who frees his worshippers from
every law.

Dionysus: Your insult to Dionysus is a compliment.

Pentheus: [*To attendant* GUARDS]
Go round the walls and tell them to close every gate.

Dionysus: And why? Or cannot gods pass even over
walls?

Pentheus: Oh, you know everything—save what you
ought to know.

Dionysus: The things most needful to be known, those
things I know.
But listen first to what this man has to report;
He comes from the mountain, and he has some news for
you.
I will stay here; I promise not to run away.

[*Enter a* HERDSMAN]

Herdsman: Pentheus, great king of Thebes! I come
from Mount Cithaeron,
Whose slopes are never free from dazzling shafts of snow.

Pentheus: And what comes next? What urgent message
do you bring?

Herdsman: I have seen the holy Bacchae, who like a
flight of spears
Went streaming bare-limbed, frantic, out of the city gate.
I have come with the intention of telling you, my lord,
And the city, of their strange and terrible doings—things
Beyond all wonder. But first I would learn whether
I may speak freely of what is going on there, or
If I should trim my words. I fear your hastiness,
My lord, your anger, your too potent royalty.

Pentheus: From me fear nothing. Say all that you have
to say;
Anger should not grow hot against the innocent.
The more dreadful your story of these Bacchic rites,
The heavier punishment I will inflict upon
This man who enticed our women to their evil ways.

Herdsman: At dawn today, when first the sun's rays
warmed the earth,
My herd of cattle was slowly climbing up towards
The high pastures; and there I saw three separate
Companies of women. The leader of one company
Was Autonoe; your mother Agaue was at the head
Of the second, Ino of the third; and they all lay
Relaxed and quietly sleeping. Some rested on beds
Of pine-needles, others had pillows of oak-leaves.
They lay just as they had thrown themselves down on the
ground,
But modestly, not—as you told us—drunk with wine
Or flute-music, seeking the solitary woods
For the pursuit of love.
When your mother Agaue
Heard the horned cattle bellowing, she stood upright
Among the Bacchae, and called to them to stir themselves
From sleep; and they shook off the strong sleep from their
eyes
And leapt to their feet. They were a sight to marvel at
For modest comeliness; women both old and young,
Girls still unmarried. First they let their hair fall free
Over their shoulders; some tied up the fastenings
Of fawnskins they had loosened; round the dappled fur
Curled snakes that licked their cheeks. Some would have
in their arms
A young gazelle, or wild wolf-cubs, to which they gave
Their own white milk—those of them who had left at
home
Young children newly born, so that their breasts were
full.
And they wore wreathes of ivy-leaves, or oak, or flowers
Of bryony. One would strike her thyrsus on a rock,
And from the rock a limpid stream of water sprang.

Another dug her wand into the earth, and there
The god sent up a fountain of wine. Those who desired
Milk had only to scratch the earth with finger-tips,
And there was the white stream flowing for them to drink,
While from the thyrsus a sweet ooze of honey dripped.
Oh! if you had been there and seen all this, you would
Have offered prayers to this god whom you now
        condemn.
We herdsmen, then, and shepherds gathered to exchange
Rival reports of these strange and extraordinary
Peformances; and one, who had knocked about the town,
And had a ready tongue, addressed us: 'You who live
On the holy mountain heights,' he said, 'shall we hunt
        down
Agaue, Pentheus' mother, and bring her back from these
Rituals, and gratify the king? What do you say?'
This seemed a good suggestion; so we hid ourselves
In the leafy bushes, waiting. When the set time came,
The women began brandishing their wands, preparing
To dance, calling in unison on the son of Zeus,
'Iacchus! Bromius!' And with them the whole mountain,
And all the creatures there, joined in the mystic rite
Of Dionysus, and with their motion all things moved.
Now, Agaue as she danced passed close to me; and I
At once leapt out from hiding, bent on capturing her.
But she called out, 'Oh, my swift-footed hounds, these
        men
Are hunting us. Come, follow me! Each one of you
Arm herself with the holy thyrsus, and follow me!'
So we fled, and escaped being torn in pieces by
Those possessed women. But our cattle were there,
        cropping
The fresh grass; and the women attacked them, with their
        bare hands.
You could see one take a full-uddered bellowing young
        heifer
And hold it by the legs with her two arms stretched wide;
Others seized on our cows and tore them limb from limb;
You'd see some ribs, or a cleft hoof, tossed high and low;
And rags of flesh hung from pine-branches, dripping
        blood.
Bulls, which one moment felt proud rage hot in their
        horns,
The next were thrown bodily to the ground, dragged
        down
By hands of girls in thousands; and they stripped the flesh
From the bodies faster than you could wink your royal
        eyes.
Then, skimming bird-like over the surface of the ground,
They scoured the plain which stretches by Asopus' banks
And yields rich crops for Thebes; and like an enemy force
They fell on Hysiae and Erythrae, two villages
On the low slopes of Cithaeron, and ransacked them
        both;
Snatched babies out of the houses; any plunder which
They carried on their shoulders stayed there without
        straps—
Nothing fell to the ground, not bronze or iron; they
        carried
Fire on their heads, and yet their soft hair was not burnt.
The villagers, enraged at being so plundered, armed
Themselves to resist; and then, my lord, an amazing sight
Was to be seen. The spears those men were throwing
        drew
No blood; but the women, hurling a thyrsus like a spear,
Dealt wounds; in short, those women turned the men to
        flight.

There was the power of a god in that. Then they went
        back
To the place where they had started from, to those
        fountains
The god had caused to flow for them. And they washed off
The blood; and snakes licked clean the stains, till their
        cheeks shone.
So, master, whoever this divinity may be,
Receive him in this land. His powers are manifold;
But chiefly, as I hear, he gave to men the vine
To cure their sorrows; and without wine, neither love
Nor any other pleasure would be left for us.
Chorus: I shrink from speaking freely before the king;
        yet I
Will say it: there is no greater god than Dionysus.
Pentheus: This Bacchic arrogance advances on us like
A spreading fire, disgracing us before all Hellas.
We must act now. [*To the* HERDSMAN] Go quickly to the
        Electran gate;
Tell all my men who carry shields, heavy or light,
All riders on fast horses, all my archers with
Their twanging bows, to meet me there in readiness
For an onslaught on these maniacs. This is beyond
All bearing, if we must let women so defy us.
Dionysus: You refuse, Pentheus, to give heed to what I
        say
Or change your ways. Yet still, despite your wrongs to me,
I warn you: stay here quietly; do not take up arms
Against a god. Dionysus will not tolerate
Attempts to drive his worshippers from their holy hills.
Pentheus: I'll not have you instruct me. You have
        escaped your chains;
Now be content—or must I punish you again?
Dionysus: I would control my rage and sacrifice to him
If I were you, rather than kick against the goad.
Can you, a mortal, measure your strength with a god's?
Pentheus: I'll sacrifice, yes—blood of women,
        massacred
Wholesale, as they deserve, among Cithaeron's glens.
Dionysus: Your army will be put to flight. What a
        disgrace
For bronze shields to be routed by those women's wands!
Pentheus: How can I deal with this impossible
        foreigner?
In prison or out, nothing will make him hold his tongue.
Dionysus: My friend, a happy settlement may still be
        found.
Pentheus: How? must I be a slave to my own slave-
        women?
Dionysus: I will, using no weapons, bring those
        women here.
Pentheus: Hear that, for the gods' sake! You're playing
        me some trick.
Dionysus: What trick?—if I am ready to save you by my
        skill.
Pentheus: You've planned this with them, so that the
        rituals can go on.
Dionysus: Indeed I have planned this—not with them,
        but with the god.
Pentheus: Bring out my armour, there!—That is
        enough from you.
Dionysus: [*With an authoritative shout*]
Wait! [*Then quietly*] Do you want to *see*
Those women, where they sit together, up in the hills?
Pentheus: Why, yes; for that, I'd give a weighty sum of
        gold.
Dionysus: What made you fall into this great desire to
        see?

Pentheus: It would cause me distress to see them drunk with wine.

Dionysus: Yet you would gladly witness this distressing sight?

Pentheus: Of course—if I could quietly sit under the pines.

Dionysus: They'll track you down, even if you go there secretly.

Pentheus: Openly, then. Yes, what you say is very true.

Dionysus: Then shall I lead you? You will undertake to go?

Pentheus: Yes, lead me there at once; I am impatient.

Dionysus: Then,
You must first dress yourself in a fine linen gown.

Pentheus: Why in a linen gown? Must I then change my sex?

Dionysus: In case they kill you, if you are seen there as a man.

Pentheus: Again you are quite right. How you think of everything!

Dionysus: It was Dionysus who inspired me with that thought.

Pentheus: Then how can your suggestion best be carried out?

Dionysus: I'll come indoors with you myself and dress you.

Pentheus: What?
Dress me? In woman's clothes? But I would be ashamed.

Dionysus: Do you want to watch the Maenads? Are you less eager now?

Pentheus: What kind of dress did you say you would put on me?

Dionysus: First I'll adorn your head with locks of flowing hair.

Pentheus: And after that? What style of costume shall I have?

Dionysus: A full-length robe; and on your head shall be a snood.

Pentheus: Besides these, is there anything else you'll put on me?

Dionysus: A dappled fawnskin round you, a thyrsus in your hand.

Pentheus: I could not bear to dress myself in woman's clothes.

Dionysus: If you join battle with the Maenads, blood will flow.

Pentheus: You are right; I must first go to spy on them.

Dionysus: That way
Is better than inviting force by using it.

Pentheus: And how shall I get through the town without being seen?

Dionysus: We'll go by empty streets; I will show you the way.

Pentheus: The Maenads must not mock me; better anything
Than that. Now I'll go in, and think how best to act.

Dionysus: You may do so. My preparations are all made.

Pentheus: I'll go in, then; and either I'll set forth at the head
Of my armed men—or else I'll follow your advice.

[*Exit* PENTHEUS]

Dionysus: Women, this man is walking into the net. He will
Visit the Bacchae; and there death shall punish him.

Dionysus!—for you are not far distant—all is now
In your hands. Let us be revenged on him! And first
Fill him with wild delusions, drive him out of his mind.
While sane, he'll not consent to put on woman's clothes;
Once free from the curb of reason, he will put them on.
I long to set Thebes laughing at him, as he walks
In female garb through all the streets; to humble him
From the arrogance he showed when first he threatened me.
Now I will go, to array Pentheus in the dress
Which he will take down with him to the house of Death,
Slaughtered by his own mother's hands. And he shall know
Dionysus, son of Zeus, in his full nature God,
Most terrible, although most gentle, to mankind.

[DIONYSUS *follows* PENTHEUS *into the palace.*]

Chorus: O for long nights of worship, gay   *Strophe*
With the pale gleam of dancing feet,
With head tossed high to the dewy air—
Pleasure mysterious and sweet!
O for the joy of a fawn at play
In the fragrant meadow's green delight,
Who has leapt out free from the woven snare,
Away from the terror of chase and flight,
And the huntsman's shout, and the straining pack,
And skims the sand by the river's brim
With the speed of wind in each aching limb,
To the blessed lonely forest where
The soil's unmarked by a human track,
And leaves hang thick and the shades are dim.

What prayer should we call wise?   *Refrain*
What gift of Heaven should man
Count a more noble prize,
A prayer more prudent, than
To stretch a conquering arm
Over the fallen crest
Of those who wished us harm?
And what is noble every heart loves best.

Slow, yet unfailing, move the Powers   *Antistrophe*
Of heaven with the moving hours.
When mind runs mad, dishonours God,
And worships self and senseless pride,
Then Law eternal wields the rod.
Still Heaven hunts down the impious man,
Though divine subtlety may hide
Time's creeping foot. No mortal ought
To challenge Time—to overbear
Custom in act, or age in thought.
All men, at little cost, may share
The blessing of a pious creed;
Truths more than mortal, which began
In the beginning, and belong
To very nature—these indeed
Reign in our world, are fixed and strong.

What prayer should we call wise?   *Refrain*
What gift of heaven should man
Count a more noble prize,
A prayer more prudent, than
To stretch a conquering arm
Over the fallen crest
Of those who wished us harm?
And what is noble every heart loves best.

Blest is the man who cheats the stormy sea   *Epode*
And safely moors beside the sheltering quay;
So, blest is he who triumphs over trial.

One man, by various means, in wealth or strength
Outdoes his neighbour; hope in a thousand hearts
Colours a thousand different dreams; at length
Some find a dear fulfillment, some denial.
      But this I say,
      That he who best
      Enjoys each passing day
      Is truly blest.
[*Enter* DIONYSUS. *He turns to call* PENTHEUS.]
Dionysus: Come, perverse man, greedy for sights you
      should not see,
Eager for deeds you should not do—Pentheus! Come out
Before the palace and show yourself to me, wearing
The garb of a frenzied Bacchic woman, and prepared
To spy on your mother and all her Bacchic company.
[*Enter* PENTHEUS *dressed as a Bacchic devotee. He is
      dazed and entirely subservient to* DIONYSUS.]
You are the very image of one of Cadmus' daughters.
Pentheus: Why now! I seem to see two suns; a double
      Thebes;
Our city's wall with seven gates appears double.
[DIONYSUS *takes* PENTHEUS *by the hand and leads him
      forward.*]
You are a bull I see leading me forward now;
A pair of horns seems to have grown upon your head.
Were you a beast before? You have become a bull.
Dionysus: The god then did not favour us; he is with
      us now,
We have made our peace with him; you see as you should
      see.
Pentheus: How do I look? Tell me, is not the way I
      stand
Like the way Ino stands, or like my mother Agaue?
Dionysus: Looking at you, I think I see them both.
      Wait, now;
Here is a curl has slipped out of its proper place,
Not as I tucked it carefully below your snood.
Pentheus: Indoors, as I was tossing my head up and
      down
Like a Bacchic dancer, I dislodged it from its place.
Dionysus: Come, then; I am the one who should look
      after you.
I'll fix it in its place again. There; lift your head.
Pentheus: You dress me, please; I have put myself in
      your hands now.
Dionysus: Your girdle has come loose; and now your
      dress does not
Hang, as it should, in even pleats down to the ankle.
Pentheus: That's true, I think—at least by the right leg,
      on this side;
But on the other side the gown hangs well to the heel.
Dionysus: You'll surely count me chief among your
      friends, when you
Witness the Maenads' unexpected modesty.
Pentheus: Ought I to hold my thyrsus in the right
      hand—so,
Or in the left, to look more like a Bacchanal?
Dionysus: In the right hand; and raise it at the same
      time as
Your right foot. I am glad you are so changed in mind.
Pentheus: Could I lift up on my own shoulders the
      whole weight
Of Mount Cithaeron, and all the women dancing there?
Dionysus: You could, if you so wished. The mind you
      had before
Was sickly; now your mind is just as it should be.

Pentheus: Shall we take crowbars? Or shall I put my
      shoulder under
The rocks, and heave the mountain up with my two arms?
Dionysus: Oh, come, now! Don't destroy the dwellings
      of the nymphs,
And the quiet places where Pan sits to play his pipes.
Pentheus: You are right. We ought not to use force to
      overcome
Those women. I will hide myself among the pines.
Dionysus: Hide—yes, you'll hide, and find the proper
      hiding-place
For one who comes by stealth to spy on Bacchic rites.
Pentheus: Why, yes! I think they are there now in their
      hidden nests,
Like birds, all clasped close in the sweet prison of love.
Dionysus: What you are going to watch for is this very
      thing!
Perhaps you will catch them—if you are not first caught
      yourself.
Pentheus: Now take me through the central streets of
      Thebes; for I
Am the one man among them all that dares do this.
Dionysus: One man alone, you agonise for Thebes;
      therefore
It is your destined ordeal that awaits you now.
Come with me; I will bring you safely to the place;
Another shall conduct you back.
Pentheus: My mother—yes?
Dionysus: A sight for all to witness.
Pentheus: To this end I go.
Dionysus: You will return borne high—
Pentheus: Royal magnificence!
Dionysus: In your own mother's arms.
Pentheus: You insist that I be spoiled.
Dionysus: One kind of spoiling.
Pentheus: Yet I win what I deserve.
                                    [*Exit* PENTHEUS]
Dionysus: Pentheus, you are a man to make men fear;
      fearful
Will be your end—an end that shall lift up your fame
To the height of heaven.
Agaue, and you her sisters, daughters of Cadmus,
Stretch out your hands! See, I am bringing this young man
To his great battle; and I and Bromius shall be
Victors. What more shall happen, the event will show.
                                    [*Exit* DIONYSUS]
Chorus: Hounds of Madness, fly to the mountain,
      fly   *Strophe*
Where Cadmus' daughters are dancing in ecstasy!
Madden them like a frenzied herd stampeding,
Against the madman hiding in woman's clothes
To spy on the Maenad's rapture!
First his mother shall see him craning his neck
Down from a rounded rock or a sharp crag.
And shout to the Maenads. 'Who is the man, you Bacchae,
Who has come to the mountain, come to the mountain
      spying
On the swift wild mountain—dances of Cadmus'
      daughters?
Which of you is his mother?
No, that lad never lay in a woman's womb;
A lioness gave him suck, or a Libyan Gorgon!'
Justice, now be revealed! Now let your sword
Thrust—through and through—to sever the throat
Of the godless, lawless, shameless son of Echion,
Who sprang from the womb of Earth!

See! With contempt of right, with a reckless rage *Antistrophe*
To combat your and your mother's mysteries, Bacchus,
With maniac fury out he goes, stark mad,
For a trial of strength against *your* invincible arm!
His proud purposes death shall discipline.
He who unquestioning gives the gods their due,
And knows that his days are as dust, shall live untouched.
I have no wish to grudge the wise their wisdom;
But the joys *I* seek are greater, outshine all others,
And lead our life to goodness and loveliness:
The joy of the holy heart
That night and day is bent to honour the gods
And disown all custom that breaks the bounds of right.

Justice, now be revealed! Now let your sword
Thrust—through and through—to sever the throat
Of the godless, lawless, shameless son of Echion,
Who sprang from the womb of Earth!

[*Then with growing excitement, shouting in unison, and
    dancing to the rhythm of their words.*]

    Come, Dionysus!   *Epode*
    Come, and appear to us!
    Come like a bull or a
    Hundred-headed serpent,
    Come like a lion snorting
    Flame from your nostrils!
    Swoop down, Bacchus, on the
    Hunter of the Bacchae;
    Smile at him and snare him;
    Then let the stampeding
    Herd of the Maenads
    Throw him and throttle him,
    Catch, trip, trample him to death!

[*Enter a* MESSENGER]

Messenger: O house that once shone glorious
    throughout Hellas, home
Of the old Sidonian king who planted in this soil
The dragon's earth-born harvest! How I weep for you!
Slave though I am, I suffer with my master's fate.

Chorus: Are you from the mountain, from the Bacchic
    rites? What news?

Messenger: Pentheus, son of Echion, is dead.

Chorus: Bromius, lord! Your divine power is revealed!

Messenger: What, woman? What was that you said? Do
    you exult
When such a cruel fate has overtaken the king?

Chorus: I am no Greek.
I sing my joy in a foreign tune.
Not any more do I cower in terror of prison!

Messenger: Do you think Thebes has no men left who
    can take command?

Chorus: Dionysus commands *me;*
Not Thebes, but Dionysus.

Messenger: Allowance must be made for you; yet, to
    rejoice
At the accomplishment of horrors, is not right.

Chorus: Tell us everything, then: this tyrant king
Bent on cruelty—how did he die?

Messenger: When we had left behind the outlying parts
    of Thebes
And crossed the river Asopus, we began to climb
Toward the uplands of Cithaeron, Pentheus and I—
I went as his attendant—and the foreigner
Who was our guide to the spectacle we were to see.
Well, first we sat down in a grassy glade. We kept
Our footsteps and our talk as quiet as possible,
So as to see without being seen. We found ourselves
In a valley full of streams, with cliffs on either side.

There, under the close shade of branching pines, the
    Maenads
Were sitting, their hands busy at their happy tasks;
Some of them twining a fresh crown of ivy-leaves
For a stripped thyrsus; others, gay as fillies loosed
From painted yokes, were singing holy Bacchic songs,
Each answering other. But the ill-fated Pentheus saw
None of this; and he said, 'My friend, from where we
    stand
My eyes cannot make out these so-called worshippers;
But if I climbed a towering pine-tree on the cliff
I would have a clear view of their shameful practices.'

And then I saw that foreigner do an amazing thing.
He took hold of a pine-tree's soaring, topmost branch,
And dragged it down, down, down to the dark earth. It
    was bent
In a circle as a bow is bent, as a wheel's curve,
Drawn with a compass, bends the rim to its own shape;
The foreigner took that mountain-pine in his two hands
And bent it down—a thing no mortal man could do.
Then seating Pentheus on a high branch, he began
To let the tree spring upright, slipping it through his
    hands
Steadily, taking care he should not be flung off.
The pine-trunk, straightened, soared into the soaring sky,
Bearing my master seated astride, so that he was
More visible to the Maenads than they were to him.
He was just coming into view on his high perch,
When out of the sky a voice—Dionysus, I suppose;
That foreigner was nowhere to be seen—pealed forth:
'Women, here is the man who made a mock of you,
And me, and of my holy rites. Now punish him.'
And in the very moment the voice spoke, a flash
Of dreadful fire stretched between earth and high heaven.
The air fell still. The wooded glade held every leaf
Still. You could hear no cry of any beast. The women,
Not having caught distinctly what the voice uttered,
Stood up and gazed around. Then came a second word
Of command. As soon as Cadmus' daughters recognised
The clear bidding of Bacchus, with the speed of doves
They darted forward, and all the Bacchae after them.
Through the torrent-filled valley, over the rocks,
    possessed
By the very breath of Bacchus they went leaping on.
Then, when they saw my master crouched high in the
    pine,
At first they climbed the cliff which towered opposite,
And violently flung at him pieces of rocks, or boughs
Of pine-trees which they hurled as javelins; and some
Aimed with the thyrsus; through the high air all around
Their wretched target missiles flew. Yet every aim
Fell short, the tree's height baffled all their eagerness;
While Pentheus, helpless in this pitiful trap, sat there.
Then, with a force like lightning, they tore down
    branches
Of oak, and with these tried to prize up the tree's roots.
When all their struggles met with no success, Agaue
Cried out, 'Come, Maenads, stand in a circle round the
    tree
And take hold of it. We must catch this climbing beast,
Or he'll disclose the secret dances of Dionysus.'
They came; a thousand hands gripped on the pine and
    tore it
Out of the ground. Then from his high perch plunging,
    crashing
To the earth Pentheus fell, with one incessant scream
As he understood what end was near.

His mother first,
As priestess, led the rite of death, and fell upon him.
He tore the headband from his hair, that his wretched
        mother
Might recognise him and not kill him. 'Mother,' he cried,
Touching her cheek, 'it is I, your own son Pentheus,
        whom
You bore to Echion. Mother, have mercy; I have sinned,
But I am still your own son. Do not take my life!'
Agaue was foaming at the mouth; her rolling eyes
Were wild; she was not in her right mind, but possessed
By Bacchus, and she paid no heed to him. She grasped
His right arm between wrist and elbow, set her foot
Against his ribs, and tore his arm off by the shoulder.
It was no strength of hers that did it, but the god
Filled her, and made it easy. On the other side
Ino was at him, tearing at his flesh; and now
Autonoe joined them, and the whole maniacal horde.
A single and continuous yell arose—Pentheus
Shrieking as long as life was left in him, the women
Howling in triumph. One of them carried off an arm,
Another a foot, the boot still laced on it. The ribs
Were stripped, clawed clean; and women's hands, thick
        red with blood,
Were tossing, catching, like a plaything, Pentheus' flesh.

His body lies—no easy task to find—scattered
Under hard rocks, or in the green woods. His poor
        head—
His mother carries it, fixed on her thyrsus-point,
Openly over Cithaeron's pastures, thinking it
The head of a young mountain-lion. She has left her
        sisters
Dancing among the Maenads, and herself comes here
Inside the walls, exulting in her hideous prey,
Shouting to Bacchus, calling him her fellow-hunter,
Her partner in the kill, comrade in victory.
But Bacchus gives her bitter tears for her reward.

Now I will go. I must find some place far away
From this horror, before Agaue returns home.
A sound and humble heart that reverences the gods
Is man's noblest possession; and the same virtue
Is wisest too, I think, for those who practise it.

                                    [*Exit the* MESSENGER]
Chorus: Let us dance a dance to Bacchus, shout and
        sing
For the fall of Pentheus, heir of the dragon's seed,
Who hid his beard in a woman's gown,
And sealed his death with the holy sign
Of ivy wreathing a fennel-reed,
When bull led man to the ritual slaughter-ring.
Frenzied daughters of Cadmus, what renown
Your victory wins you—such a song
As groans must stifle, tears must drown!

Emblem of conquest, brave and fine!—
A mother's hand, defiled
With blood and dripping red
Caresses the torn head
Of her own murdered child!

But look! I see her—there, running towards the palace—
Agaue, Pentheus' mother, her eyes wildly rolling.
Come, welcome them—Dionysus' holy company.

[AGAUE *appears, frenzied and panting, with* PENTHEUS'
        *head held in her hand. The rest of her band of
        devotees, whom the* CHORUS *saw approaching with
        her, do not enter; but a few are seen standing by the
        entrance, where they wait until the end of the play.*]

Agaue: Women of Asia! Worshippers of Bacchus!
[AGAUE *tries to show them* PENTHEUS' *head; they shrink
        from it.*]
Chorus: Why do you urge me? Oh!
Agaue: I am bringing home from the mountains
A vine-branch freshly cut,
For the gods have blessed our hunting.
Chorus: We see it . . . and welcome you in fellowship.
Agaue: I caught him without a trap,
A lion-cub, young and wild.
Look, you may see him: there!
Chorus: Where was it?
Agaue: On Cithaeron;
The wild and empty mountain—
Chorus: Cithaeron!
Agaue: . . . spilt his life-blood.
Chorus: Who shot him?
Agaue: I was first;
All the women are singing,
'Honour to great Agaue!'
Chorus: And then—who next?
Agaue: Why, Cadmus' . . .
Chorus: What—Cadmus?
Agaue: Yes, his daughters—
But after me, after me—
Laid their hands to the kill.
To-day was a splendid hunt!
Come now, join in the feast!
Chorus: What, wretched woman? *Feast?*
Agaue: [*Tenderly stroking the head as she holds it*] This
        calf is young: how thickly
The new-grown hair goes crisping
Up to his delicate crest!
Chorus: Indeed, his long hair makes him
Look like some wild creature.
Agaue: The god is a skilled hunter?
And he poised his hunting women,
And hurled them at the quarry.
Chorus: True, our god is a hunter.
Agaue: Do you praise me?
Chorus: Yes, we praise you.
Agaue: So will the sons of Cadmus . . .
Chorus: And Pentheus too, Agaue?[47]
Agaue: Yes he will praise his mother
For the lion-cub she killed.
Chorus: Oh, fearful!
Agaue: Ay, fearful!
Chorus: You are happy?
Agaue: I am enraptured;
Great in the eyes of the world,
Great are the deeds I've done,
And the hunt that I hunted there!

---

47. *And Pentheus too, Agaue?* The chorus are physically shocked
by the sight of Agaue and her prey; but their attitude does not
change to pity. Agaue has been (in their view, justly) punished
for her blasphemy against Dionysus, by being tricked into
performing the usual Bacchic rite of slaughter, not upon the
usual victim, a beast, but upon a man, and that her own son. She
is now an abhorred and polluted creature, unfit for the company
of the 'pure' Bacchae. Hence, though they welcome the
punishment of Pentheus, their tone towards Agaue is one not of
admiration but of contempt. This line in particular indicates the
complete absence of pity.

Chorus: Then show it, poor Agaue—this triumphant spoil
You've brought home; show it to all the citizens of Thebes.
Agaue: Come, all you Thebans living within these towered walls,
Come, see the beast we, Cadmus' daughters, caught and killed;
Caught not with nets or thonged Thessalian javelins,
But with our own bare arms and fingers. After this
Should huntsmen glory in their exploits, who must buy
Their needless tools from armourers? We with our hands
Hunted and took this beast, then tore it limb from limb.
Where is my father? Let old Cadmus come. And where
Is my son Pentheus? Let him climb a strong ladder
And nail up on the cornice of the palace wall
This lion's head that I have hunted and brought home.
[*Enter* CADMUS *with attendants bearing the body of* PENTHEUS.]
Cadmus: Come, men, bring your sad burden that was Pentheus. Come,
Set him at his own door. By weary, endless search
I found his body's remnants scattered far and wide
About Cithaeron's glens, or hidden in thick woods.
I gathered them and brought them here.
I had already
Returned with old Teiresias from the Bacchic dance,
And was inside the walls, when news was brought me of
My daughters' terrible deed. I turned straight back; and now
Return, bringing my grandson, whom the Maenads killed.
I saw Autonoe, who bore Actaeon to Aristaeus,
And Ino with her, there among the trees, still rapt
In their unhappy frenzy; but I understood
That Agaue had come dancing on her way to Thebes—
And there indeed she is, a sight for misery!
Agaue: Father! Now you may boast as loudly as you will
That you have sired the noblest daughters of this age!
I speak of all three, but myself especially.
I have left weaving at the loom for greater things,
For hunting wild beasts with my bare hands. See this prize,
Here in my arms; I won it, and it shall be hung
On your palace wall. There, father, take it in your hands.
Be proud of my hunting; call your friends to a feast; let them
Bless you and envy you for the splendour of my deed.
Cadmus: Oh, misery unmeasured, sight intolerable!
Oh, bloody deed enacted by most pitiful hands!
What noble prize is this you lay at the gods' feet,
Calling the city, and me, to a banquet? Your wretchedness
Demands the bitterest tears; but mine is next to yours.
Dionysus has dealt justly, but pursued justice
Too far; born of my blood, he has destroyed my house.
Agaue: What an ill-tempered creature an old man is! How full
Of scowls! I wish my son were a great hunter like
His mother, hunting beasts with the young men of Thebes;
But *he* can only fight with gods. Father, you must
Correct him.—Will not someone go and call him here
To see me, and to share in my great happiness?
Cadmus: Alas, my daughters! If you come to understand
What you have done, how terrible your pain will be!
If you remain as you are now, though you could not
Be happy, at least you will not feel your wretchedness.

Agaue: Why not happy? What cause have I for wretchedness?
Cadmus: Come here. First turn your eyes this way. Look at the sky.
Agaue: I am looking. Why should you want me to look at it?
Cadmus: Does it appear the same to you, or is it changed?
Agaue: Yes, it is clearer than before, more luminous.
Cadmus: And this disturbance of your mind—is it still there?
Agaue: I don't know what you mean; but—yes, I feel a change;
My mind is somehow clearer than it was before.
Cadmus: Could you now listen to me and give a clear reply?
Agaue: Yes, father. I have forgotten what we said just now.
Cadmus: When you were married, whose house did you go to then?
Agaue: You gave me to Echion, of the sown race, they said.
Cadmus: Echion had a son born to him. Who was he?
Agaue: Pentheus. His father lay with me; I bore a son.
Cadmus: Yes; and whose head is that you are holding in your arms?
Agaue: A lion's—so the women said who hunted it.
Cadmus: Then look straight at it. Come, to look is no great task.
[AGAUE *looks; and suddenly screams.*]
Agaue: What am I looking at? What is this in my hands?
Cadmus: Look at it steadily; come closer to the truth.
Agaue: I see—O gods, what horror! Oh, what misery!
Cadmus: Does this appear to you to be a lion's head?
Agaue: No! I hold Pentheus' head in my accursed hand.
Cadmus: It is so. Tears have been shed for him, before you knew.
Agaue: But who killed him? How did he come into my hands?
Cadmus: O cruel hour, that brings a bitter truth to light!
Agaue: Tell me—my heart is bursting, I must know the rest.
Cadmus: It was you, Agaue, and your sisters. You killed him.
Agaue: Where was it done? Here in the palace? Or where else?
Cadmus: Where, long ago, Actaeon was devoured by hounds.
Agaue: Cithaeron, But what evil fate took Pentheus there?
Cadmus: He went to mock Dionysus and your Bacchic rites.
Agaue: Why were we on Cithaeron? What had brought us there.
Cadmus: You were possessed. All Thebes was in a Bacchic trance.
Agaue: Dionysus has destroyed us. Now I understand.
Cadmus: He was insulted. You refused to call him god.
Agaue: Father, where is the beloved body of my son?
Cadmus: Here. It was I who brought it, after painful search.
Agaue: And are his limbs now decently composed?
Cadmus: Not yet.
We came back to the city with all possible haste.
Agaue: How could I touch his body with these guilty hands?

Cadmus: Your guilt, my daughter, was not heavier than his.

Agaue: What part did Pentheus have, then, in my insanity?

Cadmus: He sinned like you, refusing reverence to a god.
Therefore the god has joined all in one ruin—you,
Your sisters, Pentheus—to destroy my house and me.
I have no son; and now, my unhappy child, I see
This son of yours dead by a shameful, hideous death.
You were the new hope of our house, its bond of strength,
Dear grandson. And Thebes feared you; no one dared insult
Your old grandfather if he saw you near; you would
Teach him his lesson. But now I shall live exiled,
Dishonoured—I, Cadmus the great, who planted here,
And reaped, that glorious harvest of the Theban race.
O dearest son—yes, even in death you shall be held
Most dear—you will never touch my beard again, and call
Me Grandfather, and put your arm around me and say,
'Who has wronged you or insulted you? Who is unkind,
Or vexes or disturbs you? Tell me, Grandfather,
That I may punish him.' Never again. For me
All that remains is pain; for you, the pity of death;
For your mother, tears; torment for our whole family.

If any man derides the unseen world, let him
Ponder the death of Pentheus, and believe in gods.

Chorus: I grieve for your fate, Cadmus; though your grandson's death
Was justly merited, it falls cruelly on you.

Agaue: Father, you see how one disastrous day has shattered
My whole life . . .

[At this point the two MSS on which the text of this play depends show a lacuna of considerable extent; it covers the end of this scene, in which Agaue mourns over Pentheus' body, and the appearance of Dionysus manifested as a god. The MSS resume in the middle of a speech by Dionysus. A number of quotations by ancient authors, together with less than 20 lines from *Christus Patiens* (an anonymous A.D. 4th-century work consisting largely of lines adapted from Greek tragedies) make it possible to attempt a guess at the content of the missing lines. Since this play is often performed, it seems worthwhile to provide here a usable text. In the lines that follow, the words printed in italics are mere conjecture, and have no value except as a credible completion of the probable sense; while those in Roman type represent the sources available from *Christus Patiens* and elsewhere.]

. . . my whole life, *turned my pride to shame, my happiness*
To horror. Now my only wish is to compose
My son's body for burial, and lament for him;
And then die. But this is not lawful; for my hands
Are filthy with pollution of their own making.
When I have spilt the blood I bore, and torn the flesh
That grew in my own womb, how can I after this
Enfold him to my breast, or chant his ritual dirge?
And yet, I beg you, pity me, and let me touch
My son, and say farewell to that dear body which
I cherished, and destroyed unknowning. It is right
That you should pity, for your hands are innocent.

Cadmus: *My daughter, you and I and our whole house are crushed*

And broken by the anger of this powerful god.
It is not for me to keep you from your son. Only
Be resolute, and steel your heart against a sight
Which must be fearful to any eyes, but most of all
To a mother's. (To attendants) Men, put down your burden on the ground
Before Agaue, and remove the covering.

Agaue: *Dear child, how cruel, how unnatural are these tears,*
Which should have fallen from your eyes on my dead face.
Now I shall die with none to mourn me. This is just;
For in my pride I did not recognise the god,
Nor understand the things I ought to have understood.
You too are punished for the same impiety;
But which is the more terrible, your fate or mine,
I cannot tell. Since you have suffered too, you will
Forgive both what I did, not knowing what I did,
And what I do now, touching you with unholy hands—
At once your cruellest enemy and your dearest friend.
I place your limbs as they should lie; I kiss the flesh
That my own body nourished and my own care reared
To manhood. Help me, father; lay his poor head here.
Make all exact and seemly, with what care we can.
O dearest face, O young fresh cheek? O kingly eyes,
Your light now darkened! O my son! See, with this veil
I now cover your head, your torn and bloodstained limbs.
Take him up, carry him to burial, a king
Lured to a shameful death by the anger of a god.
[*Enter* DIONYSUS]

Chorus: *But look! Who is this, rising above the palace door?*
It is he—Dionysus comes himself, no more disguised
As mortal, but in the glory of his divinity!

Dionysus: *Behold me, a god great and powerful, Dionysus,*
The son whom Theban Semele bore to immortal Zeus.
I come to the city of seven gates, to famous Thebes,
Whose people slighted me, denied my divinity,
Refused my ritual dances. Now they reap the fruit
Of impious folly. The royal house is overthrown;
The city's streets tremble in guilt, as every Theban
Repents too late his blindness and his blasphemy.
Foremost in sin was Pentheus, who not only scorned
My claims, but put me in fetters and insulted me.
Therefore death came to him in the most shameful way,
At his own mother's hands. This fate he justly earned;
No god can see his worship scorned, and hear his name
Profaned, and not take vengeance to the utmost limit.
Thus men may learn that gods are more powerful than they.

Agaue and her sisters must immediately
Depart from Thebes; their exile will be just penance
For the pollution which this blood has brought on them.
Never again shall they enjoy their native land;
That such defilement ever should appear before
The city's altars, is an offence to piety.

Now, Cadmus, hear what suffering Fate appoints for you.
[Here the MSS resume.]
You shall transmute your nature, and become a serpent.
Your wife Harmonia, whom her father Ares gave
To you, a mortal, likewise shall assume the nature
Of beasts, and live a snake. The oracle of Zeus
Foretells that you, at the head of a barbaric horde,
Shall with your wife drive forth a pair of heifers yoked,

And with your countless army destroy many cities;
But when they plunder Loxias' oracle, they shall find
A miserable homecoming. However, Ares shall
At last deliver both you and Harmonia,
And grant you immortal life among the blessed gods.
I who pronounce these fates am Dionysus, begotten
Not by a mortal father, but by Zeus. If you
Had chosen wisdom, when you would not, you would have lived
In wealth and safety, having the son of Zeus your friend.

Cadmus: Have mercy on us, Dionysus. We have sinned.

Dionysus: You know too late. You did not know me when you should.

Cadmus: We acknowledge this; but your revenge is merciless.

Dionysus: And rightly; I am a god, and you insulted me.

Cadmus: Gods should not be like mortals in vindictiveness.

Dionysus: All this my father Zeus ordained from the beginning.

Agaue: No hope, father. Our harsh fate is decreed: exile.

Dionysus: Then why put off a fate which is inevitable?

[*Exit* DIONYSUS]

Cadmus: Dear child, what misery has overtaken us all—
You, and your sisters, and your old unhappy father!
I must set forth from home and live in barbarous lands;
Further than that, it is foretold that I shall lead
A mixed barbarian horde to Hellas. And my wife,
Harmonia, Ares' daughter, and I too, must take
The brutish form of serpents; and I am to lead her thus
At the head of an armed force, to desecrate the tombs
And temples of our native land. I am to reach
No respite from this curse; I may not even cross
The downward stream of Acheron to find peace in death.

Agaue: And I in exile, father, shall live far from you.

Cadmus: Poor child, why do you cling to me, as the young swan
Clings fondly to the old, helpless and white with age?

Agaue: Where can I turn for comfort, homeless and exiled?

Cadmus: I do not know. Your father is little help to you.

Agaue: Farewell, my home; farewell the land I know.
Exiled, accursed and wretched, now I go
Forth from this door where first I came a bride.

Cadmus: Go, daughter, find some secret place to hide
Your shame and sorrow.

Agaue: Father, I weep for you.

Cadmus: I for your suffering, and your sisters' too.

Agaue: There is strange tyranny in the god who sent
Against your house this cruel punishment.

Cadmus: Not strange: our citizens despised his claim,
And you, and they, put him to open shame.

Agaue: Father, farewell.

Cadmus: Poor child! I cannot tell
How you can *fare well;* yet I say, Farewell.

Agaue: I go to lead my sisters by the hand
To share my wretchedness in a foreign land.

[*She turns to the Theban women who have been waiting
at the edge of the stage.*]

Come, see me forth.
Gods, lead me to some place
Where loath'd Cithaeron may not see my face,
Nor I Cithaeron. I have had my fill
Of mountain-ecstasy; now take who will
My holy ivy-wreath, my thyrsus-rod,
All that reminds me how I served this god!

[*Exit, followed by* CADMUS]

Chorus: Gods manifest themselves in many forms,
Bring many matters to surprising ends;
The things we thought would happen do not happen;
The unexpected God makes possible:
And that is what has happened here to-day.

[*Exeunt*]

One Question for Discussion

1. In a world governed by a god like Dionysus, where is justice? How can people plan their lives?

6

Greece: From Hellenic to Hellenistic World

"The name Greek is no longer a mark of race, but of outlook, and is accorded to those who share our culture rather than our blood," said the Athenian orator Isokrates in 380 B.C. By then the Greek city-states no longer exercised political and military dominance in the Hellenic world of the eastern Mediterranean, but their culture spread not only throughout the Mediterranean but into Egypt and the vast Persian empire as well. What caused the decline of the Greek city-states? Their contentious fervor and pride had enabled them to soundly defeat the much larger forces of the Persian empire. However, this was because they were, for the first and last time, united against a common foe. Afterwards their pride and aggressive independence caused endless squabbles with each other, culminating in the disastrous war between Athens and Sparta and assorted allies on both sides. The Persian Wars (490–479 B.C.) inspired confidence but the internecine Peloponnesian War (431–404 B.C.) left despair and decay in its wake. Not one city-state was strong enough to take control, so a federation was impossible. Sparta dominated for a time, followed by Thebes, Athens,[1] and Corinth, but always with the tireless Persians in the background manipulating events through bribery and coercion.

By the middle of the fourth century in a backwater of Greek civilization, King Philip of Macedonia began to move toward an empire that united all of Greece. Some purposes were gained by military strategy; however, most were through a series of wily political and diplomatic moves, accomplished despite repeated warnings by the Athenian orator Demosthanes (fig. 6.1). Upon Philip's assassination in 336 his brilliant young son, Alexander (fig. 6.2), who was a student of Aristotle's, became king. In one remarkable campaign Alexander brought all of Persia (including the territory of modern Turkey) as far east as India, Egypt, and all of Greece into one vast empire. In doing so he carried Greek culture

---

1. After ineffectual Spartan rule, Athens underwent a reign of terror under Kritias and the Thirty Tyrants, followed by a brief civil war. Democracy was restored in 401 B.C. It was the insecure government of a reestablished Athens that tried and condemned Sokrates in 399 B.C. (See the *Apology* on p. 130 for Plato's account of the trial.)

Figure 6.1 Portrait bust of Demosthanes. Roman marble copy, probably after a original bronze of 280/279 B.C. Ashmolean Museum, Oxford. This last great champion of Athenian liberty lived to see Athens free itself from Macedonia after Alexander's death in 323 B.C.

Figure 6.2 Portrait bust of Alexander the Great (356–323 B.C.) by Leochares (?). Original marble of 450–425 B.C., Akropolis Museum, Athens. The greatest military genius in history, Alexander conquered and Hellenized the then-known world in just twelve years.

as it had been influenced by many foreign sources throughout that vast territory. Significantly he established at least a half-dozen new cities named Alexandria throughout the empire, and in these he built libraries and other centers of culture. The Alexandria he built in Egypt was to supplant Athens as the cultural center of the world for centuries. Remnants of Alexander's empire survived until 146 B.C., when Rome finally conquered the last Achaean League, but the influence of Hellenistic art and thought was to flourish throughout most of the Roman period.

Our concern during this time must limit itself to the developments in art, which are discussed in chapter 7, and to the contributions of two philosophers, Plato and Aristotle.

Plato

Born in 427 B.C., two years after the death of Perikles, Plato (fig. 6.3) was a young man at the time of the Athenian defeat in the Peloponnesian War and an ardent student of Sokrates. It is impossible to distinguish between the thought of Plato and Sokrates in the early writings of Plato, for most of these are dialogues in which Sokrates is the principal speaker. It is probable that Plato included much of his own thought in these dialogues, or certainly that he reported the ideas of Sokrates with which he was in agreement. Only in the latter part of his life did he speak entirely for himself, as in the *Laws*.

Figure 6.3 Portrait bust of Plato. Boeringer Collection, Geneva. Roman copy (one of eighteen) of a bronze probably created by Silanion. Apparently the original was dedicated in the Academy after Plato's death in 347 B.C. Though his real name was Aristokles, Plato has always been known by his nickname, which means "the Broad."

Plato's thought about that-which-is-real is perhaps his most significant contribution to modern thought. In developing this he started with the work of Pythagoras and the Eleatic philosophers in that he accepted permanence and unchangeability as the basic criteria for reality, and he accepted the mind as the only way to approach a knowledge of the real. In so doing, he denied the reality of all the sense-apparent objects around us, whether they be trees, animals, humans, or even such abstract concepts as the various manifestations of love or justice. All sense-apparent things he regarded as shadows of the Real, made imperfect by an alliance with material stuff. (See his illustration of this in "The Allegory of the Cave" in the excerpts from the *Republic* later in this chapter.)

For Plato, reality consisted of ideas or essences of all basic things that had their existence beyond the grasp of the human senses or even of the human mind. These ideas had no physical attributes, no material substance, but were the "pure form" for all things we see and know in our earthly existence. One must bear in mind that these forms are not ideas-in-the-minds-of-people. Thus when one imagines the perfect tree or the perfect human being, we are not dealing with Plato's essences. The ideas had existence, they were unchanging, and they were the source, in that they gave form, of all material things. But the material thing, because it is allied with matter or flesh, is always a distorted or impure shadow of its essence.

Probably this is clear enough, but a homely illustration might not be out of order. We can imagine that an architect is commissioned to design a building. Probably it does not happen this way, but assume that one morning, after wrestling with the problems for some time, he suddenly sees the building in his mind perfectly, exactly as it should be. "Eureka," he cries. "This is *it*." So he dashes off to the drawing board. In drawing the plans, he has to make some changes in his original idea. For example, he has to stack the plumbing on the various levels directly above what is below. By the time the blueprints are finished, the building is no longer the same as it was when it was idea. Then comes the construction. Perhaps the builder faces a steel strike, and another material must be substituted for some of the steel members. The costs for the planned building may go beyond the money available, so sections must be cut out, and cheaper materials substituted for those in the original plan. But finally the building is complete and stands in its material form for people to see and use. When was the structure most real? A good argument can be made that it was most real when it was pure idea, and that it has become less real each time it became involved with substance or material. One suspects that the architect, at least, looking at the final product, will see it as only a shadow of what he had once seen in his mind. To avoid argument, let us accept these last statements as true. The physical building is but a clumsy manifestation of the "real" idea. Can we take another step now? Assume that the architect is God, and that the building is the universe.

The ideas for all things existed in God's mind, and these forms, essences, or immaterial patterns exist forever, but as they are mixed with material substance—wood, mineral, flesh—they become distorted and changed. Now, perhaps, we have Plato's belief about reality with but one more step needed. From our last picture subtract the picture of God, for although Plato frequently spoke of the gods, and often of God, he did not believe that these ideas were created; they simply existed eternally.

For a further illustration of this concept of reality, the student is referred to Plato's dialogue, *The Symposium,* where the nature of love is discussed. The discussion turns on the thought that in the realm of ideas, there is one that is beauty—not a beautiful sunset, or a beautiful person, just pure beauty. Many physical things can reflect this idea, among them a person. So that when someone says, "I am in love with Isabella (or Henry)" what they really mean is, "I am attracted by beauty, and Henry (or Isabella) reflects that idea to me."

There are a great many important philosophic repercussions from this Platonic belief about reality. One of the most important is the separation of the soul from the body, and the belief that soul was related to the realm of the essences, and that body was evil because it imprisoned and distracted the soul. This has been a major bone of contention in all Christian religion, for St. Augustine, in formulating the first unified Christian theology, borrowed a great deal from Platonism. Specifically, Plato believed that in the realm of ideas a hierarchy existed, starting at the bottom with the essences of plants and animals, and ending at the top with the idea of the good (the light or fire one encounters in "The Allegory of the Cave"). This good, translated into early Christian theology, became the concept of God as the highest and best pattern for all things, and the goal toward which all Christians should strive. The method of reaching it can easily become the method of despising the flesh as a hindrance to the soul in its aspiration.

The dialogue called the *Republic* gives us our best view of the Sokratic-Platonic idea of the nature of man on earth, and the nature of his government. A much later treatise, the *Laws,* gives the purely Platonic view of the same matter, differing somewhat from the beliefs stated in the *Republic.* In the first place, it should be made clear that the *Republic* is not Plato's formation of an ideal state as such. Instead, it is a discussion between Sokrates and his students concerning the nature of justice. Justice is not necessary when one has only an isolated individual, but it becomes more and more necessary within an ever-larger group. So in the *Republic,* the discussants formulate a picture of the luxurious state (one that goes beyond the provision of the barest physical needs of humans) in order to seek out the illusive quality, justice, that exists to a greater or lesser degree in the interrelationship of people.

In regard to humans themselves, Plato felt that people were dominated by one of three qualities: appetite, spirit, or intellect. For this reason he divided people into three classes, those of iron (or brass), those of silver, and those of gold. Those who were essentially people of appetite, iron, were to be the workers, including all who followed commercial pursuits. The silver, people of spirit, were to form the auxiliaries or soldier class, who had no property or money to distract them from their duty—the maintenance of order at home and protection from foreign enemies. The men or women of intellect, or the people of gold, were to be carefully educated to become the guardians of the state, the rulers, the philosopher-kings.

Education was to be the force that gave form to this state. The lowest class was to receive little or no education. The soldier or auxiliary group was to be taught gymnastics (to give them strong bodies, fit for their duties at all times), and music to make their personalities gentle toward their fellow citizens. In the discussion of this point, Sokrates uses the example of the good watchdog as an illustration of his point, for such a dog is gentle toward his master and friends, but fierce toward enemies. The soldier class should have such a nature, with their quality of spirit tempered by the study of music. The guardian class should have all of the education of the soldiers, then study methods of reasoning, and finally philosophy. After their years of study they were to be subjected to all sorts of trials and temptations to test their strength of character and their ability to make decisions on an unselfish basis, in terms of the general good. At about the age of fifty, after passing through this period of testing, the guardians would be called upon to rule the city. They would become the famous "philosopher-kings," and they would rule the state absolutely.

One notices immediately that this is a totalitarian state, with the exception that no lunatic would ever be able to rule. But the society is divided into strict classes; and Sokrates advocates a strict censorship of all stories and music the students are to hear, so that only the best and finest will enter into their souls. The classes of citizens are not controlled by birth or wealth, however, for Sokrates proposes the "great lie," which will be perpetrated on the citizens: all children will be told that the state is their mother, and they will be reared as wards of the city until they are about seven years of age. During these formative years they will be carefully observed in all their activities and their chief characteristics noted. At the end of this time they will be divided into the three classes according to their natural ability.

Insofar as the ultimate question of the nature of justice is concerned, Plato and Sokrates take the middle ground, the Golden Mean, which was ever a Greek ideal. In the qualities of men and women, wisdom should control the other qualities, so that appetite would be curbed to the point of temperance, spirit should be limited to the point of courage, and intellect should become wisdom. When these conditions are met, justice emerges. These—temperance, courage, wisdom, and justice were the great Platonic virtues. Later on, the Christians were to add faith, hope, and love to these to establish the seven cardinal virtues. The difference between the Platonic intellectual virtues and the Christian emotional and spiritual virtues illustrates a fundamental difference between the hopes and aspirations of the two cultures.

Aristotle

Aristotle came from a very different background than that of Plato, and although he studied with Plato at the academy, his answers to the important questions are quite different, perhaps because of the difference in youthful experience. Aristotle's father was a physician in northern Greece and early in Aristotle's life was called to the city of Pella to serve as a physician in the court of King Philip. Perhaps Aristotle's inquiring mind about sense-apparent things, his interest in experimentation, his concern in change rather than permanence, and his inability to accept the mind alone as a guide to truth came from his father's interest in similar things. As a matter of fact, exactly as Plato's thought had its source in the Eleatics and Pythagoras, Aristotle's mature conclusions have their roots in the Ionians.

Aristotle is one of the most extraordinary minds of all time; the keenness of his intellect, the range of his interests and studies, and the staggering amount of information and speculation in his enormous collection of writings, rouse the admiration and awe of any who read his work. Not the least of his distinctions was the fact that he served as tutor to the youthful Prince Alexander, and must have had a great influence on the brilliant career of that monarch. After this period of tutoring, Aristotle went to Athens and founded his own school, the Lyceum. With Plato, he was to shape the course of Western thought: these two men are probably the most powerful influences from our Greek heritage.

As we have seen, Plato's quest for the permanent, the idea or form, rather than the actuality of experience, led him into a dualism that separates form from substance, soul from body. Aristotle, profoundly interested in the changing life about him, tried to reconcile the two. Perhaps the difference could be expressed in this way: when Plato wished to discuss his ideas of the state, he wrote the *Republic,* and later the *Laws,* theoretical speculations that construct the wholly imaginary idea of a state. When Aristotle wished to discuss his ideas of the state, he and his students collected and studied the constitutions of 158 Greek city-states as a prelude to the work known as *Politics.*

It is an impossible task, and not to the present purpose, to even mention the multitude of Aristotle's writings. His speculations ranged all the way from his logic, the proper process of thought, through biology, physics, metaphysics, ethics, law and politics, and literary criticism (see his *Poetics* at the end of this chapter). Only two of his ideas concern us here: one is his view of the nature of reality; the other is his idea of the conduct of life in the light of that view. These last are drawn from the *Nicomachean Ethics* and the *Eudemian Ethics,* summaries of his thought about the proper conduct of life as written by his son and one of his students.

For Aristotle, the abstract idea or form of Plato's teaching could not be separated from the matter or substance by which it was known; the two must somehow come together as different aspects of the same thing. Thus Plato's "ideal" chair did not exist for Aristotle apart from the actual wood and metal that composed it. A brick is a brick only when the "idea" brick and the clay composing it come together; then the brick is "real." The brick then may become the matter or substance of another "idea," and become house; and the house, in turn, may be substance to the idea of town or city. At every stage, the union of substance and form, of matter and idea, is necessary to constitute "reality"; but there is a progression, upwards or downwards. The substance that Plato is not concerned with becomes for Aristotle the basis for higher, more complex realities when it is informed by idea or form. Such, at least, is the direction of the difference between the two men; Plato's static view becomes more dynamic in Aristotle's teaching.

The process of change (which Plato never satisfactorily explains) is accounted for, by Aristotle, in his theory of enteleche (en–TEL–uh–kee; the Greek word is made of the particles en, "within"; telos, "purpose or end"; and echaia, "having, possessing"). That is to say, it is in the nature of things that they have within them a goal, a destiny, to fulfill: the seed becomes the plant, for that is its "enteleche"; the clay becomes the brick, for that is its "enteleche." The movement upward through increasing complexity is the "enteleche" of the universe; and the cause of the process, drawing all things toward their own perfection, is God, the First Cause, who moved all things without being moved: the "Unmoved Mover," in Aristotle's phrase.

The motive power of Aristotle's God is apparently not love, as Christianity might contend, nor will, as Judaism might argue; it is rather that there seems to be a cosmic yearning toward perfection, and that perfection is, by definition, God. Aristotle's customary view of the necessity for the union of both form and matter to constitute reality here breaks down (or more kindly, "transcends itself"?) for such a God must be pure form, with none of the inherent weakness or imperfection of the material.[2] God is the only instance where pure form is separated from matter.

How does one lead the good life? It is interesting to note that Aristotle makes no apology for thinking that it must begin with sufficient means; he holds no ascetic views on the matter, and quite matter-of-factly begins with an assumption of enough material possession to allow one the choice of doing as he would. Granted, however, the adequate wealth, what does one do? The enteleche of which he speaks implies that there is a goal, or end, reached when the person or thing is functioning properly—that is, in accord with its own inner purposes; when conditions permit such functioning, there is a highest good, a summum bonum, attained. The enteleche of humans, then, would lead them to their own summum bonum, their own best functioning, the worthy and proper fulfillment of their humanity. And since humans are for Aristotle the "rational animal," that fulfillment would be the life of reason. When they are living harmoniously, using their minds, functioning in family and state (for Aristotle also calls humans a "political," i.e., social animal), they have achieved their greatest good. Such a life has two implications, among many others, that concern us here.

One is that such a life will be a life of virtue, or excellence. But virtues may fail by being deficient, or by being carried to excess; the middle ground between is what is to be desired. Courage, for instance, is a virtue; but it may be perverted through deficiency into cowardice, or no less perverted by being carried to the excess of foolhardiness, mere rashness. Generosity is a virtue, but it can be carried to the excess of prodigality and wastefulness, or perverted through deficiency to stinginess. To mediate between extremes, to discover the "Golden Mean"—which it is to be noted is a relative and not an absolute matter— that is to achieve virtue.

The other implication, then, is that people's best use of reason is in the life of contemplation. They must have time to read, to talk, to think about the whole idea of excellence, that they may achieve the high-mindedness that is their summum bonum; the word that Aristotle uses is "magnanimity." Such a quality is not to be won in the heat and dust of the marketplace; though good persons will perform their duties as a member of society, still the life of action is not as good as the life of contemplation.

With this brief discussion of a few of the ideas of Aristotle, we come to the end of our background of Greek civilization in Greece itself. The Hellenistic culture was to flourish for many years in such centers as Egyptian Alexandria and Pergamum in Asia Minor. Indeed, much of Roman culture formed itself around Hellenistic principles.

Greek civilization had started within the shadow of superstition and tradition in archaic times. Slowly those bondages had been cut away until a very delicate balance was achieved between the freedom of each individual person and the welfare of the group in Athens early in the reign of Perikles. The philosophers, the authors, and the artists of the time took an active part in politics, and conducted their affairs in the Agora, the marketplace.

---

2. "Such then is the principle upon which depend the heavens and the world of nature. And its life (i.e., the principle, or God) is like the best that we enjoy, and enjoy but for a short time; for it is ever in this state, which we cannot be. And if then God is always in that good state in which we sometimes are, this compels our wonder; and if in a better state, then this compels it yet more. And God is in a better state. We say therefore, that God is a living being, eternal, most good; so that life and a continual eternal existence belong to God; for this is God." (Aristotle, *Metaphysics,* XII, 7.)

But change is inevitable. In Athens it would seem that the knife-edge between individuality and the welfare of the group was too thin, the balance on it too precarious, for a group of people to maintain an equilibrium for a long period of time. The skeptical sophists taught that complete individuality was the goal—violating Aeschylus's doctrine of the mean between autocracy and anarchy. The original strength of the city was sapped, but to give rise to a new and different kind of strength in the broadened horizons of Hellenistic culture. It is interesting that both Plato and Aristotle (except for their brief efforts to educate a king: Plato as tutor for the Syracusan Dionysius, Aristotle as Alexander's tutor) stood apart from politics and the vigorous life of the time; they deserted the active marketplace. They were contemplatives, aware that something had gone wrong, that the dream had somehow failed, and each in his own way, introspected into himself and his culture to discover what had failed. Probably nothing had really gone "wrong." Change had simply taken place in the cultural milieu, leading to new forms of life, new types of exploration into human existence, new forms of freedom.

The Romans brought about a different type of balance in civilization, and this will be discussed in the next unit of our work.

Bibliography

Translations of Original Material

Aristophanes. *The Comedies of Aristophanes.* Fitts and Fitzgerald, eds. Excellent translations, done with a real sense of humor appropriate to the subject. For example, in Lysistrata, the girl from Sparta speaks with a fine Texas drawl.

Aristotle. *Nicomachean Ethics.* Any recent edition.

Plato. *Great Dialogues of Plato.* Translated by W.H.D. Rouse. New York: New American Library.

Xenophon. *The Persian Expedition.* Rex Warner's translation of the *Anabasis*.

Fiction

Renault, Mary. *The Mask of Apollo.* New York: Bantam Books, 1974. Using a traveling actor as the central figure of the novel, Renault gives a lively picture of the times of Plato. See also her last two novels dealing with Alexander the Great, *The Persian Boy* and *Fire from Heaven*.

Literary Selections

APOLOGY

Plato (427–347 B.C.)

Sokrates was tried in 399 B.C. before a generally hostile jury of 501 citizens on vague charges of impropriety towards the gods and corruption of the young. Long regarded as a suspicious character because of his relentless questioning of fellow Athenians, Sokrates, because of a general amnesty, could not be charged for any offenses prior to the defeat of Athens

Figure 6.4 Portrait bust of Sokrates. Roman marble copy of an original bronze supposedly created by Lysippos in ca. 350 B.C. Museo della Terme, Rome.

in 404 B.C. The unspoken charges were: (1) being the teacher of Alkbiades the traitor (interpreted as a corruptor of the young), (2) association with the Thirty Tyrants (viewed as possible collaboration), (3) accepting money for teaching argumentation (mistakenly taking him for a Sophist), and (4) causing general intellectual unrest. Sokrates (fig. 6.4) cheerfully admits to causing unrest, contending that the gods had commanded him to search into himself and other men to find the truth. This trial is his apology for his philosophical life. The translation is by F. J. Church and R. D. Cumming, whose spelling of proper names has been retained.

CHARACTERS
Socrates
Meletus

SCENE—The Court of Justice

Socrates. I cannot tell what impression my accusers have made upon you, Athenians. For my own part, I know that they nearly made me forget who I was, so persuasive were they; and yet they have scarcely uttered one single word of truth. But of all their many falsehoods, the one which astonished me most was when they said that I was a clever speaker, and that you must be careful not to let me deceive you. I thought that it was most shameless of them not to be ashamed to talk in that way; for as soon as I open my mouth they will be refuted, and I shall prove that I am not a clever speaker in any way at all—unless, indeed, by a clever speaker they mean a man who speaks the truth. If that is their meaning, I agree with them that I am an orator not to be compared with them. My accusers, then I repeat, have said little or nothing that is true; but from me you shall hear the whole truth. Certainly you will not hear an elaborate speech, Athenians, dressed up, like theirs, with words and phrases. I will say to you what I have to say, without preparation, and in the words which come first, for I believe that my cause is just; so let none of you expect anything else. Indeed, my friends, it would hardly be seemly for me, at my age, to come before you like a young man with his specious phrases. But there is one thing, Athenians, which I do most earnestly beg and entreat of you. Do not be surprised and do not interrupt with shouts if in my defense I speak in the same way that I am accustomed to speak in the market-place, at the tables of the money-changers, where many of you have heard me, and elsewhere. The truth is this. I am more than seventy years old, and this is the first time that I have ever come before a law-court; so your manner of speech here is quite strange to me. If I had been really a stranger, you would have forgiven me for speaking in the language and the manner of my native country; and so now I ask you to grant me what I think I have a right to claim. Never mind the manner of my speech—it may be better or it may be worse—give your whole attention to the question, Is what I say just, or is it not? That is what makes a good judge, as speaking the truth makes a good orator.

I have to defend myself, Athenians, first against the old false accusations of my old accusers, and then against the later ones of my present accusers. For many men have been accusing me to you, and for very many years, who have not uttered a word of truth; and I fear them more than I fear Anytus and his associates, formidable as they are. But, my friends, those others are still more formidable; for they got hold of most of you when you were children, and they have been more persistent in accusing me untruthfully and have persuaded you that there is a certain Socrates, a wise man, who speculates about the heavens, and who investigates things that are beneath the earth, and who can make the worse argument appear the stronger. These men, Athenians, who spread abroad this report are the accusers whom I fear; for their hearers think that persons who pursue such inquiries never believe in the gods. Then they are many, and their attacks have been going on for a long time, and they spoke to you when you were at the age most readily to believe them, for you were all young, and many of you were children, and there was no one to answer them when they attacked me. And the most unreasonable thing of all is that I do not even know their names: I cannot tell you who they are except when one happens to be a comic poet. But all the rest who have persuaded you, from motives of resentment and prejudice, and sometimes, it may be, from conviction, are hardest to cope with. For I cannot call any one of them forward in court to cross-examine him. I have, as it were, simply to spar with shadows in my defense, and to put questions which there is no one to answer. I ask you, therefore, to believe that, as I say, I have been attacked by two kinds of accusers—first, by Meletus and his associates, and, then, by those older ones of whom I have spoken. And, with your leave, I will defend myself first against my old accusers; for you heard their accusations first, and they were much more forceful than my present accusers are.

Well, I must make my defense, Athenians, and try in the short time allowed me to remove the prejudice which you have been so long a time acquiring. I hope that I may manage to do this, if it be good for you and for me, and that my defense may be successful; but I am quite aware of the nature of my task, and I know that it is a difficult one. Be the outcome, however, as is pleasing to God, I must obey the law and make my defense.

Let us begin from the beginning, then, and ask what is the accusation which has given rise to the prejudice against me, which was what Meletus relied on when he brought his indictment. What is the prejudice which my enemies have been spreading about me? I must assume that they are formally accusing me, and read their indictment. It would run somewhat in this fashion: "Socrates is a wrongdoer, who meddles with inquiries into things beneath the earth and in the heavens, and who makes the worse argument appear the stronger, and who teaches others these same things." That is what they say; and in the comedy of Aristophanes[3] you yourselves saw a man called Socrates swinging round in a basket and saying that he walked the air, and sputtering a great deal of nonsense about matters of which I understand nothing, either more or less. I do not mean to disparage that kind of knowledge if there is any one who is wise about these matters. I trust Meletus may never be able to prosecute me for that. But the truth is, Athenians, I have nothing to do with these matters, and almost all of you are yourselves my witnesses of this. I beg all of you who have ever heard me discussing, and they are many, to inform your neighbors and tell them if any of you have ever heard me discussing such matters, either more or less. That will show you that the other common statements about me are as false as this one.

But the fact is that not one of these is true. And if you have heard that I undertake to educate men, and make money by so doing, that is not true either, though I think that it would be a fine thing to be able to educate men, as Gorgias of Leontini, and Prodicus of Ceos, and Hippias of Elis do. For each of them, my friends, can go into any city, and persuade the young men to leave the society of their fellow citizens, with any of whom they might associate for nothing, and to be only too glad to be allowed to pay money for the privilege of associating with themselves. And I believe that there is another wise man from Paros residing in Athens at this moment. I happened to meet Callias, the son of Hipponicus, a man who has spent more money on sophists than every one else put together. So I said to him (he has two sons), Callias, if your two sons had been foals or calves, we could have hired a trainer for them who would have made them perfect in the virtue which belongs to their nature. He would have been either a groom or a farmer. But whom do you intend to take to train them, seeing that they are men? Who understands the virtue which belongs to men and to citizens? I suppose that you must have thought of this, because of your sons. Is there such a person, said I, or not? Certainly there is, he replied. Who is he, said I, and where does he come from, and what is his fee? Evenus, Socrates, he replied, from Paros, five minae. Then I thought that Evenus was a fortunate person if he really understood this art and could teach so cleverly. If I had possessed knowledge of that kind, I should have been conceited and disdainful. But, Athenians, the truth is that I do not possess it.

Perhaps some of you may reply: But, Socrates, what is the trouble with you? What has given rise to these prejudices against you? You must have been doing

---

3. *The Clouds.* The basket was satirically assumed to facilitate Socrates' inquiries into things in the heavens.

something out of the ordinary. All these rumors and reports of you would never have arisen if you had not been doing something different from other men. So tell us what it is, that we may not give our verdict in the dark. I think that that is a fair question, and I will try to explain to you what it is that has raised these prejudices against me and given me this reputation. Listen, then. Some of you, perhaps, will think that I am joking, but I assure you that I will tell you the whole truth. I have gained this reputation, Athenians, simply by reason of a certain wisdom. But by what kind of wisdom? It is by just that wisdom which is perhaps human wisdom. In that, it may be, I am really wise. But the men of whom I was speaking just now must be wise in a wisdom which is greater than human wisdom, or else I cannot describe it, for certainly I know nothing of it myself, and if any man says that I do, he lies and speaks to arouse prejudice against me. Do not interrupt me with shouts, Athenians, even if you think that I am boasting. What I am going to say is not my own. I will tell you who says it, and he is worthy of your respect. I will bring the god of Delphi to be the witness of my wisdom, if it is wisdom at all, and of its nature. You remember Chaerephon. From youth upwards he was my comrade; and also a partisan of your democracy, sharing your recent exile[4] and returning with you. You remember, too, Chaerephon's character—how impulsive he was in carrying through whatever he took in hand. Once he went to Delphi and ventured to put this question to the oracle—I entreat you again, my friends, not to interrupt me with your shouts—he asked if there was any one who was wiser than I. The priestess answered that there was no one. Chaerephon himself is dead, but his brother here will witness to what I say.

Now see why I tell you this. I am going to explain to you how the prejudice against me has arisen. When I heard of the oracle I began to reflect: What can the god mean by this riddle? I know very well that I am not wise, even in the smallest degree. Then what can he mean by saying that I am the wisest of men? It cannot be that he is speaking falsely, for he is a god and cannot lie. For a long time I was at a loss to understand his meaning. Then, very reluctantly, I turned to investigate it in this manner: I went to a man who was reputed to be wise, thinking that there, if anywhere, I should prove the answer wrong, and meaning to point out to the oracle its mistake, and to say, "You said that I was the wisest of men, but this man is wiser than I am." So I examined the man—I need not tell you his name, he was a politician—but this was the result, Athenians. When I conversed with him I came to see that, though a great many persons, and most of all he himself, thought that he was wise, yet he was not wise. Then I tried to prove to him that he was not wise, though he fancied that he was; and by so doing I made him indignant, and many of the bystanders. So when I went away, I thought to myself, "I am wiser than this man: neither of us knows anything that is really worthwhile, but he thinks that he has knowledge when he has not, while I, having no knowledge, do not think that I have. I seem, at any rate, to be a little wiser than he is on this point: I do not think that I know what I do not know." Next I went to another man who was reputed to be still wiser than the last, with exactly the same result. And there again I made him, and many other men, indignant.

Then I went on to one man after another, seeing that I was arousing indignation every day, which caused me much grief and anxiety. Still I thought that I must set the god's command above everything. So I had to go to every man who seemed to possess any knowledge, and

investigate the meaning of the oracle. Athenians, I must tell you the truth; by the dog, this was the result of the investigation which I made at the god's bidding: I found that the men whose reputation for wisdom stood highest were nearly the most lacking in it, while others who were looked down on as common people were much more intelligent. Now I must describe to you the wanderings which I undertook, like Heraclean labors, to prove the oracle irrefutable. After the politicians, I went to the poets, tragic, dithyrambic, and others, thinking that there I should find myself manifestly more ignorant than they. So I took up the poems on which I thought that they had spent most pains, and asked them what they meant, hoping at the same time to learn something from them. I am ashamed to tell you the truth, my friends, but I must say it. Almost any one of the bystanders could have talked about the works of these poets better than the poets themselves. So I soon found that it is not by wisdom that the poets create their works, but by a certain natural power and by inspiration, like soothsayers and prophets, who say many fine things, but who understand nothing of what they say. The poets seemed to me to be in a similar situation. And at the same time I perceived that, because of their poetry, they thought that they were the wisest of men in other matters, too, which they were not. So I went away again, thinking that I had the same advantage over the poets that I had over the politicians.

Finally, I went to the artisans, for I knew very well that I possessed no knowledge at all worth speaking of, and I was sure that I should find that they knew many fine things. And in that I was not mistaken. They knew what I did not know, and so far they were wiser than I. But, Athenians, it seemed to me that the skilled artisans had the same failing as the poets. Each of them believed himself to be extremely wise in matters of the greatest importance because he was skilful in his own art: and this presumption of theirs obscured their real wisdom. So I asked myself, on behalf of the oracle, whether I would choose to remain as I was, without either their wisdom or their ignorance, or to possess both, as they did. And I answered to myself and to the oracle that it was better for me to remain as I was.

From this examination, Athenians, has arisen much fierce and bitter indignation, and from this a great many prejudices about me, and people say that I am "a wise man." For the bystanders always think that I am wise myself in any matter wherein I refute another. But, gentlemen, I believe that the god is really wise, and that by this oracle he meant that human wisdom is worth little or nothing. I do not think that he meant that Socrates was wise. He only made use of my name, and took me as an example, as though he would say to men, "He among you is the wisest who, like Socrates, knows that in truth his wisdom is worth nothing at all." Therefore I still go about testing and examining every man whom I think wise, whether he be a citizen or a stranger, as the god has commanded me; and whenever I find that he is not wise, I point out to him, on the god's behalf, that he is not wise. I am so busy in this pursuit that I have never had leisure to take any part worth mentioning in public matters or to look after my private affairs. I am in great poverty as the result of my service to the god.

---

4. During the totalitarian regime of *The Thirty* which remained in power for eight months (404 B.C.), five years before the trial.

Besides this, the young men who follow me about, who are the sons of wealthy persons and have the most leisure, take pleasure in hearing men cross-examined. They often imitate me among themselves; then they try their hands at cross-examining other people. And, I imagine, they find plenty of men who think that they know a great deal when in fact they know little or nothing. Then the persons who are cross-examined get angry with me instead of with themselves, and say that Socrates is an abomination and corrupts the young. When they are asked, "Why, what does he do? what does he teach?" they do not know what to say; but, not to seem at a loss, they repeat the stock charges against all philosophers, and allege that he investigates things in the air and under the earth, and that he teaches people to disbelieve in the gods, and to make the worse argument appear the stronger. For, I suppose, they would not like to confess the truth, which is that they are shown up as ignorant pretenders to knowledge that they do not possess. So they have been filling your ears with their bitter prejudices for a long time, for they are ambitious, energetic, and numerous; and they speak vigorously and persuasively against me. Relying on this, Meletus, Anytus, and Lycon have attacked me. Meletus is indignant with me on the part of the poets, Anytus on the part of the artisans and politicians, and Lycon on the part of the orators. And so, as I said at the beginning, I shall be surprised if I am able, in the short time allowed me for my defense, to remove from your minds this prejudice which has grown so strong. What I have told you, Athenians, is the truth: I neither conceal nor do I suppress anything, small or great. Yet I know that it is just this plainness of speech which rouses indignation. But that is only a proof that my words are true, and that the prejudice against me, and the causes of it, are what I have said. And whether you investigate them now or hereafter, you will find that they are so.

What I have said must suffice as my defense against the charges of my first accusers. I will try next to defend myself against Meletus, that "good patriot," as he calls himself, and my later accusers. Let us assume that they are a new set of accusers, and read their indictment, as we did in the case of the others. It runs thus. He says that Socrates is a wrongdoer who corrupts the youth, and who does not believe in the gods whom the state believes in, but in other new divinities. Such is the accusation. Let us examine each point in it separately. Meletus says that I do wrong by corrupting the youth. But I say, Athenians, that he is doing wrong, for he is playing a solemn joke by casually bringing men to trial, and pretending to have a solemn interest in matters to which he has never given a moment's thought. Now I will try to prove to you that it is so.

Come here, Meletus. Is it not a fact that you think it very important that the young should be as good as possible?

Meletus. It is.

Socrates. Come then, tell the judges who is it who improves them? You care so much,[5] you must know. You are accusing me, and bringing me to trial, because, as you say, you have discovered that I am the corrupter of the youth. Come now, reveal to the gentlemen who improves them. You see, Meletus, you have nothing to say; you are silent. But don't you think that this is shameful? Is not your silence a conclusive proof of what I say—that you have never cared. Come, tell us, my good man, who makes the young better?

Mel. The laws.

Socr. That, my friend, is not my question. What man improves the young, who starts with the knowledge of the laws?

Mel. The judges here, Socrates.

Socr. What do you mean, Meletus? Can they educate the young and improve them?

Mel. Certainly.

Socr. All of them? or only some of them?

Mel. All of them.

Socr. By Hera, that is good news! Such a large supply of benefactors! And do the listeners here improve them, or not?

Mel. They do.

Socr. And do the senators?

Mel. Yes.

Socr. Well then, Meletus, do the members of the assembly corrupt the young or do they again all improve them?

Mel. They, too, improve them.

Socr. Then all the Athenians, apparently, make the young into good men except me, and I alone corrupt them. Is that your meaning?

Mel. Most certainly; that is my meaning.

Socr. You have discovered me to be most unfortunate. Now tell me: do you think that the same holds good in the case of horses? Does one man do them harm and every one else improve them? On the contrary, is it not one man only, or a very few—namely, those who are skilled with horses—who can improve them, while the majority of men harm them if they use them and have anything to do with them? Is it not so, Meletus, both with horses and with every other animal? Of course it is, whether you and Anytus say yes or no. The young would certainly be very fortunate if only one man corrupted them, and every one else did them good. The truth is, Meletus, you prove conclusively that you have never thought about the youth in your life. You exhibit your carelessness in not caring for the very matters about which you are prosecuting me.

Now be so good as to tell us, Meletus, is it better to live among good citizens or bad ones? Answer, my friend. I am not asking you a difficult question. Do not the bad harm their associates and the good, good?

Mel. Yes.

Socr. Is there any one who would rather be injured than benefited by his companions? Answer, my good sir; you are obliged by the law to answer. Does any one like to be injured?

Mel. Certainly not.

Socr. Well then, are you prosecuting me for corrupting the young and making them worse, voluntarily or involuntarily?

Mel. For doing it voluntarily.

Socr. What, Meletus? Do you mean to say that you, who are so much younger than I, are yet so much wiser than I that you know that bad citizens always do evil, and that good citizens do good, to those with whom they come in contact, while I am so extraordinarily ignorant as not to know that, if I make any of my companions evil, he will probably injure me in some way, and as to commit this great evil, as you allege, voluntarily? You will not

---

5. Throughout the following passage Socrates plays on the etymology of the name "Meletus" as meaning "the man who cares."

make me believe that, nor anyone else either, I should think. Either I do not corrupt the young at all or if I do I do so involuntarily: so that you are lying in either case. And if I corrupt them involuntarily, the law does not call upon you to prosecute me for an error which is involuntary, but to take me aside privately and reprove and educate me. For, of course, I shall cease from doing wrong involuntarily, as soon as I know that I have been doing wrong. But you avoided associating with me and educating me; instead you bring me up before the court, where the law sends persons, not for education, but for punishment.

The truth is, Athenians, as I said, it is quite clear that Meletus has never cared at all about these matters. However, now tell us, Meletus, how do you say that I corrupt the young? Clearly, according to your indictment, by teaching them not to believe in the gods the state believes in, but other new divinities instead. You mean that I corrupt the young by that teaching, do you not?

Mel. Yes, most certainly I mean that.

Socr. Then in the name of these gods of whom we are speaking, explain yourself a little more clearly to me and to these gentlemen here. I cannot understand what you mean. Do you mean that I teach the young to believe in some gods, but not in the gods of the state? Do you accuse me of teaching them to believe in strange gods? If that is your meaning, I myself believe in some gods, and my crime is not that of complete atheism. Or do you mean that I do not believe in the gods at all myself, and that I teach other people not to believe in them either?

Mel. I mean that you do not believe in the gods in any way whatever.

Socr. You amaze me, Meletus! Why do you say that? Do you mean that I believe neither the sun nor the moon to be gods, like other men?

Mel. I swear he does not, judges; he says that the sun is a stone, and the moon earth.

Socr. My dear Meletus, do you think that you are prosecuting Anaxagoras? You must have a very poor opinion of these men, and think them illiterate, if you imagine that they do not know that the works of Anaxagoras of Clazomenae are full of these doctrines. And so young men learn these things from me, when they can often buy them in the theatre for a drachma at most, and laugh at Socrates were he to pretend that these doctrines, which are very peculiar doctrines, too, were his own. But please tell me, do you really think that I do not believe in the gods at all?

Mel. Most certainly I do. You are a complete atheist.

Socr. No one believes that, Meletus, not even you yourself. It seems to me, Athenians, that Meletus is very insolent and reckless, and that he is prosecuting me simply out of insolence, recklessness and youthful bravado. For he seems to be testing me, by asking me a riddle that has no answer. "Will this wise Socrates," he says to himself, "see that I am joking and contradicting myself? or shall I deceive him and every one else who hears me?" Meletus seems to me to contradict himself in his indictment: it is as if he were to say, "Socrates is a wrongdoer who does not believe in the gods, but who believes in the gods." But this is joking.

Now, my friends, let us see why I think that this is his meaning. Do you answer me, Meletus; and do you, Athenians, remember the request which I made to you at the start, and do not interrupt me with shouts if I talk in my customary manner.

Is there any man, Meletus, who believes in the existence of things pertaining to men and not in the existence of men? Make him answer the question, gentlemen, without these interruptions. Is there any man who believes in the existence of horsemanship and not in the existence of horses? or in flute-playing and not in flute-players? There is not, my friend. If you will not answer, I will tell both you and the judges. But you must answer my next question. Is there any man who believes in the existence of divine things and not in the existence of divinities?

Mel. There is not.

Socr. I am very glad that these gentlemen have managed to extract an answer from you. Well then, you say that I believe in divine things, whether they be old or new ones, and that I teach others to believe in them; at any rate, according to your statement, I believe in divine things. That you have sworn in your indictment. But if I believe in divine things, I suppose it follows necessarily that I believe in divinities. Is it not so? It is. I assume that you grant that, as you do not answer. But do we not believe that divinities are either gods themselves or the children of the gods? Do you admit that?

Mel. I do.

Socr. Then you admit that I believe in divinities. Now, if these divinities are gods, then, as I say, you are joking and asking a riddle, and asserting that I do not believe in the gods, and at the same time that I do, since I believe in divinities. But if these divinities are the illegitimate children of the gods, either by the nymphs or by other mothers, as they are said to be, then, I ask, what man could believe in the existence of the children of the gods, and not in the existence of the gods? That would be as absurd as believing in the existence of the offspring of horses and asses, and not in the existence of horses and asses. You must have indicted me in this manner, Meletus, either to test me or because you could not find any crime that you could accuse me of with truth. But you will never contrive to persuade any man with any sense at all that a belief in divine things and things of the gods does not necessarily involve a belief in divinities, and in the gods, and in heroes.

But in truth, Athenians, I do not think that I need say very much to prove that I have not committed the crime for which Meletus is prosecuting me. What I have said is enough to prove that. But I repeat it is certainly true, as I have already told you, that I have aroused much indignation. That is what will cause my condemnation if I am condemned; not Meletus nor Anytus either, but that prejudice and resentment of the multitude which have been the destruction of many good men before me, and I think will be so again. There is no fear that I shall be the last victim.

Perhaps some one will say: "Are you not ashamed, Socrates, of leading a life which is very likely now to cause your death?" I should answer him with justice, and say: "My friend, if you think that a man of any worth at all ought to reckon the chances of life and death when he acts, or that he ought to think of anything but whether he is acting rightly or wrongly, and as a good or a bad man would act, you are mistaken. According to you, the demigods who died at Troy would be foolish, and among them the son of Thetis, who thought nothing of danger when the alternative was disgrace. For when his mother—and she was a goddess—addressed him, when he was resolved to slay Hector, in this fashion, "My son, if you avenge the death of your comrade Patroclus and slay

Hector, you will die yourself, for 'fate awaits you straightway after Hector's death' "; when he heard this, he scorned danger and death; he feared much more to live a coward and not to avenge his friend. "Let me punish the evildoer and straightway die," he said, "that I may not remain here by the beaked ships jeered at, encumbering the earth."[6] Do you suppose that he thought of danger or of death? For this, Athenians, I believe to be the truth. Wherever a man's station is, whether he has chosen it of his own will, or whether he has been placed at it by his commander, there it is his duty to remain and face the danger without thinking of death or of any other thing except disgrace.

When the generals whom you chose to command me, Athenians, assigned me my station at Potidaea and at Amphipolis and at Delium, I remained where they stationed me and ran the risk of death, like other men. It would be very strange conduct on my part if I were to desert my station now from fear of death or of any other thing when God has commanded me—as I am persuaded that he has done—to spend my life in searching for wisdom, and in examining myself and others. That would indeed be a very strange thing. Then certainly I might with justice be brought to trial for not believing in the gods, for I should be disobeying the oracle, and fearing death and thinking myself wise when I was not wise. For to fear death, my friends, is only to think ourselves wise without really being wise, for it is to think that we know what we do not know. For no one knows whether death may not be the greatest good that can happen to man. But men fear it as if they knew quite well that it was the greatest of evils. And what is this but that shameful ignorance of thinking that we know what we do not know? In this matter, too, my friends, perhaps I am different from the multitude; and if I were to claim to be at all wiser than others, it would be because, not knowing very much about the other world, I do not think I know. But I do know very well that it is evil and disgraceful to do wrong, and not to be persuaded by my superior, whether man or god. I will never do what I know to be evil, and shrink in fear from what I do not know to be good or evil. Even if you acquit me now, and do not listen to Anytus' argument that, if I am to be acquitted, I ought never to have been brought to trial at all, and that, as it is, you are bound to put me to death because, as he said, if I escape, all your sons will be utterly corrupted by practising what Socrates teaches. If you were therefore to say to me, "Socrates, this time we will not listen to Anytus; we will let you go, but on this condition that you give up this investigation of yours, and philosophy; if you are found following those pursuits again, you shall die." I say, if you offered to let me go on these terms, I should reply: "Athenians, I hold you in the highest regard and affection, but I will be persuaded by the god rather than you; and as long as I have breath and strength I will not give up philosophy and exhorting you and declaring the truth to every one of you whom I meet, saying, as I am accustomed, "My good friend, you are a citizen of Athens, a city which is very great and very famous for its wisdom and power—are you not ashamed of caring so much for the making of money and for fame and prestige, when you neither think nor care about wisdom and truth and the improvement of your soul?" And if he disputes my words and says that he does care about these things, I shall not at once release him and go away: I shall question him and cross-examine him and test him. If I think that he does not possess virtue, though he says that

he does, I shall reproach him for under-valuing the most valuable things, and over-valuing those that are less valuable. This I shall do to every one whom I meet, young or old, citizen or stranger, but especially to citizens, for they are more closely related to me. For know that the god has commanded me to do so. And I think that no greater good has ever befallen you in the state than my service to the god. For I spend my whole life in going about and persuading you all to give your first and greatest care to the improvement of your souls, and not till you have done that to think of your bodies or your wealth; and telling you that virtue does not come from wealth, but that wealth, and every other good thing which men have, whether in public or in private, comes from virtue. If then I corrupt the youth by this teaching, these things must be harmful; but if any man says that I teach anything else, there is nothing in what he says. And therefore, Athenians, I say, whether you are persuaded by Anytus or not, whether you acquit me or not, I shall not change my way of life; no, not if I have to die for it many times.

Do not interrupt me, Athenians, with your shouts. Remember the request which I made to you, and do not interrupt my words. I think that it will profit you to hear them. I am going to say something more to you, at which you may be inclined to protest, but do not do that. Be sure that if you put me to death, who am what I have told you that I am, you will do yourselves more harm than me. Meletus and Anytus can do me no harm: that is impossible, for I am sure it is not allowed that a good man be injured by a worse. He may indeed kill me, or drive me into exile, or deprive me of my civil rights; and perhaps Meletus and others think those things great evils. But I do not think so: I think it is a much greater evil to do what he is doing now, and to try to put a man to death unjustly. And now, Athenians, I am not arguing in my own defense at all, as you might expect me to do, but rather in yours in order you may not make a mistake about the gift of the god to you by condemning me. For if you put me to death, you will not easily find another who, if I may use a ludicrous comparison, clings to the state as a sort of gadfly to a horse that is large and well-bred but rather sluggish from its size, and needing to be aroused. It seems to me that the god has attached me like that to the state, for I am constantly alighting upon you at every point to rouse, persuade, and reproach each of you all day long. You will not easily find anyone else, my friends, to fill my place; and if you are persuaded by me, you will spare my life. You are indignant, as drowsy persons are, when they are awakened, and, of course, if you are persuaded by Anytus, you could easily kill me with a single blow, and then sleep on undisturbed for the rest of your lives unless the god in his care for you sends another to arouse you. And you may easily see that it is the god who has given me to your city; for it is not human the way in which I have neglected all my own interests and endured seeing my private affairs neglected now for so many years, while occupying myself unceasingly in your interests, going to each of you privately, like a father or an elder brother, trying to persuade him to care for virtue. There would have been a reason for it, if I had gained any advantage by this, or if I had been paid for my

---

6. Homer, Iliad, xviii, 96, 98.

exhortations; but you see yourselves that my accusers, though they accuse me of everything else without shame, have not had the shamelessness to say that I ever either exacted or demanded payment. To that they have no witness. And I think that I have sufficient witness to the truth of what I say—my poverty.

Perhaps it may seem strange to you that, though I go about giving this advice privately and meddling in others' affairs, yet I do not venture to come forward in the assembly and advise the state. You have often heard me speak of my reason for this, and in many places: it is that I have a certain divine sign, which is what Meletus has caricatured in his indictment. I have had it from childhood. It is a kind of voice which, whenever I hear it, always turns me back from something which I was going to do, but never urges me to act. It is this which forbids me to take part in politics. And I think it does well to forbid me. For, Athenians, it is quite certain that, if I had attempted to take part in politics, I should have perished at once and long ago without doing any good either to you or to myself. And do not be indignant with me for telling the truth. There is no man who will preserve his life for long, either in Athens or elsewhere, if he firmly opposes the multitude, and tries to prevent the commission of much injustice and illegality in the state. He who would really fight for justice must do so as a private citizen, not as an office-holder, if he is to preserve his life, even for a short time.

I will prove to you that this is so by very strong evidence, not by mere words, but by what you value more—actions. Listen then to what has happened to me, that you may know that there is no man who could make me consent to do wrong from the fear of death, but that I would perish at once rather than give way. What I am going to tell you may be a commonplace in the lawcourt; nevertheless it is true. The only office that I ever held in the state, Athenians, was that of Senator. When you wished to try the ten generals who did not rescue their men after the battle of Arginusae, as a group, which was illegal, as you all came to think afterwards, the tribe Antiochis, to which I belong, held the presidency. On that occasion I alone of all the presidents opposed your illegal action and gave my vote against you. The orators were ready to impeach me and arrest me; and you were clamoring against me, and crying out to me to submit. But I thought that I ought to face the danger, with law and justice on my side, rather than join with you in your unjust proposal, from fear of imprisonment or death. That was when the state was democratic. When the oligarchy came in, the Thirty sent for me, with four others, to the council-chamber, and ordered us to bring Leon the Salaminian from Salamis, that they might put him to death. They were in the habit of frequently giving similar orders to many others, wishing to implicate as many as possible in their crimes. But, then, I again proved, not by mere words, but by my actions, that, if I may speak bluntly, I do not care a straw for death; but that I do care very much indeed about not doing anything unjust or impious. That government with all its power did not terrify me into doing anything unjust; but when we left the council-chamber, the other four went over to Salamis and brought Leon across to Athens; and I went home. And if the rule of the Thirty had not been overthrown soon afterwards, I should very likely have been put to death for what I did then. Many of you will be my witnesses in this matter.

Now do you think that I could have remained alive all these years if I had taken part in public affairs, and had always maintained the cause of justice like a good man, and had held it a paramount duty, as it is, to do so? Certainly not, Athenians, nor could any other man. But throughout my whole life, both in private and in public, whenever I have had to take part in public affairs, you will find I have always been the same and have never yielded unjustly to anyone; no, not to those whom my enemies falsely assert to have been my pupils.[7] But I was never anyone's teacher. I have never withheld myself from anyone, young or old, who was anxious to hear me discuss while I was making my investigation; neither do I discuss for payment, and refuse to discuss without payment. I am ready to ask questions of rich and poor alike, and if any man wishes to answer me, and then listen to what I have to say, he may. And I cannot justly be charged with causing these men to turn out good or bad, for I never either taught or professed to teach any of them any knowledge whatever. And if any man asserts that he ever learned or heard anything from me in private which everyone else did not hear as well as he, be sure that he does not speak the truth.

Why is it, then, that people delight in spending so much time in my company? You have heard why, Athenians. I told you the whole truth when I said that they delight in hearing me examine persons who think that they are wise when they are not wise. It is certainly very amusing to listen to that. And, I say, the god has commanded me to examine men, in oracles and in dreams and in every way in which the divine will was ever declared to man. This is the truth, Athenians, and if it were not the truth, it would be easily refuted. For if it were really the case that I have already corrupted some of the young men, and am now corrupting others, surely some of them, finding as they grew older that I had given them bad advice in their youth, would have come forward today to accuse me and take their revenge. Or if they were unwilling to do so themselves, surely their relatives, their fathers or brothers, or others, would, if I had done them any harm, have remembered it and taken their revenge. Certainly I see many of them in Court. Here is Crito, of my own deme and of my own age, the father of Critobulus; here is Lysanias of Sphettus, the father of Aeschines; here is also Antiphon of Cephisus, the father of Epigenes. Then here are others whose brothers have spent their time in my company—Nicostratus, the son of Theozotides and brother of Theodotus—and Theodotus is dead, so he at least cannot entreat his brother to be silent; here is Paralus, the son of Demodocus and the brother of Theages; here is Adeimantus, the son of Ariston, whose brother is Plato here; and Aeantodorus, whose brother is Aristodorus. And I can name many others to you, some of whom Meletus ought to have called as witnesses in the course of his own speech; but if he forgot to call them then, let him call them now—I will yield the floor to him—and tell us if he has any such evidence. No, on the contrary, my friends, you will find all these men ready to support me, the corrupter, the injurer, of their relatives, as Meletus and Anytus call me. Those of them who have been already corrupted might perhaps have some reason for supporting me, but what reason can their relatives

---

7. E.g. Critias, a leader of The Thirty, and Alcibiades.

have who are grown up, and who are uncorrupted, except the reason of truth and justice—that they know very well that Meletus is lying, and that I am speaking the truth?

Well, my friends, this, and perhaps more like this, is pretty much all I have to offer in my defense. There may be some one among you who will be indignant when he remembers how, even in a less important trial than this, he begged and entreated the judges, with many tears, to acquit him, and brought forward his children and many of his friends and relatives in Court in order to appeal to your feelings; and then finds that I shall do none of these things, though I am in what he would think the supreme danger. Perhaps he will harden himself against me when he notices this: it may make him angry, and he may cast his vote in anger. If it is so with any of you—I do not suppose that it is, but in case it should be so—I think that I should answer him reasonably if I said: "My friend, I have relatives, too, for, in the words of Homer,[8] "I am not born of an oak or a rock but of flesh and blood"; and so, Athenians, I have relatives, and I have three sons, one of them a lad, and the other two still children. Yet I will not bring any of them forward before you and implore you to acquit me. And why will I do none of these things? It is not from arrogance, Athenians, nor because I lack respect for you—whether or not I can face death bravely is another question—but for my own good name, and for your good name, and for the good name of the whole state. I do not think it right, at my age and with my reputation, to do anything of that kind. Rightly or wrongly, men have made up their minds that in some way Socrates is different from the multitude of men. And it will be shameful if those of you who are thought to excel in wisdom, or in bravery, or in any other virtue, are going to act in this fashion. I have often seen men of reputation behaving in an extraordinary way at their trial, as if they thought it a terrible fate to be killed, and as though they expected to live for ever if you did not put them to death. Such men seem to me to bring shame upon the state, for any stranger would suppose that the best and most eminent Athenians, who are selected by their fellow citizens to hold office, and for other honors, are no better than women. Those of you, Athenians, who have any reputation at all ought not to do these things, and you ought not to allow us to do them; you should show that you will be much more ready to condemn men who make the state ridiculous by these pitiful pieces of acting, than to men who remain quiet.

But apart from the question of reputation, my friends, I do not think that it is right to entreat the judge to acquit us, or to escape condemnation in that way. It is our duty to teach and persuade him. He does not sit to give away justice as a favor, but to pronounce judgment; and he has sworn, not to favor any man whom he would like to favor, but to judge according to law. And, therefore, we ought not to encourage you in the habits of breaking your oaths; and you ought not to allow yourselves to fall into this habit, for then neither you nor we would be acting piously. Therefore, Athenians, do not require me to do these things, for I believe them to be neither good nor just nor pious; and, more especially, do not ask me to do them today when Meletus is prosecuting me for impiety. For were I to be successful and persuade you by my entreaties to break your oaths, I should be clearly teaching you to believe that there are no gods, and I should be simply accusing myself by my defense of not believing in them. But, Athenians, that is very far from the truth. I do believe in the gods as no one of my accusers

believes in them: and to you and to god I commit my cause to be decided as is best for you and for me.

(He is found guilty by 281 votes to 220.)

I am not indignant at the verdict which you have given, Athenians, for many reasons. I expected that you would find me guilty; and I am not so much surprised at that as at the numbers of the votes. I certainly never thought that the majority against me would have been so narrow. But now it seems that if only thirty votes had changed sides, I should have escaped. So I think that I have escaped Meletus, as it is; and not only have I escaped him, for it is perfectly clear that if Anytus and Lycon had not come forward to accuse me, too, he would not have obtained the fifth part of the votes, and would have had to pay a fine of a thousand drachmae.

So he proposes death as the penalty. Be it so. And what alternative penalty shall I propose to you, Athenians?[9] What I deserve, of course, must I not? What then do I deserve to pay or to suffer for having determined not to spend my life in ease? I neglected the things which most men value, such as wealth, and family interests, and military commands, and popular oratory, and all the political appointments, and clubs, and factions, that there are in Athens; for I thought that I was really too honest a man to preserve my life if I engaged in these matters. So I did not go where I should have done no good either to you or to myself. I went, instead, to each one of you privately to do him, as I say, the greatest of benefits, and tried to persuade him not to think of his affairs until he had thought of himself and tried to make himself as good and wise as possible, nor to think of the affairs of Athens until he had thought of Athens herself; and to care for other things in the same manner. Then what do I deserve for such a life? Something good, Athenians, if I am really to propose what I deserve; and something good which it would be suitable to me to receive. Then what is a suitable reward to be given to a poor benefactor who requires leisure to exhort you? There is no reward, Athenians, so suitable for him as a public maintenance in the prytaneum. It is a much more suitable reward for him than for any of you who has won a victory at the Olympic games with his horse or his chariots. Such a man only makes you seem happy, but I make you really happy; and he is not in want, and I am. So if I am to propose the penalty which I really deserve, I propose this—a public maintenance in the prytaneum [town hall].

Perhaps you think me stubborn and arrogant in what I am saying now, as in what I said about the entreaties and tears. It is not so, Athenians; it is rather that I am convinced that I never wronged any man voluntarily, though I cannot persuade you of that, for we have discussed together only a little time. If there were a law at Athens, as there is elsewhere, not to finish a trial of life and death in a single day, I think that I could have persuaded you; but now it is not easy in so short a time to clear myself of great prejudices. But when I am persuaded that I have never wronged any man, I shall certainly not wrong myself, or admit that I deserve to suffer any evil, or propose any evil for myself as a penalty. Why should I?

---

8. Homer, Odyssey, xix, 163.
9. For certain crimes no penalty was fixed by Athenian law, and, having reached a verdict of guilty, the court had still to decide between the alternative penalties proposed by the prosecution and the defense.

Lest I should suffer the penalty which Meletus proposes when I say that I do not know whether it is a good or an evil? Shall I choose instead of it something which I know to be an evil, and propose that as a penalty? Shall I propose imprisonment? And why should I pass the rest of my days in prison, the slave of successive officials? Or shall I propose a fine, with imprisonment until it is paid? I have told you why I will not do that. I should have to remain in prison, for I have no money to pay a fine with. Shall I then propose exile? Perhaps you would agree to that. Life would indeed be very dear to me if I were unreasonable enough to expect that strangers would cheerfully tolerate my discussions and arguments when you who are my fellow citizens cannot endure them, and have found them so irksome and odious to you that you are seeking now to be relieved of them. No, indeed, Athenians, that is not likely. A fine life I should lead for an old man if I were to withdraw from Athens and pass the rest of my days in wandering from city to city, and continually being expelled. For I know very well that the young men will listen to me wherever I go, as they do here; and if I drive them away, they will persuade their elders to expel me; and if I do not drive them away, their fathers and kinsmen will expel me for their sakes.

Perhaps some one will say, "Why cannot you withdraw from Athens, Socrates, and hold your peace?" It is the most difficult thing in the world to make you understand why I cannot do that. If I say that I cannot hold my peace because that would be to disobey the god, you will think that I am not in earnest and will not believe me. And if I tell you that no greater good can happen to a man than to discuss virtue every day and the other matters about which you have heard me arguing and examining myself and others, and that an unexamined life is not worth living, then you will believe me still less. But that is so, my friends, though it is not easy to persuade you. And, what is more, I am not accustomed to think that I deserve anything evil. If I had been rich, I would have proposed as large a fine as I could pay: that would have done me no harm. But I am not rich enough to pay a fine unless you are willing to fix it at a sum within my means. Perhaps I could pay you a mina, so I propose that. Plato here, Athenians, and Crito, and Critobulus, and Apollodorus bid me propose thirty minae, and they will be sureties for me. So I propose thirty minae.[10] They will be sufficient sureties to you for the money.

(He is condemned to death.)

You have not gained very much time, Athenians, and, as the price of it, you will have an evil name for all who wish to revile the state, and they will say that you put Socrates, a wise man, to death. For they will certainly call me wise, whether I am wise or not, when they want to reproach you. If you would have waited for a little while, your wishes would have been fulfilled in the course of nature; for you see that I am an old man, far advanced in years, and near to death. I am saying this not to all of you, only to those who have voted for my death. And to them I have something else to say. Perhaps, my friends, you think that I have been convicted because I was wanting in the arguments by which I could have persuaded you to acquit me, if, that is, I had thought it right to do or to say anything to escape punishment. It is not so. I have been convicted because I was wanting, not in arguments, but in impudence and shamelessness—because I would not plead before you as you would have liked to hear me plead, or appeal to you with weeping and wailing, or say

and do many other things which I maintain are unworthy of me, but which you have been accustomed to from other men. But when I was defending myself, I thought that I ought not to do anything unworthy of a free man because of the danger which I ran, and I have not changed my mind now. I would very much rather defend myself as I did, and die, than as you would have had me do, and live. Both in a lawsuit and in war, there are some things which neither I nor any other man may do in order to escape from death. In battle, a man often sees that he may at least escape from death by throwing down his arms and falling on his knees before the pursuer to beg for his life. And there are many other ways of avoiding death in every danger if a man is willing to say and to do anything. But, my friends, I think that it is a much harder thing to escape from wickedness than from death, for wickedness is swifter than death. And now I, who am old and slow, have been overtaken by the slower pursuer: and my accusers, who are clever and swift, have been overtaken by the swifter pursuer—wickedness. And now I shall go away, sentenced by you to death; and they will go away, sentenced by truth to wickedness and injustice. And I abide by this award as well as they. Perhaps it was right for these things to be so; and I think that they are fairly balanced.

And now I wish to prophesy to you, Athenians, who have condemned me. For I am going to die, and that is the time when men have most prophetic power. And I prophesy to you who have sentenced me to death that a far more severe punishment than you have inflicted on me will surely overtake you as soon as I am dead. You have done this thing, thinking that you will be relieved from having to give an account of your lives. But I say that the result will be very different. There will be more men who will call you to account, whom I have held back, though you did not recognize it. And they will be harsher toward you than I have been, for they will be younger, and you will be more indignant with them. For if you think that you will restrain men from reproaching you for not living as you should, by putting them to death, you are very much mistaken. That way of escape is neither possible nor honorable. It is much more honorable and much easier not to suppress others, but to make yourselves as good as you can. This is my parting prophecy to you who have condemned me.

With you who have acquitted me I should like to discuss this thing that has happened, while the authorities are busy, and before I go to the place where I have to die. So, remain with me until I go: there is no reason why we should not talk with each other while it is possible. I wish to explain to you, as my friends, the meaning of what has happened to me. An amazing thing has happened to me, judges—for you I am right in calling judges.[11] The prophetic sign has been constantly with me all through my life till now, opposing me in quite small

---

10. [One mina was a trifling sum, Sokrates's honest opinion of his just deserts but insulting to the court. A thirty minae fine was comparable to the dowry of a moderately rich man's daughter, as Plato later mentioned, but, by this time, totally unacceptable to the court.]

11. The form of address hitherto has always been "Athenians," or "my friends."

matters if I were not going to act rightly. And now you yourselves see what has happened to me—a thing which might be thought, and which is sometimes actually reckoned, the supreme evil. But the divine sign did not oppose me when I was leaving my house in the morning, nor when I was coming up here to the court, nor at any point in my speech when I was going to say anything; though at other times it has often stopped me in the very act of speaking. But now, in this matter, it has never once opposed me, either in my words or my actions. I will tell you what I believe to be the reason. This thing that has come upon me must be a good; and those of us who think that death is an evil must needs be mistaken. I have a clear proof that that is so; for my accustomed sign would certainly have opposed me if I had not been going to meet with something good.

And if we reflect in another way, we shall see that we may well hope that death is a good. For the state of death is one of two things: either the dead man wholly ceases to be and loses all consciousness or, as we are told, it is a change and a migration of the soul to another place. And if death is the absence of all consciousness, and like the sleep of one whose slumbers are unbroken by any dreams, it will be a wonderful gain. For if a man had to select that night in which he slept so soundly that he did not even dream, and had to compare with it all the other nights and days of his life, and then had to say how many days and nights in his life he had spent better and more pleasantly than this night, I think that a private person, nay, even the great King[12] himself, would find them easy to count, compared with the others. If that is the nature of death, I for one count it a gain. For then it appears that all time is nothing more than a single night. But if death is a journey to another place, and what we are told is true that there are all who have died—what good could be greater than this, my judges? Would a journey not be worth taking, at the end of which, in the other world, we should be delivered from the pretended judges here and should find the true judges who are said to sit in judgment below, such as Minos and Rhadamanthus and Aeacus and Triptolemus, and the other demigods who were just in their own lives? Or what would you not give to discuss with Orpheus and Musaeus and Hesiod and Homer? I am willing to die many times if this be true. And for my own part I should find it wonderful to meet there Palamedes, and Ajax, the son of Telamon, and the other men of old who have died through an unjust judgment, and in comparing my experiences with theirs. That I think would be no small pleasure. And, above all, I could spend my time in examining those who are there, as I examine men here, and in finding out which of them is wise, and which of them thinks himself wise when he is not wise. What would we not give, my judges, to be able to examine the leader of the great expedition against Troy, or Odysseus, or Sisyphus, or countless other men and women whom we could name? It would be an infinite happiness to discuss with them and to live with them and to examine them. Assuredly there they do not put men to death for doing that. For besides the other ways in which they are happier than we are, they are immortal, at least if what we are told is true.

And you, too, judges, must face death hopefully, and believe this as a truth that no evil can happen to a good man, either in life or after death. His fortunes are not neglected by the gods; and what has happened to me today has not happened by chance. I am persuaded that it was better for me to die now, and to be released from

trouble; and that was the reason why the sign never turned me back. And so I am not at all angry with my accusers or with those who have condemned me to die. Yet it was not with this in mind that they accused me and condemned me, but meaning to do me an injury. So far I may blame them.

Yet I have one request to make of them. When my sons grow up, punish them, my friends, and harass them in the same way that I have harassed you, if they seem to you to care for riches or for any other thing more than virtue; and if they think that they are something when they are really nothing, reproach them, as I have reproached you, for not caring for what they should, and for thinking that they are something when really they are nothing. And if you will do this, I myself and my sons will have received justice from you.

But now the time has come, and we must go away—I to die, and you to live. Which is better is known to god alone.

Exercises

1. Sokrates could have saved his life by paying a moderate fine. Why didn't he do this? What is implied if he pays a fine?
2. Refusing to pay a reasonable rather than a token fine is one thing, but proposing lifetime maintenance at public expense is another matter. Why did Sokrates antagonize the court with this proposal? Was he serious?
3. Would Sokrates have taken this uncompromising position had he been, say, twenty years younger?

REPUBLIC
Plato

The *Republic* is discussed on page 127. At this point in the dialogue the conversation is mainly between the narrator, Sokrates, and Plato's brother, Glaucon. The translation is by F. M. Cornford, whose spelling of proper names has been retained.

Book IV

For the moment, we had better finish the inquiry which we began with the idea that it would be easier to make out the nature of justice in the individual if we first tried to study it in something on a larger scale. That larger thing we took to be a state, and so we set about constructing the best one we could, being sure of finding justice in a state that was good. The discovery we made there must now be applied to the individual. If it is confirmed, all will be well; but if we find that justice in the individual is something different, we must go back to the state and test our new result. Perhaps if we brought the two cases into contact like flint and steel, we might strike out between them the spark of justice, and in its light confirm the conception in our own minds.

---

12. Of Persia.

A good method. Let us follow it.

Now, I continued, if two things, one large, the other small, are called by the same name, they will be alike in that respect to which the common name applies. Accordingly, in so far as the quality of justice is concerned, there will be no difference between a just man and a just society.

No.

Well, but we decided that a society was just when each of the three types of human character it contained performed its own function; and again, it was temperate and brave and wise by virtue of certain other affections and states of mind of those same types.

True.

Accordingly, my friend, if we are to be justified in attributing those same virtues to the individual, we shall expect to find that the individual soul contains the same three elements and that they are affected in the same way as are the corresponding types in society.

That follows.

Here, then, we have stumbled upon another little problem: Does the soul contain these three elements or not?

Not such a very little one, I think. It may be a true saying, Socrates, that what is worth while is seldom easy.

Apparently; and let me tell you, Glaucon, it is my belief that we shall never reach the exact truth in this matter by following our present methods of discussion; the road leading to that goal is longer and more laborious. However, perhaps we can find an answer that will be up to the standard we have so far maintained in our speculations.

Is not that enough? I should be satisfied for the moment.

Well, it will more than satisfy me, I replied.

Don't be disheartened, then, but go on.

Surely, I began, we must admit that the same elements and characters that appear in the state must exist in every one of us; where else could they have come from? It would be absurd to imagine that among peoples with a reputation for a high-spirited character, like the Thracians and Scythians and northerners generally, the states have not derived that character from their individual members; or that it is otherwise with the love of knowledge, which would be ascribed chiefly to our own part of the world, or with the love of money, which one would specially connect with Phoenicia and Egypt.

Certainly.

So far, then, we have a fact which is easily recognized. But here the difficulty begins. Are we using the same part of ourselves in all these three experiences, or a different part in each? Do we gain knowledge with one part, feel anger with another, and with yet a third desire the pleasures of food, sex, and so on? Or is the whole soul at work in every impulse and in all these forms of behaviour? The difficulty is to answer that question satisfactorily.

I quite agree.

Let us approach the problem whether these elements are distinct or identical in this way. It is clear that the same thing cannot act in two opposite ways or be in two opposite states at the same time, with respect to the same part of itself, and in relation to the same object. So if we find such contradictory actions or states among the elements concerned, we shall know that more than one must have been involved.

Very well.

Consider this proposition of mine, then. Can the same thing, at the same time and with respect to the same part of itself, be at rest and in motion?

Certainly not.

We had better state this principle in still more precise terms, to guard against misunderstanding later on. Suppose a man is standing still, but moving his head and arms. We should not allow anyone to say that the same man was both at rest and in motion at the same time, but only that part of him was at rest, part in motion. Isn't that so?

Yes.

An ingenious objector might refine still further and argue that a peg-top, spinning with its peg fixed at the same spot, or indeed any body that revolves in the same place, is both at rest and in motion as a whole. But we should not agree, because the parts in respect of which such a body is moving and at rest are not the same. It contains an axis and a circumference; and in respect of the axis it is at rest inasmuch as the axis is not inclined in any direction, while in respect of the circumference it revolves; and if, while it is spinning, the axis does lean out of the perpendicular in all directions, then it is in no way at rest.

That is true.

No objection of that sort, then, will disconcert us or make us believe that the same thing can ever act or be acted upon in two opposite ways, or be two opposite things, at the same time, in respect of the same part of itself, and in relation to the same object.

I can answer for myself at any rate.

Well, anyhow, as we do not want to spend time in reviewing all such objections to make sure that they are unsound, let us proceed on this assumption, with the understanding that, if we ever come to think otherwise, all the consequences based upon it will fall to the ground.

Yes, that is a good plan.

Now, would you class such things as assent and dissent, striving after something and refusing it, attraction and repulsion, as pairs of opposite actions or states of mind—no matter which?

Yes, they are opposites.

And would you not class all appetites such as hunger and thirst, and again willing and wishing, with the affirmative members of those pairs I have just mentioned? For instance, you would say that the soul of a man who desires something is striving after it, or trying to draw to itself the thing it wishes to possess, or again, in so far as it is willing to have its want satisfied, it is giving its assent to its own longing, as if to an inward question.

Yes.

And, on the other hand, disinclination, unwillingness, and dislike, we should class on the negative side with acts of rejection or repulsion.

Of course.

That being so, shall we say that appetites form one class, the most conspicuous being those we call thirst and hunger?

Yes.

Thirst being desire for drink, hunger for food?

Yes.

Now, is thirst, just in so far as it is thirst, a desire in the soul for anything more than simply drink? Is it, for instance, thirst for hot drink or for cold, for much drink or for little, or in a word for drink of any particular kind? Is it not rather true that you will have a desire for cold drink only if you are feeling hot as well as thirsty, and for hot drink only if you are feeling cold; and if you want much drink or little, that will be because your thirst is a great thirst or a little one? But, just in itself, thirst or hunger is a desire for nothing more than its natural object, drink or food, pure and simple.

Yes, he agreed, each desire, just in itself, is simply for its own natural object. When the object is of such and such a particular kind, the desire will be correspondingly qualified.[13]

We must be careful here, or we might be troubled by the objection that no one desires mere food and drink, but always wholesome food and drink. We shall be told that what we desire is always something that is good; so if thirst is a desire, its object must be, like that of any other desire, something—drink or whatever it may be—that will be good for one.[14]

Yes, there might seem to be something in that objection.

But surely, wherever you have two correlative terms, if one is qualified, the other must always be qualified too; whereas if one is unqualified, so is the other.

I don't understand.

Well, "greater" is a relative term; and the greater is greater than the less; if it is much greater, then the less is much less; if it is greater at some moment, past or future, then the less is less at that same moment. The same principle applies to all such correlatives, like "more" and "fewer," "double" and "half"; and again to terms like "heavier" and "lighter," "quicker" and "slower," and to things like hot and cold.

Yes.

Or take the various branches of knowledge: is it not the same there? The object of knowledge pure and simple is the knowable—if that is the right word—without any qualification; whereas a particular kind of knowledge has an object of a particular kind. For example, as soon as men learnt how to build houses, their craft was distinguished from others under the name of architecture, because it had a unique character, which was itself due to the character of its object; and all other branches of craft and knowledge were distinguished in the same way.

True.

This, then, if you understand me now, is what I meant by saying that, where there are two correlatives, the one is qualified if, and only if, the other is so. I am not saying that the one must have the same quality as the other—that the science of health and disease is itself healthy and diseased, or the knowledge of good and evil is itself good and evil—but only that, as soon as you have a knowledge that is restricted to a particular kind of object, namely health and disease, the knowledge itself becomes a particular kind of knowledge. Hence we no longer call it merely knowledge, which would have for its object whatever can be known, but we add the qualification and call it medical science.

I understand now and I agree.

Now, to go back to thirst: is not that one of these relative terms? It is essentially thirst for something.

Yes, for drink.

And if the drink desired is of a certain kind, the thirst will be correspondingly qualified. But thirst which is just simply thirst is not for drink of any particular sort—much or little, good or bad—but for drink pure and simple.

Quite so.

We conclude, then, that the soul of a thirsty man, just in so far as he is thirsty, has no other wish than to drink. That is the object of its craving, and towards that it is impelled.

That is clear.

Now if there is ever something which at the same time pulls it the opposite way, that something must be an element in the soul other than the one which is thirsting and driving it like a beast to drink; in accordance with our principle that the same thing cannot behave in two opposite ways at the same time and towards the same object with the same part of itself. It is like an archer drawing the bow: it is not accurate to say that his hands are at the same time both pushing and pulling it. One hand does the pushing, the other the pulling.

Exactly.

Now, is it sometimes true that people are thirsty and yet unwilling to drink?

Yes, often.

What, then, can one say of them, if not that their soul contains something which urges them to drink and something which holds them back, and that this latter is a distinct thing and overpowers the other?

I agree.

And is it not true that the intervention of this inhibiting principle in such cases always has its origin in reflection; whereas the impulses driving and dragging the soul are engendered by external influences and abnormal conditions.[15]

Evidently.

We shall have good reason, then, to assert that they are two distinct principles. We may call that part of the soul whereby it reflects, rational; and the other, with which it feels hunger and thirst and is distracted by sexual passion and all the other desires, we will call irrational appetite, associated with pleasure in the replenishment of certain wants.

Yes, there is good ground for that view.

Let us take it, then, that we have now distinguished two elements in the soul. What of that passionate element which makes us feel angry and indignant? Is that a third, or identical in nature with one of those two?

It might perhaps be identified with appetite.

I am more inclined to put my faith in a story I once heard about Leontius, son of Aglaion. On his way up from the Piraeus outside the north wall, he noticed the bodies of some criminals lying on the ground, with the

---

13. The object of the following subtle argument about relative terms is to distinguish thirst as a mere blind craving for drink from a more complex desire whose object includes the pleasure or health expected to result from drinking. We thus forestall the objection that all desires have "the good" (apparent or real) for their object and include an intellectual or rational element, so that the conflict of motives might be reduced to an intellectual debate, in the same "part" of the soul, on the comparative values of two incompatible ends.

14. If this objection were admitted, it would follow that the desire would always be correspondingly qualified. It is necessary to insist that we do experience blind cravings which can be isolated from any judgement about the goodness of their object.

15. Some of the most intense bodily desires are due to morbid conditions, e.g. thirst in fever, and even milder desires are caused by a departure from the normal state, which demands "replenishment."

executioner standing by them. He wanted to go and look at them, but at the same time he was disgusted and tried to turn away. He struggled for some time and covered his eyes, but at last the desire was too much for him. Opening his eyes wide, he ran up to the bodies and cried, "There you are, curse you; feast yourselves on this lovely sight!"

Yes, I have heard that story too.

The point of it surely is that anger is sometimes in conflict with appetite, as if they were two distinct principles. Do we not often find a man whose desires would force him to go against his reason, reviling himself and indignant with this part of his nature which is trying to put constraint on him? It is like a struggle between two factions, in which indignation takes the side of reason. But I believe you have never observed, in yourself or anyone else, indignation make common cause with appetite in behaviour which reason decides to be wrong.

No, I am sure I have not.

Again, take a man who feels he is in the wrong. The more generous his nature, the less can he be indignant at any suffering, such as hunger and cold, inflicted by the man he has injured. He recognizes such treatment as just, and, as I say, his spirit refuses to be roused against it.

That is true.

But now contrast one who thinks it is he that is being wronged. His spirit boils with resentment and sides with the right as he conceives it. Persevering all the more for the hunger and cold and other pains he suffers, it triumphs and will not give in until its gallant struggle has ended in success or death; or until the restraining voice of reason, like a shepherd calling off his dog, makes it relent.

An apt comparison, he said; and in fact it fits the relation of our Auxiliaries to the Rulers: they were to be like watch-dogs obeying the shepherds of the commonwealth.

Yes, you understand very well what I have in mind. But do you see how we have changed our view? A moment ago we were supposing this spirited element to be something of the nature of appetite; but now it appears that, when the soul is divided into factions, it is far more ready to be up in arms on the side of reason.

Quite true.

Is it, then, distinct from the rational element or only a particular form of it, so that the soul will contain no more than two elements, reason and appetite? Or is the soul like the state, which had three orders to hold it together, traders, Auxiliaries, and counsellors? Does the spirited element make a third, the natural auxiliary of reason, when not corrupted by bad upbringing?

It must be a third.

Yes, I said, provided it can be shown to be distinct from reason, as we saw it was from appetite.

That is easily proved. You can see that much in children: they are full of passionate feelings from their very birth; but some, I should say, never become rational, and most of them only late in life.

A very sound observation, said I, the truth of which may also be seen in animals. And besides, there is the witness of Homer in that line I quoted before: "He smote his breast and spoke, chiding his heart." The poet is plainly thinking of the two elements as distinct, when he makes the one which has chosen the better course after reflection rebuke the other for its unreasoning passion.

I entirely agree.

The Virtues in the Individual

And so, after a stormy passage, we have reached the land. We are fairly agreed that the same three elements exist alike in the state and in the individual soul.

That is so.

Does it not follow at once that state and individual will be wise or brave by virtue of the same element in each and in the same way? Both will possess in the same manner any quality that makes for excellence.

That must be true.

Then it applies to justice: we shall conclude that a man is just in the same way that a state was just. And we have surely not forgotten that justice in the state meant that each of the three orders in it was doing its own proper work. So we may henceforth bear in mind that each one of us likewise will be a just person, fulfilling his proper function, only if the several parts of our nature fulfil theirs.

Certainly.

And it will be the business of reason to rule with wisdom and forethought on behalf of the entire soul; while the spirited element ought to act as its subordinate and ally. The two will be brought into accord, as we said earlier, by that combination of mental and bodily training which will tune up one string of the instrument and relax the other, nourishing the reasoning part on the study of noble literature and allaying the other's wildness by harmony and rhythm. When both have been thus nurtured and trained to know their own true functions, they must be set in command over the appetites, which form the greater part of each man's soul and are by nature insatiably covetous. They must keep watch lest this part, by battening on the pleasures that are called bodily, should grow so great and powerful that it will no longer keep to its own work, but will try to enslave the others and usurp a dominion to which it has no right, thus turning the whole of life upside down. At the same time, those two together will be the best of guardians for the entire soul and for the body against all enemies from without: the one will take counsel, while the other will do battle, following its ruler's commands and by its own bravery giving effect to the ruler's designs.

Yes, that is all true.

And so we call an individual brave in virtue of this spirited part of his nature, when, in spite of pain or pleasure, it holds fast to the injunctions of reason about what he ought or ought not to be afraid of.

True.

And wise in virtue of that small part which rules and issues these injunctions, possessing as it does the knowledge of what is good for each of the three elements and for all of them in common.

Certainly.

And, again, temperate by reason of the unanimity and concord of all three, when there is no internal conflict between the ruling element and its two subjects, but all are agreed that reason should be ruler.

Yes, that is an exact account of temperance, whether in the state or in the individual.

Finally, a man will be just by observing the principle we have so often stated.

Necessarily.

Now is there any indistinctness in our vision of justice, that might make it seem somehow different from what we found it to be in the state?

I don't think so.

Because, if we have any lingering doubt, we might make sure by comparing it with some commonplace notions. Suppose, for instance, that a sum of money were entrusted to our state or to an individual of corresponding character and training, would anyone imagine that such a person would be specially likely to embezzle it?

No.

And would he not be incapable of sacrilege and theft, or of treachery to friend or country; never false to an oath or any other compact; the last to be guilty of adultery or of neglecting parents or the due service of the gods?

Yes.

And the reason for all this is that each part of his nature is exercising its proper function, of ruling or of being ruled.

Yes, exactly.

Are you satisfied, then, that justice is the power which produces states or individuals of whom that is true, or must we look further?

There is no need; I am quite satisfied.

And so our dream has come true—I mean the inkling we had that, by some happy chance, we had lighted upon a rudimentary form of justice from the very moment when we set about founding our commonwealth. Our principle that the born shoemaker or carpenter had better stick to his trade turns out to have been an adumbration of justice; and that is why it has helped us. But in reality justice, though evidently analogous to this principle, is not a matter of external behaviour, but of the inward self and of attending to all that is, in the fullest sense, a man's proper concern. The just man does not allow the several elements in his soul to usurp one another's functions; he is indeed one who sets his house in order, by self-mastery and discipline coming to be at peace with himself, and bringing into tune those three parts, like the terms in the proportion of a musical scale, the highest and lowest notes and the mean between them, with all the intermediate intervals. Only when he has linked these parts together in well-tempered harmony and has made himself one man instead of many, will he be ready to go about whatever he may have to do, whether it be making money and satisfying bodily wants, or business transactions, or the affairs of state. In all these fields when he speaks of just and honourable conduct, he will mean the behaviour that helps to produce and to preserve this habit of mind; and by wisdom he will mean the knowledge which presides over such conduct. Any action which tends to break down this habit will be for him unjust; and the notions governing it he will call ignorance and folly.

That is perfectly true, Socrates.

Good, said I. I believe we should not be thought altogether mistaken, if we claimed to have discovered the just man and the just state, and wherein their justice consists.

Indeed we should not.

Shall we make that claim, then?

Yes, we will.

So be it, said I. Next, I suppose, we have to consider injustice.

Evidently.

This must surely be a sort of civil strife among the three elements, whereby they usurp and encroach upon one another's functions and some one part of the soul rises up in rebellion against the whole, claiming a supremacy to which it has no right because its nature fits it only to be the servant of the ruling principle. Such turmoil and aberration we shall, I think, identify with injustice, intemperance, cowardice, ignorance, and in a word with all wickedness.

Exactly.

And now that we know the nature of justice and injustice, we can be equally clear about what is meant by acting justly and again by unjust action and wrongdoing.

How do you mean?

Plainly, they are exactly analogous to those wholesome and unwholesome activities which respectively produce a healthy or unhealthy condition in the body; in the same way just and unjust conduct produce a just or unjust character. Justice is produced in the soul, like health in the body, by establishing the elements concerned in their natural relations of control and subordination, whereas injustice is like disease and means that this natural order is inverted.

Quite so.

It appears, then, that virtue is as it were the health and comeliness and well-being of the soul, as wickedness is disease, deformity, and weakness.

True.

And also that virtue and wickedness are brought about by one's way of life, honourable or disgraceful.

That follows.

So now it only remains to consider which is the more profitable course: to do right and live honourably and be just, whether or not anyone knows what manner of man you are, or to do wrong and be unjust, provided that you can escape the chastisement which might make you a better man.

But really, Socrates, it seems to me ridiculous to ask that question now that the nature of justice and injustice has been brought to light. People think that all the luxury and wealth and power in the world cannot make life worth living when the bodily constitution is going to rack and ruin; and are we to believe that, when the very principle whereby we live is deranged and corrupted, life will be worth living so long as a man can do as he will, and wills to do anything rather than to free himself from vice and wrongdoing and to win justice and virtue?

Yes, I replied, it is a ridiculous question.

The Equality of Women

Nevertheless, I continued, we are now within sight of the clearest possible proof of our conclusions, and we ought not to slacken our efforts.

No, anything rather than that.

If you will take your stand with me, then, on this point of vantage to which we have climbed, you shall see all the forms that evil takes, or at least all that it seems worth while to look at.

Lead the way and tell me what you see.

What I see is that, whereas there is only one form of excellence, imperfection exists in innumerable shapes, of which there are four that specially deserve notice.

What do you mean?

It looks as if there were as many types of character as there are distinct varieties of political constitution.

How many?

Five of each.

Will you define them?

Yes, I said. One form of constitution will be the form we have been describing, though it may be called by two names: monarchy, when there is one man who stands out above the rest of the Rulers; aristocracy, when there are more than one.[16]

True.

That, then, I regard as a single form; for, so long as they observe our principles of upbringing and education, whether the Rulers be one or more, they will not subvert the important institutions in our commonwealth.

Naturally not.

Such, then, is the type of state or constitution that I call good and right, and the corresponding type of man. By this standard, the other forms in which a state or an individual character may be organized are depraved and wrong. There are four of these vicious forms.

What are they?

Here I was going on to describe these forms in the order in which, as I thought, they develop one from another, when Polemarchus, who was sitting a little way from Adeimantus, reached out his hand and took hold of his garment by the shoulder. Leaning forward and drawing Adeimantus towards him, he whispered something in his ear, of which I only caught the words: What shall we do? Shall we leave it alone?

Certainly not, said Adeimantus, raising his voice.

What is this, I asked, that you are not going to leave alone?

You, he replied.

Why, in particular? I inquired.

Because we think you are shirking the discussion of a very important part of the subject and trying to cheat us out of an explanation. Everyone, you said, must of course see that the maxim "friends have all things in common" applies to women and children. You thought we should pass over such a casual remark!

But wasn't that right, Adeimantus? said I.

Yes, he said, but "right" in this case, as in others, needs to be defined. There may be many ways of having things in common, and you must tell us which you mean. We have been waiting a long time for you to say something about the conditions in which children are to be born and brought up and your whole plan of having wives and children held in common. This seems to us a matter in which right or wrong management will make all the difference to society; and now, instead of going into it thoroughly, you are passing on to some other form of constitution. So we came to the resolution which you overheard, not to let you off discussing it as fully as all the other institutions.

I will vote for your resolution too, said Glaucon.

In fact, Socrates, Thrasymachus added, you may take it as carried unanimously.

You don't know what you are doing, I said, in holding me up like this. You want to start, all over again, on an enormous subject, just as I was rejoicing at the idea that we had done with this form of constitution. I was only too glad that my casual remark should be allowed to pass. And now, when you demand an explanation, you little know what a swarm of questions you are stirring up. I let it alone, because I foresaw no end of trouble.

Well, said Thrasymachus, what do you think we came here for—to play pitch-and-toss or to listen to a discussion?

A discussion, no doubt, I replied; but within limits.

No man of sense, said Glaucon, would think the whole of life too long to spend on questions of this importance. But never mind about us; don't be faint-hearted yourself. Tell us what you think about this question: how our Guardians are to have wives and children in common, and how they will bring up the young in the interval between their birth and education, which is thought to be the most difficult time of all. Do try to explain how all this is to be arranged.

I wish it were as easy as you seem to think, I replied. These arrangements are even more open to doubt than any we have so far discussed. It may be questioned whether the plan is feasible, and even if entirely feasible, whether it would be for the best. So I have some hesitation in touching on what may seem to be an idle dream.

You need not hesitate, he replied. This is not an unsympathetic audience; we are neither incredulous nor hostile.

Thank you, I said; I suppose that remark is meant to be encouraging.

Certainly it is.

Well, I said, it has just the opposite effect. You would do well to encourage me, if I had any faith in my own understanding of these matters. If one knows the truth, there is no risk to be feared in speaking about the things one has most at heart among intelligent friends; but if one is still in the position of a doubting inquirer, as I am now, talking becomes a slippery venture. Not that I am afraid of being laughed at—that would be childish—but I am afraid I may miss my footing just where a false step is most to be dreaded and drag my friends down with me in my fall. I devoutly hope, Glaucon, that no nemesis will overtake me for what I am going to say; for I really believe that to kill a man unintentionally is a lighter offence than to mislead him concerning the goodness and justice of social institutions. Better to run that risk among enemies than among friends; so your encouragement is out of place.

Glaucon laughed at this. No, Socrates, he said, if your theory has any untoward effect on us, our blood shall not be on your head; we absolve you of any intention to mislead us. So have no fear.

Well, said I, when a homicide is absolved of all intention, the law holds him clear of guilt; and the same principle may apply to my case.

Yes, so far as that goes, you may speak freely.

We must go back, then, to a subject which ought, perhaps, to have been treated earlier in its proper place; though, after all, it may be suitable that the women should have their turn on the stage when the men have quite finished their performance, especially since you are so insistent. In my judgement, then, the question under what conditions people born and educated as we have described should possess wives and children, and how they should treat them, can be rightly settled only by keeping to the course on which we started them at the outset. We undertook to put these men in the position of watch-dogs guarding a flock. Suppose we follow up the analogy and imagine them bred and reared in the same sort of way. We can then see if that plan will suit our purpose.

---

16. The question whether wisdom rules in the person of one man or of several is unimportant. In the sequel the ideal constitution is called kingship or aristocracy (the rule of the best) indifferently.

How will that be?

In this way. Which do we think right for watch-dogs: should the females guard the flock and hunt with the males and take a share in all they do, or should they be kept within doors as fit for no more than bearing and feeding their puppies, while all the hard work of looking after the flock is left to the males?

They are expected to take their full share, except that we treat them as not quite so strong.

Can you employ any creature for the same work as another, if you do not give them both the same upbringing and education?

No.

Then, if we are to set women to the same tasks as men, we must teach them the same things. They must have the same two branches of training for mind and body and also be taught the art of war, and they must receive the same treatment.

That seems to follow.

Possibly, if these proposals were carried out, they might be ridiculed as involving a good many breaches of custom.

They might indeed.

The most ridiculous—don't you think?—being the notion of women exercising naked along with the men in the wrestling-schools; some of them elderly women too, like the old men who still have a passion for exercise when they are wrinkled and not very agreeable to look at.

Yes, that would be thought laughable, according to our present notions.

Now we have started on this subject, we must not be frightened of the many witticisms that might be aimed at such a revolution, not only in the matter of bodily exercise but in the training of women's minds, and not least when it comes to their bearing arms and riding on horseback. Having begun upon these rules, we must not draw back from the harsher provisions. The wits may be asked to stop being witty and try to be serious; and we may remind them that it is not so long since the Greeks, like most foreign nations of the present day, thought it ridiculous and shameful for men to be seen naked. When gymnastic exercises were first introduced in Crete and later at Sparta, the humorists had their chance to make fun of them; but when experience had shown that nakedness is better uncovered than muffled up, the laughter died down and a practice which the reason approved ceased to look ridiculous to the eye. This shows how idle it is to think anything ludicrous but what is base. One who tries to raise a laugh at any spectacle save that of baseness and folly will also, in his serious moments, set before himself some other standard than goodness of what deserves to be held in honour.

Most assuredly.

The first thing to be settled, then, is whether these proposals are feasible; and it must be open to anyone, whether a humorist or serious-minded, to raise the question whether, in the case of mankind, the feminine nature is capable of taking part with the other sex in all occupations, or in none at all, or in some only; and in particular under which of these heads this business of military service falls. Well begun is half done, and would not this be the best way to begin?

Yes.

Shall we take the other side in this debate and argue against ourselves? We do not want the adversary's position to be taken by storm for lack of defenders.

I have no objection.

Let us state his case for him. "Socrates and Glaucon," he will say, "there is no need for others to dispute your position; you yourselves, at the very outset of founding your commonwealth, agreed that everyone should do the one work for which nature fits him." Yes, of course; I suppose we did. "And isn't there a very great difference in nature between man and woman?" Yes, surely. "Does not that natural difference imply a corresponding difference in the work to be given to each?" Yes. "But if so, surely you must be mistaken now and contradicting yourselves when you say that men and women, having such widely divergent natures, should do the same things?" What is your answer to that, my ingenious friend?

It is not easy to find one at the moment. I can only appeal to you to state the case on our own side, whatever it may be.

This, Glaucon, is one of many alarming objections which I foresaw some time ago. That is why I shrank from touching upon these laws concerning the possession of wives and the rearing of children.

It looks like anything but an easy problem.

True, I said; but whether a man tumbles into a swimming-pool or into mid-ocean, he has to swim all the same. So must we, and try if we can reach the shore, hoping for some Arion's dolphin or other miraculous deliverance to bring us safe to land.[17]

I suppose so.

Come then, let us see if we can find the way out. We did agree that different natures should have different occupations, and that the natures of man and woman are different; and yet we are now saying that these different natures are to have the same occupations. Is that the charge against us?

Exactly.

It is extraordinary, Glaucon, what an effect the practice of debating has upon people.

Why do you say that?

Because they often seem to fall unconsciously into mere disputes which they mistake for reasonable argument, through being unable to draw the distinctions proper to their subject; and so, instead of a philosophical exchange of ideas, they go off in chase of contradictions which are purely verbal.

I know that happens to many people; but does it apply to us at this moment?

Absolutely. At least I am afraid we are slipping unconsciously into a dispute about words. We have been strenuously insisting on the letter of our principle that different natures should not have the same occupations, as if we were scoring a point in a debate; but we have altogether neglected to consider what sort of sameness or difference we meant and in what respect these natures and occupations were to be defined as different or the same. Consequently, we might very well be asking one another whether there is not an opposition in nature between bald and long-haired men, and, when that was admitted, forbid one set to be shoemakers, if the other were following that trade.

---

17. The musician Arion, to escape the treachery of Corinthian sailors, leapt into the sea and was carried ashore at Taenarum by a dolphin.

That would be absurd.

Yes, but only because we never meant any and every sort of sameness or difference in nature, but the sort that was relevant to the occupations in question. We meant, for instance, that a man and a woman have the same nature if both have a talent for medicine; whereas two men have different natures if one is a born physician, the other a born carpenter.

Yes, of course.

If, then, we find that either the male sex or the female is specially qualified for any particular form of occupation, then that occupation, we shall say, ought to be assigned to one sex or the other. But if the only difference appears to be that the male begets and the female brings forth, we shall conclude that no difference between man and woman has yet been produced that is relevant to our purpose. We shall continue to think it proper for our Guardians and their wives to share in the same pursuits.

And quite rightly.

The next thing will be to ask our opponent to name any profession or occupation in civic life for the purposes of which woman's nature is different from man's.

That is a fair question.

He might reply, as you did just now, that it is not easy to find a satisfactory answer on the spur of the moment, but that there would be no difficulty after a little reflection.

Perhaps.

Suppose, then, we invite him to follow us and see if we can convince him that there is no occupation concerned with the management of social affairs that is peculiar to women. We will confront him with a question: When you speak of a man having a natural talent for something, do you mean that he finds it easy to learn, and after a little instruction can find out much more for himself; whereas a man who is not so gifted learns with difficulty and no amount of instruction and practice will make him even remember what he has been taught? Is the talented man one whose bodily powers are readily at the service of his mind, instead of being a hindrance? Are not these the marks by which you distinguish the presence of a natural gift for any pursuit?

Yes, precisely.

Now do you know of any human occupation in which the male sex is not superior to the female in all these respects? Need I waste time over exceptions like weaving and watching over saucepans and batches of cakes, though women are supposed to be good at such things and get laughed at when a man does them better?

It is true, he replied, in almost everything one sex is easily beaten by the other. No doubt many women are better at many things than many men; but taking the sexes as a whole, it is as you say.

To conclude, then, there is no occupation concerned with the management of social affairs which belongs either to woman or to man, as such. Natural gifts are to be found here and there in both creatures alike; and every occupation is open to both, so far as their natures are concerned, though woman is for all purposes the weaker.

Certainly.

Is that a reason for making over all occupations to men only?

Of course not.

No, because one woman may have a natural gift for medicine or for music, another may not.

Surely.

Is it not also true that a woman may, or may not, be warlike or athletic?

I think so.

And again, one may love knowledge, another hate it; one may be high-spirited, another spiritless?

True again.

It follows that one woman will be fitted by nature to be a Guardian, another will not; because these were the qualities for which we selected our men Guardians. So for the purpose of keeping watch over the commonwealth, woman has the same nature as man, save in so far as she is weaker.

So it appears.

It follows that women of this type must be selected to share the life and duties of Guardians with men of the same type, since they are competent and of a like nature, and the same natures must be allowed the same pursuits.

Yes.

We come round, then, to our former position, that there is nothing contrary to nature in giving our Guardians' wives the same training for mind and body. The practice we proposed to establish was not impossible or visionary, since it was in accordance with nature. Rather, the contrary practice which now prevails turns out to be unnatural.

So it appears.

Well, we set out to inquire whether the plan we proposed was feasible and also the best. That it is feasible is now agreed; we must next settle whether it is the best.

Obviously.

Now, for the purpose of producing a woman fit to be a Guardian, we shall not have one education for men and another for women, precisely because the nature to be taken in hand is the same.

True.

What is your opinion on the question of one man being better than another? Do you think there is no such difference?

Certainly I do not.

And in this commonwealth of ours which will prove the better men—the Guardians who have received the education we described, or the shoemakers who have been trained to make shoes?[18]

It is absurd to ask such a question.

Very well. So these Guardians will be the best of all the citizens?

By far.

And these women the best of all the women?

Yes.

Can anything be better for a commonwealth than to produce in it men and women of the best possible type?

No.

And that result will be brought about by such a system of mental and bodily training as we have described?

Surely.

We may conclude that the institution we proposed was not only practicable, but also the best for the commonwealth.

---

18. Elementary education will be open to all citizens, but presumably carried further (to the age of 17 or 18) in the case of those who show special promise.

Yes.

The wives of our Guardians, then, must strip for exercise, since they will be clothed with virtue, and they must take their share in war and in the other social duties of guardianship. They are to have no other occupation; and in these duties the lighter part must fall to the women, because of the weakness of their sex. The man who laughs at naked women, exercising their bodies for the best of reasons, is like one that "gathers fruit unripe," for he does not know what it is that he is laughing at or what he is doing. There will never be a finer saying than the one which declares that whatever does good should be held in honour, and the only shame is in doing harm.

That is perfectly true.

Book V

Philosophers Must Be Kings

But really, Socrates, Glaucon continued, if you are allowed to go on like this, I am afraid you will forget all about the question you thrust aside some time ago: whether a society so constituted can ever come into existence, and if so, how.

Well, said I, let me begin by reminding you that what brought us to this point was our inquiry into the nature of justice and injustice.

True; but what of that?

Merely this: suppose we do find out what justice is, are we going to demand that a man who is just shall have a character which exactly corresponds in every respect to the ideal of justice? Or shall we be satisfied if he comes as near to the ideal as possible and has in him a larger measure of that quality than the rest of the world?

That will satisfy me.

If so, when we set out to discover the essential nature of justice and injustice and what a perfectly just and perfectly unjust man would be like, supposing them to exist, our purpose was to use them as ideal patterns: we were to observe the degree of happiness or unhappiness that each exhibited, and to draw the necessary inference that our own destiny would be like that of the one we most resembled. We did not set out to show that these ideals could exist in fact.

That is true.

Then suppose a painter had drawn an ideally beautiful figure complete to the last touch, would you think any the worse of him, if he could not show that a person as beautiful as that could exist?

No, I should not.

Well, we have been constructing in discourse the pattern of an ideal state. Is our theory any the worse, if we cannot prove it possible that a state so organized should be actually founded?

Surely not.

That, then, is the truth of the matter. But if, for your satisfaction, I am to do my best to show under what conditions our ideal would have the best chance of being realized, I must ask you once more to admit that the same principle applies here. Can theory ever be fully realized in practice? Is it not in the nature of things that action should come less close to truth than thought? People may not think so; but do you agree or not?

I do.

Then you must not insist upon my showing that this construction we have traced in thought could be reproduced in fact down to the last detail. You must admit that we shall have found a way to meet your demand for realization, if we can discover how a state might be constituted in the closest accordance with our description. Will not that content you? It would be enough for me.

And for me too.

Then our next attempt, it seems, must be to point out what defect in the working of existing states prevents them from being so organized, and what is the least change that would effect a transformation into this type of government—a single change if possible, or perhaps two; at any rate let us make the changes as few and insignificant as may be.

By all means.

Well, there is one change which, as I believe we can show, would bring about this revolution—not a small change, certainly, nor an easy one, but possible.

What is it?

I have now to confront what we called the third and greatest wave. But I must state my paradox, even though the wave should break in laughter over my head and drown me in ignominy. Now mark what I am going to say.

Go on.

Unless either philosophers become kings in their countries or those who are now called kings and rulers come to be sufficiently inspired with a genuine desire for wisdom; unless, that is to say, political power and philosophy meet together, while the many natures who now go their several ways in the one or the other direction are forcibly debarred from doing so, there can be no rest from troubles, my dear Glaucon, for states, nor yet, as I believe, for all mankind; nor can this commonwealth which we have imagined ever till then see the light of day and grow to its full stature. This it was that I have so long hung back from saying; I knew what a paradox it would be, because it is hard to see that there is no other way of happiness either for the state or for the individual.

Socrates, exclaimed Glaucon, after delivering yourself of such a pronouncement as that, you must expect a whole multitude of by no means contemptible assailants to fling off their coats, snatch up the handiest weapon, and make a rush at you, breathing fire and slaughter. If you cannot find arguments to beat them off and make your escape, you will learn what it means to be the target of scorn and derision.

Well, it was you who got me into this trouble.

Yes, and a good thing too. However, I will not leave you in the lurch. You shall have my friendly encouragement for what it is worth; and perhaps you may find me more complaisant than some would be in answering your questions. With such backing you must try to convince the unbelievers.

I will, now that I have such a powerful ally.

The Philosopher; The Worlds
of Knowledge and Belief

Now, I continued, if we are to elude those assailants you have described, we must, I think, define for them whom we mean by these lovers of wisdom who, we have dared to assert, ought to be our rulers. Once we have a clear view of their character, we shall be able to defend our position by pointing to some who are naturally fitted to combine philosophic study with political leadership, while the rest of the world should accept their guidance and let philosophy alone.

Yes, this is the moment for a definition.

Here, then, is a line of thought which may lead to a satisfactory explanation. Need I remind you that a man will deserve to be called a lover of this or that, only if it is clear that he loves that thing as a whole, not merely in parts?

You must remind me, it seems; for I do not see what you mean.

That answer would have come better from someone less susceptible to love than yourself, Glaucon. You ought not to have forgotten that any boy in the bloom of youth will arouse some sting of passion in a man of your amorous temperament and seem worthy of his attentions. Is not this your way with your favourites? You will praise a snub nose as piquant and a hooked one as giving a regal air, while you call a straight nose perfectly proportioned; the swarthy, you say, have a manly look, the fair are children of the gods; and what do you think is that word 'honey-pale,' if not the euphemism of some lover who had no fault to find with sallowness on the cheek of youth? In a word, you will carry pretence and extravagance to any length sooner than reject a single one that is in the flower of his prime.

If you insist on taking me as an example of how lovers behave, I will agree for the sake of argument.

Again, do you not see the same behaviour in people with a passion for wine? They are glad of any excuse to drink wine of any sort. And there are the men who covet honour, who, if they cannot lead an army, will command a company, and if they cannot win the respect of important people, are glad to be looked up to by nobodies, because they must have someone to esteem them.

Quite true.

Do you agree, then, that when we speak of a man as having a passion for a certain kind of thing, we mean that he has an appetite for everything of that kind without discrimination?

Yes.

So the philosopher, with his passion for wisdom, will be one who desires all wisdom, not only some part of it. If a student is particular about his studies, especially while he is too young to know which are useful and which are not, we shall say he is no lover of learning or of wisdom; just as, if he were dainty about his food, we should say he was not hungry or fond of eating, but had a poor appetite. Only the man who has a taste for every sort of knowledge and throws himself into acquiring it with an insatiable curiosity will deserve to be called a philosopher. Am I not right?

That description, Glaucon replied, would include a large and ill-assorted company. It is curiosity, I suppose, and a delight in fresh experience that gives some people a passion for all that is to be seen and heard at theatrical and musical performances. But they are a queer set to reckon among philosophers, considering that they would never go near anything like a philosophical discussion, though they run round at all the Dionysiac festivals in town or country as if they were under contract to listen to every company of performers without fail. Will curiosity entitle all these enthusiasts, not to mention amateurs of the minor arts, to be called philosophers?

Certainly not; though they have a certain counterfeit resemblance.

And whom do you mean by the genuine philosophers?

Those whose passion it is to see the truth.

That must be so; but will you explain?

It would not be easy to explain to everyone; but you, I believe, will grant my premiss.

Which is—?

That since beauty and ugliness are opposite, they are two things; and consequently each of them is one. The same holds of justice and injustice, good and bad, and all the essential Forms: each in itself is one; but they manifest themselves in a great variety of combinations, with actions, with material things, and with one another, and so each seems to be many.

That is true.

On the strength of this premiss, then, I can distinguish your amateurs of the arts and men of action from the philosophers we are concerned with, who are alone worthy of the name.

What is your distinction?

Your lovers of sights and sounds delight in beautiful tones and colours and shapes and in all the works of art into which these enter; but they have not the power of thought to behold and to take delight in the nature of Beauty itself. That power to approach Beauty and behold it as it is in itself, is rare indeed.

Quite true.

Now if a man believes in the existence of beautiful things, but not of Beauty itself, and cannot follow a guide who would lead him to a knowledge of it, is he not living in a dream? Consider: does not dreaming, whether one is awake or asleep, consist in mistaking a semblance for the reality it resembles?

I should certainly call that dreaming.

Contrast with him the man who holds that there is such a thing as Beauty itself and can discern that essence as well as the things that partake of its character, without ever confusing the one with the other—is he a dreamer or living in a waking state?

He is very much awake.

So may we say that he knows, while the other has only a belief in appearances; and might we call their states of mind knowledge and belief?

Certainly.

But this person who, we say, has only belief without knowledge may be aggrieved and challenge our statement. Is there any means of soothing his resentment and converting him gently, without telling him plainly that he is not in his right mind?

We surely ought to try.

Come then, consider what we are to say to him. Or shall we ask him a question, assuring him that, far from grudging him any knowledge he may have, we shall be only too glad to find that there is something he knows? But, we shall say, tell us this: When a man knows, must there not be something that he knows? Will you answer for him, Glaucon?

My answer will be, that there must.

Something real or unreal?

Something real; how could a thing that is unreal ever be known?

Are we satisfied, then, on this point, from however many points of view we might examine it: that the perfectly real is perfectly knowable, and the utterly unreal is entirely unknowable?

Quite satisfied.

Good. Now if there is something so constituted that it both *is* and *is not,* will it not lie between the purely real and the utterly unreal?

It will.

Well then, as knowledge corresponds to the real, and absence of knowledge necessarily to the unreal, so, to correspond to this intermediate thing, we must look for something between ignorance and knowledge, if such a thing there be.

Certainly.

Is there not a thing we call belief?

Surely.

A different power from knowledge, or the same?

Different.

Knowledge and belief, then, must have different objects, answering to their respective powers.

Yes.

And knowledge has for its natural object the real—to know the truth about reality. However, before going further, I think we need a definition. Shall we distinguish under the general name of "faculties"[19] those powers which enable us—or anything else—to do what we can do? Sight and hearing, for instance, are what I call faculties, if that will help you to see the class of things I have in mind.

Yes, I understand.

Then let me tell you what view I take of them. In a faculty I cannot find any of those qualities, such as colour or shape, which, in the case of many other things, enable me to distinguish one thing from another. I can only look to its field of objects and the state of mind it produces, and regard these as sufficient to identify it and to distinguish it from faculties which have different fields and produce different states. Is that how you would go to work?

Yes.

Let us go back, then, to knowledge. Would you class that as a faculty?

Yes; and I should call it the most powerful of all.

And is belief also a faculty?

It can be nothing else, since it is what gives us the power of believing.

But a little while ago you agreed that knowledge and belief are not the same thing.

Yes; there could be no sense in identifying the infallible with the fallible.[20]

Good. So we are quite clear that knowledge and belief are different things?

They are.

If so, each of them, having a different power, must have a different field of objects.

Necessarily.

The field of knowledge being the real; and its power, the power of knowing the real as it is.

Yes.

Whereas belief, we say, is the power of believing. Is its object the same as that which knowledge knows? Can the same things be possible objects both of knowledge and of belief?[21]

Not if we hold to the principles we agreed upon. If it is of the nature of a different faculty to have a different field, and if both knowledge and belief are faculties and, as we assert, different ones, it follows that the same things cannot be possible objects of both.

So if the real is the object of knowledge, the object of belief must be something other than the real.

Yes.

Can it be the unreal? Or is that an impossible object even for belief? Consider: if a man has a belief, there must be something before his mind; he cannot be believing nothing, can he?

No.

He is believing something, then; whereas the unreal could only be called nothing at all.

Certainly.

Now we said that ignorance must correspond to the unreal, knowledge to the real. So what he is believing cannot be real nor yet unreal.

True.

Belief, then, cannot be either ignorance or knowledge.

It appears not.

Then does it lie outside and beyond these two? Is it either more clear and certain than knowledge or less clear and certain than ignorance?

No, it is neither.

It rather seems to you to be something more obscure than knowledge, but not so dark as ignorance, and so to lie between the two extremes?

Quite so.

Well, we said earlier that if some object could be found such that it both *is* and at the same time *is not,* that object would lie between the perfectly real and the utterly unreal; and that the corresponding faculty would be neither knowledge nor ignorance, but a faculty to be found situated between the two.

Yes.

And now what we have found between the two is the faculty we call belief.

True.

It seems, then, that what remains to be discovered is that object which can be said both to be and not to be and cannot properly be called either purely real or purely unreal. If that can be found, we may justly call it the object of belief, and so give the intermediate faculty the intermediate object, while the two extreme objects will fall to the extreme faculties.

Yes.

On these assumptions, then, I shall call for an answer from our friend who denies the existence of Beauty itself or of anything that can be called an essential Form of Beauty remaining unchangeably in the same state for ever, though he does recognize the existence of beautiful things as a plurality—that lover of things seen who will not listen to anyone who says that Beauty is one, Justice is one, and so on. I shall say to him, Be so good as to tell us: of all these many beautiful things is there one which will not appear ugly? Or of these many just or righteous actions, is there one that will not appear unjust or unrighteous?

No, replied Glaucon, they must inevitably appear to be in some way both beautiful and ugly; and so with all the other terms your question refers to.

---

19. The Greek here uses only the common word for "power" (*dynamis*), but Plato is defining the special sense we express by "faculty."

20. This marks one distinction between the two states of mind. Further, even if true, belief, unlike knowledge, is (1) produced by persuasion, not by instruction; (2) cannot "give an account" of itself; and (3) can be shaken by persuasion.

21. If "belief" bore its common meaning, we might answer, yes. But in this context it is essentially belief in *appearances*. It includes perception by the senses, and these can never perceive objects of thoughts, such as Beauty itself.

And again the many things which are doubles are just as much halves as they are doubles. And the things we call large or heavy have just as much right to be called small or light.

Yes; any such thing will always have a claim to both opposite designations.

Then, whatever any one of these many things may be said to be, can you say that it absolutely *is* that, any more than that it *is not* that?

They remind me of those punning riddles people ask at dinner parties, or the child's puzzle about what the eunuch threw at the bat and what the bat was perched on. These things have the same ambiguous character, and one cannot form any stable conception of them either as being or as not being, or as both being and not being, or as neither.

Can you think of any better way of disposing of them than by placing them between reality and unreality? For I suppose they will not appear more obscure and so less real than unreality, or clearer and so more real than reality.

Quite true.

It seems, then, we have discovered that the many conventional notions of the mass of mankind about what is beautiful or honourable or just and so on are adrift in a sort of twilight between pure reality and pure unreality.

We have.

And we agreed earlier that, if any such object were discovered, it should be called the object of belief and not of knowledge. Fluctuating in that half-way region, it would be seized upon by the intermediate faculty.

Yes.

So when people have an eye for the multitude of beautiful things or of just actions or whatever it may be, but can neither behold Beauty or Justice itself nor follow a guide who would lead them to it, we shall say that all they have is beliefs, without any real knowledge of the objects of their belief.

That follows.

But what of those who contemplate the realities themselves as they are for ever in the same unchanging state? Shall we not say that they have, not mere belief, but knowledge?

That too follows.

And, further, that their affection goes out to the objects of knowledge, whereas the others set their affections on the objects of belief; for it was they, you remember, who had a passion for the spectacle of beautiful colours and sounds, but would not hear of Beauty itself being a real thing.

I remember.

So we may fairly call them lovers of belief rather than of wisdom—not philosophical, in fact, but philodoxical. Will they be seriously annoyed by that description?

Not if they will listen to my advice. No one ought to take offence at the truth.

The name of the philosopher, then, will be reserved for those whose affections are set, in every case, on the reality.

By all means.

Book VI

Knowledge of the Good

One difficulty, then, has been surmounted. It remains to ask how we can make sure of having men who will preserve our constitution. What must they learn, and at what age should they take up each branch of study?

Yes, that is the next point.

I gained nothing by my cunning in putting off those thorny questions of the possession of wives and children and the appointment of Rulers. I knew that the ideal plan would give offence and be hard to carry out; none the less I have had to discuss these matters. We have now disposed of the women and children, but we must start all over again upon the training of the Rulers. You remember how their love for their country was to be proved, by the tests of pain and pleasure, to be a faith that no toil or danger, no turn of fortune could make them abandon. All who failed were to be rejected; only the man who came out flawless, like gold tried in the fire, was to be made a Ruler with privileges and rewards in life and after death. So much was said, when our argument turned aside, as if hoping, with veiled face, to slip past the danger that now lies in our path.

Quite true, I remember.

Yes, I shrank from the bold words which have now been spoken; but now we have ventured to declare that our Guardians in the fullest sense must be philosophers. So much being granted, you must reflect how few are likely to be available. The natural gifts we required will rarely grow together into one whole; they tend to split apart.

How do you mean?

Qualities like ready understanding, a good memory, sagacity, quickness, together with a high-spirited, generous temper, are seldom combined with willingness to live a quiet life of sober constancy. Keen wits are apt to lose all steadiness and to veer about in every direction. On the other hand, the steady reliable characters, whose impassivity is proof against the perils of war, are equally proof against instruction. Confronted with intellectual work, they become comatose and do nothing but yawn.

That is true.

But we insist that no one must be given the highest education or hold office as Ruler, who has not both sets of qualities in due measure. This combination will be rare. So, besides testing it by hardship and danger and by the temptations of pleasure, we may now add that its strength must be tried in many forms of study, to see whether it has the courage and endurance to pursue the highest kind of knowledge, without flinching as others flinch under physical trials.

By all means; but what kinds of study do you call the highest?

You remember how we deduced the definitions of justice, temperance, courage, and wisdom by distinguishing three parts of the soul?

If I had forgotten that, I should not deserve to hear any more.

Do you also remember my warning you beforehand that in order to gain the clearest possible view of these qualities we should have to go round a longer way, although we could give a more superficial account in keeping with our earlier argument. You said that would do; and so we went on in a way which seemed to me not sufficiently exact; whether you were satisfied, it is for you to say.

We all thought you gave us a fair measure of truth.

No measure that falls in the least degree short of the whole truth can be quite fair in so important a matter. What is imperfect can never serve as a measure; though people sometimes think enough has been done and there is no need to look further.

Yes, indolence is common enough.

But the last quality to be desired in the Guardian of a commonwealth and its laws. So he will have to take the longer way and work as hard at learning as at training his body; otherwise he will never reach the goal of the highest knowledge, which most of all concerns him.

Why, are not justice and the other virtues we have discussed the highest? Is there something still higher to be known?

There is; and of those virtues themselves we have as yet only a rough outline, where nothing short of the finished picture should content us. If we strain every nerve to reach precision and clearness in things of little moment, how absurd not to demand the highest degree of exactness in the things that matter most.

Certainly. But what do you mean by the highest degree of knowledge and with what is it concerned? You cannot hope to escape that question.

I do not; you may ask me yourself. All the same, you have been told many a time; but now either you are not thinking or, as I rather suspect, you mean to put me to some trouble with your insistence. For you have often been told that the highest object of knowledge is the essential nature of the Good, from which everything that is good and right derives its value for us. You must have been expecting me to speak of this now, and to add that we have no sufficient knowledge of it. I need not tell you that, without that knowledge, to know everything else, however well, would be of no value to us, just as it is of no use to possess anything without getting the good of it. What advantage can there be in possessing everything except what is good, or in understanding everything else while of the good and desirable we know nothing?

None whatever.

Well then, you know too that most people identify the Good[22] with pleasure, whereas the more enlightened think it is knowledge.

Yes, of course.

And further that these latter cannot tell us what knowledge they mean, but are reduced at last to saying, "knowledge of the Good."

That is absurd.

It is; first they reproach us with not knowing the Good, and then tell us that it is knowledge of the Good, as if we did after all understand the meaning of that word "Good" when they pronounce it.

Quite true.

What of those who define the Good as pleasure? Are they any less confused in their thoughts? They are obliged to admit that there are bad pleasures; from which it follows that the same things are both good and bad.

Quite so.

Evidently, then, this is a matter of much dispute. It is also evident that, although many are content to do what seems just or honourable without really being so, and to possess a mere semblance of these qualities, when it comes to good things, no one is satisfied with possessing what only seems good: here all reject the appearance and demand the reality.

Certainly.

A thing, then, that every soul pursues as the end of all her actions, dimly divining its existence, but perplexed and unable to grasp its nature with the same clearness and assurance as in dealing with other things, and so missing whatever value those other things might have—a thing of such supreme importance is not a matter

about which those chosen Guardians of the whole fortunes of our commonwealth can be left in the dark.

Most certainly not.

At any rate, institutions or customs which are desirable and right will not, I imagine, find a very efficient guardian in one who does not know in what way they are good. I should rather guess that he will not be able to recognize fully that they are right and desirable.

No doubt.

So the order of our commonwealth will be perfectly regulated only when it is watched over by a Guardian who does possess this knowledge.

That follows. But, Socrates, what is your own account of the Good? Is it knowledge, or pleasure, or something else?[23]

There you are! I exclaimed; I could see all along that you were not going to be content with what other people think.

Well, Socrates, it does not seem fair that you should be ready to repeat other people's opinions but not to state your own, when you have given so much thought to this subject.

And do you think it fair of anyone to speak as if he knew what he does not know?

No, not as if he knew, but he might give his opinion for what it is worth.

Why, have you never noticed that opinion without knowledge is always a shabby sort of thing? At the best it is blind. One who holds a true belief without intelligence is just like a blind man who happens to take the right road, isn't he?

No doubt.

Well, then, do you want me to produce one of these poor blind cripples, when others could discourse to you with illuminating eloquence?

No, really, Socrates, said Glaucon, you must not give up within sight of the goal. We should be quite content with an account of the Good like the one you gave us of justice and temperance and the other virtues.

So should I be, my dear Glaucon, much more than content! But I am afraid it is beyond my powers; with the best will in the world I should only disgrace myself and be laughed at. No, for the moment let us leave the question of the real meaning of good; to arrive at what I at any rate believe it to be would call for an effort too ambitious for an inquiry like ours. However, I will tell you, though only if you wish it, what I picture to myself as the offspring of the Good and the thing most nearly resembling it.

Well, tell us about the offspring, and you shall remain in our debt for an account of the parent.

I only wish it were within my power to offer, and within yours to receive, a settlement of the whole account. But you must be content now with the interest only; and you must see to it that, in describing this offspring of the Good, I do not inadvertently cheat you with false coin.

We will keep a good eye on you. Go on.

First we must come to an understanding. Let me remind you of the distinction we drew earlier and have

---

22. Here "the Good" obviously means "the Human Good" or end of human life.

23. Here it begins to appear that the discussion is not confined to the "Human Good" but extends to the supreme Form, "Goodness itself."

often drawn on other occasions, between the multiplicity of things that we call good or beautiful or whatever it may be and, on the other hand, Goodness itself or Beauty itself and so on. Corresponding to each of these sets of many things, we postulate a single Form or real essence, as we call it.

Yes, that is so.

Further, the many things, we say, can be seen, but are not objects of rational thought; whereas the Forms are objects of thought, but invisible.

Yes, certainly.

And we see things with our eyesight, just as we hear sounds with our ears and, to speak generally, perceive any sensible thing with our sense-faculties.

Of course.

Have you noticed, then, that the artificer who designed the senses has been exceptionally lavish of his materials in making the eyes able to see and their objects visible?

That never occurred to me.

Well, look at it in this way. Hearing and sound do not stand in need of any third thing, without which the ear will not hear nor sound be heard; and I think the same is true of most, not to say all, of the other senses. Can you think of one that does require anything of the sort?

No, I cannot.

But there is this need in the case of sight and its objects. You may have the power of vision in your eyes and try to use it, and colour may be there in the objects; but sight will see nothing and the colours will remain invisible in the absence of a third thing peculiarly constituted to serve this very purpose.

By which you mean—?

Naturally I mean what you call light; and if light is a thing of value, the sense of sight and the power of being visible are linked together by a very precious bond, such as unites no other sense with its object.

No one could say that light is not a precious thing.

And of all the divinities in the skies is there one whose light, above all the rest, is responsible for making our eyes see perfectly and making objects perfectly visible?

There can be no two opinions: of course you mean the Sun.

And how is sight related to this deity? Neither sight nor the eye which contains it is the Sun, but of all the sense-organs it is the most sun-like; and further, the power it possesses is dispensed by the Sun, like a stream flooding the eye. And again, the Sun is not vision, but it is the cause of vision and also is seen by the vision it causes.

Yes.

It was the Sun, then, that I meant when I spoke of that offspring which the Good has created in the visible world, to stand there in the same relation to vision and visible things as that which the Good itself bears in the intelligible world to intelligence and to intelligible objects.

How is that? You must explain further.

You know what happens when the colours of things are no longer irradiated by the daylight, but only by the fainter luminaries of the night: when you look at them, the eyes are dim and seem almost blind, as if there were no unclouded vision in them. But when you look at things on which the Sun is shining, the same eyes see distinctly and it becomes evident that they do contain the power of vision.

Certainly.

Apply this comparison, then, to the soul. When its gaze is fixed upon an object irradiated by truth and reality, the soul gains understanding and knowledge and is manifestly in possession of intelligence. But when it looks towards that twilight world of things that come into existence and pass away, its sight is dim and it has only opinions and beliefs which shift to and fro, and now it seems like a thing that has no intelligence.

That is true.

This, then, which gives to the objects of knowledge their truth and to him who knows them his power of knowing, is the Form or essential nature of Goodness. It is the cause of knowledge and truth; and so, while you may think of it as an object of knowledge, you will do well to regard it as something beyond truth and knowledge and, precious as these both are, of still higher worth. And, just as in our analogy light and vision were to be thought of as like the Sun, but not identical with it, so here both knowledge and truth are to be regarded as like the Good, but to identify either with the Good is wrong. The Good must hold a yet higher place of honour.

You are giving it a position of extraordinary splendour, if it is the source of knowledge and truth and itself surpasses them in worth. You surely cannot mean that it is pleasure.

Heaven forbid, I exclaimed. But I want to follow up our analogy still further. You will agree that the Sun not only makes the things we see visible, but also brings them into existence and gives them growth and nourishment; yet he is not the same thing as existence.[24] And so with the objects of knowledge: these derive from the Good not only their power of being known, but their very being and reality; and Goodness is not the same thing as being, but even beyond being, surpassing it in dignity and power.

Glaucon exclaimed with some amusement at my exalting Goodness in such extravagant terms.

It is your fault, I replied; you forced me to say what I think.

Yes, and you must not stop there. At any rate, complete your comparison with the Sun, if there is any more to be said.

There is a great deal more, I answered.

Let us hear it, then; don't leave anything out.

I am afraid much must be left unspoken. However, I will not, if I can help it, leave out anything that can be said on this occasion.

Please do not.

Four Stages of Cognition: The Line

Conceive, then, that there are these two powers I speak of, the Good reigning over the domain of all that is intelligible, the Sun over the visible world—or the heaven as I might call it; only you would think I was showing off my skill in etymology. At any rate you have these two orders of things clearly before your mind: the visible and the intelligible?

---

24. The ambiguity of *genesis* can hardly be reproduced. The Sun "gives things their *genesis*" (generation, birth), but "is not itself *genesis*" (becoming, the existence in time of things which begin and cease to exist, as opposed to the real being of eternal things in the intelligible world).

I have.

Now take a line divided into two unequal parts, one to represent the visible order, the other the intelligible; and divide each part again in the same proportion, symbolizing degrees of comparative clearness or obscurity. Then (A) one of the two sections in the visible world will stand for images. By images I mean first shadows, and then reflections in water or in close-grained, polished surfaces, and everything of that kind, if you understand.

Yes, I understand.

Let the second section (B) stand for the actual things of which the first are likenesses, the living creatures about us and all the works of nature or of human hands.

So be it.

Will you also take the proportion in which the visible world has been divided as corresponding to degrees of reality and truth, so that the likeness shall stand to the original in the same ratio as the sphere of appearances and belief to the sphere of knowledge?

Certainly.

Now consider how we are to divide the part which stands for the intelligible world. There are two sections. In the first (C) the mind uses as images those actual things which themselves had images in the visible world; and it is compelled to pursue its inquiry by starting from assumptions and travelling, not up to a principle, but down to a conclusion. In the second (D) the mind moves in the other direction, from an assumption up towards a principle which is not hypothetical; and it makes no use of the images employed in the other section, but only of Forms, and conducts its inquiry solely by their means.

I don't quite understand what you mean.

Then we will try again; what I have just said will help you to understand. (C) You know, of course, how students of subjects like geometry and arithmetic begin by postulating odd and even numbers, or the various figures and the three kinds of angle, and other such data in each subject. These data they take as known; and, having adopted them as assumptions, they do not feel called upon to give any account of them to themselves or to anyone else, but treat them as self-evident. Then, starting from these assumptions, they go on until they arrive, by a series of consistent steps, at all the conclusions they set out to investigate.

Yes, I know that.

You also know how they make use of visible figures and discourse about them, though what they really have in mind is the originals of which these figures are images: they are not reasoning, for instance, about this particular square and diagonal which they have drawn, but about *the* Square and *the* Diagonal; and so in all cases. The diagrams they draw and the models they make are actual things, which may have their shadows or images in water; but now they serve in their turn as images, while the student is seeking to behold those realities which only thought can apprehend.[25]

True.

This, then, is the class of things that I spoke of as intelligible, but with two qualifications: first, that the mind, in studying them, is compelled to employ assumptions, and, because it cannot rise above these, does not travel upwards to a first principle; and second, that it uses as images those actual things which have images of their own in the section below them and

which, in comparison with those shadows and reflections, are reputed to be more palpable and valued accordingly.

I understand: you mean the subject-matter of geometry and of the kindred arts.

(D) Then by the second section of the intelligible world you may understand me to mean all that unaided reasoning apprehends by the power of dialectic, when it treats its assumptions, not as first principles, but as *hypotheses* in the literal sense, things "laid down" like a flight of steps up which it may mount all the way to something that is not hypothetical, the first principle of all; and having grasped this, may turn back and, holding on to the consequences which depend upon it, descend at last to a conclusion, never making use of any sensible object, but only of Forms, moving through Forms from one to another, and ending with Forms.

I understand, he said, though not perfectly; for the procedure you describe sounds like an enormous undertaking. But I see that you mean to distinguish the field of intelligible reality studied by dialectic as having a greater certainty and truth than the subject-matter of the "arts," as they are called, which treat their assumptions as first principles. The students of these arts are, it is true, compelled to exercise thought in contemplating objects which the senses cannot perceive; but because they start from assumptions without going back to a first principle, you do not regard them as gaining true understanding about those objects, although the objects themselves, when connected with a first principle, are intelligible. And I think you would call the state of mind of the students of geometry and other such arts, not intelligence, but thinking, as being something between intelligence and mere acceptance of appearances.

You have understood me quite well enough, I replied. And now you may take, as corresponding to the four sections, these four states of mind: *intelligence* for the highest, *thinking* for the second, *belief* for the third, and for the last *imagining*.[26] These you may arrange as the terms in a proportion, assigning to each a degree of clearness and certainty corresponding to the measure in which their objects possess truth and reality.

I understand and agree with you. I will arrange them as you say.

Book VII

The Allegory of the Cave

Next, said I, here is a parable to illustrate the degrees in which our nature may be enlightened or unenlightened. Imagine the condition of men living in a sort of cavernous chamber underground, with an entrance open to the light and a long passage all down the cave.[27] Here

---

25. Conversely, the fact that the mathematician can use visible objects as illustrations indicates that the realities and truths of mathematics are embodied, though imperfectly, in the world of visible and tangible things; whereas the counterparts of the moral Forms can only be beheld by thought.

26. Plato never uses hard and fast technical terms. The four here proposed are not defined or strictly employed in the sequel.

27. The *length* of the "way in" (*eisodos*) to the chamber where the prisoners sit is an essential feature, explaining why no daylight reaches them.

they have been from childhood, chained by the leg and also by the neck, so that they cannot move and can see only what is in front of them, because the chains will not let them turn their heads. At some distance higher up is the light of a fire burning behind them; and between the prisoners and the fire is a track[28] with a parapet built along it, like the screen at a puppet-show, which hides the performers while they show their puppets over the top.

I see, said he.

Now behind this parapet imagine persons carrying along various artificial objects, including figures of men and animals in wood or stone or other materials, which project above the parapet. Naturally, some of these persons will be talking, others silent.[29]

It is a strange picture, he said, and a strange sort of prisoners.

Like ourselves, I replied; for in the first place prisoners so confined would have seen nothing of themselves or of one another, except the shadows thrown by the fire-light on the wall of the Cave facing them, would they?

Not if all their lives they had been prevented from moving their heads.

And they would have seen as little of the objects carried past.

Of course.

Now, if they could talk to one another, would they not suppose that their words referred only to those passing shadows which they saw?[30]

Necessarily.

And suppose their prison had an echo from the wall facing them? When one of the people crossing behind them spoke, they could only suppose that the sound came from the shadow passing before their eyes.

No doubt.

In every way, then, such prisoners would recognize as reality nothing but the shadows of those artificial objects.

Inevitably.

Now consider what would happen if their release from the chains and the healing of their unwisdom should come about in this way. Suppose one of them set free and forced suddenly to stand up, turn his head, and walk with eyes lifted to the light; all these movements would be painful, and he would be too dazzled to make out the objects whose shadows he had been used to see. What do you think he would say, if someone told him that what he had formerly seen was meaningless illusion, but now, being somewhat nearer to reality and turned towards more real objects, he was getting a truer view? Suppose further that he were shown the various objects being carried by and were made to say, in reply to questions, what each of them was. Would he not be perplexed and believe the objects now shown him to be not so real as what he formerly saw?

Yes, not nearly so real.

And if he were forced to look at the fire-light itself, would not his eyes ache, so that he would try to escape and turn back to the things which he could see distinctly, convinced that they really were clearer than these other objects now being shown to him?

Yes.

And suppose someone were to drag him away forcibly up the steep and rugged ascent and not let him go until he had hauled him out into the sunlight, would he not suffer pain and vexation at such treatment, and,

when he had come out into the light, find his eyes so full of its radiance that he could not see a single one of the things that he was now told were real?

Certainly he would not see them all at once.

He would need, then, to grow accustomed before he could see things in that upper world. At first it would be easiest to make out shadows, and then the images of men and things reflected in water, and later on the things themselves. After that, it would be easier to watch the heavenly bodies and the sky itself by night, looking at the light of the moon and stars rather than the Sun and the Sun's light in the day-time.

Yes, surely.

Last of all, he would be able to look at the Sun and contemplate its nature, not as it appears when reflected in water or any alien medium, but as it is in itself in its own domain.

No doubt.

And now he would begin to draw the conclusion that it is the Sun that produces the seasons and the course of the year and controls everything in the visible world, and moreover is in a way the cause of all that he and his companions used to see.

Clearly he would come at last to that conclusion.

Then if he called to mind his fellow prisoners and what passed for wisdom in his former dwelling-place, he would surely think himself happy in the change and be sorry for them. They may have had a practice of honouring and commending one another, with prizes for the man who had the keenest eye for the passing shadows and the best memory for the order in which they followed or accompanied one another, so that he could make a good guess as to which was going to come next. Would our released prisoner be likely to covet those prizes or to envy the men exalted to honour and power in the Cave? Would he not feel like Homer's Achilles, that he would far sooner "be on earth as a hired servant in the house of a landless man" or endure anything rather than go back to his old beliefs and live in the old way?

Yes, he would prefer any fate to such a life.

Now imagine what would happen if he went down again to take his former seat in the Cave. Coming suddenly out of the sunlight, his eyes would be filled with darkness. He might be required once more to deliver his opinion on those shadows, in competition with the prisoners who had never been released, while his eyesight was still dim and unsteady; and it might take

---

28. The track crosses the passage into the cave at right angles, and is *above* the parapet built along it.

29. A modern Plato would compare his Cave to an underground cinema, where the audience watch the play of shadows thrown by the film passing before a light at their backs. The film itself is only an image of "real" things and events in the world outside the cinema.

For the film Plato has to substitute the clumsier apparatus of a procession of artificial objects carried on their heads by persons who are merely part of the machinery, providing for the movement of the objects and the sounds whose echo the prisoners hear. The parapet prevents these persons' shadows from being cast on the wall of the Cave.

30. Adam's text and interpretation. The prisoners, having seen nothing but shadows, cannot think their words refer to the objects carried past behind their backs. For them shadows (images) are the only realities.

some time to become used to the darkness. They would laugh at him and say that he had gone up only to come back with his sight ruined; it was worth no one's while even to attempt the ascent. If they could lay hands on the man who was trying to set them free and lead them up, they would kill him.[31]

Yes, they would.

Application of the Cave Allegory

Every feature in this parable, my dear Glaucon, is meant to fit our earlier analysis. The prison dwelling corresponds to the region revealed to us through the sense of sight, and the fire-light within it to the power of the Sun. The ascent to see the things in the upper world you may take as standing for the upward journey of the soul into the region of the intelligible; then you will be in possession of what I surmise, since that is what you wish to be told. Heaven knows whether it is true; but this, at any rate, is how it appears to me. In the world of knowledge, the last thing to be perceived and only with great difficulty is the essential Form of Goodness. Once it is perceived, the conclusion must follow that, for all things, this is the cause of whatever is right and good; in the visible world it gives birth to light and to the lord of light, while it is itself sovereign in the intelligible world and the parent of intelligence and truth. Without having had a vision of this Form no one can act with wisdom, either in his own life or in matters of state.

So far as I can understand, I share your belief.

Then you may also agree that it is no wonder if those who have reached this height are reluctant to manage the affairs of men. Their souls long to spend all their time in that upper world—naturally enough, if here once more our parable holds true. Nor, again, is it at all strange that one who comes from the contemplation of divine things to the miseries of human life should appear awkward and ridiculous when, with eyes still dazed and not yet accustomed to the darkness, he is compelled, in a law-court or elsewhere, to dispute about the shadows of justice or the images that cast those shadows, and to wrangle over the notions of what is right in the minds of men who have never beheld Justice itself.

It is not at all strange.

No; a sensible man will remember that the eyes may be confused in two ways—by a change from light to darkness or from darkness to light; and he will recognize that the same thing happens to the soul. When he sees it troubled and unable to discern anything clearly, instead of laughing thoughtlessly, he will ask whether, coming from a brighter existence, its unaccustomed vision is obscured by the darkness, in which case he will think its condition enviable and its life a happy one; or whether, emerging from the depths of ignorance, it is dazzled by excess of light. If so, he will rather feel sorry for it; or, if he were inclined to laugh, that would be less ridiculous than to laugh at the soul which has come down from the light.

That is a fair statement.

If this is true, then, we must conclude that education is not what it is said to be by some, who profess to put knowledge into a soul which does not possess it, as if they could put sight into blind eyes. On the contrary, our own account signifies that the soul of every man does possess the power of learning the truth and the organ to see it with; and that, just as one might have to turn the whole body round in order that the eye should see light instead of darkness, so the entire soul must be turned away from this changing world, until its eye can bear to contemplate reality and that supreme splendour which we have called the Good. Hence there may well be an art whose aim would be to effect this very thing, the conversion of the soul, in the readiest way; not to put the power of sight into the soul's eye, which already has it, but to ensure that, instead of looking in the wrong direction, it is turned the way it ought to be.

Yes, it may well be so.

It looks, then, as though wisdom were different from those ordinary virtues, as they are called, which are not far removed from bodily qualities, in that they can be produced by habituation and exercise in a soul which has not possessed them from the first. Wisdom, it seems, is certainly the virtue of some diviner faculty, which never loses its power, though its use for good or harm depends on the direction towards which it is turned. You must have noticed in dishonest men with a reputation for sagacity the shrewd glance of a narrow intelligence piercing the objects to which it is directed. There is nothing wrong with their power of vision, but it has been forced into the service of evil, so that the keener its sight, the more harm it works.

Quite true.

And yet if the growth of a nature like this had been pruned from earliest childhood, cleared of those clinging overgrowths which come of gluttony and all luxurious pleasure and, like leaden weights charged with affinity to this mortal world, hang upon the soul, bending its vision downwards; if, freed from these, the soul were turned round towards true reality, then this same power in these very men would see the truth as keenly as the objects it is turned to now.

Yes, very likely.

Is it not also likely, or indeed certain after what has been said, that a state can never be properly governed either by the uneducated who know nothing of truth or by men who are allowed to spend all their days in the pursuit of culture? The ignorant have no single mark before their eyes at which they must aim in all the conduct of their own lives and of affairs of state; and the others will not engage in action if they can help it, dreaming that, while still alive, they have been translated to the Islands of the Blest.

Quite true.

It is for us, then, as founders of a commonwealth, to bring compulsion to bear on the noblest natures. They must be made to climb the ascent to the vision of Goodness, which we called the highest object of knowledge; and, when they have looked upon it long enough, they must not be allowed, as they now are, to remain on the heights, refusing to come down again to the prisoners or to take any part in their labours and rewards, however much or little these may be worth.

Shall we not be doing them an injustice, if we force on them a worse life than they might lead?

You have forgotten again, my friend, that the law is not concerned to make any one class specially happy, but to ensure the welfare of the commonwealth as a whole.

---

31. An allusion to the fate of Socrates.

By persuasion or constraint it will unite the citizens in harmony, making them share whatever benefits each class can contribute to the common good; and its purpose in forming men of that spirit was not that each should be left to go his own way, but that they should be instrumental in binding the community into one.

True, I had forgotten.

You will see, then, Glaucon, that there will be no real injustice in compelling our philosophers to watch over and care for the other citizens. We can fairly tell them that their compeers in others states may quite reasonably refuse to collaborate: there they have sprung up, like a self-sown plant, in despite of their country's institutions; no one has fostered their growth, and they cannot be expected to show gratitude for a care they have never received. "But," we shall say, "it is not so with you. We have brought you into existence for your country's sake as well as for your own, to be like leaders and king-bees in a hive; you have been better and more thoroughly educated than those others and hence you are more capable of playing your part both as men of thought and as men of action. You must go down, then, each in his turn, to live with the rest and let your eyes grow accustomed to the darkness. You will then see a thousand times better than those who live there always; you will recognize every image for what it is and know what it represents, because you have seen justice, beauty, and goodness in their reality; and so you and we shall find life in our commonwealth no mere dream, as it is in most existing states, where men live fighting one another about shadows and quarrelling for power, as if that were a great prize; whereas in truth government can be at its best and free from dissension only where the destined rulers are least desirous of holding office."

Quite true.

Then will our pupils refuse to listen and to take their turns at sharing in the work of the community, though they may live together for most of their time in a purer air?

No; it is a fair demand, and they are fair-minded men. No doubt, unlike any ruler of the present day, they will think of holding power as an unavoidable necessity.

Yes, my friend; for the truth is that you can have a well-governed society only if you can discover for your future rulers a better way of life than being in office; then only will power be in the hands of men who are rich, not in gold, but in the wealth that brings happiness, a good and wise life. All goes wrong when, starved for lack of anything good in their own lives, men turn to public affairs hoping to snatch from thence the happiness they hunger for. They set about fighting for power, and this internecine conflict ruins them and their country. The life of true philosophy is the only one that looks down upon offices of state; and access to power must be confined to men who are not in love with it; otherwise rivals will start fighting. So whom else can you compel to undertake the guardianship of the commonwealth, if not those who, besides understanding best the principles of government, enjoy a nobler life than the politician's and look for rewards of a different kind?

There is indeed no other choice.

Exercises

1. In ancient Greece, women were generally considered inferior beings who were necessarily subordinate to men, and they are so treated in all of Plato's dialogues, that is except the *Republic*. What changes has Plato made in his ideal state that give women equality and equal opportunity to become guardians and philosopher-kings? What does this imply in regard to equal opportunity for women of today?
2. In the "Allegory of the Cave," why does Plato insist that the one who has come to know the true light *must* return to the cave, that he or she must partake of the labors and honors of the people in the cave, even though they are recognized as foolish?

POETICS
Aristotle (384–322 B.C.)

Aristotle's *Poetics*[32] is a critical examination of the nature of art and what constitutes good art. Specifically, the treatise is directed to the problems of poetry in the writing of tragedy, which Aristotle feels is the highest form of art. With no word for *fine art,* the Greek term for art is *techne,* which also translates as "craft" or "skill." Art is therefore the "making" of a thing that in its highest form is crafted with exceptional skill. The *Poetics* is the first clear statement in the history of aesthetics correlating the experience of a work of art with the skill of making the work itself.

For Aristotle, all art is an imitation of nature, and tragedy is

> the imitation of an action that is serious and also, as having magnitude, complete in itself; in language with pleasurable accessories, each kind brought in separately in the parts of the work; in a dramatic, not a narrative form; with incidents arousing pity and fear, wherewith to accomplish a katharsis of such emotions.

The theoretical perfect plot of a tragedy must have a single issue, which should be resolved within a twenty-four-hour day. Further, a good man will be reduced from happiness to misery because of some great error on his part, his so-called "fatal flaw."

The six elements of a tragedy are:

Plot (Fable). The action, what happens.
Character. Moral qualities of the agents.
Diction. Metrical structure of the poetry as revealed in speech, recitation, chant, or song.

---

32. Aristotle, *De Arte Poetika.* Translated by Ingram Bywater, 1911, with omissions.

Thought. Implied themes and theses (universal truths) as exposed by all the elements together.

Spectacle. The stage appearance of set, costumes, movement, dance.

Melody. Aristotle takes this for granted, i.e., it is "too completely understood to require explanation." Melody refers to tunes played on the aulos (see p. 196) and the musical reciting, chanting, and singing of the actors and the chorus. With the statement that "melody is the greatest of the pleasurable accessories of tragedy," Aristotle acknowledges the sensual elements of tragedy.

The *Poetics* ends with the discussion of tragedy, although Aristotle had earlier stated that he would also deal with comedy and other kinds of poetry. Even as an incomplete work, this has been one of the most influential of Aristotle's treatises.

The objects the imitator represents are actions, with agents who are necessarily either good men or bad—the diversities of human character being nearly always derivative from this primary distinction, since the line between virtue and vice is one dividing the whole of mankind. It follows, therefore, that the agents represented must be either above our own level of goodness, or beneath it, or just such as we are. It is clear that each of the arts will admit of these differences, and that it will become a separate art by representing objects with this point of difference. Even in dancing, flute-playing, and lyre-playing such diversities are possible; and they are also possible in the nameless art that uses language, prose or verse without harmony, as its means. This difference it is that distinguishes Tragedy and Comedy also; the one would make its personages worse, and the other better, than the men of the present day.

A third difference in these arts is in the manner in which each kind of object is represented. Given both the same means and the same kind of object for imitation, one may either (1) speak at one moment in narrative and at another as an assumed character, as Homer does; or (2) one may remain the same throughout, without any such change; or (3) the imitators may represent the whole story dramatically, as though they were actually doing the things described. Therefore, the differences in the imitation of these arts comes under three heads, their means, their objects, and their manner.

It is clear that the general origin of poetry was due to two causes, each of them part of human nature. Imitation is natural to man since childhood, one of his advantages over the lower animals being this, that he is the most imitative creature in the world, and learns at first by imitation. And it is also natural for all to delight in works of imitation. The truth of this second point is shown by experience: though the objects themselves may be painful to see, we delight to view the most realistic representations of them in art, the forms for example of the lowest animals and of dead bodies. The explanation is to be found in a further fact: to be learning something is the greatest of pleasures not only to the philosopher but also to the rest of mankind, however small their capacity for it; the reason of the delight in seeing the picture is that one is at the same time learning—gathering the meaning of things, e.g. that the man there is so-and-so; for if one has not seen the things before, one's pleasure will not be in the picture as an imitation of it, but will be due to the execution or coloring or some similar cause. Imitation, then, being natural to us—as also the sense of harmony and rhythm, the meters being obviously species of rhythms—it was through their original aptitude, and by a series of improvements for the most part gradual on their first efforts, that they created poetry out of their improvisations.

Poetry, however, soon broke up into two kinds according to the differences of character in the individual poets; for the graver among them would represent noble actions, and those of noble personages; and the meaner sort the actions of the ignoble. The latter class produced invectives at first, just as others did hymns and panegyrics. We know of no such poem by any of the pre-Homeric poets, though there were probably many such writers among them; instances, however, may be found from Homer downwards, e.g. his *Margites,* and similar poems of others. In this poetry of invectives its natural fitness brought an iambic meter into use; hence our present term "iambic," because it was the meter of their "iambs" or invectives against one another. The result was that the old poets became some of them writers of heroic and others of iambic verse. Homer's position, however, is peculiar: just as he was in the serious style the poet of poets, standing alone not only through the literary excellence, but also through the dramatic character of his imitations, so too he was the first to outline for us the general forms of Comedy by producing not a dramatic invective, but a dramatic picture of the Ridiculous; his *Margites* in fact stands in the same relation to our comedies as the *Iliad* and the *Odyssey* to our tragedies. As soon, however, as Tragedy and Comedy appeared in the field, those naturally drawn to the one line of poetry became writers of comedies instead of iambs, and those naturally drawn to the other, writers of tragedies instead of epics, because these new modes of art were grander and of more esteem than the old. If it be asked whether Tragedy is now all that it need be in its formative elements, to consider that, and decide it theoretically and in relation to the theatres, is a matter for further inquiry.

It certainly began in improvisations—as did also Comedy; the one originating with the authors of the Dithyramb, the other with those of the phallic songs, which still survive as institutions in many of our cities. And its advance after that was little by little, through their improving on whatever they had before them at each stage. It was in fact only after a long series of changes that the movement of Tragedy stopped on attaining its natural form. (1) The number of actors was first increased to two by Aeschylus, who curtailed the Business of the Chorus, and made the dialogue, or spoken portion, take the leading part in the play. (2) A third actor and scenery were due to Sophokles. (3) Tragedy acquired also its magnitude. Discarding short stories and a ludicrous diction, through its passing out of its satyric stage, it assumed, though only at a late point in its progress, a tone of dignity; and its meter changed from trochaic to iambic. The reason for their original use of the trochaic tetrameter was that their poetry was satyric and more connected with dancing than it now is. As soon, however, as a spoken part came in, nature herself found the appropriate meter. The iambic, we know, is the most speakable of meters, as is shown by the fact that we very often fall into it in conversation, whereas we rarely talk hexameters, and only when we do depart from the speaking tone of voice. (4) Another change was a plurality of episodes or acts.

As for Comedy, it is (as has been observed) an imitation of men worse than the average; worse, however, not as regards any and every sort of fault, but only as regards one particular kind, the Ridiculous, which is a species of the Ugly. The Ridiculous may be defined as a mistake or deformity not productive of pain or harm to others; the mask, for instance, that excites laughter, is something ugly and distorted without causing pain.

Though the successive changes in Tragedy and their authors are not unknown, we cannot say the same of Comedy; its early stages passed unnoticed, because it was not as yet taken up in a serious way. It was only at a late point in its progress that a chorus of comedians was officially granted by the archon; they used to be mere volunteers. It had also already certain definite forms at the time when the record of those termed comic poets begins. Who it was who supplied it with masks, or prologues, or a plurality of actors and the like, has remained unknown.

Epic poetry has been seen to agree with Tragedy to this extent, that of being an imitation of serious subjects in a grand kind of verse. It differs from it, however, (1) in that it is in one kind of verse and in narrative form; and (2) in its length—which is due to its action having no fixed limit of time, whereas Tragedy endeavors to keep as far as possible within a single circuit of the sun, or something near that. This, I say, is another point of difference between them, though at first the practice in this respect was just the same in tragedies as in epic poems. They differ also (3) in their constituents, some being common to both and others peculiar to Tragedy—hence a judge of good and bad in Tragedy is a judge of that in epic poetry also. All of the parts of an epic are included in Tragedy; but those of Tragedy are not all of them to be found in the Epic.

Let us proceed now to the discussion of Tragedy; before doing so, however, we must gather up the definition resulting from what has been said. A tragedy, then, is the imitation of an action that is serious and also, as having magnitude, complete in itself; in language with pleasurable accessories, each kind brought in separately in the parts of the work; in a dramatic, not a narrative form; with incidents arousing pity and fear, wherewith to accomplish its katharsis of such emotions. Here by "language with pleasurable accessories" I mean that with rhythm and harmony or song superadded; and by "the kinds separately" I mean that some portions are worked out with verse only, and others in turn with song.

As they act the stories, it follows that in the first place the Spectacle (or stage-appearance of the actors) must be some part of the whole; and in the second Melody and Diction; these two being the means of their imitation. Here by "Diction" I mean merely this, the composition of the verses; and by "Melody," what is too completely understood to require explanation. But further: the subject represented also is an action; and the action involves agents, who must necessarily have their distinctive qualities both of character and thought, since it is from these that we ascribe certain qualities to their actions. There are in the natural order of things, therefore, two causes, Thought and Character, of their actions, and consequently of their success or failure in their lives. Now the action (that which was done) is represented in the play by the Fable or Plot. The Fable, in our present sense of the term is simply this, the combination of the incidents, or things done in the story; whereas Character is what makes us ascribe certain moral

qualities to the agents; and Thought is shown in all they say when proving a particular point or, it may be, enunciating a general truth. There are six parts consequently of every tragedy, as a whole (that is) of such or such quality, viz. a Fable or Plot, Characters, Diction, Thought, Spectacle, and Melody; two of them arising from the means, one from the manner, and three from the objects of the dramatic imitation; and there is nothing else besides these six. Of these, its formative elements, then, not a few of the dramatists have made due use, as every play, one may say, admits of Spectacle, Character, Fable, Diction, Melody, and Thought.

The most important of the six is the combination of the incidents of the story. Tragedy is essentially an imitation not of persons but of action and life, of happiness and misery. All human happiness or misery takes the form of action; the end for which we live is a certain kind of activity, not a quality. Character gives us qualities, but it is in our actions—what we do—that we are happy or the reverse. In a play accordingly they do not act in order to portray the Characters; they include the Characters for the sake of the action. So that it is the action in it, i.e. its Fable or Plot, that is the end and purpose of the tragedy; and the end is everywhere the chief thing. Besides this, a tragedy is impossible without action, but there may be one without Character.

The first essential, the life and soul, so to speak, of Tragedy is the Plot; the Characters come second—compare the parallel in painting, where the most beautiful colors laid on without order will not give one the same pleasure as a simple black-and-white sketch of a portrait. We maintain that Tragedy is primarily an imitation of action, and that it is mainly for the sake of the action that it imitates the personal agents. Third comes the element of Thought, i.e. the power of saying whatever can be said, or what is appropriate to the occasion. One must not confuse it with Character. Character in a play is that which reveals the moral purpose of the agents, i.e. the sort of thing they seek or avoid, where that is not obvious—hence there is no room for Character in a speech on a purely indifferent subject. Thought, on the other hand, is shown in all they say when proving or disproving some particular point, or enunciating some universal proposition. Fourth among the literary elements is the Diction of the personages, the expression of their thoughts in words, which is practically the same thing with verse as with prose. As for the two remaining parts, the Melody is the greatest of the pleasurable accessories of Tragedy. The Spectacle, though an attraction, is the least artistic of all the parts, and has least to do with the art of poetry. The tragic effect is quite possible without a public performance and actors; and besides, the getting-up of the Spectacle is more a matter for the costumier than the poet.

Let us now consider the proper construction of the Fable or Plot, as that is at once the first and the most important thing in Tragedy. We have laid it down that a tragedy is an imitation of an action that is complete in itself, as a whole of some magnitude; for a whole may be of no magnitude to speak of. Now a whole is that which has beginning, middle, and end. A beginning is that which is naturally after something itself, either as its necessary or usual consequent, and with nothing else after it; and a middle, that which is by nature after one thing and has also another after it. A well-constructed Plot, therefore, cannot either begin or end at any point one likes; beginning and end in it must be of the forms just described. Again: to be beautiful, a living creature, and every whole made up of parts, must not only present a certain order in its arrangement of parts, but also be of a certain definite magnitude. Beauty is a matter of size and order, and therefore impossible either (1) in a very minute creature, since our perception becomes indistinct as it approaches instantaneity; or (2) in a creature of vast size, so large that its unity and wholeness is lost to the beholder. Just in the same way, then, as a beautiful whole made up of parts, or a beautiful living creature, must be of some size, but a size to be taken in by the eye, so a story or Plot must be of some length, but of a length to be taken in by the memory. The limit set by the actual nature of the thing is this: the longer the story, consistently with its being comprehensible as a whole, the finer it is by reason of its magnitude. As a rough general formula, a length which allows of the hero passing by a series of probable or necessary stages from misfortune to happiness, or from happiness to misfortune, may suffice as a limit for the magnitude of the story.

The Unity of a Plot does not consist, as some suppose, in its having one man as its subject. An infinity of things befall that one man, some of which it is impossible to reduce to unity; and in like manner there are many actions of one man which cannot be made to form one action. The truth is that, just as in the other imitative arts one imitation is always of one thing, so in poetry the story, as an imitation of action, must represent one action, a complete whole, with its several incidents so closely connected that the transposal or withdrawal of any one of them will disjoin and dislocate the whole. For that which makes no perceptible difference by its presence or absence is no real part of the whole.

From what we have said it will be seen that the poet's function is to describe, not the thing that has happened, but a kind of thing that might happen, i.e. what is possible as being probable or necessary. The distinction between historian and poet is not in the one writing prose and the other verse—you might put the work of Herodotus into verse, and it would still be a species of history; it consists really in this, that the one describes the thing that has been, and the other a kind of thing that might be. Hence poetry is something more philosophic and of graver import than history, since its statements are of the nature rather of universals, whereas those of history are singulars. By a universal statement I mean one as to what such or such a kind of man will probably or necessarily say or do—which is the aim of poetry, though it affixes proper names to the characters. It is evident that the poet must be more the poet of his stories or Plots than of his verses, inasmuch as he is a poet by virtue of the imitative element in his work, and it is actions that he imitates. And if he should come to a subject from actual history, he is none the less a poet for that; since some historic occurrences may very well be in the probable and possible order of things; and it is in that aspect of them that he is their poet.

Tragedy is an imitation not only of a complete action but also of incidents arousing pity and fear. Such incidents have the very greatest effect on the mind when they occur unexpectedly and at the same time in consequence of one another; there is more of the marvelous in them then than if they happened of themselves or by mere chance. Even matters of chance seem most marvelous if there is an appearance of design as it were in them. A Plot, therefore, of this sort is necessarily finer than others.

The next points after what we have said above will be these: (1) What is the poet to aim at, and what is he to avoid, in constructing his Plots? and (2) What are the conditions on which the tragic effect depends?

We assume that, for the finest form of Tragedy, the Plot must be not simple but complex; and further, that it must imitate actions arousing fear and pity, since that is the distinctive function of this kind of imitation. It follows, therefore, that there are three forms of Plot to be avoided. (1) A good man must not be seen passing from happiness to misery, or (2) a bad man from misery to happiness. The first situation is not fear-inspiring or piteous, but simply odious to us. The second is the most untragic that can be; it has no one of the requisites of Tragedy; it does not appeal either to the human feeling in us, or to our pity, or to our fears. Nor, on the other hand, should (3) an extremely bad man be seen falling from happiness into misery. Such a story may arouse the human feeling in us, but it will not move us to either pity or fear; pity is occasioned by undeserved misfortune, and fear by that of one like ourselves; so that there will be nothing either piteous or fear-inspiring in the situation. There remains, then, the intermediate kind of personage, a man not pre-eminently virtuous and just, whose misfortune, however, is brought upon him not by vice or depravity but by some error of judgement, of the number of those in the enjoyment of great reputation and prosperity, e.g.: Oedipus, Thyestes, and the men of note of similar families. The perfect Plot, accordingly, must have a single, and not (as some tell us) a double issue; the change in the hero's fortunes must be not from misery to happiness, but on the contrary from happiness to misery; and the cause of it must lie not in any depravity, but in some great error on his part; the man himself being either such as we have described, or better, not worse than that. The theoretically best tragedy, then, has a Plot of this description. The critics, therefore, are wrong who blame Euripides for taking this line in his tragedies, and giving many of them an unhappy ending. It is, as we have said, the right line to take.

The tragic fear and pity may be aroused by the Spectacle; but they may also be aroused by the very structure and incidents of the play—which is the better way and shows the better poet. The Plot in fact should be so framed that, even without seeing the things take place, he who simply hears the account of them shall be filled with horror and pity at the incidents; which is just the effect that the mere recital of the story in *Oedipus* would have on one. To produce the same effect by means of the Spectacle is less artistic, and requires extraneous aid. Those, however, who make use of the Spectacle to put before us that which is merely monstrous and not productive of fear, are wholly out of touch with Tragedy; not every kind of pleasure should be required of a tragedy, but only its own proper pleasure.

The tragic pleasure is that of pity and fear, and the poet has to produce it by a work of imitation; it is clear, therefore, that the causes should be included in the incidents of his story. Let us see, then, what kinds of incident strike one as horrible, or rather as piteous. In a deed of this description the parties must necessarily be either friends, or enemies, or indifferent to one another. Now when enemy does it on enemy, there is nothing to move us to pity either in his doing or in his meditating the deed, except so far as the actual pain of the sufferer is concerned; and the same is true when the parties are indifferent to one another. Whenever the tragic deed, however, is done within the family—when murder or the like is done or meditated by brother on brother, by son on father, by mother on son, or son on mother—these are the situations the poet should seek after. The traditional stories, accordingly, must be kept as they are, e.g. the murder of Klytemnestra by Orestes.

In the Characters there are four points to aim at. First and foremost, that they shall be good. There will be an element of character in the play, if (as has been observed) what a personage says or does reveals a certain moral purpose; and a good element of character, if the purpose so revealed is good. Such goodness is possible in every type of personage, even in a woman or a slave, though the one is perhaps an inferior, and the other a wholly worthless being. The second point is to make them appropriate. The Character before us may be, say, manly; but it is not appropriate in a female Character to be manly, or clever. The third is to make them like the reality, which is not the same as their being good and appropriate, in our sense of the term. The fourth is to make them consistent and the same throughout; even if inconsistency be part of the man before one for imitation as presenting that form of character, he should still be consistently inconsistent.

There should be nothing improbable among the actual incidents. If it be unavoidable, however, it should be outside the tragedy, like the improbability in the *Oedipus* of Sophocles. But to return to the Characters. As Tragedy is an imitation of personages better than the ordinary man, we in our way should follow the example of the good portrait-painters, who reproduce the distinctive features of a man, and at the same time, without losing the likeness, make him handsomer than he is. The poet in like manner, in portraying men quick or slow to anger, or with similar infirmities of character, must know how to represent them as such, and at the same time as good men, as Agathon and Homer have represented Akhilleus.

The Plot and Characters having been discussed, it remains to consider the Diction and the Thought. As for the Thought, we may assume what is said of it in our Art of Rhetoric, as it belongs more properly to that department of inquiry. The Thought of the personages is shown in everything to be effected by their language—in every effort to prove or disprove, to arouse emotion (pity, fear, anger, and the like) or to maximize or minimize things. It is clear, also, that their mental procedure must be on the same lines in their actions likewise, whenever they wish them to arouse pity or horror, or to have a look of importance or probability. The only difference is that with the act the impression has to be made without explanation; whereas with the spoken word it has to be produced by the speaker, and result from his language. What, indeed, would be the good of the speaker, if things appeared in the required light even apart from anything he says?

As regards the diction, one subject for inquiry under this head is the turns given to the language when spoken; e.g. the difference between command and prayer, simple statement and threat, question and answer, and so forth. The theory of such matters, however, belongs to Elocution and the professors of that art. Whether the poet knows these things or not, his art as a poet is never seriously criticized on that account. What fault can one see in Homer's "Sing of the wrath, Goddess"?—which Protagoras has criticized as being a command where a prayer was meant, since to bid one do or not do, he tells us, is a command. Let us pass over this, then, as appertaining to another art, and not to that of poetry.

Let this, then, suffice as an account of Tragedy, the art imitating by means of action on the stage.

Exercises

1. Aristotle contends that the ultimate aim of tragedy is to inspire pity and fear, which will be removed through a *katharsis* (Gk., to purify). Does he mean a kind of religious experience that will purge the soul? Or is the implication medical, like cleansing the body of poisons? Is there another explanation? Can the katharsis theory be applied to any one of the four tragedies that are included in chapter 5? Which ones? Why? Note: *Agamemnon* and the *Eumenides* should be considered as the beginning and end of a trilogy, with the katharsis theory applied to the *Eumenides*.

2. Review the six elements of tragedy and apply them to each of the four tragedies. Which play most closely resembles Aristotle's basic elements?

3. Consider *Oedipus* and *The Bacchae* in terms of Aristotle's "unities." Is there a single, complete issue that is resolved? Does the time span conform to Aristotle's dictum?

4. What is the "fatal flaw" of Oedipus? Of Pentheus?

5. In the *Poetics* Aristotle uses the phrase "even in a woman or a slave, though one is perhaps an inferior, and the other a wholly worthless being." What does this say about the status of women (and slaves) in Athenian society? Why does he qualify the reference to women, i.e., "perhaps inferior"? Is there some doubt in his mind? Could this doubt have something to do with dramatic characters such as Klytemnestra, Antigone, Medea, and Lysistrata?

6. What is the "improbability" in *Oedipus* that Aristotle allows because it is outside the time frame of the play?

7

Greek Art: Gods, Temples, and the Greeks

According to Greek mythology, Daidalos (DED–uh–los) was the first and greatest of artists, a legendary Minoan artificer who created amazing figures in wood, bronze, and stone, and who even invented the mysterious Minoan maze that housed the fabled Minotaur. Although the story is fascinating, it is immaterial whether or not Daidalos actually existed, because the central idea the myth celebrates is the Greek commitment to creative activity: to invent, design, sculpt, and build. Daidalean Greeks studied nature and used their discoveries to create dynamic new images and structures radiating the illusion of vitality and life. This urge to create is the hallmark of Greek genius.

While the story of Daidalos has an unhappy ending, it does point to a primary artistic consideration of Greek artists. According to the legend, Daidalos had an undisciplined son named Ikarus, who prevailed upon his father to invent wings made of wax and feathers that enabled the lad to soar birdlike in the air. Disregarding the sober advice of his father not to fly too near the sun, the reckless aviator soared so high that his wings melted, plummeting him to his death in a sea that now bears his name. A charming fabrication that reveals a higher truth, this myth symbolizes Greek respect for the laws of nature. Thus, through the story of Daidalos and his hubristic son, Ikarus, we see reflected the Greek search for freedom in the arts through the study of nature, invention, and obedience to reason.

The Aegean Heritage

Chronological Overview

	Egyptian Civilization
2850–2200 B.C.	Old Kingdom[1]
2040–1786 B.C.	Middle Kingdom
1558–1075 B.C.	New Kingdom
3000–2000 B.C.	Cycladic Civilization
2000–1100 B.C.	Minoan Civilization
1550–1100 B.C.	Mycenaean Civilization
	(late Helladic)

Keenly aware of all the cultures of the eastern Mediterranean and the Middle East, the Greeks were influenced by all, especially by Egypt and the Aegean civilizations: Cycladic, Minoan, and the Greek-speaking Mycenaeans. Egyptian civilization, for the Greeks and the Romans, was unique in its longevity and continuity. When in the fifth century B.C. the Greek historian Herodotus gazed upon the two-thousand-year-old Sphinx and the pyramids (fig. 7.1), he was as awed by their antiquity as by their engineering and aesthetic effect. Though pyramid building was already part of Egypt's distant past, Egyptian artists did adhere to other long-established traditions, leading Plato to remark that Egyptian art had not changed in "ten thousand years" (*Laws* 656D–E).

The tenacity of Egyptian artistic conventions provided a large and compelling framework that influenced pre-Greek and Greek art down through the age of Alexander, albeit with uniquely Greek refinements. (An art "convention" is a consistent manner of seeing and depicting things that is generally understood and accepted: commonly held values that have taken form. The sum of all localized conventions is "culture.")

Figure 7.1 Sphinx, ca. 2540–2514 B.C., original height 95′; top of the Great Pyramid of Khufu, ca. 2590–2568 B.C., original height 482′, Giza, Egypt.

Figure 7.2 *Mycerinus and His Queen,* ca. 2599–2571 B.C., Old Kingdom, Fourth Dynasty, from Giza. Slate schist, height 54½″. Shaw Collection. Museum of Fine Arts, Boston.

Egyptian artistic conventions can be seen in the statue of *Mycerinus* (MY–sir–reen–us) *and His Queen* (fig. 7.2), which shares qualities common to practically every Egyptian sculpture depicting life-sized standing or seated figures. Egyptian sculptors took a cubic view of the human form and prepared the statue by drawing its front and side views on the faces of a rectangular block, then working inward until the angular views met. The resultant image is one of startling clarity, but one that demands a 90° change of position every time the viewer desires another perspective. Egyptian statuary has a monumental frozen quality that can be observed from directly in front, directly in back, or squarely from the sides. Symbolizing the total control of an absolute ruler, this

---

1. Of prime concern throughout all art chapters is the evolution of artistic styles; thus the various forms of the visual arts will be considered within the context of the historical development of Western civilization, as reflections of an overall cultural evolution. Careful attention should therefore be paid to all dates, particularly those given with the illustrations. Dates are historical guideposts, and they *are* important.

immobility is a visual counterpart of Egyptian belief in unalterable laws that govern man and nature. Also characteristic of Egyptian portraiture is the rectangularity of the figures, as if they were standing in a rectangular frame within a similar box, thus reinforcing the impression of calmly composed immobility. The illusion of massiveness is heightened by leaving as much stone intact as possible; as, for example, in the stone webbing that binds the rigid arms and clenched fists to the figure. By carving what amounted to very high reliefs, Egyptian sculptors consistently avoided openings in the stone. Finally, the conventions of portraiture required formal depictions of persons of high rank, as here in the figure of the pharaoh, while less-exalted personages are portrayed more realistically. The queen's clasping of her husband's waist and the touching hand on his left arm symbolizes, in a society in which property was inherited through the female line, the transfer of her power to the pharaoh.

In Egyptian painting, as illustrated by *Offering Bearers* (fig. 7.3), we see an even more pervasive convention. Egyptian painters and relief carvers almost invariably depicted the human body with the eyes and torso as viewed from the front, but with the face and legs in profile. This arrangement shows key body parts in their most telling and easily understood view, the way artists "know" rather than how they actually "see" the parts. Further, by avoiding specific settings and placing the boldly two-dimensional figures on a frontal plane, the artists emphasized the timelessness that characterizes Egyptian art.

Despite strong artistic influences, there were significant differences between Egypt and Greece, particularly in religion, government, topography, and climate (see "Geography of Greece," p. 36). In Egypt, with an absolute monarch and a powerful clergy, there was no power and no freedom for the common people. As the inventors of democracy, with neither an organized religion nor a lifetime clergy, the citizens of Greece, particularly the Athenians, enjoyed the only political freedom in the ancient world. Differences in topography and climate were also influential. Egypt was a vast, arid land with its agriculture, and thus its culture, confined to narrow fertile bands hugging the life-giving Nile. Greece was a semiarid land of pastures and olive groves, with rugged mountains guarding broad valleys that were closely linked to a seemingly endless seacoast.

Egyptian culture was immeasurably influenced by the geography and climate of the Nile Valley. Literally a "gift of the Nile," Egypt was generally only as stable as the smoothly flowing river that dictated the pattern of Egyptian life through predictable cycles of flood and retreat. Protected by mountains, the sea, and trackless deserts, inhabited Egypt averaged some 10 miles in width along 650 miles of the mighty river. Herodotus succinctly described Egypt as "all the country covered by innundations of the Nile" and Egyptians as "all men who drink Nile water" (*Histories,* II). Since their prosperous economy was based on the dependably bountiful river, it is no wonder that Egyptians viewed nature's laws and those of the gods as immutable and the afterlife as a continuation of the good life in the Nile Valley.

Once two warring kingdoms, Upper and Lower Egypt were united (in ca. 3100 B.C.) by a powerful ruler (King Menes?) who declared himself a god and claimed ownership of the river, land, and people as gifts of the gods. The exalted position of the pharaoh, which was never disputed by the people, is symbolized by the two statues of Amenhotep III (fig. 7.4) that originally flanked his funerary temple. Necessitated perhaps by the vastness of the desert landscape, the giant figures represented the significance of the pharaoh, while also serving to awe the subjects of the royal power.

Figure 7.3 *Offering Bearers* from Tomb of Sebekhotep, ca. 1500–1300 B.C., New Kingdom, Eighteenth Dynasty. Tempera on mud plaster, width ca. 30″, Thebes. Rogers Fund. Metropolitan Museum of Art, New York.

Figure 7.4 *Colossi of Memnon,* ca. 1400 B.C., New Kingdom, Eighteenth Dynasty. Quartzsite, originally 68′ high, Thebes.

Greek Art: Gods, Temples, and the Greeks **163**

Figure 7.5 Temple of Amon, dating from the twentieth century B.C. but constructed mainly from the sixteenth to twelfth centuries, New Kingdom, Karnak.

Figure 7.6 Mortuary Temple of Queen Hatshepsut, ca. 1480 B.C., New Kingdom, Eighteenth Dynasty, Deir el-Bahari.

Figure 7.7 Temple of Amon-Mut-Khonsu, ca. 1390–1260 B.C., New Kingdom, Eighteenth Dynasty, Luxor.

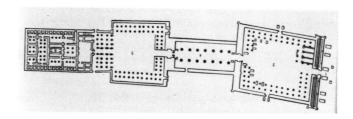

Figure 7.8 Floor plan of Temple of Amon-Mut-Khonsu: (1) entrance, (2) first court, (3) earlier sanctuaries, (4) great hall, (5) second court, and (6) sanctuaries of Amon, Mut, and Khonsu.

Egyptian temples were not only designed on an enormous scale to make a distinctive statement in the vast landscape, but also as visual symbols of the power of the gods and the authority of the priests who served the pharaoh and the gods. Towering over the foreground figure, the Temple of Amon at Karnak (fig. 7.5) was the seat of the throne of Amon and the center of religious administration. It was the most extensive temple in Egypt and one of the largest sanctuaries in the ancient world, containing 134 columns in the Great Hall alone.

Constructed at the foot of sandstone cliffs on the western bank of the Nile at Thebes, the mortuary temple of Queen Hatshepsut (fig. 7.6) is a brilliantly conceived complex designed as a memorial to the first woman to rule Egypt, the first illustrious female ruler

of whom there is any record. In order to make the structure impressive, given the enormity of the setting, the architect Senmet has thrust the upper courtyard into the cliff face so that the towering mass can serve as a kind of natural pyramid.

Even in its ruined condition the Temple of Amon-Mut-Khonsu (fig. 7.7) clearly illustrates the nature of Egyptian religious architecture. Missing from the temple complex is the high wall that originally enclosed the entire aggregate of courts, halls, and temples. Egyptian temples were designed as a succession of spaces of increasing holiness, entered through a main portal flanked by ponderous slanting masses of stone called pylons (extreme left, fig. 7.7), which led to the first inner court (no. 1 in fig. 7.8). Passing through the 74' columns of the Great Hall (right center of fig. 7.7, no. 4 in fig. 7.8) ordinary worshippers assembled in the sequestered inner court (no. 5 in fig. 7.8), but were forbidden to go any farther. From here they could only marvel at the mysterious forest of columns that darkened the inner recesses, the exclusive preserve of the priesthood (far right of fig. 7.7, no. 6 of fig. 7.8). There the all-powerful clergy administered the temples of the local deity Amon, his wife Mut, and their son Khonsu. (In fig. 7.7 the structures to the right of the pylon are the dome and minaret of a medieval mosque.)

To summarize, the cubic view of Egyptian sculptors and the simultaneous profile/frontality of painting and relief carving strongly influenced Greek art. On the other hand, Egyptian geographical, political, and religious factors accounted for their monumental structures and sculptures, which were so vastly different from their Greek counterparts, as will be discussed later in this chapter.

Cycladic Civilization 3000–2000 B.C.

In the Aegean Sea north of Crete (see map on p. 37) lies a group of islands that are called the Cyclades because they "cycle" around the hub of the sacred island of Delos, birthplace of Apollo and his twin sister Artemis. A late Neolithic culture flourished here of which little remains beyond some remarkable marble idols. These strangely modern figures are characterized by rectangular angularity and an abstract, sophisticated simplicity. They include heads and, primarily, standing female figures, all carved of pure white Parian marble. The monumentally proportioned head in figure 7.9 can be favorably compared with the work of modern abstract sculptors. Here we have an artistic truth: all figurative art is essentially abstract, or a restatement of what the artist actually saw. Obviously this artist saw a nose as a dominant feature, and so we too are very aware of the nose. In addition, there are two tiny ears, an opened mouth, and two dimly perceived eyes. An abstracted version of the artist's perception, this is not the head of a specific person but rather an image of everyone, particularly all those with prominent noses.

Because the Cycladic figures as well as the entire Minoan and Mycenaean civilizations were all rediscovered during the past century or so, we have no way of knowing the full extent of their influence on Greek culture. We can only suggest that because of their proximity, the intensely curious Greeks knew more about Aegean civilizations than is indicated by current evidence.

Minoan Civilization, ca. 2000–1100 B.C.

Remarkably different from all other civilizations, the Minoans built no monumental showplace palaces for divine monarchs, no temples, and no fortifications of any kind. (See chap. 4 for an overview of Minoan history.) Minoan palaces were designed to be lived in comfortably and enjoyed. The palaces featured

Figure 7.9 Cycladic Head, ca. 2500 B.C. Marble, height 11½". National Archeological Museum, Athens.

Figure 7.10 Detail of the south front of the Palace at Knossos, ca. 1600–1400 B.C.

hundreds of small rooms, rambling corridors and staircases, walls gaily decorated with colorful murals, running water, bathtubs, a sewage system, terraces, open galleries, and numerous light wells to convey natural illumination to lower levels of the three- to five-story structures. They probably functioned also as administrative centers for the Minoan trade empire.

Probably the most important of the many palaces on Crete was that of the legendary King Minos at Knossos (fig. 7.10), the vastness of which can only be

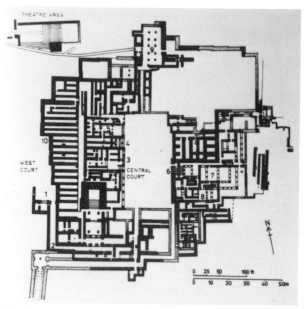

The Palace at Knossos

1. West Porch	7. Hall of the Double Axes
2. Corridor of the Procession	8. "Queen's Megaron"
3. Palace Shrine	9. Pillar Hall
4. Stepped Porch	10. Store-rooms
5. Throne Room	11. Royal Road, to Little
6. Grand Staircase	Palace

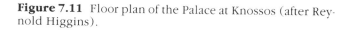

Figure 7.11 Floor plan of the Palace at Knossos (after Reynold Higgins).

Figure 7.12 Throne Room, Palace of Minos, Knossos

Figure 7.13 Queen's Megaron, Palace of Minos, Knossos

hinted at in the partial reconstruction by Sir Arthur Evans. The multiple levels, wandering corridors, and countless rooms (fig. 7.11) probably inspired the Greek legend of the labyrinth of Minos, which was guarded by the fearful Minotaur (half man, half bull). The monster was imprisoned there by Minos after his wife gave birth to it. The earthshaking roars attributed to the awesome beast can undoubtedly be linked to the earthquakes that periodically wracked Crete.

Totally unlike that of an Egyptian king's, for instance, the Throne Room (fig. 7.12) is a small chamber at ground level containing a simple, high-backed alabaster throne with stone benches around three walls, including the wall with the throne. The fanciful griffin mural (white on red) is a modern reconstruction based on fragments found in the ruins. Opposite the throne is a colonnade separating the throne room from an open atrium, which adds air and light to an intimate and unpretentious setting.

Known as the legendary friend to all sailors, five dolphins frolic contentedly in a seascape mural in the Queen's Megaron (fig. 7.13). The queen's apartment, which is illuminated by a light well, also features ornamental floral designs on the door frames and an adjoining bathroom complete with bathtub. Even now there is an air of understated elegance, an ambience of good taste.

Whether she was a priestess, goddess, or queen, the so-called *Snake Goddess* (fig. 7.14) is typical of diminutive Minoan sculpture. A culture with neither divine monarch nor priesthood has no compelling need for monumental sculpture, and indeed none has been found. Though the rigid frontal pose of this small figure indicates an Egyptian influence, the raised arms plus the small animal on her head (panther?) lighten the mood to one akin to playfulness. Characteristic of feminine attire at the time, the colorful tiered skirt, tight bodice, and bared breasts are very stylish for a cult figure. Whatever her position or function was, she is a delightful work of art.

Mycenaean Civilization, ca. 1550–1100 B.C.

Occupying Crete after the sudden destruction of Minoan civilization in ca. 1450 B.C. (see chap. 4), the Mycenaean invaders adapted Minoan styles to their more robust tastes. The Mycenaeans were the Akhaians (uh–KAY–uns) of the fabled Trojan War depicted in

Figure 7.14 *Snake Goddess,* ca. 1600 B.C., faience, height 17½″. Archeological Museum, Heraklion, Crete.

Figure 7.15 Mask from Mycenae, ca. 1500 B.C. Funeral mask from the royal tombs. Beaten gold, ca. 12″ high. National Archeological Museum, Athens.

Figure 7.16 Lion Gate, citadel at Mycenae, ca. 1250 B.C. Limestone, height of relief 9′6″.

Homer's *Iliad* and represented the final and highest stage of Helladic culture (after Hellas, the Greek mainland). Until the last century, historians had dismissed the *Iliad* as fanciful fiction, albeit a brilliant epic poem. They contended that Troy, Mycenae, and the epic heroes were products of Homer's fertile imagination. But in 1871, a wealthy German merchant named Heinrich Schliemann astounded everyone by announcing the discovery of Troy in northwest Turkey, just where his painstaking study of Homer indicated it would be.

Schliemann further astonished archeologists by discovering the Mycenaean civilization, including the great citadel at Mycenae with its grave circles full of precious jewelry and gold death masks, one of which Schliemann attributed to Agamemnon himself (fig. 7.15). It was soon determined, however, that this Mycenae predated the Homeric king, that the remains of "Agamemnon" were of someone from an earlier civilization. The undaunted German, realizing that argument was futile and acknowledging the lack of positive identification, jokingly renamed his Agamemnon "Schulze." Regardless of the appropriate name, the Mask from Mycenae is a superb example of the highly developed metal craftmanship called toreutics (to–RUE–tiks), the hammering of metals into representational form. The death mask (and weapons and jewelry) represents a Mycenaean adaptation of the Egyptian funeral practice of burying their illustrious dead with items that were commensurate with their status in life.

The citadel of Mycenae, which is today in ruins, is a massive structure whose gigantic stones were placed, according to legend, by the Cyclopes (sigh–KLO–peas), a mythical race of one-eyed giants. A highly efficient fortress, its single entrance is protected by high walls on three sides. The lintel of this ponderous gate is topped by a stone relief of two lions, now headless, flanking a symbolic Minoan column (fig. 7.16). It is from this striking carving that the giant portal takes the name Lion Gate. Unlike the Minoans with their island isolation and protective seawall, closed palaces were a distinct necessity on the Greek mainland.

Greek Civilization, ca. 800–30 B.C.

The complexity and productivity of the Greek arts make it necessary to subdivide the balance of this chapter into the following artistic periods (all dates approximate):

Chronological Overview

800–660 B.C.	Geometric Period
660–480 B.C.	Archaic Period
480–323 B.C.	Classical Period
	Early 480–450
	High 450–400
	Late 400–323
323–30 B.C.	Hellenistic Period

Following a fairly strict chronology, the different media (sculpture, architecture, pottery) will be examined as manifestations of the evolving artistic styles of ancient Greece.

Geometric Period, ca. 800–660 B.C.

The invasions of Greek-speaking Dorians (ca. 1100–800 B.C.) not only abruptly terminated Mycenaean dominance and thoroughly disrupted the lives of all the Hellenes, but it also had a devastating effect on the arts of sculpture and architecture. Military invasions always disturb the arts, as political and economic turmoil is not conducive to the commissioning of such major works as temples and life-sized statues. While probably impoverishing many artists and interfering with the transmission of technology, the waves of Dorian invaders made relatively little impact upon the utilitarian arts of furniture, textiles, glassware, and, above all, pottery. Because most of the pottery produced during this chaotic period emphasized geometric decoration, this era is known as the Geometric period.

Even though it had been practiced since the Stone Age, the craft of making pots made a great leap forward with the invention (probably in Sumer—Iran—ca. 3250 B.C.) of the potter's wheel. The wheel was introduced into Crete around 2000 B.C. and enabled Minoan potters to lead the Aegean world in transforming the craft of making utilitarian vessels into an art form that reached its apex with the classic Greek vase.

As early as the ninth century, geometric conventions of pottery decoration had evolved into a vocabulary of meanders, concentric circles, horizontal bands, wheel patterns, shaded triangles, swastikas, and zigzags. Abstract animal and figure patterns were used in a two-dimensional form in either full front or profile views. Sophisticated, aesthetically appealing, and utilitarian, the *Amphora of the Dipylon* (fig. 7.17) is a masterwork of the potter's art. Because cremation had been abandoned, these monumental vases served as

Figure 7.17 *Amphora of the Dipylon,* ca. 750 B.C. Terra-cotta, height 61″ with base. National Archeological Museum, Athens.

grave markers and also as receptacles for liquid offerings, which filtered down to the honored dead through openings in the base. The representational scene is a *prothesis* (PROTH–uh–sis), or lying-in-state of the deceased, flanked by triangulated geometric figures of mourners with their arms raised in grief. Alternating bands separate different versions of the meander[2] motif (also known as the Greek fret), with a band of grazing antelope highlighting the neck. Created about a quarter century after the inauguration of the Olympic Games in 776 B.C., this heroic vase can symbolically mark the beginning of the Homeric Age of ca. 750–700 B.C.

Though it achieved its final form during the Archaic Period (ca. 600 B.C.), it is apparent that the Greek temple was known to Homer (*Iliad,* I, 39). Fragmentary terra-cotta models from the eighth century display three of the elements of the temple canon: rectangular floor plan, enclosed inner shrine, and porch supported by columns. The "canon" (Gk., *kanon,* rule) of Greek temples refers to fundamental

---

2. From the name of a winding river in Asia Minor. In Greek decoration it is a mazelike pattern of lines that wind in and out or cross one another.

volume, modeling, and some anatomical details, design elements that place this work on the borderline between the Geometric and Archaic periods.

Based on the surviving pottery and statuettes, the Geometric can be viewed as an interlude rather than a major artistic period. The fact that Homer's *Iliad* and *Odyssey* were the greatest achievements of this era makes one wonder, however. Did the visual arts lag behind epic poetry, or have some important artworks been lost? In any event, the Geometric was a period in which the Greeks began to see and think and create as a Greek, not as an Egyptian or a Minoan or a Mycenaean. Borrowings from these civilizations are evident, but the unique forms introduced during the Geometric period clearly indicate an elementary process of producing art forms not bound to traditional conventions but subject to experimentation and invention, and above all, art that was dynamic rather than static.

Archaic Period, 600–480 B.C.

Archaic is a term derived from a Greek word meaning *ancient* and is not to be confused with such contemporary definitions as antiquated, outdated, or old-fashioned. The sixth century saw Greek genius blossom with the production of brilliant works of art. This was one of the exalted periods in world art, a vigorous era that also produced the world's first democracy.

Throughout Greek art, beginning with the Archaic period, Greek sculptors evolved new representational modes that were different from all previous artistic conceptions. They were fascinated by the complex mechanics of the human body; this led to the creation of fully three-dimensional sculpture that more nearly represented the natural world. The ideal, as illustrated in the Pygmalion legend, was the creation of a marble figure that would step down from the platform and speak to its creator.

Two main subjects preoccupied sculptors throughout the sixth century: the standing nude male and the standing fully clothed female. Apparently serving as votive or commemorative statues, these figures were not personalized portraits but rather idealized representations placed somewhere between humankind and the gods. No one really knows why the men were always nude and the women fully clothed and, moreover, we can apply only vague and unsatisfactory names to these freestanding figures: *kouros* (KOO–rose; youth) and *kore* (KORE–ay; maiden). Probably adapted from Egypt and Mesopotamia, these two subjects were repeated again and again, never with the intention of exact repetition but rather with the competitive drive that leads to constant innovation. It is the degree of this ceaseless striving for something different, something better, that sets the Greeks apart from other cultures.

Figure 7.18 Statuette of Youth, "Mantiklos dedicated me . . . , ca. 700–680 B.C. Bronze, height 8″. Francis Bartlett Donation. Courtesy, Museum of Fine Arts, Boston.

procedures that help convert a concept into reality, in this case, buildings that look precisely like what they are: temples for the gods.

Among the most popular products of the Greek artisans were statuettes, which were produced throughout Greek history. Though they were not as impressive as life-sized statuary, the very smallness of miniature figures enables one to hold and turn them around in one's hands—a very personal relationship. The statuette shown in figure 7.18 is a votive offering bearing on its thighs the inscription, "Mantiklos dedicated me to the Far Darter of the silver bow, as part of his tithe. Do thou, Phoibos, grant him gracious recompence." As obvious as the geometric elements are, the unknown artist also demonstrates a concern for

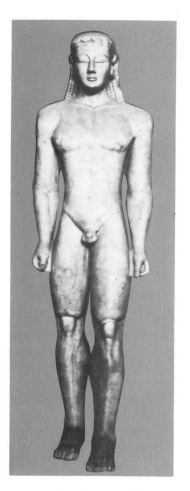

Figure 7.19 *Kore of Auxerre,* ca. 630–600 B.C. Limestone with traces of paint, height 24″. The Louvre, Paris.

Figure 7.20 *Kouros of Sounion,* ca. 600 B.C. Marble, height 10′. National Archeological Museum, Athens.

An early work, the *Kore of Auxerre* (fig. 7.19) stands as stiffly as an Egyptian statue, but compared with Egyptian conventions shows some significant differences (see fig. 7.2). Unlike his Egyptian predecessor, the sculptor has cut away some needless stone to outline the figure rather than encasing it. The hair is braided in the geometric manner, but a very human touch is conveyed by the way the waist is cinched by a wide belt. From the light shoulder covering to the swelling hips, there is a skillful contrast between curved and straight lines.

Compare the colossal statue of the *Kouros of Sounion* (fig. 7.20) with the pharaoh (fig. 7.2). We see that the Egyptian figure is "imprisoned" in stone in the manner of a very high relief, whereas the kouros statue has been liberated from unnecessary stone, with the exception of the hands. The pharaoh stands in repose with his weight on the back foot. The equal distribution of weight of the kouros figure gives the illusion that he is striding forward, an effect that is heightened by the taut thigh muscles. Vestiges of geometric ornamentation remain in the rosette hair with meticulous braids and, especially, in the scrolls (volutes) that serve as ears. The most critical differ-

ence between the Egyptian and Greek sculptures lies in the eyes and facial expression. Displaying the typical relaxed serenity of Egyptian portraiture, the pharaoh gazes dreamily into an undefined distance. The *Kouros of Sounion* manifests the characteristic dynamism of Greek art, with tension present in every line of the face. Egyptian figures seem never to have known stress, whereas tension and striving are hallmarks of the restless Greeks.

Created shortly after the Greek triumphs over the Persians at Salamis and Plataea, the *Calf-Bearer* (fig. 7.21) was something new in Greek art, a composition of two figures so unified that neither figure is conceivable without the other. A bearded man with a cloak draped over his upper body is gently balancing a bull calf on his shoulders as he strides confidently forward. With the corners of his mouth lifted slightly in the so-called Archaic smile, he stares ahead with hollow eyes that once contained inlays, probably making them quite realistic. Characteristic of the Archaic style, his braided hair and close-cropped beard are highly stylized, in contrast with the naturalistic depiction of the calf.

Figure 7.21 *Calf-Bearer (Moschophoros),* ca. 575–550 B.C. Marble, height 66″. Akropolis Museum, Athens.

Figure 7.22 *Hera of Samos,* ca. 560 B.C. Marble, height 76″. The Louvre, Paris.

Larger than life size, the figure of *Hera of Samos* (fig. 7.22) is both subtle and strong. Basically cylindrical in shape, she was probably created by an Ionian sculptor who, among other things, was very interested in the interrelationship of the airy drapery of Ionian dress with the body underneath. Notice the contrast between the diagonal draping across the breasts and the delicate folds dropping lightly from the hips in a slightly concave mirroring of a Greek column.

Painting was, for the Greeks, one of the supreme art forms, and yet very little of it survives. We must focus instead on the superb achievements of Archaic vase painters, who raised that form of pictorial art to a level comparable to the best sculpture and architecture. That the Greeks themselves valued their vases is attested to by the number of painters (and potters) who signed their creations, which incidentally raised the value (and price) of the vase. They concentrated on lively interaction between individual gods, goddesses, and heroes; and using an incisive black-figure technique (silhouetted figures on a reddish background), vase painters like Exekias (e–ZEE–ki–as) set a standard that has not been surpassed (fig. 7.23). In

Figure 7.23 Exekias, amphora: "Akhilleus Slaying Penthesiles," ca. 540 B.C. Height 16¼″. British Museum, London. Reproduced by courtesy of the Trustees of the British Museum.

Figure 7.24 Temple of Hera I, ca. 550 B.C. Paestum, Italy.

Figure 7.25 *Kore in Dorian Peplos,* ca. 530 B.C. Marble with traces of paint, height 48″. Akropolis Museum, Athens.

this incident from the Trojan War, not related in the *Iliad,* Akhilleus is in the act of killing Penthesilea, Queen of the Amazons. At the very moment of his spear thrust, we can see that he has fallen in love with her. The hulking silhouette of the mighty hero looms over the vanquished but still proud queen, forming a tight and compact composition of striking power and intensity that contrasts with the delicate spirals. A tall, two-handled jar for wine or oil, the amphora itself was made by Exekias, who signed eleven vases but only two paintings, implying that he took more pride in making vases than in painting them. Exekias managed to misspell his own name on one of his two surviving paintings, possibly confirming the judgment of Plato and Aristotle that craftsmen were manifestly inferior to philosophers.

By the sixth century, Greek city-states had established colonies in North Africa and from Byzantium (Istanbul) westward to Italy, Sicily, France, and Spain. Magna Graecia (southern Italy) was particularly important, for it was here that Pythagoras founded his religious brotherhood (see chap. 4) and Parmenides and Empedokles established the Eleatic School of philosophy (see chap. 5). One of the better-preserved of the surviving Archaic temples is that of Hera at Paestum (fig. 7.24), the site of two religious centers of Magna Graecia. Though employing an unusual nine-column front, this structure has all the elements of the basic Greek temple: rectangular floor plan, columns on four sides, three steps rising from the foundation to the top level on which the columns rest, and an enclosed inner shrine. (As far as we know the odd number of columns was never tried again. Regularity was an important Greek concept, as exemplified in the six- or eight-column fronts of classical temples; see figs. 7.41 and 7.44.) Other archaic features are heavy, bulging columns that taper sharply as they near the oversize, pillowlike capitals. The whole effect is heavy because these features seem to create a sense of physical strain, unlike the Parthenon (see fig. 7.44), which appears to be light and free of stress.

By comparing the *Kore in Dorian Peplos* (fig. 7.25) with the *Kore of Auxerre* (fig. 7.19), one can observe a basic continuity while also noting significant changes. This is the last known archaic kore statue to wear the Dorian *peplos,* a heavy tunic reaching to the ground that was fastened at each shoulder and belted at the waist. It was commonly worn over a light, sleeved tunic called a *chiton.* Though there is still a rectangular frontality about this figure, there is no doubt about the presence of a young, nubile body beneath the woolen peplos. With its lovely natural smile and arched eyebrows, the softly rounded face exudes a serene kind of happiness. The remaining paint on the graceful braids indicates that the young woman was a redhead, a valued hue in ancient Athens.

The Ionian *himation* worn by the *Kore from Chios* (fig. 7.26) contrasts sharply with the severe Dorian peplos. This elegant mantle, which was worn over the chiton, was of much lighter material than the peplos and could be draped over the body in a variety of

Figure 7.26 *Kore from Chios* (?), ca. 520 B.C. Marble with traces of paint, ca. 22″ high (lower part missing). Akropolis Museum, Athens.

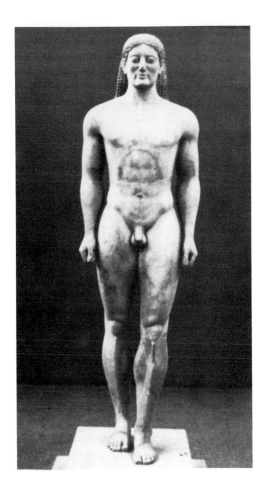

Figure 7.27 *Anavyssos Kouros,* ca. 525 B.C. Marble with traces of paint, height 76″. National Archeological Museum, Athens.

graceful arrangements. Based on the number of surviving works, it is obvious that artists were entranced with the challenge of sculpting the sinuous lines of the garment. Moreover, the wholesale adoption by Athenian women of the stylish himation (see other styles in fig. 8.6) symbolizes the individualistic, pleasure-loving Ionian orientation of Athenian society, as compared with the sober peplos and stolid, group-oriented society of the Dorian city of Sparta. As we have already seen (p. 125), the clash of these disparate cultures was apparently inevitable.

The *Anavyssos Kouros* (fig. 7.27), which was placed over the grave of a warrior named Kroisos, signals a major advance towards *naturalism,* fidelity to the actual appearance of the natural world. The revolutionary changes were already apparent in the *Kouros of Sounion* (see fig. 7.20), but were realized in what is now more nearly a portrait of the finely tuned body of a youthful wrestler who had the misfortune to die on some unknown battlefield. Though the knees and calves are emphasized according to earlier conventions, the muscles of the powerful thighs and taut arms swell with lifelike vitality. Based on an increasing knowledge of skeletal structure and anatomical details, the sculptor has concentrated on portraying

the body. Greek artists, from the very first efforts at monumental sculpture, were never interested in portrait busts, but instead were concerned with the depiction of the body. This does not imply that the head was secondary—far from it. It simply means that Greek artists were intent on portraying the whole person, especially the vibrantly healthy body the Greeks so admired.

The ancient Greeks also seemed to possess a unique visual sensibility. Many factors may account for this, and a few will be mentioned. Meticulous observation was basic to Greek science, itself an area in which the Greeks had no rivals. In medical practice as exemplified by Hippokrates, there was an emphasis on the accumulation of sensory information. The Greek gods were conceived in the images of men and women and were thus immediately accessible for artistic representation. Perhaps most important, however, is the fact that the Greeks were not subjected to views of reality imposed from above by either a divine-right monarch or an organized religion.

During the discussion of the *Anavyssos Kouros* (fig. 7.27) it was pointed out that Greek sculptors portrayed the entire person, concentrating on the body,

Figure 7.28 *Kore* (*La Delicata;* detail), ca. 500 B.C. Marble with traces of paint. Akropolis Museum, Athens.

Figure 7.29 Sosias painter, cup (detail): "Akhilleus Bandaging Patrokles' Wound," ca. 500 B.C. Attic red-figure cup, ca. 7″ high. Antikenmuseum Staatliche Museen Preussischer Kulturbesitz Berlin.

but without de-emphasizing the head. By deliberately selecting only the enchanting head of the kore figure that is sometimes called *La Delicata* (fig. 7.28), it is clearly apparent that the creator of this masterful portrait of a beautiful woman wished to highlight her pensive, almost melancholy, mood. Also known as "the girl with the almond eyes," this work epitomizes the Archaic style at its best.

Around 530 B.C. vase painters began working with a color scheme of red figures against a black background, the reverse of black-figure technique. The luminous new *red-figure* technique permitted secondary markings like hair, muscles, details of dress, and even discreet shadings. The two styles coexisted for thirty or forty years, but the red-figure technique, with its greater opportunities for delicacy and subtlety, became the dominant style of the classical period. In the red-figure cup by the Sosias painter (fig. 7.29), we see the first example of eyes painted just the way they actually appear in profile. This significant advance marks a phase out of the Egyptian convention of always depicting the eyes as they are viewed frontally. In the painting Akhilleus is intent upon tending the wound, while in a very human reaction, Patrokles has turned his head away as if he were not even a party to this unhappy event—or wishes he weren't. Below the platform are three palmettes, a decorative motif invented by the Greeks based on a stylized rendering of a palm leaf. Some basic differences between red-figure and black-figure technique become apparent when this painting is compared with that of Exekias

(fig. 7.23). It cannot be said that one of these works is better than another, only that different techniques lead to dissimilar styles. Black-figure painting is characteristic of the vigorous Archaic period, while red-figure vases typify the later Classical style.

Classical Period, 480–323 B.C.

The year 480 marked a critical turning point in the history of Athens. Invaded and humiliated by Xerxes' Persian forces, their city ravaged, and their culture in ruins, the Athenians and their allies struck back by destroying the Persian fleet at Salamis and defeating the army the following year. A resurgent Athens moved unerringly towards power, prosperity, and a legendary Golden Age epitomized by the confident Classical style.

The *Kritios Boy* (fig. 7.30), a prime example of the Severe style of early classicism, was created at about the same time as Aeschylus was gaining fame as a playwright. Somewhat like the innovations of Aeschylus, this statue represents a new principle in art. It is wearing an expression of composed, classical solemnity (compare this with the Archaic smile) and is truly a standing figure. Archaic sculptures were limited to a striding pose with an equal distribution of weight; here we have a formal composition with a fine balance of tense and relaxed muscles, the head turned slightly, one hip a bit elevated, and the weight on one leg with the other at rest. This is how any of us might stand in natural repose.

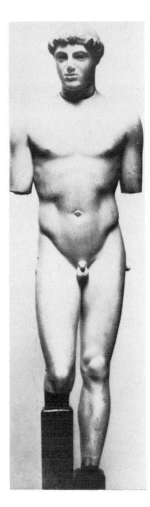

Figure 7.30 *Kritios Boy,* 481/480 B.C. marble, height 34″. Akropolis Museum, Athens.

Figure 7.31 *Delphi Charioteer,* ca. 470 B.C. Bronze, height 71″. Archeological Museum, Delphi.

Also representing the Severe style is the *Delphi Charioteer* (fig. 7.31), which was once part of a large composition of a chariot and four horses. Chariot races were entered by the owners of racing teams and driven by highly skilled charioteers, much like thoroughbred horses today are ridden by professional jockeys. Overlooking the disheveled, dusty condition of a charioteer after a grueling race, the artist idealizes a proud champion, with his chiton falling in fluted folds like those of a Doric column (see fig. 7.39). Included, however, are such realistic details as a device to keep the chiton from billowing in the wind—a cord that passed over the shoulders, under the armpits, and crossed in back. The headband performed exactly the same function as a tennis player's sweatband (fig. 7.32).

Figure 7.32 *Delphi Charioteer,* rear view, detail.

Greek Art: Gods, Temples, and the Greeks **175**

Figure 7.33 *Poseidon (Zeus?),* ca. 460 B.C. Bronze, height 82″. National Archeological Museum, Athens.

Figure 7.34 Myron, *Discobolus (Discus Thrower),* reconstructed Roman marble copy of a bronze original of ca. 450 B.C. Height 60″. Museo della Terme, Rome.

One of the finest original Greek bronzes, *Poseidon* (*Zeus* according to some; fig. 7.33) stands majestically, prepared to hurl his trident (or thunderbolt). The figure is stridently asymmetrical: arms, legs, even the head, turn in different angles from the torso, which in turn shows the competing muscular strains and tensions. Unlike even the most naturalistic archaic statues, this body has rippling muscles functioning beneath taut skin. The various concavities and convexities of the bronze surface reflect a shimmering light that further animates the figure. It matters little that if Poseidon's arms were lowered his hands would dangle at the knees; that the eyes are hollow sockets that were once filled with colored stones; or that the hair, beard, and eyebrows are highly stylized; the work exudes a kinetic energy never achieved in earlier sculptures.

The High Classical period (the Age of Perikles) was marked in part by the beginning of construction on the Akropolis, the early fame of Sophokles, and notable sculptures by Myron and Polykleitos. The *Discobolus* (*Discus Thrower;* fig. 7.34) is intended to be viewed when standing to the left of the figure in order to become totally involved with the moment leading to explosive action. Though a celebrated classical statue, the figure follows Egyptian conventions. It is designed on a frontal plane with head and legs in profile and the upper torso turned towards the front. It is balanced by the arced arms and the head and left leg, a formal composition that displays the harmonious proportions characteristic of the classical style. With simplified anatomical details and a stylized pose, all is in readiness for the athlete to wheel about and hurl the discus. Excellence of form, which counted as half of the scoring, was as important as marking the distance of the throw, a procedure comparable to the scoring in modern competitive diving. An athlete could win the olive wreath with a second-place throw, provided he displayed a form comparable to that of the *Discobolus.* (See also the discussion of the Olympic Games beginning on p. 220.)

One of the most highy acclaimed artists of the Golden Age was Polykleitos (polly–KLY–toss) of Argos, who is known today only through Roman copies of his work. This copy of his *Doryphoros* (dory–FOR–os; fig. 7.35) is of sufficiently high quality for us to see how it exemplified a "canon" (system of proportions), which became a model for several generations of artists. Displaying the powerful body of a finely conditioned athlete, the young man rests his full weight on the right leg with the left bent at the knee and his toes lightly touching the ground. With the head barely turned to the right and the right shoulder dropped slightly, the whole body can be traced as a long **S** curve from the feet to the head. At rest as no sculpted figure had ever been before, the composition is still dynamic, a balance of tension and relaxation throughout the entire body. Harmoniously proportioned and with a classic balance of artistic and natural form, this is the confident style of the Golden Age.

Figure 7.35 Polykleitos, *Doryphoros (Spear Bearer),* Roman marble copy after a bronze original of ca. 450–440 B.C. Height 78″. National Museum, Naples.

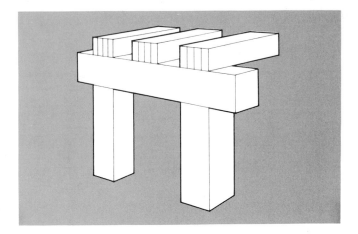

Figure 7.36 Post and lintel system

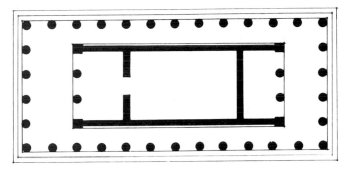

Figure 7.37 Typical Greek temple floor plan

Figure 7.38 Typical Greek temple facade

Let us turn now to developments in architecture leading to the classical temples of the Age of Perikles. As discussed earlier, Greek temples had evolved into their canonical form during the early Archaic period (ca. 600). Fundamental to the temple canon is the architectural system of post and lintel (fig. 7.36). After planting a post at all four corners of the space to be enclosed, the builder then placed a beam (lintel) on top of and across the posts. Roof beams (joists) were placed at regular intervals to link the opposite lintels, and were then covered with a roof. Spaces between the posts were filled, as needed, with walls, windows, and doors. First employed in wood, then in brick, and eventually in stone construction, the post and lintel system was used for all major Greek buildings. The greater strength of arches and the arched vault (see Roman architecture, chap. 10) was known and used, but only for such minor works as the long arched corridor leading into the stadium at Nemea.

A typical temple floor plan (fig. 7.37) shows a *cella,* a central room where the statue of the diety was placed. This basic core was provided with a columned porch at the front and, usually, one at the back, with the latter sometimes enclosed to function as a treasury. Large, important temples had exterior columns on all four sides forming a colonnade or peristyle.

The plan appears to be simple, but a diagram of a facade (fig. 7.38) reveals a progression beyond the basic post and lintel. Because the Mediterranean area

Figure 7.39 Greek orders of columns: (a) Doric, (b) Ionic, and (c) Corinthian.

is subject to heavy winter rains, a sloping or saddle-back roof was developed to facilitate drainage. It was covered with terra-cotta or marble tiles, equipped with gutters and rain spouts, and adorned with decorative sculpture. The triangular space at each end, the *pediment,* was usually decorated with large-scale high reliefs or freestanding sculpture. Heavily ornamented pediments increased the weight of the superstructure and thus necessitated additional carefully spaced columns.

The Greeks constructed steps (usually three) on a stone foundation called a *stereobate* with the top level, the *stylobate,* forming the floor of the temple. (For the Greeks "three" was the perfect number because it represented a beginning, middle, and end.) From the stylobate rose columns (shafts with capitals) that supported the lintel, also called an *architrave.* The ends of the roof joists are *triglyphs* (TRY–glifs), a term derived from the three vertical grooves that had become a decorative stone adaptation of the natural grain of wood joist ends. The spaces between the triglyphs were filled by plain, painted, or relief rectangles called *metopes* (MET–o–pays).

Determining the general mode of the basic temple plan was a problem that was brilliantly resolved with the inspired conception of three orders of columns, the classic Greek orders: Doric, Ionic, and Corinthian (fig. 7.39). The first to be invented, the Doric

order, is simple, solid, and serene. Placed directly upon the stylobate, the Doric column (shaft and capital) was about seven times as tall as its diameter, a ratio probably derived from the height of a man in relation to foot size. The column was fluted to provide visual depth and swelling in subtle convex curves (*entasis;* EN–ta–sis); it then rose to a capital (*echinus;* eh–KY–nus), or curved block under an *abacus* (AB–a–kus), which was a square block that joined the architrave. Surmounting the columns was a Doric frieze of alternating triglyphs and metopes. (For examples of Doric temples see figs. 7.41, 7.44, and 7.55.)

The contrasting Ionic order, the second temple style to be developed, is lighter than the Doric and more graceful, with a slender shaft about eleven times its diameter (approximately a woman's height in proportion to the size of her foot). Its components are a tiered base, softer flutes separated by narrow bands of stone, and a delicate shaft that terminates in a capital with paired scrolls (volutes) capped by a minute but highly decorated abacus. Usually subdivided into three projecting bands, the Ionic architrave normally consists of a continuous sculptural frieze. (For Ionic temples see figs. 7.52 and 7.54.)

A variant of the Ionic, the Corinthian order, adored by the Romans, is considerably more decorative, even opulent. Taller and more slender than the Ionic, its column culminates in an inverted bell shape encrusted with stylized acanthus leaves, an ingenious transition from a circular shaft to a rectangular architrave. (See fig. 7.71 for the only Corinthian temple in Greece.)

As illustrated by figure 7.40, the columns are made up of stone sections or drums, like multiple layers of a cake. Roughed out in the quarry, the drums were transported to the site, fitted with metal pegs that had been coated with lead to resist corrosion, and stacked into columns. The assembled columns were then finished under the supervision of the architect.

With only one form and three modes of expression, Greek architecture might appear to be a rather limited achievement, but the attainment of perfection or near perfection is slow, tedious, and seldom achieved by *any* culture. For perfection of proportion and clarity of outline, subtlety of refinement, and visual appearance of solids and spaces in equilibrium, the Greek temple has never been excelled. Moreover, no two Dorian (or Ionian) temples are exactly alike; each is as distinctive and individualistic as the Greeks themselves.

Comparatively well preserved, possibly because it was out of the paths of marauding armies and barbarian incursions, the Temple of Hera II (fig. 7.41) is a Doric hexastyle (six-column front) structure of the Early Classical period. It stands next to the earlier Temple of Hera I (fig. 7.24), and although it is quite heavy and somewhat stolid, it nevertheless has the harmonious proportions so necessary to the classic unity of the Greek temple.

Figure 7.40 Marble drum, Eleusis

Figure 7.41 Temple of Hera II, ca. 460 B.C. Limestone. Paestum, Italy.

Figure 7.42 View from the west of the akropolis at Athens

Figure 7.43 Model of the classical akropolis at Athens. American School of Classical Studies at Athens: Agora Excavations.

Most ancient Greek cities developed around an *akra* (high place), a fortified hilltop. As cities grew more prosperous and powerful, this people's high place *(akropolis)* became the center of religious and civic activity, suitably adorned with governmental buildings, libraries, and temples dedicated to the proprietary god or gods. According to legend the akropolis of Athens (fig. 7.42), the burial place of the fabled hero-king Erechtheus, was the site where Poseidon and Athena contended for authority over the city.

Under the leadership of Perikles, the Athenians completed a building and art program on the akropolis surpassing in splendor and artistic quality anything the world had ever seen. It signified the beginning of the Golden Age, in about 450 B.C., when Pheidias was appointed overseer of all works on the akropolis. By 405 the Parthenon, Erechtheion, Propylaia, and Temple of Athena Nike had been built, and

the brief period of glory was at an end. These four buildings can be identified in the model (fig. 7.43): Temple of Athena Nike, tiny building on the right parapet above the stairs; Propylaia, at the top of the steps; Parthenon, largest building; and Erechtheion, two-part structure at the upper left near the wall. No other buildings have survived.

For a half century this small rocky plateau (ca. 1000' long and 445' wide) was a center of creative activity for the greatest painters, sculptors, and architects of the time, and one should not overlook the most skillful stonemasons in the Greek world. The ample funds of the Delian Treasury, which were entrusted to Athens for military preparedness, were lavished on an Athenian building project supposedly dedicated to the goddess Athena, but in reality devoted to proclaiming the power and glory of Athens.

Figure 7.44 Iktinus and Kallikrates, Parthenon (view from the northwest), ca. 447–432 B.C. Akropolis, Athens.

Figure 7.45 Stereobate and stylobate, north side of the Parthenon.

Figure 7.46 Schematic drawing of Parthenon refinements

Built under the direction of architects Iktinus (ik–TIE–nus) and Kallikrates (ka–LIK–kra–teas), the temple of Athena Parthenos (Parthenon; fig. 7.44) was created as the crowning glory of the akropolis, complete with sculptural reliefs and a massive gold and ivory statue of Athena created by Pheidias. Although it is the largest Doric temple ever built on the Greek mainland, with refinements so subtle that the building symbolized the Periklean ideal of "beauty in simplicity," its basic plan was still that of the sixth-century archaic temple. Even though they invented nothing new, its architects clearly saw just how refined the temple form could be. Despite the great size (228' × 101' with 34' columns) this was still a rectangular box surrounded by columns and surmounted by a triangular prism. A temple in which the Doric order achieved perfection, the Parthenon is so unified and harmonious that its immense size is belied by its lightly poised serenity.

That the building has virtually no straight lines or true right angles is at first surprising. By using slight deviations from mathematical regularity, presumably to correct optical distortions, the architects succeeded in creating a building that gave the appearance of mathematical precision. This bothered Plato, who could not reconcile the discrepancy between perfection and the illusion of perfection that was projected by the masterful design.

Thus the cella walls lean slightly inwards; the stylobate rises 4¼" at the center of the 228' sides (fig. 7.45) and 2¾" at the center of the other two sides. All columns lean inward about 2½", except the corner columns, which lean diagonally, so much so that if they were extended, all four would meet at a point about a mile above the temple. Echoing the stylobate, the cornice, frieze, and architrave are all slightly higher in the center. The schematic drawing of some of the refinements (fig. 7.46) seems strange indeed, but through exaggeration it reflects these subtleties.

Further adjustments are found in the corner columns, each of which is of greater diameter and about two feet closer to its neighbors than the other columns. It is probable that these deviations were adopted so that the corner columns, which are seen most directly against the sky, would seem more supportive. Practically all Doric buildings show some signs of "correction," for the Doric column always had a slight outward curve called the entasis. In early Doric temples the entasis looks like a bulge about a third of the way up the column; but with the entire 34' Parthenon column, the deviation from a straight line is only 11/16". Established as a convention long before, fluted Doric columns were not only visually attractive but they also made an optical correction; from a distance smooth-surfaced columns appear to be flat and without sufficient solidity and rigidity to perform support functions.

Figure 7.47 Reconstruction of east pediment of Parthenon, central section. Akropolis Museum, Athens.

Figure 7.48 *Dionysos,* from east pediment of Parthenon, ca. 438–432 B.C. British Museum, London. Reproduced by courtesy of the Trustees of the British Museum.

Figure 7.49 Three Goddesses: Hestia, Dione, Aphrodite, from east pediment of Parthenon, ca. 438–432 B.C. British Museum, London. Reproduced by courtesy of the Trustees of the British Museum.

Adorned with some of the greatest marble carvings of antiquity, the Parthenon was virtually a visual encyclopedia of activities of the gods and of the Athenians themselves. A reconstruction of the east pediment (fig. 7.47) illustrates the story of the miraculous birth of Athena, who has just emerged from the brow of Zeus. All the gods at the center are astir, but Dionysos (fig. 7.48) is just awakening at the left corner as the sun god Apollo drives his chariot onto the scene. At the opposite end, three goddesses (fig. 7.49) are about to hear the good tidings, as Artemis, the moon goddess, begins her nightly travels. Dionysos and the goddesses are freestanding; larger than life size; and carved in broad, clear planes and sharply delineated lines so that they could be seen from ground level. Whether they were carved by Pheidias or his assistants is of little concern. What is important is that these are masterpieces of monumentalized human form; graceful despite their amplitude; and animated, in the case of the goddesses, by garments that reveal as well as decorate the bodies.

Greek Art: Gods, Temples, and the Greeks   **181**

Figure 7.50 *Combat between a Lapith and a Centaur,* metope from the Parthenon, ca. 447–443 B.C. Height 56". British Museum, London. Reproduced by courtesy of the Trustees of the British Museum.

Figure 7.51 *Horsemen,* from the west frieze of the Parthenon, ca. 440 B.C. Marble, ca. 42" high. British Museum, London. Reproduced by courtesy of the Trustees of the British Museum.

A Parthenon metope depicting the *Combat between a Lapith and a Centaur* (fig. 7.50) is a skillfully executed high relief symbolizing the ascendancy of human ideals over the bestial side of human nature. Detailed studies of the ninety-two outer metopes reveal consistent improvement in quality from the early, rather crude carvings to the exceptional work of later pieces, like the metope of figure 7.50. The stonemasons obviously benefitted from some kind of on-the-job training under the direction of Pheidias.

The inner frieze, about 3¾' in height and over 500' in length, ran along the outer walls of the cella. This marble bas-relief[3] depicted the gods and Athenians in the Greater Panathenaea celebration that took place every four years. This contemporary scene portrays a procession carrying a peplos, woven for the occasion, to the statue of Athena in the Parthenon. Apparently at the very moment that the procession is getting underway, the horsemen (fig. 7.51) ready their mounts to escort the singing maidens to the temple. With its six hundred persons and countless horses, this scene depicts but one moment of activity; this is "simultaneous narration," a sculptural version of the classic unities of Greek drama. Probably the most interesting aspect of this frieze is the fact that Athenians, hundreds of them, are depicted, in idealized versions, on a temple frieze, something unthinkable in other cultures of the ancient world. Of the few surviving portrayals of mortal activity on a temple wall, all of them Greek, this is the most significant example. One has only to think of the dark and forbidden recesses of the Temple of Amon-Mut-Khonsu at Luxor (see fig. 7.7) to understand some fundamental differences between the Egyptian and Greek civilizations.

The complex design of the Erechtheion (AIR–ek–thee–on; fig. 7.52) probably results from two

Figure 7.52 Mnesikles (ne–SEE–kleez), Erechtheion, ca. 421–405 B.C. View from the east. Akropolis, Athens.

3. The degree of projection of the sculpture from the surface is described as high, medium, or *bas* (the French word for low). High relief is almost detached from the surface and a bas-relief (BA–ri–leef) is only slightly raised. Seen from ground level as a bas-relief, the upper portion of the Parthenon frieze actually projected farther from the surface. This was, of course, one more optical refinement.

Figure 7.53 Porch of the Maidens (view from the southwest), Erechtheion. Akropolis, Athens.

Figure 7.54 Kallikrates, Temple of Athena Nike, ca. 427–424 B.C. Akropolis, Athens.

factors: an uneven building site and the legendary contest between Athena and Poseidon. With both gods competing for the guardianship of the city, Poseidon struck a rock on the akropolis with his trident and sea water, symbol of Athenian sea power, gushed forth. Athena then struck the ground with her spear and a full-grown olive tree appeared. Judging olives more important because they were so useful, the other Olympians awarded the city to Athena. The cautious Athenians dedicated shrines to both within the same temple, however, and to cover all bets, named the building after the mythical King Erechtheus who had supposedly lived on the site.

The higher (eastern) level of this graceful Ionic temple was dedicated to Athena, while the lower level (right background) was the sanctuary of Poseidon. Three porticos, each of different dimensions and design, project from three sides. It is the south porch (fig. 7.53) with its six caryatids (karry–AT–ids; female figures used as columns) that is best known. Only 10′ × 15′, the porch, which is actually a veranda, has an architrave supported by young women whose drapery suggests the fluting of columns. They are grouped as if in a procession toward the Parthenon, with three figures on one side slightly bending their right legs and those on the other side bending their left legs to give the appearance of life and animation. All columns suggest physical strain; despite the individual beauty of these figures, substituting a human form for a supporting column tends to place an undue burden on our imagination. One might characterize these caryatids as an excellent solution for a less than satisfactory idea. The caryatid to the right of the figure on the left corner is a copy of the figure Lord Elgin carried off to England (along with considerable booty from the Parthenon and other buildings) as part of a questionable attempt to "save" Greek art.[4] Compounding the irony, all of the figures have now been moved to a protected environment and replaced with fiberglass copies, including a copy of the copy. Air pollution, rather than the Turks or an English lord, is the latest and most deadly threat to the Athenian akropolis.

A classic example of architectural unity, the exquisite Temple of Athena Nike (fig. 7.54) is a tiny building (17′9″ × 26′10″) of pentelic marble. Though architecture is usually defined as the art of enclosing space, Greek temples embody more than this. Each temple was designed as a series of receding planes from steps to columns to cella wall, with temple reliefs in comparable planes from surface to deepest recesses. Both a strongly defined form and a four-sided sculptural relief, the Greek temple is architectural but it is also a large sculptural composition. Rather than just enclosing space the temple also fills space, and none any better than the elegant temple of Nike, goddess of victory. Originally the temple housed a statue of the victory goddess with her wings clipped so that she could never leave Athens. Some twenty years after the completion of the building (in 404 B.C.) Athens fell to Sparta, never again to regain her political and military supremacy. Demolished by the Turks in the eighteenth century in order to build a fort, the Temple of Athena Nike was later reconstructed by retrieving the stone from the demolished fort. That the temple dedicated to the victory goddess could be reconstituted in something like its original form symbolizes the enduring quality of Athenian culture, which has survived invasions by Persians, Spartans, Romans, Venetians, and Turks.

---

4. See Theodore Vrettos' *A Shadow of Magnitude; The Acquisition of the Elgin Marbles* (1974) about which Lawrence Durrell wrote, "So thoroughly researched and energetically executed, this is the first portrait in depth of that ignoble monomaniac Lord Elgin who lives in history as the man who despoiled the Parthenon." The Greek government has repeatedly pressed for the return of the Elgin Marbles.

Figure 7.55 Temple of Poseidon, ca. 440 B.C., Sounion.

Figure 7.56 Akhilleus Painter, white-ground lekythos (detail): "Muse on Mount Helicon," ca. 440–430 B.C. Height of vase 14½". Staatliche Antikensammlungen und Glyptothek, Munich.

The Classical style of the Golden Age, or Age of Perikles, was manifested not only in all the visual arts, and in literature, philosophy, music, drama, and dance but also in the finely balanced education and training of mind and body of Athenian citizens. Whenever the word *classical* is used, the basic reference point is Athens during the second half of the fifth century B.C., though the word may also be used to mean the best of its kind in any style. Whether considering original artworks, Roman copies, or even their ruined temples, we can feel some of the maturity, poise, and confidence of the Golden Age. Consider, for example, the Temple of Poseidon (fig. 7.55). Built to honor the god of the sea in grateful acknowledgement of the epochal victory at Salamis, the Doric temple is situated high on the promontory of Cape Sounion, where it replaced an earlier temple destroyed by the Persians. With 20′ columns that are considerably more slender than those of the Parthenon, the temple is poised lightly and elegantly, as if still awaiting the triumphant return of Theseus after the slaying of the dreaded Minotaur. Totally unlike ponderous Egyptian temples that attempt to fill desert landscapes, the Temple of Poseidon is more like a crown jewel placed, just so, on the tip of the hill.

Vase painters of this period were just as skilled as the architects and sculptors, and their best work can, in fact, be favorably compared with paintings by Renaissance artists. Though red-figure paintings were preferred by most artists (see figs. 8.4, 8.5, and 8.6), some favored using a variety of colors on a white background in what is called the *white-ground* technique. Before being fired in the kiln, a white clay was added in the area to be decorated and the painting was done after firing. Though they were subject to fading because the color was not baked into the vase as in the red-figure technique, white-ground paintings are similar to easel paintings, but with the additional complication of working on curved surfaces. Some artists chose the permanency of red-figure painting, while others, like the Akhilleus Painter (fig. 7.56), favored the color range of white-ground decorations. Though he did not sign his work, the distinctive style of the Akhilleus Painter has been recognized in over two hundred vase paintings. Here, sitting quietly on the sacred mountain of the muses, Polyhymnia, the muse of solemn hymn and religious dance, is reverently plucking her seven-string kithara. Lightly decorated at top and bottom, the vase has nothing to draw our attention from the solitary figure with a lone bird at her feet. Through graceful line and harmonious composition we see a superb example of the Classical style.

In the relief of *Victory Untying Her Sandal* (fig. 7.57), we have a fine illustration of the celebrated wet drapery effect of Greek sculpture. Sculptors apparently dipped a filmy material in a starchlike substance, draped the female model, and arranged the folds for best artistic effect. Portrayed here is a rather awkward human action, but one accomplished so

Figure 7.57 *Victory Untying Her Sandal,* from the parapet of the Temple of Athena Nike, ca. 410 B.C. Marble, height 42″. Akropolis Museum, Athens.

Figure 7.58 Paionios, *Nike,* ca. 421 B.C. Marble, height 76¾″ (85″ including base). Archeological Museum, Olympia.

gracefully that the work is a marvel of softly flowing lines in a perfectly balanced design.

In a strikingly different portrait of Nike (fig. 7.58), we see the goddess descending so rapidly from the sky that the startled eagle has not yet made its escape. Wearing the diaphanous Ionic himation, Nike is moving so fast that the material covering her body is almost like a second skin. Originally balanced by a pair of large wings, the material billowing out behind is so skillfully carved that it appears to be undulating drapery rather than hard marble. Note also the exceptional skill that was used to create the illusion of an airborne figure not yet in contact with the ground. Discovered at Olympia in 1875, this is one of the all-too-scarce original marbles from the Periklean Age.

A sculptured gravestone known as the *Stele* (STEE–lee) *of Hegesco* (fig. 7.59) shows a serving maid offering her seated mistress, the deceased who is commemorated, a casket of jewels. Common to Greek sculpture of the classical period is the serenity of facial expressions, whether the subjects are depicted as participating in a procession, a battle, or a meeting of the gods. Moreover, note that the heads of the standing servant and seated mistress are close to the same level; this same convention may also be noted in the Parthenon frieze (see fig. 7.51) whether the participants are standing, sitting, or riding horses.

Figure 7.59 *Stele of Hegesco,* ca. 400–390 B.C. Marble grave-relief, height 58½″. National Archeological Museum, Athens.

Figure 7.60 *Mausolos,* from the Mausoleum at Halikarnassos, ca. 359–351 B.C. Marble, height 9'10". British Museum, London. Reproduced by courtesy of the Trustees of the British Museum.

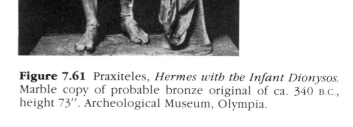

Figure 7.61 Praxiteles, *Hermes with the Infant Dionysos.* Marble copy of probable bronze original of ca. 340 B.C., height 73". Archeological Museum, Olympia.

This isocephalic (I–so–se–FALL–ik) convention, that is, the tradition of keeping all heads on approximately the same level, brings to Greek relief art of the Classical period exceptional clarity; it is so subtly done that one's sense of rightness remains undisturbed.

With the defeat of Athens by Sparta in 404 B.C. the Golden Age came to an end. That both Sophokles and Euripides died at about the same time further marked the end of an era. Throughout the following century, until the death of Alexander in 323 B.C., the classical tradition was maintained, though in a somewhat more theatrical manner. Greek artists prided themselves on adhering to the high standards of the preceding century; although Athens no longer ruled the seas, it was still the center of the artistic world.

The imposing statue usually identified as *Mausolos* (fig. 7.60) is possibly the earliest Greek portrait to survive in the original. No longer an idealized version of a general type, we see in the small mouth, heavy jaws, massive neck, and heavy body a portrait of a specific individual—and a dramatic one at that. Apparently the bunching of the drapery portrays how this person actually wore the clothing. Already famous in its own time, the tomb of Mausolos provided posterity with an appropriate name for an imposing tomb: mausoleum.

The more pleasing and personal qualities of Late Classical sculpture and the superbly executed naturalism are due, in large part, to Praxiteles (prax–SIT–uh–leas) of Athens, the most celebrated of all ancient Greek sculptors. In his *Hermes with the Infant Dionysos* (fig. 7.61) we see an example of the artist's exceptional skill in working marble. Praxiteles was apparently among the first to exploit the shimmering, translucent quality of marble. There are no sharp angles; everything is smooth, rounded, polished. Compare, for example, the striking clarity of the *Doryphoros* (fig. 7.35) with the softly sensuous treatment of the *Hermes.* Slimmer and certainly more relaxed, the *Hermes* looks positively decadent compared with the earnest Spear Bearer. Among today's experts the argument continues as to the correct attribution of the *Hermes.* Long regarded as the sole surviving original by Praxiteles, the current consensus is that this lovely sculpture is most likely a Hellenistic copy of what was possibly a bronze original. The head of the infant is proportionately too small and the rumpled drapery is inconsistent with the Late Classical style. The most telling discrepancy, however, is the marble bar that braces the hip of Hermes.

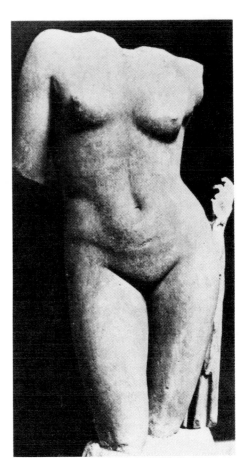

Figure 7.62 Praxiteles, *Aphrodite of Knidos.* Roman marble copy of marble original of ca. 350 B.C., height 80″. Vatican Museums, Rome.

Figure 7.63 Marble torso. Roman copy of a fourth century original, height 41″. National Museum, Naples.

Greek sculptors usually designed their works to be self-supporting, but a marble copy of an inherently strong bronze original would need to be braced. The ongoing controversy over the 2500-year-old work points up the cogent definition of culture as what remains after the society that created it has vanished.

Definitely a copy, and quite a good one, the *Aphrodite of Knidos* by Praxiteles (fig.7.62) is a revolutionary work. The single most popular statue in all antiquity, the *Aphrodite* was lavishly praised by the Roman historian Pliny (XXXVI, 20) as the finest statue in the world, so marvelous that it was placed in a shrine to be universally admired. (Pliny was equally enthusiastic about the Laokoön—fig. 7.74—and called *it* the finest sculpture in the world.) Abandoning the traditional concept of a figure occupying a rectangular space, Praxiteles designed a slender goddess with sinuous lines rising all the way from her feet to the quizzical tilt of her head. The slight outward lean of the right leg increases the sensuous curvature of the right hip. Echoing the swelling curve of the hip, the left leg is flexed so that the thighs are pressed gently together with the knees nearly touching. From the knees—the narrowest part of the composition—the figure ascends in an hourglass configuration to the slightly startled reaction of a woman surprised in the act of bathing. In line, pose, proportion, and structure Praxiteles has created an incomparable idealization of femininity, the essence of womanhood. It should be noted that although nude males were portrayed in a variety of activities, Greek artists invariably depicted women in normal situations that justified nudity: bathing, making love, functioning as flute girls, or as hetairai.

Though only a fragment of a copy, the marble torso in figure 7.63 is perhaps the most delightful of all the female nudes of the ancient world. Remarkably modern with its saucy tilt of the hips, the torso's closely positioned knees and clinging thighs are reminiscent, in a slimmer version, of the *Aphrodite of Knidos.*

Figure 7.64 *Boy from the Bay of Marathon,* ca. 340–300 B.C. Bronze, height 51″. National Archeological Museum, Athens.

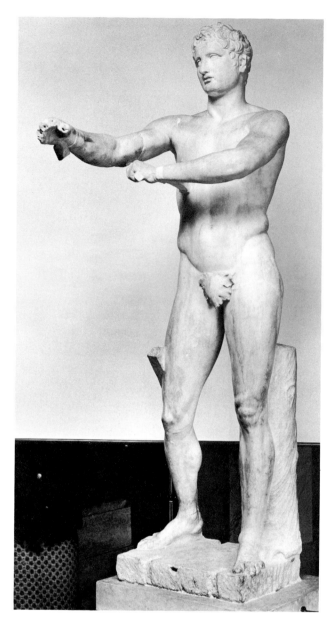

Figure 7.65 Lysippos, *Apoxyomenos (Scraper).* Roman marble copy of a bronze original of ca. 330 B.C., height 6′9″. Vatican Museums, Rome.

Looking somewhat like a male version of the marble torso, the original bronze found in the Bay of Marathon (fig. 7.64) was probably derived from the work of Praxiteles. The innate strength of bronze enabled the anonymous artist to dispense with visually irritating supports like the marble bar previously discussed (*Hermes,* fig. 7.62). The lightly poised figure, difficult to achieve in bronze but virtually impossible to reproduce in marble, is similar to the Hermes, especially in the modeling of the surfaces and the melting gaze of the eyes.

Lysippos, who was sculptor for the court of Alexander the Great, was probably the most revolutionary artist of the Late Classical period. His *Apoxyomenos* (apox–e–o–MAY–nos) in figure 7.65 was as important for the fourth century as the *Doryphoros* of Polykleitos (fig. 7.35) was for the fifth century; both works established new sculptural canons. Departing from the canon of Polykleitos, Lysippos introduced a new system of proportions in which the head was smaller, the body taller and more slender, and the limbs lithe and

long. Using an **S**-shaped tool called a strigil, the athlete is scraping oil, dust, and sweat from his body, a standard procedure at the conclusion of athletic contests. Utilizing the space in front of the body, the extended arms break through the invisible barrier of the frontal plane, violating a convention dating back to the art of Egypt's Old Kingdom. There is a new sense of movement with trunk, head, and limbs turned in different directions; this is sculpture conceived, executed, and meant to be viewed in the round—all 360 degrees. As epitomized in the *Apoxyomenos,* these revolutionary ideas were not to be fully understood until the Italian Renaissance some seventeen centuries later.

Figure 7.66 *The Dying Gaul.* Roman marble copy of bronze original from Pergamon, ca. 230–220 B.C. Life-size. Capitoline Museum, Rome.

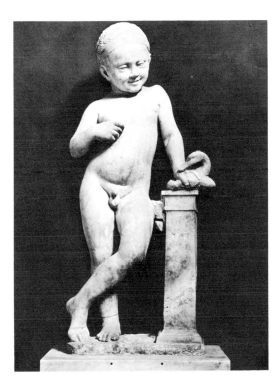

Figure 7.67 *Child with a Goose,* ca. 200 B.C. Marble, life-size. National Archeological Museum, Athens.

Hellenistic Period, 323–30 B.C.

Symbolized by the death of Alexander, the long and enormously productive classical age had come to an end. Artists were no longer concerned with idealized portraits and classical harmony, but instead became increasingly interested in actual appearances and in the infinite varieties of human nature and experience. In the midst of the rapid disintegration of the Alexandrian empire, the emphasis was upon basic survival in a world beset by constant sectional strife. Sometimes described as decadent, Hellenistic art did indeed include banalities, trivialities, pathos, and empty virtuosity. Greek genius was not yet exhausted, however, for the age also saw the production of exceptional works of art that were no less admirable than those of the classical era but were certainly different.

A Celtic tribe that ravaged Asia Minor until subdued by Attalos I of Pergamon, the Gauls were immortalized in the remarkable figure of *The Dying Gaul* (fig. 7.66). Also known as the *Dying Trumpeter* because of the discarded battle trumpet in the right foreground, the hair, facial features, and ornamental collar about the neck realistically convey the idea of a Gallic tribesman. The figure, however, is in the heroic Greek tradition of the nude warrior; and the treatment of the vanquished barbarian is sympathetic, portraying a certain poignant nobility as the dying man braces his right arm against the ground in a futile effort to ward off an ignoble death.

Genre sculptures—works depicting everyday activities—were produced by the thousands for what today would be called a mass market. Sometimes charming, more often sentimental, favorite subjects were frisky cupids, children at play, cute children playing with adorable animals, and the like. Typical of these popular knickknacks is the *Child with a Goose* (fig. 7.67), quite charming in its own way but a far cry from the classical tradition.

At the other extreme is the *Nike of Samothrace* (fig. 7.68), not only one of the most dramatic and compelling works ever created but a prime example of the continuing power of classical themes. Attributed to Pythokritos (py–THOCK–ri–toss) and erected in a sanctuary on Rhodes in honor of a naval victory over King Antiochus III of Syria, Victory is portrayed at the moment of alighting on the symbolic prow of a ship. With her great wings still extended, she is

Figure 7.68 Pythokritos of Rhodes, *Nike of Samothrace,* ca. 190 B.C. Marble, height 8′. The Louvre, Paris.

Figure 7.69 Altar of Zeus, west front, from Pergamon, ca. 180 B.C. (restored). Berlin State Museums.

moving into a wind that becomes a tangible presence as it shapes the flowing draperies into deep diagonal folds, carrying our eyes restlessly over the entire surface. Victory, who is aptly characterized as poetry in motion, communicates both the immediacy of the moment and a feeling for ongoing action in a pervasive atmosphere of wind and sea.

One of the wonders of the ancient world, the great Altar of Zeus (fig. 7.69), was built by the son and successor of Attalos I to commemorate his father's military victories. Even though it was designed as an Ionic structure for a site in Ionia, there is none of the delicacy of the classic Ionic style. With a base 100′ square, this truly monumental altar is intended to impress rather than inspire. The immense frieze around the base is over 400′ long and 7–8′ high (fig. 7.70). Using the traditional Greek device of portraying actual historical events in mythological terms, this is a highly emotional and dramatic work. Here is a world of giants, an exaggeration of physical and emotional force that, in its own way, accomplishes its goals fully as well as the classic Parthenon frieze (see fig. 7.51).

Figure 7.70 *The Battle of the Gods and Giants,* relief segment from the Altar of Zeus at Pergamon, ca. 180 B.C. Berlin State Museums.

Figure 7.71 Cossutius, Temple of the Olympian Zeus, ca. 174 B.C.–A.D. 131, Athens.

Figure 7.72 Signed by . . . andros of Antioch on the Maeander, *Aphrodite of Melos,* ca. 120 B.C. Marble, height 80″. The Louvre, Paris.

A comparison of the two friezes clearly defines the significant differences between the Classical and Hellenistic styles.

As dramatic as the Altar of Zeus and of equally monumental proportions, Hellenistic public buildings stressed sheer size over classic restraint and harmonious proportions. Even in the scanty remains of the Temple of the Olympian Zeus (fig. 7.71) one can detect some of the grandeur of a temple that originally had 104 columns over 56′ in height. Built in the Corinthian order and entirely of pentelic marble, the temple measured 130′ × 340′, as compared with the 101′ × 228′ dimensions of the Parthenon. In view of the Roman preference for the ornate Corinthian order, it is fitting that this architect was of Italic origin and that the grandiose project was completed by the Roman Emperor Hadrian.

The *Aphrodite of Melos* (fig. 7.72), formerly known by her Roman name of *Venus de Milo* and once highly praised, is a fleshy counterpart of the three goddesses

Figure 7.73 *Portrait Head,* from Delos, ca. 80 B.C. Bronze, height 12¾″. National Archeological Museum, Athens.

Figure 7.74 Hagesandros, Polydoros, and Athenodoros of Rhodes, *Laokoön and His Sons,* 1st century A.D. Marble, height 8′. Vatican Museums, Rome.

from the Parthenon pediment (see fig. 7.49). She was once a fixture in pretentious Victorian parlors of the past century, usually cast in plaster and with a clock in her tummy. Drawing more attention than her body, the abundant fabric and heavy folds of her gown demonstrate the awkwardness of a clothes-falling-off-a-figure motif.

The bronze head from Delos (fig. 7.73), originally part of a full-length statue, is a penetrating study of an apparently unhappy, fleshy-faced man who seems to be overwhelmed by doubt and anxiety. Though by no means limited to the Hellenistic age, this very private portrait seems to epitomize the predicament of helpless individuals in a chaotic and often violent world. A comparison of this face with that of the *Doryphoros* (see fig. 7.35) sums it up; the Golden Age has receded to the distant past.

The *Laokoön and His Sons* (lay–OK–o–on; fig. 7.74) is an extravagantly dramatic version of the fate of the Trojan priest. Supposedly punished by Poseidon's sea serpents because he warned his people of the Trojan horse strategy, the three Trojans writhe and struggle, their faces distorted with terror. Despite his powerful muscles the priest is helpless before the power of the gods. When this work was discovered during the High Renaissance (in 1506), its impressive virtuosity made an enormous impression on Michelangelo and other Renaissance artists. It is quite possible that the *Laokoön* was imported by the Romans because it represented an important episode in pre-Roman history. Supposedly forewarned of the fall

of Troy by the punishment of the priest, Aeneas escaped from Troy to fulfill his destiny as the legendary founder of mighty Rome.

The Legacy of Greece

The Greeks of antiquity established the foundation for the development of Western art. During a cultural epoch of approximately a thousand years, they developed in many media a viable, complex art that changed constantly but generally in a rational and humanistic direction. Their achievements were by no means restricted to the sculpture, architecture, reliefs, and pottery and vase painting discussed in the limited space in this chapter. They also excelled in jewelry, coins, engraved gems, decorative metalwork, painting and mosaics, furniture, textiles, and glassware. When their contributions in philosophy, music, and the literary arts are added to this, we see a marvelously rounded culture. They established standards that serve as thesis or antithesis for contemporary judgments and achievements throughout our cultural life.

A skeptical, resilient, and frequently cantankerous people, the Greeks respected excellence and despised mediocrity. Constantly seeking an understanding of the world and everything in it, they not only asked "Why?" but they also asked "Why not?" And they expected sane, reasonable, and logical answers. There has never been anyone else quite like them.

Bibliography

Andronicos, Manolis, et al. *The Greek Museums* (in English). Athens: Ekdotike Athenion S. A., 1975. Superb color illustrations.

Biers, William R. *The Archeology of Ancient Greece: An Introduction.* Ithaca: Cornell University Press, 1980. In addition to major monuments the author includes minor objects found at archeological sites, showing that "stylistic development is to be seen in artifacts as well as in the major arts."

Carpenter, Rhys. *The Architects of the Parthenon.* Middlesex, England: Penguin Books, 1970. Intriguing and controversial theory about who built what and why.

Charbonneaux, Jean, et al. *Grèce Archaique (620–480 avant J. C.).* Paris: Gallimard, 1968.

———. *Grèce Classique (480–330 avant J. C.).* Paris: Gallimard, 1968.

———. *Hellenistic Art (330–50 B.C.)* (in English). The three books by Charbonneaux are from the series *The Arts of Mankind,* edited by Andre Malraux and Andre Parrot. New York: George Braziller, 1973. The black-and-white and color illustrations are superb.

Dinsmoor, William B. *The Architecture of Ancient Greece.* London: B. T. Batsford, Ltd., 1950. Broad coverage and excellent bibliography.

Hampe, Roland and Erika Simon. *The Birth of Greek Art: From the Mycenaean to the Archaic Period.* New York: Oxford University Press, 1981. Detailed and thorough, it also includes metalwork, weapons, pottery, jewelry, engraving, ivory, bone, and wood.

Lullies, Reinhard, and Max Hirmer. *Greek Sculpture.* New York: Henry N. Abrams, 1960. This includes 282 magnificent photographs by Hirmer with fine notes on all plates.

Onians, John. *Art and Thought in the Hellenistic Age: The Greek World View 350–50 B.C.* London: Thames and Hudson, 1979. Valuable interdisciplinary approach.

Pollitt, J. J. *The Ancient View of Greek Art: Criticism, History, and Terminology.* New Haven: Yale University Press, 1974. Observations on contemporary art by Greeks and Romans of the ancient world. Paperback.

Ragghianti, Licia Collubi. *The Magnificent Heritage of Ancient Greece: 3,000 Years of Hellenic Art.* New York: Newsweek, 1979. Rich color plates with detailed descriptions of each.

Richter, Gisela M. A. *Handbook of Greek Art.* 7th ed. New York: E. P. Dutton, 1980. Well-illustrated and concise. Invaluable. Paperback.

Robertson, Martin. *A History of Greek Art.* 2 vols. New York: Cambridge University Press, 1975. Interesting reading, and considered by many to be a definitive study. Also available in paperback as *A Shorter History of Greek Art.* New York: Cambridge University Press, 1981.

Smith, W. Stevenson. *The Art and Architecture of Ancient Egypt.* Baltimore: Penguin Books, 1958. Comprehensive.

Music in Greek Life and Thought

Music was a requisite for the good life in ancient Greece. The education of the young men of Athens was not complete without extensive instruction in the ethical qualities of music with approximately equal time devoted to the performance of music. Further, there must be instruction in gymnastics roughly equal to the time and effort expended on music. The question Glaucon posed for Sokrates was rhetorical: "After music our youth are to be educated by gymnastics?" For the record the Sokratic reply was a terse "Certainly."

The balanced regimen of music and gymnastics encouraged a harmonious adjustment of body and soul: a sound mind in a healthy body. According to Plato, overemphasizing gymnastics made men "more brutal than they should be." Conversely, overstressing music made men "softer than is good for them."

The Greek word for music encompassed at least five different meanings. Music was:

1. The art of singing and playing music, an art enjoyed by all free men. Public performance, however, was relegated to professionals, who were much less esteemed than educated amateurs.
2. "Of the muses," thus including all of the arts presided over by the nine muses. Misinterpretation of this particular reference has led to the false assumption that music was merely a minor art.
3. Music for the purpose of education; that is, performing and listening to music as a vital part of the ethical training necessary to inculcate virtue and "sobriety in the soul" (Plato). This is the *ethos* of music that occupied such a prominent place in Greek philosophy.
4. The study of the scientific basis of music with the attendant emphasis upon acoustics and mathematics.
5. Music and mathematics as a key to understanding the harmony of the universe: the Pythagorean "music of the spheres."

All free Athenian males were involved in music performance and music education. Scientists and speculative thinkers were concerned with the scientific, mathematical, and metaphysical implications of music.

195

Figure 8.1 Lyre Player "The Boston Throne" ca. 470–450 B.C. Three-sided marble relief, height 38". H. L. Pierce Fund. Courtesy, Museum of Fine Arts, Boston. The lyre was always played from a sitting position (also see fig. 8.4).

Figure 8.2 Aulos Player of the Ludovisi Throne, ca. 460 B.C. Museo della Terme, Rome. One of the few female nudes from the Classical period, this lovely work is also notable for the relaxed and casual pose. Unlike the lyre, the aulos could be played standing or sitting.

Musical Instruments

The principal instruments were the *lyre,* a larger version of the lyre called the *kithara,* and the *aulos* (see table 8.1). According to mythology the infant Hermes, son of Zeus, killed a turtle and strung gut strings across the hollow shell. That the strings were made from intestines of oxen stolen from his brother Apollo complicated the situation. Hermes craftily avoided further trouble by permitting Apollo to play his lyre. Thus the beginning of the legendary lyre and with it the lyre-playing tradition of the cult of Apollo (fig. 8.1).

The seat of the Apollonian cult was the island of Delos and subsequently Delphi. The myths extol the virtues of the early musical life of the Greek mainland untouched by alien influences. Marvelous were the deeds of heroes and of divinely endowed musicians such as Orpheus, Amphion, Musaeus, and others, all with names connected with ancient tribes in the northern part of the mainland.

As the tribes migrated they carried their music with them. The Dorians moved as far south as Crete, the Aeolians settled in the eastern Aegean, and the Ionians moved from the west to the east central mainland and to Asia Minor.

The Ionians brought with them their music and their national instrument, the lyre. The influence of Oriental elements led to a synthesis of the two cultures which, in turn, led to the founding of Greek classical music, poetry, and dance. Mythology, characteristically, depicts the Ionian migration by relating how Orpheus accidentally dropped his lyre, which drifted eastward across the Aegean to the island of Lesbos.

The Near East produced the other national instrument, the reed pipe, or aulos (fig. 8.2). The inventors of this pungent-toned instrument came from Phrygia in Asia Minor. The aulos was associated with the Phrygian mode[1] or scale and with the cult of Dionysos. The lyre became associated with the Dorian mode or scale and with the Apollonian cult.

There was a notable conflict between the cult of the two instruments. The lyre was not fully accepted in the East, possibly because its tone quality was too delicate when compared with the nasal quality of the aulos. Legend recounts the musical competition between Olen the Lycian on the lyre and Olympos the Phrygian on the aulos. The results of that contest were inconclusive, indicating that the competing instruments attained a state of parity. The whole of Greek musical culture reflected this kind of balance of power between the Apollonian lyre and the Dionysian aulos, that is, the intellect versus the passions.

---

1. An approximation of the Phrygian mode can be made by playing the white notes on the piano from *d* to the next *d* above or below. The Dorian mode is found from *e* to *e* on the white notes.

Table 8.1 Greek Musical Instruments

Instrument	Lyre	Kithara	Aulos
Basic form			
Tone production	string instrument	string instrument	wind instrument
Played	plucking	plucking	blowing through double reed into twin pipes
Size	small, hand-held	larger than lyre, hand-held	small, hand-held
Number of strings or air columns	usually seven strings	usually eleven strings	two pipes with up to eleven tone holes
Performance by	amateurs (usually aristocrats)	professional musicians	professionals and amateurs
Function	primarily to accompany solo songs	accompany solo and group singing	solo instrument and accompany group singing
Location	home, school	social and public gatherings	plays, orgiastic religious ceremonies, elegies
Tone quality	light, delicate, serene	louder than lyre but still delicate	loud, nasal, penetrating
Ethos (ethical quality)	intellectual, Dorian, Apollonian	intellectual, Dorian, Apollonian	emotional, Phrygian, Dionysian

The earliest musicians were apparently the blind singers who performed the Homeric epics. Greek legends abound with accounts of singers who foolishly persisted in challenging the gods. Thamyris was blinded by the muses because of his boasting; the blind singer Tiresias (cf. Sophokles's *Oedipus*) had suffered the same penalty by revealing things men should not know; Misenis lost a musical contest to the sea gods and was drowned in the Aegean. The satyr Marsyas was a spectacular loser. First, he picked up the aulos that Athena had discarded because she felt she looked undignified while playing it. She had Marsyas beaten for his impudence. Failing to take the celestial hint, he then challenged Apollo to a playing contest, for which presumption he was flayed alive (fig. 8.3).

Figure 8.3 *Apollo and Marsyas,* marble relief from Manitinea, ca. 400–350 B.C. Width, ca. 4'. From the workshop of Praxiteles. National Archeological Museum, Athens. Marsyas is on the right, frantically playing, while a slave waits patiently with a knife. Holding a kithara, Apollo sits serenely at the left, waiting to execute the satyr for his hubris.

Figure 8.4 Orpheus Painter, red-figure krater (detail): "Orpheus Among the Thracians," ca. 440 B.C. Antikenmuseum Staatliche Museen Preussischer Kulturbesitz Berlin. The power of Orpheus's music obviously failed to charm the vulgar Thracians. They murdered him, which tends to confirm the Greek thesis that their music was too sophisticated for barbarians to appreciate.

The most famous singer-poet was Orpheus, reputedly the son of Apollo and Calliope. The powers attributed to Orpheus were staggering. In order to rescue Eurydice (you–RID–uh–sea), he enchanted the underworld with his lyre (fig. 8.4). He cast spells on all aspects of nature, and he was credited with inventing poetic meter and even the alphabet. The last attribute may refer to the fact that the Greeks used an elaborate musical notation based on their alphabet.

The earliest historical figure to emerge from the legendary past personified by the mythical Olympos is the kithara-player, Terpander of Lesbos (ca. 675 B.C.). His musical powers were so great that he was ordered to Sparta by the Delphic Oracle to help quell dissension within the state. As the first known musician, Terpander is regarded as the founder of Greek classical music.

Terpander's successors competed in the Olympic Games (776 B.C.–A.D. 393) in poetry and music. They sang variations on the *nomos* (nomos = law), or sung strains using fundamental melodic and rhythmic phrases. In his *Laws,* Plato described distinct classes of songs, such as kitharodic nomes, hymns, dirges, paeans, and dithyrambs, including the information that each type of song had its own special rules that even precluded the interchange of poetic texts. Terpander was credited with increasing the sections of the kitharodic nomes to the hallowed number of seven (cf. the seven-stringed lyre, the seven gates of Thebes and the—at that time—seven muses). Archilochos (are–ki–LOW–kos) of Paros, another seventh-century musician, advanced the art of lyric music—music sung to the lyre—by introducing rhythmic variety. Much of his inspiration may have been drawn from folk song. Folk art was apparently widespread because literary sources mention a variety of work songs: songs for stamping barley, treading grapes, throwing pots, spinning wool; songs for watchmen, shepherds, drawers of water, and makers of rope.

The lyric works of the poet-musicians—Sappho, Alkaios, and Anakreon—were probably inspired by folk influences, as were many of the works performed at the great contests in Olympia and Delphi. Festival performances, however, were not limited to the lyre. At the Pythian Games at Delphi in 586 B.C., Sakadas of Argos won a celebrated victory with his *Nomos Pythikos* (*Pythian Nome*) for the aulos, depicting Apollo's triumph over the Python. While most nomes were written in praise of Apollo, the poet-musician Pindar won a measure of fame for odes written in praise of victorious athletes.

From the Homeric age until the decline of Greek civilization, the lyre was the preferred instrument for the performance of epic and lyric poetry. The reedy and colorful aulos was used to accompany elegies and dramatic choruses.

Poetry and Music

When the arts of poetry and music were combined, which was the usual practice, the text dominated the music. The instruments were always designated as participants. Thus, *kitharodia* meant singing with the accompaniment of the kithara and *aulodia* meant singing with aulos accompaniment.

The principal musical-poetic type of composition was the *nomos,* which held a position analogous to the *epos* in literature. The nome was probably a melody originally, or perhaps a whole composition, but it later developed into a rather fixed style of words and music.

The nome is best understood by comparing it with architecture. A Doric temple, for example, is a kind of architectural nome. Architects were bound to a basic scheme and ornamentation called Doric but could assert their individuality by different organizations of the same elements.

The nome was usually associated with the name of one particular master but it was further developed, with certain restrictions, by other musicians without losing its basic melodic profile or rhythmic skeleton. The chief exponents of the nome from the mythic past were Olympos for the aulos nome and Terpander for the kithara nome.

Archilochos (fl. ca. 660 B.C.) must be added as the third major figure in Greek musical history. He instituted technical reforms that had far-reaching effects. Before his time, each note of the music was closely allied with the words. He added all sorts of embellishments that were improvised upon between songs. The musical accompaniment of the nomes followed the text, while instrumental solo playing now took place between the strophes or sections.

Archilochos even had the accompaniment play "dissenting" notes that were not in unison with the melody. These differing notes added considerable complexity to an already intricate musical style limited to three elements of music: melody, rhythm, and tone color. Harmony as we know it was never a part of Greek musical practice.

The profuse theoretical literature of classical antiquity did not deal with the laws of lyric poetry, that is, with rules about the metric structure of lyric verse. For the Greeks the union of lyric poetry and music was so complete that prosody and metrics did not belong to the domain of linguistics and poetry but rather formed part of the musical sciences practiced by the musician-poets.

The illustrious musician-poet (or poet-musician) Sappho was born on the Aegean island of Lesbos around 630 B.C. and lived most of her long life there. At a time when Solon was legislating in Athens and Jeremiah was prophesying in Palestine, she was at the height of her fame and, moreover, fully aware of her reputation:

The Muses have made me happy
And worthy of the world's envy,
So that even beyond death
I shall be remembered.

Celebrated in both the Greek and Roman worlds, her poems were preserved until the third century A.D. by Alexandrian editors but were later almost totally destroyed along with other so-called pagan literature. The three surviving poems and numerous fragments remain to testify to the beauty of her lyric poetry, that is, poetry sung to the delicate sounds of the lyre.

Lead off, my lyre,
And we shall sing together.

Revolving mostly around Aphrodite, Sappho's themes focus on her passions and jealousies, but there are references to two brothers and to her daughter Kleïs. Though knowledge of her personal life is scanty, Sappho certainly enjoyed the social and domestic freedom of a society in which highly educated women mixed freely with men as their equals. Not confined to a haremlike existence like Ionian women or subject to a military discipline like the Dorians of Sparta, Aeolian women were devoted to the arts of beauty, especially poetry and music (fig. 8.5).

In the following complete poem, Sappho appeals to Aphrodite to help her win the affections of a reluctant girl. Aphrodite's response is good-natured but a bit impatient; Sappho has made this kind of request before and she will certainly make it again. Moreover, as Aphrodite points out, the girl refuses your gifts today but you will refuse hers tomorrow.

God's wildering daughter deathless Aphródita,
A whittled perplexity your bright abstruse chair,
With heartbreak, lady, and breathlessness
Tame not my heart.

Figure 8.5 "Alkaios and Sappho with Lyres," detail of red-figure vase, ca. 450 B.C. Glyptothek und Museum Antiker Kleinkunst, Munich. Standing as tall as her colleague, the poet Alkaios, Sappho is depicted as a poised and beautiful woman, fully the equal of a male poet-musician.

But come down to me, as you came before,
For if ever I cried, and you heard and came,
Come now, of all times, leaving
Your father's golden house

In that chariot pulled by sparrows reined and bitted,
Swift in their flying, a quick blur aquiver,
Beautiful, high. They drew you across steep air
Down to the black earth;

Fast they came, and you behind them, O
Hilarious heart, your face all laughter,
Asking, What troubles you this time, why again
Do you call me down?

Asking, In your wild heart, who now
Must you have? Who is she that persuasion
Fetch her, enlist her, and put her into bounden love?
Sappho, who does you wrong?

If she balks, I promise, soon she'll chase,
If she's turned from gifts, now she'll give them.
And if she does not love you, she will love,
Helpless, she will love.

Come, then, loose me from cruelties.
Give my tethered heart its full desire.
Fulfill, and, come, lock your shield with mine
Throughout the siege.

The next poem is also complete except for the last four words added by the translator. The theme is jealousy, a recital of physical torments brought about by the loved one's interest in conversing with a man. The emotions are strong but recollected in tranquility in carefully chosen words. Translated into Latin by Catullus, this work was praised by Plutarch as "a masterpiece among poems of passionate love."

He seems to be a god, that man
Facing you, who leans to be close,
Smiles, and, alert and glad, listens
To your mellow voice

And quickens in love at your laughter.
That stings my breasts, jolts my heart
If I dare the shock of a glance.
I cannot speak,

My tongue sticks to my dry mouth,
Thin fire spreads beneath my skin,
My eyes cannot see and my aching ears
Roar in their labyrinths.

Chill sweat slides down my body,
I shake, I turn greener than grass.
I am neither living nor dead and cry
From the narrow between.

But endure, even (this grief of love.)

The Art of Dance

The third art associated with music and poetry was that of dance. In fact, the three arts were so mutually interconnected that it is difficult to consider any one of them in isolation.

Human beings seem to have always enjoyed dance, and few people appreciated dance more than the ancient Greeks. Greek dance probably began as a form of worship, ritual, witchcraft, enchantment, and sex symbolism in association with fertility rites. Plato believed that dance was a natural expression of emotions and that it might have grown out of the use of gestures to imitate words and phrases.

All of our knowledge of steps and movements is based on the figures on vases, on architectural friezes, and, to some extent, on various writings referring to dance. The dancing figures in Greek art display a variety of design and gesture, but over many centuries certain positions occur consistently. Arm movements were built either upon a straight line of the arm from shoulder to fingertip or upon the angularity of bending the arm at the elbow to form a right angle. The designs could be somewhat curved by increasing the angle at the elbow, by adding a curve at the waist, or both at the same time. The basic design, however, was maintained. The straight lines and curves were normally associated with light and delicate dances (fig. 8.6). The angular designs were used in strongly dramatic dances.

Dionysian dances were invariably dramatic and frequently frenzied. Dancers sometimes wore the animal skins of the Dionysian cult: bull, fawn, goat, fox, and panther. For the wild mountain dances the

Figure 8.6 "Young Girls Dancing Around the Altar," interior of red-figure bowl, ca. 450 B.C. The Hermitage, Leningrad. Note the elegantly curved chair (a Greek invention) on which the aulos player sits. The kithara player stands at the altar, while the girls circle about in a light and graceful dance. Note also the different hair styles and the variety of dress design and decoration.

dancers carried snakes. The dancers were called Maenads, Thyiades, Bacchantes, and Satyrs.

The four Dionysian festivals held every year influenced everyday Greek life as well as the arts and literature. These festivals included much dancing, sacrificial processions, banquets, choruses conducted by the poets, and, most especially, performances of the tragedies and comedies.

Greek Theatre

Music played an important role in the theatre but the precise nature of that role is not clear. There is no question about the chorus; it performed vocal functions. On occasion, the individual actors sang their lines, and the aulos sounded at various times throughout the play. The aulos was the exclusive instrument for the theatre, never used except as a solo instrument and never replaced by the lyre.

Greek drama was, to a considerable degree, a musical experience and yet hardly comparable to an operatic production. In fact, nothing in our culture compares with the Greek amalgam of choric songs, spoken dialogues, solo songs, and aulos playing. Like other conventions of Greek tragedy—masks, stylized movement and speech, platform shoes—this unique form of theatre must be accepted on its own merits, which according to the Greeks themselves were quite sufficient.

Figure 8.7 Theatre at Epidauros, ca. 350 B.C. Designed by Polykleitos the Younger. This view from the top row shows the great size (13,000 capacity) typical of Greek theatres. Nevertheless, actors and chorus could be understood even from this height.

Greek dramatic productions always utilized a circular or semicircular space in front of the stage on which the chorus danced. The theatre at Epidauros (fig. 8.7) exemplifies the classical Greek theatre where the chorus sang and danced in the circular *orkhestra* (from *orkheisthai,* to dance).

Greek plays are no longer performed in their original versions because all of the music has been lost. Over a long period of time, those who copied and recopied the manuscripts began omitting the musical notation because they were unable to read it. As a consequence, the words were transmitted to future generations but the music is gone forever.

Choric passages were an integral part of the plays of Aeschylus and were almost as important throughout the plays of Sophokles and Euripides. Towards the end of classical antiquity, however, tragedies were often performed without the choral parts. The reasons for this diminution of a major musical element are not clear but could be attributed to a decline in musical expertise in the chorus or lack of audience sophistication or both.

The high point of Greek drama, musically speaking, occurred with the plays of Aeschylus. Sophokles was a dramatist with a strong sense of plot and action, while Aeschylus was a musician, a choral lyricist, who composed his words and his music as inseparable parts of the whole. His *Agamemnon* was considered in his time to be a consummate example of tragedy because the two elements of choral song and narrative speech were combined into a powerful artistic unity.

The Doctrine of Ethos

Because music exerted a strong influence on the mood and spirits of the Greeks, the city-state assumed control of music education rather than leave such an important matter in the hands of performing artists.

Sparta became the leader in this endeavor with Lycurgus ordering regular, supervised music education. No Spartan, regardless of age, sex, or rank, was to be excluded, and each was to do his or her part to further the moral, social, and political well-being of the state.

The songs to be sung must not offend the spirit of Sparta but rather praise the fatherland and lead to a sense of order, lawfulness, and dignity. The melodies should be in the Dorian mode because this evokes poise, temperance, and simplicity.

In Athens, the champion of music was Solon. All Athenian citizens received musical training until they were thirty, and all could be expected to sing on proper social, political, or religious occasions. Musical training was mandatory and universal but prohibited for slaves because it was considered a mark of nobility and of education reserved for free Athenians.

Plato was, next to Aristoxenus, the greatest writer on music in antiquity. The philosopher saw an analogy between movements of the soul and musical progressions and therefore felt the aim of music must be more than mere amusement; the goal must be harmonic education and perfection of the soul.

The primary role of music was a pedagogical one that implied the building of character and morals. The practice of music was therefore public rather than private, an affair of state rather than of the home. Every melody, rhythm, and instrument had its unique effect on the moral nature of man and therefore upon the morality of the state. Good music promoted the welfare of the state while bad music was harmful to the individual and to society.

The emphasis upon moral imperatives led to the Greek doctrine of ethos, a doctrine that brought order into the domain of music. This doctrine was derived from the effect that music had upon the will. According to the philosophers, music influenced the will in three ways: (1) it could prompt action; (2) it could strengthen character just as, conversely, it could undermine mental health; and (3) it could suspend normal willpower and thus make the person unaware of his actions.

Plato was the most eloquent and powerful exponent of the doctrine of ethos. In the *Republic,* he recognized the balance of music and gymnastics in the education of free men, but he felt that music should precede and dominate gymnastics. Music first enobles the soul, after which the soul should then build up the body.

Plato recommended the consistent practice of music by all generations. The entire male population was to be divided into choruses with a first chorus of boys, a second of men up to the age of thirty, and a third composed of men from thirty to sixty years of age.

The Dorian and Phrygian modes were considered by Plato and Aristotle to be morally superior to the other modes, but given a preference of both philosophers for rigor and austerity the Dorian might be

Seikolos Song (A.D. 1st century)² Phrygian mode

Phrygian mode

As long as you live, be cheerful; let nothing grieve you. For life is short, and time claims its tribute.

considered superior because it was strong and dignified. Phrygian was ecstatic and religious and exerted a strong influence on the soul. Other modes were, respectively, piercing and suitable for lamentations or intimate and lascivious.

The two national instruments were naturally included in these ethical doctrines. The lyre was restrained and elegant and therefore proper for the performance of Dorian melodies. The aulos was strong and colorful and thus particularly suitable for the emotional intensity of Phrygian melodies.

In the final analysis, the doctrine of ethos, the lyre and the aulos, poetry, dance, drama, and music were all manifestations of the cults of Apollo and Dionysos. The Apollonian virtues of reason and rationality were balanced by the emotional drive of the Dionysian. As realists, the Greeks fully recognized the dualism, as they saw it, of the mind and body. As idealists, they preferred the dominance of the intellect over the passions.

Musical Example

Unfortunately no music has come down to us from the Periklean age. In fact, only a few scattered works and some fragments have survived even from Hellenistic times. At the top of this page, in modern notation, is a brief composition that was found engraved on a tombstone in Asia Minor. Something akin to the sound of Greek music can be heard if the song is played on a guitar.

Summary

The Greeks yearned for reassurance that they lived in a rational and orderly universe in which there were certain eternal truths and, most important, an appropriate place for humanity. They based their rather unique realistic idealism quite heavily upon the multifarious approaches to music in terms of education, emotional communication, the ethical life, applied science, and metaphysics.

A proper balance of instruction in music and gymnastics provided the educational foundation for the citizens of ancient Greece. The study of music included the arts in general and music in particular, with special reference to its scientific basis (acoustics) and the comprehensive theory and tuning of music built on that basis. Music was also expected to further ethical instruction, which was designed to encourage rational behavior and intellectual control.

Through acoustics the Greeks determined the mathematical relationships of sounding bodies and built a theory resting on the conception of the unity and perfection of the vibrating string. This eventually led to the metaphysical concept of a universe that could be comprehended by the intellects of those philosophers who could go beyond the sensory data of the material world.

Music performance was allied with drama, dance, and especially poetry. Principal tone colors were the golden sounds of lyre or kithara (the instruments of Apollo) and the dark and pungent tone of the aulos (the instrument of Dionysos). Rhythm was almost entirely dependent on the rhythm and meter of poetry. Melody was developed to a fine art of subtle nuances. Harmony as such was unknown, but the melodic element has reigned supreme and unmatched by developments in Western music up to the present day.

The specialized art and craft of music notation achieved a notable degree of clarity and precision, almost all of which was lost during the centuries of copying and recopying Greek manuscripts. The precious little Greek music remaining can do no more than provide a tantalizing glimpse of the richness of Greek musical culture. Modern instruments distort beyond all recognition even this hint of past achievements. Only performances on lyre, kithara, and aulos in the original Greek tunings and in conjunction with poetry and drama can actually bring to life the glory that was Greece in the tonal art known as music.

Record List

1. "Seikolos Song." On vol. 1 of *The Theory of Classical Greek Music.* Musurgia Records. This album represents a valiant attempt to recreate the actual sounds of some ancient Greek music. It is difficult to obtain but may be available through large record outlets in major cities. The "Seikolos Song" is also recorded in *History of Music in Sound,* vol. 1, RCA Victor LM–6057.
2. *Folk Music of Greece.* Folkways Album P–454. *Folk Music of Greece* is relatively contemporary but it does provide the listener with some of the character of ancient Greek music, though lyre, kithara, and aulos are not used. It does indicate the general flavor of Greek music as it might have been performed during the Hellenic and Hellenistic periods.

2. T. Reinach, *La Musique Grecque,* 1926, p. 193.

3. *Harps of the Ancient Temples.* Gail Laughton. The Hebrews A.D. 425; Japan A.D. 375; Pompeii A.D. 76; Greece 300 B.C.; the Mayans 700 B.C.; Crete 1400 B.C.; Babylon 1500 B.C.; Stonehenge 1600 B.C.; Egypt 1700 B.C.; Lemuria 16000 B.C.; Atlantis 21000 B.C. Laurel Records 111.

Bibliography

Barbour, J. Murray. *Tuning and Temperament: A Historical Survey.* East Lansing, Mich.: Michigan State University Press, 1953. Necessarily technical but the best survey of tuning, performance practices, and music theory.

Levarie, Siegmund, and Ernest Levy. *Tone: A Study in Musical Acoustics.* Kent, Ohio: Kent State University Press, 1968. Acoustics as applied to musical practices. No more technical than necessary and thus quite useful and helpful.

Reese, Gustave. *Music in the Middle Ages.* New York: W.W. Norton & Company, Inc., 1940. Technical but good material on Greek music, modes, performance practices, and music theory.

Sachs, Curt. *The Rise of Music in the Ancient World, East and West.* New York: W.W. Norton & Company, Inc., 1943. Detailed, complex, technical.

Schlesinger, K. *The Greek Aulos.* New York: Methaun, 1939. The musical instrument of Greek tragedies.

Strunk, Oliver, ed. *Source Readings in Music History.* New York: W.W. Norton & Company, Inc., 1940. Primary sources (in English) selected from Plato, Aristotle, Aristoxenus, Cleonides, Athenaeus, Boethius, and Cassiodorus. Topics include music and the state, music education and the doctrine of ethos, and Greek music theory.

Wellesz, Egon. *Ancient and Oriental Music.* New York: Oxford University Press, 1960. Thorough and necessarily technical.

Time Chart for Greek Civilization

Time	Government and Politics	Philosophers-Scientists	Literature and Art
2000 B.C.	Cretan-Minoan culture. About 2600 to 1125 B.C.	Worshippers of earth mother.	Highly sophisticated frescoes. Octopus designs on pots.
1500 B.C.	About 1600 B.C. onward, infiltration of Mycenaean Greeks. Between 1400 and 1125 these people conquered Crete. The heroic age of the Trojan War.	Worshippers of the sky gods— the traditional Greek gods. Spoke a true Greek language.	Gold death masks and other gold ornaments date from this period.
1184 B.C.	Traditional date for the fall of Troy.		
1000 B.C.	Dorian infiltration. Colonization of cities on Ionian coast. "Dark Ages" from about 1050 to 850, merging into Archaic period. Towns ruled by traditions of blood-related clans.		1000 to 700 B.C. Geometric period in Greek art.
900 B.C.	Lycurgus molds Spartan law; two kings; young men in constant military training.		
800 B.C.	Land poverty causes colonization throughout Mediterranean world.		*Iliad* and *Odyssey* of Homer. Hesiod writes *Works and Days* and *Theogony*.
700 B.C.	Revision of Spartan Constitution. Ephors rule.		
650–550 B.C.	Draco's Code: Written law, 621 B.C. Solon (638–558). Cancelled all debt; freed debt-slaves; established graduated income tax.	Ionian Philosophers. a. Thales (water as world-stuff). b. Anaximandros (the Boundless; separating out). c. Anaximenes.	660 to 480 B.C. Archaic period in Greek art. Sappho: female lyric poet.
	Pisistratus (605–527 B.C.). Redistributed land. Homeric poems form Hellenic cultural tradition.	Pythagoras (580–500 B.C.). Form found in numerical relationships.	Form of Greek temple fully established. Thespis: original dramatist.
550–500 B.C.	Kleisthenes (ca. 507). Abolished blood clans, substituting political demes. Assembly of all free Athenians. Senate of five hundred members; ten generals administer law.	Herakleitos (535–475 B.C.) "No thing abides." Fire as world-element. Logos or Reason rules change.	
500–450 B.C.	Persian Wars 490–480 B.C. Themistokles (514–449 B.C.) Income from silver mines used for fleet which defeated Persia and made Athens supreme sea power. Delian League founded, later to be transformed into Athenian empire.	The Eleatic Philosophers. a. Parmenides (510–?). b. Zeno (488–?). Nothing changes. Our senses lie to us. Only reason can be trusted. The Mediators: Many elements. Change occurs by combination.	Classical Age (480 B.C.–ca. 350). Charioteer of Delphi. Pindar (522–448). Odes to victors in Olympic Games. Aeschylus (525–456). First tragic dramatist. Celebrated greatness of men and Athens.

Time Chart for Greek Civilization (continued)

Time	Government and Politics	Philosophers-Scientists	Literature and Art
450–400 B.C.	Perikles (490–429). Ruled in Athens 443–429. The height of Athenian glory. Rebuilt city after Persian Wars.	Demokritos (460?–362?). All things made of atoms which drift through space following no law but necessity. Completely materialistic. Sokrates (469–399). Teacher of Plato.	Sophokles (496–406). Second tragic dramatist. Euripides (484–406). Third tragic dramatist. Herodotos (484–425). Historian of Persian Wars. Parthenon built, 447–438 B.C. Ictinus and Kallikrates, architects. Phidias directed or executed sculpture. Thucydides (471–400). Historian of Peloponnesian Wars.
	Peloponnesian Wars (431–404).		Myron (480–407). Famed sculptor.
		The Sophists. Plato (427–347). Reality lies in the idea or essence of things. Virtues of temperance, courage, wisdom, from which comes highest good, justice.	Polykleitos (460–412). Famed sculptor. Aristophanes (448–380). Writer of comic drama satirizing life of Athens.
400–350 B.C.		Aristotle (384–322). Collected and wrote down all wisdom of his time. Principle of enteleche or purposivity. All things exist as they are, but move into higher forms. There must be a *summum bonum* or highest good.	Praxiteles (390–330). *Hermes.*
	Philip, King of Macedon, 359–336 B.C.	Epicureans—Pleasure the highest good.	Demosthenes (383–322). Orations to arouse Athenians against Philip. Hellenistic art.
350–146 B.C.	Alexander the Great, King of Macedon, 336–323 B.C. Rome conquers Greece 146 B.C.	Stoics—Virtue the highest good.	*Laokoön.* *Aphrodite of Melos.* *Victory of Samothrace.*

Unit 3

Rome
The International Culture

9

A Thousand Years of Rome

The Roman Virtues

"So great a labor," wrote Virgil, "was it to found the Roman race." And it all began, according to legend, with Romulus and Remus, the twin sons of Mars, god of war, and of Rhea Silvia, daughter of King Numitor. It seems that Amulius, the wicked brother of Numitor, usurped the throne, forced his niece into service as a Vestal Virgin[1] and, to secure his rule against future claimants, ordered the infants placed in a flimsy basket and set adrift on the Tiber River. Rescued and suckled by a she-wolf, the ancient symbol of Rome, they were discovered by a shepherd couple and raised to vigorous manhood (fig. 9.1). Upon learning their true identity, they demonstrated their straightforward Roman nature by immediately killing Amulius and restoring Numitor to the throne. Choosing to ignore an omen of birds that pointed to Romulus as the sole founder of Rome, they resolutely set off to fulfill their destiny: to establish a mighty city on the seven hills by the Tiber. The inevitable quarrel between Romulus, the serious twin, and the light-hearted Remus led to the death of the latter; one version of the story has Remus making fun of a wall constructed by Romulus and falling victim to his brother's self-righteous anger. Subsequently, Romulus gathered an army about him, supplied them with Sabine wives (the Rape of the Sabines), and, to make a long story short, founded Rome right on schedule in 753 B.C. And, much as Moses received the tablets of law on the mountain, he accepted the first constitution from the gods and completed his imperative by becoming the first king of the Romans.

Establishing the Roman Republic was but the first step; the Roman Empire had its own legendary beginning as related by Virgil in his epic poem the *Aeneid* (see Book VI of the *Aeneid* in this chapter). "It is the nature," boasted Ovid, "of a Roman to do and suffer bravely," and Aeneas

---

1. Selected daughters of the best families served the goddess Vesta in chastity and obedience. Amulius undoubtedly forced Rhea Silvia into the arms of the goddess so that she would not bear a legitimate heir to the throne.

Figure 9.1 *The Capitoline She-Wolf* depicts Romulus, Remus, and an Etruscan wolf on Capitoline Hill in Rome. The figures were created during the Renaissance, but the wolf is a copy of an Etruscan original. Completing the symbolic representation of the Eternal City, the Colosseum looms in the background, accompanied by an early Christian bell tower and modern lighting fixtures.

was the prototype of the stoic Roman hero. After Troy fell to the Greeks under Agamemnon, Aeneas and a loyal band of Trojan warriors escaped the debacle and sailed to the west to confront their destiny. After a mighty storm at sea they found themselves on the coast of North Africa, from whence they made their way to the nearby city of Carthage where Dido (DIE–doe), the queen, received them with full honors while promptly falling in love with Aeneas. As much as stern duty would permit, Aeneas responded in kind while always knowing that, sooner or later, he would have to abandon her in order to fulfill his sacred mission of founding Rome. A despairing Dido chose suicide and, while she lay on her funeral pyre, still hopeful of a last-ditch rescue, Aeneas sailed resolutely to Sicily and finally to the banks of the Tiber. There he fought and defeated Turnus; married Lavinia, the beautiful daughter of King Latinus; and dutifully established "first among cities, the home of gods, golden Rome" (Ausonius).

Rome was fated to be a city of warriors, and of grandeur and glory; the legends of Romulus and Remus and of Aeneas were actually self-fulfilling prophecies. Romulus was descended from the god of war and Aeneas was the progenitor of the stalwart city that would restore Trojan honor by conquering the wily Greeks of the wooden horse. Rome was nourished by the forces of nature, symbolized by the she-wolf, and elevated to maturity by the good people of the soil, the peasant couple who had reared the twins. Rome pursued her imperative by seizing the Sabine lands and women, and established her legitimacy with a god-given constitution.

The Romans saw themselves as destined for world leadership; as Cicero said, "We were born to unite with our fellowmen, and to join in community with the human race." They would triumph because they were a no-nonsense, practical people with the exemplary virtues of thrift, honesty, loyalty, and dedication to hard work. Little interested in abstractions or theory, they had two questions: "Does it work?" and "How can we get the job done?" As Remus discovered, the task of building an illustrious city was no laughing matter, and obligations to the city took precedence over everything else, even passion, a lesson that was lost on the ill-fated Queen of Carthage. Duty to the state, in the final analysis, was the noblest virtue of all.

The legend of Aeneas was apparently based to a great extent on the Etruscans, the mysterious people who appeared in north central Italy during the ninth century B.C. Though the Etruscans used the Greek alphabet, their language was not an Indo-European dialect; according to the Greek historian Herodotos, they were an advanced culture from Asia Minor, a view modern historians have been unable to contradict. Leaving only partially deciphered inscriptions and no body of literature, their origins may never be known.

The Etruscans conquered most of central and northern Italy and ruled Rome itself during the sixth century B.C. From them Rome derived street plans for cities, the idea of the triumphal procession, divinations for foretelling the future, gladiatorial combat, and the masonry arch. But Rome did not accept all things Etruscan. Such Etruscan concerns as life after death, elaborate tombs, and, most especially, a luxurious style of living did not suit sober Roman sensibilities. Moreover, the Romans were so outraged about the nearly equal status of Etruscan women that they accused them of gross promiscuity including copulating in the streets, a judgment that says more about self-righteous Roman males than about Etruscan morality.

Rome came under Greek influence very early, in the eighth century B.C., when Greek colonies were established in southern Italy and Sicily in what the Romans called Magna Graecia. Syracuse, Naples, Paestum, Elea, the Pythagoreans of Krotona, the pleasure-loving Greeks of Sybaris—all were flourishing under the stern gaze of Rome. Throughout their long history the Romans were ambivalent about the Greeks. On one hand they were awed by a civilization so obviously superior, and yet there was hostility, for Greek culture amounted to a reversal of Roman values: literate, artistic, intellectual, sophisticated, delighting always in the pleasurable life, the good life. Roman enmity was not unexpected from an austere, rigid, and self-righteous society that stressed manly virtues, physical prowess, and duty to the state. From this point of view the Greeks were obviously effeminate and decadent.

Landmarks of Roman History

According to still another Roman tradition, the Republic began in 509 B.C. with the expulsion of the Etruscan king, Tarquin the Proud. In the absence of the deposed ruler the Romans were forced to devise a viable government. Never interested in abstractions or political theory, they pragmatically accepted the existing situation and made adjustments when they became necessary. It might be called the let's-try-it-this-way-and-see-if-it-stops-hurting theory of government. What existed after the hurried departure of Tarquin was an oligarchy (government by the few), and so this became the basis of the new state. The oligarchs, the land-owning aristocrats, established a republic with full citizenship reserved for the land-owning class, the patricians (Latin, *pater*, father). The other ninety percent or so of the population, the plebeians (pluh–BEE–uns; Latin, *plebs,* the multitude), could neither hold office nor marry into the patrician class. They could make money, however, which meant that political adjustments were inevitable.

The patrician class supplied the executive heads of state, two consuls who governed with full power for one year (except that each had veto power over the other). The consuls appointed patricians to life terms in the three-hundred-member Senate and were, of course, senators themselves. The other legislative body, the Centuriate Assembly, had less power than the Senate but it did elect the consuls and passed on laws submitted to it by the consuls or Senate. From among the exconsuls the Assembly elected two censors who determined eligibility for military service and ruled on the moral qualifications of Senate nominees.

Consuls also served as commanders of the army, which meant that in time of war their mutual veto power could jeopardize the state. Of course the Romans invented another adjustment, a *dictator,* a supreme military commander who received his authority constitutionally and who relinquished it at the end of his six-month term. When Julius Caesar had himself voted dictator for life, his enemies had their worst fears confirmed.

The Roman oligarchy kept the plebes in an intolerable situation; in effect they were minority stockholders in a closed corporation. Growing financial power, however, forced the Senate to create the new office of tribune, protector of the people. Later in the century (fifth century B.C.) plebeian forces accused the judges of abusing their power; there were no written laws and thus a made-to-order situation for the party in power. The Roman response was most uncharacteristic; the Senate decreed that the best legal code in existence should be studied, and accordingly sent a commission to Athens to observe the rational legal

system of Solon, the notable law-giver. The commission returned to compose the Twelve Tables of Law, at which point Roman conservatism reasserted itself; the adopted laws were fully as harsh as the fierce legal code of Draco of nearly two centuries earlier, the very system the Greeks had thankfully discarded in favor of the humane reforms of Solon.

Accomplished Roman pragmatists never solved the problem of ownership of the land, a failure that had much to do with the demise of the Empire. From the beginning of the Republic absentee landlords controlled a large part of the agricultural market, leaving the working farmer, with his small acreage, struggling to make ends meet. Competition from estate holders plus drought and pestilence forced him into debt and, finally, into a slavery decreed by the severe Twelve Tables. Large estates grew larger, operating with lower overhead because they used war booty slaves. The inexorable price for noncompetitive farmers was bankruptcy. (There were strikingly similar dilemmas in the American South prior to the Civil War.) Even after reforms barring debt-slavery and attempts to redistribute the land, many farmers ended up as urban poor: landless and unemployed. Unable to work on the land their ancestors had farmed for centuries and unfit for employment in a city that relied on slave labor, they became part of the permanent welfare program. It is estimated that by the first century B.C. about eighty percent of Rome's population was either slave laborers or subsisting on "bread and circuses." The welfare program was a failure because, as Plutarch observed, "The man who first ruined the Roman people was he who first gave them treats and gratuities."

Roman talent for organization was most spectacularly evidenced by their awesome military power. Reducing the ponderous 8,000-man phalanx to 3,600 men armed with javelin and short Roman sword, they created a mobile striking force that could march twenty-four miles in five hours, each man carrying a sixty-pound pack. Steely discipline honed a war machine that gave no quarter and asked none.

It has been said that Rome inadvertently became an empire, much as England did in the nineteenth century, but this is doubtful, because Roman conquest clearly became an end in itself during Republican days. The point at which Rome set out to deliberately conquer the world was probably 146 B.C., the final year of the Punic Wars with Carthage (264–146 B.C.). The First Punic War began when Carthage, the powerful Phoenician colony in North Africa, attempted to expand its trading empire in eastern Sicily. Responding to the appeals of their Greek allies, Roman armies found themselves opposing the Carthaginian navy. Hurriedly building their first fighting fleet, the Romans managed to defeat Carthage even though ineptness cost them more ships than did enemy action.

Spain, which had resisted Roman domination for two centuries, became the Carthaginian base for the Second Punic War (218–201 B.C.). Stating that "we will either find a way or make one," the remarkable general Hannibal negotiated the Alps with his elephants and attacked Rome from the rear. Unable to compete with his brilliant tactics, Rome, in desperation, attacked his vulnerable homeland and thus ended Carthage's dominance of the western Mediterranean. The Third Punic War, however, was a different kind of conflict.

Marcus Porcius Cato (Cato the Elder, the Censor; 234–149 B.C.) was a senator, consul, censor, and writer and, even more importantly, one of the prime instigators of the final attack on Carthage. Renowned for his devotion to Roman ideals of simplicity, honesty, courage, ability to endure hardship, rigorous sexual morality, and loyalty to Rome and the family, Cato opposed luxury, cultivation of the arts, and extravagance in any form; he hated the Greeks. He believed all children should be educated in the home and boasted of teaching his son reading, Roman law, and history, and training him in the arts of the javelin, riding, armoured combat, boxing, and swimming. Cato's maxim for slaves was that they should either be working or sleeping and they should be worked to death. Why not? Replacements were abundant and cheap.

Long since recovered from the Second Punic War but no longer a military threat to Rome, Carthage was another kind of target for Cato and other land-hungry Romans who lusted after her fertile soil and abundant harvests. After returning from a fact-finding mission to Carthage, Cato delivered an impassioned speech in the Senate about a resurgent foe that concluded, as did all subsequent speeches and writings, with a call to arms: "Delenda est Carthago!" (Carthage must be destroyed!). In 149 B.C. Rome launched an unprovoked attack upon an astonished and unprepared Carthage.

The conflict with Carthage was described by Rome as preventive warfare, but a more appropriate term would be armed robbery.[2] Carthage was not only captured but demolished and the area sown with salt. The men were killed and the women and children sold into slavery, actions that prompted Tacitus to write, "they make a desert and call it peace." This was in 146 B.C., the fateful year in which another rapacious Roman army administered the same treatment to Corinth, the richest city in Greece. "To the victors belong the spoils" is Ovid's comment, but Seneca wrote: "We are mad, not only individually, but nationally. We check manslaughter and isolated murders; but what of war and the much vaunted crime of slaughtering whole peoples?"

A new and very rich class of war-profiteering contractors, merchants, estate owners, province governors, and generals arose; they were known as *equites* (knights) because they could afford to buy equipment for the cavalry, the most expensive branch of the military. The city bulged with plunder, slaves, and increasing numbers of landless, jobless Romans. Reform was long overdue and, in the 130s and 120s, the patrician brothers Tiberius and Gaius Gracchus attempted to speak for the dispossessed. Although no one knew it then, it was the last opportunity the Senate would have to salvage the integrity of the state. The Senatorial response was to murder Tiberius and force Gaius into suicide, thus unwittingly setting the stage for one-man rule.

The first of the generals to seize power, Marius, won victories against North African and Celtic tribes, but his reorganization of the army was the critical change. The requirement that Roman citizens had to pay for their own equipment was abolished. With the state furnishing battle gear, full-time professional soldiers began replacing the citizen-soldiers who returned to their peacetime occupations between campaigns. With the beginning of Rome's war against King Mithridates in 88 B.C., Marius emerged from retirement to claim command. When the Senate chose Sulla instead, a bloody civil war ensued, ending in 84 B.C. with Sulla's conquest of Mithridates in Asia Minor. The arrogant and ruthless Pompey, a veteran of Sulla's campaigns, next rose to power and eventually formed a ruling triumvirate with Crassus and Julius Caesar.

Gaius Julius Caesar (ca. 102–44 B.C.)[3] obviously viewed himself as the best-qualified man to rescue the foundering Republic. Not everyone agreed with him, then or now, because Caesar remains one of the most controversial figures in history. A man of enormous energy and even greater ambition, his mastery of power politics can be considered a textbook example on how to take over a state. He enjoyed spectacular success in war, politics, oratory, and statesmanship. Caesar's *Commentaries* on the Gallic campaigns were masterpieces of concise and lucid Latin and his social graces were remarkable. Cicero, who hated him, remarked that he would rather spend an evening conversing with Caesar than in any other way.

In tradition-minded Rome, family background was still important and Caesar had impressive credentials; the Julian *gens* (clan, family) was one of the oldest and most powerful in Rome. The patrician Caesar cast his lot, however, with the popular (democratic) party because he astutely saw the need to identify himself with those who opposed an entrenched and unpopular aristocracy. He passed rapidly through the usual offices, made dazzling orations, and, with a daring speech in defense of the legal rights of a treasonous conspirator, secured in one bold stroke the enmity of the Senate and the adulation of the people. He utilized a public office in Spain to add gloss to his growing reputation while also attempting to reduce some of his staggering debts which, it was said, resulted from his methodical program of paying huge

---

2. "From the Punic Wars on, [Rome's] internal history is that of a successful gang of cutthroats quarreling over the division of the swag." Basil Davenport, *The Portable Roman Reader* (Baltimore, Md.: Penguin Books, 1977), p. 7.

3. All Romans had three names: first name, family name, last name.

bribes to the right people. He married his daughter to Pompey, the most successful general of the time, and completed an unbeatable combination by forming an alliance with Crassus, the richest man in Rome. The next step was by now inevitable: Caesar, Pompey, and Crassus became a ruling coalition called the First Triumvirate, a short-lived association, however, because, as Lucan pointed out, "It is a law of nature that every great man inevitably resents a partner in greatness."

Caesar's self-improvement program was not yet complete because political power in Rome was necessarily based on military power. He had himself appointed governor of the portion of Gaul that the Romans had conquered, forged a seemingly invincible army to conquer the rest of Gaul, and established his reputation as one of history's remarkable troop commanders. What Tacitus referred to as "the terror of the Roman name" was confirmed by Caesar's statement that, "It is the right of war for conquerors to treat those whom they have conquered according to their pleasure." Though his military prowess was only too apparent to the Gauls, Caesar needed strong support back in Rome. His inspired solution was the carefully composed *Commentaries on the Gallic Wars* (what would Latin classes do without Caesar?), which received wide distribution in Rome, becoming a veritable best-seller.

By 49 B.C. Gaul was secured according to Caesar's pleasure, Crassus was dead in Parthia, Pompey had gone over to the Senate, and Caesar and his intensely loyal army were poised on the banks of the Rubicon in northern Italy. An apprehensive Senate reminded him of the standing order that all field commanders had to return to Rome without their troops whereupon Caesar, never known for indecisiveness, observed that "the die is cast," and invaded and conquered all of Italy in several weeks. Following his triumphant return to a wildly enthusiastic Rome (except the Senate and aristocracy, obviously), he won a war in Spain and then defeated his rival, Pompey, in Greece. He further solidified his power and filled his purse by campaigning in Egypt where he stabilized the reign of Cleopatra, Queen of Egypt (also fathering a child by her), and guaranteed almost the entire tax revenues of Egypt for himself. In four brief, brilliant years after crossing the Rubicon, Julius Caesar had triumphed in Italy, Spain, Greece, Syria, Egypt, and North Africa, strengthening and consolidating the Empire as he went. When he returned to Rome in 45 B.C. he was undisputed master of the Roman world and a legend in his, and our, time. Less than a year later, on the Ides of March, he died of multiple stab wounds on the Senate floor at the base of Pompey's statue. There were about sixty assassins.

The motives for murder ranged from genuinely patriotic concerns over constitutional violations to plain jealousy. Moreover, some of Caesar's reforms interfered with corrupt practices of the bloated aristocracy, providing additional incentive for murder. On the other hand the people, who supported Caesar throughout his meteoric career, regarded him as a martyr to the rapacity and greed of the aristocracy. (According to Shakespeare, Caesar was "the noblest Roman of them all.") A curious and puzzling fact about the whole affair is that Caesar was almost certainly aware of the conspiracy and yet did nothing to protect himself.

Caesar's will left three-quarters of an enormous fortune to his adopted grandnephew, Octavian, but Octavian's true legacy was the opportunity to acquire Rome itself. Though only eighteen when Caesar died (and unaware of the will), Octavian reacted like a veteran politician. He formed a Second Triumvirate with Mark Antony and Lepidus, brutally suppressed all dissent and used terror and the threat of death to raise some fighting money. To his everlasting discredit he failed to stop Mark Antony from having Cicero murdered. In Macedonia he avenged Caesar by defeating and driving to suicide two of his assassins, Brutus and Cassius. (Shakespeare has Brutus say, "Not that I loved Caesar less, but that I loved Rome more.") After Lepidus was dropped from the triumvirate Antony and Cleopatra tried to use Caesar's son in their own bid for empire. After all the machinations and intrigue the final showdown was almost anticlimactic. In a naval battle off the northwest coast of Greece, near Actium, Octavian triumphed and the losers returned to Egypt to commit suicide.

Octavian became, in effect, the second emperor of the Roman Empire without most Romans even realizing that constitutional government had ended with Caesar. While prudently maintaining the appearance of restoring the Republic, Octavian orchestrated his power by redesigning the creaky governmental machinery to try to control the business of a vast empire. Careful to avoid the appellation of emperor, he did accept from the Senate the titles of Augustus (revered one) and *princeps* (first citizen). Although he ruled indirectly, he was just as much in control as any titled emperor.

Among many significant innovations, Augustus created a civil service based on merit, endowed a veterans pension fund from his own capital (secured by the taxes of Egypt), added a sales tax, rebuilt Rome ("I found Rome brick and left it marble"), created the first police and fire departments, overhauled the armed forces, and sponsored army construction of public works projects throughout the Empire. He adjusted the bureaucratic machinery of imperial Rome so it could continue to function under good, mediocre, or incompetent leadership. It survived even the tenures of murderous tyrants: Caligula, Nero, Commodus, and Caracalla (see box 9.1).

Box 9.1 Major Emperors of Rome

Julius Caesar (dictator)
(49–44 B.C.)

Caesar Augustus (princeps)
(27 B.C.–A.D. 14)

Julian Caesars
Tiberius (A.D. 14–37)
Caligula (37–41)
Claudius (41–54)
Nero (54–68)
Galba, Otho, Vitellius (69)

Flavian Caesars
Vespasian (69–79)
Titus (79–81)
Domitian (81–96)

Antoninus Caesars
Nerva (96–98)
Trajan (98–117)
Hadrian (117–138)
Antoninus Pius (138–161)
Marcus Aurelius (161–180)

Decline and Fall
Commodus (180–192)
Septimus Severus (193–211)
Caracalla (211–217)
Alexander Severus (222–235)
26 emperors (235–284)
Diocletian (284–305)
Constantine (312–337)
Constantius (353–361)
Julian (361–363)
Jovian (363–364)
Valens (364–378)
Theodosios (379–395)
Honorius (395–403)

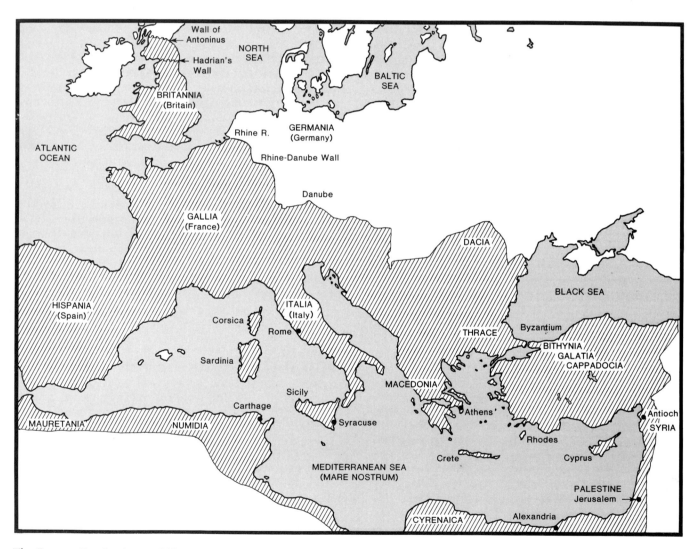

The Roman Empire in A.D. 180.

Figure 9.2 Roman coin, 17 B.C. Obverse: head of Augustus with the inscription "S.P.Q.R. IMP CAESARI." The reverse is characteristically Roman (more is better), featuring the emperor, Victory, and an elephant standing on a triumphal arch placed upon an aqueduct.

The *Pax Romana* (Roman peace) began with Caesar Augustus in 27 B.C. and ended with Marcus Aurelius in A.D. 180. (See the map of the Roman Empire in A.D. 180 on page 214.) For over two centuries the Roman world was relatively peaceful because there were no major wars. The Western world was stable and orderly for the first time in history, and people felt quite safe in their homes and even when traveling over the roads and sea routes of the prosperous Empire. Roman coins (fig. 9.2) replaced the "owls of Athena" (see fig. 5.3) as the monetary standard of the ancient world. All was not rosy, however, because as Juvenal pointed out, "We are suffering the evils of a long peace. Luxury, more deadly than war, broods over the city, and avenges a conquered world."

After Marcus Aurelius, the position of emperor was usually decided by the army, with the legions supporting any general who would offer the largest benefits to the military. The problems all the emperors faced were very much the same: an increasing national debt because of military expense, a declining population in Italy, a growing disinclination to take public office in the cities outside Rome (the officers were held responsible for paying the cities' taxes to the central government, and with increasing rural poverty no one wanted to bankrupt himself by holding office), and growing rebellion on the borders of the Empire. A vast population movement from the north and east pushed Germanic, Gothic, and Vandal peoples west and south until they overran all of Italy and Spain.

The century of decline from Commodus to Diocletian (180–284) marked the beginning of the end even though the reforms of Diocletian temporarily halted the deterioration. The growth of Christianity posed an additional challenge to which Constantine responded with the Edict of Milan (313), granting freedom of worship throughout the Empire. Constantine also divided the Empire into west and east and located the capital of the Eastern Empire in the new city of Constantinople, built on the site of the old Greek colony of Byzantium. Theodosios made Christianity the official religion of the Empire, a decision that marked the beginning of vigorous Christian persecution of other religions. As the barbarian invasions intensified, the western emperor Honorius (395–403) moved to Ravenna, leaving the Pope to defend Rome as best he could. Rome was sacked in 410 and again in 455; in 476 the first non-Roman occupied the throne of Caesar and the Roman Empire passed into history. The painfully protracted decline led Emerson to comment, "The barbarians who broke up the Roman Empire did not arrive a day too soon."

Some Achievements of Rome

Rome's major and most enduring contribution to Western civilization was her legal system: the art and science of law. Administration of justice was an art, while science (jurisprudence) defined justice and injustice. There is no clearer evidence of Roman preference for facts as opposed to abstractions than in a body of law founded, as Cicero stated, "not on theory but on nature." Justice was a process rather than a concept, a way of dealing with practical problems in everyday life. "Law is nothing but a correct principle drawn from the inspiration of the gods, commanding what is honest and forbidding the contrary" (Cicero). Venality and rapacity were human characteristics the state had to control so that, "the stronger might not in all things have their way" (Ovid). Bertrand Russell once stated that an ideal society, for him, would be one in which everyone was honest and he was the only thief. Roman law stood guard against the thief in all of us. Moreover, Roman law used its experience of empire to build up a body of international law based on a rational appraisal of consistent human behavior in a variable environment.

Modern research has shown that, contrary to popular belief, the Romans were not masters of the arts of governance; that their legal system worked need not imply, by inference, a government of comparable efficiency. Until the time of Caesar Augustus government was a chaotic mess of inefficiency and corruption caused not by a Republic trying to administer an empire but by time-honored inequities and improbities. Augustus did institute some reforms, but he followed the Roman habit of shuffling parts around when what he needed was a new engine. Diocletian (284–305) did design an efficient new system, but by this time it was like installing a new motor in a disintegrating vehicle.

Province management was a permanent problem because there was little governing; the governors were responsible primarily for sending money to Rome. Charging whatever taxes the traffic would bear and rendering "unto Caesar that which is Caesar's," they pocketed the rest. Moreover, the vaunted Roman toleration of provincial cultures was more pragmatic than magnanimous: don't do anything that will jeopardize the tax-potential of conquered territories. Except for

Figure 9.3 Main thoroughfare, Ostia Antica. Leading from Rome to its port city, this three-lane highway is a typical Roman road. Even when driving in Europe today a Roman route can be recognized by the way it rolls on and on without a curve.

Figure 9.4 Great Bath, Roman bath complex, Bath, England, 54 A.D. Part of the finest group of Roman remains in England, this sumptuous pool is still fed by natural hot springs.

Figure 9.5 Snack bar, Ostia Antica. Located across the street from a large apartment house, this cozy bar featured a common room adjoined by a roomy patio. Fast foods were undoubtedly one of the specialties.

Greece,[4] Rome treated all foreign cultures with equal indifference.

Roman science dealt entirely with empirical data; theoretical science was something left to the Greeks. For example, Eratosthenes (air–uh–TOSS–thuh–neez), an Alexandrian Greek, used his reason rather than empirical data to theorize that the world was round. Pliny the Elder began with sensory evidence when he observed that the masts of ships approaching shore were visible before the hulls could be seen; from this he deduced that the world had a curved surface. Roman medical science benefitted when their organizational talent was combined with their passion for war to produce the field hospital, a predecessor of the general hospital.

A fifty-thousand-mile network of paved roads linked Rome to all parts of the Empire. All roads did, in fact, lead to Rome. Originally designed as military roads, they carried the efficient postal service plus peripatetic Romans. Guidebooks, highway patrols, a stable every ten miles, and an inn every thirty miles made traveling easier and safer than at any other time prior to the late nineteenth century (fig. 9.3). Skillful engineering also produced the aqueducts that supplied the huge amounts of water needed for the luxurious public baths (fig. 9.4) and for the many affluent households that used water for cooking and sanitary facilities. Only a few aqueducts remain, such as the one still serving Segovia in Spain, and some of the plumbing—in the Pantheon, at Pompeii, and at Bath—still works. Almost everything else has vanished, like, for example, the vast irrigation system that watered productive farms in the northern Sahara.

As urbanization gradually supplanted Rome's early agrarian society, city building became a new specialty. Many residential units were five- and six-story apartment houses with such built-in services as nurseries, convenience markets, and neighborhood snack bars (fig. 9.5). Rome and other large cities always had extensive forums that served as civic centers (suitable backdrops for Roman pomp and ceremony) and open-air markets comparable to our shopping malls. Rome was not, however, a neat and orderly city. Except for several thoroughfares there were no names for the fifty-four miles of streets nor any house numbers. (Sample conversation: "See Marius in the leather shop behind the Pantheon; he knows where your friend, Sepulvius, lives.") There was pollution ("cease to admire the smoke, wealth and noise of prosperous Rome."—Horace) and, as Sallust observed, corruption: "A city for sale and doomed to speedy destruction, if it finds a purchaser." City facilities always included public baths, but emperors who wished to improve their public image, which included most of those who stayed alive long enough, built elaborate

---

4. The love-hate relationship with Greece was largely involuntary. As Horace wrote, "Greece, taken captive, captured her savage conqueror, and carried her arts into clownish Latium."

facilities larger than several Grand Central Stations[5]; these hedonistic temples contained, in addition to the standard baths, indoor and outdoor swimming pools, gymnasiums, libraries, lounges, restaurants, bars, and numerous gardens. Sometimes included, apparently when in short supply in the community, were efficiently designed brothels. The center of each city featured a large amphitheatre, like the Colosseum, where the entertainment was highlighted by gladiatorial combat; wild animal hunts; naval battles; and an occasional gladiator, in a bid for freedom, single-handedly killing an elephant.

Rome's bequest to the Western world was a curious compound of justice under law, military conquest, the Latin language, and Greek culture. Implicit in the laws that recognized the constitutional rights of citizens was the germinal idea that laws required the consent of the governed. Military conquest, on the other hand, was a devastating legacy of which the world has no need. In particular, Horace's pious statement, *dolce et decorum est pro patria mori* (it is sweet and glorious to die for one's country) has been used time and time again to justify enormous crimes against humanity.

In the final analysis, law and Greek culture were Rome's finest contributions to Western civilization. More imitative than inventive, Rome had the great good sense to copy Greek culture. The Greek temple style was adopted, though mainly the ornate Corinthian order; Greek sculpture was copied so often that most of what we know of Greek work exists only as Roman copies. The work of Greek artists, serving Roman tastes, appeared in the frescoes, murals, and mosaics of their houses and public buildings. Greek slaves tutored Roman children in the Greek language and the classics: Homer, Hesiod, and the plays of Aeschylus, Sophokles, and Menander. Roman tourists made the obligatory pilgrimage to Greece to view the centuries-old wonders of the Akropolis and to consult the oracle at Delphi. Rome contributed the language, organization, and law upon which the Church of Rome and the Middle Ages were built; at the same time, Rome preserved and transmitted the Greek humanism, which inspired the Renaissance and edified the Age of Reason.

Roman Religion and Philosophy

During the early days of the Republic, Roman religion encompassed household gods and earthly spirits appropriate to the simple life of a farmer. This traditional religion remained viable for those who clung to the land; the word *pagan* (literally, *countryman*) described those who adhered to the old religion of the city-state. Agrarian beliefs became inadequate, however, for urban life in an expanding empire, and the Romans again looked to Greece for suitable models. The Greek pantheon was adopted and given Roman names, albeit with somewhat different characteristics (see box 4.1 on page 40). For example, playfully amorous Aphrodite, who represented beauty and the pleasures of eroticism, became Venus, the mother of Aeneas, bringer of good fortune and victory and protector of female chastity; Athena, the Greek goddess of wisdom and patroness of the arts was transformed into Minerva, the goddess of learning and handicrafts; Poseidon, the powerful earthshaker and god of the sea became, for the Romans, Neptune, the god of water.

> Jupiter, tho' called the best and the greatest, he was never, like Zeus, the supreme arbiter of the universe and the governor of the world. Zeus reigned from the heights of Mt. Olympus, Jupiter from a low and easily accessible hill. Zeus belonged to the shining space of the air, while Jupiter, as represented by the Romans, belonged to the earth as much as to the sky. Zeus was free. Jupiter was rigid. When we compare the two gods, we find we are comparing the imagination of the Greeks to the imagination of the Romans; they had almost nothing in common.[6]

The practical mind-set of the Romans also manifested itself in their religious practices. Dedicated pragmatist that he was, Ovid commented that "it is expedient that there should be gods, and as it is expedient, let us believe that they exist." In the interest of efficiency and the glory of the state, the Pantheon (from the Greek, meaning "of all gods") housed in one sumptuous structure the seven planetary gods (see fig. 10.21). Patriotism was promoted by elevating the emperors, usually during their lifetime, to godly status. After Caesar Augustus, most emperors were deified by Senate action and emperor worship became the official religion of the Empire.[7] When the Emperor Vespasian was at the point of death he wryly remarked, "Oh dear, I think I'm becoming a god."

Emperor worship and the adopted gods of the Greek city-states gradually evolved into Romanism, the worship of the state. Seneca noted that, "Religion is regarded by the common people as true, by the wise as false, and by the rulers as useful." The more personal spiritual needs of the common people, however, plus the diverse cultures within the Empire led to a variety of imported religious beliefs. Egypt contributed Isis, the wife of Osiris (fig. 9.6) and mother of Horus, the dynamic goddess who raised her husband from the dead. Much more than Diana or Minerva, she appealed to Roman women because she was a giver of health, beauty, wisdom, and love and, moreover, she needed priestesses as well as priests.

---

5. The New York landmark was modelled after Rome's Baths of Caracalla.

6. Robert Payne et al., *Horizon Book of Ancient Rome* (New York: American Heritage Publishing Company, 1966), p. 68.

7. Little interested in the religions of other cultures, Rome was deeply concerned over the Christians who refused to place the emperor above their God; this threatened the state and was therefore heretical.

Figure 9.6 Priest of Serapis, ca. 170–180 A.D. J. Paul Getty Museum, Santa Monica, California. The sacred bull in Egyptian religion, Serapis was ruler of the underworld and supposedly the incarnation of Osiris. The priest is identified by the diadem and rosette.

Cybele, the Great Mother goddess of Phrygia (in Asia Minor), turned up in Rome during the war with Hannibal. According to the legend she loved the glorious youth Attis, who like Osiris was raised from the dead (the rebirth motif was standard for fertility cults). Her frantic grief over his death and abandoned delirium at his rebirth were followed by his unfaithfulness, at which point she castrated him. All of this dramatic spectacle was echoed in the ecstatic and bloody (including self-castration) rites of Cybele's followers. Even the Romans were sometimes aghast at the orgies and blood baths and attempted to regulate the mayhem.

The Eleusian mysteries and Dionysian rites, both Greek mystery religions, had their Roman adherents, but the vows of silence of both sects have been frustratingly effective. Dionysian ritual celebrated the nonrational but the particulars are obscure. The Eleusian mysteries are particularly intriguing because it appears that the worshippers were able to overcome their fear of death. Eventually the ceremonies at Eleusis (near Athens) were suppressed by Christianity; any religion that could conquer humanity's deepest fear could not be permitted to exist. Imported from Persia was the resolutely virtuous worship of Mithras, the unconquered intermediary between Ahura-Mazda, lord of life and light, and Ahriman, lord of death and darkness. Mithras was the protector of humanity whose believers had to be courageous and morally pure. Soldiers were strongly attracted to this male-oriented religion, which in the third century A.D. was Christianity's greatest rival.

Figure 9.7 Portrait bust of Epicurus. Roman marble copy, probably after a bronze original of ca. 275–250 B.C. Rogers Fund. Metropolitan Museum of Art. This is one of the finest of many copies. The long face marked by time and poor health is obviously an actual likeness, but in the wrinkled brow and deep-set eyes we also see "the philosopher."

Millions of believers looked to the stars as powerful deities on a par with Jupiter, Isis, and Cybele; astrology was the champion superstition of an age in which countless numbers preferred to believe the movements of heavenly bodies controlled their lives. Astrology, originating in Babylonia, had been known as early as Plato (he found it amusing) but it was not until Alexander's conquest of the Middle East that this persistent nonsense penetrated the Greek world and, ultimately, the entire Roman spectrum. The Eastern religions attracted different sectors of the populace but astrology fascinated all classes, from slaves to emperors. Greek skeptics asked how it was that people fated to die at different times all went down in the same shipwreck, or how one-twelfth of humankind could share the basic characteristics of a Capricorn, but these rational queries simply bored true believers. Augustus and Tiberius, never ones to take chances, banned astrologers from Rome, not to put a stop to larceny, but out of fear of rivals whose horoscopes might predict an enticing throne in the offing. Practitioners of magic also did a thriving business. Spells, incantations, charms, curses, and hexes were for sale to an endless procession of fervently gullible Romans. Fraud flourished on its customary grand scale.

Epicureanism and Stoicism, two eminent Athenian schools of philosophy of the third century B.C., developed ethical systems that would assist individuals in feeling more secure in an unstable and hostile world. Materialistic and practical, both philosophies were suited to thoughtful, educated Romans who chose to face up to the problems of living an ethical life in a society plagued by dissension, vice, and corruption.

The philosophy of Epicurus (341–270 B.C.; fig. 9.7) was designed primarily to secure tranquility. He considered pleasure to be the ultimate good and adhered, with remarkable consistency, to the consequences of this view. "Pleasure," he said, "is the beginning and the end of the blessed life." And further, "I know not how I can conceive the good if I withdraw the pleasures of love and those of hearing and sight. The beginning and the root of all good is the pleasure of the stomach; even wisdom and culture must be referred to this." The pleasure of the mind is therefore the contemplation of the pleasures of the body. Sokrates and Plato would disagree of course, because of their insistence upon intellectual development as the chief good, but they did not have to contend with the unsettling problems of a violent age. For Epicurus one acquired virtue by "prudence in the pursuit of pleasure." Justice was not an abstract ideal as in Plato's *Republic* but a practical matter of acting so as not to cause fear and resentment in other people. Rather than a virtue in its own right, justice was essentially a defense mechanism against pain.

Epicureanism was on a considerably higher level than mere hedonism, the pursuit of physical pleasures. All materialistic philosophies contain elements of hedonism but Epicurus advocated intellectual pleasures as superior to purely sensual pleasures. He preferred quiet pleasures to violent joys. Eat moderately for fear of indigestion; drink moderately for fear of the morning after; avoid politics, love, and other turmoil; do not present hostages to fortune by marrying and having children; above all live so as to avoid fear. For Epicurus the safest social pleasure was friendship. Holding public office was dangerous because a man multiplied envious enemies as he achieved power. "The wise man will try to live unnoticed so that he will have no enemies."

Epicurus identified two of the greatest sources of fear as religion and the dread of death. He preferred to believe that the gods, if they existed, did not interfere in human affairs and that the soul perished with the body. Religion was not a consolation but a threat; supernatural interference with nature seemed to him to be a source of terror because immortality denied the hope of being released from pain. Death was both extinction and liberation.

In his long poem, *De Rerum Nature* (*On the Nature of Things;* included later in this chapter), the Latin poet and philosopher Lucretius (loo–KREE–shus; ca. 96–55 B.C.) explained the workings of the universe as seen by the Epicurean: a rational, materialistic interpretation of the ways in which all things came to be. The poet Horace (65–8 B.C.), known for his odes, exemplified Epicureanism in his life-style and recorded the ethical results of the philosophy in his poetry. He advocated moderation in all things though he did warn against the inconvenience of poverty; above all, he said, avoid high positions because lightning strikes the tallest trees and highest mountains. A lively sense of humor was Horace's chief Epicurean pleasure. As a sophisticated man he recognized the foibles of his time, laughed at most of them, and unashamedly participated in a goodly number. As the creed of a cultivated majority, Epicureanism survived about six hundred years, though with diminishing vigor.

Stoicism was taught by Zeno the Stoic (335?–263? B.C.), a Phoenician who lived and taught in Athens. He believed totally in *common sense* which, in Greece, meant *materialism.* He trusted his senses and had no patience with metaphysical subtleties. When the skeptic asked Zeno what he meant by the real world the reply was, "I mean solid and material, like this table." "And God," asked the skeptic, "and the soul?" "Perfectly solid," answered Zeno, "more solid than the table." In response to further questioning Zeno added virtue and justice to his list of solid matter. Later Stoics like the Emperor Marcus Aurelius (A.D. 121–180) abandoned materialism but retained the ethical doctrines in virtually the same form. Stoicism was less Greek than any other doctrine because it was emotionally limited and somewhat fanatical. Moreover, its sober austerity contained religious elements the Greeks seemed unable to supply or endorse. In short, it had qualities that appealed to the Romans.

The main doctrines of Stoicism are concerned with cosmic determinism and human freedom. "There is no such thing as chance," said Zeno, "and the course of nature is determined by natural law." The natural world was originated by a Lawgiver, a supreme power called, variously, God or Zeus or Jupiter, who is the soul of the world. Each person has within a part of the Divine Fire. All things are part of a single system called Nature and the individual life is good when it is in harmony with nature. People are in harmony with nature, in one sense, because they cannot violate natural laws but in another, the stoic sense, a human life harmonizes with nature when the individual *will* is directed to ends that agree with nature. *Virtue*, therefore, is a *will* that is in agreement with nature. The wicked obey God's laws involuntarily, like a horse driven by a charioteer.

In an individual's life, virtue is the sole good; such things as health, happiness, possessions are of no account. Since virtue resides in the will, everything good or bad in a person's life depends entirely on that person. A person may be poor but virtuous; one can be sentenced to death, like Sokrates, who was looked upon as a patron saint by the Stoics. Other people may have power over externals; virtue, the only true good, is internal. Every person, therefore, has perfect freedom providing they free themselves from all mundane desires. The doctrine has a certain, non-Greek coldness; not only are bad passions condemned but all passions. The Stoic sage does not feel bereft when his wife and children die because his virtue is not disturbed. Friendship is all very well but don't let the misfortunes of your friend interfere with your detached calm. Participation in politics is permitted but helping other people does nothing for virtue.

Stoic doctrine does have some logical difficulties. If virtue is the only good then the Lawgiver must promote virtue; why, then, are there more sinners than saints? Also, how can injustice be wrong if, as Stoics liked to point out, it provided Stoics with more opportunities to endure and therefore more chances to be virtuous?

The Romans were acquainted with Stoicism mainly through the writings of Cicero, but the three most influential Roman Stoics were Seneca, Epictetus, and Marcus Aurelius: a minister, a slave, and an emperor, in that order. Seneca (ca. 3 B.C.–A.D. 65) was the teacher of Nero and also a multimillionaire, which casts some doubt on his reputation as a teacher and as a Stoic. Falsely accused of plotting Nero's assassination, he was ordered to commit suicide. His final words to his grieving family were, "Never mind, I leave you what is far more valuable than earthly riches, the example of a virtuous life."

Epictetus (ep–ik–TEE–tus; ca. A.D. 60–110) was a Greek and a slave though he did achieve his freedom. The Greek slave and Emperor Marcus Aurelius were in nearly complete agreement about the elements of Stoicism but their lives displayed some ironic contrasts. Marcus Aurelius was devoted to Stoic virtue, of which he had great need, since his reign was an endless procession of wars, insurrections, pestilence, and a few earthquakes. He was conscientious in his efforts but mainly unsuccessful and certainly frustrated. Out of political necessity he tried vainly to stamp out the Christian sect because their rejection of the state religion was an intolerable threat to the stability of the Empire. On the other hand, Epictetus lived a relatively short and uneventful life but his teachings had a profound effect on early Christianity. Consider, for example, the implications of the following:

On earth we are prisoners in an earthly body.
God is the Father of all men and we are all brothers.
Slaves are the equal of other men because all are alike in the eyes of God.
We must submit to God as a good citizen submits to the law.
The soldier swears to respect no man above Caesar but we are to respect ourselves first of all.
We must love our enemies.

Late Stoicism, in the philosophy of Epictetus and Marcus Aurelius, emphasized the idea of the brotherhood of all mankind; since the great intelligence (divine spark) is within each person, and each person is a necessary part of the rational scheme of things, then all men are brothers in the changing universe. Roman law interpreted this concept as all men being equal in the eyes of the law.

A third imported Greek philosophy was Neoplatonism, which became even more of a religion than did Stoicism. Its picture of an afterlife offered comfort to those Romans who enjoyed little satisfaction or self-fulfillment in their earthly existence. Neoplatonism was based on the doctrines of Plato and came to Rome from the Academy founded by Plato, the still-flourishing school in Athens (till A.D. 529). The Neoplatonists began with the Platonic concept of ideas as the true reality. Now, said the Neoplatonists, people can never know ideas in their pure form. For example, we always know and appreciate beauty in some of its manifestations in a beautiful person, or beautiful landscape or picture, but we can never imagine pure beauty apart from any of these things. To use another example, we can never imagine pure mind; we can only approach a knowledge of the mind as we see people acting according to the dictates of their mind. We see only the manifestations of the mind, never the reality. By the same token, the true reality of Good (God or Pure Idea) is something people can never conceive of on earth. A person's goal, therefore, is to approach as near as possible to an understanding of reality while on earth so that they may, upon death, be fit to enter the City of Good and finally contemplate the True Reality. With Neoplatonism there is the beginning of an idea of salvation and eternal life for those who lived their earthly lives in contemplation and with a desire for true wisdom. The influence of these ideas on Christianity can scarcely be overemphasized, for it was St. Augustine (354–430), a Neoplatonist in his youth, who laid the foundation for the doctrine of the early Christian church in his monumental volume, *The City of God*.

Games and Contests in Greece and Rome

This chapter has referred to the differences between Greek and Roman cultures. Consider now the athletic contests in the ancient world as a way of highlighting the differences. The Olympic Games and gladiatorial combat were both athletic contests, though we might refer to the Olympics as "games" and call battling gladiators something quite different, which already tells us something significant about the Greeks and the Romans. First we shall describe the games the Greeks played and then take a look at the Roman versions. By comparing the radically different approaches to athletics (sports), the reader can draw some conclusions about the two cultures in question.

The Greeks staged many festivals that featured contests in drama, music, poetry, and athletics, especially athletics. It seems that the cities of Sparta, Elis, and Pisa were always squabbling and, rather than settling their difficulties by the usual fractious methods, they decided upon a truce built around a footrace to determine superiority. This worked so well that by 776 B.C. almost the entire Hellenic world was involved in footracing and other contests at the sacred site of Olympia. In fact, 776 was felt to be so significant that the Greeks began dating their entire history from that date. The contests were held every four years (the Olympiad) and so 776 was the first Olympiad, 772 the second Olympiad, and so on through the three hundred and twentieth Olympiad in A.D. 392: 1,168 years of Greek history.

From the beginning the truce was the critical factor and it was unique to the Olympic Games. The conditions were simple: no one was to bear arms in Elis (the province of the games); all athletes and spectators were guaranteed safe access to Elis from anywhere in the Greek world; all fighting would cease throughout that world. It is now thought that the truce lasted for ten months and probably included travel time to and from the games. True to style, the Greeks pledged on their honor to abide by these rules. The one time that Sparta violated the truce the entire Greek-speaking world was called upon to witness their shame; there were no further violations.

Athletic contests were staged throughout Greece and the greatest of these was at Olympia, not just because of the caliber of competition but because Olympia symbolized peace, the only extended periods of peace in the ancient world. Sportsmanship and brotherhood were also basic components of the games. Cheating was simply not permitted even though the Greeks were realistic enough to require from each athlete an oath of fair play. The kinship of all Greeks was recognized and competition was therefore open to all of Greek descent regardless of rank, class, or the city from which they came. Brotherhood was national rather than universal, however, because barbarians (from the Greek word for foreigner) could not compete. The dominating spirit of the games was precisely the same as it was for all Greek culture: *kalos k'agathos,* the beautiful and the good.

The best athletes in each city (selected by competition) started training exactly ten months before the festival; no one contestant had an unfair advantage. Because training was not permitted at the sacred site, final warm-ups were scheduled at Elis, after which everyone moved to Olympia for five days of competition dedicated to Zeus and Hera. Since the Olympiad was Greece's top event it had to be scheduled for both good weather and maximum attendance. Consequently, competition began on the third full moon of summer (in July or August), which placed the festivities after the grain and olive harvests and before the demands of fall planting. Adapting to the natural world was a consistent characteristic of Greek life.

The basic events of the games were footraces, primarily because all Greeks took great pride in their speed and stamina as runners.[8] The unit of distance was based on the length of the stadium at Olympia, which was about 200 yards (fig. 9.8). There were sprints of one-stade (200 yards), two-stade (400 yards), and so on up to distances of about three miles. There were no places (2d, 3rd) in the Olympics; there was one winner and everyone else was an also-ran. The prize, a simple olive wreath,[9] was the most sought after in Greece; though the leaves soon withered and fell, the winner's name was recorded in the roll of the Olympics and, ever after, his descendents would recall his name.

Figure 9.8 Stadium at Delphi. About the same length as the Olympic stadium, this is a fairly well-preserved site, whereas the Olympic facility was destroyed along with the statues and temples. This is a view from the semicircular end to the starting gates at the other end. The marble slabs with their etched starting line are still in place in the ground awaiting the next runners to "come up to scratch."

The winner of a footrace in the modern Olympics is, as everyone knows, the first to break the tape, unless disqualified because of a foul. The Greeks were more sophisticated; in the judging the position of finish counted only fifty percent. The other half was evaluated independently by judges who searched for that something special: grace, poise, rhythm, what we might call, in one word, style.[10] As usual, the Greeks had a word for it: *arete* (ARE–uh–tay), which can be translated as skill, or stylish grace or, more precisely, diligence in the pursuit of excellence.[11] Besides the quality of *arete,* the games differed from the modern version in one other significant respect. Though the Greeks honored tradition they were not bound by the past, preferring instead to live enthusiastically in the present. They kept meticulous records of each Olympiad but they never recorded winning distances or times; athletes competed with each other, not with the past.

8. Cross-country running was, surprisingly, not one of the Olympic events. The marathon, based on the Marathon-to-Athens run of Pheidippides to announce the wondrous victory over the Persians, was introduced at the modern Olympics which began at Athens in 1896.

9. The other games of the sacred circuit awarded the laurel at Delphi (Pythian), pine at Corinth (Isthmian), and wild celery at Nemea (Nemean). The olive branch of the Olympic Games remains as a nearly universal symbol of peace.

10. Athletes competed in the nude so that judges could better evaluate their performance. It should also be noted that women were forbidden to attend the games under penalty of death, a prohibition based on religious reasons rather than the fact of nudity, which was not a problem for the Greeks, who looked upon their readiness to strip in public as one of the traits that separated them from barbarians.

11. Style is a factor in judging modern Olympic events like diving, gymnastics, and ice skating.

Figure 9.9 *Runner at the Starting Point, Two Wrestlers, Javelin Thrower.* Bas-relief, marble, ca. 500 B.C., 12¼″ × 26½″. National Museum, Athens. Originally decorating the base of a kouros, this illustrates the bound hair and heavily muscled bodies of the athletes.

Figure 9.10 Temple of Hera, ca. 600 B.C., Olympia. The column drums still lie where they were pushed over on orders of Theodosios or, as some would claim, toppled by an earthquake.

Except for chariot racing the ancient Olympic events are still a basic part of the modern Olympics: footracing, broad jump, discus, javelin, and boxing and wrestling (fig. 9.9). The composite event, the pentathlon,[12] featured the kind of individual the Greeks especially admired, a well-rounded person who could do many things well. The Romans admired specialists; Greeks, generalists.

During the 1,169 years of the Olympic Games the high point was reached, not unexpectedly, during the Golden Age of Perikles. There was a slight decline in quality and integrity after that time, which accelerated rapidly beginning in 146 B.C., the year in which Carthage and Corinth were razed, the year in which the Romans took over Olympia. Typical of the Roman way was the behavior of Nero, who had himself declared winner of any event he entered; there was no one who could deny him. The games came to an end in A.D. 393, after the three hundred and twentieth Olympiad, when the Emperor Theodosios, in the name of Christianity, issued an edict forbidding the games because they "promoted the worship of heathen and false gods." No mention was made of the ancient truce when the emperor completed his work by ordering the destruction of the statues and temples. *Arete, kalos k'agathos* (skill, beauty, and goodness) vanished from the sacred groves of the peaceful river valley at Olympia (fig. 9.10).

Roman games were originally conceived and produced to honor the gods but, by the time of the Empire, private individuals were sponsoring extravagant spectacles honoring themselves, with just passing references to the gods. While the Romans had frequent athletic contests the public was far more entranced by the giant spectacles staged in the Colosseum and Circus Maximus (see figures 10.11, 10.12, and 10.13). When the Romans discussed the *ludi* (games, from which we get the word *ludicrous*), they referred specifically to five types of extravaganzas produced for immense arenas: chariot races, gladiatorial combat, wild animal hunts, naval battles, and mythological pantomimes. These *ludi* were not competitive in the Greek sense nor was there any concern for style or beauty. They were intended for the entertainment of vast crowds, and so we can credit the Romans with the invention of mass entertainment. As a part of the welfare program that also supplied food to the unemployed, the games were free. The familiar phrase "bread and circuses" aptly describes the Roman manner of controlling their constituency.

Most popular were the *ludi circenses* (games in a ring), the chariot races held at six racetracks in and about Rome. Racing was a frenzied and dangerous sport, if one can call driving four-horse chariots on a tight oval track that had only one rule—to the victor goes the spoils—a sport. The stakes were certainly high enough; the best drivers made a great deal of money and also enjoyed a status exceeding the combined charisma of a pro football star and a Grand Prix champion. There is no contemporary equivalent for a day at the races at the Circus Maximus in ancient Rome. Try to imagine an oval track 2,000 feet in circumference, four tense and tough racing teams (blues, greens, whites, reds) and 250,000 fanatical spectators who had millions riding on every race. Moreover, the races provided the ideal setting for the intrigues and assignations that were so much a part of Roman life (see Ovid's *The Art of Love* in "Literary Selections").

Gladiatorial combat calls for a more extensive discussion, not only because it was unique to Roman civilization but also because it was so characteristic of Roman values. There has been a tendency, probably dating back to Napoleon, to ascribe the Roman

---

12. Five events: sprint, broad jump, wrestling and boxing, discus, and javelin. The decathlon (ten events) of the modern Olympics dropped the wrestling and boxing and added shot put, pole vault, high jump, 110-meter hurdles, and 100-, 400-, and 1500-meter races.

virtues of nobility, courage, and honesty to the austere days of the Republic, and thus blame the Empire for much of the brutality and decadence for which Rome is justly infamous. It was the Republic, however, that brutally destroyed Carthage and Corinth in 146 B.C. and it was the Republic that bred gladiatorial combat, beginning in 264 B.C.

The ritual of mortal combat always began with the ceremonial march of the gladiators into the arena and the famous words to the royal box: *Ave, Caesar, morituri te salutant* (Hail, Caesar, we who are about to die salute you). Then there was the drawing of lots and the inspection of arms. A typical match-up, to start the show, would be a gladiator of the Thracian type versus one of the *hoplomachi* fighting style. The Thracian wore a heavy helmet, had leather and metal covering much of his body, and carried a small shield and curved sword. The *hoplomachi* wore a heavy helmet, was nearly naked, and carried a large, oblong shield and a Roman sword. Bodies were guarded by a variety of clothing and armament, all designed to protect the combatant from disabling minor wounds. What the crowd wanted was a skillful, courageous, and relatively even fight; given this kind of battle, public sentiment tended towards a thumbs-up verdict for the loser, who could then fight another day. The *editor,* the sponsor of the day's games, had the final say, however, and the verdict could just as well be thumbs-down. The loser was then expected to display his superb training and discipline (he was also trained in how to die) by presenting his naked throat to his conqueror's sword. Anguish and gore enough it would seem, but the Romans further embellished the bloody scene with an actor dressed as a god and brandishing a white-hot staff, which he pressed into the flesh of the fallen man to make certain he was dead. The tattered body was then hooked behind a horse and dragged away and the entire arena sprayed with perfume, after which the crowd settled contentedly back for the next contest.

The next pair, perhaps a *retiarius* and a *secutor,* were always great crowd pleasers. Possessing neither helmet nor shield, the *retiarius* had a dagger in his belt, while one hand gripped a net and the other a trident. His opponent, the *secutor,* wore a helmet and carried a long rectangular shield and a sword plus the standard dagger in his belt. The *retiarius* had to be very mobile because the contest amounted to a swift runner attacking a human tank; the advantage usually lay with the tank. Although the two pairs described above appeared at most spectacles, there was also fighting from chariots, dwarf gladiators, female combatants, and whatever else could be concocted to stimulate the interest of the common people in the upper tiers. Staging these extravaganzas was so expensive that the government had to assume the responsibility for special schools, which in Rome alone trained and housed some two thousand gladiators. Amphitheatre combat was probably scheduled only several times a year; this kept expenses down, helped maintain a full complement of gladiators (about six hundred pairs fought in each production) and, most importantly, heightened expectations for the next spectacular event.

Other spectacles involved elaborately staged hunts, which featured an African jungle, for example, in the Colosseum with hunters and assorted lions and tigers stalking each other, though it is doubtful the starved, frightened creatures wanted anything more than a place to hide from their tormentors. Many thousands of wild animals were slaughtered in this manner, so many in fact, that whole species were annihilated. Fought in pools built for the occasion, naval battles were reenactments of famous engagements, bloody reminders of the power of Roman arms at sea. Finally, there were dramatic pantomimes based on familiar mythological plots and starring condemned criminals in their first and last performance. Treated to mythology in action, audiences witnessed Herakles being consumed by flames, Dirce lashed to the horns of a maddened bull, Ikarus of the failing wings falling among wild beasts, and other edifying splendors. Roman efficiency was well-served; the mob was entertained and enlightened while, at the same time, justice was served.

The Roman games were so appallingly brutal that some apologists have tried to rationalize the whole bloody business into justifiable and necessary entertainment for restless and potentially dangerous mobs. Others have sought evidence that educated Romans disapproved of the institution; they have looked in vain, however, since Romans of every class and station attended and enjoyed the games. With the possible exception of Seneca and Pliny the Younger, we know of not a single Roman who ever voiced any concerns, humane or otherwise, about the events staged in the Colosseum. Death, in this ancient time, was not a significant consideration for those in power, particularly when the lower classes were doing the dying. Ironically, the one event that was vigorously denounced was the *sparsio,* the bonus episode that usually followed the final gladiatorial contest. While the upper class beat a hasty retreat, a machine with a rotating arm that hurled clay or wooden tablets in the general direction of the upper tiers was wheeled into the arena. Whatever was depicted on the tally was redeemable in kind: a water buffalo, ten pounds of ostrich feathers, an occasional elephant, two tickets in the lower tier for the next attraction, and so on. Horace spoke for the upper class when he wrote: "I hate the vulgar herd and hold it far."

It should be noted, in conclusion, that Roman spectacles were enthusiastically adopted throughout the Mediterranean world. Roman games, however, were never staged in Athens, Delphi, Delos, Epidauros, or, most especially, Olympia.

The Best of the Roman Ideal

Artistically and creatively, Rome reached its peak during the reign of Augustus. Virgil and Horace both lived during these years. The great orator, Cicero, had just died, and the passionate poet Catullus (kuh–TUL–us) had died only a few years before. Virgil, by the way, was almost adopted by Christianity, and during the Middle Ages was the only classic author who was read, largely because of his *Fourth Eclogue* (included in this chapter) in which he celebrated the birth of a child who, he predicted, would bring the world back to the Golden Age. His fame, however, rests on his celebrated epic poem the *Aeneid* (i–NEE–id; Book VI is included in this chapter).

To cut through the superficial judgments that may be made about the *Aeneid* is difficult. The first such judgment is that the poem provided "instant mythology" for the Roman empire, for it was apparent to Virgil that much of the greatness of Athenian life resulted from the tradition furnished by Homer's *Iliad* and *Odyssey*. Virgil knew these poems well and patterned his epic upon them to give Rome the same kind of golden past Greece had had, and to provide inspiration for the carrying on of great and noble works. Too clearly the reader gets the picture of Virgil thinking to himself, "Tomorrow we are going to start the old tradition of Roman greatness."

A second quick judgment is that the *Aeneid* presents a picture of the dutiful Stoic as epic hero, and somehow, the over-thoughtful, rather pompous figure of the middle-aged Aeneas (i–NEE–us) falls short of the glory-bound Akhilleus or Hektor, and especially the wily and resourceful Odysseus.

The good reader will accept these first judgments and then feel beyond them. The *Aeneid is* literature as propaganda for a great nation. But what's the matter with propaganda for a good cause? The hero is middle-aged and has gained the wisdom of maturity. Aeneas sees clearly that a kind of sadness underlies all heroic acts, and that many things people do result from choices that are forced upon them. Compared with Homer, Virgil loses much in dash; what he gains is a sad and chastened wisdom.

The poem recounts the legend of the founding of Rome by the Trojan hero Aeneas after the fall of Troy to Agamemnon and the Greeks. Aeneas, commanded by Jupiter and Aeneas's goddess mother, escaped from Troy with his aged father, his son Askanius (a–SKAY–nee–us; also called Ilus, and later Iulus to relate him to the Julian line of Caesars), and with the household gods that are to be the gods of the new city, Rome. The voyage is full of epic incident, storms at sea, battles, rather pleasant interludes, and the final war on Italian soil to conquer the kingdom of Latium and arrange for the marriage that will produce the Roman line.

Only two or three incidents need be mentioned to suggest the flavor of the epic. At the first of the book Aeneas, storm-tossed, landed on the shore near Carthage where he and his companions were made welcome by Dido, the queen of the city. As he recounted his adventures, Dido fell in love with him, and he with her. So satisfying was the affair that Aeneas lingered for a long time, while Dido tried to persuade him to settle there and make Carthage the city he was supposed to found. Aeneas, prodded by his stoic sense of duty, knew that he must push on, and so one morning before daybreak he and his companions set sail. Aeneas as a person hated his decision, but he was honor-bound to make it; Dido was so devastated that she had a great funeral pyre built and committed suicide in the flames. One of the ironies of the poem lies in the meeting of the lovers in the underworld in Book VI, when Aeneas tries to rekindle their love and she turns against him. Aeneas knew all there was to know about the founding of cities, but he understood little about the human heart.

Another of the little incidents occurs when the Trojans land on Sicily. The land is so beautiful that a number of Aeneas's group suggest that the city be founded there, but the hero knows that this is not the place, so he allows some of his party to stay while he again sails away to make war and cause death so that the city might be properly founded. Once again he realized the tragedy of his choice, but Duty, stern daughter of the voice of god, would not let him make the easy choice.

Many other events could be cited to illustrate the same point. Aeneas's chief adversary in Italy is a hero named Turnus, a thoroughly noble person; probably a better man than Aeneas. Turnus was patterned on the character of Hektor in the *Iliad*. Turnus must be destroyed, and Aeneas does it. Hektor, too, had to be killed. The difference is that Akhilleus, the youthful hero, fought his battle fiercely and killed his enemy in passion. Aeneas simply knew that the better man must be killed, and he did the job in full knowledge and for a greater good (the founding of the city of Rome) than would be accomplished by the saving of one good man.

Such is the tone of the whole poem except for some interludes, such as the funeral games for Ankhises when Virgil allows himself to relax and enjoy the deeds of physical strength and skill. The *Aeneid,* like the stoic philosophy, sees duty as the highest way of life, and the true Roman hero places duty above all other human values. Virgil wonderfully gave Rome its best and highest creed, when in the underworld, Ankhises told his son Aeneas:

Others, no doubt, will better mould the bronze
To the semblance of soft breathing, draw from marble,
The living countenance; and others plead
With greater eloquence, or learn to measure,
Better than we, the pathways of the heaven,
The risings of the stars: remember, Roman,
To rule the people under law, to establish
The way of peace, to battle down the haughty,
To spare the meek. Our fine arts, these, forever.

This was the highest of the Roman ideal. While it sacrificed much in the realm of human value, while it denigrated such qualities as imagination and joy, it furnished a noble code of conduct as long as the Romans adhered to it.

Bibliography

General
Auguet, Roland. *Cruelty and Civilization: The Roman Games.* London: (George) Allen and Unwin, Ltd., 1972. Excellent overview of a subject that is both fascinating and repulsive.

Balsdon, J.P.V.D. *Life and Leisure in Ancient Rome.* London: Bodley Head, Ltd., 1969.

Boren, Henry. *Roman Society from Nero to Marcus Aurelius.* Lexington, Mass.: D.C. Heath & Company, 1977. Classic social history now published by Heath.

Casson, Lionel. *Daily Life in Ancient Rome.* New York: American Heritage, 1975. Outstanding series, which also includes ancient Egypt, the Renaissance, Victorian England, and the Middle Ages.

Clarke, M.L. *The Roman Mind: Studies in the History of Thought from Cicero to Marcus Aurelius.* New York: W.W. Norton & Company, Inc., 1968.

Grant, Michael. *The World of Rome.* New York: Mentor Books, New American Library, N.D. Historical sketches plus fine discussions of the arts, politics, religion, and society.

Hadas, Moses. *Imperial Rome.* New York: Time-Life Books, 1965. Good overview from the *Great Ages of Man* series.

Hamilton, Edith. *The Roman Way.* New York: W.W. Norton & Company, Inc., 1932. A companion piece to the author's *Greek Way,* though she clearly favors the latter.

Rostovtzeff, Mikhail. *Social and Economic History of the Roman Empire.* 2d ed. New York: Oxford University Press, 1957. The standard work.

Translations of Original Material
Arrowsmith, William. *The Satyricon of Petronius.* Ann Arbor, Mich.: University of Michigan Press, 1959. Good contemporary English but somewhat marred by some outdated slang.

Davenport, Basil. *The Portable Roman Reader.* New York: Viking Press, 1959. The best cross section of Roman literature in a single volume.

Duckworth, George E. *The Complete Roman Drama.* New York: Random House, 1942.

Graves, Robert. *Lucan: Pharsalia.* Baltimore, Md.: Penguin Books, 1959.

————. *Suetonius, The Lives of the Twelve Caesars.* Baltimore, Md.: Penguin Books, 1957. The author of *I, Claudius* also does superb translations.

Hadas, Moses. *The Basic Works of Cicero.* New York: Modern Library, 1951.

————. *The Complete Works of Tacitus.* New York: Modern Library, 1942.

————. *Livy: A History of Rome.* New York: Modern Library, 1963.

————. *The Stoic Philosophy of Seneca.* New York: Doubleday & Co., 1958.

Humphries, Rolfe. *The Aeneid of Virgil.* New York: Charles Scribner's Sons, 1951.

————. *Ovid: The Art of Love.* Bloomington, Ind.: Indiana University Press, 1957. Humphries is a superb translator.

————. *The Satires of Juvenal.* Bloomington, Ind.: Indiana University Press, 1958. Contemporary idiomatic translation.

Kraemer, Casper J., Jr. *The Complete Works of Horace.* New York: Modern Library, 1936.

Lindsay, Jack. *Apuleius: The Golden Ass.* Bloomington, Ind.: Indiana University Press, 1961.

Marcellino, Ralph. *Martial: Selected Epigrams.* Indianapolis, Ind.: The Bobbs-Merrill Co., 1968.

Michie, James. *The Poems of Catullus.* London: Hart-Davis, MacGibbon Ltd., 1969. There are so many translations of Catullus that the reader would be well advised to sort through all of them.

Mills, Barriss. *Epigrams from Martial: A Verse Translation.* Lafayette, Ind.: Purdue University Studies, 1969. Skillful contemporary translation.

Radice, Betty. *The Letters of Pliny.* Baltimore, Md.: Penguin Books, 1963.

Schuckburgh, Evelyn. *Polybius: Histories.* 6 vols. Bloomington, Ind.: Indiana University Press, 1962.

Sesar, Carl. *Selected Poems of Catullus.* New York: Mason & Lipscomb, 1974. Idiomatic, profane, erotic, and scatalogical and thus close to the style and spirit of the original.

Sisson, C.H. *The Poetry of Catullus.* New York: The Orion Press, 1967. Contemporary idiom but not for every poem.

Turner, Paul. *Lucian: Satirical Sketches.* Baltimore, Md.: Penguin Books, 1961. Stylish translation in the contemporary idiom.

————. *Plutarch's Lives.* Carbondale, Ill.: Southern Illinois University Press, 1963.

Whigham, Peter. *The Poems of Catullus.* New York: Penguin Books, 1966. Probably the only recent translation that manages to avoid using the English equivalent of Catullus's candid vocabulary.

Chronological Overview

	PROSE	**POETRY**
Early Republic **ca. 300–80 B.C.**	Polybius (205–133 B.C.) Plautus (254?–184 B.C.) (Drama) Terence (190?–159 B.C.) (Drama)	Theocritus (310?–250 B.C.)
Age of Cicero **80–43 B.C.**	Cicero (106–43 B.C.) Caesar (102–44 B.C.) Sallust (86–34 B.C.)	Lucretius (ca. 96–55 B.C.) Catullus (84–54 B.C.)
Augustan Golden Age **42 B.C.–A.D. 17**	Livy (59 B.C.–A.D. 17)	Virgil (70–19 B.C.) Horace (65–8 B.C.) Ovid (43 B.C.–A.D. 17)
Silver Age **A.D. 17–130**	Seneca (4 B.C.–A.D. 65) Petronius (d. 66 A.D.) Pliny the Elder (23–79) Quintilian (35–ca. 100) Plutarch (46–120) Tacitus (55–120) Epictetus (ca. 60–110) Pliny the Younger (62–114) Suetonius (ca. 70–160) Lucian (ca. 117–180)	Lucan (39–65 A.D.) Martial (40–104 A.D.) Juvenal (ca. 60–140)
Decline and Fall **140–476**	Apuleius (fl. 155) Marcus Aurelius (121–180)	
Christian	Tertullian (160–230) St. Jerome (340–420) St. Ambrose (340–397) St. Augustine (353–430) Boethius (475–524)	

The pragmatic Romans cherished their flawed institutions and their proclivity for war, plunder, and profits, but they did have the saving grace of being able to laugh at themselves. Enthusiastically adapting satire to Roman tastes, they lambasted all that they held dear: politics, material possessions, manners, and morals. The Romans were, in the final analysis, rational and civilized people, and nowhere is there clearer evidence of this than in their literature. No more given to profundities than their society, Roman writers were, collectively, sophisticated, worldly-wise, and sometimes jaded. They sought to entertain and to inform rather than to enlighten, and they accomplished this with great style and a kind of lusty elegance. The literature is consistently entertaining, often irreverent, frequently lewd; it certainly makes lovely reading.[13]

---

13. Though much too long for inclusion here, it is strongly recommended that you read the rest of the *Aeneid* and all of Ovid's *Metamorphoses*. Further, reading all of the latter's *Art of Love* (plus *Amores* and *Remedy of Love*) clearly reveals why Ovid was so important to the medieval troubadour-trouvère tradition (see chap. 16) and the Age of Chivalry.

ON THE REPUBLIC

from Book VI, *Scipio's Dream*
Marcus Tullius Cicero (106–43 B.C.)

In both his political career and his writing Cicero is the perfect embodiment of the noble Roman statesman and cultured man of letters. Metaphysics and aesthetics are Greek concerns and of no interest for a patriot committed to the austere business of being a Roman. Rather, practicality and devotion to the state are his central concerns; these support a Rome whose destiny is to establish order and to civilize the world.

In his *On the Republic* (54–51 B.C.), Cicero follows Stoic teaching on promoting the welfare of the state, but adopts some details from Plato's *Republic.* Although patterned after Plato's *Myth of Er* (*Republic,* Book X), Cicero's *Scipio's Dream* is unequivocally Roman. Plato's myth is a vision of aspiration towards the state as an absolute ideal; Cicero uses a dream device to illustrate duty, honor, and patriotism, for as Scipio is told, "the noblest of pursuits . . . are those undertaken for the safety of your country."

The narrator is Scipio Africanus the Younger, the adopted grandson of Scipio Africanus the Elder, the general who defeated Hannibal at Carthage (Second Punic War, 218–201 B.C.). Scipio the Younger totally destroyed Carthage at the end of the Third Punic War (149–146 B.C.). In this essay he is an officer under the consul Manius Manilius, whom he later replaced. Widely read in the Middle Ages, this essay influenced both Chaucer and Dante; the geography and cosmology of the latter's *Hell* (see chap. 14) can be compared with Cicero's summary of the science of his day.

I served in Africa as military tribune of the Fourth Legion under Manius Manilius, as you know. When I arrived in that country my greatest desire was to meet King Masinissa, who had good reasons to be attached to my family. The old man embraced me tearfully when I called, and presently looked up to heaven and said, "I thank thee, sovereign sun, and ye lesser heavenly beings, that before I depart this life I behold in my realm and beneath my roof Publius Cornelius Scipio, whose very name refreshes my strength, so inseparable from my thought is the memory of that noble and invincible hero who first bore it." Then I questioned him about his kingdom, and he me about our commonwealth, and the day wore away with much conversation on both sides.

After I had been royally entertained we continued our conversation late into the night, the old man talking of nothing but Africanus and rehearsing his sayings as well as his deeds. When we parted to take our rest I fell into a deeper sleep than usual, for the hour was late and I was weary from travel. Because of our conversation, I suppose—our thoughts and utterances by day produce an effect in our sleep like that which Ennius speaks of with reference to Homer, of whom he used frequently to think and speak in his waking hours—Africanus appeared to me, in the shape that was familiar to me from his bust rather than from his own person. I shuddered when I recognized him, but he said: "Courage, Scipio, lay aside your dread and imprint my words on your memory. Do you see yonder city which I forced to submit to Rome but which is now stirring up the old hostilities and cannot remain at rest (from a lofty eminence bathed in brilliant starlight he pointed to Carthage), the city which you have come to attack, slightly more than a private? Within two years you shall be consul and overthrow it, and so win for yourself that which you now bear by inheritance. When you shall have destroyed Carthage, celebrated your triumph, been chosen censor, have traversed Egypt, Syria, Asia, and Greece as ambassador, you will be chosen consul a second time in your absence and will put an end to a great war by extirpating Numantia. But when you shall be borne into the capitol in your triumphal chariot, you shall find the government thrown into confusion by the machinations of my grandson; and here, Africanus, you must display to your country the lustre of your spirit, genius, and wisdom.

"But at this period I perceive that the path of your destiny is a doubtful one; for when your life has passed through seven times eight oblique journeys and returns of the sun; and when these two numbers (each of which is regarded as complete, one on one account and the other on another) shall, in their natural circuit, have brought you to the crisis of your fate, then will the whole state turn itself toward thee and thy glory; the senate, all virtuous men, our allies, and the Latins, shall look up to you. Upon your single person the preservation of your country will depend; and, in short, it is your part, as dictator, to settle the government, if you can but escape the impious hands of your kinsmen."—Here, when Laelius uttered an exclamation, and the rest groaned with great excitement, Scipio said, with a gentle smile, "I beg that you will not waken me out of my dream; listen a few moments and hear what followed.

"But that you may be more earnest in the defense of your country, know from me, that a certain place in heaven is assigned to all who have preserved, or assisted, or improved their country, where they are to enjoy an endless duration of happiness. For there is nothing which takes place on earth more acceptable to that Supreme Deity who governs all this world, than those councils and assemblies of men bound together by law, which are termed states; the governors and preservers of these go from hence, and hither do they return." Here, frightened as I was, not so much from the dread of death as of the treachery of my friends, I nevertheless asked him whether my father Paulus, and others, whom we thought to be dead, were yet alive? "To be sure they are alive (replied Africanus), for they have escaped from the fetters of the body as from a prison; that which is called life is really death. But behold your father Paulus approaching you."— No sooner did I see him than I poured forth a flood of tears; but he, embracing and kissing me, forbade me to weep. And when, having suppressed my tears, I regained the faculty of speech, I said: "Why, thou most sacred and excellent father, since this is life, as I hear Africanus affirm, why do I tarry on earth, and not hasten to come to you?"

"Not so, my son," he replied; "unless that God, whose temple is all this which you behold, shall free you from this imprisonment in the body, you can have no admission to this place; for men have been created under this condition, that they should keep that globe called earth which you see in the middle of this temple. And a soul has been supplied to them from those eternal fires which you call constellations and stars, and which, being globular and round, are animated with divine spirit, and complete their cycles and revolutions with amazing rapidity. Therefore you, my Publius, and all good men, must preserve your souls in the keeping of your bodies; nor are you, without the order of that Being who bestowed them upon you, to depart from mundane life, lest you seem to desert the duty assigned you by God. But, Scipio, like your grandfather here, like me who begot you, cherish justice and duty, a great obligation to parents and kin but greatest to your country. Such a life is the way to heaven and to this assembly of those who have already lived, and, released from the body, inhabit the place which you now see" (it was the circle of light which blazed most brightly among the other fires), "which you have learned from the Greeks to call the Milky Way." And as I looked on every side I saw other things transcendently glorious and wonderful. There were stars which we never see from the earth, and all were vast beyond what we have ever imagined. The least was that farthest from heaven and nearest the earth which shone with a borrowed light. The starry spheres were much larger than the earth; the earth itself looked so small as to make me ashamed of our empire, which was a mere point on its surface.

As I gazed more intently on earth, Africanus said: "How long will your mind be fixed on the ground? Do you not see what lofty regions you have entered? These are the nine circles, or rather spheres, by which all things are held together. One, the outermost, is the celestial; it contains all the rest and is itself the Supreme God, holding and embracing within itself the other spheres. In this are fixed those stars which ever roll in an unchanging course. Beneath it are seven other spheres which have a retrograde movement, opposite to that of the heavens. Of these, the globe which on earth you call Saturn, occupies one sphere. That shining body which you see next is called Jupiter, and is friendly and salutary to mankind. Next the lucid one, terrible to the earth, which you call Mars. The Sun holds the next place, almost under the middle region; he is the chief, the leader, and the director of the other luminaries; he is the soul and guide of the world, and of such immense bulk, that he illuminates and fills all other objects with his light. He is followed by the orbit of Venus, and that of Mercury, as attendants; and the Moon rolls in the lowest sphere, enlightened by the rays of the Sun. Below this there is nothing but what is mortal and transitory, excepting those souls which are given to the human race by the goodness of the gods. Whatever lies above the Moon is eternal. For the earth, which is the ninth sphere, and is placed in the center of the whole system, is immovable and below all the rest; and all bodies, by their natural gravitation, tend toward it."

When I had recovered from my amazement at these things I asked, "What is this sound so strong and sweet that fills my ears?" "This," he replied, "is the melody which, at intervals unequal, yet differing in exact proportions, is made by the impulse and motion of the spheres themselves, which, softening shriller by deeper tones, produce a diversity of regular harmonies. It is impossible that such prodigious movements should pass in silence; and nature teaches that the sounds which the spheres at one extremity utter must be sharp, and those on the other extremity must be grave; on which account

that highest revolution of the star-studded heaven, whose motion is more rapid, is carried on with a sharp and quick sound; whereas this of the moon, which is situated the lowest and at the other extremity, moves with the gravest sound. For the earth, the ninth sphere, remaining motionless, abides invariably in the innermost position, occupying the central spot in the universe. But these eight revolutions, of which two, those of Mercury and Venus, are in unison, make seven distinct tones, with measured intervals between, and almost all things are arranged in sevens. Skilled men, copying this harmony with strings and voice, have opened for themselves a way back to this place, as have others who with excelling genius have cultivated divine sciences in human life. But the ears of men are deafened by being filled with this melody; you mortals have no duller sense than that of hearing. As where the Nile at the Falls of Catadupa pours down from lofty mountains, the people who live hard by lack the sense of hearing because of the cataract's roar, so this harmony of the whole universe in its intensely rapid movement is so loud that men's ears cannot take it in, even as you cannot look directly at the sun, your sense of sight being overwhelmed by its radiance." While I marveled at these things I was ever and anon turning my eyes back to earth, upon which Africanus resumed:

"I perceive that even now you are fixing your eyes on the habitation and abode of men, and if it seems to you diminutive, as it in fact is, keep your gaze fixed on these heavenly things and scorn the earthly. What fame can you obtain from the speech of men, what glory worth the seeking? You perceive that men dwell on but few and scanty portions of the earth, and that amid these spots, as it were, vast solitudes are interposed! As to those who inhabit the earth, not only are they so separated that no communication can circulate among them from the one to the other, but part lie upon one side, part upon another, and part are diametrically opposite to you, from whom you assuredly can expect no glory. You observe that the same earth is encircled and encompassed as it were by certain zones, of which the two that are most distant from one another and lie as it were toward the vortexes of the heavens in both directions, are rigid as you see with frost, while the middle and the largest zone is burned up with the heat of the sun. Two of these are habitable. The southern, whose inhabitants imprint their footsteps in an opposite direction to you, has no relation to your race. As to this other, lying toward the north, which you inhabit, observe what a small portion of it falls to your share; for all that part of the earth which is inhabited by you, which narrows toward the south and north but widens from east to west, is no other than a little island surrounded by that sea which on earth you call the Atlantic, sometimes the great sea, and sometimes the ocean; and yet with so grand a name, you see how diminutive it is! Now do you think it possible for your renown, or that of any one of us, to move from those cultivated and inhabited spots of ground, and pass beyond that Caucasus, or swim across yonder Ganges? What inhabitant of the other parts of the east, or of the extreme regions of the setting sun, of those tracts that run toward the south or toward the north, shall ever hear of your name? Now supposing them cut off, you see at once within what narrow limits your glory would fain expand itself. As to those who speak of you, how long will they speak?

"Let me even suppose that a future race of men shall be desirous of transmitting to their posterity your renown or mine, as they received it from their fathers; yet when we consider the convulsions and conflagrations that must necessarily happen at some definite period, we are unable to attain not only to an eternal, but even to a lasting fame. Now of what consequence is it to you to be talked of by those who are born after you, and not by those who were born before you, who certainly were as numerous and more virtuous; especially, as amongst the very men who are thus to celebrate our renown, not a single one can preserve the recollections of a single year? For mankind ordinarily measure their year by the revolution of the sun, that is of a single heavenly body. But when all the planets shall return to the same position which they once had, and bring back after a long rotation the same aspect of the entire heavens, then the year may be said to be truly completed; I do not venture to say how many ages of mankind will be contained within such a year. As of old the sun seemed to be eclipsed and blotted out when the soul of Romulus entered these regions, so when the sun shall be again eclipsed in the same part of his course and at the same period of the year and day, with all the constellations and stars recalled to the point from which they started on their revolutions, then count the year as brought to a close. But be assured that the twentieth part of such a year has not yet elapsed.

"Consequently, should you renounce hope of returning to this place where eminent and excellent men find their reward, of what worth is that human glory which can scarcely extend to a small part of a single year? If, then, you shall determine to look on high and contemplate this mansion and eternal abode, you will neither give yourself to the gossip of the vulgar nor place your hope of well-being on rewards that man can bestow. Virtue herself, by her own charms, should draw you to true honor. What others may say of you regard as their concern, not yours. They will doubtless talk about you, but what they say is limited to the narrow regions which you see; nor does talk of anyone last into eternity—it is buried with those who die, and lost in oblivion for those who come afterward."

When he had finished I said: "Truly, Africanus, if the path to heaven lies open to those who have deserved well of their country, though from my childhood I have ever trod in your and my father's footsteps without disgracing your glory, yet now, with so noble a prize set before me, I shall strive with much more diligence."

"Do so strive," replied he, "and do not consider yourself, but your body, to be mortal. For you are not the being which this corporeal figure evinces; but the soul of every man is the man, and not that form which may be delineated with a finger. Know also that you are a god, if a god is that which lives, perceives, remembers, foresees, and which rules, governs, and moves the body over which it is set, just as the Supreme God rules the universe. Just as the eternal God moves the universe, which is in part mortal, so does an everlasting soul move the corruptible body.

"That which is always in motion is eternal; but that which, while communicating motion to another, derives its own movement from some other source, must of necessity cease to live when this motion ends. Only what moves itself never ceases motion, for it is never deserted by itself; it is rather the source and first cause of motion in whatever else is moved. But the first cause has no beginning, for everything originates from the first cause; itself, from nothing. If it owed its origin to anything else, it would not be a first cause. If it has no beginning, it has no end. If a first cause is extinguished, it will neither be reborn from anything else, nor will it create anything else from itself, for everything must originate from a first cause. It follows that motion begins with that which is moved of itself, and that this can neither be born nor die—else the heavens must collapse and nature perish, possessing no force from which to receive the first impulse to motion.

"Since that which moves of itself is eternal, who can deny that the soul is endowed with this property? Whatever is moved by external impulse is soulless; whatever possesses soul is moved by an inner impulse of its own, for this is the peculiar nature and property of soul. And since soul is the only force that moves itself, it surely has no beginning and is immortal. Employ it, therefore, in the noblest of pursuits; the noblest are those undertaken for the safety of your country. If it is in these that your soul is diligently exercised, it will have a swifter flight to this, its proper home and permanent abode. Even swifter will be the flight if, while still imprisoned in the body, it shall peer forth, and, contemplating what lies beyond, detach itself as far as possible from the body. For the souls of those who have surrendered themselves to the pleasures of the body and have become their slaves, who are goaded to obedience by lust and violate the laws of gods and men—such souls, when they pass out of their bodies, hover close to earth, and do not return to this place till they have been tossed about for many ages."

He departed; I awoke from sleep.

THE LOWER WORLD (THE AENEID, BOOK VI)
Virgil (Publius Virgilius Maro) (70-19 B.C.*)*

In the story of the journey of Aeneas (i-NEE-us), the Trojan hero has fled from Troy, and, after a great storm at sea caused by Juno, he and his people landed on the coast of North Africa. They made their way to Carthage, a land ruled by Queen Dido (DIE-doe). In her court he told the story of the last days of the Trojan War and of the fall of Troy. He told how he gathered a group around him including his aged father, Ankhises (an-KI-sees), son Askanius (A-SKAY-nee-us), and the household gods and fled from the coast of Asia Minor. He also told of their subsequent wanderings and of the death of Ankhises.

In the meantime Dido has fallen in love with Aeneas, and he, as much as his duty will allow, with her. Fearful of what might come of this, Aeneas and his band fled to Sicily, and Dido built a great funeral pyre and cast herself upon it. In Sicily Aeneas left a good part of his group who were tired of wandering, and with a select band he pushed on to fulfill his destiny—the founding of the City of Rome. The group arrived in Italy after Palinurus (pal–uh–NOOR–us), the steersman, was lost overboard. Long before, Aeneas had been told that he should consult the Kumean Sibyl (kyoo–MEE–an si–bil), a prophetess of Apollo, on his arrival, and that he should visit the underworld where he would meet the spirit of his father. This visit is presented here in full. After the visit, the little group sailed up the Tiber and established a village and fort. They became engaged in a war with the Italian hero Turnus, and finally vanquished him. Then Aeneas was ready to follow his destiny further by marrying Lavinia, daughter of King Latinus (la–TIE–nus), and establishing the Roman Empire.

The selection given here presents the best of the Roman spirit. Notice first the difficulty of Aeneas' mission; yet his sense of duty drives him on. Notice the pathos this professional spirit evokes in the meeting with Dido's spirit. Pride of race and family are present as Ankhises points out the spirits who are to return to earth to found the great Roman families. Virgil is, for all practical purposes, writing the *Social Register* for the Rome of his own time. Finally, one should notice the nine lines in which Ankhises gives what seems to be the highest statement of the Roman ideal.

Since Dante used Virgil as his guide through Hell and Purgatory, it is interesting to note Virgil's influence on the *Divine Comedy*.

The translation given here was made by the twentieth-century poet and scholar Rolfe Humphries. His spelling of proper names is unchanged.

Mourning for Palinurus, he drives the fleet
To Cumae's coast-line; the prows are turned, the anchor
Let down, the beach is covered by the vessels.
Young in their eagerness for the land in the west,
They flash ashore; some seek the seeds of flame
Hidden in veins of flint, and others spoil
The woods of tinder, and show where water runs.
Aeneas, in devotion, seeks the heights
Where stands Apollo's temple, and the cave
Where the dread Sibyl dwells, Apollo's priestess,
With the great mind and heart, inspired revealer
Of things to come. They enter Diana's grove,
Pass underneath the roof of gold.
                                            The story
Has it that Daedalus fled from Minos' kingdom[14]
Trusting himself to wings he made, and travelled
A course unknown to man, to the cold north,
Descending on this very summit; here,
Earth-bound again, he built a mighty temple,
Paying Apollo homage, the dedication
Of the oarage of his wings. On the temple doors
He carved, in bronze, Androgeos' death, and the payment
Enforced on Cecrops' children, seven sons
For sacrifice each year: there stands the urn,
The lots are drawn—facing this, over the sea,
Rises the land of Crete: the scene portrays
Pasiphae in cruel love, the bull
She took to her by cunning, and their offspring,
The mongrel Minotaur, half man, half monster,
The proof of lust unspeakable; and the toil
Of the house is shown, the labyrinthine maze

Which no one could have solved, but Daedalus
Pitied a princess' love, loosened the tangle,
Gave her a skein to guide her way. His boy,
Icarus, might have been here, in the picture,
And almost was—his father had made the effort
Once, and once more and dropped his hands; he could
    not
Master his grief that much. The story held them;
They would have studied it longer, but Achates[15]
Came from his mission; with him came the priestess,
Deiphobe, daughter of Glaucus, who tends the temple
For Phoebus and Diana; she warned Aeneas:
"It is no such sights the time demands; far better
To offer sacrifice, seven chosen bullocks,
Seven chosen ewes, a herd without corruption."
They were prompt in their obedience, and the priestess
Summoned the Trojans to the lofty temple.

The rock's vast side is hollowed into a cavern,
With a hundred mouths, a hundred open portals,
Whence voices rush, the answers of the Sibyl.
They had reached the threshold, and the virgin cried:
"It is time to seek the fates; the god is here,
The god is here, behold him." And as she spoke
Before the entrance, her countenance and color
Changed, and her hair tossed loose, and her heart was
    heaving,
Her bosom swollen with frenzy; she seemed taller,
Her voice not human at all, as the god's presence
Drew nearer, and took hold on her. "Aeneas,"
She cried, "Aeneas, are you praying?
Are you being swift in prayer? Until you are,
The house of the gods will not be moved, nor open
Its mighty portals." More than her speech, her silence
Made the Trojans cold with terror, and Aeneas
Prayed from the depth of his heart: "Phoebus Apollo,
Compassionate ever, slayer of Achilles
Through aim of Paris' arrow, helper and guide
Over the seas, over the lands, the deserts,
The shoals and quicksands, now at last we have come
To Italy, we hold the lands which fled us:
Grant that thus far, no farther, a Trojan fortune
Attend our wandering. And spare us now;
All of you, gods and goddesses, who hated
Troy in the past, and Trojan glory. I beg you,
Most holy prophetess, in who foreknowing
The future stands revealed, grant that the Trojans—
I ask with fate's permission—rest in Latium
Their wandering storm-tossed gods. I will build a temple,
In honor of Apollo and Diana,
Out of eternal marble, and ordain
Festivals in their honor, and for the Sibyl
A great shrine in our Kingdom, and I will place there
The lots and mystic oracles for my people
With chosen priests to tend them. Only, priestess,
This once, I pray you, chant the sacred verses

---

14. .Daedalus (DED–uh–lus) was a mythical artist and inventor. Imprisoned by King Minos of Crete, he constructed wings for himself and his son Icarus (IK–ar–us) and flew away. Icarus flew too near the sun and melted the wax wings. The other pieces of sculpture mentioned here show other incidents in Daedalus' life.
15. The companion of Aeneas (a–KOT–eez).

With your own lips; do not trust them to the leaves,[16]
The mockery of the rushing wind's disorder."

But the priestess, not yet subject to Apollo,
Went reeling through the cavern, wild, and storming
To throw the god, who presses, like a rider,
With bit and bridle and weight, tames her wild spirit,
Shapes her to his control. The doors fly open,
The hundred doors, of their own will, fly open,
And through the air the answer comes:—"O Trojans,
At last the dangers of the sea are over;
That course is run, but graver ones are waiting
On land. The sons of Dardanus[17] will reach
The kingdom of Lavinia[18]—be easy
On that account—the sons of Dardanus, also,
Will wish they had not come there. War, I see,
Terrible war, and the river Tiber foaming
With streams of blood. There will be another Xanthus,
Another Simois,[19] and Greek encampment,
Even another Achilles, born in Latium,
Himself a goddess' son. And Juno further
Will always be there: you will beg for mercy,
Be poor, turn everywhere for help. A woman
Will be the cause once more of so much evil,
A foreign bride, receptive to the Trojans,
A foreign marriage. Do not yield to evil,
Attack, attack, more boldly even than fortune
Seems to permit. An offering of safety,—
Incredible!—will come from a Greek city."

So, through the amplifiers of her cavern,
The hollow vaults, the Sibyl cast her warnings,
Riddles confused with truth; and Apollo rode her,
Reining her rage, and shaking her, and spurring
The fierceness of her heart. The frenzy dwindled,
A little, and her lips were still. Aeneas
Began:—"For me, no form of trouble, maiden,
Is new, or unexpected; all of this
I have known long since, lived in imagination.
One thing I ask: this is the gate of the kingdom,
So it is said, where Pluto reigns, the gloomy
Marsh where the water of Acheron[20] runs over.
Teach me the way from here, open the portals
That I may go to my beloved father,
Stand in his presence, talk with him. I brought him,
Once, on these shoulders, through a thousand weapons
And following fire, and foemen. He shared with me
The road, the sea, the menaces of heaven,
Things that an old man should not bear; he bore them,
Tired as he was. And he it was who told me
To come to you in humbleness. I beg you
Pity the son, the father. You have power,
Great priestess, over all; it is not for nothing
Hecate[21] gave you this dominion over
Avernus' groves. If Orpheus could summon
Eurydice from the shadows with his music,
If Pollux could save his brother, coming, going,
Along this path,—why should I mention Theseus,
Why mention Hercules?[22] I, too, descended
From the line of Jupiter." He clasped the altar,
Making his prayer, and she made answer to him:
"Son of Anchises, born of godly lineage,
By night, by day, the portals of dark Dis[23]
Stand open: it is easy, the descending
Down to Avernus. But to climb again,
To trace the footsteps back to the air above,
There lies the task, the toil. A few, beloved

By Jupiter, descended from the gods,
A few, in whom exalting virtue burned,
Have been permitted. Around the central woods
The black Cocytus glides, a sullen river;
But if such love is in your heart, such longing
For double crossing of the Stygian lake,
For double sight of Tartarus, learn first
What must be done. In a dark tree there hides
A bough, all golden, leaf and pliant stem,
Sacred to Proserpine.[24] This all the grove
Protects, and shadows cover it with darkness.
Until this bough, this bloom of light, is found,
No one receives his passport to the darkness
Whose queen requires this tribute. In succession,
After the bough is plucked, another grows,
Gold-green with the same metal. Raise the eyes,
Look up, reach up the hand, and it will follow
With ease, if fate is calling; otherwise,
No power, no steel, can loose it. Furthermore,
(Alas, you do not know this!), one of your men
Lies on the shore, unburied, a pollution
To all the fleet, while you have come for counsel
Here to our threshold. Bury him with honor;
Black cattle slain in expiation for him
Must fall before you see the Stygian kingdoms,
The groves denied to living men."
                    Aeneas,
With sadness in his eyes, and downcast heart,
Turned from the cave, and at his side Achates
Accompanied his anxious meditations.
They talked together: who could be the comrade
Named by the priestess, lying there unburied?
And they found him on dry sand; it was Misenus,[25]
Aeolus' son, none better with the trumpet
To make men burn for warfare. He had been
Great Hector's man-at-arms; he was good in battle
With spear as well as horn, and after Hector
had fallen to Achilles, he had followed
Aeneas, entering no meaner service.
Some foolishness came over him; he made

---

16. The prophecies of this Cumaean Sibyl were usually written on leaves which the winds in the cave might scatter and confuse (v. Book III).

17. The mythical founder of Troy.

18. The daughter of the Italian King Latinus. Aeneas was later to marry her to establish his kingdom.

19. Rivers near Troy that ran with blood during the Trojan War.

20. This is the river (AK–uh–ron) that leads to Hades. Other rivers in the lower world are the Styx, which forms a boundary for the region, Cocytus (ko–SI–tus), and Phlegethon (FLEG–uh–thon), which serves as a barrier between the mild punishments and the more severe.

21. Hecate (HEK–uh–tee) is a very powerful goddess who, among many responsibilities, controlled the spirits of the dead. Avernus is a very deep pool surrounded by gloomy woods. Its depth and gloom inspired the idea that it led to the underworld.

22. All of these are the names of mythical heroes who had descended into Hades and returned.

23. Dis is another name for the underworld.

24. Proserpine (pro–SUR–pi–nee), as wife of Pluto, is queen of the underworld.

25. mi–SEEN–us.

The ocean echo to the blare of his trumpet
That day, and challenged the sea-gods to a contest
In martial music, and Triton, jealous, caught him,
However unbelievable the story,
And held him down between the rocks, and drowned him
Under the foaming waves. His comrades mourned him,
Aeneas most of all, and in their sorrow
They carry out, in haste, the Sibyl's orders,
Construct the funeral altar, high as heaven,
They go to an old wood, and the pine-trees fall
Where wild beasts have their dens, and holm-oak rings
To the stroke of the axe, and oak and ash are riven
By the splitting wedge, and rowan-trees come rolling
Down the steep mountain-side. Aeneas helps them,
And cheers them on; studies the endless forest,
Takes thought, and prays: "If only we might see it,
That golden bough, here in the depth of the forest,
Bright on some tree. She told the truth, our priestess,
Too much, too bitter truth, about Misenus."
No sooner had he spoken than twin doves
Came flying down before him, and alighted
On the green ground. He knew his mother's birds,[26]
And made his prayer, rejoicing,—"Oh, be leaders,
Wherever the way, and guide me to the grove
Where the rich bough makes rich the shaded ground.
Help me, O goddess-mother!" And he paused,
Watching what sign they gave, what course they set.
The birds flew on a little, just ahead
Of the pursuing vision; when they came
To the jaws of dank Avernus, evil-smelling,
They rose aloft, then swooped down the bright air,
Perched on the double tree, where the off-color
Of gold was gleaming golden through the branches.
As mistletoe, in the cold winter, blossoms
With its strange foliage on an alien tree,
The yellow berry gilding the smooth branches,
Such was the vision of the gold in leaf
On the dark holm-oak, so the foil was rustling,
Rattling, almost, the bract in the soft wind
Stirring like metal. Aeneas broke it off
With eager grasp, and bore it to the Sibyl.

Meanwhile, along the shore, the Trojans mourned,
Paying Misenus' dust the final honors.
A mighty pyre was raised, of pine and oak,
The sides hung with dark leaves, and somber cypress
Along the front, and gleaming arms above.
Some made the water hot, and some made ready
Bronze caldrons, shimmering over fire, and others
Lave and anoint the body, and with weeping
Lay on the bier his limbs, and place above them
Familiar garments, crimson color; and some
Take up the heavy burden, a sad office,
And, as their fathers did, they kept their eyes
Averted, as they brought the torches nearer.
They burn gifts with him, bowls of oil, and viands,
And frankincense; and when the flame is quiet
And the ashes settle to earth, they wash the embers
With wine, and slake the thirsty dust. The bones
Are placed in a bronze urn by Corynaeus,
Who, with pure water, thrice around his comrades
Made lustral cleansing, shaking gentle dew
From the fruitful branch of olive; and they said
Hail and farewell! And over him Aeneas
Erects a mighty tomb, with the hero's arms,
His oar and trumpet, where the mountain rises
Memorial for ever, and named Misenus.

These rites performed, he hastened to the Sibyl.
There was a cavern, yawning wide and deep,
Jagged, below the darkness of the trees,
Beside the darkness of the lake. No bird
Could fly above it safely, with the vapor
Pouring from the black gulf (the Greeks have named it
Avernus, or A-Ornos, meaning *birdless*),
And here the priestess for the slaughter set
Four bullocks, black ones, poured the holy wine
Between the horns, and plucked the topmost bristles
For the first offering to the sacred fire,
Calling on Hecate, a power in heaven,
A power in hell. Knives to the throat were driven,
The warm blood caught in bowls. Aeneas offered
A lamb, black-fleeced, to Night and her great sister,
A sterile heifer for the queen; for Dis
An altar in the night, and on the flames
The weight of heavy bulls, the fat oil pouring
Over the burning entrails. And at dawn,
Under their feet, earth seemed to shake and rumble,
The ridges move, and bitches bay in darkness,
As the presence neared. The Sibyl cried a warning,
"Keep off, keep off, whatever is unholy,
Depart from here! Courage, Aeneas; enter
The path, unsheathe the sword. The time is ready
For the brave heart." She strode out boldly, leading
Into the open cavern, and he followed.

Gods of the world of spirit, silent shadows,
Chaos and Phlegethon, areas of silence,
Wide realms of dark, may it be right and proper
To tell what I have heard, this revelation
Of matters buried deep in earth and darkness!

Vague forms in lonely darkness, they were going
Through void and shadow, through the empty realm
Like people in a forest, when the moonlight
Shifts with a baleful glimmer, and shadow covers
The sky, and all the colors turn to blackness.
At the first threshold, on the jaws of Orcus,
Grief and avenging Cares have set their couches,
And pale Diseases dwell, and sad Old Age,
Fear, evil-counselling Hunger, wretched Need,
Forms terrible to see, and Death, and Toil,
And Death's own brother, Sleep, and evil Joys,
Fantasies of the mind, and deadly War,
The Furies' iron chambers, Discord, raving,
Her snaky hair entwined in bloody bands.
An elm-tree loomed there, shadowy and huge,
The aged boughs outspread, beneath whose leaves,
Men say, the false dreams cling, thousands on thousands.
And there are monsters in the dooryard, Centaurs,
Scyllas, of double shape, the beast of Lerna,
Hissing most horribly, Briareus,
The hundred-handed giant, a Chimaera
Whose armament is fire, Harpies, and Gorgons,
A triple-bodied giant. In sudden panic
Aeneas drew his sword, the edge held forward,
Ready to rush and flail, however blindly,
Save that his wise companion warned him, saying
They had no substance, they were only phantoms
Flitting about, illusions without body.

---

26. Aeneas' mother was Venus.

From here, the road turns off to Acheron,
River of Hell; here, thick with muddy whirling,
Cocytus boils with sand. Charon[27] is here,
The guardian of these mingling waters, Charon,
Uncouth and filthy, on whose chin the hair
Is a tangled mat, whose eyes protrude, are burning,
Whose dirty cloak is knotted at the shoulder.
He poles a boat, tends to the sail, unaided,
Ferrying bodies in his rust-hued vessel.
Old, but a god's senility is awful
In its raw greenness. To the bank come thronging
Mothers and men, bodies of great-souled heroes,
Their life-time over, boys, unwedded maidens,
Young men whose fathers saw their pyres burning,
Thick as the forest leaves that fall in autumn
With early frost, thick as the birds to landfall
From over the seas, when the chill of the year compels
     them
To sunlight. There they stand, a host, imploring
To be taken over first. Their hands, in longing
Reach out for the farther shore. But the gloomy boatman
Makes choice among them, taking some, and keeping
Others far back from the stream's edge. Aeneas,
Wondering, asks the Sibyl, "Why the crowding?
What are the spirits seeking? What distinction
Brings some across the livid stream, while others
Stay on the farther bank?" She answers, briefly:
"Son of Anchises, this is the awful river,
The Styx,[28] by which the gods take oath; the boatman
Charon; those he takes with him are the buried,
Those he rejects, whose luck is out, the graveless.
It is not permitted him to take them over
The dreadful banks and hoarse-resounding waters
Till earth is cast upon their bones. They haunt
These shores a hundred restless years of waiting
Before they end postponement of the crossing."
Aeneas paused, in thoughtful mood, with pity
Over their lot's unevenness; and saw there,
Wanting the honor given the dead, and grieving,
Leucaspis, and Orontes, the Lycian captain,
Who had sailed from Troy across the stormy waters,
And drowned off Africa, with crew and vessel,
And there was Palinurus, once his pilot,
Who, not so long ago, had been swept over,
Watching the stars on the journey north from Carthage.
The murk was thick; Aeneas hardly knew him,
Sorrowful in that darkness, but made question:
"What god, O Palinurus, took you from us?
Who drowned you in the deep? Tell me. Apollo
Never before was false, and yet he told me
You would be safe across the seas, and come
Unharmed to Italy; what kind of promise
Was this, to fool me with?" But Palinurus
Gave him assurance:—"It was no god who drowned me,
No falsehood on Apollo's part, my captain,
But as I clung to the tiller, holding fast
To keep the course, as I should do, I felt it
Wrenched from the ship, and I fell with it, headlong.
By those rough seas I swear, I had less fear
On my account than for the ship, with rudder
And helmsman overboard, to drift at the mercy
Of rising seas. Three nights I rode the waters,
Three nights of storm, and from the crest of a wave,
On the fourth morning, sighted Italy,
I was swimming to land, I had almost reached it, heavy
In soaking garments; my cramped fingers struggled

To grasp the top of the rock, when barbarous people,
Ignorant men, mistaking me for booty,
Struck me with swords; waves hold me now, or winds
Roll me along the shore. By the light of heaven
The lovely air, I beg you, by your father,
Your hope of young Iulus,[29] bring me rescue
Out of these evils, my unconquered leader!
Cast over my body earth—you have the power—
Return to Velia's harbor,—or there may be
Some other way—your mother is a goddess,
Else how would you be crossing this great river,
This Stygian swamp?—help a poor fellow, take me
Over the water with you, give a dead man
At least a place to rest in." But the Sibyl
Broke in upon him sternly:—"Palinurus,
Whence comes this mad desire? No man, unburied,
May see the Stygian waters, or Cocytus,
The Furies' dreadful river; no man may come
Unbidden to this bank. Give up the hope
That fate is changed by praying, but hear this,
A little comfort in your harsh misfortune:
Those neighboring people will make expiation,
Driven by signs from heaven, through their cities
And through their countryside; they will build a tomb,
Thereto bring offerings yearly, and the place
Shall take its name from you, Cape Palinurus."
So he was comforted a little, finding
Some happiness in the promise.
                    And they went on,
Nearing the river, and from the stream the boatman
Beheld them cross the silent forest, nearer,
Turning their footsteps toward the bank. He
     challenged:—
"Whoever you are, O man in armor, coming
In this direction, halt where you are, and tell me
The reason why you come. This is the region
Of shadows, and of Sleep and drowsy Night;
I am not allowed to carry living bodies
In the Stygian boat; and I must say I was sorry
I ever accepted Hercules and Theseus
And Pirithous, and rowed them over the lake,
Though they were sons of gods and great in courage.
One of them dared to drag the guard of Hell,
Enchained, from Pluto's throne, shaking in terror,
The others to snatch our queen from Pluto's chamber."
The Sibyl answered briefly: "No such cunning
Is plotted here; our weapons bring no danger.
Be undisturbed: the hell-hound in his cavern
May bark forever, to keep the bloodless shadows
Frightened away from trespass; Proserpine,
Untouched, in pureness guard her uncle's threshold.
Trojan Aeneas, a man renowned for goodness,
Renowned for nerve in battle, is descending
To the lowest shades; he comes to find his father.
If such devotion has no meaning to you,
Look on this branch at least, and recognize it!"

---

27. KARE–on.

28. STICKS.

29. This is Aeneas' son, also known as Askanius.

And with the word she drew from under her mantle
The golden bough; his swollen wrath subsided.
No more was said; he saw the bough, and marvelled
At the holy gift, so long unseen; came sculling
The dark-blue boat to the shore, and drove the spirits,
Lining the thwarts, ashore, and cleared the gangway,
And took Aeneas aboard; as that big man
Stepped in, the leaky skiff groaned under the weight,
And the strained seams let in the muddy water,
But they made the crossing safely, seer and soldier,
To the far margin, colorless and shapeless,
Grey sedge and dark-brown ooze. They heard the baying
Of Cerberus,[30] that great hound, in his cavern crouching,
Making the shore resound, as all three throats
Belled horribly; and serpents rose and bristled
Along the triple neck. The priestess threw him
A sop with honey and drugged meal; he opened
The ravenous throat, gulped, and subsided, filling
The den with his huge bulk. Aeneas, crossing
Passed on beyond the bank of the dread river
Whence none return.

   A wailing of thin voices[31]
Came to their ears, the souls of infants crying,
Those whom the day of darkness took from the breast
Before their share of living. And there were many
Whom some false sentence brought to death. Here
  Minos[32]
Judges them once again; a silent jury
Reviews the evidence. And there are others,
Guilty of nothing, but who hated living,
The suicides. How gladly, now, they would suffer
Poverty, hardship, in the world of light!
But this is not permitted; they are bound
Nine times around by the black unlovely river;
Styx holds them fast.
   They came to the Fields of
  Mourning,
So-called, where those whom cruel love had wasted
Hid in secluded pathways, under myrtle,
And even in death were anxious. Procris, Phaedra,
Eriphyle, displaying wounds her son
Had given her, Caeneus, Laodamia,
Caeneus, a young man once, and now again
A young man, after having been a woman.
And here, new come from her own wound, was Dido,[33]
Wandering in the wood. The Trojan hero,
Standing near by, saw her, or thought he saw her,
Dim in the shadows, like the slender crescent
Of moon when cloud drifts over. Weeping, he greets
  her:—
"Unhappy Dido, so they told me truly
That your own hand had brought you death. Was I—
Alas!—the cause? I swear by all the stars,
By the world above, by everything held sacred
Here under the earth, unwillingly, O queen,
I left your kingdom. But the gods' commands,
Driving me now through these forsaken places,
This utter night, compelled me on. I could not
Believe my loss would cause so great a sorrow.
Linger a moment, do not leave me; whither,
Whom, are you fleeing? I am permitted only
This last word with you."
   But the queen, unmoving
As flint or marble, turned away, her eyes
Fixed on the ground: the tears were vain, the words,
Meant to be soothing, foolish; she turned away,
His enemy forever, to the shadows

Where Sychaeus, her former husband, took her
With love for love, and sorrow for her sorrow.
And still Aeneas wept for her, being troubled
By the injustice of her doom; his pity
Followed her going.
   They went on. They came
To the farthest fields, whose tenants are the warriors,
Illustrious throng. Here Tydeus came to meet him,
Parthenopaeus came, and pale Adrastus,
A fighter's ghost, and many, many others,
Mourned in the world above, and doomed in battle,
Leaders of Troy, in long array; Aeneas
Sighed as he saw them: Medon; Polyboetes,
The priest of Ceres; Glaucus; and Idaeus
Still keeping arms and chariot; three brothers,
Antenor's sons; Thersilochus; a host
To right and left of him, and when they see him,
One sight is not enough; they crowd around him,
Linger, and ask the reasons for his coming.
But Agamemnon's men, the Greek battalions,
Seeing him there, and his arms in shadow gleaming,
Tremble in panic, turn to flee for refuge,
As once they used to, toward their ships, but where
Are the ships now? They try to shout, in terror;
But only a thin and piping treble issues
To mock their mouths, wide-open.
   One he knew
Was here, Deiphobus,[34] a son of Priam,
With his whole body mangled, and his features
Cruelly slashed, and both hands cut, and ears
Torn from his temples, and his nostrils slit
By shameful wounds. Aeneas hardly knew him,
Shivering there, and doing his best to hide
His marks of punishment; unhailed, he hailed him:—
"Deiphobus, great warrior, son of Teucer,
Whose cruel punishment was this? Whose license
Abused you so? I heard, it seems a story
Of that last night, how you had fallen, weary
With killing Greeks at last; I built a tomb,
Although no body lay there, in your honor,
Three times I cried, aloud, over your spirit,
Where now your name and arms keep guard. I could not,
Leaving my country, find my friend, to give him
Proper interment in the earth he came from."
And Priam's son replied:—"Nothing, dear comrade,
Was left undone; the dead man's shade was given
All ceremony due. It was my own fortune
And a Spartan woman's[35] deadliness that sunk me
Under these evils; she it was who left me
These souvenirs. You know how falsely happy
We were on that last night; I need not tell you.

---

30. SIR–bur–us.

31. Here and about 190 lines later you might compare the sins and their punishments with the disposition Dante makes of the souls in Hell in Canto XI of the *Inferno*.

32. MI–nus.

33. Dido, Queen of Carthage, filled with rage and guilt had committed suicide when Aeneas sailed away from her city.

34. dee–IF–uh–bus.

35. This is Helen of Troy. Virgil believes that she was married to Deiphobus after Paris' death.

When that dread horse came leaping over our walls,
Pregnant with soldiery, she led the dancing,
A solemn rite, she called it, with Trojan women
Screaming their bacchanals; she raised the torches
High on the citadel; she called the Greeks.
Then—I was worn with trouble, drugged in slumber,
Resting in our ill-omened bridal chamber,
With sleep as deep and sweet as death upon me—
Then she, that paragon of helpmates, deftly
Moved all the weapons from the house; my sword,
Even, she stole from underneath my pillow,
Opened the door, and called in Menelaus,
Hoping, no doubt, to please her loving husband,
To win forgetfulness of her old sinning.
It is quickly told: they broke into the chamber,
The two of them, and with them, as accomplice,
Ulysses came, the crime-contriving bastard.
O gods, pay back the Greeks; grant the petition
If goodness asks for vengeance! But you, Aeneas,
A living man—what chance has brought you here?
Vagrant of ocean, god-inspired,—which are you?
What chance has worn you down, to come, in sadness,
To these confusing sunless dwelling-places?''

    While they were talking, Aurora's rosy car
Had halfway crossed the heaven; all their time
Might have been spent in converse, but the Sibyl
Hurried them forward:—"Night comes on, Aeneas;
We waste the hours with tears. We are at the cross-road,
Now; here we turn to the right, where the pathway leads
On to Elysium, under Pluto's ramparts.
Leftward to Tartarus, and retribution,
The terminal of the wicked, and their dungeon.''
Deiphobus left them, saying, "O great priestess,
Do not be angry with me; I am going;
I shall not fail the roll-call of the shadows.
Pride of our race, go on; may better fortune
Attend you!'' and, upon the word, he vanished.

    As he looked back, Aeneas saw, to his left,
Wide walls beneath a cliff, a triple rampart,
A river running fire, Phlegethon's torrent,
Rocks roaring in its course, a gate, tremendous,
Pillars of adamant, a tower of iron,
Too strong for men, too strong for even gods
To batter down in warfare, and behind them
A Fury, sentinel in bloody garments,
Always on watch, by day, by night. He heard
Sobbing and groaning there, the crack of the lash,
The clank of iron, the sound of dragging shackles.
The noise was terrible; Aeneas halted,
Asking, "What forms of crime are these, O maiden?
What harrying punishment, what horrible outcry?''
She answered:—"O great leader of the Trojans,
I have never crossed that threshold of the wicked;
No pure soul is permitted entrance thither,
But Hecate, by whose order I was given
Charge of Avernus' groves, my guide, my teacher,
Told me how gods exact the toll of vengeance.
The monarch here, merciless Rhadamanthus,
Punishes guilt, and hears confession; he forces
Acknowledgment of crime; no man in the world,
No matter how cleverly he hides his evil,
No matter how much he smiles at his own slyness,
Can fend atonement off; the hour of death
Begins his sentence. Tisiphone, the Fury,
Leaps at the guilty with her scourge; her serpents
Are whips of menace as she calls her sisters.

Imagine the gates, on jarring hinge, rasp open,
You would see her in the doorway, a shape, a sentry,
Savage, implacable. Beyond, still fiercer,
The monstrous Hydra dwells; her fifty throats
Are black, and open wide, and Tartarus
Is black, and open wide, and it goes down
To darkness, sheer deep down, and twice the distance
That earth is from Olympus. At the bottom
The Titans crawl, Earth's oldest breed, hurled under
By thunderbolts; here lie the giant twins,
Aloeus' sons, who laid their hands on heaven
And tried to pull down Jove; Salmoneus here
Atones for high presumption,—it was he
Who aped Jove's noise and fire, wheeling his horses
Triumphant through his city in Elis, cheering
And shaking the torch, and claiming divine homage,
The arrogant fool, to think his brass was lightning,
His horny-footed horses beat out thunder!
Jove showed him what real thunder was, what lightning
Spoke from immortal cloud, what whirlwind fury
Came sweeping from the heaven to overtake him.
Here Tityos, Earth's giant son, lies sprawling
Over nine acres, with a monstrous vulture
Gnawing, with crooked beak, vitals and liver
That grow as they are eaten; eternal anguish,
Eternal feast. Over another hangs
A rock, about to fall; and there are tables
Set for a banquet, gold with royal splendor,
But if a hand goes out to touch the viands,
The Fury drives it back with fire and yelling.
Why name them all, Pirithous, the Lapiths,
Ixion? The roll of crime would take forever.
Whoever, in his lifetime, hated his brother,
Or struck his father down; whoever cheated
A client, or was miserly—how many
Of these there seem to be!—whoever went
To treasonable war, or broke a promise
Made to his lord, whoever perished, slain
Over adultery, all these, walled in,
Wait here their punishment. Seek not to know
Too much about their doom. The stone is rolled,
The wheel keeps turning; Theseus forever
Sits in dejection; Phlegyas, accursed,
Cries through the halls forever: *Being warned,
Learn justice; reverence the gods!* The man
Who sold his country is here in hell; the man
Who altered laws for money; and a father
Who knew his daughter's bed. All of them dared,
And more than dared, achieved, unspeakable
Ambitions. If I had a hundred tongues,
A hundred iron throats, I could not tell
The fullness of their crime and punishment.''
And then she added:—"Come: resume the journey,
Fulfill the mission; let us hurry onward.
I see the walls the Cyclops made, the portals
Under the archway, where, the orders tell us,
Our tribute must be set.'' They went together
Through the way's darkness, came to the doors, and
    halted,
And at the entrance Aeneas, having sprinkled
His body with fresh water, placed the bough
Golden before the threshold. The will of the goddess
Had been performed, the proper task completed.

    They came to happy places, the joyful dwelling,
The lovely greenery of the groves of the blessed.
Here ampler air invests the fields with light,

Rose-colored, with familiar stars and sun.
Some grapple on the grassy wrestling-ground
In exercise and sport, and some are dancing,
And others singing; in his trailing robe
Orpheus strums the lyre; the seven clear notes
Accompany the dance, the song. And heroes
Are there, great-souled, born in the happier years,
Ilus,[36] Assaracus; the city's founder,
Prince Dardanus. Far off, Aeneas wonders,
Seeing the phantom arms, the chariots,
The spears fixed in the ground, the chargers browsing,
Unharnessed, over the plain. Whatever, living,
The men delighted in, whatever pleasure
Was theirs in horse and chariot, still holds them
Here under the world. To right and left, they banquet
In the green meadows, and a joyful chorus
Rises through groves of laurel, whence the river
Runs to the upper world. The band of heroes
Dwell here, all those whose mortal wounds were suffered
In fighting for the fatherland; and poets,
The good, the pure, the worthy of Apollo;
Those who discovered truth and made life nobler;
Those who served others—all, with snowy fillets
Binding their temples, throng the lovely valley.
And these the Sibyl questioned, most of all
Musaeus,[37] for he towered above the center
Of that great throng:—"O happy souls, O poet,
Where does Anchises dwell? For him we come here,
For him we have traversed Erebus' great rivers."
And he replied:—"It is all our home, the shady
Groves, and the streaming meadows, and the softness
Along the river-banks. No fixed abode
Is ours at all; but if it is your pleasure,
Cross over the ridge with me; I will guide you there
By easy going." And so Musaeus led them
And from the summit showed them fields, all shining,
And they went on over and down.

    Deep in a valley of green, father Anchises
Was watching, with deep earnestness, the spirits
Whose destiny was light, and counting them over,
All of his race to come, his dear descendants,
Their fates and fortunes and their works and ways,
And as he saw Aeneas coming toward him
Over the meadow, his hands reached out with yearning,
He was moved to tears, and called:—"At last, my son,—
Have you really come, at last? and the long road nothing
To a son who loves his father? Do I, truly,
See you, and hear your voice? I was thinking so,
I was hoping so, I was counting off the days,
And I was right about it. O my son!
What a long journey, over land and water,
Yours must have been! What buffeting of danger!
I feared, so much, the Libyan realm would hurt you."
And his son answered:—"It was your spirit, father,
Your sorrowful shade, so often met, that led me
To find these portals. The ships ride safe at anchor,
Safe in the Tuscan sea. Embrace me, father;
Let hand join hand in love; do not forsake me."
And as he spoke, the tears streamed down. Three times
He reached out toward him, and three times the image
Fled like the breath of the wind or a dream on wings.

    He saw, in a far valley, a separate grove
Where the woods stir and rustle, and a river,
The Lethe,[38] gliding past the peaceful places,
And tribes of people thronging, hovering over,
Innumerable as the bees in summer
Working the bright-hued flowers, and the shining

Of the white lilies, murmuring and humming.
Aeneas, filled with wonder, asks the reason
For what he does not know, who are the people
In such a host, and to what river coming?
Anchises answers:—"These are spirits, ready
Once more for life; they drink of Lethe's water
The soothing potion of forgetfulness.
I have longed, for long, to show them to you, name them,
Our children's children; Italy discovered,
So much the greater happiness, my son."
"But, O my father, is it thinkable
That souls would leave this blessedness, be willing
A second time to bear the sluggish body,
Trade Paradise for earth? Alas, poor wretches,
Why such a mad desire for light?" Anchises
Gives detailed answer: "First, my son, a spirit
Sustains all matter heaven and earth and ocean,
The moon, the stars; mind quickens mass, and moves it.
Hence comes the race of man, of beast, of winged
Creatures of air, of the strange shapes which ocean
Bears down below his mottled marble surface.
All these are blessed with energy from heaven;[39]
The seed of life is a spark of fire, but the body
A clod of earth, a clog, a mortal burden.
Hence humans fear, desire, grieve, and are joyful,
And even when life is over, all the evil
Ingrained so long, the adulterated mixture,
The plagues and pestilences of the body
Remain, persist. So there must be a cleansing,
By penalty, by punishment, by fire,
By sweep of wind, by water's absolution,
Before the guilt is gone. Each of us suffers
His own peculiar ghost. But the day comes
When we are sent through wide Elysium,
The Fields of the Blessed, a few of us, to linger
Until the turn of time, the wheel of ages,
Wears off the taint, and leaves the core of spirit
Pure sense, pure flame. A thousand years pass over
And the god calls the countless host to Lethe
Where memory is annulled, and souls are willing
Once more to enter into mortal bodies."

    The discourse ended; the father drew his son
And his companion toward the hum, the center
Of the full host; they came to rising ground
Where all the long array was visible,
Anchises watching, noting, every comer.
"Glory to come, my son, illustrious spirits
Of Dardan lineage, Italian offspring,
Heirs of our name, begetters of our future!
These I will name for you and tell our fortunes:
First, leaning on a headless spear, and standing
Nearest the light, that youth, the first to rise
To the world above, is Silvius; his name
Is Alban; in his veins Italian blood
Will run with Trojan; he will be the son
Of your late age; Lavinia will bear him,
A king and sire of kings; from him our race

---

36. These are all ancestors of Aeneas, all former kings of Troy.

37. A mythical poet and singer.

38. LEE–thee.

39. You might compare this with Dante's ideas on the same thing. See, for example, Purgatory, Cantos XVI and XVIII.

Will rule in Alba Longa.[40] Near him, Procas,
A glory to the Trojan race; and Capys,
And Numitor, and Silvius Aeneas,
Resembling you in name, in arms, in goodness,
If ever he wins the Alban kingdom over.
What fine young men they are! What strength, what
    prowess!
The civic oak already shades their foreheads.
These will found cities, Gabii, Fidenae,
Nomentum; they will crown the hills with towers
Above Collatia, Inuus fortress, Bola,
Cora, all names to be, thus far ungiven.

"And there will be a son of Mars; his mother
Is Ilia, and his name is Romulus,
Assaracus' descendant. On his helmet
See, even now, twin plumes; his father's honor
Confers distinction on him for the world.
Under his auspices Rome, that glorious city,
Will bound her power by earth, her pride by heaven,
Happy in hero sons, one wall surrounding
Her seven hills, even as Cybele, riding
Through Phrygian cities, wears her crown of towers,
Rejoicing in her offspring, and embracing
A hundred children of the gods, her children,
Celestials, all of them, at home in heaven.
Turn the eyes now this way; behold the Romans,
Your very own. These are Iulus' children,
The race to come. One promise you have heard
Over and over: here is its fulfillment,
The son of a god, Augustus Caesar, founder
Of a new age of gold, in lands where Saturn
Ruled long ago; he will extend his empire
Beyond the Indies, beyond the normal measure
Of years and constellations, where high Atlas
Turns on his shoulders the star-studded world.
Maeotia[41] and the Caspian seas are trembling
As heaven's oracles predict his coming,
And all the seven mouths of Nile are troubled
Not even Hercules, in all his travels,
Covered so much of the world, from Erymanthus
To Lerna; nor did Bacchus, driving his tigers
From Nysa's summit. How can hesitation
Keep us from deeds to make our prowess greater?
What fear can block us from Ausonian land?

"And who is that one yonder, wearing the olive,
Holding the sacrifice? I recognize him,
That white-haired king of Rome, who comes from Cures,
A poor land, to a mighty empire, giver
Of law to the young town. His name is Numa.
Near him is Tullus; he will rouse to arms
A race grown sluggish, little used to triumph.
Beyond him Ancus, even now too boastful,
Too fond of popular favor. And then the Tarquins,
And the avenger Brutus, proud of spirit,
Restorer of the balance. He shall be
First holder of the consular power; his children
Will stir up wars again, and he, for freedom
And her sweet sake, will call down judgment on them,
Unhappy, however future men may praise him,
In love of country and intense ambition.

"There are the Decii,[42] and there the Drusi,
A little farther off, and stern Torquatus,
The man with the axe, and Camillus, the regainer
Of standards lost. And see those two, resplendent
In equal arms, harmonious friendly spirits
Now, in the shadow of night, but if they ever

Come to the world of light, alas, what warfare,
What battle-lines, what slaughter they will fashion,
Each for the other, one from Alpine ramparts
Descending, and the other ranged against him
With armies from the east, father and son
Through marriage, Pompey and Caesar. O my children,
Cast out the thoughts of war, and do not murder
The flower of our country. O my son,
Whose line descends from heaven, let the sword
Fall from the hand, be leader in forbearing!

"Yonder is one who, victor over Corinth,
Will ride in triumph home, famous for carnage
Inflicted on the Greeks; near him another,
Destroyer of old Argus and Mycenae
Where Agamemnon ruled; he will strike down
A king descended from Achilles; Pydna
Shall be revenge for Pallas' ruined temple,
For Trojan ancestors. Who would pass over,
Without a word, Cossus, or noble Cato,
The Gracchi, or those thunderbolts of warfare,
The Scipios, Libya's ruin, or Fabricius
Mighty with little, or Serranus, ploughing
The humble furrow; My tale must hurry on:
I see the Fabii next, and their great Quintus
Who brought us back an empire by delaying.
Others, no doubt, will better mould the bronze[43]
To the semblance of soft breathing, draw, from marble,
The living countenance; and others plead
With greater eloquence, or learn to measure,
Better than we, the pathways of the heaven,
The risings of the stars: remember, Roman,
To rule the people under law, to establish
The way of peace, to battle down the haughty,
To spare the meek. Our fine arts, these, forever."

Anchises paused a moment, and they marvelled,
And he went on:—"See, how Marcellus triumphs,
Glorious over all, with the great trophies
Won when he slew the captain of the Gauls,
Leader victorious over leading foeman.
When Rome is in great trouble and confusion
He will establish order, Gaul and Carthage
Go down before his sword, and triple trophies
Be given Romulus in dedication."

There was a young man going with Marcellus,
Brilliant in shining armor, bright in beauty,
But sorrowful, with downcast eyes. Aeneas
Broke in, to ask his father: "Who is this youth
Attendant on the hero? A son of his?
One of his children's children? How the crowd
Murmurs and hums around him! what distinction,
What presence, in his person! But dark night
Hovers around his head with mournful shadow.
Who is he, father?" And Anchises answered:—
"Great sorrow for our people! O my son,
Ask not to know it. This one fate will only

---

40. One of the earliest of the Italian cities, near Rome.
Supposedly founded by Askanius.

41. These names merely signify that the empire will extend from
one end to the other of the known world.

42. These are the names of families who produced famous men
in Rome's history.

43. Probably these nine lines are a better expression of the best
of the Roman spirit than can be found in any other place.

Show to the world; he will not be permitted
Any long sojourn. Rome would be too mighty,
Too great in the gods' sight, were this gift hers.
What lamentation will the field of Mars
Raise to the city! Tiber, gliding by
The new-built tomb, the funeral state, bear witness!
No youth from Trojan stock will ever raise
His ancestors so high in hope, no Roman
Be such a cause for pride. Alas for goodness,
Alas for old-time honor, and the arm
Invincible in war! Against him no one,
Whether on foot or foaming horse, would come
In battle and depart unscathed. Poor boy,
If you should break the cruel fates; if only—
You are to be Marcellus. Let me scatter
Lilies, or dark-red flowers, bringing honor
To my descendant's shade; let the gift be offered,
However vain the tribute."

     So through the whole wide realm they went together,
Anchises and his son; from the fields of air
Learning and teaching of the fame and glory,
The wars to come, the toils to face, or flee from,
Latinus' city and the Latin peoples,
The love of what would be.

          There are two portals,
Twin gates of Sleep, one made of horn, where easy
Release is given true shades, the other gleaming
White ivory, whereby the false dreams issue
To the upper air. Aeneas and the Sibyl
Part from Anchises at the second portal.
He goes to the ships, again, rejoins his comrades,
Sails to Caieta's harbor, and the vessels
Rest on their mooring-lines.

ECLOGUE IV
Virgil (Pubilius Virgilius Maro)

Virgil's *Fourth Eclogue* (EK–log, a pastoral or idyllic poem), known as the "Pollio" from the name of the friend to whom it was addressed and known also as "The Messianic Eclogue," was written in 40 B.C. to commemorate the birth of a child; but the identity of the child has eluded the scholars—there is no agreement among them. However, the high praise and the mystical allusions of the poet, strongly reminiscent of the very phrases of Isaiah in his prophecies of the Messiah, have connected the poem in the minds of many with the coming of the Christ. Early Christians found in the Eclogue corroboration of the biblical prophecies, and consequently thought of Virgil as a "virtuous Pagan," one to whom had been vouchsafed some gleams of the advent of Christ. Virgil's reputation as a good, even holy, man, grew as the Middle Ages remembered his poem; his reputation increased, in folklore, as a magician and seer—possibly because of his birthplace, where witchcraft, necromancy, and magic were always a matter of popular concern. So strong was his reputation as a foreteller of Christ's birth that Dante saw fit to make him his "guide, philosopher, and friend" in the *Divine Comedy;* he was led by Virgil as far as the pagan could take him, to the very entrance of the earthly Paradise.

The student would do well to refresh the memory with the verses of Isaiah, especially in Chapters vii, ix, and xi, that have to do with vines and briers, "unto us a child is born," the concord among living things, and the like. There is no evidence that Virgil was acquainted with the writings of the Hebrew prophet.

Pastoral[44] Muses of Sicily,
    now let us sing a loftier song;
    not all are pleased with country themes
        of orchard trees and lowly shrubs:
    if we sing in pastoral style,
        let it be a style still worthy of a consul's ear!
Now, even now, the last great age is coming in,
    foretold in the Cumaean Sybil's book;
The great cycle of the ages[45] starts anew,
    as from the beginning;
Astraea returns, the maiden Justice;
    the Golden Age of Saturn comes again;
    a new generation is sent us from high heaven.
Diana,—Lucina, Light-Bringer—chaste goddess,
    look favorably upon the coming birth,
    the child for whom the old bad Iron Race yields
        to a new Golden one, rising over all the world:
    your brother Apollo begins his reign.
Pollio,[46] in your term of office, even while you are consul,
    this Wonder of Time will begin his being;
    the majestic months commence their progress;
    under your leadership, Pollio.
    even if traces remain of our human guilt,
    new times will free earth from its abiding terror.
This child will live like a god;
    he will see gods and heroes mingling together,
    and himself will be seen of them a god and a hero;
    he will rule over a world made peaceful,
        with ancestral virtues.

---

44. "Pastoral"—it is interesting to note that the more sophisticated the civilization, the more urban and artificial the life of time, the greater the appeal of pastoral poetry, "the simple life," "back to nature." Virgil's age is a case in point; torn with the dissensions of civil strife and the growing importance of metropolitan Rome, the Italy of his day found satisfaction in "getting away from it all" thru the medium of the pastoral.

45. "the cycle of the ages"—it is unnecessary to go into the ancient (Etruscan?) notion that the world-cycle moved thru successive stages back to a point identical with the beginning; the "Platonic Year," when even the stars and planets would return to their position as at Creation. Suffice it to say, Virgil does have some sort of cycle of world history in mind; the Ages of Gold, Silver, Brass, and Iron, returning eventually to a new Golden Age.

46. "Pollio"—C. Asinus Pollio, Virgil's friend to whom the Eclogue is addressed, was a well-known public figure of the times; a general and adherent of Julius Caesar, he became consul in 40 B.C., and concluded the peace treaty between Octavian and Antony, known as the Treaty of Brundisium. It has been suggested (but not proved) that the child of the Eclogue may have been one of Pollio's sons.

For you, little child, the earth untilled
    will pour forth, as your first birthday-gifts,
    her plants and herbs; twining ivy,
    and valerian, and the arum lily,
        intermingling with the gay acanthus.
Of themselves the goats, untended, will return home,
    their udders swollen with milk;
    the herds will have no fear of mighty lions;
    your very cradle will run over with lovely flowers.
        The serpent will die, poison's treacherous plant
            will die;
        Oriental spice will spring up everywhere.
When you are old enough to read of great men,
    and the deeds of your fathers before you,
    when you understand the meaning of manliness,
    then will the harvest field turn yellow with volunteer
        grain,
    the reddening grape-cluster hang in the place of the
        profitless bramble,
    and tough old oaks will drip with honey-dew.
(Even then will linger some last vestiges
    of the wickedness of man;
    the lusting passion that delights
    to dare the sea with ships,
    to ring towns about with high walls,
    to scar the earth with furrows:
there will still be another Tiphys,[47]
    piloting a new Argo that carries its chosen heroes;
there will still be wars; once again
    some great Achilles will be sent against another
        Troy . . .)
But when the maturing years find you fully grown,
    then even the trader will abandon the sea;
    no pine-masted vessels will barter wares,
    instead, everywhere the whole earth
        will of itself yield all things needful.
    No more will the ground suffer the harrow,
        nor the vine the pruning-hook;
    the stalwart plowman will remove the yoke from his
        oxen.
Wool will not have to learn the deception of lying dyes,
    for the ram in the meadows will himself
    change the color of his fleece,
    sometimes to soft purple, like the murex,
    sometimes to saffron yellow;
    of its own volition
        crimson will clothe the grazing lamb.
"Run on, such times as these!"
    —thus say the Gray Sisters over their spindles,
    agreeing in the fixed decree of destiny.
Go on, little child, to great honors;
    your hour is at hand, dear offspring of divinity,
    great fulfillment of Jove.
    See, earth bows its vaulted weight,
        the lands, the expanse of the sea, even the deep
            heavens;
    see how everything rejoices in the time that is to be!
With you for my theme, Orpheus, singer of Thrace, could
        not overcome me,
    though he were helped by his mother Calliope;
    nor Linus,[48] howevermuch comely Apollo, his father,
        assisted him;
    even Pan, if Arcadia his homeland judged him with
        me,

even Pan, with Arcadia judging, would admit him-
    self beaten!
Begin, then, little boy, by greeting your mother with a
        smile;
    she has waited thru the long weariness of many
        months.
    Learn to smile, little child—[49]
    for one whom his parents have not smiled upon
    no god deems worthy of his table, nor goddess of
        her couch.

ON THE NATURE OF THINGS
Titus Lucretius Carus (ca. 96–55 B.C.*)*

Nothing at all is known of Lucretius (Titus Lucretius
Carus) beyond the fact that he is credited with a poem
(excerpted below) extolling materialism and the philosophy of Epicurus, under whose disciples he probably studied. This is the most complete exposition of
the materialistic basis of Epicureanism as well as being
one of the world's outstanding poems.

In the following passage, Lucretius discusses the
rise of ambition, of republican forms of government,
of religions, the discovery of metals, of garments, of
agriculture, of singing and dancing, and finally of the
total development of luxurious civilization. Notice
how carefully he suggests a materialistic origin for all
of these things.

At several points during the selection he makes
general statements about the nature of men and of
human motives. Can you piece these together to discover Lucretius's basic thoughts about human nature
and human motives, and about the nature of the best
life? From these would you say that the author was
essentially an optimist, a pessimist, or something in
between? Compare the ideas with some of those expressed by Marcus Aurelius.

More and more every day men who excelled in intellect
and were of vigorous understanding, would kindly show
others how to exchange their former way of living for new
methods. Kings began to build towns and lay out a citadel
as a place of strength and of refuge for themselves, and
divided cattle and lands and gave to each man in
proportion to his personal beauty and strength and
intellect; for beauty and vigorous strength were much
esteemed. Afterwards wealth was discovered and gold
found out, which soon robbed of their honors strong and
beautiful alike, for men however valiant and beautiful of
person generally follow in the train of the richer man. But
were a man to order his life by the rules of true reason, a
frugal subsistence joined to a contented mind is for him

---

47. "Tiphys"—the pilot of the Argo: Jason and the Argonauts,
sailing after the Golden Fleece, suggest to the reader at once
adventurousness and cupidity, bravery and selfishness.

48. Orpheus, Linus, and Pan; the greatest singers of classical
antiquity.

49. The ending is apparently a mildly humorous good luck
charm: "Smile, baby, so that your parents will smile at you;
unwanted, unwelcome children are Bad Luck, but smiling,
happy, wanted ones are blessed."

great riches; for never is there any lack of a little. But men desired to be famous and powerful, in order that their fortunes might rest on a firm foundation and they might be able by their wealth to lead a tranquil life; but in vain, since in their struggle to mount up to the highest dignities they rendered their path one full of danger; and even if they reach it, yet envy like a thunderbolt sometimes strikes and dashes men down from the highest point with ignominy into noisome Tartarus; since the highest summits and those elevated above the level of other things are mostly blasted by envy as by a thunderbolt, so that far better it is to obey in peace and quiet than to wish to rule with power supreme and be the master of kingdoms. Therefore let men wear themselves out to no purpose and sweat drops of blood, as they struggle on along the straight road of ambition, since they gather their knowledge from the mouths of others and follow after things from hearsay rather than the dictates of their own feelings; and this prevails not now nor will prevail by and by any more than it has prevailed before.

Kings therefore being slain, the old majesty of thrones and proud sceptres were overthrown and laid in the dust, and the glorious badge of the sovereign head bloodstained beneath the feet of the rabble mourned for its high prerogative; for that is greedily trampled on which before was too much dreaded. It would come then in the end to the lees of uttermost disorder, each man seeking for himself empire and sovereignty. Next a portion of them taught men to elect legal officers, and drew up codes, to induce men to obey the laws. For mankind, tired out with a life of brute force, lay exhausted from its feuds; and therefore the more readily it submitted of its own free will to laws and stringent codes. For as each one moved by anger took measures to avenge himself with more severity than is now permitted by equitable laws, for this reason men grew sick of a life of brute force. Thence fear of punishment mars the prizes of life; for violence and wrong enclose all who commit them in their meshes and do mostly recoil on him whom they began; and it is not easy for him who by his deeds transgresses the terms of the public peace to pass a tranquil and a peaceful existence. For though he eludes God and man, yet he cannot but feel a misgiving that his secret can be kept forever; seeing that many by speaking in their dreams or in the wanderings of disease have often we are told betrayed themselves and have disclosed their hidden deeds of evil and their sins.

And now what cause has spread over great nations the worship of the divinities of the gods and filled towns with altars and led to the performance of stated sacred rites, rites not in fashion on solemn occasions and in solemn places, from which even now is implanted in mortals a shuddering awe which raises new temples of the gods over the whole earth and prompts men to crowd them on festive days, all this is not so difficult to explain in words. Even then in sooth the races of mortal men would see in waking mind glorious forms, would see them in sleep of yet more marvellous size of body. To these then they would attribute sense, because they seemed to move their limbs and to utter lofty words suitable to their glorious aspects and surpassing powers. And they would give them life everlasting, because their face would appear before them and their form abide; yes, and yet without all this because they would not believe that beings possessed of such powers could lightly be overcome by any force. And they would believe them to be pre-eminent in bliss, because none of them was ever

troubled with the fear of death, and because at the same time in sleep they would see them perform many miracles, yet feel on their part no fatigue from the effort. Again they would see the system of heaven and the different seasons of the years come round in regular succession, and could not find out by what cause this was done; therefore they would seek a refuge in handing over all things to the gods and supposing all things to be guided by their nod. And they placed in heaven the abodes and realms of the gods, because night and moon are seen to roll through heaven; moon, day and night, and night's austere constellations and night-wandering of the sky and flying bodies of flame, clouds, sun, rains, snow, winds, lightnings, hail, and rapid rumblings and loud threatful thunderclaps.

O hapless race of men, when that they charged the gods with such acts and coupled with them bitter wrath! What groanings did they then beget for themselves, what wounds for us, what tears for our children's children! No act is it of piety to be often seen with veiled head to turn to a stone and approach every altar and fall prostrate on the ground and spread out the palms before the statues of the gods and sprinkle the altars with much blood of beasts and link vow on vow, but rather to be able to look on all things with a mind at peace. For when we turn our gaze on the heavenly quarters of the great upper world and ether fast above the glittering stars, and direct our thoughts to the courses of the sun and moon, then into our breasts burdened with other ills that fear as well begins to exalt its reawakened head, the fear that we may haply find the power of the gods to be unlimited, able to wheel the bright stars in their varied motion; for lack of power to solve the question troubles the mind with doubts, whether there was ever a birth-time of the world, and whether likewise there is to be any end; how far the walls of the world can endure this strain of restless motion; or whether gifted by the grace of gods with an everlasting existence they may glide on through a never-ending tract of time and defy the strong powers of immeasurable ages. Again who is there whose mind does not shrink into itself with fear of the gods, whose limbs do not cower in terror, when the parched earth rocks with the appalling thunder-stroke and rattling runs through the great heaven? Do not people and nations quake, and proud monarchs shrink into themselves smitten with fear of the gods, lest for any foul transgression or overweening work the heavy time of reckoning has arrived at its fullness? When, too, the utmost fury of the headstrong wind passes over the sea and sweeps over its waters the commander of a fleet together with his mighty legions and elephants, does he not draw near with vows to seek the mercy of the gods and ask in prayer with fear and trembling a lull in the winds and propitious gales; but all in vain, since often caught up in the furious hurricane he is borne none the less to the shoals of death? So constantly does some hidden power trample on human grandeur and is seen to tread under its heel and make sport for itself of the renowned rods and cruel axes.[50] Again when the whole earth rocks under their feet and towns tumble with the shock or doubtfully threaten to

---

50. A bundle of rods enclosing an axe was the emblem of magisterial authority at Rome.

fall, what wonder that mortal men abase themselves and make over to the gods in things here on earth high prerogatives and marvelous powers, sufficient to govern all things?

To proceed, copper and gold and iron were discovered and at the same time weighty silver and the substance of lead, when fire with its heat had burnt up vast forests on the great hills, either by a discharge of heaven's lightning, or else because men waging with one another a forest-war had carried fire among the enemy in order to strike terror, or because drawn on by the goodness of the soil they would wish to clear rich fields, and bring the country into pasture, or else to destroy wild beasts and enrich themselves with the booty; for hunting with pitfall and with fire came into use before the practice of enclosing the lawn with nets and stirring it with dogs. Whatever the fact is, from whatever cause the heat of flame had swallowed up the forests with a frightful crackling from their very roots and had thoroughly baked the earth with fire, there would run from the boiling veins and collect into the hollows of the ground a stream of silver and gold, as well as of copper and lead. And when they saw these afterwards cool into lumps and glitter on the earth with a brilliant gleam, they would lift them up attracted by the bright and polished lustre, and they would see them to be moulded in a shape the same as the outline of the cavities in which each lay. Then it would strike them that these might be melted by heat and cast in any form or shape soever, and might by hammering out be brought to tapering points of any degree of sharpness and fineness, so as to furnish them with tools and enable them to cut the forests and hew timber and plane smooth the planks, and also to drill and pierce and bore, and they would set about these works just as much with silver and gold at first as with the overpowering strength of stout copper, but in vain, since their force would fail and give way and not be able like copper to stand the severe strain. At that time copper was in higher esteem and gold would be neglected on account of its uselessness, with its dull blunted edge; now copper lies neglected, gold has mounted up to the highest place of honor. Thus time as it goes round changes the seasons of things. That which was in esteem, falls at length into utter disrepute; and then another thing mounts up and issues out of its degraded state and every day is more and more coveted and blossoms forth high in honor when discovered and is in marvelous repute with men.

And now to find out by yourself in what way the nature of iron was discovered. Arms of old were hands, nails, and teeth, and stones and boughs broken off from the forest, and flame and fire, as soon as they had become known. Afterwards the force of iron and copper was discovered, and the use of copper was known before that of iron, as its nature is easier to work and it is found in greater quantity. With copper they would labor the soil of the earth, with copper stir up the billows of war and deal about the wide gaping wounds and seize cattle and lands; for everything defenseless and unarmed would readily yield to them with arms in hand. Then by slow steps the sword of iron gained ground and the make of the copper sickle became a by-word; and with iron they began to plough through the earth's soil, and the struggles of wavering war were rendered equal. . . .

A garment tied on the body was in use before a dress of woven stuff. Woven stuff comes after iron, because iron is needed for weaving a web; and in no other way can such finely polished things be made, as heddles and spindles, shuttles and ringing yarnbeams. And nature impelled men to work up the wool before womankind; for the male sex in general far excels the other in skill and is much more ingenious; until the rugged countrymen so upbraided them with it, that they were glad to give it over into the hands of the women and take their share in supporting hard toil, and in such hard work hardened body and hands.

But nature parent of things was herself the first model of sowing and first gave rise to grafting, since berries and acorns dripping from the trees would put forth in due season swarms of young shoots underneath; and hence also came the fashion of inserting grafts in their stocks and planting in the ground young saplings over the fields. Next they would try another and yet another kind of tillage for their loved piece of land and would see the earth better the wild fruits through genial fostering and kindly cultivation, and they would force the forests to recede every day higher and higher up the hillside and yield the ground below to tilth, in order to have on the uplands and plains, meadows, tanks, runnels, cornfields, and glad vineyards, and allow a gray-green strip of olives to run between and mark divisions, spreading itself over hillocks and valleys and plains; just as you now see richly dight with varied beauty all the ground which they lay out and plant with rows of sweet fruit-trees, and enclose all round with plantations of other goodly trees.

But imitating with the mouth the clear notes of birds was in use long before men were able to sing in tune smooth-running verses and give pleasure to the ear. And the whistlings of the zephyr through the hollows of reeds first taught peasants to blow into hollow stalks. Then step by step they learned sweet plaintive ditties, which the pipe pours forth pressed by the fingers of the players, heard through pathless woods and forests and lawns, through the unfrequented haunts of shepherds and abodes of unearthly calm. These things would soothe and gratify their minds when sated with food; for then all things of this kind are welcome. Often therefore stretched in groups on the soft grass beside a stream of water under the boughs of a high tree at no great cost they would pleasantly refresh their bodies, above all when the weather smiled and the seasons of the year painted the green grass with flowers. Then went round the jest, the tale, the peals of merry laughter; for the peasant muse was then in its glory; then frolick mirth would prompt to entwine head and shoulders with garlands plaited with flowers and leaves, and to advance in the dance out of step and move the limbs clumsily and with clumsy feet beat mother earth; which would occasion smiles and peals of merry laughter, because all these things then from their greater novelty and strangeness were in high repute, and the wakeful found a solace for want of sleep in this, in drawing out a variety of notes and going through tunes and running over the reeds with curving lip; whence even at the present day watchmen observe these traditions and have lately learned to keep the proper tune; and yet for all this receive not a jot more of enjoyment than erst the rugged race of sons of earth received. For that which we have in our hands, if we have known before nothing pleasanter, pleases above all and is thought to be the best;[51] and as a rule the later discovery

---

51. Notice throughout this piece the philosophic generalization which Lucretius makes. Try reading them together without the intervening descriptions and see if you can get a fairly complete picture of his philosophy.

of something better spoils the taste for the former things and changes the feelings in regard to all that has gone before. Thus began distaste for the acorn, thus were abandoned those sleeping places strawn with grass and enriched with leaves. The dress too of wild beasts' skin fell into neglect; though I can fancy that in those days it was found to arouse such jealousy that he who first wore it met his death by an ambuscado, and after all it was torn in pieces among them and drenched in blood, was utterly destroyed and could not be turned to any use. In those times therefore skins, now gold and purple plague men's lives with cares and wear them out with war. And in this methinks the greater blame rests with us; but us it harms not in the least to do without a robe of purple, spangled with gold and large figures, if only we have a dress of the people to protect us. Mankind therefore ever toils vainly and to no purpose wastes life in groundless cares, because sure enough they have not learnt what is the true end of getting and up to what point genuine pleasure goes on increasing: this by slow degrees has carried life out into the deep sea and stirred up from their lowest depths the mighty billows of war.

But those watchful guardians sun and moon traversing with their light all around the great revolving sphere of heaven taught men that the seasons of the year came round and that the system was carried on after a fixed plan and fixed order.

Already they would pass their life fenced about with strong towers, and the land, portioned out and marked off by boundaries, be tilled; the sea would be filled with ships scudding under sail; towns have auxiliaries and allies as stipulated by treaty, when poets began to consign the deeds of men to verse; and letters had not been invented long before. For this reason our age cannot look back to what has gone before, save where reason points out any traces.

Ships and tillage, walls, laws, roads, dress, and all such like things, all the prizes, all the elegancies too of life without exception, poems, pictures, and chiselling of fine-wrought statues, all these things practiced together with the acquired knowledge of the untiring mind taught men by slow degrees as they advanced on the way step by step. Thus time by degrees brings each several thing forth before men's eyes and reason raises it up into the borders of light; for things must be brought to light one after the other and in due order in the different arts, until these have reached their highest point of development.

Gaius Valerius Catullus (ca. 84–54 B.C.), the leading Latin lyric poet, composed his love poetry for the enchanting Clodia (Lesbia in the poems), wife of Quintus Metellus. She became the most notoriously faithless beauty in Rome, while Catullus struggled with a virulent passion for her that slowly shriveled to despair before subsiding into bitter maledictions. Poems 5, 51, 58, 72, and 75 testify to the stages of his infatuation. The first three stanzas of poem 51 are a partial translation by Catullus of a poem by Sappho, the seventh-century Greek poet from the island of Lesbos. Poems 1, 22, 40, and 42 are concerned with poets and poetry; poem 42 refers to the stubborn muse of poetry who frustrates the best of poets by failing to provide the requisite inspiration.

1

Who do I give this neat little book to
all new and polished up and ready to go?
You, Cornelius, because you always thought
there was something to this stuff of mine,
and were the one man in Italy with guts enough
to lay out all history in a couple of pages,
a learned job, by god, and it took work.
So here's the book, for whatever it's worth
I want you to have it. And please, goddess,
see that it lasts for more than a lifetime.

5

Let's you and me live it up, my Lesbia,
and make some love, and let old cranks
go cheap talk their damn fool heads off.
Maybe suns can set and come back up again,
but once the brief light goes out on us
the night's one long sleep forever.
First give me a kiss, a thousand kisses,
then a hundred, and then a thousand more,
then another hundred, and another thousand,
and keep kissing and kissing me so many times
we get all mixed up and can't count anymore,
that way nobody can give us the evil eye
trying to figure how many kisses we've got.

22

Take Suffenus, now you know the guy, Varus,
handsome, good talker, knows his way around,
well he writes poetry also, in big shipments.
I think he's got thousands, maybe millions
copied out, I don't mean in rough draft either:
fancy imperial stock, new rolls, new pegs,
thongs of red leather, sheepskin slip covers,
lines ruled, edges trimmed, the whole works.
Then you read them. Suddenly your suave and
sophisticated Suffenus turns into a goat milker,
a shit shoveler from the mountains. It's grim!
What's going on anyway? Here he is, sharp,
looks like he could slice you down in a word,
but the minute he starts fooling with poetry,
watch out, he's clumsier than a hick is clumsy.
And he's never happier than when writing a poem,
or more pleased, he thinks he's just wonderful!
Okay, it's true, we all do it, there's nobody
who isn't a Suffenus in one thing or another.
Everybody has a pack of faults on his shoulders,
if heads were on backwards we'd all see our own.

40

Lost your mind Ravidus, you poor ass,
landing smack into one of my poems like this?
Is some god getting you into trouble
because you didn't say your prayers right?
Or are you just out to get talked about?
What do you want? To be famous, never mind how?
Okay you will, and being that it's my girl you're after,
you're going to suffer for a long, long time.

42

Calling all syllables! Calling all syllables!
Let's go! I need all the help I can get!
Some filthy whore's playing games with me
and won't give me back my manuscripts with

your pals inside! Are you going to let her?
Who is she, you ask? Well go take a look,
she's over there shaking her ass all around
and flashing smiles like a Pomeranian bitch.
Ready? Okay, line up and let her have it!
'O foul adulteress, O lascivious witch,
give me back my notebooks, you dirty bitch!'
What? Up yours, you say? You slut, tramp,
you've sunk so low you look up to see down!
Still, we can't let her get away like this,
if all else fails, at least let's see whether
we can force a blush from the hard-faced beast.
Try again, fellas, good and loud this time!
'O FOUL ADULTERESS, O LASCIVIOUS WITCH,
GIVE ME BACK MY NOTEBOOKS, YOU DIRTY BITCH!'
No use. It won't work. Nothing moves her.
We've got to switch to different tactics,
almost anything will work better than this.
'O maiden so modest, O virgin so pure . . .'

51

To me, that man seems to be one of the gods,
or to tell the truth, even more than a god,
sitting there face to face with you, forever
looking, listening

to you laughing sweetly, while poor me, I take
one look at you and I'm all torn up inside,
Lesbia, there's nothing left of me. I can't
make a sound, my tongue's

stuck solid, hot little fire flashes go
flickering through my body, my ears begin
ringing around in my head, my eyes black out,
shrouded in darkness . . .

This soft life is no good for you. Catullus,
you wallow in it, you don't know when to stop.
A soft life's already been the ruin of both
great kings and cities.

58

Caelius, our Lesbia, that Lesbia,
the Lesbia Catullus once loved
more than himself and all he owns,
now works streets and back alleys
groping big-hearted sons of Remus.

72

Time was you said only Catullus could touch you,
that God in heaven couldn't have you before me.
I loved you then, not just as a guy does a girl,
but the way a father loves his sons and grandsons.
Now I know you, Lesbia, and if my passion grows,
you're also much cheaper to me and insignificant.
How's that? Because, hurt a man in love and he
lusts for you more, but the less he really cares.

75

My mind's sunk so low, Lesbia, because of you,
wrecked itself on your account so bad already,
I couldn't like you if you were the best of women,
or stop loving you, no matter what you do.

Horace (Quintus Horatius Flaccus; 65–8 B.C.) specialized in writing odes. Given below are two odes in contemporary translations by M. A. Crane. The first is a wry commentary about Pyrrha, his former mistress, while the second ode is an expression of Horace's Epicurean philosophy.

1

On the bulletin board there's a picture of me
Luckily saved from disaster at sea
Donating my gear to the God of the Ocean.

Tonight, some boy smelling of after-shave lotion
Is making a play for you, Pyrrha, my fair,
Trying that innocent look with your hair.

His turn will come soon to complain of foul weather
If he thinks that after you're going together
You'll stay bland and easy as on this first date.

Until you up anchor, all dinghys look great!

2

The peace that the sailor seeks in the storm
And the rest that's the warrior's aim
Can't be purchased with wealth in any form
Nor, Grosphus, with power or fame.
The pauper who wants only what he can afford
Sleeps soundly. But he who would fly
To new fortunes, although he hastens aboard
Speedy vessels, sees his troubles stand by.

Fools nourish dreams of perfect joy;
I'll take less, having witnessed a hero
Die young and watched rotting old age destroy
Tithonus, reduced to a jibbering zero.
It may be *I* have just those things that *you* need
Amidst your horses, fine clothing, and cattle-
Subsidence, and joy from the poems I read,
And no jealous mob doing me battle.

THE ART OF LOVE
Publius Ovidius Naso (43 B.C.–A.D. 17)

Ovid was the most popular poet of antiquity. His engaging versions of Greek and Roman myths, the *Metamorphoses,* is unique; no classic is easier or more pleasant to read. Included here is an excerpt from the *Art of Love,* a sophisticated guide to seduction, which also includes deft descriptions of everyday life in Rome. As you read Ovid's "manual" you might ask yourself if times or techniques have really changed.

This is a book for the man who needs instruction in
    loving.
        Let him read it and love, taught by the lines he has
        read.
Art is a thing one must learn, for the sailing, or rowing, of
    vessels,
        Also for driving a car: love must be guided by art.
Automedon excelled with the reins in the car of Achilles,
        Tiphys in Jason's craft, crafty with rudder and sail;

Thanks be to Venus, I too deserve the title of master,
    Master of Arts, I might say, versed in the precepts of
    love.
Love, to be sure, is wild and often inclined to resent me;
    Still, he is only a boy, tender and easily swayed.
When Achilles was young, Chiron could tame his wild
    spirit,
    Even could teach his hands how to move over a lyre.
He, who frightened his foes, and frightened his friends
    just as often,
    Dreaded one aged man, so all the ages believe.
He would reach out his hands, submissive and meek, for
    a lashing:
    Those were the violent hands Hector was later to
    know.
Chiron instructed Achilles, and I am Cupid's preceptor,
    Each of them savage and rough, each one a
    goddess's son.
Yet, in good time, as bulls accept the yoke and the
    ploughshare,
    As the wild horses submit, taking the bridle and bit,
So will Love yield to me, though he wounds my heart
    with his arrows,
    Whirls his torch in the air, showering sparks from the
    brand.
So much the worse for him: the more he pierces and
    burns me,
    I shall avenge all the more all of the wounds he has
    made.
I am no liar to claim that my art has come from Apollo,
    Nor am I taught my song by the voices of birds in the
    air,
Neither has Clio appeared at my side, with all of her
    sisters,
    While I was tending my flocks out in some
    countryside vale.
No: I have learned what I know from experience, take my
    word for it.
    It is the truth you will hear. Venus, give aid to my
    song!
Keep far away, stern looks and all of modesty's emblems,
    Headdresses worn by the pure, skirts hiding feet in
    their folds.
What is the theme of my song? A little pleasant
    indulgence.
    What is the theme of my song? Nothing that's very far
    wrong.
First, my raw recruit, my inexperienced soldier,
    Take some trouble to find the girl whom you really
    can love.
Next, when you see what you like your problem will be
    how to win her.
    Finally, strive to make sure mutual love will endure.
That's as far as I go, the territory I cover,
    Those are the limits I set: take them or leave them
    alone.
While you are footloose and free to play the field at your
    pleasure,
    Watch for the one you can tell, "I want no other but
    you!"
She is not going to come to you floating down from the
    heavens:
    For the right kind of a girl you must keep using your
    eyes.

Hunters know where to spread their nets for the stag in
    his covert,
    Hunters know where the boar gnashes his teeth in
    the glade.
Fowlers know brier and bush, and fishermen study the
    waters
    Baiting the hook for the cast just where the fish may
    be found.
So you too, in your hunt for material worthy of loving.
    First will have to find out where the game usually
    goes.
I will not tell you to sail searching far over the oceans,
    I will not tell you to plod any long wearisome road.
Perseus went far to find his dusky Indian maiden:
    That was a Grecian girl Paris took over the sea.
Rome has all you will need, so many beautiful lovelies
    You will be bound to say, "Here is the grace of the
    world!"
Gargara's richness of field. Methymna's abundance of
    vineyard.
    All the fish of the sea, all the birds in the leaves.
All the stars in the sky, are less than the girls Rome can
    offer;
    Venus is mother and queen here in the town of her
    son.
If you are fond of them young, you will find them here by
    the thousands,
    Maids in their teens, from whom you will have
    trouble to choose.
Maybe a bit more mature, a little bit wiser? Believe me.
    These will outnumber the first as they come trooping
    along.
Take your time, walk slow, when the sun approaches the
    lion.
    There are porticoes, marbled under the shade,
Pompey's Octavia's, or the one in Livia's honor.
    Or the Danaids' own, tall on the Palatine hill.
Don't pass by the shrine of Adonis, sorrow to Venus,
    Where, on the Sabbath day, Syrians worship, and
    Jews.
Try the Memphian fane of the Heifer, shrouded in linen;
    Isis makes many a girl willing as Io for Jove.
Even the courts of the law, the bustle and noise of the
    forum.
    (This may be hard to believe) listen to whispers of
    love.
Hard by the marble shrine of Venus, the Appian fountain,
    Where the water springs high in its rush to the air.
There, and more than once, your counsellor meets with
    his betters,
    All his forensic arts proving of little avail:
Others he might defend; himself he cannot; words fail
    him,
    Making objections in vain; Cupid says, *Overruled!*
Venus, whose temple is near, laughs at the mortified
    creature,
    Lawyer a moment ago, in need of a counsellor now.
Also, the theater's curve is a very good place for your
    hunting,
    More opportunity here, maybe, than anywhere else.
Here you may find one to love, or possibly only have fun
    with,
    Someone to take for a night, someone to have and to
    hold.

Just as a column of ants keeps going and coming forever,
  Bearing their burdens of grain, just as the flight of
  the bees
Over the meadows and over the fields of the thyme and
  the clover,
  So do the women come, thronging the festival
  games.
Elegant, smart, and so many my sense of judgment is
  troubled.
  Hither they come, to see; hither they come, to be
  seen.
This is a place for the chase, not the chaste, and Romulus
  knew it,
  Started it all, in fact; think of the Sabine girls.
There were no awnings, then, over the benches of
  marble,
  There were no crimson flowers staining the
  platform's floor,
Only the natural shade from the Palatine trees, and the
  stage-set
  Quite unadorned, and the folk sitting on steps of
  sod,
Shading their foreheads with leaves, studying, watching
  intently,
  Each for the girl he would have, none of them saying
  a word.
Then, while the Tuscan flute was sounding its primitive
  measure,
  While the dancer's foot thrice beat the primitive
  ground,
While the people roared in uninhibited cheering,
  Romulus gave the sign. They had been waiting. They
  knew.
Up they leaped, and their noise was proof of their
  vigorous spirit.
  Never a virgin there was free from the lust of a hand.
Just as the timid doves fly from the swooping of eagles,
  Just as the newest lamb tries to escape from the wolf,
So those girls, fearing men, went rushing in every
  direction;
  Every complexion, through fright, turning a different
  hue.
Though their fear was the same, it took on different
  guises;
  Some of them tore their hair; some of them sat
  stricken dumb.
One is silent in grief, another calls for her mother,
  One shrieks out, one is still; one runs away, and one
  stays.
So, they are all carried off, these girls, the booty of
  husbands,
  While, in many, their fear added endowments of
  charm.
If one struggled too much, or refused to go with her
  captor,
  He'd pick her up from the ground, lift her aloft in
  his arms,
Saying, "Why do you spoil your beautiful eyes with that
  crying?
  Wasn't your mother a wife? That's all I want you to
  be."
Romulus, you knew the way to give rewards to your
  soldiers!
  Give me rewards such as these, I would enlist for the
  wars.

So, to this very day, the theater keeps its tradition:
  Danger is lurking there still, waiting for beautiful
  girls.
Furthermore, don't overlook the meetings when horses
  are running;
  In the crowds at the track opportunity waits.
There is no need for a code of finger-signals or nodding.
  Sit as close as you like; no one will stop you at all.
In fact, you will have to sit close—that's one of the rules,
  at a race track.
  Whether she likes it or not, contact is part of the
  game.
Try to find something in common, to open the
  conversation;
  Don't care too much what you say, just so that every
  one hears.
Ask her, "Whose colors are those?"—that's good for an
  opening gambit.
  Put your own bet down, fast, on whatever she plays.
Then, when the gods come along in procession, ivory,
  golden,
  Outcheer every young man, shouting for Venus, the
  queen.
Often it happens that dust may fall on the blouse of the
  lady.
  If such dust should fall, carefully brush it away.
Even if there's no dust, brush off whatever there isn't.
  Any excuse will do: why do you think you have
  hands?
If her cloak hangs low, and the ground is getting it dirty,
  Gather it up with care, lift it a little, so!
Maybe, by way of reward, and not without her indulgence,
  You'll be able to see ankle or possibly knee.
Then look around and glare at the fellow who's sitting
  behind you,
  Don't let him crowd his knees into her delicate
  spine.
Girls, as everyone knows, adore these little attentions:
  Getting the cushion just right, that's in itself quite an
  art;
Yes, and it takes a technique in making a fan of your
  program
  Or in fixing a stool under the feet of a girl.
Such is the chance of approach the race track can offer a
  lover.
  There is another good ground, the gladiatorial
  shows.
On that sorrowful sand Cupid has often contested,
  And the watcher of wounds often has had it himself.
While he is talking, or touching a hand, or studying
  entries,
  Asking which one is ahead after his bet has been
  laid.
Wounded himself, he groans to feel the shaft of the arrow;
  He is a victim himself, no more spectator, but show.
Parties are also fine, not only for food on the tables.
  Something more than the wine you will find there if
  you look.
Often Bacchus lies there at his ease, and bright-colored
  Cupid,
  Soft-armed Cupid, near by, coaxes with wheedling
  charm,
Finds that his thirsty wings are suddenly sprinkled with
  wine-drops,
  Stands in his place, weighed down, almost unable to
  move,

Shakes out his dripping plumes, to be sure, in all kinds of
    a hurry—
    This may hurt more than you think, getting a
    dousing from love.
Wine sets the spirit afire, and wine brings passionate
    ardor;
    When there is plenty of wine, sorrow and worry take
    wing,
Then the laughter comes, and even the poor man has
    plenty,
    Wrinkles and frowns depart, grief is gone from the
    heart,
Then simplicity comes, and the inhibitions are banished,
    Slyness dispelled by a grace all too rare in our day.
That is the time when the girls can capture the hearts of
    their young men:
    When you have Venus in wine, then you have fire in
    fire.
Don't, at any such time, put too much faith in the
    lamplight.
    Judgment of beauty can err, what with the wine and
    the dark.
In the full light of the day the judgment of Paris was
    given:
    That was the time when he said, "Venus, no doubt
    that you win."
Flaws are hidden at night, and every flaw is forgiven;
    When the cats are all gray, then are the woman all
    fair.
Take the advice of the light when you're looking at linens
    or jewels;
    Looking at faces or forms, take the advice of the day.
Why should I mention them all, the gathering-places of
    women?
    They are as many—no, more than all the sands of the
    shore,
Baiae, for instance, or Bath (as the British barbarians call
    it),
    Where the waters steam sulphurous out of the
    ground.
    And the drops from the tree are called by her name,
    the myrrh.
Once in the shadowy vales, the wooded uplands of Ida,
    Roamed a snow-white bull, glory and pride of the
    herd.
There was one black spot between the horns of his
    forehead,
    That was his only mark, all of the rest white as milk.
All the heifers of Cnossus, and all the Cydonean heifers
    Wanted him riding their backs—that was their prayer
    and desire.
Pasiphae, the queen, desired this bull for her lover,
    Jealous, with hate in her heart for all the beautiful
    cows.
I sing of things well-known, and Crete can never deny
    them,
    Liar though Crete may be through all her hundreds
    of towns.
Pasiphae, I say, with hands not used to such labors,
    Gathered new leaves and young grass, holding them
    out to the beast,
Went where the heifers would go, and had no thought of
    her husband,
    Minos, the lord of Crete. (He, too, was horned, it
    appears.)

Ah, what good did it do to put on her costliest dresses?
    To such a lover as hers riches meant nothing at all.
Why take a mirror along, seeking the herds on the
    mountains?
    Why, in your foolishness, constantly tend to your
    hair?
Still, the mirror is right in telling you that you're no
    heifer,
    Not however you wish, can you grow horns on your
    brow.
Does not Minos suffice? Why seek an adulterous lover?
    If he must be deceived, then let it be with a man.
Leaving her bower, the queen goes to the glades and the
    woodlands,
    As the Bacchanals go when the Aonian calls.
Often she looked at a cow, and frowned with a jealous
    expression,
    "How in the world," she says, "can he find pleasure
    in her?
Look how she lumbers and leaps before him over the
    meadows,
    Nor do I doubt the damn fool thinks she's a beautiful
    sight."
Then she would order the beast, poor thing, to be led
    from the pasture,
    Put the yoke on her neck, set her to hauling the
    plough,
Or, on some pretense of sacrificial devotion,
    Have her struck down, and hold entrails in jubilant
    hands,
Pleasing the altars of gods with the slaughtered corpse of
    a rival,
    "Go now, and please our lord!" her benediction
    would be.
Sometimes she wished she had been Io, and sometimes
    Europa;
    One was a cow for a while, one carried off by a bull.
Finally had her way, devising a heifer of maple,
    So her Minotaur son proved the success of the sire.
Had Aerope abstained from her guilty love of Thyestes
    (Pleasing one man alone seems such a lesson to
    learn!)—
Never would Phoebus have turned his car from the town
    of Mycenae,
    Wheeling his steeds around, reining them back to
    the East.
Scylla, the daughter of Nisus, stole from the head of her
    father
    That one precious lock: now the hounds rage in her
    womb.
Agamemnon survived the wars and the violent oceans,
    Victim in his own halls, slain by a murderous wife.
Who has not mourned for the flames of Ephyrean Creusa
    Or the mother's hands, stained with the blood of her
    sons?
Phoenix, the son of Amyntor, weeping from eyes that
    were blinded,
    Theseus' dismembered son, torn by his horses in
    fright,
Phineus, blinding his sons, the victims of false accusation,
    Suffering in his turn torments of hunger and doom—
All of these crimes, every one, arose from the lust of a
    woman,
    Keener in their desire, fiercer, more wanton than
    ours.

So, you need have little doubt when it comes to winning
  them over;
    Out of the many there are, hardly a one will refuse.
If they say Yes, or say No, they're pleased with the
  invitation:
    Even suppose you guess wrong, it costs you nothing
    to try.
But why should you be wrong? Untried delights are a
  pleasure:
    Those which we do not own tempt with attraction
    and charm.
In the fields of our neighbor the grass forever is greener;
    Always the other man's herd offers the richer reward.
Take some trouble, at first, to make her handmaiden's
  acquaintance:
    She, more than any one else, really can lighten your
    way.
She must be one you can trust, if she knows of the tricks
  you are playing,
    Confidante. wise and discreet, high in her mistress'
    regard.
Spoil her by promising much, and spoil her by pleading a
  little,
    What you seek you will find, if she is willing you
    should.
She will choose the right time—a maid is as good as a
  doctor—
    When she is in the right mood, all the more ripe to
    be had.
When she is in the right mood, you will know it because
  she is happy,
    Like the flowers in the field, seeming to burst into
    bloom.
When the hearts are glad, and sorrow does not confine
  them,
    Then they are open wide, and Venus steals coaxingly
    in.
Troy, in her days of gloom, was well defended by armor;
    When she rejoiced, the horse entered with Greeks in
    its womb.
It is worth making a try when she's grieving because of a
  rival,
    Vengeance can quickly be hers if you're
    conveniently there.
While her maid is at work, combing her hair in the
  morning,
    Let her keep urging her on, let her add oars to the
    sail,
Let her say with a sigh, or the softest murmuring whisper,
    "I don't suppose, after all, there is a thing you can
    do,"
Then let her talk about you, and add some words of
  persuasion,
    Let her swear that she knows you must be dying of
    love.
Hurry! before the sails are furled and the breezes grown
  milder;
    Anger, like brittle ice, dies with a little delay.
"Do you think it would do any good to seduce the maid?"
  What a question!
    Any such notions involve, always, too much of a risk.
One gets up from the bed too anxious, another too lazy,
    One aids her mistress's cause, one wants you all for
    her own.
Maybe it works, maybe not: it might be amusing to try it,
    Still, my advice would be, let it completely alone.

I would not show you the way over steep and precipitous
  passes,
    No young man in my school ever will ride for a fall,
Yet, if she seems to please, while giving and taking your
  letters,
    By her figure and face, not by her service alone,
Go for the lady first, and let the servant come second;
    When you are making love, do not begin with the
    maid.
One final warning word: if you have any faith in my
  teaching,
    If my words are not swept over the sea by the gale,
Either succeed, or don't try—she never will be an
  informer,
    If she is guilty herself: how could she tattle on you?
Birds, with the lime on their wings, cannot take flight to
  the heavens,
    Boars cannot plunge to their dens, caught in the
    mesh of the net.
Don't let your fish get away after the bait has been taken:
    Press the attack, keep on; don't go away till you've
    won.
Then she can never betray you, because you were guilty
  together;
    All of her mistress's acts, all of her words you will
    know.
Do not give her away: if she knows you are keeping her
  secrets,
    She will be yours any time, knowing and willingly
    known.

Martial (Marcus Valerius Martialis; ca. A.D. 40 104)
wrote hundreds of epigrams, which are brief poems,
often satiric, ending in a surprise twist or climax. His
style can be described as terse, sardonic, sparse, as-
cerbic, sarcastic, witty, and, withal, strikingly and de-
lightfully modern.

I, i

Here he is—the one you read,
the one you ask for—Martial,
recognized the world over
for his witty books of epigrams.
Learned reader, you've given him
(while he's still alive to enjoy it)
the glory poets rarely get
after they've turned to ashes.

I, xxxv

You take me to task for writing
poems that aren't as prissy
and prim as they might be, Cornelius.
Not the kind a schoolmaster
would read aloud in the classroom.
But my little books wouldn't satisfy
(anymore than husbands can
their wives) without a little sex.
Would you want me to write a wedding-song
without using the words that wedding-songs
always use? Would you cover up
Flora's nymphs with a lot of clothing
or let prostitutes hide their shamefulness
under ladies' robes? There's a rule
that merry songs can't be merry
unless they're a bit indecent.

So forget your prudishness, please,
and spare my jokes and my naughtiness,
and don't try to castrate my poems.
Nothing's worse than Priapus posing
as a eunuch of Cybele.

II, xxxvi

I don't say you should curl your hair,
but you could comb it.
I don't say your body should be oiled,
but you could take a bath.
You needn't have a eunuch's beard
or a jailbird's. I don't insist
upon too much manliness,
Pannychus, or too little.
As it is, your legs are hairy
and your chest is shaggy with bristles,
but your mind, Pannychus, is bald.

II, lxviii

Don't think me insolent, Olus,
for calling you by your name
nowadays instead of "Patron"
or "Master" as I used to do.
I've bought my freedman's cap
with everything I possessed.

A man needs patrons and masters
if he isn't master of himself
and covets the same things patrons
and masters covet. But once
he can get along without a slave,
he can get along without a master.

III, xxxviii

Tell me, what brings you to Rome
so self-confidently, Sextus?
What are you after, and what
do you expect to find there?

"First of all, I'll plead cases
more eloquently than Cicero
himself. There won't be anyone
in the three forums to touch me."

Atestinus and Civis
(you know them both) pled cases,
but neither one of them took in
enough to pay the rent.

"Well, if nothing comes of that,
I'll write poems. When you hear them,
you'll say they're Vergil's work."

You're crazy. Wherever you look
you'll see Ovids and Vergils—all of them
shivering in their thin cloaks.

"Then I'll cultivate rich men."

That sort of thing has supported
maybe three or four. The rest
of the crowd are pale with hunger.

"What *will* I do? Advise me.
I'm determined to live in Rome."

Well, Sextus, if you're honest,
you'll be lucky to stay alive.

IV, xlix

Believe me, Flaccus—anyone
who calls epigrams mere trifles
and frivolities doesn't understand
what they are. It's more frivolous,
really, when somebody writes
about Tereus' revolting dinner
or that undigestible meal
of yours, Thyestes, or Daedalus
fitting the meltable wings
to his son, or Polyphemus
grazing his Sicilian sheep.
That kind of windiness
won't be found in any of my poems.
My Muse doesn't puff herself up
with such tragic nonsense.

    "Still,
everybody praises that kind
of thing—admires it—worships it!"

Granted. They praise it, but
it's my kind of poem they read.

V, xiii

I'll admit I'm poor, Callistratus,
and always have been. And yet
two Emperors gave me a knighthood
and I'm not altogether unknown,
and my reputation isn't bad.

I've got a great many readers
everywhere in the world who will say
"That's Martial," and recognition
such as few receive after they're dead
has come to me while I'm alive.

On the other hand, your house-roof
is supported by a hundred columns,
and your money-boxes contain
a freedman's wealth, and wide fields
near Syene on the River Nile
call you master, and Parma in Gaul
shears its countless flocks for you.
That's what we are, you and I.
But you can never be what I am,
while anyone at all can be like you.

V, lvi

You've been wondering and worrying
and asking me every day
whom you ought to hand over your son to
for instruction, Lupus. I warn you:
stay away from all those grammarians
and professors of rhetoric.

Don't let him have anything to do
with Cicero's writings, or Vergil's,
and let Tutilius, the author
and advocate, earn his reputation
somewhere else. If the boy writes poems,
disown the young versifier!

Does he want to learn to make money?
Then have him take lessons in harping
or fluting. Or if the young fellow's
not too bright, you can turn him into
a salesman or an architect.

VI, xiv

You keep insisting, Labierus,
that you know how to write fine poems.
Then why is it you're unwilling
to try? Knowing how to write
fine poems and never doing it!
What will power, Labierus!

VI, xxxi

You know your wife's playing around
with your physician, Charidemus,
but you don't do anything about it.
My guess is you won't have to wait
for a fever to carry you off.

VIII, xii

Why don't I marry a rich wife?
Because I won't make my wife
my master. A wife should be
submissive to her husband, Priscus.
There's no other way to give men
an equal chance with their women.

XI, lxvi

You're a spy and a blackmailer,
a forger, a pimp, a pervert,
and a trainer of gladiators,
Vacerra. I can't understand
why you aren't rich.

On the Dedication of the Colosseum in Rome

Barbaric Egypt, boast no more
    The wonders of your pyramids!
Babylon, vaunt no longer now
    The gardens of Semiramis!
Let not the soft Ionians swell
    With pride for their great Artemis
Whose temple splendor long has been
    The claim and fame of Ephesus.
Let Delos hide its head in shame
    And say no more Apollo
Himself did rear the altar there
    (A claim both weak and hollow).
Let not the Carians wildly praise
    The wondrous, sculptured tomb
The Queen at Halicarnassus raised
    When Mausolus met his doom.
Let every wonder of the past
    Yield now to this great wonder.
Fame shall cling to this at last,
    Her applause as loud as thunder.

(Mills, 1969)

DISCOURSES OF EPICTETUS, BOOK I, CHAPTER 1

Arrian (b. A.D. 108)

This lecture of Epictetus (ca. A.D. 60–110), as recorded by his student Arrian, together with the meditations of Marcus Aurelius (121–180), which follows, present the Stoic point of view. This philosophy assumes that the great *Logos* (Intelligence) pervades the entire world and directs all that happens. Therefore, as will be seen in the selections, it is essentially a stern philosophy of acceptance, duty, and brotherhood of all men.

On Things in Our Power and Things Not in Our Power

Of our faculties in general you will find that none can take cognizance of itself; none therefore has the power to approve or disapprove its own action. Our grammatical faculty for instance: how far can that take cognizance? Only so far as to distinguish expression. Our musical faculty? Only so far as to distinguish tune. Does any one of these then take cognizance of itself? By no means. If you are writing to your friend, when you want to know what words to write grammar will tell you; but whether you should write to your friend or should not write grammar will not tell you. And in the same way music will tell you about tunes, but whether at this precise moment you should sing and play the lyre or should not sing nor play the lyre it will not tell you. What will tell you then? That faculty which takes cognizance of itself and of all things else. What is this? The reasoning faculty: for this alone of the faculties we have received is created to comprehend even its own nature; that is to say, what it is and what it can do, and with what precious qualities it has come to us, and to comprehend all other faculties as well. For what else is it that tells us that gold is a goodly thing? For the gold does not tell us. Clearly it is the faculty which can deal with our impressions. What else is it which distinguishes the faculties of music, grammar, and the rest, testing their uses and pointing out the due seasons for their use? It is reason and nothing else.

The gods then, as was but right, put in our hands the one blessing that is best of all and master of all, that and nothing else, the power to deal rightly with our impressions, but everything else they did not put in our hands. Was it that they would not? For my part I think that if they could have entrusted us with those other powers as well they would have done so, but they were quite unable. Prisoners on the earth and in an earthly body and among earthly companions, how was it possible that we should not be hindered from the attainment of these powers by these external fetters?

But what says Zeus? 'Epictetus, if it were possible I would have made your body and your possessions (those trifles that you prize) free and untrammelled. But as things are—never forget this—this body is not yours, it is but a clever mixture of clay. But since I could not make it free, I gave you a portion in our divinity, this faculty of impulse to act and not to act, of will to get and will to avoid, in a word the faculty which can turn impressions to right use. If you pay heed to this, and put your affairs in its keeping, you will never suffer let nor hindrance, you will not groan, you will blame no man, you will flatter none. What then? Does all this seem but little to you?'

Heaven forbid!

'Are you content then?'

So surely as I hope for the gods' favour.

But, as things are, though we have it in our power to pay heed to one thing and to devote ourselves to one, yet instead of this we prefer to pay heed to many things and to be bound fast to many—our body, our property, brother and friend, child and slave. Inasmuch then as we are bound fast to many things, we are burdened by them and dragged down. That is why, if the weather is bad for sailing, we sit distracted and keep looking continually and ask, 'What wind is blowing?' 'The north wind.' What have we to do with that? 'When will the west wind blow?' When it so chooses, good sir, or when Aeolus chooses. For God made Aeolus the master of the winds, not you. What follows? We must make the best of those things that are in our power, and take the rest as nature gives it. What do you mean by 'nature'? I mean, God's will.

'What? Am I to be beheaded now, and I alone?'

Why? Would you have had all beheaded, to give you consolation? Will you not stretch out your neck as Lateranus did in Rome when Nero ordered his beheadal? For he stretched out his neck and took the blow, and when the blow dealt him was too weak he shrank up a little and then stretched it out again. Nay more, on a previous occasion, when Nero's freedman Epaphroditus came to him and asked him the cause of his offence, he answered, 'If I want to say anything, I will say it to your master.'

What then must a man have ready to help him in such emergencies? Surely this: he must ask himself, 'What is mine, and what is not mine? What may I do, what may I not do?'

I must die. But must I die groaning? I must be imprisoned. But must I whine as well? I must suffer exile. Can any one then hinder me from going with a smile, and a good courage, and at peace?

'Tell the secret!'

I refuse to tell, for this is in my power.

'But I will chain you.'

What say you, fellow? Chain me? My leg you will chain—yes, but my will—no, not even Zeus can conquer that.

'I will imprison you.'

My bit of a body, you mean.

'I will behead you.'

Why? When did I ever tell you that I was the only man in the world that could not be beheaded?

These are the thoughts that those who pursue philosophy should ponder, these are the lessons they should write down day by day, in these they should exercise themselves.

Thrasea used to say 'I had rather be killed to-day than exiled tomorrow'. What then did Rufus say to him? 'If you choose it as the harder, what is the meaning of your foolish choice? If as the easier, who has given you the easier? Will you not study to be content with what is given you?'

It was in this spirit that Agrippinus used to say—do you know what? 'I will not stand in my own way!' News was brought him, 'Your trial is on in the Senate!' 'Good luck to it, but the fifth hour is come'—this was the hour when he used to take his exercise and have a cold bath—'let us go and take exercise.' When he had taken his exercise they came and told him, 'You are condemned.' 'Exile or death?' he asked. 'Exile.' 'And my property?' 'It is not confiscated.' 'Well then, let us go to Aricia and dine.'

Here you see the result of training as training should be, of the will to get and will to avoid, so disciplined that nothing can hinder or frustrate them. I must die, must I? If at once, then I am dying: if soon, I dine now, as it is time for dinner, and afterwards when the time comes I will die. And die how? As befits one who gives back what is not his own.

MEDITATIONS, BOOK II
Marcus Aurelius (121–180)

Begin the morning by saying to thyself, I shall meet with the busybody, the ungrateful, arrogant, deceitful, envious, unsocial. All these things happen to them by reason of their ignorance of what is good and evil. But I who have seen the nature of the good that it is beautiful, and of the bad that it is ugly, and the nature of him who does wrong, that it is akin to me, not only of the same blood or seed, but that it participates in the same intelligence and the same portion of the divinity, I can neither be injured by any of them, for no one can fix on me what is ugly, nor can I be angry with my kinsman, nor hate him. For we are made for cooperation, like feet, like hands, like eyelids, like the rows of the upper and lower teeth. To act against one another then is contrary to nature; and it is acting against one another to be vexed and to turn away.

2. Whatever this is that I am, it is a little flesh and breath, and the ruling part. Throw away thy books; no longer distract thyself: it is not allowed; but as if thou wast now dying, despise the flesh; it is blood and bones and a network, a contexture of nerves, veins, and arteries. See the breath also, what kind of a thing it is, air, and not always the same, but every moment sent out and again sucked in. The third then is the ruling part: consider thus: Thou art an old man; no longer let this be a slave, no longer be pulled by the strings like a puppet to unsocial movements, no longer be either dissatisfied with thy present lot, or shrink from the future.

5. Every moment think steadily as a Roman and a man to do what thou hast in hand with perfect and simple dignity, and feeling of affection, and freedom, and justice; and to give thyself relief from all other thoughts. And thou wilt give thyself relief, if thou doest every act of thy life as it were the last, laying aside all carelessness and passionate aversion from the commands of reason, and all hypocrisy, and self-love, and discontent with the portion which has been given to thee. Thou seest how few the things are, that which if a man lays hold of, he is able to live a life which flows in quiet, and is like the existence of the gods; for the gods on their part will require nothing more from him who observes these things.

9. This thou must always bear in mind, what is the nature of the whole, and what is my nature, and how this is related to that, and what kind of a part it is of what kind of a whole; and that there is no one who hinders thee from always doing and saying the things which are according to the nature of which thou art a part.

11. Since it is possible that thou mayest depart from life this very moment, regulate every act and thought accordingly. But to go away from among men, if there are gods, is not a thing to be afraid of, for the gods will not involve thee in evil; but if indeed they do not exist, or if they have no concern about human affairs, what is it to me to live in a universe devoid of gods or devoid of Providence? But in truth they do exist, and they do care for human things, and they have put all the means in man's power to enable him not to fall into real evils. And as to the rest, if there was anything evil, they would have provided for this also, that it should be altogether in a man's power not to fall into it. Now that which does not make a man worse, how can it make a man's life worse? But neither through ignorance, nor having the

knowledge, but not the power to guard against or correct these things, is it possible that the nature of the universe has overlooked them; nor is it possible that it has made so great a mistake, either through want of power or want of skill, that good and evil should happen indiscriminately to the good and the bad. But death certainly, and life, honour and dishonour, pain and pleasure, all these things equally happen to good men and bad, being things which make us neither better nor worse. Therefore they are neither good nor evil.

16. The soul of man does violence to itself, first of all, when it becomes an abscess and, as it were, a tumour on the universe, so far as it can. For to be vexed at anything which happens is a separation of ourselves from nature, in some part of which the natures of all other things are contained. In the next place, the soul does violence to itself when it turns away from any man, or even moves towards him with the intention of injuring, such as are the souls of those who are angry. In the third place, the soul does violence to itself when it is overpowered by pleasure or by pain. Fourthly, when it plays a part, and does or says anything insincerely and untruly. Fifthly, when it allows any act of its own and any movement to be without an aim, and does anything thoughtlessly and without considering what it is, it being right that even the smallest things be done with reference to an end; and the end of rational animals is to follow the reason and the law of the most ancient city and polity.

17. Of human life the time is a point, and the substance is in a flux, and the perception dull, and the composition of the whole body subject to putrefaction, and the soul a whirl, and fortune hard to divine, and fame a thing devoid of judgement. And, to say all in a word, everything which belongs to the body is a stream, and what belongs to the soul is a dream and vapour, and life is a warfare and a stranger's sojourn, and after-fame is oblivion. What then is that which is able to conduct a man? One thing and only one, philosophy. But this consists in keeping the daemon within a man free from violence and unharmed, superior to pains and pleasures, doing nothing without a purpose, nor yet falsely and with hypocrisy, not feeling the need of another man's doing or not doing anything; and besides, accepting all that happens, and all that is allotted, as coming from thence, wherever it is, from whence he himself came; and, finally, waiting for death with a cheerful mind, as being nothing else than a dissolution of the elements of which every living being is compounded. But if there is no harm to the elements themselves in each continually changing into another, why should a man have any apprehension about the change and dissolution of all the elements? For it is according to nature, and nothing is evil which is according to nature.

AGAINST THE CITY OF ROME
Decimus Junius Juvenalis (ca. 60–140)

Juvenal (Decimus Junius Juvenalis) was the last and best of the remarkable Roman satirists. As a brilliant social critic who was scarred by abrasive poverty, he saw through the glass darkly. The bitter tone, merciless barbs, and blatant prejudices (against Greeks and the "inferior" sex) are directed against a Rome he despises because it has become foolish and wicked.

Troubled because my old friend is going, I still must commend him
For his decision to settle down in the ghost town of Cumae,[52]
Giving the Sibyl one citizen more. That's the gateway to Baiae
There, a pleasant shore, a delightful retreat, I'd prefer
Even a barren rock in that bay to the brawl of Subura.
Where have we ever seen a place so dismal and lonely
We'd not be better off there, than afraid, as we are here, of fires,
Roofs caving in, and the thousand risks of this terrible city
Where the poets recite all through the dog days of August?

While they are loading his goods on one little four-wheeled wagon,
Here he waits, by the old archways which the aqueducts moisten.
This is where Numa, by night, came to visit his goddess.
That once holy grove, its sacred spring, and its temple,
Now are let out to the Jews, if they have some straw and a basket.
Every tree, these days, has to pay rent to the people.
Kick the Muses out; the forest is swarming with beggars.
So we go down to Egeria's vale, with its modern improvements.
How much more close the presence would be, were there lawns by the water,
Turf to the curve of the pool, not this unnatural marble!
Umbricius has much on his mind. "Since there's no place in the city,"
He says, "For an honest man, and no reward for his labors,
Since I have less today than yesterday, since by tomorrow
That will have dwindled still more, I have made my decision. I'm going
To the place where, I've heard, Daedalus put off his wings,[53]
While my white hair is still new, my old age in the prime of its straightness,
While my fate spinner still has yarn on her spool, while I'm able
Still to support myself on two good legs, without crutches.
Rome, good-bye! Let the rest stay in the town if they want to,
Fellows like A, B, and C, who make black white at their pleasure,
Finding it easy to grab contracts for rivers and harbors,
Putting up temples, or cleaning out sewers, or hauling off corpses,
Or, if it comes to that, auctioning slaves in the market.
Once they used to be hornblowers, working the carneys;
Every wide place in the road knew their puffed-out cheeks and their squealing.
Now they give shows of their own. Thumbs up! Thumbs down! And the killers
Spare or slay, and then go back to concessions for private privies.

---

52. Cumae was the oldest Greek colony in Italy.
53. Daedalus, according to Virgil, ended his flight at Cumae.

Nothing they won't take on. Why not?—since the
    kindness of Fortune
(Fortune is out for laughs) has exalted them out of the
    gutter.
"What should I do in Rome? I am no good at lying.
If a book's bad, I can't praise it, or go around ordering
    copies.
I don't know the stars; I can't hire out as assassin
When some young man wants his father knocked off for a
    price; I have never
Studied the guts of frogs, and plenty of others know
    better
How to convey to a bride the gifts of the first man she
    cheats with.
I am no lookout for thieves, so I cannot expect a
    commission
On some governor's staff. I'm a useless corpse, or a
    cripple.
Who has a pull these days, except your yes men and
    stooges
With blackmail in their hearts, yet smart enough to keep
    silent?
No honest man feels in debt to those he admits to his
    secrets,
But your Verres must love the man who can tattle on
    Verres[54]
Any old time that he wants. Never let the gold of the
    Tagus,
Rolling under its shade, become so important, so
    precious
You have to lie awake, take bribes that you'll have to
    surrender,
Tossing in gloom, a threat to your mighty patron forever.
"Now let me speak of the race that our rich men dote on
    most fondly.
These I avoid like the plague, let's have no coyness about
    it.
Citizens, I can't stand a Greekized Rome. Yet what
    portion
Of the dregs of our town comes from Achaia only?
Into the Tiber pours the silt, the mud of Orontes,
Bringing its babble and brawl, its dissonant harps and its
    timbrels,
Bringing also the tarts who display their wares at the
    Circus.
Here's the place, if your taste is for hat-wearing whores,
    brightly colored!
What have they come to now, the simple souls from the
    country
Romulus used to know? They put on the *trechedipna*
(That might be called, in our tongue, their running-to-
    dinner outfit),
Pin in their *niketeria* (medals), and smell *ceromatic*
(Attar of wrestler). They come, trooping from Samos and
    Tralles,
Andros, wherever that is, Azusa and Cucamonga,
Bound for the Esquiline or the hill we have named for the
    vineyard,
Termites, into great halls where they hope, some day, to
    be tyrants.
Desperate nerve, quick wit, as ready in speech as Isacus,
Also a lot more long-winded. Look over there! See that
    fellow?
What do you take him for? He can be anybody he
    chooses,

Doctor of science or letters, a vet or a chiropractor,
Orator, painter, masseur, palmologist, tightrope walker.
If he is hungry enough, your little Greek stops at nothing.
Tell him to fly to the moon, and he runs right off for his
    space ship.
Who flew first? Some Moor, some Turk, some Croat, or
    some Slovene?
Not on your life, but a man from the very center of
    Athens.
"Should I not run away from these purple-wearing
    freeloaders?
Must I wait while they sign their names? Must their
    couches always be softer?
Stowaways, that's how they got here, in the plums and figs
    from Damascus.
I was here long before they were: my boyhood drank in
    the sky
Over the Aventine hill; I was nourished by Sabine olives.
Agh, what lackeys they are, what sycophants! See how
    they flatter
Some ignoramus's talk, or the looks of some horrible
    eyesore,
Saying some Ichabod Crane's long neck reminds them of
    muscles
Hercules strained when he lifted Antaeus aloft on his
    shoulders,
Praising some cackling voice that really sounds like a
    rooster's
When he's pecking a hen. We can praise the same objects
    that they do,
Only, they are believed. Does an actor do any better
Mimicking Thais, Alcestis, Doris without any clothes on?
It seems that a woman speaks, not a mask; the illusion is
    perfect
Down to the absence of bulge and the little cleft under
    the belly.[55]
Yet they win no praise at home, for all of their talent.
Why?—Because Greece is a stage, and every Greek is an
    actor.
Laugh, and he splits his sides; weep, and his tears flow in
    torrents
Though he's not sad; if you ask for a little more fire in the
    winter
He will put on his big coat; if you say 'I'm hot,' he starts
    sweating.
We are not equals at all; he always has the advantage,
Able, by night or day, to assume, from another's
    expression,
This or that look, prepared to throw up his hands, to
    cheer loudly
If his friend gives a good loud belch or doesn't piss
    crooked,
Or if a gurgle comes from his golden cup when inverted
Straight up over his nose—a good deep swig, and no
    heeltaps!
"Furthermore, nothing is safe from his lust, neither
    matron nor virgin,

---

54. Verres was the corrupt governor of Sicily against whom
Cicero delivered his famous prosecution speeches. The name
passed into the language as the emblem of rapacious
administrators.
55. In Greek-style comedies women's roles were played by men.

Nor her affianced spouse, or the boy too young for the razor.
If he can't get at these, he would just as soon lay his friend's grandma.
(Anything, so he'll get in to knowing the family secrets!)
Since I'm discussing the Greeks, let's turn to their schools and professors,
The crimes of the hood and gown. Old Dr. Egnatius, informant,
Brought about the death of Barea, his friend and his pupil,
Born on that riverbank where the pinion of Pegasus landed.
No room here, none at all, for any respectable Roman
Where a Protogenes rules, or a Diphilus, or a Hermarchus,
Never sharing their friends—a racial characteristic!
Hands off! He puts a drop of his own, or his countryside's poison
Into his patron's ear, an ear which is only too willing
And I am kicked out of the house, and all my years of long service
Count for nothing. Nowhere does the loss of a client mean less.

"Let's not flatter ourselves. What's the use of our service?
What does a poor man gain by hurrying out in the nighttime,
All dressed up before dawn, when the praetor nags at his troopers
Bidding them hurry along to convey his respects to the ladies,
Barren, of course, like Albina, before any others can get there?
Sons of men freeborn give right of way to a rich man's
Slave; a crack, once or twice, at Calvina or Catiena
Costs an officer's pay, but if you like the face of some floozy
You hardly have money enough to make her climb down from her high chair.
Put on the stand, at Rome, a man with a record unblemished,
No more a perjurer than Numa was, or Metellus,
What will they question? His wealth, right away, and possibly, later,
(Only possibly, though) touch on his reputation.
'How many slaves does he feed? What's the extent of his acres?
How big are his platters? How many? What of his goblets and wine bowls?'
His word is as good as his bond—if he has enough bonds in his strongbox.
But a poor man's oath, even if sworn on all altars
All the way from here to the farthest Dodecanese island,
Has no standing in court. What has he to fear from the lightnings
Of the outraged gods? He has nothing to lose; they'll ignore him.

"If you're poor, you're a joke, on each and every occasion.
What a laugh, if your cloak is dirty or torn, if your toga
Seems a little bit soiled, if your shoe has a crack in the leather,
Or if more than one patch attests to more than one mending!
Poverty's greatest curse, much worse than the fact of it, is that
It makes men objects of mirth, ridiculed, humbled, embarrassed.

'Out of the front-row seats!' they cry when you're out of money,
Yield your place to the sons of some pimp, the spawn of some cathouse,
Some slick auctioneer's brat, or the louts some trainer has fathered
Or the well-groomed boys whose sire is a gladiator.
Such is the law of place, decreed by the nitwitted Otho:
All the best seats are reserved for the classes who have the most money.
Who can marry a girl if he has less money than she does?
What poor man is an heir, or can hope to be? Which of them ever
Rates a political job, even the meanest and lowest?
Long before now, all poor Roman descendants of Romans
Ought to have marched out of town in one determined migration.
Men do not easily rise whose poverty hinders their merit.
Here it is harder than anywhere else: the lodgings are hovels,
Rents out of sight; your slaves take plenty to fill up their bellies
While you make do with a snack. You're ashamed of your earthenware dishes—
Ah, but that wouldn't be true if you lived content in the country,
Wearing a dark-blue cape, and the hood thrown back on your shoulders.
"In a great part of this land of Italy, might as well face it,
No one puts on a toga unless he is dead. On festival days
Where the theater rises, cut from green turf, and with great pomp
Old familiar plays are staged again, and a baby,
Safe in his mother's lap, is scared of the grotesque mask,
There you see all dressed alike, the balcony and the front-rows,
Even His Honor content with a tunic of simple white.
Here, beyond our means, we have to be smart, and too often
Get our effects with too much, an elaborate wardrobe, on credit!
This is a common vice; we must keep up with the neighbors,
Poor as we are. I tell you, everything here costs you something.
How much to give Cossus the time of day, or receive from Veiento
One quick glance, with his mouth buttoned up for fear he might greet you?
One shaves his beard, another cuts off the locks of his boyfriend,
Offerings fill the house, but these, you find, you will pay for.
Put this in your pipe and smoke it—we have to pay tribute
Giving the slaves a bribe for the prospect of bribing their masters.
"Who, in Praeneste's cool, or the wooded Volsinian uplands,
Who, on Tivoli's heights, or a small town like Gabii, say,
Fears the collapse of his house? But Rome is supported on pipestems,
Matchsticks; it's cheaper, so, for the landlord to shore up his ruins,
Patch up the old cracked walls, and notify all the tenants
They can sleep secure, though the beams are in ruins above them.

No, the place to live is out there, where no cry of *Fire!*
Sounds the alarm of the night, with a neighbor yelling for water,
Moving his chattels and goods, and the whole third story is smoking.
This you'll never know: for if the ground floor is scared first,
You are the last to burn, up there where the eaves of the attic
Keep off the rain, and the doves are brooding over their nest eggs.
Codrus owned one bed, too small for a midget to sleep on,
Six little jugs he had, and a tankard adorning his sideboard,
Under whose marble (clay), a bust or a statue of Chiron,
Busted, lay on its side; an old locker held Greek books
Whose divinest lines were gnawed by the mice, those vandals.
Codrus had nothing, no doubt, and yet he succeeded, poor fellow,
Losing that nothing, his all. And this is the very last straw—
No one will help him out with a meal or lodging or shelter.
Stripped to the bone, begging for crusts, he still receives nothing.
"Yet if Asturicus' mansion burns down, what a frenzy of sorrow!
Mothers dishevel themselves, the leaders dress up in black,
Courts are adjourned. We groan at the fall of the city, we hate
The fire, and the fire still burns, and while it is burning,
Somebody rushes up to replace the loss of the marble,
Some one chips in toward a building fund, another gives statues,
Naked and shining white, some masterpiece of Euphranor
Or Polyclitus' chef d'oeuvre; and here's a fellow with bronzes
Sacred to Asian gods. Books, chests, a bust of Minerva,
A bushel of silver coins. *To him that hath shall be given!*
This Persian, childless, of course, the richest man in the smart set,
Now has better things, and more, than before the disaster.
How can we help but think he started the fire on purpose?

"Tear yourself from the games, and get a place in the country!
One little Latian town, like Sora, say, or Frusino,
Offers a choice of homes, at a price you pay here, in one year,
Renting some hole in the wall. Nice houses, too, with a garden,
Springs bubbling up from the grass, no need for windlass or bucket,
Plenty to water your flowers, if they need it, without any trouble.
Live there, fond of your hoe, an independent producer,
Willing and able to feed a hundred good vegetarians.
Isn't it something, to feel, wherever you are, how far off,
You are monarch? At least, lord of a single lizard.
"Here in town the sick die from insomnia mostly.
Undigested food, on a stomach burning with ulcers,
Brings on listlessness, but who can sleep in a flophouse?
Who but the rich can afford sleep and a garden apartment?

That's the source of infection. The wheels creak by on the narrow
Streets of the wards, the drivers squabble and brawl when they're stopped,
More than enough to frustrate the drowsiest son of a sea cow.
When his business calls, the crowd makes way, as the rich man,
Carried high in his car, rides over them, reading or writing,
Even taking a snooze, perhaps, for the motion's composing.
Still, he gets where he wants before we do; for all of our hurry
Traffic gets in our way, in front, around and behind us.
Somebody gives me a shove with an elbow, or two-by-four scantling.
One clunks my head with a beam, another cracks down with a beer keg.
Mud is thick on my shins, I am trampled by somebody's big feet.
Now what?—a soldier grinds his hobnails into my toes.
"Don't you see the mob rushing along to the handout?
There are a hundred guests, each one with his kitchen servant.
Even Samson himself could hardly carry those burdens,
Pots and pans some poor little slave tries to keep on his head, while he hurries
Hoping to keep the fire alive by the wind of his running.
Tunics, new-darned, are ripped to shreds; there's the flash of a fir beam
Huge on some great dray, and another carries a pine tree,
Nodding above our heads and threatening death to the people.
What will be left of the mob, if that cart of Ligurian marble
Breaks its axle down and dumps its load on these swarms?
Who will identify limbs or bones? The poor man's cadaver,
Crushed, disappears like his breath. And meanwhile, at home, his household
Washes the dishes, and puffs up the fire, with all kinds of a clatter
Over the smeared flesh-scrapers, the flasks of oil, and the towels.
So the boys rush around, while their late master is sitting,
Newly come to the bank of the Styx, afraid of the filthy
Ferryman there, since he has no fare, not even a copper
In his dead mouth to pay for the ride through the muddy whirlpool.

"Look at other things, the various dangers of nighttime.
How high it is to the cornice that breaks, and a chunk beats my brains out,
Or some slob heaves a jar, broken or cracked, from a window.
Bang! It comes down with a crash and proves its weight on the sidewalk.
You are a thoughtless fool, unmindful of sudden disaster,
If you don't make your will before you go out to have dinner.
There are as many deaths in the night as there are open windows
Where you pass by; if you're wise, you will pray, in your wretched devotions,
People may be content with no more than emptying slop jars.

"There your hell-raising drunk, who has had the bad luck
    to kill no one,
Tosses in restless rage, like Achilles mourning Patroclus,
Turns from his face to his back, can't sleep, for only a
    fracas
Gives him the proper sedation. But any of these young
    hoodlums,
All steamed up on wine, watches his step when the
    crimson
Cloak goes by, a lord, with a long, long line of attendants,
Torches and brazen lamps, warning him, *Keep your
    distance!*
Me, however, whose torch is the moon, or the feeblest
    candle
Fed by a sputtering wick, he absolutely despises.
Here is how it all starts, the fight, if you think it is fighting
When he throws all the punches, and all I do is absorb
    them.
He stops. He tells me to stop. I stop. I have to obey him.
What can you do when he's mad and bigger and stronger
    than you are?
'Where do you come from?' he cries, 'you wino, you bean-
    bloated bastard?
Off what shoemaker's dish have you fed on chopped leeks
    and boiled lamb-lip?
What? No answer? Speak up, or take a swift kick in the
    rear.
Tell me where you hang out—in some praying-house
    with the Jew-boys?'
If you try to talk back, or sneak away without speaking,
All the same thing: you're assaulted, and then put under a
    bail bond
For committing assault. This is a poor man's freedom.
Beaten, cut up by fists, he begs and implores his assailant,
Please, for a chance to go home with a few teeth left in
    his mouth.
"This is not all you must fear. Shut up your house or your
    store,
Bolts and padlocks and bars will never keep out all the
    burglars,
Or a holdup man will do you in with a switch blade.
If the guards are strong over Pontine marshes and
    pinewoods
Near Volturno, the scum of the swamps and the filth of
    the forest
Swirl into Rome, the great sewer, their sanctuary, their
    haven.
Furnaces blast and anvils groan with the chains we are
    forging:
What other use have we for iron and steel? There is
    danger
We will have little left for hoes and mattocks and
    ploughshares.
Happy the men of old, those primitive generations
Under the tribunes and kings, when Rome had only one
    jailhouse!
"There is more I could say, I could give you more of my
    reasons,
But the sun slants down, my oxen seem to be calling,
My man with the whip is impatient, I must be on my way.
So long! Don't forget me. Whenever you come to Aquino
Seeking relief from Rome, send for me. I'll come over
From my bay to your hills, hiking along in my thick boots
Toward your chilly fields. What's more, I promise to listen
If your satirical verse esteems me worthy the honor."

PHILOSOPHIES GOING CHEAP
Lucian (ca. 117–180)

Skepticism about academic philosophy and traditional religious beliefs was increasingly prevalent
during the second century of the Roman peace
(80–180). One of the most influential doubters was a
Hellenized Syrian, Lucian, who composed stinging
satires in classical Greek in the style of Aristophanes.
Known throughout the Graeco-Roman world for his
witty and scathing dialogues, Lucian attacked fraud
and hypocrisy with malevolent glee. In the following
dialogue he demolishes prominent beliefs by selling
philosophers to the highest bidder.

The translation is by Paul Turner, whose spelling
has been retained.

*Scene: A large auction-room with a platform at one end.
The proprietors, Zeus and Hermes, and two of their
employees are preparing for a sale.*
Zeus: [*to one of the assistants*] Here, you! Put out the
chairs and get the place ready for the customers. [*Turning
to the other*] And you bring in the philosophers and line
them up on the platform. Only do tidy them up a bit first,
so that they look reasonably attractive. Try and give them
as much sales-appeal as possible.
[*The assistants carry out his orders.*]
Hermes, would you act as auctioneer? Collect as many
customers as you can, and ask them to step inside. Say
we've got a wide selection of philosophical systems for
sale, in fact all the brands available. If anyone can't pay
cash, he can do it by instalments spread over the next
twelve months—with suitable security, of course.
[*Hermes goes out into the street, and customers soon start
streaming into the auction-room and sitting down on the
chairs. Finally Hermes returns and closes the door.*]
Hermes: [*quietly, to Zeus*] Well, we've got a full house.
We'd better not hang about and keep them waiting.
Zeus: All right, let's start the sale.
Hermes: Who do you want put up first?
Zeus: That long-haired type from Ionia. He's the most
impressive to look at.
Hermes: Hey, you! Pythagoras! Come down and let the
gentlemen take a look at you.
[*A lean, bearded man, badly in need of a hair-cut, steps
down off the platform and starts parading slowly round
the room.*]
Zeus: [*to Hermes*] Go on, give them a little sales talk.
Hermes: [*raising his voice*] Now here's a first-rate
philosophy, a really grand specimen! Any offers,
gentlemen? Who wants to be superhuman? Who wants to
hear the music of the spheres?
A Customer: He doesn't look too bad, but what's his
speciality?
Hermes: Arithmetic, astronomy, tall stories, geometry,
music, and confidence-tricks. You also see before you a
top-notch fortune-teller.
Customer: May I ask him a few questions?
Hermes: By all means.
Customer: Where do you come from?
Pythagoras: Samos.
Customer: And where were you educated?
Pythagoras: In Egypt was I taught the wisdom of the
East.

Customer: Well now, if I buy you, what'll you teach me?

Pythagoras: Nothing. I will only bring things back from your unconscious.

Customer: How will you do that?

Pythagoras: First, by purifying your psyche, and washing out your dirty mind.

Customer: All right, let's assume that it's no longer dirty. What's the next stage?

Pythagoras: First, a long silence. You must not speak a word for five years.

Customer: My dear chap, you need a pupil who's a deaf mute! Personally I like talking, and I've no wish to turn myself into a statue. Still, what comes after the five-year period of silence?

Pythagoras: You will be instructed in music and geometry.

Customer: It's a fine thing if I can't acquire a philosophy without taking music-lessons!

Pythagoras: After that you must learn to count.

Customer: But I know how to count already.

Pythagoras: Let me hear you count.

Customer: One, two, three, four—

Pythagoras: What did I tell you? What you think is four, is actually ten—an equilateral triangle, and the oath by which we swear.

Customer: By Four, then, I swear I've never heard anything so mysterious and holy in my life!

Pythagoras: After that, my friend, you will learn the shapes and motions of earth, air, water, and fire.

Customer: But have fire, or air, or water *got* any shapes?

Pythagoras: Clearly they have. For what does not exist in any shape or form is incapable of motion. Moreover you will learn that God is Arithmetic, Intelligence, Harmony.

Customer: That sounds marvellous.

Pythagoras: Furthermore, in addition to what I have said, you will learn that you are not one person as you think, nor are you the same as you appear to be.

Customer: I'm not me, you mean? I'm not the person who's talking to you at this moment?

Pythagoras: At this moment, yes, you are he. But once you had another body and another name.

Customer: Do you mean to say I'm going to live for ever, and keep changing bodies all the time? But never mind about that. What are your views on diet?

Pythagoras: I am a vegetarian, except that I eat no Beans.

Customer: Whyever not? Do they turn you up or something?

Pythagoras: No, but the Bean is holy, Its nature is truly wonderful. For first It is one hundred per cent reproductive. If you peel a Bean while It is still green, you will see that It closely resembles the male genital organs. If you boil It and expose It to the moon for precisely the right number of nights, It will turn to blood. What is more, Beans are used at Athens to register votes at elections.

Customer: That all sounds very fine and religious. But now take off your clothes—I want to see what you're like stripped.

[*Pythagoras undresses.*]
Good Lord, he's got a golden thigh! He's not a human being at all—he's a god! I must certainly buy him. [*To Hermes*] How much do you want for him?

Hermes: Ten minas.

Customer: I'll take him.

Zeus: [*to an assistant*] Make a note of the buyer's name and address.

Hermes: [*to Zeus*] I think he's an Italian. Comes from Croton, or Tarentum, or somewhere in Magna Graecia. But he's not on his own. He represents a syndicate of three hundred members.

Zeus: Well, they can have him. Bring down the next one.

Hermes: Which do you suggest? That filthy creature from Pontus?

Zeus: Yes, he'll do.

Hermes: Hoy, you there! The half-naked one with the knapsack! Come and walk round the room.
[*Diogenes descends from the platform. He is dressed in a dirty old blanket, and carries a stick and a knapsack.*]
Now here's a good manly type, a noble type, a free type. What will you bid me?

A Customer: I say, what exactly do you mean by a free type? You're not selling a free man, are you?

Hermes: Certainly I am.

Customer: Aren't you afraid of being had up before the Areopagus for kidnapping?

Hermes: It's all right, he doesn't mind being sold. He thinks himself perfectly free whatever happens.

Customer: But what could one do with a dirty creature like that? Look what a wretched state he's in! Though I dare say one could use him for hedging and ditching, or carrying buckets of water.

Hermes: You could also employ him as a janitor. You'd find him a most reliable watch-dog. In fact he's called a Cynic, which is only another word for dog-like.

Customer: And where does he come from? What sort of life does he recommend?

Hermes: You'd better ask him that.

Customer: I hardly like to speak to him. He looks so sulky and bad-tempered that I'm afraid he might bark at me, or even bite me.

[*Diogenes shows signs of exasperation.*]
There you are, he's scowling at me and threatening me with his stick.

Hermes: Don't worry, he's perfectly tame.

Customer: [*nervously*] Well, first of all, my dear sir, where do you come from?

Diogenes: Everywhere.

Customer: What do you mean?

Diogenes: [*irritably*] Can't you see? I'm a citizen of the world.

Customer: And who's your favourite character?

Diogenes: Heracles.

Customer: Then why aren't you wearing a lion-skin? You've got his club all right!

Diogenes: [*not amused*] This old blanket's my lion-skin. Like Heracles I belong to the Anti-Pleasure Brigade. And I'm not a conscript either—I'm a volunteer. Cleaning things up—that's my line.

Customer: And a very good line too. But what exactly are you an expert at? What's your actual trade?

Diogenes: I'm a Human Emancipator. I cure people of their feelings. In short, I aim to be the champion of truth and sincerity.

Customer: Good for you, Champ! But suppose I buy you, what course of treatment will you prescribe?

Diogenes: Well, the first stage will be to eliminate all luxuries, reduce you to poverty, and make you wear a blanket. After that I'll order plenty of hard labour, sleeping on the ground, and a diet of water and any old food that happens to come along. If you have any money, I'll recommend you to go and throw it into the sea, and on my advice you'll lose all interest in your wife, your children, and your country, and regard all that sort of thing as a lot of nonsense. You'll leave your family residence and go and live in a tomb or a lonely tower, or even in a tub. You'll have a knapsack full of lupine seeds and dog-eared books, and with that amount of property you'll claim to be as happy as a king. And if you get flogged or tortured, you won't consider it at all unpleasant.

Customer: You say it won't hurt if I'm flogged? What do you think I am? A tortoise or a lobster?

Diogenes: Don't you remember that line of Euripides?

'It was my mouth and not my mind that swore.'

Well, that must be your motto—in a slightly adapted form, of course.

Customer: How do you mean?

Diogenes: You'll mind it all right, but you'll keep your mouth shut. Otherwise, the chief requirements are as follows. You must have immense assurance and be rude to everybody, irrespective of rank. That's the way to make people admire you, and think you very brave. Then you must cultivate a hideous accent and speak in a grating voice, just like a dog snarling. You must pull a long face, and adopt the sort of walk that goes with it, and generally make yourself as savage and beastly as possible. To hell with all modesty, decency, and sense of proportion. Be barefaced and completely unblushing. Pick out the most crowded place you can find to be a recluse in, and refuse to have anything to do with either friends or strangers, for that's the way to bring down the government. Cheerfully do things in public that no decent person would do even in private, and specialize in the more ridiculous forms of sexual intercourse. Finally, if you feel like it, commit suicide by eating a raw octopus or squid. There! That's the part of happiness I can give you.

Customer: Get away from me! Your programme's so inhuman it's quite disgusting.

Diogenes: Ah, but a very easy one to follow, my good man. Anyone can do it. You don't need to have any training, or go to any lectures, or any nonsense of that sort. It's a real short cut to fame. Even if you're a perfectly ordinary person, a cobbler, a fishmonger, a carpenter, or a bank clerk, there's nothing to stop you being a huge success, so long as you're shameless enough, and learn the technique of vulgar abuse.

Customer: Well, I certainly don't want you for anything like that—but you might come in useful as a deck-hand or a gardener—that is, if this gentleman's not asking more than a couple of obols.

Hermes: He's all yours. We're only too glad to get rid of him. He's been a frightful nuisance, always shouting and jeering at everyone.

Zeus: [to Hermes] Now let's have that character from Cyrene, the one in evening dress with the flowers round his neck.

[Hermes beckons to Aristippus, who staggers down from the platform, smiling and hiccuping in a drunken stupor, and zigzags unsteadily round the room.]

Hermes: Now listen, everybody. Here's a very expensive model—only millionaires need apply. Here's something really pleasant, really enjoyable. Who wants to live in the lap of luxury? What am I offered for this dainty creature?

A Customer: [to Aristippus] Come over here, my man, and tell me what you can do. If you're any use to me, I'll buy you.

Hermes: Oh, please don't worry him with questions, sir. He's far too drunk to answer. He'd never get his tongue round the words.

Customer: Well, I don't see much sense in buying a degenerate alcoholic like that. Phew! How he stinks of scent! And just look at the way he's lurching about! However, perhaps you can tell me what he's good at, Hermes, and what he does with himself.

Hermes: Well, briefly, he's an experienced cohabiter, excellent at parties and nights out with girls, just the thing for a highly-sexed and dissolute employer. Apart from that he knows all about cooking and pastry-making, and is generally an expert at self-indulgence. He was educated at Athens, and got his first job with a dictator in Sicily who gave him a splendid reference. The main features of his doctrine are despising everything, making use of everything, and extracting pleasure from everything.

Customer: You'd better try someone else—someone with plenty of money to throw around. A gay life like that isn't quite in my line.

Hermes: [to Zeus] It looks as if we're going to have him left on our hands.

Zeus: Well, send him away and bring down the next one—or rather the next two, the man from Abdera and the man from Ephesus, for I want them sold as a pair.

Hermes: [beckoning to them] Come down, you two, and take the floor.

[Democritus and Heraclitus descend from the platform.] Now here we have two real paragons of wisdom.

A Customer: Good Lord, what a contrast! One of them never stops laughing, and the other must be in mourning for someone—he's streaming with tears! [To Democritus] Well, my good man, what's the joke? Why are you laughing?

Democritus: Why do you think? Because all your activities are so ridiculous, of course—and so are you.

Customer: What's that? You dare to make fun of us and the things we do?

Democritus: That's right. It's not really a very serious subject, you know. Why the universe itself is merely a lot of empty space with a few atoms rushing about in it.

Customer: That description would be better applied to the contents of your head.

[Democritus roars with laughter.]

Oh, stop laughing, can't you? I never heard of such impudence!

[Democritus goes on laughing.]

[Turning to Heraclitus] And why are you crying, my poor fellow? I'm sure I'll get more sense out of you.

Heraclitus: I am in mourning, sir, for human life. It seems to me such a wretched and lamentable thing—all its goods are so very perishable, I feel so sorry for you that I can't help crying. I can't say much for your present situation, but your future prospects are absolutely appalling—nothing but conflagrations and universal catastrophe. That's why I'm in mourning—because nothing has any stability—everything gets thrown into the melting-pot, where pleasure is indistinguishable from pain, knowledge from ignorance, great from small, up from down. Everything keeps churning round and changing places with everything else, for they're all the playthings of Eternity.

Customer: Eternity? What's that?

Heraclitus: A child playing with its toys, and flinging them about the nursery.

Customer: And what are human beings?

Heraclitus: Dying gods.

Customer: And gods?

Heraclitus: Undying human beings.

Customer: My good man, you're talking in riddles. Are you deliberately trying to muddle me? Why, you're as bad as an oracle—I can't make head or tail of you.

Heraclitus: I don't much care if you can't.

Customer: Then nobody in his senses is going to buy you.

Heraclitus: Whether you buy me or not, I strongly advise you all to spend your whole lives being miserable.

Customer: [*to the man sitting next him*] He must be a manic depressive. I'm not having either of them.

Hermes: [*to Zeus*] Now they're going to be left on our hands too.

Zeus: Try another one.

Hermes: What about that Athenian over there who's always shooting his mouth off?

Zeus: All right.

Hermes: [*beckoning*] Here, you!

[*Socrates comes down from the platform. He has a squashed nose, thick lips, pop-eyes, and a very large stomach.*]

Now here's a good sensible one. Any offers for this saintly specimen?

A Customer: [*to Socrates*] Tell me, what's your special subject?

Socrates: Sexology and homosexuality.

Customer: Then you're no use to me. I want a private tutor for my son—and he happens to be rather good-looking.

Socrates: [*licking his lips*] Private tutor to a good-looking boy? You won't find anyone better qualified for the job than I am. You see, I'm quite Platonic—it's only their minds I'm interested in. Why, even when I go to bed with them, they'll tell you nothing very terrible happens.

Customer: That's a bit much to believe—a homosexual who only messes about with people's minds, even when he has a chance to go further!

Socrates: I swear to Dog and Plane-tree it's perfectly true.

Customer: What a very curious oath!

Socrates: Why, do you doubt the divinity of Dog? Haven't you ever heard of the great god Anubis in Egypt, or Sirius up in the sky, or Cerberus down below?

Customer: Quite right. My mistake. But what sort of life do you lead?

Socrates: I live in a strange *Republic* of my own invention, and abide by my own *Laws*.

Customer: Could you tell me one of them?

Socrates: The most important one is the Nationalization of Women Act, which abolished private ownership, and ensured that the Means of Reproduction were shared by all the males in the community.

Customer: Do you mean to say there's no law against adultery?

Socrates: Certainly not. We've done away with all nonsense of that sort.

Customer: And what are the regulations about attractive boys?

Socrates: They're reserved as special rewards for gallantry, or any type of social distinction.

Customer: Talk about a generous government! But what are the chief features of your philosophy?

Socrates: The Ideas, the prototypes of all objects in the Phenomenal world. Every visible object, like the earth, the things on the earth, the sky, the sea, has an invisible prototype outside the universe.

Customer: But where, exactly?

Socrates: Nowhere. For if they were anywhere, they wouldn't really exist.

Customer: I don't quite see the idea of these prototypes.

Socrates: Of course you don't. Your mind's eye isn't strong enough. But I can see all the Ideas. I see another invisible You and another invisible Me—in fact, I see everything double.

Customer: You must be very clever and have remarkably good eyesight. You're obviously well worth buying. [*Turning to Hermes*] Let's see, how much are you asking for him?

Hermes: Two talents.

Customer: I'll take him. Put it down on my account.

Hermes: What name, please?

Customer: Dion of Syracuse.

Hermes: Well, I wish you luck with him. Now you, Epicurus.

[*Epicurus steps down.*]

Any offers for this one? He's an ex-pupil of two previous items on the catalogue—the laughing one and the drunk one—and he gets higher marks than either of them for impiety. In other respects he's quite a pleasant character, and something of a gourmet.

A Customer: What's his price?

Hermes: Two minas.

Customer: [*handing over the money*] There you are. By the way, what sort of food does he like?

Hermes: Oh, anything sweet, like honey—and he's particularly fond of figs.

Customer: That's easy enough. I'll send for a packet of dried ones from Caria.

Zeus: [*to Hermes*] Now let's have that Stoic, the one with the close-cropped hair and the gloomy look on his face.

Hermes: Good idea. As far as I can see, he's the one that most of the customers are waiting for.

[*He beckons to Chrysippus, who steps down.*]

Now here we have virtue itself—absolute perfection. Who wants to have a monopoly of knowledge?

A Customer: How do you mean?

Hermes: I mean, here we have the only person in the world who's really wise, just, and brave—the only genuine specimen extant of a king, an orator, a millionaire, a legislator, etc., etc.

Customer: Then presumably he's also the only genuine cook, cobbler, carpenter, etc., etc.?

Hermes: Presumably.

Customer: [*to Chrysippus*] Come here, my good fellow, and tell a prospective customer what sort of person you are. First of all, don't you mind being sold as a slave?

Chrysippus: Certainly not. A thing like that is quite beyond my control, and so a matter of complete Indifference to me.

Customer: I don't understand what you mean?

Chrysippus: Why, don't you understand that some things are Preferable, and others Non-Preferable?

Customer: No, I don't understand that either.

Chrysippus: That's probably because you're not used to our terminology, and have no Imaginative Grasp—whereas a serious student who has mastered Logical Theory not only knows about that, but can also explain the important distinction between a Primary and a Secondary Accident.

Customer: Oh, be a good philosopher and tell me what Primary and Secondary Accidents are. There's something so attractive about the rhythm of those words.

Chrysippus: I'll be only too glad to. Suppose someone has a gammy leg and accidentally bangs that gammy leg against a stone and cuts it open. Well, the gamminess is a Primary Accident, and the cut is a Secondary Accident.

Customer: What a clever example to think up on the spur of the moment! But what else are you good at?

Chrysippus: I'm very good at tying people in knots when they try to talk to me. I can put a gag on them which shuts them up and stops them saying another word. The secret of my power is the famous Syllogism.

Customer: My goodness, that must be a pretty deadly weapon!

Chrysippus: I'll just show you. Have you a baby?

Customer: [*mystified already*] Why do you want to know?

Chrysippus: Suppose that child was crawling about beside a river, and a crocodile got hold of it. Suppose the crocodile then promised to give it back provided you stated correctly whether the crocodile had decided to give the baby back or not. What would you say the crocodile had decided to do?

Customer: That's a very difficult question. I really can't think what would be the best thing to say in the circumstances. But for God's sake do tell me the right answer and save my baby's life, quick, before the crocodile gobbles it up!

Chrysippus: Don't you worry. I can teach you some far more remarkable things than that.

Customer: Such as?

Chrysippus: Oh, logical fallacies like the Reaper, the Master, and above all the Electra, and the Man Under The Sheet.

Customer: Tell me about the last two.

Chrysippus: Well, the Electra in question is the famous daughter of Agamemnon, and the point is that she's simultaneously in a state of ignorance and knowledge about the same subject. For when Orestes turns up in disguise, she knows that Orestes is her brother, but she doesn't know that this stranger is Orestes. The Man Under The Sheet's a very good one too. Tell me, do you know your own father?

Customer: Yes.

Chrysippus: Well, suppose I put someone in front of you with a sheet all over him, and asked if you recognized him, what would you say?

Customer: That I didn't, of course.

Chrysippus: But the man under the sheet is your father. So if you don't recognize him, you obviously don't know your own father.

Customer: Maybe not. But I'd know him all right if I took off the sheet. Anyway, what's the ultimate object of your system? What will you do when you've reached the top of the Hill of Virtue?

Chrysippus: I shall then concentrate on things like health and wealth, which are naturally of the first importance. But before that I'll have a lot of hard work to do, straining my eyes to read books in very small writing, collecting masses of footnotes, and filling myself up with ungrammatical paradoxes. And of course there's no hope of ever becoming a Wise Man, unless one takes three doses of hellebore.

Customer: What a splendid programme! It all sounds so terribly virile. But I gather you're also a bit of a skinflint and lend money at exorbitant interest. Is that quite the kind of thing one expects from a man who's had his three doses and perfected his moral character?

Chrysippus: Certainly it is. In fact the Wise Man is the obvious person to go in for moneylending. It's his business to be logical and it's only logical to be businesslike, therefore the Good Man has a good head for business. He's a man of many interests, and his interests are never simple, like other people's, but invariably compound—for, as you know, some interests are Primary and others Secondary. The former give birth, as it were, to the latter. You can put it in the form of a syllogism, if you like. Primary Interest gives rise to Secondary Interest. But the Wise Man charges Primary Interest. Therefore he charges Secondary Interest. Q.E.D.

Customer: I suppose the same argument would apply to the fees that you charge your students? Clearly the Good Man is the only person who makes virtue pay.

Chrysippus: You're getting the idea. You see, I don't charge fees for my own benefit, but for the benefit of my students. It's more blessed to give than to receive, so I force myself to do the receiving, and leave all the giving to my students.

Customer: Yet it really ought to be the other way round, because you're the only genuine millionaire.

Chrysippus: Oh, very funny—but mind I don't shoot you down with an Indemonstrable Syllogism.

Customer: Why, what harm would that do me?

Chrysippus: It would induce frustration and aphasia, and leave you with a permanent kink in the brain. What's more, if I care to, I can instantaneously turn you into stone.

Customer: My dear chap, how could you? You're hardly my idea of Perseus!

Chrysippus: Like this. A stone is a solid body, isn't it?

Customer: Yes.

Chrysippus: And what about a living creature? Isn't that a solid body?

Customer: Yes, it is.

Chrysippus: And are you a living creature?

Customer: I certainly thought I was.

Chrysippus: Then you're a solid body, and therefore a stone.

Customer: Oh, please don't say that! For God's sake give me some reductive analysis and turn me back into a human being!

Chrysippus: No difficulty about that. Just answer my questions. Is every solid body a living creature?

Customer: No.

Chrysippus: What about a stone? Is that a living creature?

Customer: No.

Chrysippus: But you're a solid body?

Customer: Yes.

Chrysippus: And you're a solid body which is also a living creature?

Customer: Yes.

Chrysippus: Then if you're a living creature, you're not a stone.

Customer: Oh, thanks awfully. My legs were beginning to feel all cold and stiff, like Niobe's. Well, I'll buy you. [*To Hermes*] How much do I pay for him?

Hermes: Twelve minas.

Customer: [*handing it over*] There you are.

Hermes: Are you the only purchaser?

Customer: Good Lord, no! [*Waving his hand round the room*] All these gentlemen are buying him too.

Hermes: Well, there are certainly enough of them, and they seem to have good strong arms—I should think the Reaper will be very glad of their help.

Zeus: [*to Hermes*] Don't waste time. Let's have that Peripatetic now.

[*Hermes beckons to the Peripatetic, who affects not to know that he is wanted until he is properly addressed.*]

Hermes: Yes, I mean you, the rich, handsome one.

[*The Peripatetic comes down from the platform.*]

Now, gentlemen, here's a chance to buy supreme intelligence and universal knowledge.

A Customer: What sort of character can you give him?

Hermes: Oh, he's a very moderate, reasonable, adaptable type, and what's more, there are two of him.

Customer: What can you mean?

Hermes: Apparently his exterior is quite different from what he's like inside. So if you buy him, you must remember to call one of him Exoteric and the other Esoteric.

Customer: And what exactly does he know?

Hermes: That happiness depends on three things, one's mind, one's body, and one's circumstances.

Customer: Well, that sounds fairly sensible. How much is he?

Hermes: Twenty minas.

Customer: That's rather expensive.

Hermes: Oh no, it isn't, my dear sir, for it seems he's got private means of his own—so you'd better hurry up and buy him. Besides, he can tell you right away the life-span of a gnat, the depth to which sunlight penetrates into the sea, and all about the psychology of oysters.

Customer: Good Lord, what an eye for detail he must have!

Hermes: That's nothing. You should hear him on the subject of reproduction, and the development of the embryo in the womb—he goes into far more microscopic detail there. He can also tell you that Man is a risible animal, whereas donkeys are non-risible and incapable of carpentry or navigation.

Customer: How very impressive! Now that's what I call really useful information. Yes, I must certainly have him, even if he does cost twenty minas.

[*He pays over the money to Hermes.*]

Hermes: Right.

Zeus: [*to Hermes*] Who have we got left?

Hermes: Only that Sceptic. Come on, Pyrrho, get a move on. Nearly all the customers seem to have left, and there isn't likely to be much demand for you.

[*Pyrrho steps down off the platform, carrying a pair of scales.*]

Still—does anybody want to buy this one?

A Customer: Yes, I do. But tell me first of all [*turning to Pyrrho*] what do you know about?

Pyrrho: I don't know about anything.

Customer: Why, what do you mean?

Pyrrho: I doubt if anything exists at all.

Customer: Then none of us are actually here?

Pyrrho: That I can't say.

Customer: Can't you even say if you exist yourself?

Pyrrho: No, that's even more problematical.

Customer: What an extraordinary state of indecision! But what are those scales for?

Pyrrho: I use them for weighing hypotheses and balancing them against one another. I make quite sure that the arguments on both sides have precisely the same weight, and then—I simply don't know what to believe.

Customer: But is there anything you're really good at?

Pyrrho: I'm good at everything except travelling.

Customer: What's so difficult about that?

Pyrrho: Well, sir, it's just that I never seem to get anywhere.

Customer: I'm not surprised. You don't look as if you could go very fast. But what exactly are you aiming at?

Pyrrho: A state of ignorance, hearing and seeing nothing.

Customer: Then to all intents and purposes you're blind and deaf?

Pyrrho: Also incapable of judgement or perception, and generally no better than a worm.

Customer: In that case I must certainly buy you. [*To Hermes*] What's he supposed to be worth?

Hermes: One mina.

Customer: [*handing over the money*] There you are. [*To Pyrrho*] Well, my man, have I bought you?

Pyrrho: I'm not quite sure.

Customer: Nonsense, of course I've bought you. I've actually handed over the money.

Pyrrho: I prefer to suspend judgement on that point.

Customer: Well anyway, come with me. You've got to, now you're my slave.

Pyrrho: Who knows if that's true or not?

Customer: The auctioneer knows. That mina knows. Everybody in the room knows.

Pyrrho: Is there anybody in the room?

Customer: Well, as a crude method of convincing you that I'm your master, I'm going to put you to work in my treadmill.

Pyrrho: Oh, do suspend judgement on that point!

Customer: Too late! I've already passed sentence.

Hermes: [*to Pyrrho*] Here, you, stop arguing and go along with your master. [*To the remaining customers*] And may I invite you, gentlemen, to come back tomorrow? We'll be selling off our stock of ordinary, unenlightened common sense—just the thing for the man in the street.

10

Roman Art and Music: The Arts of Megalopolis

Etruscan Civilization

Chronological Overview

800s B.C.	Etruscans in Italy
ca. 800–700 B.C.	Conquest of central Italy
ca. 650–550 B.C.	Conquest of Rome
509 B.C.	Romans expel Tarquin the Proud and begin final destruction of the Etruscan city-states

Although strongly influenced by their constant contacts and conflicts with Greek city-states but generally lagging behind Greek innovations, the Etruscans developed a distinctive kind of art. Provincial, sometimes homespun, their work has an earthy vigor, which in turn influenced their Roman conquerors. With no literature and little more than some massive stone walls remaining of their fortified hilltop cities, our scanty knowledge of Etruscan culture is based almost entirely on the contents of the thousands of tombs found throughout central Italy. Etruscan skill in making terra-cotta objects is exemplified by the funerary sculpture (fig. 10.1) found in the *necropolis* (city of the dead) outside Cerveteri, northwest of Rome. A deceased couple is shown resting their left elbows on a couch as if they are attending a celestial banquet. The smooth bodies, braided hair, and archaic smiles in the Greek manner are typical of the Etruscan style, as is the display of mutual affection and the individualized features of the couple. The exact meaning of festive banquet scenes in tomb paintings and as depicted on numerous sarcophagi is unknown, but continuation of the good life after death may have been intended.

Constantly at war with the Phoenicians and the Greeks over trade routes in the western Mediterranean, the Etruscans nevertheless valued the arts of Greece, especially Greek vases; most Greek pottery recovered

Figure 10.1 Etruscan sarcophagus, from Cerveteri, Italy, ca. 510 B.C. Painted terra-cotta, length ca. 80″. Museo Nazionale della Villa Giulia, Rome.

to date has been found in Etruscan tombs. Unconcerned with art objects, the Romans apparently learned utilitarian skills from the Etruscans: how to plan cities and how to build fortifications, monumental gateways, bridges, and aqueducts.

Roman Civilization, ca. 753 B.C.–A.D. 476

Chronological Overview

753 B.C.	Traditional date of the founding of Rome
ca. 509 B.C.	Founding of the Republic
264–146 B.C.	Three Punic Wars with Carthage and (214–146 B.C.) four wars with Macedonia and Dyria
133–27 B.C.	Disintegration of the Republic
27 B.C.– A.D. **180**	*Pax Romana*
27 B.C.– A.D. **17**	Augustan (Gold) Age
A.D. **17–130**	Silver Age
180–284	Age of Revolutions
284–337	Reorganization and division into East and West Empires.
330	Constantine transfers the capital to New Rome (Constantinople)
337–476	Decline and Fall of Western Empire

For the stern Romans, art was a corrupting influence that could undermine the moral fiber of the people, especially the citizen-soldiers of the republic. As late as the third century B.C., Rome was, according to Plutarch, a drab and dreary city full of battle trophies, barbarous weapons, triumphal monuments, and bloodstained hostages—a metropolis devoid of refinement and beauty. The penetration of Greek culture, especially Greek art, was a slow process that gathered momentum with Roman triumphs over Greek territories. During the conquest of the luxurious cities of Magna Graecia (southern Italy) in 212 B.C., for example, one general returned bearing Greek statues and paintings with which to adorn the city, while another general displayed gold and jewels, which according to the old guard was the only proper kind of booty. With the conquest of the Greek mainland in 146 B.C., a huge volume of confiscated artworks flooded the city, overwhelming the hostility of the die-hard conservatives and establishing Rome as the prime custodian of the Hellenic artistic tradition. Geared more to copying than creating, doing rather than theorizing, the native arts in Rome were produced by an army of anonymous artisans, with most efforts directed at a burgeoning mass market.

Though much of what we call Roman art is derived from Greek models and often created by Greek artists, the Romans did make some significant and original contributions with their realistic portrait busts, landscape painting, and, especially, their architecture. Justly famous for the monumental architecture of the imperial period, the Romans must also be credited with developing the "art" of civilized living. During the early days of the Republic, more attention was paid to the efficient design of military camps than to the urban planning of Rome and other growing cities of the rapidly expanding Republic.

Figure 10.2 West portico of the forum, Pompeii

Figure 10.3 Atrium, House of the Vetti, Pompeii

With the shift from a simple rural to an affluent urbanized society, the Romans had to come to grips with the problems of city planning. Taking their cue from Etruscan hill towns, they learned how to design and build the basic requirements for urban life: fortifications; streets; bridges; aqueducts; sewers; town houses; apartment houses; and recreational, shopping, and civic centers.

With no art and very little architecture remaining from the early centuries of the Republic, we will begin our study of the arts of Rome with Pompeii, which through an accident of history is the only surviving city of the Roman Republic. The eruption of Mount Vesuvius in A.D. 79 buried Pompeii under cinders and ashes that, in effect, preserved the city as a museum of Roman civilization. Probably founded in the sixth century B.C., Pompeii was inhabited by Italic Oscans and Samnites, plus some Greeks, until its conquest by Rome in about 80 B.C. Containing the earliest extant amphitheatre and public baths, Pompeii was built in a modified Greek grid plan around the most important early forum outside Rome (fig. 10.2). Reflecting Greek influence, the Doric colonnade with superimposed Ionic columns was a device that was later extended to four levels in the design of the Colosseum (see fig. 10.14). There are, in fact, so many different elements of Etruscan, Greek, and Italic contributions to Pompeiian decoration that it is impossible to precisely determine who did what. The civic center, or forum, is, however, typically Roman. Combining religious, commercial, and civic functions, forums are found in every Roman city, reflecting Roman concerns for centralized authority and control.

Because the city-center forum was always closed to vehicular traffic, the network of streets began at the perimeter and expanded outward to the suburbs. Much as old Italian towns are today, the streets nearer the forum were lined by shops, which were flanked by houses of shopkeepers and other citizens. The *domus*, single-family residence, was entered through a front doorway set in a windowless wall that guaranteed privacy and shut out city noise and dirt. An entrance hall led to the *atrium* (fig. 10.3), a typical Italic-Roman design for larger houses and for the still more elaborate villas in the surrounding countryside. A rectangular, windowless court that kept out heat while admitting light and air, the atrium had an inwardly sloping roof that drained rainwater into the pool below, from which it was piped to a cistern. Surrounding the central atrium were the kitchen, parlors, and other rooms for everyday living. Beyond the atrium were the bedrooms, with porches fronting on an open courtyard surrounded by a peristyle of, in this case, Doric columns. As was customary with Roman houses, the numerous blank walls were either brightly painted or decorated with murals like those on the two square columns and exterior bedroom walls in figure 10.3. The combination of Roman atrium and Hellenistic Greek peristyle court, which was adopted in the second century B.C., makes the Roman house or villa an ideal design for hot Mediterranean summers.

Maintaining a strong sense of identity was a major concern for Roman families; they preserved collections of exact portrait masks in wax of their ancestors.

Figure 10.4 Bust of Julius Caesar, first century B.C. Marble, height 38″. National Museum, Naples.

Figure 10.6 Three portrait busts of Caesar Augustus. British Museum, London. Reproduced by courtesy of the Trustees of the British Museum.

Figure 10.5 *Augustus of Primaporta,* ca. 20 B.C. **Marble,** height 81″. Vatican Museums, Rome.

Recognizable portrayals were therefore required, accounting for the long tradition of starkly realistic marble portrait busts as represented, for example, by the bust of Julius Caesar (fig. 10.4). As the man responsible for the final demise of the embattled Republic, Caesar is depicted as history has revealed him to be: imperious, ruthless, a charismatic leader of men. With their no-nonsense approach to reality, the Romans insisted upon an exactitude that included every wart, pimple, line, and blemish. This bust may have been done from life; if so, it is possible that Caesar relished the portrait, particularly the commanding tilt of the head.

There are no blemishes on the commanding statue of Caesar Augustus from the Imperial Villa at Primaporta (fig. 10.5). Idealized in the Greek manner, this is how Augustus intended to be seen and to be remembered—a noble ruler. Based on the *Doryphoros* (see fig. 7.35), with the commanding gesture probably derived from Near Eastern art, this is an official portrait. With his likeness on Roman coins and with thousands of busts like those in figure 10.6 distributed throughout the Empire, Augustus created the imperial image of powerful Rome. Based on Virgil's tracing of his ancestry to Aeneas, founder of Rome, Augustus's divine origins are revealed here in the cupid and the dolphin, symbols of Venus, mother of Aeneas. Indicating the secular history, the statue's cloak has fallen low enough to reveal the relief sculpture on the armor detailing the emperor's road to power. The only realistic elements are the tactile illusions of leather, metal, and cloth that give the feeling of actuality prized by Romans but considered trite by Greeks. Becoming a stock device for depicting kings, emperors, and dictators, the commanding gesture will also be seen in the figure of Christ in the Royal Portal of Chartres Cathedral (see fig. 15.39) and

Figure 10.7 Maison Carrée, ca. 19 B.C., Nîmes, France.

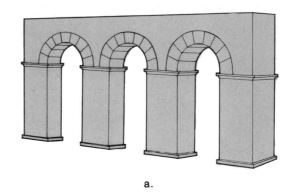

a.

Figure 10.8 Corinthian capital

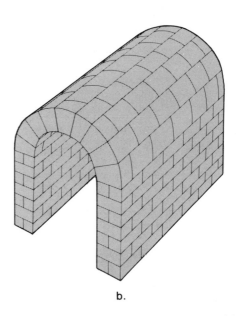

b.

Figure 10.9 (a) Semicircular arch arcade (b) Semicircular arch vault.

in Michelangelo's Christ of the *Last Judgment* in the Sistine Chapel. The *Augustus of Primaporta* is a superb example of a didactic art form, probably forever after destined to serve church and state.

Though no intact Augustan temples remain in Rome, the remarkably well preserved temple nicknamed the Maison Carrée (marble house; fig. 10.7) embodies the qualities advocated by the emperor. Unlike their Greek counterparts, Roman temples stand on high podiums and are entered from the front by a single flight of steps. The open form of the Greek temple, with a walkway and three steps on all four sides, has been converted to the closed form of buildings designed to enclose space. This temple uses the rich Corinthian order (fig. 10.8) favored by most Roman architects and engaged columns attached to the cella walls in a decorative device from Republican days. A small building measuring 59′ × 117′ with 30′ columns, the Maison Carrée became a prototype of temples honoring notable emperors, much as the Jefferson Memorial in Washington memorializes an illustrious president. This building, in fact, inspired

Thomas Jefferson to utilize the classic style of Rome in his neoclassic designs of the Virginia State Capitol, the University of Virginia, and his own home of Monticello.

Rome made a lasting contribution to the development of the rounded arch and vault as structural architectural principles. Used for centuries in Asia Minor and Greece for lesser works like gates, storage areas, corridors, and sewers, the arch was exploited by Roman engineers on a massive scale. They were concerned with spanning and enclosing space, and thus used arches to build bridges, aqueducts, baths, and basilicas, the secular structures necessary for the efficient operation of Roman cities. A semicircle of stone blocks, or bricks and mortar (fig. 10.9), spanning spaces between piers or walls, the arch was better suited to the utilitarian needs of Roman engineering than the post and lintel system. Not intended to bridge large spaces, the lintel is the weaker portion of the system because it can support a limited amount of weight. To bear greater loads it must be enlarged, the columns moved closer together, or both.

Figure 10.10 Pont du Gard, ca. 20–10 B.C., near Nîmes, France.

Figure 10.11 Roman Mausoleum, ca. A.D. 40, St.-Rémy-du-Provence, France.

In the arch, the wedge-shaped blocks called *voussoirs* (voo–SWAHR) curve up to the keystone at the apex of the arch, giving strength and stability because of the mutually supporting pressures from pier to keystone. From the keystone the thrust is transmitted through the voussoirs down through the pier, or wall, to the ground. When the arches are side by side they form an arcade, as in the Pont du Gard (see fig. 10.10). When extended longitudinally along its axis, the arch is called a barrel or tunnel vault, as in the Arch of Titus (see fig. 10.18).

Representing Roman engineering and power, aqueducts were a highly visible portion of the network of waterways and roadways that interconnected the empire. Built by Agrippa, a lieutenant under Augustus, the Pont du Gard (fig. 10.10) is 180' high and in its present condition about 900' long. It carried water some twenty-five miles from the mountains, across the gorge of the Gard River, and into Nîmes. Spanning over 80', each massive arch supports an arch of similar dimensions but with much less masonry, which in turn undergirds the watercourse itself. Supported by three small arches for each large one, the water flowed steadily down an approximate 1 percent grade, dropping about one foot every hundred feet. Using stones weighing up to six tons each and assembled without mortar, the bridge of the lowest arcade has been in continuous use for two thousand years.

The best-preserved of all Roman funerary memorials, the so-called Mausoleum (fig. 10.11) is actually a cenotaph that honors the dead but does not contain the remains. Erected in honor of two grandsons of Augustus who died in childhood, the three-stage structure has reliefs on the solid base and engaged Corinthian columns flanking the second-level arches. Statues of the two children are within the circular third level. The combination of reliefs, projecting cornices, squared-off arches, and rounded forms is eclectic rather than classical and illustrates how far removed Roman opulence is from Greek restraint.

In *Herakles Discovering the Infant Telephos in Arcadia* (fig. 10.12) we see an example of the continuing interest in classical themes, which formed one of the bridges between Greek and Roman cultures. The powerful nude figure stands before a classically conceived woman representing the mythical Arcadia, where everyone lived at peace with one another and with nature. The lion is painted in a vaguely impressionistic manner, while the doe in the left foreground is light, lovely, and graceful. The disparate figures look like they have been placed in a preexisting space with little concern for how they relate to each other or to the overall unity of the painting. In common with much Roman painting, the work does display, however, great technical skill in the manipulation of light, lines, and shapes, and in the illusion of three-dimensional space.

Figure 10.12 *Herakles Discovering the Infant Telephos in Arcadia,* wall painting from Herculaneum, ca. A.D. 70, approximately 86" × 74". Roman copy of a Hellenistic painting of second century B.C. National Museum, Naples.

Figure 10.13 Reconstruction of fourth-century Rome (detail) by I. Gismondi. Museum of Roman Civilization, Rome.

A comparison of the assemblage of visual images of the *Herakles* with the figure of the *Doryphoros* (see fig. 7.35) illustrates some fundamental differences between Greek and Roman cultures. More concerned with practice than theory, the Romans itemized rather than conceptualized. The *Herakles* is a kind of visual catalog of a specific event: Herakles finding his son in Arcadia. The *Doryphoros* is not a specific person but a realization of the ideal athlete, the embodiment of a concept against which individual athletes measured themselves. The Romans portrayed people as they were and the Greeks depicted them as they should be. The Romans were practical, the Greeks theoretical. It is no wonder that the Romans viewed the Greeks with awe, contempt, envy, and suspicion. The Romans accepted the world, with its imperfections as it was; the Greeks wanted something better. The quarreling Greek city-states were forcibly united by Alexander; Rome conquered the world.

That Greek culture was generally superior to any other was acknowledged by the Romans, and Greek literature, art, and architecture became basic strands in the fabric of Roman civilization. The empire was, in fact, administered in both languages—the Latin of the ruling Romans and the Greek of the conquered Hellenes. (Try to imagine Napoleon administering the French Empire in French *and* German.) Where the two cultures differed significantly was in sheer size. Athens of the Golden Age had a population of about 100,000; Imperial Rome had a much larger population and greater wealth. It also had the endless problems that plague large cities in any culture. Shown in figure 10.13 is part of the central section of a city with over fifty miles of streets, almost none with names, and a population in the second century A.D. of about 1,200,000. Much of the area shown was constructed by the Flavian emperors (A.D. 69–96); the monumental civic structures were completed by Nerva, Trajan, and Hadrian (A.D. 96–138).

In the far upper left of the model can be seen the Baths of Trajan; with a central complex of thermal rooms surrounded by thermal rooms further enclosed by peripheral rooms, this became the model for all subsequent imperial baths. Near the bottom of the model is the Circus Maximus, the primary stadium for chariot racing and the common meeting ground for all levels of Roman society (see the selection from Ovid on p. 243). Achieving its final form in about 329 B.C. the stadium enclosed a race course measuring 220 yards × 650 yards. Seating about 250,000 spectators and operating a full racing program on 240 days of the year, the Circus Maximus could, with full houses, total about seventy million admissions a year. Thinking big was the Roman way.

Figure 10.14 Colosseum, A.D. 72–80, 513′ × 620′ × 161′ high, Rome.

Figure 10.15 Colosseum, Rome (aerial view)

Directly above the Circus Maximus are the Imperial Forums and the Claudius Aqueduct leading to the Palatine, highest of the seven hills of Rome and urban abode of the aristocracy. Seen at the upper left is the Colosseum, the single most representative building of the Roman Empire, then and now. Designed for the staging of battles between various combinations of animals and gladiators, the Colosseum seated about 50,000 spectators around an arena measuring 156′ × 258′. With underground corridors for gladiators, animals, and technicians, and elaborate stage equipment for crowd-pleasing effects, the Colosseum was a complete entertainment center. Built on four levels, the exterior is unified by four superimposed orders of columns (fig. 10.14). Beginning with a simplification of the Doric column called Tuscan, the columns mount upwards through the Ionic and Corinthian orders to flat Corinthian piers called *pilasters.* Topping the wall are sockets for pennants and for a removable canvas covering that helped keep off the sun and rain. A key design unit in the exterior wall is the characteristic combination of a Roman arch flanked by a Greek order. Called the Roman arch order, the basic elements are a Roman arch set in a Greek post and lintel frame. Used in triumphal arches and other structures, this device was revived in the Italian Renaissance and can be seen today in neoclassic building facades in Europe and America.

Invented by the Romans as a derivation of Greek theatre design, the Colosseum is an amphitheatre (Gk., *amphi,* both; *theatron,* theatre). As the name indicates, this building is actually two theatres facing each other to form an oval-shaped bowl (fig. 10.15). Brilliantly designed and executed, the Colosseum exemplifies the qualities the Roman architect Vitruvius (first century B.C.) considered basic for superior design: firmness, commodity, and delight. Structurally sound in its own day (firmness), the Colosseum functioned exceptionally well as a grand arena with eighty portals for easy ingress and egress, comfortable seating, and unobstructed sightlines (commodity). Though not a prime Roman concern, it does have a quality of "delight," an aesthetic appeal that makes a work of art exalted and memorable.

Erected by the Flavian emperors, the Colosseum, also known as the Flavian Amphitheatre, was largely built by prisoners of the Jewish Wars, which had ended in A.D. 70 with the conquest of Jerusalem and the destruction of the Temple of Solomon. Dedicated by Titus in A.D. 80, the Colosseum opened with inaugural ceremonies that lasted 100 days and that were, according to contemporary accounts, very successful, costing the lives of some 9,000 wild animals and 2,000 gladiators.

The Colosseum was the largest Roman amphitheatre (see Martial's "On the Dedication of the Colosseum in Rome" on p. 249), but its basic design was anything but innovative. Apparently the amphitheatre concept was first realized at Pompeii in about 80 B.C. and copied throughout the empire before finally appearing in Rome. The Roman procedure was to develop a workable design and then to increase the efficiency of later structures through improved engineering. Amphitheatres are still used today in Verona, Italy and in France at Nîmes and Arles (fig. 10.16), testifying to the remarkable stability of Roman structural engineering. The amphitheatre at Verona is used for operatic productions, but the one at Arles is mainly a bullring.

With stability restored after the murderous excesses of Caligula and Nero, the Flavian emperors (Vespasian, Titus, and Domitian, 69–96) presided over an ever larger and richer empire. Despite attempts, especially by Vespasian, to return to the austerity of sober Republican days, Flavian artists became highly proficient in the dynamic sculptural techniques of Praxiteles and the Hellenistic sculptors. Representative of the high fashion of the Flavian age, the portrait

Figure 10.16 Roman amphitheatre, ca. 46 B.C., 21,000 capacity. Arles, France.

Figure 10.17 *Flavian Woman,* ca. A.D. 80. Marble, life-size. J. Paul Getty Museum, Santa Monica, California.

of a Flavian woman (fig. 10.17) is notable both for the towering coiffure and for its relentless Roman realism. Undoubtedly a Flavian aristocrat, the lady is as homely as she is stylish.

Julius Caesar contended that the only truly effective way of controlling conquered people was to execute every man, woman, and child. However, the practical Roman alternative to extermination was the conversion of prisoners of war into a tractable slave labor force. One of the most effective propaganda devices for impressing their bondage on the slaves was the triumphal arch, a symbolic representation of the yoke of oxen. In a ritualistic dramatization of Roman might, victorious generals marched their prisoners through hastily erected temporary arches to the accompaniment of Roman battle trumpets and drums. The overall effect was meant to be awesome and intimidating.

To commemorate his brother Titus's destruction of Jerusalem in A.D. 70, Domitian had a permanent version of the triumphal arch erected where the Via Sacra enters the Roman Forum (fig. 10.18). (By the end of the empire there would be over sixty triumphal arches in Rome and many more throughout the empire.) Constructed of concrete with a marble facing, the Arch of Titus utilized a Roman arch order similar to that of the Colosseum. Massive piers with dual-engaged columns provided a post and lintel frame for a deep Roman arch vault (see fig. 10.9). With a superstructure called the *attic* bearing the commemorative inscription, the walls of the vault were decorated with high reliefs depicting Titus's successful campaign against the Jews. Symbolizing a major Roman victory, the arch was also a graphic reminder for all slaves, especially the Jews who labored on the Colosseum, of the futility of opposing the might of Rome.

Figure 10.18 Arch of Titus, A.D. 81, Rome

Figure 10.19 Column of Trajan, ca. A.D. 106–113. Marble, height 125′ with base, Rome.

Figure 10.20 Column of Trajan, detail

The assassination of Domitian in A.D. 96 ended the Flavian dynasty and ushered in the era of the so-called good emperors: Nerva, Trajan, Hadrian, Antoninus Pius, and Marcus Aurelius (96–180). The first non-Italian to occupy the throne, the brilliant Spanish general, Trajan, led Rome to the maximum expansion of her empire. Among the monuments commemorating his phenomenal successes is the Column of Trajan (fig. 10.19), an unprecedented conception. Carved in low relief in 150 scenes, the 658′ frieze narrates the highlights of Trajan's two campaigns into Dacia (modern Romania and Hungary). To "read" the story it is necessary to walk around and around the column, but it soon becomes impossible to read it without binoculars. How and if this story was read in its entirety has never been satisfactorily explained. Perhaps there were special viewing balconies or perhaps slaves were stationed at the base of the monument delivering illuminating lectures and selling guidebooks.

Though the inspiration for this unusual monument is unknown, it is perhaps significant that it was placed between the Latin and Greek libraries of Trajan; the column is quite similar to library books of the time—*rotuli* (scrolls), which were wound on two spindles. The basic inspiration, however, is the "continuous narration" technique, which is so typically Roman, as opposed to Greek "simultaneous narration." The Greek unities of time, place, and action as observed in the Parthenon frieze (see fig. 7.51) were apparently not suitable for the day-to-day world of empire building. Reflected in the Column of Trajan

is Roman interest in biography and history; the basic unity is the focus on the leadership of Trajan while history is served by the unfolding scenes of campaigns. A detail from the bottom of the column (fig. 10.20) depicts a river god, symbolizing the Danube, and landscapes as stylized stage sets. Artistic details are minimized, making the soldiers the prime figures of the Roman conquest. Executed under the direction of a single artist, the frieze is a masterpiece of didactic art in the tradition of the *Augustus of Primaporta* (see fig. 10.5). The column was originally topped by a statue of Trajan, which was destroyed during the Middle Ages; the figure now standing at the top is a sixteenth-century statue of St. Peter. The first pope of the Church of Rome is positioned over a visual record of two bloody Roman campaigns, symbolizing the Church's triumph over Rome.

Probably the best educated of all Roman emperors and certainly the most cosmopolitan, Hadrian (117–138) was more interested in improving the cultural life of the empire than in extending political frontiers. Indicating the extent of the Roman Empire at that time, Hadrian lived and worked in Britain, southern France, Spain, Morocco, Asia Minor, Greece, Tunisia, Greece (again), Syria, Palestine, and Egypt. He finally returned after ten years abroad to build Hadrian's Villa at Tivoli near Rome. A student of all things Greek, Hadrian was more concerned with supporting the intellectual life of Greece than with whatever took place in the mercantile environment of Rome. He did, however, strongly support the most advanced concepts of Roman architects in their designs of interior space.

One of the most revolutionary and authoritative structures ever built, the Pantheon (fig. 10.21) has influenced the architecture of every age since from ancient Rome to the present day. The inscription on the frieze, "M. AGRIPPA L.F. COS TERTIUM FECIT"

Figure 10.21 The Pantheon, ca. A.D. 118–125, Rome.

Figure 10.22 *Equestrian Statue of Marcus Aurelius,* ca. A.D. 161–180. Bronze, over life size. Piazza del Campidoglio, Rome.

(Marcus Agrippa, son of Lucius, consul for the third time, built this), does not refer to this building but to previous structures erected in 27–25 B.C. by Agrippa, son-in-law of Augustus. Because the original buildings included baths and a temple called Pantheon (Gk., to all the gods), Hadrian, displaying his fine sense of Roman history, had the original inscription repeated on the new temple. With a portico 59′ high and measuring 143′ in the interior (diameter and height), the Pantheon is topped by one of the largest domes ever built. (St. Peter's dome is 140′ in diameter and that of Florence Cathedral averages 137½′.) Twenty feet thick at the outside edge, the poured concrete dome decreases to less than five feet at the center. Resting on eight enormous piers and providing interior lighting with a circular opening *(oculus)* that is nearly 30′ in diameter, the dome is coffered (indented panels) to decrease the weight without sacrificing structural strength. The water from rainstorms can be drained away in a matter of minutes by a plumbing system that still works. The Pantheon is the best preserved of all Roman buildings because it was converted into a Christian church early in the history of the Church of Rome.

The eight-column front of Corinthian capitals topping polished granite columns is, in effect, a Greek portico opening into a massive drum derived from the circular Greek tholos. One of the most astounding spatial accomplishments in architecture, the impressiveness of the interior is communicated better by the Panini painting (colorplate 8) than by any contemporary photograph. Originally painted blue, the hemisphere of concrete was highlighted with rosettes of gilded bronze set into each coffer. Softly colored columns alternate with marble panels, pilasters, and niches, forming a harmonious blend within a single, self-sufficient, uninterrupted space. Dedicated to the worship of the seven planetary gods, the Pantheon is a stunning human version of the sky itself, the Dome of Heaven.

The bronze head of Hadrian (colorplate 9), which wears a trim beard in the Greek manner, was probably created during the enlightened reign of that remarkable monarch. A combination of the staid portrait style of Republican tradition and the glamorous, more sensuous Hellenistic imperial style, the bust was found in the Thames River under London Bridge. That a masterful portrait of this most urbane of Roman rulers should be found in the outermost reaches of empire symbolizes the international culture of Rome. Writing during the reign of Trajan, the Greek biographer Plutarch remarked, "I am a citizen, not of Athens or of Greece, but of the world."

The last of the illustrious Antonine emperors,[1] Marcus Aurelius (161–180) was an unusual combination of distinguished general and Stoic philosopher. Most un-Roman in his detestation of war, he confined his military activities to defending the borders against barbarian incursions, particularly in the Balkans. It was on that distant frontier that the philosopher-king died in the performance of his stoic duty towards the state. As depicted in the only equestrian statue surviving from the ancient world (fig. 10.22), the emperor wore a beard in the Greek style first adopted by Hadrian. With his right arm extended in the characteristic gesture of a general about to address his troops, the emperor is both commanding and resigned to the necessity of fulfilling his responsibilities. Vigorous and impatient, the high-spirited warhorse displays the artist's exceptional knowledge of equine anatomy. Originally the head of a conquered

---

1. The very last Antonine was Commodus (180–192), the son of Marcus Aurelius. Anything but illustrious, he was corrupt, demented, and, ultimately, the victim of a household conspiracy.

Figure 10.23 *Head of a Bearded Man,* ca. A.D. 250. Marble, life size. J. Paul Getty Museum, Santa Monica, California.

Figure 10.24 Arch of Constantine, A.D. 312–315, Rome.

Figure 10.25 *Constantine the Great,* ca. A.D. 330. Marble, height 8′. Palazzo dei Conservatori, Rome.

warrior was under the raised right hoof of the charger as a symbol of Roman dominance. That the imperial bronze survived at all was due to a case of mistaken identity; Christians mistook it for a depiction of the Emperor Constantine.

After the death of Marcus Aurelius in 180, the empire was in an almost continual state of disruption. Between 235 and 284 there were no less than 26 "barracks emperors" sponsored by various army factions. The accession of Diocletian in 284 replaced anarchy with a rigid despotism under which the Roman Senate lost the last vestige of its by then ephemeral powers. A time of agony and despair, the chaotic third century saw the flourishing of many mystery cults as people sought spiritual salvation in the midst of nihilism. Representative of the malaise of the time, the *Head of a Bearded Man* (fig. 10.23) is a study in ambivalence: hopefulness coupled with despair, spiritual aspirations conflicting with the problem of sheer physical survival. It was the worst of times.

Seizing power from his corulers, Constantine (312–337) represented the last effective authority in an empire doomed to destruction from external assaults and from internal corruption and decadence. Built to celebrate his assumption of sole imperial power, the Arch of Constantine (fig. 10.24) was wholly dependent on its predecessors for its impressive appearance. In an attempt to recapture the glorious past, the three-arch design was copied from the Arch of Septimus Severus (ca. 203) in the Roman Forum, while the eight Corinthian columns are literally from the time of Domitian (81–96). The freestanding statues, with heads recarved to resemble Constantine, were lifted from monuments to Trajan, Hadrian, and Marcus Aurelius. Despite the borrowed design and transferred columns and statues, there is little trace of the Hellenic tradition. The inferior craftsmanship of the carved reliefs can be explained by a shortage of skilled artists; there had been no official relief sculpture in nearly a century. Despite the technical inadequacies, the shift from classical to a new Constantinian style appears, however, to have been deliberate. Compare, for example, the classical style of the Augustus of Primaporta (see fig. 10.5) with the head of Constantine the Great (fig. 10.25). In addition to

Colorplate 8 Giovanni Paolo Panini, *The Interior of the Pantheon.* Samuel H. Kress Collection. National Gallery of Art, Washington, D.C.

Colorplate 9 *Head of Emperor Hadrian*. Bronze, height 16″. Roman provincial work of second century A.D. British Museum, London. Reproduced by permission of the Trustees of the British Museum.

Colorplate 10 Interior, San Vitale, Ravenna

Colorplate 11 *Emperor Justinian and His Courtiers*, ca. 547. Mosaic, San Vitale, Ravenna

Colorplate 12 *Empress Theodora and Retinue,* ca. 547. Mosaic, San Vitale, Ravenna

the notable stylistic differences, it is clear that the latter is intended as a much more obvious symbol of imperial majesty *and* spiritual superiority. Part of a colossal statue enthroned in his basilica, the masterful modeling of the head demonstrates a total awareness of the Hellenistic tradition with the significant exception of the remarkably large eyes. Carved even with a marble fleck representing light reflecting from the cornea, these are not the eyes of a mere man; this is an exalted being, unique in authority and vision, with godlike eyes fixed upon infinity. Symbolizing sanctity and sometimes saintliness, oversized eyes become a convention in Early Christian and Byzantine art.

Though a miniature in fact and truly miniscule when compared with the head of Constantine, the *Diptych of Consul Boethius* (bow–E–thi–us; fig. 10.26) is similar to the bust in that the artist has denied the physical reality of Boethius and emphasized instead his authority and spirit. Costume, body, and space are reduced to patterned lines that are more emotional than representational. One of the last Roman consuls and the author of *Consolation of Philosophy* (A.D. 524), the other-worldliness of Boethius can be compared to the physical reality of the *Augustus of Primaporta* (see fig. 10.5). Both share the commanding arm gesture—a symbol of authority—but all else has changed. In the *Augustus* we see a man with supreme authority and in the *Boethius* there is depicted supreme authority that happens to be a man.

The Artistic Legacy of Rome

Roman achievements in architecture were notable and still act upon the modern world. The first to achieve mastery of enclosing space, Roman prototypes are visible today in grandiose train stations, monumental public buildings, and the ubiquitous football and soccer stadiums patterned after the Colosseum. In fact, one essential difference between the Astrodome and the Colosseum is that the latter had a removable canvas roof. With their superbly designed roads, bridges, and aqueducts, Roman engineers made essential contributions to civilizing and humanizing people that were fully as important as their monuments, buildings, and stadiums. Indeed, roads, bridges, and sewers may be as essential for the development of civilization as art, music, and literature.

Sculpture was as common in the Roman world as billboards are in the United States, but considerably more attractive. Streets, buildings, and homes were filled with portrait busts and freestanding statues or reliefs of the gods of all major and minor religions. Included were masterpieces confiscated from Greece and Egypt and mass-produced copies of Greek works of all periods. A compelling urge to create was characteristic of Greek artists, while the Romans were often content to copy. It was in portraiture and historical narrative that Roman artists excelled, precisely because they were copyists of the world as they saw it.

Figure 10.26 *Diptych of Consul Boethius,* ca. A.D. 487. Ivory miniature. Brescia Museum, Italy.

The little that is left of Roman painting was found mainly in the ruins of Pompeii and Herculaneum (see fig. 10.12), which were buried by the eruption of Vesuvius in A.D. 79. Excavations beginning in the eighteenth century have revealed at least four major styles of painting. Whether this work was accomplished by Greek, Hellenistic, or Roman artists cannot be determined. Furthermore, later development of painting during the enlightened regimes of the Antonines may never be known. Deeply indebted to Greek developments in painting techniques, it is safe to assume that Roman painters produced works comparable to the Pantheon and the *Augustus of Primaporta.*

Roman Music

No Roman music survives nor are there any extant musical documents or theoretical treatises. With nothing original to contribute, the Romans were content to use the brass instruments of the Etruscans and to adopt the whole of Greek musical culture. Though some musical instruments have survived, our knowledge of Roman music has been derived from sculptures, mosaics, wall paintings, and references to music by Cicero, Seneca, and Quintilian. According to the evidence, music was highly esteemed, particularly in association with poetry. Interested in the visual arts mainly as collectors, the patrician class left the messy business of painting and sculpting to artisans and slaves. Writing verse and singing to lute accompaniment was, however, a worthy pursuit for wealthy amateurs of both sexes. The arts of poetry and music added to the social graces of patricians and emperors alike. Hadrian wrote poetry in Latin and Greek and, like Antoninus Pius and the tyrant Caracalla, was an accomplished performer on the kithara and the hydraulis.[2] A kind of chamber instrument with clear and delicate tones, the effect of the hydraulis was described by Cicero as a "sensation as delectable to the ears as the most delicious fish to the palate."

Music of a public nature provided appropriate settings for acrobats, pantomime, popular theatre, dancing, chariot racing, gladiatorial combat, and the maneuvers of Roman troops. Commensurate with Roman ideas of grandeur, instruments were increased in number and size, particularly the trumpets and drums that relayed battle commands to the Roman legions. Quintilian, in fact, equated the brassy loudness of Roman trumpets with the supremacy of Roman arms. Audiences in amphitheatres were treated to musical spectacles featuring huge choral and instrumental groups that sometimes outnumbered the spectators. The limpid-toned hydraulis was converted to an advertising medium for the proclaiming of gladiatorial contests. Traveling on a large wagon and with vastly increased air pressure supplied by hordes of toiling slaves, the now strident tone had a reputed range of over three miles.[3]

Roman drama omitted the Greek choruses but used musical interludes throughout, all of which were composed by specialists rather than by the dramatists themselves, as had been the case with Greek drama. The aulos, called *tibia* in Latin, and the kithara were still employed much as they were in Greek plays and generally played by Greek musicians, who were usually more skilled than Roman musicians. Nero fancied himself an outstanding instrumentalist and had coins minted depicting him playing the kithara. He did not start the great fire that burned most of Rome in 64 nor, contrary to legend, did he "fiddle while Rome burned." He was blamed for the fire, however, and launched the first persecution of the new Christian sect to divert attention from himself.

Using a variety of drums plus trumpetlike instruments such as the buccina, lituus, and tuba, official bands were important components of military establishments throughout the empire. With their ceremonial music they effectively proclaimed the magnificence of the state, much as military bands have done in just about every culture since ancient times.

Bibliography

Brilliant, Richard. *Roman Art: From the Republic to Constantine.* New York: Praeger Publishers, 1974. Good overall survey.

Brown, Frank A. *Roman Architecture.* 7th ed. New York: George Braziller, Inc., 1979. Many photographs of Roman structures plus reconstructions, building plans, and city plans. Paperback.

Grant, Michael. *The Art and Life of Pompeii and Herculaneum.* New York: Newsweek, 1979. Everyday living.

Hanfmann, George M. *Roman Art: A Modern Survey of the Art of Ancient Rome.* New York: W. W. Norton & Co., 1975. Includes recent archeological discoveries.

Kraus, Theodor. *Pompeii and Herculaneum.* Milano: Silvana Editoriale d'Arte, 1973. The text is Italian but the illustrations are gorgeous.

Maiuri, Amadeo. *Roman Painting.* New York: Skira, 1953. Superbly done, especially the colorplates.

Smith, E. Baldwin. *Architectural Symbolism in Imperial Rome and the Middle Ages.* Princeton: Princeton University Press, 1956. An impressive work that makes architecture comprehensible in terms of politics, economics, and religion.

Wheeler, Mortimer. *Roman Art and Architecture.* New York: Frederick A. Praeger, Inc., 1964. Lucid and comprehensive account. Invaluable. Paperback.

2. Hydraulis (Gk., *hydor,* water; *aulos,* pipe) invented ca. 300 B.C. Of Near Eastern origin and improved on by the Greeks, this was actually a pipe organ. Air was pumped into an inverted bowl with air pressure controlled by the volume of water holding the bowl in place. Adding water increased the pressure of the air supplied to the pipes and thus the volume of sound. Though no instruments have survived, a precise clay model found in the ruins of Carthage has provided enough information for modern reconstructions.

3. The association of the hydraulis with the so-called games in the arena, especially those with assorted lions and Christians, delayed for many centuries the introduction of the pipe organ into Christian services.

Unit **4**

Judaism and Christianity
The Star and the Cross

11

Faith, Hope, and Love: The Judeo-Christian Tradition

It was pointed out in the preceding unit on Rome that life in the later years of the Empire was a matter of increasing disillusionment and pessimism. Epicureanism is grounded on pessimism; Stoicism is at best a resignation to the evil of the world; popular cults provided little abiding satisfaction. The discontent and dissatisfaction were not found only among thinkers and philosophers, but were shared by the common people. A Roman epitaph found rather frequently reveals the spirit of cynicism and disillusion; it reads

I was not
I was
I am not
I do not care

One could scarcely go further in general world-weariness; yet the sentiment was not uncommon.

There were two conflicting tendencies during this period and earlier. One was the general disbelief in the old Olympian religion, and a cynical attitude toward emperor-worship; the intellectual element in the population was skeptical about religion in general. The other was, contradictorily, the appeal of mystical cults and religions, usually of oriental origin: Mithraism, the worship of Isis, the cult of Cybele, and the like. However much scoffing or indifferent disregard there may have been at the upper level of society, the poor and uneducated were ready for the emotional appeal of any religiosity that softened their uncertainties and insecurities; there was a need for comfort and reassurance.

The genius of the Greeks was intellectual rather than moral or spiritual, and the Romans had little to add on the latter score to what they inherited from the Greeks. Both peoples had advocated the life lived according to reason. For a Plato, an Aristotle, a Cato, such a life could be worthy and satisfying, but not many men in any generation are of such caliber, and even those few are often felt to be wanting in human warmth. At best, the God whom Aristotle finds the sum of perfection is cold, distant, and aloof from human affairs: a noble concept, but again lacking warmth.

Reason, important as it is, has never been the only tool in man's possession. Call it emotion, belief, faith, there is something that is not in the same category. No one will seriously give six good reasons why he or she loves the beloved, for love is not "reasonable." That is not to say that it is necessarily contrary to reason; it simply moves in another category. That "something" beyond reason may be considered the compulsion of a moral ideal, or a yearning for spiritual satisfaction; it is more pronounced in some people than in others, but hardly ever totally absent in any individual. It is precisely such a range of human experience that the perhaps overly-intellectualized philosophical traditions of Greece and Rome failed to satisfy.

While the Greek and Roman cultures were developing—cultures devoted to two forms of rationalism—a third and entirely different type of society had come into being in Palestine. A vast amount of pure intellectual power has gone into the development of Jewish doctrine, but the core of Judaism is faith, as faith is different from, though not opposed to, reason. The Hebrew religion itself, and as it has had wider influence through Christianity, wove another strand into the great amalgam we call Western civilization.[1]

The Chosen People

The Hebrews would have been just another set of Near Eastern tribes, small in number and lacking talent for art and invention, had it not been for their remarkable religion. Other civilizations have come and gone; they alone have maintained their culture essentially intact for four thousand years.

Following the leadership of Abraham, the Hebrews emigrated (ca. 1950 B.C.) from the Sumerian city of Ur in the Euphrates valley to the west, eventually arriving in the "Land of Canaan" (later called Palestine). Probably prompted by famine, many Hebrews followed Joseph to Egypt and into slavery, from which they were delivered by Moses. Leading the Children of Israel into Sinai (ca. 1300 B.C.), Moses gave them the concept of a single tribal God, Yahweh (or Jehovah), and a covenant with the deity based on their acceptance of his commandments.

The Promised Land of "milk and honey" was taken by conquest, with the key city of Jericho falling to Joshua in 1230 B.C. By 1020 they had formed a monarchy with Saul as king. The height of Hebrew political power was reached with the United Kingdom of Palestine under David (1000–960) and Solomon (960–922), followed by a division into Israel (933–722) and Judah (933–586). Conquered by the Assyrians in 722 B.C., they were later carried into exile by King Nebuchadnezzar (Babylonian Captivity, 586–538 B.C.). Allowed to return to Jerusalem by the Persian king Cyrus the Great, they rebuilt the Temple of Solomon but were politically subservient to three successive empires: Persian, Hellenistic, and Roman.

During the first century A.D. the Jews rebelled against Rome. Jerusalem was totally destroyed and much of the population was killed or driven from the land, a Diaspora (Dye–AS–po–ra; "scattering") that was to last nearly two thousand years.

The will to resist and to survive was based on their religion, Judaism,[2] four aspects of which were different from all other Near Eastern religions.

1. Monotheism: There was only one God and he came to be viewed as universal.
2. Covenant: God chose Israel to be his people and they accepted him as their God.
3. Graven images: Images of God or of any living thing were prohibited.
4. The name of God (Yahweh, meaning "he causes to be" or "the creator") was not to be taken "in vain," i.e., was not to be spoken.

Let us examine each of these concepts. Beginning with the Mosaic period in the Sinai, Yahweh was the primary God among many: "You shall have no other gods before me" (Exodus 20:3). This concept gradually evolved into a monotheism in which there was one Hebrew God and, later, one universal God. The first people to insist upon monotheism, the Jews found this to be, throughout their history, their greatest source of strength.

The covenant was a religious bond that the Hebrews made of their own free will with Yahweh. Moses climbed the mountain and returned with knowledge of God's will—"commandments" inscribed on tablets of stone and subsequently amplified in the Torah. In a narrow sense the Torah consists of the first five books of the Bible, the so-called Pentateuch, or Books of Moses. Torah means Law but it also means "teaching" or "direction." In the broad modern sense, Torah refers to the total content of God's unending revelation to and through Israel.

The prohibition of graven images separated Judaism from all other religions, which represented their gods in a variety of ways. This stricture, designed to guard against idolatry, had the effect of nullifying any significant artistic development.

The injunction against using the Lord's name in vain emphasized a reverence unknown to other ancient religions.

In sum, Judaism was a People in covenant with God, a Book (the Hebrew Scriptures), a Way of Life, and a Hope grounded in Faith.

---

1. See chap. 15 for an overview of Islam and its culture.
2. A term coined by Greek-speaking Jews to distinguish their religious way of life from that of the Hellenes. Though the term is late, the religion to which it refers goes back to the beginnings of Jewish spiritual life.

Prophecy

The Hebrew prophets of the eighth to fifth centuries B.C. emerged from a tradition of augurs and seers who, as they did in other religions, sought to ascertain the divine will and to forecast the future through dreams, divinations, and induced ecstasy. Eventually these professionals were denounced as "false prophets" and replaced by a succession of preachers, mystics, moralists, and poets who felt themselves to be speaking for Yahweh. Prophets like Amos and Isaiah spoke as instruments of Yahweh's creative purpose in the lives of his people. Ethical considerations were primary and the predictive element secondary, an extension of ethical and religious tendencies into a foreseeable future. Stressing righteousness and justice, the prophets spoke and, more importantly, wrote as restorers and conservators of Israel's inspiring spiritual heritage. Not always accepted by various classes of society, they preached an uncompromising and lofty doctrine of ethical monotheism.

The first and perhaps most important of the notable eighth-century prophets, Amos preached against luxury, corruption, and selfishness, pointing the way to altruism and a higher form of religion.

¹¹Therefore because you trample upon the poor
    and take from him exactions of wheat,
you have built houses of hewn stone,
    but you shall not dwell in them;
you have planted pleasant vineyards,
    but you shall not drink their wine.
¹²For I know how many are your transgressions,
    and how great are your sins—
you who afflict the righteous, who take a bribe,
    and turn aside the needy in the gate.
¹³Therefore he who is prudent will keep silent in such a
      time;
    for it is an evil time.
¹⁴Seek good, and not evil,
    that you may live;
and so the LORD, the God of hosts, will be with you,
    as you have said.
¹⁵Hate evil, and love good,
    and establish justice in the gate;
it may be that the LORD, the God of hosts,
    will be gracious to the remnant of Joseph.

                        Amos 5:11–15

⁴"Woe to those who lie upon beds of ivory,
    and stretch themselves upon their couches,
and eat lambs from the flock,
    and calves from the midst of the stall;
⁵who sing idle songs to the sound of the harp,
    and like David invent for themselves instruments of
      music;
⁶who drink wine in bowls,
    and anoint themselves with the finest oils,
    but are not grieved over the ruin of Joseph!
⁷Therefore they shall now be the first of those to go into
      exile,
    and the revelry of those who stretch themselves shall
      pass away."

⁸The Lord GOD has sworn by himself
(says the LORD, the God of hosts):
"I abhor the pride of Jacob,
    and hate his strongholds;
    and I will deliver up the city and all that is in it."

                        Amos 6:4–8

Active around 740–700 B.C., Isaiah[3] was the prophet of faith, preaching an abiding trust in the providence of God. Also a prophet of doom like the other preachers, Isaiah saw that a purging was necessary in the interest of spiritual betterment in a kindlier and more loving world. He was among the first to picture a warless world under the benign rule of a Prince of Peace, a Messiah ("anointed one") descended from the House of David.

¹There shall come forth a shoot from the stump of Jesse,
    and a branch shall grow out of his roots.
²And the Spirit of the LORD shall rest upon him,
    the spirit of wisdom and understanding,
    the spirit of counsel and might,
    the spirit of knowledge and the fear of the LORD.
³And his delight shall be in the fear of the LORD.
He shall not judge by what his eyes see,
    or decide by what his ears hear;
⁴but with righteousness he shall judge the poor,
    and decide with equity for the meek of the earth;
and he shall smite the earth with the rod of his mouth,
    and with the breath of his lips he shall slay the
      wicked.
⁵Righteousness shall be the girdle of his waist,
    and faithfulness the girdle of his loins.
⁶The wolf shall dwell with the lamb,
    and the leopard shall lie down with the kid,
and the calf and the lion and the fatling together,
    and a little child shall lead them.
⁷The cow and the bear shall feed;
    their young shall lie down together;
    and the lion shall eat straw like the ox.
⁸The sucking child shall play over the hole of the asp,
    and the weaned child shall put his hand on the
      adder's den.
⁹They shall not hurt or destroy
    in all my holy mountain;
for the earth shall be full of the knowledge of the LORD
    as the waters cover the sea.

                        Isaiah 11:1–9

For unto us a child is born,
    to us a son is given;
and the government will be upon his shoulder,
    and his name will be called
"Wonderful Counselor, Mighty God,
Everlasting Father, Prince of Peace."

                        Isaiah 9:6

During the Babylonian Captivity when his people were far from home, their city and Temple destroyed, Ezekiel preached the universality of the faith

---

3. The Book of Isaiah contains prophecies attributed to Isaiah (chaps. 1–39) and those by an unknown prophet of the fifth century, known today as Second Isaiah (chaps. 40–66).

and of the personal relationship between the individual Jew and his God. God existed wherever the people were; the city and the Temple were not indispensable. Each person had the option of selecting good over evil or even turning from evil ways to a righteous life.

²⁵"Yet you say,'The way of the Lord is not just.' Hear now, O house of Israel: Is my way not just? Is it not your ways that are not just? ²⁶When a righteous man turns away from his righteousness and commits iniquity, he shall die for it; for the iniquity which he has committed he shall die. ²⁷Again, when a wicked man turns away from the wickedness he has committed and does what is lawful and right, he shall save his life. ²⁸Because he considered and turned away from all the transgressions which he had committed, he shall surely live, he shall not die. ²⁹Yet the house of Israel says,'The way of the Lord is not just.' O house of Israel, are my ways not just? Is it not your ways that are not just?

³⁰"Therefore I will judge you, O house of Israel, every one according to his ways, says the Lord GOD. Repent and turn from all your transgressions, lest iniquity be your ruin. ³¹Cast away from you all the transgressions which you have committed against me, and get yourselves a new heart and a new spirit! Why will you die, O house of Israel? ³²For I have no pleasure in the death of any one, says the Lord GOD; so turn, and live."

Ezekiel 18:25–32

The celebrated unknown prophet of the exile, known as Second Isaiah, was the great architect of Jewish ethical monotheism. Climaxing the prophetic movement, his ethical and religious insight set the sufferings of the Jews against a background of God's eventual redemption of the entire world. He saw the Jews as a people chosen to exemplify in their characters and lives the spiritual presence of the Lord. "A light to the nations" (Isaiah 42:1), their suffering had not been in vain. The world would say of Israel:

³He was despised and rejected by men;
    a man of sorrows, and acquainted with grief,
and as one from whom men hide their faces
    he was despised, and we esteemed him not.
⁴Surely he has borne our griefs
    and carried our sorrows,
yet we esteemed him stricken,
    smitten by God, and afflicted.
⁵But he was wounded for our transgressions,
    he was bruised for our iniquities;
upon him was the chastisement that made us whole,
    and with his stripes we are healed.
⁶All we like sheep have gone astray;
    we have turned every one to his own way;
and the LORD has laid on him
    the iniquity of us all.

Isaiah 53:3–6

They were to return to the New Jerusalem where the work of redemption would be a model for all the world.

¹Comfort, comfort my people,
    says your God.
²Speak tenderly to Jerusalem,
    and cry to her

that her warfare is ended,
    that her iniquity is pardoned,
that she has received from the LORD's hand
    double for all her sins.
³A voice cries:
    "In the wilderness prepare the way of the LORD,
    make straight in the desert a highway for our God.
⁴Every valley shall be lifted up,
    and every mountain and hill be made low;
the uneven ground shall become level,
    and the rough places a plain.
⁵And the glory of the LORD shall be revealed,
    and all flesh shall see it together,
    for the mouth of the LORD has spoken."
⁶A voice says, "Cry!"
    And I said, "What shall I cry?"
All flesh is grass,
    and all its beauty is like the flower of the field.
⁷The grass withers, the flower fades,
    when the breath of the LORD blows upon it;
    surely the people is grass.
⁸The grass withers, the flower fades;
    but the word of our God will stand for ever.
⁹Get you up to a high mountain,
    O Zion, herald of good tidings,
lift up your voice with strength,
    O Jerusalem, herald of good tidings,
lift it up, fear not;
say to the cities of Judah,
    "Behold your God!"

Isaiah 40:1–9

The profound insights of Second Isaiah strongly influenced later Judaism but were even more significant for early Christianity. His writings were studied and pondered by those who awaited the coming of the Messiah. In particular the story of the sufferings of Israel (see Isaiah 53:3–6 above) was so specific and individualized that later generations came to believe that he was speaking of a particular person, a Messiah who would redeem the world through his suffering. In Jesus of Nazareth the early Christians found that Messiah.

Some of the Teachings of Jesus

Jesus was born in the year we now call 4 B.C., or possibly 6 B.C.,⁴ a time that was ripe for his message of hope and love. He preached for possibly three years, but in the two thousand years since that time—whether people have believed his teachings or not, whether they have acted upon them or not—men and women throughout what was once called "Christendom" have been hearing the teachings of Jesus. What are the cardinal points of his teaching? These: that One God (a Personal Spirit, not an abstract idea nor a principle) is not only the Creator, but also the living Father of all humankind; that all people are

—————

4. The idea of denominating the years of the Christian era was introduced in A.D. 525 by Dionysius Exiguus; the B.C. sequence extending backwards from the birth of Christ was not added until the seventeenth century.

consequently the children of God, and that as a result all men and women are brothers and sisters; that as children of God, human beings are capable of better lives than they lead; that their human inadequacies, imperfections, and shortcomings can be forgiven if they are repentant; that life is eternal, and death is not extinction; that "all the Law and the Prophets" hangs upon the joint commandment to "Love thy God, and thy neighbor as thyself"; and that the intention—the act of the personality—is of greater importance than the deed—the act of the person.

Not the least of the appeals of Christianity is the joy and hope that it carries with it because of its doctrine of Christ as Redeemer. Theologically, one of several explanations may be stated in this way: because of the sin of Adam, humankind as a whole carried with it the taint of original sin, a sort of moral disease. But God, loving all people, sought to redeem them. This was accomplished through the mystery of Incarnation in which God became man, taking to himself all of humankind's inherent guilt. Then, in Christ's death as a mortal, the guilt is atoned, and human beings are set free. The possibility of salvation and eternal life with God, from that moment on, lies before each person. In a world-weary and guilt-ridden time like that of the late Roman Empire, even as in our own time, such a possibility can bring hope and joy to the believer.

All of these teachings affect the world of here and now, for Christianity is a "social" religion; that is, its effects are seen in the daily acts of people in relation to other people. It is not essentially a religion in which the believers isolate themselves from others and seek individual salvation through private contemplation. It is a religion of involvement for most Christians. Love must prompt the worshipper to present acts of love, mercy, and compassion as evidence of an inward change. The act of the believer in Christ cannot wait upon another world. If three words could be used to sum up this teaching, those three, with their many implications, might be those Jesus addressed to Peter: "Feed my sheep."

Early Christianity

Jesus left no written record of his work nor are there any surviving accounts contemporary with his ministry. A collection of his sayings, written in Aramaic, disappeared before A.D. 60, and scholars are still debating some of the references to Jesus in the Dead Sea Scrolls. His life, character, and message inspired hope and joy but this, coupled with the absence of documentation, was not sufficient for a theology. By definition, Christian theology is a discipline concerned with God and God's relation to the world. It remained for the followers of Jesus to construct a systematic theology as a solid foundation for the propagation of the new faith.

Written accounts in Greek began to appear several decades after Christ's death: Saint Paul's epistles to the Corinthians (ca. A.D. 55); the Acts of the Apostles (ca. 60); the four Gospels telling the story of Jesus: Mark (ca. 70); Matthew and Luke (ca. 80–85); and John (ca. 100–120). By about A.D. 200 the texts were revised in Alexandria into a canonical Christian text.

An upper-class Jew of Orthodox parentage, Saint Paul (Saul of Tarsus) was first a persecutor of Christians and later one of the most ardent missionaries of the faith. A Hellenized Jew, Paul took the position that "there is neither Jew nor Greek" (Galatians 3:28). Contending at first with Paul, Saint Peter believed instead that the Christian message was intended only for Jews and converted Gentiles. Paul argued (and Peter later agreed) that the Law was no longer valid, even for Jews; it could only bring people to an understanding of their dependence on Christ in a new covenant with Christ the Saviour. Sweeping aside Jewish rituals and practices, Paul, the "apostle to the Gentiles," carried the message of salvation through faith in Christ throughout the eastern Mediterranean and into Rome itself.

An enthusiastic teacher, organizer, and administrator, Paul was neither a theologian nor a logician. He was convinced that Christian faith was not a matter of reasoning but rather an act of faith. Confirmed by his own conversion experience on the road to Damascus, Paul believed that faith was a gift of God. Christians had only to accept the discipline of the Church and to lead quiet, faithful, and firmly Christian lives.

A synthesis of Judaic, Greek, and Christian ideas, Christian theology developed separately from the work of the Apostle Paul. In his Prologue, which introduces the fourth Gospel, John states that:

In the beginning was the Word, and the Word was with God, and the Word was God. ²He was in the beginning with God; ³all things were made through him, and without him was not anything made that was made. ⁴In him was life, and the life was the light of men. ⁵The light shines in the darkness, and the darkness has not overcome it.

John 1:1–5

In the Greek of the New Testament, "word" is a translation of *logos,* a word as old as the Greek language. Introduced by Herakleitos in the fifth century B.C., logos was a principle of cosmic interpretation. Constantly changing, the cosmos was a total process becoming controlled by an agency called logos. To avoid chaos, change had to conform to fixed patterns; logos was thus an intelligent and eternal agent that imposed an orderly process upon change.

Though the concept of logos is vague and unspecified in Plato and Aristotle, the Stoics took it from them but used logos to designate a divine element present in all men. It remained for Philo Judaeus of Alexandria (ca. 30 B.C.–A.D. 50) to go beyond the Stoics and to consciously construct a synthesis of Hebraic and Hellenic philosophy. Philo saw logos as a mediator between God and man and as a translation of the Hebrew word for "wisdom." As a personal agent of God in the creation of the world, logos was not identical with God but distinctly separate from him.

The Prologue of John is thus a creation story; Jesus is a divine being whose existence antedates the world itself. God's relation to this imperfect world was through the intervention of the logos; in Christ "the Word became flesh and dwelt among us, full of grace and truth" (John 1:14). It can be said that Herakleitos and Second Isaiah meet in John, representing two contrasting civilizations, which are synthesized into a Christian philosophy of history.[5]

The Impact of Christianity

Objective study of the historical Jesus and the facts about his life and death yields no clear-cut answers to some basic questions. Was he the Messiah, "Son of God," "son of man," a religious reformer, prophet, humanitarian, inspired teacher? Or was he, as his Jewish critics claim, a blasphemer and an imposter? Based on currently available sources there has been no final answer acceptable to everyone. The multiplicity of Christian beliefs (Catholic, Orthodox, varieties of Protestantism) testifies to the different interpretations of the evidence.

Nevertheless, the Christian emphasis on the importance of the human personality carries a religious sanction weightier than the speculations of the philosophers. The worth and dignity of the individual soul, and its responsibility to itself, has been a shaping influence in Western thought.

It is small wonder that Christianity spread from an obscure, remote province of the Roman Empire to practically throughout the known world within the first century of its existence; its message of hope, joy, salvation, and a merciful and loving God in a world that knew only the sterner aspects of justice made its welcome assured. Encompassing the whole of life, and able to take to itself the good things of any civilization, Christianity could appropriate to itself the best of Greek thought, as well as the most notable product of Rome: its law and organization. With the passage of time, it produced such diverse offshoots as the elegance and beauty of Chartres Cathedral and the horror and brutality of the Inquisition; but its impact upon the Western world is fundamental.

Bibliography

The Bible. Obviously the best source of information for both Judaism (The Old Testament) and Christianity (The New Testament). The authors personally prefer the King James Version, but recommend a modern translation like the Revised Standard Version, New York, 1946, 1952.

Chase, Mary Ellen. *The Bible and the Common Reader.* New York: Macmillan Co., 1945. In conjunction with the Bible reading, this book is recommended so that the student can be aware of the background and purposes of the various books.

Herzberg, Arthur, ed. *Judaism.* New York: George Braziller, Inc., n.d. A systematic account of Jewish belief with appropriate quotations from Jewish scholars from early times to the present.

Michener, James. *The Source.* New York: Random House, 1965. A fictional history of Judaism from preagricultural times to the present, the book gives an emotional identification with Jews that is not found elsewhere.

Noss, John B. *Man's Religions.* New York: Macmillan Co., 1969. Designed for undergraduate Religious Studies courses, this is a nontechnical and quite comprehensive survey of the world's major religions. There are many objective books on world religions, most with extensive bibliographies similar to those in this textbook.

Literary Selections

The Bible (Greek, Ta Biblia, The Books) has exercised a more profound and continuous influence upon Western civilization than has any other literary work. By its style alone it has burnished the tongues of poets and writers from Chaucer to Shakespeare to Lincoln, and its ethical tenets have become basic to the codes and customs of Western culture. Of its two main divisions, the Old Testament (thirty-nine books in the King James Version) was written almost entirely in Hebrew (with a little Aramaic) from the eleventh to the second century B.C. The New Testament (twenty-seven books in the King James Version) was written in Greek from about A.D. 40 to 150.

Divided into three parts, the Hebrew Scripture (Old Testament) consists of the Law (Pentateuch or Torah), the Prophets, and the Hagiographa (Writings). The Book of Job is from the Hagiographa.

THE BOOK OF JOB

Because the Book of Job is not included in this text, the reader is referred to any version of the Bible that may be available.[6] The following comments and "Some Topics for Discussion" may be used in conjunction with your Old Testament reading about the incredible trials of Job.

The problem of human suffering, particularly the suffering of the innocent, the just, and the good, has confused humankind since the beginning of time, particularly when people believe in a just and benevolent God. The Book of Job, written sometime after the seventh century B.C., tackles this problem as few books do. The author is unknown (indeed there is a strong possibility that the prose, prologue, and epilogue were originally a unit, and that the poetic drama is an interpolation), and the hero, Job, may or may not have been a historical character. It seems probable that

---

5. See chap. 13 for subsequent developments in Christian theology.

6. The translations included in this chapter are all from the American Revised Standard Version (RSV).

the book is addressed to all of Israel after one of the frequent persecutions of the Jews. Perhaps the author is attempting to explain to his people the nature of their suffering. If one considers the final answer from a completely rational point of view—as the Greeks, the Romans, and twentieth-century Americans would—one is left unsatisfied, for the attempt to probe God's secrets with the unaided human mind has seldom brought satisfactory results. If the reader can somehow translate his or her questioning into the realm of faith and mystery, an intuitive understanding may be reached.

From verses 1–5 in chapter 1, we must accept the fact that Job is a completely good man, and totally loyal to God. Job's comforters hold to an old religious concept of a simple cause-and-effect relationship between God and man: if man is upright, God will reward him; if he is evil, God will punish him. The generation gap is quite apparent when the youth, Elihu, speaks in chapter 32 and begins to introduce a totally new idea of the nature of the God-man relationship, an idea that is developed as God speaks out of the whirlwind.

The reader should not expect a logical development of ideas up to chapter 32. Rather, Job's searing doubts are explored with ever-greater intensity, and the arguments for the old religious idea are reiterated by the three comforters. Although this is not a drama in the strict sense of the word, the reader should try to imagine the tone of voice of the speakers. Notice, for example, the timid way in which Eliphaz begins his argument in chapter 4 after sitting on the ground for seven days and seven nights, or how Bildad's argument in chapter 25 sputters to a quick conclusion. What is Elihu's tone after listening to the lengthy discussions of Job?

Some Topics for Discussion

1. The reader might question the role of Satan at the first of the book. As one of the children of God, what force does he represent? A force for evil, almost as powerful as God himself?

2. One of the central arguments of Job's comforters is that the wicked are always destroyed, while the good prosper. In chapter 21 Job answers this argument. What is the basis for the argument of the comforters? What is the basis for Job's final answer?

3. In all the discussion up to Elihu's outburst the four men are searching for something not understood in the governing of the world. Sometimes this takes the form of sinfulness, which Job does not recognize, sometimes a question about the ways of God in determining the course of the universe. Using this search for the "something not understood" as a key question, follow all of the speeches.

4. How does Elihu's rebuke to the three old men foreshadow the revelation given from God in the voice out of the whirlwind? Question very carefully God's answer to the problem that is faced in the book. What is He really saying?

5. Do you find the final rewarding of Job with the twofold return of everything that he has lost a satisfactory conclusion to the book?

6. This Hebrew book and the play *Oedipus the King* have much in common in that both represent the downfall of a good man through the intervention of God or gods. Do you see any difference in the spirit of the inquiry between the Hebrew and the Greek exploration of the problem?

PSALMS OF DAVID

The third part of the Hebrew Bible is a collection of late writings, including the Psalms, a hymnal (Psalter) reflecting the whole history of Hebrew worship. The Psalmists sing Israel's praise of God the creator, intone their sorrow for national guilt and tribulations, and carol the songs of salvation. Following are two Psalms of salvation and glory.

24 The earth is the Lord's and the fulness thereof,
the world and those who dwell therein;
²for he has founded it upon the seas,
    and established it upon the rivers.
³Who shall ascend the hill of the Lord?
    And who shall stand in his holy place?
⁴He who has clean hands and a pure heart,
    who does not lift up his soul to what is false,
    and does not swear deceitfully.
⁵He will receive blessing from the Lord,
    and vindication from the God of his salvation.
⁶Such is the generation of those who seek him,
    who seek the face of the God of Jacob.   *Selah*
⁷Lift up your heads, O gates!
    and be lifted up, O ancient doors!
    that the King of glory may come in.
⁸Who is the King of glory?
    The Lord, strong and mighty,
    the Lord, mighty in battle!
⁹Lift up your heads, O gates!
    and be lifted up, O ancient doors!
    that the King of glory may come in!
¹⁰Who is this King of glory?
    The Lord of hosts,
    he is the King of glory!   *Selah*

150 Praise the Lord!
Praise God in his sanctuary;
    praise him in his mighty firmament!
²Praise him for his mighty deeds;
    praise him according to his exceeding greatness!
³Praise him with trumpet sound;
    praise him with lute and harp!
⁴Praise him with timbrel and dance;
    praise him with strings and pipe!
⁵Praise him with sounding cymbals;
    praise him with loud clashing cymbals!
⁶Let everything that breathes praise the Lord!
Praise the Lord!

Apparently composed during the Babylonian Captivity (586–538 B.C.), Psalm 137 is a Lamentation. Though the condition of the Jews in Babylon was relatively favorable, the mourning is caused by the destruction of Jerusalem and by their own separation from the homeland. This magnificent poem was especially prominent in the worship services of American slaves, who viewed slavery as Babylonian or Egyptian captivity, an enforced exile from the African homeland.

137 By the waters of Babylon,
there we sat down and wept,
    when we remembered Zion.
²On the willows there
    we hung up our lyres.
³For there our captors
    required of us songs,
and our tormentors, mirth, saying,
    "Sing us one of the songs of Zion!"
⁴How shall we sing the LORD's song
    in a foreign land?
⁵If I forget you, O Jerusalem,
    let my right hand wither!
⁶Let my tongue cleave to the roof of my
      mouth,
    if I do not remember you,
if I do not set Jerusalem
    above my highest joy!
⁷Remember, O LORD, against the E'dom-
      ites
    the day of Jerusalem,
how they said, "Rase it, rase it!
    Down to its foundations!"
⁸O daughter of Babylon, you devastator!
    Happy shall he be who requites you
    with what you have done to us!
⁹Happy shall he be who takes your little
      ones
    and dashes them against the rock!

ECCLESIASTES

From the Writings part of the Old Testament, Ecclesiastes (Greek, the preacher) is representative of pessimistic Oriental wisdom (teaching) literature. It dates from the third century B.C. and reflects some of the inroads of Greek civilization, but not enough to disturb the basic philosophy that all is vanity and that a young man should enjoy his youth.

3 For everything there is a season, and a time for every
    matter under heaven:
²a time to be born, and a time to die;
a time to plant, and a time to pluck up what is planted;
³a time to kill, and a time to heal;
a time to break down, and a time to build up;
⁴a time to weep, and a time to laugh;
a time to mourn, and a time to dance;
⁵a time to cast away stones, and a time to gather stones
    together;
a time to embrace, and a time to refrain from embracing;
⁶a time to seek, and a time to lose;
a time to keep, and a time to cast away;
⁷a time to rend, and a time to sew;

a time to keep silence, and a time to speak;
⁸a time to love, and a time to hate;
a time for war, and a time for peace.
⁹What gain has the worker from his toil?
¹⁰I have seen the business that God has given to the sons of men to be busy with. ¹¹He has made everything beautiful in its time; also he has put eternity into man's mind, yet so that he cannot find out what God has done from the beginning to the end. ¹²I know that there is nothing better for them than to be happy and enjoy themselves as long as they live; ¹³also that it is God's gift to man that every one should eat and drink and take pleasure in all his toil. ¹⁴I know that whatever God does endures for ever; nothing can be added to it, nor anything taken from it; God has made it so, in order that men should fear before him. ¹⁵That which is, already has been; that which is to be, already has been; and God seeks what has been driven away.

¹⁶Moreover I saw under the sun that in the place of justice, even there was wickedness, and in the place of righteousness, even there was wickedness. ¹⁷I said in my heart, God will judge the righteous and the wicked, for he has appointed a time for every matter, and for every work. ¹⁸I said in my heart with regard to the sons of men that God is testing them to show them that they are but beasts. ¹⁹For the fate of the sons of men and the fate of beasts is the same; as one dies, so dies the other. They all have the same breath, and man has no advantage over the beasts; for all is vanity. ²⁰All go to one place; all are from the dust, and all turn to dust again. ²¹Who knows whether the spirit of man goes upward and the spirit of the beast goes down to the earth? ²²So I saw that there is nothing better than that a man should enjoy his work, for that is his lot; who can bring him to see what will be after him?

THE SERMON ON THE MOUNT
Matthew 5–7

The New Testament contains four sections: (1) the Gospels and Acts of the Apostles, (2) the Epistles of Paul, (3) the pastoral and general Epistles, and (4) the Book of Revelations. Mark's Gospel emphasizes the human aspect of Jesus, while Matthew and Luke include substantial additions dealing mainly with the birth and teaching of Jesus, including the Sermon on the Mount and the parables. The basic ethical teachings of Christ are presented in the Sermon on the Mount, in which the Mosaic Ten Commandments are compared with a new ethic. Beginning with the statement "You have heard that it was said to the men of old," Jesus takes each commandment in turn and contrasts it with his own commandment. As presented by Matthew, Jesus is the new Moses expounding a new Torah, which commands a higher righteousness than that found even in the best of Judaism.

Seeing the crowds, he went up on the mountain, and when he sat down his disciples came to him. And he opened his mouth and taught them, saying:

    "Blessed are the poor in spirit, for theirs is the kingdom of heaven.

    "Blessed are those who mourn, for they shall be comforted.

"Blessed are the meek, for they shall inherit the earth.

"Blessed are those who hunger and thirst for righteousness, for they shall be satisfied.

"Blessed are the merciful, for they shall obtain mercy.

"Blessed are the pure in heart, for they shall see God.

"Blessed are the peacemakers, for they shall be called sons of God.

"Blessed are those who are persecuted for righteousness' sake, for theirs is the kingdom of heaven.

"Blessed are you when men revile you and persecute you and utter all kinds of evil against you falsely on my account. Rejoice and be glad, for your reward is great in heaven, for so men persecuted the prophets who were before you.

"You are the salt of the earth; but if salt has lost its taste, how can its saltness be restored? It is no longer good for anything except to be thrown out and trodden under foot by men.

"You are the light of the world. A city set on a hill cannot be hid. Nor do men light a lamp and put it under a bushel, but on a stand, and it gives light to all in the house. Let your light so shine before men, that they may see your good works and give glory to your Father who is in heaven.

"Think not that I have come to abolish the law and the prophets; I have come not to abolish them but to fulfill them. For truly, I say to you, till heaven and earth pass away, not an iota, not a dot, will pass from the law until all is accomplished. Whoever then relaxes one of the least of these commandments and teaches men so, shall be called least in the kingdom of heaven; but he who does them and teaches them shall be called great in the kingdom of heaven. For I tell you, unless your righteousness exceeds that of the scribes and Pharisees, you will never enter the kingdom of heaven.

"You have heard that it was said to the men of old, 'You shall not kill; and whoever kills shall be liable to judgment.' But I say to you that every one who is angry with his brother shall be liable to judgment; whoever insults his brother shall be liable to the council, and whoever says, 'You fool!' shall be liable to the hell of fire. So if you are offering your gift at the altar, and there remember that your brother has something against you, leave your gift there before the altar and go; first be reconciled to your brother, and then come and offer your gift. Make friends quickly with your accuser, while you are going with him to court, lest your accuser hand you over to the judge, and the judge to the guard, and you be put in prison; truly, I say to you, you will never get out till you have paid the last penny.

"You have heard that it was said, 'You shall not commit adultery.' But I say to you that every one who looks at a woman lustfully has already committed adultery with her in his heart. If your right eye causes you to sin, pluck it out and throw it away; it is better that you lose one of your members than that your whole body be thrown into hell. And if your right hand causes you to sin, cut it off and throw it away; it is better that you lose one of your members than that your whole body go into hell.

"It was also said, 'Whoever divorces his wife, let him give her a certificate of divorce.' But I say to you that every one who divorces his wife, except on the ground of unchastity, makes her an adulteress; and whoever marries a divorced woman commits adultery.

"Again you have heard that it was said to the men of old, 'You shall not swear falsely, but shall perform to the Lord what you have sworn.' But I say to you, do not swear at all, either by heaven, for it is the throne of God, or by the earth, for it is his footstool, or by Jerusalem, for it is the city of the great King. And do not swear by your head, for you cannot make one hair white or black. Let what you say be simply 'Yes' or 'No'; anything more than this comes from evil.

"You have heard that it was said, 'An eye for an eye and a tooth for a tooth.' But I say to you, Do not resist one who is evil. But if any one strikes you on the right cheek, turn to him the other also; and if any one would sue you and take your coat, let him have your cloak as well; and if any one forces you to go one mile, go with him two miles. Give to him who begs from you, and do not refuse him who would borrow from you.

"You have heard that it was said, 'You shall love your neighbor and hate your enemy.' But I say to you, Love your enemies and pray for those who persecute you, so that you may be sons of your Father who is in heaven; for he makes his sun rise on the evil and on the good, and sends rain on the just and on the unjust. For if you love those who love you, what reward have you? Do not even the tax collectors do the same? And if you salute only your brethren, what more are you doing than others? Do not even the Gentiles do the same? You, therefore, must be perfect, as your heavenly Father is perfect.

"Beware of practicing your piety before men in order to be seen by them; for then you will have no reward from your Father who is in heaven.

"Thus, when you give alms, sound no trumpet before you, as the hypocrites do in the synagogues and in the streets, that they may be praised by men. Truly, I say to you, they have their reward. But when you give alms, do not let your left hand know what your right hand is doing, so that your alms may be in secret; and your Father who sees in secret will reward you.

"And when you pray, you must not be like the hypocrites; for they love to stand and pray in the synagogues and at the street corners, that they may be seen by men. Truly, I say to you, they have their reward. But when you pray, go into your room and shut the door and pray to your Father who is in secret; and your Father who sees in secret will reward you.

"And in praying do not heap up empty phrases as the Gentiles do; for they think that they will be heard for their many words. Do not be like them, for your Father knows what you need before you ask him. Pray then like this:
'Our Father who art in heaven,
Hallowed be thy name.
Thy kingdom come,
Thy will be done,
    On earth as it is in heaven.
Give us this day our daily bread;
And forgive us our debts,
    As we also have forgiven our debtors;
And lead us not into temptation,
    But deliver us from evil.'

"For if you forgive men their trespasses, your heavenly Father also will forgive you; but if you do not forgive men their trespasses, neither will your Father forgive your trespasses.

"And when you fast, do not look dismal, like the hypocrites, for they disfigure their faces that their fasting may be seen by men. Truly, I say to you, they have their reward. But when you fast, anoint your head and wash your face, that your fasting may not be seen by men but by your Father who is in secret; and your Father who sees in secret will reward you.

"Do not lay up for yourselves treasures on earth, where moth and rust consume and where thieves break in and steal, but lay up for yourselves treasures in heaven, where neither moth nor rust consumes and where thieves do not break in and steal; for where your treasure is, there will your heart be also.

"The eye is the lamp of the body. So, if your eye is sound, your whole body will be full of light; but if your eye is not sound, your whole body will be full of darkness. If then the light in you is darkness, how great is the darkness!

"No one can serve two masters; for either he will hate the one and love the other, or he will be devoted to the one and despise the other. You cannot serve God and mammon.

"Therefore I tell you, do not be anxious about your life, what you shall eat or what you shall drink, nor about your body, what you shall put on. Is not life more than food, and the body more than the clothing? Look at the birds of the air: they neither sow nor reap nor gather into barns, and yet your heavenly Father feeds them. Are you not of more value than they? And which of you by being anxious can add one cubit to his span of life? And why be anxious about clothing? Consider the lilies of the field, how they grow; they neither toil nor spin; yet I tell you, even Solomon in all his glory was not arrayed like one of these. But if God so clothes the grass of the field, which today is alive and tomorrow is thrown into the oven, will he not much more clothe you, O men of little faith? Therefore do not be anxious, saying, 'What shall we eat?' or 'What shall we drink?' or 'What shall we wear?' For the Gentiles seek all these things; and your heavenly Father knows that you need them all. But seek first his kingdom and his righteousness, and all these things shall be yours as well.

"Therefore do not be anxious about tomorrow, for tomorrow will be anxious for itself. Let the day's own trouble be sufficient for the day.

"Judge not, that you be not judged. For with the judgment you pronounce you will be judged, and the measure you give will be the measure you get. Why do you see the speck that is in your brother's eye, but do not notice the log that is in your own eye? Or how can you say to your brother, 'Let me take the speck out of your eye,' when there is the log in your own eye? you hypocrite, first take the log out of your own eye, and then you will see clearly to take the speck out of your brother's eye.

"Do not give dogs what is holy; and do not throw your pearls before swine, lest they trample them underfoot and turn to attack you.

"Ask, and it will be given you; seek, and you will find; knock, and it will be opened to you. For every one who asks receives, and he who seeks finds, and to him who knocks it will be opened. Or what man of you, if his son asks him for a loaf, will give him a stone? Or if he asks for a fish, will give him a serpent? If you then, who are evil, know how to give good gifts to your children, how much more will your Father who is in heaven give good things to those who ask him? So whatever you wish that men would do to you, do so to them; for this is the law and the prophets.

"Enter by the narrow gate; for the gate is wide and the way is easy, that leads to destruction, and those who enter by it are many. For the gate is narrow and the way is hard, that leads to life, and those who find it are few.

"Beware of false prophets, who come to you in sheep's clothing but inwardly are ravenous wolves. You will know them by their fruits. Are grapes gathered from thorns, or figs from thistles? So, every sound tree bears good fruit, but the bad tree bears evil fruit. A sound tree cannot bear evil fruit, nor can a bad tree bear good fruit. Every tree that does not bear good fruit is cut down and thrown into the fire. Thus you will know them by their fruits.

"Not every one who says to me, 'Lord, Lord,' shall enter the kingdom of heaven, but he who does the will of my Father who is in heaven. On that day many will say to me, 'Lord, Lord, did we not prophesy in your name, and cast out demons in your name, and do many mighty works in your name?' And then will I declare to them, 'I never knew you; depart from me, you evil-doers.'

"Every one then who hears these words of mine and does them will be like a wise man who built his house upon the rock; and the rain fell, and the floods came, and the winds blew and beat upon that house, but it did not fall, because it had been founded on the rock. And everyone who hears these words of mine and does not do them will be like a foolish man who built his house upon the sand; and the rain fell, and the floods came, and the winds blew and beat against the house, and it fell; and great was the fall of it."

And when Jesus finished these sayings, the crowds were astonished at his teaching, for he taught them as one who had authority, and not as their scribes.

The Apostle Paul wrote his letters to the Corinthians during the years A.D. 54 to 56. Perhaps the most familiar of all his Epistles is chapter 13 of 1 Corinthians in which Paul speaks eloquently of the place of love in Christian living.

13 If I speak in the tongues of men and of angels, but have not love, I am a noisy gong or a clanging cymbal. And if I have prophetic powers, and understand all mysteries and all knowledge, and if I have all faith, so as to remove mountains, but have not love, I am nothing. [3]If I give away all I have, and if I deliver my body to be burned, but have not love, I gain nothing.

[4]Love is patient and kind; love is not jealous or boastful; [5]it is not arrogant or rude. Love does not insist on its own way; it is not irritable or resentful; [6]it does not rejoice at wrong, but rejoices in the right. [7]Love bears all things, believes all things, hopes all things, endures all things.

[8]Love never ends; as for prophecy, it will pass away; as for tongues, they will cease; as for knowledge, it will pass away. [9]For our knowledge is imperfect and our prophecy is imperfect; [10]but when the perfect comes, the imperfect will pass away. [11]When I was a child, I spoke like a child, I thought like a child, I reasoned like a child; when I became a man, I gave up childish ways. [12]For now we see in a mirror dimly, but then face to face. Now I know in part; then I shall understand fully, even as I have been fully understood. [13]So faith, hope, love abide, these three; but the greatest of these is love.

FIVE PARABLES

I

(Matthew 18:23–35)

"Therefore the kingdom of heaven may be compared to a king who wished to settle accounts with his servants. When he began the reckoning, one was brought to him who owed him ten thousand talents; and as he could not pay, his lord ordered him to be sold, with his wife and children and all that he had, and payment to be made. So the servant fell on his knees, imploring him, 'Lord, have patience with me, and I will pay you everything.' And out of pity for him the lord of that servant released him and forgave him the debt. But that same servant, as he went out, came upon one of his fellow servants who owed him a hundred denarii; and seizing him by the throat he said, 'Pay what you owe.' So his fellow servant fell down and besought him, 'Have patience with me, and I will pay you.' He refused and went and put him in prison till he should pay the debt. When his fellow servants saw what had taken place, they were greatly distressed, and they went and reported to their lord all that had taken place. Then his lord summoned him and said to him, 'You wicked servant! I forgave you all that debt because you besought me; and should not you have had mercy on your fellow servant, as I had mercy on you?' And in anger his lord delivered him to the jailers, till he should pay all his debt. So also my heavenly Father will do to every one of you, if you do not forgive your brother from your heart."

II

(Matthew 20:1–16)

"For the kingdom of heaven is like a householder who went out early in the morning to hire laborers for his vineyard. After agreeing with the laborers for a denarius a day, he sent them into his vineyard. And going out about the third hour he saw others standing idle in the market place; and to them he said, 'You go into the vineyard too, and whatever is right I will give you.' So they went. Going out again about the sixth hour and the ninth hour, he did the same. And about the eleventh hour he went out and found others standing; and he said to them, 'Why do you stand here idle all day?' They said to him, 'Because no one has hired us.' He said to them, 'You go into the vineyard too.' And when evening came, the owner of the vineyard said to his steward, 'Call the laborers and pay them their wages, beginning with the last, up to the first.' And when those hired about the eleventh hour came, each of them received a denarius. Now when the first came, they thought they would receive more; but each of them also received a denarius. And on receiving it they grumbled at the householder, saying, 'These last worked only one hour, and you have made them equal to us who have borne the burden of the day and the scorching heat.' But he replied to one of them, 'Friend, I am doing you no wrong; did you not agree with me for a denarius? Take what belongs to you, and go; I choose to give to this last as I give to you. Am I not allowed to do what I choose with what belongs to me? Or do you begrudge my generosity?' So the last will be first, and the first last."

III

(Luke 10:30–37)

"A man was going down from Jerusalem to Jericho and he fell among robbers, who stripped him and beat him, and departed, leaving him half-dead. Now by chance a priest was going down that road; and when he saw him he passed by on the other side. So likewise a Levite, when he came to the place and saw him, passed by on the other side. But a Samaritan, as he journeyed, came to where he was; and when he saw him, he had compassion, and went to him and bound up his wounds, pouring on oil and wine; then he set him on his own beast and brought him to an inn, and took care of him. And the next day he took out two denarii and gave them to the innkeeper, saying, 'Take care of him; and whatever more you spend, I will repay you when I come back.' Which of these three, do you think, proved neighbor to the man who fell among the robbers?" He said, "The one who showed mercy on him." And Jesus said to him, "Go and do likewise."

IV

(Luke 15:11–32)

"There was a man who had two sons; and the younger of them said to his father, 'Father, give me the share of property that falls to me.' And he divided his living between them. Not many days later, the younger son gathered all he had and took his journey into a far country, and there he squandered his property in loose living. And when he had spent everything, a great famine arose in that country, and he began to be in want. So he went and joined himself to one of the citizens of that country, who sent him into his fields to feed swine. And he would gladly have fed on the pods that the swine ate; and no one gave him anything. But when he came to himself he said, 'How many of my father's hired servants have bread enough and to spare, but I perish here with hunger! I will arise and go to my father, and I will say to him, "Father, I have sinned against heaven and before you; I am no longer worthy to be called your son; treat me as one of your hired servants."' And he arose and came to his father. But while he was yet at a distance, his father saw him and had compassion, and ran and embraced him and kissed him. And the son said to him, 'Father, I have sinned against heaven and before you; I am no longer worthy to be called your son.' But the father said to his servants, 'Bring quickly the best robe, and put it on him; and put a ring on his hand, and shoes on his feet; and bring the fatted calf and kill it, and let us eat and make merry; for this my son was dead, and is alive again; he was lost, and is found.' And they began to make merry.

"Now his elder son was in the field; and as he came and drew near to the house, he heard music and dancing. And he called one of the servants and asked what this meant. And he said to him, 'Your brother has come, and your father has killed the fatted calf, because he has received him safe and sound.' But he was angry and refused to go in. His father came out and entreated him, but he answered his father, 'Lo, these many years I have served you, and I never disobeyed your command; yet you never gave me a kid, that I might make merry with my friends. But when this son of yours came, who has devoured your living with harlots, you killed for him the fatted calf!' And he said to him, 'Son, you are always with me, and all that is mine is yours. It was fitting to make merry and be glad, for this your brother was dead, and is alive; he was lost, and is found.' "

V

(Matthew 25:14–30)

"For it [the Kingdom of Heaven] will be as when a man going on a journey called his servants and entrusted to them his property; to one he gave five talents, to another two, to another one, to each according to his ability. Then he went away. He who had received the five talents went at once and traded with them; and he made five talents more. So too, he who had the two talents made two talents more. But he who had received the one talent, went and dug in the ground and hid his master's money. Now after a long time the master of those servants came and settled accounts with them. And he who had received the five talents came forward, bringing five talents more, saying, 'Master, you delivered to me five talents; here I have made five talents more.' His master said to him, 'Well done, good and faithful servant; you have been faithful over a little, I will set you over much; enter into the joy of your master.' And he also who had the two talents came forward, saying, 'Master, you delivered to me two talents; here I have made two talents more.' His master said to him, 'Well done, good and faithful servant; you have been faithful over a little, I will set you over much; enter into the joy of your master.' He also who had received the one talent came forward, saying, 'Master, I knew you to be a hard man, reaping where you did not sow, and gathering where you did not winnow; so I was afraid, and I went and hid your talent in the ground. Here you have what is yours.' But his master answered him, 'You wicked and slothful servant! You knew that I reap where I have not sowed, and gather where I have not winnowed? Then you ought to have invested my money with the bankers, and at my coming I should have received what was my own with interest. So take the talent from him, and give it to him who has the ten talents. For to every one who has will more be given, and he will have abundance; but from him who has not, even what he has will be taken away. And cast the worthless servant into the outer darkness; there men will weep and gnash their teeth.' "

Exercises

The East has always been fond of teaching by parable, the brief narrative that by comparison provides a way of getting at a truth. It is not quite like an algebraic problem, to be solved by substituting terms: "x = y," "a = b," and the like. It is rather a way of stimulating the imagination, of getting at the point by *insight*. Jesus was following an ancient, well-established tradition in teaching by parables. These stories must be understood on an exceedingly literal level; they mean what they say; but they do not stop there—the mind goes on to seize upon the inherent likenesses, the points to be compared. Here are some questions over the parables in the text.

1. "The Wicked Servant." What prompted the action of the servant's lord, at the beginning and at the end? What is the specific fault of the servant? What was the point that Jesus was trying to convey?

2. "The Vineyard." Imagine a disciple of Plato, who wrote the whole treatise of the *Republic* in order to consider the question "What is Justice?", commenting upon this story. In two or three sentences, what would his opinion be? Imagine a disciple of Jesus trying to answer, again in two or three sentences. Where is the point of departure between the two?

3. "The Good Samaritan." Why does Jesus make a *Samaritan* the subject of his tale? In trying to modernize it, what word would you pick instead? (On second thought—better *not* answer that question!) What fault or shortcoming among his contemporaries was Jesus pointing out?

4. "The Prodigal Son." It is always tempting to feel a great deal of sympathy for the elder brother in this story. When you do so (or when you side with the workers in the vineyard who had worked all day), what *basis* of judgment are you using? How does this measuring rod of what is just differ from that of Jesus?

5. "The Talents." Which of the other parables is this most like? As a story it is harsh and forbidding; how would you answer the argument that it does not portray a merciful and loving God?

REVELATION

For several centuries before and after Christ, there flourished a distinctive writing known as apocalypse or revelation. Apocalyptic thought was based on the Jewish eschatological[7] view of history. A portion of the Book of Daniel is an apocalypse, and Paul included several apocalyptic verses in 2 Thessalonians. The last book of the Bible, called Revelation or Apocalypse of John, is the only full apocalypse in the New Testament. Writing to seven beseiged churches around A.D. 93 during Domitian's savage persecution of Christians, John of Patmos declares, in visionary terms, the ultimate triumph over the empire and his perception of a new heaven, a new earth, and a new Jerusalem after all souls have been raised from the dead for the Last Judgment. In the early Church there was a widespread belief that the Second Coming of Christ was imminent.

In the following selection, Christ opens four of the seven seals, releasing the Four Horsemen of the Apocalypse: Conquest, War, Famine, and Death (fig. 11.1).

---

7. Eschatology (Gk., *eschatos,* furthest) is a branch of theology dealing with the last things, such as death, judgment, resurrection, and immortality.

6 Now I saw when the Lamb opened one of the seven seals, and I heard one of the four living creatures say, as with a voice of thunder, "Come!" ²And I saw, and behold, a white horse, and its rider had a bow; and a crown was given to him, and he went out conquering and to conquer.

³When he opened the second seal, I heard the second living creature say, "Come!" ⁴ And out came another horse, bright red; its rider was permitted to take peace from the earth, so that men should slay one another; and he was given a great sword.

⁵When he opened the third seal, I heard the third living creature say, "Come!" And I saw, and behold, a black horse, and its rider had a balance in his hand; ⁶and I heard what seemed to be a voice in the midst of the four living creatures saying, "A quart of wheat for a denarius, and three quarts of barley for a denarius, but do not harm oil and wine!"

⁷When he opened the fourth seal, I heard the voice of the fourth living creature say, "Come!" ⁸And I saw, and behold, a pale horse, and its rider's name was Death, and Hades followed him; and they were given power over a fourth of the earth, to kill with sword and with famine and with pestilence and by wild beasts of the earth.

Revelation 6:1–8

Following the Last Judgment, John presents a golden vision of the world to come.

21 Then I saw a new heaven and a new earth; for the first heaven and the first earth had passed away, and the sea was no more. ²And I saw the holy city, new Jerusalem, coming down out of heaven from God, prepared as a bride adorned for her husband; ³and I heard a great voice from the throne saying, "Behold, the dwelling of God is with men. He will dwell with them, and they shall be his people, and God himself will be with them; ⁴he will wipe away every tear from their eyes, and death shall be no more, neither shall there be mourning nor crying nor pain any more, for the former things have passed away."

Revelation 21:1–4

Figure 11.1 *The Fourth Horseman of the Apocalypse*, Angers Tapestries, Angers Castle, France. Height ca. 8′. Woven by Nicolas Bataillel in 1375/80 in Paris, this is the oldest known French tapestry.

12

The Beginnings of Christian Art

Chronological Overview

306–337	Reign of Constantine
313	Edict of Milan guaranteed Christians freedom of worship
325	First Council of Nicea condemned Arian heresy
330	Constantine established a new capital at Constantinople
410; 455	Rome sacked by Visigoths and by Vandals
476	Last Roman emperor deposed
ca. 493–527	Theodoric and Ostrogothic Kingdom
527–565	Emperor Justinian; First Byzantine Golden Age
726–843	Iconoclastic Controversy
ca. 900–1100	Second Byzantine Golden Age
1204	Destruction of Constantinople by Fourth Crusade
1453	Constantinople falls to Ottoman Turks; end of Eastern Roman Empire

The first two centuries of Christianity had little need for art in any form. Meeting in small groups in private homes, early Christians conducted simple services centered around the Eucharist, the consecrated bread and wine commemorating Christ's sacrifice on the cross. Dating from about 250, the earliest known church building is a Greek peristyle house in Dura-Europos, Syria. Suitable for a congregation of no more than sixty, this was a private home converted to liturgical use though it possessed neither decorations nor architectural distinction. There is, in fact, no surviving Christian art from the first two centuries and very little from the third century, and that almost entirely from the catacombs of Rome.

Christianity in Rome

Initially and during most of the first two centuries, Christians were buried in regular Roman cemeteries. Rejecting cremation (the usual procedure for the lower classes) because of their belief in the Resurrection, Christians continued burying their dead in surface cemeteries except in the outskirts of Rome, Naples, and Syracuse, where porous stone (tufa) was easily excavated for subterranean tombs. During the late second century Christian communities became increasingly interested in separate burial areas where they could, in privacy, perform rites for the dead and also safeguard the tombs. Because Roman law permitted no burials within city limits, Christian families or groups bought land on hillsides alongside the major highways leading into Rome, sites that already contained the funerary monuments of wealthy Roman families. Utilizing surface buildings and subterranean passages, these cemeteries were ideally suited to Christian concerns for seclusion and security. At no time, however, were the catacombs exclusively Christian nor were they used as secret meeting places; Roman officials knew the location and extent of the burial grounds. There were, after all, some thirty-eight subterranean cemeteries outside Rome in which were interred about four million bodies.

The Roman catacombs had up to five subterranean levels with superimposed niches for sarcophagi eight to ten deep in each passage. Each cemetery included small chapels for burial and commemorative services. In the chapels and sometimes over the burial niches are found the earliest examples of Christian figurative art. Executed by artisans working by lamplight in a dark, dank, and undoubtedly malodorous environment, the representations were generally simple and often hastily executed. However, neither the client nor the artist was preoccupied with aesthetics; Christians were mainly interested in conveying a message or a prayer that would be understood by the Christian community and, above all, by God.

The most common representation in the catacombs was the *orant* (OR–an; from the Latin word for *praying*; fig. 12.1), a figure presented in full frontality, standing with arms raised in prayer or supplication. The orant can symbolize the soul of the deceased praying for salvation or it can reflect the Hellenistic view, a personification in human form of abstract ideas like resurrection or salvation.

The figure of Jesus as *The Good Shepherd* (fig. 12.2), a commonly used representation of Christ throughout the centuries, appears frequently in catacomb frescoes. As might be expected, the Good Shepherd motif can be found in most cultures in which sheepherding is an important occupation. There is, for example, the *Calf-Bearer* (see fig. 7.21) of Archaic Greek sculpture and, in the Hebraic tradition, David the shepherd boy, giant-killer, psalmist, and king. Christ as the Good Shepherd is a symbol of

Figure 12.1 *Orant,* ca. A.D. 300. Catacombs of St. Priscilla, Rome.

Figure 12.2 *The Good Shepherd,* ca. A.D. 250. Ceiling painting, Catacombs of St. Callixtus, Rome.

$$
\begin{array}{l}
\mathrm{I}\eta\sigma o\upsilon s \\
\mathrm{X}\rho\iota\sigma\tau o s \\
\Theta\varepsilon o\upsilon \\
\mathrm{'Y}\iota o s \\
\Sigma\omega\tau\eta\rho
\end{array}
$$

Figure 12.3 Anagram as derived from the Greek for "Jesus Christ, the Son of God, Savior."

Figure 12.4 *Crucifixion,* from the west door of the Church of Santa Sabina, ca. A.D. 430, Rome. Wood, 11″ × 15¾″.

the guardian of the faithful of his church; further, Jesus was a descendent of the David who tended sheep in Palestine.

Artistic representation of the concepts inherent in the new religion caused difficulties never dreamed of by Egyptian, Greek, and Roman artists. The Greeks, for example, had created the gods in their own image, thus making the divinities instantly available for artistic representation: Zeus with a thunderbolt symbolizing the power principle; Poseidon with his trident; Aphrodite as the Goddess of Love, and so forth. How, then, was the Christian artist to depict such abstractions as the Trinity, the Holy Spirit, salvation, redemption, the Eucharist, immortality? In time, artists worked out a variety of solutions using biblical stories, parables, and symbols. The idea of immortality, for example, could be represented through biblical scenes of salvation: Moses leading his people out of Egypt; Jonah released from the whale; Daniel escaping from the lion's den; Lazarus rising from his tomb. The anchor came to represent hope, the dove was peace or the Holy Spirit, and the palm meant victory through martyrdom. Symbolizing Christ is the Khi–Rho (KYE–ro) monogram, which superimposes the first two letters of Christ's name (Khristos) in Greek: ☧ . The first and last letters of the Greek alphabet, Alpha (**A**) and Omega (**Ω**), symbolize infinity as in Christ's statement, "I am Alpha and Omega, the Beginning and the End." Multiple meanings are found in the symbol of the fish: (1) the Last Supper; (2) Christian evangelism as represented in Christ's exhortation to his fishermen disciples to be "fishers of men"; and (3) an anagram upon a Greek phrase, the initial letters of which form the Greek word *ikhthys,* or *fish* (fig. 12.3).

The one event that was not symbolized in catacombs paintings was the Crucifixion. The most ignoble and horrible method of Roman execution, crucifixion was reserved for criminals judged guilty of foul and heinous acts; Christ was crucified by the Romans as an "enemy of the state," treason being the worst of all crimes. For early Christians, the simple geometric form of the cross was all that was needed to symbolize Christ's sacrifice. Perhaps the earliest extant crucifixion scene produced for a public place is a small, wooden, low relief panel on one of the doors of the Church of Santa Sabina (fig. 12.4). Set amidst a door rich with elaborately carved panels this, the simplest panel, appears to be a deliberate attempt to tone down the horror of the crucifixion.

Early Christians also refrained from producing sculpture in the round, especially life-size figures. God's commandment to Moses that "Thou shall not make unto thee any graven images" remained basic to Christianity though religious conservatives chose to interpret this injunction literally. The recognition by the early church fathers of the didactic and educational value of art was summed up by Pope Gregory the Great (ruled 590–604): "Pictures are used in the church in order that those who are ignorant of letters may, merely by looking at the walls, read there what they were unable to read in books." Supplementing this realistic position was the theological argument that since Jesus was "made flesh and dwelt among us," he had a human likeness and nature that could be represented in art. Conservatives were nevertheless suspicious of freestanding statues because they associated these with the gods of other religions, which is the main reason why there was very little monumental sculpture between the fourth and tenth centuries.

Two very rare three-dimensional sculptures do survive from fourth-century Rome. Classical in pose and reminiscent of the catacomb painting in figure

Figure 12.5 *Good Shepherd,* ca. A.D. 350. Marble, height 39″. Vatican Museums, Rome.

Figure 12.6 *Christ Enthroned,* ca. A.D. 350–360. Marble, smaller than life size. National Museum, Rome.

12.2, the *Good Shepherd* (fig. 12.5) is as carefully detailed as the finest Hellenistic genre sculpture. Stylistically it still relates to the *Calf-Bearer* (see fig. 7.21) that was created about a thousand years earlier.

The statue of *Christ Enthroned* (fig. 12.6) depicts Christ as a young, clean-shaven philosopher or emperor. Features, clothing, and gestures are classical, as is the smooth, idealized face. Not accepted until the Byzantine era, though certainly the universal image today, the concept of a bearded Christ was probably Syrian in origin. Because this was art of the spirit rather than the flesh, literal depiction was not the goal; this is Christ the symbol, the Son of God. Just as the image of Christ is venerated as if it were the person, so too can a cross or relic be venerated. Nevertheless, the existence of these two sculptures is unusual and might even be construed as images from another religion if very similar figures did not also appear on innumerable early Christian sarcophagi.

By the middle of the third century important church leaders were entombed in stone sarcophagi, but the practice was not widely accepted until Christianity was legalized in the fourth century. Drawing on both classical sources and catacomb paintings, the superb *Jonah Sarcophagus* (fig. 12.7) depicts the Jonah story in a continuous narration, a series of successive episodes in which Jonah appears three times and the strangely serpentine whale twice. Reading

from left to right: Jonah is cast naked into a swirling sea by the sailors and heads directly into the mouth of the waiting whale; after the confused whale disgorges Jonah, the latter ends up sleeping nude under a protective arbor of gourds. Noah appears in a miniscule box floating on the sea to the right of the second whale, while in the upper left-hand corner Jesus addresses a tiny mummy standing in front of a tomb, thus paralleling the raising of Lazarus with the Noah and Jonah stories. Though using biblical material to communicate the idea of salvation, the artist was clearly influenced by classical sculptors.

By the middle of the fourth century, sarcophagi began to emphasize New Testament scenes, as evidenced in the *Sarcophagus of Junius Bassus* (fig. 12.8). The front panel, illustrated here, is divided into ten reliefs on two levels. The top level includes: (1) the Sacrifice of Isaac, (2) the Arrest of St. Peter, (3) Christ Enthroned between St. Peter and St. Paul, and (4–5) Christ before Pilate. The bottom level shows: (1) the Misery of Job, (2) Adam and Eve after the Fall, (3) Christ's Entry into Jerusalem, (4) Daniel in the Lion's Den, and (5) St. Paul Led to His Martyrdom. Many interpretations are possible for a series this complex: The sacrifice of Isaac is in response to God's

Figure 12.7 *The Jonah Sarcophagus,* late third century A.D. Lateran Museum, Rome.

Figure 12.8 *The Sarcophagus of Junius Bassus,* ca. A.D. 359. Marble, 46½″ × 96″, St. Peter's, Rome.

command, as is the testing of Job; Daniel, Abraham, and Job represent salvation; the fall of Adam and Eve represents the condition of humanity that is redeemed by Christ's sacrifice; the triumphal entry into Jerusalem signals the eternal triumph of the Resurrected Christ, depicted directly above. The implications are endless. All of the Old and New Testament figures look like Romans of the time and, indeed, the central top panel shows the Roman sky god Caelus holding up the firmament on which Christ is resting his feet.

The Age of Constantine

For a document of such critical importance, the Edict of Milan is a typical example of the urbane and low-keyed Roman approach to affairs of state:

When we, Constantine Augustus and Licinius Augustus, met so happily at Milan, and considered together all that concerned the interest and security of the State, we decided . . . to grant to Christians and to everybody the free power to follow the religion of their choice, in order that all that is divine in the heavens may be favorable and propitious towards us and towards all who are placed under our authority.

From a rescript issued at Nicomedia by Licinius, June 13, 313.[1]

---

1. Laotantius, *De mortibus persecutorum,* xlviii. Constantine did not assume sole leadership of the empire until 324, when he had Licinius, his coregent, executed.

Figure 12.9 Roman basilica, Volubilis, Morocco, third century A.D.

Figure 12.10 Basilica of St. Clement, interior of lower church, fourth century A.D., Rome.

Though it came soon after the two most severe and methodical persecutions of Christians, by Decius in 249–251 and by Diocletian in 303–305, this declaration of religious freedom found organized Christianity ready to build churches and otherwise assume a prominent role in the empire. For centuries the Romans had constructed basilicas, large buildings that served as meeting halls, mercantile centers, halls of justice, and the like. The basilica was a prototype of the kind of large, dignified structure Christians needed for worship services. For example, the basilica at Volubilis (fig. 12.9) originally had five aisles and four rows of arcades like the one pictured here. Serving as a hall of justice for a large Roman colony, the building has the usual Roman arches with Corinthian pilasters punctuating the heavy columns. By removing the pillar and letting the column carry the thrust of the arch (fig. 12.10), Christian architects developed a lighter and more graceful setting for the Christian liturgy. St. Clement, one of the smaller early churches, has only one aisle on each side and a single triumphal arch framing the altar. It is called a basilica because it contains the relics of a saint; it is not, however, a true basilica as an architectural type.

None of the great basilica-type churches erected in Constantine's Rome have survived as such. Old St. Peter's was replaced by the present church, and hardly anything original remains of St. John Lateran after numerous restorations. St. Paul's Outside the Walls was destroyed by fire in 1823 and faithfully reconstructed by 1854, insofar as that was possible. However, the etching by Piranesi (fig. 12.11) is of the original church and clearly illustrates a basic design used for nearly all Western churches throughout the entire medieval period. The secular basilica was usually entered from its longitudinal sides, but Christians shifted the entrances to a shorter side, usually the western end, thus orienting the building along a longitudinal axis. The interior space was divided into a large area called the *nave,* because it seemed to symbolize a ship (*navis,* the ship of souls), flanked by two aisles on each side (see fig. 12.12). The nave joins a secondary space, the *transept,* which is placed at right angles to the nave proper and forms an interior Latin cross. Later churches would lengthen the transept so that even the exterior walls assumed a cruciform shape, the most characteristic church design in Western Christendom. Behind the transept is a semicircular space called an *apse* (aps) in which the altar is placed on a raised platform. The nave was covered with an A-shaped truss roof; at a level well below the nave roof the aisles were covered by lean-to truss roofs so that the clerestory, or clearstory, windows could be set in the upper nave wall to illuminate the interior. Corinthian columns connected a nave arcade above which was the *triforium,* usually painted or covered with mosaics; above that was the clerestory area with alabaster windows. Aesthetically, the basilica interior is complex and stimulating, for there is no single point from which one can comprehend the space. The strong rhythm of the nave arcade seems to march inexorably towards the eastern end and the triumphal arch that frames the ultimate focus of the design: the high altar where the sacraments are celebrated.

An obvious choice for Christian use, the basilica had imperial associations that suited the triumph of Christianity and a spacious interior that could accommodate thousands of worshipers; Old St. Peter's was said to have a capacity of 40,000. In addition to the interior space, large churches like St. Paul's and Old St. Peter's were fronted by an open courtyard called an *atrium,* which was surrounded on three sides by a covered arcade called an *ambulatory,* or walkway.

Figure 12.11 Interior, St. Paul's Outside the Walls, begun 386 A.D., Rome. Etching by Giambattista Piranesi, 1749.

On the fourth side of the atrium was a porch, or *narthex,* that led to the front doors of the church. Adapted from Roman house plans (see fig. 10.3), the atrium was later moved to the south side of monastic churches to become the medieval cloister. Traversing the entire complex from the ambulatory into the arcaded courtyard (atrium), going through the narthex, entering the church proper, and walking down the nave to the altar is curiously suggestive of the layout of Egyptian temples (see figs. 7.7 and 7.8).

With a deliberately plain exterior of brick or rubble construction, Christian churches reserved glorious interiors—embellished structural materials, marble panels, paintings, and mosaics—for their congregations. Very little of early Christian mural painting has survived, and what remains is not as striking as the incredibly beautiful mosaics. As created by Hellenistic and Roman artists, mosaics were composed of small bits of marble called *tesserae* (TES–ser–ay). Almost always designed as floor mosaics, artists incorporated subtle gradations of color into designs, some of which were reproductions of existing paintings. Early Christian mosaics were, on the other hand, unprecedented. Designed entirely as wall or ceiling decorations, the tesserae were made of bits of glass cubes that had a wide range of color

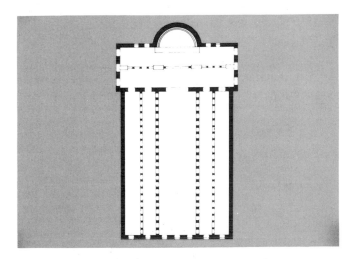

Figure 12.12 Schematic floor plan of St. Paul's, Rome

and intensity, including transparent pieces backed with glittering gold leaf. With shiny, irregular glass faces, the tesserae were set into plaster at slightly varying angles, turning a flat wall surface into a shimmering screen of color. Depicting Christ enthroned and raised above the Apostles, the much renovated

Figure 12.13 *Christ Teaching the Apostles in the Heavenly Jerusalem,* mosaic in the apse of Santa Pudenziana, ca. A.D. 401–407, Rome.

Figure 12.14 *Abraham and the Celestial Visitors,* mosaic from the second quarter of the fifth century, Church of Santa Maria Maggiore, Rome.

mosaic of Santa Pudenziana (fig. 12.13), asserts Christ's authority and, by implication, the institutional authority of the church. In the background are buildings representing the Heavenly Jerusalem, while in the sky are winged symbols of the four evangelists: the lion of St. Mark, the ox of St. Luke, the eagle of St. John, and the winged man of St. Matthew. Of unknown origin but widely employed by this time, these evangelical images continued throughout Christian iconography. Not meant to be read as a historical event, this scene is an essay on salvation as assured by Christ's death on the cross, of which we have been informed by the evangelists, and which is available through the church, the representative of God on earth.

What is believed to be the oldest cycle of evangelical and biblical mosaics is found in the fifth-century church of Santa Maria Maggiore in Rome. One scene depicts, on two levels, the encounter of Abraham with the three celestial visitors at Mamre and his subsequent vision of the Trinity (fig. 12.14). On the lower level Sarah prepares food, which Abraham then sets before the three young men, whose celestial status is marked by halos. On the upper level Abraham bows before his visitors, who now appear in a vision; this time the central figure of Christ is completely surrounded by an oval field of light called an *aureole* (OR–e–ol). This manner of representing the Holy Trinity was common in the West into the Gothic period and even in today's Byzantine world.

Figure 12.15 *The Good Shepherd,* mosaic; Mausoleum of Galla Placidia, ca. 425–450, Ravenna, Italy.

Ravenna

Serving briefly as an imperial city for the Romans, Ostrogoths, and the Byzantine Empire, provincial Ravenna was, when compared with Rome, a most unlikely capital. Located south of Venice in the midst of extensive swamps, the port of Ravenna did provide the Western emperors with an easily defensible site and, perhaps more importantly, a low profile compared with the once mighty city of Rome, now the natural target of every barbarian invader. Becoming the capital of the West under Honorius in 404, Ravenna fell to Odoacer in 476 but emerged as the capital of Theodoric's Ostrogothic Kingdom (489–526), and concluded its royal career as the Western capital of Justinian's Byzantine Empire (527–565). Modern Ravenna contains notable artworks from all three imperial periods.

The mausoleum Empress Galla Placidia, half sister of Honorius, built for members of her family contains some of the best-preserved and splendid mosaics of the fifth century. Set in a *lunette* (lew–NET), a semicircular wall of a vaulted room, the mosaic of *The Good Shepherd* (fig. 12.15) depicts a majestic Christ watching over six attentive sheep, who balance him in pyramid formations of three on each side, thus symbolizing the Trinitarian doctrine. The regal pose spirals upwards from the right hand feeding a sheep to the left hand, which grasps a knob-ended cross signifying the earthly death of the King of Kings. In the Hellenic tradition of classical painting, the forms are positioned in a real space and give the illusion of having three-dimensional bulk. Particularly notable is the rocky landscape, which though increasingly stylized remained in the repertoire of landscape painting throughout the Byzantine tradition and into the late medieval style of such painters as Giotto. Often overlooked are the funnel-shaped tubes along the lower border that represent footlights illuminating a liturgical tableau.

Figure 12.16 Interior, Church of Sant' Apollinare Nuovo, ca. 493–526, Ravenna.

Theodoric, King of the Ostrogoths, built some notable churches in Ravenna. Originally dedicated by Theodoric to "Our Lord Jesus Christ" to serve his Arian sect, the Church of Sant' Apollinare Nuovo (fig. 12.16) was later renamed by the Orthodox church after Apollinarus, a disciple of St. Peter and the patron saint of Ravenna. Though the teaching of Arius of Alexandria (ca. 256–336) was condemned by the 325 Council of Nicea over which Constantine presided, many Germanic tribes like the Ostrogoths persisted in the Arian heresy. Briefly, the Arians held to the rationalistic belief that since Christ was created by God the Father, he must be subordinate and not of the same divine substance as his creator. Jesus was therefore the highest of created beings but human rather than divine. The orthodox Byzantine view was that Christ, as the Word Incarnate, was of single substance with the Father and thus wholly divine. The popes of the Western church held to a middle ground: the Word was made flesh, and so Christ was both divine and human and a full member of the Holy Trinity. Reflecting the controversy between Arianism and Byzantine orthodoxy, the mosaics of Sant' Apollinare Nuovo are arranged in three levels. Created by Roman artists for Theodoric, the top band includes scenes from the life of Christ, while the figures between the clerestory windows represent Old Testament patriarchs and prophets. After the Byzantine conquest of Ravenna, Bishop Angellus ordered the lowest band removed, presumably because Arian beliefs were depicted. These were replaced with Byzantine-style saints in procession, women on the north wall (left in fig. 12.16) and men on the south. The nave itself has an

Figure 12.17 San Vitale, ca. 526–547, Ravenna

arcade of columns with ornate capitals topped by blocks from which spring the semicircular arches. With only one side aisle and no transepts, the plan is that of a small and unpretentious basilica, which further highlights the splendid mosaics.

The Byzantine World

Marking the true beginning of the Byzantine style, the reign of Justinian (527–565) was notable for artistic production and for the Justinian Legal Code, plus the dubious distinction of closing, after a thousand years, Plato's Academy in Athens. Operating from his capitals of Constantinople in the East and Ravenna in the West, Justinian was both an emperor in the Roman tradition and an Oriental potentate in what was to later become the Byzantine Empire. Except for some architecture in Constantinople, most Byzantine art created prior to 1402 can be found in Ravenna. The rape of Constantinople by the Fourth Crusade (1204) destroyed most of the art and much of the city, which was not retaken from the Latins until 1261.

The most "Byzantine" of the many religious buildings in Ravenna is the octagonal domed church of San Vitale (fig. 12.17), a prototype of the central-plan churches that were to dominate the world of Orthodox Christianity just as the basilica plan prevailed throughout Western Christendom. The brick exterior is a complex and subtle interplay of angular patterns around a central core, marred only by the addition of a Renaissance doorway. The interior is a veritable jewel box (colorplate 10), with walls of polychromed marble, pierced marble screens, hundreds of decorative and pictorial mosaics, marble floor mosaics, and numerous carved alabaster columns. San Vitale is an octagonal structure surmounted by an octagonal drum on which the circular dome rests. The transition from the octagonal drum to the round dome was accomplished by using *squinches,* stone lintels placed diagonally across corners formed by the octagonal walls. Topping the aisle that surrounds the nave is a vaulted triforium gallery reserved for women, as was customary for Orthodox Christianity. Compact and intimate, San Vitale functioned for the imperial court somewhat like a diminutive, luxurious theatre.

Facing the altar from opposite sides are the two justly celebrated mosaics of Emperor Justinian (colorplate 11) and Empress Theodora (colorplate 12). Though extensively reconstructed, these ceremonial works are still the best extant examples of early Byzantine mosaics. Illustrating the new ideal of the Byzantine style, the figures are tall and slim with small feet, solemn faces, and large oval eyes. Frozen in time without a hint of movement, the grave figures are depicted in full frontality, highly stylized, but nevertheless revealing individual differences. Flanked by twelve companions suggesting the twelve Apostles, Justinian stands in the exact center holding the offering of bread for the mass. He is crowned with both the imperial diadem and a halo, representative of the unity of the spiritual force of the church and of the temporal power of the state. At Justinian's left is Bishop Maximianus, who was responsible for the completion of San Vitale and whose importance is signified by the label over his head. The composition of the work delineates the threefold structure of the empire: the six soldiers represent the army, the three staff members the state, and the three clergymen the church. One of the soldiers holds a shield with the Chrismon insignia that symbolizes not only the name of Christ but allegorically becomes a combination of the cross and shepherd's crook, indicating Christ's death and his pastoral mission.

Unlike the emperor, Theodora is depicted in a more specific setting, probably the narthex of San Vitale. About to pass through a doorway to which she is beckoned by an attendant, she is carrying the offering of wine in a gold chalice encrusted with precious stones. With her huge diadem, ropes of pearls, and luxurious ceremonial gown in royal purple, Theodora is portrayed as the strong-willed, intelligent, and beautiful empress history has revealed her to be, and considerably removed from her early career as circus performer and courtesan. Pictured on her gown are the Magi bringing their offerings to the infant Jesus, suggesting a parallel with her gift-bearing activity. Both mosaics achieve some of their clarity by conforming to the Greek isocephalic convention of placing all heads on about the same level.

Figure 12.18 *Christ Pantocrater,* dome mosaic, ca. 532, Church of St. Irene, Constantinople (Istanbul).

Figure 12.19 Anthemius of Tralles and Isodorus of Miletos, Hagia Sophia, 532–537, Constantinople (Istanbul).

The City of Constantine

Dedicated by Constantine in 330 as "New Rome," Constantinople, as the city quickly came to be known, was the sumptuous center of Byzantine civilization for over a thousand years. Typical of central-plan churches, St. Irene was only one of Justinian's many building projects for the imperial city. Contrasting with the extended longitudinal axis of the basilica plan, central-plan churches are built around a vertical axis which extends from the floor to the ceiling mosaic of the central dome. Figure 12.18 illustrates the psychological impact of the head of Christ as the ultimate focus of the vertical axis, and symbolizes the total dominance of the Orthodox faith under the aegis of the emperor who built the churches and appointed the patriarch of Constantinople.

Justinian's building program for Constantinople began in 532 as a matter of necessity. It was in that year that the Blues and Greens, rival chariot-racing factions, had combined in a powerful revolt against the autocratic rule of Justinian and Theodora. Before the imperial troops put down the revolution by slaughtering about 30,000 people, most of the public buildings had been destroyed, including the Constantinian Basilica of Hagia Sophia (HA–jeh SO–fee–ah; Church of Holy Wisdom).

Disdaining the usual procedure of selecting an architect for a building project, Justinian appointed the noted mathematician Anthemius of Tralles to design the new Hagia Sophia. Assisted by Isodorus of Miletos and possibly Justinian himself, Anthemius invented a revolutionary new design unlike anything in either the Roman or Byzantine world (fig. 12.19). Combining the longitudinal axis of the basilica plan with the domed structure of a central plan, abutted on east and west by half domes, the new Hagia Sophia was a beautiful and inspiring building, truly a majestic architectural achievement. No wonder Justinian is said to have exclaimed as he rode up to the church for its consecration, "O Solomon, I have excelled thee!"

The interior of Hagia Sophia is breathtaking (fig. 12.20). The dome seems to float on light, as it rests upon a tightly spaced ring of forty windows. The entire interior is, in fact, flooded with light from hundreds of windows in the thin, shell-like walls. Adding to the magical effect of all this light were thousands of tesserae that were set into the walls, but later covered with plaster and paint when the Turks converted the building into a mosque. With an interior measuring 240' x 270', crowned by a dome 112' in diameter and extending to 184' above the pavement, this is one of the largest space enclosures achieved prior to this century. At the corners of a 100' square area under the dome are 70' piers that support massive arches. They in turn are connected by *pendentives* (pen–DEN–tivs), which effect the transition from the basic square to the circular rim of the dome. Best described as concave spherical triangles, two of the four pendentives can be seen in figure 12.20. A more graceful transition from a square base to a round dome than squinches, pendentives also facilitate the covering of more floor space. Their origin remains unknown and their use on the monumental scale of Hagia Sophia is unprecedented. Henceforth used in most Byzantine architecture, pendentives became standard structural devices from the Renaissance to the present day.

Figure 12.20 Interior of Hagia Sophia, Constantinople (Istanbul).

Figure 12.21 Greek Orthodox church, from the fourth century A.D. Naxos, Greece.

Figure 12.22 Aerial view of St. Mark's Cathedral, begun 1063, Venice.

As sometimes happens with highly original buildings, there were some technical problems, the most serious being the collapse of the dome twenty-one years after its completion. The present higher-arched dome solved that problem. Byzantium never produced another structure to equal Hagia Sophia. Though it inspired similar designs that can be seen all over Istanbul, it remains unique—the first and best of its kind. First a church and then a mosque, Hagia Sophia is now a museum.

Typical of the more modest churches throughout the empire is the small Orthodox church on the Greek island of Naxos (fig. 12.21). It was built of local field-stone and displays the Byzantine central-dome plan at the left, but this diminutive church also features domes over the other arms of the Greek cross plan, such as those used much later and on a far-greater scale in the Cathedral of St. Mark's in Venice (see fig. 12.22).

Brutally terminating the first Byzantine golden age, the Iconoclastic Controversy lasted off and on, mostly on, from 726 to 843. Issuing an imperial decree forbidding idolatry, Leo III ordered the destruction of all images of Christ, saints, prophets, and the like. Representations of all sorts, including mosaics in Hagia Sophia, were destroyed along with the entire legacy of pictorial art of Justinian's age, except in Byzantine Italy and on Mount Sinai. Iconoclasts (image-destroyers) mutilated, blinded, tortured, and sometimes executed those who tried to protect sacred images. Ostensibly a religious issue based on the biblical commandment forbidding graven images, the controversy was essentially a conflict between Church and State. The monastic movement had achieved great wealth and power and won considerable respect from the faithful, much to the consternation of the emperors; furthermore, monasteries were diverting revenue from the state and paying little or no taxes. As principal repositories for sacred images, monasteries were attacked, sometimes confiscated, and their resident monks executed, without, however, stamping out the image-worshipping monks (iconodules) in the West. A later Empress Theodora allowed images again in 843, but the Western and Eastern branches of Christianity were already launched on a parting of the ways, which led, in 1054, to a schism that has yet to be healed. Though the extent of the loss of priceless artworks can never be known the disaster was not total. The controversy did help to spark a renewed interest in secular art and Late Classical motifs, setting the stage for the Second Byzantine Golden Age of ca. 900–1100.

The Second Golden Age

The largest and most profusely decorated church of the Second Golden Age, St. Mark's of Venice is also the most ambitious structure outside the empire. St. Mark's differs from Hagia Sophia in that the Greek cross form is clearly visible from within and that in addition to the central dome, each arm of the cross is capped by a full dome. From the exterior and especially from the air (fig. 12.22), St. Mark's, with each of its five domes encased in wood covered by gilt copper sheathing and topped by ornate lanterns, is the splendid showcase the Republic of Venice intended it to be. As required by law, every ship's captain had to return to Venice with something of value for construction or decoration of the cathedral. Because of the law many treasures from the 1204 sack of Constantinople found their way to Venice. Despite Romanesque and Gothic elements, the Greek cross plan, multiple domes, strong interior lighting, and glittering mosaics make St. Mark's a Byzantine masterpiece.

After the victory of the iconophiles (image-lovers) in 843, Byzantine painting and mosaics began to blend the otherworldly beauty of Justinian's time with a renewed interest in classical Greek art. Perhaps the finest examples of art of the Second Golden Age are to be found in the monastery church at Daphne, Greece. In the *Crucifixion* mosaic (fig. 12.23) there are no Apostles, soldiers, or thieves, only the grief-stricken Mary looking up at Christ and John gazing on in sorrow. The suffering is intense but restrained, reflecting an adaptation of classical Greek sculptural elements to the linear Byzantine style. The skull at the base of the cross represents Golgotha, the "place of the skull." Symbolizing the sacraments of the Eucharist and Baptism, the blood spilling from Christ's side also nourishes the flowers, which represent a new life in Christ. Controlled and compassionate, this is not a historical representation but a humanized portrayal of the Passion of Jesus Christ, his ultimate sacrifice for all of humankind.

The Byzantine style spread throughout the Balkans, Russia, and as far west as Sicily. Strongly influencing some of the Western art of the Middle Ages, it flourished in Eastern Europe for centuries beyond the demise of the Byzantine empire in 1453.

Figure 12.23 *Crucifixion,* mosaic. ca. 1100, Monastery Church, Daphné, Greece.

Bibliography

Grabar, Andre. *Byzantine Painting.* New York: Skira International Corp, 1953. The title is misleading, for most of the book is devoted to mosaics. The illustrations are all in color and they are exceptionally beautiful.

Grabar, Andre, and Carl Nordenfalk. *Early Medieval Painting.* New York: Skira International Corp., 1964. A superb book with illustrations of very high quality.

Krautheimer, Richard. *Early Christian and Byzantine Architecture.* Baltimore: Praeger Books, 1965. Part of the Scholarly Pelican History of Art Series.

Morey, Charles Rufus. *Early Christian Art.* 2d ed. Princeton: Princeton University Press, 1953. This is the classic work in this area of study. Read its text while referring to the illustrations used in any of the books listed here for an enjoyable and informative experience.

Rice, David Talbot. *The Art of Byzantium.* New York: Praeger Books, 1963. Fine illustrations and available in paperback.

Volbach, Wolfgang F., and Max Hirmer. *Early Christian Art.* New York: Harry N. Abrams, Inc., 1962. Excellent, succinct text with superb photographs of key works.

Unit

5

The Age of Faith

13

Building Medieval Walls

The so-called Middle Ages extended for approximately a thousand years from about A.D. 410 to around 1400. Furthermore, they divide themselves sharply at about the year 1000, for reasons that will become apparent. This long period constitutes an amalgamation of various cultures—some features of the Arabic and Moslem, the Eastern civilization that had its source in Byzantium (Constantinople), and principally the crude northern way of life of Germany and the Scandinavian countries—into the old Graeco-Roman institutions. As such, the gestation of the Middle Ages constitutes an almost new start for Western culture, with only a memory of past glories, with written records that lay dormant for centuries, and with the Roman Church as foci of centralizing forces. The rather glorious medieval culture, which reached maturity during the twelfth and thirteenth centuries, represents a fusion of seemingly contradictory ways of life, and of opposition in ways of feeling and thought. Once again we can witness a testimony to the toughness of the human spirit, which lives, survives, changes itself, and finally triumphs over darkness and confusion, expressing itself in magnificent symbols of new growth.

We have already said that Rome "fell" sometime in the fifth century—the arbitrary dates of 410 or 476 do not make much difference. It should be remarked, however, that the average Roman citizen living at the time did not know that Rome had fallen. Life went on much as it had before; life got tougher and tougher, but the government and the Emperor, whether he be Italian or Ostrogoth, were still there. For example, the philosopher Boethius (Bo–EE–thi–us; ca. 475–524), who wrote the famous *Consolation of Philosophy* during the last year of his life, held the office of Roman consul about fifty years after the final "official" date for the fall of Rome.

As a matter of fact, the power of Rome dwindled until it was virtually nonexistent. For centuries the Roman legions had been replaced by barbarian mercenaries, and Rome, unable to defend its borders, either pulled back the soldiers who had been stationed on the extreme boundaries of the Empire or allowed them to become integrated with the local peoples. An ever-increasing number of tribesmen were settled in Italy when the original Italian peoples deserted the land. The capital of the Empire was moved, once to Milan and later to Ravenna, and under the Emperor Constantine the Empire was split into an eastern and a western section, with a growing sense of independence in each area. The "fall" was simply a slow disintegration of power, not a sudden cataclysm. But as civil power failed, the Church gained in strength until it became the great unifying power in Western civilization. The development of this power needs to be considered.

The Early Church: St. Augustine

Christianity had its source in the teachings of Christ, but it became an institutionalized church largely through the efforts of two men. The first of these was the apostle Paul, who traveled widely and kept up a very active correspondence with the communities of Christians throughout the Roman world. Largely through his efforts, the various congregations in the important cities were held together. After his work, a centralized doctrine and a widely accepted institution for the preservation and the propagation of the faith was still lacking. This last work was accomplished in large measure by St. Augustine (354–430).

Augustine was a North African who was very well educated in the arts of logic and dialectic in his native town of Thagaste and in Carthage. The chief Christianizing influence on the young man was his mother, Monica, who admonished him and prayed for him so much that she must have been a real millstone around the neck of the high-spirited young man. He was not baptized until he came under the influence of St. Ambrose and other Christians in Milan in 387. The following year he returned to North Africa, where he founded a monastic order, was made Bishop of Hippo in 396, and spent the rest of his life in that post, writing and preaching in defense of the faith against various heretical groups and against pagans, particularly those who attacked Christianity after the sack of Rome in the year 410. His greatest work, *The City of God*, was written in part as a refutation of the pagan claim that Rome's failure resulted from the Christian influence.

All of his life Augustine was a searcher for a firm belief. As a young man he became a Manichaean, a sect with a strong dualistic belief in a power of good and a power of evil conflicting in the world and in people. His logical mind could not, however, accept all the doctrine of this sect, and later, in Rome, he became a skeptic, a believer in nothing, not even his own existence. Finally he read some of the Neoplatonists and was strongly influenced by them, so much so that he regarded his Neoplatonic period as the most important stepping stone to his acceptance of Christianity, for his doctrine incorporated much of Neoplatonism (minus Greek rationalism). This was in Milan, where he was serving as a municipally appointed teacher (his students in Carthage had been too unruly for him to put up with; the students were better behaved in Rome but they seldom paid their tuition), where his Christian mother, Monica, had joined him, and where he heard the impressive preaching of Bishop Ambrose, a critical influence on his eventual conversion to Christianity. After experiencing his famous mystical experience in the garden (as recounted in his noted autobiography, *The Confessions*), he was baptized in 387 by St. Ambrose. Although he preferred to lead a contemplative life, his later duties as Bishop of Hippo forced him into vigorous activity as a powerful advocate of the Roman Church against the Manichaeans, the Arians and, especially, against the Donatist heresy, which he energetically persecuted.

The Arian and Donatist heresies represented practical and philosophical problems of the early Christian church, problems that were still of great concern to Augustine and his contemporaries. Roman persecution of Christians after A.D. 303 forced many priests to collaborate with authorities by handing over sacred texts. After Constantine's edicts of toleration in 311 and 313, these "handers-over" (*traditores*) resumed their roles as priests only to be challenged by Donatus, bishop of Carthage. Donatus advocated punishing weak, collaborationist priests by declaring their administration of the sacraments invalid, a politically dangerous position because it gave believers opportunities to judge which priests were dispensing valid sacraments. Because of the political nature of the controversy, Constantine utilized his imperial prerogative by ruling that once a priest has been properly ordained, his administration of the sacraments remains valid even though his actions may become reprehensible. The problems of dissent and violence over the Donatist heresy continued to plague North Africa even after Augustine's tenure as Bishop of Hippo.

Heresy also involved such philosophical principles as Arianism, named after Arius, an Alexandrian priest who maintained that God the Son could not be precisely of the *same* essence as God the Father because the begetter must be somehow superior to, as well as necessarily earlier in time than, the begotten. This view threatened to diminish the divinity of Christ and to break up the Holy Trinity, as emphasized by Arius's bitter opponent, Athanasius, bishop of Alexandria. Disdaining logic and espousing mystery, Athanasius and his followers exhorted Christians to simply accept on faith that the Trinity of Father, Son, and Holy Ghost was both equal and contemporary. Unable to settle the quarrel, in 325 Constantine called the first meeting to involve the whole church, an ecumenical council (Greek, *oikoumene*, the inhabited world). Meeting at Nicaea, across the straits from Constantinople, the assembled bishops backed Athanasius's view, resulting in the famous Nicene Creed ("We believe in one God"), which was issued by Constantine with all the force of an imperial decree.

Augustine was not only a theologian but also a very busy administrator as Bishop of Hippo and propagandist for the Roman Church. In this respect he was faced with the problem of the efficacy of the sacraments when performed by priests who belonged to heretical sects or who led impure lives. His judgment in the matter was that the efficacy of the sacraments (it must be remembered that only through the sacraments did one find salvation) lay in the office of the priesthood, not in the man who performed them. The basis for this decision rested in the argument that if the benefit of the sacraments lay in the quality of the man who performed them, then people themselves would be placed in judgment of God's grace. The promulgation of this doctrine did much to establish the concept of the infallibility of the Church, since its power was inherent within its offices. This power, it was argued, descended directly from the apostles, who were the original bishops of the Church. From them it passed to other bishops, and from the bishops to the priests through the "laying on of hands." Through this act, the power to administer the sacraments was given and could not be revoked.

When considering Augustine as a philosopher and theologian we are confronted with the vast number of books written about the whole body of his thought. Here we shall give a very summary treatment of his ideas about the nature of God, of the creation, of free will, his philosophy of history, and the infallibility of the Church, for these beliefs provide the backbone for European civilization up to the late Middle Ages.

Earlier in our study we made the point that a culture is based upon the idea of Reality that is held by that culture. According to Augustine, God was the only reality, who created the world out of nothingness. This God was a mystic being, not an intellectual principle as was the case with the Neoplatonists, so that knowledge of God and life in him was available to all human beings, whether they were philosophers or not. Although Augustine regarded his own early philosophic speculations as stepping stones to belief, he felt that his conversion came about through the grace of God, not through human efforts, and that this grace is available to all people. For Augustine and all believers throughout the Middle Ages, union with God is the only true goal and the only true happiness for people, all of which takes place in the hereafter.

The process of creation-from-nothingness took place because of two aspects of the mind of God, roughly corresponding to the Platonic essences, but with significant differences. One such aspect corresponds to the eternal truths, such as the truth that the sum of the angles of a triangle always equals 180°. Such truths, existing before creation and after the destruction of the world, constitute the basic patterns and harmonies of the universe. Another aspect of God's mind consists of the "seminal (or seed) reasons" for created things. These are the patterns that acquire physical substance and form the visible things of the world: the visible people, trees, earth, and the myriad things that are apparent to our senses. These sense-apparent things exist in time; they rise, disintegrate, and pass away, and because of their transitory nature are the least important of God's creations.

Implicit in the last statement is Augustine's dualistic concept of time. He believed in a direct flow of time in which humanity's activities (never repeating themselves in spiral or circular patterns) moved upward toward eventual perfection, toward the godlike. The flow of time and all the changes that occur within it are characteristic of the temporal world. God, however, with all the attributes of his mind, dwells in eternity, which is really a timeless instant. In this realm past and future have no meaning; all is present.

In this way, Augustine reconciled the problem of God's foreknowledge of all events and humanity's free will. He asserted that people, with the exception of original sin that could be washed away with baptism, had free will; yet God knew every event that would take place. How does one avoid fatalism and the idea of predestination if all of a person's actions are known in advance? The answer is that God's seeing all things as present-time allows for foreknowledge in what *we* call time, yet the "seeing" of things does not influence them. All events are simultaneous for God, and thus he can know them without influencing them. A person's vision is shackled by past, present, and an inscrutable future, but in the temporal world there is complete free will.

In his attitude toward the body and the whole world of matter, Augustine was somewhat ambivalent. If this world is God's creation then it must be good. On the other hand, being overly concerned with the acquisition of worldly goods can turn a person away from God, and that is of course sinful. The matter of bodily pleasures was especially disturbing. Before his conversion Augustine had lived a lusty life of fleshly pleasures; his proclivities were dramatized in his famous prayer: "O Lord, make me chaste, but not yet." He shifted to the other extreme after his conversion and condemned sexual pleasure (music was included in this censure because, like the sex act, it kept the mind from contemplating God).

His view of the material world was strongly influenced by Platonic doctrine, but not entirely. He believed that the physical things of the world are all passing away and changing. For example, in *The City of God* he makes the point that in Rome in 410 many people lost all of their worldly possessions, yet Christians remained happy since their "possessions" were in their spirit and could not be taken away. The conclusion is that a concern with worldly things is a concern with nothing, since these things are ephemeral. The only vital concern is with the things of the spirit, which have their existence in the realm of eternity. This type of thought is not completely dualistic in that it does not despise the flesh and the things of the world, yet it tends in that direction. Many later Christian thinkers were to turn completely against the world and the flesh, asserting even more strongly than Plato and Augustine that these things were traps for the mind and the spirit of humanity. Much of the puritanical thought of our time comes from this basic reasoning.

Augustine, in the first complete formulation of a Christian philosophy of history, viewed the story of humanity as a conflict between two cities. (He used the word *city* as we might use the word *community* in such a phrase as the "business community.") One of these was the City of God, the other the City of Man. In the beginning, when time was created, he stated, everything belonged to the good city, yet with the revolt of the angels and Satan's expulsion from heaven, the other city came into being. From that time until the birth of Christ, almost all of humanity belonged to the Earthly City. Only a few Hebrews who had faith in the coming of a Savior belonged to the City of God. With Christ's coming for the redemption of mortals, and with the formation of the Church, the membership in the two cities was more sharply divided, since all members of the City of God were also members of the Church. This, he was careful to assert, did not work conversely—all members of the Church were not necessarily members of God's City. The end of history will come with the Last Judgment and the final and complete separation of the two cities. The saved will be reclothed in their perfect bodies and take their place with God; the damned will undergo eternal torture with Satan. Since the members of the good city are already known to God, we find here the basis for the doctrine of the elect, a tenet that was to be completely enunciated by Calvin after the Reformation.

This philosophy of history has at least one other important consequence. If the original members of the City of God are to be found only among the Hebrews, they alone knew truth. Thus all pagan learning, that of the Greeks, for example, is falsehood and is not to be studied. The loss of the Graeco-Roman heritage had an incalculable effect on the course of Western civilization.

Sometime after the death of Augustine final authority of the Church in Rome was achieved, for the bishops of Rome had asserted their supremacy over the other bishops. The argument for this was that St. Peter had founded the Church in Rome, and that he was Christ's spiritual successor. Biblical authority was given for this claim from Christ's words concerning Peter, "Upon this rock *(petras)* will I build my church." Leo, Bishop of Rome from 440 to 461, first made this claim to ecclesiastical authority, and Pope Gregory the Great, slightly more than a century later, was such an able diplomat and churchman that the primacy of the Pope became universally accepted for the Western Church.

These were the moves that established a body of doctrine incorporating the infallibility of the Church, and a strong and revered institution that was able to maintain its authority throughout the troubled and confused years of the early Middle Ages as the only source of order throughout all of Europe. Very early on the Church was divided into two branches: the regular clergy (from the Latin *regula* or *rule*) composed of the monks and those who retreated from the active life, and the secular clergy, the Pope, the bishops, and parish priests who lived among the people and sought to lead them to a better life. During the time of the decline of the Roman authority, a very great number of men, particularly among the intellectual class, retreated from the world to live and work in the communal life of monasteries leading the contemplative existence. This is not an unusual phenomenon during any time of cultural upheaval, including our own.

Feudalism and Manorialism

Following the withdrawal of Roman military and governmental stability, the people of western Europe had to find ways by which they could govern themselves with some semblance of justice, and by which they could make a living. The governmental system, feudalism, did not develop fully until the tenth century, but it can be described here as the slowly evolving political system of the Middle Ages. Manorialism, the economic arrangement by which the people made a living, actually had its beginnings during late Roman times when the peasants were forced to stay on the land and became serfs. Furthermore, the two systems, at the lowest level—the demesne, or land-holding of a single knight—are so intertwined that they are scarcely distinguishable.

In its essence, feudalism is simply an arrangement by which the whole territory of the former empire was divided up into small enough units so that a single man could rule each one. It also created a fighting society, since the lords constantly raided adjoining territories, and all of them were subject to the forays of the northern tribes from Germany and Scandinavia.

In what had once been the civilized Roman Empire, we find a number of kings who lacked both the money and the power to hold their kingdoms together. These rulers proceeded to split up their kingdoms among the nobility, the highest ranking of which were the barons. The barons accepted the land from the king, and in return swore allegiance to him and agreed to furnish a certain number of fighting men when the kingdom was attacked. Thus a baron became a *vassal* of the king. But since the barons also lacked power to administer their lands, they took vassals under them, further subdividing the land. This successive division of land continued down to the knight, who owned one estate or demesne consisting of a village and the rather extensive farmlands surrounding it. Each member of the nobility was thus a despotic ruler over the land that he actually controlled, subject only to the oaths of loyalty he swore to the lord immediately over him. One knight could control his one small village and the farms that surrounded it and provide some form of rough justice for the inhabitants.

The manorial system was simply the totality of the life within one of these villages. Here, unless he was away at war, resided the lord in his manor house. A priest took care of the spiritual needs of the community, and the church and parish house usually occupied the center of the village. In addition to these

Figure 13.1 Aigues-Mortes, France. Located on the Mediterranean coast, this perfectly preserved medieval town was founded as a staging area and supply base for the crusades. Medieval walls were a common denominator throughout Europe.

Figure 13.2 Inside the walls, Carcassonne, France. When inside the restored walls of this fortified town, the overwhelming masses of masonry give a comforting feeling of security and community.

buildings, one usually found a community bake-oven, a winepress, and a mill for grinding grain. The farming land (one can assume that an average demesne comprised about a thousand acres) was divided into three main sections, two of which were planted each year and the third allowed to lie fallow. The lord retained a certain area as his personal property (though it was farmed by the serfs), the priest was given a small allotment of land, a section was retained as common woodland, and another section was used as a common meadow. Each farmer or serf was given certain strips of land in each of the three fields—each strip was usually an eighth of a mile in length and about seventeen feet wide.[1] The serf and his family were "attached" to the land, that is, they could not leave, but neither could they be turned away. The serf gave a certain portion of his produce to the lord and was also obligated to work a certain number of days on the lord's land. The lord, in his turn, was obliged to protect his villagers and to provide justice, though he was the only judge in the case of disputes, and his word was final.

The manorial system gives us a picture of a poverty-stricken and almost totally isolated life. All of the bare necessities were provided within the single manor, and the serf scarcely ever traveled beyond it. No news of the world came in except when the lord returned from a war, or when an occasional itinerant peddler came through. One can safely assume that none of the peasants could read, and that formal education was unknown. Life on the manor slowed to the regular round of work, religious holidays, births, marriages, and deaths. Life was maintained at a minimal level behind medieval walls, which shut out hostile forces but also, figuratively speaking, kept out ideas that might disturb the rigid order enforced by the church and the barons (figs. 13.1 and 13.2). It is little wonder that the people came to regard this world as a vale of tears and that they lived in anticipation of a glorious afterlife in heaven.

Charlemagne

The most important political and humanistic period of the early Middle Ages was the reign of Charlemagne (Charles the Great, ruled 768–814). The first bright spark in the so-called Dark Ages, the Carolingian Renaissance proved that the light of civilization had not been entirely extinguished.

Charles was the second of the Carolingian Kings of the Franks, and his father had already gained the support of the Roman Church by defeating the Lombards in Italy and granting a very considerable area of land to the Papacy. When Charles came to the throne he set about to expand and solidify the kingdom of the Franks, fighting the Moslems in Spain, the Norsemen up to the border of Denmark, and against the Lombards in Italy. The battle of Roncevaux in 778 in

---

1. Replacing the scratch plow, a new kind of plow was invented (late seventh century) which was equipped with a vertical knife to cut the furrow, a horizontal plowshare to slice under the sod, and a moldboard to turn it over. Pulled by eight oxen (communally owned), it attacked the land with such violence that cross-plowing was unnecessary and fields tended to be shaped in long strips. Found nowhere else in the world (for centuries to come), this plow marked the beginning of a technological revolution that would change the European from nature's partner to an exploiter of natural resources, leading to today's ecological problems.

Figure 13.3 Aachen, Germany. Four periods of history are represented here. At the right is a modern building constructed after Aachen was almost totally demolished during World War II. The tower is twelfth century Romanesque, to the left of which is Charlemagne's eighth century domed chapel, with the fourteenth century Gothic choir at the far left.

which Charles's knight, Count Roland, was ambushed and killed furnished the kernel for the great cycle of songs and stories relating to the exploits of Charles. In return for this warring activity against the pagans, and as a shrewd political move, the Pope crowned Charles as "Emperor of the Romans" on Christmas day in the year 800.

Important as these political events are, they cannot be our main concern. The significant factor here is that Charles had a great respect for learning and brought scholars from all Europe to his court at Aachen (Aix-la-Chapelle). The architecture of this court itself is a landmark in Western culture, for Charles had been to Ravenna where he had seen the magnificent architecture and the gleaming mosaics, the ideas for which had come directly from Byzantium. The chapel at Aachen is modeled after the Church of San Vitale in Ravenna, and it was responsible for introducing Eastern ideas of beauty and Roman stone construction to the Western world (fig. 13.3; also see fig. 12.17, colorplate 10, and fig. 15.10).

Most important of all in this revival of learning was the establishment of the Palace (or Palatine) School. To direct it, Charles imported the English scholar Alcuin from the cathedral school at York, and in addition to teaching and directing the school itself, Alcuin collected a considerable number of manuscripts of ancient learning and revived the monastic practice of copying manuscripts, both for the palace library and for distribution to other seats of learning. The Palatine School did not generate much original thought, but it was the first center of scholarship since the collapse of classical civilization and thus very important in terms of later intellectual development.

Under Charles, all of Italy, northern Spain, all of modern France, and southern Germany were united under a single rule, though Charles did not attempt to impose a single code of law on the diverse people. He did, however, have all of his counties inspected regularly to see that the lands were well governed and that justice was administered. Further than that he strengthened the power of the Church, since he forcibly Christianized all of the pagans whom he conquered. One consequence of his being crowned as emperor by the Pope lay in the development of the idea that the Church was superior to all secular authority, an idea that was to give all sorts of trouble in later centuries.

After Charlemagne's death in 814, and the short rule of his ineffective son Louis the Pious, his empire was divided among his three grandsons, none of whom was able to continue the tradition that each had inherited. The empire rapidly fell apart, particularly under the invasions of the Norsemen, the Vikings, who ravaged all of Europe and even sailed to the continent that was later to be named America.

The Assimilation of Cultures

Earlier in this chapter it was pointed out that the most important development during the early Middle Ages was the digestion of several very different and opposed cultures. No one can deny that the old classic tradition of Greece and Rome had run its full course and that it was no longer fruitful. If life was to become meaningful, new ideas, new ways of life, new blood needed to be transfused into the cultural body. The dark period from the fifth to the tenth centuries, full of fear, doubt, confusion, and strife was the result of these clashing cultures. From the vantage point of not having to live in those times, this can now be seen as a period of transition leading to a new culture.

In the main, Byzantine and Moslem cultures remained as storehouses that would be drawn upon by European civilization in the later Middle Ages. Except for a brief conquest of Italy and North Africa under the Eastern emperor Justinian and the influence we have already noted during the rule of Charlemagne, Byzantium was chiefly important as a bastion against eastern infringement upon Europe by the Persians, and by the Slavic and Magyar peoples who settled in what is now Hungary, the Balkans, and southern Russia. These peoples were Christianized and civilized chiefly by missionaries from the Eastern Catholic Church. Another and rather unusual influence of the East came through the Christianizing of Ireland according to the Eastern ritual. For a time at least, Ireland enjoyed a higher and more enlightened culture than did the rest of Europe, and subtle influences of this civilization reached the mainland.

The strongest influence on Western culture was the rise of Islamic religion and culture, a powerful movement that threatened to engulf all of Europe. Originally the Arabs were an uncultured polytheistic people, and they, in themselves, did little to produce enlightenment, but under the general peace and stability of their rule, Hellenistic, Persian, and Syrian art and intellect were permitted to expand.

Mohammed was born in Mecca in about the year 570 and worked as a merchant there until his then unpopular religious beliefs forced him to flee the city in 622. This last date is accepted as the beginning of the Muslim faith. Very soon after this flight, he returned to Mecca in triumph and succeeded in converting many Arabs to his belief.

Mohammed regarded his religious insight as an extension and culmination of the Judeo-Christian tradition, and the faith shares much with those two religious beliefs. Islam stresses the oneness of God and the equality of all men before God. For this reason, it developed no priesthood and no central institutional authority other than the political rulers, the caliphs, under whose rule and warlike spirit the faith was propagated. Particularly important for the development of Western culture was the Muslim banning of statues and images, which was to send many refugee artists to Europe when the Muslims captured Constantinople in 1453.

The Arabs, united for the first time in their new religious belief, set out to conquer most of the world, and were remarkably successful. Very early they overran Persia and the lands to the east, including India. They also occupied Egypt and all of North Africa, and by 720 had conquered all of Spain. They crossed the Pyrenees and invaded France. Here they were met by Charles Martel, grandfather of Charlemagne, near the city of Poitiers in 732, and driven back to Spain. Much of Charlemagne's time was spent fighting in Spain in his attempt to drive the Moors out of Europe.

The contribution of Islam lay not in the wars, but in the peace and prosperity that followed them. Trade routes were opened clear to China so that material goods and immaterial ideas flowed freely through the Islamic world. They were great builders, synthesizing the Roman dome with features of Persian architecture to produce the pointed dome, which we usually associate with Islamic construction. Because images were banned for religious reasons, they developed decorative forms based on geometric designs, which we now call *arabesques*. Most important of all, learning flourished under the rule of these people, and such great universities as those at Cairo and Toledo came into being, both preserving older knowledge and developing new. The works of Plato and Aristotle were translated into Arabic and studied with great zeal; mathematics was developed, particularly with the use of the Arabic system of numbers rather than the clumsy Roman system; and the study of medicine was greatly advanced. While Italy and northern Europe were slogging along in the mud, a very high culture flourished in Asia, Africa, and Spain, the riches of which would not be known until after the Crusades began.

By far the greatest cultural fusion in the early Middle Ages was that of the Celto-Germanic peoples of the north with the Graeco-Romans of the south. We have already become well acquainted with the balanced and intellectual culture of the Greeks and Romans, whose horizontal-linear architecture and predictable designs in art and architecture give a clue, at least, to their reposeful, rational character. We have already seen, too, that many of the northern people had come into the Roman Empire either by invitation, infiltration, or military conquest. But these people were vastly different in basic character from the Romans. Their architectural line was energetic, vertical, and angular; their decorations were twisted and unpredictable. Just about the time of the removal of Roman authority, we witness a great folk-wandering of these peoples, with tribes from the east pressing upon the Germanic tribes, and they, in turn, moving outward both as colonizers and as warlike raiders through all of the continent of Europe. This restless movement of peoples was to continue for centuries, with an inevitable clash and subsequent fusion of the two cultures.

The basic social organization of these northern peoples was the *comitatus,* which was the banding together of a group of fighting men under the leadership of a warrior chieftain. The men pledged their loyalty and their strength to the chief, and he, in turn, promised to give them rewards from captured plunder. Thus in the early Germanic poem of *Beowulf,* both the hero and another leader, Hrothgar, are frequently called "ringgivers" from their roles as leaders distributing gold to their fighting men. Once the comitatus was formed, it had only one function: to fight, to capture, and to plunder. The dragonships of the Norsemen were frequent and fearful visitors in England and all Europe.

But there is another aspect to these people that is revealed in their religion. The contemporary philosopher Lewis Mumford has spoken of the Graeco-Romans as "pessimistic of the body and optimistic for the soul," and of the Celto-Germanic peoples as "optimistic of the body but pessimistic for the spirit." The distinction is a valid one. The classic and Christian southern peoples regarded life here on earth only as a short period of pain and sorrow to be followed, they hoped, by a joyous afterlife in heaven. The Celto-Germanics ate greatly, drank deeply, raped widely, but were ultimately pessimistic about the afterlife. Theirs was perhaps the only religion that pictures the ultimate defeat of the "good" gods by the forces of evil and darkness.

The Norsemen worshipped a group of anthropomorphic "good" gods who lived in a celestial residence called Valhalla. Wotan was the king of the gods; the most active, certainly, was Thor, the thunder god. Baldur represented the idea of beauty, springtime, and warmth; Loki was the trickster. Even in the heavenly abode the pessimistic nature of these gods appears, for, through a trick of Loki's, Baldur was slain. For the fighting men on earth, an afterlife among the gods was promised, but far different from any heaven conceived of by Christians, Muslims, or Jews.

If a warrior were killed in battle, semidivine maidens (the Valkyrie) swooped over the battlefield to take him to Valhalla. Here the hero simply continued his earthly life of fighting, eating, and drinking.

For the gods and heroes, however, an awful fate was predicted, for Valhalla was surrounded by the land of the giant Jotuns, probably representing the cold and the darkness of the northern climate. The gods and the Jotuns were engaged in constant small warfare and trickery, but in the Norse religion, the future held a great battle between the two forces, with the Jotuns winning and bringing about the downfall of the gods. Thus the ultimate and total pessimism of the spirit of the Scandinavian-Germanic people.

The difference between the Graeco-Roman and the Celto-Germanic personalities has been suggested earlier with a comparison between the structural line and the type of ornamentation that each found beautiful and which, therefore, may give a clue to the differences in character. A comparison between the type of literature each culture produced may strengthen our awareness of the clash of cultures. No better example of the Graeco-Roman literature of the very early Middle Ages can be found than Boethius's *Consolation of Philosophy*. Boethius, one remembers, was a Roman consul, serving under the Roman emperor (actually an Ostrogoth) Theodoric. The *Consolation* was written in the year 524 while he was languishing in prison awaiting death after being accused by his emperor of treason.

Boethius gives his work the form of a highly rational dialogue between himself as a man who is deeply distressed by his fate in the world, and a vision of philosophy as a stately woman. The dialogue is interspersed with poetical passages that serve to sum up the previous discussion and form a bridge into their next topic. The subjects for discussion range from the nature of fortune and chance, of happiness, the existence of evil, of free will, and the paradox of humanity's free will and an all-knowing God. In reading the whole discussion, one is reminded of a Sokratic dialogue, and indeed Boethius draws heavily on Platonic thought. While the ideas themselves are not new, the reader is constantly aware of a classic coolness and dignified withdrawal from the passions of life. Perhaps a brief quotation may make this clear. The excerpt is drawn from book III, prose X. Philosophy speaks first:

> "But it has been conceded that the highest Good is happiness?"
>
> "Yes," I said.
>
> "Therefore," she said, "it must be confessed that God is Happiness itself."
>
> "I cannot gainsay what you premised before," said I, "and I perceive that this follows necessarily from those premises."
>
> "Look, then," she said, "whether the same proposition is not proved more strongly by the following argument: there cannot be two different highest Goods. For it is clear that where there are two different goods the one cannot be the other; wherefore neither one can be the perfect Good while each is wanting to the other. And that which is not perfect is manifestly not the highest; therefore, if two things are the highest Good, they can by no means be different. Further, we have concluded that both God and happiness are the highest Good; therefore the highest Deity must be identical with the highest happiness."
>
> "No conclusion," said I, "could be truer in fact or stronger in theory or worthier of God."
>
> "Over and above this," she said, "let me give you a corollary such as geometricians are wont to do when they wish to derive a deduction from the propositions they have demonstrated. Since men become happy by attaining happiness, and happiness is identical with divinity, it is plain that they become happy by attaining divinity. And as men become just by attaining justice and wise by attaining wisdom, so by the same reasoning they become godlike by attaining divinity. Every happy man, then, is Godlike; but, while there is nothing to prevent as many men as possible for being God-like, only one is God by nature: men are God-like by participation."[2]

Nothing could be more urbane, civilized, classic, or rational than the discussion cited above. To become aware of the difference in spirit between this and the Celto-Germanic personality, one may look briefly at two of the hero-epics from the northern people. *Beowulf* and the *Nibelungenlied* will serve as examples. The very sound of the harsh lines, much smoothed and rounded in modern English translation, reveals something of the lusty vigor of the people. Consider, for example, the alliteration of crashing consonants in the line, "Bit his bone-frame, drank blood from his veins." This is a far cry from the epics of Greece and Rome in its very tone.

The story of Beowulf is almost equally harsh. It tells of Beowulf, a warrior from the south of Sweden who went to the court of his uncle in Denmark. There he slew a monster, Grendel, who had been devastating the uncle's kingdom. As a trophy of the fight, Beowulf brought home the arm and shoulder of the monster as it had been wrenched from the giant's torso. Following the victory, a great banquet was held in the hero's honor. Having eaten and drunk until they could hold no more, Beowulf and his men lay down on the floor of the banquet hall, their war gear hanging by them, for the night's rest. But when all was quiet, Grendel's mother entered the hall, killed some of the men, and took the bloody arm and shoulder of her son back to the home she had beneath the waters of a dismal fen.

On the next morning Beowulf set out and tracked Grendel's mother to the shore of a swamp. Fearlessly he donned his armor and plunged into the water, down to the opening of the cave. Here he grappled

---

2. Boethius, *The Consolation of Philosophy,* ed. James J. Buchanan (New York: Frederick Ungar Publishing Co., Inc., 1957), 31–32.

with the hag-monster and finally killed her with a weapon forged by the giants of old. (See the Literary Selections.)

The last episode of the poem tells of Beowulf's last days when, as king or chief of his Swedish tribe, his own land was threatened by a dragon. As a warrior hero and leader, he went forth, killed the dragon, and was mortally wounded himself. The poem ends with his funeral pyre as a Viking chieftain, and the construction of his tomb as a monument that would serve as a landmark for Viking ships at sea.

Beowulf was never tender, never kind, never sympathetic. When his friends were slain in battle or in the great hall of Heorot, he never wept for them or extolled their virtues. Rather, he swore vengeance and went forth to do it. He was the mighty warrior, the great adventurer. Such was the Germanic hero.

Another example is at once older and younger; it is the German tale called the *Niebelungenlied, or Song of the Niblungs*. It was not written down in its present form until the 1200s, but its materials hark back to the days of Attila the Hun, in the fifth century. The Scandinavian version of the tale is known as the *Volsunga saga;* Wagner freely adapted the tale in his four music-dramas, *The Ring of the Nibelung.*

The epic is concerned with the hero Siegfried, who loved Kriemhild, sister of the Burgundian king, Gunther. In order to win her, Siegfried promised his help in Gunther's wooing of Brunhild, the warlike queen of a distant country. By magical means Siegfried assisted him in the feats of strength that won her. On their wedding night, Brunhild tied Gunther up in knots, and hung him behind the door; again it was Siegfried who came to the rescue, and on the second night, wrapped in his cloak of invisibility, wrestled with her and subdued her, without Brunhild's being aware that her adversary was Siegfried, not Gunther. How he took from her then a ring and a girdle, giving them to Kriemhild; how the two queens quarreled; how Kriemhild, in haughty anger, revealed the trick of Brunhild's conquest; and how Brunhild plotted revenge, is quickly recounted. The climax of the first part is the treacherous murder of Siegfried by Hagen, the loyal henchman of Gunther, and the villain of the piece. The last half of the story concerns Kriemhild's revenge against the Burgundians. Married, after many years, to Etzel (Attila), King of the Huns, she invited the Burgundians to visit her, and there follows a general massacre in which they are all slain, including Kriemhild.

One sees in these epics the warrior's world of the first half of the medieval period, its spirit of adventure, courage, bravery, harshness, and blood.

Perhaps these examples can help one to visualize the difference between the character of the two peoples who encountered each other during the early Middle Ages. So important was it that Dorothy Sayers in her introduction to the translation of the *Divine Comedy* attributes the origin of the two great political factions that tore Italy apart in late medieval times, the Guelfs and the Ghibellines, to this cultural difference. She contends that the Ghibellines represented the descendants of the northern stock with all of their vigorous energy, and that the Guelfs were essentially the native Italian land-owning, placid southern people.

Be that as it may, by the tenth century the two cultures achieved a physical amalgamation. Many of the northerners had moved to the south, had become Christianized, and had given up some of their savage ways. The Angles and Saxons settled in England, other Norsemen took over the great province of Normandy in France. Throughout all of Europe the Germanic people settled and took land, so that the northern chieftain moved into the already evolving feudal system, becoming a baron or a count, a duke or a knight, holding land from his suzerain and granting fiefs to those under him. It was still a warlike society, the difference being chiefly in its fairly settled nature. The leader gave up his wooden hall for a castle built of stone. The highest virtue became a mutual loyalty between the lord and his vassals. The *Song of Roland* furnishes a good example of this new civilization. This minor epic was written in French at about the time of the first crusade (the 1090s), but the written version simply records a hero-story that had been sung and recited concerning the events that happened (legendarily) three centuries before in the days of Charlemagne. The persons of the story are Franks, the Germanic conquerors who gave their name to France; the central figure is Roland, the emperor's nephew. The great event of the poem is the ambush by Saracens of the rear guard of Charlemagne's army in the passes of the Pyrenees at Roncevaux. The ambush was arranged by Roland's treacherous kinsman Ganelon, inspired by envy and revenge. Roland and his companion, Oliver, together with the militant Archbishop Turpin, are the last survivors of the Frankish host; they too are killed, facing overwhelming odds. One of the best-known episodes is that of Roland's refusal to blow his ivory horn (oliphant), despite the urging of Oliver, to recall Charlemagne's host before the battle begins. When he realizes that he and his Franks are doomed, he does at last blow three mighty blasts that Charlemagne hears, thirty leagues away, and the Emperor returns to rout the Saracens and avenge the death of Roland and his companions. The epic concludes with the trial and punishment of Ganelon.

It is a truly feudal poem, full of the vigorous, active, restless spirit of the northern warrior. Roland is the man-at-arms, the warrior, unsoftened by the chivalry of later knighthood; he is a splendid barbarian, courageous in the face of overwhelming odds, loyal to his friends, utterly devoted to God, his spiritual overlord, and to Charlemagne, his temporal one. He is blood brother to his earlier northern kinsmen, Beowulf; both heroes represent the all-out, do-or-die, go-for-broke spirit of the heroic age.

There are many magnificent scenes: the pathetic one in which the wounded Oliver, dazed and blinded by blood, strikes his best friend Roland, and the two are immediately reconciled; the striking one in which Roland tries to shatter his sword, "Durendal," against a rock lest its hilt, which is a reliquary with sacred relics in it, fall into pagan hands. Let us read only one, the one hundred and seventy-sixth stanza, or "laisse," of the poem:

Count Roland lies under a pine tree,
Towards Spain has he turned his face.
Many things he recalls to remembrance:
How many lands, hero-like, he has won;
Sweet France; the men of his lineage;
Charlemagne his lord, who reared him.
At this he sighs and weeps, nor can he restrain himself.
But he does not wish to go into oblivion;
He confesses his fault, and prays God's mercy:
"True Father, Who never lies,
Who raised St. Lazarus from the dead,
Who preserved Daniel from the lions,
Keep my soul from all dangers,
Despite all the sins I have committed in my life!"
He raises towards God the glove from his right hand;
St. Gabriel from his hand receives it.
On his arms his head falls back;
His hands clasped, he goes to his end.
God sends his angel Cherubin
And St. Michael of the Peril;
Together with these comes St. Gabriel.
The count's soul they carry into Paradise.

The similarities and differences between this story and that of *Beowulf* are immediately apparent. Roland, with its heavy Christian overlay, is much more "civilized" than the early epic. But it is still a very masculine, savagely militaristic poem, extolling the glories of war, of bravery, and of loyalty. Not least interesting in the poem is the role of the Archbishop Turpin, who is a great Church leader, at least in title. Throughout the battle, however, he ranges through the ranks of fighting men, wielding his great mace (at this time it was illegal for a churchman to wield a sword) and breaking heads with the best of them. We see here a new role of the Church, with churchmen active in feudal society, holding great areas of land, and as much concerned with battle and secular affairs as with the religious life. The final act of Roland reveals much of the spirit of the time, for his offer of his glove to God is the very act of pledging loyalty to a feudal lord. Roland, always a vassal of Charlemagne, has now accepted a new suzerain in God, and the acceptance of the glove signifies God's acceptance of Roland as a vassal in the celestial feudal system.

Summary

It is almost symbolic that the people of the early Middle Ages built walls around their villages; wooden palisades in the early days, later, with feudalism, the walls were constructed of stone and the lord's house and the whole village became a fortified enclave. The total way of life at the time paralleled those confining fortifications, because early medieval people built battlements of equal strength around their minds.

The universe was based on the Church of Rome, which allowed no questioning of its tenets or of its actions. Further, the Church, through a contraction of the Augustinian doctrine, took a very dim view of all worldly pleasure and carefully restrained any questioning of the physical world. Science as we know it was lost completely, so that the natural world was a closed book, to be interpreted only as a vague shadow of the intention and mind of God. Life here and now was viewed as a brief and transitory journey through a dismal land, with true life and true happiness coming only after death. Furthermore, as is particularly apparent in the morality play of *Everyman* (see the Literary Selections), the only way to reach the blissful afterlife lay in the faithful acceptance of the doctrines and the sacraments of the Church.

The economic system of manorialism bound the greatest part of the population to the thousand acres or so of the manor itself. They could not escape; the few who traveled any distance at all had to have special permission. In fact, the average serf never strayed as much as one mile from the demesne. Food, clothing, and meager physical comforts were limited to what the manor could produce. Not even the mind could escape the narrow confines; reading was almost unknown because there was so little literacy (not even all of the clergy could read and write). Illiteracy and minimal travel meant also that news of the outside world almost never penetrated the closed miniworld of the manor.

The political system of feudalism was equally narrowing. Justice lay entirely in the hands of the feudal lord or, more often, his deputy. Except for the specific obligations of serf to lord and vassal to suzerain, which were generally known and accepted, the law was made up on the spot, and the individual never knew what to expect.

The narrow confines of Church, manorialism, and feudalism provided the walls that closed in upon the human spirit. Creativity and freedom of thought were almost unknown. But, with the withdrawal of Roman protection and with all the dangers from bands of marauders, these walls provided protection for the individual. If ordinary serfs could not live well, they could at least live safely.

Perhaps Elinor Wylie's twentieth-century poem "Sanctuary" expresses the same problem:

This is the bricklayer; hear the thud
Of his heavy load dumped down on stone,
His lustrous bricks are brighter than blood,
His smoking mortar whiter than bone.

Set each sharp-edged, fire-bitten brick
Straight by the plumb-line's shivering length;
Make my marvelous wall so thick
Dead nor living may shake its strength.

Full as a crystal cup with drink
Is my cell with dreams, and quiet, and cool . . .
Stop, old man! You must leave a chink;
How can I breathe? *You can't, you fool!*

But the human spirit is never content with mere security. Particularly with gaining of a little freedom as it did in the tenth century, it clamors more and more for expansion. (The twentieth-century movement towards equality of opportunity is a similar phenomenon.) The seeds that were to germinate and eventually break down medieval walls were already planted. Some of the directions for that growth may be indicated.

First, the human spirit has never long been content to *not* examine the world around it. The varied forms of the world, its beauties, and reason for being demand attention. Both art and science express this quest for an exploration of the world of the senses.

Second, the two personality types of Europe, the rational Graeco-Roman and the emotional and energetic Germanic lived side by side but not in unison by the year 1000. Some form of synthesis between these two personality types, almost exactly opposite each other, needed to be found.

Third, a problem limited largely to politics: the question of supremacy of church or state demanded settlement. At a time when the secular power was so weak as to be almost nonexistent, the Church could and did assert its authority over kings and lords. But with the growth of the powers of the world a struggle was inevitable, a bitter conflict of church and state that has been waged all over the Western world and which is still not fully resolved.

Fourth, and perhaps most important, people demand and need joy in the present life, but this was sternly denied by the Church. A desire for immediate physical and intellectual pleasure in life now would necessarily conflict with the doctrine that life here was nothing, the afterlife was everything. The pull of life as opposed to the Church-dictated pull of death was bound to tear the human personality apart until some synthesis could be effected.

These are the latent problems one sees at the end of the early Middle Ages. Their solutions will be dealt with in subsequent chapters.

Bibliography

General

Clark, Kenneth. *Civilisation: A Personal View.* New York: Harper & Row, Publishers, 1970. This sophisticated and urbane book might well be a companion piece to *The Search* from this point on through the discussion of the twentieth century. It will not be listed in succeeding bibliographies, but Clark's comments on art and life are worth reading and rereading.

Special Studies

Kelly, A. R. *Eleanor of Aquitane and the Four Kings.* Cambridge, Mass.: Harvard University Press, 1950. Also available in a Vintage edition. Lively treatment of one of the most fascinating women in history.

Stephenson, Carl. *Medieval Feudalism.* Ithaca, N.Y.: Cornell University Press, 1967. An excellent but uncomplicated introduction.

Philosophy

St. Augustine. *Confessions.* Translated by Edward Pusey. New York: Pocket Books, 1957.

Boethius. *Consolations of Philosophy.* Translated by James Buchanan. New York: Frederick Ungar Publishing Company, 1957.

Coplestone, Frederick. *A History of Philosophy.* Vol. 2. New York: Doubleday, n.d.

Freemantle, Anne, ed. *The Age of Belief* (through chapter 5). New York: Arno Press, 1954. The two histories of philosophy listed here present some pretty tough reading for the student, but so does all pure philosophy, and medieval thought in particular.

Literature

The Song of Roland. The Isabel Butler translation (Houghton Mifflin Company, 1904) is a standard; Dorothy Sayers has a newer translation (Penguin Books, 1957).

Trapp, J. B. *Medieval English Literature.* New York: Oxford University Press, 1973. Fine anthology that includes *Beowulf, The Wakefield Second Shepherd's Play,* popular ballads, and middle English lyrics.

Historical Fiction

Bryher, W. *The Fourteenth of October.* New York: Pantheon Books, 1952. Accurate and interesting novel about the Norman Conquest of England.

Muntz, H. *The Golden Warrior.* New York: Charles Scribner's Sons, 1949. Another good novel about the Norman Conquest.

Oldenbourg, Zoe. *The World Is Not Enough.* New York: Pantheon Books, 1948. The life, color, and violence of twelfth-century France. See also her book *The Crusades.*

Literary Selections

Beowulf's Fight with Grendel's Dam from BEOWULF

The oldest of English epics, *Beowulf* probably dates from early in the eighth century. Written by an unknown author of exceptional talent, the poem is a brilliant example of the masculine code, the embodiment of the heroic tradition.[3] In the brief excerpt given below (see p. 314 for a synopsis of the plot), Beowulf tracks Grendel's hag-mother to her cave in the depths of a swamp where he battles her to the death. The modern translation in alliterative verse is by Charles W. Kennedy; the line numbers are from Klaeber's Old English text.

> Beowulf spoke, the son of Ecgtheow:
> 'Sorrow not, brave one! Better for man
> To avenge a friend than much to mourn.
> All men must die; let him who may
> Win glory ere death. That guerdon is best
> For a noble man when his name survives him.
> Then let us rise up, O ward of the realm,
> And haste us forth to behold the track
> Of Grendel's dam. And I give you pledge
> She shall not in safety escape to cover,
> To earthy cavern, or forest fastness,
> Or gulf of ocean, go where she may.
> This day with patience endure the burden
> Of every woe, as I know you will.'
> Up sprang the ancient, gave thanks to God
> For the heartening words the hero had spoken.
>
> Quickly a horse was bridled for Hrothgar,
> A mettlesome charger with braided mane;
> In royal splendor the king rode forth
> Mid the trampling tread of a troop of shieldmen.

---

3 The warrior code of *Beowulf* should be compared with the courtly code of the age of chivalry in chapter 14 *(The Art of Courtly Love, Morte Darthur)* and in chapter 16 (troubadour-trouvère tradition).

The tracks lay clear where the fiend had fared
Over plain and bottom and woodland path,
Through murky moorland making her way
With the lifeless body, the best of thanes
Who of old with Hrothgar had guarded the hall.
By a narrow path the king pressed on

[1384–1408]

Through rocky upland and rugged ravine,
A lonely journey, past looming headlands,
The lair of monster and lurking troll.
Tried retainers, a trusty few,
Advanced with Hrothgar to view the ground.
Sudden they came on a dismal covert
Of trees that hung over hoary stone,
Over churning water and blood-stained wave.
Then for the Danes was the woe the deeper,
The sorrow sharper for Scylding earls,
When they first caught sight, on the rocky sea-cliff,
Of slaughtered Æschere's severed head.
The water boiled in a bloody swirling
With seething gore as the spearmen gazed.
The trumpet sounded a martial strain;
The shield-troop halted. Their eyes beheld
The swimming forms of strange sea-dragons,
Dim serpent shapes in the watery depths,
Sea-beasts sunning on headland slopes;
Snakelike monsters that oft at sunrise
On evil errands scour the sea.
Startled by tumult and trumpet's blare,
Enraged and savage, they swam away;
But one the lord of the Geats brought low,
Stripped of his sea-strength, despoiled of life,
As the bitter bow-bolt pierced his heart.
His watery-speed grew slower, and ceased,
And he floated, caught in the clutch of death.
Then they hauled him in with sharp-hooked boar-spears,
By sheer strength grappled and dragged him ashore,
A wondrous wave-beast; and all the array

[1409–1440]

Gathered to gaze at the grisly guest.
  Beowulf donned his armor for battle,
Heeded not danger; the hand-braided byrny,
Broad of shoulder and richly bedecked,
Must stand the ordeal of the watery depths.
Well could that corselet defend the frame
Lest hostile thrust should pierce to the heart.
Or blows of battle beat down the life.
A gleaming helmet guarded his head
As he planned his plunge to the depths of the pool
Through the heaving waters—a helm adorned
With lavish inlay and lordly chains,
Ancient work of the weapon-smith
Skillfully fashioned, beset with the boar,
That no blade of battle might bite it through.
Not the least or the worst of his war-equipment
Was the sword the herald of Hrothgar loaned
In his hour of need—Hrunting its name—
An ancient heirloom, trusty and tried;
Its blade was iron, with etched design,
Tempered in blood of many a battle.
Never in fight had it failed the hand
That drew it daring the perils of war,
The rush of the foe. Not the first time then
That its edge must venture on valiant deeds.
But Ecglaf's stalwart son was unmindful
Of words he had spoken while heated with wine,
When he loaned the blade to a better swordsman.

He himself dared not hazard his life
In deeds of note in the watery depths;
And thereby he forfeited honor and fame.

[1440–1471]

Not so with that other undaunted spirit
After he donned his armor for battle.
Beowulf spoke, the son of Ecgtheow:
'O gracious ruler, gold-giver to men,
As I now set forth to attempt this feat,
Great son of Healfdene, hold well in mind
The solemn pledge we plighted of old,
That if doing your service I meet my death
You will mark my fall with a father's love.
Protect my kinsmen, my trusty comrades,
If battle take me. And all the treasure
You have heaped on me bestow upon Hygelac,
Hrothgar beloved! The lord of the Geats,
The son of Hrethel, shall see the proof,
Shall know as he gazes on jewels and gold,
That I found an unsparing dispenser of bounty,
And joyed, while I lived, in his generous gifts.
Give back to Unferth the ancient blade,
The sword-edge splendid with curving scrolls,
For either with Hrunting I'll reap rich harvest
Of glorious deeds, or death shall take me.'
  After these words the prince of the Weders
Awaited no answer, but turned to the task,
Straightway plunged in the swirling pool.
Nigh unto a day he endured the depths
Ere he first had view of the vast sea-bottom.
Soon she found, who had haunted the flood,
A ravening hag, for a hundred half-years,
Greedy and grim, that a man was groping
In daring search through the sea-troll's home.
Swift she grappled and grasped the warrior

[1471–1501]

With horrid grip, but could work no harm,
No hurt to his body; the ring-locked byrny
Cloaked his life from her clutching claw;
Nor could she tear through the tempered mail
With her savage fingers. The she-wolf bore
The ring-prince down through the watery depths
To her den at the bottom; nor could Beowulf draw
His blade for battle, though brave his mood.
Many a sea-beast, strange sea-monsters,
Tasked him hard with their menacing tusks,
Broke his byrny and smote him sore.
  Then he found himself in a fearsome hall
Where water came not to work him hurt,
But the flood was stayed by the sheltering roof.
There in the glow of firelight gleaming
The hero had view of the huge sea-troll.
He swung his war-sword with all his strength,
Withheld not the blow, and the savage blade
Sang on her head its hymn of hate.
But the bold one found that the battle-flasher
Would bite no longer, nor harm her life.
The sword-edge failed at his sorest need.
Often of old with ease it had suffered
The clash of battle, cleaving the helm,
The fated warrior's woven mail.
That time was first for the treasured blade
That its glory failed in the press of the fray.
But fixed of purpose and firm of mood
Hygelac's earl was mindful of honor;
In wrath, undaunted, he dashed to earth
The jewelled sword with its scrolled design,

[1502–1532]

The blade of steel; staked all on strength,
On the might of his hand, as a man must do
Who thinks to win in the welter of battle
Enduring glory; he fears not death.
The Geat-prince joyed in the straining struggle,
Stalwart-hearted and stirred to wrath,
Gripped the shoulder of Grendel's dam
And headlong hurled the hag to the ground.
But she quickly clutched him and drew him close,
Countered the onset with savage claw.
The warrior staggered, for all his strength,
Dismayed and shaken and borne to earth.
She knelt upon him and drew her dagger,
With broad bright blade, to avenge her son,
Her only issue. But the corselet's steel
Shielded his breast and sheltered his life
Withstanding entrance of point and edge.
  Then the prince of the Geats would have gone his
    journey,
The son of Ecgtheow, under the ground;
But his sturdy breast-net, his battle-corselet,
Gave him succor, and holy God,
The Lord all-wise, awarded the mastery;
Heaven's Ruler gave right decree.
  Swift the hero sprang to his feet;
Saw mid the war-gear a stately sword,
An ancient war-brand of biting edge,
Choicest of weapons worthy and strong,
The work of giants, a warrior's joy,
So heavy no hand but his own could hold it,
Bear to battle or wield in war.

            [1533–1562]

Then the Scylding warrior, savage and grim,
Seized the ring-hilt and swung the sword,
Struck with fury, despairing of life,
Thrust at the throat, broke through the bone-rings;
The stout blade stabbed through her fated flesh.
She sank in death; the sword was bloody;
The hero joyed in the work of his hand.
The gleaming radiance shimmered and shone
As the candle of heaven shines clear from the sky.
Wrathful and resolute Hygelac's thane
Surveyed the span of the spacious hall;
Grimly gripping the hilted sword
With upraised weapon he turned to the wall.
The blade had failed not the battle-prince;
A full requital he firmly planned
For all the injury Grendel had done
In numberless raids on the Danish race,
When he slew the hearth-companions of Hrothgar,
Devoured fifteen of the Danish folk
Clasped in slumber, and carried away
As many more spearmen, a hideous spoil.
All this the stout-heart had stern requited;
And there before him bereft of life
He saw the broken body of Grendel
Stilled in battle, and stretched in death,
As the struggle in Heorot smote him down.
The corpse sprang wide as he struck the blow,
The hard sword-stroke that severed the head.
  Then the tried retainers, who there with Hrothgar
Watched the face of the foaming pool,
Saw that the churning reaches were reddened,

            [1563–1593]

The eddying surges stained with blood.
And the gray, old spearmen spoke of the hero,
Having no hope he would ever return

Crowned with triumph and cheered with spoil.
Many were sure that the savage sea-wolf
Had slain their leader. At last came noon.
The stalwart Scyldings forsook the headland;
Their proud gold-giver departed home.
But the Geats sat grieving and sick in spirit,
Stared at the water with longing eyes,
Having no hope they would ever behold
Their gracious leader and lord again.
  Then the great sword, eaten with blood of battle,
Began to soften and waste away
In iron icicles, wonder of wonders,
Melting away most like to ice
When the Father looses the fetters of frost,
Slackens the bondage that binds the wave,
Strong in power of times and seasons;
He is true God! Of the goodly treasures
From the sea-cave Beowulf took but two,
The monster's head and the precious hilt
Blazing with gems; but the blade had melted,
The sword dissolved, in the deadly heat,
The venomous blood of the fallen fiend.

EVERYMAN

Medieval drama began in the tenth century as liturgical drama (discussed in detail in chap. 16), out of which grew plays in the vernacular called mysteries or mystery plays (a corruption of the Latin *ministerium*, service). Performed by trade guilds, mystery plays were cycles depicting the history of humanity from damnation to redemption. The various guilds enacted episodes associated with their own craft; thus, the shipwright's guild was responsible for the building of the ark, the water drawers for Noah's flood, the goldsmiths for the story of the magi, and so on.

Performed outdoors from dawn to dusk on "pageants" (L. *paginae),* wagons consisting of roofed platforms on wheels, the plays used scanty scenery but often elaborate costumes. Cycles like, for example, *The Second Shepherd's Play* included a large repertoire of acting conventions, comic elaboration, and considerable opportunity for improvisation. During the sixteenth century the plays became more and more secular, with increasing elements of comedy and outright buffoonery until, during the reign of Elizabeth I, they were suppressed. By this time they had been superseded by the plays of Marlowe and Shakespeare.

On the continent miracle plays dealt with miracles worked by the saints; in England the word was interchangeable with mystery. A completely separate category, but developing along with mystery plays, the morality play was a single work rather than a cycle. Mystery plays dramatized biblical events to show their relevance to everyday life; morality plays were more directly didactic, enacting the conflict between good and evil, the constant struggle within each person between virtue and vice.

The contest was presented as an allegory with virtues and vices personified: Patience vs. Anger, Pride vs. Humility, and so forth. A key element was penance, the recognition and confession of sin to the priest followed by absolution, on condition of the performance of assigned penances. One of the primary themes of *Everyman* is the necessity of penitence for sin before death within the discipline of the church.

Everyman was written about 1485 and may be a translation of a Dutch play on the same theme or possibly the Dutch play was a translation from the English. The most famous of its type, *Everyman* is not a battle between opposites but rather a somber stripping of worldly goods from a man, concentrating on his increasing isolation as he descends into the grave. Only Good Deeds is left as a mediator between him and Judgment. *Everyman* is a moral allegory of preparation for death, a solemn statement of the human predicament, and, no less important, an exposition of church doctrine.

CHARACTERS:

Messenger
God (Adonai)
Death
Everyman
Fellowship
Kindred
Cousin
Goods
Good-Deeds
Knowledge
Confession
Beauty
Strength
Discretion
Five-Wits
Angel
Doctor

HERE BEGINNETH A TREATISE HOW THE HIGH FATHER OF HEAVEN SENDETH DEATH TO SUMMON EVERY CREATURE TO COME AND GIVE ACCOUNT OF THEIR LIVES IN THIS WORLD AND IS IN MANNER OF A MORAL PLAY.

Messenger: I pray you all give your audience,
And hear this matter with reverence,
By figure a moral play—
The *Summoning of Everyman* called it is,
That of our lives and ending shows
How transitory we be all day.
This matter is wondrous precious,
But the intent of it is more gracious,
And sweet to bear away.
The story saith,—Man, in the beginning,
Look well, and take good heed to the ending,
Be you never so gay!
Ye think sin in the beginning full sweet,
Which in the end causeth thy soul to weep,
When the body lieth in clay.
Here shall you see how *Fellowship* and *Jollity*,
Both *Strength, Pleasure,* and *Beauty,*
Will fade from thee as flower in May.
For ye shall hear, how our heaven king
Calleth *Everyman* to a general reckoning:
Give audience, and hear what he doth say.
God: I perceive here in my majesty,
How that all creatures be to me unkind,
Living without dread in worldly prosperity:
Of ghostly sight the people be so blind,

Drowned in sin, they know me not for their God:
In worldly riches is all their mind,
They fear not my right wiseness, the sharp rod:
My law that I shewed, when I for them died,
They forget clean, and shedding of my blood red:
I hanged between two, it cannot be denied:
To get them life I suffered to be dead:
I healed their feet, with thorns hurt was my head:
I could do no more than I did truly,
And now I see the people do clean forsake me,
They use the seven deadly sins damnable;
As pride, covetise, wrath, and lechery,
Now in the world be made commendable;
And thus they leave of angels the heavenly company;
Everyman liveth so after his own pleasure,
And yet of their life they be nothing sure:
I see the more that I them forbear
The worse they be from year to year;
All that liveth appaireth[4] fast,
Therefore I will in all the haste
Having a reckoning of Everyman's person
For and I leave the people thus alone
In their life and wicked tempests,
Verily they will become much worse than beasts;
For now one would by envy another up eat;
Charity they all do clean forget.
I hoped well that Everyman
In my glory should make his mansion,
And thereto I had them all elect;
But now I see, like traitors deject,
They thank me not for the pleasure that I to them meant
Nor yet for their being that I them have lent;
I proffered the people great multitude of mercy,
And few there be that asketh it heartily;
They be so combered with worldly riches,
That needs of them I must do justice,
On Everyman living without fear.
Where art thou, Death, thou mighty messenger?
Death: Almighty God, I am here at your will,
Your commandment to fulfil.
God: Go thou to Everyman,
And show him in my name
A pilgrimage he must on him take,
Which he in no wise may escape;
And that he bring with him a sure reckoning
Without delay or any tarrying.
Death: Lord, I will in the world go run over all,
And cruelly outsearch both great and small;
Every man will I beset that liveth beastly
Out of God's laws, and dreadeth not folly:
He that loveth riches I will strike with my dart,
His sight to blind, and from heaven to depart,
Except that alms be his good friend,
In hell for to dwell, world without end.
Lo, yonder I see Everyman walking;
Full little he thinketh on my coming;
His mind is on fleshly lusts and his treasure,
And great pain it shall cause him to endure
Before the Lord Heaven King.
Everyman, stand still; whither art thou going
Thus gaily? Hast my Maker forgot?
Everyman: Why askst thou?
Wouldest thou wete?[5]

---

4. Is impaired.

5. Know.

Death: Yea, sir, I will show you;
In great haste I am sent to thee
From God out of his majesty.
Everyman: What, sent to me?
Death: Yea, certainly.
Though thou have forget him here,
He thinketh on thee in the heavenly sphere,
As, or we depart, thou shalt know.
Everyman: What desireth God of me?
Death: That shall I show thee;
A reckoning he will needs have
Without any longer respite.
Everyman: To give a reckoning longer leisure I crave;
This blind matter troubleth my wit.
Death: On thee thou must take a long journey:
Therefore thy book of count with thee thou bring;
For turn again thou can not by no way,
And look thou be sure of thy reckoning:
For before God thou shalt answer, and show
Thy many bad deeds and good but a few;
How thou hast spent thy life, and in what wise,
Before the chief lord of paradise.
Have ado that we were in that way,
For, wete thou well, thou shalt make none attournay.[6]
Everyman: Full unready I am such reckoning to give.
I know thee not: what messenger art thou?
Death: I am Death, that no man dreadeth.
For every man I rest and no man spareth;
For it is God's commandment
That all to me should be obedient.
Everyman: O Death, thou comest when I had thee
  least in mind,
In thy power it lieth me to save,
Yet of my good will I give thee, if ye will be kind,
Yea, a thousand pound shalt thou have,
And defer this matter till another day.
Death: Everyman, it may not be by no way;
I set not by gold, silver, nor riches,
Ne by pope, emperor, king, duke, ne princes.
For and I would receive gifts great,
All the world I might get;
But my custom is clean contrary.
I give thee no respite: come hence, and not tarry.
Everyman: Alas, shall I have no longer respite?
I may say Death giveth no warning:
To think on thee, it maketh my heart sick,
For all unready is my book of reckoning.
But twelve year and I might have abiding,
My counting book I would make so clear,
That my reckoning I should not need to fear.
Wherefore, Death, I pray thee, for God's mercy,
Spare me till I be provided of remedy.
Death: Thee availeth not to cry, weep, and pray:
But haste thee lightly that you were gone the journey.
And prove thy friends if thou can.
For, wete thou well, the tide abideth no man,
And in the world each living creature
For Adam's sin must die of nature.
Everyman: Death, if I should this pilgrimage take,
And my reckoning surely make,
Show me, for saint charity,
Should I not come again shortly?
Death: No, Everyman; and thou be once there,
Thou mayst never more come here,
Trust me verily.

Everyman: O gracious God, in the high seat celestial,
Have mercy on me in this most need;
Shall I have no company from this vale terrestrial
Of mine acquaintance that way me to lead?
Death: Yea, if any be so hardy,
That would go with thee and bear thee company.
Hie thee that you were gone to God's magnificence,
Thy reckoning to give before his presence.
What, weenest thou thy life is given thee,
And they worldly goods also?
Everyman: I had wend so, verily.
Death: Nay, nay; it was but lent thee;
For as soon as thou art go,
Another awhile shall have it, and then go therefro
Even as thou has done.
Everyman, thou art mad; thou hast thy wits five,
And here on earth will not amend thy life,
For suddenly I do come.
Everyman: O wretched caitiff, whither shall I flee,
That I might scape this endless sorrow!
Now, gentle Death, spare me till to-morrow,
That I may amend me
With good advisement.
Death: Nay, thereto I will not consent,
Nor no man will I respite,
But to the heart suddenly I shall smite
Without any advisement.
And now out of thy sight I will me nie;
See thou make thee ready shortly,
For thou mayst say this is the day
That no man living may scape away.
Everyman: Alas, I may well weep with sighs deep;
Now have I no manner of company
To help me in my journey, and me to keep;
And also my writing is full unready.
How shall I do now for to excuse me?
I would to God I had never be gete![7]
To my soul a full great profit it had be;
For now I fear pains huge and great.
The time passeth; Lord, help that all wrought;
For though I mourn it availeth nought.
The day passeth, and is almost a-go;
I wot not well what for to do.
To whom were I best my complaint to make?
What, and I to Fellowship thereof spake,
And showed him of this sudden chance?
For in him is all mine affiance;
We have in the world so many a day
Be on good friends in sport and play.
I see him yonder, certainly;
I trust that he will bear me company;
Therefore to him will I speak to ease my sorrow.
Well met, good Fellowship, and good morrow!
Fellowship: Everyman, good morrow by this day.
Sir, why lookest thou so piteously?
If any thing be amiss, I pray thee, me say,
That I may help to remedy.
Everyman: Yea, good Fellowship, yea.
I am in great jeopardy.
Fellowship: My true friend, show to me your mind;
I will not forsake thee, unto my life's end,
In the way of good company.

------

6. Mediator.
7. Been gotten, been born.

Everyman: That was well spoken, and lovingly.
Fellowship: Sir, I must needs know your heaviness;
I have pity to see you in any distress;
If any have ye wronged he shall revenged be,
Though I on the ground be slain for thee—
Though that I know before that I should die.
Everyman: Verily, Fellowship, gramercy.
Fellowship: Tush! by thy thanks I set not a straw;
Show me your grief, and say no more.
Everyman: If I my heart should to you break,
And then you to turn your mind from me,
And would not me comfort, when you hear me speak,
Then should I ten times sorrier be.
Fellowship: Sir, I say as I will do in deed.
Everyman: Then be you a good friend at need:
I have found you true here before.
Fellowship: And so ye shall evermore;
For, in faith, and thou go to Hell,
I will not forsake thee by the way!
Everyman: Ye speak like a good friend; I believe you
    well;
I shall deserve it, and I may.
Fellowship: I speak of no deserving, by this day.
For he that will say and nothing do
Is not worthy with good company to go;
Therefore show me the grief of your mind,
As to your friend most loving and kind.
Everyman: I shall show you how it is;
Commanded I am to go a journey,
A long way, hard and dangerous,
And give a strait count without delay
Before the high judge Adonai.[8]
Wherefore I pray you, bear me company,
As ye have promised, in this journey.
Fellowship: That is matter indeed! Promise is duty,
But, and I should take such a voyage on me,
I know it well, it should be to my pain:
Also it make me afeard, certain.
But let us take counsel here as well as we can,
For your words would fear a strong man.
Everyman: Why, ye said, If I had need,
Ye would me never forsake, quick nor dead,
Though it were to hell truly.
Fellowship: So I said, certainly,
But such pleasures be set aside, thee sooth to say:
And also, if we took such a journey,
When should we come again?
Everyman: Nay, never again till the day of doom.
Fellowship: In faith, then will not I come there!
Who hath you these tidings brought?
Everyman: Indeed, Death was with me here.
Fellowship: Now, by God that all hath bought,
If Death were the messenger,
For no man that is living today
I will not go that loath journey—
Not for the father that begat me!
Everyman: Ye promised other wise, pardie.
Fellowship: I wot well I say so truly
And yet if thou wilt eat, and drink, and make good cheer,
Or haunt to women, the lusty company,
I would not forsake you, while the day is clear,
Trust me verily!
Everyman: Yea, thereto ye would be ready;
To go to mirth, solace, and play
Your mind will sooner apply
Than to bear me company in my long journey.

Fellowship: Now, in good faith, I will not that way.
But and thou wilt murder, or any man kill,
In that I will help thee with a good will!
Everyman: O that is a simple advice indeed!
Gentle fellow, help me in my necessity;
We have loved long, and now I need,
And now, gentle Fellowship, remember me.
Fellowship: Whether ye have loved me or no,
By Saint John, I will not with thee go.
Everyman: Yet I pray thee, take the labour, and do so
    much for me
To bring me forward, for saint charity,
And comfort me till I come without the town.
Fellowship: Nay, and thou would give me a new gown,
I will not a foot with thee go;
But and you had tarried I would not have left thee so.
And as now, God speed thee in thy journey,
For from thee I will depart as fast as I may.
Everyman: Whither away, Fellowship? Will you forsake
    me?
Fellowship: Yea, by my fay, to God I betake thee.
Everyman: Farewell, good Fellowship; for this my
    heart is sore;
Adieu for ever, I shall see thee no more.
Fellowship: In faith, Everyman, farewell not at the end;
For you I will remember that parting is mourning.
Everyman: Alack! shall we thus depart indeed?
Our Lady, help, without any more comfort,
Lo, Fellowship forsaketh me in my most need:
For help in this world whither shall I resort?
Fellowship herebefore with me would merry make;
And now little sorrow for me doth he take.
It is said, in prosperity men friends may find,
Which in adversity be full unkind.
Now whither for succour shall I flee,
Sith that Fellowship hath forsaken me?
To my kinsmen I will truly,
Praying them to help me in my necessity:
I believe that they will do so,
For kind will creep where it may not go,
Where be ye now, my friends and kinsmen?
Kindred: Here be we now at your commandment.
Cousin, I pray you show us your intent
In any wise, and not spare.
Cousin: Yea, Everyman, and to us declare
If ye be disposed to go any whither,
For wete you well, we will live and die together.
Kindred: In wealth and woe we will with you hold,
For over his kin a man may be bold.
Everyman: Gramercy, my friends and kinsmen kind.
Now shall I show you the grief of my mind:
I was commanded by a messenger,
That is an high king's chief officer;
He bade me go a pilgrimage to my pain,
And I know well I shall never come again;
Also I must give a reckoning straight,
For I have a great enemy, that hath me in wait,
Which intendeth me for to hinder.
Kindred: What account is that which ye must render?
That would I know.
Everyman: Of all my works I must show
How I have lived and my days spent;
Also of ill deeds, that I have used

---

8. God.

In my time, sith life was me lent;
And of all virtues that I have refused.
Therefore I pray you go thither with me,
To help to make mine account, for saint charity.
Cousin: What, to go thither? Is that the matter?
Nay, Everyman, I had liefer fast bread and water
All this five year and more.
Everyman: Alas, that ever I was bore![9]
For now shall I never be merry
If that you forsake me.
Kindred: Ah, sir; what, ye be a merry man!
Take good heart to you, and make no moan.
But one thing I warn you, by Saint Anne,
As for me, ye shall go alone.
Everyman: My Cousin, will you not with me go?
Cousin: No, by our Lady; I have the cramp in my toe.
Trust not to me, for, so God me speed,
I will deceive you in your most need.
Kindred: It availeth not us to tice.
Ye shall have my maid with all my heart;
She loveth to go to feasts, there to be nice,
And to dance, and abroad to start:
I will give her leave to help you in that journey,
If that you and she may agree.
Everyman: Now show me the very effect of your mind.
Will you go with me, or abide behind?
Kindred: Abide behind? Yea, that I will and I may!
Therefore farewell until another day.
Everyman: How should I be merry or glad?
For fair promises to me make,
But when I have most need, they me forsake.
I am deceived; that maketh me sad.
Cousin: Cousin Everyman, farewell now,
For verily I will not go with you;
Also of mine own an unready reckoning
I have to account; therefore I make tarrying.
Now, God keep thee, for now I go.
Everyman: Ah, Jesus, is all come hereto?
Lo, fair words maketh fools feign;
They promise and nothing will do certain.
My kinsmen promised me faithfully
For to abide with me steadfastly,
And now fast away do they flee:
Even so Fellowship promised me.
What friend were best me of to provide?
I lose my time here longer to abide.
Yet in my mind a thing there is:—
All my life I have loved riches;
If that my goods now help me might,
He would make my heart full light.
I will speak to him in this distress.—
Where art thou, my Goods and riches?
Goods: Who calleth me? Everyman? What haste thou
    hast!
I lie here in corners, trussed and piled so high,
And in chests I am locked so fast,
Also sacked in bags, thou mayst see with thine eye,
I cannot stir; in packs low I lie,
What would ye have, lightly me say.
Everyman: Come hither, Good, in all the haste thou
    may,
For of counsel I must desire thee.
Goods: Sir, and ye in the world have trouble or
    adversity,
That can I help you to remedy shortly.
Everyman: It is another disease that grieveth me;
In this world it is not, I tell thee so.

I am sent for another way to go,
To give a straight account general
Before the highest Jupiter of all;
And all my life I have had joy and pleasure in thee.
Therefore I pray thee go with me,
For, peradventure, thou mayst before God Almighty
My reckoning help to clean and purify;
For it is said ever among,
That money maketh all right that is wrong.
Goods: Nay, Everyman, I sing another song,
I follow no man in such voyages;
For and I went with thee
Thou shouldst fare much the worse for me;
For because on me thou did set thy mind,
Thy reckoning I have made blotted and blind
That thine account thou cannot make truly;
And that hast thou for the love of me.
Everyman: That would grieve me full sore,
When I should come to that fearful answer.
Up, let us go thither together.
Goods: Nay, not so, I am too brittle, I may not endure;
I will follow no man one foot, be ye sure.
Everyman: Alas, I have thee loved, and had great
    pleasure
All my life-days on good and treasure.
Goods: That is to thy damnation without lesing,
For my love is contrary to the love everlasting
But if thou had me loved moderately during,
As, to the poor give part of me,
Then shouldst thou not in this dolour be,
Nor in this great sorrow and care.
Everyman: Lo, now was I deceived or I was ware,
And all I may wyte[10] my spending of time.
Goods: What, weenest thou that I am thine?
Everyman: I had wend so.
Goods: Nay, Everyman, I say no;
As for a while I was lent thee,
A season thou hast had me in prosperity;
My condition is man's soul to kill;
If I save one, a thousand I do spill;
Weenest thou that I will follow thee?
Nay, from this world, not verily.
Everyman: I had wend otherwise.
Goods: Therefore to thy soul Good is a thief;
For when thou art dead, this is my guise
Another to deceive in the same wise
As I have done thee, and all to his soul's reprief.
Everyman: O false Good, cursed thou be!
Thou traitor to God, that has deceived me,
And caught me in thy snare.
Goods: Marry, thou brought thyself in care,
Whereof I am glad,
I must needs laugh, I cannot be sad.
Everyman: Ah, Good, thou hast had long my heartly
    love;
I gave thee that which should be the Lord's above.
But wilt thou not go with me in deed?
I pray thee truth to say.
Goods: No, so God me speed,
Therefore farewell, and have good day.

---

9. Born.
10. Blame.

Everyman: O, to whom shall I make moan
For to go with me in that heavy journey?
First Fellowship said he would with me gone;
His words were very pleasant and gay,
But afterward he left me alone.
Then spake I to my kinsmen all in despair,
And also they gave me words fair,
They lacked no fair speaking,
But all forsake me in the ending.
Then went I to my Goods that I loved best,
In hope to have comfort, but there had I least:
For my Goods sharply did me tell
That he bringeth many into hell.
Then of myself I was ashamed,
And so I am worthy to be blamed;
Thus may I well myself hate,
Of whom shall I now counsel take?
I think that I shall never speed
Till that I go to my Good-Deed,
But alas, she is so weak,
That she can neither go nor speak,
Yet will I venture on her now.—
My Good-Deeds, where be you?
Good-Deeds: Here I lie cold on the ground;
Thy sins hath me sore bound,
That I cannot stir.
Everyman: O, Good-Deeds, I stand in fear;
I must you pray of counsel,
For help now should come right well.
Good-Deeds: Everyman, I have understanding
That ye be summoned account to make
Before Messias, of Jerusalem King;
And you by me[11] that journey what[12] you will I take.
Everyman: Therefore I come to you, my moan to make;
I pray you, that ye will go with me.
Good-Deeds: I would full fain, but I cannot stand
verily.
Everyman: Why, is there anything on you fall?
Good-Deeds: Yea, sir, I may thank you of all;
If ye had perfectly cheered me,
Your book of account now full ready had be.
Look, the books of your works and deeds eke;
Oh, see how they lie under the feet,
To your soul's heaviness.
Everyman: Our Lord Jesus, help me!
For one letter here I can not see.
Good-Deeds: There is a blind reckoning in time of
distress!
Everyman: Good-Deeds, I pray you, help me in this
need,
Or else I am for ever damned indeed;
Therefore help me to make reckoning
Before the redeemer of all thing,
That king is, and was, and ever shall.
Good-Deeds: Everyman, I am sorry of your fall,
And fain would I help you, and I were able.
Everyman: Good-Deeds, your counsel I pray you give
me.
Good-Deeds: That shall I do verily;
Though that on my feet I may not go,
I have a sister, that shall with you also,
Called Knowledge, which shall with you abide,
To help you to make that dreadful reckoning.
Knowledge: Everyman, I will go with thee, and be thy
guide,
In thy most need to go by thy side.

Everyman: In good condition I am now in every thing,
And am wholly content with this good thing;
Thanked be God my Creator.
Good-Deeds: And when he hath brought thee there,
Where thou shalt heal thee of thy smart,
Then go you with your reckoning and your Good-Deeds
together
For to make you joyful at heart
Before the blessed Trinity.
Everyman: My Good-Deeds, gramercy;
I am well content, certainly,
With your words sweet.
Knowledge: Now go we together lovingly,
To Confession, that cleansing river.
Everyman: For joy I weep; I would we were there;
But, I pray you, give me cognition
Where dwelleth that holy man, Confession.
Knowledge: In the house of salvation:
We shall find him in that place,
That shall us comfort by God's grace.
Lo, this is Confession: kneel down and ask mercy,
For he is in good conceit with God almighty.
Everyman: O glorious fountain that all uncleanness
doth clarify,
Wash from me the spots of vices unclean,
That on me no sin may be seen;
I come with Knowledge for my redemption,
Repent with hearty and full contrition;
For I am commanded a pilgrimage to take,
And great accounts before God to make.
Now, I pray you, Shrift, mother of salvation,
Help my good deeds for my piteous exclamation.
Confession: I know your sorrow well, Everyman;
Because with Knowledge ye come to me,
I will you comfort as well as I can,
And a precious jewel I will give thee,
Called penance, wise voider of adversity;
Therewith shall your body chastised be,
With abstinence and perseverance in God's service:
Here shall you receive that scourge of me,
Which is penance strong, that ye must endure,
To remember thy Savior was scourged for thee
With sharp scourges, and suffered it patiently;
So must thou, or thou scape that painful pilgrimage;
Knowledge, keep him in this voyage,
And by that time Good-Deeds will be with thee.
But in any wise, be sure of mercy,
For your time draweth fast, and ye will saved be;
Ask God mercy, and He will grant truly,
When with the scourge of penance man doth him bind,
The oil of forgiveness then shall he find.
Everyman: Thanked be God for his gracious work!
For now I will my penance begin;
This hath rejoiced and lighted my heart,
Though the knots be painful and hard within.
Knowledge: Everyman, look your penance that ye fulfil,
What pain that ever it to you be,
And Knowledge shall give you counsel at will,
How your accounts ye shall make clearly.

---

11. If you go by me.
12. With.

Everyman: O eternal God, O heavenly figure,
O way of rightwiseness, O goodly vision,
Which descended down in a virgin pure
Because he would Everyman redeem,
Which Adam forfeited by his disobedience:
O blessed Godhead, elect and high-divine,
Forgive my grievous offence;
Here I cry thee mercy in this presence.
O ghostly treasure, O ransomer and redeemer
Of all the world, hope and conductor,
Mirror of joy, and founder of mercy,
Which illumineth heaven and earth thereby,
Here my clamorous complaint, though it late be;
Receive my prayers; unworthy in this heavy life,
Though I be, a sinner most abominable,
Yet let my name be written in Moses' table;
O Mary, pray to the Maker of all thing,
Me for to help at my ending,
And save me from the power of my enemy,
For Death assaileth me strongly;
And, Lady, that I may be means of thy prayer
Of your Son's glory to be partaker,
By the means of his passion I it crave,
I beseech you, help my soul to save.—
Knowledge, give me the scourge of penance;
My flesh therewith shall give a quittance:
I will now begin, if God give me grace.
Knowledge: Everyman, God give you time and space:
Thus I bequeath you in the hands of our Saviour,
Thus may you make your reckoning sure.
Everyman: In the name of the Holy Trinity,
My body sore punished shall be:
Take this, body, for the sin of the flesh;
Also thou delightest to go gay and fresh,
And in the way of damnation thou did me bring;
Therefore suffer now strokes and punishing.
Now of penance I will wade the water clear,
To save me from purgatory, that sharp fire.
Good-Deeds: I thank God, now I can walk and go;
And am delivered of my sickness and woe.
Therefore with Everyman I will go, and not spare;
His good works I will help him to declare.
Knowledge: Now, Everyman, be merry and glad;
Your Good-Deeds cometh now; ye may not be sad;
Now is your Good-Deeds whole and sound,
Going upright upon the ground.
Everyman: My heart is light, and shall be evermore;
Now will I smite faster than I did before.
Good-Deeds: Everyman, pilgrim, my special friend,
Blessed be thou without end;
For thee is prepared the eternal glory.
Ye have me made whole and sound,
Therefore I will bide by thee in every stound.[13]
Everyman: Welcome, my Good-Deeds; now I hear thy
voice,
I weep for very sweetness of love.
Knowledge: Be no more sad, but ever rejoice,
God seeth thy living in his throne above;
Put on this garment to thy behove,
Which is wet with your tears,
Or else before God you may it miss,
When you to your journey's end come shall.
Everyman: Gentle Knowledge, what do you it call?
Knowledge: It is a garment of sorrow:
From pain it will you borrow;
Contrition it is,
That getteth forgiveness;
It pleaseth God passing well.

Good-Deeds: Everyman, will you wear it for your heal?
Everyman: Now blessed be Jesu, Mary's Son!
For now have I on true contrition.
And let us go now without tarrying;
Good-Deeds, have we clear our reckoning?
Good-Deeds: Yea, indeed I have it here.
Everyman: Then I trust we need not fear;
Now, friends, let us not part in twain.
Knowledge: Nay, Everyman, that will we not, certain.
Good-Deeds: Yet must thou lead with thee
Three persons of great might.
Everyman: Who should they be?
Good-Deeds: Discretion and Strength they hight,
And thy Beauty may not abide behind.
Knowledge: Also ye must call to mind
Your Five-wits as for your counsellors.
Good-Deeds: You must have them ready at all hours.
Everyman: How shall I get hither?
Knowledge: You must call them all together,
And they will hear you incontinent.
Everyman: My friends, come hither and be present,
Discretion, Strength, my Five-wits, and Beauty.
Beauty: Here at your will we be all ready.
What will ye that we should do?
Good-Deeds: That ye would with Everyman go,
And help him in his pilgrimage,
Advise you, will ye with him or not in that voyage?
Strength: We will bring him all thither,
To his help and comfort, ye may believe me.
Discretion: So will we go with him all together.
Everyman: Almighty God, loved thou be,
I give thee laud that I have hither brought
Strength, Discretion, Beauty, and Five-wits; lack I nought;
And my Good-Deeds, with Knowledge clear,
All be in my company at my will here;
I desire no more to my business.
Strength: And I, Strength, will by you stand in distress,
Though thou would in battle fight on the ground.
Five-Wits: And though it were through the world
round,
We will not depart for sweet nor sour.
Beauty: No more will I unto death's hour,
Whatsoever thereof befall.
Discretion: Everyman, advise you first of all;
Go with a good advisement and deliberation;
We all give you virtuous monition
That all shall be well.
Everyman: My friends, hearken what I will tell:
I pray God reward you in his heavenly sphere.
Now hearken, all that be here
For I will make my testament
Here before you all present.
In alms half my good I will give with my hands twain
In the way of charity, with good intent,
And the other half still shall remain
In quiet to be returned there it ought to be.
This I do in despite of the fiend of hell
To go quite out of his peril
Ever after and this day.
Knowledge: Everyman, hearken what I say;
Go to priesthood, I you advise,
And receive of him in any wise
The holy sacrament and ointment together;
Then shortly see ye turn again hither;
We will all abide you here.

---

13. Season.

Five-Wits: Yea, Everyman, hie you that ye ready were,
There is no emperor, king, duke, ne baron,
That of God hath commission,
As hath the least priest in the world being;
For of the blessed sacraments pure and benign,
He beareth the keys and thereof hath the cure
For man's redemption, it is ever sure;
Which God for our soul's medicine
Gave us out of his heart with great pine;
Here in this transitory life, for thee and me
The blessed sacraments seven there be.
Baptism, confirmation, with priesthood good,
And the sacrament of God's precious flesh and blood,
Marriage, the holy extreme unction, and penance;
These seven be good to have in remembrance,
Gracious sacraments of high divinity.
Everyman: Fain would I receive that holy body
And meekly to my ghostly father I will go.
Five-Wits: Everyman, that is the best that ye can do:
God will you to salvation bring,
For priesthood exceedeth all other thing;
To us Holy Scripture they do teach,
And converteth man from sin heaven to reach;
God hath to them more power given,
Than to any angel that is in heaven;
With five words he may consecrate
God's body in flesh and blood to make,
And handleth his maker between his hands;
The priest bindeth and unbindeth all bands,
Both in earth and in heaven;
Thou ministers all the sacraments seven;
Though we kissed thy feet thou were worthy;
Thou art surgeon that cureth sin deadly:
No remedy we find under God
But all only priesthood.
Everyman, God gave priests that dignity,
And setteth them in his stead among us to be;
Thus be they above angels in degree.
Knowledge: If priests be good it is so surely;
But when Jesus hanged on the cross with great smart
There he gave, out of his blessed heart,
The same sacrament in great torment:
He sold them not to us, that Lord Omnipotent.
Therefore Saint Peter the apostle doth say
That Jesu's curse hath all they
Which God their Saviour do buy or sell,
Or they for any money do take or tell.
Sinful priests giveth the sinners example bad;
Their children sitteth by other men's fires, I have heard;
And some haunteth women's company,
With unclean life, as lusts of lechery:
These be with sin made blind.
Five-Wits: I trust to God no such may we find;
Therefore let us priesthood honour,
And follow their doctrine for our souls' succour;
We be their sheep, and they shepherds be
By whom we all be kept in surety.
Peace, for yonder I see Everyman come,
Which hath made true satisfaction.
Good-Deeds: Methinketh it is he indeed.
Everyman: Now Jesu be our alder speed.[14]
I have received the sacrament for my redemption,
And then mine extreme unction:
Blessed be all they that counselled me to take it!
And now, friends, let us go without longer respite;
I thank God that ye have tarried so long.

Now set each of you on this rod your hand,
And shortly follow me:
I go before, there I would be; God be our guide.
Strength: Everyman, we will not from you go,
Till ye have gone this voyage long.
Discretion: I, Discretion, will bide by you also.
Knowledge: And though this pilgrimage be never so
  strong,
I will never part you fro:
Everyman, I will be as sure by thee
As ever I did by Judas Maccabee.
Everyman: Alas, I am so faint I may not stand,
My limbs under me do fold;
Friends, let us not turn again to this land,
Not for all the world's gold,
For into this cave must I creep
And turn to the earth and there to sleep.
Beauty: What, into this grave? Alas!
Everyman: Yea, there shall you consume more and
  less.
Beauty: And what, should I smother here?
Everyman: Yea, by my faith, and never more appear.
In this world live no more we shall,
But in heaven before the highest Lord of all.
Beauty: I cross out all this; adieu by Saint John;
I take my cap in my lap and am gone.
Everyman: What, Beauty, whither will ye?
Beauty: Peace, I am deaf; I look not behind me,
Not and thou would give me all the gold in thy chest.
Everyman: Alas, whereto may I trust?
Beauty goeth fast away hie;
She promised with me to live and die.
Strength: Everyman, I will thee also forsake and deny;
Thy game liketh me not at all.
Everyman: Why, then ye will forsake me all.
Sweet Strength, tarry a little space.
Strength: Nay, sir, by the rood of grace
Though thou weep till thy heart brast.
Everyman: Ye would ever bide by me, ye said.
Strength: Yea, I have you far enough conveyed;
Ye be old enough, I understand,
Your pilgrimage to take on hand;
I repent me that I hither came.
Everyman: Strength, you to displease I am to blame;
Will you break promise that is debt?
Strength: In faith, I care not;
Thou art but a fool to complain,
You spend your speech and waste your brain;
Go thrust thee into the ground.
Everyman: I had wend surer I should you have found.
He that trusteth in his Strength
She him deceiveth at the length.
Both Strength and Beauty forsaketh me,
Yet they promised me fair and lovingly.
Discretion: Everyman, I will after Strength be gone,
As for me I will leave you alone.
Everyman: Why, Discretion, will ye forsake me?
Discretion: Yea, in faith, I will go from thee,
For when Strength goeth before
I follow after evermore.
Everyman: Yet I pray thee, for the love of the Trinity,
Look in my grave once piteously.

---

14. Speed in help of all.

Discretion: Nay, so nigh will I not come.
Farewell, every one!
Everyman: O all thing faileth, save God alone;
Beauty, Strength, and Discretion;
For when Death bloweth his blast,
They all run from me full fast.
Five-Wits: Everyman, my leave now of thee I take;
I will follow the other, for here I thee forsake.
Everyman: Alas! then may I wail and weep,
For I took you for my best friend.
Five-Wits: I will no longer thee keep;
Now farewell, and there an end.
Everyman: O Jesu, help, all hath forsaken me!
Good-Deeds: Nay, Everyman, I will bide with thee,
I will not forsake thee indeed;
Thou shalt find me a good friend at need.
Everyman: Gramercy, Good-Deeds; now may I true
    friends see;
They have forsaken me every one;
I loved them better than my Good-Deeds alone.
Knowledge, will ye forsake me also?
Knowledge: Yea, Everyman, when ye to death do go:
But not yet for no manner of danger.
Everyman: Gramercy, Knowledge, with all my heart.
Knowledge: Nay, yet I will not from hence depart,
Till I see where ye shall be come.
Everyman: Methinketh, alas, that I must be gone
To make my reckoning and my debts pay,
For I see my time is nigh spent away.
Take example, all ye that this do hear or see,
How they that I loved best do forsake me,
Except my Good-Deeds that bideth truly.
Good-Deeds: All earthly things is but vanity:
Beauty, Strength, and Discretion, do man forsake,
Foolish friends and kinsmen, that fair spake,
All fleeth save Good-Deeds, and that am I.
Everyman: Have mercy on me, God most mighty;
And stand by me, thou Mother and Maid, holy Mary.
Good-Deeds: Fear not, I will speak for thee.
Everyman: Here I cry God mercy.
Good-Deeds: Short our end, and minish our pain;
Let us go and never come again.
Everyman: Into thy hands, Lord, my soul I commend;
Receive it, Lord, that it be not lost;
As thou me boughtest, so me defend,
And save me from the fiend's boast,
That I may appear with that blessed host
That shall be saved at the day of doom.
In manus tuas—of might's most
For ever—*commendo spiritum meum.*[15]
Knowledge: Now hath he suffered that we all shall
    endure;
The Good-Deeds shall make all sure.
Now hath he made ending;
Methinketh that I hear angels sing
And make great joy and melody,
Where Everyman's soul received shall be.
Angel: Come, excellent elect spouse to Jesu:
Hereabove thou shalt go
Because of thy singular virtue:
Now the soul is taken the body fro;
Thy reckoning is crystal-clear.
Now shalt thou into the heavenly sphere,
Unto the which all ye shall come
That liveth well before the day of doom.
Doctor: This moral men may have in mind;
Ye hearers, take it of worth, old and young,
And forsake pride, for he deceiveth you in the end,

And remember Beauty, Five-wits, Strength, and
    Discretion,
They all at the last do Everyman forsake,
Save his Good-Deeds, there doth he take.
But beware, and they be small
Before God, he hath not help at all.
None excuse may be there for Everyman:
Alas, how shall he do then?
For after death amends may no man make,
For then mercy and pity do him forsake.
If his reckoning be not clear when he do come,
God will say—*ite maledicti in ignem aeternum.*[16]
And he that hath his account whole and sound,
High in heaven he shall be crowned;
Unto which place God brings us all thither
That we may live body and soul together.
Thereto help the Trinity,
Amen, say ye, for saint Charity.
THUS ENDETH THIS MORALL PLAY OF EVERYMAN.

AUCASSIN AND NICOLETTE

Contrasting sharply with *Everyman,* the *chant-fable* of *Aucassin and Nicolette*[17] points up the conflicts in medieval life represented by the somber morality play and the charming fable of the young lovers. One smiles with pleasure at the sensuous description of Nicolette, or the piling up of ludicrous incidents: Aucassin riding forth to battle like every stereotype of the medieval knight, only to forget what he should be doing, and ending as a captive; or again, falling off his horse and breaking his collarbone. Meanwhile Nicolette hides behind a bush and waits until he drags himself most painfully into her little bower before she gives him comfort and love which is more potent than penicillin. One could list many incidents, or call attention to the gracefulness of the verse as opposed to the earnest tone and sober rhythms of *Everyman.* The *chant-fable* not only speaks of the joy of life, it *is* that joy. The two as a side-by-side contrast ask the question, "Which way is this civilization to go?"

Who will deign to hear the song,
Solace of a captive's wrong,
Telling how two children met,
Aucassin and Nicolette;
How by grievous pains distraught,
Noble deeds the varlet wrought
For his love, and her bright face!
Sweet my rhyme, and full of grace,
Fair my tale, and debonair.
He who lists—though full of care,
Sore astonied, much amazed,
All cast down, by men mispraised,
Sick in body, sick in soul,
Hearing, shall be glad and whole,
So sweet the tale.
Now they say and tell and relate:

---

15. Into your hands I commend my spirit.
16. Be damned to the eternal fire.
17. The names are pronounced oh–kah–SAN and ni–koh–LET.

How the Count Bougars of Valence made war on Count Garin of Beaucaire, war so great, so wonderful, and so mortal, that never dawned the day but that he was at the gates and walls and barriers of the town, with a hundred knights and ten thousand men-at-arms, on foot and on horse. So he burned the Count's land, and spoiled his heritage, and dealt death to his men. The Count Garin of Beaucaire was full of years, and frail; he had long outworn his day. He had no heir, neither son nor daughter, save one only varlet, and he was such as I will tell you. Aucassin was the name of the lad. Fair he was, and pleasant to look upon, tall and shapely of body in every whit of him. His hair was golden, and curled in little rings about his head; he had grey and dancing eyes, a clear, oval face, a nose high and comely, and he was so gracious in all good graces that nought in him was found to blame, but good alone. But love, that high prince, so utterly had cast him down, that he cared not to become knight, neither to bear arms, nor to tilt at tourneys, nor yet to do aught that it became his name to do.

His father and his mother spake him thus, "Son, don now thy mail, mount thy horse, keep thy land, and render aid to thy men. Should they see thee amongst them, the better will the men-at-arms defend their bodies and their substance, thy fief[18] and mine."

"Father," said Aucassin, "why speakest thou in such fashion to me? May God give me nothing of my desire if I become knight, or mount to horse, or thrust into the press to strike other or be smitten down, save only that thou give me Nicolette, my sweet friend, whom I love so well."

"Son," answered the father, "this may not be. Put Nicolette from mind. For Nicolette is but a captive maid, come hither from a far country, and the Viscount of this town bought her with money from the Saracens, and set her in this place. He hath nourished and baptized her, and held her at the font. On a near day he will give her to some young bachelor, who will gain her bread in all honor. With this what hast thou to do? Ask for a wife, and I will find thee the daughter of a king, or a count. Were he the richest man in France, his daughter shalt thou have, if so thou wilt."

"Faith, my father," said Aucassin, "what honor of this world would not Nicolette, my very sweet friend, most richly become! Were she Empress of Byzantium or of Allemaigne, or Queen of France, or England, low enough would be her degree, so noble is she, so courteous and debonair, and gracious in all good graces."

Now is sung:
Aucassin was of Beaucaire,
Of the mighty castle there,
But his heart was ever set
On his fair friend, Nicolette.
Small he heeds his father's blame,
Or the harsh words of his dame:
"Fool, to weep the livelong day,
Nicolette trips light and gay.
Scouring she from far Carthage,
Bought of Paynims for a wage.
Since a wife beseems thee good,
Take a wife of wholesome blood."
"Mother, nought for this I care,
Nicolette is debonair;
Slim the body, fair the face,
Make my heart a lighted place;
Love has set her as my peer,
    Too sweet, my dear."
Now they say and tell and relate:

When the Count Garin of Beaucaire found that in nowise could he withdraw Aucassin his son from the love of Nicolette, he sought out the Viscount of the town, who was his man, and spake him thus, "Sir Count, send Nicolette your godchild straightly from this place. Cursed be the land wherefrom she was carried to this realm; for because of her I lose Aucassin, who will not become knight, nor do aught that it becometh knight to do. Know well that, were she once within my power, I would hurry her to the fire; and look well to yourself for you stand in utmost peril and fear."

"Sire," answered the Viscount, "this lies heavy upon me, that ever Aucassin goes and he comes seeking speech with my ward. I have bought her with my money, and nourished and baptized her, and held her at the font. Moreover, I am fain to give her to some young bachelor, who will gain her bread in all honor. With this Aucassin your son had nought to do. But since this is your will and your pleasure, I will send her to so far a country that nevermore shall he see her with his eyes."

"Walk warily," replied the Count Garin, "for great evil easily may fall to you of this." So they went their ways.

Now the Viscount was a very rich man, and had a rich palace standing within a garden. In a certain chamber of an upper floor he set Nicolette in ward, with an old woman to bear her company, and to watch; and he put there bread and meat and wine and all things for their need. Then he placed a seal upon the door, so that none might enter in, nor issue forth, save only that there was a window looking on the garden, strictly close, whereby they breathed a little fresh air.

Now is sung:
Nicolette is prisoned fast,
In a vaulted chamber cast,
Shaped and carven wondrous well,
Painted as by miracle.
At the marble casement stayed
On her elbow leaned the maid;
Golden showed her golden hair,
Softly curved her eyebrows rare,
Fair her face, and brightly flushed,
Sweeter maiden never blushed.
In the garden from her room
She might watch the roses bloom,
Hear the birds make tender moan;
Then she knew herself alone.
" 'Lack, great pity 'tis to place
Maid in such an evil case.
Aucassin, my liege, my squire,
Friend, and dear, and heart's desire,
Since thou dost not hate me quite,
Men have done me foul despite,
Sealed me in this vaulted room,
Thrust me to this bitter doom.
But by God, Our Lady's Son,
Soon will I from here begone.
    So it be won."
Now they say and tell and relate:
Nicolette was prisoned in the chamber, as you have heard and known. The cry and the haro[19] went through all the land that Nicolette was stolen away. Some said that

_____
18. Fief—the demesne of the Count.
19. Protest against injustice.

she had fled the country, and some that the Count Garin of Beaucaire had done her to death. Whatever man may have rejoiced, Aucassin had no joy therein, so he sought out the Viscount of the town and spake him thus, "Sir Viscount, what have you done with Nicolette, my very sweet friend, the thing that most I love in all the world? Have you borne her off, or hidden her from my sight? Be sure that should I die hereof, my blood will be required of you, as is most just, for I am slain of your two hands; since you steal from me the thing that most I love in all the world."

"Fair sire," answered the Viscount, "put this from mind. Nicolette is a captive maid whom I brought here from a far country. For her price I trafficked with the Saracens, and I have bred and baptized her, and held her at the font. I have nourished her duly, and on a day will give her to some young bachelor who will gain her bread in honorable fashion. With this you have nought to do; but only to wed the daughter of some count or king. Beyond this, what profit would you have, had you become her lover, and taken her to your bed? Little enough would be your gain therefrom, for your soul would lie tormented in Hell all the days of all time, so that to Paradise never should you win."

"In Paradise what have I to do? I care not to enter, but only to have Nicolette, my very sweet friend, whom I love so dearly well. For into Paradise go none but such people as I will tell you of. There go those aged priests, and those old cripples, and the maimed, who all day long and all night cough before the altars, and in the crypts beneath the churches; those who go in worn old mantles and old tattered habits; who are naked, and barefoot, and full of sores; who are dying of hunger and of thirst, of cold and of wretchedness. Such as these enter in Paradise, and with them have I nought to do. But in Hell will I go. For to Hell go the fair clerks and the fair knights who are slain in the tourney and the great wars, and the stout archer and the loyal man. With them will I go. And there go the fair and courteous ladies, who have friends, two or three, together with their wedded lords. And there pass the gold and the silver, the ermine and all rich furs, harpers and minstrels, and the happy of the world. With these will I go, so only that I have Nicolette, my very sweet friend, by my side."

"Truly," cried the Viscount, "you talk idly, for never shall you see her more; yea, and if perchance you spoke together, and your father heard thereof, he would burn both me and her in one fire and yourself might well have every fear."

"This lies heavy upon me," answered Aucassin. Thus he parted from the Viscount making great sorrow.

Now is sung:

Aucassin departed thus
Sad at heart and dolorous;
Gone is she, his fairest friend,
None may comfort give or mend,
None by counsel make good end.
To the palace turned he home,
Climbed the stair, and sought his room.
In the chamber all alone
Bitterly he made his moan,
Presently began to weep
For the love he might not keep.
"Nicolette, so gent, so sweet,
Fair the faring of thy feet,
Fair thy laughter, sweet thy speech,
Fair our playing each with each,

Fair thy clasping, fair thy kiss,
Yet it endeth all in this.
Since from me my love is ta'en
I misdoubt that I am slain;
Sister, sweet friend."

Now they say and tell and relate:

Whilst Aucassin was in the chamber lamenting Nicolette, his friend, the Count Bougars of Valence, wishful to end the war, pressed on his quarrel, and setting his pikemen and horsemen in array, drew near the castle to take it by storm. Then the cry arose and the tumult; and the knights and the men-at-arms took their weapons, and hastened to the gates and the walls to defend the castle, and the burgesses climbed to the battlements, flinging quarrels[20] and sharpened darts upon the foe. Whilst the siege was so loud and perilous, the Count Garin of Beaucaire sought the chamber where Aucassin lay mourning, assotted upon[21] Nicolette, his very sweet friend, whom he loved so well.

"Ha, son," cried he, "craven art thou and shamed, that seest thy best and fairest castle so hardly beset. Know well that if thou lose it, thou art a naked man. Son, arm thyself lightly, mount the horse, keep thy land, aid thy men, hurtle into the press. Thou needest not to strike together, neither to be smitten down, but if they see thee amongst them, the better will they defend their goods and their bodies, thy land and mine; and thou art so stout and strong that very easily thou canst do this thing, as is but right."

"Father," answered Aucassin, "what sayest thou now? May God give me naught that I require of Him if I become a knight, or mount to horse, or thrust into the press to strike knight or to be smitten down, save only thou givest me Nicolette, my sweet friend, whom I love so well!"

"Son," replied the father, "this can never be. Rather will I suffer to lose my heritage, and go bare of all, than that thou shouldst have her, either as woman or as dame."

So he turned without farewell; but when Aucassin saw him part, he stayed him, saying, "Father, come now; I will make a true bargain with thee."

"What bargain, fair son?"

"I will arm me, and thrust into the press on such bargain as this: that if God bring me again safe and sound, thou wilt let me look on Nicolette, my sweet friend, so long that I may have with her two words or three, and kiss her only one time."

"I pledge my word to this," said the father. Of this covenant had Aucassin much joy.

Now is sung:

Aucassin the more was fain
Of the kiss he sought to gain,
Rather than his coffers hold
A hundred thousand marks of gold.
At the call his squire drew near,
Armed him fast in battle gear;
Shirt and hauberk donned the lad,
Laced the helmet on his head,
Girt his golden-hilted sword—
Came the war-horse at his word—

---

20. Square-headed crossbow-bolt.
21. Infatuated with.

Gripped the buckler and the lance,
At the stirrups cast a glance;
Then, most brave from plume to heel,
Pricked the charger with the steel,
Called to mind his absent dear,
Passed the gateway without fear
    Straight to the fight.

Now they say and tell and relate:

Aucassin was armed and horsed as you have heard.
God, how bravely showed the shield about his neck, the
helmet on his head, and the fringes of the baldric upon
his left thigh! The lad was tall and strong, slender and
comely to look upon; and the steed he bestrode was great
and speedy, and fiercely had he charged clear of the gate.
Now think not that he sought spoil of oxen and cattle, nor
to smite others and himself escape. Nay, but of all this he
took no heed. Another was with him; and he thought so
dearly upon Nicolette, his fair friend, that the reins fell
from his hand, and he struck never a blow. Then the
charger, yet smarting from the spur, bore him into the
battle, amidst the thickest of the foe, so that hands were
laid upon him from every side, and he was made prisoner.
Thus they spoiled him of shield and lance, and forthwith
led him from the field a captive, questioning amongst
themselves by what death he should be slain.

When Aucassin marked their words, "Ha, God!"
cried he. "Sweet Creature, these are my mortal foes who
lead me captive, and who soon will smite off my head;
and when my head is smitten, never again may I have fair
speech with Nicolette, my sweet friend, whom I hold so
dear. Yet have I a good sword; and my horse is yet
unblown. Now if I defend me not for her sake, may God
keep her never, should she love me still!" The varlet was
hardy and stout, and the charger he bestrode was right
fierce. He plucked forth his sword, and smote suddenly
on the right hand and on the left, cutting sheer through
nasal and headpiece, gauntlet and arm, making such ruin
around him as the wild boar deals when brought to bay
by hounds in the wood, until he had struck down ten
knights, and hurt seven more, and won clear of the *melee*,
and rode back at utmost speed, sword in his hand.

The Count Bougars of Valence heard tell that his
men were about to hang Aucassin, his foe, in shameful
wise, so he hastened to the sight; and Aucassin passed
him not by. His sword was yet in hand, and struck the
Count so fiercely upon the helm that the headpiece was
cleft and shattered upon the head. So bewildered was he
by the stroke that he tumbled to the ground, and Aucassin
stretched forth his hand, and took him, and led him
captive by the nasal of the helmet, and delivered him to
his father. "Father," said Aucassin, "behold the foe who
wrought such war and mischief upon you! Twenty years
hath this war endured, and none was there to bring it to
an end."

"Fair son," replied his father, "better are such deeds
as this than foolish dreams!"

"Father," returned Aucassin, "preach me no
preachings; but carry out our bargain."

"Ha! What bargain, fair son?"

"How now, father, hast thou returned from the
market? By my head, I will remember—whosoever may
forget—so close is it to my heart! Didst thou not bargain
with me, when I armed me and fared into the press, that
if God brought me again safe and sound, thou wouldst
grant me sight of Nicolette, my sweet friend, so long that
I might have with her two words or three, and kiss her
once? Such was the bargain; so be thou honest dealer."

"I!" cried the father. "God aid me never, should I
keep such terms. Were she here, I would set her in the
flames; and thou thyself might well have every fear."

"Is this the very end?" said Aucassin.

"So help me God," said his father, "yea!"

"Certès," said Aucassin, "grey hairs go ill with a
lying tongue."

"Count of Valence," said Aucassin, "thou art my
prisoner?"

"Sire," answered the Count, "it is verily and truly
so."

"Give me thy hand," said Aucassin.

"Sire, as you wish!" So each took the other's hand.

"Plight me thy faith," said Aucassin, "that so long as
thou drawest breath, never shall pass a day but thou shalt
deal with my father in shameful fashion, either in goods
or in person, if so thou canst."

"Sire, for God's love make me not a jest, but name
me a price for my ransom. Whether you ask gold or silver,
steed or palfrey, pelt or fur, hawk or hound, it shall be
paid."

"What!" said Aucassin; "art thou not my prisoner?"

"Truly, sire," said the Count Bougars.

"God aid me never," quoth Aucassin, "but I send thy
head flying, save thou plight me such faith as I said."

"In God's name," cried he, "I plight such affiance as
seems most meet to thee." He pledged his troth; so
Aucassin set him upon a horse, and brought him into a
place of surety, himself riding by his side.

Now is sung:

When Count Garin knew his son
Aucassin still loved but one,
That his heart was ever set
Fondly on fond Nicolette,
Straight a prison he hath found,
Paved with marble, walled around,
Where in vault beneath the earth
Aucassin made little mirth,
But with wailing filled his cell
In such wise as now I tell
"Nicolette, white lily-flow'r,
Sweetest lady found in bow'r,
Sweet as grape that brimmeth up
Sweetness in the spiced cup,
On a day this chanced to you:
Out of Limousin there drew
One, a pilgrim, sore adread—
Lay in pain upon his bed,
Tossed, and took with fear his breath,
Very dolent, near to death—
Then you entered, pure and white,
Softly to the sick man's sight,
Raised the train that swept adown,
Raised the ermine-bordered gown
Raised the smock, and bared to him,
Daintily, each lovely limb.
Then a wondrous thing befell.
Straight he rose up, sound and well,
Left his bed, took cross in hand,
Sought again his own dear land.
Lily-flow'r, so white, so sweet,
Fair the faring of thy feet,
Fair thy laughter, fair thy speech,
Fair our playing each with each!
Sweet thy kisses, soft thy touch!
All must love thee overmuch.

'Tis for thee that I am thrown
In this vaulted cell alone;
'Tis for thee that I attend
Death, that comes to make an end—
　　For thee, sweet friend!

　　Now they say and tell and relate:

　　Aucassin was set in prison as you have heard tell, and
Nicolette for her part was shut in the chamber. It was in
the time of summer heat, in the month of May, when the
days are warm, long and clear, and the night still and
serene. Nicolette lay one night sleepless on her bed, and
watched the moon shine brightly through the casement,
and listened to the nightingale plain in the garden. Then
she bethought her of Aucassin, her friend, whom she
loved so well. She called also to mind the Count Garin of
Beaucaire, her mortal foe, and feared greatly to remain,
lest her hiding-place should be told to him, and she be
put to death in some shameful fashion. She made certain
that the old woman who held her in ward was sound
asleep. So she rose, and wrapped herself in a very fair silk
mantle, the best she had, and taking the sheets from her
bed and the towels of her bath, knotted them together to
make so long a rope as she was able, tied it about a pillar
of the window, and slipped down into the garden. Then
she took her skirt in both hands, the one before, and the
other behind, and kilted her lightly against the dew
which lay thickly upon the grass, and so passed through
the garden. Her hair was golden, with little lovelocks; her
eyes blue and laughing; her face most dainty to see, with
lips more vermeil than ever was rose or cherry in the time
of summer heat; her teeth white and small; her breasts so
firm that they showed beneath her vesture like two
rounded nuts. So frail was she about the girdle that your
two hands could have spanned her, and the daisies that
she brake with her feet in passing showed altogether
black against her instep and her flesh, so white was the
fair young maiden.

　　She came to the postern, and unbarring the gate,
issued forth upon the street of Beaucaire, taking heed to
keep within the shadows, for the moon shone very bright,
and thus she fared until she chanced upon the tower
where her lover was prisoned. The tower was buttressed
with pieces of wood in many places, and Nicolette hid
herself amongst the pillars, wrapped close in her mantle.
She set her face to a crevice of the tower, which was old
and ruinous, and there she heard Aucassin weeping
within, making great sorrow for the sweet friend whom he
held so dear; and when she had hearkened awhile, she
began to speak.

　　Now is sung:

Nicolette, so bright of face,
Leaned within this buttressed place,
Heard her lover weep within,
Marked the woe of Aucassin.
Then in words her thought she told:
"Aucassin, fond heart and bold,
What avails thine heart should ache
For a Paynim maiden's sake?
Ne'er may she become thy mate,
Since we prove thy father's hate,
Since thy kinsfolk hate me too;
What is left for me to do?
Nothing, but to seek the strand,
Pass o'er sea to some far land."
Shore she then one golden tress,

Thrust it in her love's duress;
Aucassin hath seen the gold
Shining bright in that dark hold,
Took the lock at her behest,
Kissed and placed it in his breast;
Then once more his eyes were wet
　　For Nicolette.

　　Now they say and tell and relate:

　　When Aucassin heard Nicolette say that she would
fare into another country, he was filled with anger. "Fair
sweet friend," said he, "this be far from thee, for then
wouldst thou have slain me. And the first man who saw
thee, if so he might, would take thee forthwith and carry
thee to his bed, and make thee his leman. Be sure that if
thou wert found in any man's bed, save it be mine, I
should not need a dagger to pierce my heart and slay me.
Certes, no; wait would I not for a knife; but on the first
wall or the nearest stone would I cast myself, and beat out
my brains altogether. Better to die so foul a death as this
than know thee to be in any man's bed, save mine."

　　"Aucassin," said she, "I doubt that thou lovest me
less than thy words; and that my love is fonder than
thine."

　　"Alack," cried Aucassin, "fair sweet friend, how can
it be that thy love should be so great? Woman can not
love man, as man loves woman; for woman's love is in the
glance of her eye, and the blossom of her breast, and the
tip of the toe of her foot; but the love of man is set deep
in the hold of his heart, from whence it can not be torn
away."

　　Whilst Aucassin and Nicolette were thus at odds
together, the town watch entered the street, bearing
naked swords beneath their mantles, for Count Garin had
charged them strictly, once she were taken, to put her to
death. The warder from his post upon the tower marked
their approach, and as they drew near, heard them
speaking of Nicolette, menacing her with death.

　　"God," said he, "it is great pity that so fair a damsel
should be slain, and a rich alms should I give if I could
warn her privily, and so she escape the snare; for of her
death Aucassin, my liege, were dead already, and truly
this were a piteous case."

　　Now is sung:

Brave the warder, full of guile,
Straight he sought some cunning wile:
Sought and found a song betime,
Raised this sweet and pleasant rhyme.
"Lady of the loyal mind,
Slender, gracious, very kind,
Gleaming head and golden hair,
Laughing lips and eyes of vair!
Easy, Lady, 'tis to tell
Two have speech who love full well.
Yet in peril are they met,
Set the snare, and spread the net.
Lo, the hunters draw this way,
Cloaked, with privy knives, to slay.
Ere the huntsmen spy the chase[22]
Let the quarry haste apace
　　And keep her well."

　　Now they say and tell and relate:

---

22. Quarry.

"Ah," said Nicolette, "may the soul of thy father and of thy mother find sweetest rest, since in so fair and courteous a manner hast thou warned me. So God please, I will indeed keep myself close, and may He keep me too."

She drew the folds of her cloak about her, and crouched in the darkness of the pillars till the watch had passed beyond; then she bade farewell to Aucassin, and bent her steps to the castle wall. The wall was very ruinous, and mended with timber, so she climbed the fence, and went her way till she found herself between wall and moat. Gazing below, she saw the fosse was very deep and perilous, and the maid had great fear.

"Ah, God," cried she, "sweet Creature, should I fall, my neck must be broken; and if I stay, tomorrow shall I be taken, and men will burn my body in a fire. Yet were it better to die, now, in this place, than to be made a show tomorrow in the market."

She crossed her brow, and let herself slide down into the moat, and when she reached the bottom, her fair feet and pretty hands, which had never learned that they could be hurt, were so bruised and wounded that the blood came from them in places a many; yet knew she neither ill nor dolor because of the mightiness of her fear. But if with pain she had entered in, still more it cost her to issue forth. She called to mind that it were death to tarry, and by chance found there a stake of sharpened wood, which those within the keep had flung forth in their defense of the tower. With this she cut herself a foothold, one step above the other, till with extreme labor she climbed forth from the moat. Now the forest lay but the distance of two bolts from a crossbow, and ran some thirty leagues in length and breadth; moreover, within were many wild beasts and serpents. She feared these greatly, lest they should do her a mischief; but presently she remembered that should men lay hands upon her, they would lead her back to the city to burn her at the fire.

Now is sung:

Nicolette the fair, the fond,
Climbed the fosse and won beyond;
There she kneeled her, and implored
Very help of Christ the Lord.
"Father, King of majesty,
Where to turn I know not, I.
So, within the woodland gloom
Wolf and boar and lion roam,
Fearful things, with rav'ning maw,
Rending tusk and tooth and claw.
Yet, if all adread I stay,
Men will come at break of day,
Treat me to their heart's desire,
Burn my body in the fire.
But by God's dear majesty
Such a death I will not die;
Since I die, ah, better then
Trust the boar than trust to men.
Since all's evil, men and beast,
     Choose I the least."

Now they say and tell and relate:

Nicolette made great sorrow in such manner as you have heard. She commended herself to God's keeping, and fared on until she entered the forest. She kept upon the fringes of the woodland, for dread of the wild beasts and reptiles; and hiding herself within some thick bush, sleep overtook her, and she slept fast until six hours of the morn, when shepherds and herdsmen came from the city to lead their flocks to pasture between the wood and the river. The shepherds sat by a clear, sweet spring, which bubbled forth on the outskirts of the greenwood, and spreading a cloak upon the grass, set bread thereon. Whilst they ate together, Nicolette awoke at the song of the birds and the laughter, and hastened to the well.

"Fair children," said she, "God have you in His keeping."

"God bless you also," answered one who was more fluent of tongue than his companions.

"Fair child," said she, "do you know Aucassin, the son of Count Garin of this realm?"

"Yes, we know him well."

"So God keep you, pretty boy," said she, "as you tell him that within this wood there is a fair quarry for his hunting; and if he may take her, he would not part with one of her members for a hundred golden marks, nor for five hundred, nay, nor for aught that man can give."

Then looking upon her steadfastly, their hearts were troubled, the maid was so beautiful. "Will I tell him?" cried he who was readier of words than his companions. "Woe to him who speaks of it ever, or tells Aucassin what you say. You speak not truth but faery, for in all this forest there is no beast neither stag, nor lion, nor boar—one of whose legs would be worth two pence, or three at very best, and you talk of five hundred marks of gold! Woe betide him who believes your story, or shall spread it abroad! You are a fay, and no fit company for such as us; so pass upon your road."

"Ah, fair child," answered she, "yet you will do as I pray; for this beast is the only medicine that may heal Aucassin of his hurt. And I have here five sous in my purse; take them, and give him my message. For within three days must he hunt this chase and if within three days he find not the quarry, never may he cure him of his wound."

"By my faith," cried he, "we will take the money and if he comes this way, will give him your message; but certainly we will not go and look for him."

"As God pleases!" answered she. So she bade farewell to the shepherds, and went her way.

Now is sung:

Nicolette, as you heard tell,
Bade the shepherd lads farewell;
Through deep woodlands warily
Fared she 'neath the leafy tree,
Till the grass-grown way she trod
Brought her to a forest road,
Whence, like fingers on a hand,
Forked sev'n paths throughout the land.
There she called to heart her love,
There bethought her she would prove
Whether true her lover's vows.
Plucked she then young sapling boughs,
Grasses, leaves that branches yield,
Oak shoots, lilies of the field—
Built a lodge with frond and flow'r—
Fairest mason, fairest bow'r!
Swore then, by the truth of God,
Should her lover come that road,
Nor for love of her who made
Dream a little in its shade,
'Spite his oath, no true love, he
     Nor fond heart, she!

Now they say and tell and relate:

Nicolette built the lodge, as you have heard; very pretty it was and very dainty, and well furnished, both outside and in, with a tapestry of flowers and of leaves. Then she withdrew herself a little way from the bower, and hid within a thicket to spy what Aucassin would do. And the cry and the haro went through all the realm that Nicolette was lost; some had it that she was stolen away, and others that Count Garin had done her to death. Whoever had joy thereof, Aucassin had little pleasure. His father, Count Garin, brought him out of his prison, and sent letters to the lords and ladies of those parts bidding them to a very rich feast, so that Aucassin, his son, might cease to dote. When the feast was at its merriest, Aucassin leaned against the musicians' gallery, sad and all discomforted. No laugh had he for any jest, since she whom most he loved was not amongst the ladies set in hall.

A certain knight marked his grief, and coming presently to him, said, "Aucassin, of such fever as yours, I, too, have been sick. I can give you good counsel, if you are willing to listen."

"Sir knight," said Aucassin, "great thanks! Good counsel, above all things, I would hear."

"Get to horse," said he; "take your pleasure in the woodland amongst flowers and bracken and the songs of the birds. Perchance (who knows?) you may hear some word of which you will be glad."

"Sir knight," answered Aucassin, "great thanks! This will I do." He left the hall privily, and went down-stairs to the stable where was his horse. He caused the charger to be saddled and bridled, then put foot in stirrup, mounted, and left the castle, riding till he entered the forest, and so by adventure came upon the well whereby the shepherd lads were sitting; and it was then about three hours after noon. They had spread a cloak upon the grass, and were eating their bread, with great mirth and jollity.

Now is sung:

Round about the well were set
Martin, Robin, Esmeret—
Jolly shepherds, gaily met—
Frulin, Jack, and Aubriet.
Laughed the one, "God keep in ward
Aucassin, our brave young lord—
Keep besides the damsel fair,
Blue of eye and gold of hair,
Gave us wherewithal to buy
Cate and sheath-knife presently,
Horn and quarter-staff and fruit,
Shepherd's pipe and country flute;
God make him well!"

Now they say and tell and relate:

When Aucassin marked the song of the herdboys he called to heart Nicolette, his very sweet friend, whom he held so dear. He thought she must have passed that way, so he struck his horse with the spurs and came quickly to the shepherds.

"Fair children, God keep you!"

"God bless you!" replied he who was readier of tongue than his fellows.

"Fair children," said he, "tell over again the song that you told but now."

"We will not tell it," answered he who was more fluent of speech than the others. "Sorrow be his who sings it to you, fair sir!"

"Fair children," returned Aucassin, "do you not know me?"

"Oh, yes; we know that you are Aucassin, our young lord. But we are not your men; we belong to the Count."

"Fair children, sing me the song once more, I pray you!"

"By the Wounded Heart, what fine words! Why should I sing for you if I have no wish to do so? Why, the richest man in all the land—saving the presence of Count Garin—would not dare to drive my sheep and oxen and cows from out his wheatfield or his pasture, for fear of losing his eyes! Wherefore, then, should I sing for you if I have no wish to do so?"

"God keep you, fair children; yet you will do this thing for me. Take ten sous that I have in my purse."

"Sire, we will take the money; but I will not sing for you, since I have sworn not to do so. But I will tell it in plain prose, if such be your pleasure."

"As God pleases!" answered Aucassin. "Better the tale in prose than no story at all!"

"Sire, we were in this glade between six and nine of the morn, and were breaking our bread by the well, just as we are doing now, when a girl came by, the loveliest thing in all the world, so fair that we doubted her a fay, and she brimmed our wood with light. She gave us money, and made a bargain with us that if you came here we would tell you that you must hunt in this forest; for in it is such a quarry that if you may take her you would not part with one of her members for five hundred silver marks, nor for aught that man can give. For in the quest is so sweet a salve that if you take her you shall be cured of your wound; and within three days must the chase be taken, for if she be not found by then, never will you see her more. Now go to your hunting if you will, and if you will not, let it go; for truly have I carried out my bargain with her."

"Fair children," cried Aucassin, "enough have you spoken; and may God set me on her track!"

Now is sung:

Aucassin's fond heart was moved
When this hidden word he proved
Sent him by the maid he loved.
Straight his charger he bestrode,
Bade farewell, and swiftly rode
Deep within the forest dim,
Saying o'er and o'er to him:
"Nicolette, so sweet, so good,
'Tis for you I search this wood—
Antler'd stag nor boar I chase—
Hot I follow on your trace.
Slender shape and deep blue eyes,
Dainty laughter, low replies,
Fledge the arrow in my heart.
Ah, to find you—ne'er to part!
Pray God give so fair an end,
    Sister, sweet friend!"

Now they say and tell and relate:

Aucassin rode through the wood in search of Nicolette, and the charger went right speedily. Do not think that the spines and the thorns were pitiful to him. Truly, it was not so; for his raiment was so torn that the least tattered of his garments could scarcely hold to his body, and the blood ran from his arms and legs and flanks in forty places, or at least in thirty, so that you could have followed after him by the blood which he left upon the grass. But he thought so fondly of Nicolette, his sweet friend, that he felt neither ill nor dolor. Thus all day long he searched the forest in his fashion, but might learn no news of her, and when it drew towards dusk, he commenced to weep because he had heard nothing. He rode at adventure down an old grass-grown road, and looking before him, saw a young man standing, such as I will tell you. Tall he was, and marvelously ugly and hideous. His head was big and blacker than smoked meat; the palm of your hand could easily have gone between his two eyes; he had very large cheeks and a monstrous flat nose with great nostrils; lips redder than uncooked flesh; teeth yellow and foul; he was shod with shoes and gaiters of bull's hide, bound about the leg with ropes to well above the knee; upon his back was a rough cloak; and he stood leaning on a huge club. Aucassin urged his steed towards him, but was all afeared when he saw him as he was.

"Fair brother, God keep you."

"God bless you too," said he.

"As God keeps you, what do you here?"

"What is that to you?" said he.

"Truly, naught," answered Aucassin. "I asked with no wish to do you wrong."

"And you, for what cause do you weep?" asked the other, "and make such heavy sorrow? Certainly, were I so rich a man as you are, not the whole world should make me shed a tear."

"Do you know me, then?" said Aucassin.

"Yes, well I know you to be Aucassin, the son of the Count, and if you will tell me why you weep, well, then I will tell what I do here."

"Certes," said Aucassin, "I will tell you with all my heart. I came this morning to hunt in the forest, and with a white grey-hound, the swiftest in the whole world. I have lost him, and that is why I weep."

"Hear him," cried he, "by the Sacred Heart, and you make all this lamentation for a filthy dog! Sorrow be his who shall esteem you more. Why, there is not a man of substance in these parts who would not give you ten or fifteen or twenty hounds—if so your father wishes—and be right glad to make you the gift. But for my part I have full reason to weep and cry aloud."

"And what is your grief, brother?"

"Sire, I will tell you. I was hired by a rich farmer to drive his plough, with a yoke of four oxen. Now three days ago, by great mischance, I lost the best of my bullocks, Roget, the very best ox in the plough. I have been looking for him ever since, and have neither eaten nor drunk for three days; since I dare not go back to the town, because men would put me into prison, as I have no money to pay for my loss. Of all the riches of the world I have nought but the rags upon my back. My poor old mother, too, who had nothing but one worn-out mattress, why, they have taken that from under her, and left her lying on the naked straw. That hurts me more than my own trouble. For money comes and money goes; if I have lost today, why, I may win tomorrow; and I will pay for my ox when pay I can. Not for this will I wring my hands. And you—you weep aloud for a filthy cur. Sorrow take him who shall esteem you more."

"Certes, thou art a true comforter, fair brother, and blessed may you be. What is the worth of your bullock?"

"Sire, the villein demands twenty sous for his ox. I can not beat the price down by a single farthing."

"Hold out your hand," said Aucassin, "take these twenty sous which I have in my purse, and pay for your ox."

"Sire," answered the hind, "many thanks, and God grant you find that for which you seek."

So they parted from each other, and Aucassin rode upon his way. The night was beautiful and still, and so he fared along the forest path until he came to the seven crossroads where Nicolette had builded her bower. Very pretty it was, and very dainty, and well furnished both outside and in, ceiling and floor, with arras and carpet of freshly plucked flowers; no sweeter habitation could man desire to see. When Aucassin came upon it, he reined back his horse sharply, and the moonbeams fell within the lodge.

"Dear God," cried Aucassin, "here was Nicolette, my sweet friend, and this has she builded with her fair white hands. For the sweetness of the house and for love of her, now will I dismount, and here will I refresh me this night."

He withdrew his foot from the stirrup, and the charger was tall and high. He dreamed so deeply on Nicolette, his very sweet friend, that he fell heavily upon a great stone, and his shoulder came from its socket. He knew himself to be grievously wounded, but he forced him to do all that he was able, and fastened his horse with the other hand to a thorn. Then he turned on his side, and crawled as best he might into the lodge. Looking through a crevice of the bower, he saw the stars shining in the sky, and one brighter than all the others, so he began to repeat—

Now is sung:

Little Star I gaze upon
Sweetly drawing to the moon.
In such golden haunt is set
Love, and bright-haired Nicolette.
God hath taken from our war
Beauty, like a shining star.
Ah, to reach her, though I fell
From her Heaven to my Hell!
Who were worthy such a thing,
Were he emperor or king?
Still you shine, oh perfect Star,
    Beyond, afar.

Now they say and tell and relate:

When Nicolette heard Aucassin speak these words, she hastened to him from where she was hidden near by. She entered in the bower, and clasping her arms about his neck, kissed and embraced him straitly. "Fair sweet friend, very glad am I to find you."

"And you, fair sweet friend, glad am I to meet." So they kissed, and held each other fast, and their joy was lovely to see.

"Ah, sweet friend," cried Aucassin, "it was but now that I was in grievous pain with my shoulder, but since I hold you close I feel neither sorrow nor wound."

Nicolette searched his hurt, and perceived that the shoulder was out of joint. She handled it so deftly with her white hands and used such skillful surgery, that by the grace of God (who loveth all true lovers) the shoulder came back to its place. Then she plucked flowers, and fresh grass and green leafage, and bound them tightly about the setting with the hem torn from her shift, and he was altogether healed.

"Aucassin," said she, "Fair sweet friend, let us take thought together as to what must be done. If your father beats the wood tomorrow, and men take me, whatever may chance to you, certainly I shall be slain."

"Certes, fair sweet friend, the sorer grief would be mine. But so I may help, never shall you come to his hands." So he mounted to horse, and setting his love before him, held her fast in his arms, kissing her as he rode, and thus they came forth to the open fields.

Now is sung:

Aucassin, that loving squire,
Dainty fair to heart's desire,
Rode from out the forest dim
Clasping her he loved to him.
Placed upon the saddlebow
There he kissed her, chin and brow,
There embraced her, mouth and eyes.
But she spake him, sweetly wise:
"Love, a term to dalliance;
Since for us no home in France
See we Rome or far Byzance?"
"Sweet my love, all's one to me,
Dale or woodland, earth or sea;
Nothing care I where we ride
So I hold you at my side."
So, enlaced, the lovers went,
Skirting town and battlement,
Rocky scaur,[23] and quiet lawn;
Till one morning, with the dawn,
Broke the cliffs down to the shore,
Loud they heard the surges roar,
    Stood by the sea.

(From this point Aucassin and Nicolette were separated. After some adventures Aucassin returned to his home where he became Count of Beaucaire. Nicolette was taken to Carthage where she was recognized as the king's daughter and was to be married to a Moorish Prince. She ran away, however, and made her way to Beaucaire disguised as a minstrel.)

Now is sung:

'Neath the keep of strong Beaucaire
On a day of summer fair,
At his pleasure, Aucassin
Sat with baron, friend and kin.
Then upon the scent of flow'rs,
Song of birds, and golden hours,
Full of beauty, love, regret,
Stole the dream of Nicolette,
Came the tenderness of years;
So he drew apart in tears.
Then there entered to his eyes
Nicolette, in minstrel guise,
Touched the viol with the bow,
Sang as I will let you know.
"Lords and ladies, list to me,
High and low, of what degree;
Now I sing, for your delight,
Aucassin, that loyal knight,
And his fond friend, Nicolette.
Such the love betwixt them set
When his kinsfolk sought her head,
Fast he followed where she fled.
From their refuge in the keep
Paynims bore them o'er the deep.
Nought of him I know to end.
But for Nicolette, his friend,
Dear she is, desirable,
For her father loves her well;
Famous Carthage owns him king,
Where she has sweet cherishing.
Now, as lord he seeks for her,
Sultan, Caliph, proud Emir.

But the maid of these will none,
For she loves a dansellon,
Aucassin, who plighted troth.
Sworn has she some pretty oath
Ne'er shall she be wife or bride,
Never lie at baron's side
    Be he denied."

Now they say and tell and relate:

When Aucassin heard Nicolette sing in this fashion, he was glad at heart; so he drew her aside, and asked, "Fair sweet friend," said Aucassin, "know you nought of this Nicolette, whose ballad you have sung?"

"Sire, truly, yea; well I know her for the most loyal of creatures, and as the most winning and modest of maidens born. She is daughter to the King of Carthage, who took her when Aucassin also was taken, and brought her to the city of Carthage, till he knew for certain that she was his child, whereat he rejoiced greatly. Any day he would give her for husband one of the highest kings in all Spain; but rather would she be hanged or burned than take him, however rich he be."

"Ah, fair sweet friend," cried the Count Aucassin, "if you would return to that country and persuade her to have speech with me here, I would give you of my riches more than you would dare to ask of me or to take. Know that for love of her I choose not to have a wife, however proud her race, but I stand and wait; for never will there be wife of mine if it be not she, and if I knew where to find her I should not need to grope blindly for her thus."

"Sire," answered she, "if you will do these things, I will go and seek her for your sake, and for hers too; because to me she is very dear."

He pledged his word, and caused her to be given twenty pounds. So she bade him farewell, and he was weeping for the sweetness of Nicolette. And when she saw his tears, "Sire," said she, "take it not so much to heart; in so short a space will I bring her to this town, and you shall see her with your eyes."

When Aucassin knew this, he rejoiced greatly. So she parted from him, and fared in the town to the house of the Viscountess, for the Viscount, her godfather, was dead. There she lodged, and opened her mind fully to the lady on all the business; and the Viscountess recalled the past, and knew well that it was Nicolette whom she had cherished. So she caused the bath to be heated, and made her take her ease for fully eight days. Then Nicolette sought an herb that was called celandine, and washed herself therewith, and became so fair as she had never been before. She arrayed her in a rich silken gown from the lady's goodly store, and seated herself in the chamber on a rich stuff of broidered sendal; then she whispered the dame, and begged her to fetch Aucassin, her friend. This she did. When she reached the palace, lo, Aucassin in tears, making great sorrow for the long tarrying of Nicolette, his friend; and the lady called to him, and said, "Aucassin, behave not so wildly; but come with me, and I will show you that thing you love best in all the world; for Nicolette, your sweet friend, is here from a far country to seek her love." So Aucassin was glad at heart.

---

23. Isolated cliff.

Now is sung:

When he learned that in Beaucaire
Lodged his lady, sweet and fair,
Aucassin arose, and came
To her hostel, with the dame;
Entered in, and passed straightway
To the chamber where she lay.
When she saw him, Nicolette
Had such joy as never yet;
Sprang she lightly to her feet,
Swiftly came with welcome meet.
When he saw her, Aucassin
Oped both arms, and drew her in,
Clasped her close in fond embrace,
Kissed her eyes and kissed her face.
In such greeting sped the night,
Till, at dawning of the light,
Aucassin, with pomp most rare,
Crowned her Countess of Beaucaire.
Such delight these lovers met,
Aucassin and Nicolette.
Length of days and joy did win,
Nicolette and Aucassin;
Endeth song and tale I tell
    With marriage bell.

14

The Late Middle Ages: Expansion and Synthesis

It is impossible to pinpoint any particular reason for the liberation of a whole social structure, but as we look back over the centuries, we know that it happened in eleventh-century Europe. Perhaps not the least of the reasons was a release from a sense of doom; the end of the world had been predicted for the year 1000 and the prediction was widely believed by the peasantry. One must imagine the wonder of a whole culture when people woke up on New Year's morning of the year 1001, pinched themselves, and found that they were still alive in the flesh, and felt the pangs of hunger, not for spiritual food, but for a very physical breakfast. Such a reprieve may have been one of the causative factors in the general awakening of Europe. The people were still in the Middle Ages; God was still the accepted Reality, but what a difference was soon to be discovered in the lives and the thoughts of men and women!

The difference expresses itself in various ways. One can notice a change from the masculine code of feudalism to the feminine code of chivalry, closely associated with the rising Cult of the Virgin, which became the dominant popular religious force in late medieval times. Another factor to be considered is the rise of cities. The Crusades, still another leavening influence, brought about an increasing knowledge of the relatively luxurious life of Islamic culture. Within the new cities we also witness the revival of humanistic learning with the rise of the great universities. Last to be mentioned, though perhaps basic to the whole movement, was the philosophic ferment about the nature of reality itself, which culminated in the "Battle of Universals" in philosophic circles.

Historians attribute the rise of cities to a number of causes, all of which were probably significant. One reason lay in the increase of land available for agriculture because of the drainage of swamps, for it must be remembered that cities need agriculture to supply food. The needs of the great nobility for central fighting forces gave another impetus to the gathering of people, for as wars became bigger and landholdings wider, the barons needed men in a central place who could be mobilized immediately. Perhaps the most important force in the development of cities was the rise of trade and commerce (though one who asks for the causative force in this development cannot find a specific answer except that it happened). At any rate, the itinerant peddler, traveling from manor to manor, had been known throughout the early Middle Ages. Sometime about the eleventh century this trade became somewhat stabilized as the peddlers-become-merchants set up stalls under the protection of the great churches or abbeys, and the Church law that governed the place insured peaceful transactions. This brought about another change. If trade were to flourish, the old barter system was no longer adequate, and money was reintroduced to Europe. The nobility was quick to seize upon this change and to foster it. For centuries they had collected their feudal dues in produce and goods, but money offered them much greater freedom in carrying on their activities. They were willing, therefore, to grant charters to the cities, giving them varying degrees of freedom from feudal responsibilities in return for tax money. Thus did the towns grow, and whatever the immediate forces that made them flourish, their development was but a symptom of a general stirring of the human spirit.

Throughout Europe the word went around, "City air is free air," for in free cities the custom was established that a serf who could maintain his residence for a year and a day became a free man. The more adventurous and intelligent serfs flocked to the city. Here men of common interests—interests centered in their trades—formed themselves into guilds to regulate the quality and price of their goods and to provide insurance and a measure of social life for the members and their families.

As these guilds—first craft guilds, later merchant guilds—became wealthy, the grand guildhalls flanked the great church to form a quadrangle about the open marketplace; these became the distinguishing feature of the medieval city. After the towns were founded, came the great expansion of the merchants, plying their trade with the East and returning to Europe with the silks and spices they were able to buy there. In 1241, nearly three centuries after the first movement toward city growth, came the great Hanseatic League, the guild of merchants of the German coastal towns, uniting to carry on their trade. The cities, already founded, formed a safe outlet for their goods. Trade could be carried on. The increase in wealth, for the Church, for the producers of goods in the craft guilds, and for the merchants, was such that it found an outlet in drama, processions, and parades—one answer to the need for beauty in a world that had for centuries been sparse and bare.

The Crusades were another of the forces that enlightened the Middle Ages. The first Crusade took place at the end of the eleventh century, and was followed by many others even into the Renaissance. The last Crusade was led by Don John of Austria (1571). In carrying on these holy wars to free the Holy Land from the Muslims, various groups of crusading knights (the Knights of St. John, for example) set up permanent bases on such islands as Rhodes and Malta, and even on the eastern shores of the Mediterranean. As

was noted in the consideration of the early Middle Ages, a flourishing culture and a luxurious civilization had been alive in the Near East, parts of North Africa, and Spain during the first five hundred years of medieval times in Europe.

Well before the Crusades, Europe had been influenced by contacts with Islam in Sicily and Spain. Its agriculture and commerce, already expanding rapidly, were further stimulated by crusader encounters with the heart of Islamic culture. The luxurious booty carted home by the soldiers, as is the ancient custom of all soldiers, contributed to the rising expectations for a better life. First imported as luxuries, food (sugar, saffron, rice, citrus, melon) and manufactured goods (silk, damask, muslin, cotton) quickly became necessities. More important than food and textiles, however, was the rich reservoir of Islamic science, medicine, and mathematics and the carefully tended heritage of ancient Greece. The way was still long and tortuous but semibarbaric Europe began, finally, to develop the arts of civilized living.

One of the most interesting transformations was that from feudalism to chivalry, a movement from a masculine to a feminine code of behavior. Feudalism, according to the historian Henry Adams, was the code of men-at-arms. With the later Middle Ages, however, especially in France, women assumed a more prominent role in matters of taste and manners. Men were away from home for great stretches of time, trading, fighting, and crusading. In their absence their wives had opportunities to expand their limited roles by introducing poetry and music to the courts and elevating the standards of behavior, dress, and manners. If we must have one name to fix this movement in our memory, Adams gives us that of the remarkable Eleanor of Aquitaine (1122–1204), Queen of France and then of England. Insisting on accompanying her husband, King Louis VII of France, on the Second Crusade in 1147, Eleanor was especially impressed by the sophistication of Constantinople, and undoubtedly incorporated elements of Byzantine and Muslim culture into her already extensive education. Along with her daughter, Marie of Champagne, and granddaughter, Blanche of Castile, Eleanor established Courts of Love that were to write legal-sounding codes of etiquette. Epic tales of bloody battles and mighty heroes were replaced by lyrical love songs composed and performed by aristocratic troubadours and trouvères (fig. 14.1; see also chap. 16). This change may be seen in the contrast between Roland's lament over the fallen Franks at Roncevaux, representative of the ideals of feudalism, and the lament over the dead Lancelot, representative of the chivalrous knight. Roland, surveying the field of death where lie his comrades in arms, says:

> Lords and barons, now may God have mercy upon you, and grant Paradise to all your souls that you may rest among the blessed flowers. Man never saw better men of arms that ye were. Long and well, year in and year out, have ye served me, and many wide lands have ye won for the glory of Charles. Was it to such an end that he nourished you? O France, fair land,

Figure 14.1 "Music and Her Attendants" from Boethius, *De Arithmetica*, Biblioteca Nazionale, Naples. Holding a portable pipe organ, the elegant lady who symbolizes the civilized art of courtly music is surrounded by an ensemble of female court musicians. In the circle at the top King David plays a psaltery, the instrument named after the Psalms (Psaltery) of David.

today art thou made desolate by rude slaughter. Ye Frankish barons, I see you die through me, yet I can do naught to save and defend you. May God, who knows no lie, aid you!

Yet when Lancelot, the almost perfect knight of chivalry, lies dead, we hear the following lament:

> Thou wert the courtliest knight that ever bare shield, and thou were the truest friend to thy lover that ever bestrode horse, and thou wert the truest lover among sinful men that ever loved woman, and thou wert the kindest man that ever struck with sword, and thou wert the goodliest person that ever came among the crowd of knights, and thou wert the meekest man and the gentlest that ever are in hall among ladies, and thou wert the sternest knight to thy mortal foe that ever put spear in breast.

From this we see the transformation from a fighting code to a courtly and courteous one. Both are found in the lament over Lancelot, but the virtues of mildness, of love, and of humility always stand before the virtues of strength or the recognition of human weakness.

Given the vagaries of human nature, the elaborate codes of courtly love were undoubtedly violated about as often as they were observed, there being few Lancelots in this world. They assisted nevertheless in the long process of civilizing barbaric Europe.

Closely allied to the evolution of chivalry was the development of beauty and warmth within the Church. As has already been pointed out, the official doctrine of the Church was a vast intellectual monument. It centered in the Trinity—the Father, the Son, and the Holy Ghost—a Three who were always One, administering the rigid justice found in the development of doctrine from the time of Augustine. For sinful people, justice is the last thing to be desired, and medieval men and women, guilt-ridden by the absolutism of the time, were convinced that they were sinful. They sought not justice, but mercy, turning to the Virgin, the highest of the Saints, the Queen of Heaven. She was the essence of purity, an idealized version of love, warmth, and beauty. A manifestation of the polarized medieval view of women, the Cult of the Virgin venerated one woman, pure in body and soul, possessor of all the womanly virtues. Her diametric opposite was Eve the temptress, the "fallen" woman who had been beguiled by Satan, a concept that was to have disastrous consequences in later centuries, including our own.

The Virgin was nevertheless the loving Mother who could mercifully intercede for the faithful, and it was to her that the great cathedrals were dedicated. Indeed, in France one asks not how to get to the cathedral, but how to get to Notre Dame, the church of "Our Lady." The two are almost synonymous. As Adams points out:

> The measure of this devotion [to the Virgin], which proves to any religious American mind, beyond possible cavil, its serious and practical reality, is the money it cost. According to statistics, in the single century between 1170 and 1270, the French built 80 cathedrals and nearly five hundred churches of the cathedral class, which would have cost, according to an estimate made in 1840, more than five thousand millions to replace. Five thousand million francs is a thousand million dollars,[1] and this covered only the great churches of a single century. . . . The share of this capital which was—if one may use a commercial figure—invested in the Virgin cannot be fixed . . . but in a spiritual and artistic sense, it was almost the whole. . . .
>
> Expenditure like this rests invariably on an economic idea. . . . In the thirteenth [century] they trusted their money to the Queen of Heaven—because of their belief in her power to repay it with interest in the life to come.

Therein lay the power of the Virgin in bringing human understanding and human sympathy into the cold philosophic structure of Church doctrine. While

---

1. This is the money values of 1840. If we multiplied the figure by fifty, it would still be low for the late twentieth century.

the philosophers wrangled about the nature of the universal substance, the common people found comfort and a release of pent-up energies in the addition of a Person with human sympathy and warmth to the austere Trinity. Such faith reveals itself in the great body of stories of the mysteries of the Virgin, one of the most widely known and touching of which is "Our Lady's Juggler," given on page 349.

Most important of all in terms of a basic way of life were the continual attacks and modifications of the doctrine of the Church itself, for the Church insisted upon absolute authority. In spite of his early philosophic gropings, St. Augustine had finally said, "I believe in order that I may know." Thus *faith* in the Scripture and the writings of the early churchmen and total submission to these sources was the first necessity for Christian life. Knowledge came second, and if at any point the doctrine seemed contrary to reason or inexplicable by it, the doctrine was to be believed and intellect was to be denied.

Upon this basis was built the great structure of Christian Scholasticism, the way of thought of the late Middle Ages. Most simply, Scholasticism can be explained in this way: If a thinker had any question for which he wanted an answer, he went first to the Bible and the writings of the Church Fathers to discover all the passages that pertained to his subject. This was his only source for basic data; experimentation in the world of his senses was not permitted. Then, as a second step, he used Aristotelian logic to work on his source material. Such logic is built upon the three-part syllogism: a major premise, *all men are mortal;* a minor premise, *Sokrates is a man;* a conclusion, *therefore Sokrates is mortal.* Then this conclusion can be used as a major or minor premise in further syllogisms until the thinker reaches an answer to his problems.[2]

As early as the ninth century the conflict between faith and reason had been pointed up by John Scotus Erigena who insisted that both reason and the Scriptures had come from God, and that there could be no conflict between them. After his time, the Church's stand on faith alone had been reaffirmed, particularly by Anselm of Canterbury in the eleventh century.

This reaffirmation was not to stand unchallenged for long. In the late eleventh century a philosophic conflict broke out that was called the Battle of Universals. The "battle" involved a lengthy philosophic dispute, greatly simplified here, about the nature of reality. Twentieth-century students may view this as a dry wrangle between a number of ivory-towered philosophers, but it was not. In the first place it has been pointed out that the idea of reality that is held at any time determines the nature of civilization, and that a change in this idea will bring about a change in the way people think and live. We are dealing with thinkers as important to their time as Einstein and Freud have been to ours. Second, the philosophers were important Churchmen, and since the Church was the central institution of the time, any change in its position would and did have a very great effect on life

itself. True, the peasant on the farm or the craftsman in his shop neither knew nor cared about the Battle of Universals, but the men concerned in it were the men who made and moved society as a whole.

To see the nature of this "battle" we may remember that one of the strongest foundations of Church doctrine was a Christian adaption of the Neoplatonist belief that reality was permanent, unchanging, without any body or material substance, existing in the mind of God. This position sprang from Plato's belief in essences (forms, ideas) as the ultimate reality. Thus body and substance, all physical things subject to change were only illusory shadows, imperfect copies, of the Idea (see Plato's "Allegory of the Cave" for a full explanation). According to this accepted doctrine, the human body was to be disregarded and a study of the physical world wasted time that should be spent seeking eternal truths. This Neoplatonic, Augustinian doctrine was accepted, up to the eleventh century, by the "Establishment" and became known as the *Realist* position.

The philosopher Roscellinus first challenged this doctrine and established what was called the *Nominalist* position, very close to the belief of most people today. He said that physical things were the only reality. For example, each sense-apparent tree is real and as far as trees are concerned, no higher reality exists. The question then arises, "How can we know the 'idea' tree?" Certainly we know these insubstantial ideas, for we can speak of trees, or people, or elephants, or justice when no specific one is present to our senses. Roscellinus answered that these "ideas" were only names (hence the word *Nominalist*), and that we form the idea as a generalization only after experience with a great number of individual things. We experience, he said, specific examples of elms, pines, palms, and all kinds of trees. In our mind we then generalize and form the "idea" tree so that we can talk about the species—and understand each other—in the middle of the ocean, with no specific tree within a thousand miles.

The two positions in the battle were thus established, as opposite as any two opposites can be. William of Champeaux stoutly defended the Realist position, the standard doctrine of the Church. If he should fail, the Church itself would be in danger, and indeed it was.

---

2. Modern students tend to scoff at this type of reasoning until they remember that *every* culture sets similar limits to its thought process. For example, in the early twentieth century, the searcher for truth drew the basic material for investigation from the world of the senses (one was not encouraged to go outside of this realm) and then used the scientific method to refine the raw data and find answers to the questions. The type of knowledge found through the use of this technique of research is totally different from that found in the Middle Ages, but the limitations are equally severe. A God-centered society results from one method, a completely materialistic society comes from the other.

A middle position was suggested by the brilliant thinker Peter Abelard, probably the most popular teacher in the early University of Paris. (Abelard is shown as a hero for the twentieth century as well as a brilliant thinker of the eleventh and twelfth centuries in the contemporary play, *Abelard and Heloise.*) Abelard had studied with both Roscellinus and William of Champeaux and knew their arguments thoroughly and, as a matter of interest, he defeated William in a public debate on the nature of the universals. (Henry Adams in *Mont-St. Michel and Chartres* gives an imaginary debate between the two, which is not too difficult to follow.) Abelard's compromise became known as the *Conceptualist* position, and anticipates an Aristotelian view of the problem even before the whole body of Aristotle's works was known to Europe. The Conceptualist view can be stated rather quickly, for it will become much better developed with the work of St. Thomas a century or so later. Briefly, Abelard held that the *idea* is *real,* but that it does not exist either before a particular physical thing or after it. That is, reality as idea exists only in the physical, sense-apparent object.

Abelard's intellectual daring was condemned by the Church, but the Battle of Universals was debated without conclusion for a century. The Realist, the Nominalist, and the Conceptualist positions remained at loggerheads and were a sore point in Church doctrine until the great synthesis, which was to be made by St. Thomas, who established what was to become the official dogma of the Church.

Abelard not only developed one of the sides in the Battle of Universals, but he threw another bombshell into the religious thought of the time when he published his book *Sic et non* (Yes and No). One remembers that the source of all knowledge at the time lay in the Scriptures and the writings of the early commentators on the Bible, the Church Fathers. In *Sic et non* Abelard proposed a number of important religious questions, then in opposite columns set down what the Fathers had written on the subject. In doing so, he demonstrated that one could find contradictory answers in this body of writings. If this body was the source of knowledge, and if contradictions existed within it, as Abelard clearly showed, how wrong must conclusions be that were based on this writing. The whole way of thought of Scholasticism was threatened if its original source of knowledge was self-contradictory, and all answers to questions that had been derived by the method must be suspect.

Still another fire broke out in the structure of the Church with the rediscovery of all of Aristotle's works in the last part of the twelfth century. Because his logic had been universally used as the method of thinking, Aristotle, though a pagan, was perhaps the most venerated name among all of the world's philosophers throughout the early Middle Ages, but only his work on logic was known to the philosophers of the time. About the year 1200 almost the entire corpus of his works was brought into Europe through a curious process. Aristotle had written in Greek, Syrian scholars had translated him into Syriac, then Arabic writers had converted those translations into Arabic. Finally, through the Muslims in Spain, the body of thought was discovered, turned into medieval Latin, and made available to all of Europe. The discovery of this trove of scientific knowledge posed several touchy questions, but the most important was that it revealed that Aristotle had developed considerable knowledge of the world by investigating and classifying *physical* things. The Church had stood against any studies of the physical world, yet here was a man more revered by scholars than were most of the saints, who had developed his knowledge by such investigation. The impact was about as great as if we discovered that one of our most revered scientists received his knowledge and made his discoveries by consulting a witch doctor. What was the Church to do?

The first reaction was to ban the newly discovered works entirely, and in 1210 and for the next few years we have records of the books being banned at the University of Paris. The discovery of the books was sufficiently well known, however, that they could not so conveniently be done away with. The next step was the publication of "authorized" versions from which all of Aristotle's ideas that were directly contradictory to Church doctrine had been expurgated. Since the minds of the scholars were hungry for new material, this step did not work either, and finally the entire body of knowledge was made available to the scholars of the late Middle Ages.

The Church had preached complete otherworldliness and disdained earthly knowledge except as it seemed to be a symbol or testimony of scriptural knowledge and heavenly life. Yet these books revealed that the most revered mind of the Middle Ages had dissected animals to discover similarities and differences between species; had classified plants according to their structure. Thus another problem was presented, demanding synthesis if the Church were to maintain its authority.

The rise of the universities is the last of the symptoms of new life we will consider here. Actually their origin is very obscure, for we have little knowledge of them until their formal charters were issued. In Christian Europe (as different from Spain) the University of Salerno, which specialized in medicine, was probably the earliest, for we have records of its existence in the middle of the eleventh century, yet situated in southern Italy, it had little influence on the general dawn of culture. The University of Bologna with its great law school was given a formal grant of rights in 1158; the University of Paris was granted a royal charter in 1200 and a Papal license in 1231. Oxford was formed in the twelfth century when a group of teachers and students seceded from Paris, and Cambridge came into being somewhat later when a dissident group left Oxford. The growth was so rapid that by the end of the Middle Ages we find eighty universities scattered throughout Europe. The actual founding dates for the universities are of relatively little importance, since it is probable that schools had existed in connection with cathedrals and abbeys where the universities were founded at least a century before formal charters were granted; this, at least, was the case with the University of Paris, which had a long history as the Cathedral School of Notre Dame before it was licensed as a university. Nor did the schools have a smooth course throughout; the occasion for the Papal license of the University of Paris in 1231 was the reopening of the University that had been closed for two years following a riot between students and the city authorities. Few things are new under the sun!

The word *universitas* is Latin for a corporation such as a trade guild. When teachers (or students) joined together as a legal body, a university came into existence. Operating under the protection of a charter granted usually by the pope or a king, universities were generally freed from local jurisdiction, though they could not avoid "town and gown" conflicts that seem to be endemic to university communities. Their operation paralleled that of craft guilds, with guild masters (professors) awarding qualifying certificates (degrees) to apprentices (students), who were working to become masters in the teaching corporation (university). Graduation of the apprentices marked their "commencement" as certified teachers.

Offering instruction in all recognized fields of knowledge, the University of Paris was the leading institution of the time, with faculties of medicine, law, theology, and liberal arts. As a prerequisite for professional courses, the liberal arts curriculum followed the seven liberal arts pattern of monastic schools: trivium (grammar, rhetoric, logic) and quadrivium (arithmetic, geometry, astronomy, and music, plus the works of Aristotle). In today's terms the subjects of the trivium were humanistic and those of the quadrivium mathematical.

Initial studies were devoted to the trivium (including analyses of works of philosophy, literature, and history) but with no prescribed hours or units of credit. Achievement was measured solely by comprehensive oral examinations, after which the bachelor of arts (B.A.) degree was awarded as the necessary prerequisite for studying the quadrivium. Passing the second set of examinations certified the student as a master of arts (M.A.), and thus qualified to teach the liberal arts curriculum. The higher degrees of doctor (in law, medicine, and theology) were also teaching degrees, with the doctor of philosophy (Ph.D.) added later for advanced study in the liberal arts. Usually based upon four years of study beyond the M.A., doctorates were awarded after passing another set of rigorous examinations and successfully defending a "thesis," or proposition, before a faculty board. The comparative few who survived this ordeal were granted not only a doctorate but also the opportunity to put on a banquet for the examiners.

Though some women had been admitted to Plato's Academy and some Hellenistic scholars were women, medieval universities were operated solely by and for the masculine sex. The medieval assumption that women had no need for formal education resulted, of course, in an incalculable loss of the brain power of half the human race, a cultural deprivation still not entirely rectified.

As guilds of teachers and scholars, universities at first had no campus and no buildings. With classes meeting wherever rooms could be found, usually in churches, early regulations specified charges for room and board, the price of books (usually rented because manuscripts were expensive), the minimum number of classes students had to attend to be "official" (usually two a week), and the number of lectures and their length that a professor had to give to collect his fees. Students could fine professors for absences or for lecturing too long and, by not attending his classes, cost him a portion of his fees.

The *collegium* (L., community, society) was a residence hall that private benefactors began providing for students who were too poor to pay room and board. Robert de Sorbon, royal chaplain to Louis IX, endowed a hall in 1257 called the College de Sorbonne, now the college of arts and sciences of the University of Paris.

This was a new group of people who had been unknown in the early Middle Ages. They were eager for all sorts of knowledge and questing for experience. Their motto may well have been Abelard's famous teaching, "for by doubting we come to inquiry, by inquiry we discover the truth." These people would not tolerate a culture that walled itself in by authority and allowed no questioning of that authority. Here, as in most areas of life in the late Middle Ages, we see life bursting out at the seams.

At the end of the preceding chapter we saw that medieval men and women had sheltered themselves within the narrow walls of the authoritarian church and of feudalism and manorialism. These provided a measure of physical and psychological safety but little room in which to grow. With the rise of cities and the increasing intellectual ferment in the universities, we see the breeching of medieval walls in the search for knowledge of the physical world. Contacts with Muslim and Byzantine cultures and the civilizing effects of chivalry and the courts of love indicated that life here on this earth could be made immeasurably better. In the ferment of city life and in the idea-ferment of the universities all established modes of existence were called into question, a questioning that is revealed in the literature of the time.

Life's Questions as Seen in Literature

In the preceding chapter the morality play *Everyman* and the French chante-fable *Aucassin and Nicolette* were presented. *Everyman*, to review briefly, faced either eternal damnation or eternal bliss; there is no middle ground and the fear of death hangs like a pall over all of life. *Aucassin and Nicolette*, on the other hand, speaks not only of the joy of life but *is* itself that joy. As a side-by-side contrast the question is reiterated: "Which way is this civilization to go?"

Chaucer, in his "Prolog" to *The Canterbury Tales,* illustrates this problem, though his tone and outlook are essentially realistic. While he is not seeking to illustrate anything, while he is trying only to describe an assortment of people with their too human weakness, he poses the problem nevertheless. The basic nature of the gathering of the pilgrims is a case in point. The pilgrimage to the Shrine of St. Thomas is, or should be, a religious exercise. Yet these people, or some of them at any rate, seem to be there for an extended picnic and nothing else. In the characters, again, we see the division of personality. On the one hand we have the poor and virtuous Parson; on the other we see the Friar, the Summoner, and the Pardoner, who are devoted entirely to the gratification of the flesh, and all of whom exploit their religious affiliation to make these gratifications possible.

In some instances we see the city men, the new class of merchants, lawyers, doctors, and guildsmen. Their aim is profit and they will achieve their purpose regardless of any nice concerns about religion. They partake of the upsurging spirit that denies the balance of the old Graeco-Roman tradition. Chaucer draws no moral from this collection of people, nor does he attempt to state a problem with the exactness of a mathematician or a social worker. What does the reader make of this collection of medieval men and women?

Nowhere is the spiritual conflict of the time better illustrated than in the student songs, for the universities themselves were products of the new and stirring life. The pulls upon the personality are particularly evident in one of the student creeds in which the dying goliard burlesques the creed of the Church. With almost savage vigor he takes each word of the Church's creed and turns it to a flaunting of his vices. Then the student faces the last moment and is gripped by a fear of the unknown to which he is committing himself: a fear that is supported by five hundred years of religious tradition. With an anguish that strikes home to the reader, he commits his soul to God and begs for the last sacrament of the Church.

The Medieval Synthesis

To summarize the conflicts in the late Middle Ages, which have been suggested, the clash of the times came about in new secular ways of thinking and living that challenged the older religious and mystic ways. Where was the art that could bring these together in a new synthesis? Where were the people who could define new relationships between human beings and the universe, human beings and God, the individual person and society as a whole? Where could be found artists to suggest new purposes for life since the old were so sorely challenged?

It would seem that this new synthesis came about in three places. In philosophy, it was St. Thomas Aquinas who built a new philosophic structure that could accommodate the divergent points of view. In art, the medieval Gothic cathedral furnished a synthesis at the point when the artist's skill and the function came together. Chartres Cathedral is the prime example of such a structure. In literature, the new balance was suggested by Dante Alighieri in *The Divine Comedy*. Let us look briefly at the ways in which the synthesis was achieved in these three forms.

It cannot be our purpose here to go into detail in a discussion of the doctrines of St. Thomas. Rather, we shall show how he reconciled some of the contradictions of the time. In discussing Thomas's thought, one can scarcely avoid using the symbol of the equilateral triangle as a representation of the individual person, of the nation, and of the universe, for all of his ideas seem to shape themselves around that symbol. It was no accident that this is also the symbol of the Trinity of God; it may have been accident that it is also a shape that suggests both stability and upward motion. In its visual form it unifies the energy of the Celto-Germanic spirit with the desire for stability of the Graeco-Roman world where it first appeared as the perfect two-dimensional figure of Pythagoras (see pp. 344 and 48).

In Thomas's unification of Aristotelian thought with that of the Church, he accepted the central Aristotelian doctrine, similar to that of the Conceptualists. This doctrine was that matter and form (or idea) cannot exist separately. Matter, he said, had only potentiality, that is the possibility of being itself, until it was entered into by the idea of the thing. Then it became that thing. For example, "clay" is not "brick," nor is there "brick" without "clay"; but when "clay," which has only potentiality by itself, is joined with the form or idea of "brick," then the "brick" exists. Next, he said, lower forms of existence are only matter in the formation of higher forms. And everything, he said, was moving, changing, growing, turning into something else. This movement is the movement toward perfection, which is God. Thus the First Mover, God, does not move things from behind, but is the purpose toward which all things are moving. Since things must desire the thing toward which they move, then the motive force is the love of God.

This argument involves the most important of Thomas's proofs of the existence of God. (He proposed five such proofs, bearing out his belief that all things accepted by faith could be proved by reason.) His most famous proof is that of motion. Very briefly stated, this proof proceeds in this way: We see motion. If there is motion, there must be a mover. If we think backward, for example, I roll a stone; something causes me to move to roll it; but something causes the mover which moves me, etc.; we have an endless and infinite series of movers. On the other hand, consider the first mover as a force that attracts rather than pushes from behind. Then we can come to a first "attracting force" (like a magnet), which sets all other things in motion. This First Mover, or if you will, the Unmoved Mover, is God, pulling all things toward himself.

Furthermore, in the idea that both *form* and *matter* are necessary for reality, Thomas brought together the conflicting arguments in the Battle of Universals. Here we may consider the question of whether form (or Idea) has existence *before,* or only *in* a specific thing, and whether it exists *after* the specific has vanished. All three, said Thomas. The Idea exists (as potentiality) before the thing; it exists in the thing, and in its continuing progress upward, it exists after the particular thing. Thus, borrowing heavily from the Conceptualist view, he brought the three positions into harmony.

It was with the doctrine of lower and higher forms, all in motion toward perfection, that Thomas brought together the conflict between the growing desire of people for natural knowledge and the doctrine of the Church that such knowledge was a study of nothingness, for, said Thomas, the highest human studies are philosophy and law. He considered philosophy as a study of the humanly knowable laws for the discipline of the spirit, and law, of course, as the study of the rules for the governing of our physical nature. Both, according to the Aristotelian concept of reality, are necessary and equal. To reach a knowledge of these subjects, a study of all forms and all matter is necessary. It is in this way that people attain their highest perfection—through knowledge.

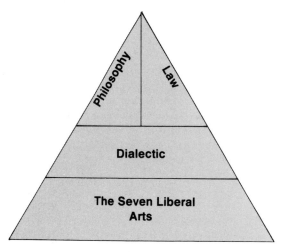

Thomas's Plan of Education

Then, he continued, there is another realm of knowledge, complementary to philosophy. This is theology, which has its source in God. It cannot be understood through natural learning, but only by revelation. The two, however, are not opposed to each other. Rather, a knowledge of philosophy leads to the possibility of receiving revelation and revelation presupposes a knowledge of philosophy. Finally, he said that true knowledge, the union with the divine science, came only after death. It was the duty of people, therefore, during their lifetimes to acquire as much natural knowledge as possible that they might be fit to receive the final revelation of God after their death.

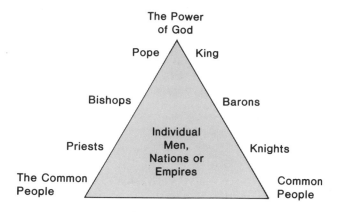

The Separate, Equal Roles of Church and State

The settlement of the opposition of Church and State came with a justification of feudalism on the basis of the lower forms constantly seeking the higher. However, in the governing of people he believed Church and State equal, with both the king and the pope receiving their power directly from God. It was the duty of the king to administer God's laws for the physical nature of human beings; of the pope and the Church to administer the law for the spirit of humankind. This solution, which justified the status quo, ran contrary to the secular spirit of the time and the growing nationalism. Thomas's argument would not stand for long against the moving social and political forces.

The pull of life and death, perhaps the greatest question of all, was solved by St. Thomas, first with the Aristotelian doctrine of matter and form existing only when they were together and in each other. With this, and with Thomas's insistence that natural knowledge, gained through the use of human senses, was necessary for the perfection of the human being, he banished the dualism that had existed since the time of Augustine and the idea of the City of God. Hereafter, both body and soul were necessary for earthly perfection, the one as important as the other.

Thus it was that the Middle Ages, in this final great synthesis, found freedom and opened the way for people to develop themselves, like the medieval city, outside of its early walls, yet still in keeping with the fundamental pattern. The way for science was now open, hate for the body was banished, the State was recognized as one of the forms of order leading to the highest order, that of the kingdom of God.

Without becoming too technical, this may suggest the kind of synthesis that was made in philosophy. For the common people, however, the involved thinking of philosophers has little meaning. In the Middle Ages, it was the common person, as well as the serious thinker, who needed a solution to the problems that were splitting the personality.

For these common people it is probable that the Gothic cathedral effected this synthesis. The thrust of the cathedral was upward. Standing before it, the beholder's eye moved up its great towers, impelled by the pointed arches, until the eye reached the spire, which directed it even farther upward—toward heaven. In this way was the need for the otherworldly satisfied. So, too, did the figures in the stained-glass windows tell the stories of the Bible and the lives of saints and satisfy the religious needs of the time. It is foolish to argue that people could "read" the stories told in the windows. Even with binoculars we cannot clearly read the upper pictures. However, the profuse beauty of colored light, like the echo of the unintelligible Latin ecclesiastical chants echoing through the arches, filled the onlooker with a sense of beauty and awe (see colorplate 18).

So there was more to the cathedral than lessons, for here was beauty. Not only did the windows preach the gospel, but their colors also brought joy to the beholder. The pageantry of the Church was a thing of splendor made colorful by the rich garments of the bishop and those who assisted him at the mass, by the heaviness of the incense, and by the chant of the choir. All these brought richness to the life of the medieval person who sought such satisfaction in day-to-day living. Even the task of building these cathedrals, a great communal effort shared alike by nobility, wealthy burghers, and common people, furnished a creative outlet for the energies of these people of the Middle Ages.

Architecturally, the Gothic cathedral furnished a symbol of balance between classic and energetic. It achieved balanced tension and unity, yet it had the thrust, the upward push, which we have remarked as characteristic of the northern personality. The elongated statuary of the portals, the pointed arches, the flying buttresses, beautiful in themselves and symbolic of the desire to go upward beyond the limits wall and column could support, all these are marks of the Gothic style.

Among the thousands of symbols connected with the Gothic cathedral, one significance of the tower deserves mention. The lower, heavy square tower represented earthly life. The spire signified human aspiration toward the divine. And finally, the elevation of the eye from the last point of physical stone toward the sky suggested union with God. The architect of the south tower at Chartres (see fig. 15.38) had the right idea when he created a transition between the square tower and the octagonal spire that is almost imperceptible. In a truly Thomistic sense, the things of this world blend perfectly with those of the next; the physical and the spiritual are united. The transition triumphs both as architecture and as symbol of the best thought of the time.

In one other aspect the cathedral was the symbol of the synthesis of the Middle Ages, for it was here that the Cult of the Virgin reached its height. The sudden flowering of this cult may be ascribed to the sense of sin that obsessed the people, convinced as they were of their moral deformity from Adam, and of their weakness to withstand the pulls of the world around them. For them, the justice of the Trinity was a thing to flee from, and they fell back upon the mercy of the Mother. Miracles were needed to insure their salvation, and a whole body of literature has grown up to tell of the miracles wrought by the Gracious Lady. Mary provided comfort, solace, and understanding for nobility and common people alike. Thus people could believe that a juggler doing his act for her amusement was as important as the learned friar writing scholarly books according to the formulas of Scholasticism.

A three-dimensional medieval synthesis, the Gothic cathedral was church, school, meeting place, concert hall, a place of beauty in the present life, and an inspiration to heaven. It represented the golden moment in the development of an art form when artists were masters of achieving what they had envisioned. In addition to the cathedral, there were other great syntheses of medieval life. We have already spoken of the notable work of St. Thomas, which brought the doctrines of the church together into a coherent whole. Still another synthesis, in the realm of literature, was the *Commedia* of Dante.

For the present study, the important aspect of the *Commedia* was the removal of restrictions that earlier centuries had imposed upon people. The goal and final purpose of human beings was still the attainment of heaven and the bliss of that afterlife, but people were left free to achieve this goal through their own power and through the discipline of their own will. Dante's God was no accountant; rather, he was perfect wisdom, which in Dante's mind was almost synonymous with love. The purpose and goal of humankind, like the enteleche of Aristotle, was perfect union with this God. For Dante, this heavenly state is the true home of humankind, which must ever be earned anew because of Adam's fall from grace. Furthermore, people, while they are alive, cannot know the wisdom or order or love of God; for salvation, the final union was still a matter of God's grace rather than a result of human effort. It was as if God's wisdom were a different category of wisdom from that of human beings, one to which people may aspire, but to which they can be admitted only by the will of God.

While people may not achieve union with God through their own efforts, they may prepare themselves for it by gaining the maturity that accompanies earthly wisdom. This mature nature is called innocence by Dante, by which he meant the happy state of Adam and Eve before the fall. It is for this reason that Dante places the Garden of Eden, the Earthly Paradise, at the top of the mountain of Purgatory. It is here that men and women, after having attained their full maturity, the totality of human wisdom, may await the act of God that will transport them into the category beyond.

Mystery plays represented an emotional approach to God, while morality plays like *Everyman* were didactic. Dante's vision, on the other hand, was intellectual. For him human beings were part of God's rational order, which was love; so it was through the pull of the love of God that individual human beings, exercising their own free will, ascended the ladder of love. The choice was made on earth and that choice, expressed in faith and good works, determined the destiny of each person in the afterlife.

What were the choices? Since the way of God is discipline and orderliness, the way of Satan is disorder and lack of proportion. God himself is perfect freedom, and the way toward him is the constant increase of one's personal freedom. Essential sin is the loss of freedom. This idea can be illustrated with the simple and not *too* sinful example of smoking—or any other addiction.

At first—in relation to cigarettes—the individual is ignorant, knowing neither the pleasures or the harms of smoking. So, for one reason or another, the person tries one. *The act in itself is not sinful,* nor are subsequent experiences with smoking. The person always says, "I can quit any time." And, for a time, that is true. A time comes, however, when given a choice of smoking or not smoking, true addicts will always choose to smoke; they have lost the power to say no, and if cigarettes are denied, they will end up climbing the wall. Thus they have sacrificed one aspect of their freedom of choice, and this, for Dante, is sin. Godlike freedom is the ability to say yes, no, or any of the choices between. Sin is loss of that ability, and in Dante's Hell we see that the degree of sin is measured by the extent to which the person consciously twists a body or an intellect away from free choice. The person who loses hope of making free choices is destined for Hell, and the inscription Dante envisions over the mouth of Hell, "Abandon hope, all ye that enter here," is an expression of the state the condemned ones have reached. In their choice, they have abandoned all hope and all desire to be anything or anywhere else. The punishments Dante saw for the souls in Hell are symbolic of the nature they have made for themselves. With the body removed, in other words, we see them exactly as they have made themselves to be. Step by descending step we traverse the cone of Hell, in each lower depth viewing the souls who are deeper and deeper in sin. Step by descending step we see these souls deprived of more and more freedom, until at the very bottom of the pit we find Satan, the greatest sinner of all, deprived of movement, frozen, as he is, in ice. So is he bound by his sins.

Emerging with Dante at the base of the mountain of Purgatory, we find another picture. Here are the souls who have erred, who have somehow strayed in their earthly lives from the path of wisdom. The difference is that these people still have hope; they aspire toward their own true selves and toward God. Their labors are difficult as they expiate their sin, but through all the labor they are joyous, for they know that the end will be full wisdom and maturity, the Garden of Eden, and the state of Earthly Paradise. It is of utmost importance to realize that each soul decides for itself when it is completely purged of any sin and is ready to move upward to another cornice of the mountain. The decision is never made by an angel or any other outside force. So free of envy are all the souls on the mountain that they chant *Gloria in excelsis* in unison when an individual moves upward.

This is explicitly stated when Dante and Virgil, toiling up the mountain, encounter the spirit of the Latin poet Statius, who has just moved from a lower cornice to a higher one. The occasion is so momentous that the whole mountain has shaken, and all the souls have shouted the *Gloria.* (The word *inn* in the fifth line quoted simply means "resting place.") It is of great importance to note that while the soul moves upward through its own free choice, it disciplines itself so that the movement is never made until it feels that the stain of former sin is completely removed (see the seventh through the thirteenth quoted lines).

But when some spirit, feeling purged and sound,
    Leaps up or moves to seek a loftier station,
    The whole mount quakes and the great shouts resound.
The will itself attests its own purgation;
    Amazed, the soul that's free to change its inn
    Finds its mere will suffice for liberation;
True, it wills always, but can nothing win
    So long as heavenly justice keeps desire
    Set toward the pain as once 'twas toward the sin;
Thus I, who've languished in this torment dire
    Five hundred years and more, felt only now
    The enfranchised will urge me to thresholds higher;
Then didst thou feel the shock, then heardest how—
    God send them happy—the kind souls to speed me
    Gave praise from mountain-foot to mountain-brow.

Finally in Heaven, and guided by Beatrice, Dante receives instruction in theology, the science of God. It is here that he sees the perfect order of the whole universe, both of humans and of angels. He sees the Church and its officers as the guardians of the human spirit and he sees the kings' importance to God, for they maintain temporal order on earth. Here, too, he finds freedom, as opposed to the ever-increasing bondage he witnessed in Hell, for in Heaven, though the souls are symbolically assigned to different spheres as a result of their different capacities for joy and love, yet they are actually free to pass through all the spheres and to approach the throne of God itself. There is no bondage here. In the final Cantos of the *Paradiso,* Dante comes as close as any human being can to communicating the mystic union of the soul with God as actual living experience.

Is this only a poem of death, or does Dante have something to say for living people? We believe that he has much to say to us. He says that people must make their choice, for which they have their own wills. If they choose wisely, they will choose a life of order and discipline. Throughout their life, they will gain knowledge, for that and its resultant wisdom will make them free. Finally, he tells us, our studies should turn to philosophy and law, the fields of knowledge that represent the best possible concepts of order on earth; the former disciplines and instructs the spirit, the latter has the same function in our temporal dealings with each other. This life will be one that is joyously led, and leads to the final realization of the true self when, by the will of God, the soul is united with the perfect wisdom.

These ideas, too, are stated clearly in Canto 27 of the *Purgatory* with Virgil's farewell to Dante. The mountain has been climbed and we have reached the point of perfect *human* wisdom. Since Virgil was a pagan, he can go no farther, and the "fair eyes" of Beatrice will guide Dante farther on his way. Incidentally, the "temporal fire" referred to is that of Purgatory; the "eterne" is that of Hell. Further, the mitre is the hat worn by a bishop; the crown is a king's hat. Thus from this point onward, Dante, through his free choices, has complete control over both his spiritual and physical natures, in accordance with his own and St. Thomas's philosophy.

So when the stair had dropped, long flight on flight,
    Away beneath us, then did Virgil turn
    On the top step and fix me with his eyes,
Saying: "The temporal fire and the eterne
    Thou hast beheld, my son, and reached a place
    Where, of myself, no further I discern.
I've brought thee here by wit and by address;
    Make pleasure now they guide—thou art well sped
    Forth of the steep, forth of the narrow ways.
See how the sun shines here upon thy head;
    See the green sward, the flowers, the boskages
    That from the soil's own virtue here are bred.
While those fair eyes are coming, bright with bliss,
    Whose tears sent me to thee, thou may'st prospect
    At large, or sit at ease to view all this.
No word from me, no further sign expect;
    Free, upright, whole, thy will henceforth lays down
    Guidance that it were error to neglect,
Whence o'er thyself I mitre thee and crown."

What has Dante brought together here? In the first place, he envisions a life at once balanced and aspiring. These are the Gothic and classic elements of the Middle Ages. He brings together the desire for broad worldly knowledge and religion, for his poem itself is scientific according to the science of his time, and he counsels the widest possible earthly knowledge as a necessary condition for heavenly bliss. He brings together the pulls of life and death, for his concept of the full life is one that is joyous and in which people use their full powers, yet use them as they aspire to the greatest possible happiness and freedom both now and in the hereafter. Finally, he unites the rival claims of pope and king as he sees each working God's will and God's order on earth, each in his own way and in his own place.

This is the final answer of the Middle Ages to the great question of the search for freedom. It started with the building of walls, for people needed their protection. It has progressed through the stage where they found their walls no longer necessary for protection and found them cramping in the human desire for the good life. It emerges in a great synthesis in which human nature is free, by nature divine, but in which human beings have freedom of choice. The *Commedia* unites body and soul in the process of discipline—one individuals must choose for themselves, a discipline that must occur in the present life.

This discipline, in its order, produces freedom here and prepares the spirit for freedom in the afterlife. Particularly in the cathedrals and in the *Commedia* we see the artist at work, proposing new answers to the great questions of humankind. It is upon these answers that the institutions are to be reshaped, and upon them that a new pattern for existence is to be built.

What was the nature of human freedom within this new design? The period of synthesis during the late Middle Ages was brief. Dante lived from 1265 to 1321. St. Thomas lived from 1225 to 1274. Chartres dates from the thirteenth century. Yet by the beginning of the fifteenth century, the Renaissance had burst upon Europe. The forces that had challenged the old walls of life that had been built during the Dark Ages (the years 500 to 1000) were too strong to be held in check, and the secular spirit was to go ahead to new triumphs. But in those 200 years, we can witness a new freedom toward which many world-weary people of the twentieth century look back with longing. It is worthy of at least a brief examination.

The single and fundamental characteristic of medieval freedom lies in the sense of unity that provided strict rules for all types of human behavior, and yet furnished complete individual freedom to create within those rules. This seems to be a paradox, a contradiction. At least it can be seen as a most delicate balance between individual aspiration and endeavor and community solidarity, which offers stability.

Perhaps better than anywhere else, this balance can be seen in the art of the late Middle Ages. Consider, for example, the cathedral. Its pattern was extremely strict. It had to be oriented with the altar toward the east. It had to be cruciform. Each part of the structure carried some symbolic meaning, so that the symbols had to be exactly treated. All this was a part of the strict rule that governed art and life in the period of balance.

Yet consider the freedom of the individual within this rule. The stonecarver was free to do as he wanted. If he wanted to carve little fat angels or animals he had seen or imagined, that was his decision. One sees much of this type of work on the miserere seats in the choir stall. Here a woodcarver thought that it would be fun to carve a pig playing a fiddle. No sooner thought of than started! Or somewhere else, the carver wished to caricature a fat burgher of the town. He could do it because he was a free man, working within the limits of the grand design. These were no machine-made units to be put up as they came from the factory. They were the work of free and independent craftsmen.

This same freedom, within strict limits, is found in all spheres of activity during the late Middle Ages. For example, the craftsman necessarily belonged to his guild. It was the association that regulated the quality of his work, the price that could be charged, and many other things. Beyond that, the guild served as an insurance and burial society for its members, a social group, and a dramatic society, since the mystery and miracle plays that amused and inspired the city-dwellers were functions of the guilds. The guild-hall was not only a place of business, but was also a social center where banquets, weddings, and balls were held. The guild also very strictly regulated the membership within itself and established stringent rules for the training of the craftsmen. All these point to the strict communal regulation of the individual.

But within those limits, the member of a guild, the shoemaker, let us say, was absolutely free. He had his own shop, which was part of his home. He did his work only on order, so that when there was no business, he could lock up and take the members of his family, together with the apprentices and journeymen in his shop, and go for an outing in the country. Furthermore, and one suspects that this is the important aspect of the whole system, each pair of shoes was an individual creation. The pride of craft and of creation entered into all of the work done, and the master craftsman developed a sense of pride in each item of his work. The very fact that he did the whole job, from heel to toe, from sole to the very top of the uppers, gave him a sense of responsibility and of pride.

The story of "Our Lady's Juggler" reveals the same type of freedom within religion. The Catholic creed was strict, and its rules were absolute. But within them people were free. There was sufficient opportunity for individual practice of the religious observances to satisfy each person. Dante's idea of freedom as participation in the wisdom, the order, and the love of God are of great importance here. The person who was not free was the one who, by his or her own choices, had become inhuman in outward form and in nature. The order of God, however, was of sufficient latitude that people could make a comfortable life within it. In addition to this, there was the one provision of the Christian scheme of things that has always been a source of strength for that faith. This was the idea that a mistake does not mean inevitable damnation. Such an error may need purging, but it is only when one comes to a conscious desire for the way of evil that one is damned.

The concept of freedom in this period of balance in the Middle Ages, then, was one in which all the forces of the culture grouped themselves around the individual to provide support. Yet they did not hamper freedom, individuality, or creativity as long as he or she stayed within the rules of that culture.

This balance, like all others we have seen, was too delicate to last. Within a brief time, the secular forces we saw born during the Middle Ages were to triumph, breaking down the new designs that had been made by St. Thomas, by the architects of the great cathedrals, and by Dante. The fundamental beliefs of the culture were to change in a new epoch, which we call the Renaissance.

Bibliography

General

Adams, Henry. *Mont-Saint-Michael and Chartres.* New York: Houghton-Mifflin, 1933.

Armstrong, Edward A. *Saint Francis: Nature Mystic.* Berkeley, Calif.: University of California Press, 1975.

Barber, Richard. *King Arthur in Legend and History.* Totowa, N.J.: Rowman & Littlefield, 1974.

Branner, Robert, ed. *Chartres Cathedral.* New York: W. W. Norton & Co., 1969.

Clark, Mary T., ed. *Aquinas Reader.* New York: Doubleday & Co., n.d.

Durrell, Lawrence. *Pope Joan.* New York: Penguin Books, 1974. The legend of the Joan who became Pope John is very persistent and, in this account, very interesting.

Luciano. *Stained Glass Window Art.* New York: Quick Fox, 1974.

Malory, Thomas. *King Arthur and His Knights.* New York: Oxford University Press, 1975.

Robinson, Ian. *Chaucer and the English Tradition.* New York: Cambridge University Press, 1974.

Strayer, Joseph P. *Albigensian Crusades.* New York: The Dial Press, 1971.

Taylor, H. O. *The Medieval Mind.* New York: Macmillan, 1950.

Philosophy

Fremantle, Anne, ed. *The Age of Belief* (chap. 6 to the end). New York: Arno Press, 1954.

Literature

Chaucer. *The Canterbury Tales.* The student will enjoy reading all the tales and their introductions, but if a selection must be made, we recommend "The Knight's Tale," the "Franklin's Tale," and the "Reeve's Tale" (p. 359) as samples of different types of medieval literature.

Dante. *Divine Comedy.* The *Purgatory* and *Paradise.* After an exploration of the possibilities for evil in the human soul (Hell), it is good to see the way of redemption and the soul's potentiality for good, culminating in the mystic union with God. (Canto 33 of the *Paradiso* is given in full on p. 404.) One can easily find a whole library of scholarly works on Dante; Dorothy Sayers's *Further Papers on Dante* is very helpful.

St. Francis. *The Little Flowers of St. Francis.* Translated by L. Sherley-Price. Baltimore, Md: Penguin Books, Inc. The universal empathy of this mystic saint is revealed in these poems.

Literary Selections

Songs and Poems of the Wandering Scholars

The pull of life was strong in the time when new ideas were breaking down the old medieval walls. And students (even those who were to become learned clergymen) were much the same in those days as they are now.

GAUDEAMUS IGITUR

Let us live, then, and be glad
　　While young life's before us!
After youthful pastime had,
After old age, hard and sad,
　　Earth will slumber o'er us.

Where are they who in this world
　　Ere we kept, were keeping?
Go ye to the gods above;
Go to hell; inquire thereof;
　　They are not; they are sleeping.

Brief is life, and brevity
　　Briefly shall be ended;
Death comes like a whirlwind strong,
Bears us with his blast along;
　　None shall be defended.

Live this university,
　　Men that learning nourish;
Live each member of the same,
Long live all that bear its name,
　　Let them ever flourish!

Live the commonwealth also,
　　And the men that guide it!
Live our town in strength and health,
Founders, patrons, by whose wealth
　　We are here provided!

Live all gods! A health to you,
　　Melting maids and beauteous;
Live the wives and women too,
Gentle, loving, tender, true,
　　Good, industrious, duteous!

Perish cares that pule and pine!
　　Perish envious blamers!
Die the Devil, thine and mine!
Die the starch-neck Philistine!
　　Scoffers and defamers!

LAURIGER HORATIUS

Horace with your laurel crowned,
Truly have you spoken:
Time, a-rush with leap and bound,
Devours and leaves us broken.

Where are now the flagons, full
Of sweet wine, honey-clear?
Where the smiles and shoves and frowns
Of blushing maiden dear?

Swift the young grape grows and swells;
So do comely lasses!
Lo, on the poet's head, the snows
Of the Time that passes!

What's the good of lasting fame,
If people think it sinful
Here and now to kiss a dame
And drink a jolly skinful!

A GOLIARD'S CREED

A *goliard* is dying; the priest sent for in haste speaks comfortable words; have comfort, good son; let him but recite his Credo.[3]

That I will, Sir, and hear me now.

Credo—in dice I well believe,
That got me often bit and sup,
And many a time hath had me drunk,
And many a time delivered me
From every stich and every penny.

In Deum—never with my will
Gave Him a thought nor ever will.
The other day I took a shirt
From a ribald and I diced it,
And lost, and never gave it back.
If I die, he can have mine.
Put it in writing, 'tis my will,
I would not like it were forgot.
Patrem—at St. Denis in France,
Good sir, I had a father once,
Omnipotentem in his having,
Money and horses and fine wearing,
And by the dice that thieveth all things
I lost and gamed it all away. . . .

Creatorem who made all
I've denied—He has His will
Of me now, I know I'm dying,
Nothing here but bone and hide.

Coeli—of Heaven ever think?
Nay, but the wine that I could drink.

Et terrae—there was all my joy. . . .
(The burlesque recitation goes on to the final phrase)

Et corporis—the body's lust
I do perform. Sir Priest, I chafe
At thinking of that other life.
I tell you, 'tis not worth a straw.
And I would pray to the Lord God
That He will in no kind of way

Resurrectionem make of me,
So long as I may drench the place
With good wine where I'll be laid
And so pray I of all my friends
That if I can't, themselves will do't,
And leave me a full pot of wine
Which I may to the Judgment bring.

Vitam aeternam wilt Thou give,
O Lord God? wilt Thou forgive
All my evil, well I know it,

Amen. Priest, I now am through with't.
Through with life. Death hath its pain.
Too much . . . . too much . . . . This agony . . . .
I'm dying. I to God commend you.
I ask it of you—Pray for me."

OUR LADY'S JUGGLER

In this simple story one can see the hold and the charm of the Cult of the Virgin, especially for the simple people for whom chivalry and philosophy had no meaning (fig. 14.2).

　　In the days of King Louis there lived a poor juggler by the name of Barnabas, a native of Compiegne, who wandered from city to city performing tricks of skill and prowess.

---

3. The Creed being recited is as follows: I believe (credo) in God (in Deum) the Father (Patrem), Omnipotent (Omnipotentem), the Creator (Creatorem) of heaven (coeli) and earth (et terrae) . . . and in the resurrection (et . . . resurrectionem) of the body (corporis) and life everlasting (vitam aeternam). Amen.

Figure 14.2 "King David Playing Harp under the Inspiration of the Holy Ghost, while One Attendant Juggles and Others Play the Rebec, Trumpet and Oliphant." British Museum, London, eleventh century, English. Reproduced by the courtesy of the Trustees of the British Museum. This curious juxtaposition of David the Psalm Singer with common people juggling and playing musical instruments was a standard medieval practice. At the lower right the ivory oliphant is like the one Roland blew (too late) to summon Charlemagne to his rescue. Of Arab origin, the rebec was an early precursor of the violin (see chap. 16).

On fair days he would lay down in the public square a worn and aged carpet, and after having attracted a group of children and idlers by certain amusing remarks which he had learned from an old juggler, and which he invariably repeated in the same fashion without altering a word, he would assume the strangest postures and balance a pewter plate on the tip of his nose. At first the crowd regarded him with indifference, but when, with his hands and head on the ground he threw into the air and caught with his feet six copper balls that glittered in the sunlight, or when, throwing himself back until his neck touched his heels, he assumed the form of a perfect wheel and in that position juggled with twelve knives, he elicited a murmur of admiration from his audience, and small coins rained on his carpet.

Still, Barnabas of Compiegne, like most of those who exist by their accomplishments, had a hard time making a living. Earning his bread by the sweat of his brow, he bore rather more than his share of those miseries we are all heir to through the fault of our Father Adam.

Besides, he was unable to work as much as he would have liked, for in order to exhibit his wonderful talents, he required—like the trees—the warmth of the sun and the heat of the day. In winter time he was no more than a tree stripped of its leaves, in fact, half-dead. The frozen earth was too hard for the juggler. Like the cicada mentioned by Marie de France, he suffered during the bad season from hunger and cold. But, since he had a simple heart, he suffered in silence.

He had never thought much about the origin of wealth nor about the inequality of human conditions. He firmly believed that if this world was evil the next could not but be good, and this faith upheld him. He was not like the clever fellows who sell their souls to the devil; he never took the name of God in vain; he lived the life of an honest man, and though he had no wife of his own, he did not covet his neighbor's, for woman is the enemy of strong men, as we learn by the story of Samson which is written in the Scriptures.

Verily, his mind was not turned in the direction of carnal desire, and it caused him far greater pain to renounce drinking than to forgo the pleasure of women. For, though he was not a drunkard, he enjoyed drinking when the weather was warm. He was a good man, fearing God, and devout in his adoration of the Holy Virgin. When he went into a church he never failed to kneel before the image of the Mother of God and to address her with his prayer:

"My Lady, watch over my life until it shall please God that I die, and when I am dead, see that I have the joys of Paradise."

One evening, after a day of rain, as he walked sad and bent with his juggling balls under his arm and his knives wrapped up in his old carpet seeking some barn where he might go supperless to bed, he saw a monk going in his direction, and respectfully saluted him. As they were both walking at the same pace, they fell into conversation.

"Friend," said the monk, "how does it happen that you are dressed all in green? Are you perchance going to play the part of the fool in some mystery?"[4]

"No, indeed, father," said Barnabas. "My name is Barnabas, and my business is that of juggler. It would be the finest calling in the world if I could eat every day."

"Friend Barnabas," answered the monk, "be careful what you say. There is no finer calling than the monastic. The priest celebrates the praise of God, the Virgin, and the saints; the life of a monk is a perpetual hymn to the Lord."

And Barnabas replied: "Father, I confess I spoke like an ignorant man. My estate cannot be compared to yours, and though there may be some merit in dancing and balancing a stick with a denier[5] on top of it on the end of your nose, it is in no wise comparable to your merit. Father, I wish I might, like you, sing the Office every day, especially the Office of the Very Holy Virgin, to whom I am specially and piously devoted. I would willingly give up the art by which I am known from Soissons to Beauvais, in more than six hundred cities and villages, in order to enter the monastic life."

---

4. Mystery—one of the religious dramas of the time.
5. Denier—a small coin.

The monk was touched by the simplicity of the juggler, and as he was not lacking in discernment, he recognized in Barnabas one of those well-disposed men of whom Our Lord has said, "Let peace be with them on earth." And he made answer therefore:

"Friend Barnabas, come with me and I will see that you enter the monastery of which I am the Prior. He who led Mary the Egyptian through the desert put me across your path in order that I might lead you to salvation."

Thus did Barnabas become a monk. In the monastery which he entered, the monks celebrated most magnificently the Cult of the Holy Virgin, each of them bringing to her service all the knowledge and skill which God had given him.

The Prior, for his part, wrote books, setting forth, according to the rules of scholasticism, all the virtues of the Mother of God. Brother Maurice copied these treatises with a cunning hand on pages of parchment, while Brother Alexandre decorated them with delicate miniatures representing the Queen of Heaven seated on the throne of Solomon, with four lions on guard at the foot of it. Around her head, which was encircled by a halo, flew seven doves, the seven gifts of the Holy Spirit: fear, piety, knowledge, power, judgment, intelligence, and wisdom. With her were six golden-haired virgins: Humility, Prudence, Retirement, Respect, Virginity, and Obedience. At her feet two little figures, shining white and quite naked, stood in suppliant attitudes. They were souls imploring, not in vain, Her all-powerful intercession for their salvation. On another page Brother Alexandre depicted Eve in the presence of Mary, that one might see at the same time sin and its redemption, woman humiliated, and the Virgin exalted. Among the other much prized pictures in his book were the Well of Living Waters, the Fountain, the Lily, the Moon, the Sun, and the Closed Garden, of which much is said in the Canticle; the Gate of Heaven and the City of God. These were all images of the Virgin.

Brother Marbode, too, was one of the cherished children of Mary. He was ever busy cutting images of stone, so that his beard, his eyebrows, and his hair were white with the dust, and his eyes perpetually swollen and full of tears. But he was a hardy and a happy man in his old age, and there was no doubt that the Queen of Paradise watched over the declining days of Her child. Marbode represented Her seated in a pulpit. Her forehead encircled by a halo, with an orb of pearls. He was at great pains to make the folds of Her robe cover the feet of Her of whom the prophet has said, "My beloved is like a closed garden."

At times he represented Her as a graceful child, and Her image seemed to say, "Lord, Thou art My Lord!"

There were also in the monastery poets who composed prose writings in Latin and hymns in honor of the Most Gracious Virgin Mary; there was, indeed, one among them—a Picard—who translated the Miracles of Our Lady into rimed verses in the vulgar tongue.

Perceiving so great a competition in praise and so fine a harvest of good works, Barnabas fell to lamenting his ignorance and simplicity.

"Alas!" he sighed as he walked by himself one day in the little garden shaded by the monastery wall, "I am so unhappy because I cannot, like my brothers, give worthy praise to the Holy Mother of God to whom I have consecrated all the love in my heart. Alas, I am a stupid fellow, without art, and for your service, Madame, I have no edifying sermons, no fine treatises nicely prepared according to the rules, no beautiful paintings, no cunningly carved statues, and no verses counted off by feet and marching in measure! Alas, I have nothing."

Thus did he lament and abandon himself to his misery.

One evening when the monks were talking together by way of diversion, he heard one of them tell of a monk who could not recite anything but the *Ave Maria*. He was scorned for his ignorance, but after he died there sprang from his mouth five roses, in honor of the five letters in the name Maria. Thus was his holiness made manifest.

In listening to this story, Barnabas was conscious once more of the Virgin's beneficence, but he was not consoled by the example of the happy miracle, for his heart was full of zeal and he wanted to celebrate the glory of his Lady in Heaven.

He sought for a way in which to do this, but in vain, and each day brought him greater sorrow, until one morning he sprang joyously from his cot and ran to the chapel, where he remained alone for more than an hour. He returned thither again after dinner, and from that day onward he would go into the chapel every day the moment it was deserted, passing the greater part of the time which the other monks dedicated to the pursuit of the liberal arts and the sciences. He was no longer sad and he sighed no more. But such singular conduct aroused the curiosity of the other monks, and they asked themselves why Brother Barnabas retired alone so often, and the Prior, whose business it was to know everything that his monks were doing, determined to observe Barnabas. One day, therefore, when Barnabas was alone in the chapel, the Prior entered in company with two of the oldest brothers, in order to watch, through the bars of the door, what was going on within.

They saw Barnabas before the image of the Holy Virgin, his head on the floor and his feet in the air, juggling with six copper balls and twelve knives. In honor of the Holy Virgin he was performing the tricks which had in former days brought him the greatest fame. Not understanding that he was thus putting his best talents at the service of the Holy Virgin, the aged brothers cried out against such sacrilege. The Prior knew that Barnabas had a simple soul, but he believed that the man had lost his wits. All three set about to remove Barnabas from the chapel, when they saw the Virgin slowly descend from the altar and, with a fold of her blue mantle, wipe the sweat that streamed over the juggler's forehead.

Then the Prior, bowing his head down to the marble floor, repeated these words:

"Blessed are the pure in heart, for they shall see God."

"Amen," echoed the brothers, bowing down to the floor.

The Prolog to THE CANTERBURY TALES
Geoffrey Chaucer (1340?–1400)

Chaucer was exceptionally well read for his time, learned in French, Italian, and Latin literature. Having visited Italy where he acquired a fair knowledge of Italian, he knew the works of Dante but was more influenced by the writings of Boccaccio, especially the

Decameron. Though he may have been influenced by earlier collections of stories like the *Decameron* and Ovid's *Metamorphoses* (which he also knew well), Chaucer invented the scheme of a pilgrimage as a device to frame his stories and develop the interplay of his characters.

The following excerpt from the "Prolog" (lines 1–18) is given in the original Middle English (*Beowulf* is in Old English), the language in use from early in the twelfth century until late in the fifteenth century, when it was superseded by Early Modern English. For the modern reader, the prime difficulty with Middle English is in the spelling, which can be described as a phonetic system. Therefore, the flavor and some of the meaning of Chaucer's language can be best appreciated by reading these lines aloud, pronouncing each syllable distinctly and with gusto. This version is based on the Hengwrt Manuscript.

Whan that Aprille with his shoures soot
The droghte of Marche hath perced to the roote,
And bathed every veyne in swich licour,
Of which vertu engendred is the flour;
When Zephyrus eek with his swete breeth
Inspired hath in every holt and heeth
The tendre croppes, and the yonge sonne
Hath in the Ram his halfe cours yronne,
And smale fowles maken melodye,
That slepen al the night with open yë,
(So priketh hem Nature in hir corages):
That longen folk to goon on pilgrimages,
(And palmeres for to seken straunge strondes)
To ferne halwes, couthe in sondry londes;
And specially, from every shires ende
Of Engelond, to Caunterbury they wende,
The holy blisful martyr for to seke,
That hem hath holpen, whan that they were seke.

Following now is the complete "Prolog," translated into modern English by Leslie Dae Lindou. Here we are introduced to a fascinating cast of characters representing a panorama of life in the late Middle Ages. Note the shrewdness of Chaucer's descriptions, deft touches that reveal the personality of each individual.

When April with its sweet and welcome showers
The drought of March has pierced, and to the flowers
And every vein of growing things has sent
Life-giving moisture, wholesome nourishment;
When Zephyr,[6] too, has with his own sweet breath
Revived again in every wood and heath
The tender shoots, and when the northering sun
Has half his course into the Ram[7] now run,
And little song-birds make their melody
That sleep all thru the night with open eye
—So Nature urges them with her commands—
Then people long to go in pilgrim bands,
And palmers[8] once again to seek far strands
And distant shrines, well known in many lands:
Especially, from every county's end
Of England, Canterbury-ward they wend,
The holy blessed martyr[9] there to seek
Who was their help when they were ill or weak.

It happened in that season, on a day,
In Southwerk at the Tabard as I lay,
Ready my pilgrimage to undertake
To Canterbury, for my own soul's sake,
At night there came into that hostelry
Some nine-and-twenty in a company
Of various folk, who came by chance to fall
Into one group, and pilgrims were they all;
To Canterbury they all planned to ride.
The chambers and the stables there were wide,
And we were lodged in comfort, with the best.
And very soon—the sun now gone to rest—
So had I spoken with them, every one,
That I was of their fellowship anon,
And planned with them quite early to arise
To take our way, as I shall you advise:

    —Nevertheless, while I have time and space,
Before I further in this story pace,
It seems to me both sensible and sound
To tell you in detail of all I found
About each one, just as it seemed to me,
And what they were, and what was their degree,
And tell what kind of costume they were in;
And at a knight, then, will I first begin.

Knight

A knight there was, a worthy man,
Who from the time when that he first began
To ride on quests, had well loved chivalry,
Truth and honor, freedom and courtesy.
Full worthy was this man in his lord's war,
And therein had he ridden—none so far—
Thru Christendom, and heathen lands no less,
Always honored for his worthiness.
At Alexandria was he when it was won;
Many a time he had the board begun[10]
Above all other guests, in distant Prussia;
In Latvia[11] he fought, again in Russia,
No Christian man so oft, of his degree.
Against the Moors in Spain he fought, and he
In Africa and Asia Minor warred
Against the infidel; his mighty sword
Found service all about the Inland Sea;
At any noble action, there he'd be.
At mortal battles had he been—fifteen;
And for the faith he fought, at Tramyssene,
In tourney thrice, and each time slew his foe.

---

6. Zephyr—the west wind: here, the life-giving breath of Spring.

7. Ram—the third sign of the zodiac, which the sun enters ca. March 12 and leaves ca. April 11 to enter Taurus. Chaucer is only saying that April is well advanced; the date is about April 18.

8. Palmers—pilgrims who had visited the Holy Lands bore palms as token of their pilgrimage.

9. Martyr—Thomas à Becket, murdered in the cathedral at Canterbury in 1170, was canonized in 1173. His shrine was the great national shrine, and many stories of miraculous cures were told of it.

10. He sat in the seat of honor, at the head of the table: a mark of distinction and worth.

11. Probably he had fought in Latvia or Lithuania, with the Order of Teutonic Knights. Chaucer lists by name other scenes of the Knights's exploits: the main point is, they were associated with fighting for the faith rather than for gain. The Knight is very nearly the ideal knight of chivalry.

And this same worthy knight had been also
At one time with the lord of Palatye
Against another heathen land—Turkey;
And every time he held the topmost prize.
And yet, with all his courage, he was wise—
His conduct, meek as that of any maid.
No villainy had this man ever said
In all his life to any sort of wight.
He was a true, a perfect, gentle knight.
　　—But, to tell you briefly his array,
His horse was good, but certainly not gay;
He wore a fustian garment (a gypoun)
All rust-and-armor stained (his haubergeon),
For he had just completed the last stage
Of travel, and at once made pilgrimage.

Squire

With him was his son, a fine young Squire,
A lover and a lusty bachelor,
With locks as curly as if laid in press;
Near twenty years of age he was, I guess.
His stature was of ordinary length,
But agile, and revealing a great strength.
And he had ridden in the cavalry
In Flanders, in Artois, and Picardy,
And born him well, within his life's short space,
In hope that he might win his lady's grace.
Fancily clad in fashion's newest whim,
—One thought of flowering fields, on seeing him!—
Singing he was, or whistling, all the day:
He was as fresh as is the month of May.
His gown was short, with sleeves both long and wide;
He knew just how to sit a horse and ride,
To make up songs, and fit the words aright,
To joust, and dance, and draw, and even write.
So hot he loved (at least, so goes the tale)
He slept o'nights less than the nightingale!
Courteous was he, meek, in service able,
And carved before his father at the table.

Yeoman

A yeoman had he—no other servants, tho,
As at that time; it pleased him to ride so—
And he was clad in coat and hood of green.
A sheaf of peacock arrows, bright and keen,
Under his belt he carried, gay but grim;
(He well knew how to keep his gear in trim—
His arrow never drooped with feathers low)
And in his hand he bore a mighty bow.
His head was cropped; his face the sun had burned;
Of woodcraft, every subtle trick he'd learned.
Upon his arm a bracer gay he wore
And by his side a sword and buckler bore,
And on the other side, a dagger gay,
As sharp as point of spear, well sheathed away.
A Christopher medal gleamed upon his breast;
His horn's green sling was hung across his chest.
He must have been a forester, I guess.

Prioress

There was also a nun, a Prioress,
Whose smile was sweetly simple, but coy;[12]
Her greatest oath was but by good St. Loy;
And she was known as Madam Eglantine.
Full well she sang the services divine
Intoning thru her nose right properly.

And French she spoke, both well and carefully,
But Stratford-fashion, if the truth be told;
Parisian French she knew not—hers was old.
Her table-manners were well taught, withal;
She never from her lips let morsels fall,
Nor wet her fingers in the sauce too deep;
She knew just how to lift her food, to keep
A single drop from falling on her breast.
In etiquette she found the greatest zest.
Her upper lip she always wiped so clean
That in her cup there never could be seen
A speck of grease, when she had drunk her fill;
Fine manners at the table were her will.
And truly she was fond of harmless sport,
Pleasant, friendly, and of good report;
She took great pains the court to imitate,
Her manner formal, an affair of state;
For she would have men do her reverence.
But now, to tell about her moral sense,
So kindly was she and so piteous,
She wept, if ever that she saw a mouse
Caught in a trap, if it were dead, or bled.
Some little dogs she had, and these she fed
With roasted meat, or milk and good white bread.
But sore she wept if one of them were dead,
Or if men hit one with a stick, to smart;
And all for her was conscience, tender heart.
Becomingly her wimple fell in pleat;
As blue as glass her eyes, her nose right neat;
Her mouth was very small, and soft, and red;
But certainly she had a fine forehead;
It was almost a span in breadth, I'd say—
She was not under-sized, in any way!
Quite stylish was the cloak the lady wore;
About her arm small coral beads she bore,
And they were interspersed with gauds[13] of green,
And therefrom hung a brooch of golden sheen,
Whereon was written first a crowned "A,"
And after, "Amor Vincit Omnia."
She had another nun, for company,
Who was her chaplain; and her priests were three.

Monk

A monk there was—th' administrative sort—
Outrider,—hunting was his favorite sport—
A manly man, to be an abbott able.
Full many a fancy horse he had in stable,
And when he rode, men could his bridle hear
Jingling in the whistling wind as clear
And just as loud as does the chapel bell
Where this good lord was Keeper of the Cell.
The rule of Maurus or St. Benedict[14]
This monk considered old and over-strict.
He'd rather let the old things go their way.
And follow fashions of a newer day.

---

12. In Chaucer's text the word meant "bashful" or "modest."

13. Gauds—the large Paternoster beads marking off the sections of a rosary.

14. St. Benedict and his disciple Maurus, founders of the Benedictine Order; St. Benedict established the famous monastery at Monte Cassino in 529.

For texts he didn't give a well-plucked hen
That say that hunters are not holy men,
Nor that a monk, who leaves his cloister's bounds
Is like a fish that's out of water—zounds!
—Why shouldn't monks go out of cloister?
Texts like that aren't worth an oyster!
And I said his views were good thereon.
Why should he study till his wits were gone
Upon a book in cloister, like a clerk,
Or labor with his hands, always at work,
As old St. Austin[15] bids? What good is served?
Let Austin have his work to him reserved!
And so this monk his hunting much preferred.
Greyhounds had he, swift as any bird;
In riding, and in hunting of the hare,
Was his delight—and for no cost he'd spare.
I saw his sleeves were fur-trimmed at the hand,
Expensively, the finest in the land;
And, to fasten up his hood beneath his chin.
He had a rich, elaborate, golden pin;
A love-knot in the larger end there was.
His head was bald, and shone as bright as glass;
As if anointed shone his ruddy face.
He was a lord right fat, and in good case.
His eyes were staring, rolling in his head,
Gleaming like the furnace-fires red.
His boots were supple, and his horse was great;
Now certainly, he was a fine prelate!
He was not pale as some poor starveling ghost.
A fat swan loved he best of any roast.
His palfrey was as brown as any berry.

Friar

A friar there was, a wanton man and merry;
A Limiter,[16] a most impressive one;
Indeed in all four orders there was none
Who knew so much of small talk, fine language;
And he had made right many a marriage
Of young girls at his own expense and hire;
A pillar of his order was this friar!
Familiar and full well beloved was he
With franklins[17] over all in his county,
For as confessor he had won renown
Far more than curates had in their possession
—His order licensed him to hear confession.
His hearing of confession was a pleasure,
His absolution always within measure;
The penance he imposed was never stern—
If something for himself he'd thereby earn!
For when to his poor order gifts were given,
It must be sign the givers were well shriven;
For such gifts, said this friar for his part,
Show clearly that a man is changed at heart.
For many men are hardened, it appears,
So that they find no outlet thru their tears;
Instead of tears and useless weeping, then,
The silver that they give will save such men.
He always kept his tippet[18] stuffed with knives
And pins to give to young attractive wives.
Certainly he had a merry note;
He knew well how to sing, and play a rote,[19]
At song-fests he would win the prize outright.
As any lily flower his neck was white.
And like a champion wrestler he was strong.
All the taverns, as he went along,
And every hostler, and barmaid, he knew,

Better than outcasts and the beggar-crew;
Because, to such a worthy man as he,
It was not fitting, you will all agree,
To have acquaintance with such worthless wretches;
Such contact brings no profit, nothing fetches. . . .
There is no gain in dealing with *canaille,*[20]
But with rich men, of social station high.
And thus, whenever profit would arise,
This friar was humble, courteous, and wise.
So virtuous a man was nowhere found;
And what a beggar, as he made his round!
Why, if a widow had no shoe to show,
So pleasant was his "In principio . . ."[21]
He'd have the widow's mite, before he went!
His income always went beyond his rent.
And he could play around like any whelp;
On love-days[22] he knew how to be of help.
He was not like a needy monk or scholar,
Threadbare, shabby, down to his last dollar;
But he was like a great man or a pope.
Of finest woolen was his semicope,[23]
That rounded like a bell out of its mold.
He lisped a little, if the truth he told,
To make his speech sound sweeter on his tongue;
And in his harping, after he had sung,
His twinkling eyes shone in his head as bright
As do the stars on cold and frosty night.
This worthy Limiter was called Hubert.

Merchant

The merchant, next:—with forked beard, and girt
In livery, high on his horse he sat,
Upon his head a Flemish beaver hat;
His boots were clasped up in the latest mode;
He spoke in serious fashion as he rode,
Referring always to his gains in gold.
He wished, he said, to have the sea patrolled
From Middleburgh across to Orewell.[24]
A money-changer, he could buy or sell;
This worthy man knew how his wits to set:
No one ever knew he was in debt,
So well he managed all the deals he made,
His sales and bargains, and his tricks of trade.
He was a worthy man, in every way;
But what his name, I never heard men say!

---

15. St. Augustine, Bishop of Hippo, was a great proponent of labor as part of the monastic life.

16. A "Limiter" was a friar licensed to beg within a definite ("limited") region.

17. Franklins were landholders of free, but not of noble, birth; they ranked below the gentry.

18. Tippet—a long scarf; a handy substitute for pockets.

19. Rote—a stringed instrument, sometimes played with a bow, sometimes with a fixed wheel like a hurdy-gurdy. (See fig. 16.3.)

20. Canaille—riff-raff, rabble.

21. "In principio . . ."—the beginning of the Last Gospel. These verses were thought to have supernatural powers, and were used as greeting, blessing, and the like.

22. "Love-days" were days set aside for settlement of disputes by arbitration; the clergy were often the judges.

23. A short cape or cloak.

24. The port of Middleburgh, just off the coast of Netherlands, was just opposite the English port of Harwich (then called "Orewell"). The merchant was probably engaged (among other things!) in the wool trade, and desired protection for his shipping.

Clerk

A clerk of Oxford rode with us also,
Who turned to logic-study long ago;
His horse was lean and skinny as a rake,
And he was not so fat, I'll undertake!
But hollow-looking, hungry evermore;
Quite threadbare were the shabby clothes he wore,
For he had found as yet no benefice,
Nor was so worldly as to hold office.
For he had rather have, at his bed's head,
A score of books, all bound in black or red,
Of Aristotle and philosophy
Than rich robes, fiddle, or gay psaltery.
And yet philosophy, if truth be told,
Had brought him in but very little gold,
But all that willing friends to him had lent
On books and learning eagerly he spent;
When friends helped with his schooling, then for those
He'd pray in earnest, for their souls' repose.
Of study he took every care and heed;
Not a word he spoke more than was need;
Then what he said was formal, reverent,
Short and to the point, of high intent;
Pertaining unto virtue was his speech;
And gladly would he learn, and gladly teach.

Sergeant-at-law

A sergeant of the law, who used to go
Full many a time to St. Paul's portico,[25]
There was also, of richest excellence;
Discreet he was and of great reverence.
—At least he seemed so, for his words were wise.
He often sat as justice in assize,[26]
By full commission or in his own right.
His learning and his fame were more than slight,
So he had fees, and robes, abundantly.
Nowhere a greater purchaser[27] than he.
Provisions of the law so well he knew
That none could quibble with the deeds he drew.
But no one does as much as this man does—
And yet, he seemed much busier than he was . . .
From William's day[28] he knew each court decision
In every case, by heart, and with precision.
His documents were drawn up so that none
Could find a fault or loop-hole—not a one;
The Statutes he'd recite, and all by rote.
He rode quite simply in a medley coat,
Girt with a belt of striped silk. No more
I have to tell of what this Sergeant wore.

Franklin

With him a franklin rode, whose beard was white
As any daisy, and his face was bright
And ruddy: sanguine, one would call the man.
He loved a wine-sop as the day began.
He liked to live in comfort and in joy;
Truly, he was Epicurus' boy,
Who stoutly held that comfort—that is, pleasure—
Was of happiness the only measure.
A householder, and a great, was he;
He was St. Julian[29] in his own country.
His bread and ale were uniformly fine;
No man was better stocked than he with wine;
Baked meats were never lacking at his place—
Both fish and flesh—or he'd have felt disgrace!
It snowed in his house both of meat and drink,
Of every good thing that a man can think.

According to the season of the year,
So changed his food, and all his table-cheer;
Fat partridges he kept on his preserve,
And fishponds stocked, his table well to serve.
Woe to the cook, unless his sauce were fine,
And sharp and tasty, and the meal on time!
His covered table was not put away
But stood in readiness the live-long day.
At session,[30] he was lord—no man stood higher—
And many a time he served as Knight-of-Shire.
He wore a knife, and purse—made all of silk—,
Hung from his girdle, white as morning milk.
He'd served as sheriff, and county auditor;
Nowhere was a more worthy vavasour.[31]

The Five Tradesmen

A haberdasher, and a carpenter,
A weaver, dyer, and an arras-maker,
—All these were clad in the same livery
Of one great dignified fraternity;
All fresh and new the gear they wore, it seemed;
Not with brass their knives and trimmings gleamed,
But silver, and fine work in every part;
Their belts and purses were in style, and smart.
Important citizens, enough, were all
These men, to sit on dais in guild-hall,
And anyone of them, it's safe to state,
Was wise enough to be a magistrate;
They certainly had goods enough, and rent;
And, I'm sure, their wives would give assent,
For otherwise they would have been in blame;
It's good to hear a "Madam" with one's name,
And lead the way at church, and to be seen
With mantle borne, as royal as a queen!

Cook

A cook was in their party, to prepare
Their favorite dishes, foods both rich and rare:
Chickens, marrow-bones, and tarts well-flavored.
Many a draught of London ale he'd savored.
He knew how to roast, boil, broil, and fry,
Make soups and sauces hot, and bake a pie.
A pity was it, so it seemed to me,
That on his shin an ulcerous sore had he.
His blanc-mange[32] would be rated with the best.

---

25. The porch of St. Paul's Cathedral was a traditional meeting-place for lawyers.

26. Assize: session of the court.

27. Purchaser—a buyer of land. Does Chaucer imply that the Sergeant is desirous of becoming a landed gentleman, or that he is a land-speculator?

28. The Sergeant knew the law clear back to the conquest—the statutes of William the Conqueror.

29. St. Julian is the patron saint of hospitality.

30. These were probably sessions of the Justices of the Peace, not the big assizes.

31. Vavasour—a substantial landholder.

32. Not like the modern pudding, but a compound of minced capon, almonds, cream, sugar, and flour!

Shipman

A shipman was there, living far to west
—For all I know he came from Dartmouth town.
He rode as best he could a nag; his gown
Of falding[33] rough hung clear down to his knee;
A dagger hanging on a lace had he
About his neck, beneath his arm and down.
Hot summer suns had made his hue all brown;
A boon companion was this salty tar.
He'd helped himself to many a good wine jar
From Bordeaux, while below his owners slept.
Fine scruple was a thing he never kept.
In sea-fights, if he got the upper hand,
By water he sent them home to every land.
But no man, in his skill to reckon tides,
His streams, his chance and all besides,
His harbors, and his moons, and navigation;
From Hull to Carthage had his reputation.
Bold he was, but wise, in undertaking;
Many a tempest set his beard to shaking!
And he knew all the havens as they were
From Gotland to the Cape of Finisterre,[34]
And every creek in Brittany and Spain.
His barge was called the good ship "Madeleine."

Physician

A doctor of physic, known both far and near,
Was with us; nowhere could you find his peer,
In surgery or physic; what is more,
Well-grounded in astrology's deep lore,
He treated patients for the better part
By horoscope and such-like magic art.
For he knew how to forecast, by his spell,
The ascendant planets that would make them well.
He knew the cause of every malady,
Whether of cold or hot or moist or dry,[35]
Where engendered, from what humor traced;
He was a doctor of much skill and taste.
The cause once known, and of the source once sure,
He quickly brought the sick man to his cure.
And he had ready his apothecaries
To send him potent drugs and lectuaries[36]—
For each assisted other, gold to gain;
Their friendship was no new one, that is plain!
—This doctor knew old Esculapius,
The Greek Deiscorides, and ancient Rufus,
Hippocrates, Galen, Hali the Saracen,
Serapion, and Rhazes, Avicen,
Averroes, Bernard, Constantine,
Gatesden, Gilbert, John the Damascene.[37]
And in his diet temperate was he;
It was not full of superfluity,
But wholesome, one of healthful nourishment.
Bible-study was not this man's bent.
He dressed in costly colors, red and blue,
With taffeta and silken linings, too;
And yet he was a man to hate expense.
He kept what he had earned in pestilence;
And since, in physic, gold's a cordial, he
Found gold was what he loved especially!

Wife of Bath

A goodwife came from Bath, that ancient city,
But she was rather deaf; and that's a pity.
Her skill in making cloth, I hear, was such
That, as they say, she wove "to beat the Dutch."[38]

In all the parish never a woman came
To offering before this worthy dame—
But if there did, so much enraged was she
That she lost all her Christian charity!
Her kerchiefs were of finest weave, and dear;
They must have weighed a full ten pounds, or near,
That on a Sunday covered up her head.
Her hose[39] were fancy-fine, of scarlet red,
And tightly tied, her shoes were soft and new.
Her face was bold, and fair, and red of hue.
She was a worthy woman all her life;
To husbands five this woman had been wife,
Not counting other company in youth;
There's no need now to speak of that, in truth!
Three times to Jerusalem she'd been;
Full many a distant stream her feet were in . . .
To Rome she'd been, and gone to far Boulogne,
In Spain to Santiago, to Cologne;
She knew a lot of wandering by the way.
Gap-toothed this goodwife was, the truth to say.
Easily her ambling horse she sat,
With flowing wimple—on her head a hat
As broad as is a buckler or a shield;
A foot-mantle left her ample hips concealed;
And on her feet she wore well-sharpened spurs.
The gift of laughter and of fun was hers.
Love's remedies she knew, and not by chance;
She knew first-hand the art of that old dance.

Parson

A good religious man went on this ride,
A parish priest, who served the countryside;
Poor in money, rich in holy work,
A very learned scholar was this clerk.
The gospel of Our Lord he strove to preach,
And tried his poor parishioners to teach.
Benign he was, hard-working, diligent,
In adverse seasons patiently content,
As he had proved on more than one occasion.
He did not threaten excommunication
When poor folk could not pay their tithes; instead,
The little that he had he'd share, his bread
As well as money, with a cheerful heart.
Contentment with a little was his art.
Tho wide his parish, houses far asunder,
He'd not neglect, in spite of rain or thunder,
The afflicted in mind, body, or estate,
The farthest in his parish, small or great;
Staff in hand, he'd visit them, on foot.

---

33. Falding—coarse woolen cloth with shaggy nap.

34. That is, from Sweden to the western tip of France.

35. The reference is to the theory of the "bodily humors," or fluids, and their effect on the health and temperament of the person.

36. Lectuaries—more properly, electuaries. Medicine in a sticky or sirupy base, originally meant to be "licked up" by the patient!

37. This impressive list is to indicate that the doctor was thoroughly versed in all the medical authorities, ancient and "modern." It seems curious to a modern reader to find among his qualifications that he is an excellent astrologer.

38. Chaucer says "She passed hem of Ypres and of Gaunt"—the Low Countries were famous for textiles.

39. Not stockings, but gaiters or leggings.

This fine example to his flock he put,
That first he acted; afterward he taught.
From out the Gospel these words he had caught.
This figure he had added thereunto:
"If fine gold rust, what shall poor iron do?"
For if the priest be foul, in whom we trust,
No wonder if the ignorant people rust;
A shame it is, and brings the priest to mock—
A shitty shepherd, tending a clean flock!
Rather should a priest example give,
By his clean living, how his sheep should live.
He never set his benefice to hire
And left his sheep encumbered in the mire,
Running up to London, to St. Paul's,
Singing paid requiems within those walls;
Nor in some brotherhood withdrew, alone;
But caring for his flock he stayed at home,
So that no wolf his helpless sheep might harry;
He was a shepherd, not a mercenary.
A virtuous man and holy was he, then,
Not arrogant in scolding sinful men,
Not haughty in his speech, or too divine,
But prudent in his teaching and benign.
To draw the folk to heaven by kindliness
And good example was his business.
But then, if any one were obstinate,
Whoever he was, of high or low estate,
He'd scold him sharply, raise a mighty row;
Nowhere was there a better priest, I vow.
No hankering after pomp and reverence,
No putting on of airs, and no pretence;
The lore of Christ and His apostles true
He taught; but what he preached, he'd do.

Plowman

With him there was a plowman, his own brother,
Who'd loaded many a cart with dung; no other
Was a worker good and true as he,
Living in peace and perfect charity.
God he loved best, with his entire soul,
At all times, whether he knew joy or dole;
And next, as Christ commands, he loved his neighbor.
For he would thresh, or ditch, or dig, and labor
For Jesus' sake, without a thot of pay,
To help poor folk, if in his power it lay.
Cheerfully, in full, his tithes he paid
Both on his goods, and what by work he made.
In tabard clad, he rode an old gray mare.
—(A miller and a reeve were also there,
A summoner, also, and a pardoner,
A manciple and I—that's all there were.)

Miller

The miller was a big and hefty lout,
Brawny, burly, big of bone, and stout.
Against all comers, as events turned out,
He won the ram[40] at every wrestling-bout,
Stocky, broad-shouldered, in build a battering-ram,
There was no door he couldn't tear from jamb
Or break it, running at it with his head.
His beard like any sow or fox was red,
And broad as any spade, and cut off short,
Right atop his nose he had a wart;
In it stood a little tuft of hairs,
Red as the bristles in an old sow's ears.
As for his nostrils, they were black and wide;
A sword and buckler bore he by his side.

His big mouth like a furnace needed stoking:
He was a jesting clown whose bawdy joking
Mostly ran to sin: it wasn't nice.
From the grain he ground he'd steal—and then toll
    thrice;
Good millers have a golden thumb, it's said . . .
A white coat, and a blue hood on his head,
He wore; and with his bagpipe's merry sound
He cheered us as we started, outward-bound.

Manciple

There was a manciple[41] from the Inns of Court[42]
To whom all purchasers could well resort
To learn to buy supplies in large amount;
For whether he bought by cash, or on account,
He watched his dealings with so close an eye
That he came out ahead in every try.
Now is it not indeed by God's own grace
That he, uneducated, could outface
His masters—that heap of learned men?
His employers numbered three times ten,
Legal experts, with good sense endowed:
—There must have been a dozen in the crowd
Worthy to be stewards of rent or land
Of any lord in England, to help him stand
Within his income, if he only would,
In honor, out of debt, all to the good,
Or help him live as sparsely as desired:
Why, they could help a county, as required,
In any kind of case that might befall:—
And yet this manciple could beat them all.

Reeve

The reeve, a scrawny, peevish man was he;
His beard was shaved as close as close could be;
His hair was shorn off short around his ears,
His top docked like a priest's, so it appears.
His legs were very long and very lean,
Thin as a stick; no calf could there be seen.
He managed well the granary and bin;
No auditor could get ahead of him.
And he could estimate, by drought and rain,
The yield he could expect of seed and grain.
His lord's sheep, cows, and other stock,
The swine and horses, and the poultry-flock,
Were wholly in his hands to manage well,
And on his oath the reckoning to tell,
Ever since his lord reached twenty years.
No man could ever find him in arrears.
There was no agent, shepherd, hired hand,
Whose tricks he didn't know or understand;
They feared him, everyone, as they feared death.
His dwelling place stood fair upon the heath,
But sheltered was his place with green trees' shade.
Far better bargains than his lord he made;
Richly he had feathered his own nest.
He knew the way to please his master best,
By giving him, or lending, his own goods,
And getting not mere thanks, but coats and hoods.

---

40. The customary wrestling prize.
41. Steward, or purchasing agent.
42. The lodgings of the lawyers.

In youth, he'd learned a trade—he was a wright;
In carpentry he was a skillful wight.
This reeve's good horse rode at an easy trot;
A dapple-gray he was; his name was Scot.
His long surcoat of Persian blue was made,
And by his side he bore a rusty blade.
Of Norfolk was this reeve of whom I tell,
From just outside a town called Baldeswell.
He tucked up all his garments like a friar,
And rode the hindmost: Such was his desire.

Summoner

A summoner[43] was there with us in that place,
Who had a fire-red cherubic face,
All pimply, full of whelks; his eyes were narrow,
And he was hot and lecherous as a sparrow,
With black and scabby brows, and scanty beard:
His was the sort of face that children feared.
There was no mercury nor brimstone, salve
Of tartar, lead, or borax, that could have
The strength to rid him of the lumps and knobs
Disfiguring his face in ugly gobs;
These acneous pimples covered both his cheeks.
And he was fond of garlic, onions, leeks;
He loved to drink strong wine, as red as blood;
Then spoke and cried as one demented would.
And having drunk his wine, and feeling gay,
Then not a word but Latin would he say;
—He knew a few expressions—two or three—
That he had picked up, out of some decree—
No wonder, for he heard it every day:
And everybody knows that even a jay
Can learn to call out "Wat!" as well as the Pope!
But when he tried with other things to cope,
His slender stock of learning would give out:
"Questio quid juris!"[44] he would shout.
He was a noble rascal, and a kind;
A better fellow would be hard to find.
He would arrange it, for a quart of wine,
For a friend of his to keep a concubine
The whole year thru, and never get in trouble;
Oh, he was very good at dealings double!
And if he liked a person whom he saw,
He'd teach that person not to stand in awe
Nor fear, for what he did, the archdeacon's curse—
Why, does a man's soul live within his purse?
Yet purse alone can suffer penalty:
"Purse is the archdeacon's hell," said he.
(But well I know he lied in saying so;
Such curses ought the guilty men forego.
As absolution saves, so curses slay;
From all Significavits,[45] stay away!)
And at his mercy, in his tender charge,
Were young folks of the diocese at large;
He knew their secrets; they were easily led.
He had set a garland on his head
So large it would have served for an ale-stake.[46]
A buckler he had made him of a cake.

Pardoner

With him a noble pardoner rode, his pal
And peer (his patron-house was Ronceval),[47]
Who straight from Rome had come—or so said he—
And loud he sang, "Come hither, love, to me!"
The summoner added, in the bass, a ground:
No trumpet had one half so loud a sound.

The pardoner had yellow hair, like wax,
That hung as limp as does a bunch of flax;
Stringily his locks hung from his head,
So that his shoulders were all overspread.
But thin it lay, in hanks there, one by one.
No hood he wore; he left it off, for fun,
Trussed up in his bag. It seemed to him
That thus he rode in fashion's latest whim,
Uncovered—save for cap—his head all bare.
Staring eyes he had, just like a hare.
A vernicle he'd sewed upon his cap.
His wallet lay before him, in his lap,
Brimful of pardons, hot from Rome, please note!
Small the voice he had, just like a goat.
He had no beard: nor ever would, in truth:
As it were fresh-shaved, his face was smooth;
I think he was a gelding—or a mare.
But of his trade, from Berwyck clear to Ware
Was never such a pardoner as this lad!
In his bag a pillow-case he had
Which—so he claimed—was once Our Lady's veil—
He said he had a fragment of the sail
That once St. Peter used, in days of yore,
Before Our Lord gave him new work, ashore!
He had a cross of latten,[48] set with stones,
And in a glass jar carried some pig's bones.
But with these silly "relics," when he spied
Some simple priest out in the country-side,
On such a day more money would he win
Than in two months the parson could fetch in;
And thus, with flattery and lying mock,
He'd fool the priest and all his simple flock.
But give the devil his due; for, when all's past,
In church he was a great ecclesiast;
Well knew he how to read a Bible story,
But especially well he sang the offertory;
For well he knew that when the song was sung,
He then would preach, and sharpen up his tongue,
To win their money from the gullible crowd;
That's why he sang so merrily and loud.
Now I've told you briefly, clause by clause,
The state, the number and array and cause
In which assembled was this company
In Southwerk at this noble hostelry
That's called the Tabard Inn, right near the Bell.

---

43. Process-server or bailiff for the ecclesiastical court, usually presided over by the archdeacon.

44. "The question is, what part of the law applies?"—a lawyer's technicality.

45. *Significavit*—the opening word in a summons to appear before the ecclesiastical court.

46. Ale was advertised by a bunch of greens, hanging on a stake or pole above the door.

47. A London hospital.

48. Cheap metal.

The Reeve's Tale from
THE CANTERBURY TALES
Chaucer

Just as Chaucer gave a very wide view of the population of the people of the late Middle Ages in his Prolog, in the stories that they tell during the pilgrimage, he presents many of the types of literature of the time. "The Reeve's Tale," like the preceding "Miller's Tale," is a *fabliau,* a type of boisterous and bawdy story popular at the time and, in fact, most any other time. A manager on a large country estate, Oswald the Reeve is shrewd, cunning, and bad tempered. In his early days he was a carpenter, which explains why he became incensed by the Miller's version of a foolish old carpenter who was cuckolded by his young and lively wife. Furthermore, the Reeve was old and, as he said in his Prologue (not given here), is now like everyone else who "knows that when a man no longer has the ability to do a certain thing, he spends his time talking about it." Prodded by the Host to cease his sermonizing, the Reeve begins his story, warning that his language will be just as rough as that used by the Miller. Not surprisingly, the foolish victim of the Reeve's tale is a miller. The modern English translation is by Neville Coghill.

At Trumpington, not far from Cambridge town,
    A bridge goes over where the brook runs down
And by that brook there stands a mill as well.
And it's God's truth that I am going to tell.
    There was a miller lived there many a day
As proud as any peacock and as gay;
He could play bag-pipes too, fish, mend his gear,
And turn a lathe, and wrestle, and poach deer.
And at his belt he carried a long blade,
Trenchant it was as any sword that's made,
And in his pouch a jolly little knife.
No one dared touch him, peril of his life.
He had a Sheffield dagger in his hose.
Round was his face and puggish was his nose;
Bald as an ape he was. To speak more fully,
He was a thorough-going market bully
Whom none dared lay a hand on or come near
Without him swearing that they'd buy it dear.
    He was a thief as well of corn and meal,
And sly at that; his habit was to steal.
Simpkin the Swagger he was called in scorn.
He had a wife and she was nobly born;
Her father was the parson of the town;
A dowery of brass dishes he put down
In order to have Simpkin his relation.
The nuns had given her an education.
Simpkin would take no woman, so he said,
Unless she were a virgin and well-bred,
To save the honour of his yeoman stock;
And she was proud, pert as a magpie cock.
    It was a proper sight to see the pair
On holidays, what with him strutting there
In front of her, his hood about his head,
And she behind him all decked out in red,
Like Simpkin's hose, for scarlet-red he had 'em.

No one dared call her anything but 'Madam',
And there was no one bold enough to try
A bit of fun with her or wink an eye,
Unless indeed he wanted Sim the Swagger
To murder him with cutlass, knife or dagger,
For jealous folk are dangerous, you know,
At least they want their wives to think them so.
And then her birth was smirched to say the least;
Being the daughter of a celibate priest
She must maintain her dignity, of which
She had as much as water in a ditch.
She was a sneering woman and she thought
That ladies should respect her, so they ought,
What with her well-connected family,
And education in a nunnery.
    They had a daughter too between them both,
She was a girl of twenty summers' growth;
But that was all except a child they had
Still in the cradle, but a proper lad.
The wench was plump, well-grown enough to pass,
With a snub nose and eyes as grey as glass;
Her rump was broad, her breasts were round and high;
She'd very pretty hair, I will not lie.
The parson of the town, for she was fair,
Intended to appoint the girl as heir
To all his property in house and land
And he was stiff with suitors to her hand.
He purposed to bestow her if he could
Where blood and ancient lineage made it good.
For Holy Church's goods should be expended
On Holy Church's blood, so well-descended,
And holy blood should have what's proper to it
Though Holy Church should be devoured to do it.
    This miller levied toll beyond a doubt
On wheat and malt from all the land about,
Particularly from a large-sized College
In Cambridge, Solar Hall. 'Twas common knowledge
They sent their wheat and malt to him to grind it.
Happened one day the man who ought to mind it,
The college manciple, lay sick in bed,
And some reported him as good as dead.
On hearing which the miller robbed him more
A hundred times than he had robbed before;
For up till then he'd only robbed politely,
But now he stole outrageously, forthrightly.
    The Warden scolded hard and made a scene,
But there! The miller didn't give a bean,
Blustered it out and swore it wasn't so.
    Two poor young Bible-clerks or students, though,
Lived in this College (that of which I spoke).
Headstrong they were and eager for a joke
And simply for the chance of sport and play
They went and plagued the Warden night and day
Just for a little leave to spend the morn
Watching the miller grind their meal and corn,
And each was ready to engage his neck
The miller couldn't rob them half a peck
Of corn by trickery, nor yet by force;
And in the end he gave them leave of course.
    One was called John and Alan was the other,
Both born in the same village, name of Strother,
Far in the north, I cannot tell you where.
    Alan collected all his gear with care,
Loaded his corn upon a horse he had,
And off he went with John the other lad,
Each with his sword and buckler by his side.

John knew the way—he didn't need a guide—
Reaches the mill and down the sack he flings.
    Alan spoke first: 'Well, Simon, lad, how's things?
And how's your canny daughter and your wife?'
Says Simpkin, 'Welcome, Alan! Odds my life,
It's John as well! What are you up to here?'
'By God,' said John. 'Needs-must has got no peer,
And it behoves a man that has nie servant
To work, as say the learned and observant.
Wor[49] Manciple is like enough to dee,
Such aches and torments in his teeth has he;
So Alan here and I have brought wor sack
Of corn for grinding and to bring it back.
Help us get home as quickly as ye can.'
'It shall be done,' said he, 'as I'm a man.
What'll you do while I've the job in hand?'
'By God,' said John, 'I have a mind to stand
Right by the hopper here and watch the corn
As it gans in. Never since I was born
Saw I a hopper wagging to and fro.'
    Alan spoke up: 'Eh, John, and will ye so?
Then I shall stand below a short way off
And watch the meal come down into the trough;
I need no more than that by way of sport,
For John, in faith, I'm one of the same sort
And diven't knaa nowt of milling, same as ye.'
    The miller smiled at their simplicity
And thought, 'It's just a trick, what they're about
They think that nobody can catch them out,
But by the Lord I'll blear their eyes a bit
For all their fine philosophy and wit.
The more they try to do me on the deal,
When the time comes, the more I mean to steal.
Instead of flour they shall be given bran.
''The greatest scholar is not the wisest man'',
As the wolf said in answer to the mare.
Them and their precious learning! Much I care.'
    And when he saw his chance he sidled out
Into the yard behind and looked about
Without their noticing until at last
He found their horse where they had made him fast
Under an arbour just behind the mill.
    Up to the horse he goes with quiet skill
And strips the bridle off him there and then.
And when the horse was loose, off to the fen
Through thick and thin, and whinneying 'Weehee!'
He raced to join the wild mares running free.
    The miller then went back, and did not say
A word of this, but passed the time of day
With John and Alan till their corn was ground;
And when the meal was fairly sacked and bound,
John wandered out and found their horse was gone.
'Good Lord! Help! Help! Come quickly!' shouted John,
'Wor horse is lost, Alan! The devil's in it!
God's bones, man, use you legs! Come out this minute!
Lord save us all, the Warden's palfrey's lost.'
    Alan forgot his meal and corn and cost,
Abandoning frugality and care.
'What's that?' he shouted, 'Palfrey? Which way? Where?'
    The miller's wife ran clucking like a hen
Towards them, saying, 'Gone off to the fen
To the wild mares as fast as he can go.
Curse on the clumsy hand that tied him so!
Should have known better how to knit the reins.'
John said, 'Bad luck to it. Alan, for Christ's pains,
Put down your sword, man; so will I; let's gan!
We'll rin him like a roe together, man!

God's precious heart! He cannot scape up all!
Why didn't you put the palfrey in the stall?
You must be daft, bad luck to you! Haway!'
And off ran John and Alan in dismay,
Towards the fen as fast as they could go.
    And when the miller saw that this was so,
A good half-bushel of their flour he took
And gave it over to his wife to cook.
'I think,' he said, 'these lads have had a fright.
I'll pluck their beards. Yes, Let 'em read and write,
But none the less a miller is their match.
Look at them now! Like children playing catch.
Won't be an easy job to get him, though!'
    These foolish Bible-clerks ran to and fro
And shouted, 'Woa, lad, stand! . . . Look out behind!
Whistle him up . . . I've got him . . . watch it . . . *mind!*'
But to be brief, it wasn't until night
They caught the palfrey, hunt him as they might
Over the fens, he ran away so fast;
But in a ditch they captured him at last.
    Weary and wet, like cattle in the rain,
Came foolish John and Alan back again.
Said John, 'Alas the day that I was born!
We've earned nowt here but mockery and scorn.
Wor corn is stolen and they'll call us fools,
Warden and all wor meäts in the Schools,
And most of all the miller. What a day!'
    So back they went, John grousing all the way,
Towards the mill and put the horse in byre.
They found the miller sitting by the fire,
For it was night, too late for going home,
And, for the love of God, they begged a room
For shelter and they proffered him their penny.
'A room?' the miller said. 'There isn't any.
There's this, such as it is; we'll share it then.
My house is small, but you are learned men
And by your arguments can make a place
Twenty foot broad as infinite as space.
Take a look round and see if it will do,
Or make it bigger with your parley-voo.'
'Well, Simon, you must have your little joke
And, by St. Cuthbert, that was fairly spoke!
Well, people have a proverb to remind them
To bring their own, or take things as they find them,'
Said John. 'Dear host, do get us out the cup;
A little meat and drink would cheer us up.
We'll give ye the full payment, on my word.
No empty-handed man can catch a bird;
See, here's the silver, ready to be spent.'
    Down into Trumpington the daughter went
For bread and ale; the miller cooked a goose,
And tied their horse up lest it should get loose
Again, and in his chamber made a bed
With clean white sheets and blankets fairly spread,
Ten foot from his, upon a sort of shelf,
His daughter had a bed all by herself
Quite close in the same room; they were to lie
All side by side, no help for it, and why?
Because there was no other in the house.
    They supped and talked and had a fine carouse
And drank a lot of ale, the very best.
Midnight or thereabout they went to rest.

---

49. *Wor* means 'our.' John is speaking the north of England dialect.

Properly pasted was this miller's head,
Pale-drunk he was, he'd passed the stage of red;
Hiccupping through his nose he talked and trolled
As if he'd asthma or a heavy cold.
To bed he goes, his wife and he together;
She was as jolly as a jay in feather,
Having well wet her whistle from the ladle.
And by her bed she planted down the cradle
To rock the baby or to give it sup.
    When what was in the crock had been drunk up,
To bed went daughter too, and thereupon
To bed went Alan and to bed went John.
That was the lot; no sleeping-draught was needed.
The miller had taken so much booze unheeded,
He snorted like a cart-horse in his sleep
And vented other noises, loud and deep.
His wife joined in the chorus hot and strong;
Two furlongs off you might have heard their song.
The wench was snoring too, for company.
    Alan the clerk in all this melody
Gave John a poke and said, 'Are ye awake?
Did ye ever hear sich sang for guidness sake?
There's family prayers for ye among they noddies!
Wild fire come doon and burn them up, the bodies!
Who ever heard a canny thing like that?
The devil take their souls for what they're at!
All this lang neet I shall na get nie rest.
    'But never ye mind, all shall be for the best;
I tell ye, John, as sure as I'm a man,
I'm going to have that wench there, if I can!
The law grants easement when things gan amiss,
For, John, there is a law that gans like this:
"If in one point a person be aggrieved,
Then in another he shall be relieved."
    'Wor corn is stolen, nivvor doubt of that;
Ill-luck has followed us in all we're at,
And since no compensation has been offered
Against wor loss, I'll take the easement proffered.
God's soul, it shall be so indeed, none other?'
    John whispered back to him, 'Be careful, brother,
The miller is a torble man for slaughter;
If he should wake and find ye with his daughter
He might do injury to you and me.'
'Injury? Him! I coont him nat a flea!'
    Alan rose up; towards the wench he crept.
The wench lay flat upon her back and slept,
And ere she saw him, he had drawn so nigh
It was too late for her to give a cry.
To put it briefly, they were soon at one.
Now, Alan, play! For I will speak of John.
    John lay there still for quite a little while,
Complaining and lamenting in this style:
'A bloody joke . . . Lord, what a chance to miss!
I shall be made a monkey of for this!
My meät has got some comfort for his harms,
He has the miller's daughter in his arms;
He took his chance and now his needs are sped,
I'm but a sack of rubbish here in bed.
And when this jape is told in time to come
They'll say I was a softie and a bum!
I'll get up too and take what chance I may,
For God helps those that help theirsels, they say.'
    He rises, steals towards the cradle, lifts it,
And stepping softly back again, he shifts it
And lays it by his bed upon the floor.

    The miller's wife soon after ceased to snore,
Began to wake, rose up, and left the room,
And coming back she groped about in gloom,
Missing the cradle, John had snatched away.
'Lord, Lord,' she said, 'I nearly went astray
And got into the student's bed. . . . How dreadful!
There would have been foul doings. What a bed-ful!'
    At last she gropes to where the cradle stands,
And so by fumbling upwards with her hands
She found the bed and thinking nought but good,
Since she was certain where the cradle stood,
Yet knew not where she was, for it was dark,
She well and fairly crept in with the clerk,
Then lay quite still and tried to go to sleep.
John waited for a while, then gave a leap
And thrust himself upon this worthy wife.
It was the merriest fit in all her life,
For John went deep and thrust away like mad.
It was a jolly life for either lad
Till the third morning cock began to sing.
    Alan grew tired as dawn began to spring;
He had been hard at work the long, long night.
'Bye-bye,' he said, 'sweet Molly. . . . Are ye a'right?
The day has come, I cannot linger here,
But ever mair in life and death, my dear,
I am your own true clerk, or strike me deid!'
'Good-bye, my sweet,' she whispered, 'take good
        heed . . .
But first I'll tell you something, that I will!
When you are riding homewards past the mill
By the main entrance-door, a bit behind it,
There's the half-bushel cake—you're sure to find it—
And it was made out of the very meal
You brought to grind and I helped father steal. . . .
And, dearest heart, God have you in his keeping!'
And with that word she almost burst out weeping.
    Alan got up and thought, 'Dawn's coming on,
Better get back and creep in beside John.'
But there he found the cradle in his way.
'By God,' he thought, 'I nearly went astray!
My heed is tottering with my work to-neet,
That'll be why I cannot gan areet!
This cradle tells me I have lost my tether;
You must be miller and his wife together.'
    And back he went, groping his weary way
And reached the bed in which the miller lay,
And thinking it was John upon the bed
He slid in by the miller's side instead,
Grabbing his neck, and with no more ado
Said, 'Shake yourself, wake up, you pig's-head, you!
For Christ's soul, listen! O such noble games
As I have had! I tell you, by St. James,
Three times the neet, from midnight into morn,
The miller's daughter helped me grind my corn
While you've been lying in your cowardly way . . .'
'You scoundrel!' said the miller, 'What d'you say?
You beast! You treacherous blackguard! Filthy rat!
God's dignity! I'll murder you for that!
How dare you be so bold as to fling mud
Upon my daughter, come of noble blood?'
    He grabbed at Alan by his Adam's apple,
And Alan grabbed him back in furious grapple
And clenched his fist and bashed him on the nose.
Down miller's breast a bloody river flows
Onto the floor, his nose and mouth all broke;
They wallowed like two porkers in a poke,

And up and down and up again they go
Until the miller tripped and stubbed his toe,
Spun round and fell down backwards on his wife.

    She had heard nothing of this foolish strife,
For she had fallen asleep with John the clerk,
Weary from all their labours in the dark.
The miller's fall started her out of sleep.
'Help!' she screamed. 'Holly cross of Bromeholme keep
Us! Lord! Into thy hands! To Thee I call!
Simon, wake up! The devil's among us all!
My heart is bursting, help! I'm nearly dead,
One's on my stomach, and another's on my head.
Help, simpkin, help! These nasty clerks are fighting!'

    Up started John, he needed no inciting,
And groped about the chamber to and fro
To find a stick; she too was on the go
And, knowing the corners better than them all,
Was first to find one leaning by the wall;
And by a little shaft of shimmering light
That shone in through a hole—the moon was bright—
Although the room was almost black as pitch
She saw them fight, not knowing which was which;
But there was something white that caught her eye
On seeing which she peered and gave a cry,
Thinking it was the night-cap of the clerk.

    Raising her stick, she crept up in the dark
And, hoping to hit Alan, it was her fate
To smite the miller on his shining pate,
And down he went, shouting, 'O God, I'm dying!'

    The clerks then beat him well and left him lying
And throwing on their clothes they took their horse
And their ground meal and off they went, of course,
And as they passed the mill they took the cake
Made of their meal the girl was told to bake.

    And thus the bumptious miller was well beaten
And done out of the supper they had eaten,
And done out of the money that was due
For grinding Alan's corn, who beat him too.
His wife was plumbed, so was his daughter. Look!
That comes of being a miller and a crook!

    I heard this proverb when I was a kid,
'Do evil and be done by as you did'.
Tricksters will get a tricking, so say I;
And God that sits in majesty on high
Bring all this company, great and small, to Glory!
Thus I've paid out the Miller with my story!

THE ART OF COURTLY LOVE
Andreas Capellanus (fl. 1174–1186)

Countess Marie of Champagne established a Court of
Love at Troyes where Andreas was probably chaplain
to the court, or so he claimed. Andreas was an accomplished writer whose treatise on love provides us with
a vivid and probably accurate picture of courtly life.
Specifically, Andreas intended his manual as a portrayal of the Poitiers court of Marie's mother, Queen
Eleanor of Aquitaine, as it was between 1170 and 1174.

    Undoubtedly written by direction of Countess
Marie, the manual is a codification of the etiquette of
love. Andreas combines quotations from classic Latin
writers (mainly Ovid) and the spirit of lyric love poetry by troubadours like Bernart de Ventadorn (see

chap. 16) with his own observation of actual practices, producing a unique work known throughout
Europe in a variety of translations.

Book One
Introduction to the Treatise on Love

We must first consider what love is, whence it gets its
name, what the effect of love is, between what persons
love may exist, how it may be acquired, retained,
increased, decreased, and ended, what are the signs that
one's love is returned, and what one of the lovers ought
to do if the other is unfaithful.

Chapter I. What Love Is

Love is a certain inborn suffering derived from the sight of
and excessive meditation upon the beauty of the opposite
sex, which causes each one to wish above all things the
embraces of the other and by common desire to carry out
all of love's precepts in the other's embrace.

    That love is suffering is easy to see, for before the
love becomes equally balanced on both sides there is no
torment greater, since the lover is always in fear that his
love may not gain its desire and that he is wasting his
efforts. He fears, too, that rumors of it may get abroad, and
he fears everything that might harm it in any way, for
before things are perfected a slight disturbance often
spoils them. If he is a poor man, he also fears that the
woman may scorn his poverty; if he is ugly, he fears that
she may despise his lack of beauty or may give her love to
a more handsome man; if he is rich, he fears that his
parsimony in the past may stand in his way. To tell the
truth, no one can number the fears of one single lover.[50]
This kind of love, then, is a suffering which is felt by only
one of the persons and may be called "single love." But
even after both are in love the fears that arise are just as
great, for each of the lovers fears that what he has
acquired with so much effort may be lost through the
effort of someone else, which is certainly much worse for
a man than if, having no hope, he sees that his efforts are
accomplishing nothing, for it is worse to lose the things
you are seeking than to be deprived of a gain you merely
hope for. The lover fears, too, that he may offend his
loved one in some way; indeed he fears so many things
that it would be difficult to tell them.

    That this suffering is inborn I shall show you clearly,
because if you will look at the truth and distinguish
carefully you will see that it does not arise out of any
action; only from the reflection of the mind upon what it
sees does this suffering come. For when a man sees some
woman fit for love and shaped according to his taste, he
begins at once to lust after her in his heart; then the more
he thinks about her the more he burns with love, until he
comes to a fuller meditation. Presently he begins to think
about the fashioning of the woman and to differentiate
her limbs, to think about what she does, and to pry into
the secrets of her body, and he desires to put each part of
it to the fullest use.[51] Then after he has come to this
complete meditation, love cannot hold the reins; but he

---

50. Ovid *Art of Love* II. 517 ff.
51. Compare Ovid *Metamorphoses* VI. 490–93.

proceeds at once to action; straightway he strives to get a helper and to find an intermediary. He begins to plan how he may find favor with her, and he begins to seek a place and a time opportune for talking; he looks upon a brief hour as a very long year, because he cannot do anything fast enough to suit his eager mind. It is well known that many things happen to him in this manner. This inborn suffering comes, therefore, from seeing and meditating. Not every kind of meditation can be the cause of love, an excessive one is required; for a restrained thought does not, as a rule, return to the mind, and so love cannot arise from it.

In Chapter VIII (Book Two), Andreas presents the Rules of Love as the climax of a properly romantic mission. It seems that a knight of Britain cannot win the love of "a certain British lady" until he has brought her the hawk sitting on a golden perch in King Arthur's court. And, he is told,

> you can't get this hawk that you are seeking unless you prove, by a combat in Arthur's palace, that you enjoy the love of a more beautiful lady than any man at Arthur's court has; you can't even enter the palace until you show the guards the hawk's gauntlet, and you can't get this gauntlet except by overcoming two mighty knights in a double combat.

After defeating the pugnacious keeper of a golden bridge, the Briton then vanquishes a giant and rides on to Camelot where he manfully accomplishes the assigned tasks. While seizing the hawk he discovers a written parchment and is told that "This is the parchment on which are written the rules of love which the King of Love . . . pronounced for lovers. You should take it with you and make these rules known to lovers."

These are the rules.

 I. Marriage is no real excuse for not loving.
 II. He who is not jealous cannot love.
 III. No one can be bound by a double love.
 IV. It is well known that love is always increasing or decreasing.
 V. That which a lover takes against the will of his beloved has no relish.
 VI. Boys do not love until they arrive at the age of maturity.
 VII. When one lover dies, a widowhood of two years is required of the survivor.
 VIII. No one should be deprived of love without the very best of reasons.
 IX. No one can love unless he is impelled by the persuasion of love.
 X. Love is always a stranger in the home of avarice.
 XI. It is not proper to love any woman whom one would be ashamed to seek to marry.
 XII. A true lover does not desire to embrace in love anyone except his beloved.
 XIII. When made public love rarely endures.
 XIV. The easy attainment of love makes it of little value; difficulty of attainment makes it prized.
 XV. Every lover regularly turns pale in the presence of his beloved.

 XVI. When a lover suddenly catches sight of his beloved his heart palpitates.
 XVII. A new love puts to flight an old one.[52]
 XVIII. Good character alone makes any man worthy of love.
 XIX. If love diminishes, it quickly fails and rarely revives.
 XX. A man in love is always apprehensive.
 XXI. Real jealousy always increases the feeling of love.
 XXII. Jealousy, and therefore love, are increased when one suspects his beloved.
 XXIII. He whom the thought of love vexes eats and sleeps very little.
 XXIV. Every act of a lover ends in the thought of his beloved.
 XXV. A true lover considers nothing good except what he thinks will please his beloved.
 XXVI. Love can deny nothing to love.
 XXVII. A lover can never have enough of the solaces of his beloved.
 XXVIII. A slight presumption causes a lover to suspect his beloved.
 XXIX. A man who is vexed by too much passion usually does not love.
 XXX. A true lover is constantly and without intermission possessed by the thought of his beloved.
 XXXI. Nothing forbids one woman being loved by two men or one man by two women.

These rules, as I have said, the Briton brought back with him on behalf of the King of Love to the lady for whose sake he endured so many perils when he brought her back the hawk. When she was convinced of the complete faithfulness of this knight and understood better how boldly he had striven, she rewarded him with her love. Then she called together a court of a great many ladies and knights and laid before them these rules of Love, and bade every lover keep them faithfully under threat of punishment by the King of Love. These laws the whole court received in their entirety and promised forever to obey in order to avoid punishment by Love. Every person who had been summoned and had come to the court took home a written copy of the rules and gave them out to all lovers in all parts of the world.

MORTE DARTHUR
Sir Thomas Malory (ca. 1410–1471)

Arthur, the representative of goodness and order, is killed by the forces of evil and disorder but, either in his own person or as a later English king, he shall return. He is the "once and future king," lord of Camelot, England, and the world, the embodiment of the noble virtues of chivalry. No discussion of the medieval world would be complete without some of the romance of King Arthur, his Knights of the Round Table, and Camelot, the original Court of Love.

---

52. Compare Cicero *Tusculan Disputations* IV. XXXV.

The Sword in the Stone

Then the queen Igraine drew daily near her time when the child Arthur should be born, and it fell, within half a-year, that king Uther asked her by the faith she owed unto him, who was father to her child? Then was she sore abashed to give an answer. "Fear you not," said the king; "but tell me the truth, and I shall love you the better by that faith of my body." "Sir," said she, "I shall tell you the truth. The same night that my lord was dead, that hour of his death, there came unto my castle of Tintagil a man like my lord in speech and countenance, and two knights with him in likeness of his two knights, Brastias and Jordains; and so I received him as I ought to do my lord; and that same night, as I shall answer unto God, the child was begotten." "That is truth," said the king, "as you say, for it was I myself that came in his likeness; and, therefore, fear you not, for I am father to the child." And there he told her all the cause how it was by Merlin's counsel. Then the queen made great joy when she knew who was the father of her child. Soon came Merlin unto the king, and said, "Sir you must provide you for the nourishing of your child." "As thou wilt," said the king, "be it." "Well," said Merlin, "I know a lord of yours, in this land, that is a passing true man, and faithful, and he shall have the nourishing of your child; his name is Sir Ector, and he is a lord of fair livelihood, in many parts of England and Wales. And this lord, Sir Ector, let him be sent for, for to come and speak with you, and desire him yourself, as he loveth you, that he will put his own child to nourishing to another woman, and that his wife nourish yours; and when the child is born, let it be delivered unto me, at yonder postern, unchristened." As Merlin had devised, so it was done. And when Sir Ector was come, he made affiance to the king for to nourish the child, like as the king desired; and there the king granted Sir Ector great rewards. Then when the queen was delivered, the king commanded two knights and two ladies to take the child, bound in rich cloth of gold, "And deliver him to what poor man you meet at the postern gate of the castle." So the child was delivered unto Merlin, and so he bore it forth unto Sir Ector, and made a holy man to christen him, and named him Arthur; and so Sir Ector's wife nourished him with her own breasts.

Then within two years king Uther fell sick of a great malady; and in the meanwhile his enemies usurped upon him, and did a great battle upon his men, and slew many of his people. "Sir," said Merlin, "you may not lie so as you do, for you must to the field, though you ride in a horse-litter; for you shall never have the better of your enemies but if your person be there, and then shall you have the victory." So it was done as Merlin had devised, and they carried the king forth in a horse-litter, with a great host towards his enemies. And at St. Alban's there met with the king a great host of the north; and that day Sir Ulfius and Sir Brastias did great deeds of arms, and king Uther's men overcame the northern battle, and slew much people, and put the remnant to flight; and then the king returned to London, and made great joy of his victory. And within a while after he was passing sore sick, so that three days and three nights he was speechless, wherefore all the barons made great sorrow, and asked Merlin what counsel were best? "There is none other remedy," said Merlin, "but God will have his will; but look ye all his barons be before him to-morrow, and God and I shall make him to speak." So on the morrow all the barons, with Merlin, came before the king; then Merlin said aloud unto king Uther, "Sir, shall your son

Arthur be king after your days of this realm, with all the appurtenances?" Then Utherpendragon turned him and said, in hearing of them all, "I give him God's blessing and mine, and bid him pray for my soul, and righteously and worshipfully that he claim the crown upon forfeiture of my blessing." And therewith he yielded up the ghost. And then he was interred as belonged unto a king; wherefore Igraine, the queen, made great sorrow, and all the barons. Then stood the realm in great jeopardy a long while, for every lord that was mighty of men made him strong, and many weened to have been king. Then Merlin went to the Archbishop of Canterbury, and counselled him to send for all the lords of the realm, and all the gentlemen of arms, that they should come to London before Christmas, upon pain of cursing; and for this cause, that as Jesus was born on that night, that He would of His great mercy show some miracle as He was come to be king of all mankind, for to show some miracle who should be rightwise king of this realm. So the archbishop, by the advice of Merlin, sent for all the lords and gentlemen of arms, that they should come by Christmas eve to London; and many of them made them clean of their lives, that their prayer might be the more acceptable to God. So in the greatest church of London (whether it were Paul's or not the French book maketh no mention) all the estates and lords were long or it was day in the church for to pray. And when matins and the first mass was done, there was seen in the churchyard, against the high altar, a great stone, four-square, like to a marble stone, and in the midst thereof was an anvil of steel, a foot of height, and therein stuck a fair sword, naked by the point, and letters of gold were written about the sword that said thus: "Whoso pulleth out this sword of this stone and anvil is rightwise king born of England." Then the people marvelled and told it to the archbishop. "I command you," said the archbishop, "that you keep you within your church; and pray unto God still that no man touch the sword till the high mass be all done." So when all the masses were done, all the estates went for to behold the stone and the sword, and when they saw the scripture, some assayed, such as would have been king; but none might stir the sword, nor move it. "He is not yet here," said the archbishop, "that shall achieve the sword, but doubt not God will make him to be known. "But this is my counsel," said the archbishop "that we let purvey ten knights, men of good fame, and they to keep this sword." And so it was ordained, and then there was made a cry, that every man should assay that would for to win the sword. And, upon new year's day, the barons let make a joust and tournament, that all knights that would joust and tourney there might play; and all this was ordained for to keep the lords together, and the commons, for the archbishop trusted that God would make him known that should win the sword. So, upon new year's day, when the service was done, the barons rode to the field, some to joust, and some to tourney. And so it happened that Sir Ector, that had great livelihood about London, rode to the jousts, and with him rode Sir Kaye, his son, and young Arthur, that was his nourished brother; and Sir Kaye was made knight at Allhallowmas afore. So as they rode towards the jousts, Sir Kaye had lost his sword, for he had left it at his father's lodging; and so he prayed young Arthur to ride for his sword. "I will with a good will," said Arthur, and rode fast after the sword; and when he came home, the lady and all were gone out to see the jousting. Then was Arthur wrath, and said to himself, "I will ride to the churchyard and take the sword with me that sticketh in the stone, for my brother, Sir Kaye, shall not be without a sword this day." And so, when he came to the churchyard, Arthur alighted, and tied his horse to the stile, and so went to the tent, and found no knights there, for they were all at the jousting; and so he handled the sword by the handles, and lightly and fiercely he pulled it out of the stone, and took his horse, and rode his way till he came to his brother, Sir Kaye, and delivered him the sword. And, as soon as Sir Kaye saw the sword, he wist well that it was the sword of the stone; and so he rode to his father, Sir Ector, and said, "Sir, lo! here is the sword of the stone; wherefore I must be king of this land." When Sir Ector beheld the sword, he returned again, and came to the church, and there they alighted all three, and went into the church; and anon he made Sir Kaye to swear upon a book how he came to that sword. "Sir," said Sir Kaye, "by my brother, Arthur, for he brought it to me." "How gat you this sword?" said Sir Ector to Arthur. "Sir, I will tell you; when I came home for my brother's sword I found nobody at home for to deliver me his sword; and so I thought my brother, Sir Kaye, should not be swordless, and so I came thither eagerly, and pulled it out of the stone without any pain." "Found ye any knights about this sword?" said Sir Ector. "Nay," said Arthur. "Now," said Sir Ector to Arthur, "I understand that you must be king of this land." "Wherefore I?" said Arthur, "and for what cause?" "Sir," said Sir Ector, "for God will have it so; for there should never no man have drawn out this sword, but he that shall be rightwise king of this land. Now, let me see whether ye can put the sword there as it was, and pull it out again." "That is no mastery," said Arthur; and so he put it in the stone. Therewith Sir Ector assayed to pull out the sword, and failed.

IV.

"Now assay you," said Sir Ector to Sir Kaye. And anon he pulled at the sword with all his might, but it would not be. "Now shall ye assay," said Sir Ector to Arthur. "With a good will," said Arthur, and pulled it out easily. And therewithal Sir Ector kneeled down to the earth, and Sir Kaye also. "Alas!" said Arthur, "mine own dear father, and my brother, why kneel you to me?" "Nay, nay, my lord Arthur, it is not so. I was never your father, nor of your blood, but I wot well that you are of an higher blood than I weened you were?" And then Sir Ector told him all how he was betaken him to nourish and by whose commandment, and by Merlin's deliverance. Then Arthur made great moan when he understood that Sir Ector was not his father. "Sir," said Sir Ector unto Arthur, "will you be my good and gracious lord when you are king?" "Else were I to blame," said Arthur, "for you are the man in the world that I am most beholden unto, and my good lady and mother, your wife, that, as well as her own, hath fostered and kept me; and, if ever it be God's will that I be king, as you say, ye shall desire of me what I may do, and I shall not fail you; God forbid I should fail you." "Sir," said Sir Ector, "I will ask no more of you but that you will make my son, your fostered brother, Sir Kaye, seneschal of all your lands." "That shall be done, sir," said Arthur, "and more by the faith of my body, and that never man shall have that office but he while that he and I live." Therewithal they went unto the archbishop, and told him how the sword was achieved, and by whom. And, upon the twelfth day, all the barons came thither for

to assay to take the sword who that would assay. But there before them all there might none take it out but only Arthur, wherefore there were many great lords wrath, and said, "It was great shame unto them all and the realm, to be governed with a boy of no high blood born." And so they fell out at that time that it was put off til Candlemas, and then all the barons should meet there again. But always the ten knights were ordained for to watch the sword both day and night; and so they set a pavilion over the stone and the sword, and five always watched. And at Candlemas many more great lords came thither for to have won the sword, but none of them might prevail; and right as Arthur did at Christmas he did at Candlemas, and pulled out the sword easily, whereof the barons were sore aggrieved, and put it in delay till the high feast of Easter; and, as Arthur sped before, so did he at Easter; and yet there were some of the great lords had indignation that Arthur should be their king, and put it off in delay till the feast of Pentecost. Then the Archbishop of Canterbury, by Merlin's providence, let purvey of the best knights that might be gotten, and such knights as king Uther-pendragon loved best, and most trusted in his days; and such knights were put about Arthur, as Sir Boudwine, of Britain; Sir Kaye, Sir Ulfias, and Sir Brastias; all these, with many others, were always about Arthur, day and night, till the feast of Pentecost.

V.

And, at the feast of Pentecost, all manner of men assayed for to pull at the sword that would assay; and none might prevail but Arthur, and he pulled it out before all the lords and commons that were there; wherefore all the commons cried at once, "We will have Arthur unto our king, we will put him no more in delay, for we all see that it is God's will that he shall be our king, and who that holdeth against it we will slay him," and therewithal they all kneeled down all at once, and cried Arthur mercy because they had delayed him so long. And Arthur forgave it them, and took the sword between both his hands, and offered it up to the altar, where the archbishop was, and was made knight of the best man that was there. And so anon was the coronation made, and there was he sworn to the lords and commons for to be a true king, to stand with true justice from thenceforth all the days of his life; and then he made all the lords that held off the crown, to come in and do him service as they ought to do. And many complaints were made unto king Arthur, of great wrongs that were done since the death of king Utherpendragon, of many lands that were bereaved of lords, knights, ladies, and gentlemen; wherefore king Arthur made the lands for to be rendered again unto them that owed them. When this was done, that the king had established all the countries about London, then he did make Sir Kaye seneschal of England, and Sir Boudwine, of Britain, was made constable, and Sir Ulfias was made chamberlain, and Sir Brastias was made warden, for to wait upon the north from Trent forward; for it was that time, for the most part, enemy unto the king. But within few years after, king Arthur won all the north, Scotland, and all that were under their obeisance; also a part of Wales held against king Arthur, but he overcame them all, as he did the remnant, and all through the noble prowess of himself and his knights of the Round Table.

The Book of the Queen's Maying

I.

And thus it passed on from Candlemas until after Easter, that the month of May was come, when every lusty heart beginneth to blossom, and to bring forth fruit. For, like as herbs and trees bring forth fruit, and flourish in May, in likewise every lusty heart, that is in any manner a lover, springeth and flourisheth in lusty deeds; for it giveth unto all lovers courage that lusty month of May in some thing, for to constrain him in some manner of thing; more in that month than in any other month, for divers causes; for then all herbs and trees renew a man and woman. And, in likewise, lovers call again to their mind old gentleness and old service, and many kind deeds that were forgotten by negligence. For, like as winter rasure doth always rase and deface green summer; so fareth it by unstable love in a man, and in woman, for in many persons there is no stability. For we may see all day a little blast of winter's rasure, anon we shall deface and put away true love for little or naught, that cost much thing; this is no wisdom no stability, but is feebleness of nature, and great disworship, whosoever useth this. Therefore, like as May month flowereth and flourisheth in many gardens, so in likewise let every man of worship flourish his heart in this world; first unto God, and next unto the joy of them that he promiseth his faith unto. For there was never worshipful woman, but they loved one better than another. And worship in arms may never be defiled. But first, reserve the honour unto God; and secondly, the quarrel must come of thy lady; and such love I call virtuous love. But now-a-days men cannot love, may not endure by reason; for where they be soon accorded, and hasty heat soon cooleth; right so fareth love now-a-days, soon hot, soon cold. This is no stability, but the old love was not so. Men and women could love together seven years, and no lusts were between them; and then was love, truth and faithfulness. And so in likewise was love used in King Arthur's days; wherefore, I liken love now-a-days unto summer and winter: for, like as the one is hot and the other cold, so fareth love now-a-days. Therefore, all ye that be lovers, call unto your remembrance the month of May, like as did Queen Guenever, for whom I make here a little mention, that while she lived she was a true lover, and there she had a good end.

II.

Now it befell in the month of lusty May that Queen Guenever called unto her knights of the Round Table, and she gave them warning, that early in the morning she should ride a-maying into woods and fields beside Westminster; "and I warn you that there be none of you but that he be well horsed, and that ye all be clothed in green; and I shall bring with me ten ladies, and every knight shall have a lady behind him, and every knight shall have a squire and two yeomen, and I will that ye and all be well horsed." So they made them ready in the freshest manner, and these were the names of the knights: Sir Kaye, Sir Agravaine, Sir Brandiles, Sir Sagramore, Sir Donidas, Sir Ozanna, Sir Ladinas, Sir Persuant, Sir Ironside, and Sir Pelleas. And those ten knights made them ready in the most freshest manner to ride with the Queen. So on the morrow they took their horses and rode a-maying with the Queen in great joy and delight; and the Queen purposed to have been again with the King at the furthest by ten of the clock, and so was her purpose at that time. Then there was a knight, the which hight Sir Meliagraunce, and he was son unto King Bagdemagus; and this knight had at that time a castle of the gift of King Arthur, within seven miles of Westminster. And this knight, Sir Meliagraunce, loved passing well Queen Guenever, and so he had done long and many years; and he had laid long in wait for to steal away the Queen, but evermore he forbear, because of Sir Launcelot du Lake, for in nowise he would meddle with the Queen if Sir Launcelot were in her company, or else and he were near hand her; and that time there was such a custom, that the Queen rode never without a great fellowship of men of arms about her; and there were many good knights, and the most part were young men that would have worship, and they were called the Queen's knights, and never in no battle, tournament, or jousts, they never bear none of them no manner of knowledge of their own arms, but plain white shields, and thereby they were called the Queen's knights. And then when it happened any of them to be of great worship by his noble deeds, then at the next high feast of Pentecost, if there were any slain or dead, as there was no year that failed but some were dead, then was there chosen in their stead that were dead the most men of worship, that were called the Queen's knights. And thus they came up all first, or they were renowned men of worship, both Sir Launcelot and all the remnant of them. But this knight, Sir Meliagraunce, had fullwell espied the Queen and her purpose, and how Sir Launcelot was not with her, and how she had no men of arms with her, but the ten knights all arrayed in green for maying. Then he purveyed him twenty men of arms, and a hundred archers to destroy the Queen and her knights, for he thought that time was the best season to take the Queen.

III.

So as the Queen had mayed and all her knights, all were bedecked with herbs and flowers, in the best manner and freshest. Right so came out of a wood Sir Meliagraunce, with eight score men well armed, as they should fight in battle of arrest, and bade the Queen and her knights abide, for mauger there heads they should abide. "Traitor knight," said Queen Guenever, "what thinkest thou to do? wilt thou shame thyself? Bethink thee how thou art a king's son, and knight of the Round Table, and thou to be about for to dishonour the noble king that made thee knight; thou shamest the high order of knighthood and thyself! and me, I let the wit, shalt thou never shame, for I had rather cut my throat in twain, rather than thou shouldst dishonour me." "As for all this language," said Sir Meliagraunce, "be it as it may, for wit ye well, madam, that I have loved you many years, and never or now could I get you at such advantage as I do now, and therefore I will take you as I find you." Then spake the ten knights all with one voice, and said, "Sir Maliagraunce, wit ye well ye are about to jeopard your worship to dishonour, also ye cast for to jeopard our persons; howbeit we be unarmed, ye have us at a great advantage, for it seemeth by you that ye have laid watch on us; but rather than ye should put the Queen to shame and us all, we had as leave to depart from our lives, for and if we otherwise did we were shamed for ever." Then Sir Meliagraunce said, "Dress you as well as ye can, and keep the Queen." Then the ten knights of the Round Table drew their swords, and the others let run at them with their spears; and the ten knights manly abode them, and smote away their spears, that no spear did them harm. Then they lashed together with their swords, and anon Sir Kaye, Sir Griflet, Sir Agravaine, Sir Dodinas, and Sir Ozanna were smitten to the earth with grimly wounds. Then Sir Brandiles and Sir Persuant, Sir Ironside and Sir Pelleas, fought long, and they were full sore wounded; for these knights, or ever they were laid to the ground, slew forty men of the best of them. So when the Queen saw her knights thus dolefully wounded, and needs must be slain at the last, then for pity and sorrows she cried and said, "Sir Meliagraunce, slay not my knights, and I will go with thee upon this convenant, that thou save them, and suffer them to be no more hurt; with this, that they be led with me wheresoever thou leadest me, for I will rather slay myself than I go with thee, unless that these, my noble knights, may be in presence." "Madam," said Sir Meliagraunce, "for your sake they shall be led with you into my castle, with that ye will be ruled and ride with me."

Then Queen Guenever prayed the four knights to leave their fight, and she and they would not depart. "Madam," said Sir Pelleas, "we will do as ye do; for as for me, I take no force of my life nor death." For Sir Pelleas gave such buffets there, that no armour might hold them.

IV.

Then by the Queen's command they left battle, and dressed the wounded knights on horseback, some sitting and some athward, that it was pity to behold them. And then Sir Meliagraunce charged the Queen and all the knights, that none of her fellowship should depart from her; for full sore he dreaded Sir Launcelot du Lake, lest he should have any knowledge. All this espied the Queen, and privily she called unto her a child of her chamber, which was swiftly horsed, to whom she said, "Go thou, when thou seest thy time, and bear this ring unto Sir Launcelot du Lake, and pray him as he loveth me that he will come and see me, and that he rescue me if ever he will have joy of me, and spare not thou thy horse," said the Queen, "neither for water nor yet for land." And so the child espied his time, and lightly he mounted upon his horse, and smote him with his spurs, and so departed from there as fast as ever his horse might run. And when Sir Meliagraunce saw the child so flee, he understood well it was by the Queen's command, for to warn Sir Launcelot. Then they that were best horsed chased him, and shot at him; but the child went from them all. And then Sir Meliagraunce said unto Queen Guenever, "Madam, ye be about to betray me; but I shall ordain for Sir Launcelot, that he shall not lightly come at you." And then he rode with her and they all to his castle, in all the haste that they might; and by the way Sir Meliagraunce laid in an ambushment the best archers that he might get in his country, to the number of thirty, for to wait upon Sir Launcelot, charging them, that if they saw such a manner of knight come by the way upon a white horse, in anywise to slay his horse; but in no manner of wise not to have to do with him bodily, for he is overhard to be overcome. So this was done, and they were come to his castle; but in nowise the Queen would never let none of the ten knights and her ladies be out of her sight, but alway they were in her presence: for that Sir Meliagraunce durst make no masteries for dread of Sir Launcelot, inasmuch as he deemed that he had warning. So when the child was departed from the fellowship of Sir Meliagraunce, within a while he came to Westminster, and anon he found Sir Launcelot; and when he had told his message, and delivered him the Queen's ring, "Alas!" said Sir Launcelot, "now am I ashamed for ever only that I

may rescue that noble lady from dishonour." "Then eagerly he asked his armour, and ever the child told Sir Launcelot how the ten knights fought marvellously, and how Sir Pelleas, Sir Ironside, Sir Brandiles, and Sir Persuant of Inde fought strongly, but mainly Sir Pelleas; for there was none might withstand him, and how they all fought till at the last they were laid to the earth. And then the Queen made appointment for to save their lives, and went with Sir Meliagraunce. "Alas!" said Sir Launcelot, "that that most noble knight should be destroyed; I had rather," said Sir Launcelot, "than all the realm of France, that I had been there well armed." So when Sir Launcelot was all armed and upon his horse, he prayed the child of the Queen's chamber for to warn Sir Lavaine how suddenly he was departed, and for what cause; and pray him that, as he loveth me, that he will hie him fast after me, and that he stint not till that he come to me unto the castle whereas Sir Meliagraunce abideth or dwelleth. "For there," said Sir Launcelot, "shall he hear of me, if I be a man living! and rescue the queen, and the ten knights, the which full traitorously have been taken, that shall I prove upon his head, and all them that holdeth with him."

V.

Then Sir Launcelot rode as fast as he might, and then he took the water at Westminster bridge, and made his horse for to swim over the Thames to Lambeth. And then within a while he came to the place whereas the ten knights had fought with Sir Meliagraunce. And then Sir Launcelot followed the trace until he came unto a wood, and there was a straight way, and therein the thirty archers bade Sir Launcelot to turn again and follow no longer the trace. "What command have ye thereto," said Sir Launcelot, "to cause me, that am a knight of the Round Table, to leave my right way?" "This way shalt thou leave, or else thou shalt go it upon thy feet; for wit thou well, thy horse shall be slain." "That is little mastery," said Sir Launcelot, "for to slay my horse; but as for myself, when my horse is slain, I give right nought for you, not and ye were five hundred more." So then they shot Sir Launcelot's horse, and smote him with many arrows. And then Sir Launcelot avoided his horse and went on foot; but there were so many ditches and hedges between them and him, that he might not meddle with one of them. "Alas! for shame," said Sir Launcelot, "that ever one knight should betray another knight; but it is an old saying, 'A good man is never in danger but when he is in danger of a coward.'" Then Sir Launcelot went awhile on foot, and then was he foul cumbered with his armour, shield, and spear, and all that belonged to him; wit ye well he was full sore annoyed, and full loth he was to leave any thing that belonged unto him, for he dread right sore the treason of Sir Meliagraunce. And then by fortune there came by a chariot, the which came thither for to fetch wood. "Tell me, carter," said Sir Launcelot, "what shall I give thee for to suffer me to leap into the chariot, and that thou bring me unto a castle within these two miles." "Thou shalt not come within my chariot," said the carter; "for I am sent for to fetch wood for my lord, Sir Meliagraunce." "With him would I fain speak," said Sir Launcelot. "Thou shalt not go with me," said the carter. Then Sir Launcelot leapt to him, and gave him such a buffet, that he fell to the ground stark dead. Then the other carter, his fellow, was afraid, and thought to have gone the same way, and then he cried and said, "Fair lord, save my life, and I will bring you where you will." "Then I charge thee," said Sir

Launcelot, "that thou drive me and this chariot even unto Sir Meliagraunce Castle." "Leap up into the chariot," said the carter, "and ye shall be there anon." So the carter drove forth as fast as he could; and Sir Launcelot's horse followed the chariot with more than forty arrows broad and rough in him. And more than an hour and a half Queen Guenever was in a bye window waiting with her ladies, and espied an armed knight standing in a chariot, "See, madam" said a lady, "whereas rideth in a chariot a goodly armed knight; I suppose that he rideth to hanging." "Where?" said the Queen. And then the Queen espied by his shield that he was there himself, Sir Launcelot du Lake. And then she was aware where came his horse after that chariot. "Alas!" said the Queen, "now I see well and prove, that well is him that hath a trusty friend. Ah! most noble knight." said Queen Guenever, "I see well that thou hast been hard bestead, when thou ridest in a cart," Then she rebuked that lady that likened him to ride in a chariot to hanging. "It was foul mouthed," said the Queen, "and evil likened, so for to liken the most noble knight in the world in such a shameful death. Oh! Jesu, defend him and keep him," said the Queen, "from all mischievous end." By this was Sir Launcelot come unto the gate of the castle, and he descended down, and cried, that all the castle rang of it: "Where art thou, false traitor, Sir Meliagraunce, and knight of the Round Table? Now come forth here, thou false traitor knight, thou and thy fellowship with thee, for here I am, Sir Launcelot du Lake; I shall fight with thee." And therewithal he bear the gate wide open upon the porter, and smote him under his ear with his gauntlet, that his neck brake asunder.

VI.

So when Sir Meliagraunce heard that Sir Launcelot was come, he ran to the Queen, and fell upon his knees, and said, "Mercy, madam! now I put me wholly in your grace." "What aileth you now?" said Queen Guenever: "forsooth, ye might well wit that some good knight would revenge me, though my lord King Arthur wist not of this your work." "Madam," said Sir Meliagraunce, "all that is done amiss on my part shall be amended, right as yourself will devise, and wholly I put me in your grace." "What would ye that I did?" said the Queen. "I would no more," said Sir Meliagraunce, "but that ye would take into your own hands, and that ye will rule my lord, Sir Launcelot; and such cheer as may be made him in this poor castle ye shall have until to-morrow. And then may ye and all your knights and ladies return to Westminster, and my body, and all that I have, shall I put into your rule." "Ye say well," said the Queen; "and better is peace than always war; and the less strife is made, the more is my worship." Then the Queen and her fair ladies went down unto the knight, Sir Launcelot, which stood wroth out of measure in the inner court for to abide battle, and ever he said, "Thou traitor knight, come forth here!" Then the Queen came unto him, and said, "Sir Launcelot, why be ye so moved?" "Ah! madam," said Sir Launcelot, "wherefore ask ye me that question? Me seemeth," said Sir Launcelot, "ye ought to be more displeased that I am, for ye have the hurt and the dishonour; for wit ye well, madam, my hurt is but little for the killing of a mare's son, but the despite grieveth me much more than all my hurt." "Truly," said Queen Guenever, "ye say truth: but heartily I thank you," said the Queen, "but ye must come in with me peaceably, for all things is put in my hands, and all that is evil shall be for the best, for the knight full sore repenteth him for

the misadventure that is befallen him." "Madam," said Sir Launcelot, "sith it is so that ye are accorded with him: as for me, I may not be against it, howbeit Sir Meliagraunce hath done full shamefully to me and full cowardly. Madam," said Sir Launcelot, "if I had wist that ye would have been so soon accorded with him, I would not have made such haste to you." "Why say you so?" said the Queen: "do you forethink yourself of your good deeds? Wit ye well," said the Queen, "I accorded never unto him for favour, nor love that I have unto him, but for to lay down every shameful noise." "Madam," said Sir Launcelot, "ye understand full well that I was never willing nor glad of shameful slander nor noise; and there is neither king, queen, nor knight that beareth life, except my lord King Arthur and you, madam, that should let me, but that I should make Sir Meliagraunce's heart full cold or I depart from hence." "That wot I well," said the Queen, "but what will ye more; ye shall have all things ruled as ye like to have it." "Madam," said Sir Launcelot, "so that ye be pleased, I care not; as for my part, ye shall full soon please." Right so the Queen took Sir Launcelot by the bare hand, for he had put off his gauntlet, and so she went with him to her chamber. And then she commanded him to be unarmed; and then Sir Launcelot asked where the ten knights were, that were sore wounded. So she showed them unto Sir Launcelot, and there they made great joy of his coming; and Sir Launcelot made great dole for their hurts, and bewailed them greatly. And there Sir Launcelot told them how cowardly and traitorously Sir Meliagraunce had set archers to slay his horse, and how he was fain to put himself in a chariot. Thus they complained the one unto the other: and full fain they would have been revenged, but they appeased themselves because of the Queen. Then Sir Launcelot was called many a day after Le Chevalier du Chariot, and did many deeds, and great adventures he had.

And so leave we off this tale of Chevalier du Chariot, and return we unto our tale. So Sir Launcelot had great cheer with the Queen; and then Sir Launcelot made a promise with the Queen, that the same night he should come into a window, outward into a garden, and that window was barred with iron. And there Sir Launcelot promised to meet her, when all folks were asleep. So then came Sir Lavaine driving to the gate crying, "Where is my lord, Sir Launcelot du Lake?" Then was he forthwith sent for, and when Sir Lavaine saw Sir Launcelot he said, "My lord, I found well how ye were hard bestead, for I have found your horse, the which was slain with arrows." "As for that," said Sir Launcelot, "I pray you, Sir Lavaine, speak ye of other matters, and let this pass; and we shall right it another time, when we best may."

VII.

Then the knights that were wounded were searched, and soft salves were laid to their wounds, and so it passed on till supper time; and all the cheer that might be made them, there it was showed unto the Queen and her knights. Then, when season was, they went to their chamber: but in no wise the Queen would not suffer the wounded knights to be from her, but that they were laid within draughts, upon beds and pillows, that she herself might see to them, that they lacked nothing. So when Sir Launcelot was in his chamber, that was assigned unto him, he called unto him Sir Lavaine, and told him, that that night he must go speak with his lady, Dame

Guenever. "Sir," said Sir Lavaine, "let me go with you, and it please you, for I dread me sore of the treason of Sir Meliagraunce." "Nay," said Sir Launcelot, "I thank you; I will have no person with me at this time." And then Sir Launcelot took his sword in his hand, and privily went unto a place whereas he had espied a ladder beforehand, and that he took under his arm, and bear it through the garden, and set it up in a window, and there anon the Queen was ready to meet him; and then they made either to other their complaints of divers things: and then Sir Launcelot wished that he might come in. "Wit ye well," said the Queen, "I would as fain as ye that ye might come in." "Would ye, madam," said Sir Launcelot, "with your heart that I were with you?" "Yea, truly," said the Queen. "Now shall I prove my might," said Sir Launcelot, "for the love of you." And then he set his hand upon the bars of iron, and pulled at them with such a great might, that he break them clean out of the stone walls; and therewithal one of the bars of iron cut the brawn of Sir Launcelot's hand throughout to the bone, and then he leapt into the chamber to the Queen. "Make ye no noise," said the Queen, "for my wounded knights lie here fast by me." And so, to pass forth upon this tale, Sir Launcelot took no force of his hurt hand, but took his pleasure and his liking until it was in the dawning of the day; and wit ye well he slept not, but watched. And when he saw the time that he might tarry no longer he took his leave and departed at the window, and put it together as well he might again, and so departed unto his own chamber; and there he told Sir Lavaine how he was hurt. Then Sir Lavaine dressed his hand and staunched it, and put upon it a glove, that it should not be espied; and so the queen lay long in her bed, until it was nine of the clock. Then Sir Meliagraunce went to the Queen's chamber, and found her ladies there ready clothed. "Jesu, mercy!" said Sir Meliagraunce, "what aileth you, madam, that ye sleep thus long?" And so forthwithal he opened the curtains for to behold her; and then was he ware where she lay, and all the sheet and pillow was all bloody, with the blood of Sir Launcelot's hurt hand: and when Sir Meliagraunce espied that blood, then he deemed in himself that she was false unto the King, and that some of the wounded knights had been with her all that night. "Ah! madam," said Sir Meliagraunce, "Now I have found you false traitoress unto my lord, King Arthur; for now I prove it well, that it was not for nought ye laid these wounded knights within the bounds of your chamber. Therefore I will accuse you of treason before my liege lord, King Arthur, and now I have proved you, madam, with a shameful deed, and that they be all false, or some of them, and that I will make good; for a wounded knight this night hath been with you." "That is false," said the Queen, "and that I report me to them all." Then, when the ten knights heard Sir Meliagraunce's words, they spake all with one voice, and said to Sir Meliagraunce, "Thou sayeth falsely, and wrongfully puttest upon us such a deed; and that we will make good, any of us, choose which thou list of us, when we are whole of our wounds." "Ye shall not," said Sir Meliagraunce, "say nay, with proud language: for here ye may all see," said Sir Meliagraunce, "that by the Queen this night a wounded knight hath lain." Then were they all ashamed when they saw the blood. And wit ye well that Sir Meliagraunce was passing glad that he had the Queen at such advantage, for he deemed that should hide his treason. So in this rumour came in Sir Launcelot, and found them all at a great array.

VIII.

"Aha! what array is this?" said Sir Launcelot. Then Sir Meliagraunce told him what he had found, and showed him the Queen's bed. "Truly," said Sir Launcelot, "ye did not your part, nor knightly, to touch a queen's bed, the while it was drawn, and she lying therein. For I dare say, and make good, that my lord King Arthur himself would not have displaced her curtains, she being within her bed, unless that it had pleased him to have lain down by her; and therefore have ye done unworshipfully and shamefully to yourself." "I wot not what you mean," said Sir Meliagraunce: "but well I am sure there hath one of her wounded knights lain with her this night; and therefore I will prove it, by my hands, that she is a traitoress unto my lord, King Arthur." "Beware what ye do," said Sir Launcelot, "for and ye say so, and that he will prove it, it shall be taken at your hands." "My lord, Sir Launcelot," said Sir Meliagraunce, "be you aware also what ye do; for though ye are never so good a knight, as wot ye well that ye are renowned the best knight of the world, yet should ye be advised to do battle in a wrong quarrel. For God will have a stroke in every battle that is done." "As for that," said Sir Launcelot, "God is to be dreaded. But as to that I say nay plainly, that this night there was none of these ten wounded knights with my lady, Queen Guenever, and that will I prove with my hands, that ye say untruly in that now." "Hold!" said Sir Meliagraunce, "here is my glove, that she is a traitoress unto my lord, King Arthur." "And I receive your glove," said Sir Launcelot. And so they were sealed with their signets, and delivered to the ten knights. "Upon what day shall we do battle together?" said Sir Launcelot. "This day eight days," said Sir Meliagraunce, "in the field beside Westminster." "I am agreed," said Sir Launcelot. "But now," said Meliagraunce, "sith it is that we must do battle together, I beseech you, as ye are a noble knight, await me with no treason, nor no villainy, in the meanwhile." "Nor none for you, so God me help," said Sir Launcelot: "ye shall right well wit I was never of these conditions, for I report me unto all knights that ever knew me, I used never no treason; nor I loved never to be in the fellowship of no man that used treason." "Then let us go to dinner," said Sir Meliagraunce, "and after dinner ye and the Queen, and ye all, may ride unto Westminster." "I will well," said Sir Launcelot. And then Sir Meliagraunce said unto Sir Launcelot, "Please it you to see the features of this castle?" "With a good will," said Sir Launcelot. And then they went together from chamber to chamber: for Sir Launcelot dreaded no perils. For ever a man of worship and of prowess dreadeth always perils least; for they ween that every man is as they be; but always he that dealeth with treason putteth a man oft in great danger. So it befell Sir Launcelot that no peril dreaded. And, as he went with Sir Meliagraunce, he trod on a trap, and the board rolled, and therewith Sir Launcelot fell down more than ten fathoms into a cave, upon straw. And then Sir Meliagraunce departed, and made semblance as though he had not wist where he was. And when Sir Launcelot was thus missed, they marvelled where he was become; and then Queen Guenever, and many of them, deemed that he had departed, as he was wont to do suddenly. For Sir Meliagraunce made suddenly to put out of the way Sir Launcelot's horse, that they might all understand that Sir Launcelot was departed suddenly. So it past forth until after dinner, and then Sir Lavaine would not stint until that he had ordained horse-litters for the wounded knights, that they might be laid in them; and so with the Queen, and them all, both ladies and gentlewomen, and many other went to Westminster. And the knights told unto King Arthur how Sir Meliagraunce had appealed the Queen of high treason; and how Sir Launcelot had received the glove of him, and this day eight days they shall do battle together afore you. "By my head," said King Arthur, "I am afraid that Sir Meliagraunce hath taken upon him a great charge: but where is Sir Launcelot?" said the King. "Sir," said they all, "we wit not where he is; but we deem he is ridden to some adventures, as he is oftentimes wont to do, for he hath Sir Lavaine's horse." "Let him be," said the King; "he will be found, unless he be trapped with some treason."

IX.

Now return we unto Sir Launcelot, lying within that cave, in great pain. And every day there came a lady and brought him his meat and his drink, and wooed him to have his love; and ever the noble knight, Sir Launcelot, said her nay. "Sir Launcelot," said she, "ye are not wise, for ye may never come out of this prison, but if ye have my help; and also your lady, Queen Guenever, shall be burnt in your default, unless that you be there at the day of battle." "God defend it," said Sir Launcelot, "that she should be burnt in my default; and if that be so," said Sir Launcelot, "that I may not be there, it shall be well understood, of both the King and of the Queen, and with all men of worship, that I am dead, or sick, or else in prison; for all men that know me will say for me, that I am in some evil case, if I be not there that day: and well I wot there is some good knight, either of my blood, or else some other that loveth me, that will take my quarrel in hand; and, therefore," said Sir Launcelot, "wit ye well that ye shall not fear me: and if there were no more women in this land but you, I would not have your love." "Then art thou shamed and destroyed for ever," said the lady. "As for world's shame," said Sir Launcelot, "Jesu defend me; and as for my distress, it is welcome whatsoever it be that God sendeth me." So she came unto Sir Launcelot that same day that the battle should be, and said to him, "Sir Launcelot, me thinketh ye are too strong hearted; but wouldest thou kiss me once, I would deliver thee and thine armour, and the best horse that is within Sir Meliagraunce's stable." "As for to kiss you," said Sir Launcelot, "I may do that and lose no worship; and wit you well, and I understand there was any disworship for to kiss you, I would not do it." Then he kissed her, and then she gat him, and brought him to his armour. And when he was armed she brought him to a stable, whereas stood twelve good coursers, and bade him choose the best. Then Sir Launcelot looked upon a white courser which liked him best; and anon he commanded the keeper fast to saddle him with the best saddle of war that was there: and so it was done as he commanded. Then gat he his spear in his hand, and his sword by his side, and commended the lady to God, and said, "Lady, for this good deed I shall do you service, if ever it be in my power."

X.

Now leave we Sir Launcelot galloping all that he might, and speak we of Queen Guenever that was brought to a fire to have been burnt; for Sir Meliagraunce was sure him thought that Sir Launcelot should not be at that battle; and, therefore, he ever cried upon King Arthur for to do him justice, or else for to bring forth Sir Launcelot. Then

was the King and all the court full sore abashed and shamed, that the Queen should be burnt in the default of Sir Launcelot. "My good lord, King Arthur," said Sir Lavaine, "ye may right well understand that it is not well with my lord, Sir Launcelot, for and he were alive, so that he be not sick or in prison, wit ye well that he would be here, for never heard ye that ever he failed his part for whom he should do battle; and, therefore, now," said Sir Lavaine, "my lord, King Arthur, I beseech you give me license to do battle here this day for my lord and master, and for to save my lady, the Queen." 'Gramercy, gentle knight, Sir Lavaine, said King Arthur, "for I dare say that Sir Meliagraunce putteth upon my lady, Queen Guenever, is wrong; for I have spoken with all the ten wounded knights, and there is not one of them, and he were whole, and able to do battle, but that he would prove upon Sir Meliagraunce's body that it is false that he putteth upon the Queen." "So shall I," said Sir Lavaine, "in defending my lord, Sir Launcelot, and ye will give me leave." "Now I give you leave," said King Arthur, "and do your best; for I dare well say there is some treason done to Sir Launcelot." Then was Sir Lavaine horsed, and suddenly at the list's end he rode to perform this battle. And right as the heralds should cry, "*Laissez les aller,*" right so came in Sir Launcelot, driving with all the force of his horse. And so King Arthur cried, "Go and abide." Then was Sir Launcelot called before King Arthur on horseback, and there he told openly before the King, and all them that were present, how Sir Meliagraunce had served him first and last. And when the King and the Queen and all the lords knew of the treason of Sir Meliagraunce, they were all ashamed on his behalf. And then was Queen Guenever sent for, and set by the King in great trust of her champion. And so then there was no more to say, but Sir Launcelot and Sir Meliagraunce dressed them unto battle, and took their spears, and so they came together as thunder, and there Sir Launcelot bore him down quite over his horse's croup: and then Sir Launcelot alighted and dressed his shield on his shoulder, with his sword in his hand: and Sir Meliagraunce in the same wise dressed him unto Sir Launcelot. And there they smote many strokes together; and at the last Sir Launcelot smote him such a buffet upon the helm, that he fell on the one side to the ground, and then he cried upon him aloud, "Most noble knight, Sir Launcelot du Lake, I pray you save my life, for I yield me unto you; and I beseech you, as ye be a knight and fellow of the Round Table, slay me not, for I yield me as an overcome knight; and, whether I shall live or die, I put me in the King's hands and yours." Then Sir Launcelot wist not what to do, for he had rather than all the good of the world he might have been revenged upon Sir Meliagraunce. And then Sir Launcelot looked towards Queen Guenever if he might espy, by any sign or countenance, what he should have done: and then the Queen wagged her head upon Sir Launcelot, as though she should say, slay him. Full well knew Sir Launcelot by the wagging of the head, that she would have him dead. Then Sir Launcelot bade him "arise for shame, and perform that battle to the uttermost." "Nay," said Sir Meliagraunce, "I will never arise until that ye take me as yielden and recreant." "I shall proffer you large proffers," said Sir Launcelot; "that is to say, I shall unarm my head, and the left quarter of my body, all that may be unarmed, and I shall let bind my left hand behind me, so that it shall not help me; and right so I shall do battle with you." When Sir Meliagraunce heard that, he started up on his legs, and said on high, "My lord, King Arthur, take heed to this proffer, for I will take it, and let him be disarmed and bound according unto his proffer." "What say ye," said King Arthur unto Sir Launcelot; "will ye abide by your proffer?" "Yea, my lord," said Sir Launcelot, "I will never go from that I have once said." Then the knights' porters of the field disarmed Sir Launcelot, first his head, and after his left arm, and his left side; and then they bound his left arm behind his back, without shield or any thing, and then were they put together. Wit ye well, there was many a lady and knight marvelled that Sir Launcelot would jeopard himself in such wise. Then Sir Meliagraunce came with his sword all on high, and Sir Launcelot showed him openly his bare head, and the bare left side; and when he weened to have smitten him upon the head, then lightly he avoided the left leg and the left side, and put his right hand and his sword to that stroke, and so put it aside with great sleight; then with great force, Sir Launcelot smote him upon the helmet such a buffet, that the stroke carved the head in two parts. Then there was no more to do, but he was drawn out of the field; and, at the instance of the knights of the Round Table, the King suffered him to be buried, and the mention made upon him, and for what cause he was slain. And then the King and the Queen made much of Sir Launcelot, and more he was cherished than ever he was before.

THE DIVINE COMEDY, HELL
Dante Alighieri (1265–1321)

At the outset, let us agree that reading the *Commedia* is no easy task. Dante himself recognized this when, in writing to a friend and patron, he said:

> The meaning of this work is not simple . . . for we obtain one meaning from the letter of it, and another from that which the letter signifies; and the first is called *literal,* but the other *allegorical* or *mystical.* . . .
>
> The subject of the whole work, then, taken in the literal sense is "the state of the soul after death straightforwardly affirmed," for the development of the whole work hinges on and about that. But, if, indeed, the work is taken *allegorically,* its subject is: "Man, as by good or ill deserts, in the exercise of his free choice, he becomes liable to rewarding or punishing justice."

On two scores, the rewards of reading the *Commedia* justify the effort. First, it represents the finest statement of the medieval synthesis that we have; it is comparable to Chartres Cathedral or the *Summa Theologica* of St. Thomas. Second, and more important, it presents one of the half-dozen very great insights into the nature and meaning of human life in all of literature or art. It is meaningful to us in the twentieth century not only as a great historical document, but as living literature.

Its form represents as tight a discipline as we know in literature, for it takes its shape around the number three. It is written in *terza rima,* a form preserved in the translations taken from the Hell and Paradiso as excerpts from those sections are given here.

Figure 14.3 Florentine school, *Allegorical Portrait of Dante,* ca. 1575–1585, 50″ × 47¼″. Samuel H. Kress Collection. National Gallery of Art, Washington, D.C. On the open book are inscribed the first forty-eight lines of Canto XXV of *Paradise* in which Dante yearns to return from exile to be honored by the Florentines. In the right background is the mountain of Purgatory, behind which is the divine glow of Paradise. With his right hand over the dome of Florence Cathedral, the poet tries to protect his beloved city from the flames of Hell.

It is written in three great sections: Hell, Purgatory, and Heaven (fig. 14.3). Within the first of these sections we find one introductory canto, followed by thirty-three more cantos, and in each of the following sections thirty-three cantos are to be found. The sum is the number one hundred, the perfect and complete number.

Insofar as its meaning is concerned, the great poem will speak for itself, aided by the notes. We must understand, however, that Dante accepts the idea that all of nature is in motion, following the laws, the love, and the wisdom of God. Of all the orders of being, humans alone have both free will and the potentiality of turning from the way of God. With free will comes the responsibility of choosing and accepting the consequences of choice. No one can say that they are the irresponsible victims of heredity or environment. With the gift of intellect and free will, each person must assume the full weight of making choices, and must, as well, accept the idea that the choices are important and that they do make a difference for others, and most particularly for oneself.

The translation was made by the twentieth-century writer and Dante scholar, Dorothy Sayers.

The translation of *Paradiso*, Canto 33 was made by the equally important Dante scholar, Barbara Reynolds, following the death of Dorothy Sayers.

The Greater Images

Dante in the *story* is always himself—the Florentine poet, philosopher, and politician, and the man who loved Beatrice. In the *allegory*, he is the image of every Christian sinner, and his pilgrimage is that which every soul must make, by one road or another, from the dark and solitary Wood of Error to the City of God.

Virgil is in the *story* the shade of the poet who, in the *Aeneid*, celebrated the origin and high destiny of the Roman Empire and its function in unifying the civilized world. In the Middle Ages he was looked upon as having been an unconscious prophet of Christianity and also (in popular tradition) as a great "White Magician," whose natural virtue gave him power among the dead. Dante's portrait of him has preserved traces of these medieval fancies, and also agrees very well with what we know of the gentle and charming characteristics of the real Virgil. In the *allegory*, Virgil is the image of Human Wisdom—the best that man can become in his own strength without the especial grace of God. He is the best of human philosophy, the best of human morality; he is also poetry and art, the best of human feeling and imagination. Virgil, as the image of these things, cannot himself enter Heaven or bring anyone else there (art and morality and philosophy cannot be made into substitutes for religion), but he can (and they can), under the direction of the Heavenly Wisdom, be used to awaken the soul to a realization of its own sinfulness, and can thereafter accompany and assist it towards that state of natural perfection in which it is again open to receive the immediate operation of Divine Grace.

Beatrice remains in the *story* what she was in real life: the Florentine girl whom Dante loved from the first moment that he saw her, and in whom he seemed (as is sometimes the case with lovers) to see Heaven's glory walking the earth bodily. Because, for him, she was thus in fact the vehicle of the Glory—the earthly vessel in which the divine experience was carried—she is, in the *allegory*, from time to time likened to, or equated with, those other "God-bearers": the Church, and Divine Grace in the Church; the Blessed Virgin; even Christ Himself. She is the image by which Dante perceives all these, and her function in the poem is to bring him to that state in which he is able to perceive them directly; at the end of the *Paradiso* the image of Beatrice is—not replaced by, but—taken up into the images, successively, of the Church Triumphant; of Mary, the historic and universal God-bearer; and of God, in whom Image and Reality are one and the same. Beatrice thus represents for every man that person—or, more generally that experience of the Notself—which by arousing his adoring love, has become for him the God-bearing image, the revelation of the presence of God.

Hell in the *story* is the place or condition of lost souls after death; it is pictured as a huge funnel-shaped pit, situated beneath the Northern Hemisphere and running down to the centre of the earth. In the *allegory*, it is the image of the deepening possibilities of evil within the soul. Similarly, the sinners who there remain fixed forever in the evil which they have obstinately chosen are also images of the perverted choice itself. For the *story*, they are historical or legendary personages, external to Dante (and to us); for the *allegory* they figure his (and our) disordered desires, seen and known to us as we plunge ever deeper into the hidden places of the self: every condemned sinner in the poem is thus the image of a self-condemned sin (actual or potential) in every man. Neither in the *story* nor in the *allegory* is Hell a place of punishment to which anybody is arbitrarily *sent*: it is the condition to which the soul reduces itself by a stubborn determination to evil, and in which it suffers the torment of its own perversions.

We must be careful to distinguish between Hell itself, taken literally, and the *vision of Hell* which is offered to Dante. Hell itself is not remedial; the dead who have chosen the "eternal exile" from God, and who thus experience the reality of their choice, cannot profit by that experience. In that sense, no living soul can enter Hell, since, however great the sin, repentance is always possible while there is life, even to the very moment of dying.[53] But the *vision of Hell*, which is remedial, is the soul's self-knowledge in all its evil potentialities—"the revelation of the nature of impenitent sin."[54]

Purgatory in the *story*, as in Catholic theology, is the place or condition of redeemed souls after death, and is imagined by Dante as a lofty mountain on an island in the Southern Hemisphere. On its seven encircling cornices, the souls are purged successively of the taint of the seven deadly sins, and so made fit to ascend into the presence of God in Paradise. In the *allegory*, it is the image of repentance, by which the soul purges the guilt of sin in *this* life; and, similarly, the blessed spirits who willingly embrace its purifying pains figure the motions of the soul, eagerly confessing and making atonement for its sins.

Paradise, in the same way, is, in the *story*, the place or condition, after death, of beatified souls in Heaven. Dante pictures it, first, under the figure of the ten Heavens of medieval astronomy and, secondly, under that of the Mystical Rose. He explains that, although the souls are shown as enjoying ascending degrees of bliss in the ten successive Heavens, all these are, in reality, one Heaven; nor is the bliss unequal, each soul being filled, according to its capacity, with all the joy it is able to experience. In the *allegory*, Paradise is the image of the soul in a state of grace, enjoying the foretaste of the Heaven which it knows to be its true home and city; and in the inhabitants of Paradise we may recognize the figure of the ascending stages by which it rises to the contemplation of the Beatific Vision.

---

53. Unless, indeed, the will is so hardened in sin that the power to repent is destroyed, in which case the condition of the soul, even in this world, is literally a "living hell."

54. See P.H. Wicksteed: *From Vita Nuova to Paradiso*, from which the last few words are quoted.

The Empire and the City. Throughout the poem, we come across various images of the Empire or the City (Florence, Rome, and other cities of Italy, as well as the City and Empire of Dis in Hell, and the Eternal City or Heavenly Rome in Paradise). All these may be taken as expressing, in one way or another, what today we should perhaps more readily think of as the Community. Indeed, the whole *allegory* may be interpreted politically, in the widest sense of the word, as representing the way of salvation, not only for the individual man, but for Man-in-community. Civilizations, as well as persons, need to know the Hell within them and purge their sins before entering into a state of Grace, Justice, and Charity and so becoming the City of God on earth.

Canto I

The Story

Dante finds that he has strayed from the right road and is lost in a Dark Wood. He tries to escape by climbing a beautiful Mountain, but is turned aside, first by a gambolling Leopard, then by a fierce Lion, and finally by a ravenous She-Wolf. As he is fleeing back into the Wood, he is stopped by the shade of Virgil, who tells him that he cannot hope to pass the Wolf and ascend the Mountain by that road. One day a Greyhound will come and drive the Wolf back to Hell; but the only course at present left open to Dante is to trust himself to Virgil, who will guide him by a longer way, leading through Hell and Purgatory. From there, a worthier spirit than Virgil (Beatrice) will lead him on to see the blessed souls in Paradise. Dante accepts Virgil as his "master, leader, and lord," and they set out together.

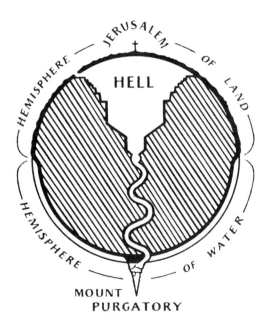

Midway this way of life we're bound upon,
  I woke to find myself in a dark wood,
  Where the right road was wholly lost and gone.

Ay me! how hard to speak of it—that rude   4
  And rough and stubborn forest! the mere breath
  Of memory stirs the old fear in the blood;

It is so bitter, it goes nigh to death;   7
  Yet there I gained such good, that, to convey
  The tale, I'll write what else I found therewith.

How I got into it I cannot say,   10
  Because I was so heavy and full of sleep
  When first I stumbled from the narrow way;

But when at last I stood beneath a steep   13
  Hill's side, which closed that valley's wandering maze
  Whose dread had pierced me to the heart-root deep,

Then I looked up, and saw the morning rays   16
  Mantle its shoulder from that planet bright
  Which guides men's feet aright on all their ways;

And this a little quieted the affright   19
  That lurking in my bosom's lake had lain
  Through the long horror of that piteous night.

And as a swimmer, panting, from the main   22
  Heaves safe to shore, then turns to face the drive
  Of perilous seas, and looks, and looks again,

So, while my soul yet fled, did I contrive   25
  To turn and gaze on that dread pass once more
  Whence no man yet came ever out alive.

Weary of limb I rested a brief hour,   28
  Then rose and onward through the desert hied,
  So that the fixed foot always was the lower;

And see! not far from where the mountain-side   31
  First rose, a Leopard, nimble and light and fleet,
  Clothed in a fine furred pelt all dapple-dyed,

Came gambolling out, and skipped before my feet,   34
  Hindering me so, that from the forthright line
  Time and again I turned to beat retreat.

The morn was young, and in his native sign   37
  The Sun climbed with the stars whose glitterings
  Attended on him when the Love Divine

---

l. 1: *midway:* i.e., at the age of 35, the middle point of man's earthly pilgrimage of three-score and ten years.

l. 17: *that planet bright:* the Sun. In medieval astronomy, the Earth was looked upon as being the centre of the universe, and the sun counted as a planet. In the *Comedy,* the Sun is often used as a figure for "the spiritual sun, which is God." (Dante: *Convivio,* iv. 12.)

l. 27: *whence no man yet came ever out alive:* Dante, as we shall see, is by no means "out" as yet; nor will he be, until he has passed through the "death unto sin."

l. 30: *so that the fixed foot always was the lower:* i.e., he was going uphill. In walking, there is always one fixed foot and one moving foot; in going uphill, the moving foot is brought *above,* and in going downhill *below,* the fixed foot.

l. 37: *in his native sign:* According to tradition the Sun was in the Zodiacal sign of Aries (the Ram) at the moment of the creation. The Sun is in Aries from 21 March to 21 April: therefore the "sweet season" is that of spring. Later, we shall discover that the day is Good Friday, and that the moon was full on the previous night. These indications do not precisely correspond to the actual Easter sky of 1300; Dante has merely described the astronomical phenomena typical of Eastertide.

First moved those happy, prime-created things: 40
    So the sweet season and the new-born day
    Filled me with hope and cheerful augurings

Of the bright beast so speckled and so gay;   43
    Yet not so much but that I fell to quaking
    At a fresh sight—a Lion in the way.

I saw him coming, swift and savage, making   46
    For me, head high, with ravenous hunger raving
    So that for dread the very air seemed shaking.

And next, a Wolf, gaunt with the famished craving   49
    Lodged ever in her horrible lean flank,
    The ancient cause of many men's enslaving;—

She was the worst—at that dread sight a blank   52
    Despair and whelming terror pinned me fast,
    Until all hope to scale the mountain sank.

Like one who loves the gains he has amassed,   55
    And meets the hour when he must lose his loot,
    Distracted in his mind and all aghast,

Even so was I, faced with that restless brute   58
    Which little by little edged and thrust me back,
    Back, to that place wherein the sun is mute.

Then, as I stumbled headlong down the track,   61
    Sudden a form was there, which dumbly crossed
    My path, as though grown voiceless from long lack

Of speech; and seeing it in that desert lost,   64
    "Have pity on me!" I hailed it as I ran,
    "Whate'er thou art—or very man, or ghost!"

It spoke: "No man, although I once was man;   67
    My parents' native land was Lombardy
    And both by citizenship were Mantuan.

Sub Julio born, though late in time, was I,   70
    And lived at Rome in good Augustus' days,
    When the false gods were worshipped ignorantly.

Poet was I, and tuned my verse to praise   73
    Anchises' righteous son, who sailed from Troy
    When Ilium's pride fell ruined down ablaze.

But thou—oh, why run back where fears destroy   76
    Peace? Why not climb the blissful mountain
      yonder,
    The cause and first beginning of all joy?"

"Canst thou be Virgil? thou that fount of splendour   79
    Whence poured so wide a stream of lordly
      speech?"
    Said I, and bowed my awe-struck head in wonder;

"Oh honour and light of poets all and each,   82
    Now let my great love stead me—the bent brow
    And long hours pondering all thy book can teach!

Thou art my master, and my author thou,   85
    From thee alone I learned the singing strain,
    The noble style, that does me honour now.

See there the beast that turned me back again—   88
    Save me from her, great sage—I fear her so,
    She shakes my blood through every pulse and
      vein."

"Nay, by another path thou needs must go   91
    If thou wilt ever leave this waste," he said,
    Looking upon me as I wept, "for lo!

The savage brute that makes thee cry for dread   94
    Lets no man pass this road of hers, but still
    Trammels him, till at last she lays him dead.

Vicious her nature is, and framed for ill;   97
    When crammed she craves more fiercely than
      before;
    Her raging greed can never gorge its fill.

With many a beast she mates, and shall with more,   100
    Until the Greyhound come, the Master-hound,
    And he shall slay her with a stroke right sore.

He'll not eat gold nor yet devour the ground;   103
    Wisdom and love and power his food shall be,
    His birthplace between Feltro and Feltro found;

Saviour he'll be to that low Italy   106
    For which Euryalus and Nisus died,
    Turnus and chaste Camilla, bloodily.

He'll hunt the Wolf through cities far and wide,   109
    Till in the end he hunt her back to Hell,
    Whence Envy first of all her leash untied.

But, as for thee, I think and deem it well   112
    Thou take me for thy guide, and pass with me
    Through an eternal place and terrible

Where thou shalt hear despairing cries, and see   115
    Long-parted souls that in their torments dire
    Howl for the second death perpetually.

---

l. 87: *the noble style:* Dante, in 1300, was already a poet of considerable reputation for his love-lyrics and philosophic odes, though he had not as yet composed any narrative verse directly modelled upon the *Aeneid*. When he says that he owes to Virgil the "*bello stilo* which has won him honour," he can scarcely be referring to the style of his own *prose* works, whether in Latin or Italian, still less to that of the as yet unwritten *Comedy*. Presumably he means that he had studied to imitate, in his poems written in the vernacular, the elegance, concise power, and melodious rhythms of the Virgilian line.

l. 105: *between Feltro and Feltro:* This is a much-debated line. If the Greyhound represents a political "saviour," it may mean that his birthplace lies between Feltre in Venetia and Montefeltro in Romagna (i.e., in the valley of the Po). But some commentators think that "feltro" is not a geographical name at all, but simply that of a coarse cloth (felt, or frieze); in which case Dante would be expecting salvation to come from among those who wear the robe of poverty, and have renounced "gold and ground"—i.e., earthly possessions. We should perhaps translate: "In cloth of frieze his people shall be found."

l. 106: *low Italy:* The Italian word is *umile*, humble, which may mean either "low-lying," as opposed to "high Italy" among the Alps, or "humiliated," with reference to the degradation to which the country had been brought. In either case, the classical allusions which follow show that Dante meant Rome.

l. 114: *an eternal place and terrible:* Hell.

l. 117: *the second death:* this might mean "cry for a second death to put an end to their misery," but more probably means "cry out because of the pains of Hell," in allusion to *Rev.* xx. 14.

---

ll. 63–64: *as though grown voiceless from long lack of speech:* i.e., the form is trying to speak to Dante, but cannot make itself heard. From the point of view of the *story*, I think this means that, being in fact that of a ghost, it cannot speak until Dante has established communication by addressing it first. *Allegorically,* we may take it in two ways: (1) on the historical level, it perhaps means that the wisdom and poetry of the classical age had been long neglected; (2) on the spiritual level, it undoubtedly means that Dante had sunk so deep into sin that the voice of reason, and even of poetry itself, had become faint and almost powerless to recall him.

l. 70: *sub Julio:* under Julius (Caesar). Virgil was born in 70 B.C. and had published none of his great poems before the murder of Julius in 41 B.C., so that he never enjoyed his patronage.

Next, thou shalt gaze on those who in the fire   118
    Are happy, for they look to mount on high,
    In God's good time, up to the blissful quire;

To which glad place, a worthier spirit than I   121
    Must lead thy steps, if thou desire to come,
    With whom I'll leave thee then, and say good-bye;

For the Emperor of that high Imperium   124
    Wills not that I, once rebel to His crown,
    Into that city of His should lead men home.

Everywhere is His realm, but there His throne,   127
    There is His city and exalted seat:
    Thrice-blest whom there He chooses for His own!"

Then I to him: "Poet, I thee entreat,   130
    By that great God whom thou didst never know,
    Lead on, that I may free my wandering feet

From these snares and from worse; and I will go   133
    Along with thee, St. Peter's Gate to find,
    And those whom thou portray'st suffering so."

So he moved on; and I moved on behind.   136

The Images

The Dark Wood is the image of Sin or Error—not so much of any specific act of sin or intellectual perversion as of that spiritual condition called "hardness of heart," in which sinfulness has so taken possession of the soul as to render it incapable of turning to God, or even knowing which way to turn.

The Mountain, which on the mystical level is the image of the Soul's Ascent to God, is thus on the moral level the image of Repentance, by which the sinner returns to God. It can be ascended directly from "the right road," but not from the Dark Wood, because there the soul's cherished sins have become, as it were, externalized, and appear to it like demons or "beasts" with a will and power of their own, blocking all progress. Once lost in the Dark Wood, a man can only escape by so descending into himself that he sees his sin, not as an external obstacle, but as the will to chaos and death within him (Hell). Only when he has "died to sin" can he repent and purge it. Mount Purgatory and the Mountain of Canto I are, therefore, really one and the same mountain, as seen on the far side, and on this side, of the "death unto sin."

The Beasts. These are the images of sin. They may be identified with Lust, Pride, and Avarice respectively, or with the sins of Youth, Manhood, and Age; but they are perhaps best thought of as the images of the three *types* of sin which, if not repented, land the soul in one or other of the three main divisions of Hell (*v*. Canto XI).

    The gay *Leopard* is the image of the self-indulgent sins—*Incontinence; the fierce *Lion,* of the violent sins—*Bestiality;* the *She-Wolf* of the malicious sins, which involve *Fraud.*

The Greyhound has been much argued about. I think it has both a historical and a spiritual significance. Historically, it is perhaps the image of some hoped-

for political saviour who should establish the just World-Empire. Spiritually, the Greyhound, which has the attributes of God ("wisdom, love, and power"), is probably the image of the reign of the Holy Ghost on earth—the visible Kingdom of God for which we pray in the Lord's Prayer (cf. *Purg.* xi. 7–9).

Canto II

The Story

Dante's attempts to climb the Mountain have taken the whole day and it is now Good Friday evening. Dante has not gone far before he loses heart and "begins to make excuse." To his specious arguments Virgil replies flatly: "This is mere cowardice"; and then tells how Beatrice, prompted by St. Lucy at the instance of the Virgin Mary herself, descended into Limbo to entreat him to go to Dante's rescue. Thus encouraged, Dante pulls himself together, and they start off again.

Day was departing and the dusk drew on,
    Loosing from labour every living thing
    Save me, in all the world; I—I alone—

Must gird me to the wars—rough travelling,   4
    And pity's sharp assault upon the heart—
    Which memory shall record, unfaltering;

Now, Muses, now, high Genius, do your part!   7
    And Memory, faithful scrivener to the eyes,
    Here show thy virtue, noble as thou art!

I soon began: "Poet—dear guide—'twere wise   10
    Surely, to test my powers and weigh their worth
    Ere trusting me to this great enterprise.

Thou sayest, the author of young Silvius' birth,   13
    Did to the world immortal, mortal go,
    Clothed in the body of flesh he wore on earth—

Granted; if Hell's great Foeman deigned to show   16
    To *him* such favour, seeing the vast effect,
    And what and who has destined issue—no,

That need surprise no thoughtful intellect,   19
    Since to Rome's fostering city and empery
    High Heaven had sealed him as the father-elect;

Both these were there established, verily,   22
    To found that place, holy and dedicate,
    Wherein great Peter's heir should hold his See;

So that the deed thy verses celebrate   25
    Taught him the road to victory, and bestowed
    The Papal Mantle in its high estate.

---

ll. 118–19: *those who in the fire are happy:* the redeemed in Purgatory.

l. 134: *St. Peter's Gate:* the gate by which redeemed souls are admitted to Purgatory (*Purg.* ix. 76 *sqq.*); not the gate of Heaven.

---

l. 7: Canto I forms, as it were a prologue to the whole *Divine Comedy*. The actual *Inferno* (Hell) begins with Canto II; and here we have the invocation which, in each of the three books, prefaces the journey to Hell, Purgatory, and Paradise respectively. It is addressed, in the classic manner, to the Muses, to Genius, and to Memory, the Mother of the Muses. (As the story proceeds, Dante will invoke higher, and still higher aid; till the final invocation towards the end of the *Paradiso*, is made to God, the "supreme light" Himself.)

l. 13: *the author of young Silvius' birth:* Aeneas; the allusion is to the sixth book of the *Aeneid*, which describes how Aeneas visits Hades and is told that he is to settle in Italy and so bring about the foundation of Rome, the seat both of the Empire and the Papacy. (See Chap. 9.)

l. 16: *Hell's great Foeman:* God.

Thither the Chosen Vessel, in like mode, 28
    Went afterward, and much confirmed thereby
    The faith that sets us on salvation's road.

But how should *I* go there? Who says so? Why? 31
    I'm not Aeneas, and I am not Paul!
    Who thinks me fit? Not others. And not I.

Say I submit, and go—suppose I fall 34
    Into some folly? Though I speak but ill,
    Thy better wisdom will construe it all."

As one who wills, and then unwills his will, 37
    Changing his mind with every changing whim,
    Till all his best intentions come to nil,

So I stood havering in that moorland dim, 40
    While through fond rifts of fancy oozed away
    The first quick zest that filled me to the brim.

"If I have grasped what thou dost seem to say," 43
    The shade of greatness answered, "these doubts breed
    From sheer black cowardice, which day by day

Lays ambushes for men, checking the speed 46
    Of honourable purpose in mid-flight,
    As shapes half-seen startle a shying steed.

Well then, to rid thee of this foolish fright, 49
    Hear why I came, and learn whose eloquence
    Urged me to take compassion on thy plight.

While I was with the spirits who dwell suspense, 52
    A Lady summoned me—so blest, so rare,
    I begged her to command my diligence.

Her eyes outshone the firmament by far 55
    As she began, in her own gracious tongue,
    Gentle and low, as tongues of angels are:

'O courteous Mantuan soul, whose skill in song 58
    Keeps green on earth a fame that shall not end
    While motion rolls the turning spheres along!

A friend of mine, who is not Fortune's friend, 61
    Is hard beset upon the shadowy coast;
    Terrors and snares his fearful steps attend,

Driving him back; yea, and I fear almost 64
    I have risen too late to help—for I was told
    Such news of him in Heaven—he's too far lost.

But thou—go thou! Lift up thy voice of gold; 67
    Try every needful means to find and reach
    And free him, that my heart may rest consoled.

Beatrice am I, who thy good speed beseech; 70
    Love that first moved me from the blissful place
    Whither I'd fain return, now moves my speech.

Lo! when I stand before my Lord's bright face 73
    I'll praise thee many a time to Him.' Thereon
    She fell on silence; I replied apace:

'Excellent lady, for whose sake alone 76
    The breed of men exceeds all things that dwell
    Closed in the heaven whose circles narrowest run

To do thy bidding pleases me so well 79
    That were't already done, I should seem slow;
    I know thy wish, and more needs not to tell.

Yet say—how can thy blest feet bear to know 82
    This dark road downward to the dreadful centre,
    From that wide room which thou dost yearn for so?'

'Few words will serve (if thou desire to enter 85
    Thus far into our mystery),' she said,
    'To tell thee why I have no fear to venture.

Of hurtful things we ought to be afraid, 88
    But of no others, truly, inasmuch
    As these have nothing to give cause for dread;

My nature, by God's mercy, is made such 91
    As your calamities can nowise shake,
    Nor these dark fires have any power to touch.

Heaven hath a noble Lady, who doth take 94
    Ruth of this man thou goest to disensnare
    Such that high doom is cancelled for her sake.

She summoned Lucy to her side, and there 97
    Exhorted her: "Thy faithful votary
    Needs thee, and I commend him to thy care."

Lucy, the foe to every cruelty, 100
    Ran quickly and came and found me in my place
    Beside ancestral Rachel, crying to me:

"How now, how now, Beatrice, God's true praise! 103
    No help for him who once they liegeman was,
    Quitting the common herd to win thy grace?

Dost thou not hear his piteous cries, alas? 106
    Dost thou not see death grapple him, on the river
    Whose furious rage no ocean can surpass?"

When I heard that, no living wight was ever 109
    So swift to seek his good or flee his fear
    As I from that high resting-place to sever

And speed me down, trusting my purpose dear 112
    To thee, and to thy golden rhetoric
    Which honours thee, and honours all who hear.'

She spoke; and as she turned from me the quick 115
    Tears starred the lustre of her eyes, which still
    Spurred on my going with a keener prick.

---

l. 28: *the Chosen Vessel:* St. Paul (*Acts* ix. 15). His vision of Hell is described in the fourth-century apocryphal book known as *The Apocalypse of Paul,* which Dante had evidently read. (See M.R. James: *The Apocryphal New Testament.*) There is probably also an allusion to 2 *Cor.* xii. 2.

l. 52: *the spirits who dwell suspense:* those of the virtuous pagans, who taste neither the bliss of salvation nor the pains of damnation, but dwell forever suspended between the two, in Limbo, the uppermost circle of Hell. (We shall meet them in Canto IV.)

l. 70: Of all this passage, Charles Williams says: "Beatrice has to ask [Virgil] to go; she cannot command him, though she puts her trust in his 'fair speech.' Religion itself cannot order poetry about; the grand art is wholly autonomous. . . . We should have been fortunate if the ministers of religion and poetry had always spoken to each other with such courtesy as these." (*The Figure of Beatrice,* p. 112.)

---

l. 78: *the heaven whose circles narrowest run:* The heaven of the Moon, the smallest and nearest to the Earth.

l. 91: *my nature, by God's mercy, is made such:* The souls of the blessed can still pity the self-inflicted misery of the wicked, but they can no longer be hurt or infected by it: "the action of pity will live for ever; the passion of pity will not." (C.S. Lewis: *The Great Divorce,* p. 111, where the subject is handled in a very illuminating way.)

l. 102: *ancestral Rachel:* Leah and Rachel, the two wives of Jacob, figure respectively the active and the contemplative life.

l. 107: *the river:* no literal river is intended; it is only a metaphor for human life.

Therefore I sought thee out, as was her will, 118
    And brought thee safe off from that beast of prey
    Which barred thee from the short road up the hill.

What ails thee then? Why, why this dull delay? 121
    Why bring so white a liver to the deed?
    Why canst thou find no manhood to display

When three such blessed ladies deign to plead 124
    Thy cause at that supreme assize of right,
    And when my words promise thee such good
      speed?''

As little flowers, which all the frosty night 127
    Hung pinched and drooping, lift their stalks and
      fan
    Their blossoms out, touched by the warm white
      light,

So did my fainting powers; and therewith ran 130
    Such good, strong courage round about my heart
    That I spoke boldly out like a free man:

"O blessed she that stooped to take my part! 133
    O courteous thou, to obey her true-discerning
    Speech, and thus promptly to my rescue start!

Fired by thy words, my spirit now is burning 136
    So to go on, and see this venture through.
    I find my former stout resolve returning.

Forward! henceforth there's but one will for two, 139
    Thou master, and thou leader and thou lord.''
    I spoke; he moved; so, setting out anew,

I entered on that savage path and froward. 142

The Images

Mary, The Blessed Virgin, whom the Church calls
Theotokos (Mother of God), is the historical and
universal God-bearer, of whom Beatrice, like any
other God-bearing image, is a particular type. Mary is
thus, in an especial and supreme manner, the vessel
of Divine Grace, as experienced in, and mediated
through, the redeemed creation. (Note that the name
of Mary, like the name of Christ, is never spoken in
Hell.)

Lucia (St. Lucy), a virgin martyr of the third century, is
the patron saint of those with weak sight, and chosen
here as the image of Illuminating Grace. Mary,
Beatrice, and Lucia are a threefold image of Divine
Grace in its various manifestations.

Virgil's Mission. Dante is so far gone in sin and error
that Divine Grace can no longer move him directly;
but there is still something left in him which is
capable of responding to the voice of poetry and of
human reason; and this, under Grace, may yet be
used to lead him back to God. In this profound and
beautiful image, Dante places Religion, on the one
hand, and human Art and Philosophy, on the other,
in their just relationship.

---

l. 120: *the short road up the hill:* this line shows clearly that the
"blissful Mountain" and Mount Purgatory are in reality one and
the same; since the Beasts prevent Dante from taking "the short
road," he is obliged to go by the long road—i.e., through Hell—
to find the mountain again on the other side of the world.

Canto III
The Story

*Arriving at the gate of Hell, the Poets read the inscription
upon its lintel. They enter and find themselves in the
Vestibule of Hell, where the Futile run perpetually after a
whirling standard. Passing quickly on, they reach the
river Acheron. Here the souls of all the damned come at
death to be ferried across by Charon, who refuses to take
the living body of Dante till Virgil silences him with a
word of power. While they are watching the departure of
a boatload of souls the river banks are shaken by an
earthquake so violent that Dante swoons away.*

UPPER HELL

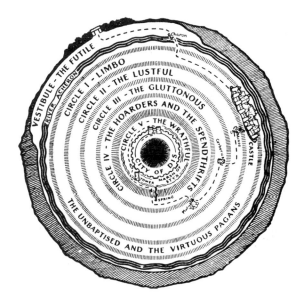

INCONTINENCE –
THE SINS OF THE LEOPARD

THROUGH ME THE ROAD TO THE CITY OF DESOLATION,
    THROUGH ME THE ROAD TO SORROWS DIUTURNAL,
    THROUGH ME THE ROAD AMONG THE LOST CREATION.

JUSTICE MOVED MY GREAT MAKER; GOD ETERNAL 4
    WROUGHT ME: THE POWER, AND THE UNSEARCHABLY
    HIGH WISDOM, AND THE PRIMAL LOVE SUPERNAL.

---

l. 1: *the City of Desolation* (*la citta dolente;* lit.: *the sorrowful
city*). Hell, like Heaven, is represented under the figure
sometimes of a city, and sometimes of an empire. Later on (Canto
IX) we shall come to the actual city itself, which has its
fortifications on the edge of the Sixth Circle, and comprises the
whole of Nether Hell. At present we are only in Upper Hell,
forming as it were the suburbs of the city and made up of the
Vestibule and the first five circles.

ll. 4–6: *power . . . wisdom supreme and primal love:* the
attributes of the Trinity. "If there is God, if there is freewill, then
man is able to choose the opposite of God. Power, Wisdom,
Love, gave man freewill; therefore Power, Wisdom, Love, created
the gate of hell and the possibility of hell." (Charles Williams:
The Figure of Beatrice, p. 113.)

NOTHING ERE I WAS MADE WAS MADE TO BE   7
  SAVE THINGS ETERNE, AND I ETERNE ABIDE;
  LAY DOWN ALL HOPE, YOU THAT GO IN BY ME.

These words, of sombre colour, I descried   10
  Writ on the lintel of a gateway; "Sir,
  This sentence is right hard for me," I cried.

And like a man of quick discernment: "Here   13
  Lay down all thy distrust," said he, "reject
  Dead from within thee every coward fear;

We've reached the place I told thee to expect,   16
  Where thou shouldst see the miserable race,
  Those who have lost the good of intellect."

He laid his hand on mine, and with a face   19
  So joyous that it comforted my quailing,
  Into the hidden things he led my ways.

Here sighing, and here crying, and loud railing   22
  Smote on the starless air, with lamentation,
  So that at first I wept to hear such wailing.

Tongues mixed and mingled, horrible execration,   25
  Shrill shrieks, hoarse groans, fierce yells and
    hideous blether
  And clapping of hands thereto, without cessation

Made tumult through the timeless night, that hither   28
  And thither drives in dizzying circles sped,
  As whirlwind whips the spinning sands together.

Whereat, with horror flapping round my head: 31
  "Master, what's this I hear? Who can they be,
  These people so distraught with grief?" I said.

And he replied: "The dismal company   34
  Of wretched spirits thus find their guerdon due
  Whose lives knew neither praise nor infamy;

They're mingled with that caitiff angel-crew   37
  Who against God rebelled not, nor to Him
  Were faithful, but to self alone were true;

Heaven cast them forth—their presence there would   40
  dim
  The light; deep Hell rejects so base a herd,
  Lest sin should boast itself because of them.

Then I: "But, Master, by what torment spurred   43
  Are they driven on to vent such bitter breath?"
  He answered: "I will tell thee in a word:

This dreary huddle has no hope of death,   46
  Yet its blind life trails on so low and crass
  That every other fate it envieth.

No reputation in the world it has,   49
  Mercy and doom hold it alike in scorn—
  Let us not speak of these; but look, and pass."

So I beheld, and lo! an ensign borne   52
  Whirling, that span and ran, as in disdain
  Of any rest; and there the folk forlorn

Rushed after it, in such an endless train,   55
  It never would have entered in my head
  There were so many men whom death had slain.

And when I'd noted here and there a shade   58
  Whose face I knew, I saw and recognized
  The coward spirit of the man who made

The great refusal; and that proof sufficed;   61
  Here was that rabble, here without a doubt,
  Whom God and whom His enemies despised.

This scum, who'd never lived, now fled about   64
  Naked and goaded, for a swarm of fierce
  Hornets and wasps stung all the wretched rout

Until their cheeks ran blood, whose slubbered   67
  smears,
  Mingled with brine, around their footsteps fell,
  Where loathly worms licked up their blood and
  tears.

Then I peered on ahead, and soon quite well   70
  Made out the hither bank of a wide stream,
  Where stood much people. "Sir," said I, "pray tell

Who these are, what their custom, why they seem   73
  So eager to pass over and be gone—
  If I may trust my sight in this pale gleam."

And he to me: "The whole shall be made known;   76
  Only have patience till we stay our feet
  On yonder sorrowful shore of Acheron."

Abashed, I dropped my eyes; and, lest unmeet   79
  Chatter should vex him, held my tongue, and so
  Paced on with him, in silence and discreet,

To the riverside. When from the far bank lo!   82
  A boat shot forth, whose white-haired boatman old
  Bawled as he came: "Woe to the wicked! Woe!

Never you hope to look on Heaven—behold!   85
  I come to ferry you hence across the tide
  To endless night, fierce fires and shramming cold.

And thou, the living man there! stand aside   88
  From these who are dead!" I budged not, but
  abode;
  So, when he saw me hold my ground, he cried:

"Away with thee! for by another road   91
  And other ferries thou shalt make the shore,
  Not here; a lighter skiff must bear thy load."

Then said my guide: "Charon, why wilt thou roar   94
  And chafe in vain? Thus it is willed where power
  And will are one; enough; ask thou no more."

This shut the shaggy mouth up of that sour   97
  Infernal ferryman of the livid wash,
  Only his flame-ringed eyeballs rolled a-glower.

---

l. 8: *things eterne:* In Canto XXXIV Dante tells how Hell was made when Satan fell from Heaven: it was created "for the devil and his angels" (*Matt.* XXV. 41) and before it nothing was made except the "eternal things," i.e., the Angels and the Heavens.

l. 9: *lay down all hope:* For the soul that literally enters Hell there is no return, nor any passage to Purgatory and repentance. Dante is naturally disturbed (l. 12) by this warning. But what he is entering upon, while yet in this life, is not Hell but the vision of Hell, and for him there is a way out, provided he keeps his hope and faith. Accordingly, Virgil enjoins him (ll. 14–15) to reject doubt and fear.

l. 18: *the good of intellect:* In the *Convivio* Dante quotes Aristotle as saying: "truth is the good of the intellect." What the lost souls have lost is not the intellect itself, which still functions mechanically, but the *good* of the intellect: i.e., the knowledge of God, who is Truth. (For Dante, as for Aquinas, "intellect" does not mean what we call, colloquially, "braininess": it means the whole "reasonable soul" of man.)

l. 61: *the great refusal:* Probably Celestine V, who, in 1294, at the age of 80, was made Pope, but resigned the papacy five months later. His successor was Pope Boniface VIII, to whom Dante attributed many of the evils which had overtaken the Church.

ll. 91–92: *another road and other ferries:* souls destined for Heaven never cross Acheron; they assemble at the mouth of Tiber and are taken in a boat piloted by an angel to Mount Purgatory at the Antipodes (*Purg,* ii). Charon recognizes that Dante is a soul in Grace (see ll. 127–29).

But those outwearied, naked souls—how gash 100
And pale they grew, chattering their teeth for
dread,
When first they felt his harsh tongue's cruel lash.

God they blaspheme, blaspheme their parents' bed, 103
The human race, the place, the time, the blood,
The seed that got them, and the womb that bred;

Then, huddling hugger-mugger, down they scud, 106
Dismally wailing, to the accursed strand
Which waits for every man that fears not God.

Charon, his eyes red like a burning brand, 109
Thumps with his oar the lingerers that delay,
And rounds them up, and beckons with his hand.

And as, by one and one, leaves drift away 112
In autumn, till the bough from which they fall
Sees the earth strewn with all its brave array,

So, from the bank there, one by one, drop all 115
Adam's ill seed, when signalled off the mark,
As drops the falcon to the falconer's call.

Away they're borne across the waters dark, 118
And ere they land that side the stream, anon
Fresh troops this side come flocking to embark.

Then said my courteous master: "See, my son, 121
All those that die beneath God's righteous ire
From every country come here every one.

They press to pass the river, for the fire 124
Of heavenly justice stings and spurs them so
That all their fear is changed into desire;

And by this passage, good souls never go; 127
Therefore, if Charon chide thee, do thou look
What this may mean—'tis not so hard to know."

When he thus said, the dusky champaign shook 130
So terribly that, thinking on the event,
I feel the sweat pour off me like a brook.

The sodden ground belched wind, and through the 133
rent
Shot the red levin, with a flash and sweep
That robbed me of my wits, incontinent;

And down I fell, as one that swoons on sleep. 136

The Images

Hell-Gate. High and wide and without bars (*Inf.* viii.
126), the door "whose threshold is denied to none"
(*Inf.* xiv. 87) always waits to receive those who are
astray in the Dark Wood. Anyone may enter if he so
chooses, but if he does, he must abandon hope,
since it leads nowhere but to the *Città Dolente,* the
City of Desolation. In the *story,* Hell is filled with the
souls of those who died with their wills set to enter
by that gate; in the *allegory,* these souls are the
images of sin in the self or in society.

The Vestibule was presumably suggested to Dante by
the description in *Aeneid* vi. (where, however, it is
tenanted by rather a different set of people). It does
not, I think, occur in any previous Christian
eschatology. Heaven and Hell being states in which

choice is permanently fixed, there must also be a
state in which the refusal of choice is itself fixed,
since to refuse choice is in fact to choose indecision.
The Vestibule is the abode of the weather-cock
mind, the vague tolerance which will neither
approve nor condemn, the cautious cowardice for
which no decision is ever final. The spirits rush
aimlessly after the aimlessly whirling banner, stung
and goaded, as of old, by the thought that, in doing
anything definite whatsoever, they are missing doing
something else.

Acheron, "the joyless," first of the great rivers of Hell
whose names Dante took from Virgil and Virgil from
Homer.

Charon, the classical ferryman of the dead. Most of the
monstrous organisms by which the functions of Hell
are discharged are taken from Greek and Roman
mythology. They are neither devils nor damned
souls, but the images of perverted appetites,
presiding over the circles appropriate to their
natures.

Canto IV

The Story

*Recovering from his swoon, Dante finds himself across
Acheron and on the edge of the actual Pit of Hell. He
follows Virgil into the First Circle—the Limbo where the
Unbaptized and the Virtuous Pagans dwell "suspended,"
knowing no torment save exclusion from the positive bliss
of God's presence. Virgil tells him of Christ's Harrowing of
Hell, and then shows him the habitation of the great men
of antiquity—poets, heroes, and philosophers.*

A heavy peal of thunder came to waken me
Out of the stunning slumber that had bound me,
Startling me up as though rude hands had shaken me.

I rose, and cast my rested eyes around me, 4
Gazing intent to satisfy my wonder
Concerning the strange place wherein I found me.

Hear truth: I stood on the steep brink whereunder 7
Runs down the dolorous chasm of the Pit,
Ringing with infinite groans like gathered thunder.

Deep, dense, and by no faintest glimmer lit 10
It lay, and though I strained my sight to find
Bottom, not one thing could I see in it.

"Down must we go, to that dark world and blind," 13
The poet said, turning on me a bleak
Blanched face; "I will go first—come thou
behind."

---

l. 126: *all their fear is changed into desire:* This is another of the
important passages in which Dante emphasizes that Hell is the
soul's choice. The damned fear it and long for it, as in this life a
man may hate the sin which makes him miserable, and yet
obstinately seek and wallow in it.

---

l. 7: *I stood on the steep brink:* It is disputed how Dante passed
Acheron; the simplest explanation is that Charon, obedient to
Virgil's "word of power," ferried him across during his swoon.
Technically speaking, Dante had to describe a passage by boat in
Canto VIII, and did not want to anticipate his effects; I think,
however, he had also an allegorical reason for omitting the
description here (see Canto VII. *Images: Path down Cliff*). Note
that the "peal of thunder" in l. 1 is not that which followed the
lightning-flash at the end of Canto III, but (l. 9) the din issuing
from the mouth of the Pit—an orchestra of discord, here blended
into one confused roar, which, resolved into its component
disharmonies, will accompany us to the bottom circle of Hell.

Then I, who had marked the colour of his cheek: 16
  "How can I go, when even thou art white
  For fear, who art wont to cheer me when I'm
    weak?"

But he: "Not so; the anguish infinite   19
  They suffer yonder paints my countenance
  With pity, which thou takest for affright;

Come, we have far to go; let us advance."   22
  So, entering, he made me enter, where
  The Pit's first circle makes circumference.

We heard no loud complaint, no crying there,   25
  No sound of grief except the sound of sighing
  Quivering for ever through the eternal air;

Grief, not for torment, but for loss undying,   28
  By women, men, and children sighed for so,
  Sorrowers thick—thronged, their sorrows
    multiplying.

Then my good guide: "Thou dost not ask me who   31
  These spirits are," said he, "whom thou
    perceivest?
  Ere going further, I would have thee know

They sinned not; yet their merit lacked its chiefest   34
  Fulfilment, lacking baptism, which is
  The gateway to the faith which thou believest;

Or, living before Christendom, their knees   37
  Paid not aright those tributes that belong
  To God; and I myself am one of these.

For such defects alone—no other wrong—   40
  We are lost; yet only by this grief offended:
  That, without hope, we ever live, and long."

Grief smote my heart to think, as he thus ended,   43
  What souls I knew, of great and sovran
  Virtue, who in that Limbo dwelt suspended.

"Tell me, sir—tell me, Master," I began   46
  (In hope some fresh assurance to be gleaning
  Of our sin-conquering Faith), "did any man

By his self-merit, or on another leaning,   49
  Ever fare forth from hence and come to be
  Among the blest?" He took my hidden meaning.

"When I was newly in this state," said he,   52
  "I saw One come in majesty and awe,
  And on His head were crowns of victory.

Our great first father's spirit He did withdraw,   55
  And righteous Abel, Noah who built the ark,
  Moses who gave and who obeyed the Law,

King David, Abraham the Patriarch,   58
  Israel with his father and generation,
  Rachel, for whom he did such deeds of mark,

With many another of His chosen nation;   61
  These did He bless; and know, that ere that day
  No human soul had ever seen salvation."

---

l. 53: *I saw One come:* The episode, based upon I *Peter* iii. 19, of Christ's descent into Limbo to rescue the souls of the patriarchs (the "Harrowing of Hell") was a favourite subject of medieval legend and drama. The crucifixion is reckoned as having occurred in A.D. 34, when Virgil had been dead fifty-three years. Note that the name of Christ is never spoken in Hell—He is always referred to by some periphrasis.

l. 55: *our great first father:* Adam.

While he thus spake, we still made no delay,   64
  But passed the wood—I mean, the wood (as
    'twere)
  Of souls ranged thick as trees. Being now some
    way—

Not far—from where I'd slept, I saw appear   67
  A light, which overcame the shadowy face
  Of gloom, and made a glowing hemisphere.

'Twas yet some distance on, yet I could trace   70
  So much as brought conviction to my heart
  That persons of great honour held that place.

"O thou that honour'st every science and art,   73
  Say, who are these whose honour gives them claim
  To different customs and a sphere apart?"

And he to me: "Their honourable name,   76
  Still in thy world resounding as it does,
  Wins here from Heaven the favour due to fame."

Meanwhile I heard a voice that cried out thus: 79
  "Honour the most high poet! his great shade,
  Which was departed, is returned to us."

It paused there, and was still; and lo! there made   82
  Toward us, four mighty shadows of the dead,
  Who in their mien nor grief nor joy displayed.

"Mark well the first of these," my master said,   85
  "Who in his right hand bears a naked sword
  And goes before the three as chief and head;

Homer is he, the poets' sovran lord;   88
  Next, Horace comes, the keen satirical;
  Ovid the third; and Lucan afterward.

Because I share with these that honourable   91
  Grand title the sole voice was heard to cry
  They do me honour, and therein do well."

Thus in their school assembled I, even I,   94
  Looked on the lords of loftiest song, whose style
  O'er all the rest goes soaring eagle-high.

When they had talked together a short while   97
  They all with signs of welcome turned my way,
  Which moved my master to a kindly smile;

And greater honour yet they did me—yea,   100
  Into their fellowship they deigned invite
  And make me sixth among such minds as they.

So we moved slowly onward toward the light   103
  In talk 'twere as unfitting to repeat
  Here, as to speak there was both fit and right.

And presently we reached a noble seat—   106
  A castle, girt with seven high walls around,
  And moated with a goodly rivulet

O'er which we went as though upon dry ground;   109
  With those wise men I passed the sevenfold gate
  Into a fresh green meadow, where we found

Persons with grave and tranquil eyes, and great   112
  Authority in their carriage and attitude,
  Who spoke but seldom and in voice sedate.

So here we walked aside a little, and stood   115
  Upon an open eminence, lit serene
  And clear, whence one and all might well be
    viewed.

---

l. 106: *a noble seat:* The scene is, I think, a medievalized version of the Elysian Fields, surrounded by "many-watered Eridanus." (*Aen.* vi. 659.) Detailed allegorical interpretations of the seven gates, walls, etc., have no great value.

Plain in my sight on the enamelled green   118
   All those grand spirits were shown me one by
     one—
   It thrills my heart to think what I have seen!

I saw Electra, saw with her anon   121
   Hector, Aeneas, many a Trojan peer,
   And hawk-eyed Caesar in his habergeon;

I saw Camilla and bold Penthesilea,   124
   On the other hand; Latinus on his throne
   Beside Lavinia his daughter dear;

Brutus, by whom proud Tarquin was o'erthrown,   127
   Marcia, Cornelia, Julia, Lucrece—and
   I saw great Saladin, aloof, alone.

Higher I raised my brows and further scanned,   130
   And saw the Master of the men who know
   Seated amid the philosophic band;

All do him honour and deep reverence show;   133
   Socrates, Plato, in the nearest room
   To him; Diogenes, Thales and Zeno,

Democritus, who held that all things come   136
   By chance; Empedocles, Anaxagoras wise,
   And Heraclitus, him that wept for doom;

Dioscorides, who named the qualities,   139
   Tully and Orpheus, Linus, and thereby
   Good Seneca, well-skilled to moralize;

Euclid the geometrician, Ptolemy,   142
   Galen, Hippocrates, and Avicen,
   Averroës who made the commentary—

Nay, but I tell not all that I saw then;   145
   The long theme drives me hard, and everywhere
   The wondrous truth outstrips my staggering pen.

The group of six dwindles to two; we fare   148
   Forth a new way, I and my guide withal,
   Out from that quiet to the quivering air,

And reach a place where nothing shines at all.   151

The Images

After those who refused choice come those without
   opportunity of choice. They could not, that is,
   choose Christ; they could, and did choose human
   virtue, and for that they have their reward. (Pagans
   who chose evil by their own standards are judged by
   these standards—cf. *Rom.* ii. 8–15—and are found
   lower down.) Here again, the souls "have what they
   chose"; they enjoy that kind of after-life which they
   themselves imagined for the virtuous dead; their
   failure lay in not imagining better. They are lost (as
   Virgil says later, *Purg* vii. 8) because they "had not
   faith"—primarily the Christian Faith, but also, more
   generally, faith in the nature of things. The *allegory*
   is clear: it is the weakness of Humanism to fall short
   in the imagination of ecstasy; at its best it is noble,

reasonable, and cold, and however optimistic about a
balanced happiness in this world, pessimistic about a
rapturous eternity. Sometimes wistfully aware that
others claim the experience of this positive bliss, the
Humanist can neither accept it by faith, embrace it
by hope, nor abandon himself to it in charity. Dante
discusses the question further in the *Purgatory* (esp.
Cantos VII and XXII) and makes his full doctrine
explicit in *Paradise*, Cantos XIX–XX.

Canto V

The Story

*Dante and Virgil descend from the First Circle to the
Second (the first of the Circles of Incontinence). On the
threshold sits Minos, the judge of Hell, assigning the souls
to their appropriate places of torment. His opposition is
overcome by Virgil's word of power, and the Poets enter
the Circle, where the souls of the Lustful are tossed for
ever upon a howling wind. After Virgil has pointed out a
number of famous lovers, Dante speaks to the shade of
Francesca da Rimini, who tells him her story.*

From the first circle thus I came descending
   To the second, which, in narrower compass
     turning,
   Holds greater woe, with outcry loud and rending.

There in the threshold, horrible and girning,   4
   Grim Minos sits, holding his ghastly session,
   And, as he girds him, sentencing and spurning;

For when the ill soul faces him, confession   7
   Pours out of it till nothing's left to tell;
   Whereon that connoisseur of all transgression

Assigns it to its proper place in hell,   10
   As many grades as he would have it fall,
   So oft he belts him round with his own tail.

Before him stands a throng continual;   13
   Each comes in turn to abye the fell arraign;
   They speak—they hear—they're whirled down one
     and all.

"Ho! thou that comest to the house of pain,"   16
   Cried Minos when he saw me, the appliance
   Of his dread powers suspending, "think again

How thou dost go, in whom is thy reliance;   19
   Be not deceived by the wide open door!"
   Then said my guide: "Wherefore this loud
     defiance?

Hinder not thou his fated way; be sure   22
   Hindrance is vain; thus it is willed where will
   And power are one; enough; ask now no more."

And now the sounds of grief begin to fill   25
   My ear; I'm come where cries of anguish smite
   My shrinking sense, and lamentation shrill—

---

l. 121: *Electra etc.:* Pride of place is given to the Trojans,
founders of the Roman line; (Julius) Caesar is grouped with
them as a descendant of Aeneas.

l. 129: *Saladin:* His inclusion here, along with Lucan, Averroes,
and other A.D. personages who were not, strictly speaking,
without opportunity of choice, perhaps tacitly indicates Dante's
opinion about all those who, though living in touch with
Christianity and practicing all the moral virtues, find themselves
sincerely unable to accept the Christian revelation.

l. 131: *the Master of the men who know:* Aristotle.

---

l. 6: *as he girds him, sentencing:* as Dante explains in ll. 11–12,
Minos girds himself so many times with his tail to indicate the
number of the circle to which each soul is to go.

A place made dumb of every glimmer of light, 28
    Which bellows like tempestuous ocean birling
    In the batter of a two-way wind's buffet and fight.

The blast of hell that never rests from whirling 31
    Harries the spirits along in the sweep of its swath,
    And vexes them, for ever beating and hurling.

When they are borne to the rim of the ruinous path 34
    With cry and wail and shriek they are caught by
      the gust,
    Railing and cursing the power of the Lord's wrath.

Into this torment carnal sinners are thrust, 37
    So I was told—the sinners who make their reason
    Bond thrall under the yoke of their lust.

Like as the starlings wheel in the wintry season 40
    In wide and clustering flocks wing-borne, wind-
      borne,
    Even so they go, the souls who did this treason,

Hither and thither, and up and down, outworn, 43
    Hopeless of any rest—rest, did I say?
    Of the least minishing of their pangs forlorn.

And as the cranes go chanting their harsh lay, 46
    Across the sky in long procession trailing,
    So I beheld some shadows borne my way,

Driven on the blast and uttering wail on wailing; 49
    Wherefore I said: "O Master, art thou able
    To name these spirits thrashed by the black wind's
      flailing?"

"Among this band," said he, "whose name and fable 52
    Thou seek'st to know, the first who yonder flies
    Was empress of many tongues, mistress of Babel.

She was so broken to lascivious vice 55
    She licensed lust by law, in hopes to cover
    Her scandal of unnumbered harlotries.

This was Semiramis; 'tis written of her 58
    That she was wife to Ninus and heiress, too,
    Who reigned in the land the Soldan now rules
      over.

Lo! she that slew herself for love, untrue 61
    To Sychaeus' ashes. Lo! tost on the blast,
    Voluptuous Cleopatra, whom love slew.

Look, look on Helen, for whose sake rolled past 64
    Long evil years. See great Achilles yonder,
    Who warred with love, and that war was his last.

See Paris, Tristram see!" And many—oh, wonder 67
    Many—a thousand more, he showed by name
    And pointing hand, whose life love rent asunder.

And when I had heard my Doctor tell the fame 70
    Of all those knights and ladies of long ago,
    I was pierced through with pity, and my head
      swam.

---

l. 28: *a place made dumb of every glimmer of light*—(cf. Canto
I. 60, "wherein the sun is mute"): Nevertheless, Dante is able to
see the spirits. This is only one of many passages in which the
poet conveys to us that the things he perceives during his
journey are not perceived altogether by the mortal senses, but
after another mode. (In *Purg*, xxi. 29, Virgil explains to another
spirit that Dante "could not come alone, because he does not see
after our manner, wherefore I was brought forth from Hell to
guide him.") So, in the present case, Dante recognizes that the
darkness is total, although he can see in the dark.

l. 61: *she that slew herself for love:* Dido.

"Poet," said I, "fain would I speak those two 73
    That seem to ride as light as any foam,
    And hand in hand on the dark wind drifting go."

And he replied: "Wait till they nearer roam, 76
    And thou shalt see; summon them to thy side
    By the power of the love that leads them, and they
      will come."

So, as they eddied past on the whirling tide, 79
    I raised my voice: "O souls that wearily rove,
    Come to us, speak to us—if it be not denied."

And as desire wafts homeward dove with dove 82
    To their sweet nest, on raised and steady wing
    Down-dropping through the air, impelled by love,

So these from Dido's flock came fluttering 85
    And dropping toward us down the cruel wind,
    Such power was in my affectionate summoning.

"O living creature, gracious and so kind, 88
    Coming through this black air to visit us,
    Us, who in death the globe incarnadined,

Were the world's King our friend and might we thus 91
    Entreat, we would entreat Him for thy peace,
    That pitiest so our pangs dispiteous!

Hear all thou wilt, and speak as thou shalt please, 94
    And we will gladly speak with thee and hear,
    While the winds cease to howl, as they now cease.

There is a town upon the sea-coast, near 97
    Where Po with all his streams comes down to rest
    In ocean; I was born and nurtured there.

---

l. 88: *O living creature:* The speaker is Francesca da Rimini.
Like many of the personages in the *Comedy,* she does not
directly name herself, but gives Dante particulars about her
birthplace and history which enable him to recognize her. She
was the daughter of Guido Vecchio di Polenta of Ravenna, and
aunt to Guido Novello di Polenta, who was Dante's friend and
host during the latter years of his life; so that her history was of
topical interest to Dante's readers. For political reasons, she was
married to the deformed Gianciotto, son of Malatesta da
Verrucchio, lord of Rimini, but fell in love with his handsome
younger brother Paolo, who became her lover. Her husband,
having one day surprised them together, stabbed them both to
death (1285).

l. 94: *hear all thou wilt:* Tender and beautiful as Dante's
handling of Francesca is, he has sketched her with a deadly
accuracy. All the good is there; the charm, the courtesy, the
instant response to affection, the grateful eagerness to please; but
also all the evil; the easy yielding, the inability to say No, the
intense self-pity.

Of this, the most famous episode in the whole *Comedy,*
Charles Williams writes: "It is always quoted as an example of
Dante's tenderness. So, no doubt, it is, but it is not here for that
reason. . . . It has a much more important place; it presents the
first tender, passionate, and half-excusable consent of the soul to
sin. . . . [Dante] so manages the description, he so heightens the
excuse, that the excuse reveals itself as precisely the sin . . . the
persistent parleying with the occasion of sin, the sweet
prolonged laziness of love, is the first surrender of the soul to
Hell—small but certain. The formal sin here is the adultery of
the two lovers; the poetic sin is their shrinking from the adult
love demanded of them, and their refusal of the opportunity of
glory," (*The Figure of Beatrice,* p. 118).

l. 97: *a town upon the sea-coast:* Ravenna.

Love, that so soon takes hold in the gentle breast,   100
    Took this lad with the lovely body they tore
    From me; the way of it leaves me still distrest.

Love, that to no loved heart remits love's score,   103
    Took me with such great joy of him, that see!
    It holds me yet and never shall leave me more.

Love to a single death brought him and me;   106
    Cain's place lies waiting for our murderer now."
    These words came wafted to us plaintively.

Hearing those wounded souls, I bent my brow   109
    Downward, and thus bemused I let time pass,
    Till the poet said at length: "What thinkest thou?"

When I could answer, I began: "Alas!   112
    Sweet thoughts how many, and desire how great,
    Brought down these twain unto the dolorous
        pass!"

And then I turned to them: "Thy dreadful fate,   115
    Francesca, makes me weep, it so inspires
    Pity," said I, "and grief compassionate.

Tell me—in that time of sighing-sweet desires,   118
    How, and by what, did love his power disclose
    And grant you knowledge of your hidden fires?"

Then she to me: "The bitterest woe of woes   121
    Is to remember in our wretchedness
    Old happy times; and this thy Doctor knows:

Yet, if so dear desire thy heart possess   124
    To know that root of love which wrought our fall,
    I'll be as those who weep and who confess.

One day we read for pastime how in thrall   127
    Lord Lancelot lay to love, who loved the Queen;
    We were alone—we thought no harm at all.

As we read on, our eyes met now and then,   130
    And to our cheeks the changing colour started,
    But just one moment overcame us—when

We read of the smile, desired of lips long-thwarted,   133
    Such smile, by such a lover kissed away,
    He that may never more from me be parted

Trembling all over, kissed my mouth. I say   136
    The book was Galleot, Galleot the complying
    Ribald who wrote; we read no more that day."

---

l. 102: *the way of it leaves me still distrest:* Either (1) the way of the murder, because the lovers were killed in the very act of sin and so had no time for repentance; or (2) the way in which their love came about. The story went that Paolo was sent to conduct the marriage negotiations, and that Francesca was tricked into consenting by being led to suppose that he, and not Gianciotto, was to be her bridegroom. In the same way, in the Arthurian romances, Queen Guinevere falls in love with Launcelot when he is sent to woo her on King Arthur's behalf; and it is this parallel which makes the tale of Launcelot so poignant for her and Paolo.

l. 107: *Cain's place:* Caina, so called after Cain; the first ring of the lowest circle in Hell, where lie those who were treacherous to their own kindred.

l. 123: *thy Doctor:* Virgil (see l. 70). Dante is probably thinking of Aeneas' words to Dido: *infandum, regina, jubes renovare dolorem* . . . (O queen, thou dost bid me renew an unspeakable sorrow . . .), *Aeneid* ii. 3.

l. 137: *the book was Galleot:* In the romance of *Launcelot du Lac,* Galleot (or Galehalt) acted as intermediary between Launcelot and Guinevere, and so in the Middle Ages his name, like that of Pandarus in the tale of *Troilus and Cressida,* became a synonym for a go-between. The sense of the passage is: "The book was a pander and so was he who wrote it."

While the one spirit thus spoke, the other's crying   139
    Wailed on me with a sound so lamentable,
    I swooned for pity like as I were dying.

And, as a dead man falling, down I fell.   142

The Images

The Circles of Incontinence. This and the next three circles are devoted to those who sinned less by deliberate choice of evil than by failure to make resolute choice of the good. Here are the sins of self-indulgence, weakness of will, and easy yielding to appetite—the "sins of the Leopard."

The Lustful. The image here is sexual, though we need not confine the *allegory* to the sin of unchastity. Lust is a type of *shared* sin; at its best, and so long as it remains a sin of incontinence only, there is mutuality in it and exchange: although, in fact, mutual indulgence only serves to push both parties along the road to Hell, it is not, in intention, wholly selfish. For this reason Dante, with perfect orthodoxy, rates it as the least hateful of the deadly sins. (Sexual sins in which love and mutuality have no part find their place far below.)

Minos, a medievalized version of the classical Judge of the Underworld (see *Aen.* vi. 432). He may image an accusing conscience. The souls are damned on their own confession, for, Hell being the place of self-knowledge in sin, there can be no more self-deception here. (Similarly, even in the circles of Fraud, all the shades tell Dante the truth about themselves; this is poetically convenient, but, given this conception of Hell, it must be so.) The *literally* damned, having lost "the good of the intellect," cannot profit by their self-knowledge; *allegorically,* for the living soul, this vision of the Hell in the self is the preliminary to repentance and restoration.

The Black Wind. As the lovers drifted into self-indulgence and were carried away by their passions, so now they drift for ever. The bright, voluptuous sin is now seen *as it is*—a howling darkness of helpless discomfort. (The "punishment" for sin is simply the sin itself, experienced without illusion—though Dante does not work this out with mathematical rigidity in every circle.)

Canto VI

The Story

Dante now finds himself in the Third Circle, where the Gluttonous lie wallowing in the mire, drenched by perpetual rain and mauled by the three-headed dog Cerberus. After Virgil has quieted Cerberus by throwing earth into his jaws, Dante talks to the shade of Ciacco, a Florentine, who prophesies some of the disasters which are about to befall Florence, and tells him where he will find certain other of their fellow-citizens. Virgil tells Dante what the condition of the spirits will be, after the Last Judgment.

Canto VII

The Story

At the entrance to the Fourth Circle, the poets are opposed by Pluto, and Virgil is again obliged to use a "word of power." In this circle, the Hoarders and the Spendthrifts roll huge rocks against one another, and here Virgil explains the nature and working of Luck (or Fortune).

Then, crossing the circle, they descend the cliff to the Marsh of Styx, which forms the Fifth Circle and contains the Wrathful. Skirting its edge, they reach the foot of a tower.

Canto VIII

The Story

From the watch-tower on the edge of the marsh a beacon signals to the garrison of the City of Dis that Dante and Virgil are approaching, and a boat is sent to fetch them. Phlegyas ferries them across Styx. On the way they encounter Filippo Argenti, one of the Wrathful, who is recognized by Dante and tries to attack him. They draw near to the red-hot walls of the City and after a long circuit disembark at the gate. Virgil parleys with the Fallen Angels who are on guard there, but they slam the gate in his face. The two poets are obliged to wait for Divine assistance.

Canto IX

The Story

Dante, alarmed by Virgil's anxiety, tactfully inquires of him whether he really knows the way through Hell, and gets a reassuring answer. The Furies appear and threaten to unloose Medusa. A noise like thunder announces the arrival of a Heavenly Messenger, who opens the gates of Dis and rebukes the demons. When he has departed, the Poets enter the City and find themselves in a great plain covered with the burning tombs of the Heretics.

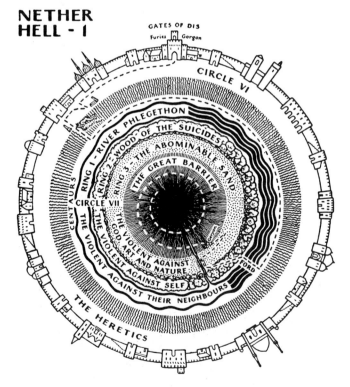

NETHER HELL - I

**HERESY : VIOLENCE —
THE SINS OF THE LION**

Seeing my face, and what a coward colour
  It turned when he came back, my guide was quick
  To put away his own unwonted pallor.

He stood and leaned intent, as who should prick   4
  His ear to hear, for far one could not see,
  So black the air was, and the fog so thick.

"Nay, somehow we must win this fight," said he;   7
  "If not . . . That great self-proffered aid is lent;
  But oh! how long his coming seems to be!"

I saw too clearly how his first intent   10
  Was cloaked by what came after; what he said
  Was not what he'd designed, but different.

But none the less his speech increased my dread—   13
  For maybe I pieced out the broken phrase
  To a worse ending than was in his head.

"Did any ever, descending from that place   16
  Where loss of hope remains their only woe,
  Thread to its depth this hollow's dreary maze?"

I put this question. He replied: "Although   19
  'Tis rare that one of us should come this way
  Or undertake the journey I now go,

Yet once before I made it, truth to say,   22
  Conjured by cruel Erichtho, she whose spell
  Wont to call back the shades to their dead clay.

I was not long stripped of my mortal shell   25
  When she compelled me pass within yon wall
  To fetch a spirit from Judas' circle of Hell;

That is the deepest, darkest place of all,   28
  And farthest from high Heaven's all-moving gyre;
  I know the way; take heart—no ill shall fall.

On every side, the vast and reeking mire   31
  Surrounds this city of the woe-begot,
  Where now's no entering, save with wrath and
  ire . . ."

And he went on, saying I know not what,   34
  For my whole being was drawn up with my eyes
  To where the tower's high battlements burned
  red-hot:

For there of a sudden I saw three shapes arise,   37
  Three hellish Furies, boltered all with blood;
  Their form and bearing were made woman-wise;

Vivid green hydras girt them, and a brood   40
  Of asps and adders, each a living tress,
  Writhed round the brows of that fell sisterhood.

And, knowing well those handmaids pitiless   43
  Who serve the Queen of everlasting woe:
  "Behold," said he, "the fierce Erinyes.

---

l. 8: *that great self-proffered aid is lent:* How Virgil summons this aid or knows of its coming is not stated; presumably he is aware that the help of Him who harrowed Hell is always available for a Christian soul in need.

l. 16: *descending from that place,* etc.: i.e., from Limbo.

l. 29: *high Heaven's all-moving gyre:* i.e., the *Primum Mobile*, the highest of the revolving heavens, which imparts motion to all the rest.

l. 44: *the Queen of everlasting woe:* Proserpine, or Persephone, queen of the classical underworld.

There on the right Alecto howls, and lo! 46
    Mcgaera on the left; betwixt them wails
    Tisiphone." And he was silent so.

They beat their breasts, and tore them with their 49
    nails,
    Shrieking so loud that, faint and tremulous,
    I clutched the poet; and they, with fiercer yells,

Cried: "Fetch Medusa!", glaring down on us, 52
    "Turn him to stone! Why did we not requite—
    Woe worth the day!—the assault of Theseus?"

"Turn thee about, and shut thine eyelids tight: 55
    If Gorgon show her face and thou thereon
    Look once, there's no returning to the light."

Thus cried the master; nor to my hands alone 58
    Would trust, but turned me himself, and urgently
    Pressed my palms close and covered them with his
    own.

O you whose intellects keep their sanity, 61
    Do you mark well the doctrine shrouded o'er
    By the strange verses with their mystery.

Then o'er that dull tide came the crash and roar 64
    Of an enormous and appalling sound,
    So that the ground shuddered from shore to shore;

A sound like the sound of a violent wind, around 67
    The time of opposing heats and the parched
    weather,
    When it sweeps on the forest and leaps with a
    sudden bound,

Shattering and scattering the boughs hither and 70
    thither;
    Superb with a tower of dust for harbinger
    It goes, while the wolves and herdsmen flee
    together,

He loosed my eyes: "Now look," said he, "see there, 73
    Yonder, beyond the foam of the ancient lake,
    Where the harsh marsh mist hangs thickest upon
    the air."

And so the frogs, spying the foeman snake, 76
    Go squattering over the pond, and dive, and sit
    Huddled in the mud, even so I saw them break

Apart, whole shoals of ruined spirits, and flit 79
    Scudding from the path of one who came to us,
    Walking the water of Styx with unwet feet.

His left hand, moving, fanned away the gross 82
    Air from his face, nor elsewise did he seem
    At all to find the way laborious.

And when I saw him, right well did I deem 85
    Him sent from Heaven, and turned me to my
    guide,
    Who signed me to be still and bow to him.

What scorn was in his look! He stood beside 88
    The gate, and touched it with a wand; it flew
    Open; there was no resistance; all stood wide.

"Outcasts of Heaven, despicable crew," 91
    Said he, his feet set on the dreadful sill,
    "Why dwells this foolish insolence in you?

Why kick against the pricks of that great Will 94
    Whose purpose never can be overborne,
    And which hath oft increased your sorrows still?

Or say, what boots it at the Fates to spurn? 97
    Think how your Cerberus tried it, and yet bears
    The marks of it on jowl and throttle torn."

Then back he went by those foul thoroughfares, 100
    And unto us said nothing, but appeared
    Like one much pressed with weightier affairs

Than the cares of those before him. So we stirred 103
    Our footsteps citywards with hearts reposed,
    Safely protected by the heavenly word.

Through the great ward we entered unopposed, 106
    And I, being all agog to learn what state
    Of things these huge defensive works enclosed,

Gazed round, the moment I had passed the gate, 109
    And saw a plain, stretched spacious on both sides,
    Filled with ill woes and torments desolate.

For as at Arles, where soft the slow Rhones slide, 112
    Or as at Pola, near Quarnaro's bay,
    That fences Italy with its washing tides,

The ground is all uneven with the array, 115
    On every hand, of countless sepulchres,
    So here; but in a far more bitter way:

For strewn among the tombs tall flames flared fierce, 118
    Heating them so white-hot as never burned
    Iron in the forge of any artificers.

The grave-slabs all were thrown back and upturned, 121
    And from within came forth such fearful crying,
    'Twas plain that here sad tortured spirits mourned.

"Or Sir," said I, "who are the people lying 124
    In these grim coffers, whose sharp pains disclose
    Their presence to the ear by their sad sighing?"

And he: "The great heresiarchs, with all those, 127
    Of every sect, their followers; and much more
    The tombs lie laden than thou wouldst suppose.

Here like with like is laid; and their flames roar 130
    More and less hot within their monuments."
    Then we moved onward, and right-handed bore

Between those fires and the high battlements. 133

The Images

The Furies (Erinyes) in Greek mythology were the
    avenging goddesses who haunted those who had
    committed great crimes. In the *allegory,* they are the
    image of the fruitless remorse which does not lead to
    penitence.

---

l. 54: *the assault of Theseus:* Theseus, king of Athens, tried to
carry off Persephone from Hell; he failed, but was rescued by
Hercules. The Furies mean that, if they had succeeded in
punishing Theseus, other living men would have been deterred
from venturing into the underworld, and they had better make an
example of Dante.

l. 88: *what scorn was in his look!* In Hell, God's power is
experienced only as judgment, alien and terrible.

---

l. 97: *what boots it at the Fates to spurn?* The Angel uses two
forms of speech—one Christian, "that great Will," the other
classical, "the Fates"—to denote the Divine power. The evil
powers which he is addressing belong both to the Christian and
to the pre-Christian mythology.

l. 98: *Cerberus:* As the last of his labours, Hercules brought
Cerberus out of Hell, mauling his throat in the process.

l. 112: *Arles:* where in Dante's time the Rhone spread into a
stagnant lake, contains many ancient tombs, said to be those of
Charlemagne's soldiers slain in battle against the Saracens at
Aleschans. *Pola* (on the Adriatic) is said to have formerly
contained about 700 tombs of Slavonians, buried on the
seashore.

Medusa was a *Gorgon* whose face was so terrible that anyone who looked upon it was turned to stone. In the *allegory*, she is the image of the despair which so hardens the heart that it becomes powerless to repent.

The Heavenly Messenger. He is, I think, the image of Divine revelation, *(a)* stirring the conscience, *(b)* safeguarding the mind against false doctrine.

Canto X

The Story

As the Poets are passing along beneath the city walls, Dante is hailed by Farinata from one of the burning tombs, and goes to speak to him. Their conversation is interrupted by Cavalcante dei Cavalcanti with a question about his son. Farinala prophesies Dante's exile and explains how the souls in Hell know nothing of the present, though they can remember the past and dimly foresee the future.

Canto XI

The Story

While the Poets pause for a little on the brink of the descent to the Seventh Circle, Virgil explains to Dante the arrangement of Hell.

The Images

The only image here is that of Hell itself. Dante's classification of sins is based chiefly on Aristotle, with a little assistance from Cicero. Aristotle divided wrong behaviour into three main kinds:
(A) *Incontinence* (uncontrolled appetite);
(B) *Bestiality* (perverted appetite); (C) *Malice* or *Vice* (abuse of the specifically human faculty of reason). Cicero declared that all injurious conduct acted by either (a) *Violence* or (b) *Fraud*. Combining these two classifications, Dante obtains three classes of sins: I. *Incontinence*; II. *Violence* (or *Bestiality)*; III. *Fraud* (or *Malice)*. These he subdivides and arranges in 7 Circles: 4 of Incontinence, 1 of Violence, and 2 of Fraud.

To these purely ethical categories of wrong *behaviour* he, as a Christian, adds 2 Circles of wrong *belief*: 1 of *Unbelief* (Limbo) and 1 of *Mischief* (the Heretics), making 9 Circles in all. Finally, he adds the Vestibule of the Futile, who have neither faith nor works; this, not being a Circle, bears no number.

Thus we get the 10 main divisions of Hell. In other books of the *Comedy* we shall find the same numerical scheme of 3, made up by subdivision to 7; plus 2 (= 9); plus 1 (= 10). Hell, however, is complicated by still further subdivision. The Circle of *Violence* is again divided into 3 Rings; the Circle of Fraud Simple into 10 Bowges; and the Circle of Fraud Complex into 4 Regions. So that Hell contains a grand total of 24 divisions (see section map).

Canto XII

The Story

At the point where the sheer precipice leading down to the Seventh Circle is made negotiable by a pile of tumbled rock, Virgil and Dante are faced by the Minotaur. A taunt from Virgil throws him into a fit of

blind fury, and while he is thrashing wildly about, the Poets slip past him. Virgil tells Dante how the rocks were dislodged by the earthquake which took place at the hour of Christ's descent into Limbo. At the foot of the cliff they come to Phlegethon, the river of boiling blood, in which the Violent against their Neighbours are immersed, and whose banks are guarded by Centaurs. At Virgil's request, Chiron, the chief Centaur, sends Nessus to guide them to the ford and carry Dante over on his back. On the way, Nessus points out a number of notable tyrants and robbers.

The place we came to, to descend the brink from.
    Was sheer crag; and there was a Thing there—making.
    All told, a prospect any eye would shrink from.

Like the great landslide that rushed downward, shaking   4
    The bank of Adige on this side Trent,
    (Whether through faulty shoring or the earth's quaking)

So that the rock, down from the summit rent   7
    Far as the plain, lies strewn, and one might crawl
    From top to bottom by that unsure descent.

Such was the precipice; and there we spied,   10
    Topping the cleft that split the rocky wall,
    That which was wombed in the false heifer's side,

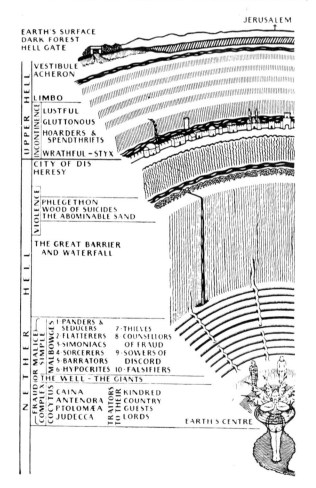

---

1. 5: *the bank of Adige:* Dante likens the fall of rock to the Slavini di Marco on the Adige between Trent and Verona. An early commentator (Benvenuto da Imola) says that the comparison is very apt, since before the landslide the bank was as sheer as the wall of a house and absolutely unscalable; but afterwards it was just possible to scramble down it.

The infamy of Crete, stretched out a-sprawl;   13
   And seeing us, he gnawed himself, like one
   Inly devoured with spite and burning gall.

Then cried my Wisdom: "How now, hellion!   16
   Thinkst thou the Duke of Athens comes anew,
   That slew thee in the upper world? Begone,

Monster! not guided by thy sister's clue   19
   Has this man come; only to see and know
   Your punishments, he threads the circle through."

Then, as a bull pierced by the mortal blow   22
   Breaks loose, and cannot go straight, but reels in
     the ring
   Plunging wildly and staggering to and fro,

I saw the Minotaur fall a-floundering,   25
   And my wary guide called: "Run! run for the pass!
   Make good thy going now, while his rage has its
     fling."

So down we clambered by that steep crevasse   28
   Of tumbled rock; and oft beneath my tread
   The stones slipped shifting with my unwonted
     mass.

I went bemused; wherefore: "Perchance thy head   31
   Puzzles at this great fissure here, watched o'er
   By the furious brute I quelled just now," he said.

"I'd have thee know, when I went down before,   34
   That other time, into Deep Hell this way,
   The rock had not yet fallen; but now for sure

'Twas thus, if I judge rightly: on the day   37
   When that great Prince to the First Circle above
   Entered, and seized from Dis the mighty prey,

Shortly ere He came, the deep foul gulf did move   40
   On all sides down to the centre, till I thought
   The universe trembled in the throes of love,

Whereby, as some believe, the world's been brought   43
   Oft-times to chaos; in that moment, here
   And elsewhere, was these old rocks' ruin wrought.

But now look to the vale, for we draw near   46
   The river of blood, where all those wretches boil
   Whose violence filled the earth with pain and
     fear."

O blind, O rash and wicked lust of spoil,   49
   That drives our short life with so keen a goad,
   And steeps our life eternal in such broil!

I saw a river, curving full and broad   52
   Arewise, as though the whole plain's girth
     embracing.
   Just as my guide had told me on the road;

And 'twixt the bank and it came centaurs racing   55
   By one and one, their bows and quivers bearing
   As when through the woods of the world they
     went a-chasing.

They checked their flight to watch us downward   58
     faring,
   And three of the band wheeled out and stood
     a-row,
   Their bows and chosen arrows first preparing;

And one cried out from far: "Hey! whither go   61
   You on the cliff there? What's your penalty?
   Speak where you stand; if no, I draw the bow."

The master shouted back: "That word shall be   64
   For Chiron there; headstrong thou dost remain,
   And so thou ever wast—the worse for thee."

Then, nudging me: "That's Nessus, who was slain   67
   For fair Deïanira, and in the aftermath
   With his own blood avenged his blood again.

Gazing upon his breast, betwixt them both,   70
   Achilles' tutor, the great Chiron, stands;
   The third is Pholus, once so full of wrath.

All round the fosse they speed in myriad bands,   73
   Shooting at every soul that tries to lift
   Higher out of the blood than doom demands."

We were near them now, those creatures snell and   76
     swift,
   And Chiron took an arrow, and with the notch
   Put back upon his jaws his snowy drift

Of beard, and having freed his great mouth: "Watch,"   79
   Said he to those who stood with him; "mark you
   How the feet of the one behind move what they
     touch?

Those of the dead are not used so to do,"   82
   And my good guide, now standing at his breast
   Where the two natures join, replied: "Quite true,

---

l. 13: *the infamy of Crete:* the Minotaur was the offspring of
Pasiphae (wife of Minos, king of Crete), who became enamoured
of a beautiful bull, and was brought to him in the effigy of a cow
("the false heifer") made for her by the cunning artificer
Daedalus. Minos kept the Minotaur in the labyrinth at Cnossos.
Later, having waged a successful war against Athens, he
compelled the Athenians to send him a yearly tribute of seven
youths and seven maidens to be devoured by the monster. The
Minotaur was slain by Theseus, "the Duke of Athens," who made
his way back from the labyrinth by the aid of a clue of thread
given to him by Ariadne, daughter of Minos and Pasiphaë.

l. 34: *when I went down before:* Virgil's previous journey (Canto
IX. 22) was made before the death of Christ.

l. 39: *the mighty prey:* i.e., the souls of the patriarchs (Canto IV.
55 *sqq.*).

l. 42: *the universe trembled in the throes of love,* etc.:
Empedocles taught that the universe was held together in
tension by discord among the elements; but that from time to
time the motions of the heavens brought about a state of
harmony (love). When this happened, like matter flew to like,
and the universe was once more resolved into its original
elements and so reduced to chaos.

l. 47: *river of blood:* Phlegethon.

---

l. 62: *what's your penalty?* The Centaurs mistake Dante and
Virgil for damned souls going to their allotted place of torment.

l. 65: *Chiron:* the great Centaur to whom Achilles, Peleus,
Theseus, and other Greek heroes went to be tutored. He was
famous for his skill in hunting, gymnastics, medicine, music, and
prophecy, and was accounted the wisest and most just of the
Centaurs. Accordingly, though placing him among the guardians
of Phlegethon, Dante has given him the most amiable character
of all the inhabitants of Hell.

l. 67: *Nessus:* This Centaur attempted to carry off Deïanira, the
wife of Hercules, while taking her over a river on his back.
Hercules killed him with an arrow, and the dying Nessus told
Deïanira to take some of his blood, since it would act upon
Hercules as a love-charm. Deïanira did so, and later, fearing that
Hercules was falling in love with another woman, put on him a
shirt steeped in the blood of Nessus. The blood was poisonous
and, after suffering intolerable agonies, Hercules placed himself
on a pyre of wood and had himself burned to death.

l. 72: *Pholus:* Little is known of him except that he also was
killed by Hercules. The three Centaurs possibly typify three
passions which may lead to violence: wrath, lust, and the will to
dominate.

He is alive; so, on his lonely quest, 85
    Needs must I lead him through the vales of night;
    Necessity brings him here, not sport nor jest;

From the singing of alleluias in the light 88
    Came she who laid on me this novel charge;
    The man's no poacher, I'm no thievish spite.

Now by the power that moves my steps at large 91
    On this wild way, lend us a courier
    Whom we may follow by the river's marge,

To show us where the ford is, and to bear 94
    This other upon his back across the tide,
    For he's no spirit to walk the empty air."

Then Chiron turned on his right flank, and cried: 97
    "Wheel round and guide them, Nessus; if you're met
    By another patrol, see that it stands aside."

So with this trusty escort, off we set 100
    Along the bank of the bubbling crimson flood,
    Whence the shrieks of the boiled rose shrill and desperate.

There saw I some—plunged eyebrow-deep they stood; 103
    And the great centaur said to me: "Behold
    Tyrants, who gave themselves to ravin and blood.

Here they bewail oppressions manifold; 106
    Alexander's here; Dionysius too, whose brute
    Fury long years vexed Sicily uncontrolled.

That forehead there, with locks as black as soot, 109
    Is Azzolino, and that fair-haired one
    Obizzo d'Este, he whose light was put

Out, up above there, by his stepson son." 112
    I turned here to the poet, who said, "Why, yes,
    He first, I second now, must guide thee on."

Further along, the centaur checked his pace 115
    Beside a second gang, who seemed to start
    Far as the throat from the stream's boiling race.

He showed one shade set by itself apart, 118
    Saying: "There stands the man who dared to smite,
    Even in the very bosom of God, the heart

They venerate still on Thames." Next, reared upright 121
    Both head and chest from the stream, another horde
    Appeared, full many known to me by sight.

Thus shallow and shallower still the red blood poured 124
    Till it was only deep enough to cook
    The feet; and here it was we passed the ford.

And the centaur said to me: "Now, prithee, look: 127
    Just as, this side, it ever grows less deep,
    On that, I'd have thee know, the boiling brook

Lowers its rocky bed, down-shelving steep, 130
    Until it comes full circle, and joins its ring
    There where the tyrants are condemned to weep.

Here doth the heavenly justice rack and wring 133
    Pyrrhus and Sextus; here it overbears
    That scourge of earth called Attila the King;

And here for ever it milks the trickling tears 136
    Squeezed by the scald from those rough highwaymen
    The Pazzian and Cornetan Riniers."

With this he turned and crossed the ford again. 139

The Images

The Circle of Violence. From now to the end of Canto XVII we are in the circle devoted to *Violence* or *Bestiality* (the "sins of the Lion") which, together with the Circle of the Heretics, makes up the first division of Nether Hell.

The Minotaur and The Centaurs. In this and the next ring we find demon-guardians compounded of man and brute. They are the types of perverted appetite—the human reason subdued to animal passion. The Minotaur had the body of a man and the head of a bull; the Centaurs were half-man, half-horse.

Phlegethon—"the fiery"—is the third chief river of Hell. Like Acheron and Styx, it forms a complete circuit about the abyss, and it is deep at one side and shallow at the other. The sinners whose fiery passions caused them to shed man's blood are here plunged in that blood-bath for ever.

Canto XIII

The Story

The Poets enter a pathless Wood. Here Harpies sit shrieking among the withered trees, which enclose the souls of Suicides. Pier delle Vigne tells Dante his story, and also explains how these shades come to be changed into trees and what will happen to their bodies at the Last Day. The shades of two Profligates rush through the wood, pursued and torn by black hounds. Dante speaks to a bush containing the soul of a Florentine.

Canto XIV

The Story

In a desert of Burning Sand, under a rain of perpetual fire, Dante finds the Violent against God, Nature, and Art. The Violent against God lie supine, facing the Heaven which they insulted; among these is Capaneus, blasphemous and defiant in death as in life. The Poets pick their way carefully between the forest and the hot sand till they come to the edge of a boiling, red stream. Here Virgil explains the origin of all the rivers of Hell.

Canto XV

The Story

While crossing the Sand upon the dyke banking Phlegethon, Dante sees the Violent against Nature, who run perpetually, looking towards the human body against which they offended. He meets his old teacher, Brunetto

---

l. 88: *from the singing of alleluias . . . came she:* i.e., Beatrice.

l. 90: *no poacher, and . . . no thievish sprite:* Virgil means that he and Dante have not come, like Theseus or Orpheus, to try and rob Hell of any of its victims.

l. 112: *stepson son:* Actually his son; Dante calls him "stepson" because of his unnatural behaviour.

l. 120: *the heart they venerate still on Thames:* Prince Henry, son of Richard, Duke of Cornwall, and nephew to Henry III of England, was killed in the Cathedral at Viterbo, during High Mass ("in the very bosom of God"), by Guy, son of Simon de Montfort (1270). A statue of him, holding in its right hand the casket containing his heart, is said to have been placed on London Bridge.

---

l. 131: *until it comes full circle:* Apparently Dante and Virgil have made the full half-circle of Phlegethon, from the deep side where the tyrants stand to the shallow ford.

Latini, whom he addresses with affectionate regret and deep gratitude for past benefits. Brunetto predicts Dante's ill-treatment at the hands of the Florentines.

Canto XVI

The Story

Dante is already within earshot of the waterfall at the end of the path, when he meets the shades of three distinguished Florentine noblemen and gives them news of their city. At the edge of the cliff, Virgil throws Dante's girdle into the gulf below, and in answer to this signal a strange form comes swimming up towards them.

Canto XVII

The Story

Geryon, the monster called up from the Circles of Fraud, alights on the edge of the precipice. While Virgil talks to him, Dante goes to look at the shades of Usurers seated on the Burning Sand. The Poets then mount on Geryon's shoulders and are carried down over the Great Barrier to the Eighth Circle.

Canto XVIII

The Story

Dante now finds himself in the Eighth Circle (Malbowges), which is divided into ten trenches (bowges) containing those who committed Malicious Frauds upon mankind in general. The Poets walk along the edge of Bowge i, where Panders and Seducers run, in opposite directions, scourged by demons; and here Dante talks with Venedico Caccianemico of Bologna. As they cross the bridge over the bowge, they see the shade of Jason. Then they go on to the bridge over Bowge ii, where they see Thais, and Dante converses with another of the Flatterers who are here plunged in filth.

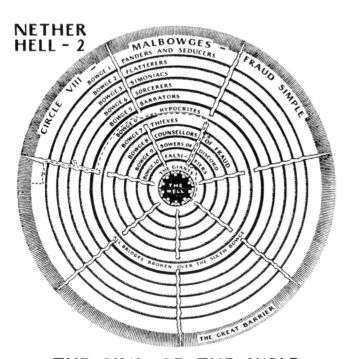

NETHER HELL - 2

THE SINS OF THE WOLF

There is in Hell a region that is called
    Malbowges; it is all of iron-grey stone,
    Like the huge barrier-rock with which it's walled.

Plumb in the middle of the dreadful cone   4
    There yawns a well, exceeding deep and wide.
    Whose form and fashion shall be told anon.

That which remains, then, of the foul Pit's side,   7
    Between the well and the foot of the craggy steep,
    Is a narrowing round, which ten great chasms divide.

As one may see the girding fosses deep   10
    Dug to defend a stronghold from the foe,
    Trench within trench about the castle-keep,

Such was the image here; and as men throw   13
    Their bridges outward from the fortress-wall,
    Crossing each moat to the far bank, just so

From the rock's base spring cliffs, spanning the fall   16
    Of dyke and ditch, to the central well, whose rim
    Cuts short their passage and unites them all.

When Geryon shook us off, 'twas in this grim   19
    Place that we found us; and the poet then
    Turned to the left, and I moved after him.

There, on our right, more anguished shades of men,   22
    New tortures and new torturers, I espied,
    Cramming the depth of this first bowge of ten.

In the bottom were naked sinners, who, our side   25
    The middle, moved to face us; on the other,
    Along with us, though with a swifter stride.

Just as the Romans, because of the great smother   28
    Of the Jubilee crowds, have thought of a good device
    For controlling the bridge, to make the traffic smoother,

So that on one side all must have their eyes   31
    On the Castle, and go to St. Peter's; while all the throng
    On the other, towards the Mount moves contrariwise.

I saw horned fiends with heavy whips and strong   34
    Posted each side along the dismal rock,
    Who scourged their backs, and drove them on headlong.

---

l. 2: *Malbowges (Maleholge):* The Italian word *bolgia* means *(a)* a trench in the ground; *(b)* a purse or pouch, *Malebolge* can thus be interpreted as either "evil pits" or "evil pouches;" and Dante puns on this double meaning. There is no English word which combines the two meanings; there is, however, an old word "bowge" meaning "pouch." This makes it possible to English *Malebolge* as "Malbowges" (which is, in all probability, the form which a medieval translator would have given it), and so to retain a suggestion of the pun about "pouching."

l. 6: *shall be told anon:* see Canto XXXI.

ll. 23–33: The fact that traffic control appears to Dante as a startling and ingenious novelty probably brings home to us, far more than his theology or his politics, the six hundred years which separate his times from ours. The year 1300 (the year of his vision) had been proclaimed by Pope Boniface VIII a Jubilee Year, and Rome was consequently crowded with pilgrims. For the better avoidance of congestion, the authorities (whose organization seems to have been remarkably efficient) adopted a rule of the road on the Bridge of Castello Sant' Angelo, so-called from the castle which stood at one end of it. The "Mount" at the other end was either the Janiculum or Monte Giordano. It will be noticed that in the First Bowge the rule is "keep to the right," as it is on the Continent today.

Hey! how they made them skip at the first shock!   37
  How brisk they were to lift their legs and prance!
  Nobody stayed for the second or third stroke.

And as I was going, one of them caught my glance,   40
  And I promptly said to myself: "How now! who's
    he?
  Somewhere or other I've seen that countenance."

I stopped short, figuring out who this might be;   43
  And my good lord stopped too; then let me go
  Back a short way, to follow him and see.

The whipped shade hung his head, trying not to   46
    show
  His face; but little good he got thereby,
  For: "Hey, there! thou whose eyes are bent so low,

Thy name's Venedico—or thy features lie—   49
  Caccianemico, and I know thee well;
  What wormwood pickled such a rod," said I,

"To scrub thy back?" And he: "I would not tell,   52
  But for that voice of thine; those accents clear
  Remind me of the old life, and compel

My answer. I am the man who sold the fair   55
  Ghisola to the Marchese's lust; that's fact,
  However they tell the ugly tale up there.

I'm not alone here from Bologna; packed   58
  The place is with us; one could scarcely find
  More tongues saying 'Yep' for 'Yes' in all the tract

'Twixt Reno and Savena. Art inclined   61
  To call for proof? What witness need I join
  To the known witness of our covetous mind?"

And one of the fiends caught him a crack on the loin   64
  With the lash, even as he spoke, crying: "Away,
  Pander! there are no women here to coin!"

So to my escort I retraced my way,   67
  And soon we came, a few steps further wending,
  To where a great spur sprang from the barrier grey.

-----

ll. 49–50: *Venedico Caccianemico:* A Bolognese Guelf. Ghisola was his own sister, and the Marchese was Obizzo d' Este (Canto XII. 111).

l. 51: *what wormwood:* lit.: "what has got thee into such a pickle (*pungenti salse*)?" The word *salse* means *"sauce"*; but it was also the name of a place near Bologna where criminals were flogged and executed, so that Dante's sauce is punning as well as pungent. I have done my best to supply a parallel allusion of a native and contemporary kind.

l. 57: *however they tell the ugly tale:* Presumably other, whitewashing, versions of the story, less disagreeable to the feelings of the powerful d' Este family, had been assiduously put about.

l. 60: *"yep" (sipa) for "yes" (si):* an allusion to the Bolognese dialect. The Savena and Reno are rivers running west and east of Bologna.

l. 63: *the known witness of our covetous mind:* The Bolognese seem to have had a reputation for venality.

ll. 67: *sqq.: retraced my way,* etc.: The poets had turned left on entering Malbowges and walked along the edge of Bowge i. Then Dante retraced his steps to go after Caccianemico. Now he returns to where Virgil is waiting for him, and they continue their original course till they come to where the first rock-spur runs across their path at right angles and forms a bridge over the bowge. To cross the bridge they have to *climb* on to this spur and turn right so as to walk *along* it till they are over the spot where the rock is tunnelled out to let the bowge pass below it. From this, the crest of the arch, they look down on the sinners passing below, as one would watch trains from the middle of railway bridge (see illustration, p. 386). Once this procedure has been clearly visualized, the reader will have very little trouble with the geography of Malbowges.

This we climbed lightly, and right-handed bending,   70
  Crossed its rough crest, departing from the rout
  Of shades who run their circuits never-ending.

But, coming above the part that's tunnelled out   73
  To let the flogged past under, "Stay" said he;
  "Let those who go the other way about

Strike on thine eyes; just now thou couldst not see   76
  Their faces, as we passed along the verge,
  For they were travelling the same road as we."

So from that ancient bridge we watched the surge   79
  Sweep on towards us of the wretched train
  On the farther side, chased likewise by the
    scourge.

"Look who comes here," my good guide said again   82
  Without my asking, "that great spirit of old,
  Who will not shed one tear for all his pain.

Is he not still right royal to behold?   85
  That's Jason, who by valour and by guile
  Bore from the Colchian strand the fleece of gold.

He took his way past Lemnos, where, short while   88
  Before, the pitiless bold women achieved
  The death of all the menfolk of their isle;

And there the young Hypsipyle received   91
  Tokens and fair false words, till, snared and
    shaken,
  She who deceived her fellows was deceived;

And there he left her, childing and forsaken;   94
  For those deceits he's sentenced to these woes,
  And for Medea too revenge is taken.

And with him every like deceiver goes.   97
  Suffice thee so much knowledge of this ditch
  And those whom its devouring jaws enclose."

Already we'd come to where the narrow ridge   100
  Crosses the second bank, and makes of it
  An abutment for the arch of the next bridge.

Here we heard people in the farther pit   103
  Make a loud whimpering noise, and heard them
    cough,
  And slap themselves with their hands, and snuffle
    and spit.

The banks were crusted with foul scum, thrown off   106
  By the fume, and caking there, till nose and eye
  Were vanquished with sight and reek of the
    noisome stuff.

So deep the trench, that one could not espy   109
  Its bed save from the topmost cliff, which makes
  The keystone of the arch. We climbed; and I,

-----

l. 86: *Jason:* the Greek hero who led the Argonauts to fetch the Golden Fleece from the hands of Aietes, king of Colchis. He was helped by the king's daughter, Medea, whom he persuaded to accompany him home to Iolcus. He married her, but afterwards deserted her for Creusa.

l. 88: *Lemnos:* When the women of Lemnos killed all the men on the island because they had brought home some Thracian concubines, Hypsipyle, the daughter of King Thosa, saved her father by a ruse (l. 93). On their way to Colchis, the Argonauts landed at Lemnos and Jason seduced Hypsipyle.

ll. 100–101; *the narrow ridge,* etc.: The spur runs straight on, forming bridges over all the bowges in succession (see map, p. 386).

Thence peering down, saw people in the lake's   112
    Foul bottom, plunged in dung, the which appeared
    Like human ordure running from a jakes.

Searching its depths, I there made out a smeared   115
    Head—whether clerk or lay was hard to tell,
    It was so thickly plastered with the merd.

"Why stand there gloating?" he began to yell,   118
    "Why stare at me more than the other scum?"
    "Because," said I, "if I remember well,

I've seen thy face, dry-headed, up at home;   121
    Thou art Alessio Interminei, late
    Of Lucca—so, more eagerly than on some,

I look on thee." He beat his pumpkin pate,   124
    And said: "The flatteries I spewed out apace
    With tireless tongue have sunk me to this state."

Then said my guide: "Before we leave the place,   127
    Lean out a little further, that with full
    And perfect clearness thou may'st see the face

Of that uncleanly and dishevelled trull   130
    Scratching with filthy nails, alternately
    Standing upright and crouching in the pool.

That is the harlot Thaïs. 'To what degree,'   133
    Her leman asked, 'have I earned thanks, my love?'
    'O, to a very miracle,' said she.

And having seen this, we have seen enough."   136

The Images

The Eighth and Ninth Circles. These are the Circles of *Fraud* or *Malice*—the "Sins of the Wolf."

Malbowges. The Eighth Circle is a huge funnel of rock, round which run, at irregular intervals, a series of deep, narrow trenches called "bowges" *(bolge).* From the foot of the Great Barrier at the top to the Well which forms the neck of the funnel run immense spurs of rock (like the ribs of an umbrella) raised above the general contour of the slope and forming bridges over the bowges. The maps and the sketch on p. 386 show the arrangement, except, of course, that the distances from bowge to bowge are greater, and the rock-surfaces much steeper and craggier, than it is possible to suggest in small diagrams.

    Malbowges is, I think, after a rather special manner, the image of the City in corruption: the progressive disintegration of every social relationship, personal and public. Sexuality, ecclesiastical and civil office, language, ownership, counsel, authority, psychic influence, and material interdependence—all the media of the community's exchange are perverted and falsified, till nothing remains but the descent into the final abyss where faith and trust are wholly and forever extinguished.

---

l. 122: *Allessio Interminei:* Little is known of him, except that he was a member of a White Guelf family, and was notorious for his oily manners.

l. 133: *Thais:* The fulsome reply here quoted really belongs, not to the historical Thais, the Athenian courtesan, but to a character in Terence's play, *Eunuchus,* of the same name and profession. It is mentioned by Cicero, and Dante presumably took it from him, under the impression that it was historical. Note that Thais is not here because she is personally a harlot; the sin which has plunged her far below the Lustful, and even below the traffickers in flesh, is the prostitution of words—the medium of *intellectual* intercourse.

The Panders and Seducers. In the Circles of Fraud (the abuse of the specifically human faculty of reason) the ministers of Hell are no longer mere embodied *appetites,* but actual devils, images of the perverted *intellect.* In the First Bowge, those who deliberately exploited the passions of others and so drove them to serve their own interests, are themselves driven and scourged. The image is a sexual one; but the Panders and Seducers *allegorically* figure the stimulation and exploitation of every kind of passion—e.g., rage or greed—by which one may make tools of other people.

The Flatterers. These, too, exploit others by playing upon their desires and fears; their especial weapon is that abuse and corruption of language which destroys communication between mind and mind. Here they are plunged in the slop and filth which they excreted upon the world. Dante did not live to see the full development of political propaganda, commercial advertisement, and sensational journalism, but he has prepared a place for them.

Canto XIX

The Story

In the Third Bowge of Malbowges, Dante sees the Simoniacs, plunged head-downwards in holes of the rock, with flames playing upon their feet. He talks to the shade of Pope Nicholas III, who prophesies that two of his successors will come to the same bad end as himself. Dante rebukes the avarice of the Papacy.

Canto XX

The Story

In the Fourth Bowge of the Eighth Circle Dante sees the Sorcerers, whose heads are twisted so that they can only look behind them, and who are therefore compelled to walk backwards. Virgil tells him about the origin of Mantua. The moon is setting as the Poets leave the bowge.

Canto XXI

The Story

In the Fifth Bowge, Barrators, who made money by trafficking in public offices, are plunged in Boiling Pitch, guarded by demons with sharp hooks. Virgil crosses the bridge and goes down to parley with the demons. Belzecue, the chief demon, says that the spur of rock which the Poets have been following was broken by an earthquake (at the moment of Christ's entry into Hell) and no longer bridges the Sixth Bowge; but he will give them an escort of ten demons to "see them safe as far as the bridge which is still unbroken." In this disagreeable company, Virgil and Dante set off along the lower brink of the Bowge.

Cantos XXI and XXII. The mood of these two cantos—a mixture of savage satire and tearing high spirits—is unlike anything else in the *Comedy,* and is a little disconcerting to the more solemn-minded of Dante's admirers. Artistically, this grim burlesque is of great value as an interlude in the ever-deepening descent from horror to horror; but Dante had also personal reasons for letting his pen rip at this point, since an accusation of barratry was the pretext upon which he was banished from Florence. (I have translated rather more freely here than elsewhere, in order to keep up the pace of the original.)

And so we passed along from bridge to bridge,
  With other talk, whereof my Comedy
  Cares not to tell, until we topped the ridge;

And there we stayed our steps awhile, to see   4
  Malbowges' next ravine, and wailings all
  Vain: and most marvellous dark it seemed to be.

For as at Venice, in the Arsenal   7
  In winter-time, they boil the gummy pitch
  To caulk such ships as need an overhaul,

Now that they cannot sail—instead of which   10
  One builds him a new boat, one toils to plug
  Seams strained by many a voyage, others stitch

Canvas to patch a tattered jib or lug,   13
  Hammer at the prow, hammer at the stern, or
    twine
  Ropes, or shave oars, refit and make all snug—

So, not by fire, but by the art divine,   16
  A thick pitch boiled down there, spattering the
    brink
  With viscous glue; I saw this, but therein

Nothing; only great bubbles black as ink   19
  Would rise and burst there; or the seething tide
  Heave up all over, and settle again, and sink.

And while I stood intent to gaze, my guide,   22
  Suddenly crying to me, "Look out! look out!"
  Caught me where I stood, and pulled me to his
    side.

O then I turned, as one who turns about,   25
  Longing to see the thing he has to shun,
  Dares not, and dares, and, dashed with hideous
    doubt,

Casts a look back and still goes fleeing on;   28
  And there behind us I beheld a grim
  Black fiend come over the rock-ridge at a run.

Wow! what a grisly look he had on him!   31
  How fierce his rush! And, skimming with spread
    wing,
  How swift of foot he seemed! how light of limb!

On high-hunched shoulders he was carrying   34
  A wretched sinner, hoist by haunch and hip,
  Clutching each ankle by the sinew-string.

"Bridge ho!" he bawled, "Our own Hellrakership!   37
  Here's an alderman of St. Zita's coming down;
  Go souse him, while I make another trip

For more; they're barrators all in that good town—   40
  Except Bonturo, hey?—I've packed it stiff
  With fellows who'd swear black's white for half-a-
    crown."

He tossed him in, and over the flinty cliff   43
  Wheeled off; and never did mastiff run so hot
  And hard on the trail, unleashed to follow a thief.

Down bobbed the sinner, then up in a writhing knot;   46
  But the fiends beneath the archway yelled as he
    rose up:
  "No Sacred Face will help thee here! it's not

A Serchio bathing-party! Now then, toes up   49
  And dive! 'Ware hooks! To save thyself a jabbing,
  Stay in the pitch, nor dare to poke thy nose up!"

Then, with a hundred prongs clawing and stabbing: 52
  "Go cut thy capers! Try down there to do
  Subsurface deals and secret money-grabbing!"

Just so, cooks make their scullions prod the stew   55
  With forks, to thrust the flesh well down within
  The cauldron, lest it float above the brew.

Then the good master: "Better not be seen,"   58
  Said he; "so crouch well down in some embrasure
  Behind a crag, to serve thee for a screen;

And whatsoever outrage or displeasure   61
  They do to me, fear nothing; I have faced
  Frays of this sort before, and have their measure."

He passed the bridgehead then; but when he placed   64
  His foot on the sixth bank, good need had he
  Of a bold front; for with such furious haste

And concentrated venom of savagery   67
  As dogs rush out upon some harmless tramp
  Who stops, alarmed, to falter out his plea,

Out dashed the demons lurking under the ramp,   70
  Each flourishing in his face a hideous hook;
  But he: "Hands off! ere grappling-iron or cramp

Touch me, send one to hear me speak; then look   73
  You take good counsel, before any of you
  Try to dispose of me by hook or crook!"

This checked them; and they cried: "Send Belzecue!"   76
  And one moved forward, snarling as he went:
  "What good does he imagine this will do?"

"Dost thou think, Belzecue, that I had bent   79
  My footsteps thus far hither," the master said,
  "Safe against all your harms, were I not sent

By will divine, by fates propitious led?   82
  Let me pass on; 'tis willed in Heaven that I
  Should guide another by this pathway dread."

At this the fiend, crestfallen utterly,   85
  Let fall his grappling-iron at his feet,
  Crying to the rest: "Strike not! he must go by."

---

l. 7: **at Venice, in the Arsenal:** Venice, in the Middle Ages, was a great sea-power, and the old Arsenal, built in 1104, was one of the most important shipyards in Europe.

l. 35: **a wretched sinner:** One old commentator identifies him as an alderman called Martino Bottaio, who died in 1300.

l. 37: **our own Hellrakership** (lit.: *Malebranche* of our bridge): Dante calls the demons in this bowge *Malebranche* = Evil Claws, which I have rendered "Hellrakers."

l. 38: **St. Zita's:** i.e., Lucca, whose patron saint was St. Zita.

l. 41: **except Bonturo:** This is sarcasm, since Bonturo Dati was especially notorious for his barratry.

l. 48: **Sacred Face:** an ancient wooden figure of Christ, revered at Lucca, and invoked in time of need.

l. 49: **Serchio:** a river near Lucca.

l. 65: **the sixth bank:** i.e., the lower bank of the Fifth Bowge, which is also the upper bank of the Sixth.

l. 76: **Belzecue:** In Italian, *Malacoda* = Evil Tail. The names of the demons in the Fifth Bowge are thought by some to contain allusions to various Florentine officials who were Dante's enemies; but even if they do, the average English reader cannot get much fun out of it at this time of day. I have therefore Englished most of the names for the greater convenience of rhyme and metre.

l. 82: **by will divine, by fates propitious:** Notice once again the double terminology, as in Canto IX. 94–97.

My guide called up: "Thou, cowering there discreet,　　　88
　　Hid mousey-mouse among the splintery, cracked
　　Crags of the bridge, come down! all's safe for it."

I rose and ran to him, and sure I slacked　　　91
　　Not speed; for the fiends pressed forward, and
　　　grave doubt
　　Seized me, for fear they might not keep the pact.

So I once saw the footmen, who marched out　　　94
　　Under treaty from Caprona, look and feel
　　Nervous, with all their foes ringed round about.

I pressed close to my guide from head to heel,　　　97
　　Cringing, and keeping a sharp eye upon
　　Their looks, which were by no means amiable.

They lowered their hooks to the ready, and, "Just for　　　100
　　fun,"
　　Says one, shall I tickle his rump for him?" "Yes,
　　　try it,"
　　Says another, "nick him and prick him, boy—go
　　　on!"

But the other devil, the one that stood in diet　　　103
　　Still with my escort, turned him instant round,
　　Saying: "Now Scaramallion! quiet, quiet!"

And then to us: "By this cliff 'twill be found　　　106
　　Impossible to proceed, for the sixth arch
　　Lies at the bottom, shattered to the ground.

If you're determined to pursue your march,　　　109
　　Follow the bank; a span quite free from block
　　Or fall, lies handy to reward your search;

But this—why, yesterday, five hours by the clock　　　112
　　From now, 'twas just twelve hundred, sixty and six
　　Years since the road was rent by earthquake shock.

I'm sending a squad your way, to fork and fix　　　115
　　Any rash soul who may be taking the air;
　　Why not go with them? They will play no tricks.

Stand forward, Hacklespur and Hellkin there!"　　　118
　　He then began, "and Harrowhound as well,
　　And your decurion shall be Barbiger;

Let Libbicock go too, and Dragonel,　　　121
　　Guttlehog of the tusks, and Grabbersnitch
　　And raving Rubicant and Farfarel

Take a good look all round the boiling pitch;　　　124
　　See these two safe, as far as to the spit
　　That runs unbroken on from ditch to ditch."

---

l. 88: *cowering there:* Dante's comic terror in this bowge is,
characteristically, a double-edged gibe at himself and his
accusers.

l. 95: *Caprona:* This Pisan fortress was taken by the Tuscan
Guelfs in 1289, and Dante, apparently, took part in the operation.

ll. 112–14: *five hours by the clock from now,* etc.: The earthquake
is that which followed the Crucifixion and is mentioned by Virgil
as having heralded Christ's entry into Hell and caused the
landslide on the cliff between the Sixth and Seventh Circles
(Canto XII. 34–45). According to the Synoptists, it took place at
the ninth hour (3 P.M.); this would make the conversation with
Belzecue take place five hours earlier, i.e., at 10 A.M.

l. 113: *twelve hundred, sixty and six:* The Crucifixion is
reckoned as having taken place A.D. 34.

ll. 125–26: *safe, as far as to the spit that runs unbroken:* The
safe-conduct is less valuable than it might appear, and the
malicious grimaces of the demons show that they have taken
these instructions in the spirit in which they were meant.

"Sir, I don't like the looks of this one bit,"　　　127
　　Said I; "no escort, please; let's go alone,
　　If thou know'st how—for I've no stomach to it!

Where is thy wonted caution? Ugh! they frown,　　　130
　　They grind their teeth—dost thou not see them?
　　　Lo,
　　How they threat mischief, with their brows drawn
　　　down!"

But he: "I'd have thee firmer-minded; no,　　　133
　　Let them go grind and gnash their teeth to suit
　　Their mood; 'tis the broiled souls they glare at
　　　so."

They by the left bank wheeling chose their route;　　　136
　　But first in signal to their captain each
　　Thrust out his tongue; and, taking the salute,

He promptly made a bugle of his breech.　　　139

The Images

The Barrators and the Pitch. The Barrators are to the
　　City what the Simoniacs are to the Church: they
　　make profit out of the trust reposed in them by the
　　community; and what they sell is justice. As the
　　Simoniacs are imbedded in the burning rock, so
　　these are plunged beneath the black and boiling
　　stream, for their dealings were secret. Money stuck to
　　their fingers: so now the defilement of the pitch
　　sticks fast to them.

Canto XXII

The Story

*As the party proceeds along the bank of the bowge, the
devils fork a Barrator up out of the pitch, who tells the
Poets who he is and mentions the names of some of his
fellow-sinners. By a trick he eludes the devils who are
preparing to tear him to pieces; whereupon his captors
quarrel among themselves and two of them fall into the
pitch.*

I have seen horsemen moving camp, and beating
　　The muster and assault, seen troops advancing,
　　And sometimes with uncommon haste retreating,

Seen forays in your land, and coursers prancing,　　　4
　　O Aretines! and I've beheld some grandish
　　Tilts run and tourneys fought, with banners
　　　dancing,

And fife and drum, and signal-flares a-brandish　　　7
　　From towers, and cars with tintinnabulation
　　Of bells, and things both native and outlandish;

---

ll. 1 *sqq.: I have seen horsemen,* etc.: The Battle of Camp-
aldino (1289) was fought between the Guelfs (headed by
Florence) and the Ghibellines (headed by Arezzo). The
Florentine forces, among whom Dante was, were thrown into
confusion by the first charge of the Aretines; but the Guelfs
rallied and eventually defeated the Ghibellines with great
slaughter, and the rest of the campaign was fought on Aretine
territory.

l. 6: *tilts run and tourneys fought:* A *tilt* was an encounter
between two knights across a barrier; a *tourney* or *tournament*
was an "all-in" encounter between equal parties of knights in
open field.

l. 8: *cars with tintinnabulation of bells:* In Dante's time, each
Italian city had a car (*carroccio*), or war-chariot. It was gaily
painted, drawn by oxen, and furnished with a bell, and served as
a rallying-point in battle.

But to so strange a trumpet's proclamation 10
    I ne'er saw move or infantry or cavalry,
    Or ship by sea-mark or by constellation.

Well, off we started with that bunch of devilry; 13
    Queer company—but there! "with saints at
        church,
    And at the inn with roisterers and revelry."

Meanwhile, my eyes were wholly bent to search 16
    The pitch, to learn the custom of that moat
    And those who wallowed in the scald and smirch.

And very like the dolphins, when they float 19
    Hump-backed, to warn poor seamen of the
        heightening
    Storm, that they may prepare to save the boat,

So now and then, to get a little slightening 22
    Of pain, some miserable wretch would hulk
    His back up, and pop down again like lightning.

Others lay round about like frogs, that skulk 25
    At the stream's edge, just noses out of shelter,
    The water hiding all their limbs and bulk,—

Till Barbiger arrived; then, in a welter 28
    Of fear, with unanimity quite clannish,
    They shot into the hot-pot helter-skelter.

I saw—and from my memory cannot banish 31
    The horrid thrill—one soul remain a squatter,
    As one frog will at times, when others vanish;

And Grabbersnitch, the nearest truant-spotter, 34
    Hooked him by the clogged hair, and up he came,
    Looking to me exactly like an otter.

(I could pick all the fiends out now by name; 37
    I'd watched while they were chosen, noted how
    They called each other, and made sure of them.)

"Claws, claws there, Rubicant! we've got him now! 40
    Worry him, worry him, flay him high and low!"
    Yelled all the demon-guardians of the slough.

"O master, if thou canst, contrive to know 43
    Who is this wretched criminal." I said,
    "Thus fallen into the clutches of the foe."

My guide drew near to him thus hard-bested, 46
    And asked him whence he came; he said:
        "Navarre;
    In that same kingdom was I born and bred.

My mother placed me servant to a peer, 49
    For he that got me was a ribald knave,
    A spendthrift of himself and of his gear.

Next, I was good King Tibbald's man, and gave 52
    My mind to jobbery; now, I job no more,
    But foot the bill this hotter side the grave."

Here Guttlehog, who, like a savage boar, 55
    Carried great tushes either side his jaws,
    Let the wretch feel how deep the fangs could
        score.

'Twas cat and mouse—ten cats with cruel claws! 58
    But Barbiger, with both arms seizing him,
    Cried: "Back! I'll do the grabbing!" In the pause

He leered round at my lord, and said with grim 61
    Relish: "Any further questions? Ask away!
    Quick—before some one tears him limb from
        limb!"

So then my guide: "Name if thou canst, I pray, 64
    Some Latian rogues among these tarry throngs."
    And he: "But now, I left one such—or, nay,

One that to a near-neighbouring isle belongs; 67
    Would I lay hid beside him still!—I'd mock
    At threatening claws, and ugly tusks, and prongs."

"We've stood too much of this!" cried Libbicock, 70
    And from his arm, making a sudden snatch,
    Ripped off a sinewy gobbet with his hook.

Then Dragonel was fain to have a catch 73
    At the dangling legs; which made their leader spin
    Round with ferocious haste, and looks to match.

When they were somewhat calmer, and the din 76
    Died down, my guide, turning to him who still
    Stared upon his own mangled flesh and skin,

Asked promptly: "Who was he, whom in an ill 79
    Hour thou didst quit, thou sayest, to seek the
        brink?"
    " 'Twas Fra Gomitta, the ineffable

Scamp of Gallura, corruption's very sink," 82
    Said he; "he held his lord's foes in his power,
    And earned their praise—earned it right well, I
        think;

'The golden key,' says he, 'undid the door'; 85
    But all his jobs were jobbed; no petty jobbery
    For him—he was a sovereign barrator.

With him's Don Michael Zanche, artist in robbery 88
    From Logodor'; their tongues, going clack-clack-
        clack
    About Sardinia, kick up a ceaseless bobbery.

O look! that fiend there grinning at me! alack, 91
    He frightens me!—I've plenty more to tell,
    But sure he'll flay my scalp or skin my back!"

Then their huge prefect turned on Farfarel, 94
    Whose eyes were rolling in the act to pounce,
    Crying: "Hop off, thou filthy bird of hell!"

"Are there no souls from other lands or towns," 97
    The quivering wretch went on, "you'd like to see?
    Tuscans? or Lombards? I'll get them here at once.

Let but the Hellrakers draw back a wee 100
    Bit from the shore, so that they need not fear
    Reprisals, and for one poor little me

I'll fetch up seven, just sitting quietly here 103
    And whistling, as it is our wont to do
    When one pops out and finds the coast is clear."

---

ll. 19–21: *dolphins:* This common belief about dolphins is mentioned in a popular Italian version of Brunetto Latini's *Thesauruss,* and elsewhere.

l. 44: *who is this wretched criminal:* Tradition says that this is a certain Spaniard, named Ciampolo, or Gian Polo.

l. 52: *King Tibbald:* Teobaldo II (Count Thibaut V of Champagne), king of Navarre (1253–1270).

---

l. 65: *Latian:* a native of Lower Italy. (Dante never uses the word "Italian," but speaks only of Tuscans, Lombards, etc., in the north and Latians in the south.)

l. 67: *a near-neighbouring isle:* Sardinia.

l. 81: *Fra Gomita:* Sardinia at that time belonged to Pisa, and Gomita was judge of the province of Gallura, under Nino Visconti of Pisa, who put up with his peculations until he found that he had been bribed to let some prisoners escape, whereupon he had him hanged.

l. 88: *Michael Zanche:* Vicar of Logodoro under Enzo, king of Sardinia, who was a natural son of Frederick II. About 1290 he was murdered by his son-in-law, Branca d'Oria.

Harrowhound shook his head and scornful threw 106
    His snout up: "That's a dirty trick," said he,
    "He's thought of, to get back beneath the brew."

"Trickster I am, and what a trick 'twill be," 109
    Said he who had every dodge at his command,
    "Luring my neighbours to worse misery!"

Here Hellkin got completely out of hand 112
    And burst out: "If thou stoop to hit the ditch
    I need not gallop after thee by land,

I have my wings to soar above the pitch; 115
    We'll leave the crest and hide behind the bank—
    Are ten heads best, or one? We'll show thee which!"

New sport, good Reader! hear this merry prank! 118
    The silly demons turned their eyes away—
    And he who first held back now led the rank.

The Navarrese chose well the time to play; 121
    He dug his toes in hard, then, quick as thought,
    Dived; and so baulked the sportsmen of their prey.

Then all were stung with guilt, and he who taught 124
    The rest to play the fool was angriest;
    He swooped off to pursue him, shouting: "Caught!"

But all in vain; no wings could fly so fast 127
    As fear; the quarry plunged; the hunter rose,
    Skimming the surface with uplifted breast.

Just as the wild-duck, with the falcon close 130
    Upon her, all of a sudden dives down quick,
    And up he skirrs again, foiled and morose.

Hacklespur, who was furious at the trick, 133
    Went rushing after, hoping very much
    The sinner would escape, that he might pick

A quarrel; so when he saw the jobber touch 136
    Surface and vanish, he turned his claws on his brother—
    Fiend, and they grappled over the ditch in a clutch.

But Hellkin was a hawk as good as another 139
    To fight back tooth and nail; so, scratching and chewing,
    They both dropped down plumb in the boiling smother.

The heat at once unlocked them; their undoing 142
    Came when they tried to rise; they struggled, fluttering
    With helpless wings clogged stiff by the tarry glueing.

Barbiger, who with the others stood there spluttering 145
    With rage, sent four across to the farthermost
    Bank with their draghooks; so the band flew scuttering

This side and that, each to some vantage-post 148
    Whence they could reach their drags to the pair half-strangled
    And baked already beneath the scummy crust;

And there we left them, floundering and entangled. 151

The Images

The Tricked and Quarrelling Demons. Though it may present an appearance of solidarity, Satan's kingdom is divided against itself and cannot stand, for it has no true order, and fear is its only discipline. Moreover, in the long run, the devil is a fool: trickery preys on trickery and cruelty on cruelty.

Canto XXIII

The Story

The angry demons pursue the Poets, who are forced to escape by scrambling down the upper bank of Bowge vi. Here they find the Hypocrites, walking in Gilded Cloaks lined with lead. They talk to two Jovial Friars from Bologna, and see the shade of Caiaphas crucified upon the ground.

Canto XXIV

The Story

After an arduous climb from the bottom of Bowge vi, the Poets gain the arch of the seventh bridge. They hear voices from below, but it is too dark to see anything, so they cross to the far side and go down. The Seventh Bowge is filled with monstrous reptiles, among whom are the shades of Thieves. A Thief is stung by a serpent, reduced to ashes, and then restored to his former shape. He reveals himself to be Vanni Fucci of Pistoia, tells his story, and predicts the overthrow of the Florentine Whites.

Canto XXV

The Story

Vanni Fucci defies God and flees, pursued by the monster Cacus. Three more spirits arrive, and the Poets watch while one of them becomes blended with the form of a reptile containing the spirit of a fourth, and the second exchanges shapes with yet another transformed Thief.

Canto XXVI

The Story

Dante, with bitter irony, reproaches Florence. The Poets climb up and along the rugged spur to the arch of the next bridge, from which they see the Counselors of Fraud moving along the floor of the Eighth Bowge, each wrapped in a tall flame. Virgil stops the twin-flame which contains the souls of Ulysses and Diomede, and compels Ulysses to tell the story of his last voyage.

Florence, rejoice, because thy soaring fame
    Beats its broad wings across both land and sea,
    And all the deep of Hell rings with thy name!

Five of thy noble townsmen did I see 4
    Among the thieves; which makes me blush anew,
    And mighty little honour it does to thee.

But if toward the morning men dream true, 7
    Thou must ere long abide the bitter boon
    That Prato craves for thee, and others too;

Nay, were 't already here, 'twere none too soon; 10
    Let come what must come, quickly—I shall find
    The burden heavier as the years roll on.

---

l. 9: *Prato:* Cardinal Nicholas of Prato was sent to Florence in 1304 by Pope Benedict XI in hopes of reconciling the hostile factions. Finding all his efforts wasted, he said, "Since you refuse to be blessed, remain accursed," and laid the city under an interdict. Various disasters which happened shortly afterwards— the collapse of a bridge, killing a vast number of people, and a terrible fire in which over 2000 houses were destroyed and many great families ruined—were attributed to the curse of the Church.

We left that place; and by the stones that bind 13
    The brink, which made the stair for our descent,
    My guide climbed back, and drew me up behind.

So on our solitary way we went, 16
    Up crags, up boulders, where the foot in vain
    Might seek to speed, unless the hand were lent.

I sorrowed then; I sorrow now again, 19
    Pondering the things I saw, and curb my hot
    Spirit with an unwontedly strong rein

For fear it run where virtue guide it not, 22
    Lest, if kind star or greater grace have blest
    Me with good gifts, I mar my own fair lot.

Now, thickly clustered,—as the peasant at rest 25
    On some hill-side, when he whose rays illume
    The world conceals his burning countenance
    least,

What time the flies go and mosquitoes come, 28
    Looks down the vale and sees the fire-flies
    sprinkling
    Fields where he tills or brings the vintage home—

So thick and bright I saw the eighth moat twinkling 31
    With wandering fires, soon as the arching road
    Laid bare the bottom of the deep rock-wrinkling.

Such as the chariot of Elijah showed 34
    When he the bears avenged beheld it rise,
    And straight to Heaven the rearing steeds
    upstrode,

For he could not so follow it with his eyes 37
    But that at last it seemed a bodiless fire
    Like a little shining cloud high in the skies,

So through that gulf moved every flaming spire; 40
    For though none shows the theft, each, like a
    thief,
    Conceals a pilfered sinner. To admire,

I craned so tip-toe from the bridge, that if 43
    I had not clutched a rock I'd have gone over,
    Needing no push to send me down the cliff.

Seeing me thus intently lean and hover, 46
    My guide said: "In those flames the spirits go
    Shrouded, with their own torment for their cover."

"Now thou hast told me, sir," said I, "I know 49
    The truth for sure; but I'd already guessed,
    And meant to ask—thinking it must be so—

Who walks in that tall fire cleft at the crest 52
    As though it crowned the pyre where those great
    foes,
    His brother and Eteocles, were placed?"

"Tormented there," said he, "Ulysses goes 55
    With Diomede, for as they ran one course,
    Sharing their wrath, they share the avenging
    throes.

In fire they mourn the trickery of the horse, 58
    That opened up the gates through which the high
    Seed of the Romans issued forth perforce;

There mourn the cheat by which betrayed to die 61
    Deïdamia wails Achilles still;
    And the Palladium is avenged thereby."

Then I: "O Master! if these sparks have skill 64
    To speak, I pray; and re-pray that each prayer
    May count with thee for prayers innumerable,

Deny me not to tarry a moment here 67
    Until the horned flame come; how much I long
    And lean to it I think thee well aware."

And he to me: "That wish is nowise wrong, 70
    But worthy of high praise; gladly indeed
    I grant it; but do thou refrain thy tongue

And let me speak to them; for I can read 73
    The question in thy mind; and they, being Greek,
    Haply might scorn thy speech and pay no heed."

So, when by time and place the twin-fire peak, 76
    As to my guide seemed fitting, had come on,
    In this form conjuring it, I heard him speak:

"You that within one flame go two as one, 79
    By whatsoever I merited once of you,
    By whatsoever I merited under the sun

When I sang the high songs, whether little or great 82
    my due,
    Stand; and let one of you say what distant bourne,
    When he voyaged to loss and death, he voyaged
    unto."

---

ll. 20–24: Dante realizes that he, like the Counsellors, has been blessed by fate ("kind star") or Providence ("greater grace") with great intellectual gifts, and must, therefore, take particular care not to abuse them.

l. 26: *when he whose rays,* etc.: i.e., in summer, when the days are longest.

l. 28: *what time the flies go and mosquitoes come*: i.e., at dusk.

l. 35: *he the bears avenged*: Elisha. (2 *Kings* ii. 11–12, 23–24.)

l. 54: *Eteocles*: The war of the Seven against Thebes arose from the rival claims of Eteocles and his brother Polynices, the sons of Oedipus, to the throne. They killed each other in battle, and were placed on one pyre; but, even so, such was their mutual hatred that their very flames would not mingle. (Statius: *Thebaïd* xii, 429 *sqq.*)

---

ll. 55–56: *Ulysses . . . Diomede*: the Greek heroes who fought against Troy. The "crafty Ulysses" (Odysseus) advised the stratagem of the Wooden Horse, by which Greek soldiers were smuggled into Troy to open the gates to the besiegers; and also the theft of the sacred statue of Pallas (the Palladium) on which the safety of Troy was held to depend. Thetis, the mother of Achilles, knowing that he would perish if he went to Troy, concealed him at the court of the king of Scyros, disguised as a woman; but he seduced the king's daughter, Deïdamia, who bore him a son. Ulysses discovered his hiding-place and persuaded him to go to Troy; whereupon Deïdamia died of grief.

ll. 74–75: *they: being Greek . . . might scorn thy speech*: The great Greek heroes would despise Dante, as an Italian (i.e., a descendant of the defeated Trojans).

l. 78: *in this form*: Virgil is also an Italian; but he has the power, which Dante has not, of compelling the spirits. We must remember that Virgil, in the Middle Ages, was thought of as a "White Magician," and though the power he uses is not what we should nowadays call "magic" in any evil sense, what follows is in fact a *formal conjuration*. Notice that, since Virgil is here only gratifying Dante's laudable curiosity, he does not use any of those great "words of power" by which he overcame the ministers of Hell in the name of high Heaven (cf. Cantos III. 95; V. 23), but relies on his own power, which is twofold: (1) the native virtue of a good man who, though not in the Grace of Christ, is yet fulfilling a Divine commission "under the Protection"; (2) the claim of the Poet upon the souls who are indebted to him for their fame in the world.

ll. 80–83: *"By whatsoever . . . stand and . . . say"*: This is the *forma*—the form, or formula—of conjuration: a twice-repeated obsecration, "by whatsoever . . ." (naming the claim which constitutes the point of psychic contact between the master and the spirits), followed by a command: "stand . . . speak."

Then of that age-old fire the loftier horn 85
    Began to mutter and move, as a wavering flame
    Wrestles against the wind and is over-worn;

And, like a speaking tongue vibrant to frame 88
    Language, the tip of it flickering to and fro
    Threw out a voice and answered: "When I came

From Circe at last, who would not let me go, 91
    But twelve months near Caieta hindered me
    Before Aeneas ever named it so,

No tenderness for my son, nor piety 94
    To my old father, nor the wedded love
    That should have comforted Penelope

Could conquer in me the restless itch to rove 97
    And rummage through the world exploring it,
    All human worth and wickedness to prove.

So on the deep and open sea I set 100
    Forth, with a single ship and that small band
    Of comrades that had never left me yet.

Far as Morocco, far as Spain I scanned 103
    Both shores; I saw the island of the Sardi,
    And all that sea, and every wave-girt land.

I and my fellows were grown old and tardy 106
    Or ere we made the straits where Hercules
    Set up his marks, that none should prove so hardy

To venture the uncharted distances; 109
    Ceuta I'd left to larboard, sailing by,
    Seville I now left in the starboard seas.

'Brothers,' said I, 'that have come valiantly 112
    Through hundred thousand jeopardies undergone
    To reach the West, you will not now deny

To this last little vigil left to run 115
    Of feeling life, the new experience
    Of the uninhabited world behind the sun.

Think of your breed; for brutish ignorance 118
    Your mettle was not made; you were made men,
    To follow after knowledge and excellence.'

My little speech made every one so keen 121
    To forge ahead, that even if I'd tried
    I hardly think I could have held them in.

So, with our poop shouldering the dawn, we plied, 124
    Making our oars wings to the witless flight,
    And steadily gaining on the larboard side.

Already the other pole was up by night 127
    With all its stars, and ours had sunk so low,
    It rose no more from the ocean-floor to sight;

Five times we had seen the light kindle and grow 130
    Beneath the moon, and five times wane away,
    Since to the deep we had set course to go,

When at long last hove up a mountain, grey 133
    With distance, and so lofty and so steep,
    I never had seen the like on any day.

Then we rejoiced; but soon we had to weep, 136
    For out of the unknown land there blew foul
      weather,
    And a whirlwind struck the forepart of the ship;

And three times round she went in a roaring smother 139
    With all the waters; at the fourth, the poop
    Rose, and the prow went down, as pleased
      Another,

And over our heads the hollow seas closed up." 142

The Images

The Counsellors of Fraud. The sinners in Bowge viii
are not men who deceived those whom they
counselled, but men who counselled others to
practise fraud. The Thieves in the bowge above stole
material goods; these are spiritual thieves, who rob
other men of their integrity. This explains, I think,
the name which Dante gives to their punishment.

The Thievish Fire. The fire which torments also
conceals the Counsellors of Fraud, for theirs was a
furtive sin (Lat.: *furtivus,* from *fur,* thief). And as they
sinned with their tongues, so now speech has to pass
through the tongue of the tormenting and thievish
flame.

Canto XXVII

The Story

*The spirit of Guido da Montefeltro asks for news of
Romagna, and, being answered, tells his story.*

Canto XXVIII

The Story

*From the bridge over the Ninth Bowge the Poets look
down upon the Sowers of Discord, who are continually
smitten asunder by a Demon with a sword. Dante is
addressed by Mahomet and Pier da Medicina, who send
messages of warning to people on earth. He sees Curio
and Mosca, and finally Bertrand de Born.*

---

l. 83: *one of you:* i.e., Ulysses. Notice that, unlike the other
spirits with whom the poets talk, Ulysses never addresses them
personally. Compelled by the conjuration, his narrative reels off
automatically like a gramophone record and then stops.
The voyage of Ulysses, perhaps the most beautiful thing in the
whole *Inferno,* derives from no classical source, and appears to
be Dante's own invention. It may have been suggested to him by
the Celtic voyages of Maelduin and St. Brendan. It influenced
Tasso (*Ger. Lib.* Canto XV.), and furnished Tennyson with the
theme for his poem *Ulysses.* (See Chap. 24.)

l. 91: *Circe:* the sorceress who detained Ulysses on his way from
Troy to Ithaca, after turning several of his companions into swine
(see *Odyssey,* Bk. x).

l. 92: *Caieta* (Gaeta): a town on the south coast of Italy, said to
have been so named by Aeneas after his old nurse, who died and
was buried there (*Aen.* vii. 1–4).

l. 96: *Penelope:* the faithful wife of Ulysses.

l. 104: *the island of the Sardi:* Sardinia.

l. 108: *his marks:* The Pillars of Hercules were looked upon as
the limit of the habitable globe, and the sun was imagined
setting close behind them.

---

ll. 127: *sqq.: the other pole,* etc.: The voyagers had crossed the
equator and made so much leeway south that the Southern
Celestial Pole stood high in the heavens with all its attendant
constellations; consequently, not only was our Pole Star beneath
the northern horizon, but Arctic constellations (the Great and
Little Bears, etc.), which in this hemisphere never set, there
never rose.

l. 133: *a mountain:* This is the mountain of the Earthly Paradise,
which, after Christ's Harrowing of Hell, becomes Mount
Purgatory—the only land, according to Dante, in the Southern
Hemisphere (see Canto XXXIV. 122–23, note).

l. 141: *as pleased Another:* i.e., as pleased God.

Who, though with words unshackled from the rhymes,
    Could yet tell full the tale of wounds and blood
    Now shown me, let him try ten thousand times?

Truly all tongues would fail, for neither could   4
    The mind avail, nor any speech be found
    For things not to be named nor understood.

If in one single place were gathered round   7
    All those whose life-blood in the days of yore
    Made outcry from Apulia's fateful ground,

Victims of Trojan frays, and that long war   10
    Whose spoil was heaped so high with rings of
        gold,
    As Livy tells, who errs not; those that bore

The hammering brunt of battle, being bold   13
    'Gainst Robert Guiscard to make stand on stand;
    And they whose bones still whiten in the mould

Of Ceperan', where all the Apulian band   16
    Turned traitors, and on Tagliacozzo's field
    Won by old Alard, weaponless and outmanned;

If each should show his bleeding limbs unhealed,   19
    Pierced, lopt and maimed, 'twere nothing, nothing
        whatever
    To that ghast sight in the ninth bowge revealed.

No cask stove in by cant or middle ever   22
    So gaped as one I saw there, from the chin
    Down to the fart-hole split as by a cleaver.

His tripes hung by his heels; the pluck and spleen   25
    Showed with the liver and the sordid sack
    That turns to dung the food it swallows in.

I stood and stared; he saw me and stared back;   28
    Then with his hands wrenched open his own
        breast,
    Crying: "See how I rend myself! what rack

Mangles Mahomet! Weeping without rest   31
    Ali before me goes, his whole face slit
    By one great stroke upward from chin to crest.

All these whom thou beholdest in the pit   34
    Were sowers of scandal, sowers of schism abroad
    While they yet lived; therefore they now go split.

Back yonder stands a fiend, by whom we're scored   37
    Thus cruelly; and over and over again
    He puts us to the edge of the sharp sword

As we crawl through our bitter round of pain;   40
    For ere we come before him to be bruised
    Anew, the gashed flesh reunites its grain.

But who art thou that dalliest there bemused   43
    Up on the rock-spur—doubtless to delay
    Going to thy pangs self-judged and self-accused?"

"Nor dead as yet, nor brought here as a prey   46
    To torment by his guilt," my master said,
    "But to gain full experience of the Way

He comes; wherefore behoves him to be led—   49
    And this is true as that I speak to thee—
    Gyre after gyre through Hell, by me who am
        dead."

And, hearing him, stock-still to look on me   52
    Souls by the hundred stood in the valley of stone,
    And in amaze forgot their agony.

"Well, go then, thou that shalt behold the sun   55
    Belike ere long—let Fra Dolcino know,
    Unless he is in haste to follow me down,

He must well arm himself against the snow   58
    With victuals, lest the Novarese starve him out,
    Who else might find him hard to overthrow."

Thus unto me Mahomet, with one foot   61
    Lifted to leave us; having said, he straight
    Stretched it to earth and went his dreary route.

Then one with gullet pierced and nose shorn flat   64
    Off to the very eyebrows, and who bare
    Only a single ear upon his pate,

Having remained with all the rest to stare,   67
    Before the rest opened his weasand now,
    Which outwardly ran crimson everywhere,

And said: "O thou whom guilt condemns not, thou   70
    Whom I have seen up there in Italy
    Unless some likeness written in thy brow

Deceives me; if thou e'er return to see   73
    Once more the lovely plain that slopes between
    Vercelli and Marcabo, then think of me,

Of Pier da Medicina; and tell those twain,   76
    Ser Guido and Angiolello, Fano's best,
    That, if our foresight here be not all vain,

---

l. 9: *Apulia's fatal ground:* The region in south-east Italy where all the wars and battles alluded to in this passage took place.

l. 10: *Trojan frays:* Wars of the Romans (Trojans) against the Samnites (343–290 B.C.); *that long war,* etc.: the Punic Wars (264–146 B.C.).

l. 11: *rings of gold:* According to Livy, so many Romans were killed at the Battle of Cannae, in the second Punic War, that three bushels of golden rings were collected from their bodies.

l. 14: *Robert Guiscard:* combated Greeks and Saracens (1015–1085).

l. 16: *Ceperan (o):* The Apulian barons, under Manfred, deserted at the pass of Ceperano, and let Charles of Anjou through to defeat Manfred at Benevento (1266).

l. 17: *Tagliacozzo:* where Charles of Anjou defeated Manfred's nephew, Conradin; by the advice of Alard de Valery, he allowed two-thirds of his army to retreat, and then, with his reserve troops, annihilated the enemy who had scattered in search of plunder.

l. 31: *Mahomet:* classed as a Christian schismatic.

l. 32: *Ali:* the nephew of Mahomet, was himself the figure-head of an internal schism within the following of the Prophet himself.

l. 42: *the gashed flesh reunites:* We may suppose that in all cases where damned souls are mangled or mutilated (e.g., by Cerberus in the Third Circle or by the "black braches" in the Wood of the Suicides) the shadowy flesh is thus restored; but Dante, with great artistic tact, says nothing about it until, at this point, he can use it to make a ghastly and grotesque effect. He hints at it again in Canto XXXIV. 60.

l. 56: *Fra Dolcino:* Head of a sect, the "Apostolic Brethren," rightly or wrongly condemned as schismatic. In 1305 Pope Clement V ordered a crusade against the Brethren, and after holding out for a year and a day in the hills near Novara, they were forced to surrender. Dolcino was burnt at Vercelli in 1307.

l. 76: *Pier da Medicina:* whose intrigues were instrumental in fomenting the feud between the houses of Polenta and Malatesta in Romagna. His methods were to disseminate scandal and misrepresentation—hence he is shown mutilated in the eavesdropping ear, the lying throat, and the inquisitive nose.

l. 77: *Guido* (del Cassero) *and Angiolello* (da Calignano): two noblemen of Fano, were invited to a conference at La Cattolica, on the Adriatic, by Malatestino of Rimini, who had them treacherously drowned off the headland of Focara, notorious for its dangerous winds.

They'll be flung overboard and drowned, in the 79
    unblest
    Passage near La Cattolica, by the embargo
    Laid on their lives at a false lord's behest.

Neptune ne'er saw so foul a crime, such cargo 82
    Of wickedness 'twixt Cyprus and Majorca
    Ne'er passed, no pirate-crew, no men of Argo

Could show the like. That one-eyed mischief-worker 85
    Whose land there's one here with me in this vale
    Wishes he'd never seen, that smooth-tongued
    talker

Shall lure them to a parley, and when they sail 88
    Deal so with them that they shall have no need
    Of vow or prayer against Focara's gale."

Then I to him: "Tell me, so may I speed 91
    Thy message up to the world as thou dost seek,
    Who's he whose eyes brought him that bitter
    meed?"

At once he laid his hand upon the cheek 94
    Of a fellow-shade, and pulled his jaws apart,
    Saying: "Look! this is he; he cannot speak.

This outcast quenched the doubt in Caesar's heart: 97
    'To men prepared delays are dangerous';
    Thus he gave sign for civil strife to start."

O how deject to me, how dolorous 100
    Seemed Curio, with his tongue hacked from his
    throat,
    He that of speech was so adventurous!

And one that had both hands cut off upsmote 103
    The bloody stumps through the thick air and
    black,
    Sprinkling his face with many a filthy clot,

And cried: "Think, too, on Mosca, Mosca alack! 106
    Who said: 'What's done is ended,' and thereby
    For Tuscany sowed seed of ruin and wrack."

"And death to all thy kindred," added I; 109
    Whereat, heaping despair upon despair,
    He fled, like one made mad with misery.

But I remained to watch the throng, and there 112
    I saw a thing I'd hesitate to tell
    Without more proof—indeed, I should not dare,

Did not a blameless conscience stead me well— 115
    That trusty squire that harnesses a man
    In his own virtue like a coat of mail.

---

l. 84: *men of Argo:* lit.: the Argolican race, i.e., the Greeks, always famous for piracy. But there may be a specific reference to the crime of Argonauts, who murdered Absyrtus and threw his body into the sea on their return from Colchis.

l. 85: *that one-eyed mischief-worker:* Malatestino of Rimini.

l. 93: *that bitter meed:* referring back to ll. 86–87. It was by Curio's advice that Julius Caesar crossed the Rubicon (near Rimini), which at that time (49 B.C.) was the frontier between Italy and Cis-Alpine Gaul, and so declared war on the Republic.

l. 98: *to men prepared,* etc.: Quoted from Lucan: *Pharsalia* (i. 281).

l. 106: *Mosca:* The great Guelf-Ghibelline feud in Florence flared up over a family quarrel. Buondelmonte dei Buondelmonti, who was betrothed to a girl of the Amadei, jilted her for one of the Donati. When her kinsfolk were debating how best to avenge the slight, Mosca dei Lamberti said: "What's done is ended" (i.e., "stone dead hath no fellow"). Buondelmonte was accordingly murdered; the whole city took sides; and thenceforward Florence was distracted by the disputes of the rival factions.

Truly I saw—it seems to me I can 118
    See still—I saw a headless trunk that sped
    Running towards me as the others ran;

And by the hair it held the severed head 121
    Swung, as one swings a lantern, in its hand;
    And that caught sight of us: 'Ay me!' it said.

Itself was its own lamp, you understand, 124
    And two in one and one in two it was,
    But how—He only knows who thus ordained!

And when it reached our bridge, I saw it toss 127
    Arm up and head together, with design
    To bring the words it uttered near to us;

Which were: "O breathing soul, brought here to win 130
    Sight of the dead, behold this grievous thing,
    See if there be any sorrow like to mine.

And know, if news of me thou seek to bring 133
    Yonder, Bertrand de Born am I, whose fell
    Counsel, warping the mind of the Young King

Like Absalom with David, made rebel 136
    Son against father, father against son,
    Deadly as the malice of Achitophel.

Because I sundered those that should be one, 139
    I'm doomed, woe worth the day! to bear my brain
    Cleft from the trunk whence all its life should run;

Thus is my measure measured to me again." 142

The Images

The Sowers of Discord. Three types are shown: fomenters of (1) religious schism (Mahomet; Ali), (2) civil strife (de Medicina; Curio); (3) family disunion (Mosca; Bertrand).

    They appear in the Circle of Fraud because their sin is primarily of the intellect. They are the fanatics of party, seeing the world in a false perspective, and ready to rip up the whole fabric of society to gratify a sectional egotism.

The Sundering Sword. The image here is sufficiently obvious. Note how it is adapted to suit the various types of crime.

Canto XXIX

The Story

Dante lingers, expecting to see a kinsman of his in the Ninth Bowge; but Virgil says he has already passed by unnoticed. They cross the next bridge and descend into Bowge x, where the Falsifiers lie stricken with hideous diseases. Dante talks with an old friend, Capocchio.

Canto XXX

The Story

The shades of Myrrha and Gianni Schicchi are pointed out by Griffolino. Dante becomes intent upon a quarrel between Adam of Brescia and Sinon of Troy, and earns a memorable rebuke from Virgil.

---

l. 134: *Bertrand de Born:* (*ca.* 1140–1215), the warrior and troubadour, was lord of Hautefort (Altaforte) in Perigord. According to his Provencal biographers, he fomented the quarrel between Henry II of England and his son Prince Henry, "the Young King" (so-called because he was crowned during his father's lifetime). For Absalom and Achitophel, see 2 *Samuel* xv–xvii. Bertrand is decapitated because to part father and son is like severing the head from the body.

Canto XXXI

The Story

Dante and Virgil now reach the Well at the bottom of the abyss, round which stand the Giants, visible from the waist up above its rim. They see Nimrod and Ephialtes, and are lowered over the edge of the Well by Antaus.

The self-same tongue that first had wounded me,
  Bringing the scarlet blood to both my cheeks,
  Thus to my sore applied the remedy;

Even so, Achilles' lance was wont to mix   4
  Good gifts with ill, as erst his sire's had done,
  Hurting and healing; so the old tale speaks.

We went our way, turning our backs upon   7
  That mournful vale, up by its girdling bound,
  And silent paced across the bank of stone;

And less than day, and less than night, all round   10
  It gloomed; my eyes, strained forward on our course,
  Saw little; but I heard a high horn sound

So loud, it made all thunder seem but hoarse;   13
  Whereby to one sole spot my gaze was led,
  Following the clamour backward to its source:

When Charlemayn, in rout and ruin red,   16
  Lost all the peerage of the holy war
  The horn of Roland sounded not so dread.

And when I'd gazed that way a little more   19
  I seemed to see a plump of tall towers looming;
  "Master," said I, "what town lies on before?"

"Thou striv'st to see too far amid these glooming   22
  Shadows," said he: "this makes thy fancy err,
  Concluding falsely from thy false assuming;

Full well shalt thou perceive, when thou art there,   25
  How strangely distance can delude the eye:
  Therefore spur on thy steps the speedier."

But after that, he took me lovingly   28
  By the hand, and said: "Nay now, before we go,
  I'll tell thee, lest the strange reality

Surprise thee out of measure; therefore know,   31
  These are not towers, but giants, set in a ring,
  And hid from the navel down in the well below."

And, just as when a mist is vanishing,   34
  Little by little the eye reshapes anew
  The outlines hid by the crowded vapouring,

So, as that thick, gross air we journeyed through,   37
  Little by little drawing nigh the well,
  My error left me, and my terror grew.

As Montereggion's ring-shaped citadel   40
  Has all its circling rampart crowned with towers,
  Even so, with half their bodies the horrible

---

l. 4: *Achilles' lance:* Peleus, the father of Achilles, gave to his son a lance, whose wound could be healed only by sprinkling with rust from the lance-head itself (see Ovid: *Remed. Amor.* 47–48; Chaucer, *Squire's Tale,* 231–32; Shakespeare, 2 *Hen. VI.* v. i, etc.).

l. 16: *Charlemayn:* When Charlemagne was returning from fighting the Saracens in Spain, his rearguard, led by his nephew Roland and the Twelve Peers, was betrayed to the enemy by Ganelon, and slaughtered at the Pass of Roncevaux in the Pyrenees. With almost his last breath, Roland blew his horn Olifant so loud that Charlemagne, eight miles away, heard it and returned to avenge his Peerage.

l. 40: *Montereggion:* A castle about six miles from Siena, surmounted by twelve turrets.

Giants, whom Jove, when the thunder rolls and lowers,   43
  Threatens from heaven, girded the well's high rim,
  Turreting it—the tall and terrible powers.

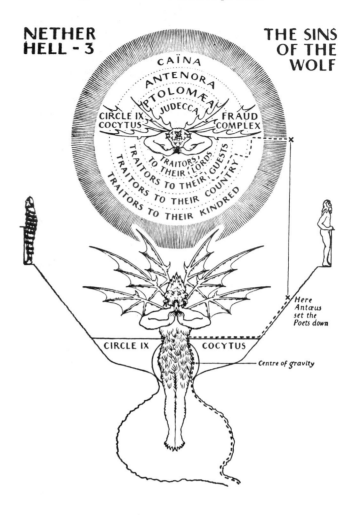

NETHER HELL - 3   **THE SINS OF THE WOLF**

Already I made out one huge face, the dim   46
  Shoulders and breast and part of the belly, and close
  Hung at his sides, both monstrous arms of him.

Nature in truth did wisely when she chose   49
  To leave off making such vast animals
  And let Mars lack executives like those;

If she repents not elephants or whales,   52
  Whoso looks subtly at the case will find
  How prudently her judgment trims the scales;

For where the instrument of thinking mind   55
  Is joined to strength and malice, man's defence
  Cannot avail to meet those powers combined.

As large and long his face seemed, to my sense,   58
  As Peter's Pine at Rome, and every bone
  Appeared to be proportionately immense,

---

l. 59: *Peter's Pine:* A bronze image of a pine-tree, about 7½ ft. high, which, in Dante's time, stood under a canopy outside the old basilica of St. Peter in Rome, but was later removed to the Vatican. Much ingenuity has been expended on calculating the height of the Giants; we may take them to average 50 or 60 ft.

So that the bank which aproned him from zone 61
    To foot, still showed so much, three Friesians
    Might vainly boast to lay a finger on

His hair; for from the place at which a man's 64
    Mantle is buckled, downward, you may call me
    Liar if he measured not fully thirty spans.

"*Rafel maï amech zabi almi*" 67
    The savage mouth began at once to howl,
    Such was the sweetest and the only psalm he

Could sing. "Stick to thy horn, thou stupid soul," 70
    My guide called up; "use that to vent thy breast
    When rage or other passions through thee roll.

Feel at thy neck and find the baldrick laced 73
    That girds it on thee; see, O spirit confused,
    The horn itself that hoops thy monstrous chest."

And then to me: "Himself he hath accused; 76
    That's Nimrod, by whose fault the gracious bands
    Of common speech throughout the world were
    loosed.

We'll waste no words, but leave him where he stands, 79
    For all speech is to him as is to all
    That jargon of his which no one understands."

So, turning to the left beside the wall, 82
    We went perhaps a cross-bow shot, to find
    A second giant, still more fierce and tall.

I do not know what master hand could bind 85
    Him thus, but there he stood, his left hand bound
    Fast down before him, and the right behind,

By an iron chain, which held him closely wound 88
    Down from the neck; and on the part displayed
    Above the brink the turns went five times round.

"So proud a spirit was this," my leader said, 91
    "He dared to match his strength against high Jove,
    And in this fashion his reward is paid.

Ephialtes is his name, who greatly strove 94
    When the giants made the gods tremble for fright;
    The arms he brandished then no longer move."

"Were it but possible, I wish my sight," 97
    Said I, "could once experience and take in
    Briareus' huge unmeasurable might."

"Not far from hence," he answered, "thou shalt win 100
    Sight of Antaeus, who speaks and wears no chain;
    And he shall bear us to the bottom of sin.

Very far off is he whom thou wouldst fain 103
    Behold; like this he's fettered, and doth look
    As this one looks, but twice as fierce again."

No terrible earthquake-trembling ever took 106
    And shook a tower so mightily as forthwith
    Huge Ephialtes in his fury shook;

And never had I been so afraid of death— 109
    For which no more was needed save the fear,
    But that I saw the chains, and dared draw breath.

So on we went; and presently drew near 112
    Antaeus; seven cloth-yards above the well,
    Without the head, his towering bulk rose sheer.

"Thou that of old within the fateful vale 115
    That made the name of Scipio ever-glorious,
    When Hannibal with all his host turned tail,

Didst ravish by thy prowess meritorious 118
    A thousand lions; thou whose aid, 'twould seem,
    Might well have made the sons of earth victorious

Hadst thou allied thee with thy brethren's team, 121
    Pray be not loth, but lower us to the deep,
    Where the great cold locks up Cocytus' stream.

Make us not go to Typhon; let not slip 124
    Thy chance to Tiryus; for this man can give
    That which is craved for here; curl not thy lip,

But stoop; for he's alive, and can retrieve 127
    Thy fame on earth, where he expects—so Grace
    Call him not early home—long years to live."

Thus spake the master; he, all eagerness, 130
    Stretched those enormous hands out to my guide
    Whence Hercules endured so great distress.

And when he felt them grasp him, Virgil cried 133
    To me: "Come here and let me take thee!" So
    He clasped me and made one bunch of us twined
    and tied.

As Carisenda looks, when one stands below 136
    On the leaning side, and watches a passing cloud
    Drift over against the slant of it, swimming slow,

Antaeus looked to me, as I watched him bowed 139
    Ready to stoop; and that was a moment such
    That I heartily wished we might travel another
    road.

---

l. 62: *Friesians:* The men of Friesland were celebrated for their immense stature.

l. 67: *Rafel mai amech zabi almi:* In view of Virgil's express warning (ll. 80–81), the strenuous efforts of commentators to make sense of this remark seem rather a waste of energy. My own impression, for what it is worth, is that if Dante did not make up this gibberish out of his own head, it may have been suggested to him by some conjuring book, for its diction and rhythm are curiously reminiscent of the garbled language of popular charms.

l. 77: *Nimrod:* "and the beginning of his kingdom was Babel" (*Gen.* x. 9–10). For the story of the building of Babel and the confusion of languages see *Genesis* xi. In making Nimrod a giant, Dante follows St. Augustine (*De Civ. Dei* xvi. 3). He is given a horn because he was "a mighty hunter before the Lord."

l. 94: *Ephialtes:* son of Neptune (the sea); one of the giants who fought against the gods, threatening to pile Mount Ossa upon Olympus, and Mount Pelion upon Ossa. They were slain by Apollo.

l. 99: *Briareus:* son of Tellus (the earth), another giant who fought against the Olympians (*Aen.* x. 565 *sqq.*). According to Homer and Virgil, he had a hundred arms and fifty heads; but Dante seems here to have followed Statius, who (*Theb.* ii. 596) merely calls him "immense," and Lucan, who (*Phars.* iv. 596) refers to "fierce Briareus."

---

ll. 101–21: *Antaeus:* son of Neptune and Tellus a giant who was invincible so long as he was in contact with his mother Earth. Hercules eventually overcame him by lifting him from the ground and squeezing him to death in mid-air (see l. 132 of this canto). Antaeus is left unchained because he was not one of the giants who fought against the gods. His exploit with the lions took place near Zama in Libya, where Hannibal was defeated by Scipio. Dante took all these details about Antaeus from Lucan's *Pharsalia* (iv. 593–660).

ll. 124–25: *Typhon . . . Tityus:* two more of the sons of Tellus, who offended against Jupiter. All these earth-giants and sea-giants seem originally to have been personifications of elemental natural forces.

l. 136: *Carisenda:* a leaning tower at Bologna. When one stands beneath one of these towers and looks up, an optical illusion is produced as though it were about to fall upon one; and this illusion is strengthened if a cloud happens to be moving across in the opposite direction to the apparent movement.

But he set us lightly down in the deep whose clutch   142
    Holds Judas and holds Lucifer pent fast;
    Nor in that stooping posture lingered much,
But swung him up, as in a ship the mast.   145

The Images

The Giants. From the point of view of the *story,* it is easy
    to see that Dante placed the Giants here, not merely
    to furnish a means of transport from Malbowges to
    the depth of the Well, but, artistically, to provide a
    little light relief between the sickening horrors of
    the last bowges of Fraud Simple and the still greater,
    but wholly different, horrors of the pit of Treachery.
    But *allegorically,* what do they signify? In one sense
    they are images of Pride; the Giants who rebelled
    against Jove typify the pride of Satan who rebelled
    against God. But they may also, I think, be taken as
    the images of the blind forces which remain in the
    soul, and in society, when the "general bond of
    love" is dissolved and the "good of the intellect"
    wholly withdrawn, and when nothing remains but
    blocks of primitive mass-emotion, fit to be the
    "executives of Mars" and the tools of treachery.
    Nimrod is a braggart stupidity; Ephialtes, a senseless
    rage; Antaeus, a brainless vanity: one may call them
    the doom of nonsense, violence, and triviality,
    overtaking a civilization in which the whole natural
    order is abrogated.

Canto XXXII

The Story

*The Ninth Circle is the frozen Lake of Cocytus, which fills
the bottom of the Pit, and holds the souls of the Traitors.
In the outermost region, Caïna, are the betrayers of their
own kindred, plunged to the neck in ice; here Dante sees
the Alberti brothers, and speaks with Camicion dei Pazzi.
In the next, Antenora, he sees and lays violent hands on
Bocca degli Abati, who names various other betrayers of
their country; and a little further on he comes upon two
other shades, frozen together in the same hole, one of
whom is gnawing the head of the other.*

Canto XXXIII

The Story

*Having heard Count Ugolino's ghastly story of his death
by famine, the Poets pass on to Ptolomaea, where Fra
Alberigo is cheated by Dante into telling him about
himself and Branca d'Oria and others who enjoy the
terrible "privilege" of Ptolomaea.*

This was not life, and yet it was not death;   25
    If thou hast wit to think how I might fare
    Bereft of both, let fancy aid thy faith.
The Emperor of the sorrowful realm was there,   28
    Out of the girding ice he stood breast-high,
    And to his arm alone the giants were
Less comparable than to a giant I;   31
    Judge then how huge the stature of the whole
    That to so huge a part bears symmetry.

---

l. 28: *the Emperor:* "Dante uses the word with the full meaning
of its perversion" (Charles Williams). In Canto II, he refers to
God as "the Emperor of the Imperium on high"; this is the
Emperor of the realm below, who gives his name to the
"sorrowful City."

If he was once as fair as now he's foul,   34
    And Dared outface his Maker in rebellion,
    Well may he be the fount of all our dole.
And marvel 'twas, out-marvelling a million,   37
    When I beheld three faces in his head;
    The one in front was scarlet like vermilion;
And two, mid-centred on the shoulders, made   40
    Union with this, and each with either fellow
    Knit at the crest, in triune junction wed.
The right was of a hue twixt white and yellow;   43
    The left was coloured like the men who dwell
    Where Nile runs down from source to sandy
      shallow.
From under each sprang two great wings that well   46
    Befitted such a monstrous bird as that;
    I ne'er saw ship with such a spread of sail.
Plumeless and like the pinions of a bat   49
    Their fashion was; and as they flapped and
      whipped
    Three winds went rushing over the icy flat
And froze up all Cocytus; and he wept   52
    From his six eyes, and down his triple chin
    Runnels of tears and bloody slaver dripped.
Each mouth devoured a sinner clenched within,   55
    Frayed by the fangs like flax beneath a brake;
    Three at a time he tortured them for sin.
But all the bites the one in front might take   58
    Were nothing to the claws that flayed his hide
    And sometimes stripped his back to the last flake.
"That wretch up there whom keenest pangs divide   61
    Is Judas called Iscariot," said my lord,
    "His head within, his jerking legs outside;
As for the pair whose heads hang hitherward: 64
    From the black mouth the limbs of Brutus
      sprawl—
    See how he writhes and utters never a word;
And strong-thewed Cassius is his fellow-thrall.   67
    But come; for night is rising on the world
    Once more; we must depart; we have seen all."
Then, as he bade, about his neck I curled   70
    My arms and clasped him. And he spied the time
    And place; and when the wings were wide
      unfurled
Set him upon the shaggy flanks to climb,   73
    And thus from shag to shag descended down
    'Twixt matted hair and crusts of frozen rime.

---

l. 38: *three faces:* The three faces, red, yellow, and black, are
thought to suggest Satan's dominion over the three races of the
world: the red, the European (the race of Japhet); the yellow, the
Asiatic (the race of Shem); the black, the African (the race of
Ham). But they are also, undoubtedly, a blasphemous anti-type
of the Blessed Trinity: Hatred, Ignorance, Impotence as against
Love, Wisdom, Power.

l. 46: *from under each sprang two great wings:* Satan was a
fallen cherub, and retains, in a hideous and perverted form, the
six wings which belong to his original rank.

l. 68: *night is rising on the world:* it is about 6 P.M.

l. 74: *from shag to shag descended:* Satan's body is shaggy like
that of a satyr, according to a well-known medieval convention.
The poets clamber down him, feet-first, as one descends a ladder,
working their way through the points where the thick pelt
prevents the ice from adhering close to the surface of his body.
(We must remember the enormous height of Satan—somewhere
about 1,000 or 1,500 ft. at a rough calculation.)

And when we had come to where the huge thigh-
bone   76
  Rides in its socket at the haunch's swell,
  My guide, with labour and great exertion,

Turned head to where his feet had been, and fell   79
  To hoisting himself up upon the hair,
  So that I thought us mounting back to Hell.

"Hold fast to me, for by so steep a stair,"   82
  My master said, panting like one forspent,
  "Needs must we quit this realm of all despair."

At length, emerging through a rocky vent,   85
  He perched me sitting on the rim of the cup
  And crawled out after, heedful how he went.

I raised my eyes, thinking to see the top   88
  Of Lucifer, as I had left him last;
  But only saw his great legs sticking up.

And if I stood dumfounded and aghast,   91
  Let those thick-witted gentry judge and say,
  Who do not see what point it was I'd passed.

"Up on thy legs!" the master said; "the way   94
  Is long, the road rough going for the feet,
  And at mid-terce already stands the day."

The place we stood in was by no means fit   97
  For a king's palace, but a natural prison,
  With a vile floor, and very badly lit.

"One moment, sir," said I, when I had risen;   100
  "Before I pluck myself from the Abyss,
  Lighten my darkness with a word in season.

Kindly explain; what's happened to the ice?   103
  What's turned him upside-down? or in an hour
  Thus whirled the sun from dusk to dawning
  skies?"

"Thou think'st," he said, "thou standest as before   106
  You side the centre, where I grasped the hair
  Of the ill Worm that pierces the world's core.

So long as I descended, thou wast there;   109
  But when I turned, then was the point passed by
  Toward which all weight bears down from
  everywhere.

The other hemisphere doth o'er thee lie—   112
  Antipodal to that which land roofs in,
  And under whose meridian came to die

The Man born sinless and who did no sin;   115
  Thou hast thy feet upon a little sphere
  Of whose far side Judecca forms the skin.

When it is evening there, it's morning here;   118
  And he whose pelt our ladder was, stands still
  Fixt in the self-same place, and does not stir.

This side the world from out high Heaven he fell;   121
  The land which here stood forth fled back
  dismayed,
  Pulling the sea upon her like a veil,

And sought our hemisphere; with equal dread,   124
  Belike, that peak of earth which still is found
  This side, rushed up, and so this void was made."

There is a place low down there underground,   127
  As far from Belzebub as his tomb's deep,
  Not known to sight, but only by the sound

Of a small stream which trickles down the steep,   130
  Hollowing its channel, where with gentle fall
  And devious course its wandering waters creep.

By that hid way my guide and I withal,   133
  Back to the lit world from the darkened dens
  Toiled upward, caring for no rest at all,

He first, I following; till my straining sense   136
  Glimpsed the bright burden of the heavenly ears
  Through a round hole; by this we climbed, and
  thence

Came forth, to look once more upon the stars.   139

---

l. 79: *turned head to . . . feet*, etc.: They have been descending feet-first; now they turn themselves topsy-turvy and go *up* again, headfirst.

l. 93: *what point it was I'd passed:* Since Dante proceeds to take the sting out of "thick-witted" by admitting that he himself was completely bewildered, we may perhaps, without offence, explain that the "point" was the centre of gravity, which was situated precisely at Satan's navel. The sketch of p. 400 will make all these geographical complexities clear.

l. 96: *mid-terce:* Terce, the first of the four canonical divisions of the day, lasted from sunrise (6 A.M. at the equinox) till 9 A.M.; mid-terce would therefore be about 7:30 A.M.

l. 103: *Kindly explain:* Dante wants to know (1) why Satan is apparently upside-down; (2) how it is that, having started their descent of Satan about 6 P.M., they have, after about an hour and a half of climbing, apparently arrived at the following morning. Virgil explains that (1) having passed the centre, they are now in the Southern Hemisphere, so that "up" and "down" are reversed, and (2) they are now going by southern time, so that day and night are reversed. Purgatory stands on the opposite meridian to Jerusalem; therefore Purgatory time is twelve hours behind Jerusalem time; i.e., it is now 7:30 A.M. on Holy Saturday, all over again.

l. 108: *the ill Worm:* Satan. At the centre of the Earth is a little sphere (see l. 116, and look at the sketch), and Satan's body is run through this, like a knitting-needle through an orange, with his head out at one end and his legs at the other.

l. 113: *that which land roofs in:* the Northern Hemisphere, which according to St. Augustine and most medieval geographers, contained all the land in the world.

l. 114: *under whose meridian:* the meridian of Jerusalem, where Christ ("the Man born sinless") was crucified.

ll. 116–17: *a little sphere*, etc.: See sketch, p. 400.

ll. 121 *sqq.: This side the world:* i.e., the southern side. When Satan fell from Heaven, two things happened. (1) The dry land, which until then had occupied the Southern Hemisphere, fled in horror from before him, and fetched up in the Northern Hemisphere; while the ocean poured in from all sides to fill the gap. (2) the inner bowels of the Earth, to avoid contact with him, rushed upwards towards the south, and there formed the island and mountain at the top of which was the Earthly Paradise, ready for the reception of Man, and which, after Hell's Harrowing became Mount Purgatory. This, according to Dante, is the only land in the Southern Hemisphere. The hollow thus left in the middle of the Earth is the core of Hell, together with the space in which Dante and Virgil are now standing—the "tomb" of Satan. From this a winding passage leads up to the surface of the Antipodes. By this passage the river Lethe descends, and up it the poets now make their way.

l. 130: *a small stream:* This is Lethe, the river of oblivion, whose springs are in the Earthly Paradise. They are moving against it— i.e., towards recollection.

The Images.

Judecca. The region of the Traitors to sworn allegiance is called Judecca after Judas, who betrayed Our Lord. Here, cut off from every contact and every means of expression, those who committed the final treason lie wholly submerged.

Judas, Brutus and Cassius. Judas, obviously enough, is the image of the betrayal of God. To us, with our minds dominated by Shakespeare and by "democratic" ideas, the presence here of Brutus and Cassius needs some explanation. To understand it, we must get rid of all political notions in the narrow sense. We should notice, first, that Dante's attitude to Julius Caesar is ambivalent. *Personally,* as a pagan, Julius is in Limbo (Canto IV. 123). *Politically,* his rise to power involved the making of civil war, and Curio, who advised him to cross the Rubicon, is in the Eighth Circle of Hell (Canto XXVIII. 97–102 and note). But, although Julius was never actually Emperor, he was the founder of the Roman Empire, and *by his function,* therefore, he images that institution which, in Dante's view, was divinely appointed to govern the world. Thus Brutus and Cassius, by their breach of sworn allegiance to Caesar, were Traitors to the Empire, i.e., to World-order. Consequently, just as Judas figures treason against God, so Brutus and Cassius figure treason against Man-in-Society; or we may say that we have here images of treason against the Divine and the Secular government of the world.

Dis, so Virgil calls him; Dis, or Pluto, being the name of the King of the Classical Underworld. But to Dante he is Satan or Lucifer or Beelzebub—or, as we say, the Devil. "He can see it now—that which monotonously resents and repels, that which despairs. . . . Milton imagined Satan, but an active Satan; this is beyond it, this is passive except for its longing. Shakespeare imagined treachery; this is treachery raised to an infinite cannibalism. Treachery gnaws treachery, and so inevitably. It is the imagination of the freezing of every conception, an experience of which neither life nor death can know, and which is yet quite certain, if it is willed." (Charles Williams: *The Figure of Beatrice,* p. 144.)

Paradiso, Canto XXXIII, Dante's Ultimate Vision

Dante has ascended the Mountain of Purgatory, and led by Beatrice has moved through the spheres of the heavens where he has been instructed in the nature of God's order for the universe, and in his own spirit he has experienced this love, order, and wisdom. Finally they have reached the Empyrean, beyond the last sphere of the heavens, which is the place of God and souls who have experienced the joy of salvation. Here St. Bernard, the special devotee of the Virgin, becomes Dante's guide (see Image I). The translation of the last twelve Cantos, including this one, was made by Barbara Reynolds, following the death of Dorothy Sayers.

The Story.

St. Bernard addresses to the Virgin a prayer for intercession for Dante that grace may be granted him to behold God. Conveying her acceptance of the prayer, the Virgin turns her eyes above and Dante, doing likewise, is enabled to penetrate with his vision to the True Light of which all other is the radiance or reflection. Therein he beholds the unity of all creation and all time, the Three Persons (manifested as three spheres), and, finally, Christ, one with the eternal being of Godhead. Here his powers of representation failed him and all that remains is the remembrance of his will and love wholly surrendered to the love of God.

"O Virgin Mother, Daughter of thy Son,
Lowliest and loftiest of created stature,
Fixed goal to which the eternal counsels run,

Thou art that She by whom our human nature   4
Was so ennobled that it might become
The Creator to create Himself His creature.

Thy sides were made a shelter to relume   7
The Love whose warmth within the timeless peace
Quickened the seed of this immortal bloom;

High noon of charity to those in bliss,   10
And upon earth, to men in mortal plight,
A living spring of hope, thy presence is.

Lady, so great thou art and such thy might,   13
The seeker after grace who shuns thy knee
May aim his prayer, but fails to wing the flight.

Not only does thy succour flow out free   16
To him who asks, but many a time the aid
Fore-runs the prayer, such largesse is in thee.

All ruth, all mercy are in thee displayed,   19
And all munificence; in thee is knit
Together all that's good in all that's made.

This man, who witnessed from the deepest pit   22
Of all the universe, up to this height,
The souls' lives one by one, doth now entreat

That thou, by grace, may grant to him such might   25
That higher yet in vision he may rise
Towards the final source of bliss and light.

And I who never burned for my own eyes   28
More than I burn for his, with all my prayers
Now pray to thee, and pray they may suffice,

That of all mortal clouding which impairs,   31
Thine own prayers may posses the power to clean
His sight, till in the highest bliss it shares.

And further do I pray thee, heavenly Queen,   34
Who canst all that thou wilt, keep his heart pure
And meet, when such great vision he has seen.

With thy protection render him secure   37
From human impulse; for this boon the saints,
With Beatrice, thronging fold hands and implore.''

---

l. 8: ". . . *within the timeless peace*": in the eternal peace of the Empyrean.

l. 9: "*this immortal bloom*": i.e., the celestial Rose.

ll. 14–15: "*The seeker after grace who shuns thy knee*," etc.: Compare Abelard's hymn to the Virgin:
    They flee to the Judge's mother
    Who flee from the Judge's wrath.
The Roman Church teaches the futility of prayer that does not invoke the intercession of the Virgin Mary.

l. 39: "*With Beatrice, thronging fold hands and implore*": This is our last glimpse of Beatrice.

The eyes which God doth love and reverence,   40
    Gazing on him who prayed, to us made plain
    How prayers, devoutly prayed, her joy enhance.

Unto the eternal light she raised them then: 43
    No eye of living creature could aspire
    To penetrate so fixedly therein.

And I, who now was drawing ever nigher   46
    Towards the end of yearning, as was due,
    Quenched in my soul the burning of desire.

Bernard conveyed to me what I should do   49
    By sign and smile; already on my own
    I had looked upwards, as he wished me to.

For now my sight, clear and yet clearer grown,   52
    Pierced through the ray of that exalted light,
    Wherein, as in itself, the truth is known.

Henceforth my vision mounted to a height   55
    Where speech is vanquished and must lag behind,
    And memory surrenders in such plight.

As from a dream one may awake to find   58
    Its passion yet imprinted on the heart,
    Although all else is cancelled from the mind,

So of my vision now but little part   61
    Remains, yet in my inmost soul I know
    The sweet instilling which it did impart.

So the sun melts the imprint on the snow,   64
    Even so the Sybil's wisdom that was penned
    On light leaves vanished on the winds that blow.

O Light supreme, by mortal thought unscanned,   67
    Grant that Thy former aspect may return,
    Once more a little of Thyself relend.

Make strong my tongue that in its words may burn   70
    One single spark of all Thy glory's light
    For future generations to discern.

For if my memory but glimpse the sight   73
    Whereof these lines would now a little say,
    Men may the better estimate Thy might.

The piercing brightness of the living ray   76
    Which I endured, my vision had undone,
    I think, if I had turned my eyes away.

And I recall this further led me on,   79
    Wherefore my gaze more boldness yet assumed
    Till to the Infinite Good it last had won.

O grace abounding, whereby I presumed   82
    So deep the eternal light to search and sound
    That my whole vision was therein consumed!

In that abyss I saw how love held bound   85
    Into one volume all the leaves whose flight
    Is scattered through the universe around;

How substance, accident, and mode unite   88
    Fused, so to speak, together, in such wise
    That this I tell of is one simple light.

Yea, of this complex I believe mine eyes   91
    Beheld the universal form—in me,
    Even as I speak, I feel such joy arise.

One moment brings me deeper lethargy   94
    Than twenty-five centuries brought the quest that
        dazed
    Neptune when Argo's shadow crossed the sea.

And so my mind, bedazzled and amazed,   97
    Stood fixed in wonder, motionless, intent,
    And still my wonder kindled as I gazed.

That light doth so transform a man's whole bent   100
    That never to another sight or thought
    Would he surrender, with his own consent;

For everything the will has ever sought   103
    Is gathered there, and there is every quest
    Made perfect, which apart from it falls short.

Now, even what I recall will be exprest   106
    More feebly that if I could wield no more
    Than a babe's tongue, yet milky from the breast;

Not that the living light I looked on wore   109
    More semblances than one, which cannot be,
    For it is always what it was before;

But as my sight by seeing learned to see,   112
    The transformation which in me took place
    Transformed the single changeless form for me.

That light supreme, within its fathomless   115
    Clear substance, showed to me three spheres,
        which bare
    Three hues distinct, and occupied one space;

The first mirrored the next, as though it were   118
    Rainbow from rainbow, and the third seemed
        flame
    Breathed equally from each of the first pair.

---

l. 40: *The eyes which God doth love and reverence:* The Virgin's
eyes are loved by the Father and reverenced by the Son.

l. 54: *Wherein, as in itself, the truth is known:* The light of God
alone is the true light, of which every other light is either the
radiation or the reflection.

ll. 65–66: *"even so the Sybil's wisdom,"* etc.: The Cumaean Sybil
wrote her oracles on leaves which were scattered in the wind (cf.
Aeneid III. 441 *et sqq.* VI. 74 *et sqq.*).

ll. 85–87: *In that abyss I saw how love held bound,* etc.: In the
Divine Essence, Dante sees that all creation and all time are
bound up, like the pages in a volume, in God.

l. 88: *. . . substance, accident, and mode:* Substances, i.e.,
things existing in themselves, accidents, i.e., qualities residing in
substances, and the relations between both are seen by Dante to
be so fused together in God as to be indistinguishable.

ll. 91–93: *Yea, of this complex I believe mine eyes beheld the
universal form,* etc.: A "substantial form" is the distinguishing
feature of a substance, that which makes it the thing it is and not
another. The "form of the universe," therefore, would be the
feature, property, or nature of the universe, that which makes it
what it is. To glimpse that would be to read in the mind of God
Himself the divine idea of all things, an experience which would
defy description in mortal words. All Dante can do is to convey
the exultation of spirit which is renewed in him when he speaks
of recalling it.

l. 94: *lethargy:* forgetfulness, oblivion.

ll. 95–96: *Than twenty-five centuries brought the quest,* etc.: The
Argo, the first ship that ever sailed, caused the stupor of Neptune
as its shadow passed over the water, on its way to Colchis for the
Golden Fleece (1200 B.C., or 25 centuries previous to Dante's
vision). A moment after Dante's experience was over, it was
plunged in deeper oblivion than an event which took place 2,500
years ago. (Dante also mentions the Argonauts in Canto II.
16–18.)

ll. 118–20: *The first mirrored the next, as though it were rainbow
from rainbow,* etc.: The Son is begotten of the Father (as a
second rainbow was thought to be "begotten" of the first; cf.
Canto XIII. 10–15); the Holy Ghost proceeds from the Father
and the Son.

How weak are words, and how unfit to frame   121
    My concept—which lags after what was shown
    So far, 'twould flatter it to call it lame!

Eternal light, that in Thyself alone   124
    Dwelling, alone dost know Thyself, and smile
    On Thy self-love, so knowing and so known!

The sphering thus begot, perceptible   127
    In Thee like mirrored light, now to my view—
    When I had looked on it a little while—

Seemed in itself, and in its own self-hue,   130
    Limned with our image; for which cause mine
      eyes
    Were altogether drawn and held thereto.

As the geometer his mind applies   133
    To square the circle, nor for all his wit
    Finds the right formula, howe'er he tries,

So strove I with that wonder—how to fit   136
    The image to the sphere; so sought to see
    How it maintained the point of rest in it.

Thither my own wings could not carry me,   139
    But that a flash my understanding clove,
    Whence its desire came to it suddenly.

High phantasy lost power and here broke off;   142
    Yet, as a wheel moves smoothly, free from jars,
    My will and my desire were turned by love,

The love that moves the sun and the other stars.   145

The Images

The Prayer to the Virgin: In his prayer to the Virgin,
St. Bernard implores her to intercede for Dante that
he may attain, now, to the vision of God and that, in
his life henceforth, he may, under her protection,
persevere in truth and righteousness, his affections
and human impulses guarded from unworthiness.

---

l. 127: *The sphering thus begot:* i.e., The Son.

ll. 130–31: *Seemed . . . limned with our image:* The human
features of Christ are perceptible to Dante within the "sphering"
(l. 127).

ll. 133–35: *As the geometer his mind applies to square the circle,*
etc.: The problem of squaring the circle was formulated by the
Greeks and was proved insoluable at the end of the last century.
The problem is to construct a square with area equal to that of a
given circle by using a straight line and compass only. The radius
of the circle can be taken as a unit of length, so that the problem
is to construct a segment of length $\sqrt{\pi}$. The point of the simile
is that just as a circle is immeasurable in terms of a square, so is
the deity inexpressible in terms of humanity.

ll. 136–38: *So strove I with that wonder—how to fit the image to
the sphere,* etc.: Dante's mind fails to grapple with the difficulty
of reconciling the circle of Deity (the Son) and the human
countenance of Christ.

ll. 140–41: *. . . a flash my understanding clove, whence its
desire came to it suddenly:* By a flash of insight, or by an
instantaneous participation of the bliss of souls in Heaven, Dante
understands how the human and the divine are joined in God.
To the souls who see Him in His essence, this union is as self-
evident as axiomatic truth (cf. Canto II. 40–45).

ll. 142–45: *High phantasy lost power and here broke off,* etc.: At
this point, the power of Dante's intellect to represent what it sees
failed, and he can describe nothing more of his experience
except to state his awareness that his will and desire were in
accord with God's love. Compare St. Paul, "I was not disobedient
unto the heavenly vision."

The prayer is also a hymn of praise to the Virgin. St.
Bernard, in life the most ardent worshipper in the
Virgin-cult, now extols her as excelling all creatures,
angelic or human, in loveliness, goodness, and
vision. On earth, the historical and universal God-
bearer, the vessel of Divine Grace, now, in Heaven,
she is the one mediator to whom man must turn in
prayer. In the *story*, the Virgin, from the very
beginning, is the gentle Lady who is so moved to
pity on Dante's account that for her sake "high doom
is cancelled" (*Inf.* II. 94–96). She it is who summons
Lucy to her side, exhorting her: "Thy faithful votary
needs thee, and I commend him to thy care"; and
Lucy, in her turn, appeals to Beatrice, who swiftly
seeks the aid of Virgil, who, alone, at this stage, can
speak to, and be heard by, Dante. Now the story has
come full circle. Grace, in its various manifestations,
has brought Dante from the depths of Hell up to this
height. As St. Bernard prays for the Virgin's supreme
intercession, all the saints, and Beatrice among them,
fold their hands in the vast fellowship of prayer—
prayer for one man's need.

The Vision of God: The final vision, the crown and
climax of the whole work, consists of two
revelations. First, Dante perceives in the Divine Light
the form, or exemplar, of all creation. All things that
exist in themselves ("substance"), all aspects or
properties of being ("accident"), all mutual relations
("mode") are seen bound together in one single
concept. The Universe is *in* God. Next, having
glimpsed the whole of creation, Dante beholds the
Creator. He sees three circles, of three colours, yet of
one dimension. One seems to be reflected from the
other, and the third, like flame, proceeds equally
from both (the Father, Son, and Holy Ghost). Then,
as he gazes, the reflected circle shows within itself
the human form, coloured with the circle's own hue.
As Dante strives to comprehend how human nature
is united with the Word, a ray of divine light so
floods his mind that his desire is at rest. At this point
the vision ceases, and the *story* ends with the poet's
will and desire moving in perfect coordination with
the love of God.

15

The Medieval Synthesis in Art

Chronological Overview

375–700	Migrations of Germanic and Asiatic tribes[1]
622–732	Islamic conquest of Middle East, western Asia, North Africa, Spain, Portugal
732	Charles Martel turns back Muslims at Poitiers
600–800	Hiberno-Saxon Period; Irish Golden Age
750–900	Carolingian Period
900–1000	Ottonian Period
1000–1150	Romanesque Period in France (until ca. 1200 outside France)
1140–1200	Early Gothic Period
1200–1300	High Gothic Period
1300–1500s	Late Gothic Period; International Style

"There is no God but Allah and Mohammed is his prophet." Not a religion of complex beliefs, Islam is based totally on that simple statement; the complexity is in the observance. The Arabic word for submission is *Islam,* the faith; he who submits is a "Muslim," a believer. Submitting unreservedly to an all-powerful God, believers make up a religious community that follows the Koran's detailed rules for every aspect of daily life. Compiled from the writings of the Prophet some twenty years after his death in 632, the Koran is the only authority, the last word in theology, law, and all social institutions. By far the most important textbook in Muslim universities, the Koran may never be translated; the faith has one language and that language is Arabic.

---

1. All dates are approximate except the Charles Martel victory.

Figure 15.1 Koca Sinan, Suleymaniye Camii Mosque, 1550–1557 (foreground); Fatih Camii Mosque, 1463 (background). Istanbul.

Figure 15.2 Ceiling designs, Suleymaniye Camii Mosque

Originating in the desert wastes of culturally backward Arabia, a religion as circumscribed as Islam could not have developed a high degree of civilization had it not been for the propagation of the faith by the sword. Unlike most faiths, Islam is a missionary religion (as is Christianity), which launched a *jihad*—a holy war—to conquer half of the known world in a single century. Unified by faith and a common language and immeasurably enriched by contacts with other civilizations, Islam developed and promoted learning and some of the arts from India to the Iberian peninsula.

Strictly limited by the Koran, artistic development was very uneven to put it mildly. Architecture was of paramount importance, particularly in the construction of mosques, but sculpture was, according to Mohammed, idolatrous, a satanic art. Figurative and monumental scale painting were forbidden for similar reasons, leaving only manuscript decoration using organic and geometric designs.

A religion that provides direct access to God through prayers, Islam has no priests, liturgy, or sacraments. Buildings were not needed because praying could be done anywhere, and Mohammed did indeed teach and pray everywhere including his own house. Based on this model, early mosque design evolved into a simple enclosure in which one wall, the *qibla,* faced towards Mecca. A sacred niche, the *mihrab,* was soon added to the qibla, to the right of which was the *minbar,* or pulpit, for readings from the Koran and the Friday sermon. A characteristic feature from the earliest days, the *sahn,* a pool for ritual ablutions, was located in the courtyard. Though *muezzins* (mu–EZ–ins; criers) could call the faithful to prayer from any high place, *minarets,* or tall, slender towers, quickly became standard features of mosque design.

The Fatih Camii Mosque (background, fig. 15.1) was built by Sultan Mehmet II in 1463, ten years after the Ottoman Turks conquered Constantinople. Built on one of the seven hills of Istanbul by Turkey's greatest architect, Koca Sinan, the Suleymaniye Camii Mosque (foreground) honors Sultan Suleyman the

Figure 15.3 Courtyard, El Attarin Medersa, 1323–1325, Fez, Morocco.

Magnificent. There is no mandatory number of minarets; the only stipulation is that no mosque may have seven minarets like the Great Mosque in Mecca. Patterned after Hagia Sophia (see fig. 12.19), as are most mosques in Istanbul, this massive structure embodies Muslim fascination with complex geometric designs (fig. 15.2). The viewpoint in the illustration is that of a spectator standing on the floor of the mosque and looking straight up at the ceiling. In this view, the central dome is at the bottom and at the top is the half-dome with its circling windows and flanking partial domes. The arches are outlined in red and white stones, and the geometric designs and Arabic calligraphy are brightly lit by the hundreds of windows similar to those in Hagia Sophia (see fig. 12.20).

With the sacred niche—the mihrab—indicating the direction of Mecca, the courtyard of El Attarin Medersa, a Muslim college (fig. 15.3), features the ritual fountain or sahn, panels of glazed faience, and mosaic floors, all with elaborate geometric designs.

Figure 15.4 Interior, The Great Mosque, 785–990, Cordoba, Spain. Now the Cathedral of Cordoba.

Figure 15.5 Portal, Great Mosque, Cordoba

Built by Sultan Abou Said near the end of the golden age of Islamic architecture, El Attarin is an elegant example of delicate, intricate design.

Begun by Caliph Abd al-Rahman in the eighth century, the mosque of the caliphs of Cordoba (fig. 15.4) is so large that a sixteenth-century Christian church was built in its midst. With no axis and thus no focus, the forest of columns—856 in all—symbolizes the worshippers who are as individual as the columns but who are all united in common prayer, part of the great community of believers. The striped arches are a Muslim invention but the columns were recycled, having been taken from Roman and Christian buildings.

The doorway of the Great Mosque (fig. 15.5) emphasizes the characteristic horseshoe arch of Mozarabic (Spanish Christian) design. Lavishly embellished with mosaics and abstract reliefs, the overall style is best described as Moorish, a synthesis of North African and Spanish styles. One of the glories of Moslem Spain, the Great Mosque was only one of the wonders of Cordoba, itself the most illustrious center of art and learning in all of Europe until its conquest by Christians in 1236.

The ponderous exterior of the palace of the caliphs of Granada, the Alhambra, shields an inner architectural fairyland resonating to the liquid murmer of running water. Because of its desert origins, Islam pictures Hell and Paradise as extensions of the natural environment; Hell is an arid and flaming inferno while Paradise is like an oasis: cool, wet, and lush. Drawing unlimited water from the snows of the Sierra Nevadas, the caliphs built an earthly paradise: delicate, intimate, cooled and soothed by playful fountains and the channels of water coursing throughout the palace, the embodiment of what an Arabian Nights setting should be. A prominent feature of the Alhambra is the Court of the Lions (fig. 15.6) at the center

Figure 15.6 Court of the Lions, 1354–1391, The Alhambra, Granada, Spain.

of the most elaborate and ethereal section of the palace. Guarded by rare, for Islam, sculptures of stylized lions, the fountain adds its bubbling sounds to the flowing waters of a fantastic courtyard of delicate columns and arches decorated with tiles and stucco. Lacy arabesques and airy stuccoed ceilings contribute to what is actually a lucid, rhythmic design. Not a single column is both perfectly tapered and precisely vertical, thus symbolizing the imperfections of earthly existence. In other words, even this manufactured Eden is but a defective version of the heavenly paradise to come. The last notable structure built in Moorish Spain, the Alhambra fell to Ferdinand and Isabella in the eventful year of 1492.

Figure 15.7 National Mosque, Kuala Lumpur, Malaysia.

Because they are not bound to a unified liturgy as, for example, Roman Catholic churches are, no two mosques are alike and some, like the Great Mosque at Cordoba, are unique. There are certain distinguishing characteristics, however, that have become conventional. Though a contemporary design in reinforced concrete and marble, the National Mosque (fig. 15.7) is still a recognizable mosque. The dome of the central plan, the freestanding minaret, and the courtyard fountain (not visible here) add up to a modern setting for a very traditional religion.

Hiberno-Saxon Period, ca. 600–800

Though never part of the Roman Empire, Ireland was known by the Latin name *Hibernia,* which later became *Ivernin* in Old Celtic and then *Erin* in Old Irish. Occupied by Celts and Christianized by St. Patrick of Gaul, Ireland was cut off from the continent by the Anglo-Saxon conquest of England. This isolation led to the development of a unique form of Christian monasticism patterned after the solitary hermits of Egypt rather than the urbanized Roman version of Christianity. Founding monasteries in the countryside, Irish monks emphasized a strict ascetic discipline and, unlike the desert saints, a deep devotion to scholarship. Preempting the power of the bishops, Irish monasteries sponsored a remarkable missionary program in England and western Europe which resulted in a spiritual and cultural dominance fittingly called the Irish Golden Age of ca. 600–800.

Manuscripts were produced in abundance to supplement these missionary activities, especially numerous copies of the Bible, all elaborately decorated to signify the supreme importance of the sacred texts. Displaying little interest in the figurative art of Roman Christianity, monks synthesized Celtic and Germanic elements to produce a richly decorated art based on geometric designs and organic abstractions derived from plant and animal forms. Created at a

Figure 15.8 "Cross Page," Bishop Eadfrith (?), *Lindisfarne Gospels,* ca. 698–721. British Museum, London. Reproduced by courtesy of the Trustees of the British Museum.

monastery on the island of Lindisfarne off the east coast of England, the *Lindisfarne Gospels* is a superb example of Hiberno-Saxon decorative art. As meticulous as printed electronic circuitry, the "Cross Page" (fig. 15.8) is a miniature maze of writhing shapes and mirror-image effects highlighted by intertwined dragons and serpents. The Celtic cross spans a page bursting with energy and vitality. With details so fine that they are best studied with a magnifying glass, one wonders how this work was accomplished.

The "X-P (khi-rho) Page" (colorplate 13) is lovely testimony to the masterful use of color to enhance but not compete with either the linear composition or the importance of the gospel text.

The last of the remarkable Hiberno-Saxon illuminated manuscripts, the *Book of Kells* is also the most elaborately decorated. Reduced to the Greek letters XPI (khri), the name of Christ dominates a page swirling with animal and abstract interlaces and geometric decoration (fig. 15.9). Whorls within circles within larger circles dazzle the eye, but closer study reveals two human faces and, on the left vertical of the X, three human figures depicted from the waist up. Near the bottom and to the right of the same vertical is a playful genre scene featuring two cats and four mice.

Figure 15.9 "XPI Page", *Book of Kells*, ca. 760–820. Reproduced by permission of the Board of Trinity College, Dublin.

Figure 15.10 Odo of Metz, Palatine Chapel of Charlemagne, 792–805, Aachen, Germany.

Hiberno-Saxon manuscripts typify the early period of intricate and painstaking Northern craftsmanship, which included weaving, ivory and stone carving, jewelry, and stained glass, a tradition that led to spectacular achievements in the Gothic age and, eventually, to machine design and the industrial revolution. An important factor in the development of Northern crafts may have been climate, for these are mainly indoor activities that could be carried on regardless of the inclement weather of long, dark winters.

Carolingian Art, ca. 750–900

Ruling from 768 to 814 as a Frankish king, Charlemagne saw himself as a successor to the Caesars of Rome, a concept that was reinforced in 800 when the pope crowned him Emperor of the Holy Roman Empire. To his capital at Aachen, Germany, he brought scholars, artists, and craftsmen to help revive classical antiquity. Short-lived but vital for later developments, the Carolingian Renaissance utilized Celtic-Germanic and Mediterranean traditions to produce a Carolingian art that combined classic forms with Christian symbols and subject matter.

Societies tend to develop an architecture based on the availability of building materials, and at that time the vast forests of northern Europe provided an endless supply of wood for the timber-frame construction of private and public buildings. Charlemagne, however, wanted impressive palaces and churches built in the Roman manner, and to do that he had to import southern principles of building in stone. Because there were no local stonemasons, he undoubtedly imported southern masons to work on his buildings and to instruct northern craftsmen, a procedure culminating in the expert stonework of Romanesque and Gothic cathedrals.

One of the few buildings to survive intact from the age of Charlemagne, the chapel of his palace at Aachen (fig. 15.10) is an impressive example of northern stone construction. Designed by Odo of Metz, the first known Northern architect, the chapel is modeled after San Vitale (see colorplate 10), which so impressed Charlemagne during a visit to Ravenna. A revision of San Vitale and not a copy, the chapel is simpler in style but still patterned after the Byzantine central plan. The central octagon is formed by arcades resting on heavy piers. Above this there are tall arches and within them are two levels of decorative columns. As might be expected during the early period of stone construction, the columns and most of the capitals were taken from existing Roman buildings. One would suspect that Charlemagne preferred using columns of the Caesars for his personal chapel.

Figure 15.11 Germigny des Pres, view from the east, 806.

Figure 15.12 Interior, Germigny des Pres

One of the oldest churches in France, Germigny des Pres (fig. 15.11) was erected by Theodolphus, a friend of Charlemagne, and by the emperor's Armenian architect. Taller than the usual Byzantine church, this brick building is topped by a square tower that is capped with a peaked tile roof. Despite destructive attacks by Viking invaders, later called Northmen, and then Normans, the mosaic and much of the structure was preserved and then restored in the nineteenth century. The interior features heavy semicircular arches with a focus from the central altar, which is modern, to the mosaic in the apse (fig. 15.12). Brought back by Charlemagne from Theodoric's palace in Ravenna and composed of 130,000 glass cubes, this is the only Byzantine mosaic in France.

The "Saint Mark" from the *Gospel Book of Archbishop Ebbo of Reimes*, which was painted shortly after Charlemagne's death, derives from a classic model (fig. 15.13). The Hiberno-Saxon influence is discernible in the draperies swirling about the torso in lines as dynamic as those in an Irish manuscript. Rather than a scholar writing a book, Mark is a man inspired by divine guidance, a transmitter of the sacred text. This follows the ancient view that poets, like Homer for example, are divinely inspired and possess superhuman powers.

Influenced possibly by Byzantine decorative arts, Carolingian book covers were made of precious metals and richly ornamented with jewels. Created during the waning influence of the Carolingian dynasty, the "Crucifixion Cover" of the *Lindau Gospels* is of gold, with the figures of Christ and angels delineated

Figure 15.13 "St. Mark" from the *Gospel Book of Archbishop Ebbo of Reims,* 816–835. Municipal Library, Epernay, France.

Figure 15.14 Interior, St. Martin du Canigou, eleventh century, near Vernet-les-Bains, France.

Figure 15.15 St.-Benoit-sur-Loire, 1004–1218. View from the southeast.

in graceful, sinuous lines (colorplate 14). Outlining the golden Greek cross in gold beads, semiprecious and precious stones, the artist has reinforced the cross motif with jeweled crosses in the four panels and all around the border. Major stones are set away from the gold surface so that reflected light can add to their brilliance. There can be no doubt of the importance of the text within this cover.

After the remarkable reign of Charlemagne (768–814) the Holy Roman Empire declined in power and influence. Nevertheless, the revival of Greek and Roman learning sparked a synthesis of classical civilization and Celtic-Germanic culture, elements of which are still discernible in modern Europe and America.

Romanesque Period, ca. 1000–1150/ 1200

By about 1000 A.D. virtually all of Europe had been Christianized. After centuries of ferocious attacks, the barbaric Vikings, Magyars, and Slavs had finally been converted to Christianity and assimilated by their victims. Stupendous building programs began all over Europe to replace damaged structures and to construct new churches and monasteries. During the eleventh century the Cluniac Order alone built nearly a thousand monastic churches; every hamlet, village, town, and city had at least one new church. Inevitably architecture and architectural sculpture became the dominant art forms of this vigorous new age.

Located high in the French Pyrenees, the tiny monastic church of St. Martin du Canigou is one of the earliest structures with a complete barrel vault of cut stone (fig. 15.14). Vaulted stone roofs became the rule for Romanesque churches in place of the wooden truss roofs of earlier buildings; whether accidental or caused by hostile invaders, fire was a constant danger. Stone roofs relieved that difficulty but brought about another: how to support the heavy roof. The solution included thick walls supported by evenly spaced columns alternating with massive piers and connected by semicircular arches. Dimly lit because large windows weaken supporting walls, Romanesque churches are characteristically heavy and solid, giving a feeling of protective walls shutting out a hostile world. Intended for the exclusive use of the religious community, the monastic church shielded the monks from all outside influences.

Christians had been making pilgrimages to scenes of Christ's life since the third century and, during Charlemagne's reign, in ever-increasing numbers. By the tenth century it was commonly believed that viewing sacred relics of Christ and the Saints secured God's pardon for sins, a belief encouraged by pilgrimage churches housing sacred relics. Featuring the relics of St. Benedict, which were supposedly rescued from Monte Cassino,[2] the Abbey of Fleury (now St.-Benoit-sur-Loire) became one of the prime destinations for organized parties of pilgrims (fig. 15.15). Rebuilt after brutal Viking raids of the ninth century, the abbey church, with its belfry-topped porch and noble crossing tower, rests in the lush French countryside like a ship in a calm sea. Ornamented by the largest surviving group of carved capitals, many of

---

2. The saint's remains were lost in the ruins of Monte Cassino during its destruction by the Lombard invasion of 577.

Figure 15.16 Capitals and piers, west porch, St.-Benoit-sur-Loire.

Figure 15.17 "Flight to Egypt" capital, St.-Benoit-sur-Loire.

Figure 15.18 Choir, looking east, St.-Benoit-sur-Loire

Figure 15.19 Collegiate Church of St. Sernin, ca. 1080–1120. Toulouse, France.

them Corinthian, the porch is supported by early examples of compound piers (fig. 15.16). Just as strong as the solid masonry piers of St. Martin du Canigou (see fig. 15.14), the clustered columns around a central core became basic to mature Romanesque architecture.

Prime examples of early architectural sculpture, the lavishly carved capitals are among the glories of St.-Benoit-sur-Loire and harbingers of a sculptural renaissance that climaxed in the Gothic Age (fig. 15.17). The "Flight to Egypt" features Joseph carrying a palm frond and leading the donkey carrying the Virgin and Child. On the left is the star and an angel slaying a dragon, as described in chapter 12 of the Apocalypse. Not nearly as naive as it might first appear, the carving relates the flight from Herod in unmistakable terms for the illiterate peasantry.

Illustrating the increasing height of Romanesque vaulting, the choir of St.-Benoit-sur-Loire features a barrel vault with ornamental ribs (fig. 15.18). The clerestory windows, which admit considerable light for a Romanesque church, are set above a blind arcade that decorates the upper wall. Adorned only with architectural details, the masonry walls are supported by majestic columns connected by Roman arches. The interiors of French Romanesque and Gothic churches are always restrained, depending for their effect on a unity of basic design and discreet architectural embellishment without recourse to mosaics, murals, frescoes, or other extraneous decorations. The result is a rational design of awesome power.

Most but not all pilgrimage churches were monastic. A major stop on the pilgrimage road from Italy and Provence to Spain's Santiago de Compostela, the church of St. Sernin is a superb example of the Burgundian Romanesque style (fig. 15.19). The view shown is of the chevet (sheh–VAY), the rounded eastern end, and the octagonal 215′ tower over the crossing. The semicircular barrel vault is punctuated by nonstructural transverse arches evenly distributed

Figure 15.20 Nave, St. Sernin

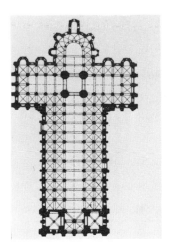

Figure 15.21 Plan of St. Sernin (after Kenneth John Conant).

Figure 15.22 West facade, Abbey of Jumièges, 1037–1067, on the lower Seine near Rouen, France.

Figure 15.23 St. Etienne (Abbaye aux Hommes), 1064–1135, Caen, France. View from the southeast.

down the nave (fig. 15.20). Constructed on the module of the crossing square under the tower, the size of each compartment between the columns, called a *bay,* is exactly half the size of the crossing square (fig. 15.21). On the side aisles each square is one-quarter of the module. The compound columns are two stories high with arches supporting a gallery that runs above the side aisles and that was probably used by some of the pilgrim throngs. Minus the triumphal arch of Early Christian churches, the evenly spaced columns and identically sized bays lead inexorably down the nave to the focal point of the altar. St. Sernin is a classic example of French Romanesque design, unified and lucid.

Now one of the most imposing ruins in France, the Abbey of Jumièges was founded in the seventh century and destroyed by Vikings in the ninth. It was reconsecrated in 1067 in the presence of William the Conqueror, a descendent of the Viking marauders (fig. 15.22). With its 141' twin towers and outward-thrust-

ing porch, Jumièges represents the impressive Norman style that was to decisively influence Gothic architecture. The present state of Jumièges typifies the fate of French monasteries after the 1789 Revolution. After the monks were dispersed, the abbey was auctioned off in 1793 to a timber merchant who quarried and sold many of the stones. The ruins now belong to the nation.

Begun shortly before the Conqueror sailed for England, St. Etienne was under the personal protection of King William (fig. 15.23). The characteristic twin towers of Norman architecture reach 295' with the aid of spires that were a Gothic addition. The seven towers are a vigorous contribution to the design as well as symbols of the Holy Trinity plus the Four Evangelists. With the Conqueror's tomb before the high altar, St. Etienne still stands as the royal church of the Norman king.

Figure 15.24 "The Battle Rages," detail from Bayeux Tapestry, ca. 1070–1080. Wool embroidery on linen. Height ca. 20",
entire length 231'. Town Hall, Bayeux, with special authorization of the Village of Bayeux.

Probably designed by a woman and embroidered
on linen by Saxon women, the Bayeux Tapestry is the
most precise medieval document which has survived
intact, providing daily life scenes and details of
clothes, customs, and weapons. In fifty-eight scenes,
the rivalry between King Harold of England and William of Normandy is depicted, culminating in the Battle of Hastings (fig. 15.24). In this episode the English,
identified by their mustaches, are beginning to suc-
cumb to the superior numbers of the French. The tri-
partite design features an ornamental band above the
violent battle scene and a lower band depicting the
casualties. Despite the stylized design, the details are
brutally realistic; warriors and horses have died in
agony.

The abbey church of Ste.-Madeleine in the village of Vézelay is intimately associated with another
kind of warfare: holy war. Originally scheduled for
Vézelay, Pope Urban II preached the First Crusade
from Clermont in 1095, calling on all Christians to free
the Holy Land from the Saracens. In 1146 Vézelay was
the site for St. Bernard's Second Crusade and, in 1190,
King Richard the Lion-Heart of England and King
Phillip Augustus of France departed from Vézelay on
the Third Crusade, a disastrous failure, as was every
Crusade from the Second in 1146 to the Eighth in
1291. Intended to support and define the Crusades as
a second mission to convert the heathen, the *Mission
of the Apostles* tympanum at Vézelay (fig. 15.25) exemplifies the revived relationship of architecture and
sculpture in the Romanesque style. Set between the
arch and lintel, the tympanum is a compendium of
sermons calling on the faithful to emulate the Apostles: save or condemn, preach the gospel, heal the sick,
and drive out devils. Following the old convention of
relating the size of a figure to its importance, Christ

Figure 15.25 *Mission of the Apostles,* tympanum of the central portal of the narthex, ca. 1120–1132, Ste.-Madeleine,
Vézelay.

dominates the composition, poised in an almond-
shaped frame wearing swirling draperies patterned
after Hiberno-Saxon manuscripts. On both sides the
Apostles are rising from their seats to commence their
evangelical mission. On the archivolts, the relief
bands that frame the tympanum, and above the lintel
are the benighted people of the world, who in their
diseased, crippled, or animalistic condition await the
enlightenment. Under the ornamented top archivolt
is an inner band of zodiac signs, the seasons, and
monthly labors, signifying the year-round Christian
mission. In its original condition, complete with
bright colors and gold embellishment, the impact of
this dynamic work must have been even greater.

Colorplate 13 Bishop Eadfrith (?), "X–P Page," *Lindisfarne Gospels.* British Library, London. Reproduced by permission of the British Library.

Colorplate 15 Reliquary in shape of head, Rhenish, early twelfth century. British Museum, London. Reproduced by courtesy of the Trustees of the British Museum.

Colorplate 14 "Crucifixion Cover," *Lindau Gospels*, ca. 870, 13¾ × 10½". The Pierpont Morgan Library, New York.

Colorplate 17 High mass, nave of Cathedral of Notre Dame, Coutances, France. Begun 1218.

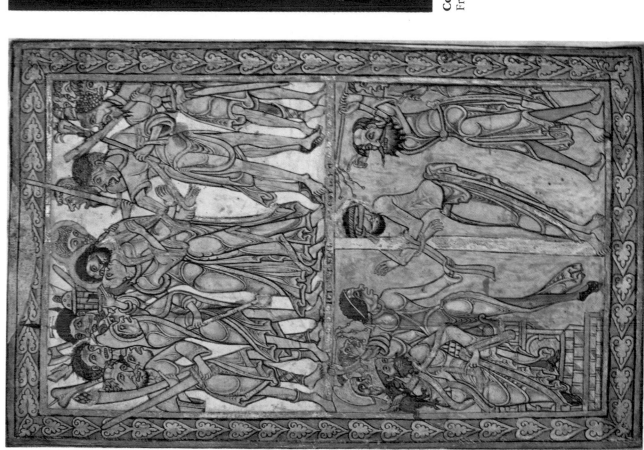

Colorplate 16 *Psalter of St. Swithin:* "Capture of Christ and the Flagellation," ca. 1250. The British Library, London. Reproduced by permission of the British Library.

Colorplate 18 Southern rose and lancets, Chartres Cathedral

Colorplate 19 Duccio, *The Calling of the Apostles Peter and Andrew,* ca. 1308. Tempera on wood, 17⅛ × 18⅛″. Samuel H. Kress Collection. National Gallery of Art, Washington, D.C.

Colorplate 20 Simone Martini, *Annunciation,* 1333. Tempera on wood, 8′8″ × 10′. (Saints in side panels by Lippo Memmi.) Uffizi Gallery, Florence.

Colorplate 21 Giotto, *Lamentation,* 1305–1306. Fresco, 7'7" × 7'9". Arena Chapel, Padua

Figure 15.26 Nave, Ste.-Madeleine, ca. 1104–1132, Véze-lay, France.

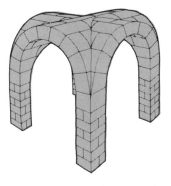

Figure 15.27 Schematic drawing of a cross-vault.

Figure 15.28 Trumeau figure of "The Prophet," Abbey Church of St. Pierre, ca. 1125–1130, Moissac.

One of the most distinctive of all Romanesque interiors, the nave of Ste.-Madeleine (fig. 15.26) is high, about 90′, with unusual transverse arches of black and white stone, probably inspired by such Islamic buildings as the Great Mosque in Cordoba (see fig. 15.4). The tunnel, or barrel, vault was no longer used because of its inherent drawback: an unbroken series of arches pressed back to back can be lighted or opened only on the opposite ends. Any and every opening in the supporting wall weakens the entire structure. One of the earliest French churches to abandon the barrel vault, Ste.-Madeleine's uses a vault that is intersected at right angles by another vault to form a "groin" or "cross" vault (fig. 15.27). Note that at this high level the groined vaults of Vézelay permit

considerable illumination from the clerestory windows. Close study of the interior also reveals that the architect used groin vaults that were too heavy for the exterior wall, vaults so massive that the upper walls are pushed outwards. External flying buttresses (see an example of the principle in fig. 15.37) had to be added to balance the thrust of the vaults, thus stabilizing this lovely nave.

An outstanding example of architectural sculpture, the strange other-worldly figure of a prophet, possibly Jeremiah, appears on the trumeau, or supporting pier, of a portal of the Abbey Church of St. Pierre at Moissac (MWA–zak; fig. 15.28). The attenuated shape, the long and slender legs, and delicate lines recall Hiberno-Saxon manuscripts. Seemingly too slight to support the mass of masonry, the gentle prophet expresses a spiritual tension and nervous vigor similar to an El Greco painting of four centuries later.

The medieval love of embellishment ranged from manuscripts to stone, including priests' vestments and such ceremonial objects as crosses, chalices, incense

Figure 15.29 Busketus, Pisa Cathedral and Campanile, 1063–1272.

Figure 15.30 Pisa Cathedral with Baptistery

burners, candlesticks, and reliquaries. A casket containing a sacred object, a reliquary was invariably made of precious materials and highly decorated. The silver Rhenish reliquary in the shape of a head (colorplate 15) is quite restrained for the period, particularly in the classical details of the hair. Embossed and incised silver figures of the twelve Apostles surround the base of what the twentieth century would label a three-dimensional composite work or "combine." In the twelfth century it was not even regarded as sculpture but as a reliquary, pure and simple.

The linear style of the Ste.-Madeleine tympanum (see fig. 15.25) and "The Prophet" (see fig. 15.28) are also prominent in the *Psalter of St. Swithin* (colorplate 16). In both manuscript scenes elegant arabesques gracefully outline the figures, thus emphasizing the grotesque faces of the brutal soldiers in comparison to the resigned passivity of Christ. Beauty and horror are effectively combined to convey a powerful spiritual message.

The basic Romanesque style of Roman arches and stone vaults supported by compound columns and heavy walls spread throughout western Europe, always displaying, however, certain variations depending on regional conventions and traditions. Adhering closely to the basilica plan of Early Christian churches, the buildings of Tuscany also evidenced an increased interest in classical art, a heritage that had never been totally forgotten. The most distinguished complex in the Tuscan Romanesque style is the cathedral group at Pisa (fig. 15.29). Constructed of readily available white marble, the cathedral resembles an Early Christian basilica, but with Romanesque characteristics: the dome over the crossing; the superimposed arcades on the west front; the blind arches encircling the entire

building. The extended trancepts with an apse at each end add to the poise and serenity of the design, which makes the famous Leaning Tower, the campanile, all the more striking. Begun in 1174 by Bonanno Pisano on an unstable foundation, the tower began to tilt well before its completion in 1350. Adjusted slightly to the left, the three upper sections were supposed to compensate for the rightward incline. Over 14′ off the perpendicular, the tower, whose bells haven't rung in years, is still moving. Engineering schemes to save the structure are complicated by the stipulation that the tower be stabilized without, however, correcting the tilt of one of Italy's prime tourist attractions.

The view from the top of the campanile clearly shows the cruciform plan of the cathedral with its clerestory windows and upper level of blind arcades (fig. 15.30). The massive baptistery, topped with a dome 115′ in diameter, was built between 1153 and 1278 and later embellished at the upper level with Gothic details, the only discordant note in a grand design.

Contrary to the notion that all medieval art is anonymous, the names of scattered individuals in Italy, France, Belgium, and Holland are known. An early work of the sculptor/architect Antelami, the *Descent from the Cross* (fig. 15.31), somewhat resembles Byzantine ivories but with some classical influence apparent in the delicate scrolls framing the scene. Contrasting sharply with the mourners on the left, the indifferent soldiers are grouped around Christ's robe, symbolizing the secular world. The spiritual world is represented on the left with the expressive curve of Christ's body, the right arm removed from the cross by the angel and extended to the mourners. Damnation is on the right, Salvation on the left.

Figure 15.31 Benedetto Antelami, *Descent from the Cross,* 1178. Relief, Cathedral of Parma, Italy.

Figure 15.32 Mont St. Michel, ca. 1017–1144; 1211–1521. Aerial view.

In all its manifestations, Romanesque art finds its unity in architecture; the church is the Fortress of God where the apocalyptic vision is ever called to mind. Exemplifying this concept, the Abbey of Mont St. Michel in the Sea of Peril (fig. 15.32), rises in awesome majesty off the coast of France. Begun about 1020 by Abbot Hildebert and Richard II of Normandy, grandfather of William the Conqueror, the building program covered five centuries as abbot succeeded abbot and crusade followed crusade. Mont St. Michel summarizes medieval architecture, a glorious mixture of Norman, Norman Romanesque and Early, High, and Late Gothic styles.

Early Gothic Period, ca. 1140–1200

Erected usually in the countryside as part of monastic communities, Romanesque churches were built by and for "regular" clergy, those who lived under the rule *(regula)* of a religious order. The rise of the great cities of Europe was paralled by the development of the new Gothic style. Staffed by the "secular" clergy, priests who lived "in the world" *(in saecula),* Gothic churches were urban establishments designed to serve city parishes. Each city's glory and chief community center, the Gothic cathedral was not only the seat *(ex cathedra)* of the bishop but a theatre, classroom, concert hall, court, and general meeting place.

Figure 15.33 Choir and ambulatory, Abbey Church of St. Denis, 1140–1144.

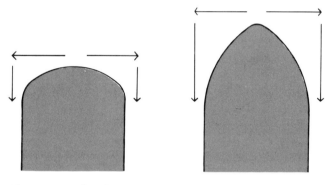

Figure 15.34 Schematic drawings of Romanesque and Gothic arch thrusts.

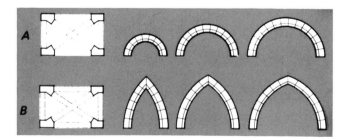

Figure 15.35 (a) Cross vault of semicircular arches over an oblong bay; (b) Cross vault of pointed arches over an oblong bay.

Though the basic structural elements of Gothic architecture were developed and used during the Romanesque period, it remained for an unknown architectural genius to put it all together at St. Denis, just north of Paris (fig. 15.33). Carried out under Abbot Suger who left a detailed account of his administration (1122–1151), the designer supported the weight of the vaults with pointed arches, which are more stable than semicircular arches. The arch principle is one of mutual support; the two halves lean against each other so that the force (gravity) that would cause either to fall actually holds them in place. But, the flatter the arch the greater the lateral thrust at the springline, that is, the outward push where the arch turns upward (fig. 15.34). The lateral thrust is significantly reduced when the pointed arch is used because the springline is angled more nearly downward. Hence, the more pointed the arch the less the tendency to push its supporting pier outwards, thus reducing the need for massive supports.

The rounded arch has a fixed diameter because it is always half of a circle. Since it has no unalterable diameter, the pointed arch can rise to almost any height and span any space (fig. 15.35). In the illustration the first rounded arch spans the short side, the second the long side, and the third the diagonal, necessitating piers of different heights. With their identical height, pointed arches simplify the engineering and improve the aesthetic effect with slender columns topped by capitals at a uniform height.

The Gothic vaulting and piers of identical height can be seen at St. Denis (see fig. 15.33). The piers on the right have less masonry to support than the main piers to the left, and are thus considerably slimmer. Still appearing bulky from the back, the primary piers are less massive than Romanesque columns, particularly when viewed from the choir, where the clustered columns now rise gracefully to the high ceiling.

The most striking difference at St. Denis is the marked increase in light. In figure 15.33 one can see, on all three levels, stained glass windows that function as light converters, transforming the interior into a hazy luminosity of shifting colors. The windows are subdivided first by mullions (carved stone posts), by stone tracery to form still smaller glass panels, and by thin lead strips to hold in place the individual pieces of colored glass. The light penetrating the stained glass provides a polychromatic effect, making the glass transparent, while the stone and metal dividers become opaque black lines separating and highlighting the colors. The mystical coloration of Gothic interiors represents the philosophical idea of light as a Neoplatonic form of ultimate beauty, an earthly manifestation of the divine light of the heavenly kingdom.

On June 11, 1144, Abbot Suger proudly presided at the dedication of the choir of St. Denis in the company of hundreds of priests and laymen, five archbishops, and Louis VII of France and his Queen, Eleanor of Aquitaine. This was a truly momentous occasion, sparking a veritable frenzy of Gothic construction in the Ile de France, the region surrounding Paris.

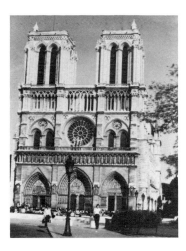

Figure 15.36 West facade, Notre Dame, Paris. Plan, 1163–1250; facade, ca. 1200–1250.

Figure 15.37 Apse with flying buttresses, Notre Dame, Paris.

The cathedral at Chartres was begun in 1142, even before the formal dedication at St. Denis, Laon in 1160, Notre Dame of Paris in 1163, Bourges in 1185, and Chartres again in 1194 after a catastrophic fire. These cathedrals, all major enterprises, were followed by hundreds of other churches in a vast building program that, in a single century, included every major city in northern Europe.

The imposing facade of Notre Dame (fig. 15.36) has been justly admired for over seven centuries as a masterpiece of rational design. Solidly buttressed at the corners, the facade rises effortlessly in three levels on which sculptural embellishment is subordinate to the architecture. Unlike the projecting porches of later Gothic cathedrals, the three portals are recessed from the frontal plane and topped by a row of carved saints. The rose window centerpiece is flanked by smaller roses over double windows, above which there is a line of lacy pointed arches. With their subtly embellished cornices and elongated windows, the square towers complete the design with restraint and dignity. This majestic west front is a fitting symbol for the ascendancy of Paris as the cultural and intellectual center of Europe.

The view of the east end of Notre Dame (fig. 15.37) displays in no uncertain terms that critical component of Gothic design, the flying buttress. Springing from heavy piers, two sets of arches curve upwards to support the piers of the exterior walls, providing the counterbalancing force needed to stabilize the structure. It is the flying buttress principle that enabled architects to utilize the curtain walls of stone pierced by numerous stained glass windows. Not visible in figure 15.36 is the Late Gothic fleche, the slender spire that rises above the crossing. Flying buttresses represent an exposed engineering which provides both the needed physical support and the psychological assurance that the building is totally solid and safe, as indeed it is.

Figure 15.38 West facade, Chartres Cathedral, ca. 1142–1507.

High Gothic Period, ca. 1200–1300

After a disastrous fire in the village of Chartres in 1194, which left intact only the Early Gothic facade of the still unfinished cathedral, the rebuilding of Chartres Cathedral commenced immediately and moved rapidly, with the basic structure completed by 1220. The idea that Gothic cathedrals took decades or even centuries to build is erroneous and probably based on the fact that these buildings were never fully completed; there was always something to be added or elaborated.

The first masterpiece of the mature period, Chartres Cathedral has been called the Queen of Cathedrals, the epitome of Gothic architecture (fig. 15.38). Typically High Gothic but unique to Chartres, the south (right) tower begins with a square base that

Figure 15.39 Central doorway, Royal Portal, ca. 1140–1150, Chartres Cathedral.

Figure 15.40 Choir, Notre Dame of Chartres

evolves smoothly into the octagonal shape of the fourth level. From here the graceful spire soars to a height of 344', the characteristic "finger pointing to God" of the Gothic age. The elaborate north tower, which was not completed until well into the Northern Renaissance, lacks the effortless verticality of the south tower. Verticality was a hallmark of Gothic; cities competed in unspoken contests to erect cathedrals with the highest vaults and the tallest towers. An inspiring House of God was also a symbol of civic achievement. With a facade 157' wide and measuring 427' in length, Chartres Cathedral is as prominent a landmark today as when it was built, thanks in part to modern zoning ordinances that control building heights throughout the village.

Incorporated into the facade when the cathedral was rebuilt, the Royal Portal (western doorways) of the earlier church emphasizes the Last Judgment theme of Romanesque portals but with significant differences (fig. 15.39). Rather than the harsh Damnation of the Last Judgment, the theme is now the Second Coming with its promise of salvation. No longer is there the inventive freedom of the Romanesque; all is unified and controlled. The outer frame is provided by the twenty-four elders of the Apocalypse on the archivolts and the lower row of twelve Apostles. Surrounded by symbols of the four Evangelists, the now benign figure of Christ raises an arm in benediction in the manner of Caesar Augustus (see fig. 10.5). Beneath the tympanum are the jamb figures, a wholly new idea in architectural sculpture.

Conceived and carved in the round, the figures were very likely fashioned after live models rather than copied from manuscripts, a further indication of the emerging this-worldly spirit of the age.

The most significant manifestation of the new age was the dedication of the cathedrals themselves. Named after apostles and saints in previous eras, the new churches were almost invariably dedicated to Our Lady *(Notre Dame)*. Mary was Queen of Heaven, interceding for her faithful who, sinners all, wanted mercy, not justice. This was the Cult of the Virgin Mary, the spiritual counterpart of the vastly enhanced status of women. The masculine Romanesque was the age of feudalism and conflict; the more feminized Gothic was the Age of Chivalry, as derived from courts of love sponsored by powerful women like Eleanor of Aquitaine, Queen of France and then of England. With the development of cathedral schools such as those at Paris and Chartres, Mary was viewed much like Athena, as patroness of arts and science. The right doorway of the Chartres Royal Portal (not illustrated) includes portraits of Aristotle, Cicero, Euclid, Ptolemy, Pythagoras and symbols of the Seven Liberal Arts. The Gothic cathedral represents the medieval synthesis of spiritual and secular life at its best.

Featuring a nave 53' in width, the most spacious of all Gothic naves, the interior of Notre Dame of Chartres is 130' in length and 122' high, the loftiest vault of its day (fig. 15.40). At the rounded end of the

Figure 15.41 West facade, Cathedral of Notre Dame of Amiens, ca. 1220–1288.

Figure 15.42 Nave, Cathedral of Notre Dame of Amiens

choir are the tall pointed arches of the arcade and the triforium gallery of the second level, culminating in the lofty and luminous stained glass windows. At the sides of the illustration can be seen two of the four enormous piers which frame the crossing and which are carved as clustered columns to minimize their bulk. Columns clustered around a central core have the same diameter as a solid pier, but their appearance gives the illusion of lightness and grace.

One of the chief glories of Gothic interiors is the kaleidoscopic color cascading from the mighty stained glass windows. Retaining most of its original windows, Chartres is a treasure house of the art, with clerestory windows 44' high, all in all some 20,000 square feet of medieval glass. Located at the south end of the transepts, the southern rose is like a gigantic multicolored jewel set above the five figurative lancet windows (colorplate 17). Because it is a southern exposure window, the predominance of color leans towards the warm part of the spectrum from roses to oranges to reds. Its counterpart, the northern rose (not illustrated), transmits the cooler colors, especially many hues of blue. Contrary to what one might expect, direct sunlight on any of the southern windows upsets the chromatic balance of the interior. All of the windows were designed to function best under the even light of the generally grey skies of northern France, enabling the warm and cool colors to effect a balance of color tones. Surpassing anything up to that time, the craftsmanship and sheer beauty of Gothic stained glass remain incomparable.

As usually seen by tourists, a Gothic cathedral is an enormous empty building, very impressive but more like a museum than a church. Despite the awesome scale of the interior, the cathedral is not at all intimidating in the manner of, say, Egyptian temples.

Rather, the church is built for people and when functioning as intended, the interior comes vibrantly alive as an inspirational setting for public worship. Colorplate 18 illustrates an actual high mass in a nave nearly filled with worshippers. A superb example of the Norman High Gothic style, Coutances has a characteristically unadorned and harmonious interior that derives its whole effect from the architecture. Not even the modern dress of the congregation or the speakers on the columns can detract from the timelessness of the setting; the scene is very nearly the same as it has been for over seven centuries.

Designed originally by one of the first known masterbuilders, Robert de Luzarches, the Cathedral of Notre Dame of Amiens marks the culmination of the best ideas of the French Gothic style. Modeled after that of Notre Dame in Paris, the west front (fig. 15.41) is not as controlled and majestic as its model. Its grandeur, however, is overwhelming. Looking like one gigantic and intricate work of sculpture, the facade is dominated by its incomparable portals. The imposing entrances thrusting outward from the facade proclaim the interior in unmistakable terms; the central portal announces the lofty nave and the two flanking doorways the side aisles. In other words, the inner structure is foretold by the exterior design.

Patterned after Chartres, the nave of Amiens is even more integrated, soaring in one breathtaking sweep to 144' above the pavement (fig. 15.42). Unfortunately minus its stained glass, the interior is still the culmination of the High Gothic style: lofty arcades with slender columns rising to the ribbed vaults. Once thought to have functioned as structural supports for the ceiling, the ribs are actually decorative extensions of columns carrying the design to the pinnacle of the ceiling, which with its groined vaults is completely self-supporting.

Figure 15.43 Sainte Chapelle, 1245–1248, Paris. View from northeast.

Figure 15.44 Interior, upper chapel, Sainte Chapelle

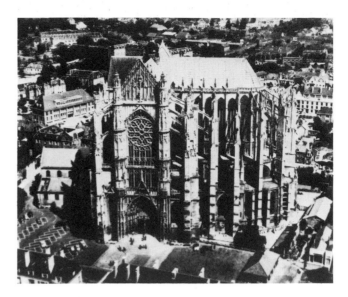

Figure 15.45 Choir of Beauvais Cathedral, France. Aerial view. Begun ca. 1225.

Completed in less than thirty-three months for Louis IX of France, later St. Louis, Sainte Chapelle (fig. 15.43) is today a small chapel set in the midst of the Palais de Justice. With virtually no stone walls the structure is a set of piers supporting walls of stained glass. Topped by a spire reaching 246' into the sky, the upper chapel, with its 49' windows, rests on a lower level intended for the use of servants. With almost 7,000 square feet of glass containing 1,134 scenes the upper chapel is a jewelbox of color dominated by brilliant reds and luminous blues (fig. 15.44). Because there are no side aisles, there are no flying buttresses to impede the penetration of light into a building whose walls are about 75 percent glass. Rivaling Chartres in the extent and quality of its original glass, Saint Chapelle managed to survive the Revolution; damaged and neglected, it became a storage area for old government files. Restored in the nineteenth century to an approximation of its original condition, the remarkable fact is that its basic structure is so flawless, so perfectly engineered that it survived completely intact for seven centuries.

With the cathedral at Beauvais, the competition to build the highest vault came to a crashing end (fig. 15.45). Reaching the incredible height of 157', the vaulting was a wonderment to all until its collapse in 1284; only the apse was left standing. Rebuilt over a period of forty years, the choir remains today as a testimonial both to Gothic vertical aspirations and the waning of enthusiasm for building enormously expensive churches; the money ran out along with the spirit. Though commonly thought that "tortured stone" could not withstand the lofty vaults of Beauvais, modern engineering research[3] points to a design

3. Robert Mark, *Experiments in Gothic Structure* (Cambridge, Mass.: MIT Press, 1982), pp. 58–77.

Figure 15.46 Nave, Canterbury Cathedral, begun 1174.

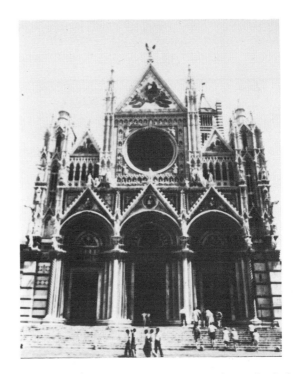

Figure 15.47 Giovanni Pisano, Facade, Cathedral of Siena, begun ca. 1285.

flaw in an exterior picr, the deterioration of which was not detected. The collapse of 1284 ironically confirmed the nature of Gothic engineering in which the stability of the vaulting depends on the proper functioning of all components. When the single pier failed due to undetected weathering, all the choir vaults came tumbling down. The apse remained standing simply because it was structurally independent. Interestingly enough, the design flaw was corrected during the rebuilding program, meaning that the entire cathedral could then have been completed as originally planned. Today one can look at the choir section and only wonder at what might have been at Beauvais.

Gothic Style outside France

By the second half of the thirteenth century the Gothic style had been accepted throughout Europe, though Italy was less than enthusiastic. Regional variations gave each area its own brand of Gothic. Taking to Gothic as if they had invented it, the English built in the style from the twelfth to the nineteenth centuries. Drawing directly upon the Ile de France style, the English utilized clearly recognizable Gothic characteristics in a manner just as distinctly non-French. The clean lines of French verticality were abandoned at the outset in favor of a multiplicity of verticals topped by veritable forests of ribs that almost obscured the groined vaults, as evidenced in Canterbury Cathedral (fig. 15.46). The nave is not seen as a majestic succession of bays but rather as a steady procession of supports and arches. Because the ribs arch up from the

triforium, the clerestory windows are not as prominent in the design as in the French style nor is the stained glass comparable in workmanship or design. A comparison of the interior of Canterbury with those of Chartres (fig. 15.40) and Amiens (fig. 15.42) reveals just how drastic the difference is, which the French are only too willing to point out. The English, on the other hand, view French interiors as cold and impersonal, while English Gothic is warmly intimate, hospitable, and comfortable. Different styles suit different people.

The Italians took up the Gothic style slowly and with many reservations; they were, after all, the ones who had labeled the new style as a barbaric creation of the Goths of the north. Distinctly unclassical, a Gothic cathedral is restless, unsettled, always incomplete, whereas a classical temple is at rest, serenely complete. Nevertheless, the Gothic spirit was on the move in Italy, becoming part of the classical and Romanesque traditions. For all its Gothic elements, the Cathedral of Siena (fig. 15.47) has square doorways, triangular pediments, and a balanced design reminiscent of the classical and Romanesque traditions. There is a Gothic rose window minus stained glass plus Gothic towers, lacy blind arches, and the three portals. Most of the statuary has been liberated from its architectural bondage and the tympanums feature colorful mosaics. Faced with multicolored marble the facade is an ensemble of Gothic elements mixed with Tuscan Romanesque, all in all a notable example of Italian reaction to the Gothic spirit.

Figure 15.48 Cimabue, *Madonna Enthroned,* ca. 1280–1290. Panel, 12'7½" × 7'4". Uffizi Gallery, Florence.

Whatever its regional variations, the Gothic cathedral epitomizes the explosive creativity and intellectual boldness of the Gothic age. Never completely finished, a process rather than an end product, it stood at the center of the storm of changes that would sweep away the medieval synthesis. It represents both the triumphant climax of the Age of Faith and the end of the Middle Ages.

Late Gothic Period, ca. 1300–1500s

An integral part of Gothic architecture, stained glass windows and relief sculpture served the pictorial purposes once provided by mosaics, murals, and frescoes. Virtually nonexistent in the Gothic north, large-scale paintings were still done in Italy, which had

maintained its contact with Byzantium. It was Italian painters who synthesized Byzantine and Gothic styles to create new procedures crucial to the future development of Western painting.

Renowned for his skill as a fresco and tempera painter[4], the Florentine Cimabue (chee–ma–BOO–uh; 1240?–1302) introduced features that were incorporated into the developing Italian style. His *Madonna Enthroned* (fig. 15.48) illustrates the new characteristics of strong, forceful figures in an atmosphere of complete serenity. The human scale of the lower figures emphasizes the towering dignity of the Madonna as she holds the mature-looking child. Distinguished from Byzantine icons by its much greater size, the gable shape and solid throne are also Gothic in origin as is the general verticality. The rigid, angular draperies and rather flat body of the Madonna are from the Byzantine tradition, but the softer lines of the angels' faces and their lightly hung draperies were inspired by works from contemporary Constantinople.

Cimabue's naturalistic, monumentally scaled work had a profound influence on his purported pupil Giotto (JOT–toe; ca. 1267–1337), the acknowledged "father of Western painting." Giotto was a one-man revolution in art, who established the illusionary qualities of space, bulk, movement, and human expression, all features of most pictorial art for the next six centuries. His indebtedness to Cimabue is obvious in his *Madonna Enthroned* (fig. 15.49), but there are significant changes that make it not necessarily better but certainly different. Giotto abandoned the Byzantine tradition and patterned his work after Western models, undoubtedly French cathedral statues. His solid human forms occupy a three-dimensional space surrounded by an architectural framework. His *Madonna Enthroned* is highlighted by the protruding knee of the Madonna, showing that there is a tangible body underneath the robe, a figure of monumental substance. When compared with Cimabue's angels, we see that Giotto's angels, especially the kneeling ones, are placed firmly at the same level on which the base of the Gothic throne rests. The ethereal, floating quality of Byzantine painting has been abandoned in favor of the illusion of tangible space occupied by three-dimensional figures.

Giotto's reputation, already imposing in his own time, rests mainly on his frescoes, most notably the biblical scenes in the Arena Chapel, which are among the most celebrated in the whole history of art. In his *Lamentation* (colorplate 21) the artist has composed a scene in the manner of a Greek tragedy. The mourning tableau is placed in the foreground so that the picture space is at eye level, making us participants in the tragedy, our involvement heightened by the

---

4. Fresco paintings are made on fresh wet plaster with pigments suspended in water; tempera uses pigments mixed with egg yolk and applied, usually, to a panel. Because the drying time for both techniques is very fast, corrections are virtually impossible without redoing entire areas. Therefore, artists had to work rapidly and with precision.

Figure 15.49 Giotto, *Madonna Enthroned,* ca. 1310. Tempera on panel, 10'8″ × 6'8″. Uffizi Gallery, Florence.

Figure 15.50. Duccio, *Rucellai Madonna,* 1285. Tempera on wood, 14'9″ × 9'6″. Uffizi Gallery, Florence.

wonderfully expressive backs of the two anonymous mourners. Grief is individualized, with each participant mourning according to his or her personality. The emotional range is vast, from the controlled intensity of the earth-bound figures to the tortured grief of the writhing angels. Giotto's achievements are summarized in this one powerful work: the creation of subtle illusions of tactile qualities; existence and movement in space; a deep psychological understanding of subject and viewer; and the establishment of a continuity of space between viewer and painting. To all of these achievements he brought a profound sense of humanity's awareness of human emotions and of their place in the world. Difficult as it is to realize today, Giotto's contemporaries saw these works as the ultimate reality, so "real" that you could walk into them. We can give proper credit to this view by comparing Giotto's work with that of his contemporaries and by remembering also that reality, or the illusion of reality, changes from epoch to epoch.

From Siena came two artists whose work was unlike that of either Cimabue or Giotto but who were instrumental in establishing the International Style,

the first international movement in Western art. Duccio (DOOT–cho; ca. 1255–1319) painted Byzantine-type faces except for the eyes, but in a style comparable to northern Gothic manuscripts and ivories. The most elegant painter of his time, his *Rucellai Madonna* (fig. 15.50) is highly decorative, with sinuous folds of background drapery and a remarkable delicacy of line for so large a work. Contrasting with the Byzantine-style flatness of the Madonna, the kneeling angels are portrayed much more in the round, combining the Hellenistic-Roman naturalistic tradition with that of French architectural sculpture. This one work is a virtual encyclopedia of the International Style synthesis of Mediterranean and northern cultures.

In his *The Calling of the Apostles Peter and Andrew* (colorplate 19), Duccio depicts a world of golden sky and translucent greenish sea where the commanding but elegant figure of Christ beckons gently to the slightly puzzled fishermen. It is a lovely creation, the world of Duccio, and this is the style the popes at Avignon and the northern kings and queens admired and called upon their artists to emulate.

Serving the pope's court in Avignon, Duccio's pupil Simone Martini (1284–1344) combined the grace of the Sienese school with the exquisite refinement of Late Gothic architecture. His *Annunciation* (colorplate 20) epitomizes the courtly style. Completely Gothic, the frame is replete with *crockets,* or ornamental leaves and flowers, and *finials,* or carved spires; signifying eternity, the gold-leaf background is Byzantine. Delineated in graceful curved lines, the Angel Gabriel kneels before the Virgin to proclaim "Hail Mary, full of grace. . . ." As the words travel literally from his lips she draws back in apprehension, her body arranged in an elaborate **S**-curve and covered by a rich blue robe. Between the two figures is an elegant vase containing white lilies symbolic of Mary's purity. As delicately executed as fine jewelry, the artistic conception is aristocratic and courtly, comparable to the polished sonnets of Petrarch, who also served the papal court at Avignon.

With its combined Classical/Byzantine/Gothic attributes, the International Style was promulgated throughout the religious and secular courts of Europe. It found an enthusiastic response wherever wealthy clients prized grace, delicacy, and refinement in art, music, manners, and dress. Aesthetic pleasure was the goal, not spiritual enlightenment.

Summary

While European civilization was descending into the Dark Ages, Islam was assimilating ancient and contemporary cultures, leading to brilliant achievements in medicine, astronomy, mathematics, scholarship, and architecture. Illustrious structures such as the Suleymaniye Mosque in Istanbul, the Great Mosque in Cordoba, and the Alhambra are enduring symbols of Islamic culture.

A curious backwater during Roman times, Christianized Ireland launched missionary activities that led to a golden age highlighted by the production of exquisite manuscripts in the Hiberno-Saxon style. Establishing a tradition of meticulous northern craftsmanship, the *Lindisfarne Gospels* and *Book of Kells* were among the first and best of a long history of illuminated manuscripts.

Charlemagne seized the opportune moment to create the Holy Roman Empire and launch the Carolingian Renaissance. Importing technology and stonemasons from the Mediterranean area, he set in motion the forces that would produce the Romanesque style and climax in the Gothic Age.

The year A.D. 1000 marked the Christianization of virtually all of Europe and the launching of a vast building program of monasteries and churches. Inspired by Roman models, builders constructed stone-vaulted churches such as the pilgrimage churches of St.-Benoir-sur-Loire, St. Sernin, and Ste.-Madeleine. Notable among the numerous monasteries built during the period were Jumièges and Mont St. Michel.

Inspired by the revolutionary design of the choir of St. Denis, French master builders erected some of the most sublime buildings ever conceived by humankind, most notably the Gothic cathedrals of Chartres and Amiens.

Though relatively immune to Gothic architecture, Italian artists synthesized Classical, Byzantine, and Gothic elements to create the first International Style in art. A medieval man like Dante and his friend and fellow Florentine Giotto carried medieval art to its final consummation. Indeed, Dante's work marks the end of the Middle Ages and sets the stage for the Renaissance.

16

Medieval Music: Sacred and Secular

The bountiful storehouse of medieval music marks the first great era of Western music, and yet little of this large repertory is heard by modern audiences. An inseparable part of everyday life, medieval music served the needs of the society: ballads to preserve tales and legends; songs of love and beauty; dances and popular tunes to celebrate the joys of life; dirges and lamentations to express the sorrows; sacred music for praise and worship. This is not the musical art of today's concert halls, but recordings of much of this rich heritage are available in authentic versions (see the Record List for this chapter and the Development of Medieval Music on p. 441).

There is a large body of sacred music but comparatively little secular music prior to the fourteenth century. In common with other nonliterate societies, secular music was passed along to later generations through oral tradition. Music of the church, on the other hand, had a status comparable to the high social position of clerics. As part of the province of the literate and the learned, music was preserved in written form as a link to the eternal. However, the sheer mass of sacred music and secular music (after the thirteenth century) has to be indicative of a comparable amount of secular music, a folk art that was rarely taken seriously and seldom written down. The survival of nearly 1,700 troubadour-trouvère melodies (discussed later in this chapter) attests to the importance of secular music in medieval life.

Sacred Music

The oldest type of music is *monophonic,* or a single melodic line with no other parts or accompaniment. The liturgical (officially authorized) music of the Church of Rome is monophonic in a style called Gregorian chant, or plainsong.

Gregorian Chant

According to legend, Pope Gregory the Great (ruled 590–604; fig. 16.1) ordered a body of liturgical music organized, priests trained in singing the music, and a common liturgy disseminated throughout the Western church. He did reorganize the church, but the chant that bears his name

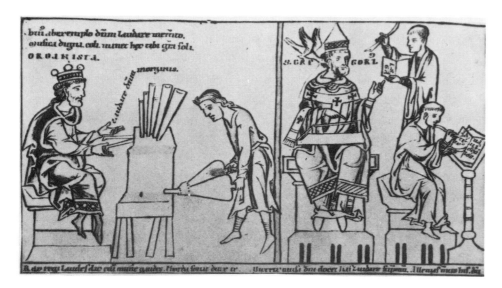

Figure 16.1 "King David as Organist (left) and Pope Gregory the Great," 1241, from Codex Lat. 17403, Bayerische Staatsbibliothek, Munich. Traditionally attributed to David, the Psalms formed a large part of the Gregorian repertory. Inspired by the dove of the Holy Spirit and holding a monochord, Gregory is depicted in his legendary role as codifier of liturgical chant.

reached its final form during and shortly after the reign of Charlemagne (ruled 768–814). Consisting today of nearly 3,000 melodies, Gregorian chant is a priceless collection of subtle and sophisticated melodies.

Gregorian chant is monophonic, *a cappella* (unaccompanied), and sung by male voices (solo and chorus) in Latin in the musical modes defined by the church. The texts determine the note values and musical accents; the rhythm of the music follows the rhythm of the words. There is no steady pulsation or beat, no division into regular acccents as there would be in a march or waltz. The undulating melodies flow smoothly, resonating through the cavernous stone churches, weaving a web of sound, and evoking in the worshipers feelings of awe and reverence.

Like secular music, Gregorian chant existed for centuries as an oral tradition. The precise musical notation of the ancient Greeks had been lost, and it was not until the eighth century that a new notational system began to evolve. Symbols for musical pitches, called *neumes*, were at first imprecise as to the actual pitch indicated, leading the monk Guido of Arezzo (ca. 990–1050) to remark that, "In our times, of all men, singers are the most foolish." Blaming the lack of precise musical notation for "losing time enough in singing to have learned thoroughly both sacred and secular letters," Guido invented a four-line musical staff on which neumes could symbolize precise pitches (fig. 16.2). Because of its limited range, chant is still scored on a four-line staff. In the following example the upper staff gives the neumes in Gregorian notation, below which the same melody is scored on the modern five-line staff. The clef sign (upper left) in Gregorian notation is C; the standard staff uses a G clef (see "clef" in chap. 3). In both notations the letter-names of the notes are F–G–E–D–F–A–G–A–G, etc.

Figure 16.2 Guido d'Arezzo, twelfth century manuscript, State Library, Vienna. Seated at the left, Guido is demonstrating on a monochord the two-octave scale (A–B–C–D–E–F–G, etc.), which was converted to neumes and placed on the staff.

Gregorian Chant: *Alleluia*

Al - le - lu - ia.

Many Gregorian melodies were adapted from Jewish Synagogue chant, especially the Alleluias (Hebrew, *Hallelujah,* praise ye the Lord). The seventh item of the mass (see table 16.1), Alleluias are characteristically *melismatic,* with many notes sung to one syllable. Following is the beginning of an Alleluia from the mass for Epiphany (visit of the Magi). The long and expressive melisma on the final syllable led eventually to innovations in texts and music called *tropes* and *sequences* (see below).

Alleluia, Vidimus stellam[1]

Gregorian chant

Solo   Chorus

Al - le - lu — ia   Al - le - lu —

ia

The Mass

The two basic types of Catholic services are the Mass and the Daily Hours of Divine Services, usually called Office Hours. The latter are celebrated eight times daily in religious communities such as monasteries. The Mass, also celebrated daily, is the principal service of the church. Essentially an elaborate reenactment of the Lord's Supper, the central theme is the consecration of the bread and the wine and the partaking of these elements by the congregation. Everything else in the service is either preparation for Communion (the Eucharist, Gk., thanksgiving) or a postscript to this commemorative act.

In a *low* Mass, the words are quietly enunciated by the priest in a low (speaking) voice in front of a silent congregation. In a *high* Mass, the service is recited and sung in a high (singing) voice using either Gregorian chant or a combination of chant and other music.

Table 16.1 The Mass

Ordinary (same text)	Proper (changing texts)
	1. *Introit*
2. *Kyrie*	
3. *Gloria*	
	4. Oratio (prayers, collect)
	5. Epistle
	6. Gradual
	7. *Alleluia* (or *Tract* during Lent)
	8. Gospel
9. *Credo*	
	10. *Offertory*
	11. Secret
	12. Preface
13. *Sanctus*	
14. Canon	
15. *Agnus dei*	
	16. *Communion*
	17. Postcommunion
18. *Ite missa est* (or *Benedicamus Domino*)	

The Mass consists of the *proper,* in which the texts vary according to the liturgical calendar, and the *ordinary,* which uses the same texts throughout the church year. Both proper and ordinary have texts that are recited or chanted by the celebrants (clergy) or sung by the choir.

The complete Mass is outlined in table 16.1 (italics indicate the sung portions of the text). Although modernization of the Mass permits the incorporation of indigenous modern language, increased layman participation, and congregational singing, the essential structure remains unchanged.

Tropes

A *trope* (Latin, *Tropus,* figure of speech) is a textual addition to an authorized text, an interpolation in the chant. Sentences or even whole poems were inserted between words of the original text. Sometimes added words were fitted to preexisting notes; at other times both words and music were injected together into the established text. For example, the chant *Kyrie eleison* (Lord have mercy upon us), with an interpolated trope, would read: Lord, *omnipotent Father, God, Creator of all,* have mercy upon us.

The practice of troping could have resulted from boredom, a desire for creativity, an inability to remember the notes, or varying combinations of all three. The authorized texts had not only remained the same for generations but many of them, particularly the texts of the ordinary, were sung countless times. Thus a need for some variety may have been one of the motivating factors.

1. Recordings of musical examples are listed at the end of each chapter on music. The Record List always follows the exact sequence in which examples are presented.

More positively, troping permitted exercises in creativity that could enliven the unvarying liturgical music. Of course one wonders, in this connection, how often creative acts are the direct result of trying to cope with monotonous repetition.

A third reason for troping may have been utilitarian. Troping originated during the time (ca. 700) when the musical liturgy was still learned by rote. Many chants had long *melismas,* that is, extended series of notes on a single syllable. (Note: The Alleluia used above as an illustration of chant has an extended melisma on the last syllable.) Attempting to remember all these melismas must have been very trying for singers who already had a large amount of liturgical music crammed into their heads. Textual additions that supplied a syllable for each note of the melisma provided additional reference points for all singers. Tropes, therefore, must have been well received by medieval choirs.

Indeed, tropes became so popular that they threatened to engulf the authorized texts. It was perhaps inevitable that the Council of Trent (1545–1563) finally abolished all tropes.

Sequences

The oldest form of trope was the last syllable, the 'ia' (ja) of the Alleluia (again see the example of the Alleluia given above). Many Alleluias, because of their Oriental origin, ended with an exotic and elaborate melisma on the final syllable. New poetry was added to this melisma and then, in time, the last section was detached from the Alleluia to become a separate composition called a *sequence*—that which follows. After separation had been accomplished, composers felt at liberty to alter the melody line.

The sequence is of special interest because it signaled the beginnings of musical composition for its own sake, a new development that was to lead to the works of composers such as Palestrina, Beethoven, and Stravinsky. The composition of sequences was a first step away from the rigidity of a prescribed musical repertoire. Composers began to explore ever more musical innovations and thus to breech and, ultimately, to break down medieval walls.

A large repertoire of sequences threatened for a time to dominate traditional Gregorian chant. The Council of Trent also tried to abolish sequences, but met with such opposition that four sequences were permitted to remain in the repertoire. Following is the oldest of the surviving sequences, the so-called Easter Sequence by Wipo (Wee-po; ca. 1024–1050), chaplain of Emperor Henry III. This melody also served as the basis for a Lutheran Easter chorale, "Christ Lay in the Bonds of Death" with text by Martin Luther.

Sequence: "Victimae paschali laudes"

Wipo

(Let Christians dedicate their praises to the Easter victim.)

Liturgical Drama

Religious ceremonies, such as the Mass, extend themselves into the realm of the theatre. The dramatic reenactment of the Last Supper in the Mass led, in time, to the development of medieval drama. The impulse was somewhat similar to that which saw classical Greek drama evolve from the cult of Dionysos. There were notable differences however; Greek tragedy dealt with ethical choices made under stress. The common people of the Middle Ages were not nearly as literate as the Greeks. They were more concerned with representations of the Nativity, the Shepherds, the Three Wise Men, and other specific events connected with their religion.

The actors were, in the beginning, priests of the Church and the plays episodes from the life of Christ, particularly the Christmas and Easter stories. During the liturgy, priests interpolated paraphrased dialogues from the Gospels, frequently using tropes. But these miniature dramas were too brief and too abstract for the unlettered congregation. Gradually the actors (clergy) enlarged the Scriptures by using Latin for the formal sections and the vernacular for the dialogues. Eventually whole plays were performed in the native language, which in the early plays was French.

Early liturgical dramas were enacted by the clergy in front of the altar. As the vernacular elements were added, the performances were moved to the church portal and the acting parts taken by laymen who, in time, formed confraternities of actors.

Liturgical dramas were mainly musical plays relying for their effects on singing and on a rich variety of accompanying instruments. Of the dozens of instruments available, favorites included the organ, harp, lyre, horn, trumpet, recorder, rebec (precursor of viols and then violins), drums, and other percussion instruments (fig. 16.3).

The following opening dialogue (sung in Latin) is from *The Play of the Three Kings,* which dates from the late eleventh century. Some of the melodies were borrowed from plainsong, but considerable music was undoubtedly composed for the occasion. This recorded performance is a cappella, but instruments could have been added to underscore the Oriental origins of the Magi.

Liturgical Drama: "Infantem Vidimus"

Shepherds
Infantem vidimus.
(We have seen the Infant.)

Figure 16.3 From the *Hortus Deliciarum* by the Abbess Herrad van Landsberg, late twelfth century. Formerly in the town library of Strasbourg, the manuscript was destroyed in the 1870 war. Hanging at the right is a rebec, a bowed string instrument of Arab origin. The female performer holds a harp while, at the left, there hangs a wheel-lyre (organistrum). This instrument has three strings set in motion by a revolving wheel operated by a hand crank, and is an ancestor of the hurdy-gurdy.

Boys
Qui sunt hi, quos stella ducit nos adeuntes, inaudita ferentes?
(Who are those whom the star leads, approaching us and bearing strange things?)
Magi
Nos sumus quos cernites reges Tharsis et Arabum et Saba, dona offerentes Christo Reginato Domino.
(We are those whom you see—the kings of Tharsis, Arabia, and Saba, offering gifts to Christ the King, the new-born Lord.)

The *conductus* was a processional used to "conduct" important characters on and off the stage. One of the most familiar of these was the "Song of the Ass," which was often used to describe Mary's flight into Egypt riding on a donkey. This song is shown as it was used in the twelfth-century *Play of Daniel*. Accompanying the Virgin as she rides into the church on a donkey, the conductus, as befits its function as processional music, is *metrical*. It has four beats to each measure in the manner of a solemn march. Only one of the seven verses is given here.

Conductus: "Song of the Ass,"[2] *The Play of Daniel*

One of the most influential religious leaders of her time, St. Hildegarde of Bingen (1098–1179) composed chants, songs, and *Play of the Virtues,* a unique liturgical drama treating spiritual material as allegory. Also involved in natural science, medicine, and political and religious debates, the Abbess Hildegarde was appointed prophetess of the Crusades by the pope on the recommendation of Bernard of Clairveaux. Her songs form a link between chant and the minnesinger tradition of Germanic literature.

After the thirteenth-century, liturgical drama developed into mystery plays (from Latin, *ministerium,* service) performed entirely in the vernacular under secular sponsorship. Using music only for processions, fanfares, and dances, these dramatic portrayals of biblical stories (life of Jesus, the Creation, and so forth) eventually evolved into European drama.

Secular Music

Goliards

The goliards of the tenth through thirteenth centuries were wandering students, vagabonds, defrocked priests, minstrels, rascals, artists, and dreamers. They were generally disenchanted with established values and entrenched institutions. They professed to take their name from a "Bishop Golias," whom they claimed as a patron—a very tolerant patron.

Their songs cover many subjects: love songs, drinking songs, spring songs, songs moral and immoral. Their songs were generally light-hearted and frequently obscene and, apparently, so was their conduct.

Though little of their music is extant, considerable poetry has survived. A thirteenth-century manuscript has been published under the title *Carmina Burana.* Selections from this collection have been set to music by the contemporary German composer Carl Orff. (See volume 2.)

---

2. G. M. Dreves, *Analecta hymnica* xx, 217, 257; H.C. Greene, *Speculum vi.*

Time: 20

O - ri-en-tis par-ti-bus Ad-ven-ta-vit a - si-nus Pulcher et
(Out from lands of Orient Was the ass divinely sent. Strong and

for - ti-si-mus Sar-ci-nis ap - tis-si-mus, Hez, Sir As-ne, hez.
very fair was he, Bearing burdens gallantly. Heigh, Sir Ass, oh heigh!)

A sampling of the opening lines from poetry in the *Carmina Burana* indicates some basic themes.

"O fortune, variable as the moon"
"I lament fortune's blows"
"Were the world all mine from the sea to the Rhine,
I would gladly forsake it all if the Queen of England
were in my arms"
"In rage and bitterness I talk to myself"
"I am the Abbot of Cluny, and I spend my time with
drinkers"
"When we are in the tavern we don't care who has
died"
"The God of Love flies everywhere"
"When a boy and a girl are alone together"
"Sweetest boy I give myself completely to you"

(Note: Three Goliard poems are printed on page 349.)

The vigorous conduct of the goliards and their assault upon established values inevitably led to conflicts with the Church. The movement died out, not because of clerical opposition, but because of the rise of the great medieval universities that replaced wandering students with resident ones.

Jongleurs

The *jongleurs* of France (and the *Gauklers,* their German counterparts) were generally not as educated as the goliards. Appearing first during the ninth century, these wandering men—and women—were seldom composers but always entertainers. They played music and sang songs that others had written, did tricks with trained animals, and, in general, helped enliven weddings and other special events. Although some of them were sufficiently talented to be socially acceptable, many were disreputable as far as a despairing clergy was concerned.

Their repertoire included *chansons de geste,* epic chronicles of the valorous deeds of heroes like Charlemagne and Roland. Because the melodies consisted of easily remembered tunes, there was no real need to notate the music and thus very little of it has survived. In a twelfth-century manuscript of the *Chanson de Roland* there are sketches that were apparently used to sing of the exploits of Roland and his horn.

The one authentic *chanson de geste* that has survived appears in the play *Le Jeu de Robin et Marion* by Adam de la Halle.

Chanson de geste: "Audiger dit Raimberge"

Au - di - gier dit Raim - ber - ge Bou - se vous di.

The *chant-fable,* part prose and part verse, was similar to the *chanson de geste* but with a slightly different form. The best-known chant-fable is *Aucassin et Nicolette* (see page 327).

Troubadours and Trouvères

Coinciding with the flowering of the age of chivalry, the troubadours of Provence and their later followers in northern France, the trouvères, produced the finest repertoire of lyric song of the Middle Ages. Educated aristocrats, both men and women, composed love poetry in the tradition of Ovid, whose love poems and *Art of Love* (see chap. 9) were undoubtedly known to the cultured nobles of the south of France. The repertoire is large (2,600 troubadour poems, ca. 300 melodies; 4,000 trouvère poems, 1,400 melodies) and covers many subjects: the Crusades, travel, adventure, but mostly romantic love. Despite the relative paucity of surviving melodies, all of the poems were meant to be sung. According to the troubadour Folquet of Marseilles (ca. 1155–1231), "A verse without music is a mill without water."

The earliest known troubadour, Duke William IX of Aquitaine (1071–1126), was a crusader, poet, and performer, whose lusty life and romantic pursuits are reflected in his poetry, of which eleven poems but only one melody have survived. The boldly masculine attitude in the following poem is comparable to Ovid's most aggressive style.

Troubadour Song

Duke William IX of Aquitaine

1. Friends, I'll write a poem that will do:
   But it'll be full of fun
   And not much sense.
   A grab-bag all about love
   And joy and youth.
2. A man's a fool if he doesn't get it
   Or deep down inside won't try
   To learn.
   It's very hard to escape from love
   Once you find you like it.
3. I've got two pretty good fillies in my corral:
   They're ready for any combat—
   They're tough.
   But I can't keep 'em both together:
   Don't get along.
4. If I could tame 'em the way I want,
   I wouldn't have to change
   This set-up,
   For I'd be the best-mounted man
   In all this world.
5. One's the fastest filly up in the hills,
   And she's been fierce and wild
   A long, long time.
   In fact, she's been so fierce and wild,
   Can't stick her in my pen.
6. The other was born here—Confolens way—
   And I never saw a better mare,
   I swear
   But she won't change her wild, wild ways
   For silver or gold.
7. I gave to her master a feeding colt;
   But I kept myself a share
   In the bargain too:
   If he'll keep her one whole year,
   I will a hundred or more.

8. Knights, your advice in this affair!
   I was never so troubled by
   Any business before.
   Which of these nags should I keep:
   Miss Agnes? Miss Arsen?
9. I've got the castle at Gimel under thumb,
   And over at Nieul I strut
   For all the folks to see.
   Both castles are sworn and pledged by oath:
   They belong to *me!*

Considerably more subtle, the next poem is designed to create a romantic, seductive atmosphere.

Troubadour Song

Duke William IX of Aquitaine

1. I'm going to write a brandnew song
   Before the wind and rain start blowing.
   My lady tries and tests me
   To see the way I love her.
   Yet despite the trials that beset me,
   I'd never break loose from her chain.
2. No, I put myself in her bondage,
   Let her write me into her charter.
   And don't think that I'm a drunkard
   If I love my good lady thus,
   For without her I couldn't live.
   I'm so hungry for her love.
3. O, she's whiter than any ivory statue.
   How could I worship any other?
   But if I don't get reinforcements soon
   To help me win my lady's love,
   By the head of St. George, I'll die!—
   Unless we kiss in bower or bed.
4. Pretty lady, what good does it do you
   To cloister up your love?
   Do you want to end up a nun?
   Listen: I love you so much
   I'm afraid that grief will jab me
   If your wrongs don't become the rights I beg.
5. What good will it do if I'm a monk
   And don't come begging round your door?
   Lady, the whole world's joy could be ours,
   If we'd just love each other.
   Over there at my friend Daurostre's
   I'm sending this song to be welcomed and sung.
6. Because of her I shake and tremble,
   Since I love her with the finest love.
   I don't think there's been a woman like her
   In the whole grand line of Lord Adam.

William's son governed the duchy for a few years, followed by his granddaughter, the celebrated Eleanor of Aquitaine (1122–1204), who established a Court of Love in Poitiers and later in Normandy and possibly England. Eleanor sponsored several troubadours and trouvères, the most notable of which was Bernart de Ventadorn (d. 1195). Dante conferred the title of master singer on Arnaut Daniel and consigned another troubadour, Bertran de Born, to Hell (see Canto XXVIII, lines 130–142), but modern critics have ceded the palm to the poet-musician from Ventadorn as the finest lyric poet of the age.

Forty poems, eighteen with music, by Bernart de Ventadorn are known today. Lively, witty, and eminently singable, the subject is always the same: love rewarded, unrequited, noble, sacred, or profane, but always love. In the following *canso* (love song; *chanson* in northern France) the first of six verses is given in both Provençal, the language of the troubadors, and in English.

Troubadour Canso: "Be m'an perdut"[3]

Bernart de Ventadorn (d. 1195)

Musical theme

Be ma'an perdut lai enves Ventadorn tuih meo amic,
(I am indeed lost from the region of Ventadorn/ To all my friends,

pois ma domna no m'ama; et es be dreihz que jamais lai no torn
for my lady loves me not; With reason I turn not back again,

c'a des estai vas me salvatj' egrama.
For she is bitter and ill-disposed toward me.

Veus per quem fai semblan irat emorn;
See why she turns a dark and angry countenance to me;

car en s'amor me deleih e'm sojorn!
Because I take joy and pleasure in loving her!

ni de ren als no's rancura ni's clama.
Nor has she ought else with which to charge me.)

After her divorce from the king of France, Eleanor married, in 1152, Henry II, Duke of Normandy and, later, king of England. The next poem implies that Bernart has followed her Court of Love to England and that the haughty highborn lady is either Eleanor herself or a member of her court. Even without the music, the singable quality of the poetry is quite evident.

Lancan Vei per Mei la Landa

Bernart de Ventadorn

1. Whenever I see amid the plain
   The leaves are drifting down from trees
   Before the cold's expansion,
   And the gentle time's in hiding,
It's good for my song to be heard,
For I've held back more than two years
   And it's right to make amends.
2. It's hard for me to serve that woman
   Who shows me only her haughty side,
   For if my heart dares make a plea,
   She won't reply with a single word.

---

3. C. Appel, *Bernart von Ventadorn* (Halle, 1915), Plate ix (citing Milan manuscript *Chansonnier* G, folio 14). The form is AAB.

Truly this fool desire is killing me:
I follow the lovely form of Love,
    Not seeing Love won't attend me.
3. She's mastered cheating, trickery,
    So that always I think she loves me.
    Ah, sweetly she deceives me,
    As her pretty face confounds me!
Lady, you're gaining absolutely nothing:
In fact, I'm sure it's toward your loss
    That you treat your man so badly.
4. God, Who nurtures all the world,
    Put it in her heart to take me,
    For I don't want to eat any food
    And of nothing good I have plenty.
Toward the beautiful one, I'm humble,
And I render her rightful homage:
    She can keep me, she can sell me.
5. Evil she is if she doesn't call me
    To come where she undresses alone
    So that I can wait at her bidding
    Beside the bed, along the edge,
Where I can pull off her close-fitting shoes
Down on my knees, my head bent down:
    If only she'll offer me her foot.
6. This verse has been filled to the brim
    Without a single word that will tumble,
    Beyond the land of the Normans,
    Here across the wild, deep sea.
    [Apparently England.]
And though I'm kept far from Milordess,
She draws me toward her like a magnet:
    God, keep that beauty ever safe!
7. If the English king and the Norman duke
    Will it, I'll see her soon
    Before the winter overtakes us.
8. For the king I remain an English-Norman,
    And if there were no Lady Magnet,
    I'd stay here till after Christmas.

A number of female troubadours have been identified (thirteen so far) including Azalais of Porcairagues, Maria of Ventadorn, Lombarda, and the Countess Garsenda of Provence. The most notable poet-musician, whose work is comparable to that of any troubadour, was the Countess of Dia (present day Die), who lived in the Drôme valley in southern France during the twelfth century. Known as Beatritz, her voice is as distinctive as that of Sappho (see chap. 8). In the following dialogue song the lady sweeps aside male rationalizations and exacts a pledge of loyalty, devotion, and a love that was to be shared equally.

Troubadour Song

Beatritz, Countess of Dia

1. Friend, I stand in great distress
    Because of you, and in great pain;
    And I think you don't care one bit
    About the ills that I'm enduring;
    And so, why set yourself as my lover
    Since to me you bequeath all the woe?
    Why can't we share it equally?
2. Lady, love goes about his job
    As he chains two friends together
    So the ills they have and the lightness too
    Are felt by each—in his fashion.

And I think—and I'm no gabber—
That all this deepdown, heartstruck woe
I have in full on my side too.
3. Friend, if you had just one fourth
    Of this aching that afflicts me now,
    I'm sure you'd see my burden of pain;
    But little you care about my grief,
    Since you know I can't break free;
    But to you it's all the same
    Whether good or bad possess me.
4. Lady, because these glozing spies,
    Who have robbed me of my sense and breath,
    Are our most vicious warriors,
    I'm stopping: not because desire dwindles.
    No, I can't be near, for their vicious brays
    Have hedged us in for a deadly game.
    And we can't sport through frolicsome days.
5. Friend, I offer you no thanks
    Because my damnation is not the bit
    That checks those visits I yearn for so.
    And if you set yourself as watchman
    Against my slander without my request,
    Then I'll have to think you're more "true-blue"
    Than those loyal Knights of the Hospital.
6. Lady, my fear is most extreme
    (I'll lose your gold, and you mere sand)
    If through the talk of these scandalmongers
    Our love will turn itself to naught.
    And so I've got to stay on guard
    More than you—by St. Martial I swear!—
    For you're the thing that matters most.
7. Friend, I know you're changeable
    In the way you handle your love,
    And I think that as a chevalier
    You're one of that shifting kind;
    And I'm justified in blaming you,
    For I'm sure other things are on your mind,
    Since I'm no longer the thought that's there.
8. Lady, I'll never carry again
    My falcon, never hunt with a hawk,
    If, now that you've given me joy entire,
    I started chasing another girl.
    No, I'm not that kind of shyster:
    It's envy makes those two-faced talk.
    They make up tales and paint me vile.
9. Friend, should I accept your word
    So that I can hold you forever true?
10. Lady, from now on you'll have me true,
    For I'll never think of another.

More direct than most of the poetry of her male counterparts, the following song leaves no doubt about the lady's fiery passion. The slighting reference to the husband may have amused the Count, for this is after all a fictional account of a woman who has much in common with the Wife of Bath in Chaucer's *Canterbury Tales.*

Troubadour Song

Beatritz, Countess of Dia

1. I've suffered great distress
    From a knight whom I once owned.
    Now, for all time, be it known:
    I loved him—yes, to excess.
        His jilting I've regretted,
    Yet his love I never really returned.
    Now for my sin I can only burn:
        Dressed, or in my bed.

2. O, if I had that knight to caress
   Naked all night in my arms,
   He'd be ravished by the charm
   Of using, for cushion, my breast.
   His love I more deeply prize
   Than Floris did Blancheflor's.
   Take that love, my core,
   My sense, my life, my eyes!
3. Lovely lover, gracious, kind,
   When will I overcome your fight?
   O, if I could lie with you one night!
   Feel those loving lips on mine!
   Listen, one thing sets me afire:
   Here in my husband's place I want *you,*
   If you'll just keep your promise true:
   Give me everything I desire.

By the middle of the twelfth century, troubadour influences had spread to northern France where notable trouvères included Blondel de Nesles (b. ca. 1155), minstrel to Richard the Lionhearted (ruled 1189–1199 and himself a trouvère); Thibaut IV, King of Navarre (1201–1253); and Adam de la Halle (ca. 1240–1287). Like troubadour cansos, trouvère chansons were monophonic with accompaniment an option depending on available instruments. The following *virelai* is a trouvère form that begins with a refrain that repeats after each verse. Composed by an unknown trouvère, this is a superb example of the sophisticated style of northern France.

Trouvère Virelai: "Or la truix"[4]

Musical theme

In 1208 Pope Innocent III preached a crusade against the Albigensian heresy (latter-day Manicheans; see St. Augustine), stating that the church must "use against heretics the spiritual sword of excommunication, and if this does not prove effective, use the material sword." Exploiting the Albigensian Crusade as an excuse to plunder the south of France, nobles and the French Crown totally destroyed the high culture that had fostered the troubadour tradition, chivalry, and the Courts of Love.

Minnesingers and Meistersingers

The *minnesinger* (Ger., *minne,* love) of Germanic literature flourished during the twelfth and thirteenth centuries. Despite the title of "love singer" these poet-musicians were strongly influenced by Christianity and sang spiritual songs of sadness, of tears, and of thoughts of death. The *minnesong* was, in effect, a reconciliation of Christian elements with erotic-secular literature of the troubadour-trouvère tradition.

Meistersingers (master singers) were "prize" singers of the fourteenth through sixteenth centuries. The art of the minnesinger was transformed into a guild of singers who practiced the art and craft of writing and singing songs much as cabinetmakers practiced the art of woodworking. The best-known meistersinger was Hans Sachs, the protagonist of Richard Wagner's opera *Die Meistersinger von Nürnberg.*

Polyphonic Music

The high point of medieval music was the development of polyphony. Polyphony (Gk., *poly-phonos,* many voices) is a style of music in which two or more melodies are played and/or sung together. "Row, Row, Row Your Boat," when sung as a round, is an example of one kind of polyphonic music in which the same melody is sung at different times. "Jesu, Joy of Man's Desiring" by J. S. Bach combines three different melodies.

Related to polyphonic music is a style that evolved several centuries later and is called homophonic (Gk., *homo-phonos,* same voice). Homophonic music consists of a single melody plus accompaniment or, to put it another way, melody and harmony. For example, "The Star Spangled Banner" and "The Battle Hymn of the Republic" are homophonic.

Polyphonic and homophonic are the two aspects of multivoiced music. Neither style exists in a pure form. Music that emphasizes two or more melodies of roughly equal importance is termed polyphonic. Homophonic music emphasizes a predominant melody line accompanied by harmony. The two styles may be illustrated as follows:

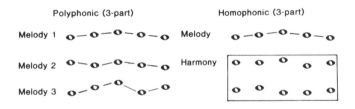

Non-Western music (Middle and Far East and Africa) never developed polyphonic or homophonic styles of music. Polyphony was spontaneous rather than planned, the result of accidental conjunctions of melodies rather than a premeditated polyphonic practice such as that developed by Western culture.

Polyphony and harmony (homophony) in Western culture are therefore unique in the world of music. Without the development of polyphonic music during the Middle Ages no subsequent expansion of musical styles could have taken place: no Bach, Beethoven, Beatles, Bob Dylan, or Rolling Stones; no blues, ragtime, jazz, country-western, rock, or pop.

---

4 Bodleian Oxford, Douce 308, folio 226 and 237. The form is ABAA.

Medieval polyphonic music probably grew out of the monophonic music of the chant. Early attempts at polyphony were quite literal and consisted of adding additional voice parts at fixed distances above and below existing chants. The added voice was referred to as the organizing voice *(vox organalis)* and the whole style of music as *organum.* Two-part music was described as *organum duplum,* three-part as *organum triplum,* and so forth. The original line of chant, now somewhat slower than in monophonic singing, was called the principal voice *(vox principalis).* Two-part organum can be illustrated as follows:

Eventually the chant melody was moved to the bottom part and referred to as the *cantus firmus* (fixed song). The chant was identified by quoting the initial phrase of the Latin text. The cantus firmus was also called the tenor (Latin, *tenere,* to hold) because it held (retained) the original chant.

All polyphonic compositions of the medieval period used a cantus firmus, usually assigned to the tenor, as a basis for writing music. The practice of using authorized liturgical music (plainsong) as a foundation for composing original music is comparable to basing a sermon on a scriptural quotation. Both procedures quote an approved source as the prerequisite for what was essentially an exercise in creativity.

Polyphonic writing developed rapidly during the twelfth century. The notation of rhythm was improved by composers associated with the cathedral of Notre Dame in Paris as they began writing three-part and even four-part compositions. Borrowing rhythmic modes from poetry (trochaic, iambic, dactylic, etc.), they wrote metrical compositions (music with a regular pulse or beat) with two or three voices above an elongated tenor. The tenor was now so drawn-out that it was usually played by an organ, the only instrument that could sustain the slow-moving notes of the cantus firmus.

Pipe organs were probably introduced into the Western church in the ninth century in response to a need for a greater volume of sound. No other instrument has the inherent ability of an organ to fill a large church with vibrant sound. The room that houses an organ necessarily becomes the sound chamber for the instrument. Thus, the increasingly large naves of Romanesque and, later, Gothic churches supplied huge resonating chambers for the brilliant sound of the king of instruments.

Following is a three-part organum by Perotin, a prominent composer at Notre Dame of Paris. The beginning measures are given in musical notation so that the two-voice lines plus tenor can be seen as well as heard. Any of the melodies can be sung, whistled, or played on an instrument. The complexity of polyphony results from the simultaneity of, in this case, rather uncomplicated melodic lines.

Organum: "Alleluya (Nativitas)"[5]

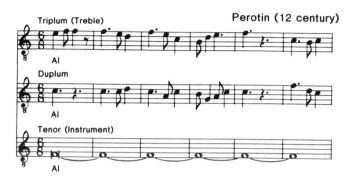

The *motet,* one of the most important forms of sacred music, was developed in the thirteenth century. In the following example, the text indicates only the source of the borrowed plainsong because an instrument was now used for the cantus firmus. Immediately above the tenor is a composed line with its own set of words, hence the name *motetus* (Fr., *le mot,* the word). The top voice also had its own set of words, which could be a different poem or even a different language. Increasing secularization led to motets, such as the one illustrated, with variations on the same love song sung in French by the *Triplum* and *Motetus.* Titles of early motets were given by indicating the beginning words of all three texts. The opening measures of notation again illustrate the uncomplicated nature of the individual melodies.

"En non Diu! Motet Quant voi; Eius in Oriente"[6]

5. Y. Rokseth, *Polyphonies du XIIIe siècle* (Paris, 1935).
6. Y. Rokseth, *Polyphonies du XIIIe siècle* (Paris, 1935).

Polyphonic Mass

Musical styles developed very rapidly during the Gothic period (thirteenth and fourteenth centuries) and some composers acquired international reputations. Paradoxically, composers came to be known by name while many of the great master builders of Gothic cathedrals remained anonymous. Guillaume de Machaut, equally proficient as poet and as a composer of both sacred and secular music, was the most acclaimed of the gifted artists of the late Middle Ages (fig. 16.4). He was the first to write a polyphonic setting of all five movements of the ordinary of the Mass, a practice that was subsequently followed by every major composer through the sixteenth century and by many composers up to the present day.

The following portion of the *Agnus Dei* is sung by the upper three voices and accompanied by an instrument on the *contratenor* part, as indicated by the absence of text. The tenor, now the next lowest voice, still sings the cantus firmus. The polyphonic Mass, as distinguished from a motet, uses the Latin text of the monophonic chant. The beginning of the movement is notated in an open score (one staff for each part) so that the more complex movement of the melodies can be compared with the examples previously given of an organum and a motet.

Notre Dame Mass: "Agnus Dei"[7]

Guillaume de Machaut (ca. 1300-1377)

Medieval Dance

Sacred Dance

Dancing as a glorification of God was widely accepted in early Christian communities. Especially popular was the "Hymn of Jesus," a round dance (or ring dance) with twelve dancers representing the twelve disciples and the twelve signs of the zodiac. The idea of zodiac dancing in order to restore order to the cosmos can be traced as far back as the ancient Egyptians. However, the most direct influence probably stemmed from the Pythagorean concept of the music of the spheres. This ring dance was also called the Ring Dance of Angels or, simply, Angel Dance.

Figure 16.4 "Machaut Receiving Honors of Royalty and Clergy." Miniature by the Master of Bocqueteaux. Biblioteque Nazionale, Paris. This first known portrait of a Western composer is indicative both of Machaut's reputation and the status of a creative artist in Gothic France.

The *tripudium* dated from early Christianity and was one of the few dance steps to survive into the medieval period. A tripudium was a three-step dance with two steps forward and one step backward. The dance symbolized both the Holy Trinity and, probably, the concept of two (spiritual) steps forward and one (human frailty) step backwards. Beginning as a solemn processional dance, the tripudium later evolved into a lively hopping dance that is still performed in modern Luxembourg in honor of a medieval saint.

"The Way to Jerusalem" was a stately dance that symbolized a pilgrimage to the Holy City. The dance was executed on the design of a labyrinth inlaid in the floor of the church nave. A leader was chosen whose function it was to determine the pace and the steps that matched the pattern of the floor tiles. This was a slow, spiraling dance that coordinated the dance steps with an accompanying chant. In order to make it all the way to Jerusalem, the leader had to arrive at the center of the labyrinth at the precise moment that the final syllable of the chant was sung. The dance was usually performed on a labyrinth modeled after the Cretan version in the palace of King Minos at Knossos. The labyrinth at the Cathedral of Chartres dates from the twelfth century and is forty feet in diameter.

The Dance of Death (*Danse Macabre*) was a phenomenon that appeared during the plague (Black Death), an epidemic that began in Constantinople in

---

7. H. Besseler, *Die Musik des Mittelalters und der Renaissance* (Bucken, *Handbuch der Musikwissenschaft)*, Potsdam, 1931, p. 149.

1347 and ravaged all of Europe. The pestilence was virulent and, at the time, inexplicable. An explanation was nevertheless forthcoming: God was punishing the wicked for their sins. The universal hysteria generated by the plague was fanned by the preaching of the Church, which called upon the sinners to repent.

The peasants, especially, suffering from plague, war, and famine, responded with repentance based on fear: fear of eternal damnation, of the plague, of the dancing ghouls from the graveyard who sought the living for the dance of death. The living, in turn, executed the dance in propitiation of their sins and in hopes of forestalling the Angel of Death.

Choreomania, a kind of dance mania, probably first appeared in England in the twelfth century. It was characterized by group psychosis and frenzied, even demented dancing. During the plague of the Black Death flagellants danced, sang, and vigorously lashed themselves in order to avert the wrath of God. Some participants died while dancing; others were mentally and/or physically crippled for the rest of their lives.

In 1374 a great dance epidemic broke out in most of Europe. Contemporary accounts of this manic behavior were medically farfetched but graphically descriptive of the pervasiveness of this kind of mass hysteria. *Choreomania* has been attributed to many causes, including psychotic reactions to the problems of war, famine, plague, and fear of death.

Secular Dance

Little is known of dancing in the early Middle Ages, but by the eighth or ninth centuries social dancing was a universal activity enjoyed by all persons at all levels of society. The frequent fairs and festivals, with the attendant vigorous dancing, enabled the peasantry to temporarily forget their otherwise bleak and meager existence. Their dances ranged from solo or lusty round dances to gaily executed couple dances.

The milkmaid's dance was an integral part of the May festival, a rite of spring that began on May 29th with a milking festival followed by games and dancing around the fertility symbol of the Maypole. Involving flirtatious milkmaids, garlands of flowers, and virile male pursuit, the milkmaid's dance appears to have been a kind of blindman's bluff set to music.

The country dance (round dance) has been a popular folk form in virtually every society. The lustiness of peasant country dancing is legendary, an exuberance that was tamed by the feudal lords and ladies to become the more genteel contre dance. In the contre dance, there was gradual entrance of couple after couple, which led to a round dance followed by couple dances, all somewhat in the manner of ballroom dancing.

The estampie (Provencal, *estamper,* to stamp) was the most popular dance of the Gothic Age and also one of the oldest forms of instrumental music.

Originally a gay open-air dance, it eventually became more compact and, by the fifteenth century was performed indoors. Although it probably began as a round dance, it was the most popular couple dance of the age.

The music for the estampie was in 3/4 time and consisted of short, rotating phrases that were repeated many times during the course of the dance. To begin the dance, couples stood side by side in a semicircle. The first part of the dance began with both starting on the same foot with a step, close, step, close to first position with heels together. The movements were first to the right, then backward, then forward, then backward once more, and then begin the pattern all over again.

Following is a two-part estampie with the parts labeled simply as Cantus Superior (C.S.) and Cantus Inferior (C.I.). They were to be played by any available instruments. An approximation of the medieval dancing mood can be attained by executing the steps of the estampie to an accompaniment of any two or more different instruments. Percussion instruments such as drum, tambourine, bells, and triangle can and should be added. Liveliness of spirit is far more important than precise execution of dance steps and music.

Estampie: "Instrumental Dance"[8]

13th century

Table 16.2, *Development of Medieval Music,* is an outline and summary of the major developments in music during the Middle Ages. Dotted lines indicate either prior development leading up to a specific musical instrument or, as with monasticism, the waning influence of that way of life. Arrows indicate continuing development or, as with the connection between feudalism and chivalry, one developing out of the other.

---

8. Wooldridge, *Early English Harmony,* London, 1897, pl. 19. Consisting of four variations on the initial section, the form is $AA^1A^2A^3A^4$.

Table 16.2 Development of Medieval Music

	600	700	800	900	1000	1100	1200	1300	1400
Stylistic Periods	Romanesque →				High Romanesque →	Early Gothic →		Late Gothic →	
General Periods		Monasticism	Feudalism			Crusades / Age of Chivalry			
Musical Periods	Early Middle Ages					School of St. Martial	Sch. of N. Dame	Ars Antiqua → Ars nova →	
Musical Styles **Monophonic Music**									
Sacred		Gregorian Chant		Sequences, Tropes		Liturgical Drama (Conductus)			
Secular				Jongleurs	Goliards		Troubadours / Trouvères / Minnesingers		Meistersingers
Polyphonic Music				Organum			Motet →	Mass →	
Instrumental Music Dances						Estampie (Ductia)			
Musical Instruments	(aulos)					Flageolet / (Drum) Tabor → Recorder			
	?					Shawm			
						Bagpipe			
						Trumpet			
							Lute		
							Gittern		
	(kithara)			Rabab		Rebec		Vielle	

The compositional school of Notre Dame was indebted to the School of St. Martial for the latter's development of organum. The Ars Antiqua (Old Art) and Ars Nova (New Art) were theoretical labels for old and new styles of music. Guillaume de Machaut was recognized in his own time as a composer of new music, that is, modern music.

The listing of musical instruments provides only a cross section of the many that were available. Other instruments that could have been listed include the psaltery, harp, rotta (Celtic lyre), fiddle, horn, and a large variety of percussion instruments.

Summary

The history of medieval music is much more than the study of the musical practices of a cultural period. Music of any era, in the playing and the singing, reflects and expresses the hopes, aspirations, frustrations, and despairs of people of all classes and stations in life. Music is still the nearest equivalent to an international language that humanity has yet devised.

Medieval music, when properly performed, can convey to us the *sound* of an era. It can bring alive the vast panorama of medieval life from Gregorian chant to liturgical drama, from troubadour love songs to peasant dances.

The sound of the music has a correlation with the architectural styles of the period. Gregorian chant, for example, was intended for participating worshipers rather than a listening audience. It is, therefore, more effective and persuasive inside the cloistered security of the monastery with its narrow windows, heavy walls, and pervasive quietude.

Polyphonic music, on the other hand, was performance oriented. The greatly expanded interior space of Romanesque churches was a proper area for the new multivoiced style. The arching melodies of organum complemented the rounded arches and high vaulting of the large Romanesque churches.

The dynamic, asymmetrical, complex mass of interreacting tension of stone structure, pointed arches, and soaring vaults that is the Gothic cathedral has its aural counterpart in the dynamic, asymmetrical, complex, and tension-packed art that is Gothic polyphonic music. That the first polyphonic mass was written for performance in the Cathedral of Notre Dame in Paris is more than coincidental. Guillaume de Machaut wrote music, whether consciously or unconsciously, to completely fill the interior of that great cathedral with vigorous and brilliant sound.

Listening Outline (Second Stage)

Note: This outline should be considered as a guide to listening; it represents the *maximum* of things to listen for. There is no expectation that everyone or even anyone can actually hear all these items; however, one can follow the music with the outline and learn to systematize and objectify listening procedures.

   I. Listening outline
   A. Medium and number of performers
      1. Vocal (specify voice parts) Text
      2. Instrumental (specify instruments)
      3. Combination (specify)
   B. Texture
      1. Monophonic, homophonic, polyphonic, combination
      2. Number of actual parts or voices (not necessarily the same as the number of performers)
   C. Construction (optional)
      1. Characteristic texts
      2. Characteristic musical phrases
   D. General type
      1. Sacred, secular
      2. Music: through-composed, repeated phrases
      3. Text: through-composed, repeated, strophic, verse-refrain, other (see the glossary)
   E. Notation (determined from the score)
      1. Clef, time signature, tempo indication (if any)
   F. Tonality (optional)
      1. Modal
      2. Major-minor
   G. Form
  II. Conclusions
   A. Possible period: ancient (600 B.C.–A.D. 100); Roman (100–600); Romanesque (600–1000); high Romanesque (1000–1150); early Gothic (1150–1350); late Gothic (1350–1450).
   B. Possible style: Greek song, Gregorian chant, sequence, trope, liturgical drama, conductus, troubadour song, trouvère song, minnesinger song, goliard song, estampie, organum, motet, mass movement.
   C. Possible national origin: Greece, Rome, western Europe, northern France, southern France (Provence), Germany, Italy, England, other.

Record List

   1. Gregorian Chant. *Alleluia:* "Vidimus Stellam." In *Masterpieces.* (see Record List for chap. 3).
   2. Sequence. "Victimae paschali laudes." In *Masterpieces.*
   3. Liturgical Drama. "Infantem vidimus." In *Treasury of Early Music,* 4 vols. Haydn Society 9100/9103; S—9100/9103 (referred to as *Treasury*) (see Record List for chap. 3).
   4. Conductus. "Song of the Ass." In *The Jolly Minstrels: Minstrel Tunes, Songs and Dances of the Middle Ages on Authentic Instruments.* Vanguard VCS—10049.
   5. Troubadour Canso. "Be m'an perdut." In *Treasury.*
   6. Trouvère Virelai. "Or la truix." In *Masterpieces.*
   7. Perotin. Organum. "Alleluya (Nativitas)." In *Masterpieces.*

8. School of Notre Dame. Motet. "En non Diu!
   Quant voi; Eius in Oriente." In *Masterpieces*.
9. Machaut. Mass. "Agnus Dei." In *Masterpieces*.
10. Estampie. "Instrumental Dance." In
    Masterpieces.

Also Recommended
1. *Music of Medieval France*, Sacred and Secular
   (1200–1400). Bach Guild BG—656.
2. *Ten Centuries of Music*. 10—DGG KL—52/61;
   SKL—152/161.
3. *The Art of Courtly Love*. EMI Box 86301.
4. *Music of the Middle Ages: Troubadour and
   Trouvère songs of the XIII Century*. Musical
   Heritage, MHS—675.
5. *Medieval Roots: Songs and Dances*. Decca DL
   79 438.
6. Bernart de Ventadorn. *Chansons d'Amore;*
   Martin Codax, *Canciones De Amigo*. Electrola C
   063—30 18.
7. Guillaume de Machaut. *Notre Dame Mass and
   Works of Perotin*. Bach Guild BGS05045.
8. ———. *Mass of Notre Dame and 9 Secular
   Works*. Archive 2533054.
9. *Chefs d'Oeuvre de la Polyphonie Francaise: de
   Machaut et de Quatris*. Barclay 995010.
10. *Estampie; Instrumental Music of the Middle
    Ages*. Electrola C 063—30 122.
11. *Antique Provençal Instruments—Instrumental
    Music of the Trouvères and Troubadours*. Arion
    90413.
12. *Ars Antiqua*. 2—Telefunken 2635010.
13. *Ars Nova*. Earl 5—83.
14. *Douce Dame—Music of Courtly Love from
    Medieval France and Italy*. Vanguard 71179.
15. *Late Medieval (1300–1400)*. Pleiades 250.
16. *Medieval Music and Songs of the Troubadours*.
    Everest 3270.
17. *Music of the Crusades*. Argo ZRG—673.
18. *Thirteenth Century Polyphony*. Pleiades P249.
19. *Voices of the Middle Ages*. Nonesuch 71171.
20. St. Pierre de Solemnes Abbey Choir
    a. *Gregorian Anthology*. Peters PLE—016.
    b. *Masses for Easter*. Peters PLE—031.
    c. *Sunday Vespers*. Peters PLE—047.
21. *Music of the Gothic Era*. 3—DG ARC—2710019.
22. *Play of Daniel*. MCA 2504.
23. *Romance of Medieval France*. MCA 2516.

Bibliography

Drinker, Sophie. *Music and Women: The Story of Women
   in Their Relation to Music*. New York: Coward
   McCann, 1948, reprinted 1980. Influential women in
   music, art, poetry, and politics from the ancient
   world to the modern era.

Harksen, Sibylle. *Women in the Middle Ages*. New York:
   Abner Schram, 1975. From anonymous women in
   everyday life to those in art, music, professions, and
   positions of power.

Liber Usualis. Tournai, Belgium: Desclee & Cie, 1952.
   The complete liturgical music (Gregorian chant) of
   the Roman Catholic church.

Parrish, Carl, and John F. Ohl. *Masterpieces of Music
   before 1750*. New York: W. W. Norton & Company,
   1951. Companion text for the record set.

Parrish, Carl. *A Treasury of Early Music*. New York: W. W.
   Norton & Company, 1958. Companion text for the
   record set.

Seay, Albert. *Music in the Medieval World*. Englewood
   Cliffs, N.J.: Prentice-Hall, Inc. (paperback), 1965. A
   survey text intended more for amateurs than for
   professional musicians.

Strunk, Oliver. *Source Readings in Music History from
   Classical Antiquity through the Romantic Era*. New
   York: W.W. Norton & Company, Inc., 1950. Useful
   primary material about music excerpted from the
   writings of Clement of Alexander, St. Basil, St.
   Jerome, St. Augustine, Boethius, Cassiodorus, Odo of
   Cluny, Guido of Arezzo, and others.

Thomson, James C. *Music through the Renaissance*.
   Dubuque, Ia.: Wm. C. Brown Publishers
   (paperback), 1965. A brief, illustrated survey of
   music from primitive peoples through the sixteenth
   century. Condensed and simplified for the
   nonmusician.

Walter, Don C. *Men and Music in Western Culture*. New
   York: Appleton-Century-Crofts (paperback), 1969. A
   very general survey from 3000 B.C. to the present day.
   Designed to give nonmusicians a broad overview of
   the importance of music in the life of man.

Wilhelm, James J. *Seven Troubadours: The Creators of
   Modern Verse*. University Park: The Pennsylvania
   State University Press, 1970. Engaging study of some
   fascinating troubadours.

Time Chart for the Middle Ages

Maps Showing a Few Significant Territorial Changes	Important Political, Historical, and Military Events	Philosophical Events	Art, Music, and Literature
The Roman Empire ca. A.D. 300	375–500—Great invasions of Roman Empire by northern and eastern tribes. Asiatic Huns harry Germanic peoples 395—Roman Empire split between East (Capital: Constantinople) and West (Capital: Rome or Ravenna) 410–476—Conventional dates for the fall of Rome. The city captured by tribes of Visigoths and Vandals	354–430—Augustine formulated doctrine of Church based on Neoplatonism 395—Christianity becomes Roman state religion under Emperor Theodosius	
Invasions of the Roman Empire ca. A.D. 500	465–511—Clovis established line of Frankish kings and (496) becomes Christian 590–604—Pope Gregory defends Rome against invaders—establishes political power of the Church	480–524—Boethius, "Consolations of Philosophy" expresses Roman world-weariness in a Christian-classical synthesis	590–604—Pope Gregory legendary founder of Gregorian chant

Time Chart for the Middle Ages (cont.)

Maps Showing a Few Significant Territorial Changes	Important Political, Historical, and Military Events	Philosophical Events	Art, Music, and Literature
Spread of Islam ca. A.D. 732 Charlemagne's Empire ca. A.D. 800	570–632—Life of Mohammed 597—St. Augustine's mission to England 600–650—First development of feudalism from northern tribal customs 732—Battle of Poitiers, Muslims checked in France, driven back to Spain 751—Pepin becomes king of Franks; establishes Carolingian rulers 800—Charlemagne crowned Roman emperor by Pope. Establishes precedent for Papal authority 850–900—Decline of Frankish kingdom. Further invasion of northmen 900—Feudalism fully established in Europe 900–1000—Towns begin to spring up in Europe 1066—Norman invasion of England	781—Charlemagne's Palace School established. Start of revival of learning	700—Beginning of Romanesque architecture developed from basilica ca. 781–850—Final form of Gregorian chant ca. 900—Organum in music discussed by Odo of Cluny 900—Approximate beginning of stave architecture in Norway

Time Chart for the Middle Ages (cont.)

Maps Showing a Few Significant Territorial Changes	Important Political, Historical, and Military Events	Philosophical Events	Art, Music, and Literature
 English and French Territories about 1154 English and French Territories about 1453	1077—Emperor Henry IV bows to Pope at Canossa 1100–1300—Main Period of Crusades 1154–1189—Rule of Henry II in England. Establishment of English common law 1150 onwards—Half Spain in Christian hands. Unification of Spain continues 1215—Magna Carta—law superior to king 1272—Rudolf of Hapsburg made Austrian king—start of the rise of the House of Hapsburg 1291—Revolt of Swiss Cantons. Start of democratic Switzerland 1295—English parliament established 1302—Estates General founded in France. A hint of democratic government 1337 to about 1440—Hundred Years War. England loses French lands. Great steps towards unification of both countries	1000–1100—The Battle of Universals; Realist-Nominalist Controversy 1079–1142—Peter Abelard teaches in Paris, *Sic et Non* 1200—The first trickle of the main body of Aristotle's works enters Europe 1270—Formal founding of University of Paris. For at least 200 years groups of students had collected at Bologna, Salerno, etc. 1270—Introduction of all of Aristotle's works in Europe 1214–1294—Roger Bacon bases knowledge on study of physical world 1225–1274—Thomas Aquinas establishes Church doctrine on Aristotelian principles	1000–1100—Full development of Romanesque architecture 1022–1084—Building of Abbey of Mont Saint Michel almost as we know it 1071–1126—First-known troubadour—but secular music was already well established 1194—The beginning of building of the present Chartres Cathedral. The height of Gothic style 1170–1270—In France alone eighty cathedrals. Five hundred great churches built, almost all devoted to the Virgin. The height of the Cult of the Virgin 1240–1302—Cimabue, begins to paint figures naturalistically 1265–1321—Dante achieves "medieval synthesis" in *The Divine Comedy* 1276–1327—Painter Giotto continues trend toward naturalism 1300 onwards—Musical development of counterpoint, polyphony. Improvement of system of musical notation 1313–1375—Boccaccio 1340–1400—Geoffrey Chaucer *The Canterbury Tales*

Glossary

Pronunciation: Approximations are given where necessary. The syllables are to be read as English words and with the capital letters accented.

Abbreviations: L., Latin; F., French; G., German; Gk., Greek; I., Italian; v., Vide (see).

Asterisks: An asterisk preceding a word or phrase indicates that a definition and/or illustration can be found under that heading.

Abbreviations: The musical abbreviations used are included here under one heading for easy reference.

Accel.   *accelerando* (ah–chel–er–AHN–doe), becoming faster.

Br.   bridge, connecting section between themes.

Bsn., Bssn.   bassoon.

C.b.   contra bass, that is, string bass.

Cl., clar.   clarinet.

Cresc.   *crescendo* (cray–SHEN–doe), becoming louder.

D.C.   *da capo* (dah–KAH–po), repeat from the beginning.

D.S.   *dal segno* (dahl–SEHN–yo), repeat from the sign.

Dim.   *diminuendo,* becoming softer.

Eng. hn.   English horn, alto oboe.

f   *forte* (FORE–tay), loud.

ff   *fortissimo,* very loud.

fff   *fortississimo,* very, very loud.

Fl.   flute.

fp   *forte piano,* loud and immediately soft.

Hn., Fr. hn.   French horn.

Low br.,   low brass, trombones and tubas (sometimes French horns).

Low stgs.   low strings, that is, cello, string bass.

Low w.w.'s   low woodwinds, that is, bass clarinet, bassoon, contra bassoon.

mf   mezzo forte (MEH–dso), half loud (medium loud).

mp   mezzo piano, half soft (medium soft).

Ob.   oboe.

Picc.   piccolo.

Pizz.   *pizzicato,* strings plucked with the fingers.

p   *piano* (pea–AHN–no), soft.

pp   *pianissimo,* very soft.

ppp   *pianississimo,* very, very soft.

Reeds   clarinet, oboe, bassoon, bass clarinet, etc.

R.h., l.h.   right hand, left hand (keyboard instruments).

Rit.   *ritardando,* become slower.

SATB   soprano, alto, tenor, bass (usually applied to vocal ensemble).

sf, sff, sfz   *sforzando* (sfor–TSAHND–o), strongly accented.

Sn. drum   snare drum, side drum.

Stgs.   strings, that is, the string section of the orchestra (violin, viola, cello, bass).

Tpt.   trumpet.

Tr.   trill.

Trans.   transition.

Trom.   trombone.

Vla.   viola.

Vlc.   violoncello, cello.

Vln.   violin.

W.w.'s   woodwinds (flute, oboe, clarinet, bassoon).

A

Abacus   The flat slab on top of a *capital.

Acanthus   A plant whose thick leaves are reproduced in stylized form on *Corinthian capitals. (See fig. 10.8.)

A cappella   (ah ka–PELL-ah; L.) Originally unaccompanied music sung "in the chapel." Term now applies to choral music without instrumental accompaniment.

Accent   In music, stress or emphasis on a tone or chord. Regular accents are assumed in metrical music. Special accent marks are used as necessary:> ∧ sfz (sforzando), etc.

Accidental   In music a sign used to add or cancel chromatic alterations, for example, ♯ (raise a semitone), ♭ (lower a semitone), x (raise a whole tone), ♭♭ (lower a whole tone), ♮ (cancel previous sharps or flats).

Acoustics   The science of sound.

Aerial perspective   See perspective.

Agnosticism   (Gk., *agnostos*, unknowing) The impossibility of obtaining knowledge of certain subjects; assertion that people cannot obtain knowledge of God.

Agnus Dei   (L., Lamb of God) Last item of the *Ordinary of the *Mass.

Agora   In ancient Greece, a marketplace/public square.

Allegory   A literary mode with a literal level of meanings plus a set of meanings above and beyond themselves. This second level may be religious, social, political, or philosophical, e.g., *The Faerie Queen* by Spenser is an allegory about Christian virtues.

Alleluia   Latinization for the Hebrew *Halleluyah* ("praise ye the Lord"). Third item of the *proper of the *Mass.

Alto, Contralto   The second highest part in choral music, that is, S A T B.

Ambulatory   A passageway around the *apse of a church. (See fig. 15.33.)

Amphora   Greek vase, usually quite large, with two handles and used to store food staples. (See fig. 7.23.)

Apocalypse   Prophetic revelation; the Book of Revelation in the New Testament.

A posteriori   (a–pos–TEER-e-or-e; L., following after) Reasoning from observed facts to conclusions; inductive; empirical.

A priori   (a–pree-OAR-e) Reasoning from general propositions to particular conclusions; deductive; nonempirical.

Apse   A recess, usually semicircular, in the east wall of a Christian church or, in a Roman *basilica, at the wall opposite to the general entrance way.

Arabesque   Literally Arab-like. Elaborate designs of intertwined flowers, foliage, and geometric patterns used in Islamic architecture. (See fig. 15.6.)

Arcade   A series of connected *arches resting on columns. (See fig. 10.9.)

Arch   A curved structure (semicircular or pointed) spanning a space, usually made of wedge-shaped blocks. Known to the Greeks, who preferred a *post and lintel system, but exploited by the Romans.

Archetype   (Gk. *arche*, first: *typos*, form) The original pattern of forms of which things in this world are copies.

Architrave   The lowest part of an *entablature, a horizontal beam or lintel directly above the *capital. (See fig. 7.20.)

Aria   (I., AHR-yah; F., air) Solo song (sometimes duet) in *operas, *oratorios, *cantatas.

Arpeggio   (ahr-PEJ-o; I., harplike) In music the playing of a *chord with the notes sounding in quick succession rather than simultaneously.

Ars antiqua   (L., old art) Music of the late twelfth and thirteenth centuries.

Ars nova   (L., new art) Music of the fourteenth century. Outstanding composers were Machaut (France) and Landini (Italy).

Art Nouveau   A style of architecture, crafts, and design of the 1890s and a bit later characterized by curvilinear patterns. Examples include Tiffany lamps and the work of Beardsley and Klimt.

Art song   Song intending an artistic combination of words and music, as distinct from popular song or folk song.

Atheism   (Gk., *a*, no; *theos*, god) The belief that there is no God; also means "not theistic" when applied to those who do not believe in a personal God.

Atonality   A type of music in which there is no tonal center, no key note. v. twelve-tone technique and serial compositon.

Atrium   The court of a Roman house, roofless, and near the entrance. Also the open, colonnaded court attached to the front of early Christian churches. (See fig. 10.3.)

Aulos   (OW-los) A shrill sounding oboelike instrument associated with the Dionysian rites of the ancient Greeks. Double-reed instrument normally played in pairs by one performer. (See fig. 8.2.)

Avant-guard   (a-vahn-GARD) A French term meaning, literally, advanced guard, and used to designate innovators and experimentalists in the various arts.

B

Bagpipe   A reed instrument with several pipes attached to a bag (skin reservoir). One or two pipes *(chanters)* have tone holes and are used for the melody. The longer pipes *(drones)* sustain the same notes throughout. Probably of Asiatic origin and imported by the Romans in first century A.D.

Baldachino   (ball-da-KEEN-o) A canopy over a tomb or altar of which the most famous is that over the tomb of St. Peter in St. Peter's in Rome; designed by Bernini.

Ballad   (L., *ballare*, to dance) Originally a dancing song. A narrative song, usually folk song but term also applied to popular songs.

Ballade   Medieval *trouvère song. In the nineteenth and twentieth centuries dramatic piano pieces, frequently inspired by romantic poetry.

Balustrade   A railing plus a supporting row of posts.

Banjo   *Guitar family instrument, probably introduced into Africa by Arab traders and brought to America on the slave ships. The body consists of a shallow, hollow metal drum with a drumhead on top and open at the bottom. It has four or more strings and is played with fingers or plectrum.

Bar   In music notation originally vertical lines through the staff (which are now called bar lines). Bar is synonymous with *measure.

Bar form Originated with German *minnesinger-*meistersinger tradition. A form of music with the first *phrase repeated followed by a different phrase, for example, A–A–B. Also see Form.

Bar Line v. Bar.

Barrel vault v. Vault.

Basilica In Roman architecture, a rectangular public building used for business or as a tribunal. (See fig. 12.9.) Christian churches that use a *cruciform plan are patterned after Roman basilicas. Though basilica is an architectural style, the Roman church calls a church a basilica if it contains the bones of a saint.

Bass "Low" musical voice as opposed to "high." Used in the following special ways: (1) lowest adult male voice; (2) bass clef has F on the fourth line; (3) short for bass viol., bass fiddle, double bass (string bass) in the orchestra; (4) prefixed to the name of an instrument to indicate the largest (and lowest) member of an instrumental family, for example, bass clarinet, bass trombone, etc.

Bass clef v. Bass (2).

Bay In Romanesque and Gothic churches the area between the columns.

Behaviorism School of psychology that restricts both animal and human psychology to the study of behavior; stress on the role of the environment and on conditioned responses to exterior stimuli.

Blank verse Unrhymed *iambic pentameter* (v. meter) in the English language, much used in Elizabethan drama.

Bourgeoisie The middle class; in Marxist theory the capitalist class, which is opposed to the proletariat, the lower or industrial working class.

Brass instruments Instruments of metal that produce a tone by vibrating the lips in a cup- or funnel-shaped mouthpiece. They include: (from high pitch to low) *trumpet, cornet, fluegelhorn, *French horn, baritone horn (euphonium), *trombone, *tuba.

Buttress Exterior support used to counter the lateral thrust of an *arch or *vault. A *pier buttress* is a solid mass of masonry added to the wall; a *flying buttress* is typically a pier standing away from the wall and from which an arch "flies" from the pier to connect with the wall at the point of outward thrust. (See fig. 15.37.)

C

Cadence Term in music applied to the concluding portion of a phrase (temporary cadence) or composition (permanent cadence).

Campanile Italian for bell tower, usually freestanding. The Leaning Tower of Pisa is a campanile. (See fig. 15.29.)

Canon (Gk., law, rule) A contrapuntal device in music in which one or more melodies strictly imitates an opening melody throughout its entire length. A canon is the strictest type of imitative *counterpoint. Canons that have no specified way to end but keep going around are called "rounds," for example, "Three Blind Mice."

Canso A *troubadour song in *"bar form," for example, A–A–B.

Cantata (I., *cantare*, to sing) A "sung" piece as opposed to a "sound" (instrumental) piece, for example, sonata. The term is now generally used for secular or sacred choral works with orchestral accompaniment, which are on a smaller scale than *oratorios.

Cantilever A self-supporting projection that needs no exterior bracing; e.g., a balcony or porch can be cantilevered.

Cantus firmus (L., fixed song) A preexisting melody used as the foundation for a *polyphonic composition. *Plainsong melodies were used for this purpose, but other sources included secular songs, Lutheran chorales, and scales. Any preexisting melody may serve as a cantus firmus.

Capital The top or crown of a column.

Cartoon A full-size preliminary drawing for a pictorial work, usually a large work such as a *mural, *fresco, or *tapestry. Also a humorous drawing.

Caryatid (care-ee-AT-id) A female figure that functions as a supporting column; male figures that function in a like manner are called *atlantes* (at-LAN-tees; plural of Atlas). (See fig. 7.51.)

Catharsis (Gk., *katharsis*, purge, purify) Purification, purging of emotions effected by tragedy (Aristotle).

Cella The enclosed chamber in a classical temple that contained the cult statue of the god or goddess after whom the temple was named.

Chamber music Term now restricted to instrumental music written for a limited number of players in which there is only one player to each part, as opposed to orchestral music, which has two or more players to some parts, for example, sixteen players on the first violin part. True chamber music emphasizes ensemble rather than solo playing.

Chanson (F., song) A major part of the *troubadour-*trouvère tradition, dating from the eleventh through the fourteenth centuries. Generic term for the general song production to a French text.

Chevet (sheh-VAY; F., pillow) The eastern end of a church, including *choir, *ambulatory, and *apse.

Chiaroscuro (kee-AR-oh-SKOOR-oh; I., light-dark) In the visual arts the use of gradations of light and dark to represent natural light and shadows.

Chinoiserie (she-nwaz-eh-REE; F.) Chinese motifs as decorative elements for craft objects, screens, wallpaper, and furniture; prominent in eighteenth-century rococo style.

Choir That part of the church where the singers and clergy are normally accommodated; usually between the *transept and the *apse; also called chancel. (See fig. 15.40.)

Chorale A hymn tune of the German Protestant (Lutheran) church.

Chord In music the simultaneous sounding of three or more tones.

Chromatic (Gk., *chroma*, color) The use of notes that are foreign to the musical scale and have to be indicated by a sharp, flat, natural, etc. The *chromatic scale* is involved in these alterations. It consists of twelve tones to an octave, each a semitone apart.

Chromatic scale v. Chromatic.

Church modes   In music the medieval scale system of four basic modes (Dorian, Phrygian, Lydian, Mixolydian) and four related modes (Hypodorian, Hypophrygian, Hypolydian, Hypomixolydian). May also include Ionian and Aeolian, which are somewhat comparable to the *major-minor system.

Cire perdue   (seer pair–DUE; F., lost wax) A metal casting method in which the original figure is modeled in wax and encased in a mold; as the mold is baked the wax melts and runs out, after which the molten metal is poured into the mold.

Clavichord   The earliest type of stringed keyboard instrument (twelfth century). Probably developed from the *monochord. It is a 2′ × 4′ oblong box with a keyboard of about three octaves. The strings run parallel to the keyboard, as opposed to harpsichords and pianos, in which the strings run at right angles to the keyboard. The keys are struck from below by metal tangents fastened to the opposite ends of elongated keys. The tone is light and delicate but very expressive because the performer can control the loudness of each note. It was sometimes called a "table *clavier" because it was portable.

Clavier   Generic term for any instrument of the stringed keyboard family: clavichord, harpsichord, and piano.

Clef   (F., key) In music a symbol placed on the staff to indicate the pitches of the lines and spaces. There are three clefs in use today: G, F, and C. The G clef is used to indicate that the note on the second line is G (treble clef). The F clef is usually used to indicate that F is on the fourth line (bass clef).

Treble Clef

Bass Clef

The C clef places middle C on either the third line (alto clef) or fourth line (tenor clef).

Alto Clef

Tenor Clef

Clerestory   In a basilica or church, the second level, the wall that rises above the roof of the other parts and has numerous windows. (See fig. 12.11.)

Cloister   An inner court bounded by covered walks; a standard feature of monastery architecture.

Collage   (F., pasting) Paper and other materials pasted on a two-dimensional surface.

Colonnade   A series of spaced columns, usually connected by lintels. (See fig. 12.11.)

Column   A vertical support, usually circular, which has a base (except in *Doric style), shaft, and *capital. (See fig. 7.37.)

Comedy   A play or other literary work in which all ends well, properly, or happily. Opposite of *tragedy.

Con   (I., with) For example, *con moto* (with motion).

Concerto   (con–CHAIR–toe; I.) A musical work for one or more solo voices with orchestral accompaniment.

Conductus   In music a twelfth- or thirteenth-century metrical (as opposed to nonmetrical plainsong) song for one or more voices in a sacred or secular style. A conductus may be *monophonic or *polyphonic.

Contrapposto   (I., set against). Figural sculpture in which parts of the body (usually hips and legs, arms and shoulders) are set against each other along a central axis, setting up an alternation of tension and relaxation.

Contrapuntal   In the style of *counterpoint.

Corinthian   The most ornate style of Greek architecture, little used by the Greeks but preferred by the Romans; tall, slender, channeled columns topped by an elaborate capital decorated with stylized acanthus leaves. (See fig.10.7.)

Cornice   The horizontal, projecting member crowning an *entablature.

Cosmology   Philosophic study of the origin and nature of the universe.

Counterpoint   The musical craft or technique of combining two or more melodies, of writing note against note *(punctus contra punctum)*. Music which consists of simultaneous melodies (two or more) is called *contrapuntal music or *polyphonic (many voiced) music.

Couplet   In poetry two successive rhymed lines in the same meter.

Credo   (L., I believe) Third item of the *Ordinary of the *Mass.

Crescendo, Decrescendo   (cray–SHEN–doe, day–cray–SHEN–doe; I.) Standard musical terminology for increasing or decreasing loudness. Also indicated by abbreviations *cresc.* and *decresc.,* or signs < and >.

Crocket   In Gothic architecture an ornamental device shaped like a curling leaf and placed on the outer angles of *gables and pinnacles. (See colorplate 20.)

Crossing   In a church, the space formed by the interception of the *nave and the *transepts.

Cruciform   The floor plan of a church in the shape of a Latin cross.

D

Daguerrotype   After L. J. M. Daguerre (1789–1851) the inventor. Photograph made on a silver-coated glass plate.

Determinism   (L., *de* + *terminus,* end) The doctrine that all events are conditioned by their causes and that people are mechanical expressions of heredity and environment; in short, we are at the mercy of blind, unknowing natural laws; the universe could care less.

Deus ex machina   (DAY–oos ex ma–KEE–na; L.) In Greek and Roman drama a deity who was brought in by stage machinery to resolve a difficult situation; any unexpected or bizarre device or event introduced to untangle a plot.

Dialectic   Associated with Plato as the art of debate by question and answer. Also dialectical reasoning using *syllogisms (Aristotle) or, according to Hegel, the distinctive characteristic of speculative thought.

Diatonic (Gk., through the tones) Applied to musical scales in which each letter name is used once only, for example, c–d–e–f–g–a–b–(c), c–d–e♭–f–g–a♭–b♭–c, etc.

Dome A hemispherical vault; may be viewed as an arch rotated on its vertical axis.

Doric The oldest of Greek temple styles, characterized by sturdy *columns with no base and an unornamented cushionlike *capital. (See fig. 7.42.)

Drum The circular sections that make up the shaft of a *column; also the circular wall on which a *dome is placed. (See fig. 7.38.)

Drums Percussion musical instruments having a skin stretched over one or both ends of a frame.
1. *Timpani* (kettledrums) The skin is stretched over a metal half-sphere. They can be tuned to definite pitch.
2. *Side drum* (snare drum) Shallow drum with metal snares (taut wire coils) on the bottom drumhead. The tone is dry and crisp.
3. *Tenor drum* A larger and deeper version of the snare drum. The tone is similar to that of a tom-tom. It does not use snares.
4. *Bass drum* The largest drum used in the orchestra. The tone is rather booming.
5. *Conga drum* One head stretched over the top of a long cylinder.
6. *Bongo drums* Small pair of single-headed drums.
7. *Tambourine* A small single-headed drum with metal discs set around the frame.

Dualism In metaphysics, a theory that admits two independent substances, e.g., Plato's dualism of the sensible and intelligible worlds, Cartesian dualism of thinking and extended subjects, Kant's dualism of the noumenal and the phenomenal.

Dynamic marks Words or symbols indicating the relative degrees of loudness or softness in a musical performance. Some of the more important markings are summarized as follows:

Term	Symbol	Meaning
pianissimo (pea-uh-NEES - see -mo)	pp	very soft
piano (pea-AHN-no)	p	soft
mezzo piano (MEH-dso)	mp	half soft
mezzo forte (FORE-tay)	mf	half loud
forte	f	loud
fortissimo	ff	very loud
forte piano	fp	loud and immediately soft
sforzando (sforr-TSAHND-o)	sfz	strongly accented
also: *crescendo, *decrescendo		

E

Elegy A meditative poem dealing with the idea of death.

Elevation The vertical arrangements of the elements of an architectural design; a vertical projection.

Empiricism A proposition that the sole source of knowledge is experience, that no knowledge is possible independent of experience.

Engaged column A nonfunctional form projecting from the surface of a wall; used for visual articulation. (See fig. 10.7.)

Engraving The process of using a sharp instrument to cut a design into a metal plate, usually copper; also the print that is made from the plate after ink has been added.

Entablature That part of a building of post and lintel construction between the capitals and the roof. In classical architecture this includes the *architrave, *frieze, and *cornice. (See fig. 7.20.)

Entasis (EN-ta-sis) A slight convex swelling in the shaft of a *column.

Epic A lengthy narrative poem dealing with protagonists of heroic proportions and issues of universal significance, e.g., Homer's *Iliad.*

Epicurean One who believes that pleasure, especially that of the mind, is the highest good.

Epistemology A branch of philosophy that studies the origin, validity, and processes of knowledge.

Eschatology (Gk., *ta eschata,* death) That part of theology dealing with last things: death, judgment, heaven, hell.

Estampie (es-TAHM-pea) A dance form popular during the twelfth to fourteenth centuries. Consists of a series of repeated sections, for example, aa, bb, cc, etc.

Etching A kind of *engraving in which the design is incised into a wax-covered metal plate, after which the exposed metal is etched by a corrosive acid; the print made from the plate is also called an etching.

Ethos In ancient Greek music the "ethical" character attributed to the various modes. The Dorian was considered strong and manly; the Phrygian, ecstatic and passionate; the Lydian, feminine, decadent, and lascivious; the Mixolydian, mournful and gloomy.

Euphemism An innocuous term substituted for one considered to be offensive or socially unacceptable, e.g., "passing away" for "dying."

F

Facade One of the exterior walls of a building, usually the one containing the main entrance.

Fenestration The arrangement of windows or other openings in the walls of a building.

Fiddle Colloquialism for the violin. Also used to designate the bowed ancestors of the violin, particularly the medieval instrument used to accompany dances.

Finial In Gothic architecture an ornament fitted to the peak of an *arch; any ornamental terminating point, such as the screw-top of a lamp. (See colorplate 20.)

Flageolet (flaj-o-LET; F.) A small wind instrument, a forerunner of the *recorder.

Flamboyant Late Gothic architecture of the fifteenth or sixteenth centuries, which featured wavy lines and flamelike forms.

Flat v. Accidental.

Fleche (flesh; F., arrow) In architecture a slender spire above the intersection of the *nave and *transepts. (See fig. 15.37.)

Flute A *woodwind instrument made of wood (originally), silver, gold, or preferably platinum. It is essentially a straight pipe with keys, is held horizontally and played by blowing across a mouth (blow) hole located near one end. The tone is mellow in the bottom octave, becoming thinner and brighter up to the top of the range. Though many thousands of years old, the flute was not used in instrumental ensembles until the early eighteenth century, when it began to replace the *recorder.

Fluting   The vertical grooves, usually semicircular, in the shaft of a *column or *pilaster.

Folk song   A song of unknown (usually) authorship preserved by means of an oral tradition. A folk song is never composed by "folk" (or a committee); it is the creation of one or two individuals (words and/or music) and tends to be remembered and transmitted because the words and music are somehow pertinent to the environment in which it was created. Folk songs about special situations (labor unions, strikes, political causes, and movements, etc.) tend to fade away in time. Folk songs having something to do with the human condition may last indefinitely.

Foot   A metrical unit in poetry such as the iamb ◡ /. Also see meter.

Foreshortening   Creating the illusion in painting or drawing that the subject is projecting out of or into the frontal plane of a two-dimensional surface.

Form, Musical form   Musical form is an intelligible structure that distinguishes music from haphazard sounds or noises. Since music is an intelligible ordering of tones all music has "form," that is, it has a beginning, middle, and end; it exists in time. "Form" is therefore any organization or structuring of any combination, or all of the four elements of music (melody, harmony, rhythm, tone color). In general, music is ordered (formed) in such a manner as to possess enough unity to achieve coherence or continuity and sufficient variety to avoid monotony (short of chaos). All musical forms consist of varying relationships of unity and variety. There are many ways of organizing musical structure; following are a few of the more important forms.
  I. Single forms (pieces or single movements).
    A. Sectional (with clearly defined [more or less] interior divisions).
    B. Continuous.
      1. Through composed (no repetition). *Organum, some medieval *motets.
      2. Imitative (contrapuntal forms): *passacaglia, *fugue, Renaissance *masses, and *motets.
  II. Composite forms are simply compositions with two or more movements, for example, *symphony, *cantata, etc.

Free verse   A verse that uses devices other than meter and rhyme.

Fresco   (I., fresh) Painting on plaster, usually wet plaster on which the colors are painted, sinking in as the plaster dries and the fresco becomes part of the wall.

Frets   Thin strips of wood or metal fastened to the fingerboard of string instruments like the *viol and *guitar (but *not* members of the violin family). The frets are placed to mark specific notes.

Frieze   In architecture decorated horizontal band, often embellished with carved figures and molding; the portion of an *entablature between the *architrave and the *cornice above.

Fugue   *Polyphonic musical composition in which a single theme is developed by the different musical voices in succession. A favorite style of Baroque composers like Bach and Handel.

Fundamental   In musical acoustics the lowest note of the overtone series. The generating tone for the series.

G

Gable   In architecture the triangular section at the end of a pitched roof, frequently with a window below.

Genre   (ZHAN-re) In the pictorial arts a depiction of scenes of everyday life.

Gittern   English name for the medieval *guitar.

Glockenspiel   A percussion instrument with rectangular metal bars laid out in a keyboard pattern. It is played with two mallets and has a sharp, bright tone.

Goliards   Wandering Bohemians of the tenth through the thirteenth centuries: students, young ecclesiastics, dreamers, and the disenchanted.

Gospels   In the Bible New Testament accounts (Matthew, Mark, Luke, and John) of the life and teachings of Christ.

Gouache   (goo-AHSH; F.) Watercolor made opaque by adding zinc white.

Graphic arts   Visual arts that are linear in character: drawing, engraving, printing, printmaking, typographic, and advertising design.

Greek cross   A cross in which the four arms are of equal length.

Gregorian chant   v. Plainsong.

Groin   In architecture the edge (groin) formed by the intersection of two *vaults. (See figs. 15.26 and 15.27.)

Guitar   A plucked string instrument with a flat body and six strings (modern guitar). Brought into Europe during the Middle Ages by the Moorish conquest of Spain.

H

Harmony   In music the vertical (simultaneous) sound of two or more pitches. Harmonic development is a major achievement of Western music while remaining secondary in the rest of the world's music.

Harp   A stringed instrument with a large triangular frame and about forty-five strings. In the modern harp the seven pedals change the pitches of the strings so that the harp can play chromatically, i.e., all twelve tones of the octave. The harp has been mentioned in recorded history since the days of the Babylonian Empire.

Harpsichord   Actually a harp turned on its side and played by means of quills or leather tongues operated by a keyboard. It was the most common keyboard instrument of the sixteenth to eighteenth centuries and is again being built today in increasing numbers.

Hatching   A series of closely spaced parallel lines in a drawing or print giving the effect of shading.

Hedonism   The doctrine that pleasure or pleasant consciousness are intrinsically good; that pleasure is the proper—and the actual—motive for every choice.

Heroic couplet Two successive lines of rhymed iambic pentameter, e.g., Pope's *Essay on Man.*

Hieratic (HYE–uh–RAT–ik) Of or used by priests; priestly.

Hieroglyphic Symbols or pictures standing for a word, syllable, or sound; writing system of ancient Egyptians.

Homophonic (Gk., same sound) Music in which a single melodic line is supported by chords or other subordinate material (percussion instruments).

Horn The modern orchestral instrument, the French Horn, is frequently referred to as a horn. Also, a generic designation for any instrument that has a mouthpiece through which the performer blows.

Hubris (HU–bris) *Tragic flaw,* i.e., excessive pride or arrogance that injures other people (not physically) and brings about the downfall of the person with the flaw.

Hue The name of a color. The chief colors of the spectrum are: red, yellow, blue (primary); green, orange, violet (secondary).

Hydraulis Ancient Greek pipe organ, probably invented in the Middle East 300–200 B.C. Air for the pipes was provided by hydraulic pressure and the pipes activated by a keyboard. Originally the tone was delicate and clear, but the Romans converted it into a noisy outdoor instrument by a large increase in air pressure.

Hymn A poem of praise. Usually, but not necessarily, sacred. The music accompanying a hymn is called the hymn tune.

I

Icon (EYE–kon; Gk., image) Two-dimensional representation of a holy person; in the Greek church a panel painting of a sacred personage. (See fig. 12.24.)

Iconography Visual imagery used to convey concepts in the visual arts; the study of symbolic meanings in the pictorial arts.

Illumination Decorative illustrations or designs, associated primarily with medieval illuminated manuscripts.

Impasto (I., paste) A painting style in which the pigment is laid on thickly, as in many of van Gogh's paintings.

Intaglio (in–TAL–yo) A graphic technique in which the design is incised; used on seals, gems, and dies for coins and also for the kinds of printing and printmaking that have a depressed ink-bearing surface.

Ionic A style of Greek classical architecture using slender, *fluted *columns and *capitals decorated with scrolls and volutes. (See fig. 7.52.)

Isocepholy (I–so–SEPH–uh–ly) In the visual arts a convention that arranges figures so that the heads are at the same height. (See figs. 7.49 and 7.59.)

J

Jamb figure Sculpted figure flanking the portal of a Gothic church. (See fig. 15.39.)

Jongleur (zhon–GLEUR) French professional musicians (minstrels) of the twelfth and thirteenth centuries who served the *troubadours and *trouvères.

K

Keystone The central wedge-shaped stone in an arch; the last stone put in place and which makes the arch stable. (See fig. 15.35.)

Kithara (KITH–a–ra) The principal stringed instrument of the ancient Greeks. Essentially a larger version of the *lyre, it has a U-shaped form and usually seven to eleven strings running vertically from the cross arm down to the sound box at the base of the instrument. The legendary instrument of Apollo. (See fig. 8.3.)

Kyrie eleison (Gk., Lord have mercy) The first item of the *Ordinary of the *Mass.

L

Lantern In architecture a small decorative structure that crowns a *dome or roof.

Latin cross A cross in which the vertical member is longer than the horizontal arm it bisects.

Legato (leh-GAH-toe; I.) Musical term meaning smooth, moving smoothly from note to note. Opposite of *staccato.

Libretto (I., little book) The text or words of an *opera, *oratorio, or other extended choral work.

Lied, Lieder (leet, LEE–der; G., song, songs). Term usually applied to the German romantic *art songs of Schubert, Schumann, Brahms, Wolf, and others. Also used for medieval songs, that is, *minnesinger and *meistersinger.

Lintel In architecture a horizontal crosspiece over an open space, which carries the weight of some of the superstructure. (See fig. 7.34.)

Lithography A printmaking process that uses a polished stone (or metal plate) on which the design is drawn with a crayon or greasy ink. Ink is chemically attracted only to the lines of the drawing, with a print made by applying paper to the inked stone.

Liturgical Pertaining to public worship, specifically to the organized worship patterns of the Christian churches.

Liturgical drama Twelfth- and thirteenth-century enactments of biblical stories, frequently with music. Developed into the "mystery plays" of the fourteenth through sixteenth centuries.

Lituus (L.) Bronze trumpet used by the Roman armies. Shaped like the letter J.

Lost wax process v. *cire perdue.*

Lute Plucked stringed instrument with a pear-shaped body and a fingerboard with *frets. It had eleven strings tuned to six notes (five sets of double strings plus a single string for the highest note). It was the most popular instrument of the sixteenth century and was used into the eighteenth century. Lutes are again being made, mainly for present-day performances of Renaissance music.

Lyre (or Lyra) Ancient Greek instrument, a simpler form of the *kithara. The sound box was often made of a tortoise shell. Used mainly by amateurs. The larger kithara was used by professional musicians. (See fig. 8.1.)

Lyric Poetry sung to the accompaniment of a lyre (Greek); troubadour and trouvère poetry intended to be sung; short poems with musical elements. (See fig. 8.1.)

M

Madrigal   Name of uncertain origin that refers to fourteenth-century vocal music or, usually, to the popular sixteenth-century type. Renaissance madrigals were free-form vocal pieces (usually set to love lyrics) in a *polyphonic style with intermixed *homophonic sections. Flemish, Italian, and English composers brought the madrigal to a high level of expressiveness in word painting and imagery. Madrigals were sometimes accompanied but mostly *a cappella.

March   Music for a parade or procession. The *meter is usually duple (simple or compound) but is sometimes quadruple.

Mass   The central service of public worship of some Christian churches, principally the Roman Catholic church. The musical portions are indicated below.

Ordinary (same text)	Proper (text varies by the liturgical calendar)
Kyrie Eleison	Introit
Gloria in Excelsis Deo	Gradual
Credo in Unum Deum	Alleluia
Sanctus	Offertory
Agnus Dei	Communion

Materialism   The doctrine that the only reality is matter; that the universe is not governed by intelligence or purpose but only by mechanical cause and effect.

Measure   In music a group of beats set off by bar lines.

Meistersinger   (G., mastersinger) The highest level in the music-poetry guilds of Germany in the fifteenth and sixteenth centuries. Succeeding the earlier *minnesinger tradition the guilds held song schools and awarded prizes, with top prizes for creating new songs going to the "mastersingers."

Melisma   A melodic unit sung to one syllable; plainsong has frequent *melismatic* passages.

Melody   A succession of musical sounds, that is, the horizontal organization of music as compared with harmony, which is a vertical organization of tones. Melody is inseparable from rhythm because it has an up and down motion of pitches and, simply stated, long and short durations of rhythm.

Metaphor   A common form of figurative language that compares two dissimilar objects by stating that the two are identical, e.g., "the moon is blue."

Metaphysics   Philosophic inquiry into the ultimate and fundamental reality; "the science of being as such."

Meter   In music a grouping of beats into patterns of two, three, or four beats or combinations thereof; in English poetry the basic rhythmic pattern of stressed (—) and unstressed (◡) syllables. Metrical patterns include: *iambic* (◡—), *trochaic* (—◡), *anapestic* (◡◡—), and *dactylic* (—◡◡).

Metope   (MET–o–pay) In classical architecture the panel between two *triglyphs in a *Doric *frieze; may be plain or carved. The Parthenon metopes are all carved.

Minnesinger   (G., from *minne,* love) German poet-musicians of noble birth of the thirteenth to fifteenth centuries (leading to the *meistersingers) who were influenced by the *troubadour-trouvère tradition of the age of chivalry. They composed *monophonic songs, usually in *bar form.

Minstrel   v. Jongleur.

Modes, rhythmic   A thirteenth-century system of music rhythmic notation based on the patterns of poetic meter. Rhythmic modes give the characteristic flavor to thirteenth-century *organum and *motets because of the constant repetition of the same rhythmic patterns. All modes were performed in so-called "perfect" meter, that is, triple.

Rhythmic Mode	Poetic Meter	Accent Pattern	Performed
I	Trochaic	— ◡	♩ ♪♩ ♪
II	Iambic	◡ —	♪♩ ♪♩
III	Dactylic	— ◡ ◡	♩. ♪♩
IV	Anapaestic	◡ ◡ —	♪♩ ♩.
V	Spondiac	— —	♩. ♩.
VI	Tribrachic	◡ ◡ ◡	♪♪♪ ♪♪♪

Monism   (Gk., *mones,* single) The philosophical position that there is but one fundamental reality. The classical advocate of extreme monism was Parmenides of Elea; Spinoza is a modern exponent.

Monochord   A device consisting of a single string stretched over a soundboard with a movable bridge. Used to demonstrate the laws of acoustics, especially the relationships between intervals and string lengths and the tuning of scales. (See fig. 16.2.)

Monophonic   (Gk., one sound) A single line of music without accompaniment or additional parts, as in *plainsong, *troubadour-trouvère-minnesinger songs, and some *folk songs, hollers, street cries, and blues.

Montage   (moan–TAHZH) A composition made of existing photographs, paintings, or drawings; in cinematography the effects achieved by superimposing images or using rapid sequences.

Mosaic   The technique of embedding bits of stone, colored glass, or marble in wet concrete to make designs or pictures for walls or floors. To achieve a complex interplay of light and shadows, the bits are set in the holding material with minute differences in the angles, as in the mosaics of San Vitale in Ravenna. (See colorplates 11 and 12.)

Motet   (from F., *mot,* word) The most important form of early *polyphonic music (ca. thirteenth to seventeenth centuries).

1. *Medieval motet* (thirteenth–fourteenth centuries). Usually 3 parts (triplum, motetus, tenor). The tenor "holds" to a *cantus firmus and the upper two voices sing different texts (sacred and/or secular).

2. *Renaissance* motet (fifteenth–sixteenth centuries). A four- or five-part composition, a cappella, generally polyphonic, with a single Latin text. A serious vocal piece intended for use in sacred services.

    There are also Baroque motets (by J. S. Bach) for mixed chorus and orchestra (German text) and some Romantic motets (Brahms), again in the *a cappella style.

Motive   The smallest musical idea, usually part of a theme, which is used in various ways to give unity to musical expressions. Motives may be melodic (and rhythmic), purely rhythmic, harmonic or different combinations of these elements. Motives can be considered as building blocks of music or as a glue that holds music together.

Mullion   A vertical member that divides a window into sections; also used to support the glass in stained-glass windows.

Mural   A painting on a wall; a *fresco is a type of mural.

Myth   Stories explaining natural phenomena, customs, institutions, religious beliefs, and so forth of a people. Usually concerned with the supernatural, gods, goddesses, heroic exploits, and the like.

N

Narthex   A porch or vestibule of a church through which one passes to enter the *nave.

Natural   In music the sign ♮ used to cancel a previous sharp or flat. Also see accidentals.

Naturalism   The view that the universe requires no supernatural cause or government, that it is self-existent, self-explanatory, self-operating, and self-directing, that the universe is purposeless, deterministic, and only incidentally productive of man. In relation to literature sometimes defined as "realism on all fours." The dominant traits of literary naturalism are biological determinism (people are what they must be because of their genes) and environmental determinism (people are what they are because of where they were nurtured). It all comes out to nature versus nurture.

Nave   The main central space of a church running from the entrance to the *crossing of the *transepts; typically flanked by one or two side aisles. Name derived from *naval* because the barrel *vault ceiling has the appearance of the inside hull of a ship.

Nomos, Nome   (Gk., law, rule) In the Homeric tradition in ancient Greece the term is used to refer to the traditional phrases and melodies singers used to recite the epics and odes.

Notation   A set, any set, of symbols used to put music into written form. It should be pointed out that musical notation (even modern notation) can only approximate the sounds the composer wants. Actual performance practices must be based not only on a reading knowledge of music but also on an awareness of performance practices and the conventions of particular periods of music. Size of audience, acoustics of a room, and capabilities of the performer also affect the conversion of musical notation into actual music.

Notes and rest values   Modern musical system based on the whole and fractional divisions of a whole note, for example:

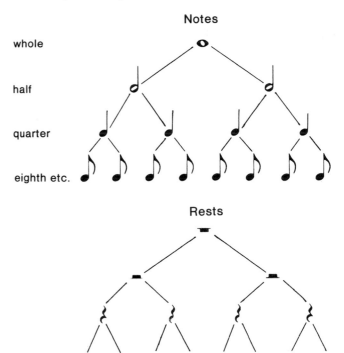

Notre Dame school   The composers of the twelfth- and thirteenth-century cathedral school at Notre Dame de Paris, most notably Leonin and Perotin. The Notre Dame school probably invented rhythmic notation for *polyphonic music.

O

Oboe   (from F., "high wind," that is, high-pitched instrument) A double-reed, soprano-range instrument with a conical bore (slightly expanding diameter from reed to bell). It has a nasal but mellow and poignant tone.

Odalisque   (oh–de–LISK) French word for a harem slave or concubine but used more broadly to refer to a reclining female figure, a favorite subject of painters like Ingres and Matisse.

Ode   A formal lyric on a usually dignified theme, in exalted language, e.g., works by Horace.

Office hours   In the Roman Catholic church the services (usually observed only in monastic churches) that take place eight times a day (every three hours): Matins, Lauds, Prime, Terce, Sext, None, Vespers, and Compline. Musically the important services are Matins, Vespers, and Compline.

Ontology   (Gk., *on,* being + *logos,* logic) Philosophic inquiry into the ultimate nature of things, what it means to be.

Opera (from I., *opera in musica,* work in music) A play in which the text is generally sung throughout to the accompaniment of an orchestra. Modern opera had its beginnings in Florence in the late sixteenth century when some musicians, poets, and scholars attempted a revival of Greek drama, which they assumed to have been sung throughout. Opera depends for its effect on communicating through song rather than other theatrical conventions such as blank verse. It is a complex synthesis of various arts: music, poetry, scenery, stagecraft, costume design, and acting. Because it is so complex it is expensive to produce (and attend) and therefore has a certain association with "society" as a prestige symbol. However, when a well-written opera is effectively staged, acted, and sung (in the language of the audience) the effect is not that of an esoteric status symbol but rather an overwhelming musical-theatrical-artistic experience.

Opus (L., work) Abbreviated as op., it generally indicates the chronological order of "works" of music. When the designation is, for example, op. 2 no. 4, the work is the fourth part or portion of a composer's second major work. This designation is usually used for a related series of short compositions, for example, twenty-four *Preludes* by Chopin in his Opus 28.

Oratorio A musical setting of a religious or epic theme for performance by soloists, chorus, and orchestra in a church or concert hall. Originally (early seventeenth century) they were similar to operas (sacred operas) with staging, costumes, and scenery. They are now usually presented in concert form, for example, *The Messiah,* by G. F. Handel.

Orchestra (from Gk., *orcheisthai,* to dance) In ancient Greek theatres the circular or semicircular space in front of the stage used by the chorus; group of instrumentalists performing ensemble music, e.g. symphony orchestra.

Ordinary of the Mass v. Mass.

Organ, Pipe organ An instrument (see Hydraulis) of ancient origin consisting of from two to seven keyboards (manuals) and a set of pedals (usually thirty-two notes) for the feet. Organs have anywhere from a few hundred up to ten thousand individual pipes, a mechanical wind supply (electric blower), and a keyboard action that is either mechanical (directly connected to pipes with wooden "trackers"), pneumatic, or electric (opening the pipes with air or with electrical action). Some modern organs are so complex that they have built-in computers to assist with "registration," that is, the selection of which ranks (or sets) of pipes to use. Many pipe organ manufacturers are operating around the clock in an effort to keep up with the demand for what has been called the king of instruments. The pipe organ is not to be confused with the numerous electronic imitations, which attempt to reproduce the sound of real pipes.

Organum (OR–ga–num; L.) The name given to the earliest types of *polyphonic music. Beginning with about the ninth century, organum was first strict, then parallel, free (contrary motion), and *melismatic. See (in the text) the section on medieval music for description and illustrations of the stages of organum.

Overture Musical introduction to an *opera, *oratorio, or other large work; an independent orchestral work in one movement.

P

Pantheism (Gk., *pan,* all, + *theos,* god) As a religious concept, the doctrine that God is immanent in all things.

Pediment In classic architecture a triangular space at the end of a building framed by the *cornice and the ends of the sloping roof (*raking cornices). (See fig. 7.36.)

Pendentive In architecture a concave triangular piece of masonry, four of which form a transition from a square base to support the circular rim of a *dome. (See fig. 12.20.)

Percussion Instruments that are played by striking, shaking, scraping, etc. See separate articles for more detailed descriptions of individual instruments. Percussion instruments can be divided into two groups:

Instruments of definite pitch
Timpani
Glockenspiel or Bells
Celesta
Xylophone
Marimba
Chimes
Vibraphone

Instruments of indefinite pitch
Snare drum (side drum)
Tenor drum
Bass drum
Tambourine
Triangle
Cymbals
Tam-Tam (gong)
Castanets
Guiro
Maracas

Period An inner division of music usually consisting of two or three *phrases.

Peristyle A series of columns that surround the exterior of a building or the interior of a court, e.g., the Parthenon has a peristyle. (See fig. 7.46.)

Perspective The illusion of a three-dimensional world on a two-dimensional surface. *Linear perspective* uses lines of projection converging on a vanishing point and with objects appearing smaller the further from the viewer. *Aerial (atmospheric) perspective* uses diminished color intensity and blurred contours for objects apparently deeper in space.

Phrase A division of music larger than a *motive but smaller than a *period. It is a unit of melody (harmony and rhythm) of no specific length that expresses at least a comprehensible portion of a musical idea. It might be compared with a phrase of speech.

Pier A mass of masonry, usually large, used to support arches or lintels; more massive than a *column and with a shape other than circular. (See fig. 15.14.)

Pieta (pyay–TA; I., pity, compassion) Representations of the Virgin mourning the body of her Son.

Pilaster A flat vertical column projecting from the wall of a building; usually furnished with a base and capital in the manner of an *engaged column, which is rounded rather than rectangular like the pilaster.

Plainsong   The term generally used for the large body of nonmetrical, *monophonic, *liturgical music of the Roman Catholic church. Also called Gregorian chant.

Polyphony   (po–LIF–o–nee) *Polyphonic* (pol–ly–PHON–ik) "Many-voiced" music, that is, melodic interest in two or more simultaneous melodic lines. Examples of polyphonic music would be *canons and *rounds.

Positivism   Philosophic inquiry limited to problems open to scientific investigation. Traditional subjects such as aesthetics and metaphysics are dismissed as "meaningless" because their content cannot be subjected to verification.

Post and lintel   A structural system in which vertical supports or columns support horizontal beams. The lintel can span only a relatively short space because the weight of the superstructure centers on the mid-point of the horizontal beam. In a structural system using *arches the thrust is distributed to the columns supporting the bases of the arches, thus allowing for a greater span. The lintel is also called an *architrave. (See fig. 7.34.)

Pragmatism   (Gk., *pragma,* things done) Philosophic doctrine that the meaning of a proposition or course of action lies in its observable consequences and that its meaning is the sum of its consequences. In everyday life the favoring of practical means over theory; if something works it's good; if not, it's bad.

Primary colors   The *hues of red, yellow, and blue with which the colors of the spectrum can be produced. Primary colors cannot be produced by mixing.

Program music   Music intended to depict ideas, scenes, or other extramusical concepts.

Proper of the Mass   v. Mass.

Proscenium   (Gk., *pro,* before; *skene,* stage) In traditional theatres the framework of the stage opening.

Psalm   A sacred song, poem, or hymn; the songs in the Old Testament book of The Psalms.

Psalter   Vernacular name for the book of The Psalms. v. Psalm.

Psaltery   Ancient or medieval instrument consisting of a flat soundboard over which a number of strings are stretched. A psaltery is plucked with the fingers. A similar instrument, the dulcimer, is played by striking the strings with hammers. The *harpsichord is a keyed psaltery. (See fig. 14.1.)

Putto   (I., plural *putti,* boy) The cherubs in Italian Renaissance painting and in rococo painting of the eighteenth century.

Q

Quatrain   A stanza of four lines, either rhymed or unrhymed.

R

Raking cornice   The end (cornice) on the sloping sides of a triangular *pediment.

Rebec   A small bowed medieval string instrument adapted from the Arabian *rebab.* It was one of the instruments from which the violin developed during the sixteenth century. (See fig. 16.3.)

Recorder   A straight, end-blown *flute, as distinct from the modern side-blown (transverse) flute. It was used from the Middle Ages until the eighteenth century and has been revived in the twentieth century.

Refrain   Recurring section of text (and usually music), e.g., verse-refrain.

Relief   In sculpture, carvings projecting from a background that is a part of the whole. Reliefs may be high (almost disengaged from the background) or low (*bas relief,* slightly raised above the background).

Reliquary   (F., remains) A receptacle for storing or displaying holy relics. (See colorplate 15.)

Rhythm   The temporal organization of music, for example, anything and everything that has to do with the motion of music, with the movement of sound in time. Rhythm is involved with pulsations (beats) that are either played or implied but it should not be confused with *meter, which is a regular pattern of beats or pulsations.

Rondo   A musical form with a primary theme alternating with several contrasting themes, e.g., ABACA.

Rotta   A medieval harp, probably originating with the Celts of western Europe. Also called a Celtic harp.

Round   In music a commonly used name for a circle *canon. At the conclusion of a melody the singer returns to the beginning, repeating the melody as often as desired. Examples: "Brother James," "Dona Nobis Pacem," and "Row, Row Your Boat."

S

Sanctuary   A sacred or holy place set aside for the worship of a god or gods; a place of refuge or protection.

Sanctus   (L., Holy) The fourth item in the *Ordinary of the *Mass.

Sarcophagus   A stone coffin.

Satire   An indictment of human foibles using humor as a weapon, e.g., the relatively mild satires of Horace and the bitter ones of Juvenal.

Scale   (L., ladder) The tonal material of music arranged in a series of rising or falling pitches. Because of the variety in the world's music there are many different scales. The basic scale of European music is the diatonic scale (C–D–E–F–G–A–B–C), i.e., the white keys of the piano. This arrangement of tones is also called a major scale or, more properly, a C major scale. Other commonly used scales are:

Minor	C–D–E♭–F–G–A♭–B♭–C
Whole tone	C–D–E–F♯–G♯–A♯–C
Pentatonic	C–D–F–G–A–C
Dorian mode	C–D–E♭–F–G–A–B♭–C
Phrygian mode	C–D♭–E♭–F–G–A♭–B♭–C

Scholasticism   The philosophy and method of medieval theologians in which speculation was separated from observation and practice, revelation was regarded as both the norm and an aid to reason, reason respected authority, and scientific inquiry was controlled by theology.

Secondary colors   Those *hues located between the *primary hues on a traditional color wheel: orange, green, and violet.

Semitone The smallest standard interval in Western music; half of a whole tone, for example, from C to C♯ on the piano keyboard.

Sempre (SEM–pra; I.) Always.

Sequence A type of chant developed in the early Middle Ages in which a freely poetic text was added to the long *melisma at the end of the Alleluias. Subsequently separated from the Alleluias, the sequences became independent syllabic chants. The composition of many original sequences finally led to the banning of all but five sequences by the Council of Trent (1545–1563).

Serial composition A general term applied to twentieth-century music that uses a tone row (v. twelve-tone technique), but which also serializes other elements of music, such as *rhythm, *dynamics, and *timbre.

Sfumato (sfoo–MAH–toe) A hazy, smoky blending of color tones in a painting to create ambiguities of line and shape, as in Leonardo's *Mona Lisa*.

Sharp v. Accidental.

Shawm A double-reed instrument that preceded the *oboe.

Simile A comparison between two quite different things, usually using "like" or "as."

Snare drum v. Drum.

Sonata (I., *sonare,* to sound) An instrumental (sounding) piece, which in the seventeenth century, denoted a composition for a single instrument. Since about 1750 the term has come to mean a composition in several movements for a keyboard instrument or for solo instrument with keyboard accompaniment. "Duet sonatas" (solo instrument plus keyboard) usually have three movements (fast-slow-fast), while solo sonatas usually have four movements (fast-slow-moderate-fast).

Sonata form A term used for a structural design in which two contrasting themes appear in an initial exposure (exposition), after which one or both are altered, fragmented, and otherwise exploited (development). The form concludes with a return to the initial material (recapitulation) followed by a concluding section (coda) when necessary. Sonata form differs from other musical forms in that it is a dual thematic form with the two themes of approximately equal importance.

Sonnet A fourteen-line poem in iambic pentameter. Petrarch, the fourteenth-century Italian poet, used a rhyming scheme of *abbaabba* followed by *cde cde* or variants thereof. Shakespeare used a rhyming scheme of *abab cdcd efef gg,* or four *quatrains followed by a *rhymed couplet.

Soprano The highest female singing voice, that is, S A T B. The term is also applied to the highest pitched instruments in a family of instruments, for example, soprano saxophones.

Spinet Originally a name for small *harpsichords with only one manual (keyboard). The term is used today for small upright pianos.

Squinch In architecture a device to effect a transition from a polygonal base to a circular dome. (See fig. 12.17 and accompanying explanation.)

Staff (musical) A set of five horizontal lines on which music is written. *Plainsong still uses a four-line staff.

Stele (STEE–lee) A carved slab of stone or pillar used especially by the Greeks as a grave marker. (See fig. 7.62.)

Still life In pictorial arts inanimate objects used as subject matter.

Stringed instruments Instruments in which the sound is produced by a stretched string. They may be divided into four main groups (see individual definitions for descriptions):

Stretched strings on a frame.
Plucked: zither.
Plucked, with keyboard: harpsichord, virginal, spinet.
Struck by hammer: dulcimer.
Struck by hammer, with keyboard: piano.
Strings touched by tangents: clavichord.

Instruments having a body and a neck.
Plucked: lute family (round back), guitar family (flat back).
Bowed: violin family, viols, vielle, rebec.

Instruments with projecting arms and crossbar: lyre, kithara.

Instrument with vertical strings: harp.

String quartet The standard chamber music ensemble of violin I and II, viola, cello. String quartets date from about 1750. In effect they are *sonatas for four instrumentalists.

Strophic A song in which the same music is used for all stanzas. When new music is used for each stanza the song is through-composed.

Stylobate The third of three steps of a Greek temple on which the *columns rest; essentially the platform on which the *cella and *peristyle are erected. (See fig. 7.49.)

Syllabic In vocal music the setting of one note for each syllable.

Syllogism A form of deductive reasoning consisting of a major premise, minor premise, and a conclusion. Example: all men are mortal; Socrates is a man; therefore Socrates is mortal.

Symphony Since the classic era (1760–1827) the term stands for a *sonata for orchestra. Symphonies are played, naturally enough, by symphony orchestras and are usually (but not always) in a four-movement form.

Syncopation Stressing a beat or portion of a beat that is usually weak or unaccented. Most commonly used in jazz.

T

Tabor A medieval drum shaped like a long cylinder. Played with one stick to accompany a small *recorder, hence the standard combination of pipe and tabor.

Teleology (Gk., *telos,* end, completion) The theory of purpose, ends, goals, final cause; opposite of materialism.

Tempera A painting technique using pigment suspended in egg yolk.

Tempo   The pace or speed of a musical composition. Since the seventeenth century, Italian terms have been used to give an approximation of the desired tempo. The invention of the metronome provides a more precise indication of a specific tempo. However, the size of an audience, the acoustics of a hall, and many other factors make the matter of tempo subject to a variety of interpretations. Some of the more common Italian tempo markings are given below, reading from slow tempo to progressively faster tempos:

Largo   Slow, broad.

Grave   (GRAH–vay) Slow, solemn.

Lento   Slow.

Adagio   (uh–DAH–jo) "At ease," slow.

Andante   (ahn–DAHN–tay) "Walking tempo," that is, moderate.

Andante cantabile   (kahn–TAH–bi–lay) In a singing manner.

Andante con moto   Andante "with motion."

Andantino   Slightly faster than andante.

Allegretto   (ahl–luh–GRET–toe) Moderately lively.

Allegro   (ahl–LEH–gro) "Cheerful," that is, fast.

Allegro appassionato   With passion.

Allegro giocoso   (joe–KO–so) Merrily.

Allegro marcato   Emphatic.

Allegro moderato   Moderately fast.

Allegro non troppo   Fast but "not too fast."

Molto allegro   "Much" fast, that is, very fast.

Vivace   (vee–VAH–chay) Very fast.

Presto   Very fast.

Presto con fuoco   Very fast, "with fire."

Prestissimo   Very, very fast.

Tenor   (L., *tenere*, to hold) (1) Originally the part that "held" the melody on which early sacred polyphonic music was based. (2) The highest male voice (S A <u>T</u> B). (3) Prefix to the name of an instrument, for example, tenor saxophone.

Terra-cotta   (I., baked earth) A baked clay used in ceramics and sculptures; a reddish color.

Tesserae   (TESS–er–ee) Bits of stone and colored glass used in *mosaics.

Tetrachord   In ancient Greek music a succession of four descending notes (a–g–f–e), which formed the nucleus of Greek music theory. Now loosely applied to any four-note segment of a scale.

Texture   The melodic (horizontal) and harmonic (vertical) fabric of music, comparable to the horizontal and vertical aspects (warp and woof) of woven fabrics. There are three basic textures: *monophonic, *homophonic, *polyphonic. All music (except monophonic music) consists of a varying combination of vertical and horizontal relationships. A polyphonic texture with two distinct melodies still has a vertical aspect brought about by the harmonic intervals formed by the two melodies. A texture with two clearly defined melodies is necessarily described as polyphonic, providing there is also a realization of the harmonic implications of simultaneous melodies.

Thrust   The outward force caused by the weight and design of an *arch or *vault, a thrust that must be countered by a *buttress. (See fig. 15.34.)

Timbre   (tambr; F., tone color) Also used in English as a term referring to the coloration of musical tones, that is, the quality that enables a listener to distinguish, for example, between a flute, an oboe, and a clarinet. Tone color is the result of the relative strengths and weakness of the tones (partials) in the overtone series. In practical terms tone color is dependent on how a tone is produced (blowing, striking, bowing, etc.), the material used (wood, silver, platinum, etc.), and the abilities of individual performers. Two different trumpet players, for example, would produce a slightly different tone color when alternating on the same instrument.

Tone   (1) In music a sound of well-defined pitch, as distinct from noise. (2) The distance of a whole step (two semitones).

Tone color   v. Timbre.

Tragedy   A serious play or other literary work with an unhappy or disastrous ending caused, in Greek drama, by *hubris on the part of the protagonist.

Transcendental   Beyond the realm of the senses; rising above common thought or ideas; exalted.

Transept   That part of a *cruciform-plan church whose axis intersects at right angles the long axis of the cross running from the entrance through the *nave to the *apse; the cross-arm of the cross.

Treble clef   v. Clef.

Triforium   In a Gothic cathedral, the gallery between the *nave arcades and the *clerestory; the triforium gallery opens on the nave with an *arcade. (See fig. 15.42.)

Triglyph   Projecting block with vertical channels that alternates with *metopes in a *Dorian *frieze of a Greek temple. The ends of the marble beams are stylized versions of the wooden beams used in early temples.

Trombone   A tenor-baritone-range brass instrument with a cylindrical bore, played with a cup-shaped mouthpiece and a movable slide. The slide is the oldest method (fifteenth century) of changing the length of air column in a brass instrument, making the trombone the oldest member of the modern brass family.

Trompe-l'oeil   (trohmp LUH–yuh; F.) Illusionistic painting designed to convince the observer that what is seen is an actual three-dimensional object rather than a two-dimensional surface; literally, "eye fooling."

Trope   Additional text and/or music added to a preexisting *plainsong. The earliest tropes were *sequences. Troping became so widespread that it was banned by the Council of Trent. *Liturgical drama was a direct outgrowth of the trope.

Troubadour   Poet-musicians, mostly of aristocratic birth, of southern France (Provence) who, during the period ca. 1100–1300, cultivated the arts of poetry and music in chivalrous service to romantic love. Their music was *monophonic in style and popular in flavor but exerted considerable influence on the development of *polyphonic music.

Trouvère Poet-musicians of central and northern France from ca. 1150–1300. Their music developed from the *troubadours and showed the same general characteristics except for the change in language from that of the south (Provençal) to the medieval forerunner of modern French.

Trumeau A pillar or column placed in the center of a portal to help support the *lintel. (See fig. 15.28.)

Trumpet A soprano-range brass instrument with basically a cylindrical bore and a cup mouthpiece. The modern trumpet lengthens the air column by using valves. The trumpet is the standard orchestral instrument and should not be confused with the instrument of shorter length and similar shape used frequently in military bands, namely, the *cornet*. The cornet has basically a conical bore and a milder and more mellow tone.

Tuba The bass instrument of the brass family with conical bore, three to five valves, and played with a cup mouthpiece.

Twelve-tone technique A twentieth-century procedure developed by Schoenberg and based on the equal tonal value of the twelve different notes within one octave. Basic to this system of *atonality is the tone row in which the twelve different notes are arranged in a nontonal pattern and used repeatedly with only mathematical variations: reverse order, change of octave, and so forth.

Tympanum The space, usually elaborately carved, enclosed by the lintel and arch of a doorway; also, the space within the horizontal and *raking cornices of a *pediment. (See fig. 15.25.)

V

Vanishing point In linear *perspective the point at which parallel lines converge on the horizon.

Vault A masonry ceiling constructed on the principle of the arch. A *barrel vault* is an uninterrupted series of arches amounting to a very deep arch. (See fig. 15.14.)

Vibrato (I., shaken) In music rapid but minute fluctuations of pitch that add a certain expressive quality to the pitch. Vocalists and string players traditionally use a vibrato on every note but other performers may or may not, depending on the circumstances.

Vielle Medieval stringed instrument (twelfth to fifteenth centuries), succeeded by the *viol (sixteenth century), which in turn was replaced by the *violin family.

Viol (VIE–ul) A family of bowed stringed instruments that were popular during the Renaissance and early Baroque periods and are being made again today. Three sizes were normally used, all with flat backs and sloping shoulders, and played sitting down with the instrument held between the knees. The string bass (bass viol) is the sole survivor of the viol family in the modern orchestra.

Viola The alto-tenor member of the violin family. Slightly larger than the violin but with a rather muffled tone, the viola has been a regular member of the orchestra since the seventeenth century.

Violin The violin emerged from the various bowed string instruments around 1600 and, with its brighter and more brilliant tone, replaced the *viols during the seventeenth century. As distinguished from the viol, it has a slightly rounded back and round shoulders. The best violins ever made were built in and around Cremona, Italy, from ca. 1600–1750 by the families Amati, Guarnierius, and Stradivarius.

Virelai A form of medieval French poetry with a refrain before and after each stanza. Virelais were used by *trouvères and exploited during the Gothic period by Machaut and others.

Virginal A *harpsichord used mainly in England and supposedly played by young ladies. The shape was frequently rectangular. When built in the standard two-keyboard form it was called a "pair of virginals."

Volute The spiral scrolls of an *Ionian *capital.

Voussoir (voo–SWAHR; F.) The wedge-shaped blocks of stone used to construct *arches and *vaults. (See fig. 15.34.)

W

Whole tone scale v. Scales.

Woodcut A wood block that has been carved so that the design stands out slightly from the block, comparable to printing type.

Woodwinds A group of instruments most of which were, at one time, built of wood. There are three general types (see separate definitions for more detailed information):

Tube open at both ends
Piccolo
Flute
Alto flute

Double-reed instruments
Oboe
English horn
Bassoon
Contra bassoon

Single-reed instruments
Clarinet
Bass clarinet
Contra bass clarinet
Saxophone family

X

Xylophone (Gk., wood sound) A percussion instrument consisting of a "keyboard" of hardwood bars and played with mallets. The tone is dry, brittle, and penetrating.

Credits

Photographs

Photographs by Robert C. Lamm except as indicated.

Figure 6.3 Boeringer Collection, Geneva.
Figure 7.2 Shaw Collection. Museum of Fine Arts, Boston.
Figure 7.9 National Archeological Museum, Athens.
Figure 7.15 National Archeological Museum, Athens.
Figure 7.18 Francis Bartlett Donation. Museum of Fine Arts, Boston.
Figure 7.33 National Archeological Museum, Athens.
Figure 7.35 National Museum, Naples.
Figure 7.43 American School of Classical Studies at Athens: Agora Excavation.
Figure 7.47 Akropolic Museum, Athens.
Figure 7.48 British Museum, London. Reproduced by the courtesy of the Trustees of the British Museum.
Figure 7.49 British Museum, London. Reproduced by the courtesy of the Trustees of the British Museum.
Figure 7.50 British Museum, London. Reproduced by the courtesy of the Trustees of the British Museum.
Figure 7.51 British Museum, London. Reproduced by the courtesy of the Trustees of the British Museum.
Figure 7.64 National Archeological Museum, Athens.
Figure 7.65 Vatican Museum, Rome.
Figure 7.66 Capitoline Museum, Rome.
Figure 7.67 National Archeological Museum, Athens.
Figure 7.69 Antikenmuseum Staatliche Museen Preussischer Kulturbesitz Berlin.
Figure 7.70 Antikenmuseum Staatliche Museen Preussischer Kulturbesitz Berlin.
Figure 7.72 The Louvre, Paris.
Figure 10.5 Vatican Museum, Rome.
Figure 10.12 Alinari/Editorial Photocolor Archives.
Figure 10.20 Alinari/Editorial Photocolor Archives.
Figure 10.26 Alinari/Editorial Photocolor Archives.
Figure 12.1 Hirmer Verlag München.
Figure 12.2 Hirmer Verlag München.
Figure 12.4 Hirmer Verlag München.
Figure 12.5 Hirmer Verlag München.
Figure 12.6 Hirmer Verlag München.
Figure 12.7 Hirmer Verlag München.
Figure 12.8 Hirmer Verlag München.
Figure 12.13 Hirmer Verlag München.

Figure 12.14   Alinari/Editorial Photocolor Archives
Figure 15.8   British Museum, London.
Figure 15.25   Bulloz-Art Reference Bureau
Figure 15.48   Alinari/Editorial Photocolor Archives
Figure 15.49   Alinari/Editorial Photocolor Archives
Figure 15.50   Alinari/Editorial Photocolor Archives
Cover illustration by Fred Otnes.

Literary Selections

The Bobbs-Merrill Company, Inc., for permission to reprint "Apology," from *Euthyphro Apology & Crito,* translated by F. J. Church and R. D. Cumming, Copyright © 1959, by the Bobbs-Merrill Co., Inc. Reprinted by permission of the publisher. For permission to reprint "On the Dedication of the Colosseum in Rome," from *Martial: Selected Epigrams,* translated by Ralph Marcellino, © 1968, by the Bobbs-Merrill Co., Inc. Reprinted by permission of the publisher.

Dell Publishing Company for two plays of Aeschylus. Copyright © 1965 by George Thomson. From *Aeschylus: The Oresteia Trilogy and Prometheus Bound,* edited by Robert Corrigan and translated by George Thomson. Reprinted by permission of the publisher.

David Higham Associates, Ltd., for permission of reprint Barbara Reynold's translation of Canto XXXIII of Dante's *Paradiso* and Dorothy Sayers's translation of Dante's *Divine Comedy.* Publishers: Victor Gollancz Ltd. and Penguin Books.

Holt, Rinehart and Winston, Inc., for Robert Frost's "Stopping by Woods on a Snowy Evening," from *The Poetry of Robert Frost,* edited by Edward Connery Lathem. © 1923, © 1969, by Holt, Rinehart and Winston. Copyright 1951 by Robert Frost. Reprinted by permission of Holt, Rinehart and Winston, Publishers. For A. E. Housman's "With rue my heart is laden," from "A Shropshire Lad," Authorized Edition from *The Collected Poems of A. E. Housman,* Copyright 1939, 1940, © 1965 by Holt, Rinehart and Winston. Copyright © 1967, 1968 by Robert E. Symons. Reprinted by permission of Holt, Rinehart and Winston, Publishers.

Indiana University Press for permission to reprint lines 1–170 and 229–399 from *Ovid: The Art of Love,* translated by Rolfe Humphries, copyright © 1957 by Indiana University Press. For permission to reprint a selection from *The Satires of Juvenal,* translated by Rolfe Humphries, copyright © 1958 by Indiana University Press.

Loeb Classical Library of the Harvard University Press for the selection from *Arrian's Discourses of Epictetus,* translated by W. A. Oldfather. Reprinted by permission.

Mason and Lipscom for permission to reprint some poems from *Selected Poems of Cattalus,* translated by Carl Sesar, © 1974.

The National Council of Churches of Christ in the U.S.A. The Scripture Quotations in this publication are from the Revised Standard Version of the Bible, copyrighted 1946, 1952, © 1971, 1973 by the Division of Christian Education of the National Council of Churches of Christ in the U.S.A., and used by permission.

W. W. Norton & Company, Inc. for permission to reprint *The Trojan Women* translated by Edith Hamilton from *Three Greek Plays,* by permission of W. W. Norton and Company, Inc. Copyright 1937 by W. W. Norton and Company, Inc. Copyright renewed 1965 by Dorian Fielding Reid.

Oxford University Press for permission to reprint "Oedipus the King" and three selections from "Antigone" from *Three Theban Plays of Sophocles,* translated by Theodore Howard Banks. Copyright 1956 by Theodore Howard Banks. Reprinted by permission of Oxford University Press, Inc. For selections from *The Republic of Plato* translated by F. M. Cornford (1941). Reprinted by permission of Oxford University Press. For selections from *Beowulf,* translated by C. W. Kennedy. Reprinted by permission of Oxford University Press.

Penguin Books Ltd. for permission to reprint "The Reeve's Tale" from Chaucer's *Canterbury Tales,* translated by Neville Coghill (Penguin Classics, 1960 ed.). Copyright © Neville Coghill, 1951, 1958, 1960. Reprinted by permission of Penguin Books, Ltd. For *The Bacchae* (complete) by Euripedes from Euripedes: *The Bacchae & Other Plays,* translated by Philip Vellacott (Penguin Classics, Revised edition 1972) pp. 191–244 Copyright © Philip Vellacott, 1954, 1972.

Pennsylvania State University Press for five troubadour songs from Wilhelm's *Seven Troubadours.* Reprinted by permission.

Purdue Research Foundation for selections from *Epigrams from Martial,* Barriss Mills, ©
1969, Purdue Research Foundation, West Lafayette, Indiana, U.S.A.

Random House, Inc. for "Scipio's Dream" from *The Basic Works of Cicero,* edited by
Moses Hadas. Copyright 1951 by Random House, Inc. Reprinted by permission of the
publisher. For Elinor Wylie's poem "Sanctuary," Copyright 1921 by Alfred A. Knopf, Inc.
and renewed 1949 by William Rose Benet. Reprinted from *Collected Poems of Elinor
Wylie,* by permission of Alfred A. Knopf, Inc.

Charles Scribner's Sons for excerpts of "Eclogue IV" and Book VI of *The Aeneid of Virgil,*
translated by Rolfe Humphries. New York: Charles Scribner's Sons, 1951.

Paul Turner for permission to reprint "Philosophies Going Cheap," from Lucian: *Satirical
Sketches,* translated by Paul Turner, 1961.

University of Michigan Press for four poems from *Sappho: Poems and Fragments,*
translated by Guy Davenport. © The University of Michigan Press, Ann Arbor, Michigan.
Reprinted by permission.

Index

All B.C. dates are specified. Titles of works are set in *italics* with the artist's name in parentheses. Page numbers of black-and-white illustrations are in boldface type; colorplates are designated. See the Glossary for definitions of technical terms.

Aachen (Aix-la-Chapelle), Germany, 312
Abacus, 178
Abbey of Jumièges, 415, **415**
Abelard, Peter, French philosopher and teacher (1079–1142), 341, 342 (quote)
Abelard and Heloise (Dronke), 341
Abraham, father of Judaism (18th c. B.C.), 278, 295, 298
Abraham and the Celestial Visitors, Church of Santa Maria Maggiore, Rome, 298, **298**
Academy of Plato, 57, 220, 300, 342
A cappella, 430, 432
Acoustics, 47–48, 202
Actium, Battle of, 213
Actors, 432
Adam, 294, 295, 345
Adams, Henry, American writer (1838–1918), 338, 339 (quote) 341
Adams, James, American historian (1878–1949), 10 (quote)
Aegean Sea, 36–38, 41, 44, 165
Aeneas, 192, 209, 210, 217, 224, 225, 229, 230, 264, 375n
Aeneid (Virgil), 209–10, 224–25, 226n, 229, 230–38 (text), 375n
Aeolians, 196, 199
Aeschylus, Greek dramatist (525–456 B.C.), 52–56, 57, 59, 61, 62–72 (text), 72–79 (text), 130, 174, 201, 217

"Against the City of Rome" (Juvenal), 251–55 (text)
Agamemnon, 38, 41, 53, 53 (box), 54, 62, 167, 210, 224
Agamemnon (Aeschylus), 53, 55, 62–72 (text), 80, 201
Agaue, 58 (box), 60, 108, 120n
Age of Reason, 217
Agora, Athens, 57, 129
Ahriman, 218
Ahura-Mazda, 218
Aigisthos, 53 (box), 54, 72
Aigues-Mortes, France, 311, **311**
Akhilleus, 38, 41, 172, 174, 224
"Akhilleus Bandaging Patrokles' Wound" (Sosias painter), 174, **174**
Akhilleus Painter, 184
"Akhilleus Slaying Penthesiles" (Exekias), **171,** 171–72
Akropolis, Athens, 55, 57, 176, 179, **179,** 180, 183, 217. *See also* Erechtheion, Parthenon, Propylaia, Temple of Athena Nike
Akrotiri, Santorini (Thira), 37, 38
Albigensian
    Crusade, 437
    Heresy, 437
Alcuin, English churchman and scholar (735?–804), 312

Alexander the Great, King of Macedonia (356–323 B.C.), 125, **126, 128,** 130, 162, 186, 188, 189, 218
Alexandria, Egypt, 126, 129, 199, 281
Alhambra, Granada, Spain, 409
Alkaios, Greek poet-musician (fl. 6th c. B.C.), 198–99
"Alkaios and Sappho with Lyres" (Greek), 199, **199**
Alkibiades, 60–61, 130, 136n
Allah, 407
Allegorical Portrait of Dante, (Florentine School) 371
Allegory of the Cave (Plato), 127, 153–55 (text), 340
Alleluias, 431, **431, 432,** 438, **438**
Altar of Zeus, Pergamon (Greek), **190,** 190–91
Ambrose, St., Bishop of Milan (340?–397), 226 (overview), 308
Ambulatory, 296, 297
Amenhotep III, Egyptian pharaoh of New Kingdom, 163
America, 312
Amiens Cathedral, France, 423, **423,** 425, 428
Amores (Ovid), 226n
Amos, Book of (Bible) 5:11–15; 6:4–8, 279 (text)
Amos, Hebrew prophet (8th c. B.C.), 279 (text)

Amphion, 196
Amphitheatres, Roman, in
  Arles, 268, **269**
  Nîmes, 268, 269
  Pompeii, 268
  Rome, **210**, 217, 222, 223, 249, 263,
    267, 268, **268**, 269
  Verona, 268
Amphora of the Dipylon (Greek), 168, **168**
Anagram: "Jesus Christ the Son of God,
  Savior," 293, **293**
Anakreon, Greek poet-musician (fl. 6th c.
  B.C.), 43, 198
Anavyssos Kouros (Greek), 173, **173**
Anaximandros, Ionian philosopher (ca.
  610–546 B.C.), 45–46
Andreas Capellanus, court chaplin and
  writer (fl. 1174–1186), 362–63
  (text)
Angel Dance, 439
Ankhises, 225, 229, 230
Annunciation (Martini), 427–28,
  colorplate 20
Anouilh, Jean, French playwright (b.
  1910), 9 (quote)
Anselm of Canterbury, prelate and
  philosopher (1033–1109), 340
Antelami, Benedetto, Italian sculptor and
  architect (late 12th, early 13th c.),
  418–19
Anthemius of Tralles, mathematician and
  architect (6th c.), 301
Antigone, 58 (box)
Antonine emperors, 214 (box), 271, 273
Antoninus Pius, Roman emperor
  (86–161), 214 (box), 270
Aphrodite, 39, 40 (box), 111n, 199, 217,
  293
Aphrodite of Knidos (Praxiteles), 187, **187**
Aphrodite of Melos (Greek), **191**, 191–92
Apocalypse, 288, 414, 422
Apollo, 39, 40 (box), 54, 55, 72, 73n, 84n,
  112n, 165, 181, 196, 197, 202, 230
Apollo, cult of, 196, 197 (box), 202
Apollo and Marsyas (Greek), 197, **197**
Apology (Plato), 61, 125n, 130–39 (text)
Apostles, 284, 297, 300, 303, 309
  in art, 416, 418, 422
Apoxyomenos (Lysippos), 188, **188**
Aqueducts, Roman, 216, 263, 265, 266,
  266, 268, 273
Aquinas, St. Thomas, theologian and
  philosopher (1225–1274), 341,
  343–44, 345, 347, 348, 371
Arabesques, 312, 409, 418
Arabian Nights, 409
Arabic, 341, 407, 408
Arabs, 312, 313, 350, 433
Arch and vault construction, **265**, 265–66,
  420, 421, 423, 425
Arch of
  Constantine, 272, **272**
  Septimus Severus, 272
  Titus, 266, 269, **269**
Arches, Roman triumphal, 268–69
Archilochos of Paros, Greek poet-musician
  (fl. 660 B.C.), 198–99

Architecture
  Byzantine, 299–303, 312
  canon of, Greek, 168–69, 177
  Carolingian, 312, 411–12
  early Christian, 296–97, 418
  Egyptian, 6, 162–65
  Gothic, 6, 298, 303, 419–26
  Greek, 56, 217
  Greek archaic, 172
  Greek classical, 6, 177–84
  Greek geometric, 168
  Hellenistic, 191
  Islamic, 408–10, 417
  Minoan, 165–66
  Mycenean, 167
  Norman, 412, 415, 423
  Roman, 261, 263, 265–72
  Romanesque, 413–19
Architrave, 178, 180, 183
Arena Chapel. *See* Giotto
Areopagus, Athens, 55, 73n
Ares, 40 (box), 83n
Arete, 221, 222
Argives, 38
Argos, 38, 53, 55, 60, 62, 72
Arian heresy, 291 (overview), 299, 308
Arians, 299, 308
Aristophanes, Greek dramatist (Old
  Comedy; ca. 448–380 B.C.), 61, 255
Aristotle, Greek philosopher (384–322
  B.C.), 9 (quote), 59, 81, 125, 126,
  128–30, 156–60 (text), 172, 201,
  277, 281, 313, 341, 342–44, 345,
  422
Aristoxenus of Tarentum, Greek music
  theorist and philosopher (fl. 4th c.
  B.C.), 201
Arius of Alexandria, Christian theologian
  (256–336), 299
Army, Roman, 211, 212, 213, 215, 274
Arnold, Matthew, English poet
  (1822–1888), 18
Arrian of Nicomedia (Flavius Arrianus),
  Greek historian and philosopher
  (ca. 100–170), 249–51 (text)
Ars Antiqua (Old Art), 441 (table), 442
Ars Nova (New Art), 441 (table), 442
Art
  Abstract, 16, 165
  aesthetics of, 11, 14, 17, 156
  Baroque, 15, 17
  basis for understanding, 9–19
  Byzantine, 16, 273, 299–303
  Carolingian, 411–13
  Cycladic, 165
  early Christianity, 273, 291–303 (chap.
    12)
  Egyptian, 15, 162–65
  Gothic, 426–28
  Greek, 161–93 (chap. 7), 217, 261–62,
    267
  Greek archaic, 169–74, 292, 294
  Greek classical, 174–89, 303
  Greek geometric, 16, 168–69
  Hellenistic, 189–92
  Hiberno-Saxon, 410–11
  how to judge, 15–17
  Islamic, 408

  medieval, 407–28 (chap. 15)
  Minoan, 166
  modern, 16, 17
  Mycenaean, 167
  Nonobjective, 16
  Roman, 261–74 (chap. 10)
  Romanesque, 416, 417, 419
Artemis, 39, 40 (box), 53, 165, 181
Arthur, King, legendary British king,
  363–71
Artist, role of, 9–11
Artistic method, 9–12, 17
Art of Courtly Love, The (Capellanus),
  317n, 362–63 (text)
Art of Love, The (Ovid), 222, 226n, 243–47
  (text), 362n, 434
Askanius (Ilus, Iulus), 224, 229
Aspasia, consort of Perikles (470?–410
  B.C.), 79–80
Astrodome, Houston, 273
Astrology, 218
Athanasius, Bishop of Alexandria
  (293?–373), 308
Athena, 38–39, 40 (box), 49, 55, 56, 57, 58
  (box), 96, 179, 180, 181, 182, 183,
  197, 215, 217, 422
Athena Nike, Temple of (Kallikrates), 179,
  183, **183**
Athena Parthenos (Pheidias), 180
Athenian empire, 36, 57, 179
Athenodoros of Rhodes, Greek sculptor
  (fl. 1st c.), 192
Athens, 4, 6, 35, 36, 42–45, 51–62, 72,
  79–80, 96, 108, 126, 128–30, 173,
  174, 179, 182–86, 195, 201, 211,
  218, 219, 220, 221n, 223. *See also*
  Attica
Atlantis, 38
Atlas, 40 (box)
Atomic theory, 52
Atreus, 53 (box), 54, 62
Atreus, House of, 53 (box), 62
Atrium
  early Christian, 296, 297
  Roman, **263**
Attalos I, King of Pergamon (fl. 200 B.C.),
  189, 190
Attica, 43, 44, 56, 60. *See also* Athens
Attila the Hun, King, invader of Europe
  (ca. 406–453), 315
Aucassin and Nicolette (chant-fable),
  327–36 (text), 342, 434
Audiger dit Raimberge (de la Halle), 434,
  434
Augustine, St., Bishop of Hippo and
  Christian theologian and
  philosopher (354–430), 127, 220,
  226 (overview), 308–10, 339, 340,
  344, 354n, 437
Augustus (Gaius Julius Caesar
  Octaviannus), Roman emperor (63
  B.C.–A.D. 14), 213, 214 (box), 215,
  217, 218, 224, 264, **264**, 266, 271
Augustus of Primaporta (Roman), 264,
  264, 265, 270, 272, 273, 422
Aulis, 53, 62
Aulodia, 198

Aulos, 110n, **196, 197,** 198, 200, 202, 274, 441 (table)
Aulos Player of the Ludovisi Throne (Greek), **196**
Ausonius, 210 (quote)
Avignon, 427, 428

Babylonia, 218, 284
Babylonian Captivity, 278, 279, 284
Bacchae, The (Euripides), 60, 108–23 (text)
Bacchantes, 109n, 200
Bach, Johann Sebastian, German composer (1685–1750), 12, 17, 26, 31, 437
Bagpipe, 441 (table)
Baldur, 313
Baptism, 303
Baptistery, 418
Basilica, 296, 300, 418
Basilica, Roman, Volubilis, Morocco, 296, **296**
Bath, England, 216
Baths, Roman, 216, **216,** 217, 263, 265, **267**
Baths of
    Caracalla, 217n
    Trajan, 267, **267**
"Battle Hymn of the Republic, The," 437
Battle of
    Actium, 213
    Hastings, 416
    Marathon, 44, 53, 57
    Platea, 45, 170
    Salamis, 45, 170, 174, 184
    Thermopylai, 44–45
    Universals, 337, 340–41, 344
Battle of the Gods and Giants, The (Greek), Altar of Zeus, 190–91, **191**
"Battle of Universals," 337, 340–41, 344
Battle Rages, The, Bayeux Tapestry, 416, **416**
Beatles, 437
Beatrice, 346, 347
Beatritz, Countess of Dia, French troubadour (12th c.), 436–37 (text)
Beauvais Cathedral, France, **424,** 424–25
Beethoven, Ludwig van, German composer (1770–1827), 6, 10, 21, 22, 23, 30, 432, 437
Be m'an perdut (Bernart de Ventadorn), **435** (text)
Benedict, St., Founder of Benedictine Order (d. ca. 547), 353n, 413
Benedictine Order, 353n
Beowulf, 314, 315, 317, 352
Beowulf, 313–16, 317–19 (text)
Bernard of Clairveaux, Saint, French monk (1091–1153), 416, 433
Bernart de Ventadorn, French troubadour (d. 1195), 362, 435–36 (text)
Bertrand de Born, French troubadour (ca. 1140–1215), 399n, 435
Bible, 39, 282, 283, 288, 340, 341, 345, 410
    Amos 5:11–15; 6:4–8, 279 (text)
    Ecclesiastes 3:1–22, 284 (text)
    Ezekial 18:25–32, 280 (text)
    I Corinthians 13:1–13, 286 (text)

Five Parables, 287–88 (text)
    Isaiah 9:6; 11:1–9, 279 (text)
    John 1:1–5, 281 (text)
    Matthew 5–7, 284–86 (text)
    Psalms 24; 137; 150, 283–84 (text)
    Revelation 6:1–8; 21:1–4, 289 (text)
    Second Isaiah 40:1–9; 53:3–6, 280 (text)
"Big Blonde" (Parker), 10
Bishop Golias, 433
Black Death, 439–40
Blondel de Nesles, French trouvère (b. ca. 1155), 437
Blues, 437
Boccaccio, Giovanni, Italian poet and humanist (1313–1375), 351–52
Boethius (Anicius Manlius Severinus), Roman consul and philosopher (ca. 475–524), 226 (overview), 273, **273,** 307, 314 (text), 339
Boniface VIII, Pope (1235–1303), 378n
Book of Kells (Hiberno-Saxon), 410, **411,** 428
"Book of the Queen's Maying, The," *Morte Darthur* (Malory), 366–71 (text)
Bourges Cathedral, France, 421
Boy from the Bay of Marathon (Greek), 188, **188**
"Bread and Circuses," 211, 222
Briseis, 38
Bruegel, Pieter, Flemish painter (1525–1569), 15, 16
Brunhild, 315
Brutus, 213
Buccina (Roman trumpet), 274
Buddha (Siddhartha Gautama), Founder of Buddhism (ca. 563–ca. 483 B.C.), 39
Bull, ceiling painting (Lascaux), 4, **4**
Bull from the Sea, The (Renault), 38
Byzantine, 298, 300, 301, 312, 338, 342, 411, 412, 418, 426, 427, 428
    churches, 300–303, 411, 412
    Empire, 299, 300, 303
    mosaics, 299–300, 302, 303
Byzantine Golden Age
    First, 291 (overview), 300–303
    Second, 291 (overview), 303
Byzantium, 36, 42, 172, 215, 302, 307, 312, 426. *See also* Constantinople

Caesar, Gaius Julius, Roman general, statesman, and historian (100–44 B.C.), 6, 211, 212–13, 214 (box), 226 (overview), 264, **264,** 269, 374n
Calf-Bearer (Greek), 170, **171,** 292, 294
Caligula (Gaius Caesar Germanicus), Roman emperor (12–41), 213, 214 (box), 268
Calling of the Apostles Peter and Andrew, The (Duccio), 427, colorplate 19
Calvin, John, French Protestant reformer (1509–1564), 310
Camelot, legendary location of King Arthur's Court, 363

Campanile, 418
Canon of architecture (Greek), 168–69, 177
Canon of sculpture, Greek (Polykleitos), 176, **177,** 188, **188**
Canterbury Cathedral, England, 425, **425**
Canterbury Tales, The (Chaucer), 343, 351, 352–62 (text), 436
Cantus firmus, 438, 439
Capitoline She-Wolf, The, **210**
"Capture of Christ and the Flagellation," *Psalter of St. Swithin,* 418, colorplate 16
Caracalla (Marcus Aurelius Antoninus), Roman emperor (188–217), 213, 214 (box)
Carcassonne, France, **311**
Carmina Burana (Orff), 433–34
Carolingian
    architecture, 411–12
    art, 411, 412–13
    Renaissance, 311–12, 411, 428
Carthage, 210, 211, 212, 222, 224, 227, 229, 262 (overview)
Carthage, Queen of. *See* Dido
Caryatids, 183, **183**
Cassius, 213
Catacombs, Rome, 291–92
Catacombs of St. Callixtus, Rome, **292**
Catacombs of St. Priscilla, Rome, **292**
Catharsis, 81
Cathedrals, 339, 347, 348
    Gothic, 343, 344, 345, 419, 420–26
    Romanesque, 418
Cato, Marcus Porcius, the Elder, Roman consul and censor (234–149 B.C.), 212, 277
Catullus, Gaius Valerius, Latin poet (87–54 B.C.), 200, 224, 226 (overview), 242–43 (text)
Cella, 177, 180, 182, 183, 265
Celto-Germanic culture, 313–16, 343, 410
Censor, Roman, 211
Central-plan churches, 300, 301, 411
Cerveteri, Etruscan city, 261
Chanson de Roland, 434. *See also Song of Roland*
Chansons de geste, 434
Chant-fable, 327, 342, 434
Chaos, 39
Chariot racing, 175, 222, 267, 274, 301
Charlemagne, Holy Roman Emperor (742–814), 311–12, 313, 316, 350, 411, 412, 413, 428, 430, 434
Chartres Cathedral (France), 282, 343, 345, 347, 371, **421,** 421–23, 424, 425, 428, 439, colorplate 17
    School of, 422
Chaucer, Geoffrey, English poet (ca. 1340–1400), 227, 282, 343, 351, 352–62 (text)
Chekhov, Anton, Russian dramatist and novelist (1860–1904), 10
Child with a Goose (Greek), 189, **189**
Chivalry, 337, 338, 339, 342, 349, 363, 422, 434, 440, 441 (table)
Chopin, Frédéric, Franco-Polish composer (1810–1849), 22, 29

Choreomania, 440
Chorus, Greek drama, 53–55, 200–201, 274
Christ, Jesus, Founder of Christianity (ca. 4 B.C.–A.D. 29), 7, 13, 39, 238, 264, 265, 280–82, 284 (quote), 288, 291, 292, 293 (quote), 294, 297, 300, 301, 302, 303, 308, 310 (quote), 432
    in art, 294, 295, 298, 299, 301, 416, 418, 422, 427
    teachings of, 284–88
Christendom, 280, 296, 300
Christ Enthroned (Roman), 294, **294**
Christianity, 6–7, 127, 128, 129, 215, 218, 220, 224, 238, 274, 278, 280–82, 291–303, 308, 408, 413, 419
    Orthodox, 299, 300, 301, 302
Christ Lay in the Bonds of Death (Luther), 432
Christ Pantocrater, St. Irene, Constantinople, 301, **301**
Christ Teaching the Apostles in the Heavenly Jerusalem, Santa Pudenziana, Rome, 297, **298**
Church, Christian
    early, 271, 291–98, 415
    medieval, 307–10, 311–16, 317–19, 320, 338, 339, 339–44, 348, 411–26
    Roman Empire, in, 215, 217, 220, 291–98, 426
Churches. *See* Architecture; *names of specific churches*
Church Fathers, 340, 341
Church of Rome, 217, 270, 271, 307, 308, 310, 311, 429
Cicero, Marcus Tullius, Roman statesman and orator (106–43 B.C.), 210 (quote), 212, 213, 215 (two quotes), 220, 226 (overview), 227–29 (text), 252n, 274, 274 (quote), 422
Cimabue, Giovanni, Italian painter (ca. 1240–1302), 19, 426, 427
Cimon, Athenian statesman and general (510–449 B.C.), 56
Circus Maximus, Rome, 222, 267, **267**
Cities, rise of, 337–38, 342, 419
City of God, The (St. Augustine), 220, 308, 309
City-states, 36, 41, 42, 52, 55, 57, 60, 125, 128, 172, 201, 217, 261, 267
Claudius (Tiberius Claudius Nero Germanicus), Roman emperor (10 B.C.–A.D. 54), 214 (box)
Clef, musical, 24, 430
Cleopatra VII, Queen of Egypt (69–30 B.C.), 213
Clerestory, 296, 414, 417, 418, 423, 425
Clergy, 434
    Regular, 310, 419
    Secular, 310, 419
Clodia (Lesbia), 242
Clouds, The (Aristophanes), 61, 131n
Cluniac Order, 413
Cocteau, Jean, French poet (1891–1963), 10 (quote), 12 (quote)
Collegiate Church of St. Sernin, Toulouse, France, 414, **414**, 415, **415**

Colosseum, Rome, **210**, 217, 222, 223, 249 (text), 263, **267**, 268, **268**, 269, 273
Colossi of Memnon (Egyptian), 163, **163**
Columns
    Carolingian, 411
    Gothic, 420, 423
    Greek, 175, **178, 179,** 180
    Islamic, 409
    Romanesque, 414–15
Combat between a Lapith and a Centaur (Greek), Parthenon, 182, **182**
Comedy, Greek
    New, 217
    Old, 61
Comitatus, 313
Commedia. See Divine Comedy
Commentaries on the Gallic Wars (Caesar), 212, 213
Commodus (Lucius Aelius Aurelius), Roman emperor (161–192), 213, 214 (box), 215, 271n
Composition
    in all arts, 10–11
    in music, 12–14, 27
    in painting, 14–17
Conceptualism, 341, 343, 344
Conductus, 433
Confessions, The (St. Augustine), 308
Consolation of Philosophy (Boethius), 273, 307, 314 (text)
Constantine I, the Great, Roman emperor (272–337), 214 (box), 215, 262 (overview), **272,** 273, 291 (overview), 295, 296, 299, 301, 308
Constantine the Great, **272**
Constantinople, 215, 262 (overview), 291 (overview), 300, 301, 303, 338, 426, 439. *See also* Byzantium; Instanbul
Consul, Roman, 211, 273, 307, 314
Contre dance, 440
Corinth, 58, 59, 81, 125, 212, 221n, 222
Corinthian architectural order, 178, **178,** 191, 217, 265, **265,** 266, **266,** 268, 271, 272, **296, 297, 414**
Corinthian capital, **265**
Council of
    Five Hundred (Athens), 44, 55
    Nicea, 291 (overview), 299, 308
    Trent, 432
Country-western music, 437
Court of Love, 338, 339, 342, 362, 363, 435, 437
Court of the Lions, Alhambra, Granada, Spain, **409**
Coutances Cathedral, France, 423, colorplate 18
Covenant, 278, 281
Crassus, Marcus Licinius, Roman statesman (ca. 115–53 B.C.), 212, 213
Crete, 35n, 36, 37, 38, 39, 58 (box), 110n, 165, 166, 168, 196, 230, 387n. *See also* Minoan culture
"Cross Page," *Lindisfarne Gospels,* **410**
Cross plan
    Greek, 302, 303
    Latin, 293, 296
Crucifixion, 293

Crucifixion, Church of Santa Sabina, Rome, **293**
Crucifixion, Monastery Church, Daphné, Greece, **303**
"Crucifixion Cover," *Lindau Gospels,* 412, 413, colorplate 14
Cruciform shape (or plan), 296, 347, 418
Crusades, 313, 315, 337, 338, 416, 433, 434, 441 (table)
Cult of the Virgin, 337, 339, 345, 349, 422
Culture-epoch theory, 5
Cybele, 110n, 218, 277
Cycladic culture, 162, 165
Cycladic head (Cycladic), 165, **165**
Cyclopes, 167
Cyrus the Great, Persian king (d. 529 B.C.), 278

Daidalos, 161, 230n, 251n
Dance
    Greek, 200, 202
    Medieval, 429, 439–40, 441 (table), 442
Dance of Death *(Danse Macabre),* 439–40
Daniel, 293, 294, **295**
Daniel, Book of (Bible), 288
Dante Alighieri, Florentine poet (1265–1321), 5, 227, 230, 234n, 236n, 238, 343, 345–48, 351, 371, 372–406 (text), 428, 435. *See also* *Allegorical Portrait of Dante*
Daphné, Monastery Church, Greece, 303
Darius I, king of Persia (ca. 558–486 B.C.), 44
Dark Ages. *See* Middle Ages
"Darling, The" (Chekhov), 10
David, king of Palestine (1000–960 B.C.), 278, 279, 292–93, 339, 350
David (Michelangelo), 5
Debussy, Claude, French composer (1862–1918), 30
Decameron (Boccaccio), 352
Decathlon, 222n
Delian
    League, 57
    Treasury, 179
Delos, 57, 165, 196, 223
Delphi, 41, 112n, 196, 221n, 223
Delphi Charioteer, 175, **175**
Delphic oracle, 41, 44, 55, 58, 58 (box), 73n, 83n, 198, 217
Demeter, 39, 40 (box), 111n
Democracy, 42–44, 45, 55, 57, 61, 80, 125n, 163, 169
Demokritos, Greek philosopher (460?–362? B.C.), 52, 57
Demosthanes, Athenian orator (384–322 B.C.), 125, **126**
Descent from the Cross (Antelami), 418, **419**
Deus ex machina, 52
Development of Medieval Music, 441 (table)
Diana, 40 (box), 217
Diaspora, 278
Dictator, Roman, 211
Dido, queen of Carthage, 210, 224, 229, 234n

Diocletian (Gaius Aurelius Valerius Diocletianus), Roman emperor (284–305), 214 (box), 215, 272, 296

Diomedes, 38

Dionysius II, tyrant of Syracuse (fl. 367 B.C.), 130

Dionysos, 40 (box), 52, 58 (box), 60, 73n, 83n, 108, 109n, 110n, 120n, 181, 196, 202

Dionysos, Cult of, 60, 108, 196, 197 (box), 200, 202, 218, 432

Dionysos (Greek), Parthenon, 181, **181**

Diptych of Consul Boethius (Roman), 273, **273**

Dirge in Woods (Meredith), 18 (text)

Discobolus (Myron), 176, **176**

"Discourses of Epictetus" (Arrian), 249–51 (text)

Divine Comedy, The (Dante), 5, 230, 238, 315, 343, 345–47, 371, 372–406 (text)
   Hell, 372–404 (text)
   Paradiso, Canto XXXIII, 404–6 (text)

Domitian (Titus Flavius Domitianus), Roman emperor (51–96), 214 (box), 268, 269, 270, 272, 288

Donatist heresy, 308

Donatus, Bishop of Carthage (4th c.), 308

Dorian mode, 196, 196n, 201–2

Dorians, 41, 168, 196
   city, 173, 199
   clothing, 172–73

Doric architectural order, 178, **178,**180–82, 184, 198, 263, 268

Doryphoros (Polykleitos), 176, **177,** 186, 188, 192, 264

Dover Beach (Arnold), 18 (text)

Drachma, Athenian, **57**

Draco, Athenian tyrant (7th c. B.C.), 43, 211

Draco's Code, 43

Drama. *See also names of individual dramas and dramatists*
   Greek, 52–56, 58–60, 61, 156–60 (text), 182, 200–201, 274, 432
   Liturgical, 319, 432–33
   medieval, 52, 319–20
   Roman, 226 (overview), 274

Drum, 274, 440, 441 (table)

Duccio di Buoninsegna, Sienese painter (1255–1319), 427

Duration, in music, 25

Dying Gaul, The (Greek), 189, **189**

Dylan, Bob, American musician (b. 1941), 437

Dyptych of Consul Boethius (Roman), 273, **273**

Eastern Sequence (Wipo), **432**

Ecclesiastes (Bible) 3:1–22, 284 (text)

Echinus, 178

Edict of Milan (Constantine), 215, 291 (overview), 295

Education
   Greek, 128, 146n, 195, 201, 202
   Roman, 212, 217

Egyptian culture, 37, 44, 45, 125, 126, 162–65, 169, 170, 174, 176, 182, 184, 188, 217, 439

Einstein, Albert, German-American physicist (1879–1955), 17, 340

El Attarin Medersa, Fez, Morocco, **408,** 408–9

Eleanor of Aquitaine, queen of France and then of England (1122–1204), 338, 362, 422, 435

Eleatic philosophy, 47, 51–52, 127, 128, 172

Electronic music, 31

Elektra, 53 (box), 55, 60, 72

Elektra (Aeschylus), 60

Elektra (Euripides), 60

Elektra (Sophokles), 60

Eleusian mysteries, 218

Eleusis, 218

Elgin, Thomas Bruce, 7th earl of (1766–1841), 183

Emerson, Ralph Waldo, American essayist and poet (1803–1882), 10 (quote), 215 (quote)

Empedokles, Greek philosopher (ca. 495–ca. 435 B.C.), 172

Emperors
   Byzantine, 299–301, 303, 312
   Holy Roman, 311–13, 315, 316
   Roman, 213, 214 (box), 215, 217, 219, 220, 222, 224, 264, 273, 295, 296, 299, 308

Engineering, Roman, 216, 265–66, 268, 273

English
   Early Modern, 352
   Middle, 352
   Modern, 352
   Old, 352

En non Diu! (School of Notre Dame), **438**

Entasis, 178, 180

Enteleche theory, 129, 345

Ephesos, Ionian city, 46

Ephialtes, Athenian statesman (d. 461 B.C.), 56

Epictetus, Stoic philosopher (60–110), 220, 226 (overview), 249–51 (text)

Epicureanism, 218, 219, 239, 277

Epicurus, Greek philosopher (ca. 342–270 B.C.), **218,** 218–19, 239

Epidauros, theatre of (Polykleitos the Younger), 52, **201**

Equestrian class, Rome, 212

Equestrian Statue of Marcus Aurelius, Rome, **271,** 271–72

Eratosthenes, Greek mathematician and astronomer (3rd c. B.C.), 216

Erechtheion (Mnesikles), Athens, 179, **182,** 182–83

Erechtheus, 179, 183

Erigena, John Scotus, Irish scholar (fl. 845–867), 340

Eros, 40 (box)

Estampie, secular dance, 440, 441 (table)

Eteokles, 58 (box)

Ethos, doctrine of, 195, 197 (box), 201–2

Etruscans, 210–12, 261–62, 263, 273

Etruscan sarcophagus, 261, **262**

Eucharist, 291, 293, 303, 431

Eudemian Ethics (Aristotle), 129

Eumenides (Aeschylus), 53, 55, 56, 72–79 (text), 80

Euripides, Greek dramatist (480–406 B.C.), 58, **59,** 59–60, 61, 96–108 (text), 108–23 (text), 186, 201

Europa, 58 (box)

Eurydice, 198

Evangelists, 415, 422

Evans, Sir Arthur, British archaeologist (1851–1941), 37, 166

Eve, 294, 295, 339, 345

Everyman, 316, 319, 320–27 (text), 342, 345

Exekias, Greek vase painter and potter (fl. 500 B.C.), 171–72, 174

Ezekial (Bible) 18:25–32, 280 (text)

Ezekial, Hebrew prophet (fl. 592–570 B.C.), 279–80 (text)

Farmers
   Greek, 41–43
   medieval, 310–11
   Roman, 211, 217

Fates, 40 (box)

Fatih Camii Mosque, Istanbul, 408, **408**

Feudalism, 310, 315, 316, 337, 338, 342, 344, 440

First Corinthians (Bible) 13:1–13, 286 (text)

Five Parables (Bible; Matthew 18:23–35; 20:1–16; 25:14–30 and Luke 10:30–37; 15:4–32), 287–88 (text)

Flavian emperors, 214 (box), 267, 268, 270

Flavian Woman, 268–69, **269**

Flight to Egypt, St.-Benoit-sur-Loire, 414, **414**

Florence, Italy, 4

Florence Cathedral, 271, 371

Flying buttress, 417, **421,** 424

Folquet of Marseilles, French troubadour (d. 1231), 434 (quote)

Form
   in art, 11
   in music, 13–14, 26–27

Forum, Pompeii, 263, **263**

Forums, Roman, 216, 263, 269, 272

Four Horsemen of the Apocalypse, 288

Fourth Crusade, 291 (overview), 300

Fourth Eclogue (Virgil), 224, 238–39 (text)

Fourth Horseman of the Apocalypse, The, **289**

Free will, 309, 314, 371

Frescoes, 292, 426–27

Freud, Sigmund, Austrian psychoanalyst (1856–1939), 340

Frieze, 178, 180, 182, 185, 190–91, 270

Frogs, The (Aristophanes), 61

Frost, Robert, American poet (1874–1963), 19

Furies, 39, 40 (box), 54, 55, 56, 78n

Gaea, 39, 40 (box)
Games
    Greek, 42, 220–22
    Roman, 222–23
Ganelon, 315
Garden of Eden, 345, 346
Gaudeamus Igitur, 349 (text)
Gauguin, Paul, French painter
    (1848–1903), 15
Gauls, 189, 213
Geometry, 47, 48, 408, 410
Germigny des Pres, France, 412, **412**
Gershwin, George, American composer
    (1898–1937), 31–32
Ghibellines, 315
Giotto, Florentine painter (1266–1336),
    299, 426, 427, 428
Girl Before a Mirror (Picasso), 17,
    colorplate 7
Gladiatorial combat, 210, 217, 220, 222,
    223, 224
Gladiators, 217, 223, 268
Gods. *See also individual names*
    Greek, 37–41, 127, 129, 130, 179–85,
      196–98, 277, 293 (*see also* Drama)
    Norse, 313
    Roman, 217–18, 219, 222, 224, 277
Goethe, Johann Wolfgang von, German
    poet and dramatist (1749–1832), 6
Golden Age
    Athens, of, 51, 174, 184, 186, 192, 222,
      267
    Byzantine
      First, 291 (overview), 300–303
      Second, 291 (overview), 303
      Irish, 407 (overview), 410–11, 428
Golden Age of Athens, 51, 174, 184, 186,
    192, 222, 267
Golden Mean, 128, 129
Golgotha, 303
Goliards, 343, 349 (text), 433–34, 441
    (table)
Goliard's Creed, A, 349 (text)
Good Shepherd (Roman), 294, **294**
Good Shepherd, The, Catacombs of St.
    Callixtus, Rome, **292,** 292–93
Good Shepherd, The, Mausoleum of
    Empress Galla Placidia, Ravenna,
    299, **299**
Gospels (Bible), 46, 281, 284, 432
Gothic, 298, 303, 312, 343, 344, 345, 347,
    407 (overview), 411, 414, 415,
    419–28
    architecture, 411, 414, 418, 420–26,
      438, 442
    music, 438–39, 441 (table)
    painting, 426–28
Government
    Greek, 36–45, 56–58, 125, 127–28
    Middle Ages, 310–12
    Minoan, 37
    Mycenaean, 38
    Roman, 211–16, 272–73, 310
Gracchus, Gaius Sempronius, Roman
    statesman (153–121 B.C.), 212
Gracchus, Tiberius Sempronius, Roman
    statesman (163–133 B.C.), 212

Graeco-Roman culture, 266, 278, 307, 310,
    312, 313, 314, 317, 343
Grand Central Station, New York, 217
Graves, Robert, English writer and critic
    (b. 1895), 37
Greater Panathenaea Celebration, 182
Great Mosque, Cordoba, Spain, **409,** 410,
    417, 428
Greco, El (Domenico Theotocopuli),
    Greek painter (1541–1613), 417
Greece, 4, 35–205 (Unit 2), 209–12, 216,
    216n, 217, 218, 220–23, 261–62,
    270, 338
    ancient (map), 37
    geography, 36, 163
    history (chronological). *See also*
      Athens; Minoan culture;
      Mycenaean culture; Sparta
      Cycladic (Aegean; ca. 3000–2000
        B.C.), 162, 165
      Minoan (ca. 2600–1125 B.C.), 36–38,
        161, 162, 165–66
      Mycenaean (ca. 1559–1100 B.C.),
        37–41, 162, 166–67
      Geometric period (ca. 1100–700
        B.C.), 168–69
      Archaic period (ca. 750–500 B.C.),
        41–45, 52, 169–74
      Classical period (Hellenic Athens;
        ca. 500–323 B.C.), 51–123 (chap. 5),
        174–89
      Hellenistic period (ca. 323–30 B.C.),
        189–92
Greek
    alphabet, 198, 210
    language, 51, 217, 255, 267, 281, 282,
      341
    musical instruments, 196, 197 (table),
      198
    musical notation, 198, 430
    Pantheon, 39, 40 (box)
    science, 173
    spelling, 35n
Greek Experience, The (Bowra), 56
    (quote)
Greek Orthodox Church, Naxos, 302, **302**
Greeks, 6, 16, 35–205 (Unit 2), 210–11,
    212, 224, 251, 264, 266, 267, 277,
    283, 310, 313
Greek temple
    facade, **177**
    floor plan, **177**
Gregorian
    chant, 12, 22, 26, 429–32, 438, 441
      (table), 442
    notation, 430, **431**
Gregory I, the Great, Saint, Pope
    (540–604), 283 (quote), 310, 429,
    430
Grendel, 317, 413
Guelfs, 315
Guido d'Arezzo, **430,** 430 (quote)
Guilds, 338, 342, 347
Gunther, 315
Gymnastics, Greek, 57, 195, 201, 202

Hades (or Pluto), 39, 40 (box), 231n
Hadrian (Publius Aelius Hadrianus),
    Roman emperor (76–132), 191, 214
    (box), 267, 270, 271, 272, 274,
    colorplate 9
Hagesandros of Rhodes, Greek sculptor
    (fl. 1st c. A.D.), 192
Hagia Sophia, Istanbul (Anthemius of
    Tralles and Isodorus of Miletos),
    301, **301,** 302, **302,** 408
Halle, Adam de la, French trouvère
    (1230–ca. 1288), 434, 437
Hamilton, Edith, British classical scholar
    (1867–1963), 53
Hamlet (Shakespeare), 10, 11
Handel, George Frederick, German
    composer (1685–1759), 10, 26, 31
Hannibal, Carthaginian general (247–ca.
    183 B.C.), 211–12, 218, 227
Hanseatic League, 338
Harmony, in music, 23, 47–48. *See also*
    Homophonic music
Harold, king of England (1022?–1066),
    416
Harp, 432, **433,** 442
"Harrowing of Hell," 380n
Hastings, Battle of, 416, **416**
Hatshepsut, queen of Egypt (15th c. B.C.),
    164
Hatshepsut, Temple of (Egyptian), 164,
    164
Haydn, Franz Joseph, Austrian composer
    (1732–1809), 30
Head of a Bearded Man (Roman), 272,
    272
Heaven (Dante), 346, 371
Hebrews, 278, 282, 310
Hedonism, 219
Hektor, 38, 224
Helen of Troy, 35n, 41, 53 (box), 96, 234n
Hell (Dante), 227, 234n, 346, 347, 371,
    372–404 (text)
Hell (Islamic), 409
Hellenes, 36, 38, 41
Henry II, king of England (1133–1189),
    435
Hephaistos, 35n, 39, 40 (box)
Hera, 39, 40 (box), 221
Herakleitos, Ionian philosopher (ca.
    535–475 B.C.), 46, 51, 281, 282
Herakles, 103n, 223, 267
*Herakles Discovering the Infant Telephos
    in Arcadia* (Roman), 266–67, **267**
Hera of Samos (Greek), 171, **171**
Herculaneum, 273
Hermes, 40 (box), 196
Hermes with the Infant Dionysos
    (Praxiteles), **186,** 186–87, 188
Herodotos, Greek historian (ca. 484–425
    B.C.), 44, 162, 163, 210
Hesiod, Greek poet (fl. 8th c. B.C.), 39,
    41–42, 43, 217
Hestia, 39, 40 (box)
Hiberno-Saxon art, 407 (overview),
    410–11, 416, 417, 428
Hildegarde of Bingen, German abbess,
    Saint (1098–1179), 433

Hippokrates, Greek physician (460–377 B.C.), 173
History of the Peloponnesian War (Thucydides), 96
Hobbema, Meindert, Dutch painter (1639–1709), 15
Holy Land, 338, 416
Homer, Greek epic poet (fl. 9th c. B.C.), 38, 41, 42, **42,** 43, 49, 135n, 167, 168, 169, 197, 217, 224, 412
Honorius, Flavius, Roman emperor (384–423), 214 (box), 215, 299
Horace (Quintus Horatius Flaccus), Latin poet (65–8 B.C.), 216 (quote), 216n (quote), 219, 223 (quote), 224, 226 (overview)
Horizon Book of Ancient Rome (Payne), 217n (quote)
Horsemen (Greek), Parthenon, 182, **182**
Hortus Deliciarum, from the (Abbess Herrad van Landsberg), **433**
Hospitals, Roman, 216
Housing, Roman, 216, 263
Housman, A. E., English poet (1859–1936), 12, 13
Hubris, 197
Hurdy-Gurdy, 354n, 433
Hydraulis, 274, 274n
"Hymn of Jesus," sacred dance, 439

Iconoclastic Controversy, 291 (overview), 302
Iconoclasts, 302
Iconophiles, 303
Ikarus, 161, 223, 230n
Iktinus, Greek architect (fl. 5th c. B.C.), 180
Iliad (Homer), 38, 42, 135n, 167, 168, 169, 172, 224
Innocent III, Pope, 437 (quote)
Inquisition, 282
Instruments, musical
    Greek, 196–98, 200–201, 274
    medieval, **339,** 432, 440, 441 (table)
    Roman, 273–74
International Style (painting), 427, 428
In the Gloaming, **27**
Ionian, 79
    cities, 44, 190
    clothing, 171–73, 185
    coast, 41
    music, 196
    philosophy, 45–46, 51
    sculpture, 171, 190
Ionic architectural order, 178, **178,** 183, **183,** 190, 263, 268
Iphigeneia 53, 53 (box), 62
Ireland, 312, 410, 428
Irish Golden Age, 407 (overview), 410–11, 428
Isaac, 294, 295
Isaiah, Book of (Bible) 9:6; 11:1–9; 40:1–9; 53:3–6, 279–80 (text)
Isaiah, Hebrew prophet (fl. ca. 740 B.C.), 238, 279 (text)
Isis, 217, 218, 277
Islam, 312, 313, 338, 407, 408, 409, 428

Islamic
    architecture, 408–10, 428
    art, 408
    culture, 337, 338, 407, 428
Ismene, 58 (box)
Isocephalic convention, 185–86, 300
Isodorus of Miletos, Greek architect (6th c. B.C.), 301
Isokrates, Greek orator (436–338 B.C.), 125 (quote)
Israel, 278, 279, 280, 283
Istanbul, 301–2, 408, 428. *See also* Constantinople
Ives, Charles, American composer (1874–1954), 31

Jason, 60, 239n, 390n
Jazz, 12, 21, 29, 437
Jefferson, Thomas, American statesman and president (1742–1826), 265
Jefferson Memorial, Washington, D.C. 265
Jeremiah, Hebrew prophet (fl. ca. 628–586 B.C.), 199, 417
Jerico, 278
Jerome, St., Christian scholar, Church Father (ca. 347–420? B.C.), 226 (overview)
Jerusalem, 268, 269, 278, 280, 284, 288, 294, 295, 298, 439
"Jesu, Joy of Man's Desiring" (Bach), 437
Jesus. *See* Christ
Jeu de Robin et Marion, Le (de la Halle), **434**
Jews, 280, 281, 283, 284, 313
Jihad, 408
Job, 283, 294, 295
Job, Book of (Bible), 282–283
Jocasta, 58, 58 (box), 59, 81
John, Gospel of (Bible) 1:1–5, 281 (text), 282
John, Saint, Apostle and evangelist (d. ca. 100), 46, 298, 303
John of Patmos, Christian visionary (1st c. A.D.), 288–89 (text)
Jonah, 294, 295
Jonah Sarcophagus (Roman), 294, **295**
Jongleurs, 434, 441 (table)
Joplin, Scott, American composer (1868–1917), 32
Joshua, 278
Jotuns, 314
"Joy to the World," **24, 25**
Judaeus, Philo, of Alexandria, Hellenistic-Judaic philosopher (ca. 30 B.C.–A.D. 50), 281–82
Judah, Kingdom of, 278
Judaism, 6–7, 129, 278–84
Judeo-Christian, 312
Julian the Apostate, Roman emperor (331?–363), 214 (box)
Julius Caesar. *See* Caesar, Gaius Julius
Jumièges, Abbey of, 415, **415**
Juno, 40 (box), 229
Jupiter, 40 (box), 217, 218, 219, 224
Justinian I, the Great, Byzantine emperor (483–565), 291 (overview), 299, 300 (colorplate 11), 301, 303, 312

Juvenal (Decimus Junius Juvenalis), Latin satiric poet (60–140), 215 (quote), 226 (overview), 251–55 (text)

Kadmus, 58 (box), 81, 93n, 108, 110n
Kadmus, House of, 58 (box)
Kalchas, 62
Kallikrates, Greek architect (fl. 5th c. B.C.), 180
Kalos k'agathos, 221, 222
Kandinsky, Wassily, Russian painter (1866–1944), 14, 16
Kassandra, 54
Khi-Rho, 293, 410
"King David as Organist and Pope Gregory the Great," **430**
"King David Playing Harp under the Inspiration of the Holy Ghost, while One Attendant Juggles and Others Play the Rebec, Trumpet and Oliphant," **350**
King Lear (Shakespeare), 9
King Must Die, The (Renault), 38
Kithara, 184, 196, **196, 197,** 198, 274, 441 (table)
Kitharodia, 198
Kleisthenes, Athenian statesman (fl. 507 B.C.), 43, 44, 56
Klytaimestra, 53, 53 (box), 54, 55, 56, 72
Knights of St. John, 338
Knights of the Round Table, at Camelot, 363
Knossos, Palace of (Minoan), 36, 37, **165,** 165–66, **166,** 439. *See also* Crete; Minoan culture
Koran, 39, 407, 408
Kore, 169–74
Kore from Chios (Greek), 172–73, **173**
Kore in Dorian Peplos (Greek), 172, **172**
Kore (La Delicata) (Greek), 174, **174**
Kore of Auxerre (Greek), 170, **170,** 172
Kouros, 169–74
Kouros of Sounion (Greek), 170, **170,** 173
Kriemhild, 315
Kritios Boy (Greek), 174, **175**
Kronos, 39, 40 (box), 109n
Kumean Sibyl, 230, 231n

Lacedemon, King of, 62
Laius, 58, 58 (box), 59, 81, 93n
Lamentation (Giotto), 426–27, colorplate 21
Lancan Vei per Mei la Landa (Bernart de Ventadorn), 435–36 (text)
Lancelot, Knight of the Round Table, 338, 339
Laokoön and His Sons (Hagesandros, Polydoros, and Athenodorus of Rhodes), 187, 192, **192**
Laon Cathedral, France, 421
Lascaux, caves of, 3, 4
Last Judgment, 288, 289, 310, 422
Last Judgment (Michelangelo), Sistine Chapel, 265
Last Supper, 293
Lauriger Horatius, 349 (text)
Law, Roman, 212, 215, 217, 220, 282, 292

Laws (Plato), 126, 127, 128, 162 (quote), 198
Lazarus, 293, 294
Leonidas, king of Sparta (d. 480 B.C.), 44
Lepidus, 213
Lesbos, 196, 198, 199
Leucippus, Greek philosopher (5th c. B.C.), 52
Libation Bearers (Aeschylus), 53, 54, 72
Lindau Gospels (Celto-Germanic), 412–13, colorplate 14
Lindisfarne Gospels (Hiberno-Saxon), 410, colorplate 13
Lindisfarne Monastery, England, 410
Linear A (Minoan), 36, 37
Linear B (Minoan), 38
Lion Gate, Mycaenae, 167, **167**
Listening Guide. *See* Music
Literary selections
    Bible, 279–80, 283–89
    Greek, 62–123, 130–60
    medieval, 317–36, 349–406
    Roman, 227–60
Literature
    basis for understanding, 12–13, 18–19
    Bible, 46, 281–83
    Greek, 52–56, 58–60, 61, 198–200, 267
    medieval, 314–16, 317, 319–20, 327, 348
    poetry, 12, 18–19, 156–57, 198–201, 338
    Roman, 224–25, 226
Liturgical drama, 432–33, 441 (table), 442
Lituus, 274
Livy (Titus Livius), Roman historian (59 B.C.–A.D. 17), 226 (overview)
Logos, 46, 249, 281–82
Loki, 313
London, 4
Louis VII, king of France (ca. 1120–1180), 338
Louis IX, king of France, Saint (1214–1270), 424
Louis XIV (Rigaud), 17, colorplate 6
Lucan (Marcus Annaeus Lucanus), Latin poet (39–65), 213, 226 (overview)
Lucian, Greek satirist (ca. 120–190), 126 (overview), 255–60 (text)
Lucretius, Latin poet and philosopher (ca. 96–55 B.C.), 219, 226 (overview), 239–42 (text)
Luke, Gospel of (Bible) 10:30–37; 15:4–32, 287 (text)
Luke, Saint, Apostle, 298
Lute, 441 (table)
Luther, Martin, German leader of Reformation (1483–1546), 432
Lyceum of Aristotle, 57, 128
Lycurgus, Spartan lawgiver (fl. 9th c. B.C.), 201
Lydia, 41
Lyre, 196, **196**, 198, 199, 200, 432
Lyre Player, "The Boston Throne," (Greek), **196**
Lysippos of Sikyon, Greek sculptor (fl. 4th c. B.C.), 188
Lysistrata, 61
Lysistrata (Aristophanes), 61

Macbeth (Shakespeare), 9
Macedonia, 60, 108, 213, 262 (overview)
Machaut, Guillaume de, French composer and poet (1300–1377), 439, 442
"Machaut Receiving Honors of Royalty and Clergy," **439**
Madeleine, Ste., Vézelay, **417**, 418, 428
Madonna della Seggiola (Raphael), 20
Madonna Enthroned (Cimabue), **426**
Madonna Enthroned (Giotto), 426, **427**
Maenads, 110n, 200
Magna Graecia, 46, 172, 210, 262
Maison Carrée, Nîmes, 265, **265**
Major Emperors of Rome, 214 (box)
Mallia, Crete, 36
Malory, Sir Thomas, English author (ca. 1410–1471), 363, 364–71 (text)
Malraux, André, French writer and statesman (1901–1976), xiii (quote)
Manicheans, 308, 437
Manorialism, 310–11, 316, 342
Manuscripts
    Carolingian, 412–13
    Gothic, 427
    Hiberno-Saxon, 410–11, 412, 428
    Islamic, 408
    Romanesque, 418
Marathon, 221n
Marathon, Battle of, 44, 53, 57
Marcel, Gabriel, French philosopher (1889–1973), 10 (quote)
Marcus Aurelius, Equestrian Statue of, Rome, **271**
Marcus Aurelius Antoninus, Roman emperor (121–180), 214 (box), 215, 219, 220, 226 (overview), 239, 249, 250–51 (text), 270, 271, 272
Marie of Champagne, French countess (12th c.), 338, 362
Marinatos, Spyridon, Greek archaeologist (1901–1974), 37
Mark, Gospel of (Bible), 281, 284
Mark, Saint, Apostle, 298
Mark Antony (Marcus Antonius), Roman general (83–30 B.C.), 213
Marlowe, Christopher, English dramatist (1564–1593), 319
Mars, 40 (box), 209
Marseilles, France, 42
Marsyas, 197, **197**
Martel, Charles, leader of the Franks (ca. 699–741), 407 (overview)
Martial (Marcus Valerius Martialis), Latin epigramist (40–104), 26 (overview), 247–49 (text), 268
Martini, Simone, Sienese painter (1284–1344), 427–28
Mary, Virgin, 339, 345, 422
    in art, 303, 414, 428
Mask from Mycaenae, 167, **167**
Mass, 431 (table), 432, **439**, 441 (table)
Mathematics, 47–49, 202, 313, 428
Matthew, Gospel of (Bible), 284–86 (text), 287–88 (text)
Matthew, Saint, Disciple, 298
Mausoleum (Cenotaph) (Roman), 266, **266**

Mausoleum of Empress Galla Placidia, 299, **299**
Mausoleum of Halikarnassos, Turkey, 186
Mausolos (Greek), 186, **186**
May festival, 440
Maypole, 440
Mecca, 408
Medea, 60, 390n
Medea (Euripides), 60
Medieval Music, Development of, 441 (table)
Meditations, Book II (Marcus Aurelius) 250–51 (text)
Meistersingers, 437, 441 (table)
Meistersinger von Nürnberg (Wagner), 437
Meletus, 133n
Melismas, 432
Melody, 23
Melos, 60
Memorial Oration (Perikles), 79, 80–81 (text)
Menander, Greek New Comedy dramatist (342?–291? B.C.), 217
Mendelssohn, Felix, German composer (1809–1847), 30
Menelaos, 41, 53 (box)
Meredith, George, English writer (1829–1909), 18
Messiah, 238, 279, 280, 282
Metamorphoses (Ovid), 226n, 243, 352, 362
Metaphysics (Aristotle), 129n (quote)
Meter, in music, 22, 433, 438
Metope, 178, 182
Michelangelo Buonarotti, Italian artist (1475–1564), 5, 6, 192, 265
Middle ages, 7, 52, 217, 224, 227, 238, 270, 307–446 (Unit 5)
    architecture, 411–15, 417–26
    art, 303, 426–28
    drama, 52, 319–20, 327, 345, 348
    history, 307–17, 337–42
    literary selections, 317–36, 348–406
    literature, 227, 343, 345–48
    music, 31, 338, 350, 429–43 (chap. 16)
    painting, 426–28
    poetry, 338, 438
Mihrab, 408
Milesian School, 45
Miletus, Ionian city, 45–46
Milkmaids dance (secular), 440
Miller, Henry, American writer (1891–1980), 4 (quote)
Miltiades, Athenian general (d. 489 B.C.), 44
Minarets, 408, 410
Minbar, 408
Minerva, 40 (box), 217
Minnesingers, 433, 441 (table)
Minoan culture, 36, 37, 38, 161–62, 165–66, 167, 168, 169
Minos, king of Crete (Minoans), 36, 58 (box), 165–66, 230n, 439
Minotaur, 161, 166, 184
Misenis, 197
Mission of the Apostles, Ste.-Madeleine, Vézelay, France, **416**

Mithraism, 218, 277
Mnesecles, Greek architect (fl. 437 B.C.),
    182–83
Modes, 201, 202
    Dorian, 196, 202
    Phrygian, 196, 202
    in poetry, 199, 202, 438
Mohammed (Mahomet), Islamic prophet
    (570?–632), 39, 313, 407, 408
Moira, 41
Mona Lisa (Leonardo da Vinci), 10
Monasteries, 302, 303, 310, 410, 415, 428,
    431, 442
Mondrian, Piet, Dutch painter
    (1872–1944), 16
Monochord, 430
Monophonic. *See* Music
Monotheism, 278, 279, 280
Mont-St. Michel, France, 419, **419**
Mont-St. Michel and Chartres (H. Adams),
    341, 419, 428
Morte Darthur (Malory), 317n, 363,
    364–71 (text)
Mosaics
    Byzantine, 299–300, 312, 412
    early Christian, 296–98
    Gothic, 425
    Mozarabic, 409
Moses, Hebrew lawgiver (fl. 13th c. B.C.),
    209, 278, 284, 293
Mosque, 165, 408, 409, 410
Motet, 438, 439, 441 (table)
Mozarabic, 409
Mozart, Wolfgang Amadeus, Austrian
    composer (1756–1791), 12, 22, 30
Muezzins, 408
Mumford, Lewis, American philosopher
    (b. 1895), 3 (quote), 313 (quote)
Musaeus, Greek musician, 196
"Muse on Mount Helicon" (Akhilleus
    Painter), 184, **184**
Muses, the, 40 (box), 112n, 195, 197
Music
    American, 31–32
    Baroque, 26, 30–31
    Basic Library of Good Music, 29–32
    basis for understanding, 10–14
    characteristics of, 22
    Classical, 30, 31
    Development of Medieval Music, 441
        (table)
    elements of, 22–23, 199
    ethos, 195, 197, 201–2
    Etruscan, 273
    fundamentals of, 24–28
    Greek, 47–48, 128, 195–202 (chap. 8),
        273–74
    Greek drama, in, 200–201
    Greek games, in, 198
    Gregorian chant, 12, 22, 26, 429–31
    harmony, 23, 47–48, 437
    Hebrew, 431
    homophonic, 26, 437, 438
    Impressionism, 30
    instrumental, 26, 196–98, 200–201, 274,
        339, 432

Listening Guide
    First Stage, 28
    Second Stage, 442
    listening to, 13–14, 22, 26–28
    medieval, 31, 338, 429–43 (chap. 16)
    melody, 23
    meter, 22, 433, 438
    modern, 31–32
    monophonic, 26, 429–37, 438, 439, 441
        (table)
    motet, 438, 439
    "music of the spheres," 48, 195, 439
    nome, 198
    notation of, 23–25, 198, 201, 202, 430
    pipe organ, 274n, 339
    polyphonic, 26, 30–31, 437–39, 441
        (table)
    Pythagoras, 47–48, 195
    Record List, 29–32, 202–3, 429, 442–43
    Renaissance, 26, 31
    response to, 12, 22
    rhythm, 22, 25, 430, 438
    Roman, 273–74
    Romanticism, 29–30
    time signatures, 22
    tone color, 23
    vocal, 26, 429–39
"Music and Her Attendants," **339**
Musicians
    Greek, 197–200
    Middle Ages, in, **339, 430,** 432,
        434–37, **439,** 442
Music of the spheres (Pythagoras), 48,
    195, 439
Muslim, 307, 311, 313, 338, 341, 342, 407,
    408, 409
Mycenae, 38, 167
Mycenaean culture, 37–42, 162, 165,
    166–67, 168, 169
Mycerinus and His Queen (Egyptian),
    162, 162–63
Myron, Greek sculptor (480–407 B.C.), 176
"Myth of Er," *Republic* (Plato), 227

Napoleon Bonaparte I, French emperor
    (1769–1821), 222, 267
Narration
    continuous (Roman), 270
    simultaneous (Greek), 182, 270
Narthex, 297, 300
National Mosque, Kuala Lumpur, Malaysia,
    410, **410**
Nave, 296, 297, 417, 422, 423, 425, 439
Nebuchadnezzar, king of Babylonia (ca.
    605–562 B.C.), 278
Nemea, 221n
Nemesis, 40 (box)
Neoplatonism, 220, 308, 309, 340
Neptune, 40 (box), 217
Nero (Claudius Caesar Drusus
    Germanicus), Roman emperor
    (37–68), 213, 214 (box), 220, 222,
    268, 274
New Testament (Bible), 281, 284, 288,
    294–95
Nibelungenlied (Volsungasaga), 314, 315
Nicene Creed, 308

Nicomachaen Ethics (Aristotle), 129
Nike, 183, 185
Nike (Paionios), 185, **185**
Nike of Samothrace (Pythokritos), 189–90,
    190
Noah, 294
Nominalism, 340, 341
Nomos Pythikos (Sakadas), 198
Norman, 412, 415, 423
Norsemen, 315
Notre Dame, Cathedral School of, 342,
    422, 441 (table), 442
Notre Dame Cathedral, Paris, **421,** 423,
    438, 442
Notre Dame Mass: "Agnus Dei"
    (Machaut), **439**

Octavian, 213. *See also* Augustus
Ode to Joy (Beethoven), **26**
Odysseus, 38–39, 41, 44, 224, 396n
Odyssey (Homer), 42, 137n, 169, 224
Oedipus, 58 (box), 58–59, 81, 91n
Oedipus (Sophokles), 197
Oedipus the King (Sophokles), 41, 58–59,
    81–96 (text)
Offering Bearers (Egyptian), 163, **163**
Office Hours, in music, 431
Old Testament (Bible), 282, 284, 295, 299
Olen the Lycian, 196
Oligarchy, 42, 211
Oliphant, 315, **350**
Olympia, 185, 198, 220, 221, 222, 223
Olympiad, 220, 221, 222
Olympian Zeus, Temple of (Cossutius),
    191, **191**
Olympic Games, 168, 176, 198, 220, 221,
    222
Olympics, modern, 221, 222n
Olympos the Phrygian, 196, 198
*On the Dedication of the Colosseum in
    Rome* (Martial), 249 (text)
On the Nature of Things (Lucretius), 219,
    239–42 (text)
Orant (Roman), 292, **292**
Oresteia (Aeschylus), 53–56, 62, 72
Orestes, 53, 53 (box), 54, 55, 60, 72
Orff, Carl, German composer
    (1895–1980), 433
Organum, 438, 441 (table), 442
Orkhestra, 201
Or La Truix, **437**
Orpheus, 196, 198, 239n
"Orpheus Among the Thracians"
    (Orpheus Painter), **198**
Osiris, 217, 218
Ostia Antica, 216
Ostrogoths, 299, 307, 314
    Kingdom, 291 (overview), 299
Ouranos, 39, 40 (box), 72
Our Lady's Juggler, 348, 349–51 (text)
Ovid (Publius Ovidius Naso), Latin poet
    (43 B.C.–A.D. 18), 209 (quote), 212
    (quote), 215 (quote), 217 (quote),
    226 (overview), 243–47 (text), 267,
    362, 434

Paestum, Italy, 172, 179, 210
Painting
    basis for understanding, 14–17
    Byzantine, 303
    Christian, 292–93, 294, 297
    Egyptian, 163
    Flemish, 15
    Gothic, 426–28
    Greek, 56, 171, 184, 262
    Roman, 262, 266, 273
Palatine Chapel of Charlemagne (Odo of
    Metz), Aachen, Germany, **312, 411**
Palatine School, 312
Palestine, 199, 278, 293
Palestrina, Giovanni Pierluigi de, Italian
    composer (ca. 1525–1595), 432
Panel (3) (Kandinsky), 16, colorplate 5
Panini, Giovanni, Italian painter (ca.
    1691–1765), 271
Pantheon, Rome, 216, 217, 270–71, **271,**
    273, colorplate 8
Pantheon, The Greek, 40 (box), 217
Paradise (Islamic), 409
Paradiso, Canto XXXIII (Dante), 404–6
    (text)
Paris of Trot, 62, 234n
Parker, Dorothy, American writer
    (1893–1967), 10
Parmenides of Elea, Greek philosopher
    (514–? B.C.), 51, 52, 172
Parthenon (Iktinus and Kallikrates),
    Athens, 5, 6, 57, 172, 179, **180,**
    180–85, 190–92, 270
    frieze, 182, 270
    pediment, 181
    schematic drawing, 180
    stereobate and stylobate, 180
Patricians, 211, 212, 274
Patroklos, 38, 174
Paul (Saul of Tarsus), Saint, Apostle (ca.
    10–ca. 64), 281, 284, 286 (text),
    288, 294, 295, 308
Pax Romana (Roman Peace), 215, 255, 262
    (overview)
Pediment, 178, 181, 192, 425
Pediment reconstruction, Parthenon, 181,
    181
Peloponnesian War, 60, 79, 125, 126
Peloponnesus, 36, 38
Pelops, 53 (box)
Pendentives, 301
Pentathlon, 222
Penthesilea, Queen of the Amazons,
    171–72
Pentheus, king of Thebes, 58 (box), 60,
    73n, 108, 110n, 120n
Pergamom, 129, 190–91
Perikles, Athenian statesman (ca. 495–429
    B.C.), 35, 56, **56,** 57, 60, 61, 79–80,
    80–81 (text), 126, 129, 176, 177,
    179, 180, 183, 185, 222
Perotin, French composer (ca. 1200), 438
Persia, 41, 60, 218
Persian Empire, 125, 278
Persians, 41, 44–45, 49, 52, 56, 61, 170,
    174, 183, 184, 221n
Persian Wars, 125

Peter (Simon Peter), Saint, Apostle (d.
    64?), 16, 270, 281, 294, 295, 299,
    310
Petrarch, Francesco, Italian humanist poet
    (1304–1374), 428
Petronius Arbiter, Gaius, Latin writer (d.
    66), 226 (overview)
Phaistos, Crete, 36
Pharaohs, 162, 163, 164, 170
Pheidias, Greek sculptor (490–432 B.C.), 6,
    10, 179, 180, 181, 182
Philip II, king of Macedonia (382–336
    B.C.), 125, 128
Philoktetes (Sophokles), 39
Philosophies Going Cheap (Lucian),
    255–60 (text)
Philosophy
    Abelard, 341, 342
    Aristotle, 59, 81, 125, 126, 128–30,
        156–60, 172, 201, 277, 281, 313,
        341–45, 422
    Atomist, 52
    Augustine, St., 127, 220, 308–10, 339,
        340, 344, 437
    Battle of Universals, 337, 340–41
    Conceptualism, 341, 343
    Demokritos, 52, 57
    Eleatic, 47, 51–52, 127, 128, 172
    Epictetus, 249–51
    Epicurean, 218–19, 239, 277
    Golden Mean, 128, 129
    Greek, 45–49, 56, 126–30, 218–20
    Herakleitos, 46, 51, 281, 282
    Ionian, 45–49, 128
    Marcus Aurelius, 250–51
    Neoplatonism, 220, 308, 309, 340
    Nominalism, 341
    Philosopher-kings, 128, 147
    Plato, 47, 52, 61, 126, 156, 172, 180,
        190, 198, 200, 201, 218–20, 227,
        277, 281, 312, 340
    Protagoras, 57
    Pythagorean, 46–49, 51, 127
    Realism, 340–41
    reality, concept of, 6, 7, 127, 129, 220,
        309, 337
    Roman, 217–20
    St. Augustine, 127, 220, 308–10, 339,
        340, 344, 437
    St. Thomas, 341, 343–44
    Scholasticism, 340–41
    Sokrates, 6, 52, 61, 80, 126–28, 130,
        139, 195, 219, 340
    Sophists, 57, 60
    Stoicism, 218–20, 224–25, 227, 249
Phrygia, 196, 218
Phrygian mode, 196, 196n, 201–2
Picasso, Pablo, Spanish artist (1881–1973),
    14, 17
Pilgrimage, 413, 414, 439
Pilgrimage churches, 413, 414, 415, 428
Pindar, Greek poet-musician (518?–ca.
    439 B.C.), 198
Pipe organ, 274n, **339,** 432, 439
Piranesi, Giovanni Battista, Italian artist
    (1720–1778), 296–97

Pisa
    Cathedral and Baptistery, **418**
    Cathedral and Campanile, **418**
Pisistratus, Athenian reformer (605–527
    B.C.), 43
Plague, 60, 439, 440
Plainsong. *See* Gregorian chant
Plataea, Battle of, 45, 170
Plato, Greek philosopher (427–347 B.C.),
    47, 52, 61, **126,** 126–28, 129,
    130–39 (text), 139–56 (text), 162
    (quote), 172, 180, 190, 198, 200,
    201, 218, 219, 220, 227, 277, 281,
    312, 340
Play of Daniel, **433**
Play of the Three Kings, The, 432–33
Play of the Virtues (Hildegarde), 433
Plays
    Miracle, 319, 348
    Morality, 319–20, 327, 345
    musical, 432
    Mystery, 319, 345, 348, 433
Plebeians, 211
Pliny the Elder, Roman naturalist and
    historian (ca. 23–79), 187, 216, 226
    (overview)
Pliny the Younger, Roman orator and
    statesman (62?–ca. 123), 223, 226
    (overview)
Plutarch, Greek biographer (ca. 46–ca.
    120), 200 (quote), 211 (quote),
    226 (overview), 262, 271 (quote)
Pluto, 40 (box)
Poetics (Aristotle), 59, 81, 128, 156–60
    (text)
Poetry, Greek, 156–57, 198–201
Politics (Aristotle), 128
Polydoros of Rhodes, Greek sculptor (fl.
    1st c. A.D.), 192
Polykleitos of Argos, Greek sculptor (fl.
    430 B.C.), 176, 188
Polynices, 58 (box)
Polyphonic. *See* Music
Pompeii, 216, 263, 273
Pompey the Great, Roman general and
    triumvir (106–48 B.C.), 212, 213
Pont du Gard, France, Roman aqueduct,
    266, **266**
Popes, 215, 270, 299, 310, 312, 344, 347,
    427, 433
Porch of the Maidens, Erechtheion,
    Athens (Mnescles), 183, **183**
Portable Roman Reader, The
    (Davenport), 212n (quote)
Portrait Head from Delos (Greek), 192,
    192
Poseidon, 39, 40 (box), 176, 179, 183, 192,
    217, 293
Poseidon (Greek), 176, **176**
Post and lintel system, 177, **177,** 265, 268,
    269
Pottery, Greek, 261
    Archaic, 171, 174
    black-figure, **171,** 171–72, 174
    Classical, 174, **174,** 184, **184, 198, 199,**
        200
    Geometric, 168, **168**

manufacture of, 43, 168
Minoan, 168
red-figure, 174, 184, **184, 198, 199, 200**
white-ground, 184, **184**
Praxiteles of Athens, Greek sculptor (fl. 340 B.C.), 186–88, 197, 268
Predestination, 309
Priest of Serapis (Roman), **218**
Prokofiev, Sergei, Russian composer (1891–1953), 31
Prolog to *The Canterbury Tales* (Chaucer), 343, 351, 352–58 (text)
Prometheus, 39, 40 (box)
Prophet, The, Abbey Church of St. Pierre, Moissac, France, **417,** 418
Prophets, Hebrew, 279–80, 282
Propylaia, Athens, 179
Proserpine, 40 (box), 131n
Protagoras, Greek sophist philosopher (ca. 481–411 B.C.), 57
Prothesis, 168
Psalms (Bible) 24; 137; 150, 283–84 (text)
Psalter of St. Swithin, 418, colorplate 16
Psaltery, **339**
Punic Wars, 211–12, 227, 262 (overview)
Purgatory (Dante), 346, 347, 371
Pygmalion, 169
Pynx Hull, Athens, 57
Pythagoras of Samos, Ionian philosopher (ca. 582–ca. 507 B.C.), 46–49, **47,** 51, 52, 127, 128, 172, 343, 422
Pythagorean Order, 49
Pythagoreans of Krotona, 46, 49, 210
Pythagorean theorem, 47
Pythian Games, 198
Pythokritos of Rhodes, Greek sculptor (fl. 200–190 B.C.), 189–90

Qibla, 408
Quadrivium, 342
Queen's Megaron, Knosses (Minoan), 166, **166**
Quintilian, Marcus Fabius, Roman rhetorician and critic (ca. 35–ca. 100), 226 (overview), 274

Rachmaninoff, Sergei, Russian composer and pianist (1873–1943), 22, 30
Raphael, Sanzio, Italian artist (1483–1520), 10, 17, 19
Ravenna, 215, 299–300, 308, 312, 411, 412
Realism, 340, 341
Rebec, **350,** 432, **433,** 441 (table)
Recordings (Discography), 29–32, 202–3, 429, 442–43
"Reeve's Tale," The *Canterbury Tales* (Chaucer), 359–62 (text)
Reformation, 310
"Regent Square," **27**
Religion. *See also* Philosophy
    Christianity, 6–7, 127–29, 215, 218, 220, 224, 238, 274, 278, 280–82, 291–303, 308, 408, 413, 439
    Cult of Cybele, 110n, 218, 277
    Cult of Isis, 217, 277
    Cult of the Virgin, 337, 339, 345, 349, 422

Egyptian, 41, 164–65, 217
Greek, 37–41, 179–87, 217. *See also* Gods
Islam, 278n, 407–8
Judaism, 6–7, 129, 278–84
Minoan, 37
Mithraism, 218, 277
Norse, 314
Pythagorean, 49
Roman, 217–20, 277
Reliquary, Rhenish, 418, colorplate 15
Remedy of Love (Ovid), 226n
Remus, 209–10
Renaissance, 7, 26, 31, 184, 188, 192, 210, 217, 268, 300, 301, 338, 347, 422, 428
Renault, Mary, English author (b. 1905), 38
Republic (Plato), 127–28, 139–56 (text), 201, 219, 227
Resurrection, 292
Return of the Hunters (Bruegel), 15, colorplate 2
Revelation (Bible), 6:1–8; 21:1–4, 289 (text)
Revolution, French, 415, 424
Rhea, 39, 40 (box)
Rhea Silvia, 209, 209n
Rhythm, 22, 25, 430, 438
Richard I the Lion-Heart, king of England (1157–1199), 416, 437
Rigaud, Hyacinthe, French painter (1659–1743), 17, colorplate 6
Ring of the Nibelung (Wagner), 315
Roads, Roman, 216, **216,** 266, 273
Roland, knight of Charlemagne (d. 778), 312, 315–16, 338, 350, 400n, 434
Rolling Stones, 437
Roman Empire in A.D. 180, 214 (map)
Romanesque, 303, 312, 407 (overview), 428, 441 (table)
    architecture, 411, 413–19, 420, 422, 425, 438, 442
    art, 416, 417, 418, 419
    music, 438, 441 (table)
Romanism, 217
Romans, 6, 129, 130, 162, 178, 183, 192, 199, 261, 277, 283, 293, 301, 310, 313, 316, 409, 411, 414, 418
Rome, 126, 192, 209–74 (Unit 3), 277, 291–98, 299, 301
    achievements of, 215–17, 224–25, 273
    Empire, 209, 212–15, 217, 220, 222–23, 230, 262 (overview), 264, 266–68, 270–74, 277, 278, 281, 296, 307, 308, 310, 313, 410
    fall of, 215, 262 (overview), 307
    founding of, 209–10, 224–25, 229, 230, 262 (overview), 264, 375n
    games and contests, 220–23
    religion and philosophy, 217–20
    Republic, 209, 211–12, 215, 217, 223, 262 (overview), 264
    sack of, 215, 291 (overview), 308, 309
Romeo and Juliet (Shakespeare), 9
Romulus, 209–10
Roncevaux, Battle of, 311–12, 315, 338

Rorem, Ned, American composer (b. 1923), 4 (quote)
Roscellinus (Roscelin), Jean, French philosopher (1050–1122), 340, 341
Rose windows, 421, 423, colorplate 17, 425
Royal Portal, Chartres Cathedral, 264, 422, **422**
Rubicon, 213
Rucellai Madonna (Duccio), 427, **427**
Runner at the Starting Point, Two Wrestlers, Javelin Thrower (Greek), 222, **222**
Russell, Bertrand, English philosopher, mathematician, and writer (1872–1970), 215

Sabines, 209
Sachs, Hans, German meistersinger (1494–1576), 437
Sahn, 408
Saint Anne, **27**
St.-Benoit-sur-Loire, 413, **413,** 414, **414,** 428
St. Clement, Rome, 296, **296**
St. Denis, Abbey Church of, **420,** 420–21, 428
Sainte Chapelle, Paris, 424, **424**
Ste.-Madeleine, Vézelay, France, **417,** 417–18, 428
St. Etienne (Abbaye aux Hommes), Caen, France, 415, **415**
St. John Lateran, Rome, 296
"St. Mark," *Gospel Book of Archbishop Ebbo of Reims,* 412, **412**
St. Mark's Cathedral, Venice, **302,** 302–3
St. Martin du Canigou, France, **413,** 413–14
St. Paul's Outside the Walls, Rome, 296–97, **297**
St. Peter's Basilica, Old, Rome, 296
St. Peter's Basilica, Rome, 271
St. Pierre, Abbey Church of, 417
St. Sernin, Collegiate Church of, France, 414, **414,** 415, **415**
Saints. *See names of individuals*
Sakadas of Argos, Greek poet-musician (fl. 6th c. B.C.), 198
Salamis, Battle of, 45, 170, 174, 184
Sallust (Caius Sallustius Crispus), Roman historian (86–ca. 34 B.C.), 216 (quote), 226 (overview)
Samos, 46, 171
"Sanctuary" (Wylie), 316 (text)
Santa Maria Maggiore, Rome, 298, **298**
Sant' Apollinare Nuovo, Ravenna, 299, **299**
Santa Pudenziana, Rome, 298, **298**
Santa Sabina, Rome, 293, **293**
San Vitale, Ravenna, 300, **300,** colorplate 10, 312, 411
Sappho of Lesbos, Greek poet-musician (fl. 6th c. B.C.), 198, **199,** 199–200 (text), 242, 436
Sarcophagi, 294–95
Sarcophagus of Junius Bassus, The (Roman), 294–95, **295**
Satan, 310, 339, 346
Satire, 61, 251

Satyrs, 110n, 197, 200
Saul, King, 278
Sayers, Dorothy L., English writer and
    translator (1893–1957), 315, 372
Scales, musical, 14, 25, 196n
Schliemann, Heinrich, German
    archaeologist (1822–1890), 167
Scholasticism, 340–41, 345
Schubert, Franz, Austrian composer
    (1797–1828), 22, 30
Schumann, Robert, German composer
    (1810–1856), 26 (quote)
Scipio Africanus the Younger, Roman
    general (ca. 185–129 B.C.), 227
"Scipio's Dream," *On the Republic*
    (Cicero), 227–29 (text)
Scriptures, 340, 341, 432
Scriptures, Hebrew, 278, 282, 283. *See also*
    Old Testament (Bible)
Sculpture
    architectural, 181–83, 413, 416, 417,
        422, 426, 427
    canon of, 176, 177
    Cycladic, 165
    early Christian, 293–94
    Egyptian, 162–65, 170
    Gothic, 422, 425
    Greek, 56, 217, 262
    Greek archaic, 169–74, 292
    Greek classical, 174–77, 181–88, 196,
        197
    Greek geometric, 169
    Hellenistic, 189–92
    Islamic, 409
    Minoan, 166, 167
    Mycenaean, 167
    relief, 163, 167, 178, 181, 182, 186, 196,
        197, 272, 295, 416, 418, 419, 426
    Roman, 262–64, 266, 268, 269, 271–73
    Romanesque, 416, 417
Second Coming of Christ, 288, 422
Second Isaiah, Hebrew prophet (6th c.
    B.C.), 279n, 280 (text)
Second Shepherd's Play, The, 319
Seikolos Song (Greek), 202, **202**
Semele, 58 (box), 108
Senate, Roman, 211, 212, 213, 217, 272
Seneca, Marcus Annaeus, Roman
    rhetorician (fl. 1st c. B.C.), 212
    (quote), 217 (quote), 223, 226
    (overview), 274
Sequences, in music, 432
Sermon on the Mount (Christ), 284–86
    (text)
Shakespeare, William, English playwright
    (1564–1616), 9, 10, 11, 213
    (quotes), 282, 319
Sic et Non (Abelard), 341
Sicily, 36, 42, 60, 210, 224, 229
Siegfried, 315
Siena Cathedral (Pisano), Italy, 425, **425**
Simonides of Keos, Greek poet-musician
    (556–468 B.C.), 43
Snake Goddess (Minoan), 166, **167**
Sokrates, Greek philosopher (469–399
    B.C.), 6, 52, 61, 80, 125n, 126, 127,
    128, 130, **130**, 131n, 133n, 138n,
    139, 155n, 195, 219, 340

Solomon, king of Palestine (960–922 B.C.),
    278
Solomon, Temple of, 268, 278, 279
Solon, Athenian lawgiver (640–558 B.C.),
    43, 44, 199, 201, 211
Song of Roland, 315–16. *See also Chanson
    de Roland*
Song of the Ass, 433, **433**
Sophists, Greek, 57, 60, 130
Sophokles, Greek dramatist (ca. 496–406
    B.C.), 39, 58, **58,** 59, 60, 61, 81–96
    (text), 176, 186, 197, 201, 217
Sorbonne, College de, Paris, 342
Sparsio, 223
Sparta, 36, 60, 125, 173, 183, 186, 198, 199,
    201, 220, 221
Spartans, 44–45
Sphinx, riddle of, 58, 81
Sphinx and Great Pyramid (Egyptian),
    162, **162**
Staff, musical, 24–25
Stained glass, 420, 421, 423, 424, 425, 426
Starry Night (van Gogh), 15, 16,
    colorplate 4
"Star Spangled Banner, The," 437
Statuette of Youth (Greek), 169, **169**
Statuettes, Greek, 169
Steele, Wilbur Daniel, American writer
    (1886–1970), 13 (quote)
Stein, Gertrude, American poet
    (1874–1946), 11–12 (quote)
Stele of Hegesco (Greek), **185,** 185–86
Stereobate, 178, **180**
Stoicism, 218, 219–20, 224–25, 227, 249,
    277
Stoics, 219–20, 224, 271, 281
Stopping by Woods on a Snowy Evening
    (Frost), 19 (text)
Strauss, Richard, Austrian composer
    (1864–1949), 23
Stravinsky, Igor, Russian-American
    composer (1882–1971), 22, 31, 432
Stylobate, 178, 180, **180**
Suger, Abbot, of St. Denis (12th c.), 420
Suleymaniye Camii Mosque (Sinan),
    Istanbul, 408, **408,** 428
Summa Theologica (Aquinas), 371
"Sword in the Stone, The," *Morte Darthur*
    (Malory), 364–65 (text)
Sybaris, Italy, 36, 210
Symposium (Plato), 127
Syracuse, Sicily, 36, 60, 210

Tacitus, Publius Cornelius, Roman
    historian (ca. 55–ca. 117), 212
    (quote), 213 (quote), 226
    (overview)
Talmud, 39
Tantalus, 53 (box)
Tarquin the Proud, Etruscan king, 210
Tartarus, 39
Tchaikovsky, Peter Ilyich, Russian
    composer (1840–1893), 22, 29
Temple of
    Amon (Egyptian), 6, 164
    Amon-Mut-Khonsu (Egyptian), 164–65,
        182

Athena (Parthenon), 5, 6, 57, 172, 179,
    180
Athena Nike (Greek), 179, 183
Hera I, Paestum (Greek), 172, 178
Hera II, Paestum (Greek), 178–79
Olympian Zeus (Greek), 191
Poseidon, Sounion (Greek), 184
Temples
    Egyptian, 164–65, 297, 423
    Greek, 172, 177–84, 191, 217, 265
    Roman, 265, 270–71
Terpander of Lesbos, Greek poet-musician
    (fl. 7th c. B.C.), 198
Tertullian, Roman Christian theologian
    (ca. 160–ca. 230), 226 (overview)
Terza rima, 371
Tetractys of the decad, 48
Texture, in music, 26
Thales, Ionian philosopher (ca. 636–546
    B.C.), 45, 46
Thames River, 271
Thamyris, Greek musician, 197
Theatre, Greek, 200–201, 268
Thebes, 58, 58 (box), 60, 81, 83n, 108, 125
Themistokles, Greek general and
    statesman (ca. 524–ca. 460 B.C.), 44,
    45
Theodora, empress, wife of Justinian I (d.
    548), 300, 301, colorplate 12
Theodoric I, Ostrogoth emperor
    (446–526), 291 (overview), 299,
    314, 412
Theodosius I, the Great, Roman emperor
    (346?–395), 214 (box), 215, 222
Theogony (Hesiod), 39
Thermopylai, Battle of, 44–45
Theseus, 184, 385n
Thespis, Greek dramatist (fl. 534 B.C.), 52
Thomas à Becket, Saint, archbishop of
    Canterbury (1118–1170), 343, 352n
Thor, 313
Three Goddesses, Parthenon, 181, **181**
Throne Room, Knossos (Minoan), 166,
    166
Thucydides, Greek historian (471–399
    B.C.), 79, 96
Thyestes, 53 (box)
Tiberius (Claudius Nero Caesar), Roman
    emperor (42 B.C.–A.D. 37), 214
    (box), 218
Tiber River, Rome, 209, 210, 230
Tibia. *See* Aulos
Time charts (chronological)
    Greek civilization, 204–5
    Middle Ages, 444–46
    Roman civilization, 226
Time signatures, in music, 22
Tiresias, Greek seer, 59, 81, 84n, 197
Titans, 39, 40 (box)
Titus (Flavius Sabinus Vespasianus),
    Roman emperor (ca. 40–81) 214
    (box), 268, 269
Tone color, in music, 23
Torah, 278, 282, 284
Toreutics (metal craftsmanship), 167
Torso, marble (Greek), 187, **187**
Trajan, Column of, 270, **270**

Trajan (Marcus Ulpius Trajanus), Roman emperor (52–117), 214 (box), 267, 270, 271, 272
Transepts, 296, 300, 418
Transmigration of souls, 49
Tribunes, Roman, 211
Triforium, 296, 425
Triglyphs, 178
Trinity, 293, 298, 299, 308, 339, 340, 343, 345, 439
Tripudium, sacred dance, 439
Trivium, 342
Trojans, 38, 192, 210, 224, 229
Trojan War, 38, 41, 53, 60, 166, 172, 229, 231n
Trojan Women, The (Euripides), 60, 96–108 (text)
Tropes, in music, 431–32
Troubadours, 26, 338, 362, 434, 435, 436, 437, 441 (table), 442
Troubadour Song (Beatritz), 436 (text), 436–37 (text)
Troubadour Song (William IX), 434–35 (text)
Troubadour-trouvère, 317n, 429, 437
Trouvères, 338, 434, 435, 437, 441 (table)
Troy, 35n, 53, 54, 60, 96, 103n, 167, 192, 210, 224, 229, 231n
Trumeau, 417
Trumpet, **350,** 432, 441 (table)
Tuba, 274
Turks, 183, 291 (overview), 301
Turnus, 224, 230
Twelve Tables of Law, Roman, 211
Tympanum, 416, 425
Tyrants, Greek, 42–44

Universities, 341–43, 434
    Bologna, 341
    Cambridge, 341
    Oxford, 341
    Paris, 341, 342
    rise of, 341, 434
    Salerno, 341

"Unmoved Mover," (Aquinas), 343
"Unmoved Mover," (Aristotle), 129
Urban II, Pope (ca. 1042–1099), 416

Valhalla, 313, 314
Valkyrie, 314
Van Gogh, Vincent, Dutch painter (1853–1890), 15, 16, 17
Vault construction
    arch, 412, 414, 420
    barrel (tunnel), 413, 414–15
    groin (cross), 417, 423, 425
    ribbed, 414, 423, 425
Venice, 299, 302, 303
Venus, 40 (box), 217, 232n, 264
Vespasian (Titus Flavius Vespasianus), Roman emperor (9–79), 214 (box), 217 (quote), 268
Vesta, 40 (box), 209n
Vestal Virgin, 209
Vesuvius, Mount, 263
Vetti, House of the, Pompeii, 263, **263**
Vézelay, 416, 417
Vibrating strings, 47–48, 202
Victory Untying Her Sandal (Greek), Temple of Athena Nike, 184–85, **185**
Vikings, 312, 315, 412, 413, 415
Violin, 350
Virgil (Publius Virgilius Maro), Latin poet (90–19 B.C.), 209, 209 (quote), 224, 226 (overview), 229, 230–39 (text), 264, 346, 347, 374n
Virginia State Capitol, Richmond, 265
Vitruvius Pollo, Marcus, Roman architect (1st c. B.C.), 268
Vivaldi, Antonio, Italian composer (1678–1741), 31

Wagner, Richard, German composer (1813–1883), 315, 437
Wasps, The (Aristophanes), 61

Watermill with the Great Red Roof (Hobbema), 15, colorplate 3
"Way to Jerusalem, The," sacred dance, 439
Wheel-lyre (organistrum), **433**
Where Do We Come From? What Are We? Where Are We Going? (Gauguin), 15, colorplate 1
Wilde, Oscar, English author (1854–1900), 10 (quote)
William of Champeaux, scholastic philosopher (ca. 1070–1121), 340, 341
William the Conqueror, duke of Normandy (1027?–1087), 415, 416
William IX, duke of Aquitaine, troubadour (1071–1126), 434, 434–35 (text)
Windows
    clerestory, 296, 414, 417, 418, 423, 425
    stained glass, 420, 421, 423–26
"With Rue My Heart Is Laden" (Housman), 12 (text)
Works and Days (Hesiod), 41–42
Wylie, Elinor, American poet (1885–1928), 316 (text)

Xenophon, Greek historian and general (434?–355? B.C.), 61
Xerxes, Persian king (519–465 B.C.), 174
XPI Page, Book of Kells (Hiberno-Saxon), 410, **411**

Yahweh, Hebrew God, 278, 279
"Young Girls Dancing Around the Altar" (Greek), 200, **200**

Zeno the Stoic, Greek philosopher (335?–263? B.C.), 219
Zeus, 39, 40 (box), 58 (box), 103n, 108, 110n, 181, 196, 217, 219, 221, 293
Zodiac, 439